The Popular Dict

En

Place-Names

A. D. Mills

PARRAGON

FOR SOLVEJG

Based on A Dictionary of English Place-Names, *Oxford University Press, first published 1991. This edition published 1996 by Parragon Book Service Ltd and Magpie Books, an imprint of Robinson Publishing Ltd, by arrangement with Oxford University Press*

British Library Cataloguing in Publication Data
Data available

ISBN 0 75251 851 8

Printed and bound in the United Kingdom

Contents

A. D. Mills is Emeritus Reader in English, University of London, and Editor of *The Place-Names of Dorset* (English Place-Name Society). He is a member of the Council of the English Place-Name Society, and of the Council for Name Studies in Great Britain and Ireland.

Preface

THE suggestions made for the origins and meanings of the place-names in this book are of course dependent on all the previous work on the subject, and acknowledgement is therefore due to the many authors and editors of the numerous monographs, books, and papers written on various aspects of English place-names over the last several decades. No book on the subject can be undertaken without frequent recourse to the detailed county volumes of the English Place-Name Society or to the monumental and still indispensable *Concise Oxford Dictionary of English Place-Names* by E. Ekwall, but many other specialized studies and papers have proved to be invaluable: a selection of these is included in the Bibliography for the reader seeking further information on individual names or interested in the many aspects of name-study outside the scope of this book.

It cannot be emphasized too strongly that in the elucidation of the original meanings of place-names the earliest available spellings are of crucial importance. The collection of suitably identified early spellings for each individual name is the basis for all place-name research, and it is only after these spellings have been carefully and systematically analysed in the light of various linguistic, historical, and geographical criteria that suggestions as to a plausible etymology can be made. Although it would be impossible in a book of this kind to present this full range of early spellings for each name, it must be stressed that the etymologies here proposed are based nevertheless on an analysis and evaluation of such spellings as are made available in the various detailed surveys, as well as on the full discussions of the names and name-types in other scholarly publications. I stand indebted to all this earlier work in the field.

My thanks are due to Professor Kenneth Cameron in his capacity as Honorary Director of the English Place-Name Society for giving permission to quote from the county surveys published by the Society, and to all my colleagues in English name studies, past and present, for our many useful discussions over the years. More personally I owe a great debt of gratitude to Professor Cameron for kindly agreeing to look over the book in page proof and for his valuable criticisms and suggestions, although it must be emphasized that the meanings and derivations proposed, together with any errors or deficiencies remaining, are my responsibility alone.

Introduction

Place-Names and their Meanings

PLACE-NAMES, those familiar but often curious labels for places that feature in all their rich diversity on map and signpost, fulfil such an essential function in our daily lives that we take them very much for granted. Yet English place-names are as much part of England's cultural heritage as the English language and the English landscape from which they spring, and almost every place-name has an older original meaning behind its modern form.

Most people will have wondered at some time or other about the original meaning of a place-name—the name of their home town or of the other familiar places encountered *en route* to work by road or rail, the names of stations and destinations and those seen on roadsigns and signposts, and the more unusual names discovered on trips into the countryside or on holiday. Why Eccles, Stoke Poges, Great Snoring, or Leighton Buzzard? What is the meaning of a name like Strangeways or Chiswick? How did Croydon, Liverpool, and Windsor get their names? What does Crick or Bootle mean?

In fact all these names, like the vast majority of the names included in this dictionary, have original meanings that are not at all apparent from their modern forms. That is because most place-names today are what could be termed 'linguistic fossils'. Although they originated as living units of speech, coined by our distant ancestors as descriptions of places in terms of their topography, appearance, situation, use, ownership, or other association, most have become, in the course of time, mere labels, no longer possessing a clear linguistic meaning. This is perhaps not surprising when one considers that most place-names are a thousand years old or more, and are expressed in vocabulary that may have evolved differently from the equivalent words in the ordinary language, or that may now be completely extinct or obscure.

Of course some place-names, even very old ones, have apparently changed very little through the many centuries of their existence, and may still convey something of their original meaning when the words from which they are composed have survived in the ordinary language (even though the features to which they refer may have changed or disappeared). Names such as Claybrooke, Horseheath, Marshwood, Nettlebed, Oxford, Saltmarshe, Sandford, and Woodbridge are shown by their early spellings to be virtually self-explanatory, having undergone little or no change in form or spelling over a very long period.

But even a casual glance at the alphabetical list of English place-names will show that such instant etymologies are usually a delusion. The modern form of a name can never be assumed to convey its original meaning without early spellings to confirm it, and indeed many names that look equally obvious and easy to interpret prove to have quite unexpected meanings in the light of the evidence of early records. Thus Easter is 'the sheep-fold', Slaughter 'the muddy place', Swine 'the creek or channel', and Wool 'the spring or springs'—the inevitable association of such names with well-known words in the ordinary vocabulary is understandable but quite misleading, for they all derive from old words which survive in fossilized form in place-names but which are no longer found in the language.

Names then can never be taken at their face value, but can only be correctly interpreted after the careful scrutiny of the earliest attested spellings in the light of the dialectal development of the sounds of the language, after wide comparisons have been made with similar or identical names, and after other linguistic, historical, and geographical factors have been taken into account. These fundamental principles of place-name etymology are most clearly illustrated by the names which now have identical forms but which prove to have quite distinct origins: for example, the name Broughton occurs several times but has no less than three different origins ('brook farmstead', 'hill farmstead', and 'fortified farmstead'), the various places called Hinton fall into two distinct groups ('high farmstead' or 'farmstead belonging to a religious community'), and even a place-name like Ashford can be deceptive and means something other than 'ash-tree ford' in two instances. On the other hand, names now with different spellings can turn out to have identical origins: thus Aldermaston and Alderminster are both 'nobleman's farmstead', Chiswick and Keswick are both 'cheese farm', Hatfield and Heathfield are both 'heathy open land', and Naunton, Newington, Newnton, Newton, and Niton are all 'new farmstead'. It goes without saying that guesswork on the basis of a modern form is of little use, and that each name must be the subject of individual scrutiny. For the same reason it should be remembered that the interpretation offered for a particular name in the list may not apply to another name with identical modern spelling occurring elsewhere, which might well have a quite different origin and meaning on the evidence of its early spellings and of other information.

Scope and Arrangement of the Dictionary

The main object of this dictionary is simple—to explain the most likely meanings and origins of over 12,000 English place-names in a clear, concise, and easily accessible form, based on the evidence and information so far available. The names included have been selected because they appear in all or several of the popular touring atlases, containing maps on a scale of three or four miles to the inch, produced by the Ordnance Survey and by the motoring organizations and other publishers. Thus the names of all the better-known places have been included: the names of England's towns and cities, of a good number of its villages and hamlets and city suburbs, together with the names of counties and districts (old and new) and of many rivers and coastal features.

The entries are strictly alphabetical, each name being referred to the post-1974 county in which the place is located. Priority in the entries is given to what the individual name 'means'. Thus wherever possible the suggested original meaning, that thought most likely as deduced from the evidence of early spellings and other information and from the fuller discussions of the name available in more detailed studies, is presented as a 'translation' into a modern English phrase of the old words or 'elements' that make up the name. The elements themselves are usually then cited in their original spelling and language, Celtic, Old English, Old Scandinavian, or other as the case may be (a Glossary of some of the most common elements being provided at the end of the book).

Most names can be satisfactorily explained with respect to the elements from which they are derived, although the precise shades of meaning of the individual elements or of a particular compound may not always be easy to ascertain. For some names the evidence so far available is not decisive, and explanations may be somewhat provisional. A few remain doubtful or obscure or partly so. It is of course possible that earlier or better evidence may still come to light for some names, especially for places in those counties like Durham, Hampshire, Kent, Lancashire, Somerset, and Suffolk for which there is as yet no English Place-Name Society survey.

Alternative explanations have often been given for names where two or more interpretations seem possible. For instance it is often difficult to say whether the first element of a compound name is a personal name or a significant word, as in names like Eversden, Hauxley, Hinxhill, Ranskill, and Yearsley. However for reasons of space some alternative explanations considered rather unlikely, problematical, or controversial have been omitted from the entries, in favour of those judged most plausible. Alternative interpretations of this kind are of course more fully rehearsed and discussed in the detailed surveys and monographs.

It should perhaps be pointed out that although the explanations suggested are considered to be the most likely, and are as accurate and reliable as possible within the limitations of scope and space imposed, final certainty in establishing the original meanings of many older place-names is unlikely to be achieved because of the nature of the materials. Given the archaic character of many place-names, and the fact that we can rarely know precisely when and by whom they were originally coined or came into use (as opposed to when they first appear in written records), there will always be an element of conjecture in their interpretation. However the study of place-names is a continually developing and evolving field, as the last few decades have shown, and further revision and refinement of etymologies is bound to come out of current and future research.

Inevitably the rather concise explanations of meaning and origin attempted in this dictionary, although based on the latest research, have meant leaving aside other important considerations. It has not been possible to enter into the complexities of philological argument, or to explore questions as to the precise nature or location of a topographical or habitative feature, or to examine the identity and status of a person associated with a place and the precise significance of that association. Such matters as these, and many other considerations bearing on the significance of a place-name in its historical, archaeological, and geographical context, are of course explored more fully in the various county surveys and studies of name-groups listed in the Bibliography, and they should be consulted by the interested reader wanting further information.

Although the scope of the present work does not allow for the presentation of a full range of early attested spellings such as would be required to provide visible support for the etymologies proposed, at least one early spelling for each name (usually the earliest known) has been cited, together with its date, to give some idea of the age of the name in question and of its original form:

Thelwall Ches. *Thelwæle* 923.

Because of the unique importance and interest of the Domesday Book of 1086 as an early source in which many English place-names are on record for the first time, the Domesday spelling of a name is always given if it occurs in that record; where several different Domesday spellings occur, only one is normally selected for inclusion:

Guisborough Cleveland. *Ghigesburg* 1086 (DB).

Even though for many names the Domesday spelling is the earliest, it should of course be borne in mind that all place-names recorded in the Domesday Book are necessarily older (some much older) than that document, and indeed many are recorded in earlier sources such as the writings of Bede (8th century), the Anglo-Saxon Chronicle (9th to 12th century), Old English charters or land-grants (from the 7th century), or even in sources as old as Ptolemy (mid 2nd century):

Tilbury Essex. *Tilaburg* 731, *Tiliberia* 1086 (DB).
York N. Yorks. *Ebórakon c.*150, *Eboracum, Euruic* 1086 (DB).

Many of the Old English charters only survive in copies made at a later date so that precise dating of early spellings can be complicated. However since the spellings included here are intended to be mainly illustrative rather than evidential or supportive of etymology, the dates cited are those at which the original documents purport to have been written, unqualified by those of the later copies:

Abingdon Oxon. *Abbandune* 968, *Ab(b)endone* 1086 (DB).

Readers needing a more accurate and critical dating for early spellings as well as details of source and document should consult the detailed county surveys and other monographs.

Where spellings from Domesday Book are followed by '(*sic*)'—Latin for 'thus'—this indicates that the spelling is given as it appears in that source even though it is apparently rather erratic or corrupt (the Norman scribes clearly had difficulty with the pronunciation and spelling of many English names!). In such cases a second, more typical, spelling from some other early source is usually included:

Testwood Hants. *Lesteorde* (*sic*) 1086 (DB), *Terstewode c.*1185.

Those names neither mentioned in Domesday Book nor recorded in sources earlier than Domesday Book are supplied with an early spelling (usually the earliest available) from some other dated source:

Harwich Essex. *Herewic* 1248.

So-called 'double-barrelled' names with manorial affixes or other distinctive additions are usually supplied with a representative early spelling incorporating that addition, again to give some idea of the date at which the fuller form of the name came into use:

Stoke Poges Bucks. *Stoches* 1086 (DB), *Stokepogeis* 1292.

Of course numerous further spellings for most names are to be found in the more detailed published surveys.

Elements and personal names cited with an asterisk are postulated or hypothetical forms, that is although there may be good evidence for their assumed existence in the early languages in question, they are either not recorded in independent use or are only found in use at a later date. To avoid unnecessary complication, the terminology for the provenance of elements and personal names has been somewhat generalized: for instance Old

English (OE) stands for all dialects, Anglian, West Saxon, etc.; Old Scandinavian (OScand.) embraces Old Norse and Old Danish as well as forms more correctly labelled Anglo-Scandinavian; Old French (OFrench) includes Norman French, Anglo-Norman, etc.; and the term Celtic is used for British, Primitive Welsh, and the other early related Brittonic languages. Similarly the term 'personal name' is used of personal names proper as well as of bynames formed in the early period.

In compound names, where both elements are from the same language the term or abbreviation for that language appears only once: e.g. OE *sand* + *wīc* for Sandwich. Where two elements are from different languages in a so-called hybrid name, each element is separately labelled, e.g. OE **wilig* + OScand. *toft* for Willitoft. Cross references to other place-names in the alphabetical list are given in small capitals. Place-names and river-names no longer in current use are printed in italics (e.g. *Ashwell* under Ashwellthorpe, *Ravenser* under Spurn Head, and River *Ann* under Amport and Andover).

Elliptical place-names of various kinds have been given the fuller meanings that seemed appropriate. Thus names of the type Byfleet and Underbarrow, consisting of preposition + noun, literally 'by stream' and 'under hill', have been translated '(place) by the stream', '(place) under the hill' to bring out the implicit meaning. So-called folk-names (originally the names of family or tribal groups rather than of places) have been similarly treated, for example Barking has been rendered '(settlement of) the family or followers of a man called *Berica'.

As already noted, names have been placed for convenience in their 'new' post-1974 counties; however lamentable one may consider the reorganization of local government to have been, it was felt that this book should acknowledge the new boundaries even though hitherto the names have usually been treated within the framework of the old historical counties (as in the volumes of the English Place-Name Society and in other monographs). It is hoped that the comparative maps of the old and new counties (pp. xxxii–xxxiii) may help in the tracing and identification of individual names subject to these changes. In order to avoid the problems encountered in some reference books, county abbreviations have been kept to a minimum.

The Chronology and Languages of English Place-Names

Place-names show an astonishing capacity for survival, as the dates alone of most of the earliest spellings testify, even though it should be remembered that every name will of course be older than its earliest occurrence in the records, often a good deal older. In general it might be claimed that most of the names included in this book are about a thousand years old, and that a good many are older than that. The various strata of English place-names reflect all the great historical migrations, conquests, and settlements of the past and the different languages spoken by successive waves of inhabitants.

Some river-names, few in number but the most ancient of all, seem to belong to an unknown early Indo-European language which is neither Celtic nor Germanic. Such pre-Celtic names, sometimes termed 'Old European', may have been in use among the very early inhabitants of these islands in Neolithic times, and it is assumed that they were passed on to Celtic settlers arriving from the Continent about the 4th century BC. Among the ancient names that possibly belong to this small but important group are Colne, Humber, Itchen, and Wey.

During the last four centuries BC there took place the invasions and settlements of the Iron-Age Celts, peoples speaking various Celtic dialects which can be divided into two main groups, Goidelic or Gaelic (later differentiated into Irish, Scots, and Manx) and Brittonic or British (later differentiated into Welsh and Cornish). Celtic place-names coined in British (really the language of the ancient Britons) were in use for several centuries and some have survived from the period when this Celtic language was spoken over the whole of what is now England as well as further west. These early place-names of Celtic or British origin were borrowed by the Anglo-Saxons when they came to Britain from the 5th century AD onwards and are found all over England, only sporadically in the east but increasing in numbers further west towards Cornwall and Wales where they are of course still predominant. Celtic place-names belong for the most part to several well-defined categories: names of tribes or territories like Devon and Leeds, names of important towns and cities like Carlisle, York, and Dover, names of hills and forests (now often transferred to places) like Crick, Mellor, Penge, and Lytchett, and most frequent of all, river-names like Avon, Exe, Frome, Thames, and Trent. There are also a good many hybrid names, consisting of a Celtic name to which an Old English element has been added, like Lichfield, Chatham, Bredon, and Manchester. Some places, important at a very early date, had Celtic names in Romano-British times which were later replaced, for instance Cambridge was *Duroliponte*, Canterbury was *Durovernum*, and Leicester was *Ratae*: for these, reference should be made to the fuller treatments of individual names in the county surveys or to the specialized study by Rivet and Smith (see Bibliography).

The Roman occupation of Britain during the first four centuries AD left little mark on place-names, for it is clear that Latin was mainly the official written language of government and administration rather than the spoken language of the countryside. Thus Celtic names, though usually Latinized in written sources, continued to be used throughout this period and were not replaced. However a few early names like Catterick and Lincoln contain Latin elements, and others like Eccles and Caterham were coined from Celtic elements that were borrowed from Latin during this early period. The small part played by Latin in place-name formation during the Romano-British period should be distinguished from the later influence of Latin on English place-names during the medieval period. In the Middle Ages, Latin was again the language of the church and administration, and this Medieval Latin was widely used in affixes like *Forum* 'market', *Magna* 'great', and *Regis* 'of the king' to distinguish places with identical names, as well as occasionally in the formation of names like Bruera, Dacorum, and Pontefract.

The Anglo-Saxon conquest and settlement of Britain began in the 5th century AD, spreading slowly from east to west and culminating in the occupation of the whole of what is now England, except for Cornwall and some areas along the Welsh border, by the 9th century. These new settlers were the Angles, Saxons, and Jutes, Germanic tribes from Northern Europe whose language was Anglo-Saxon, now usually called Old English to emphasize its continuity with Middle and Modern English. It is in this language, Old English, that the great majority of the place-names now in use in England were coined. This dominant stratum in English place-names (apart from those of Cornwall) is a result of the political domination by the Anglo-Saxons of the Celtic-speaking Britons and the gradual imposition of the Old English language on them. Many Celtic names were borrowed by the incomers as already mentioned (important evidence for the survival of a British population and for continuity and contact between the two peoples), but thousands of new names were coined in Old English during the Anglo-Saxon period between the 5th and 11th centuries. Thus the majority of English towns and villages, and a good many hamlets and landscape features, have names of Old English origin that predate the Norman Conquest. These names vary in age, and it is not always easy to tell which names belong to the earlier phases of the settlement and which to the later part of the Anglo-Saxon period, although detailed studies have shown that many of the names containing the elements *hām*, *-ingas*, *-inga-*, *ēg*, *feld*, *ford*, and *dūn* are among the earliest. It should in any case be remembered that all names are older than their earliest recorded spelling, so that names first mentioned in, for example, Domesday Book (1086) or even in a 12th-century source usually have their origins in this period.

The Scandinavian invasions and settlements took place during the 9th, 10th, and 11th centuries and resulted in many place-names of Scandinavian origin in the North and East of England. The Vikings came to Britain from two Scandinavian countries, Denmark and Norway, the Danes settling principally in East Anglia, the East Midlands, and a large part of Yorkshire, whilst the Norwegians were mainly concentrated in the North-West, especially Lancashire and Cumbria. The Germanic languages spoken by these Vikings, Old Danish and Old Norse (in this book referred to jointly as Old Scandinavian), were similar in many ways to Old English, but there were also striking differences in sound system and vocabulary which reveal themselves in the early spellings of many place-names from the areas mentioned. Although names of Scandinavian origin are rare to the south of Watling Street (because that formed the boundary of the Danelaw, which was the area subject to Danish law, established in the late 9th century), the distribution of Scandinavian names in the North and East varies greatly, parts of Norfolk, Leicestershire, Lincolnshire, and Yorkshire being among the areas with the thickest concentration. To explain such large numbers of Scandinavian place-names in these areas, recent scholarship has suggested that in addition to settlements made by Viking warriors and their descendants there was probably a large-scale migration and colonization from the Scandinavian homelands in the wake of the invasion. Many hundreds of names in the areas mentioned are completely of Scandinavian origin (Kirkby, Lowestoft, Scunthorpe, Braithwaite), others are hybrids, a mixture of Scandinavian and English (Grimston, Durham, Welby), and some (on account of the similarity of some Old English and Old Scandinavian words) could be from either language (Crook, Kettleburgh, Lytham, Snape). In addition many place-names of Old English origin were modified by Scandinavian speech in these areas, for example by the substitution of *sk* and *k* sounds for *sh* and *ch* in names like Skidbrooke, Skipton, Keswick, and Kippax.

The number of English place-names of French origin is relatively small, in spite of the far-reaching effects of the Norman Conquest on English social and political life and on the English language in general. It is clear that by 1066, most settlements and landscape features already had established names, but the new French-speaking aristocracy and ecclesiastical hierarchy often gave distinctively French names to their castles, estates, and monasteries (Battle, Belvoir, Grosmont, Montacute, Richmond), some of them transferred directly from France, and there are a few names of French origin referring to landscape and other features (Devizes, Malpas). However the French influence on English place-names is perhaps most evident in the way the names of the great French-speaking feudal families were affixed to the names of the manors they possessed. These manorial additions result in a great many hybrid 'double-barrelled' names which contribute considerable variety and richness to the map of England. Most of them serve to distinguish one manor from another with an identical name, and of course the surnames of the more powerful land-owning families occur in a good many different place-names (Kingston Lacy, Stanton Lacy, Sutton Courtenay, Hirst Courtney, Drayton Bassett, Wootton Bassett, and so on). Some place-names of this type are not easily recognizable from their modern spellings, since the manorial affixes are now compounded with the original elements (Herstmonceaux, Owermoigne, Stogursey). A further important aspect of the French influence on English place-names is the way it affected their spelling and pronunciation. Norman scribes had difficulty with some English sounds, often substituting their own (as seen for instance in the spellings of Domesday Book and other early medieval sources). Some of these Norman spellings have had a permanent effect on the names in question and have remained in use, disguising the original forms (Cambridge, Cannock, Diss, Durham, Nottingham, Salop, Trafford).

Of course not all of the names on the modern map, even names of sizeable settlements or well-known features, are as old as most of those so far mentioned. Other names besides the French names already noted originated in the Middle English period, that is between the 12th and 15th centuries inclusive. These include settlement names incorporating post-Conquest personal names and surnames like Bassenthwaite, Forston, and Vauxhall, names containing old elements but not on early record like Bournemouth and Paddock Wood, and various other names such as Broadstairs, Forest Row, Poplar, and Sacriston.

Finally there are some place-names, perhaps surprisingly few, which originate in the post-medieval period or even in quite recent times. Many of course are names of new industrial towns or of suburban developments, others are names of coastal resorts or ports or of new administrative districts. Most of these 'modern' names seem rather artificial creations compared with the earlier place-names that began life as actual descriptions of habitations or natural features. Some are in fact simply straight transfers of older names without any change of form (like the post-1974 county names Avon or Tyne and Wear, or the 'revived' district names Bassetlawe and Dacorum), some are based on rather fanciful identifications of ancient names made by early antiquarians (like Adur and Morecambe), and others are new adaptations of existing old names with some sort of addition (like Devonport, Humberside, and New Brighton). Of the newly formed modern names, some are straightforwardly descriptive of a local feature whether natural (Highcliffe) or man-made (Iron-Bridge), others are named from a building around which the settlement developed (the pub in Nelson and Queensbury, the chapel in St Helens and Chapel St Leonards), some are named from fields (Hassocks and Whyteleafe), others refer to local products (Coalville, Port Sunlight), commemorate a famous historical event (Peacehaven, Vigo, Waterloo) or even a famous novel (Westward Ho!). In addition a good number of the names coined in more recent times commemorate entrepreneurs or other notable individuals, some consisting simply of their names (Fleetwood, Peterlee, Telford), others incorporating these into a sort of spurious form that looks older than it is (Carterton, Maryport, Stewartby), others referring to landowners (Camden Town) or local families (Burgess Hill, Gerrards Cross).

Some different Types of Place-Name Formation

All English place-names, whether of Celtic, Old English, or Scandinavian origin, can be divided into three main groups: folk-names, habitative names, and topographical names.

Of the three, folk-names form the smallest group though nevertheless a very important and interesting one. Place-names in this category were originally the names of the inhabitants of a place or district. Thus tribal names came to denote the district occupied by the tribe, as with Essex and Sussex (both old Anglo-Saxon kingdoms), and Norfolk and Suffolk (divisions of the Anglo-Saxon kingdom of East Anglia). The names Jarrow, Hitchin, and Ripon also represent tribes (later their territories) from Anglo-Saxon times, and names like Clewer and Ridware must represent the settlements of smaller groups. Of particular interest, because they are to be associated with the early phases of the Anglo-Saxon settlement, are the names formed with the suffix *-ingas* ('people of', 'dwellers at') like Hastings, Reading, and Spalding, all of them originally denoting family or tribal groups, later their settlements.

Habitative names form a much larger group. They denoted inhabited places from the start, whether homesteads, farms or enclosures, villages or hamlets, strongholds, cottages, or other kinds of building or settlement. In names of this type the second element describes the kind of habitation, and among others the Old English elements *hām* 'homestead', *tūn* 'farm', *worth* 'enclosure', *wīc* 'dwelling', *cot* 'cottage', *burh* 'stronghold', and the Old Scandinavian elements *bý* 'farmstead' and *thorp* 'outlying farmstead' are particularly common, as in names like Streatham, Middleton, Lulworth, Ipswich, Didcot, Aylesbury, Grimsby, and Woodthorpe. Detailed studies of the various habitative elements have shown that they had a wide range of meanings which varied according to their use at different periods or in different parts of the country or in combination with other elements. For example Old English *tūn* may have its original elements. For example Old English *tūn* may have its original meaning 'enclosure' in some names, whereas in others 'farmstead', 'village', 'manor', or 'estate' may be more appropriate. The reader is recommended to consult the Glossary at the end of the book to discover some of the alternative meanings evidenced for other habitative elements like *bere-tūn*, *burh*, *thorp*, *wīc*, *wīc-hām*, and so on.

Topographical names also form a very large and diverse group. They consisted originally of a description of some topographical or physical feature, either natural or man-made, which was then transferred to the settlement near the feature named, probably at a very early date. Thus names for rivers and streams, springs and lakes, fords and roads, marshes and moors, hills and valleys, woods and clearings, and various other landscape features became the names of inhabited places. Typical examples of the type are Sherborne, Fulbrook, Bakewell, Tranmere, Oxford, Otmore, Stodmarsh, Swindon, Goodwood, Bromsgrove, Bexley, and Hatfield—all have second elements that originally denoted topographical features. Indeed our early ancestors made use of a vast topographical vocabulary, applied with precision and subtlety in any one period or locality to the natural and artificial features they depended upon for their subsistence and survival. However, the meanings of topographical terms can vary a good deal from name to name, for some elements used over a long period in the formation of English place-names underwent considerable changes of meaning during medieval times, for instance Old English *feld* originally 'open land' developed a later sense 'enclosed plot', Old English *wald* 'forest' came to mean 'open upland', and Old English *lēah* 'wood' became 'woodland clearing' and then 'meadow'. The choice of the most likely meaning for one of these elements in an individual name is therefore a matter of judgement, based among other things on locality, the nature of the compound, and assumptions about the age of the name. Moreover recent research has increasingly shown that what seem to be similar terms for hills or valleys, woodland or marshland, or agricultural land, had fine distinctions of meaning in early times. For instance the different Old English terms for 'hill' like *dūn*, *hyll*, *hrycg*, *hōh*, *hēafod*, and **ofer*, far from being synonymous, seem to have had their own specialized meanings. In addition these and other common topographical elements like *ēg* 'island', *hamm* 'enclosure', and *halh* 'nook' were each capable of a wide range of extended meanings according to date, region, and the character of the landscape itself. Indeed the meanings suggested for names containing these elements can often be checked and refined by those with a close knowledge of the local topography of the places in question. The Glossary at the end of the book provides a selection of the meanings found for some of these topographical elements and gives an idea of the great range and variety of this vocabulary.

From the structural point of view, most English place-names are compounds, that is they consist of two elements, the first of which usually qualifies the second. The first element in such compounds may be a noun, an adjective, a river-name, a personal name, or a tribal name. The names mentioned in the last paragraph are typical examples of compound place-names formed during the Old English period. However some place-names, known as simplex, consist of one element only, at least to begin with: examples include names like Combe ('the valley'), Hale, Lea, Stoke, Stowe, Thorpe, Worth, and Wyke. Less common are names consisting of three elements such as Claverton ('burdock ford farmstead'), Redmarley, Woodmansterne, and Wotherton; in most of these the third element has probably been added later to an already existing compound. There are also other kinds of place-name composition, one of the most frequent being the use of the medial connective particle *-ing-* in place-names like Paddington, probably best explained as 'estate associated with a man called Padda'. In addition some compound place-names in the western parts of England (especially in Cornwall, counties bordering Wales, and in Cumbria) have a different formation. They are so-called 'name-phrases' in which the usual order of elements as found in English place-names is reversed following Celtic practice. In this group are names like Aspatria ('Patrick's ash-tree'), Bewaldeth, Brigsteer, Landulph, and Tremaine.

So-called 'double-barrelled' names, usually originating as ordinary simplex or compound names but later having an affix added to distinguish them from similar or identical names, are often of the manorial type already mentioned in which the affix is the name of a land-owning individual or family (for example Langton Matravers or Leighton Buzzard). But many other kinds of affix occur, most of them dating from the 13th or 14th centuries. Some refer to the size or shape of the place as in Much Wenlock or Long Buckby, others to geographical position relative to neighbouring manors as in High Barnet or Nether and Over Haddon, others to soil conditions as in Black Callerton or Dry Doddington, or to a local product as in Iron Acton and Saffron Walden. Some affixes indicate the presence of a castle or other building or the existence of a market, as in Castle Rising, Steeple Bumpstead, Market Harborough, and Chipping Sodbury. A good number of the most notable affixes are Latin, as already noted, among them such resounding examples as Barton in Fabis, Ryme Intrinseca, Toller Porcorum, and Whitchurch Canonicorum (the last three from Dorset). But even the 'double-barrelled' names are not always what they seem: names like East Garston and Tur Langton which at face value seem to belong to this category turn out to have unexpected origins as ordinary compounds that are now completely disguised.

Many old place-names, especially compounds, have undergone some degree of reduction or contraction in the long period since they were first coined. Some names originally consisting of several syllables like Brighton or York have been considerably reduced by the centuries of use in speech. A common characteristic of compound place-names, and one which often helps to disguise their origin, is the shortening of original long vowels and diphthongs, as in compound words in the ordinary vocabulary. Just as *holi-* and *bon-* in the compounds *holiday* and *bonfire* represent *holy* and *bone* with their historically long vowels (*hālig* and *bān* in Old English), so in compound place-names Old English elements like *brād* 'broad', *brōm* 'broom', *hām* 'homestead', *stān* 'stone', and *strǣt* 'street' occur with shortened vowels in names like Bradford, Bromley, Hampstead, Stanley, Stondon, Stratford, and Stretton. The same tendency, together with weakening of stress, also affected the second elements of compound names, resulting in some originally distinct elements coinciding in form and pronunciation. Once shortened, the important Old English habitative element *hām* 'homestead, village' came to sound like the quite separate topographical element *hamm* 'enclosure, river-meadow'. As a result, without definite evidence of one kind or another, it is not possible to be sure whether a number of place-names originally contained *hām* or *hamm* (in such cases both elements will usually have been cited as possible alternatives). The same combination of shortening of vowel and weakening of stress leads to the confusion of other elements that were originally quite distinct, among them Old English *dūn* 'down, hill', *denu* 'valley', and *tūn* 'farmstead': thus the modern forms of Croydon (from *denu*), Morden (from *dūn*), and Islington (also from *dūn*) belie their origins.

Some of the archaic features of English place-names are grammatical in origin. Old English was a highly inflected language, and although certain grammatical endings of Old English nouns, adjectives, and personal names disappeared from the ordinary language by the 11th or 12th centuries, they have left their permanent mark on a good number of place-names. Thus the genitive (i.e. possessive) singular of so-called 'weak' nouns and personal names (Old English *-n*) often survives as *-n-* in names like Dagenham (Old English *Dæccan hām* '*Dæcca's homestead'), Graveney, Putney, Tottenham, and Watnall. There are also many fossilized remains of the Old English dative endings of nouns and adjectives in place-names, since place-names would often naturally occur in adverbial or prepositional contexts requiring the dative case in Old English. Thus the old dative singular ending of the 'weak' adjective (*-an*) is often preserved in the middle of a modern name, as for instance in Bradnop (Old English *brādan hope* '(at) the broad valley'), Bradenham, Henley, and Stapenhill. Even more common are modern place-names that reflect the old dative case ending of an Old English noun. Thus the names Cleeve, Hale, and Sale derive from old dative forms of the words *clif*, *halh*, and *salh*, and most examples of the name Barrow represent Old English *bearwe* '(at) the wood or grove'. The common element *burh* 'fortified place' (the word *borough* in modern English) often appears in place-names as *Bury*, *-bury* from the Old English dative singular form *byrig*, but as *Burgh*, *-borough* from the nominative case of the same word. The distinctive dative plural ending *-um* of the Old English noun has also left its trace in the modern forms of many place-names, especially in the Midlands and North. Instances include Coatham, Cotham, Coton, Cottam, and Cotton (all probably from Old English *cotum* '(at) the cottages'), Laneham (from Old English *lanum* '(at) the lanes'), and other similar names like Downholm, Newsham, and Oaken. Occasionally too, in the place-names of the old Danelaw area of the North and East, old grammatical endings from the early Scandinavian languages spoken by the Vikings have been preserved. Thus there are traces of an old genitive (possessive) ending *-ar* in names like Helperthorpe, Osmotherley, and Windermere, an Old Scandinavian plural ending *-ar* is reflected in the modern forms of Sawrey and Burton upon Stather, and the Old Scandinavian dative plural *-um* is found in names like Arram and Kelham.

It should perhaps be noted here that many of the shorter Old English and Scandinavian men's names in use in the Anglo-Saxon period and incorporated into place-names, especially those ending in *-a* or *-i*, actually resemble names used for women in modern times. For this reason particular care has been taken in the explanations of place-names to indicate the gender of the person involved. Examples of such masculine personal names liable to be misinterpreted by the modern reader include Anna (in Amble and Ancaster), Betti (in Beachley and Bettiscombe), Emma (in Emley), Hilda (in Hillingdon), Káti (in Cadeby), Lill (in Lilleshall), and Sali (in Saleby). To a more limited extent the opposite may also be true, that some Old English and Scandinavian women's names may have rather a masculine look to the modern reader, and place-names incorporating these are explained with this in mind, examples being Helperby, Kenilworth, and Wilbraham containing the feminine personal names Hjalp, Cynehild, and Wilburh respectively.

The phenomenon known as 'back-formation' accounts for a good many modern river-names. Once the original meaning of a place-name was forgotten, there was sometimes a tendency for antiquarians and others to try to reinterpret it as if it contained the name of the river or stream on which the place was situated. Thus Plym came to be the name of the river at Plympton because the village name (historically 'farmstead of the plum-tree') came to be understood as 'farmstead on the stream called Plym'. Other examples of back-formation include Arun from Arundel, Chelmer from Chelmsford, Len from Lenham, Mole from Molesey, Roch from Rochdale, Rom from Romford, Stort from Stortford, and Wandle from Wandsworth. Many of these rivers and streams are known to have had genuine earlier names which were replaced by the new back-formations, usually from about the 16th century onwards.

The wider Significance of Place-Names

It will of course already be apparent that the interest of a place-name does not stop at its meaning and derivation: rather these provide the basic and essential starting point for the fuller appreciation of a place-name's significance in its wider linguistic, historical, archaeological, or geographical context. Although the scope of the present book does not allow this fuller exploration and appraisal of individual names, a few other points will be touched upon here in addition to those already mentioned, and readers are recommended to follow up such aspects as may interest them in the various studies listed in the Bibliography.

Older names of Celtic origin (supported by place-names containing such elements as Old English *walh* 'a Briton') testify to direct communication between the Celtic Britons and the English-speaking Anglo-Saxon invaders, and indeed indicate the survival of a British population in some districts. The vast majority of English place-names reflect the steady progress from east to west and the overwhelming success of the Anglo-Saxon invasions and settlements of the 5th century onwards, certain name-types being particularly associated with the early phases of immigration and colonization and others reflecting the gradual establishment of a new administrative and manorial system and the continued exploitation of the land for agriculture. Names of French origin and those containing manorial affixes are reminders of the Norman Conquest and its political consequences, including the imposition of the feudal system, whilst in the North and East the distribution and considerable number of Scandinavian place-names suggest the extent and relative density of the Viking settlements in those areas.

A small number of place-names have pagan associations, providing evidence for the worship of the heathen deities Woden, Thunor, and Tīw in early Anglo-Saxon England before the conversion of the English to Christianity in the 7th century. Names like Wednesfield, Thundersley, and Tysoe are among the names referring to these gods, and Wye and Harrow contain words for a heathen temple. On the other hand place-names with Christian associations are extremely common, many referring to churches and other holy places (such as Hawkchurch, Ormskirk, Kidderminster, Bridstow, and Armitage), some to crosses and holy springs (as in Crosby and Holywell), and others to ownership by priests or monks or other ecclesiastics (for example Preston, Monkton, Fryerning, and Abbotsbury).

Many English place-names provide information of archaeological interest. Some are named from their situation on a Roman road (Strafford, Streatham, Street), others containing the element *ceaster* refer to old fortifications, often Roman camps or towns (as with names like Chichester and Doncaster), and those from Old English *burh* can refer to 'fortified places' ranging from Iron Age hill-forts (as with Spettisbury or Salmonbury) to Anglo-Saxon strongholds or medieval manors of a much later date (like Kingsbury and Sudbury). Particularly common are names containing Old English *hlāw*, *hlæw*, or *beorg* or Old Scandinavian *haugr* referring to burial mounds or tumuli like Taplow, Lewes, Brokenborough, and Howe.

Many place-names illustrate the social structure and legal customs of early times. All ranks of society are represented, from kings and queens and others of noble birth to the humble peasant. Such names as Kingston, Quinton, Athelington, Aldermaston, Earlstone, Hexham, Knighton, Shrewton, Charlton or Carlton, and Swanscombe reflect the early divisions of the social hierarchy. Moreover some names like Faulkland, Buckland, Fifehead, Galmpton, and Manton indicate various aspects of land tenure in Anglo-Saxon times. Others indicate meeting places (Mottram, Skirmett), boundaries (Chilmark, Meerbrook), disputes (Threapwood), or leisure activities (Hesketh, Mondrum, Playford).

Many persons and families from many different periods of history are in a sense commemorated in the place-names of England. Some of these can of course be identified with particular men and women or families known from the historical record, but about the vast majority of them nothing more is known other than what the place-names themselves tell us. Some may have been important overlords or chieftains, many must have been thegns granted their estates by kings or bishops, others may have been farmers or relatively humble peasants. A significant minority of the people named are women (in names like Abberwick, Bibury, Kimberley, and Tolpuddle). These are probably unlikely to have been secular leaders, but a few seem to have been religious persons or founders of churches and the rest were no doubt the widows or daughters of thegns who had been granted estates at some time between the 7th century and the Norman Conquest.

After 1066, many of the Old English personal names for both men and women gradually fell into disuse, being largely replaced by Christian names introduced by the Normans. Because of these drastic changes in name-giving fashions, our knowledge of the personal nomenclature of the Old English period is incomplete, for it is quite clear that only a proportion of the numerous names in use during the six centuries after the Anglo-Saxon settlement have survived in the ordinary written records. Place-names provide good evidence for the existence of many personal names of both men and women that are otherwise unrecorded. Such personal names, inferred from comparative evidence and postulated to occur with varying degrees of certainty in place-names, are customarily asterisked (like the *Dæcca in Dagenham or the *Berica in Barking) to indicate that they are not found in independent use.

The way place-names reflect the face of the landscape, utilizing a rich and diverse vocabulary to describe every undulation and type of terrain, has already been mentioned. The natural history of this landscape is also abundantly represented, as is clear from the many different species of trees and plants, wild animals and birds, fish and even insects, that are evidenced among the elements. Moreover place-names reflect every aspect of human activity over a long period, from the utilization and development of the land by our forefathers for agricultural purposes, to their exploitation of the environment for communications, trade, and industry.

The numerous place-names containing woodland terms like *bearu*, *denn*, *grāf*, *holt*, *hyrst*, *sceaga*, *skógr*, *wald*, and *wudu* provide good evidence for the distribution, use, and management of woods and groves in early times, whilst those containing elements like *lēah* and *thveit* suggest the clearing of woodland for particular purposes. Names derived from elements like *æcer*, *feld*, *hæg*, *hamm*, *land*, and *mǣd* suggest different aspects of land-use in the subsistence agriculture of our ancestors, where arable land had to be broken in to produce crops, meadowland provided hay, and pastureland and enclosures were needed for animals. Place-names give information too about the kind or quality of the soil, the crops grown and harvested, the domestic creatures reared, and the goods produced.

The importance of river valleys for early settlement, providing fertile soils and a good water supply, is reflected in the number of places named from the rivers or streams on which they are situated. Many other place-names contain words like *strǣt* or *weg* referring to the roads or routes on which they stand, essential for communications and trade. The large group of names containing the elements *ford* and *brycg* show the vital part played by river-crossings, whilst those from words like *hȳth* and *port* suggest the early importance of trade and transport by water. Many elements indicate local industries and occupations, like milling (*myln*, *cweorn*), fishing (*wer*), salt-making (*salt*, *salt-ærn*), charcoal-burning and coal-mining (*col*), pot-making (*pott*, *crocc*), hunting (*hunta*), quarrying (*pytt*, *dylf*), timber production (*timber*, *bord*, *stæf*), bee-keeping (*hunig*), and many others.

The study of place-names has made important contributions to our knowledge of the original vocabulary of Old English as well as of the vocabulary of the early Celtic and Scandinavian languages. Dozens of words once used in living speech may never have found their way into literary or historical writings before they went out of use, but such words often occur in place-names formed in the early period. This archaic vocabulary (customarily asterisked to show that it is only evidenced in place-names and not otherwise recorded) includes words like **gē* 'district' (found in the names Eastry, Ely, and Surrey), **hǣs* 'brushwood' (in Hayes, Heysham), **ofer* 'flat-topped ridge' (in Bolsover, Wentnor), **pidele* 'fen, marshland' (in Piddle and Puddletown), **wincel* 'nook, corner' (in Winchcomb and Winchelsea), **styfic* 'tree-stump' (in Stiffkey and Stukeley), **ceacga* 'broom' (in Chagford, Chailey, and Chegworth), and many others. Moreover many words are evidenced much earlier in place-names than in the ordinary language. From their occurrence in early place-name spellings we know that words such as **cingel* 'shingle' (in Chingford), **windels* 'windlass' (in Windsor), **hulfere* 'holly' (in Ulverley), and **bula* 'bull' (in Bulmer), also asterisked to show that they are only recorded in independent use in Middle English or later, are likely to date back to the Old English period. Many other old words, once part of the living language but now lost from the general vocabulary, survive in fossilized form in place-names. Words such as Old English *bærnet* 'burnt place' (found in Barnet and Burnett), *eowestre* 'sheep-fold' (in Easter, Austerfield, and Osterley), *hearg* 'heathen temple' (in Harrow), and *cīeping* 'market' (in Chipping Norton and Chipping Sodbury), are among the hundreds of examples, many of them listed in the Glossary of common elements at the end of the book.

Besides imparting information about the different languages once spoken in various parts of England, place-names and their early spellings often reveal characteristics of medieval English dialects. Thus the place-names Weald and Wool incorporate the ancient West Saxon dialect forms of the words that have become *wold* and *well* in modern English and which in fact appear as the place-names Old or Wolds and Well or Wall respectively in the old Anglian dialect areas. Synonymous pairs of names like Chalvey and Calverley, Challacott and Caldicott, Cholwell and Cauldwell, Herne and Hurn, Hulton and Hilton, Sale and Zeal, Welford and Walford, and Wilton and Welton, also reflect old dialect characteristics fossilized into their contrasting forms.

It is of course the case that the current local pronunciation of some place-names (for instance Beaulieu, Bicester, Cholmondeley, Towcester) differs from what the modern spelling might lead us to expect. Although such matters are outside the scope of the present book, the historical and linguistic reasons for these disparities are often of some interest and are dealt with in the detailed county surveys, whilst the current pronunciations themselves can be found in the specialized pronouncing dictionaries. Indeed further information of any kind about any of the names included in this dictionary, as well as information about names not included for reasons of space, should be sought in the county surveys of the English Place-Name Society or in the other monographs and studies dealing with particular name-types and groups of names, a selection of which is listed in the Bibliography.

Abbreviations

The English Counties

Avon	
Beds.	Bedfordshire
Berks.	Berkshire
Bucks.	Buckinghamshire
Cambs.	Cambridgeshire
Ches.	Cheshire
Cleveland	
Cornwall	
Cumbria	
Derbys.	Derbyshire
Devon	
Dorset	
Durham	
E. Sussex	East Sussex
Essex	
Glos.	Gloucestershire
Gtr. Manch.	Greater Manchester
Hants.	Hampshire
Heref. & Worcs.	Herefordshire and Worcestershire
Herts.	Hertfordshire
Humber.	Humberside
I. of Wight	Isle of Wight
Kent	
Lancs.	Lancashire
Leics.	Leicestershire
Lincs.	Lincolnshire
Gtr. London	Greater London
Mersey.	Merseyside
Norfolk	
N. Yorks.	North Yorkshire
Northants.	Northamptonshire
Northum.	Northumbria
Notts.	Nottinghamshire
Oxon.	Oxfordshire
Shrops.	Shropshire
Somerset	
S. Yorks.	South Yorkshire
Staffs.	Staffordshire
Suffolk	
Surrey	
Tyne & Wear	
Warwicks.	Warwickshire
W. Mids.	West Midlands
W. Sussex	West Sussex
W. Yorks.	West Yorkshire
Wilts.	Wiltshire

Other Abbreviations

c.	*circa* ('approximately')
cent.	century
DB	Domesday Book (includes *Great Domesday*, *Little Domesday*, and *Exon Domesday*)
EPNS	English Place-Name Society
ME	Middle English (the English language c.1100–c.1500)
OCornish	Old Cornish
OE	Old English (the English language c.450–c.1100)
OFrench	Old French
OGerman	Old German
OIrish	Old Irish
OScand.	Old Scandinavian (the language of the Vikings, comprising Old Danish and Old Norse)
OWelsh	Old Welsh
pers. name	personal name
Scand.	Scandinavian
St	Saint

Counties before Local Government Reorganization

Counties after Local Government Reorganization

A

Abbas Combe Somerset, see COMBE.

Abberley Heref. & Worcs. *Edboldelege* 1086 (DB). 'Woodland clearing of a man called Ēadbeald'. OE pers. name + *lēah*.

Abberton Essex. *Edburgetuna* 1086 (DB). 'Farmstead or estate of a woman called Ēadburh'. OE pers. name + *tūn*.

Abberton Heref. & Worcs. *Eadbrihtincgtun* 972, *Edbretintune* 1086 (DB). 'Estate associated with a man called Ēadbeorht'. OE pers. name + *-ing-* + *tūn*.

Abberwick Northum. *Alburwic* 1170. 'Dwelling or (dairy) farm of a woman called Aluburh or Alhburh'. OE pers. name + *wīc*.

Abbess Roding Essex, see RODING.

Abbey Dore Heref. & Worcs., see DORE.

Abbey Hulton Staffs., see HULTON.

Abbeystead Lancs. *Abbey* 1323. '(Deserted) site of the abbey', with reference to the abbey of Wyresdale. ME *abbeye* + *stede*.

Abbey Town Cumbria. *Abbey Towne* 1649. 'Estate by the abbey', with reference to the former abbey of Holme Cultram.

Abbots as affix, see main name, e.g. for **Abbots Bickington** (Devon) see BICKINGTON.

Abbotsbury Dorset. *Abbedesburie* 946, *Abedesberie* 1086 (DB). 'Fortified house or manor of the abbot'. OE *abbod* + *burh* (dative *byrig*). With reference to early possession by the abbot of Glastonbury.

Abbotsham Devon. *Hama* 1086 (DB), *Abbudesham* 1238. OE *hamm* 'enclosure' with the later addition of *abbod* 'abbot' (referring to early possession by the abbot of Tavistock).

Abbotskerswell Devon. *Cærswylle* 956, *Carsuella* 1086 (DB), *Karswill Abbatis* 1285. 'Spring or stream where water-cress grows'. OE *cærse* + *wella*. Affix from early possession by the abbot of Horton.

Abbotsley Cambs. *Adboldesle* 12th cent. 'Woodland clearing of a man called Ealdbeald'. OE pers. name + *lēah*.

Abdon Shrops. *Abetune* 1086 (DB). 'Farmstead or estate of a man called Abba'. OE pers. name + *tūn*.

Aberford W. Yorks. *Ædburford* 1176. 'Ford of a woman called Ēadburh'. OE pers. name + *ford*.

Abingdon Oxon. *Abbandune* 968, *Ab(b)endone* 1086 (DB). 'Hill of a man called Æbba or of a woman called Æbbe'. OE pers. name (genitive *-n*) + *dūn*.

Abinger Surrey. *Abinceborne (sic)* 1086 (DB), *Abingewurd* 1191. 'Enclosure of the family or followers of a man called Abba', or 'enclosure at Abba's place'. OE pers. name + *-inga-* or *-ing* + *worth*.

Abington, 'estate associated with a man called Abba', OE pers. name + *-ing-* + *tūn*: **Abington, Great & Little** Cambs. *Abintone* 1086 (DB). **Abington Pigotts** Cambs. *Abintone* 1086 (DB), *Abington Pigots* 1635. Manorial affix from the *Pykot* family, here from the 15th cent.

Ab Kettleby Leics., see KETTLEBY.

Ablington Glos. *Eadbaldingtun* 855. 'Estate associated with a man called Ēadbeald'. OE pers. name + *-ing-* + *tūn*.

Ablington Wilts. *Alboldintone* 1086 (DB). 'Estate associated with a man called Ealdbeald'. OE pers. name + *-ing-* + *tūn*.

Abram Gtr. Manch. *Adburgham* late 12th cent. 'Homestead or enclosure of a woman called Ēadburh'. OE pers. name + *hām* or *hamm*.

Abridge Essex. *Affebrigg* 1203. 'Bridge of a man called Æffa'. OE pers. name + *brycg*.

Abthorpe Northants. *Abetrop* 1190. 'Outlying farmstead or hamlet of a man called Abba'. OE pers. name + OE *throp* or OScand. *thorp*.

Aby Lincs. *Abi* 1086 (DB). 'Farmstead or village on the stream'. OScand. *á* + *bý*.

Acaster Malbis & Selby N. Yorks. *Acastre* 1086 (DB), *Acaster Malebisse* 1252, *Acastre Seleby* 1285. 'Fortification on the river'. OE *ā* or OScand. *á* + OE *ceaster*. Manorial affixes from lands here held by the *Malbis* family and by Selby Abbey.

Accrington Lancs. *Akarinton* 12th cent. 'Farmstead or village where acorns are found or stored'. OE *æcern* + *tūn*.

Achurch Northants. *Asencircan* c.980, *Asechirce* 1086 (DB). 'Church of a man called *Asa or Ási'. OE or OScand. pers. name + OE *cirice*.

Acklam, '(place at) the oak woods or clearings', OE *āc* + *lēah* (in a dative plural form *lēagum*): **Acklam** Cleveland. *Aclum* 1086 (DB). **Acklam** N. Yorks. *Aclun* 1086 (DB).

Acklington Northum. *Eclinton* 1177. Probably 'estate associated with a man called Ēadlāc'. OE pers. name + *-ing-* + *tūn*.

Ackton W. Yorks. *Aitone* (*sic*) 1086 (DB), *Aicton* c. 1166. 'Oak-tree farmstead'. OScand. *eik* + OE *tūn*.

Ackworth, High & Low W. Yorks. *Aceuurde* 1086 (DB). 'Enclosure of a man called Acca'. OE pers. name + *worth*.

Acle Norfolk. *Acle* 1086 (DB). 'Oak wood or clearing'. OE *āc* + *lēah*.

Acol Kent. *Acholt* 1270. 'Oak wood'. OE *āc* + *holt*.

Acomb, '(place at) the oak-trees', OE *āc* in a dative plural form *ācum*: **Acomb** Northum. *Akum* 1268. **Acomb** N. Yorks. *Akum* 1222.

Aconbury Heref. & Worcs. *Akornebir* 1213. 'Old fort inhabited by squirrels'. OE *āc̄weorna* + *burh* (dative *byrig*).

Acre, Castle, South & West Norfolk. *Acre* 1086 (DB), *Castelacr* 1235, *Sutacra* 1242, *Westacre* 1203. 'Newly cultivated land'. OE *æcer*. Distinguishing affixes from OFrench *castel* (with reference to the Norman castle here), OE *sūth* and *west*.

Acton, a common name, usually 'farmstead or village by the oak-tree(s)', OE *āc* + *tūn*; examples include: **Acton** Gtr. London. *Acton* 1181. **Acton Beauchamp** Heref. & Worcs. *Aactune* 727. Manorial affix from the *Beauchamp* family, here from the 12th cent. **Acton Burnell & Pigott** Shrops. *Actune* 1086 (DB), *Akton Burnill* 1198, *Acton Picot* 1255. Manorial affixes from the *Burnell* and *Picot* families, here in the 12th cent. **Acton, Iron** Avon. *Actune* 1086 (DB), *Irenacton* 1248. Affix is OE *īren* 'iron', referring to old iron-workings here. **Acton Round** Shrops. *Achetune* 1086 (DB), *Acton la Runde* 1284. Affix is ME *round* 'round in shape' or from a family name. **Acton Scott** Shrops. *Actune* 1086 (DB), *Scottes Acton* 1289. Manorial affix from the *Scot* family, here in the 13th cent. **Acton Trussell** Staffs. *Actone* 1086 (DB), *Acton Trussel* 1481. Manorial affix from the *Trussell* family, here in the 14th cent.

However some Actons have a different origin: **Acton** Dorset. *Tacatone* 1086 (DB). Probably 'farmstead or village where young sheep are reared'. OE **tacca* + *tūn*. Initial *T-* was dropped in the 16th cent. due to confusion with the preposition *at*. **Acton** Suffolk. *Acantun* c.995, *Achetuna* 1086 (DB). 'Farmstead or village of a man called Ac(c)a'. OE pers. name + *tūn*. **Acton Turville** Avon. *Achetone* 1086 (DB), *Acton Torvile* 1284. Identical in origin with the previous name. Manorial affix from the *Turville* family, here from the 13th cent.

Adbaston Staffs. *Edboldestone* 1086 (DB). 'Farmstead or village of a man called Ēadbald'. OE pers. name + *tūn*.

Adber Dorset. *Eatan beares* 956, *Ateberie* 1086 (DB). 'Grove of a man called Ēata'. OE pers. name + *bearu*.

Adderbury, East & West Oxon. *Eadburggebyrig* c.950, *Edburgberie* 1086 (DB). 'Stronghold of a woman called Ēadburh'. OE pers. name + *burh* (dative *byrig*).

Adderley Shrops. *Eldredelei* 1086 (DB). 'Woodland clearing of a woman called Althrȳth. OE pers. name + *lēah*.

Adderstone Northum. *Edredeston* 1233. 'Farmstead or village of a man called Ēadrēd'. OE pers. name + *tūn*.

Addingham W. Yorks. *Haddincham* c.972, *Odingehem* 1086 (DB). Probably 'homestead associated with a man called Adda'. OE pers. name + *-ing-* + *hām*.

Addington, 'estate associated with a man called Eadda or Æddi', OE pers. name + *-ing-* + *tūn*: **Addington** Bucks. *Edintone* 1086 (DB). **Addington** Gtr. London. *Eddintone* 1086 (DB). **Addington** Kent. *Eddintune* 1086 (DB). **Addington, Great & Little** Northants. *Edintone* 1086 (DB).

Addiscombe Gtr. London. *Edescamp* 1229. 'Enclosed land of a man called Æddi'. OE pers. name + *camp*.

Addlestone Surrey. *Attelesdene* 1241. 'Valley of a man called *Ættel'. OE pers. name + *denu*.

Addlethorpe Lincs. *Arduluetorp* 1086 (DB). 'Outlying farmstead or hamlet of a man called Eardwulf'. OE pers. name + OScand. *thorp*.

Adeney Shrops. *Eduney* 1212. 'Island, or dry ground in marsh, of a woman called Ēadwynn'. OE pers. name + *ēg*.

Adisham Kent. *Adesham* 616, *Edesham* 1086 (DB). 'Homestead of a man called *Ēad or Æddi'. OE pers. name + *hām*.

Adlestrop Glos. *Titlestrop* (*sic*) 714, *Tedestrop* 1086 (DB). 'Outlying farmstead or hamlet of a man called *Tætel'. OE pers. name + *throp*. Initial *T-* disappeared from the 14th cent. due to confusion with the preposition *at*.

Adlingfleet Humber. *Adelingesfluet* 1086 (DB). 'Water-channel or stream of the prince or nobleman'. OE *ætheling* + *flēot*.

Adlington Lancs. *Edeluinton* c.1190. 'Estate associated with a man called Ēadwulf'. OE pers. name + *-ing-* + *tūn*.

Admaston Staffs. *Ædmundeston* 1176. 'Farmstead or village of a man called Ēadmund'. OE pers. name + *tūn*.

Admington Warwicks. *Edelmintone* 1086 (DB). 'Estate associated with a man called Æthelhelm'. OE pers. name + *-ing-* + *tūn*.

Adstock Bucks. *Edestoche* 1086 (DB). 'Outlying farmstead or hamlet of a man called Æddi or Eadda'. OE pers. name + *stoc*.

Adstone Northants. *Atenestone* 1086 (DB). 'Farmstead or village of a man called *Ættīn'. OE pers. name + *tūn*.

Adur W. Sussex, district name from the River Adur, a late back-formation from *Portus Adurni* 'Adurnos's harbour', said to be at the mouth of this river by the 17th cent. antiquarian poet Drayton.

Adwell Oxon. *Advelle* 1086 (DB). 'Spring or stream of a man called Ead(d)a'. OE pers. name + *wella*.

Adwick le Street, Adwick upon Dearne S. Yorks. *Adeuuic* 1086 (DB). 'Dwelling or (dairy) farm of a man called Adda'. OE pers. name + *wīc*. Distinguishing affixes from the situation of one Adwick on a Roman road (OE *strǣt*) and of the other on the River Dearne (see BOLTON UPON DEARNE).

Affpuddle Dorset. *Affapidele* 1086 (DB). 'Estate on the River Piddle of a man called Æffa'. OE pers. name + river-name (see PIDDLEHINTON).

Agglethorpe N. Yorks. *Aculestorp* 1086 (DB). 'Outlying farmstead or hamlet of a man called Ācwulf'. OE pers. name + OScand. *thorp*.

Aikton Cumbria. *Aictun* c.1200. 'Oak-tree farmstead'. OScand. *eik* + OE *tūn*.

Ailsworth Cambs. *Ægeleswurth* 948, *Eglesworde* 1086 (DB). 'Enclosure of a man called *Ægel'. OE pers. name + *worth*.

Ainderby Steeple N. Yorks. *Eindrebi* 1086 (DB), *Aynderby wyth Stepil* 1316. 'Farmstead or village of a man called Eindrithi'. OScand. pers. name + *bý*. Affix is OE *stēpel* 'church steeple, tower'.

Ainsdale Mersey. *Einuluesdel* 1086 (DB). 'Valley of a man called *Einulfr'. OScand. pers. name + *dalr*.

Ainstable Cumbria. *Ainstapillith* c.1210. 'Slope where bracken grows'. OScand. *einstapi* + *hlíth*.

Ainsworth Gtr. Manch. *Haineswrthe*

c.1200. 'Enclosure of a man called *Ægen'. OE pers. name + *worth*.

Aintree Mersey. *Ayntre* 1220. 'Solitary tree'. OScand. *einn* + *tré*.

Airmyn Humber. *Ermenie* 1086 (DB). 'Mouth of the River Aire'. River-name + OScand. *mynni*. The river-name Aire is possibly from OScand. *eyjar* 'islands', but may be of Celtic or pre-Celtic origin with a meaning 'strongly flowing'.

Airton N. Yorks. *Airtone* 1086 (DB). 'Farmstead on the River Aire'. Old river-name (see AIRMYN) + *tūn*.

Aisby, 'farmstead or village of a man called Ási', OScand. pers. name + *bý*: **Aisby** Lincs., near Blyton. *Asebi* 1086 (DB). **Aisby** Lincs., near Sleaford. *Asebi* 1086 (DB).

Aisholt, Lower Somerset. *Æscholt* 854. 'Ash-tree wood'. OE *æsc* + *holt*.

Aiskew N. Yorks. *Echescol* (*sic*) 1086 (DB), *Aykescogh* 1235. 'Oak wood'. OScand. *eik* + *skógr*.

Aislaby N. Yorks., near Pickering. *Aslache(s)bi* 1086 (DB). 'Farmstead or village of a man called Áslákr'. OScand. pers. name + *bý*.

Aislaby N. Yorks., near Whitby. *Asulue(s)bi* 1086 (DB). 'Farmstead or village of a man called Ásulfr'. OScand. pers. name + *bý*.

Aisthorpe Lincs. *Estorp* 1086 (DB). 'East outlying farmstead or hamlet'. OE *ēast* + OScand. *thorp*.

Akeld Northum. *Achelda* 1169. 'Oak-tree slope'. OE *āc* + *helde*.

Akeley Bucks. *Achelei* 1086 (DB). 'Oak wood or clearing'. OE *ācen* + *lēah*.

Akeman Street (Roman road from Bath to St Albans). *Accemannestrete* 12th cent. 'Roman road associated with a man called *Acemann', from OE pers. name + *strǣt* (an early alternative name for BATH was *Acemannes ceastre* 10th cent., named after the same man with OE *ceaster* 'Roman town or city').

Akenham Suffolk. *Acheham* 1086 (DB). 'Homestead of a man called Aca'. OE pers. name + *hām*.

Alberbury Shrops. *Alberberie* 1086 (DB). 'Stronghold or manor of a woman called Aluburh or Alhburh'. OE pers. name + *burh* (dative *byrig*).

Albourne W. Sussex. *Aleburn* 1177. 'Stream where alders grow'. OE *alor* + *burna*.

Albrighton Shrops., near Shifnal. *Albricstone* 1086 (DB). 'Farmstead or village of a man called Æthelbeorht'. OE pers. name + *tūn*.

Albrighton Shrops., near Shrewsbury. *Etbritone* 1086 (DB). 'Farmstead or village of a man called Ēadbeorht'. OE pers. name + *tūn*.

Alburgh Norfolk. *Aldeberga* 1086 (DB). 'Old mound or hill', or 'mound or hill of a man called Alda'. OE (*e*)*ald* or OE pers. name + *beorg*.

Albury, 'old or disused stronghold', OE (*e*)*ald* + *burh* (dative *byrig*): **Albury** Herts. *Eldeberie* 1086 (DB). **Albury** Surrey. *Ealdeburi* 1062, *Eldeberie* 1086 (DB).

Alby Hill Norfolk. *Alebei* 1086 (DB). 'Farmstead or village of a man called Áli'. OScand. pers. name + *bý*.

Alcaston Shrops. *Ælmundestune* 1086 (DB). 'Farmstead or village of a man called Ealhmund'. OE pers. name + *tūn*.

Alcester Warwicks. *Alencestre* 1138. 'Roman town on the River Alne'. Celtic river-name (see ALNE) + OE *ceaster*.

Alciston E. Sussex. *Alsistone* 1086 (DB). 'Farmstead or village of a man called Ælfsige or Ealhsige'. OE pers. name + *tūn*.

Alconbury Cambs. *Acumesberie* (*sic*) 1086 (DB), *Alcmundesberia* 12th cent. 'Stronghold of a man called Ealhmund'. OE pers. name + *burh* (dative *byrig*).

Aldborough, 'old or disused stronghold', OE (*e*)*ald* + *burh*: **Aldborough** Norfolk. *Aldeburg* 1086 (DB). **Aldborough** N. Yorks. *Burg* 1086 (DB), *Aldeburg* 1145. Here referring to a Roman fort.

Aldbourne Wilts. *Ealdincburnan* *c*.970, *Aldeborne* 1086 (DB). 'Stream associated with a man called Ealda'. OE pers. name + *-ing-* + *burna*.

Aldbrough, 'old or disused stronghold', OE (*e*)*ald* + *burh*: **Aldbrough**

Humber. *Aldenburg* 1086 (DB). **Aldbrough** N. Yorks. *Aldeburne* (*sic*) 1086 (DB), *Aldeburg* 1247.

Aldbury Herts. *Aldeberie* 1086 (DB). 'Old or disused stronghold'. OE (*e*)*ald* + *burh* (dative *byrig*).

Aldeburgh Suffolk. *Aldeburc* 1086 (DB). 'Old or disused stronghold'. OE (*e*)*ald* + *burh*.

Aldeby Norfolk. *Aldebury* 1086 (DB), *Aldeby* c.1180. 'Old or disused stronghold'. OE (*e*)*ald* + *burh* (dative *byrig*) replaced by OScand. *bý* 'farmstead'.

Aldenham Herts. *Ældenham* 785, *Eldeham* 1086 (DB). 'Old homestead', or 'homestead of a man called Ealda'. OE (*e*)*ald* or OE pers. name + *hām*.

Alderbury Wilts. *Æthelware byrig* 972, *Alwarberie* 1086 (DB). 'Stronghold of a woman called *Æthelwaru'. OE pers. name + *burh* (dative *byrig*).

Alderford Norfolk. *Alraforda* 1163. 'Ford where alders grow'. OE *alor* + *ford*.

Alderholt Dorset. *Alreholt* 1285. 'Alder wood'. OE *alor* + *holt*.

Alderley Glos. *Alrelie* 1086 (DB). 'Woodland clearing where alders grow'. OE *alor* + *lēah*.

Alderley Edge Ches. *Aldredelie* 1086 (DB). 'Woodland clearing of a woman called Althrȳth'. OE pers. name + *lēah*.

Aldermaston Berks. *Ældremanestone* 1086 (DB). 'Farmstead of the chief or nobleman'. OE (*e*)*aldormann* + *tūn*.

Alderminster Warwicks. *Aldermanneston* 1167. Identical in origin with the previous name.

Aldershot Hants. *Halreshet* 1171. 'Projecting piece of land where alders grow'. OE *alor* + *scēat*.

Alderton, usually 'estate associated with a man called Ealdhere', OE pers. name + *-ing-* + *tūn*: **Alderton** Glos. *Aldritone* 1086 (DB). **Alderton** Northants. *Aldritone* 1086 (DB). **Alderton** Wilts. *Aldrintone* 1086 (DB). However two Aldertons have a different origin, 'farmstead where alders grow', OE *alor* + *tūn*: **Alderton** Shrops. *Olreton* 1309. **Alderton** Suffolk. *Alretuna* 1086 (DB).

Alderwasley Derbys. *Alrewaseleg* 1251. 'Clearing by the alluvial land where alders grow'. OE *alor* + **wæsse* + *lēah*.

Aldfield N. Yorks. *Aldefeld* 1086 (DB). 'Old (i.e. long used) stretch of open country'. OE *ald* + *feld*.

Aldford Ches. *Aldefordia* 1153. 'The old (i.e. formerly used) ford'. OE *ald* + *ford*.

Aldham, 'the old homestead', or 'homestead of a man called Ealda', OE *eald* or OE pers. name + *hām*: **Aldham** Essex. *Aldeham* 1086 (DB). **Aldham** Suffolk. *Aldeham* 1086 (DB).

Aldingbourne W. Sussex. *Ealdingburnan* c.880, *Aldingeborne* 1086 (DB). 'Stream associated with a man called Ealda'. OE pers. name + *-ing-* + *burna*.

Aldingham Cumbria. *Aldingham* 1086 (DB). Probably 'homestead of the family or followers of a man called Alda'. OE pers. name + *-inga-* + *hām*.

Aldington, 'estate associated with a man called Ealda', OE pers. name + *-ing-* + *tūn*: **Aldington** Heref. & Worcs. *Aldintona* 709, *Aldintone* 1086 (DB). **Aldington** Kent. *Aldintone* 1086 (DB).

Aldreth Cambs. *Alrehetha* 1170. 'Landing-place by the alders'. OE *alor* + *hȳth*.

Aldridge W. Midlands. *Alrewic* 1086 (DB). 'Dwelling or farm among alders'. OE *alor* + *wīc*.

Aldringham Suffolk. *Alrincham* 1086 (DB). 'Homestead of the family or followers of a man called Aldhere'. OE pers. name + *-inga-* + *hām*.

Aldsworth Glos. *Ealdeswyrthe* 1004, *Aldeswrde* 1086 (DB). 'Enclosure of a man called *Ald'. OE pers. name + *worth*.

Aldwark, 'old fortification', OE (*e*)*ald* + *weorc*: **Aldwark** Derbys. *Aldwerk* 1140. **Aldwark** N. Yorks. *Aldeuuerc* 1086 (DB).

Aldwick W. Sussex. *Aldewyc* 1235. 'Old dwelling', or 'dwelling of a man called

Ealda'. OE *eald* or OE pers. name + *wīc*.

Aldwincle Northants. *Eldewincle* 1086 (DB). 'River-bend of a man called Ealda'. OE pers. name + **wincel*.

Aldworth Berks. *Elleorde* (*sic*) 1086 (DB), *Aldewurda* 1167. 'Old enclosure', or 'enclosure of a man called Ealda'. OE *eald* or OE pers. name + *worth*.

Alfington Devon. *Alfinton* 1244. 'Estate associated with a man called Ælf'. OE pers. name + *-ing-* + *tūn*.

Alfold Surrey. *Alfold* 1227. 'Old fold or enclosure'. OE *eald* + *fald*.

Alford Lincs. *Alforde* 1086 (DB). Probably 'ford where eels are found'. OE *ǣl* + *ford*.

Alford Somerset. *Aldedeford* 1086 (DB). 'Ford of a woman called Ealdgȳth'. OE pers. name + *ford*.

Alfreton Derbys. *Elstretune* (*sic*) 1086 (DB), *Alferton* 12th cent. 'Farmstead or village of a man called Ælfhere'. OE pers. name + *tūn*.

Alfrick Heref. & Worcs. *Alcredeswike* early 13th cent. 'Dwelling or farm of a man called Ealhrǣd'. OE pers. name + *wīc*.

Alfriston E. Sussex. *Alvricestone* 1086 (DB). 'Farmstead or village of a man called Ælfrīc'. OE pers. name + *tūn*.

Alhampton Somerset. *Alentona* 1086 (DB). 'Estate on the River Alham'. Celtic river-name (of uncertain meaning) + OE *tūn*.

Alkborough Humber. *Alchebarge* 1086 (DB), *Alchebarua* 12th cent. Probably 'wood or grove of a man called Alca'. OE pers. name + *bearu*.

Alkerton Oxon. *Alcrintone* 1086 (DB). 'Estate associated with a man called Ealhhere'. OE pers. name + *-ing-* + *tūn*.

Alkham Kent. *Ealhham* c.1100. 'Homestead in a sheltered place, or by a heathen temple'. OE *ealh* + *hām*.

Alkington Shrops. *Alchetune* 1086 (DB), *Alkinton* 1256. 'Estate associated with a man called Alca'. OE pers. name + *-ing-* + *tūn*.

Alkmonton Derbys. *Alchementune* 1086 (DB). 'Farmstead or village of a man called Ealhmund'. OE pers. name + *tūn*.

All Cannings Wilts., see CANNINGS.

Allendale Town Northum. *Alewenton* 1245. 'Settlement by (in the valley of) the River Allen'. Celtic or pre-Celtic river-name (of uncertain meaning) + OE *tūn*, with the later insertion of OScand. *dalr* 'valley'.

Allenheads Northum. '(place by) the source of the River Allen'. Celtic or pre-Celtic river-name + OE *hēafod*.

Allensmore Heref. & Worcs. *More* 1086 (DB), *Aleinesmor* 1220. 'Marshy ground of a man called Ala(i)n'. OFrench pers. name + OE *mōr*.

Aller Somerset. *Alre* late 9th cent., 1086 (DB). '(Place at) the alder-tree'. OE *alor*.

Allerby Cumbria. *Aylwardcrosseby* 1260, *Aylewardby* c.1275. 'Farmstead (with crosses) of a man called Ailward (Æthelweard)'. OE pers. name + OScand. *bý* (earlier *krossa-bý*).

Allerford Somerset, near Minehead. *Alresford* 1086 (DB). 'Alder-tree ford'. OE *alor* + *ford*.

Allerston N. Yorks. *Alurestan* 1086 (DB). 'Boundary stone of a man called Ælfhere'. OE pers. name + *stān*.

Allerthorpe Humber. *Aluuarestorp* 1086 (DB). 'Outlying farmstead or hamlet of a man called Ælfweard or *Alfvarthr'. OE or OScand. pers. name + OScand. *thorp*.

Allerton, usually 'farmstead or village where alder-trees grow', OE *alor* + *tūn*: **Allerton** Mersey. *Alretune* 1086 (DB). **Allerton** W. Yorks. *Alretune* 1086 (DB). **Allerton Bywater** W. Yorks. *Alretune* 1086 (DB), *Allerton by ye water* 1430. Affix 'by the water' (OE *wæter*) refers to its situation on the River Aire. **Allerton, Chapel** W. Yorks. *Alretun* 1086 (DB), *Chapel Allerton* 1360. Affix is ME *chapele* 'a chapel'.

However some Allertons have a different origin: **Allerton, Chapel** Somerset. *Alwarditone* 1086 (DB). 'Farmstead of a man called Ælfweard'. OE pers. name + *tūn*. Affix as in previous name. **Allerton Mauleverer** N. Yorks. *Aluertone* 1086 (DB), *Aluerton Mauleuerer* 1231. 'Farmstead of a man called Ælfhere'. OE pers. name + *tūn*.

Manorial affix from the *Mauleverer* family, here from the 12th cent.

Allesley W. Mids. *Alleslega* 1176. 'Woodland clearing of a man called Ælle'. OE pers. name + *lēah*.

Allestree Derbys. *Adelardestre* 1086 (DB). 'Tree of a man called Æthelheard'. OE pers. name + *trēow*.

Allexton Leics. *Adelachestone* 1086 (DB). 'Farmstead or village of a man called *Æthellāc'. OE pers. name + *tūn*.

Allhallows Kent. *Ho All Hallows* 1285. Named from the 12th cent. church of All Saints here. For *Ho* in the early form, see HOO.

Allington, a common name, has a number of different origins: **Allington** Lincs. *Adelingetone* 1086 (DB). 'Farmstead of the princes'. OE *ætheling* + *tūn*. **Allington** Wilts., near Amesbury. *Aldintona* 1178. 'Farmstead associated with a man called Ealda'. OE pers. name + *-ing-* + *tūn*. **Allington** Wilts., near Devizes. *Adelingtone* 1086 (DB). 'Farmstead of the princes'. OE *ætheling* + *tūn*. **Allington, East** Devon. *Alintone* 1086 (DB). 'Farmstead associated with a man called Ælla or Ælle'. OE pers. name + *-ing-* + *tūn*.

Allithwaite Cumbria. *Hailiuethait* c.1170. 'Clearing of a man called Eilífr'. OScand. pers. name + *thveit*.

Allonby Cumbria. *Alayneby* 1262. 'Farmstead or village of a man called Alein'. OFrench pers. name + OScand. *bý*.

All Stretton Shrops., see STRETTON.

Allweston Dorset. *Alfeston* 1214. 'Farmstead or village of a woman called Ælfflæd or Ælfgifu'. OE pers. name + *tūn*.

Almeley Heref. & Worcs. *Elmelie* 1086 (DB). 'Elm wood or clearing'. OE *elm* + *lēah*.

Almer Dorset. *Elmere* 943. 'Eel pool'. OE *ǣl* + *mere*.

Almington Staffs. *Almentone* 1086 (DB). 'Farmstead or village of a man called Alhmund'. OE pers. name + *tūn*.

Almondbury W. Yorks. *Almaneberie* 1086 (DB). 'Stronghold of the whole community'. OScand. **almenn* (genitive plural *almanna*) + OE *burh* (dative *byrig*).

Almondsbury Avon. *Almodesberie* 1086 (DB). 'Stronghold of a man called Æthelmōd or Æthelmund'. OE pers. name + *burh* (dative *byrig*).

Alne N. Yorks. *Alna* c.1050, *Alne* 1086 (DB). A Celtic name of uncertain meaning.

Alne, Great & Little Warwicks. *Alne* 1086 (DB). Named from the River Alne, a Celtic river-name possibly meaning 'very white'.

Alnham Northum. *Alneham* 1228. 'Homestead on the River Aln'. Celtic river-name (earlier *Alaunos*, of uncertain meaning) + OE *hām*.

Alnmouth Northum. *Alnemuth* 1201. 'Mouth of the River Aln'. Celtic river-name (see ALNHAM) + OE *mūtha*.

Alnwick Northum. *Alnewich* 1178. 'Dwelling or farm on the River Aln'. Celtic river-name (see ALNHAM) + OE *wīc*.

Alperton Gtr. London. *Alprinton* 1199. 'Estate associated with a man called Ealhbeorht'. OE pers. name + *-ing-* + *tūn*.

Alphamstone Essex. *Alfelmestuna* 1086 (DB). 'Farmstead or village of a man called Ælfhelm'. OE pers. name + *tūn*.

Alpheton Suffolk. *Alflede(s)ton* 1204. 'Farmstead or village of a woman called Ælfflæd or Æthelflæd'. OE pers. name + *tūn*.

Alphington Devon. *Alfintune* c.1060, *Alfintone* 1086 (DB). 'Estate associated with a man called Ælf'. OE pers. name + *-ing-* + *tūn*.

Alport Derbys. *Aldeport* 12th cent. 'Old town'. OE *(e)ald* + *port*.

Alpraham Ches. *Alburgham* 1086 (DB). 'Homestead of a woman called Alhburh'. OE pers. name + *hām*.

Alresford Essex. *Ælesford* c.1000, *Eilesforda* 1086 (DB). 'Ford of a man called *Ægel'. OE pers. name + *ford*.

Alresford, New & Old Hants. *Alresforda* 701, *Alresforde* 1086 (DB). 'Alder-tree ford'. OE *alor* + *ford*.

Alrewas Staffs. *Alrewasse* 942, *Alrewas* 1086 (DB). 'Alluvial land where alders grow'. OE *alor* + **wæsse*.

Alsager Ches. *Eleacier* (*sic*) 1086 (DB), *Allesacher* 13th cent. 'Cultivated land of a man called Ælle'. OE pers. name + *æcer*.

Alsop en le Dale Derbys. *Elleshope* 1086 (DB), *Alsope in le dale* 1535. 'Valley of a man called Ælle'. OE pers. name + *hop*. Later affix means 'in the valley'.

Alston Cumbria. *Aldeneby* 1164–71, *Aldeneston* 1209. 'Farmstead or village of a man called Halfdan'. OScand. pers. name + OE *tūn* (earlier OScand. *bý*).

Alstone Glos. *Ælfsigestun* 969. 'Farmstead or village of a man called Ælfsige'. OE pers. name + *tūn*.

Alstonefield Staffs. *Ænestanefelt* (*sic*) 1086 (DB), *Alfstanesfeld* 1179. 'Open country of a man called Ælfstān'. OE pers. name + *feld*.

Altarnun Cornwall. *Altrenune* c.1100. 'Altar of St Nonn'. Cornish *alter* 'altar of a church' + female saint's name.

Altcar, Great (Lancs.) **& Little** (Mersey). *Acrer* (*sic*) 1086 (DB), *Altekar* 1251. 'Marsh by the River Alt'. Celtic river-name (meaning 'muddy river') + OScand. *kjarr*.

Altham Lancs. *Elvetham* c.1150. 'Enclosure or river-meadow where there are swans'. OE *elfitu* + *hamm*.

Althorne Essex. *Aledhorn* 1198. '(Place at) the burnt thorn-tree'. OE *ǣled* + *thorn*.

Althorpe Humber. *Aletorp* 1086 (DB). 'Outlying farmstead or hamlet of a man called Áli or Alli'. OScand. pers. name + *thorp*.

Altofts W. Yorks. *Altoftes* c.1090. Probably 'the old homesteads'. OE *ald* + OScand. *toft*.

Alton, usually 'farmstead at the source of a river', OE *ǣwiell* + *tūn*: **Alton** Hants. *Aultone* 1086 (DB). **Alton Pancras** Dorset. *Awultune* 1012, *Altone* 1086 (DB), *Aweltone Pancratii* 1226. Affix from the dedication of the church to St Pancras. **Alton Priors** Wilts. *Aweltun* 825, *Auuiltone* 1086 (DB), *Aulton Prioris* 1199. Affix from its early possession by the Priory of St Swithin at Winchester.
However other Altons have a different origin: **Alton** Derbys. *Alton* 1296. 'Old farmstead'. OE *ald* + *tūn*.

Alton Staffs. *Elvetone* 1086 (DB). 'Farmstead of a man called *Ælfa'. OE pers. name + *tūn*.

Altrincham Gtr. Manch. *Aldringeham* 1290. 'Homestead of the family or followers of a man called Aldhere', or 'homestead at the place associated with Aldhere'. OE pers. name + *-inga-* or *-ing* + *hām*.

Alvanley Ches. *Elveldelie* 1086 (DB). 'Woodland clearing of a man called Ælfweald'. OE pers. name + *lēah*.

Alvaston Derbys. *Alewaldestune* c.1002, *Alewoldestune* 1086 (DB). 'Farmstead or village of a man called Æthelwald or Ælfwald'. OE pers. name + *tūn*.

Alvechurch Heref. & Worcs. *Ælfgythe cyrcan* 10th cent., *Alvievecherche* 1086 (DB). 'Church of a woman called Ælfgȳth'. OE pers. name + *cirice*.

Alvecote Warwicks. *Avecote* c.1160. 'Cottage(s) of a man called Afa'. OE pers. name + *cot*.

Alvediston Wilts. *Alfwieteston* 1165. Probably 'farmstead or village of a man called Ælfgeat'. OE pers. name + *tūn*.

Alveley Shrops. *Alvidelege* 1086 (DB). 'Woodland clearing of a woman called Ælfgȳth'. OE pers. name + *lēah*.

Alverdiscott Devon. *Alveredescota* 1086 (DB). 'Cottage of a man called Ælfrēd'. OE pers. name + *cot*.

Alverstoke Hants. *Stoce* 948, *Alwarestoch* 1086 (DB). 'Outlying farmstead or hamlet of a woman called Ælfwaru or *Æthelwaru'. OE pers. name + *stoc*.

Alverstone I. of Wight. *Alvrestone* 1086 (DB). 'Farmstead or village of a man called Ælfrēd'. OE pers. name + *tūn*.

Alverton Notts. *Aluriton* 1086 (DB). 'Estate associated with a man called Ælfhere'. OE pers. name + *-ing-* + *tūn*.

Alvescot Oxon. *Elfegescote* 1086 (DB). 'Cottage of a man called Ælfhēah'. OE pers. name + *cot*.

Alveston Avon. *Alwestan* 1086 (DB). 'Boundary stone of a man called Ælfwīg'. OE pers. name + *stān*.

Alveston Warwicks. *Eanulfestun* 966, *Alvestone* 1086 (DB). 'Farmstead or village of a man called Ēanwulf'. OE pers. name + *tūn*.

Alvingham Lincs. *Aluingeham* 1086 (DB). 'Homestead of the family or followers of a man called Ælf'. OE pers. name + *-inga-* + *hām*.

Alvington Glos. *Eluinton* 1220. Probably identical in origin with the next name.

Alvington, West Devon. *Alvintone* 1086 (DB). 'Estate associated with a man called Ælf'. OE pers. name + *-ing-* + *tūn*.

Alwalton Cambs. *Æthelwoldingtun* 955, *Alwoltune* 1086 (DB). 'Estate associated with a man called Æthelwald'. OE pers. name + *-ing-* + *tūn*.

Alwinton Northum. *Alwenton* 1242. 'Farmstead or village on the River Alwin'. Celtic or pre-Celtic river-name (of uncertain meaning) + OE *tūn*.

Ambergate Derbys., a recent name, first recorded in 1836, referring to a toll-gate near the River Amber (a pre-Celtic river-name of uncertain meaning) which also gives name to the district of **Amber Valley**.

Amberley, probably 'woodland clearing frequented by a bird such as the bunting or yellow-hammer', OE *amore* + *lēah*: **Amberley** Glos. *Unberleia* 1166. **Amberley** W. Sussex. *Amberle* 957, *Ambrelie* 1086 (DB).

Ambersham, South W. Sussex. *Æmbresham* 963. 'Homestead or river-bend land of a man called *Æmbre'. OE pers. name + *hām* or *hamm*.

Amble Northum. *Ambell* 1204, *Anebell* 1256. Probably 'promontory of a man called *Amma or Anna'. OE pers. name + *bile*.

Amblecote W. Mids. *Elmelecote* 1086 (DB). Probably 'cottage of a man called *Æmela'. OE pers. name + *cot*.

Ambleside Cumbria. *Ameleseta c.*1095. 'Shieling or summer pasture by the river sandbank'. OScand. *á* + *melr* + *sǽtr*.

Ambrosden Oxon. *Ameresdone* 1086 (DB). 'Hill of a man called *Ambre'. OE pers. name + *dūn*.

Amcotts Humber. *Amecotes* 1086 (DB). 'Cottages of a man called *Amma'. OE pers. name + *cot*.

Amersham Bucks. *Agmodesham* 1066, *Elmodesham* 1086 (DB). 'Homestead or village of a man called Ealhmund'. OE pers. name + *hām*.

Amesbury Wilts. *Ambresbyrig c.*880, *Ambresberie* 1086 (DB). 'Stronghold of a man called *Ambre'. OE pers. name + *burh* (dative *byrig*).

Amington Staffs. *Ermendone* (*sic*) 1086 (DB), *Aminton* 1150. Probably 'estate associated with a man called *Earma'. OE pers. name + *-ing-* + *tūn*.

Amotherby N. Yorks. *Aimundrebi* 1086 (DB). 'Farmstead or village of a man called Eymundr'. OScand. pers. name + *bý*.

Ampleforth N. Yorks. *Ampreforde* 1086 (DB). 'Ford where dock or sorrel grows'. OE *ampre* + *ford*.

Ampney Crucis, St Mary & St Peter, Down Ampney Glos. *Omenie* 1086 (DB), *Ameneye Sancte Crucis* 1287, *Ammeneye Beate Marie* 1291, *Amenel Sancti Petri c.*1275, *Dunamenell* 1205. Named from Ampney Brook, 'stream of a man called *Amma', OE pers. name (genitive *-n*) + *ēa*. Distinguishing affixes from the dedication of the churches to the Holy Rood (Latin *crucis* 'of the cross'), St Mary and St Peter, and from OE *dūne* 'lower downstream'.

Amport Hants. *Anna de Port c.*1270. 'Estate on the River *Ann* held by a family called *de Port*'. Celtic river-name (meaning 'ash-tree stream') + manorial affix (from its Domesday owner), see ANDOVER.

Ampthill Beds. *Ammetelle* 1086 (DB). 'Ant-hill, hill infested with ants'. OE *ǣmette* + *hyll*.

Ampton Suffolk. *Hametuna* 1086 (DB). 'Farmstead or village of a man called *Amma'. OE pers. name + *tūn*.

Amwell, Great & Little Herts. *Emmewelle* 1086 (DB). 'Spring or stream of a man called *Æmma'. OE pers. name + *wella*.

Ancaster Lincs. *Anecastre* 12th cent. Probably 'Roman fort or town associated with a man called Anna'. OE pers. name + *cæster*.

Ancroft Northum. *Anecroft* 1195.

'Lonely or isolated enclosure'. OE *āna* + *croft*.

Anderby Lincs. *Andreby c.*1135. Possibly 'farmstead or village of a man called Arnthórr'. OScand. pers. name + *bý*. Alternatively the first element may be OScand. *andri* 'snow-shoe' perhaps in the sense 'billet of wood'.

Anderton Ches. *Anderton* 1184. 'Farmstead or village of a man called Ēanrēd or Eindrithi'. OE or OScand. pers. name + *tūn*.

Andover Hants. *Andeferas* 955, *Andovere* 1086 (DB). '(Place by) the ash-tree waters'. Celtic river-name *Ann* (an earlier name for the River Anton and Pillhill Brook) with the Celtic word also found in DOVER.

Andoversford Glos. *Onnan ford* 759. 'Ford of a man called Anna'. OE pers. name + *ford*.

Angersleigh Somerset. *Lega* 1086 (DB), *Aungerlegh* 1354. OE *lēah* 'woodland clearing' with manorial addition from the *Aunger* family, here in the 13th cent.

Angmering W. Sussex. *Angemæringum c.*880, *Angemare* 1086 (DB). '(Settlement of) the family or followers of a man called *Angenmǣr'. OE pers. name + *-ingas* (dative *-ingum*).

Angram, '(place at) the pastures or grasslands', OE **anger* in a dative plural form **ang(e)rum*: **Angram** N. Yorks., near Keld. *Angram* late 12th cent. **Angram** N. Yorks., near York. *Angrum* 13th cent.

Anlaby Humber. *Unlouebi* (*sic*) 1086 (DB), *Anlauebi* 1203. 'Farmstead or village of a man called Óláfr'. OScand. pers. name + *bý*.

Anmer Norfolk. *Anemere* (*sic*) 1086 (DB), *Anedemere* 1291. 'Duck pool'. OE *æned* + *mere*.

Ann, Abbots Hants. *Anne* 901, 1086 (DB), *Anne Abbatis c.*1270. 'Estate on the River *Ann* belonging to the abbot'. Celtic river-name (meaning 'ash-tree stream') with manorial affix referring to early possession by Hyde Abbey at Winchester.

Anna Valley Hants., a recent name, coined from the old river-name *Ann* as in previous name, see ANDOVER.

Annesley Woodhouse Notts. *Aneslei* 1086 (DB), *Annesley Wodehouse* 13th cent. 'Woodland clearing of a man called *Ān'. OE pers. name + *lēah*, with the later addition denoting 'woodland hamlet'.

Ansley Warwicks. *Hanslei* 1086 (DB), *Anesteleye* 1235. Probably 'woodland clearing with a hermitage'. OE *ānsetl* + *lēah*.

Anslow Staffs. *Ansedlega c.*1180. Identical in origin with the previous name.

Anstey, Ansty, a name found in various counties, from OE *ānstiga* 'narrow or lonely track', or 'track linking other routes'; examples include: **Anstey** Leics. *Anstige* 1086 (DB). **Anstey, East & West** Devon. *Anesti(n)ga* 1086 (DB). **Ansty** Warwicks. *Anestie* 1086 (DB). **Ansty** Wilts. *Anestige* 1086 (DB). **Ansty Cross, Higher Ansty** Dorset. *Anesty* 1219.

Anston, North & South S. Yorks. *Anestan, Litelanstan* 1086 (DB), *Northanstan, Suthanstan* 1297. 'The single or solitary stone'. OE *āna* + *stān*.

Anthorn Cumbria. *Eynthorn* 1279. 'Solitary thorn-tree'. OScand. *einn* + *thorn*.

Antingham Norfolk. *Antingham* 1044–7, 1086 (DB). 'Homestead of the family or followers of a man called *Anta'. OE pers. name + *-inga-* + *hām*.

Antony Cornwall. *Antone* 1086 (DB). 'Farmstead of a man called Anna or *Anta'. OE pers. name + *tūn*.

Anwick Lincs. *Amuinc* (*sic*) 1086 (DB), *Amewic* 1218. 'Dwelling or farm of a man called *Amma'. OE pers. name + *wīc*.

Apethorpe Northants. *Patorp* (*sic*) 1086 (DB), *Apetorp* 1162. 'Outlying farmstead or hamlet of a man called Api'. OScand. pers. name + *thorp*.

Apley Lincs. *Apeleia* 1086 (DB). 'Apple wood'. OE *æppel* + *lēah*.

Apperknowle Derbys. *Apelknol* 1317. 'Apple-tree hillock'. OE *æppel* + *cnoll*.

Apperley Glos. *Apperleg* 1210. 'Wood or clearing where apple-trees grow'. OE *apuldor* + *lēah*.

Appleby, 'farmstead or village where apple-trees grow', OE *æppel* (perhaps replacing OScand. *epli*) + OScand. *bý*: **Appleby** Cumbria. *Aplebi* 1130. **Appleby** Humber. *Aplebi* 1086 (DB). **Appleby Magna & Parva** Leics. *Æppelby* 1002, *Aplebi* 1086 (DB). Distinguishing affixes are Latin *magna* 'great' and *parva* 'little'.

Appledore, '(place at) the apple-tree', OE *apuldor*: **Appledore** Devon. *le Apildore* 1335. **Appledore** Kent. *Apuldre* 10th cent., *Apeldres* 1086 (DB).

Appleford Oxon. *Æppelford c.*895, *Apleford* 1086 (DB). 'Ford where apple-trees grow'. OE *æppel* + *ford*.

Appleshaw Hants. *Appelsag* 1200. 'Small wood where apple-trees grow'. OE *æppel* + *sceaga*.

Appleton, 'farmstead where apples grow, apple orchard', OE *æppel-tūn*; examples include: **Appleton** Ches. *Epletune* 1086 (DB). **Appleton** Oxon. *Æppeltune* 942, *Apletune* 1086 (DB). **Appleton, East** N. Yorks. *Apelton* 1086 (DB). **Appleton-le-Moors** N. Yorks. *Apeltun* 1086 (DB). Affix means 'near the moors'. **Appleton-le-Street** N. Yorks. *Apletun* 1086 (DB). Affix means 'on the main road'. **Appleton Roebuck** N. Yorks. *Æppeltune c.*972, *Apleton* 1086 (DB), *Appleton Roebucke* 1664. Manorial affix from the *Rabuk* family, here in the 14th cent. **Appleton Wiske** N. Yorks. *Apeltona* 1086 (DB). Affix refers to its situation on the River Wiske (from OE *wisc* 'marshy meadow').

Appletreewick N. Yorks. *Apletrewic* 1086 (DB). 'Dwelling or farm by the apple-trees'. OE *æppel-trēow* + *wīc*.

Appley Bridge Lancs. *Appelleie* 13th cent. 'Apple-tree wood or clearing'. OE *æppel* + *lēah*.

Apsley End Beds. *Aspele* 1230. 'Aspen-tree wood'. OE *æspe* + *lēah*.

Apuldram W. Sussex. *Apeldreham* 12th cent. 'Homestead or enclosure where apple-trees grow'. OE *apuldor* + *hām* or *hamm*.

Arborfield Berks. *Edburgefeld c.*1190, *Erburgefeld* 1222. Probably 'open land of a woman called Hereburh'. OE pers. name + *feld*.

Ardeley Herts. *Eardeleage* 939, *Erdelei* 1086 (DB). 'Woodland clearing of a man called *Earda'. OE pers. name + *lēah*.

Arden (old forest) Warwicks., see HENLEY-IN-ARDEN.

Ardingly W. Sussex. *Erdingelega* early 12th cent. 'Woodland clearing of the family or followers of a man called *Earda'. OE pers. name + *-inga-* + *lēah*.

Ardington Oxon. *Ardintone* 1086 (DB). Probably 'estate associated with a man called *Earda'. OE pers. name + *-ing-* + *tūn*.

Ardleigh Essex. *Erleiam* (*sic*) 1086 (DB), *Ardlega* 12th cent. Probably 'woodland clearing with a dwelling place'. OE *eard* + *lēah*.

Ardley Oxon. *Eardulfes lea* 995, *Ardulveslie* 1086 (DB). 'Woodland clearing of a man called Eardwulf'. OE pers. name + *lēah*.

Ardsley S. Yorks. *Erdeslaia* 12th cent. 'Woodland clearing of a man called Eorēd or Ēanrēd'. OE pers. name + *lēah*.

Ardsley East W. Yorks. *Erdeslawe* 1086 (DB). 'Mound of a man called Eorēd or Ēanrēd'. OE pers. name + *hlāw*.

Areley Kings Heref. & Worcs. *Erneleia c.*1138, *Kyngges Arley* 1405. 'Wood or clearing frequented by eagles'. OE *earn* + *lēah*. Affix *Kings* because it was part of a royal manor.

Arkendale N. Yorks. *Arghendene* 1086 (DB). Probably 'valley of a man called *Eorcna or *Eorcon'. OE pers. name + *denu* (replaced from the 14th cent. by OScand. *dalr*).

Arkesden Essex. *Archesdana* 1086 (DB). Possibly 'valley of a man called Arnkel'. OScand. pers. name + OE *denu*.

Arkholme Lancs. *Ergune* 1086 (DB). '(Place at) the shielings or hill-pastures'. OScand. *erg* in a dative plural form *ergum*.

Arksey S. Yorks. *Archeseia* 1086 (DB). 'Island, or dry ground in marsh, of a man called Arnkel'. OScand. pers. name + OE *ēg*.

Arlecdon Cumbria. *Arlauchdene c.*1130. 'Valley of the stream frequented by eagles'. OE *earn* + *lacu* + *denu*.

Arlesey Beds. *Alricheseia* 1062, 1086 (DB). 'Island or well-watered land of a man called Ælfrīc'. OE pers. name + *ēg*.

Arleston Shrops. *Erdelveston* 1180. 'Farmstead or village of a man called Eardwulf'. OE pers. name + *tūn*.

Arley, usually 'wood or clearing frequented by eagles', OE *earn* + *lēah*: **Arley** Warwicks. *Earnlege* 1001, *Arlei* 1086 (DB). **Arley, Upper** Heref. & Worcs. *Earnleie* 996, *Ernlege* 1086 (DB).
However the following may have a different origin: **Arley** Ches. *Arlegh* 1340. Possibly 'grey wood', or 'wood on a boundary'. OE *hār* + *lēah*.

Arlingham Glos. *Erlingeham* 1086 (DB). 'Homestead or enclosure of the family or followers of a man called *Eorl(a)'. OE pers. name + *-inga-* + *hām* or *hamm*.

Arlington Devon. *Alferdintona* 1086 (DB). 'Estate associated with a man called Ælffrith'. OE pers. name + *-ing-* + *tūn*.

Arlington E. Sussex. *Erlington* 1086 (DB). 'Estate associated with a man called *Eorl(a)'. OE pers. name + *-ing-* + *tūn*.

Arlington Glos. *Ælfredincgtune* 1004, *Alvredintone* 1086 (DB). 'Estate associated with a man called Ælfrēd'. OE pers. name + *-ing-* + *tūn*.

Armathwaite Cumbria. *Ermitethwait* 1212. 'Clearing of the hermit'. ME *ermite* + OScand. *thveit*.

Arminghall Norfolk. *Hameringahala* 1086 (DB). Possibly 'nook of land of the family or followers of a man called *Ambre or Ēanmǣr'. OE pers. name + *-inga-* + *halh*.

Armitage Staffs. *Armytage* 1520. '(Place at) the hermitage'. ME *ermitage*.

Armscote Warwicks. *Eadmundescote* 1042. 'Cottage(s) of a man called Ēadmund'. OE pers. name + *cot*.

Armthorpe S. Yorks. *Ernulfestorp* 1086 (DB). 'Outlying farmstead or hamlet of a man called Earnwulf or Arnulfr'. OE or OScand. pers. name + OScand. *thorp*.

Arncott, Upper & Lower Oxon. *Earnigcote* 983, *Ernicote* 1086 (DB). 'Cottage(s) associated with a man called *Earn'. OE pers. name + *-ing-* + *cot*.

Arne Dorset. *Arne* 1268. Probably OE *ærn* 'house or building'. Alternatively '(place at) the heaps of stones or tumuli', from OE **hær* in a dative plural form **harum*.

Arnesby Leics. *Erendesbi* 1086 (DB). 'Farmstead or village of a man called Iarund or *Erendi'. OScand. pers. name + *bý*.

Arnold, 'nook of land frequented by eagles', OE *earn* + *halh*: **Arnold** Humber. *Ærnhale* 1190. **Arnold** Notts. *Ernehale* 1086 (DB).

Arnside Cumbria. *Harnolvesheuet* 1184–90. 'Hill or headland of a man called Earnwulf or Arnulfr'. OE or OScand. pers. name + OE *hēafod*.

Arram Humber. *Argun* 1086 (DB). '(Place at) the shielings or hill-pastures'. OScand. *erg* in a dative plural form *ergum*.

Arrathorne N. Yorks. *Ergthorn* 13th cent. 'Thorn-tree by the shieling or hill-pasture'. OScand. *erg* + *thorn*.

Arreton I. of Wight. *Eaderingtune* c.880, *Adrintone* 1086 (DB). 'Estate associated with a man called Ēadhere'. OE pers. name + *-ing-* + *tūn*.

Arrington Cambs. *Earnningtone* c.950, *Erningtune* 1086 (DB). Probably 'farmstead of the family or followers of a man called *Earn(a)'. OE pers. name + *-inga-* + *tūn*.

Arrow (river) Heref. & Worcs., see STAUNTON ON ARROW.

Arrow Warwicks. *Arne (sic)* 710, *Arue* 1086 (DB). Named from the River Arrow, a Celtic or pre-Celtic river-name meaning simply 'stream'.

Arthington W. Yorks. *Hardinctone* 1086 (DB). 'Estate associated with a man called *Earda'. OE pers. name + *-ing-* + *tūn*.

Arthingworth Northants. *Arningvorde* 1086 (DB). 'Enclosure associated with a man called *Earn(a)'. OE pers. name + *-ing-* + *worth*.

Arundel W. Sussex. *Harundel* 1086 (DB). 'Valley where the plant horehound grows'. OE *hārhūne* + *dell*. The river-name Arun is a 'back-formation' from the place-name.

Asby, 'farmstead or village where ash-trees grow', OScand. *askr* + *bý*: **Asby** Cumbria, near Arlecdon. *Asbie* 1654. **Asby, Great & Little** Cumbria. *Aschaby* c.1160.

Ascot, Ascott, 'eastern cottage(s)', OE *ēast* + *cot*: **Ascot** Berks. *Estcota* 1177. **Ascott under Wychwood** Oxon. *Estcot* 1220. Affix means 'near the forest of Wychwood' (an OE name, *Huiccewudu* 840, meaning 'wood of a tribe called the *Hwicce*').

Asenby N. Yorks. *Æstanesbi* 1086 (DB). 'Farmstead or village of a man called Eysteinn'. OScand. pers. name + *bý*.

Asfordby Leics. *Osferdebie* 1086 (DB). 'Farmstead or village of a man called Ásfrøthr or Ásfrithr'. OScand. pers. name + *bý*.

Asgarby, 'farmstead or village of a man called Ásgeirr', OScand. pers. name + *bý*: **Asgarby** Lincs., near Sleaford. *Asegarby* 1201. **Asgarby** Lincs., near Spilsby. *Asgerebi* 1086 (DB).

Ash, '(place at) the ash-tree(s)', OE *æsc*; examples include: **Ash** Kent, near Sandwich. *Ece* 1086 (DB). **Ash** Surrey. *Essa* 1170. **Ash Magna** Shrops. *Magna Asche* 1285. Affix is Latin *magna* 'great'. **Ash Priors** Somerset. *Æsce* 1065, *Esse Prior* 1263. Affix from its early possession by the Prior of Taunton.

Ashampstead Berks. *Essamestede* 1155–8. 'Homestead by the ash-tree(s)'. OE *æsc* + *hām-stede*.

Ashbocking Suffolk. *Assa* 1086 (DB), *Bokkynge Assh* 1411. '(Place at) the ash-tree(s)'. OE *æsc* + manorial affix from the *de Bocking* family, here in the 14th cent.

Ashbourne Derbys. *Esseburne* 1086 (DB). 'Stream where ash-trees grow'. OE *æsc* + *burna*.

Ashbrittle Somerset. *Aisse* 1086 (DB), *Esse Britel* 1212. '(Place at) the ash-tree(s)'. OE *æsc* + manorial affix from its possession by a man called *Bretel* in 1086.

Ashburton Devon. *Essebretone* 1086 (DB). 'Farmstead or village by the stream where ash-trees grow'. OE *æsc* + *burna* + *tūn*.

Ashbury, 'stronghold where ash-trees grow', OE *æsc* + *burh* (dative *byrig*): **Ashbury** Devon. *Esseberie* 1086 (DB). **Ashbury** Oxon. *Eissesberie (sic)* 1086 (DB), *Æsseberia* 1187.

Ashby, a common name in the North and Midlands, usually 'farmstead or village where ash-trees grow', OE *æsc* or OScand. *askr* + OScand. *bý*; however 'farmstead of a man called Aski', OScand. pers. name + *bý*, is a possible alternative for some names; examples include: **Ashby** Humber. *Aschebi* 1086 (DB). **Ashby by Partney** Lincs. *Aschebi* 1086 (DB). See PARTNEY. **Ashby, Canons** Northants. *Ascebi* 1086 (DB), *Essheby Canons* 13th cent. Affix from the priory here, founded in the 12th cent. **Ashby, Castle** Northants. *Asebi* 1086 (DB), *Castel Assheby* 1361. Affix from the former castle here. **Ashby, Cold** Northants. *Essebi* 1086 (DB), *Caldessebi* c.1150. Affix is OE *cald* 'cold, exposed'. **Ashby cum Fenby** Humber. *Aschebi* 1086 (DB). Fenby is 'farmstead near a fen or marsh', OE *fenn* + *bý*; Latin *cum* is 'with'. **Ashby de la Launde** Lincs. *Aschebi* 1086 (DB). Manorial affix from the *de la Launde* family, here in the 14th cent. **Ashby de la Zouch** Leics. *Ascebi* 1086 (DB), *Esseby la Zusche* 1241. Manorial affix from the *de la Zuche* family, here in the 13th cent. **Ashby Folville** Leics. *Ascbi* 1086 (DB). Manorial affix from the *de Foleuilla* family, here in the 12th cent. **Ashby Magna & Parva** Leics. *Essebi* 1086 (DB). Affixes are Latin *magna* 'great', *parva* 'little'. **Ashby, Mears** Northants. *Asbi* 1086 (DB), *Esseby Mares* 1281. Manorial affix from the *de Mares* family, here in the 13th cent. **Ashby Puerorum** Lincs. *Aschebi* 1086 (DB). Latin affix means 'of the boys', in allusion to a bequest for the support of the choir-boys of Lincoln Cathedral. **Ashby St Ledgers** Northants. *Ascebi* 1086 (DB), *Esseby Sancti Leodegarii* c.1230. Affix from the dedication of the church to St Leger. **Ashby St Mary** Norfolk. *Ascebei* 1086 (DB). Affix from the dedication of the church. **Ashby, West** Lincs. *Aschebi* 1086 (DB).

Ashcombe Devon. *Aissecome* 1086 (DB). 'Valley where ash-trees grow'. OE *æsc* + *cumb*.

Ashdon Essex. *Æstchendune* c.1036, *Ascenduna* 1086 (DB). 'Hill overgrown with ash-trees'. OE *æscen* + *dūn*.

Ashdown Forest Sussex. *Essendon* 1207. Identical in origin with the previous name.

Asheldham Essex. *Assildeham* c.1130. 'Homestead of a woman called *Æschild'. OE pers. name + *hām*.

Ashen Essex. *Asce* 1086 (DB), *Asshen* 1344. '(Place at) the ash-trees'. OE *æsc* in a dative plural form *æscum*.

Ashendon Bucks. *Assedune* 1086 (DB). 'Hill overgrown with ash-trees'. OE *æscen* + *dūn*.

Ashfield, 'open land where ash-trees grow', OE *æsc* + *feld*: **Ashfield** Notts. *Esfeld* 1216. An old name now revived as a district name. **Ashfield** Suffolk. *Assefelda* 1086 (DB). **Ashfield, Great** Suffolk. *Eascefelda* 1086 (DB).

Ashford, usually 'ford where ash-trees grow', OE *æsc* + *ford*: **Ashford** Derbys. *Æscforda* 926, *Aisseford* 1086 (DB). **Ashford** Devon. *Aiseforda* 1086 (DB). **Ashford Bowdler & Carbonel** Shrops. *Esseford* 1086 (DB), *Asford Budlers, Aysford Carbonel* 1255. Manorial affixes from the *de Boulers* and *Carbunel* families, here at an early date.

However two Ashfords have a different origin: **Ashford** Kent. *Essetesford* 1086 (DB). 'Ford by a clump of ash-trees'. OE **æscet* + *ford*. **Ashford** Surrey. *Ecelesford* 969, *Exeforde* 1086 (DB). Possibly 'ford of a man called *Eccel', from OE pers. name + *ford*, or the first element may be an old river-name **Ecel*.

Ashill Norfolk. *Asscelea* 1086 (DB). 'Ash-tree wood'. OE *æsc* + *lēah*.

Ashill Somerset. *Aisselle* 1086 (DB). 'Hill where ash-trees grow'. OE *æsc* + *hyll*.

Ashingdon Essex. *Assandun* 1016, *Nesenduna* (*sic*) 1086 (DB). 'Hill of the ass, or of a man called *Assa'. OE *assa* or OE pers. name (genitive *-n*) + *dūn*.

Ashington Northum. *Essenden* 1205. 'Valley where ash-trees grow'. OE *æscen* + *denu*.

Ashington W. Sussex. *Essingetona* 1073. 'Farmstead of the family or followers of a man called Æsc'. OE pers. name + *-inga-* + *tūn*.

Ashleworth Glos. *Escelesuuorde* 1086 (DB). 'Enclosure of a man called *Æscel'. OE pers. name + *worth*.

Ashley, a common name, 'ash-tree wood or clearing', OE *æsc* + *lēah*; examples include: **Ashley** Cambs. *Esselie* 1086 (DB). **Ashley** Ches. *Ascelie* 1086 (DB). **Ashley** Devon. *Esshelegh* 1238. **Ashley** Dorset. *Asseleghe* 1246. **Ashley** Hants., near Lymington. *Esselie* 1086 (DB). **Ashley** Hants., near Winchester. *Asselegh* 1275. **Ashley** Northants. *Ascele* 1086 (DB). **Ashley** Staffs. *Esselie* 1086 (DB). **Ashley Green** Bucks. *Essleie* 1227, *Assheley grene* 1468.

Ashling, East & West W. Sussex. *Estlinges* 1185. Probably '(settlement of) the family or followers of a man called *Æscla'. OE pers. name + *-ingas*.

Ashmansworth Hants. *Æscmæreswierthe* 909. 'Enclosure by the ash-tree pool'. OE *æsc* + *mere* + *worth*.

Ashmore Dorset. *Aisemare* 1086 (DB). 'Pool where ash-trees grow'. OE *æsc* + *mere*.

Ashorne Warwicks. *Hassorne* 1196. 'Horn-shaped hill where ash-trees grow'. OE *æsc* + *horn*.

Ashover Derbys. *Essovre* 1086 (DB). 'Ridge or slope where ash-trees grow'. OE *æsc* + **ofer*.

Ashow Warwicks. *Asceshot* (*sic*) 1086 (DB), *Essesho* 12th cent. 'Hill spur of the ash-tree or of a man called *Æsc'. OE *æsc* or OE pers. name + *hōh*.

Ashperton Heref. & Worcs. *Spertune* (*sic*) 1086 (DB), *Aspretonia* 1144. Probably 'farmstead or village of a man called Æscbeorht or Æscbeorn'. OE pers. name + *tūn*.

Ashprington Devon. *Aisbertone* 1086 (DB). 'Estate associated with a man called Æscbeorht or Æscbeorn'. OE pers. name + *-ing-* + *tūn*.

Ashreigney Devon. *Aissa* 1086 (DB), *Esshereingni* 1238. '(Place at) the ash-tree(s)'. OE *æsc* + manorial affix from the *de Regny* family, here in the 13th cent.

Ashtead Surrey. *Stede* 1086 (DB), *Estede*

c.1150. 'Place where ash-trees grow'. OE *æsc* + *stede*.

Ashton, a common name, usually 'farmstead where ash-trees grow', OE *æsc* + *tūn*; examples include: **Ashton** Ches. *Estone* 1086 (DB). **Ashton** Heref. & Worcs. *Estune* 1086 (DB). **Ashton** Northants., near Oundle. *Ascetone* 1086 (DB). **Ashton-in-Makerfield** Gtr. Manch. *Eston* 1212. Affix is an old district name (*Macrefeld* 1121), from a Celtic word meaning 'wall, ruin' + OE *feld* 'open land'. **Ashton Keynes** Wilts. *Æsctun* 880–5, *Essitone* 1086 (DB), *Aysheton Keynes* 1572. Manorial affix from the *de Keynes* family, here from the 13th cent. **Ashton, Long** Avon. *Estune* 1086 (DB), *Longe Asshton* 1467. Affix from the length of the village. **Ashton, Steeple & West** Wilts. *Æystone* 964, *Aistone* 1086 (DB), *Westaston* 1248, *Stepelaston* 1268. Distinguishing affixes from OE *stīepel* 'church steeple' and *west*. **Ashton under Hill** Heref. & Worcs. *Æsctun* 991, *Essetone* 1086 (DB), *Assheton Underhill* 1544. Affix 'under the hill' refers to BREDON Hill. **Ashton-under-Lyne** Gtr. Manch. *Haistune c*.1160, *Asshton under Lyme* 1305. Affix is from an old Celtic district name *Lyme*, probably meaning 'elm-tree region'. **Ashton upon Mersey** Gtr. Manch. *Asshton* 1408. On the River Mersey, 'boundary river' from OE *mǣre* (genitive *-s*) + *ēa*.

However some Ashtons have a different origin: **Ashton** Northants., near Northampton. *Asce* 1086 (DB), *Asshen* 1296. '(Place at) the ash-trees'. OE *æsc* in a dative plural form *æscum*. **Ashton, Higher & Lower** Devon. *Aiserstone* 1086 (DB). 'Farmstead of a man called Æschere'. OE pers. name + *tūn*.

Ashurst, 'wooded hill growing with ash-trees', OE *æsc* + *hyrst*: **Ashurst** Kent. *Aeischerste c*.1100. **Ashurst** W. Sussex. *Essehurst* 1164.

Ashurstwood W. Sussex. *Foresta de Esseherst* 1164. Identical in origin with the previous names.

Ashwater Devon. *Aissa* 1086 (DB), *Esse Valteri* 1270. '(Place at) the ash-tree(s)'. OE *æsc* + manorial affix from its possession by a man called *Walter* in the 13th cent.

Ashwell, 'spring or stream where ash-trees grow', OE *æsc* + *wella*: **Ashwell** Herts. *Asceuuelle* 1086 (DB). **Ashwell** Leics. *Exewelle* 1086 (DB).

Ashwellthorpe Norfolk. *Aescewelle, Thorp c*.1066. 'Hamlet belonging to a place called *Ashwell* ('ash-tree spring or stream')'. OE *æsc* + *wella* + OScand. *thorp*.

Ashwick Somerset. *Escewiche* 1086 (DB). 'Dwelling or farmstead where ash-trees grow'. OE *æsc* + *wīc*.

Ashwicken Norfolk. *Wiche* 1086 (DB), *Askiwiken* 1275. '(Place at) the dwellings or buildings'. OE *wīc* in a dative plural form *wīcum* or a ME plural form *wiken*. Later addition may be OE *æsc* 'ash-tree' or a pers. name.

Askam in Furness Cumbria. *Askeham* 1535. Possibly '(place at) the ash-trees'. OScand. *askr* in a dative plural form *askum*. For the affix, see BARROW IN FURNESS.

Askern S. Yorks. *Askern c*.1170. 'House near the ash-tree'. OScand. *askr* + OE *ærn*.

Askerswell Dorset. *Oscherwille* 1086 (DB). 'Spring or stream of a man called Ōsgār'. OE pers. name + *wella*.

Askham, 'homestead or enclosure where ash-trees grow', OE *æsc* (replaced by OScand. *askr*) + OE *hām* or *hamm*: **Askham** Notts. *Ascam* 1086 (DB). **Askham Bryan & Richard** N. Yorks. *Ascham* 1086 (DB), *Ascam Bryan* 1285, *Askham Ricardi* 1291. Manorial additions from early possession by men called *Brian* and *Richard*.

Askrigg N. Yorks. *Ascric* 1086 (DB). Probably 'ash-tree ridge'. OScand. *askr* + OE **ric*.

Askwith N. Yorks. *Ascvid* 1086 (DB). 'Ash-tree wood'. OScand. *askr* + *vithr*.

Aslackby Lincs. *Aslachebi* 1086 (DB). 'Farmstead or village of a man called Áslákr'. OScand. pers. name + *bý*.

Aslacton Norfolk. *Aslactuna* 1086 (DB). 'Farmstead or village of a man called Áslákr'. OScand. pers. name + OE *tūn*.

Aslockton Notts. *Aslachetune* 1086 (DB). Identical in origin with the previous name.

Aspatria Cumbria. *Aspatric c.*1160. 'Ash-tree of St Patrick'. OScand. *askr* + Celtic pers. name. The order of elements is Celtic.

Aspenden Herts. *Absesdene* 1086 (DB). 'Valley where aspen-trees grow'. OE *æspe* + *denu*.

Aspley Guise Beds. *Æpslea* 969, *Aspeleia* 1086 (DB), *Aspeleye Gyse* 1363. 'Aspen-tree wood or glade'. OE *æspe* + *lēah*, with manorial affix from the *de Gyse* family, here in the 13th cent.

Aspull Gtr. Manch. *Aspul* 1212. 'Hill where aspen-trees grow'. OE *æspe* + *hyll*.

Asselby Humber. *Aschilebi* 1086 (DB). 'Farmstead or village of a man called Áskell'. OScand. pers. name + *bý*.

Assendon, Lower & Middle Oxon. *Assundene* late 10th cent. 'Valley of the ass, or of a man called *Assa'. OE *assa* or OE pers. name + *denu*.

Assington Suffolk. *Asetona* 1086 (DB), *Assintona* 1175. 'Estate associated with a man called *As(s)a'. OE pers. name + *-ing-* + *tūn*.

Astbury Ches. *Astbury* 1093. 'East manor or stronghold'. OE *ēast* + *burh* (dative *byrig*).

Astcote Northants. *Aviescote* 1086 (DB). 'Cottage(s) of a man called Æfic'. OE pers. name + *cot*.

Asterley Shrops. *Asterlegh* 1316. 'More easterly woodland clearing'. OE *ēasterra* + *lēah*.

Asterton Shrops. *Esthampton* 1255. 'Eastern home farm'. OE *ēast* + *hām-tūn*.

Asthall Oxon. *Esthale* 1086 (DB). 'East nook(s) of land'. OE *ēast* + *h(e)alh*.

Asthall Leigh Oxon. *Estallingeleye* 1272. 'Woodland clearing of the people of Asthall'. ASTHALL + OE *-inga-* + *lēah*.

Astley, 'east wood or clearing', OE *ēast* + *lēah*: **Astley** Heref. & Worcs. *Eslei* 1086 (DB). **Astley** Shrops. *Hesleie* 1086 (DB). **Astley** Warwicks. *Estleia* 1086 (DB). **Astley Abbots** Shrops. *Hestlee c.*1150, *Astleye Abbatis* 1327. Affix alludes to early possession by Shrewsbury Abbey. **Astley Green** Gtr. Manch. *Asteleghe c.*1210.

Aston, a common name, usually 'eastern farmstead or estate', OE *ēast* + *tūn*; examples include: **Aston** W. Mids. *Estone* 1086 (DB). **Aston Blank** or **Cold Aston** Glos. *Eastunæ* 716–43, *Estone* 1086 (DB). Affix may be OFrench *blanc* 'white, bare'. **Aston Cantlow** Warwicks. *Estone* 1086 (DB), *Aston Cantelou* 1273. Manorial affix from the *de Cantilupe* family, here in the 13th cent. **Aston Clinton** Bucks. *Estone* 1086 (DB), *Aston Clinton* 1237–40. Manorial affix from the *de Clinton* family, here in the late 12th cent. **Aston Fields** Heref. & Worcs. *Eastun* 767, *Estone* 1086 (DB), *Aston Fields* 1649. **Aston Ingham** Heref. & Worcs. *Estune* 1086 (DB), *Estun Ingan* 1242. Manorial affix from the *Ingan* family, here in the 13th cent. **Aston, Steeple** Oxon. *Estone* 1086 (DB), *Stipelestun* 1220. Affix is OE *stīepel* 'church steeple'. **Aston upon Trent** Derbys. *Estune* 1086 (DB). For the river-name, see TRENTHAM. **Aston, White Ladies** Heref. & Worcs. *Eastune* 977, *Estun* 1086 (DB), *Whitladyaston* 1481. Affix from its possession by the Cistercian nuns of Whitstones.

However the following has a different origin: **Aston on Clun** Shrops. *Assheston* 1291. 'Ash-tree farmstead'. OE *æsc* + *tūn*. For the river-name, see CLUN.

Astrop Northants. *Estrop* 1200. 'East hamlet'. OE *ēast* + *throp*.

Astwood, 'east wood', OE *ēast* + *wudu*: **Astwood** Bucks. *Estwode* 1151–4. **Astwood** Heref. & Worcs. *Estwode* 1182.

Aswarby Lincs. *Asuuardebi* 1086 (DB). 'Farmstead or village of a man called Ásvarthr'. OScand. pers. name + *bý*.

Aswardby Lincs. *Asewrdeby c.*1155. Identical in origin with the previous name.

Atcham Shrops. *Atingeham* 1086 (DB). 'Homestead of the family or followers of a man called Ætti or Ēata', or 'homestead at the place associated with Ætti or Ēata'. OE pers. name + *-inga-* or *-ing* + *hām*. Alternatively the final element may be *hamm* 'land in a river-bend'.

Atch Lench Heref. & Worcs., see LENCH.

Athelhampton Dorset. *Pidele* 1086 (DB), *Pidele Athelamston* 1285. Originally named from the River Piddle on which it stands (see PIDDLEHINTON), later 'farmstead of a man called Æthelhelm', OE pers. name + *tūn*.

Athelington Suffolk. *Alinggeton* 1219. 'Farmstead or village of the princes'. OE *ætheling* + *tūn*.

Athelney Somerset. *Æthelingaeigge* 878, *Adelingi* 1086 (DB). 'Island, or dry ground in marsh, of the princes'. OE *ætheling* + *ēg*.

Atherfield, Little I. of Wight. *Aderingefelda* 959, *Avrefel* 1086 (DB). 'Open land of the family or followers of a man called Ēadhere or Æthelhere'. OE pers. name + *-inga-* + *feld*.

Atherington Devon. *Hadrintone* 1272. 'Estate associated with a man called Ēadhere or Æthelhere'. OE pers. name + *-ing-* + *tūn*.

Atherstone Warwicks. *Aderestone* 1086 (DB), *Atheredestone* 1221. 'Farmstead or village of a man called Æthelrēd'. OE pers. name + *tūn*.

Atherstone on Stour Warwicks. *Eadrichestone* 710, *Edricestone* 1086 (DB). 'Farmstead or village of a man called Ēadrīc'. OE pers. name + *tūn*. Affix from its situation on the River Stour, a Celtic or OE river-name probably meaning 'the strong one'.

Atherton Gtr. Manch. *Aderton* 1212. 'Farmstead or village of a man called Æthelhere'. OE pers. name + *tūn*.

Atlow Derbys. *Etelawe* 1086 (DB). 'Burial-mound of a man called Eatta'. OE pers. name + *hlāw*.

Attenborough Notts. *Adinburcha* 12th cent. 'Stronghold associated with a man called Adda or Æddi'. OE pers. name + *-ing-* + *burh*.

Attleborough Norfolk. *Atleburc* 1086 (DB). 'Stronghold of a man called Ætla'. OE pers. name + *burh*.

Attleborough Warwicks. *Atteleberga* 12th cent. 'Hill or mound of a man called Ætla'. OE pers. name + *beorg*.

Attlebridge Norfolk. *Atlebruge* 1086 (DB). 'Bridge of a man called Ætla'. OE pers. name + *brycg*.

Atwick Humber. *Attingwik* 12th cent. 'Dwelling or dairy-farm of a man called Atta'. OE pers. name + *-ing-* + *wīc*.

Atworth Wilts. *Attenwrthe* 1001. 'Enclosure of a man called Atta'. OE pers. name + *worth*.

Aubourn Lincs. *Aburne* 1086 (DB), *Alburn* 1275. 'Stream where alder-trees grow'. OE *alor* + *burna*.

Auckland, Bishop & West Durham. *Alclit c.*1040. Probably a Celtic name meaning 'rock or hill on a river called *Clyde* ("the cleansing one")'. *Clyde* was probably the original name of the River Gaunless (from OScand. **gagnlauss* 'unprofitable one'). Later distinguishing affix from possession by the Bishop of Durham.

Auckley S. Yorks. *Alchelie* 1086 (DB). 'Woodland clearing of a man called Alca or *Alha'. OE pers. name + *lēah*.

Audenshaw Gtr. Manch. *Aldwynshawe c.*1200. 'Copse of a man called Aldwine'. OE pers. name + *sceaga*.

Audlem Ches. *Aldelime* 1086 (DB). 'Old *Lyme*', or 'the part of *Lyme* belonging to a man called Alda'. OE *ald* or OE pers. name + old Celtic district name *Lyme* probably meaning 'elm-tree region'.

Audley Staffs. *Aldidelege* 1086 (DB). 'Woodland clearing of a woman called Aldgȳth'. OE pers. name + *lēah*.

Aughton, 'farmstead where oak-trees grow', OE *āc* + *tūn*: **Aughton** Humber. *Actun* 1086 (DB). **Aughton** Lancs., near Lancaster. *Acheton* 1212. **Aughton** Lancs., near Ormskirk. *Achetun* 1086 (DB). **Aughton** S. Yorks. *Actone* 1086 (DB).

Ault Hucknall Derbys., see HUCKNALL.

Aunsby Lincs. *Ounesbi* 1086 (DB), *Outhenby* 1281. Probably 'farmstead or village of a man called Authunn'. OScand. pers. name + *bý*. Alternatively the first element may be OScand. *authn* 'uncultivated land, deserted farm'.

Aust Avon. *Austan* 794. Possibly from Latin *Augusta*, perhaps alluding to the crossing of the River Severn here used by the Roman Second Legion, the *Legio Augusta*. Alternatively from the Latin pers. name *Augustinus*.

Austerfield S. Yorks. *Eostrefeld c.*715, *Oustrefeld* 1086 (DB). 'Open land with a sheepfold'. OE *eowestre* + *feld*.

Austrey Warwicks. *Alduluestreow* 958, *Aldulvestreu* 1086 (DB). 'Tree of a man called Ealdwulf'. OE pers. name + *trēow*.

Austwick N. Yorks. *Ousteuuic* 1086 (DB). 'East dwelling or dairy-farm'. OScand. *austr* + OE *wīc*.

Authorpe, 'outlying farmstead or hamlet of a man called Ag(g)i', OScand. pers. name + *thorp*: **Authorpe** Lincs. *Agetorp* 1086 (DB). **Authorpe Row** Lincs. *Aghetorp* c.1115.

Avebury Wilts. *Aureberie* 1086 (DB), *Aveberia* c.1180. Probably 'stronghold of a man called Afa'. OE pers. name + *burh* (dative *byrig*).

Aveley Essex. *Aluitheleam* 1086 (DB). 'Woodland clearing of a woman called Ælfgȳth'. OE pers. name + *lēah*.

Avening Glos. *Æfeningum* 896, *Aveninge* 1086 (DB). '(Settlement of) the people living by the River *Avon*'. Celtic river-name (perhaps the original name of the stream here, meaning simply 'river') + OE *-ingas*.

Averham Notts. *Aigrun* 1086 (DB). Probably '(place by) the floods or high tides' (with reference to the Trent bore). OE *ēgor* in a dative plural form *ēgrum*.

Aveton Gifford Devon. *Avetone* 1086 (DB), *Aveton Giffard* 1276. 'Farmstead on the River Avon'. Celtic river-name (meaning simply 'river') + OE *tūn* + manorial affix from the *Giffard* family, here in the 13th cent.

Avington Berks. *Avintone* 1086 (DB). 'Estate associated with a man called Afa'. OE pers. name + *-ing-* + *tūn*.

Avon (new county), named after the River Avon (the Bristol or Lower Avon), see AVONMOUTH.

Avon Hants. *Avere* 1086 (DB). Named from another River Avon, one of several so called in England, a Celtic river-name meaning simply 'river'.

Avon Dassett Warwicks., see DASSETT.

Avonmouth Avon, a modern port at the mouth of the River Avon (*Afenemuthan* 10th cent.). Celtic river-name (meaning simply 'river') + OE *mūtha*.

Awbridge Hants. *Abedric* 1086 (DB). 'Ridge of the abbot'. OE *abbod* + *hrycg*.

Awliscombe Devon. *Aulescome* 1086 (DB). Probably 'valley near the fork of a river'. OE *āwel* + *cumb*.

Awre Glos. *Avre* 1086 (DB). Probably '(place at) the alder-tree'. OE *alor*.

Awsworth Notts. *Ealdeswyrthe* 1002, *Eldesvorde* 1086 (DB). 'Enclosure of a man called *Eald'. OE pers. name + *worth*.

Axbridge Somerset. *Axanbrycg* 10th cent. 'Bridge over the River Axe'. Celtic river-name (meaning uncertain) + OE *brycg*.

Axford Wilts. *Axeford* 1184. 'Ford by the ash-trees'. OE *æsc* + *ford*.

Axminster Devon. *Ascanmynster* late 9th cent., *Aixeministra* 1086 (DB). 'Monastery or large church by the River Axe'. Celtic river-name + OE *mynster*.

Axmouth Devon. *Axanmuthan* c.880, *Alsemuda* 1086 (DB). 'Mouth of the River Axe'. Celtic river-name + OE *mūtha*.

Aycliffe Durham. *Aclea* c.1085. 'Oak-tree wood or clearing'. OE *āc* + *lēah*.

Aylburton Glos. *Ailbricton* 12th cent. 'Farmstead or village of a man called Æthelbeorht'. OE pers. name + *tūn*.

Ayle Northum., named from the river on which it stands, Ayle Burn (*Alne* 1347), a Celtic river-name meaning 'very white'.

Aylesbeare Devon. *Ailesberga* 1086 (DB). 'Grove of a man called *Ægel'. OE pers. name + *bearu*.

Aylesbury Bucks. *Ægelesburg* late 9th cent., *Eilesberia* 1086 (DB). 'Stronghold of a man called *Ægel'. OE pers. name + *burh* (dative *byrig*).

Aylesby Humber. *Alesbi* 1086 (DB). 'Farmstead or village of a man called Áli'. OScand. pers. name + *bý*.

Aylesford Kent. *Æglesforda* 10th cent., *Ailesford* 1086 (DB). 'Ford of a man called *Ægel'. OE pers. name + *ford*.

Aylesham Kent. *Elisham* 1367. Possibly 'homestead or enclosure of a man called *Ægel'. OE pers. name + *hām* or *hamm*.

Aylestone Leics. *Ailestone* 1086 (DB).

'Farmstead or village of a man called *Ægel'. OE pers. name + *tūn*.

Aylmerton Norfolk. *Almartune* 1086 (DB). 'Farmstead or village of a man called Æthelmǣr'. OE pers. name + *tūn*.

Aylsham Norfolk. *Ailesham* 1086 (DB). 'Homestead of a man called *Ægel'. OE pers. name + *hām*.

Aylton Heref. & Worcs. *Aileuetona* 1138. 'Farmstead or village of a woman called Æthelgifu'. OE pers. name + *tūn*.

Aymestrey Heref. & Worcs. *Elmodestreu* 1086 (DB). 'Tree of a man called Æthelmund'. OE pers. name + *trēow*.

Aynho Northants. *Aienho* 1086 (DB). 'Hill-spur of a man called *Æga'. OE pers. name (genitive *-n*) + *hōh*.

Ayot St Lawrence & St Peter Herts. *Aiegete c.*1060, *Aiete* 1086 (DB). 'Gap or pass of a man called *Æga'. OE pers. name + *geat*. Distinguishing affixes from the dedications of the churches at the two places.

Aysgarth N. Yorks. *Echescard* 1086 (DB). 'Gap or open place where oak-trees grow'. OScand. *eiki* + *skarth*.

Ayston Leics. *Æthelstanestun* 1046. 'Farmstead or village of a man called Æthelstān'. OE pers. name + *tūn*.

Aythorpe Roding Essex, see RODING.

Ayton, 'farmstead or estate on a river', OE *ēa* (modified by OScand. *á*) + *tūn*: **Ayton, East & West** N. Yorks. *Atune* 1086 (DB). **Ayton, Great & Little** N. Yorks. *Atun* 1086 (DB).

Azerley N. Yorks. *Asserle* 1086 (DB). 'Woodland clearing of a man called Atsurr'. OScand. pers. name + OE *lēah*.

B

Babbacombe Devon. *Babbecumbe* c.1200. 'Valley of a man called Babba'. OE pers. name + *cumb*.

Babcary Somerset. *Babba Cari* 1086 (DB). 'Estate on the River Cary held by a man called Babba'. OE pers. name + Celtic or pre-Celtic river-name (see CARY FITZPAINE).

Babraham Cambs. *Badburgham* 1086 (DB). 'Homestead or village of a woman called *Beaduburh'. OE pers. name + *hām*.

Babworth Notts. *Baburde* 1086 (DB). 'Enclosure of a man called Babba'. OE pers. name + *worth*.

Backbarrow Cumbria. *Bakbarowe* 1537. 'Hill with a ridge'. OE *bæc* + *beorg*.

Backford Ches. *Bacfort* 1150. 'Ford by a ridge'. OE *bæc* + *ford*.

Backwell Avon. *Bacoile* (*sic*) 1086 (DB), *Bacwell* 1202. 'Spring or stream near a ridge'. OE *bæc* + *wella*.

Backworth Tyne & Wear. *Bacwrth* 12th cent. 'Enclosure of a man called Bacca'. OE pers. name + *worth*.

Baconsthorpe Norfolk. *Baconstorp* 1086 (DB). 'Outlying farmstead or hamlet of a family called *Bacon*'. Norman surname + OScand. *thorp*.

Bacton, 'farmstead of a man called Bacca', OE pers. name + *tūn*: **Bacton** Heref. & Worcs. *Bachetone* 1086 (DB). **Bacton** Norfolk. *Baketuna* 1086 (DB). **Bacton** Suffolk. *Bachetuna* 1086 (DB).

Bacup Lancs. *Fulebachope* c.1200, *Bacop* 1324. 'Valley by a ridge'. OE *bæc* + *hop* (prefixed by OE *fūl* 'foul, muddy' in the early spelling).

Badbury Wilts. *Baddeburi* 955. Probably 'stronghold of a man called Badda'. OE pers. name + *burh* (dative *byrig*).

Badby Northants. *Baddanbyrig* 944, *Badebi* 1086 (DB). Identical in origin with the previous name, though the second element was replaced at an early date by OScand. *bý* 'farmstead, village'.

Baddeley Green Staffs. *Baddilige* 1227. 'Woodland clearing of a man called Badda'. OE pers. name + *lēah*.

Baddesley, 'woodland clearing of a man called *Bæddi', OE pers. name + *lēah*: **Baddesley Ensor** Warwicks. *Bedeslei* 1086 (DB), *Baddesley Endeshouer* 1327. Manorial affix from the *de Edneshoure* family (from EDENSOR), here in the 13th cent. **Baddesley, North** Hants. *Bedeslei* 1086 (DB).

Baddow, Great & Little Essex. *Beadewan* c.975, *Baduuen* 1086 (DB). Probably a Celtic river-name (an old name for the River Chelmer), of uncertain origin and meaning.

Badger Shrops. *Beghesovre* 1086 (DB). 'Hill-spur of a man called *Bæcg'. OE pers. name + **ofer*.

Badgeworth, Badgworth, 'enclosure of a man called *Bæcga', OE pers. name + *worth*: **Badgeworth** Glos. *Beganwurthan* 862, *Beiewrda* 1086 (DB). **Badgworth** Somerset. *Bagewerre* 1086 (DB).

Badingham Suffolk. *Badincham* 1086 (DB). 'Homestead or village associated with a man called *Bēada'. OE pers. name + *-ing-* + *hām*.

Badlesmere Kent. *Badelesmere* 1086 (DB). Probably 'pool of a man called *Bæddel'. OE pers. name + *mere*.

Badminton, Great & Little Glos. *Badimyncgtun* 972, *Madmintune* (*sic*) 1086 (DB). 'Estate associated with a man called Baduhelm'. OE pers. name + *-ing-* + *tūn*.

Badsey Heref. & Worcs. *Baddeseia* 709, *Badesei* 1086 (DB). 'Island, or dry ground in marsh, of a man called *Bæddi'. OE pers. name + *ēg*.

Badsworth W. Yorks. *Badesuuorde* 1086

(DB). 'Enclosure of a man called *Bæddi'. OE pers. name + *worth*.

Badwell Ash Suffolk. *Badewell* 1254, *Badewelle Asfelde* 13th cent. 'Spring or stream of a man called Bada'. OE pers. name + *wella* + later affix from shortened form of ASHFIELD.

Bagborough, West Somerset. *Bacganbeorg* 904, *Bageberge* 1086 (DB). Probably 'hill of a man called Bacga'. OE pers. name + *beorg*.

Bagby N. Yorks. *Baghebi* 1086 (DB). 'Farmstead or village of a man called Baggi'. OScand. pers. name + *bý*.

Bag Enderby Lincs., see ENDERBY.

Bagendon Glos. *Benwedene* (*sic*) 1086 (DB), *Baggingeden* 1220. 'Valley of the family or followers of a man called *Bæcga'. OE pers. name + *-inga-* + *denu*.

Baginton Warwicks. *Badechitone* 1086 (DB). 'Estate associated with a man called Badeca'. OE pers. name + *-ing-* + *tūn*.

Bagley Shrops. *Bageleia* c.1090. Probably 'wood or clearing frequented by badgers'. OE **bagga* + *lēah*.

Bagnall Staffs. *Badegenhall* 1273. Probably 'nook of land of a man called Badeca'. OE pers. name (genitive *-n*) + *halh*.

Bagshot Surrey. *Bagsheta* 1164. 'Projecting piece of land frequented by badgers'. OE **bagga* + *scēat*.

Bagshot Wilts. *Bechesgete* 1086 (DB). 'Gate or gap of a man called *Beocc'. OE pers. name + *geat*.

Bagthorpe Norfolk. *Bachestorp* 1086 (DB). Probably 'outlying farmstead or hamlet of a man called Bakki or Bacca'. OScand. or OE pers. name + OScand. *thorp*.

Bagworth Leics. *Bageworde* 1086 (DB). 'Enclosure of a man called *Bæcga'. OE pers. name + *worth*.

Baildon W. Yorks. *Bægeltune*, *Bældune* c.1030, *Beldune* 1086 (DB). 'Circle hill'. OE **bǣgel* + *dūn*.

Bainbridge N. Yorks. *Bainebrigg* 1218. 'Bridge over the River Bain'. OScand. river-name ('the short or helpful one') + OE *brycg*.

Bainton Cambs. *Badingtun* c.980. 'Estate associated with a man called Bada'. OE pers. name + *-ing-* + *tūn*.

Bainton Humber. *Bagentone* 1086 (DB). 'Estate associated with a man called Bǣga'. OE pers. name + *-ing-* + *tūn*.

Bakewell Derbys. *Badecanwelle* 949, *Badequella* 1086 (DB). 'Spring or stream of a man called Badeca'. OE pers. name + *wella*.

Balcombe W. Sussex. *Balecumba* late 11th cent. Possibly 'valley of a man called Bealda'. OE pers. name + *cumb*. Alternatively the first element may be OE *bealu* 'evil, calamity'.

Baldersby N. Yorks. *Baldrebi* 1086 (DB). 'Farmstead or village of a man called Baldhere'. OE pers. name + OScand. *bý*.

Balderstone Lancs. *Baldreston* 1323. 'Farmstead of a man called Baldhere'. OE pers. name + *tūn*.

Balderton Notts. *Baldretune* 1086 (DB). Identical in origin with the previous name.

Baldock Herts. *Baldoce* c.1140. This place was founded in the 12th cent. by the Knights Templars, who called it *Baldac*, the OFrench form for the Arabian city of Baghdad.

Baldon, Marsh & Toot Oxon. *Balde(n)done* 1086 (DB), *Mersse Baldindon* 1241, *Totbaldindon* 1316. 'Hill of a man called Bealda'. OE pers. name + *dūn*. Distinguishing affixes from OE *mersc* 'marsh' and **tōt(e)* 'look-out hill'.

Baldwinholme Cumbria. *Baldewinholme* 1278. 'Island or water-meadow of a man called Baldwin'. OGerman pers. name + OScand. *holmr*.

Bale Norfolk. *Bathele* 1086 (DB). 'Woodland clearing where there are springs used for bathing'. OE *bæth* + *lēah*.

Balham Gtr. London. *Bælgenham* 957, *Belgeham* 1086 (DB). Probably 'smooth or rounded enclosure'. OE **bealg* + *hamm*.

Balkholme Humber. *Balcholm* 1199. 'Island on a low ridge', or 'island of a man called Balki'. OE *balca* or OScand. pers. name + OScand. *holmr*.

Ballingham Heref. & Worcs. *Badelingeham* 1215. 'Homestead of the family or followers of a man called *Badela', or 'homestead at the place associated with *Badela'. OE pers. name + *-inga-* or *-ing* + *hām*. Alternatively the second element may be OE *hamm* 'land in a river-bend'.

Balne N. Yorks. *Balne* 12th cent. Probably from Latin *balneum* 'a bathing place'.

Balsall W. Mids. *Beleshale* 1185. 'Nook of land of a man called *Bæll(i)'. OE pers. name + *halh*.

Balscott Oxon. *Berescote* (*sic*) 1086 (DB), *Belescot* c.1190. 'Cottage(s) of a man called *Bæll(i)'. OE pers. name + *cot*.

Balsham Cambs. *Bellesham* 974, *Belesham* 1086 (DB). 'Homestead or village of a man called *Bæll(i)'. OE pers. name + *hām*.

Balterley Staffs. *Baltrytheleag* 1002, *Baltredelege* 1086 (DB). 'Woodland clearing of a woman called *Baldthrȳth'. OE pers. name + *lēah*.

Baltonsborough Somerset. *Balteresberghe* 744, *Baltunesberge* 1086 (DB). 'Hill or mound of a man called Bealdhūn'. OE pers. name + *beorg*.

Bamber Bridge Lancs. *Bymbrig* in an undated medieval document. Probably 'tree-trunk bridge'. OE *bēam* + *brycg*.

Bamburgh Northum. *Bebbanburge* c.710–20. 'Stronghold of a queen called Bebbe'. OE pers. name + *burh*.

Bamford Derbys. *Banford* 1086 (DB). 'Tree-trunk ford'. OE *bēam* + *ford*.

Bampton, usually 'farmstead made of beams or by a tree', OE *bēam* + *tūn*: **Bampton** Cumbria. *Bampton* c.1160. **Bampton** Oxon. *Bemtun* 1069, *Bentone* 1086 (DB). **Bampton, Little** Cumbria. *Parua Bampton* 1227.
However the following has a different origin: **Bampton** Devon. *Badentone* 1086 (DB). 'Farmstead of the dwellers by the pool'. OE *bæth* + *hǣme* + *tūn*.

Banbury Oxon. *Banesberie* 1086 (DB). 'Stronghold of a man called *Ban(n)a'. OE pers. name + *burh* (dative *byrig*).

Banham Norfolk. *Benham* 1086 (DB). 'Homestead or enclosure where beans are grown'. OE *bēan* + *hām* or *hamm*.

Banningham Norfolk. *Banincham* 1086 (DB). 'Homestead or village of the family or followers of a man called *Ban(n)a'. OE pers. name + *-inga-* + *hām*.

Banstead Surrey. *Benestede* 1086 (DB). 'Place where beans are grown'. OE *bēan* + *stede*.

Banwell Avon. *Bananwylle* 904, *Banwelle* 1086 (DB). 'Spring or stream of the murderer, or of a man called *Bana'. OE *bana* or OE pers. name + *wella*.

Bapchild Kent. *Baccancelde* 696–716. 'Spring of a man called Bacca'. OE pers. name + *celde*.

Barbon Cumbria. *Berebrune* 1086 (DB). 'Stream frequented by bears or beavers'. OE *bere* + *burna* or OScand. *bjórr* + *brunnr*.

Barby Northants. *Berchebi* 1086 (DB). 'Farmstead or village on the hill(s)'. OScand. *berg* + *bý*.

Barcheston Warwicks. *Berricestone* 1086 (DB). 'Farmstead of a man called Beadurīc'. OE pers. name + *tūn*.

Barcombe E. Sussex. *Bercham* (*sic*) 1086 (DB), *Berecampe* 12th cent. 'Enclosed land used for barley'. OE *bere* + *camp*.

Barden N. Yorks., near Leyburn. *Bernedan* 1086 (DB). Probably 'valley where barley is grown'. OE *beren* + *denu*.

Bardfield, Great & Little, Bardfield Saling Essex. *Byrdefelda* 1086 (DB), *Berdeford Saling* 13th cent. 'Open land by a bank or border'. OE **byrde* + *feld*. Affix from the neighbouring parish of GREAT SALING.

Bardney Lincs. *Beardaneu* 731, *Bardenai* 1086 (DB). 'Island, or dry ground in marsh, of a man called *Bearda'. OE pers. name (genitive *-n*) + *ēg*.

Bardsea Cumbria. *Berretseige* 1086 (DB). 'Island of a man called Beornrǣd'. OE pers. name + *ēg* or OScand. *ey*.

Bardsey W. Yorks. *Berdesei* 1086 (DB). Probably 'island (of higher land) of a man called Beornrǣd'. OE pers. name + *ēg*.

Bardsley Gtr. Manch. *Berdesley* 1422. 'Woodland clearing of a man called Beornrǣd'. OE pers. name + *lēah*.

Bardwell Suffolk. *Berdeuuella* 1086 (DB). Probably 'spring or stream of a man called *Bearda'. OE pers. name + *wella*.

Barford, usually 'barley ford', i.e. 'ford used at harvest time', OE *bere* + *ford*; examples include: **Barford** Norfolk. *Bereforda* 1086 (DB). **Barford** Warwicks. *Bereforde* 1086 (DB). **Barford, Great** Beds. *Bereforde* 1086 (DB). **Barford St Martin** Wilts. *Bereford* 1086 (DB), *Berevord St Martin* 1304. Affix from the dedication of the church. **Barford St Michael** Oxon. *Bereford* 1086 (DB), *Bereford Sancti Michaelis* c.1250. Affix from the dedication of the church.

However the following has a different origin: **Barford, Little** Beds. *Bereforde* (*sic*) 1086 (DB), *Berkeford* 1202. 'Ford where birch-trees grow'. OE *beorc* + *ford*.

Barfreston Kent. *Berfrestone* 1086 (DB). Probably 'farmstead of a man called Beornfrith'. OE pers. name + *tūn*.

Barham Cambs. *Bercheham* 1086 (DB). 'Homestead or enclosure on a hill'. OE *beorg* + *hām* or *hamm*.

Barham Kent. *Bioraham* 799, *Berham* 1086 (DB). 'Homestead or village of a man called *Be(o)ra'. OE pers. name + *hām*.

Barham Suffolk. *Bercham* 1086 (DB). Identical in origin with BARHAM (Cambs.).

Barholm Lincs. *Berc(a)ham* 1086 (DB). 'Homestead or enclosure on a hill'. OE *beorg* + *hām* or *hamm*.

Barkby Leics. *Barchebi* 1086 (DB). 'Farmstead or village of a man called Bǫrkr or Barki'. OScand. pers. name + *bý*.

Barkestone Leics. *Barchestone* 1086 (DB). 'Farmstead of a man called Barkr or Bǫrkr'. OScand. pers. name + OE *tūn*.

Barkham Berks. *Beorchamme* 952, *Bercheham* 1086 (DB). 'Enclosure or river-meadow where birch-trees grow'. OE *beorc* + *hamm*.

Barking, '(settlement of) the family or followers of a man called *Berica', OE pers. name + *-ingas*: **Barking** Gtr. London. *Berecingum* 731, *Berchinges* 1086 (DB). **Barking** Suffolk. *Berchinges* c.1050, *Berchingas* 1086 (DB).

Barkisland W. Yorks. *Barkesland* 1246. 'Cultivated land of a man called Barkr'. OScand. pers. name + *land*.

Barkston, 'farmstead of a man called Barkr or Bǫrkr', OScand. pers. name + OE *tūn*: **Barkston** Lincs. *Barchestune* 1086 (DB). **Barkston** N. Yorks. *Barcestune* c.1030, *Barchestun* 1086 (DB).

Barkway Herts. *Bercheuuei* 1086 (DB). 'Birch-tree way'. OE *beorc* + *weg*.

Barkwith, East & West Lincs. *Barcuurde* 1086 (DB). Possibly 'enclosure of a man called Barki'. OScand. pers. name + OE *worth*.

Barlaston Staffs. *Beorelfestun* 1002, *Bernulvestone* 1086 (DB). 'Farmstead of a man called Beornwulf'. OE pers. name + *tūn*.

Barlavington W. Sussex. *Berleventone* 1086 (DB). Probably 'estate associated with a man called Beornlāf'. OE pers. name + *-ing-* + *tūn*.

Barlborough Derbys. *Barleburh* c.1002, *Barleburg* 1086 (DB). Probably 'stronghold near the wood frequented by boars'. OE *bār* + *lēah* + *burh*.

Barlby N. Yorks. *Bardulbi* 1086 (DB). 'Farmstead or village of a man called *Beardwulf or Bardulf'. OE or OGerman pers. name + OScand. *bý*.

Barlestone Leics. *Berulvestone* 1086 (DB). Probably 'farmstead of a man called Beornwulf or Berwulf'. OE pers. name + *tūn*.

Barley Herts. *Beranlei* c.1050, *Berlai* 1086 (DB). Probably 'woodland clearing of a man called *Be(o)ra'. OE pers. name + *lēah*.

Barley Lancs. *Bayrlegh* 1324. 'Woodland clearing frequented by boars, or where barley is grown'. OE *bār* or *bere* + *lēah*.

Barling Essex. *Bærlingum* 998, *Berlinga* 1086 (DB). '(Settlement of) the family or followers of a man called *Bǣrla'. OE pers. name + *-ingas*.

Barlow Derbys. *Barleie* 1086 (DB). 'Woodland clearing frequented by boars, or where barley is grown'. OE *bār* or *bere* + *lēah*.

Barlow N. Yorks. *Bernlege* c.1030, *Berlai* 1086 (DB). 'Woodland clearing with a barn, or where barley is grown'. OE *bere-ærn* or *beren* + *lēah*.

Barmby, probably 'farmstead of the children, i.e. one held jointly by a number of heirs' from OScand. *barn* + *bý*; alternatively 'farmstead of a man called Barni or Bjarni' from OScand. pers. name + *bý*: **Barmby Moor** Humber. *Barnebi* 1086 (DB), *Barneby in the More* 1371. Affix is OE *mōr* 'moor'. **Barmby on the Marsh** Humber. *Bærnabi c.*1050, *Barnebi* 1086 (DB). Affix is OE *mersc* 'marsh'.

Barmer Norfolk. *Benemara* (*sic*) 1086 (DB), *Beremere* 1202. 'Pool frequented by bears', or 'pool of a man called *Bera'. OE *bera* or pers. name + *mere*.

Barming, East Kent. *Bermelinge*, *Bermelie* 1086 (DB). Origin and meaning uncertain.

Barmston Humber. *Benestone* 1086 (DB). 'Farmstead of a man called Beorn'. OE pers. name + *tūn*.

Barnack Cambs. *Beornican c.*980, *Bernac* 1086 (DB). Probably '(place at) the oak-tree(s) of the warriors'. OE *beorn* + *āc*.

Barnacle Warwicks. *Bernhangre* 1086 (DB). 'Wooded slope by a barn'. OE *bere-ærn* + *hangra*.

Barnard Castle Durham. *Castellum Bernardi* 1200. 'Castle of a baron called Bernard'. He was here in the 12th cent.

Barnardiston Suffolk. *Bernardeston* 1194. 'Farmstead of a man called Beornheard'. OE pers. name + *tūn*.

Barnby, probably 'farmstead of the children, i.e. one held jointly by a number of heirs', OScand. *barn* + *bý*; alternatively the first element of some names may be the OScand. pers. name *Barni* or *Bjarni*; examples include: **Barnby** Suffolk. *Barnebei* 1086 (DB). **Barnby Dun** S. Yorks. *Barnebi* 1086 (DB), *Barneby super Don* 1285. Affix means 'on the River Don'. **Barnby, East & West** N. Yorks. *Barnebi* 1086 (DB). **Barnby in the Willows** Notts. *Barnebi* 1086 (DB). Affix means 'among the willow-trees'. **Barnby Moor** Notts. *Barnebi* 1086 (DB). Affix means 'on the moor'.

Barnes Gtr. London. *Berne* 1086 (DB). '(Place by) the barn or barns'. OE *bere-ærn*.

Barnet, Chipping & Friern Gtr. London. *Barneto c.*1070, *Chepyng Barnet* 1329, *Frerenbarnet* 1274. 'Land cleared by burning'. OE *bærnet*. Distinguishing affixes are OE *cīeping* 'market' and ME *freren* 'of the brothers' (referring to early possession by the Knights of St John of Jerusalem). Chipping Barnet has also been known as *High Barnet* since the 17th cent.

Barnetby le Wold Humber. *Bernodebi* 1086 (DB). 'Farmstead or village of a man called Beornnōth'. OE pers. name + OScand. *bý*. Affix means 'on the wold(s)', referring to its situation at the northern edge of the Lincolnshire WOLDS.

Barney Norfolk. *Berlei* (*sic*) 1086 (DB), *Berneie* 1198. Possibly 'island, or dry ground in marsh, of a man called *Bera'. OE pers. name (genitive *-n*) + *ēg*.

Barnham Suffolk. *Byornham c.*1000, *Bernham* 1086 (DB). 'Warrior homestead', or 'homestead of a man called Beorn'. OE *beorn* or OE pers. name + *hām*.

Barnham W. Sussex. *Berneham* 1086 (DB). 'Homestead or enclosure of the warriors, or of a man called Beorna'. OE *beorn* or OE pers. name + *hām* or *hamm*.

Barnham Broom Norfolk. *Bernham* 1086 (DB). Identical in origin with BARNHAM (Suffolk). Affix is OE *brōm* 'broom'.

Barningham, 'homestead or village of the family or followers of a man called Beorn', OE pers. name + *-inga-* + *hām*: **Barningham** Durham. *Berningham* 1086 (DB). **Barningham** Suffolk. *Bernincham* 1086 (DB). **Barningham, Little** Norfolk. *Berningeham* 1086 (DB).

Barnoldby le Beck Humber. *Bernulfbi* 1086 (DB). 'Farmstead or village of a man called Bjǫrnulfr or Beornwulf'. OScand. or OE pers. name + OScand. *bý*. Affix means 'on the stream' from OScand. *bekkr*.

Barnoldswick Lancs. *Bernulfesuuic* 1086 (DB). 'Dwelling or (dairy) farm of a man called Beornwulf or Bjǫrnulfr'. OE or OScand. pers. name + OE *wīc*.

Barnsley Glos. *Bearmodeslea c.*802, *Bernesleis* 1086 (DB). 'Woodland clearing of a man called Beornmōd'. OE pers. name + *lēah*.

Barnsley S. Yorks. *Berneslai* 1086 (DB). 'Woodland clearing of a man called Beorn'. OE pers. name + *lēah*.

Barnstaple Devon. *Beardastapol* late 10th cent., *Barnestaple* 1086 (DB). 'Bearded post', i.e. 'post marked with a besom or the like and used as a landmark or seamark'. OE *beard* + *stapol*.

Barnston Essex. *Bernestuna* 1086 (DB). 'Farmstead of a man called Beorn'. OE pers. name + *tūn*.

Barnston Mersey. *Bernestone* 1086 (DB). 'Farmstead of a man called Beornwulf'. OE pers. name + *tūn*.

Barnwell All Saints Northants. *Byrnewilla* c.980, *Bernewelle* 1086 (DB). Probably 'spring or stream of the warriors, or of a man called Beorna'. OE *beorn* or OE pers. name + *wella*. Affix from the dedication of the church.

Barnwood Glos. *Berneuude* 1086 (DB). 'Wood of the warriors, or of a man called Beorna'. OE *beorn* or OE pers. name + *wudu*.

Barr, Great W. Mids. *Bearre* 957, *Barre* 1086 (DB). Celtic **barr* 'hill-top'.

Barrasford Northum. *Barwisford* 1242. 'Ford by a grove'. OE *bearu* (genitive *bearwes*) + *ford*.

Barrington Cambs. *Barentone* 1086 (DB). Probably 'farmstead of a man called *Bāra'. OE pers. name (genitive *-n*) + *tūn*.

Barrington Somerset. *Barintone* 1086 (DB). Probably 'estate associated with a man called *Bāra'. OE pers. name + *-ing-* + *tūn*.

Barrington, Great & Little Glos. *Berni(n)tone* 1086 (DB). 'Estate associated with a man called Beorn(a)'. OE pers. name + *-ing-* + *tūn*.

Barrow, usually '(place at) the wood or grove', OE *bearu* (in a dative form *bearwe*); examples include: **Barrow** Suffolk. *Baro* 1086 (DB). **Barrow, Great & Little** Ches. *Barue* 958, *Bero* 1086 (DB). **Barrow Gurney** Avon. *Berue* 1086 (DB), *Barwe Gurnay* 1283. Affix from possession by *Nigel de Gurnai* in 1086. **Barrow, North & South** Somerset. *Berue*, *Berrowene* 1086 (DB). **Barrow upon Humber** Humber. *Ad Baruae* 731, *Barewe* 1086 (DB). For the river-name, see HUMBERSIDE. *Ad* in the early form is Latin 'at'. **Barrow upon Soar** Leics. *Barhou* 1086 (DB). Soar is a Celtic or pre-Celtic river-name probably meaning 'flowing one'. **Barrow upon Trent** Derbys. *Barewe* 1086 (DB). For the river-name, see TRENTHAM.

However some Barrows have a different origin: **Barrow** Leics., near Oakham. *Berc* 1197. '(Place at) the hill'. OE *beorg*. **Barrow in Furness** Cumbria. *Barrai* 1190. 'Promontory island'. Celtic **barr* + OScand. *ey*. The old district name Furness (*Fuththernessa* c.1150) means 'headland by the rump-shaped island', OScand. *futh* (genitive *-ar*) + *nes*.

Barrowby Lincs. *Bergebi* 1086 (DB). 'Farmstead or village on the hill(s)'. OScand. *berg* + *bý*.

Barrowden Leics. *Berchedone* 1086 (DB). 'Hill with barrows or tumuli'. OE *beorg* + *dūn*.

Barrowford Lancs. *Barouforde* 1296. 'Ford by the grove'. OE *bearu* + *ford*.

Barsby Leics. *Barnesbi* 1086 (DB). 'Farmstead or village of the child or young heir, or of a man called Barn'. OScand. *barn* or pers. name + *bý*.

Barsham, 'homestead or village of a man called Bār', OE pers. name + *hām*: **Barsham** Norfolk. *Barseham* 1086 (DB). **Barsham** Suffolk. *Barsham* 1086 (DB).

Bartestree Heref. & Worcs. *Bertoldestreu* 1086 (DB). 'Tree of a man called Beorhtwald'. OE pers. name + *trēow*.

Barthomley Ches. *Bertemeleu* (*sic*) 1086 (DB), *Bertamelegh* 13th cent. Possibly 'woodland clearing of the dwellers at a place called *Brightmead* or *Brightwell* or the like'. The first element of an older place-name (possibly OE *beorht* 'bright') + *hǣme* + *lēah*.

Bartley, 'birch-tree wood or clearing', OE *beorc* + *lēah*: **Bartley** Hants. *Berchelai* 1107. **Bartley Green** W. Mids. *Berchelai* 1086 (DB).

Bartlow Cambs. *Berkelawe* 1232. 'Mounds or tumuli where birch-trees grow'. OE *beorc* + *hlāw*.

Barton, a common name, usually OE

bere-tūn 'barley farm, outlying grange where corn is stored'; examples include: **Barton** Devon, near Torquay. *Bertone* 1333. **Barton** Glos., near Guiting. *Berton* 1158. **Barton** Lancs., near Preston. *Bartun* 1086 (DB). **Barton Bendish** Norfolk. *Bertuna* 1086 (DB), *Berton Binnedich* 1249. Affix means 'inside the ditch' (OE *binnan* + *dīc*) referring to Devil's Dyke. **Barton, Earls** Northants. *Bartone* 1086 (DB), *Erlesbarton* 1261. Affix from the Earl of Huntingdon who held the manor in the 12th cent. **Barton in Fabis** Notts. *Bartone* 1086 (DB), *Barton in le Benes* 1388. Latin affix means 'where beans are grown'. **Barton le Clay** Beds. *Bertone* 1086 (DB), *Barton-in-the-Clay* 1535. Affix means 'on clay soil'. **Barton Seagrave** Northants. *Bertone* 1086 (DB), *Barton Segrave* 1321. Manorial affix from the *de Segrave* family, here in the 13th cent. **Barton Stacey** Hants. *Bertune* c.1000, *Bertune* 1086 (DB), *Berton Sacy* 1302. Manorial affix from the *de Saci* family, here in the 12th cent. **Barton under Needwood** Staffs. *Barton* 942, *Bertone* 1086 (DB). Affix means 'near or within the forest of NEEDWOOD'. **Barton upon Humber** Humber. *Bertone* 1086 (DB). For the river-name, see HUMBERSIDE.

However the following has a different origin: **Barton on Sea** Hants. *Bermintune* 1086 (DB). 'Estate associated with a man called *Beorma'. OE pers. name + *-ing-* + *tūn*.

Barugh, Great & Little N. Yorks. *Berg, Berch* 1086 (DB). '(Place at) the hill'. OE *beorg*.

Barway Cambs. *Bergeia* 1155. 'Island, or dry ground in marsh, with barrows or tumuli on it'. OE *beorg* + *ēg*.

Barwell Leics. *Barewelle* 1086 (DB). 'Spring or stream frequented by boars'. OE *bār* + *wella*.

Barwick, 'barley farm, outlying part of an estate', OE *bere-wīc*: **Barwick** Somerset. *Berewyk* 1219. **Barwick in Elmet** W. Yorks. *Bereuuith* 1086 (DB). *Elmet* is an ancient district name, obscure in origin and meaning, first recorded in the 7th cent. as *Elmed*.

Baschurch Shrops. *Bascherche* 1086 (DB). 'Church of a man called Bas(s)a'. OE pers. name + *cirice*.

Bascote Warwicks. *Bachecota* 1174. Probably 'cottage(s) of a man called *Basuca'. OE pers. name + *cot*.

Basford Staffs. *Bechesword* (*sic*) 1086 (DB), *Barkeford* 1199. Probably 'ford of a man called Beorcol'. OE pers. name + *ford*.

Bashall Eaves Lancs. *Bacschelf* 1086 (DB). 'Ridge shelf'. OE *bæc* + *scelf*. Later addition *Eaves* (from 16th cent.) is from OE *efes* 'edge of a wood'.

Bashley Hants. *Bageslucesleia* 1053, *Bailocheslei* 1086 (DB). 'Woodland clearing of a man called Bægloc'. OE pers. name + *lēah*.

Basildon Essex. *Berlesduna* (*sic*) 1086 (DB), *Bertlesdon* 1194. 'Hill of a man called Beorhtel'. OE pers. name + *dūn*.

Basing Hants. *Basengum* 871, *Basinges* 1086 (DB). '(Settlement of) the family or followers of a man called *Basa'. OE pers. name + *-ingas*.

Basingstoke Hants. *Basingastoc* 990, *Basingestoches* 1086 (DB). 'Secondary settlement or outlying farmstead of the family or followers of a man called *Basa'. OE pers. name + *-inga-* + *stoc*.

Baslow Derbys. *Basselau* 1086 (DB). 'Burial mound of a man called Bassa'. OE pers. name + *hlāw*.

Bassenthwaite Cumbria. *Bastunthuait* c.1175. 'Clearing or meadow of a family called *Bastun*'. ME surname + OScand. *thveit*.

Bassetlaw (district) Notts. *Bernesedelaue* 1086 (DB). Possibly 'mound or hill of the dwellers on land cleared by burning'. OE *bærnet* + *sǣte* + *hlāw*.

Bassingbourn Cambs. *Basingborne* 1086 (DB). 'Stream of the family or followers of a man called Bas(s)a'. OE pers. name + *-inga-* + *burna*.

Bassingfield Notts. *Basingfelt* 1086 (DB). 'Open land of the family or followers of a man called Bas(s)a'. OE pers. name + *-inga-* + *feld*.

Bassingham Lincs. *Basingeham* 1086 (DB). 'Homestead or village of the family or followers of a man called Bas(s)a'. OE pers. name + *-inga-* + *hām*.

Bassingthorpe Lincs. *Torp* 1086 (DB), *Basewinttorp* 1202. 'Outlying farmstead or hamlet'. OScand. *thorp* + later manorial addition from possession by the *Basewin* family.

Baston Lincs. *Bacstune* 1086 (DB). 'Farmstead of a man called Bak'. OScand. pers. name + OE *tūn*.

Bastwick Norfolk. *Bastuuic* 1086 (DB). 'Farm or building where bast (the bark of the lime-tree used for rope-making) is stored'. OE *bæst* + *wīc*.

Batcombe, 'valley of a man called Bata', OE pers. name + *cumb*: **Batcombe** Dorset. *Batecumbe* 1201. **Batcombe** Somerset, near Bruton. *Batancumbæ* 10th cent., *Batecumbe* 1086 (DB).

Bath Avon. *Bathum* 796, *Bade* 1086 (DB). '(Place at) the (Roman) baths'. OE *bæth* in a dative plural form. See also AKEMAN STREET.

Bathampton Avon. *Hamtun* 956, *Hantone* 1086 (DB). OE *hām-tūn* 'home farm, homestead' with later addition from its proximity to BATH.

Bathealton Somerset. *Badeheltone* 1086 (DB). Possibly 'farmstead of a man called Beaduhelm'. OE pers. name + *tūn*.

Batheaston Avon. *Estone* 1086 (DB), *Batheneston* 1258. 'East farmstead or village'. OE *ēast* + *tūn* with later addition from its proximity to BATH.

Bathford Avon. *Forda* 957, *Forde* 1086 (DB). '(Place at) the ford'. OE *ford* with later addition from its proximity to BATH.

Bathley Notts. *Badeleie* 1086 (DB). 'Woodland clearing with springs used for bathing'. OE *bæth* + *lēah*.

Batley W. Yorks. *Bathelie* 1086 (DB). 'Woodland clearing of a man called Bata'. OE pers. name + *lēah*.

Batsford Glos. *Bæccesore* 727–36, *Beceshore* 1086 (DB). 'Hill-slope of a man called *Bæcci'. OE pers. name + *ōra*.

Battersby N. Yorks. *Badresbi* 1086 (DB). 'Farmstead or village of a man called Bǫthvarr'. OScand. pers. name + *bý*.

Battersea Gtr. London. *Badrices ege* 11th cent., *Patricesy* 1086 (DB). 'Island, or dry ground in marsh, of a man called Beadurīc'. OE pers. name + *ēg*.

Battisford Suffolk. *Betesfort* 1086 (DB). 'Ford of a man called *Bætti'. OE pers. name + *ford*.

Battle E. Sussex. *La Batailge* 1086 (DB). '(Place of) the battle'. OFrench *bataille*. The abbey here was founded to commemorate the battle of Hastings in 1066.

Battlefield Shrops. *Batelfeld* 1415. 'Field of battle'. OFrench *bataille*. A college of secular canons was founded here to commemorate the battle of Shrewsbury in 1403.

Battlesden Beds. *Badelesdone* 1086 (DB). 'Hill of a man called *Bæddel'. OE pers. name + *dūn*.

Baughurst Hants. *Beaggan hyrste* 909. 'Wooded hill of a man called *Beagga'. OE pers. name + *hyrst*. Alternatively the first element may be OE **bagga* 'a badger'.

Baumber Lincs. *Badeburg* 1086 (DB). 'Stronghold of a man called Badda'. OE pers. name + *burh*.

Baunton Glos. *Baudintone* 1086 (DB). 'Estate associated with a man called Balda'. OE pers. name + *-ing-* + *tūn*.

Baverstock Wilts. *Babbanstoc* 968, *Babestoche* 1086 (DB). 'Outlying farmstead or hamlet of a man called Babba'. OE pers. name + *stoc*.

Bavington, Great & Little Northum. *Babington* 1242. 'Estate associated with a man called Babba'. OE pers. name + *-ing-* + *tūn*.

Bawburgh Norfolk. *Bauenburc* 1086 (DB). 'Stronghold of a man called *Bēawa'. OE pers. name + *burh*.

Bawdeswell Norfolk. *Baldereswella* 1086 (DB). 'Spring or stream of a man called Baldhere'. OE pers. name + *wella*.

Bawdrip Somerset. *Bagetrepe* 1086 (DB). 'Place where badgers are trapped or snared'. OE **bagga* + *træppe*.

Bawdsey Suffolk. *Baldereseia* 1086 (DB). 'Island, or dry ground in marsh, of a man called Baldhere'. OE pers. name + *ēg*.

Bawtry S. Yorks. *Baltry* 1199. Probably 'tree rounded like a ball'. OE **ball* + *trēow*.

Baxenden Lancs. *Bastanedenecloch* 1194. 'Valley where flat stones for baking are found'. OE **bæc-stān* + *denu*, with OE **clōh* 'ravine' in the early form.

Baxterley Warwicks. *Basterleia c.*1170. 'Woodland clearing belonging to the baker'. OE *bæcestre* + *lēah*.

Baycliff Cumbria. *Belleclive* 1212. Possibly 'cliff where a signal-fire is lit'. OE *bēl* + *clif*.

Baydon Wilts. *Beidona* 1146. 'Hill where berries grow'. OE *beg* + *dūn*.

Bayford Herts. *Begesford* (*sic*) 1086 (DB), *Begeford c.*1090. 'Ford of a man called Bǣga'. OE pers. name + *ford*.

Baylham Suffolk. *Beleham* 1086 (DB). Probably 'homestead or enclosure at a river-bend'. OE **bēgel* + *hām* or *hamm*.

Bayston Hill Shrops. *Begestan* 1086 (DB). 'Stone of a woman called Bēage or of a man called Bǣga'. OE pers. name + *stān*.

Bayswater Gtr. London. *Bayards Watering Place* 1380. 'Watering place for horses, or belonging to a family called *Bayard*'. ME *bayard* (or ME surname from this word) + *water*.

Bayton Heref. & Worcs. *Betune* 1086 (DB). 'Farmstead of a woman called Bēage or of a man called Bǣga'. OE pers. name + *tūn*.

Beachampton Bucks. *Bechentone* 1086 (DB). 'Home farm by a stream'. OE *bece* + *hām-tūn*.

Beachley Avon. *Beteslega* 12th cent. 'Woodland clearing of a man called Betti'. OE pers. name + *lēah*.

Beachy Head E. Sussex. *Beuchef* 1279. 'Beautiful headland'. OFrench *beau* + *chef*, with the (strictly redundant) addition of *head* in recent times.

Beaconsfield Bucks. *Bekenesfelde* 1184. 'Open land near a beacon or signal-fire'. OE *bēacon* + *feld*.

Beadlam N. Yorks. *Bodlum* 1086 (DB). '(Place at) the buildings'. OE *bōthl* in a dative plural form *bōthlum*.

Beadnell Northum. *Bedehal* 1161. 'Nook of land of a man called Bēda'. OE pers. name (genitive *-n*) + *halh*.

Beaford Devon. *Baverdone* (*sic*) 1086 (DB), *Beuford* 1242. 'Ford infested with gadflies'. OE *bēaw* + *ford*.

Beal Northum. *Behil* 1208–10. 'Hill frequented by bees'. OE *bēo* + *hyll*.

Beal N. Yorks. *Begale* 1086 (DB). 'Nook of land in a river-bend'. OE *bēag* + *halh*.

Bealings, Great & Little Suffolk. *Belinges* 1086 (DB). Possibly '(settlement of) the dwellers in the glade, or by the funeral pyre'. OE **bel-* or *bēl* + *-ingas*.

Beaminster Dorset. *Bebingmynster* 862, *Beiminstre* 1086 (DB). 'Large church of a woman called Bebbe'. OE pers. name + *mynster*.

Beamish Durham. *Bewmys* 1288. 'Beautiful mansion'. OFrench *beau* + *mes*.

Beamsley N. Yorks. *Bedmesleia* 1086 (DB). Probably 'woodland clearing of a man called Bēdhelm'. OE pers. name + *lēah*. Alternatively the first element may be an OE **bethme* 'valley bottom'.

Beane (river) Herts., see BENINGTON.

Beanley Northum. *Benelega c.*1150. 'Clearing where beans are grown'. OE *bēan* + *lēah*.

Bearley Warwicks. *Burlei* 1086 (DB). 'Woodland clearing near a fortified place'. OE *burh* + *lēah*.

Bearpark Durham. *Beaurepayre* 1267. 'Beautiful retreat'. OFrench *beau* + *repaire*.

Bearsted Kent. *Berghamstyde* 695. 'Homestead on a hill'. OE *beorg* + *hām-stede*.

Beauchief S. Yorks. *Beuchef* 12th cent. 'Beautiful headland or hill-spur'. OFrench *beau* + *chef*.

Beaulieu Hants. *Bellus Locus Regis* 1205, *Beulu c.*1300. 'Beautiful place (of the king)'. OFrench *beau* + *lieu* (often rendered in Latin, as in the first spelling).

Beaumont, 'beautiful hill', OFrench *beau* or *bel* + *mont*: **Beaumont** Cumbria. *Beumund c.*1240. **Beaumont** Essex. *Fulepet* 1086 (DB), *Bealmont* 12th cent. The earlier name means 'foul pit' from OE *fūl* + *pytt*!

Beausale Warwicks. *Beoshelle* (*sic*) 1086 (DB), *Beausala* 12th cent. 'Nook of land of a man called *Bēaw'. OE pers. name + *halh*.

Beaworthy Devon. *Begeurde* 1086 (DB). 'Enclosure of a woman called Bēage or of a man called Bǣga'. OE pers. name + *worth*.

Bebington Mersey. *Bebinton c.*1100. 'Estate associated with a woman called Bebbe or a man called *Bebba'. OE pers. name + *-ing-* + *tūn*.

Bebside Northum. *Bibeshet* 1198. Probably 'projecting piece of land of a man called *Bibba'. OE pers. name + *scēat*.

Beccles Suffolk. *Becles* 1086 (DB). Probably 'pasture by a stream'. OE *bece* + *lǣs*.

Becconsall Lancs. *Bekaneshou* 1208. 'Burial mound of a man called Bekan'. OIrish pers. name + OScand. *haugr*.

Beckbury Shrops. *Becheberie* 1086 (DB). 'Stronghold or manor of a man called Becca'. OE pers. name + *burh* (dative *byrig*).

Beckenham Gtr. London. *Beohha hammes gemæru* 973, *Bacheham* 1086 (DB). 'Homestead or enclosure of a man called *Beohha'. OE pers. name (genitive *-n*) + *hām* or *hamm*. The early form contains OE *(ge)mǣre* 'boundary'.

Beckford Heref. & Worcs. *Beccanford* 803, *Beceford* 1086 (DB). 'Ford of a man called Becca'. OE pers. name + *ford*.

Beckham Norfolk. *Beccheham* 1086 (DB). 'Homestead or village of a man called Becca'. OE pers. name + *hām*.

Beckhampton Wilts. *Bachentune* 1086 (DB). 'Home farm near the ridge'. OE *bæc* + *hām-tūn*.

Beckingham, 'homestead or enclosure of the family or followers of a man called Becca or *Beohha', OE pers. name + *hām* or *hamm*: **Beckingham** Lincs. *Bekingeham* 1177. **Beckingham** Notts. *Bechingeham* 1086 (DB).

Beckington Somerset. *Bechintone* 1086 (DB). 'Estate associated with a man called Becca'. OE pers. name + *-ing-* + *tūn*.

Beckley, 'woodland clearing of a man called Becca', OE pers. name + *lēah*: **Beckley** E. Sussex. *Beccanlea c.*880. **Beckley** Oxon. *Beccalege* 1005–12, *Bechelie* 1086 (DB).

Becontree Gtr. London. *Beuentreu* (*sic*) 1086 (DB), *Begintre* 12th cent. 'Tree of a man called *Beohha'. OE pers. name (genitive *-n*) + *trēow*. The tree marked the Hundred meeting-place.

Bedale N. Yorks. *Bedale* 1086 (DB). 'Nook of land of a man called Bēda'. OE pers. name + *halh*.

Bedburn Durham. *Bedburn* 1291. 'Stream of a man called Bēda'. OE pers. name + *burna*.

Beddingham E. Sussex. *Beadyngham c.*800, *Bedingeham* 1086 (DB). 'Promontory of the family or followers of a man called Bēada'. OE pers. name + *-inga-* + *hamm*.

Beddington Gtr. London. *Beaddinctun* 901–8, *Beddintone* 1086 (DB). 'Estate associated with a man called *Beadda'. OE pers. name + *-ing-* + *tūn*.

Bedfield Suffolk. *Berdefelda* (*sic*) 1086 (DB), *Bedefeld* 12th cent. 'Open land of a man called Bēda'. OE pers. name + *feld*.

Bedfont, East (Gtr. London) **& West** (Surrey). *Bedefunt* 1086 (DB). Probably 'spring provided with a drinking-vessel'. OE *byden* + **funta*.

Bedford Beds. *Bedanford* 880, *Bedeford* 1086 (DB). 'Ford of a man called Bīeda'. OE pers. name + *ford*. **Bedfordshire** (OE *scīr* 'district') is first referred to in the 11th cent.

Bedhampton Hants. *Betametone* 1086 (DB). Possibly 'farmstead of the dwellers where beet is grown'. OE *bēte* + *hǣme* + *tūn*.

Bedingfield Suffolk. *Bedingefelda* 1086 (DB). 'Open land of the family or followers of a man called Bēda'. OE pers. name + *-inga-* + *feld*.

Bedlington Northum. *Bedlingtun c.*1050. Probably 'estate associated with a man called *Bēdla or *Bētla'. OE pers. name + *-ing-* + *tūn*.

Bednall Staffs. *Bedehala* 1086 (DB). 'Nook of land of a man called Bēda'. OE pers. name (genitive *-n*) + *halh*.

Bedstone Shrops. *Betietetune* 1086 (DB). 'Farmstead of a man called *Bedgēat'. OE pers. name + *tūn*.

Bedworth Warwicks. *Bedeword* 1086 (DB). 'Enclosure of a man called Bē(a)da'. OE pers. name + *worth*.

Bedwyn, Great & Little Wilts. *Bedewinde* 778, *Bedvinde* 1086 (DB). Probably 'place where bindweed or convolvulus grows'. OE **bedwinde*.

Beeby Leics. *Bebi* 1086 (DB). 'Farmstead or village where bees are kept'. OE *bēo* + OScand. *bý*.

Beech Staffs. *Le Bech* 1285. '(Place at) the beech-tree'. OE *bēce*.

Beech Hill Berks. *Le Bechehulle* 1384. 'Hill where beech-trees grow'. OE *bēce* + *hyll*.

Beechingstoke Wilts. *Stoke* 941, *Bichenestoch* 1086 (DB). 'Outlying farmstead where bitches or hounds are kept'. OE *bicce* (genitive plural *-na*) + *stoc*.

Beeding, Lower & Upper W. Sussex. *Beadingum* c.880, *Bedinges* 1086 (DB). '(Settlement of) the family or followers of a man called Bēada'. OE pers. name + *-ingas*.

Beedon Berks. *Bydene* 965, *Bedene* 1086 (DB). '(Place at) the tub-shaped valley'. OE *byden*.

Beeford Humber. *Biuuorde* 1086 (DB). '(Place) by the ford', or 'ford where bees are found'. OE *bī* or *bēo* + *ford*.

Beeley Derbys. *Begelie* 1086 (DB). 'Woodland clearing of a woman called Bēage or a man called *Bēga'. OE pers. name + *lēah*.

Beelsby Humber. *Belesbi* 1086 (DB). 'Farmstead or village of a man called Beli'. OScand. pers. name + *bý*.

Beenham Berks. *Benham* 12th cent. 'Homestead or enclosure where beans are grown'. OE *bēan* + *hām* or *hamm*.

Beer Devon. *Bera* 1086 (DB). '(Place by) the grove'. OE *bearu*.

Beer Crocombe Somerset. *Bere* 1086 (DB). 'The grove', or 'the woodland pasture'. OE *bearu* or *bǣr* + manorial affix from the *Craucombe* family, here in the 13th cent.

Beer Hackett Dorset. *Bera* 1176, *Berehaket* 1362. 'The grove', or 'the woodland pasture'. OE *bearu* or *bǣr* + manorial affix from a 12th cent. owner called *Haket*.

Beesby Lincs. *Besebi* 1086 (DB). Possibly 'farmstead or village of a man called Bōsi'. OScand. pers. name + *bý*. Alternatively the first element may be OE **bēos* 'bent-grass'.

Beeston, usually 'farmstead where bent-grass grows', OE **bēos* + *tūn*:
Beeston Beds. *Bistone* 1086 (DB).
Beeston Norfolk. *Bestone* 1254.
Beeston Notts. *Bestune* 1086 (DB).
Beeston W. Yorks. *Bestone* 1086 (DB).
Beeston Regis Norfolk. *Besetune* 1086 (DB). Affix is Latin *regis* 'of the king'.
However the following has a different origin: **Beeston** Ches. *Buistane* 1086 (DB). Probably 'stone or rock where commerce takes place'. OE *byge* + *stān*.

Beetham Cumbria. *Biedun* 1086 (DB). Probably '(place by) the embankments'. OScand. **beth* in a dative plural form **bjǫthum*.

Beetley Norfolk. *Betellea* 1086 (DB). Possibly 'clearing where beet is grown'. OE *bēte* + *lēah*.

Begbroke Oxon. *Bechebroc* 1086 (DB). 'Brook of a man called Becca'. OE pers. name + *brōc*.

Beighton Norfolk. *Begetuna* 1086 (DB). 'Farmstead of a woman called Bēage or of a man called Bǣga'. OE pers. name + *tūn*.

Beighton S. Yorks. *Bectune* c.1002, 1086 (DB). 'Farmstead by the stream'. OE *bece* + *tūn*.

Bekesbourne Kent. *Burnes* 1086 (DB), *Bekesborne* 1280. '(Place at) the stream'. OE *burna* + manorial affix from the *de Beche* family, here in the late 12th cent.

Belaugh Norfolk. *Belaga* 1086 (DB). Possibly 'enclosure where the dead are cremated'. OE *bēl* + *haga*.

Belbroughton Heref. & Worcs. *Beolne*, *Broctun* 817, *Bellem*, *Brocton* 1086 (DB), *Bellebrocton* 1292. Originally two distinct names. *Bell* is an old river-name, probably from OE *beolone* 'henbane'; *Broughton* is 'farmstead on the brook', OE *brōc* + *tūn*.

Belchamp Otten, St Paul & Walter Essex. *Bylcham* c.940, *Belcham*, *Belcamp* 1086 (DB), *Belcham Otes* 1256, *Belchampe of St Paul* 1451, *Waterbelcham* 1297. Probably 'homestead with a beamed or vaulted roof'. OE *belc* + *hām*. Distinguishing affixes from early possession by a man called *Otto*, by St Paul's Cathedral, and by a man called *Walter*.

Belchford Lincs. *Beltesford* 1086 (DB). Probably 'ford of a man called *Belt'. OE pers. name + *ford*.

Belford Northum. *Beleford* 1242. Possibly 'ford by the bell-shaped hill'. OE *belle* + *ford*.

Belleau Lincs. *Elgelo* 1086 (DB). 'Meadow of a man called Helgi'. OScand. pers. name + *ló*. The modern form, as if from a French name meaning 'beautiful water', is unhistorical.

Bellerby N. Yorks. *Belgebi* 1086 (DB). 'Farmstead or village of a man called Belgr'. OScand. pers. name + *bý*.

Bellingham Gtr. London. *Beringaham* 998, *Belingeham* 1198. 'Homestead or enclosure of the family or followers of a man called *Bera'. OE pers. name + *-inga-* + *hām* or *hamm*.

Bellingham Northum. *Bellingham* 1254. 'Homestead of the dwellers at the bell-shaped hill', or simply 'homestead at the bell-shaped hill'. OE *belle* + *-inga-* or *-ing* + *hām*.

Belmesthorpe Leics. *Beolmesthorp* c.1050, *Belmestorp* 1086 (DB). 'Outlying farmstead or hamlet of a man called Beornhelm'. OE pers. name + OScand. *thorp*.

Belper Derbys. *Beurepeir* 1231. 'Beautiful retreat'. OFrench *beau* + *repaire*.

Belsay Northum. *Bilesho* 1163. 'Hill-spur of a man called Bil(l)'. OE pers. name + *hōh*.

Belsize Herts., not on record before the mid 19th cent., but a common name-type found as Bellasis, Bellasize, etc. in other counties and meaning 'beautiful seat or residence', from OFrench *bel* + *assis*.

Belstead Suffolk. *Belesteda* 1086 (DB). 'Place in a glade' or 'place of a funeral pyre'. OE **bel-* or *bēl* + *stede*.

Belstone Devon. *Bellestam* (*sic*) 1086 (DB), *Belestan* 1167. '(Place at) the bell-shaped stone'. OE *belle* + *stān*.

Beltoft Humber. *Beltot* 1086 (DB). Possibly 'homestead near a funeral pyre, or on dry ground in marsh'. OE *bēl* or **bel-* + OScand. *toft*.

Belton, meaning uncertain, 'farmstead in a glade or on dry ground in marsh', or 'farmstead near a funeral pyre', OE **bel-* or *bēl* + *tūn*: **Belton** Humber. *Beltone* 1086 (DB). **Belton** Leics., near Shepshed. *Beltona* c.1125. **Belton** Leics., near Uppingham. *Bealton* 1167. **Belton** Lincs. *Beltone* 1086 (DB). **Belton** Norfolk. *Beletuna* 1086 (DB).

Belvoir Leics. *Belveder* 1130. 'Beautiful view'. OFrench *bel* + *vedeir*.

Bembridge I. of Wight. *Bynnebrygg* 1316. '(Place lying) inside the bridge'. OE *binnan* + *brycg*.

Bempton Humber. *Bentone* 1086 (DB). 'Farmstead made of beams, or by a tree'. OE *bēam* + *tūn*.

Benacre Suffolk. *Benagra* 1086 (DB). 'Cultivated plot where beans are grown'. OE *bēan* + *æcer*.

Benenden Kent. *Bingdene* 993, *Benindene* 1086 (DB). 'Woodland pasture associated with a man called Bionna'. OE pers. name + *-ing-* + *denn*.

Benfleet Essex. *Beamfleote* 10th cent., *Benflet* 1086 (DB). 'Tree-trunk creek', perhaps referring to a bridge. OE *bēam* + *flēot*.

Benhall Green Suffolk. *Benenhala* 1086 (DB). 'Nook of land where beans are grown'. OE *bēanen* + *halh*.

Beningbrough N. Yorks. *Benniburg* 1086 (DB). 'Stronghold associated with a man called Beonna'. OE pers. name + *-ing-* + *burh*.

Benington Herts. *Benintone* 1086 (DB). 'Farmstead by the River Beane'. Pre-English river-name (of uncertain origin and meaning) + OE *-ing-* + *tūn*.

Benington Lincs. *Benigtun* 12th cent. 'Farmstead associated with a man called Beonna'. OE pers. name + *-ing-* + *tūn*.

Bennington, Long Lincs. *Beningtun* 1086 (DB). Identical in origin with the previous name.

Benniworth Lincs. *Beningurde* 1086 (DB). 'Enclosure of the family or followers of a man called Beonna'. OE pers. name + *-inga-* + *worth*.

Benson Oxon. *Bænesingtun* c.900, *Besintone* 1086 (DB). 'Estate associated with a man called *Benesa'. OE pers. name + *-ing-* + *tūn*.

Benthall Shrops., near Broseley. *Benethala* 12th cent. 'Nook of land where bent-grass grows'. OE *beonet* + *halh*.

Bentham, 'homestead or enclosure where bent-grass grows', OE *beonet* + *hām* or *hamm*: **Bentham** Glos. *Benetham* 1220. **Bentham, High & Lower** N. Yorks. *Benetain (sic)* 1086 (DB), *Benetham* 1214.

Bentley, a common name, 'woodland clearing where bent-grass grows', OE *beonet* + *lēah*; examples include: **Bentley** Hants., near Alton. *Beonetleh c.*965, *Benedlei* 1086 (DB). **Bentley** Humber. *Benedlage* 1086 (DB). **Bentley** S. Yorks. *Benedleia* 1086 (DB). **Bentley, Fenny** Derbys. *Benedlege* 1086 (DB), *Fennibenetlegh* 1272. Affix is OE *fennig* 'marshy'. **Bentley, Great & Little** Essex. *Benetleye c.*1040, *Benetlea* 1086 (DB).

Bentworth Hants. *Binteworda* 1130. Probably 'enclosure of a man called *Binta'. OE pers. name + *worth*.

Benwick Cambs. *Beymwich* 1221. 'Farm where beans are grown', or 'farm by a tree-trunk'. OE *bēan* or *bēam* + *wīc*.

Beoley Heref. & Worcs. *Beoleah* 972, *Beolege* 1086 (DB). 'Wood or clearing frequented by bees'. OE *bēo* + *lēah*.

Bepton W. Sussex. *Babintone* 1086 (DB). 'Estate associated with a woman called Bebbe or a man called *Bebba'. OE pers. name + *-ing-* + *tūn*.

Berden Essex. *Berdane* 1086 (DB). Probably 'valley with a woodland pasture'. OE *bǣr* + *denu*.

Bere Alston Devon. *Alphameston* 1339, *Berealmiston c.*1450. 'Farmstead of a man called Ælfhelm'. OE pers. name + *tūn*, with *Bere* from BERE FERRERS.

Bere Ferrers Devon. *Birlanda (sic)* 1086 (DB), *Ber* 1242, *Byr Ferrers* 1306. 'Woodland pasture', or 'wood, grove', OE *bǣr* or *bearu* (in the first spelling with *land* 'estate'). Manorial affix from the *de Ferers* family, here in the 13th cent.

Bere Regis Dorset. *Bere* 1086 (DB), *Kyngesbyre* 1264. 'Woodland pasture', or 'wood, grove', OE *bǣr* or *bearu*. Affix is Latin *regis* 'of the king'.

Bergholt, 'wood on or by a hill', OE *beorg* + *holt*: **Bergholt, East** Suffolk. *Bercolt* 1086 (DB). **Bergholt, West** Essex. *Bercolt* 1086 (DB).

Berkeley Glos. *Berclea* 824, *Berchelai* 1086 (DB). 'Birch-tree wood or clearing'. OE *beorc* + *lēah*.

Berkhamsted, Great Herts. *Beorhthanstædæ* 10th cent., *Berchehamstede* 1086 (DB). Probably 'homestead on or near a hill'. OE *beorg* + *hām-stede*.

Berkhamsted, Little Herts. *Berchehamstede* 1086 (DB). Probably 'homestead where birch-trees grow'. OE *beorc* + *hām-stede*.

Berkley Somerset. *Berchelei* 1086 (DB). 'Birch-tree wood or clearing'. OE *beorc* + *lēah*.

Berkshire (the county). *Berrocscire* 893. An ancient Celtic name meaning 'hilly place' + OE *scīr* 'shire, district'.

Berkswell W. Mids. *Berchewelle* 1086 (DB). 'Spring or stream of a man called Beorcol'. OE pers. name + *wella*.

Bermondsey Gtr. London. *Vermundesei (sic) c.*712, *Bermundesye* 1086 (DB). 'Island, or dry ground in marsh, of a man called Beornmund'. OE pers. name + *ēg*.

Berrick Salome Oxon. *Berewiche* 1086 (DB), *Berwick Sullame* 1571. 'Barley farm', or 'outlying part of an estate'. OE *bere-wīc* + manorial affix from early possession by the *de Suleham* family.

Berrier Cumbria. *Berghgerge* 1166. 'Shieling or pasture on a hill'. OScand. *berg* + *erg*.

Berrington Northum. *Berigdon* 1208–10. 'Hill with a fortification'. OE *burh* (genitive or dative *byrig*) + *dūn*.

Berrington Shrops. *Beritune* 1086 (DB). 'Farmstead near a fortification'. OE *burh* (genitive or dative *byrig*) + *tūn*.

Berrow Somerset. *Burgh* 973, *Berges* 1196. '(Place at) the hill(s) or mound(s)'. OE *beorg*, with reference to the sand-dunes here.

Berrow Green Heref. & Worcs. *Berga* 1275. '(Place at) the hill or mound'. OE *beorg*.

Berrynarbor Devon. *Biria c.*1150, *Bery Narberd* 1244. '(Place at) the fortification'. OE *burh* (dative *byrig*) + manorial affix from the *Nerebert* family, here in the 13th cent.

Berry Pomeroy Devon. *Beri* 1086 (DB),

Bury Pomery 1281. Identical in origin with the previous name. Manorial affix from the *de Pomerei* family, here from the 11th cent.

Bersted W. Sussex. *Beorganstede* 680. Probably 'homestead by a tumulus'. OE *beorg* + *hām-stede*.

Berwick, a common name, from OE *bere-wīc* 'barley farm, outlying part of an estate'; examples include: **Berwick Bassett** Wilts. *Berwicha* 1168, *Berewykbasset* 1321. Manorial affix from the *Basset* family, here in the 13th cent. **Berwick St James** Wilts. *Berewyk Sancti Jacobi c.*1190. Affix *St James* (Latin *Jacobus*) from the dedication of the church. **Berwick St John** Wilts. *Berwicha* 1167, *Berewyke S. Johannis* 1265. Affix from the dedication of the church. **Berwick St Leonard** Wilts. *Berewica* 12th cent., *Berewyk Sancti Leonardi* 1291. Affix from the dedication of the church. **Berwick upon Tweed** Northum. *Berewich* 1167, *Berewicum super Twedam* 1229. For the river-name, see TWEEDMOUTH.

Besford Heref. & Worcs. *Bettesford* 972, *Beford* (*sic*) 1086 (DB). 'Ford of a man called Betti'. OE pers. name + *ford*.

Bessacarr S. Yorks. *Beseacra* 1182. 'Cultivated plot where bent-grass grows'. OE **bēos* + *æcer*.

Bessels Leigh Oxon., see LEIGH.

Bessingham Norfolk. *Basingeham* 1086 (DB). 'Homestead of the family or followers of a man called *Basa'. OE pers. name + *-inga-* + *hām*.

Besthorpe, 'outlying farmstead or hamlet of a man called Bōsi, or where bent-grass grows', OScand. pers. name or OE **bēos* + OScand. *thorp*: **Besthorpe** Norfolk. *Besethorp* 1086 (DB). **Besthorpe** Notts. *Bestorp* 1147.

Beswick Humber. *Basewic* 1086 (DB). 'Dwelling or (dairy) farm of a man called Bōsi or Bessi'. OScand. pers. name + OE *wīc*.

Betchworth Surrey. *Becesworde* 1086 (DB). 'Enclosure of a man called *Becci'. OE pers. name + *worth*.

Bethersden Kent. *Baedericesdaenne c.*1100. 'Woodland pasture of a man called Beadurīc'. OE pers. name + *denn*.

Bethnal Green Gtr. London. *Blithehale* 13th cent., *Blethenalegrene* 1443. 'Nook of land of a man called *Blītha'. OE pers. name (genitive *-n*) + *halh*, with the later addition of *grēne* 'village green'. Alternatively the first element may be an OE stream-name *Blīthe* meaning 'the gentle one'.

Betley Staffs. *Betelege* 1086 (DB). 'Woodland clearing of a woman called *Bette'. OE pers. name + *lēah*.

Betteshanger Kent. *Betleshangre* 1176. Probably 'wooded slope by a house or building'. OE *(ge)bytle* + *hangra*.

Bettiscombe Dorset. *Bethescomme* 1129. 'Valley of a man called Betti'. OE pers. name + *cumb*.

Betton, possibly 'farmstead of a woman called Bēage or of a man called Bǣga', OE pers. name + *tūn*: **Betton** Shrops., near Binweston. *Betune* 1086 (DB). **Betton** Shrops., near Market Drayton. *Baitune* 1086 (DB).

Bevercotes Notts. *Beurecote* 1165. 'Place where beavers have built their nests'. OE *beofor* + *cot*.

Beverley Humber. *Beferlic c.*1025, *Bevreli* 1086 (DB). Probably 'stream frequented by beavers'. OE *beofor* + **licc*.

Beverstone Glos. *Beurestane* 1086 (DB). Probably '(boundary) stone of a man called *Beofor'. OE pers. name + *stān*.

Bewaldeth Cumbria. *Bualdith* 1255. 'Homestead or estate of a woman called Aldgȳth'. OScand. *bú* + OE pers. name. The order of elements is Celtic.

Bewcastle Cumbria. *Bothecastre* 12th cent. 'Roman fort within which shelters or huts were situated'. OScand. *búth* + OE *ceaster*.

Bewdley Heref. & Worcs. *Beuleu* 1275. 'Beautiful place'. OFrench *beau* + *lieu*.

Bewerley N. Yorks. *Beurelie* 1086 (DB). 'Woodland clearing frequented by beavers'. OE *beofor* + *lēah*.

Bewholme Humber. *Begun* 1086 (DB). '(Place at) the river-bends'. OE *bēag* or OScand. **bjúgr* in a dative plural form *bēagum* or **bjúgum*.

Bexhill E. Sussex. *Bixlea* 772, *Bexelei* 1086 (DB). 'Wood or clearing where box-trees grow'. OE **byxe* + *lēah*.

Bexington Dorset. *Bessintone* 1086 (DB). 'Farmstead or village where box-trees grow'. OE *byxen* + *tūn*.

Bexley Gtr. London. *Byxlea* 814. 'Wood or clearing where box-trees grow'. OE **byxe* + *lēah*. **Bexleyheath** is a more recent name with the addition *heath*.

Bexwell Norfolk. *Bekeswella* 1086 (DB). 'Spring or stream of a man called *Bēac'. OE pers. name + *wella*.

Beyton Suffolk. *Begatona* 1086 (DB). Probably 'farmstead of a woman called Bēage or of a man called Bǣga'. OE pers. name + *tūn*.

Bibury Glos. *Beaganbyrig* 8th cent., *Begeberie* 1086 (DB). 'Stronghold or manor house of a woman called Bēage'. OE pers. name + *burh* (dative *byrig*).

Bicester Oxon. *Bernecestre* 1086 (DB). 'Fort of the warriors, or of a man called Beorna'. OE *beorn* or OE pers. name + *ceaster*.

Bickenhall Somerset. *Bichehalle* 1086 (DB). Probably 'hall of a man called Bica'. OE pers. name (genitive *-n*) + *heall*.

Bicker Lincs. *Bichere* 1086 (DB). Probably 'village marsh', from OScand. *bý* + *kjarr*. Alternatively '(place) by the marsh', with OE *bī* as first element.

Bickerstaffe Lancs. *Bikerstad* late 12th cent. 'Landing-place of the bee-keepers'. OE **bīcere* + *stæth*.

Bickerton, 'farmstead of the bee-keepers', OE **bīcere* + *tūn*: **Bickerton** Ches. *Bicretone* 1086 (DB). **Bickerton** N. Yorks. *Bicretone* 1086 (DB).

Bickington, 'estate associated with a man called Beocca', OE pers. name + *-ing-* + *tūn*: **Bickington** Devon, near Ashburton. *Bechintona* 1107. **Bickington, Abbots** Devon. *Bicatona* 1086 (DB), *Abbots Bekenton* 1580. Affix from early possession by Hartland Abbey. **Bickington, High** Devon. *Bichentona* 1086 (DB), *Heghebuginton* 1423. Affix is OE *hēah* 'high'.

Bickleigh, Bickley, probably 'woodland clearing where there are nests of bees', OE **bīc* + *lēah*: **Bickleigh** Devon, near Plymouth. *Bicheleia* 1086 (DB). **Bickleigh** Devon, near Tiverton. *Bicanleag* 904, *Bichelia* 1086 (DB). **Bickley** Gtr. London. *Byckeleye* 1279. **Bickley Moss** Ches. *Bichelei* 1086 (DB). Later addition is OE *mos* 'peat-bog'.

Bicknacre Essex. *Bikenacher* 1186. Probably 'cultivated plot of a man called Bica'. OE pers. name (genitive *-n*) + *æcer*.

Bicknoller Somerset. *Bykenalre* 1291. 'Alder-tree of a man called Bica'. OE pers. name (genitive *-n*) + *alor*.

Bicknor Kent. *Bikenora* 1186. Probably 'slope below the pointed hill'. OE **bica* (genitive *-n*) + *ōra*.

Bicknor, English Glos. *Bicanofre* 1086 (DB), *Englise Bykenore* 1248. Probably 'ridge with a point'. OE **bica* (genitive *-n*) + **ofer*. Affix from its situation on the *English* side of the River Wye.

Bicknor, Welsh Heref. & Worcs. *Bykenore Walens* 1291. Identical in origin with the previous name, with distinguishing affix from its situation on the *Welsh* side of the River Wye.

Bickton Hants. *Bichetone* 1086 (DB). Probably 'farmstead of a man called Bica'. OE pers. name + *tūn*.

Bicton Shrops., near Shrewsbury. *Bichetone* (*sic*) 1086 (DB), *Bykedon* 1248. Probably 'hill with a pointed ridge'. OE **bica* + *dūn*.

Bidborough Kent. *Bitteberga* c.1100. 'Hill or mound of a man called *Bitta'. OE pers. name + *beorg*.

Biddenden Kent. *Bidingden* 993. 'Woodland pasture associated with a man called *Bida'. OE pers. name + *-ing-* + *denn*.

Biddenham Beds. *Bidenham* 1086 (DB). 'Homestead, or land in a river-bend, of a man called Bīeda'. OE pers. name (genitive *-n*) + *hām* or *hamm*.

Biddestone Wilts. *Bedestone* 1086 (DB), *Bedeneston* 1187. Probably 'farmstead of a man called *Bīedin or *Bīede'. OE pers. name + *tūn*.

Biddisham Somerset. *Biddesham* 1065. 'Homestead or enclosure of a man called *Biddi'. OE pers. name + *hām* or *hamm*.

Biddlesden Bucks. *Betesdene* (*sic*) 1086 (DB), *Bethlesdena* 12th cent. Probably 'valley with a house or building'. OE *bythle* + *denu*. Alternatively the first element may be an OE pers. name *Byttel.

Biddlestone Northum. *Bidlisden* 1242. Probably identical in origin with the previous name.

Biddulph Staffs. *Bidolf* 1086 (DB). '(Place) by the pit or quarry'. OE *bī* + **dylf*.

Bideford Devon. *Bedeford* 1086 (DB). Possibly 'ford at the stream called *Bȳd*'. Celtic river-name (of uncertain origin and meaning) + OE *ēa* + *ford*.

Bidford on Avon Warwicks. *Budiford* 710, *Bedeford* 1086 (DB). Probably identical in origin with the previous name, but alternatively the first element may be an OE **bydic* 'trough, deep place'.

Bielby Humber. *Belebi* 1086 (DB). 'Farmstead or village of a man called Beli'. OScand. pers. name + *bý*.

Bierley W. Yorks. *Birle* 1086 (DB). 'Woodland clearing by the stronghold'. OE *burh* (genitive *byrh*) + *lēah*.

Bierton Bucks. *Bortone* 1086 (DB). 'Farmstead near the stronghold'. OE *byrh-tūn*.

Bigbury Devon. *Bicheberie* 1086 (DB). 'Stronghold of a man called Bica'. OE pers. name + *burh* (dative *byrig*).

Bigby Lincs. *Bechebi* 1086 (DB). Probably 'farmstead or village of a man called *Bekki'. OScand. pers. name + *bý*.

Biggin Hill Gtr. London. *Byggunhull* 1499. 'Hill with or near a building'. ME *bigging* + OE *hyll*.

Biggleswade Beds. *Pichelesuuade* (*sic*) 1086 (DB), *Bicheleswada* 1132. 'Ford of a man called *Biccel'. OE pers. name + *wæd*.

Bighton Hants. *Bicincgtun* 959, *Bighetone* 1086 (DB). 'Estate associated with a man called Bica'. OE pers. name + *-ing-* + *tūn*.

Bignor W. Sussex. *Bigenevre* 1086 (DB). 'Hill brow of a man called *Bicga'. OE pers. name (genitive *-n*) + *yfer*.

Bilborough Notts. *Bileburch* 1086 (DB). 'Stronghold of a man called *Bila or *Billa'. OE pers. name + *burh*.

Bilbrook Staffs. *Bilrebroch* 1086 (DB). 'Brook where watercress grows'. OE **billere* + *brōc*.

Bilbrough N. Yorks. *Mileburg* (*sic*) 1086 (DB), *Billeburc* 1167. Identical in origin with BILBOROUGH.

Bildeston Suffolk. *Bilestuna* 1086 (DB). Identical in origin with BILSTONE.

Billericay Essex. *Byllyrica* 1291. Probably from a medieval Latin word **bellerīca* meaning 'dyehouse or tanhouse'.

Billesdon Leics. *Billesdone* 1086 (DB). 'Hill of a man called Bill'. OE pers. name + *dūn*. Alternatively the first element may be OE *bill* 'sword' used of a pointed hill.

Billesley Warwicks. *Billeslæh* 704-9, *Billeslei* 1086 (DB). 'Woodland clearing of a man called Bill'. OE pers. name + *lēah*. Alternatively the first element may be OE *bill* 'pointed hill'.

Billing, Great & Little Northants. *Bel(l)inge* 1086 (DB). Probably '(settlement of) the family or followers of a man called Bill or *Billa'. OE pers. name + *-ingas*.

Billingborough Lincs. *Billingeburg* 1086 (DB). Probably 'stronghold of the family or followers of a man called Bill or *Billa'. OE pers. name + *-inga-* + *burh*.

Billinge Mersey. *Billing* 1202. Probably OE **bil(l)ing* 'a hill, a sharp ridge'.

Billingham Cleveland. *Billingham* c.1050. 'Homestead of the family or followers of a man called Bill or *Billa', or 'homestead at the place associated with Bill(a)'. OE pers. name + *-inga-* or *-ing* + *hām*. Alternatively the first element may be OE **bil(l)ing* 'a hill'.

Billinghay Lincs. *Belingei* 1086 (DB). 'Island, or dry ground in marsh, of the family or followers of a man called Bill or *Billa'. OE pers. name + *-inga-* + *ēg*.

Billingley S. Yorks. *Bilingeleia* 1086 (DB). 'Woodland clearing of the family or followers of a man called Bill or *Billa'. OE pers. name + *-inga-* + *lēah*.

Billingshurst W. Sussex. *Bellingesherst* 1202. Probably 'wooded hill of a man called Billing'. OE pers. name + *hyrst*. Alternatively the first element may be OE **bil(l)ing* 'a hill, a sharp ridge'.

Billington Beds. *Billendon* 1196. 'Hill of a man called *Billa'. OE pers. name (genitive *-n*) + *dūn*.

Billington Lancs. *Billingduna* 1196. 'Hill with a sharp ridge'. OE **bil(l)ing* + *dūn*.

Billockby Norfolk. *Bithlakebei* 1086 (DB). Possibly 'farmstead or village of a man called *Bithil-Áki'. OScand. pers. name + *bý*.

Bilney, 'island near a ridge', or 'island of a man called Bil(l)a', OE *bile* or OE pers. name (genitive *-n*) + *ēg*: **Bilney, East** Norfolk. *Billneye* 1254. **Bilney, West** Norfolk. *Bilenei* 1086 (DB).

Bilsborrow Lancs. *Billesbure* 1187. 'Stronghold of a man called Bill'. OE pers. name + *burh*.

Bilsby Lincs. *Billesbi* 1086 (DB). 'Farmstead or village of a man called Bildr'. OScand. pers. name + *bý*.

Bilsington Kent. *Bilsvitone* 1086 (DB). 'Farmstead of a woman called Bilswīth'. OE pers. name + *tūn*.

Bilsthorpe Notts. *Bildestorp* 1086 (DB). 'Outlying farmstead or hamlet of a man called Bildr'. OScand. pers. name + *thorp*. Alternatively the first element may be OScand. *bildr* 'angle' used figuratively for 'hill, promontory'.

Bilston W. Mids. *Bilsetnatun* 996, *Billestune* 1086 (DB). 'Farmstead of the dwellers at the sharp ridge'. OE *bill* + *sǣte* (genitive plural *sǣtna*) + *tūn*.

Bilstone Leics. *Bildestone* 1086 (DB). Probably 'farmstead of a man called Bildr'. OScand. pers. name + OE *tūn*. Alternatively the first element may be OScand. *bildr* 'angle' used figuratively for 'hill, promontory'.

Bilton, usually 'farmstead of a man called Bill or *Billa', OE pers. name + *tūn*: **Bilton** Humber. *Bil(l)etone* 1086 (DB). **Bilton** Northum. *Bylton* 1242. **Bilton** N. Yorks. *Biletone* 1086 (DB).
However with a different origin is: **Bilton** Warwicks. *Beltone, Bentone* 1086 (DB). Possibly 'farmstead where henbane grows'. OE *beolone* + *tūn*.

Binbrook Lincs. *Binnibroc* 1086 (DB). '(Place) enclosed by the brook', or 'brook of a man called Bynna'. OE *binnan* or OE pers. name + *brōc*.

Bincombe Dorset. *Beuncumbe* 987, *Beincome* 1086 (DB). Probably 'valley where beans are grown'. OE *bēan* + *cumb*.

Binegar Somerset. *Begenhangra* 1065. Probably 'wooded slope of a woman called Bēage'. OE pers. name (genitive *-n*) + *hangra*. Alternatively the first element may be OE **begen* 'growing with berries'.

Binfield Berks. *Benetfeld c.*1160. 'Open land where bent-grass grows'. OE *beonet* + *feld*.

Binfield Heath Oxon. *Benifeld* 1177. Probably identical in origin with the previous name, but possibly 'open land of a man called *Beona', OE pers. name + *feld*. The addition *heath* is found from the 16th cent.

Bingfield Northum. *Bingefeld* 1181. Probably 'open land of the family or followers of a man called Bynna'. OE pers. name + *-inga-* + *feld*. Alternatively in this and the following two names the first element may be an OE **bing* 'a hollow'.

Bingham Notts. *Bingheham* 1086 (DB). Probably 'homestead of the family or followers of a man called Bynna'. OE pers. name + *-inga-* + *hām*. But see BINGFIELD.

Bingley W. Yorks. *Bingelei* 1086 (DB). Probably 'woodland clearing of the family or followers of a man called Bynna'. OE pers. name + *-inga-* + *lēah*. But see BINGFIELD.

Binham Norfolk. *Binneham* 1086 (DB). 'Homestead or enclosure of a man called Bynna'. OE pers. name + *hām* or *hamm*.

Binley W. Mids. *Bilnei* 1086 (DB). 'Island near a ridge', or 'island of a man called *Bil(l)a'. OE *bile* or pers. name (genitive *-n*) + *ēg*.

Binstead I. of Wight. *Benestede* 1086 (DB). 'Place where beans are grown'. OE *bēan* + *stede*.

Binsted Hants. *Benestede* 1086 (DB). Identical in origin with the previous name.

Binton Warwicks. *Bynningtun c.*1005, *Beninton* 1086 (DB). 'Estate associated with a man called Bynna'. OE pers. name + *-ing-* + *tūn*.

Bintree Norfolk. *Binnetre* 1086 (DB).

'Tree of a man called Bynna'. OE pers. name + *trēow*.

Binweston Shrops. *Binneweston* 1292. Probably 'west farmstead of a man called Bynna'. OE pers. name + *west* + *tūn*.

Birch Essex. *Bric(ce)iam* 1086 (DB). OE *bryce* 'land newly broken up for cultivation'.

Birch, Much & Little Heref. & Worcs. *Birches* 1252. '(Place at) the birch-tree(s)'. OE *birce*. The affix *Much* is from OE *micel* 'great'.

Bircham, Great, Bircham Newton, Bircham Tofts Norfolk. *Brecham* 1086 (DB). 'Homestead by newly cultivated ground'. OE *brēc* + *hām*. Bircham Newton is *Niwetuna* 1086 (DB), 'new farmstead', OE *nīwe* + *tūn*. Bircham Tofts is *Toftes* 1205, OScand. *toft* 'homestead'.

Birchanger Essex. *Bilichangra (sic)* 1086 (DB), *Birichangre* 12th cent. 'Wooded slope growing with birch-trees'. OE *birce* + *hangra*.

Bircher Heref. & Worcs. *Burchoure* 1212. 'Ridge where birch-trees grow'. OE *birce* + **ofer*.

Birchington Kent. *Birchenton* 1240. 'Farmstead where birch-trees grow'. OE *bircen* + *tūn*.

Birchover Derbys. *Barcovere (sic)* 1086 (DB), *Birchoure* 1226. 'Ridge where birch-trees grow'. OE *birce* + **ofer*.

Birdbrook Essex. *Bridebroc* 1086 (DB). 'Brook frequented by birds'. OE *bridd* + *brōc*.

Birdham W. Sussex. *Bridham* 683, *Brideham* 1086 (DB). 'Homestead or enclosure frequented by birds'. OE *bridd* + *hām* or *hamm*.

Birdlip Glos. *Bridelepe* 1221. Probably 'steep place frequented by birds'. OE *bridd* + **hlēp*.

Birdsall N. Yorks. *Brideshala* 1086 (DB). 'Nook of land of a man called Bridd'. OE pers. name + *halh*.

Birkby N. Yorks. *Bretebi* 1086 (DB). 'Farmstead or village of the Britons'. OScand. *Bretar* + *bý*. The same name occurs in W. Yorks. and Cumbria.

Birkdale Mersey. *Birkedale c.*1200. 'Valley where birch-trees grow'. OScand. *birki* + *dalr*.

Birkenhead Mersey. *Bircheveth c.*1200. 'Headland where birch-trees grow'. OE *birce, bircen* (with Scand. *-k-*) + *hēafod*.

Birkenshaw W. Yorks. *Birkenschawe* 1274. 'Small wood or copse where birch-trees grow'. OE *bircen* (with Scand. *-k-*) + *sceaga*.

Birkin N. Yorks. *Byrcene c.*1030, *Berchine* 1086 (DB). 'Place growing with birch-trees'. OE **bircen* (with Scand. *-k-*).

Birley Heref. & Worcs. *Burlei* 1086 (DB). 'Woodland clearing near a stronghold'. OE *burh* + *lēah*.

Birling, probably '(settlement of) the family or followers of a man called *Bǣrla', OE pers. name + *-ingas*: **Birling** Kent. *Boerlingas* 788, *Berlinge* 1086 (DB). **Birling** Northum. *Berlinga* 1187.

Birlingham Heref. & Worcs. *Byrlingahamm* 972, *Berlingeham* 1086 (DB). 'Land in a river-bend of the family or followers of a man called *Byrla'. OE pers. name + *-inga-* + *hamm*.

Birmingham W. Mids. *Bermingeham* 1086 (DB). 'Homestead of the family or followers of a man called *Beorma', or 'homestead at the place associated with *Beorma'. OE pers. name + *-inga-* or *-ing* + *hām*.

Birstall Leics. *Burstelle* 1086 (DB). OE *burh-stall* 'the site of a stronghold'.

Birstall W. Yorks. *Birstale* 12th cent. Identical in meaning with the previous name, but from OE *byrh-stall*.

Birstwith N. Yorks. *Beristade* 1086 (DB). Probably 'farm built on the site of a lost farm'. OScand. *býjar-stathr*.

Birtley, 'bright clearing', OE *beorht* + *lēah*: **Birtley** Northum. *Birtleye* 1229. **Birtley** Tyne & Wear. *Britleia* 1183.

Bisbrooke Leics. *Bitlesbroch* 1086 (DB). 'Brook of a man called *Bitel or *Byttel'. OE pers. name + *brōc*.

Bishampton Heref. & Worcs. *Bisantune* 1086 (DB). Possibly 'homestead of a man called *Bisa'. OE pers. name + *hām-tūn*.

Bishop, Bishops as affix, see main

name, e.g. for **Bishop Auckland** (Durham) see AUCKLAND.

Bishopsbourne Kent. *Burnan* 799, *Burnes* 1086 (DB), *Biscopesburne* 11th cent. '(Place at) the stream belonging to the bishop'. OE *biscop* (referring to the Archbishop of Canterbury) + *burna*.

Bishop's Castle Shrops. *Bissopes Castell* 1269. 'The bishop's castle'. OE *biscop* + *castel*.

Bishopsteignton Devon. *Taintona* 1086 (DB), *Teynton Bishops* 1341. 'Farmstead on the River Teign'. Celtic river-name (see TEIGNMOUTH) + OE *tūn*, with manorial affix from its possession by the Bishop of Exeter in 1086.

Bishopstoke Hants. *Stoches* 1086 (DB), *Stoke Episcopi* c.1270. 'Outlying farmstead or hamlet (of the bishop)'. OE *stoc* with later addition from its possession by the Bishop of Winchester.

Bishopstone, 'the bishop's estate', OE *biscop* + *tūn*; examples include: **Bishopstone** Bucks. *Bissopeston* 1227. **Bishopstone** E. Sussex. *Biscopestone* 1086 (DB). **Bishopstone** Heref. & Worcs. *Biscopestone* 1166. **Bishopstone** Wilts., near Swindon. *Bissopeston* 1186. **Bishopstone** Wilts., near Wilton. *Bissopeston* 1166.

Bishopsworth Avon. *Biscopewrde* 1086 (DB). 'The bishop's enclosure'. OE *biscop* + *worth*.

Bishopthorpe N. Yorks. *Torp* 1086 (DB), *Biscupthorp* 1275. 'Outlying farmstead or hamlet held by the bishop'. OE *biscop* + OScand. *thorp*.

Bishopton Durham. *Biscoptun* 1104–8. 'The bishop's estate'. OE *biscop* + *tūn*.

Bisley Glos. *Bislege* 986, *Biselege* 1086 (DB). 'Woodland clearing of a man called *Bisa'. OE pers. name + *lēah*.

Bisley Surrey. *Busseleghe* 933. 'Woodland clearing of a man called *Byssa'. OE pers. name + *lēah*.

Bispham, 'the bishop's estate', OE *biscop* + *hām*: **Bispham** Lancs. *Biscopham* 1086 (DB). **Bispham Green** Lancs. *Biscopehaim* c.1200.

Bisterne Close Hants. *Betestre* (*sic*) 1086 (DB), *Budestorn* 1187. Probably 'thorn-tree of a man called *Bytti'. OE pers. name + *thorn*.

Bitchfield Lincs. *Billesfelt* 1086 (DB). 'Open land of a man called Bill'. OE pers. name + *feld*. Alternatively the first element may be OE *bill* 'sword' used figuratively for 'hill, promontory'.

Bittadon Devon. *Bedendone* (*sic*) 1086 (DB), *Bettenden* 1205. 'Valley of a man called *Beotta'. OE pers. name + *denu*.

Bittering Norfolk. *Britringa* 1086 (DB). '(Settlement of) the family or followers of a man called Beorhthere'. OE pers. name + *-ingas*.

Bitterley Shrops. *Buterlie* 1086 (DB). 'Pasture which produces good butter'. OE *butere* + *lēah*.

Bitterne Hants. *Byterne* c.1090. Possibly 'house near a bend'. OE *byht* + *ærn*.

Bitteswell Leics. *Betmeswelle* 1086 (DB). Probably 'spring or stream in a broad valley'. OE **bytm* + *wella*.

Bitton Avon. *Betune* 1086 (DB). 'Farmstead on the River Boyd'. Celtic river-name (of uncertain origin and meaning) + OE *tūn*.

Bix Oxon. *Bixa* 1086 (DB). '(Place at) the box-tree wood'. OE **byxe*.

Blaby Leics. *Bladi* (*sic*) 1086 (DB), *Blabi* 1175. Probably 'farmstead or village of a man called Blár'. OScand. pers. name + *bý*.

Black as affix, see main name, e.g. for **Black Bourton** (Oxon.) see BOURTON.

Blackawton Devon. *Auetone* 1086 (DB), *Blakeauetone* 1281. 'Farmstead of a man called Afa'. OE pers. name + *tūn*. Affix is OE *blæc* 'dark-coloured' (referring to soil or vegetation).

Blackborough, 'dark-coloured hill', OE *blæc* + *beorg*: **Blackborough** Devon. *Blacaberga* 1086 (DB). **Blackborough End** Norfolk. *Blakeberge* c.1150.

Blackburn Lancs. *Blacheburne* 1086 (DB). 'Dark-coloured stream'. OE *blæc* + *burna*.

Blackden Heath Ches. *Blakedene* 1287. 'Dark valley'. OE *blæc* + *denu*.

Blackfield Hants., a recent name, self-explanatory.

Blackford Somerset, near Wedmore. *Blacford* 1227. 'Dark ford'. OE *blæc* + *ford*.

Blackfordby Leics. *Blakefordebi* c.1125.

'Farmstead at the dark ford'. OE *blæc* + *ford* + OScand. *bý*.

Blackheath Gtr. London. *Blachehedfeld* 1166. 'Dark-coloured heathland'. OE *blæc* + *hǣth* (with *feld* 'open land' in the early form).

Blackland Wilts. *Blakeland* 1194. 'Dark-coloured cultivated land'. OE *blæc* + *land*.

Blackley Gtr. Manch. *Blakeley* 1282. 'Dark wood or clearing'. OE *blæc* + *lēah*.

Blackmoor Hants. *Blachemere* 1168. 'Dark-coloured pool'. OE *blæc* + *mere*.

Blackmore Essex. *Blakemore* 1213. 'Dark-coloured marshland'. OE *blæc* + *mōr*.

Blackpool Lancs. *Pul* c.1260, *Blackpoole* 1602. 'Dark-coloured pool'. OE *blæc* + **pull*.

Blackrod Gtr. Manch. *Blacherode* c.1189. 'Dark clearing'. OE *blæc* + **rodu*.

Blackthorn Oxon. *Blaketorn* 1190. '(Place at) the black-thorn'. OE **blæc-thorn*.

Blacktoft Humber. *Blaketofte* c.1160. 'Dark-coloured homestead'. OE *blæc* + OScand. *toft*.

Blackwell, 'dark-coloured spring or stream', OE *blæc* + *wella*: **Blackwell** Derbys., near Buxton. *Blachewelle* 1086 (DB). **Blackwell** Durham. *Blakewell* 1183. **Blackwell** Warwicks. *Blacwælle* 964, *Blachewelle* 1086 (DB).

Blacon Ches. *Blachehol* (*sic*) 1086 (DB), *Blachenol* 1093. 'Dark-coloured hill'. OE *blæc* + *cnoll*.

Bladon Oxon. *Blade* 1086 (DB). A pre-English river-name of uncertain origin and meaning, an old name of the River EVENLODE.

Blagdon, 'dark-coloured hill', OE *blæc* + *dūn*: **Blagdon** Avon. *Blachedone* 1086 (DB). **Blagdon** Devon. *Blakedone* 1242. **Blagdon** Somerset. *Blakedona* 12th cent.

Blaisdon Glos. *Blechedon* 1186. 'Hill of a man called *Blæcci'. OE pers. name + *dūn*.

Blakemere Heref. & Worcs. *Blakemere* 1249. 'Dark-coloured pool'. OE *blæc* + *mere*.

Blakeney, 'dark-coloured island or dry ground in marsh', OE *blæc* (dative *blacan*) + *ēg*: **Blakeney** Glos. *Blakeneia* 1196. **Blakeney** Norfolk. *Blakenye* 1242.

Blakenhall Ches. *Blachenhale* 1086 (DB). 'Dark nook of land'. OE *blæc* (dative *blacan*) + *halh*.

Blakenham, Great & Little Suffolk. *Blac(he)ham* 1086 (DB). Probably 'homestead or enclosure of a man called Blaca'. OE pers. name (genitive *-n*) + *hām* or *hamm*.

Blakesley Northants. *Blaculveslei* 1086 (DB). 'Woodland clearing of a man called *Blæcwulf'. OE pers. name + *lēah*.

Blanchland Northum. *Blanchelande* 1165. 'White woodland glade'. OFrench *blanche* + *launde*.

Blandford Forum, Blandford St Mary Dorset. *Blaneford* 1086 (DB), *Blaneford Forum* 1297, *Blaneford St Mary* 1254. Probably 'ford where blay or gudgeon are found'. OE *blǣge* (genitive plural *blǣgna*) + *ford*. Distinguishing affixes from Latin *forum* 'market' and from the dedication of the church.

Blankney Lincs. *Blachene* (*sic*) 1086 (DB), *Blancaneia* 1157. 'Island, or dry ground in marsh, of a man called *Blanca'. OE pers. name (genitive *-n*) + *ēg*.

Blaston Leics. *Bladestone* 1086 (DB). Possibly 'farmstead of a man called *Blēath'. OE pers. name + *tūn*.

Blatchington, 'estate associated with a man called Blæcca', OE pers. name + *-ing-* + *tūn*: **Blatchington, East** E. Sussex. *Blechinton* 1169. **Blatchington, West** E. Sussex. *Blacinctona* 1121.

Blatherwycke Northants. *Blarewiche* 1086 (DB). Possibly 'farm where bladder-plants grow'. OE *blǣddre* + *wīc*.

Blawith Cumbria. *Blawit* 1276. 'Dark wood'. OScand. *blár* + *vithr*.

Blaxhall Suffolk. *Blaccheshala* 1086 (DB). 'Nook of land belonging to a man called *Blæc'. OE pers. name + *halh*.

Blaxton S. Yorks. *Blacston* 1213. 'Black boundary stone'. OE *blæc* + *stān*.

Blaydon Tyne & Wear. *Bladon* 1340. Probably 'cold or cheerless hill'. OScand. *blár* + OE *dūn*.

Bleadon Avon. *Bleodun* 956, *Bledone* 1086 (DB). 'Variegated hill'. OE **blēo* + *dūn*.

Blean Kent. *Blean* 724. Probably '(place in) the rough ground'. OE **blēa* (dative *-n*).

Bleasby Notts. *Blisetune* 956, *Blesby* 1268. Probably 'farmstead or village of a man called Blesi'. OScand. pers. name + *bý* (OE *tūn* in the earliest form).

Bledington Glos. *Bladintun* 1086 (DB). 'Farmstead on the River *Bladon*'. Pre-English river-name of uncertain origin and meaning (an old name of River EVENLODE) + OE *tūn*.

Bledlow Bucks. *Bleddanhlæw* 10th cent., *Bledelai* 1086 (DB). 'Burial-mound of a man called *Bledda'. OE pers. name + *hlāw*.

Blencarn Cumbria. *Blencarn* 1159. 'Cairn or rock summit'. Celtic **blain* + **carn*.

Blencogo Cumbria. *Blencoggou* c.1190. 'Cuckoos' summit'. Celtic **blain* + *cog* (plural *cogow*).

Blencow, Great & Little Cumbria. *Blenco* 1231. Celtic **blain* 'summit' with an uncertain second element.

Blendworth Hants. *Blednewrthie* c.1170. Probably 'enclosure of a man called *Blǣdna'. OE pers. name + *worth*.

Blennerhasset Cumbria. *Blennerheiseta* 1188. Probably 'hay shieling at the hill-farm'. Celtic **blain* + *tre* + OScand. *hey* + *sætr*.

Bletchingdon Oxon. *Blecesdone* 1086 (DB). 'Hill of a man called *Blecci'. OE pers. name + *dūn*.

Bletchingley Surrey. *Blachingelei* 1086 (DB). 'Woodland clearing of the family or followers of a man called Blæcca'. OE pers. name + *-inga-* + *lēah*.

Bletchley Bucks. *Blechelai* 12th cent. 'Woodland clearing of a man called Blæcca'. OE pers. name + *lēah*.

Bletchley Shrops. *Blecheslee* 1222. 'Woodland clearing of a man called Blæcca or *Blecci'. OE pers. name + *lēah*.

Bletsoe Beds. *Blechesho* 1086 (DB). 'Hill-spur of a man called *Blecci'. OE pers. name + *hōh*.

Blewbury Oxon. *Bleobyrig* 944, *Blidberia (sic)* 1086 (DB). 'Hill-fort with variegated soil'. OE **blēo* + *burh* (dative *byrig*).

Blickling Norfolk. *Blikelinges* 1086 (DB). '(Settlement of) the family or followers of a man called *Blicla'. OE pers. name + *-ingas*.

Blidworth Notts. *Blideworde* 1086 (DB). 'Enclosure of a man called *Blītha'. OE pers. name + *worth*.

Blindcrake Cumbria. *Blenecreyc* 12th cent. 'Rock summit'. Celtic **blain* + **creig*.

Blisland Cornwall. *Bleselonde* 1284. OE *land* 'estate' with an obscure first element.

Blisworth Northants. *Blidesworde* 1086 (DB). 'Enclosure of a man called *Blīth'. OE pers. name + *worth*.

Blithbury Staffs. *Blidebire* 1200. 'Stronghold on the River Blythe'. OE river-name (from *blīthe* 'gentle, pleasant') + *burh* (dative *byrig*). The same river gives name to **Blithfield, Blythe Bridge,** and **Blythe Marsh**.

Blockley Glos. *Bloccanleah* 855, *Blochelei* 1086 (DB). 'Woodland clearing of a man called *Blocca'. OE pers. name + *lēah*.

Blofield Norfolk. *Blafelda* 1086 (DB). Possibly 'exposed open country'. OE *blāw* + *feld*.

Blo Norton Norfolk, see NORTON.

Bloomsbury Gtr. London. *Blemondesberi* 1291. 'Manor held by the *de Blemund* family'. OE *burh* (dative *byrig*).

Blore Staffs., near Ilam. *Blora* 1086 (DB). '(Place at) the swelling or hill'. OE **blōr*.

Bloxham Oxon. *Blochesham* 1086 (DB). 'Homestead of a man called *Blocc'. OE pers. name + *hām*.

Bloxholm Lincs. *Blochesham* 1086 (DB). Identical in origin with the previous name.

Bloxwich W. Mids. *Blocheswic* 1086 (DB). 'Dwelling or (dairy) farm of a man called *Blocc'. OE pers. name + *wīc*.

Bloxworth Dorset. *Blacewyrthe* 987, *Blocheshorde* 1086 (DB). 'Enclosure of a man called *Blocc'. OE pers. name + *worth*.

Blubberhouses N. Yorks. *Bluberhusum* 1172. '(Place at) the houses by the bubbling spring'. ME *bluber* + OE *hūs* (dative plural *-um*).

Blundeston Suffolk. *Blundeston* 1203. 'Farmstead of a man called *Blunt'. OE pers. name + *tūn*.

Blunham Beds. *Blunham* 1086 (DB). Possibly 'homestead, or land in a river-bend, of a man called *Blūwa'. OE pers. name (genitive *-n*) + *hām* or *hamm*.

Blunsdon St Andrew, Broad Blunsdon Wilts. *Bluntesdone* 1086 (DB), *Bluntesdon Seynt Andreu* 1281, *Bradebluntesdon* 1234. 'Hill of a man called *Blunt'. OE pers. name + *dūn*. Affixes from the dedication of the church and from OE *brād* 'broad, great'.

Bluntisham Cambs. *Bluntesham* c.1050, 1086 (DB). 'Homestead or enclosure of a man called *Blunt'. OE pers. name + *hām* or *hamm*.

Blyborough Lincs. *Bliburg* 1086 (DB). Probably 'stronghold of a man called Blígr'. OScand. pers. name + OE *burh*.

Blyford Suffolk. *Blitleford* (*sic*) c.1060, *Blideforda* 1086 (DB). 'Ford over the River Blyth'. OE river-name ('the gentle or pleasant one' from OE *blīthe*) + *ford*.

Blymhill Staffs. *Brumhelle* (*sic*) 1086 (DB), *Blumehil* 1167. Possibly 'hill where plum-trees grow'. OE *plȳme* + *hyll*.

Blyth Northum. *Blida* 1130. Named from the River Blyth (OE *blīthe* 'the gentle or pleasant one').

Blyth Notts. *Blide* 1086 (DB). Identical in origin with the previous name, *Blyth* being the old name of the River Ryton.

Blythburgh Suffolk. *Blideburh* 1086 (DB). 'Stronghold on the River Blyth'. OE river-name ('the gentle or pleasant one' from OE *blīthe*) + *burh*.

Blythe Bridge & Marsh Staffs., see BLITHBURY.

Blyton Lincs. *Blitone* 1086 (DB). Probably 'farmstead of a man called Blígr'. OScand. pers. name + OE *tūn*.

Boarhunt Hants. *Byrhfunt* 10th cent., *Borehunte* 1086 (DB). 'Spring of the stronghold or manor'. OE *burh* (genitive *byrh*) + **funta*.

Boarstall Bucks. *Burchestala* 1158. OE *burh-stall* 'the site of a stronghold'.

Boasley Cross Devon. *Borslea* c.970, *Bosleia* 1086 (DB). 'Woodland clearing where spiky plants grow'. OE **bors* + *lēah*.

Bobbing Kent. *Bobinge* c.1100. '(Settlement of) the family or followers of a man called Bobba'. OE pers. name + *-ingas*.

Bobbington Staffs. *Bubintone* 1086 (DB). 'Estate associated with a man called Bubba'. OE pers. name + *-ing-* + *tūn*.

Bocking Essex. *Boccinge(s)* c.995, *Bochinges* 1086 (DB). '(Settlement of) the family or followers of a man called *Bocca', or '*Bocca's place'. OE pers. name + *-ingas* or *-ing*.

Boddington Glos. *Botingtune* 1086 (DB). 'Estate associated with a man called Bōta'. OE pers. name + *-ing-* + *tūn*.

Boddington Northants. *Botendon* 1086 (DB). 'Hill of a man called Bōta'. OE pers. name (genitive *-n*) + *dūn*.

Bodenham Heref. & Worcs. *Bodeham* 1086 (DB). 'Homestead or river-bend land of a man called Boda'. OE pers. name (genitive *-n*) + *hām* or *hamm*.

Bodenham Wilts. *Boteham* 1249. 'Homestead or enclosure of a man called Bōta'. OE pers. name (genitive *-n*) + *hām* or *hamm*.

Bodham Norfolk. *Bodenham* 1086 (DB). 'Homestead or enclosure of a man called Boda'. OE pers. name (genitive *-n*) + *hām* or *hamm*.

Bodiam E. Sussex. *Bodeham* 1086 (DB). Identical in origin with the previous name.

Bodicote Oxon. *Bodicote* 1086 (DB). 'Cottage(s) associated with a man called Boda'. OE pers. name + *-ing-* + *cot*.

Bodmin Cornwall. *Bodmine* c.975, 1086 (DB). Probably 'dwelling by church-land'. OCornish **bod* + **meneghi*.

Bodney Norfolk. *Budeneia* 1086 (DB). 'Island, or dry ground in marsh, of a man called *Beoda'. OE pers. name (genitive *-n*) + *ēg*.

Bognor Regis W. Sussex. *Bucganora* c.975. 'Shore of a woman called Bucge'. OE pers. name + *ōra*. Latin affix *regis* 'of the king' is only recent, alluding to the stay of George V here in 1929.

Bolam, '(place at) the tree-trunks', OE **bola* or OScand. *bolr* in a dative plural form *bolum*: **Bolam** Durham. *Bolom* 1317. **Bolam** Northum. *Bolum* 1155.

Bolas, Great Shrops. *Belewas* 1198. OE **wæsse* 'alluvial land' with an uncertain first element.

Bold Heath Mersey. *Bolde* 1204. OE *bold* 'a special house or building'.

Boldon Tyne & Wear. *Boldun* c.1170. Probably 'rounded hill'. OE **bol* + *dūn*.

Boldre Hants. *Bovre* (*sic*) 1086 (DB), *Bolre* 1152. Origin and meaning uncertain, possibly an old name of the Lymington river.

Boldron Durham. *Bolrum* c.1180. 'Clearing used for bulls'. OScand. *boli* + *rúm*.

Bole Notts. *Bolun* 1086 (DB). '(Place at) the tree-trunks'. OE **bola* or OScand. *bolr* in a dative plural form *bolum*.

Bollington, 'farmstead on the River Bollin', old river-name of uncertain origin and meaning + OE *tūn*: **Bollington** Ches., near Altrincham. *Bolinton* c.1222. **Bollington** Ches., near Macclesfield. *Bolynton* 1270.

Bolney E. Sussex. *Bolneye* 1263. 'Island, or dry ground in marsh, of a man called Bola'. OE pers. name (genitive *-n*) + *ēg*.

Bolnhurst Beds. *Bulehestre* (*sic*) 1086 (DB), *Bollenhirst* 11th cent. 'Wooded hill where bulls are kept'. OE **bula* (genitive plural **bulena*) + *hyrst*.

Bolsover Derbys. *Belesovre* (*sic*) 1086 (DB), *Bolesoura* 12th cent. Probably 'ridge of a man called *Boll or *Bull'. OE pers. name + **ofer*.

Bolsterstone S. Yorks. *Bolstyrston* 1398. 'Stone on which criminals are beheaded'. OE *bolster* + *stān*.

Bolstone Heref. & Worcs. *Boleston* 1193. 'Stone of a man called Bola'. OE pers. name + *stān*.

Boltby N. Yorks. *Boltebi* 1086 (DB). 'Farmstead or village of a man called Boltr or *Bolti'. OScand. pers. name + *bý*.

Bolton, a common name in the North, from OE **bōthl-tūn* 'settlement with a special building'; examples include: **Bolton** Gtr. Manch. *Boelton* 1185. **Bolton by Bowland** Lancs. *Bodeltone* 1086 (DB). The district-name Bowland (*Boelanda* 1102) means 'district characterized by bends', OE *boga* + *land*. **Bolton, Castle** N. Yorks. *Bodelton* 1086 (DB). Affix from the castle built here in 1379. **Bolton le Sands** Lancs. *Bodeltone* 1086 (DB). Affix means 'on the sands'. **Bolton Percy** N. Yorks. *Bodeltune* 1086 (DB), *Bolton Percy* 1305. Manorial affix from its possession by the *de Percy* family (from 1086). **Bolton upon Dearne** S. Yorks. *Bodeltone* 1086 (DB). The river-name Dearne is possibly from OE *derne* 'hidden', but may be of Celtic origin.

Bonby Humber. *Bundebi* 1086 (DB). 'Farmstead or village of the peasant farmers'. OScand. *bóndi* + *bý*.

Bondleigh Devon. *Bolenei* (*sic*) 1086 (DB), *Bonlege* 1205. Probably 'woodland clearing of a man called Bola'. OE pers. name (genitive *-n*) + *lēah*.

Bonehill Staffs. *Bolenhull* 1230. Probably 'hill where bulls graze'. OE **bula* (genitive plural **bulena*) + *hyll*.

Boningale Shrops. *Bolynghale* 12th cent. Probably 'nook of land associated with a man called Bola'. OE pers. name + *-ing-* + *halh*.

Bonnington Kent. *Bonintone* 1086 (DB). 'Estate associated with a man called Buna'. OE pers. name + *-ing-* + *tūn*.

Bonsall Derbys. *Bunteshale* 1086 (DB). 'Nook of land of a man called *Bunt'. OE pers. name + *halh*.

Bookham, Great & Little Surrey. *Bocheham* 1086 (DB). 'Homestead where beech-trees grow'. OE *bōc* + *hām*.

Boothby, 'farmstead or village with booths or shelters', OScand. *bōth* + *bý*: **Boothby Graffoe** Lincs. *Bodebi* 1086 (DB). Affix is an old district name of uncertain origin. **Boothby Pagnell** Lincs. *Bodebi* 1086 (DB). Manorial affix from the *Paynel* family, here in the 14th cent.

Boothferry Humber. *Booth's Ferry* 1651. 'Ferry at Booth (near Howden)', from OScand. *ferja*. The place-name Booth (originally *Botheby* 1550) was named from a family who came from one of the places called Boothby (see previous names).

Bootle, 'the special building', OE *bōtl*: **Bootle** Cumbria. *Bodele* 1086 (DB). **Bootle** Mersey. *Boltelai* (*sic*) 1086 (DB), *Botle* 1212.

Boraston Shrops. *Bureston* 1188. Possibly 'peasant's farmstead'. OE (*ge*)*būr* + *tūn*.

Borden Kent. *Bordena* 1177. 'Valley or woodland pasture by a hill'. OE **bor* + *denu* or *denn*.

Bordley N. Yorks. *Borelaie* (*sic*) 1086 (DB), *Bordeleia* c.1140. Probably 'woodland clearing where boards are got'. OE *bord* + *lēah*.

Boreham, probably 'homestead or enclosure on or by a hill', OE **bor* + *hām* or *hamm*: **Boreham** Essex. *Borham* c.1045, 1086 (DB). **Boreham Street** E. Sussex. *Borham* 12th cent.

Borehamwood Herts. *Borham* 1188, *Burhamwode* 13th cent. Identical in origin with the previous names + OE *wudu* 'wood'.

Borley Essex. *Barlea* 1086 (DB). 'Woodland clearing frequented by boars'. OE *bār* + *lēah*.

Boroughbridge N. Yorks. *Burbrigg* 1220. 'Bridge near the stronghold'. OE *burh* + *brycg*.

Borough Green Kent. *Borrowe Grene* 1575. From OE *burh* 'manor, borough' or *beorg* 'hill, mound'.

Borrowby N. Yorks., near Leake. *Bergebi* 1086 (DB). 'Farmstead or village on the hill(s)'. OScand. *berg* + *bý*.

Borrowdale Cumbria, near Keswick. *Borgordale* c.1170. 'Valley of the fort river'. OScand. *borg* (genitive *-ar*) + *á* + *dalr*.

Borwick Lancs. *Bereuuic* 1086 (DB). 'Barley farm' or 'outlying part of an estate'. OE *bere-wīc*.

Bosbury Heref. & Worcs. *Bosanbirig* early 12th cent., *Boseberge* 1086 (DB). 'Stronghold of a man called Bōsa'. OE pers. name + *burh* (dative *byrig*).

Boscastle Cornwall. *Boterelescastel* 1302. 'Castle of a family called *Boterel*'. OFrench surname + *castel*.

Boscombe, probably 'valley overgrown with spiky plants', OE **bors* + *cumb*: **Boscombe** Dorset. *Boscumbe* 1273. **Boscombe** Wilts. *Boscumbe* 1086 (DB).

Bosham W. Sussex. *Bosanham(m)* 731, *Boseham* 1086 (DB). 'Homestead or promontory of a man called Bōsa'. OE pers. name + *hām* or *hamm*.

Bosley Ches. *Boselega* 1086 (DB). 'Woodland clearing of a man called Bōsa or Bōt'. OE pers. name + *lēah*.

Bossall N. Yorks. *Bosciale* 1086 (DB). Probably 'nook of land of a man called Bōt or *Bōtsige'. OE pers. name + *halh*.

Bossiney Cornwall. *Botcinnii* 1086 (DB). 'Dwelling of a man called Kyni'. OCornish **bod* + pers. name.

Bostock Green Ches. *Botestoch* 1086 (DB). 'Outlying farmstead or hamlet of a man called Bōta'. OE pers. name + *stoc*.

Boston Lincs. *Botuluestan* 1130. 'Stone (marking a boundary or meeting-place) of a man called Bōtwulf'. OE pers. name + *stān*. Identification of Bōtwulf with the 7th cent. missionary St Botulf is improbable.

Boston Spa W. Yorks. *Bostongate* 1799. A recent name, perhaps so called from a family called *Boston* from BOSTON (Lincs.). The affix *Spa* refers to the mineral spring discovered here in 1744.

Bosworth, Husbands Leics. *Baresworde* 1086 (DB). Probably 'enclosure of a man called Bār'. OE pers. name + *worth*. Affix probably means 'of the farmers or husbandmen' (from late OE *hūsbonda*).

Bosworth, Market Leics. *Boseworde* 1086 (DB). 'Enclosure of a man called Bōsa'. OE pers. name + *worth*. Affix (found from the 16th cent.) alludes to the important market here.

Botesdale Suffolk. *Botholuesdal* 1275. 'Valley of a man called Bōtwulf'. OE pers. name + *dæl*.

Bothal Northum. *Bothala* 12th cent.

'Nook of land of a man called Bōta'. OE pers. name + *halh*.

Bothamsall Notts. *Bodmescel* 1086 (DB). 'Shelf by a broad river-valley'. OE **bothm* + *scelf*.

Bothel Cumbria. *Bothle* c.1125. OE *bōthl* 'a special house or building'.

Bothenhampton Dorset. *Bothehamton* 1268. 'Home farm in a valley'. OE **bothm* + *hām-tūn*.

Botley Bucks. *Bottlea* 1167. 'Woodland clearing of a man called Botta'. OE pers. name + *lēah*.

Botley Hants. *Botelie* 1086 (DB). 'Woodland clearing of a man called Bōta, or where timber is obtained'. OE pers. name or OE *bōt* + *lēah*.

Botley Oxon. *Boteleam* 12th cent. Identical in origin with the previous name.

Botolph Claydon Bucks., see CLAYDON.

Botolphs W. Sussex. *Sanctus Botulphus* 1288. From the dedication of the parish church to St Botolph.

Bottesford, 'ford by the house or building', OE *bōtl* + *ford*: **Bottesford** Humber. *Budlesforde* 1086 (DB). **Bottesford** Leics. *Botesford* 1086 (DB).

Bottisham Cambs. *Bodekesham* 1060, *Bodichessham* 1086 (DB). 'Homestead or enclosure of a man called *Boduc'. OE pers. name + *hām* or *hamm*.

Botusfleming Cornwall. *Bothflumet* 1259. OCornish **bod* 'dwelling' with an obscure second element.

Boughton, found in various counties, has two distinct origins. Some are 'farmstead of a man called Bucca, or where bucks (male deer) or he-goats are kept', OE pers. name or OE *bucc* or *bucca* + *tūn*; examples include: **Boughton** Northants., near Moulton. *Buchetone* 1086 (DB). **Boughton** Notts. *Buchetone* 1086 (DB).

Other Boughtons are 'farmstead where beech-trees grow', OE *bōc* + *tūn*; examples include: **Boughton Aluph** Kent. *Boltune* (*sic*) 1086 (DB), *Botun Alou* 1237. Manorial affix from a 13th owner called *Alulf*. **Boughton Malherbe** Kent. *Boltune* (*sic*) 1086 (DB), *Boctun Malerbe* 1275. Manorial affix from early possession by the *Malherbe* family.

Bouldon Shrops. *Bolledone* 1086 (DB). OE *dūn* 'hill' with an uncertain first element, possibly **bula* 'bull'.

Boulmer Northum. *Bulemer* 1161. 'Pond used by bulls'. OE **bula* + *mere*.

Boultham Lincs. *Buletham* 1086 (DB). 'Enclosure where ragged robin or the cuckoo flower grows'. OE *bulut* + *hamm*.

Bourn, Bourne, '(place at) the spring(s) or stream(s)', OE *burna* or OScand. *brunnr*: **Bourn** Cambs. *Brune* 1086 (DB). **Bourne** Lincs. *Brune* 1086 (DB).

Bourne End Bucks. *Burnend* 1236. 'End of the stream' (here where the River Wye meets the Thames). OE *burna* + *ende*.

Bournemouth Dorset. *La Bournemowthe* 1407. 'The mouth of the stream'. OE *burna* + *mūtha*.

Bournville W. Mids. 'Town on a river called Bourne' (from OE *burna* 'stream'). A recent name incorporating French *ville*.

Bourton, usually OE *burh-tūn* 'fortified farmstead' or 'farmstead near a fortification'; examples include: **Bourton** Dorset. *Bureton* 1212. **Bourton, Black** Oxon. *Burtone* 1086 (DB). Affix possibly refers to the black habits of the canons of Osney Abbey who had lands here. **Bourton-on-the-Water** Glos. *Burchtun* 714, *Bortune* 1086 (DB). In this name reference is to the nearby hill-fort. Affix refers to the River Windrush which flows through the village.

Bovey Tracey, North Bovey Devon. *Bovi* 1086 (DB), *Bovy Tracy* 1276, *Northebovy* 1199. Named from the River Bovey, a pre-English river-name of uncertain origin and meaning. Manorial affix from the *de Tracy* family, here in the 13th cent.

Bovingdon Herts. *Bovyndon* c.1200. Probably 'hill associated with a man called Bōfa'. OE pers. name + *-ing-* + *dūn*.

Bovington Dorset. *Bovintone* 1086 (DB). 'Estate associated with a man called Bōfa'. OE pers. name + *-ing-* + *tūn*.

Bow, '(place at) the arched bridge', OE

boga: **Bow** Devon. *Limet* (*sic*) 1086 (DB), *Nymetboghe* 1270, *la Bogh* 1281. *Nymet* is the old name of the River Yeo, see NYMET. **Bow** Gtr. London. *Stratford* 1177, *Stratford atte Bowe* 1279. Its earlier name means 'ford on a Roman road', OE *strǣt* + *ford*.

Bow Brickhill Bucks., see BRICKHILL.

Bowcombe I. of Wight. *Bovecome* 1086 (DB). 'Valley of a man called Bōfa', or '(place) above the valley'. OE pers. name or OE *bufan* + *cumb*.

Bowden, Great & Little Leics. *Bugedone* 1086 (DB). 'Hill of a woman called Bucge or of a man called Bugga'. OE pers. name + *dūn*.

Bowdon Gtr. Manch. *Bogedone* 1086 (DB). 'Curved hill'. OE *boga* + *dūn*.

Bowerchalke Wilts., see CHALKE.

Bowers Gifford Essex. *Bure* 1065, *Bura* 1086 (DB), *Buresgiffard* 1315. 'The dwellings or cottages'. OE *būr* + manorial affix from the *Giffard* family, here in the 13th cent.

Bowes Durham. *Bogas* 1148. 'The river-bends'. OE *boga* or OScand. *bogi*.

Bowland (old district and forest) Lancs./N. Yorks., see BOLTON BY BOWLAND.

Bowley Heref. & Worcs. *Bolelei* 1086 (DB). 'Woodland clearing of a man called Bola, or where there are tree-trunks'. OE pers. name or **bola* + *lēah*.

Bowling W. Yorks. *Bollinc* 1086 (DB). 'Place at a hollow'. OE *bolla* + *-ing*.

Bowness-on-Solway Cumbria. *Bounes* c.1225. 'Rounded headland'. OE *boga* + *næss*, or OScand. *bogi* + *nes*. Solway (*Sulewad* 1218) probably means 'ford of the pillar or post', OScand. *súla* + *vath*, perhaps referring to the Lochmaben Stone at the Scottish end of the ford across the Solway Firth (Scottish *firth* 'estuary').

Bowness-on-Windermere Cumbria. *Bulnes* 1282. 'Bull headland'. OE **bula* + *næss*. See WINDERMERE.

Bowsden Northum. *Bolesdon* 1195. Probably 'hill of a man called *Boll'. OE pers. name + *dūn*.

Bowthorpe Norfolk. *Boethorp* 1086 (DB). 'Outlying farmstead or hamlet of a man called Búi'. OScand. pers. name + *thorp*.

Box, '(place at) the box-tree', OE *box*: **Box** Glos. *la Boxe* 1260. **Box** Wilts. *Bocza* 1144.

Boxford Berks. *Boxora* 821, *Bousore* 1086 (DB). 'Slope where box-trees grow'. OE *box* + *ōra*.

Boxford Suffolk. *Boxford* 12th cent. 'Ford where box-trees grow'. OE *box* + *ford*.

Boxgrove W. Sussex. *Bosgrave* 1086 (DB). 'Box-tree grove'. OE *box* + *grāf*.

Boxley Kent. *Boseleu* (*sic*) 1086 (DB), *Boxlea* c.1100. 'Wood or clearing where box-trees grow'. OE *box* + *lēah*.

Boxted Essex. *Bocstede* 1086 (DB). 'Place where beech-trees grow'. OE *bōc* + *stede*.

Boxted Suffolk. *Boesteda* (*sic*) 1086 (DB), *Bocstede* 1154. 'Place where beech-trees or box-trees grow'. OE *bōc* or *box* + *stede*.

Boxworth Cambs. *Bochesuuorde* 1086 (DB). 'Enclosure of a man called *Bucc'. OE pers. name + *worth*.

Boyd (river) Avon, see BITTON.

Boylestone Derbys. *Boilestun* 1086 (DB). Probably 'farmstead at the rounded hill'. OE *boga* + *hyll* + *tūn*.

Boynton Humber. *Bouintone* 1086 (DB). 'Estate associated with a man called Bōfa'. OE pers. name + *-ing-* + *tūn*.

Boyton, 'farmstead of a man called Boia', OE pers. name + *tūn*: **Boyton** Cornwall. *Boietone* 1086 (DB). **Boyton** Suffolk. *Boituna* 1086 (DB). **Boyton** Wilts. *Boientone* 1086 (DB).

Bozeat Northants. *Bosiete* 1086 (DB). 'Gate or gap of a man called Bōsa'. OE pers. name + *geat*.

Brabourne Kent. *Bradanburna* c.860, *Bradeburne* 1086 (DB). '(Place at) the broad stream'. OE *brād* + *burna*.

Braceborough Lincs. *Braseborg* 1086 (DB). Possibly 'strong fortress', or 'fortress of a man called *Bræsna'. OE *bræsen* or pers. name + *burh*.

Bracebridge Lincs. *Brachebrige* 1086 (DB). Possibly 'bridge or causeway made of small branches or brushwood'. OE **bræsc* + *brycg*.

Braceby Lincs. *Breizbi* 1086 (DB). 'Farmstead or village of a man called Breithr'. OScand. pers. name + *bý*.

Bracewell Lancs. *Braisuelle* 1086 (DB). 'Spring or stream of a man called Breithr'. OScand. pers. name + OE *wella*.

Brackenfield Derbys. *Brachentheyt* 1269. 'Bracken clearing'. OScand. **brækni* + *thveit*.

Brackley Northants. *Brachelai* 1086 (DB). Probably 'woodland clearing of a man called *Bracca'. OE pers. name + *lēah*.

Bracknell Berks. *Braccan heal* 942. 'Nook of land of a man called *Bracca'. OE pers. name (genitive *-n*) + *halh*.

Bracon Ash Norfolk. *Brachene* 1175. '(Place amid) the bracken'. ON **brækni* or OE **bræcen* with the later addition of *ash* 'ash-tree'.

Bradbourne Derbys. *Bradeburne* 1086 (DB). '(Place at) the broad stream'. OE *brād* + *burna*.

Bradden Northants. *Bradene* 1086 (DB). 'Broad valley'. OE *brād* + *denu*.

Braddock Cornwall. *Brodehoc* 1086 (DB). 'Broad oak', or 'broad hook of land'. OE *brād* + *āc* or *hōc*.

Bradenham, 'broad homestead or enclosure', OE *brād* (dative *-an*) + *hām* + *hamm*: **Bradenham** Bucks. *Bradeham* 1086 (DB). **Bradenham** Norfolk. *Bradenham* 1086 (DB).

Bradenstoke Wilts. *Bradenestoche* 1086 (DB). 'Settlement dependent on Braydon forest'. Pre-English forest-name of obscure origin and meaning + OE *stoc*.

Bradfield, 'broad stretch of open land,' OE *brād* + *feld*; examples include: **Bradfield** Berks. *Bradanfelda* 990–2, *Bradefelt* 1086 (DB). **Bradfield** Essex. *Bradefelda* 1086 (DB). **Bradfield** Norfolk. *Bradefeld* 1212. **Bradfield** S. Yorks. *Bradesfeld* 1188. **Bradfield Combust, St Clare, & St George** Suffolk. *Bradefelda* 1086 (DB). Distinguishing affixes from ME *combust* 'burnt', from early possession by the *Seyncler* family, and from dedication of the church to St George.

Bradford, a fairly common name, '(place at) the broad ford', OE *brād* + *ford*; examples include: **Bradford** W. Yorks. *Bradeford* 1086 (DB). **Bradford Abbas** Dorset. *Bradanforda* 933, *Bradeford* 1086 (DB), *Braddeford Abbatis* 1386. Affix is Latin *abbas* 'abbot', alluding to early possession by Sherborne Abbey. **Bradford on Avon** Wilts. *Bradanforda be Afne* c.900, *Bradeford* 1086 (DB). Avon is a Celtic river-name meaning simply 'river'. **Bradford Peverell** Dorset. *Bradeford* 1086 (DB), *Bradeford Peuerel* 1244. Manorial affix from the *Peverel* family, here in the 13th cent.

Brading I. of Wight. *Brerdinges* 683, *Berardinz* 1086 (DB). '(Settlement of) the dwellers on the hill-side'. OE *brerd* + *-ingas*.

Bradley, a common name, usually 'broad wood or clearing', OE *brād* + *lēah*; examples include: **Bradley** Derbys. *Braidelei* 1086 (DB). **Bradley, Maiden** Wilts. *Bradelie* 1086 (DB), *Maydene Bradelega* early 13th cent. Affix means 'of the maidens' and refers to the nuns of Amesbury who had a cell here. **Bradley, North** Wilts. *Bradlega* 1174.

However the following has a different origin: **Bradley in the Moors** Staffs. *Bretlei* 1086 (DB). 'Wood where boards or planks are got'. OE *bred* + *lēah*.

Bradmore Notts. *Brademere* 1086 (DB). 'Broad pool'. OE *brād* + *mere*.

Bradninch Devon. *Bradenese* 1086 (DB). '(Place at) the broad ash-tree or oak-tree'. OE *brād* (dative *-an*) + *æsc* or *āc* (dative *ǣc*).

Bradnop Staffs. *Bradenhop* 1219. 'Broad valley'. OE *brād* (dative *-an*) + *hop*.

Bradpole Dorset. *Bratepolle* 1086 (DB). 'Broad pool'. OE *brād* + *pōl*.

Bradshaw Gtr. Manch. *Bradeshaghe* 1246. 'Broad wood or copse'. OE *brād* + *sceaga*.

Bradstone Devon. *Bradan stane* c.970, *Bradestana* 1086 (DB). '(Place at) the broad stone'. OE *brād* + *stān*.

Bradwell, '(place at) the broad spring or stream', OE *brād* + *wella*; examples include: **Bradwell** Bucks. *Bradewelle* 1086 (DB). **Bradwell** Derbys. *Bradewelle* 1086 (DB). **Bradwell** Essex. *Bradewell* 1238. **Bradwell** Norfolk. *Bradewell* 1211. **Bradwell** Staffs.

Bradewull 1227. **Bradwell-on-Sea** Essex. *Bradewella* 1194.

Bradworthy Devon. *Brawardine* (*sic*) 1086 (DB), *Bradewurtha* 1175. 'Broad enclosure'. OE *brād* + *worthign* or *worthig*.

Brafferton, 'farmstead by the broad ford', OE *brād* + *ford* + *tūn*: **Brafferton** Durham. *Bradfortuna* 1091. **Brafferton** N. Yorks. *Bradfortune* 1086 (DB).

Brafield-on-the-Green Northants. *Bragefelde* 1086 (DB). 'Open country by higher ground'. OE **bragen* + *feld*. The affix dates from the 16th cent.

Brailes Warwicks. *Brailes* 1086 (DB). Possibly from an OE **brægels* 'burial place, tumulus'. Alternatively a Celtic name 'hill court' from **breȝ* + **līs*.

Brailsford Derbys. *Brailesford* 1086 (DB). Possibly 'ford by a burial place'. OE **brægels* + *ford*. Alternatively the first part of this name may be Celtic, see the previous name.

Braintree Essex. *Branchetreu* 1086 (DB). 'Tree of a man called *Branca'. OE pers. name + *trēow*. The river-name Brain is a 'back-formation' from the place-name.

Braiseworth Suffolk. *Briseworde* 1086 (DB). 'Enclosure infested with gadflies or belonging to a man called *Brīosa'. OE *brīosa* or pers. name + *worth*.

Braishfield Hants. *Braisfelde c.*1235. OE *feld* 'open land' with an uncertain first element, possibly an OE **bræsc* 'small branches or brushwood'.

Braithwaite, 'broad clearing', OScand. *breithr* + *thveit*: **Braithwaite** Cumbria, near Keswick. *Braithait c.*1160. **Braithwaite** S. Yorks. *Braytweyt* 1276. **Braithwaite, Low** Cumbria. *Braythweyt* 1285.

Braithwell S. Yorks. *Bradewelle* 1086 (DB). '(Place at) the broad spring or stream'. OE *brād* (replaced by OScand. *breithr*) + *wella*.

Bramber W. Sussex. *Bremre* 956, *Brembre* 1086 (DB). OE *brēmer* 'bramble thicket'.

Bramcote Notts. *Brunecote* (*sic*) 1086 (DB), *Bramcote c.*1156. 'Cottage(s) where broom grows'. OE *brōm* + *cot*.

Bramdean Hants. *Bromdene* 824, *Brondene* 1086 (DB). 'Valley where broom grows'. OE *brōm* + *denu*.

Bramerton Norfolk. *Brambretuna* 1086 (DB). Possibly 'farmstead by the bramble thicket'. OE *brēmer* + *tūn*.

Bramfield Herts. *Brandefelle* (*sic*) 1086 (DB), *Brantefeld* 12th cent. Probably 'steep open land'. OE *brant* + *feld*.

Bramfield Suffolk. *Brunfelda* (*sic*) 1086 (DB), *Bramfeld* 1166. 'Open land where broom grows'. OE *brōm* + *feld*.

Bramhall Gtr. Manch. *Bramale* 1086 (DB). 'Nook of land where broom grows'. OE *brōm* + *halh*.

Bramham W. Yorks. *Bram(e)ham* 1086 (DB). 'Homestead or enclosure where broom grows'. OE *brōm* + *hām* or *hamm*.

Bramhope W. Yorks. *Bramhop* 1086 (DB). 'Valley where broom grows'. OE *brōm* + *hop*.

Bramley, 'woodland clearing where broom grows', OE *brōm* + *lēah*: **Bramley** Hants. *Brumelai* 1086 (DB). **Bramley** S. Yorks. *Bramelei* 1086 (DB). **Bramley** Surrey. *Bronlei* 1086 (DB).

Brampford Speke Devon. *Branfort* 1086 (DB), *Bramford Spec* 1275. Possibly 'ford where broom grows'. OE *brōm* + *ford*. Manorial affix from the *Espec* family, here in the 12th cent.

Brampton, a fairly common name, 'farmstead where broom grows', OE *brōm* + *tūn*; examples include: **Brampton** Cambs. *Brantune* 1086 (DB). **Brampton** Cumbria, near Irthington. *Brampton* 1169. **Brampton Bryan** Heref. & Worcs. *Brantune* 1086 (DB), *Bramptone Brian* 1275. Manorial affix from a 12th cent. owner called *Brian*. **Brampton, Chapel & Church** Northants. *Brantone* 1086 (DB). The distinguishing affixes occur from the 13th cent.

Bramshall Staffs. *Branselle* (*sic*) 1086 (DB), *Bromschulf* 1327. 'Shelf of land where broom grows'. OE *brōm* + *scelf*.

Bramshaw Hants. *Bramessage* 1086 (DB). Probably 'wood or copse where brambles grow'. OE *brǣmel* + *sceaga*.

Bramshott Hants. *Brenbresete* 1086 (DB). 'Projecting piece of land where brambles grow'. OE *brǣmel* + *scēat*.

Bramwith, Kirk S. Yorks. *Branuuet* (*sic*) 1086 (DB), *Branwyth* 1200, *Kyrkbramwith* 1341. 'Wood overgrown with broom'. OE *brōm* + OScand. *vithr*. Affix is OScand. *kirkja* 'church'.

Brancaster Norfolk. *Bramcestria c.*960, *Broncestra* 1086 (DB). 'Roman station at *Branodunum*'. Reduced form of ancient Celtic name (probably 'crow fort') + OE *ceaster*.

Brancepeth Durham. *Brantespethe c.*1170. 'Path or road of a man called Brandr'. OScand. pers. name + OE *pæth*.

Brandesburton Humber. *Brantisburtone* 1086 (DB). 'Fortified farmstead of a man called Brandr'. OScand. pers. name + OE *burh-tūn*.

Brandeston Suffolk. *Brantestona* 1086 (DB). 'Farmstead of a man called *Brant'. OE pers. name + *tūn*.

Brandiston Norfolk. *Brantestuna* 1086 (DB). Identical in origin with the previous name.

Brandon, usually 'hill where broom grows', OE *brōm* + *dūn*: **Brandon** Durham. *Bromdune c.*1190. **Brandon** Northum. *Bremdona c.*1150, *Bromdun* 1236. Here the first element alternates with OE **brēmen* 'broomy'. **Brandon** Suffolk. *Bromdun* 11th cent., *Brandona* 1086 (DB). **Brandon** Warwicks. *Brandune* 1086 (DB). **Brandon Parva** Norfolk. *Brandun* 1086 (DB).

However the following may have a different origin: **Brandon** Lincs. *Branthon* 1060–6, *Brandune* 1086 (DB). Probably 'hill by the River Brant'. OE river-name (from OE *brant* 'steep, deep') + *dūn*.

Brandsby N. Yorks. *Branzbi* 1086 (DB). 'Farmstead or village of a man called Brandr'. OScand. pers. name + *bý*.

Branscombe Devon. *Branecescumbe* 9th cent., *Branchescome* 1086 (DB). 'Valley of a man called Branoc'. Celtic pers. name + OE *cumb*.

Bransford Heref. & Worcs. *Bregnesford* 963, *Bradnesford* 1086 (DB). Probably 'ford by the hill'. OE *brægen* + *ford*.

Branston, 'farmstead of a man called *Brant', OE pers. name + *tūn*: **Branston** Leics. *Brantestone* 1086 (DB). **Branston** Staffs. *Brontiston* 942, *Brantestone* 1086 (DB).

However the following may have a different origin: **Branston** Lincs. *Branztune* 1086 (DB). Probably 'farmstead of a man called Brandr'. OScand. pers. name + OE *tūn*.

Brant Broughton Lincs., see BROUGHTON.

Brantham Suffolk. *Brantham* 1086 (DB). Possibly 'homestead or enclosure of a man called *Branta'. OE pers. name + *hām* or *hamm*.

Branthwaite Cumbria, near Workington. *Bromthweit* 1210. 'Clearing where broom grows'. OE *brōm* + OScand. *thveit*.

Brantingham Humber. *Brentingeham* 1086 (DB). 'Homestead of the family or followers of a man called *Brant', from OE pers. name + *-inga-* + *hām*. Alternatively 'homestead of those dwelling on the steep slopes', from OE *brant* + *-inga-* + *hām*.

Branton Northum. *Bremetona c.*1150. 'Farmstead overgrown with broom'. OE **brēmen* + *tūn*.

Branton S. Yorks. *Brantune* 1086 (DB). 'Farmstead where broom grows'. OE *brōm* + *tūn*.

Branxton Northum. *Brankeston* 1195. 'Farmstead of a man called Branoc'. Celtic pers. name + OE *tūn*.

Brassington Derbys. *Branzinctun* 1086 (DB). 'Estate associated with a man called *Brandsige'. OE pers. name + *-ing-* + *tūn*.

Brasted Kent. *Briestede* (*sic*) 1086 (DB), *Bradestede c.*1100. 'Broad place'. OE *brād* + *stede*.

Bratoft Lincs. *Breietoft* 1086 (DB). 'Broad homestead'. OScand. *breithr* + *toft*.

Brattleby Lincs. *Brotulbi* 1086 (DB). 'Farmstead or village of a man called *Brotulfr'. OScand. pers. name + *bý*.

Bratton, usually 'farmstead by newly cultivated ground', OE *brǣc* + *tūn*: **Bratton** Wilts. *Bratton* 1177. **Bratton Clovelly** Devon. *Bratona* 1086 (DB), *Bratton Clavyle* 1279. Manorial affix from the *de Clavill* family, here in the 13th cent. **Bratton Fleming** Devon. *Bratona* 1086 (DB). Manorial affix from the *Flemeng* family, here in the 13th cent.

However the following have a

different origin, 'farmstead by a brook', OE *brōc* + *tūn*: **Bratton** Shrops. *Brochetone* 1086 (DB). **Bratton Seymour** Somerset. *Broctune* 1086 (DB). Manorial affix from the *Saint Maur* family, here *c.*1400.

Braughing Herts. *Breahingas* 825–8, *Brachinges* 1086 (DB). '(Settlement of) the family or followers of a man called *Breahha'. OE pers. name + *-ingas*.

Braunston, Braunstone, 'farmstead of a man called *Brant', OE pers. name + *tūn*: **Braunston** Leics. *Branteston* 1167. **Braunston** Northants. *Brantestun* 956, *Brandestone* 1086 (DB). **Braunstone** Leics. *Brantestone* 1086 (DB).

Braunton Devon. *Brantona* 1086 (DB). 'Farmstead where broom grows'. OE *brōm* + *tūn*.

Brawby N. Yorks. *Bragebi* 1086 (DB). 'Farmstead or village of a man called Bragi'. OScand. pers. name + *bý*.

Braxted, Great Essex. *Brachestedam* 1086 (DB). Probably 'place where fern or bracken grows'. OE *bracu* + *stede*.

Bray Berks. *Brai* 1086 (DB). Probably OFrench *bray(e)* 'marsh'.

Braybrooke Northants. *Bradebroc* 1086 (DB). '(Place at) the broad brook'. OE *brād* + *brōc*.

Brayfield, Cold Bucks. *Bragenfelda* 967. 'Open land by higher ground'. OE **bragen* + *feld*. Affix means 'bleak, exposed'.

Braystones Cumbria. *Bradestanes* 1247. 'Broad stones'. OE *brād* (replaced by OScand. *breithr*) + *stān*.

Brayton N. Yorks. *Breithe-tun c.*1030, *Bretone* 1086 (DB). 'Broad farmstead' or 'farmstead of a man called Breithi'. OScand. *breithr* or pers. name + OE *tūn*.

Breadstone Glos. *Bradelestan* (*sic*) 1236, *Bradeneston* 1273. '(Place at) the broad stone'. OE *brād* (dative *-an*) + *stān*.

Breage Cornwall. *Egglosbrec c.*1170. 'Church of St Breage'. From the female patron saint of the church (with Cornish *eglos* 'church' in the early form).

Breamore Hants. *Brumore* 1086 (DB). 'Moor or marshy ground where broom grows'. OE *brōm* + *mōr*.

Brean Somerset. *Brien* 1086 (DB). Possibly a Celtic name containing a derivative of **breȝ* 'hill'.

Brearton N. Yorks. *Braretone* 1086 (DB). 'Farmstead amongst the briars'. OE *brēr* + *tūn*.

Breaston Derbys. *Braidestune* 1086 (DB). 'Farmstead of a man called *Brægd'. OE pers. name + *tūn*.

Breckland (district) Norfolk. 'Area in which ground has been broken up for cultivation', from dialect *breck*.

Breckles Norfolk. *Brecchles* 1086 (DB). 'Meadow by newly-cultivated land'. OE *brēc* + *lǣs*.

Bredbury Gtr. Manch. *Bretberie* 1086 (DB). 'Stronghold or manor-house built of planks'. OE *bred* + *burh* (dative *byrig*).

Brede E. Sussex. *Brade* 1161. 'Broad stretch of land'. OE *brǣdu*.

Bredfield Suffolk. *Bredefelda* 1086 (DB). 'Broad stretch of open country'. OE *brǣdu* + *feld*.

Bredgar Kent. *Bradegare c.*1100. 'Broad triangular plot'. OE *brād* + *gāra*.

Bredhurst Kent. *Bredehurst* 1240. 'Wooded hill where boards are obtained'. OE *bred* + *hyrst*.

Bredon Heref. & Worcs. *Breodun* 772, 1086 (DB). 'Hill called *Bre*'. Celtic **breȝ* 'hill' + explanatory OE *dūn*.

Bredon's Norton Heref. & Worcs., see NORTON.

Bredwardine Heref. & Worcs. *Brocheurdie* (*sic*) 1086 (DB), *Bredewerthin* late 12th cent. OE *worthign* 'enclosure', probably with *bred* 'board, plank' or *brǣdu* 'broad stretch of land'.

Bredy, Long & Littlebredy Dorset. *Bridian* 987, *Langebride, Litelbride* 1086 (DB). Named from the River Bride, a Celtic river-name meaning 'gushing or surging stream'. Distinguishing affixes are OE *lang* 'long' and *lȳtel* 'little'.

Breedon on the Hill Leics. *Briudun* 731. 'Hill called *Bre*'. Celtic **breȝ* 'hill' + explanatory OE *dūn* 'hill'. With the more recent affix the name thus contains three different words for 'hill'.

Breighton Humber. *Bricstune* 1086 (DB). Possibly 'bright farmstead' or 'farmstead of a man called *Beorhta'. OE *beorht* or pers. name + *tūn*.

Bremhill Wilts. *Bre(o)mel* 937, *Breme* (*sic*) 1086 (DB). 'Bramble thicket'. OE *brēmel*.

Brenchley Kent. *Braencesle* c.1100. Probably 'woodland clearing of a man called *Bræncі'. OE pers. name + *lēah*.

Brendon Devon. *Brandone* 1086 (DB). 'Hill where broom grows'. OE *brōm* + *dūn*.

Brenkley Tyne & Wear. *Brinchelawa* 1178. Possibly 'hill or mound of a man called Brynca'. OE pers. name + *hlāw*. Alternatively the first element may be OE **brince* 'brink or edge'.

Brent, probably a Celtic name meaning 'high place': **Brent, East** Somerset. *Brente* 663, *Brentemerse* 1086 (DB). With OE *mersc* 'marsh' in the Domesday form. **Brent, South** Devon. *Brenta* 1086 (DB).

Brent Eleigh Suffolk, see ELEIGH.

Brentford Gtr. London. *Breguntford* 705. 'Ford over the River Brent'. Celtic river-name (meaning 'holy one') + OE *ford*. The London borough of **Brent** takes its name from the river.

Brentor Devon. *Brentetor* 1232. 'Rocky hill called *Brente*'. Celtic hill-name + OE *torr*.

Brent Pelham Herts., see PELHAM.

Brentwood Essex. *Boscus arsus* 1176, *Brendewode* 1274. 'The burnt wood'. OE **berned* (ME *brende*) + *wudu*. In the earliest form the name has been translated into Latin.

Brenzett Kent. *Brensete* 1086 (DB). 'The burnt fold or stable'. OE **berned* + *(ge)set*.

Brereton Ches. *Bretone* (*sic*) 1086 (DB), *Brereton* c.1100. 'Farmstead amongst the briars'. OE *brēr* + *tūn*.

Brereton Staffs. *Breredon* 1279. 'Hill where briars grow'. OE *brēr* + *dūn*.

Bressingham Norfolk. *Bresingaham* 1086 (DB). 'Homestead of the family or followers of a man called *Brīosa'. OE pers. name + *-inga-* + *hām*.

Bretford Warwicks. *Bretford* early 11th cent. Probably 'ford provided with planks'. OE *bred* + *ford*.

Bretforton Heref. & Worcs. *Bretfertona* 709, *Bratfortune* 1086 (DB). 'Farmstead near the plank ford'. OE *bred* + *ford* + *tūn*.

Bretherdale Head Cumbria. *Britherdal* 12th cent. 'Valley of the brother(s)'. OScand. *bróthir* + *dalr*.

Bretherton Lancs. *Bretherton* 1190. 'Farmstead of the brother(s)'. OE *brōthor* or OScand. *bróthir* + OE *tūn*.

Brettenham, 'homestead of a man called *Bretta or *Beorhta', OE pers. name (genitive *-n*) + *hām*: **Brettenham** Norfolk. *Bretham* 1086 (DB). **Brettenham** Suffolk. *Bretenhama* 1086 (DB).

Bretton, 'farmstead of the Britons', OE *Brettas* (genitive *Bretta*) + *tūn*: **Bretton, Monk** S. Yorks. *Brettone* 1086 (DB), *Munkebretton* 1225. Affix from OE *munuc* 'monk' referring to the monks of Bretton Priory. **Bretton, West** W. Yorks. *Bretone* 1086 (DB), *West Bretton* c.1200.

Brewham Somerset. *Briweham* 1086 (DB). 'Homestead or enclosure on the River Brue'. Celtic river-name (see BRUTON) + OE *hām* or *hamm*.

Brewood Staffs. *Breude* 1086 (DB). 'Wood by the hill called *Bre*'. Celtic **breȝ* 'hill' + OE *wudu*.

Briantspuddle Dorset. *Pidele* 1086 (DB), *Brianis Pedille* 1465. 'Estate on the River Piddle held by a man called Brian'. OE river-name (see PIDDLEHINTON) with manorial affix from 14th cent. lord of manor.

Bricett, Great Suffolk. *Brieseta* 1086 (DB). Possibly 'fold or stable infested with gadflies'. OE *brīosa* + *(ge)set*.

Bricket Wood Herts. *Bruteyt* 1228. 'Bright-coloured small island or piece of marshland'. OE *beorht* + *ēgeth*.

Brickhill, Bow, Great & Little Bucks. *Brichelle* 1086 (DB), *Bolle Brichulle, Magna Brikehille, Parua Brichull* 1198. 'Hill called *Brig*'. Celtic **brig* 'hill top' + explanatory OE *hyll*. Distinguishing affixes from OE pers. name *Bolla* (no doubt an early tenant), Latin *magna* 'great' and *parva* 'little'.

Bricklehampton Heref. & Worcs.

Bricstelmestune 1086 (DB). 'Estate associated with a man called Beorhthelm'. OE pers. name + *-ing-* + *tūn*.

Bride (river) Dorset, see BREDY.

Bridekirk Cumbria. *Bridekirke c.*1210. 'Church of St Bride or Brigid'. Irish saint's name + OScand. *kirkja*.

Bridestowe Devon. *Bridestou* 1086 (DB). 'Holy place of St Bride or Brigid'. Irish saint's name + OE *stōw*.

Bridford Devon. *Brideforda* 1086 (DB). 'Ford suitable for brides', i.e. a shallow ford easy to cross. OE *brȳd* + *ford*.

Bridge Kent. *Brige* 1086 (DB). '(Place at) the bridge'. OE *brycg*.

Bridge Hewick N. Yorks., see HEWICK.

Bridgerule Devon. *Brige* 1086 (DB), *Briggeroald* 1238. '(Place at) the bridge held by a man called Ruald'. OE *brycg* + manorial affix from OScand. *Róaldr* (tenant in 1086).

Bridge Sollers Heref. & Worcs. *Bricge* 1086 (DB), *Bruges Solers* 1291. '(Place at) the bridge'. OE *brycg* + manorial affix from the *de Solers* family, here in the 12th cent.

Bridgford, 'ford by the bridge', OE *brycg* + *ford*: **Bridgford, East** Notts. *Brugeford* 1086 (DB). **Bridgford, West** Notts. *Brigeforde* 1086 (DB).

Bridgham Norfolk. *Brugeham c.*1050. 'Homestead or enclosure by a bridge'. OE *brycg* + *hām* or *hamm*.

Bridgnorth Shrops. *Brug* 1156, *Brugg Norht* 1282. '(Place at) the bridge'. OE *brycg* + later affix *north*.

Bridgwater Somerset. *Brugie* 1086 (DB), *Brigewaltier* 1194. '(Place at) the bridge held by a man called Walter'. OE *brycg* + manorial affix from an early owner.

Bridlington Humber. *Bretlinton* 1086 (DB). 'Estate associated with a man called Berhtel'. OE pers. name + *-ing-* + *tūn*.

Bridport Dorset. *Brideport* 1086 (DB). 'Harbour or market town belonging to (Long) BREDY'. OE *port*.

Bridstow Heref. & Worcs. *Bridestowe* 1277. 'Holy place of St Bride or Brigid'. Irish saint's name + OE *stōw*.

Brierfield Lancs., a self-explanatory name of 19th cent. origin, no doubt influenced by the nearby **Briercliffe** (*Brerecleve* 1193) which is 'bank where briars grow', OE *brēr* + *clif*.

Brierley, 'woodland clearing where briars grow', OE *brēr* + *lēah*: **Brierley** S. Yorks. *Breselai (sic)* 1086 (DB), *Brerelay* 1194. **Brierley Hill** W. Mids. *Brereley* 14th cent.

Brigg Humber., earlier *Glanford Brigg* 1235. 'Bridge at the ford where people assemble for revelry or games'. OE *glēam* + *ford* + *brycg*.

Brigham, 'homestead or enclosure by a bridge', OE *brycg* + *hām* or *hamm*: **Brigham** Cumbria, near Cockermouth. *Briggham c.*1175. **Brigham** Humber. *Bringeham (sic)* 1086 (DB), *Brigham* 12th cent.

Brighouse W. Yorks. *Brighuses* 1240. 'Houses by the bridge'. OE *brycg* + *hūs*.

Brighstone I. of Wight. *Brihtwiston* 1212. 'Farmstead of a man called Beorhtwīg'. OE pers. name + *tūn*.

Brighthampton Oxon. *Byrhtelmingtun* 984, *Bristelmestone* 1086 (DB). 'Farmstead of a man called Beorhthelm'. OE pers. name + *tūn*.

Brightling E. Sussex. *Byrhtlingan* 1016–20, *Brislinga* 1086 (DB). '(Settlement of) the family or followers of a man called Beorhtel'. OE pers. name + *-ingas*.

Brightlingsea Essex. *Brictriceseia* 1086 (DB). 'Island of a man called Beorhtrīc or *Beorhtling'. OE pers. name + *ēg*.

Brighton E. Sussex. *Bristelmestune* 1086 (DB). 'Farmstead of a man called Beorhthelm'. OE pers. name + *tūn*.

Brighton, New Mersey., 19th cent. resort named after BRIGHTON.

Brightwalton Berks. *Beorhtwaldingtune* 939, *Bristoldestone* 1086 (DB). 'Estate associated with a man called Beorhtwald'. OE pers. name (+ *-ing-*) + *tūn*.

Brightwell, 'bright or clear spring', OE *beorht* + *wella*: **Brightwell** Oxon. *Beorhtawille* 854, *Bricsteuuelle* 1086 (DB). **Brightwell** Suffolk. *Brithwelle c.*1050, *Brihtewella* 1086 (DB). **Brightwell Baldwin** Oxon. *Berhtanwellan* 887, *Britewelle* 1086 (DB). Manorial affix from possession by Sir

Baldwin de Bereford in the late 14th cent.

Brignall Durham. *Bringhenale* 1086 (DB). Possibly 'nook of the family or followers of a man called Brȳni'. OE pers. name + *-inga-* + *halh.*

Brigsley Humber. *Brigeslai* 1086 (DB). 'Woodland clearing by a bridge'. OE *brycg* + *lēah.*

Brigsteer Cumbria. *Brigstere* early 13th cent. 'Bridge of a family called *Stere*, or one used for bullocks'. OScand. *bryggja* + ME surname or OE *stēor*. The order of elements is Celtic.

Brigstock Northants. *Bricstoc* 1086 (DB). Probably 'outlying farm or hamlet by a bridge'. OE *brycg* + *stoc.*

Brill Bucks. *Bruhella* 1072, *Brunhelle* (*sic*) 1086 (DB). 'Hill called *Bre*'. Celtic **breʒ* 'hill' + explanatory OE *hyll.*

Brilley Heref. & Worcs. *Brunlege* 1219. Probably 'woodland clearing where broom grows'. OE *brōm* + *lēah.*

Brimfield Heref. & Worcs. *Bromefeld* 1086 (DB). 'Open land where broom grows'. OE *brōm* + *feld.*

Brimington Derbys. *Brimintune* 1086 (DB). 'Estate associated with a man called Brēme'. OE pers. name + *-ing-* + *tūn.*

Brimpsfield Glos. *Brimesfelde* 1086 (DB). 'Open land of a man called Brēme'. OE pers. name + *feld.*

Brimpton Berks. *Bryningtune* 944, *Brintone* 1086 (DB). 'Estate associated with a man called Brȳni'. OE pers. name + *-ing-* + *tūn.*

Brind Humber. *Brende* 1188. OE **brende* 'place destroyed or cleared by burning'.

Brindle Lancs. *Burnhull* 1206. Probably 'hill by a stream'. OE *burna* + *hyll.*

Brineton Staffs. *Brunitone* 1086 (DB). Probably 'estate associated with a man called Brȳni'. OE pers. name + *-ing-* + *tūn.*

Bringhurst Leics. *Bruninghyrst* 1188. Probably 'wooded hill of the family or followers of a man called Brȳni'. OE pers. name + *-inga-* + *hyrst.*

Brington, 'estate associated with a man called Brȳni', OE pers. name + *-ing-* + *tūn*: **Brington** Cambs. *Brynintune* 974, *Brenincturne* 1086 (DB). **Brington, Great & Little** Northants. *Brinintone* 1086 (DB).

Briningham Norfolk. *Bruningaham* 1086 (DB). 'Homestead of the family or followers of a man called Brȳni'. OE pers. name + *-inga-* + *hām.*

Brinkhill Lincs. *Brincle* 1086 (DB). 'Woodland clearing of a man called Brynca, or on the brink of a hill'. OE pers. name or OE **brince* + *lēah.*

Brinkley Cambs. *Brinkelai* late 12th cent. 'Woodland clearing of a man called Brynca'. OE pers. name + *lēah.*

Brinklow Warwicks. *Brinckelawe* c.1155. 'Burial mound of a man called Brynca, or on the brink of a hill'. OE pers. name or OE **brince* + *hlāw.*

Brinkworth Wilts. *Brinkewrtha* 1065, *Brenchewrde* 1086 (DB). 'Enclosure of a man called Brynca'. OE pers. name + *worth.*

Brinscall Lancs. *Brendescoles* c.1200. 'Burnt huts'. ME *brende* + OScand. *skáli.*

Brinsley Notts. *Brunesleia* 1086 (DB). 'Woodland clearing of a man called Brūn'. OE pers. name + *lēah.*

Brinsop Heref. & Worcs. *Hope* 1086 (DB), *Bruneshopa* c.1130. 'Enclosed valley of a man called Brūn or Brȳni'. OE pers. name + *hop.*

Brinsworth S. Yorks. *Brinesford* 1086 (DB). 'Ford of a man called Brȳni'. OE pers. name + *ford.*

Brinton Norfolk. *Bruntuna* 1086 (DB). 'Estate associated with a man called Brȳni'. OE pers. name + *-ing-* + *tūn.*

Brisley Norfolk. *Bruselea* c.1105. 'Woodland clearing infested with gadflies'. OE *brīosa* + *lēah.*

Brislington Avon. *Brihthelmeston* 1199. 'Farmstead of a man called Beorhthelm'. OE pers. name + *tūn.*

Bristol Avon. *Brycg stowe* 11th cent., *Bristou* 1086 (DB). 'Assembly place by the bridge'. OE *brycg* + *stōw.*

Briston Norfolk. *Burstuna* 1086 (DB). 'Farmstead by a landslip or broken ground'. OE *byrst* + *tūn.*

Britford Wilts. *Brutford* 826, *Bredford* 1086 (DB). Possibly 'ford of the Britons'. OE *Bryt* + *ford.*

Britwell Salome Oxon. *Brutwelle* 1086 (DB), *Brutewell Solham* 1320. Possibly 'spring or stream of the Britons'. OE *Bryt* + *wella*. Manorial affix from the *de Suleham* family, here in the 13th cent.

Brixham Devon. *Briseham (sic)* 1086 (DB), *Brikesham* 1205. 'Homestead or enclosure of a man called Brioc'. Celtic pers. name + OE *hām* or *hamm*.

Brixton Devon. *Brisetona (sic)* 1086 (DB), *Brikeston* 1200. Probably 'farmstead of a man called Brioc'. Celtic pers. name + OE *tūn*.

Brixton Gtr. London. *Brixges stan* 1062, *Brixiestan* 1086 (DB). 'Stone (probably marking a Hundred meeting-place) of a man called Beorhtsige'. OE pers. name + *stān*.

Brixton Deverill Wilts. *Devrel* 1086 (DB), *Britricheston* 1229. 'Estate on the River *Deverill* held by a man called Beorhtrīc'. OE pers. name + *tūn* with Celtic river-name (meaning 'watery'), an old name for the River Wylye.

Brixworth Northants. *Bricleswrde* 1086 (DB). 'Enclosure of a man called Beorhtel or *Bricel'. OE pers. name + *worth*.

Brize Norton Oxon., see NORTON.

Broad as affix, see main name, e.g. for **Broad Blunsdon** (Wilts.) see BLUNSDON.

Broadbottom Gtr. Manch. *Brodebothem* 1286. 'Broad valley-bottom'. OE *brād* + **bothm*.

Broadhembury Devon. *Hanberia* 1086 (DB), *Brodehembyri* 1273. 'High or chief fortified place'. OE *hēah* (dative *hēan*) + *burh* (dative *byrig*). Later affix is OE *brād* 'broad, great'.

Broadhempston Devon. *Hamistone* 1086 (DB), *Brodehempstone* 1362. 'Farmstead of a man called *Hǣme or Hemme'. OE pers. name + *tūn*. Affix is OE *brād* 'large' to distinguish this place from LITTLEHEMPSTON.

Broadmayne Dorset. *Maine* 1086 (DB), *Brademaene* 1202. Celtic **main* 'a rock, a stone', with later affix from OE *brād* 'broad, great'.

Broads, The (district) Norfolk, named from over thirty 'broads', i.e. extensive pieces of fresh water formed by the broadening out of rivers.

Broadstairs Kent. *Brodsteyr* 1435. 'Broad stairway or ascent'. OE *brād* + *stǣger*.

Broadstone Dorset, a recent name for a parish formed in 1906, self-explanatory.

Broad Town Wilts. *Bradetun* 12th cent. 'Broad or large farmstead'. OE *brād* + *tūn*.

Broadwas Heref. & Worcs. *Bradeuuesse* 779, *Bradewesham* 1086 (DB). 'Broad tract of alluvial land'. OE *brād* + **wæsse* (with *hām* 'homestead' in the 1086 form).

Broadwater W. Sussex. *Bradewatre* 1086 (DB). '(Place at) the broad stream'. OE *brād* + *wæter*.

Broadway, '(place at) the broad way or road', OE *brād* + *weg*: **Broadway** Heref. & Worcs. *Bradanuuege* 972, *Bradeweia* 1086 (DB). **Broadway** Somerset. *Bradewei* 1086 (DB).

Broadwell, '(place at) the broad spring or stream', OE *brād* + *wella*: **Broadwell** Glos. *Bradewelle* 1086 (DB). **Broadwell** Oxon. *Bradewelle* 1086 (DB). **Broadwell** Warwicks. *Bradewella* 1130.

Broadwey Dorset. *Wai(a)* 1086 (DB), *Brode Way* 1243. Named from the River Wey, see WEYMOUTH. Affix is OE *brād* 'broad, great', referring either to the width of the river here or to the size of the manor.

Broadwindsor Dorset. *Windesore* 1086 (DB), *Brodewyndesore* 1324. 'River-bank with a windlass'. OE **windels* + *ōra*, with *brād* 'great'.

Broadwoodkelly Devon. *Bradehoda (sic)* 1086 (DB), *Brawode Kelly* 1261. 'Broad wood'. OE *brād* + *wudu* + manorial affix from the *de Kelly* family, here in the 13th cent.

Broadwoodwidger Devon. *Bradewode* 1086 (DB), *Brodwode Wyger* 1310. Identical in origin with the previous name. Manorial affix from the *Wyger* family, here in the 13th cent.

Brobury Heref. & Worcs. *Brocheberie* 1086 (DB). 'Stronghold or manor near a brook'. OE *brōc* + *burh* (dative *byrig*).

Brockdish Norfolk. *Brodise (sic)* 1086

(DB), *Brochedisc c.*1095. 'Pasture by the brook'. OE *brōc* + *edisc*.

Brockenhurst Hants. *Broceste* (*sic*) 1086 (DB), *Brocheherst* 1158. Probably 'wooded hill of a man called *Broca'. OE pers. name (genitive -*n*) + *hyrst*. Alternatively the first element may be OE *brocen* 'broken up, undulating'.

Brockford Street Suffolk. *Brocfort* 1086 (DB). 'Ford over the brook'. OE *brōc* + *ford*.

Brockhall Northants. *Brocole* 1086 (DB). OE *brocc-hol* 'a badger hole, a sett'.

Brockham Surrey. *Brocham* 1241. 'River-meadow by the brook, or frequented by badgers'. OE *brōc* or *brocc* + *hamm*.

Brockhampton, 'homestead by the brook', OE *brōc* + *hām-tūn*: **Brockhampton** Glos., near Sevenhampton. *Brochamtone* 1166. **Brockhampton** Heref. & Worcs., near Bromyard. *Brockampton* 1251.

Brocklesby Lincs. *Brochelesbi* 1086 (DB). 'Farmstead or village of a man called *Bróklauss'. OScand. pers. name + *bý*.

Brockley Avon. *Brochelie* 1086 (DB). 'Woodland clearing of a man called *Broca, or frequented by badgers'. OE pers. name or *brocc* + *lēah*.

Brockley Gtr. London. *Brocele* 1182. Identical in origin with the previous name.

Brockley Suffolk. *Broclega* 1086 (DB). 'Woodland clearing by a brook'. OE *brōc* + *lēah*.

Brockton, Brocton, 'farmstead by a brook', OE *brōc* + *tūn*: **Brockton** Shrops., near Lilleshall. *Brochetone* 1086 (DB). **Brockton** Shrops., near Madeley. *Broctone* 1086 (DB). **Brockton** Shrops., near Worthen. *Brockton* 1272. **Brocton** Staffs., near Stafford. *Broctone* 1086 (DB).

Brockweir Glos. *Brocwere c.*1145. 'Weir by the brook'. OE *brōc* + *wer*.

Brockworth Glos. *Brocowardinge* 1086 (DB). 'Enclosure by the brook'. OE *brōc* + *worthign*.

Brocton Staffs., see BROCKTON.

Brodsworth S. Yorks. *Brodesworde* 1086 (DB). 'Enclosure of a man called Broddr or Brord'. OScand. or OE pers. name + *worth*.

Brokenborough Wilts. *Brokene beregge* 956, *Brocheneberge* 1086 (DB). 'Broken barrow' (probably referring to a tumulus that had been broken into). OE *brocen* + *beorg*.

Bromborough Mersey. *Brunburg* early 12th cent. 'Stronghold of a man called Brūna'. OE pers. name + *burh*.

Brome Suffolk. *Brom* 1086 (DB). 'Place where broom grows'. OE *brōm*.

Bromeswell Suffolk. *Bromeswella* 1086 (DB). 'Rising ground where broom grows'. OE *brōm* + **swelle*.

Bromfield Cumbria. *Brounefeld c.*1125. 'Brown open land, or open land where broom grows'. OE *brūn* or *brōm* + *feld*.

Bromfield Shrops. *Brunfelde* 1086 (DB). Probably 'open land where broom grows'. OE *brōm* + *feld*.

Bromham, 'homestead or enclosure where broom grows', OE *brōm* + *hām* or *hamm*: **Bromham** Beds. *Bruneham* 1086 (DB). Alternatively the first element in this name may be the OE pers. name *Brūna*. **Bromham** Wilts. *Bromham* 1086 (DB).

Bromley, usually 'woodland clearing where broom grows', OE *brōm* + *lēah*: **Bromley** Herts. *Bromlegh* 1248. **Bromley** Gtr. London, near Beckenham. *Bromleag* 862, *Bronlei* 1086 (DB). **Bromley, Abbots** Staffs. *Bromleage* 1002. Affix from its early possession by Burton Abbey. **Bromley, Great & Little** Essex. *Brumleiam* 1086 (DB). **Bromley, Kings** Staffs. *Bromelei* 1086 (DB), *Bramlea Regis* 1167. Affix is Latin *regis* 'of the king', alluding to a royal manor.
However the following has a different origin: **Bromley** Gtr. London, near Bow. *Bræmbelege c.*1000. 'Woodland clearing where brambles grow'. OE *bræmbel* + *lēah*.

Brompton, usually 'farmstead where broom grows', OE *brōm* + *tūn*: **Brompton** N. Yorks., near Northallerton. *Bromtun c.*1050, *Bruntone* 1086 (DB). **Brompton** N. Yorks., near Snainton. *Bruntun* 1086 (DB). **Brompton on Swale** N. Yorks. *Brunton* 1086 (DB). On the River Swale (probably OE **swalwe* 'rushing water').

Brompton, Patrick N. Yorks. *Brunton* 1086 (DB), *Patricbrunton* 1157. Manorial affix from its early possession by a man called *Patric* (an OIrish pers. name). **Brompton, Potter** N. Yorks. *Brunetona* 1086 (DB). Affix probably alludes to early potmaking here.

However the following has a different origin: **Brompton Ralph & Regis** Somerset. *Burnetone, Brunetone* 1086 (DB), *Brompton Radulphi* 1274, *Brompton Regis* 1291. 'Farmstead by the brown hill'. OE *Brūna* (referring to Brendon Hills) + *tūn*. Manorial affixes from early possession by a man called Ralph (Latin *Radulphus*) and by the king (Latin *regis* 'of the king').

Bromsgrove Heref. & Worcs. *Bremesgrefan* 804, *Bremesgrave* 1086 (DB). 'Grove or copse of a man called Brēme'. OE pers. name + *grǣfe, grāf*.

Bromwich, 'dwelling or farm where broom grows', OE *brōm* + *wīc*: **Bromwich, Castle** W. Mids. *Bramewice* 1168, *Castelbromwic* 13th cent. Affix refers to a 12th cent. earthwork. **Bromwich, West** W. Mids. *Bromwic* 1086, *Westbromwich* 1322.

Bromyard Heref. & Worcs. *Bromgeard* c.840, *Bromgerde* 1086 (DB). 'Enclosure where broom grows'. OE *brōm* + *geard*.

Brondesbury Gtr. London. *Bronnesburie* 1254. 'Manor of a man called Brand'. ME pers. name or surname + *bury* (from OE *byrig*, dative of *burh*).

Brook, Brooke, '(place at) the brook', OE *brōc*: **Brook** I. of Wight. *Broc* 1086 (DB). **Brook** Kent. *Broca* 11th cent. **Brooke** Leics. *Broc* 1176. **Brooke** Norfolk. *Broc* 1086 (DB).

Brookland Kent. *Broklande* 1262. 'Cultivated land by a brook'. OE *brōc* + *land*.

Brookmans Park Herts. *Brokemanes* 1468. Named from a local family called *Brokeman*.

Brookthorpe Glos. *Brostorp* (*sic*) 1086 (DB), *Brocthrop* 12th cent. 'Outlying farmstead or hamlet by a brook'. OE *brōc* + *throp*.

Brookwood Surrey. *Brocwude* 1225. 'Wood by a brook'. OE *brōc* + *wudu*.

Broom, Broome, 'place where broom grows', OE *brōm*; examples include: **Broom** Beds. *Brume* 1086 (DB). **Broom** Durham. *Brom* c.1170. **Broom** Heref. & Worcs. *Brom* 1169. **Broom** Warwicks. *Brome* 710, 1086 (DB). **Broome** Norfolk. *Brom* 1086 (DB).

Broomfield, 'open land where broom grows', OE *brōm* + *feld*: **Broomfield** Essex. *Brumfeldam* 1086 (DB). **Broomfield** Kent, near Maidstone. *Brunfelle* (*sic*) 1086 (DB), *Brumfeld* c.1100. **Broomfield** Somerset. *Brunfelle* 1086 (DB).

Broomfleet Humber. *Brungareflet* 1150–4. 'Stretch of river belonging to a man called Brūngār'. OE pers. name + *flēot*.

Brooms, High Kent, earlier *Bromgebrug* 1270, *Bromelaregg* 1318, from OE *brōm* 'broom' with either *brycg* 'bridge' or *hrycg* 'ridge'.

Broseley Shrops. *Burewardeslega* 1177. 'Woodland clearing of the fort-keeper, or of a man called Burgweard'. OE *burh-weard* or pers. name + *lēah*.

Brotherton N. Yorks. *Brothertun* c.1030. 'Farmstead of the brother, or of a man called Bróthir'. OE *brōthor* or OScand. pers. name + OE *tūn*.

Brotton Cleveland. *Broctune* 1086 (DB). 'Farmstead by a brook'. OE *brōc* + *tūn*.

Brough, 'stronghold or fortification', OE *burh*; examples include: **Brough** Cumbria. *Burc* 1174. **Brough** Derbys. *Burc* 1195. **Brough** Humber. *Burg* c.1200. **Brough** Notts. *Burgh* 1525.

Broughton, a common name, usually 'farmstead by a brook', OE *brōc* + *tūn*; examples include: **Broughton Astley** Leics. *Broctone* 1086 (DB), *Broghton Astley* 1423. Manorial affix from the *de Estle* family, here in the 13th cent. **Broughton Gifford** Wilts. *Broctun* 1001, *Broctone* 1086 (DB), *Brocton Giffard* 1288. Manorial affix from the *Giffard* family, here in the 13th cent. **Broughton, Great & Little** Cumbria. *Broctuna* 12th cent. **Broughton Hackett** Heref. & Worcs. *Broctun* 972, *Broctune* 1086 (DB), *Broctone Haket* 1275. Manorial affix from the *Hackett* family, here in the 12th cent. **Broughton in Furness** Cumbria. *Brocton* 1196. For the district name Furness, see BARROW. **Broughton Poggs** Oxon. *Brotone* 1086 (DB), *Broughton Pouges* 1526. Manorial affix from early possession of lands here by the *Pugeys* family.

However other Broughtons have a different origin: **Broughton** Hants. *Brestone* 1086 (DB), *Burchton* 1173. 'Farmstead by a hill or mound'. OE *beorg* + *tūn*. **Broughton** Humber. *Bertone* 1086 (DB). Identical in origin with previous name. **Broughton** Northants. *Burtone* 1086 (DB). 'Fortified farmstead' or 'farmstead near a fortification'. OE *burh-tūn*. **Broughton, Brant** Lincs. *Burtune* 1086 (DB), *Brendebrocton* 1250. Identical in origin with the previous name. Affix is ME *brende* 'burnt, destroyed by fire'.

Brown Candover Hants., see CANDOVER.

Brown Edge Lancs. *Browneegge* 1551. 'Brown edge or ridge'. OE *brūn* + *ecg*.

Brownhills Staffs., a recent self-explanatory name.

Brownsea Island Dorset. *Brunkeseye* 1241. 'Island of a man called *Brūnoc'. OE pers. name + *ēg*.

Brownston Devon. *Brunardeston* 1219. 'Farmstead of a man called *Brūnweard'. OE pers. name + *tūn*.

Broxbourne Herts. *Brochesborne* 1086 (DB). 'Stream frequented by badgers'. OE *brocc* + *burna*.

Broxted Essex. *Brocheseued* c.1050, *Brocchesheuot* 1086 (DB). 'Badger's head', i.e. 'hill frequented by badgers', or 'hill resembling a badger's head'. OE *brocc* + *hēafod*.

Bruera Ches. *Bruera* c.1150. Latin *bruer(i)a* 'heath'.

Bruisyard Suffolk. *Buresiart* 1086 (DB). 'Peasant's enclosure'. OE *(ge)būr* + *geard*.

Brumby Humber. *Brunebi* 1086 (DB). 'Farmstead or village of a man called Brúni'. OScand. pers. name + *bý*. Alternatively the first element may be OScand. *brunnr* 'spring'.

Brundall Norfolk. *Brundala* 1086 (DB). Possibly 'broomy nook of land'. OE **brōmede* + *halh*.

Brundish Suffolk. *Burnedich* 1177. 'Pasture on a stream'. OE *burna* + *edisc*.

Brunton Northum. *Burneton* 1242. 'Farmstead by a stream'. OE *burna* + *tūn*.

Brushford, 'ford by the bridge', OE *brycg* + *ford*: **Brushford** Devon. *Brigeford* 1086 (DB). **Brushford** Somerset. *Brigeford* 1086 (DB).

Bruton Somerset. *Briwetone* 1086 (DB). 'Farmstead on the River Brue'. Celtic river-name (meaning 'brisk') + OE *tūn*.

Bryher Isles of Scilly, Cornwall. *Braer* 1319. Probably 'the hills'. Cornish **bre* in a plural form.

Bryn Shrops. *Bren* 1272. Celtic **brïnn* 'hill'.

Bubbenhall Warwicks. *Bubenhalle (sic)* 1086 (DB), *Bubenhull* 1211. 'Hill of a man called Bubba'. OE pers. name (genitive *-n*) + *hyll*.

Bubwith Humber. *Bobewyth* 1066–9, *Bubvid* 1086 (DB). 'Wood (or dwelling) of a man called Bubba'. OE pers. name + OScand. *vithr* (perhaps replacing OE *wīc*).

Buckby, Long Northants. *Buchebi* 1086 (DB), *Longe Bugby* 1565. 'Farmstead or village of a man called Bukki or Bucca'. OScand. or OE pers. name + OScand. *bý*. Affix refers to the length of the village.

Buckden Cambs. *Bugedene* 1086 (DB). 'Valley of a woman called Bucge'. OE pers. name + *denu*.

Buckden N. Yorks. *Buckeden* 12th cent. 'Valley frequented by bucks (male deer)'. OE *bucc* + *denu*.

Buckenham, 'homestead of a man called Bucca', OE pers. name (genitive *-n*) + *hām*: **Buckenham** Norfolk. *Buc(h)anaham* 1086 (DB). **Buckenham, New & Old** Norfolk. *Buc(he)ham* 1086 (DB).

Buckerell Devon. *Bucherel* 1165. Obscure in origin and meaning.

Buckfast Devon. *Bucfæsten* 1046, *Bucfestre* 1086 (DB). 'Place of shelter for bucks (male deer)'. OE *bucc* + *fæsten*.

Buckfastleigh Devon. *Leghe Bucfestre* 13th cent. 'Wood or woodland clearing near BUCKFAST'. OE *lēah*.

Buckhorn Weston Dorset, see WESTON.

Buckhurst Hill Essex. *Bocherst* 1135. 'Wooded hill growing with beeches'. OE *bōc* + *hyrst*.

Buckingham Bucks. *Buccingahamme* early 10th cent., *Bochingeham* 1086 (DB). 'River-bend land of the family or followers of a man called Bucca'. OE pers. name + *-inga-* + *hamm*. **Buckinghamshire** (OE *scīr* 'district') is first referred to in the 11th cent.

Buckland, a common name, from OE *bōc-land* 'charter land', i.e. 'estate with certain rights and privileges created by an Anglo-Saxon royal diploma'; examples include: **Buckland** Surrey. *Bochelant* 1086 (DB). **Buckland Brewer** Devon. *Bochelanda* 1086 (DB), *Boclande Bruere* 1290. Manorial affix from the *Briwerre* family, here in the 13th cent. **Buckland Dinham** Somerset. *Boclande* 951, *Bochelande* 1086 (DB), *Bokelonddynham* 1329. Manorial affix from the *de Dinan* family, here in the 13th cent. **Buckland, Egg** Devon. *Bochelanda* 1086 (DB), *Eckebokelond* 1221. Manorial affix from its possession by a man called Heca in 1086. **Buckland Filleigh** Devon. *Bochelan* 1086 (DB), *Bokelondefilleghe* 1333. Manorial affix from the *de Fyleleye* family, here in the 13th cent. **Buckland Monachorum** Devon. *Boclande c.*970, *Bochelanda* 1086 (DB), *Boclonde Monachorum* 1291. Latin affix 'of the monks', referring to an abbey founded here in 1278. **Buckland Newton** Dorset. *Boclonde* 941, *Bochelande* 1086 (DB), *Newton Buckland* 1576. Relatively late addition Newton is from STURMINSTER NEWTON.

Bucklebury Berks. *Borgeldeberie* 1086 (DB). 'Stronghold of a woman called Burghild'. OE pers. name + *burh* (dative *byrig*).

Bucklesham Suffolk. *Bukelesham* 1086 (DB). 'Homestead of a man called *Buccel'. OE pers. name + *hām*.

Buckminster Leics. *Bucheminstre* 1086 (DB). 'Large church of a man called Bucca'. OE pers. name + *mynster*.

Bucknall, 'nook of land of a man called Bucca, or where he-goats graze', OE pers. name or *bucca* (genitive *-n*) + *halh*: **Bucknall** Lincs. *Bokenhale* 806, *Buchehale* 1086 (DB). **Bucknall** Staffs. *Bucenhole* 1086 (DB).

Bucknell, 'hill of a man called Bucca, or where he-goats graze', OE pers. name or *bucca* (genitive *-n*) + *hyll*: **Bucknell** Oxon. *Buchehelle* 1086 (DB). **Bucknell** Shrops. *Buchehalle* (*sic*) 1086 (DB), *Bukehill* 1175.

Buck's Cross Devon. *Bochewis* 1086 (DB). 'Measure of land granted by charter'. OE *bōc* + *hīwisc*.

Buckton, 'farmstead of a man called Bucca, or where bucks (male deer) or he-goats are kept', OE pers. name or OE *bucc* or *bucca* + *tūn*: **Buckton** Heref. & Worcs. *Buctone* 1086 (DB). **Buckton** Humber. *Bochetone* 1086 (DB). **Buckton** Northum. *Buketun* 1208–10.

Buckworth Cambs. *Buchesworde* 1086 (DB). 'Enclosure of a man called *Bucc'. OE pers. name + *worth*.

Budbrooke Warwicks. *Budebroc* 1086 (DB). 'Brook of a man called Budda'. OE pers. name + *brōc*.

Budby Notts. *Butebi* 1086 (DB). 'Farmstead or village of a man called Butti'. OScand. pers. name + *bý*.

Bude Cornwall. *Bude* 1400. Perhaps originally a river-name, of uncertain origin and meaning.

Budle Northum. *Bolda* 1166. 'The special house or building'. OE *bōthl*.

Budleigh, East Devon. *Bodelie* 1086 (DB). 'Woodland clearing of a man called Budda'. OE pers. name + *lēah*.

Budleigh Salterton Devon, see SALTERTON.

Budock Water Cornwall. 'Church of *Sanctus Budocus*' 1208. From the patron saint of the church, St Budock. Later affix is *water* in the sense 'stream'.

Budworth, 'enclosure of a man called Budda', OE pers. name + *worth*: **Budworth, Great** Ches. *Budewrde* 1086 (DB). **Budworth, Little** Ches. *Bodeurde* 1086 (DB).

Buerton Ches., near Audlem. *Burtune* 1086 (DB). 'Enclosure belonging to a fortified place'. OE *byrh-tūn*.

Bugbrooke Northants. *Buchebroc* 1086 (DB). Probably 'brook of a man called Bucca'. OE pers. name + *brōc*.

Bugthorpe Humber. *Bugetorp* 1086 (DB). 'Outlying farmstead or hamlet of a man called Buggi'. OScand. pers. name + *thorp*.

Bulby Lincs. *Bolebi* 1086 (DB). Probably

'farmstead or village of a man called Boli or Bolli'. OScand. pers. name + *bý*.

Bulford Wilts. *Bulte(s)ford* 12th cent. Possibly 'ford by the island where ragged robin or the cuckoo flower grows'. OE *bulut* + *īeg* + *ford*.

Bulkeley Ches. *Bulceleia* 1170. 'Clearing or pasture where bullocks graze'. OE *bulluc* + *lēah*.

Bulkington, 'estate associated with a man called *Bulca', OE pers. name + *-ing-* + *tūn*: **Bulkington** Warwicks. *Bochintone* 1086 (DB). **Bulkington** Wilts. *Boltintone* 1086 (DB).

Bulkworthy Devon. *Buchesworde* 1086 (DB). 'Enclosure of a man called *Bulca'. OE pers. name + *worth*.

Bulley Glos. *Bulelege* 1086 (DB). 'Woodland clearing where bulls graze'. OE **bula* + *lēah*.

Bullingham, Lower Heref. & Worcs. *Boninhope (sic)* 1086 (DB), *Bullingehope* 1242. 'Marsh enclosure associated with a man called *Bulla', or 'marsh enclosure at *Bulla's place'. OE pers. name + *-ing-* or *-ing* + *hop* (later replaced by *hamm*).

Bulmer, 'pool where bulls drink', OE **bula* (genitive plural *bulena*) + *mere*: **Bulmer** Essex. *Bulenemera* 1086 (DB). **Bulmer** N. Yorks. *Bolemere* 1086 (DB).

Bulphan Essex. *Bulgeuen* 1086 (DB). 'Fen near a fortified place'. OE *burh* + *fenn*. The spelling with *-l-* is due to Norman influence.

Bulverhythe E. Sussex. *Bulwareheda* 12th cent. 'Landing-place of the town-dwellers (of Hastings)'. OE *burh-ware* + *hȳth*.

Bulwell Notts. *Buleuuelle* 1086 (DB). 'Spring or stream of a man called *Bula, or where bulls drink'. OE pers. name or OE **bula* + *wella*.

Bulwick Northants. *Bulewic* 1162. 'Farm where bulls are reared'. OE **bula* + *wīc*.

Bumpstead, Helions & Steeple Essex. *Bumesteda* 1086 (DB), *Bumpsted Helyun* 1238, *Stepilbumstede* 1261. 'Place where reeds grow'. OE *bune* + *stede*. Distinguishing affixes from *Tihel de Helion* who held one manor in 1086, and from OE *stēpel* 'steeple, tower'.

Bunbury Ches. *Boleberie (sic)* 1086 (DB), *Bonebury* 12th cent. 'Stronghold of a man called Būna'. OE pers. name + *burh* (dative *byrig*).

Bungay Suffolk. *Bunghea* 1086 (DB). Probably 'island of the family or followers of a man called Būna'. OE pers. name + *-inga-* + *ēg*.

Bunny Notts. *Bonei* 1086 (DB). Probably 'island, or dry ground in marsh, where reeds grow'. OE *bune* + *ēg*.

Buntingford Herts. *Buntingeford* 1185. 'Ford frequented by buntings or yellow-hammers'. ME *bunting* + *ford*.

Bunwell Norfolk. *Bunewell* 1198. 'Spring or stream where reeds grow'. OE *bune* + *wella*.

Burbage Derbys. *Burbache* 1417. 'Stream or ridge by a fortified place'. OE *burh* + *bece* or *bæc* (dative **bece*).

Burbage Leics. *Burhbeca* 1043, *Burbece* 1086 (DB). Probably 'ridge by a fortified place'. OE *burh* + *bæc* (dative **bece*).

Burbage Wilts. *Burhbece* 961, *Burbetce* 1086 (DB). Probably 'stream by a fortified place'. OE *burh* + *bece*.

Burcombe Wilts. *Brydancumb* 937, *Bredecumbe* 1086 (DB). Probably 'valley of a man called *Brȳda'. OE pers. name + *cumb*.

Burcot Oxon. *Bridicote* 1198. Probably 'cottage(s) associated with a man called *Brȳda'. OE pers. name (+ *-ing-*) + *cot*.

Burdale N. Yorks. *Bredhalle* 1086 (DB). 'Hall or house made of planks'. OE *bred* + *hall*.

Bures & Mount Bures Essex. *Bura* 1086 (DB), *Bures* 1198, *Bures atte Munte* 1328. 'The dwellings or cottages'. OE *būr* with later affix 'at the hill' from ME *munt*.

Burford, 'ford by the fortified place', OE *burh* + *ford*: **Burford** Oxon. *Bureford* 1086 (DB). **Burford** Shrops. *Bureford* 1086 (DB).

Burgess Hill W. Sussex. *Burges Hill* 1597. Named from a family called *Burgeys*, here in the 13th cent.

Burgh, a common name, usually OE *burh* 'fortification, stronghold, fortified manor'; examples include: **Burgh** Suffolk. *Burc* 1086 (DB). **Burgh-by-Sands** Cumbria. *Burch* *c*.1180, *Burg en le Sandes* 1292. This is an old Roman fort on the coast. **Burgh le Marsh** Lincs. *Burg* 1086 (DB). Affix means 'in the marshland'.

However the following has a different origin: **Burgh, Great & Burgh Heath** Surrey. *Berge* 1086 (DB), *Borow heth* 1545. '(Place at) the barrow(s)', from OE *beorg*, with the later addition of *hǣth* 'heath'.

Burghclere Hants. *Burclere* 1171. OE *burh* in one of its meanings 'fortification, manor, borough, market-town' added to the original name found also in HIGHCLERE.

Burghfield Berks. *Borgefel* 1086 (DB). 'Open land by the hill'. OE *beorg* + *feld*.

Burghill Heref. & Worcs. *Burgelle* 1086 (DB). 'Hill with a fort'. OE *burh* + *hyll*.

Burham Kent. *Burhham* 10th cent., *Borham* 1086 (DB). 'Homestead near the fortified place'. OE *burh* + *hām*.

Buriton Hants. *Buriton* 1227. 'Enclosure near or belonging to a fortified place'. OE *byrh-tūn*.

Burland Ches. *Burlond* 1260. 'Cultivated land of the peasants'. OE *(ge)būr* + *land*.

Burlescombe Devon. *Berlescoma* (*sic*) 1086 (DB), *Burewoldescumbe* 12th cent. 'Valley of a man called Burgweald'. OE pers. name + *cumb*.

Burleston Dorset. *Bordelestone* 934. 'Farmstead of a man called Burdel'. OE pers. name + *tūn*.

Burley, 'woodland clearing by or belonging to a fortified place', OE *burh* + *lēah*: **Burley** Hants. *Burgelea* 1178. **Burley** Leics. *Burgelai* 1086 (DB). **Burley** W. Yorks. *Burcheleia c*.1200. **Burley in Wharfedale** W. Yorks. *Burhleg c*.972, *Burghelai* 1086 (DB). Affix is 'valley of the River Wharfe', Celtic river-name (meaning 'winding one') + OScand. *dalr*.

Burleydam Ches. *Burley c*.1130, *Burleydam* 1643. 'Woodland clearing of the peasants'. OE *(ge)būr* + *lēah* with the later addition of ME *damme* 'a mill-dam'.

Burlingham Norfolk. *Berlingeham* 1086 (DB). 'Homestead of the family or followers of a man called *Bǣrla or *Byrla'. OE pers. name + *-inga-* + *hām*.

Burlton Shrops. *Burghelton* 1241. 'Farmstead by a hill with a fort'. OE *burh* + *hyll* + *tūn*.

Burmarsh Kent. *Burwaramers* 7th cent., *Burwarmaresc* 1086 (DB). 'Marsh of the town-dwellers (of Canterbury)'. OE *burh-ware* + *mersc*.

Burmington Warwicks. *Burdintone* (*sic*) 1086 (DB), *Burminton* late 12th cent. 'Estate associated with a man called Beornmund or *Beorma'. OE pers. name + *-ing-* + *tūn*.

Burn N. Yorks. *Byrne c*.1030. Probably 'place cleared by burning'. OE *bryne*.

Burnaston Derbys. *Burnulfestune* 1086 (DB). 'Farmstead of a man called *Brūnwulf or Brynjólfr'. OE or OScand. pers. name + OE *tūn*.

Burnby Humber. *Brunebi* 1086 (DB). 'Farmstead or village by a spring or stream'. OScand. *brunnr* + *bý*.

Burneside Cumbria. *Brunoluesheued c*.1180. 'Headland or hill of a man called *Brūnwulf or Brunulf'. OE or OGerman pers. name + OE *hēafod*.

Burneston N. Yorks. *Brennigston* 1086 (DB). Probably 'farmstead of a man called Brýningr'. OScand. pers. name + *tūn*.

Burnett Avon. *Bernet* 1086 (DB). 'Land cleared by burning'. OE *bærnet*.

Burnham, usually 'homestead or village on a stream', OE *burna* + *hām*: **Burnham** Bucks. *Burneham* 1086 (DB). **Burnham Deepdale & Market, Burnham Norton & Overy, Burnham Thorpe** Norfolk. *Brun(e)ham, Depedala* 1086 (DB), *Brunham Norton* 1457, *Brunham Overhe* 1457, *Brunhamtorp* 1199. Distinguishing affixes are 'deep valley' (OE *dēop* + *dæl*), 'market', 'north farm' (OE *north* + *tūn*), 'over the river' (OE *ofer* + *ēa*) and 'outlying farmstead' (OScand. *thorp*). **Burnham on Crouch** Essex. *Burneham* 1086 (DB). Affix is from the River Crouch (not recorded before 16th cent., probably from OE *crūc* 'a cross').

However two Burnhams have a different origin: **Burnham** Humber. *Brune* (*sic*) 1086 (DB), *Brunum c*.1115. '(Place at) the springs or streams'.

OScand. *brunnr* in a dative plural form *brunnum*. **Burnham on Sea** Somerset. *Burnhamm c.*880, *Burneham* 1086 (DB). 'Enclosure by a stream'. OE *burna* + *hamm*.

Burniston N. Yorks. *Brinnistun* 1086 (DB). 'Farmstead of a man called Brýningr'. OScand. pers. name + OE *tūn*.

Burnley Lancs. *Brunlaia* 1124. 'Woodland clearing by the River Brun'. OE river-name (from *brūn* 'brown' or *burna* 'stream') + *lēah*.

Burnsall N. Yorks. *Brineshale* 1086 (DB). 'Nook of land of a man called Brȳni'. OE pers. name + *halh*.

Burpham, 'homestead near the stronghold or fortified place', OE *burh* + *hām*: **Burpham** Surrey. *Borham* 1086 (DB). **Burpham** W. Sussex. *Burhham c.*920, *Bercheham* 1086 (DB).

Burradon, 'hill with a fort', OE *burh* + *dūn*: **Burradon** Northum. *Burhedon* early 13th cent. **Burradon** Tyne & Wear. *Burgdon* 12th cent.

Burrill N. Yorks. *Borel* 1086 (DB). Probably 'hill with a fort'. OE *burh* + *hyll*.

Burringham Humber. *Burringham* 1199. Probably 'homestead of the dwellers on the stream'. OE *burna* + *-inga-* + *hām*.

Burrington Avon. *Buringtune* 12th cent. 'Farmstead by a fortified place'. OE *burh* (genitive or dative *byrig*) + *tūn*.

Burrington Devon. *Bernintone* 1086 (DB). 'Estate associated with a man called Beorn'. OE pers. name + *-ing-* + *tūn*.

Burrington Heref. & Worcs. *Boritune* 1086 (DB). 'Farmstead by a fortified place'. OE *burh* (genitive or dative *byrig*) + *tūn*.

Burrough Green Cambs. *Burg c.*1045, *Burch* 1086 (DB), *Boroughegrene* 1571. 'The fortified place'. OE *burh* with the later addition of *grēne* 'village green'.

Burrough on the Hill Leics. *Burg* 1086 (DB). 'The fortified place'. OE *burh*, referring to an Iron Age hill-fort.

Burrow Bridge Somerset. *Æt tham Beorge* 1065. '(Place) at the hill'. OE *beorg*.

Burrow, Nether & Over Lancs. *Borch* 1086 (DB). 'The fortified place', here referring to a Roman fort. OE *burh*.

Burscough Lancs. *Burscogh c.*1190. 'Wood by the fort'. OE *burh* + OScand. *skógr*.

Burshill Humber. *Bristehil* 12th cent. 'Hill with a landslip or rough ground'. OE *byrst* + *hyll*.

Bursledon Hants. *Brixendona c.*1170. Probably 'hill associated with a man called Beorhtsige'. OE pers. name + *-ing-* + *dūn*.

Burslem Staffs. *Barcardeslim* (*sic*) 1086 (DB), *Borewardeslyme* 1242. 'Estate in *Lyme* belonging to the fort-keeper, or to a man called Burgweard'. OE *burh-weard* or pers. name with old Celtic district name *Lyme* probably meaning 'elm-tree region'.

Burstall Suffolk. *Burgestala* 1086 (DB). 'Site of a fort or stronghold'. OE *burh-stall*.

Burstead, Great & Little Essex. *Burgestede c.*1000, *Burghesteda* 1086 (DB). 'Site of a fort or stronghold'. OE *burh-stede*.

Burstock Dorset. *Burewinestoch* 1086 (DB). 'Outlying farmstead or hamlet of a woman called Burgwynn or of a man called Burgwine'. OE pers. name + *stoc*.

Burston Norfolk. *Borstuna* 1086 (DB). Possibly 'farmstead by a landslip or rough ground'. OE *byrst* + *tūn*.

Burston Staffs. *Burouestone* 1086 (DB). Possibly 'farmstead of a man called Burgwine or Burgwulf'. OE pers. name + *tūn*.

Burstow Surrey. *Burestou* 12th cent. 'Place by a fort or stronghold'. OE *burh* (genitive *byrh*) + *stōw*.

Burstwick Humber. *Brostewic* 1086 (DB). Probably 'dwelling or farm of a man called Bursti'. OScand. pers. name + OE *wīc*.

Burton, a common name, usually OE *burh-tūn* 'fortified farmstead', or 'farmstead near a fortification'; examples include: **Burton Agnes** Humber. *Bortona* 1086 (DB), *Burton*

Agneys 1231. Manorial affix from its possession by *Agnes de Percy* in the late 12th cent. **Burton, Cherry** Humber. *Burtone* 1086 (DB), *Cheriburton* 1444. Affix is ME *chiri* 'cherry', no doubt referring to cherry-trees growing here. **Burton, Constable** N. Yorks. *Bortone* 1086 (DB), *Burton Constable* 1301. Manorial affix from its possession by the Constables of Richmond Castle in the 12th cent. **Burton Dassett** Warwicks., see DASSETT. **Burton Fleming** Humber. *Burtone* 1086 (DB), *Burton Flemeng* 1234. Manorial affix from the *Fleming* family, here in the 12th cent. **Burton Hastings** Warwicks. *Burhtun* 1002, *Bortone* 1086 (DB), *Burugton de Hastings* 1313. Manorial affix from the *de Hasteng* family, here in the 13th cent. **Burton Latimer** Northants. *Burtone* 1086 (DB), *Burton Latymer* 1482. Manorial affix from the *le Latimer* family, here in the 13th cent. **Burton upon Stather** Humber. *Burtone* 1086 (DB), *Burtonstather* 1275. Affix means 'by the landing-places' from OScand. *stǫth* in a plural form *stǫthvar*.

However the following have a different origin: **Burton Bradstock** Dorset. *Bridetone* 1086 (DB). 'Farmstead on the River Bride'. Celtic river-name (see BREDY) + OE *tūn*. The later addition Bradstock is from the Abbey of BRADENSTOKE which held the manor from the 13th cent. **Burton Joyce** Notts. *Bertune* 1086 (DB), *Birton Jorce* 1327. OE *byrh-tūn* 'farmstead of the fortified place or stronghold'. Manorial affix from the *de Jorz* family, here in the 13th cent. **Burton Salmon** N. Yorks. *Brettona c.*1160, *Burton Salamon* 1516. 'Farmstead of the Britons'. OE *Brettas* (genitive *Bretta*) + *tūn*. Manorial affix from a man called *Salamone* who had lands here in the 13th cent. **Burton upon Trent** Staffs. *Byrtun* 1002, *Bertone* 1086 (DB). Identical in origin with BURTON JOYCE. For the river-name, see TRENTHAM.

Burtonwood Ches. *Burtoneswod* 1228. 'Wood by the fortified farmstead'. OE *burh-tūn* + *wudu*.

Burwardsley Ches. *Burwardeslei* 1086 (DB). 'Woodland clearing of the fort-keeper, or of a man called Burgweard'. OE *burh-weard* or pers. name + *lēah*.

Burwarton Shrops. *Burertone (sic)* 1086 (DB), *Burwardton* 1194. 'Farmstead of the fort-keeper, or of a man called Burgweard'. OE *burh-weard* or pers. name + *tūn*.

Burwash E. Sussex. *Burhercse* 12th cent. 'Ploughed field by the fort'. OE *burh* + *ersc*.

Burwell, 'spring or stream by the fort', OE *burh* + *wella*: **Burwell** Cambs. *Burcwell* 1060, *Buruuella* 1086 (DB). **Burwell** Lincs. *Buruelle* 1086 (DB).

Bury, '(place by) the fort or stronghold', OE *burh* (dative *byrig*): **Bury** Cambs. *Byrig* 974. **Bury** Gtr. Manch. *Biri* 1194. **Bury** W. Sussex. *Berie* 1086 (DB).

Bury St Edmunds Suffolk. *Sancte Eadmundes Byrig* 1038. 'Town associated with St Ēadmund'. OE saint's name (a 9th cent. king of East Anglia) + OE *burh* (dative *byrig*).

Burythorpe N. Yorks. *Bergetorp* 1086 (DB). Probably 'outlying farmstead or hamlet of a woman called Bjǫrg'. OScand. pers. name + *thorp*.

Busby, Great N. Yorks. *Buschebi* 1086 (DB). 'Farmstead or village of a man called *Buski, or among the bushes or shrubs'. OScand. pers. name or **buskr*, **buski* + *bý*.

Buscot Oxon. *Boroardescote* 1086 (DB). 'Cottage(s) of the fort-keeper, or of a man called Burgweard'. OE *burh-weard* or pers. name + *cot*.

Bushbury W. Mids. *Byscopesbyri* 996, *Biscopesberie* 1086 (DB). 'The bishop's fortified manor'. OE *biscop* + *burh* (dative *byrig*).

Bushey Herts. *Bissei* 1086 (DB). 'Enclosure near a thicket, or hedged with box-trees'. OE **bysce* or **byxe* + *hæg*.

Bushley Heref. & Worcs. *Biselege* 1086 (DB). 'Woodland clearing with bushes, or of a man called *Byssa'. OE **bysce* or pers. name + *lēah*.

Bushton Wilts. *Bissopeston* 1242. 'The bishop's farmstead'. OE *biscop* + *tūn*.

Buston, High & Low Northum. *Buttesdune* 1166, *Butlesdon* 1249. Possibly 'hill of a man called *Buttel', OE pers. name + *dūn*. Alternatively the first element may be OE **butt* 'stumpy hill'.

Butcombe Avon. *Budancumb c.*1000, *Budicome* 1086 (DB). 'Valley of a man called Buda'. OE pers. name + *cumb*.

Butleigh Somerset. *Budecalech* 725, *Boduchelei* 1086 (DB). 'Woodland clearing of a man called *Budeca'. OE pers. name + *lēah*.

Butley Suffolk. *Butelea* 1086 (DB). 'Woodland clearing of a man called *Butta'. OE pers. name + *lēah*. Alternatively the first element may be an OE **butte* 'mound, hill'.

Butterleigh Devon. *Buterlei* 1086 (DB). 'Clearing with good pasture'. OE *butere* + *lēah*.

Buttermere, 'lake or pool with good pasture', OE *butere* + *mere*: **Buttermere** Cumbria. *Butermere* 1230. **Buttermere** Wilts. *Butermere* 863, *Butremere* 1086 (DB).

Butterton Staffs., near Leek. *Buterdon* 1200. 'Hill with good pasture'. OE *butere* + *dūn*.

Butterwick, 'dairy farm where butter is made', OE *butere* + *wīc*: **Butterwick** Durham. *Boterwyk* 1131. **Butterwick** Lincs. *Butrvic* 1086 (DB). **Butterwick** N. Yorks., near Foxholes. *Butruid* (*sic*) 1086 (DB), *Butterwic c.*1130. **Butterwick** N. Yorks., near Hovingham. *Butruic* 1086 (DB). **Butterwick, East & West** Humber. *Butreuuic* 1086 (DB).

Buxhall Suffolk. *Bucyshealæ c.*995, *Buckeshala* 1086 (DB). 'Nook of land of a man called *Bucc'. OE pers. name + *halh*.

Buxted E. Sussex. *Boxted* 1199. 'Place where beech-trees or box-trees grow'. OE *bōc* or *box* + *stede*.

Buxton Derbys. *Buchestanes c.*1100. Probably 'the rocking stones or logan-stones'. OE **būg-stān*.

Buxton Norfolk. *Bukestuna* 1086 (DB). 'Farmstead of a man called *Bucc'. OE pers. name + *tūn*.

Byers Green Durham. *Bires* 1345. 'The byres or cowsheds'. OE *bȳre*.

Byfield Northants. *Bifelde* 1086 (DB). '(Place) by the open country'. OE *bī* + *feld*.

Byfleet Surrey. *Biflete* 933, *Biflet* 1086 (DB). '(Place) by the stream'. OE *bī* + *flēot*.

Byford Heref. & Worcs. *Buiford* 1086 (DB). 'Ford near the river-bend'. OE *byge* + *ford*.

Bygrave Herts. *Bigravan* 973, *Bigrave* 1086 (DB). '(Place) by the grove or by the trench'. OE *bī* + *grāfa* or **grafa*.

Byker Tyne & Wear. *Bikere* 1196. Identical in origin with BICKER.

Byley Ches. *Bevelei* 1086 (DB). 'Woodland clearing of a man called Bēofa'. OE pers. name + *tūn*.

Bytham, Castle & Little Lincs. *Bytham c.*1067, *Bitham* 1086 (DB). 'Valley bottom'. OE *bythme*.

Bythorn Cambs. *Bitherna c.*960, *Bierne* 1086 (DB). '(Place) by the thorn-bush'. OE *bī* + *thyrne*.

Byton Heref. & Worcs. *Boitune* 1086 (DB). 'Farmstead by the river-bend'. OE *byge* + *tūn*.

Byworth W. Sussex. *Begworth* 1279. 'Enclosure of a woman called Bēage or a man called Bǣga'. OE pers. name + *worth*.

C

Cabourne Lincs. *Caburne* 1086 (DB). 'Stream frequented by jackdaws'. OE **cā* + *burna*.

Cadbury, 'fortified place or stronghold of a man called Cada', OE pers. name + *burh* (dative *byrig*): **Cadbury** Devon. *Cadebirie* 1086 (DB). **Cadbury, North & South** Somerset. *Cadanbyrig* c.1000, *Cadeberie* 1086 (DB).

Caddington Beds. *Caddandun* c.1000, *Cadendone* 1086 (DB). 'Hill of a man called Cada'. OE pers. name (genitive *-n*) + *dūn*.

Cadeby, 'farmstead or village of a man called Káti or Kátr', OScand. pers. name + *bý*: **Cadeby** Leics. *Catebi* 1086 (DB). **Cadeby** S. Yorks. *Catebi* 1086 (DB).

Cadeleigh Devon. *Cadelie* 1086 (DB). 'Woodland clearing of a man called Cada'. OE pers. name + *lēah*.

Cadishead Gtr. Manch. *Cadewalesate* 1212. 'Dwelling or fold by the stream of a man called Cada'. OE pers. name + *wælla* + *set*.

Cadmore End Bucks. *Cademere* 1236. 'Estate boundary or pool of a man called Cada'. OE pers. name + *mǣre* or *mere*.

Cadnam Hants. *Cadenham* 1272. 'Homestead or enclosure of a man called Cada'. OE pers. name (genitive *-n*) + *hām* or *hamm*.

Cadney Humber. *Catenai* 1086 (DB). 'Island, or dry ground in marsh, of a man called Cada'. OE pers. name (genitive *-n*) + *ēg*.

Caenby Lincs. *Couenebi* 1086 (DB). Probably 'farmstead or village of a man called *Cāfna or *Kafni'. OE or OScand. pers. name + OScand. *bý*.

Caister, Caistor, 'Roman camp or town', OE *cæster*: **Caister-on-Sea** Norfolk. *Castra* 1044–7, 1086 (DB). **Caistor** Lincs. *Castre* 1086 (DB). **Caistor St Edmund** Norfolk. *Castre* c.1025, *Castrum* 1086 (DB), *Castre Sancti Eadmundi* 1254. Affix from its early possession by the Abbey of Bury St Edmunds.

Caistron Northum. *Cers* c.1160, *Kerstirn* 1202. 'Thornbush by the fen'. ME *kers* + OScand. *thyrnir*.

Calbourne I. of Wight. *Cawelburne* 826, *Cavborne* 1086 (DB). 'Stream called *Cawel*', or 'stream where cole or cabbage grows'. Celtic river-name (of uncertain meaning) or OE *cawel* + *burna*.

Calceby Lincs. *Calesbi* 1086 (DB). 'Farmstead or village of a man called Kalfr'. OScand. pers. name + *bý*.

Calcethorpe Lincs. *Cheilestorp* c.1115. 'Outlying farmstead or hamlet of a man called *Cægel'. OE pers. name + OScand. *thorp*.

Calcot Row Berks., not on record before the 18th century, but probably identical in origin with CALDECOTE.

Calcutt Wilts. *Colecote* 1086 (DB). Probably 'cottage of a man called Cola'. OE pers. name + *cot*.

Caldbeck Cumbria. *Caldebek* 11th cent. 'Cold stream'. OScand. *kaldr* + *bekkr*.

Caldbergh N. Yorks. *Caldeber* 1086 (DB). 'Cold hill'. OScand. *kaldr* + *berg*.

Caldecote, Caldecott, a place-name found in various counties, meaning 'cold or inhospitable cottage(s), or shelter(s) for travellers', from OE *cald* + *cot*; examples include: **Caldecote** Cambs. *Caldecote* 1086 (DB). **Caldecote** Herts. *Caldecota* 1086 (DB). **Caldecote** Northants. *Caldecot* 1202. **Caldecote Hill** Warwicks. *Caldecote* 1086 (DB). **Caldecott** Leics. *Caldecote* 1086 (DB). **Caldecott** Northants. *Caldecote* 1086 (DB).

Calder Bridge & Hall Cumbria. *Calder* 1178. Named from the River

Calder, an old Celtic river-name meaning 'rapid stream'.

Calder Vale Lancs., named from a stream, identical in origin with the previous name.

Caldwell N. Yorks. *Caldeuuella* 1086 (DB). 'Cold spring or stream'. OE *cald* + *wella*.

Caldy Mersey. *Calders* 1086 (DB), *Caldei* 1182. 'Cold island', earlier 'cold rounded hill'. OE *cald* + *ēg* (replacing *ears*).

Cale (river) Dorset, Somerset, see WINCANTON.

Calke Derbys. *Calc* 1132. '(Place on) the limestone'. OE *calc*.

Callaly Northum. *Calualea* 1161. 'Clearing where calves graze'. OE *calf* (genitive plural *calfra*) + *lēah*.

Callerton, 'hill where calves graze', OE *calf* (genitive plural *calfra*) + *dūn*: **Callerton, Black** Northum. *Calverdona* 1212. Affix is OE *blæc* 'dark-coloured'. **Callerton, High** Northum. *Calverdon* 1242.

Callington Cornwall. *Calwetone* 1086 (DB). Probably 'farmstead by the bare hill'. OE *calu* (in a dative form) + *tūn*.

Callow Heref. & Worcs. *Calua* 1180. 'The bare hill'. OE *calu* in a dative form.

Calmsden Glos. *Kalemundesdene* 852. 'Valley of a man called *Calumund'. OE pers. name + *denu*.

Calne Wilts. *Calnė* 955, 1086 (DB). A pre-English river-name of uncertain meaning.

Calow Derbys. *Calehale* 1086 (DB). 'Bare nook of land', or 'nook of land at a bare hill'. OE *calu* + *halh*.

Calshot Hants. *Celcesoran* 980, *Celceshord* 1011. OE *ord* 'point or spit of land' (replacing *ōra* 'shore' in the earliest spelling) with an uncertain first element, possibly OE *cælic* 'cup, chalice' used in some topographical sense.

Calstock Cornwall. *Kalestoc* 1086 (DB). The second element is OE *stoc* 'outlying farm, secondary settlement', the first is uncertain.

Calstone Wellington Wilts. *Calestone* 1086 (DB), *Caulston Wellington* 1568. Probably 'farmstead or village by CALNE', from OE *tūn*. The manorial addition is from a family called *de Wilinton*, here from the 13th century.

Calthorpe Norfolk. *Calethorp* 1044–7, *Caletorp* 1086 (DB). 'Outlying farmstead or hamlet of a man called Kali'. OScand. pers. name + *thorp*.

Calthwaite Cumbria. *Caluethweyt* 1272. 'Clearing where calves are kept'. OE *calf* or OScand. *kalfr* + *thveit*.

Calton, 'farm where calves are reared', OE *calf* + *tūn*: **Calton** N. Yorks. *Caltun* 1086 (DB). **Calton** Staffs. *Calton* 1238.

Calveley Ches. *Calueleg c.*1235. 'Clearing where calves are pastured'. OE *calf* + *lēah*.

Calver Derbys. *Calvoure* 1086 (DB). 'Slope or ridge where calves graze'. OE *calf* + **ofer*.

Calverhall Shrops. *Cavrahalle* 1086 (DB). 'Nook of land where calves graze'. OE *calf* + *halh*.

Calverleigh Devon. *Calodelie* (*sic*) 1086 (DB), *Calewudelega* 1194. 'Clearing in the bare wood'. OE *calu* + *wudu* + *lēah*.

Calverley W. Yorks. *Caverleia* 1086 (DB). 'Clearing where calves are pastured'. OE *calf* (genitive plural *calfra*) + *lēah*.

Calverton, 'farm where calves are reared', OE *calf* (genitive plural *calfra*) + *tūn*: **Calverton** Bucks. *Calvretone* 1086 (DB). **Calverton** Notts. *Caluretone* 1086 (DB).

Cam Glos. *Camma* 1086 (DB). Named from the River Cam, an old Celtic river-name meaning 'crooked'.

Cam Beck (river) Cumbria, see KIRKCAMBECK.

Camberley Surrey, an arbitrary name of recent origin, altered from *Cambridge Town* which was named in 1862 from the Duke of Cambridge.

Camberwell Gtr. London. *Cambrewelle* 1086 (DB). OE *wella* 'spring or stream' with an obscure first element.

Camblesforth N. Yorks. *Camelesforde* 1086 (DB). Possibly 'ford associated with a man called *Camel(e)'. OE pers. name + *ford*.

Cambo Northum. *Camho* 1230. 'Hill-spur with a crest or ridge'. OE *camb* + *hōh*.

Cambois Northum. *Cammes c.*1050. A Celtic name, a derivative of Celtic **camm* 'crooked' and originally referring to the bay here.

Camborne Cornwall. *Camberon* 1182. 'Crooked hill'. Cornish *camm* + *bronn*.

Cambridge Cambs. *Grontabricc c.*745, *Cantebrigie* 1086 (DB). 'Bridge on the River Granta'. Celtic river-name (see GRANTCHESTER) + OE *brycg*. The change from *Grant-* to *Cam-* is due to Norman influence. **Cambridgeshire** (OE *scīr* 'district') is first referred to in the 11th cent.

Cambridge Glos. *Cambrigga* 1200–10. 'Bridge over the River Cam'. Celtic river-name (see CAM) + OE *brycg*.

Camden Town Gtr. London, so named in 1795 from Earl *Camden* (died 1794) who came into possession of the manor of Kentish Town of which this formed part.

Camelford Cornwall. *Camelford* 13th cent. 'Ford over the River Camel'. Celtic river-name (possibly 'crooked one' from a derivative of Celtic **camm*) + OE *ford*.

Camel, Queen & West Somerset. *Cantmæl* 995, *Camelle* 1086 (DB). Possibly a Celtic name from **canto-* 'border or district' and **mēl* 'bare hill'. Affix *Queen* from its possession by Queen Eleanor in the 13th cent.

Camerton Avon. *Camelartone* 954, *Camelertone* 1086 (DB). 'Farmstead or estate on Cam Brook'. Celtic river-name (earlier *Cameler*, probably a derivative of **camm* 'crooked') + OE *tūn*.

Camerton Cumbria. *Camerton c.*1150. OE *tūn* 'farmstead, estate' with an obscure first element.

Cammeringham Lincs. *Camelingeham* (*sic*) 1086 (DB), *Cameryngham c.*1115. Possibly 'homestead of the family or followers of a man called *Cāfmǣr or *Cantmǣr'. OE pers. name + *-inga-* + *hām*.

Campden, Broad & Chipping Glos. *Campedene* 1086 (DB), *Bradecampedene* 1224, *Chepyng Campedene* 1287. 'Valley with enclosures'. OE *camp* + *denu*. Affixes are OE *brād* 'broad' and OE *cēping* 'market'.

Campsall S. Yorks. *Cansale* (*sic*) 1086 (DB), *Camshale* 12th cent. Possibly 'nook of land of a man called *Cam'. OE pers. name + *halh*. Alternatively the first element may be a derivative of Celtic **camm* 'crooked' used in some topographical sense.

Camps, Castle & Shudy Cambs. *Canpas* 1086 (DB), *Campecastel* 13th cent., *Sudekampes* 1219. 'The fields or enclosures', from OE *camp*, plural *campas*. The affix *Castle* is from a medieval castle, *Shudy* is probably an OE **scydd* 'shed, hovel'.

Campsey Ash Suffolk. *Campeseia* 1086 (DB). 'Island, or dry ground in marsh, with a field or enclosure'. OE *camp* + *ēg*. *Ash* was originally a separate place, mentioned as *Esce* in 1086 (DB), from OE *æsc* 'ash-tree'.

Campton Beds. *Chambeltone* 1086 (DB). Probably 'farmstead by a river called *Camel*'. Lost Celtic river-name (possibly 'crooked one' from a derivative of Celtic **camm*) + OE *tūn*.

Candlesby Lincs. *Calnodesbi* 1086 (DB). Probably 'farmstead or village of a man called *Cal(u)nōth'. OE pers. name + OScand. *bý*.

Candover, Brown & Preston Hants. *Cendefer c.*880, *Candovre* 1086 (DB), *Brunkardoure* 1296, *Prestecandevere c.*1270. Named from the stream here, a Celtic river-name meaning 'pleasant waters'. Distinguishing affixes are manorial, from early possession by a family called *Brun* and by priests (ME genitive plural *prestene*).

Canewdon Essex. *Carenduna* (*sic*) 1086 (DB), *Canuedon* 1181. Probably 'hill of the family or followers of a man called Cana'. OE pers. name + *-inga-* + *dūn*.

Canfield, Great Essex. *Canefelda* 1086 (DB). 'Open land of a man called Cana'. OE pers. name + *feld*.

Canford Dorset. *Cheneford* (*sic*) 1086 (DB), *Kaneford* 1195. 'Ford of a man called Cana'. OE pers. name + *ford*.

Cann Dorset. *Canna* 12th cent. OE *canne* 'a can, a cup', used topographically for 'a hollow, a deep valley'.

Cannings, All & Bishops Wilts. *Caninge* 1086 (DB), *Aldekanning* 1205, *Bisshopescanyngges* 1314. '(Settlement of) the family or followers of a man called Cana'. OE pers. name + *-ingas.* Affixes are OE *eald* 'old' and *biscop* 'bishop' (referring to early possession by the Bishop of Salisbury).

Cannington Somerset. *Cantuctun c.*880, *Cantoctona* 1086 (DB). 'Estate or village by the QUANTOCK HILLS'. Celtic hill-name + OE *tūn.*

Cannock Staffs. *Chenet* (*sic*) 1086 (DB), *Canoc* 12th cent. 'The small hill, the hillock'. OE *cnocc.*

Canon Frome Heref. & Worcs., see FROME.

Canterbury Kent. *Cantwaraburg c.*900, *Canterburie* 1086 (DB). 'Stronghold or fortified town of the people of KENT'. Ancient Celtic name + OE *-ware* + *burh.*

Cantley, probably 'woodland clearing of a man called *Canta', OE pers. name + *lēah*: **Cantley** Norfolk. *Cantelai* 1086 (DB). **Cantley** S. Yorks. *Canteleia* 1086 (DB).

Cantlop Shrops. *Cantelop* 1086 (DB). OE *hop* 'enclosed place' with an obscure first element.

Cantsfield Lancs. *Cantesfelt* 1086 (DB). Probably 'open land by the River Cant'. Celtic river-name (of uncertain meaning) + OE *feld.*

Canvey Essex. *Caneveye* 1255. Possibly 'island of the family or followers of a man called Cana'. OE pers. name + *-inga-* + *ēg.*

Canwick Lincs. *Canewic* 1086 (DB). 'Dwelling or dairy-farm of a man called Cana'. OE pers. name + *wīc.*

Capel, a place-name found in several counties, from ME *capel* 'a chapel': **Capel** Surrey. *Capella* 1190. **Capel le Ferne** Kent. *Capel ate Verne* 1377. The addition means 'at the ferny place' from OE **(ge)fierne.* **Capel St Andrew** Suffolk. *Capeles* 1086 (DB). Addition from the dedication of the chapel. **Capel St Mary** Suffolk. *Capeles* 1254. Addition from the dedication of the chapel.

Capenhurst Ches. *Capeles* (*sic*) 1086 (DB), *Capenhurst* 13th cent. Probably 'wooded hill at a look-out place'. OE **cape* (genitive *-an*) + *hyrst.*

Capernwray Lancs. *Coupmanwra* c.1200. 'The merchant's nook or corner of land'. OScand. *kaup-mathr* + *vrá.*

Capheaton Northum. *Magna Heton* 1242, *Cappitheton* 1454. 'High farmstead, farmstead situated on high land'. OE *hēah* + *tūn.* The affix *Cap-* is from Latin *caput* 'head, chief'.

Capton Devon. *Capieton* 1278. Probably 'estate of a family called *Capia*'. ME surname + OE *tūn.*

Carbrook S. Yorks. *Kerebroc* 1200–18. Probably 'stream in the marsh'. OScand. *kjarr* + OE *brōc.* Alternatively the first element may be an old Celtic river-name.

Carbrooke Norfolk. *Cherebroc* 1086 (DB). Identical in origin with the previous name.

Carburton Notts. *Carbertone* 1086 (DB). OE *tūn* 'farmstead, village' with an obscure first element.

Car Colston Notts., see COLSTON.

Carcroft S. Yorks. *Kercroft* 12th cent. 'Enclosure near the marsh'. OScand. *kjarr* + OE *croft.*

Cardeston Shrops. *Cartistune* 1086 (DB). Probably 'farm or estate of a man called *Card'. OE pers. name + *tūn.*

Cardington Shrops. *Cardintune* 1086 (DB). Probably 'estate associated with a man called *Card(a)'. OE pers. name + *-ing-* + *tūn.*

Cardinham Cornwall. *Cardinan c.*1180. Both parts of the name mean 'fort', Cornish **ker* + **dinan.*

Cardurnock Cumbria. *Cardrunnock* 13th cent. A Celtic place-name, from *cair* 'fortified town' + **durnōg* 'pebbly'.

Careby Lincs. *Careby* 1199. 'Farmstead or village of a man called Kári'. OScand. pers. name + *bý.*

Cargo Cumbria. *Cargaou c.*1178. Celtic **carreg* 'rock' + OScand. *haugr* 'hill'.

Carham Northum. *Carrum c.*1050. '(Place) by the rocks'. OE *carr* in a dative plural form *carrum.*

Carhampton Somerset. *Carrum* 9th cent., *Carentone* 1086 (DB). 'Farm at the place by the rocks'. OE *carr* (dative plural *carrum*) + *tūn.*

Carisbrooke I. of Wight. *Caresbroc* 12th

cent. Possibly 'the brook called *Cary*'. Lost Celtic river-name + OE *brōc*.

Cark Cumbria. *Karke* 1491. Celtic **carreg* 'a stone, a rock'.

Carlby Lincs. *Carlebi* 1086 (DB). Probably 'homestead or village of the peasants or freemen'. OScand. *karl* + *bý*.

Carlecotes Derbys. *Carlecotes* 13th cent. 'Cottages of the freemen'. OScand. *karl* + OE *cot*.

Carlesmoor N. Yorks. *Carlesmore* 1086 (DB). 'Moorland of the freeman or of a man called Karl'. OScand. *karl* or pers. name + *mór*.

Carleton, Carlton, a common place-name in the old Danelaw areas of the Midlands and the North, usually 'farmstead or estate of the freemen or peasants', from OScand. *karl* (often no doubt replacing OE *ceorl*) + OE *tūn*; examples include: **Carleton** Cumbria. *Karleton* 1250. **Carleton** N. Yorks. *Carlentone* 1086 (DB). **Carleton Forehoe** Norfolk. *Carletuna* 1086 (DB), *Karleton Fourhowe* 1268. Affix from the nearby Forehoe Hills, from OE *fēower* 'four' and OScand. *haugr* 'hill'. **Carleton Rode** Norfolk. *Carletuna* 1086 (DB), *Carleton Rode* 1201. Manorial addition from the *de Rode* family, here in the 14th cent. **Carlton** Beds. *Carlentone* 1086 (DB). **Carlton** N. Yorks., near Snaith. *Carletun* 1086 (DB). **Carlton** Notts. *Karleton* 1182. **Carlton Colville** Suffolk. *Carletuna* 1086 (DB), *Carleton Colvile* 1346. Manorial addition from the *de Colevill* family, here in the 13th cent. **Carlton Curlieu** Leics. *Carletone* 1086 (DB), *Carleton Curly* 1273. Manorial addition from the *de Curly* family, here in the 13th cent. **Carlton Husthwaite** N. Yorks. *Carleton* 1086 (DB), *Carlton Husthwat* 1516. Affix from its proximity to HUSTHWAITE. **Carlton in Lindrick** Notts. *Carletone* 1086 (DB), *Carleton in Lindric* 1212. Affix from the district called Lindrick, which means 'strip of land where lime-trees grow', from OE *lind* + **ric*. **Carlton le Moorland** Lincs. *Carletune* 1086 (DB). Affix from its situation 'in the moorland'. **Carlton Miniott** N. Yorks. *Carletun* 1086 (DB), *Carleton Mynyott* 1579. Manorial addition from the *Miniott* family, here in the 14th cent. **Carlton on Trent** Notts. *Carletune* 1086 (DB). For the river-name, see TRENTHAM. **Carlton Scroop** Lincs. *Carletune* 1086 (DB). Manorial addition from the *Scrope* family, here in the 14th cent.

Carlingcott Avon. *Credelincote* 1086 (DB). 'Cottage associated with a man called *Cridela'. OE pers. name + *-ing-* + *cot*.

Carlisle Cumbria. *Luguvalio* 4th cent., *Carleol* c.1106. An old Celtic name meaning '(place) belonging to a man called *Luguvalos', to which Celtic *cair* 'fortified town' was added after the Roman period.

Carlton, see CARLETON.

Carnaby Humber. *Cherendebi* 1086 (DB). Possibly 'homestead or village of a man called *Kærandi or *Keyrandi'. OScand. pers. name + *bý*.

Carnforth Lancs. *Chreneforde* 1086 (DB). Probably 'ford frequented by cranes or herons'. OE *cran* + *ford*.

Carperby N. Yorks. *Chirprebi*. Possibly 'homestead or village of a man called Cairpre'. OIrish pers. name + OScand. *bý*.

Carrington Gtr. Manch. *Carrintona* 12th cent. Possibly 'estate associated with a man called *Cāra'. OE pers. name + *-ing-* + *tūn*. Alternatively the first element may be an OE **caring* 'tending, herding' or an OE **cǣring* 'river-bend'.

Carrington Lincs. First recorded in 1812, and named after Robert Smith, Lord *Carrington* (1752–1838), who had lands here.

Carrock, Castle Cumbria. *Castelcairoc* c.1165. 'Fortified castle'. Celtic *castel* + a derivative of Celtic *cair* 'fort'.

Carshalton Gtr. London. *Aultone* 1086 (DB), *Cresaulton* 1235. 'Farm by the river-spring where watercress grows'. OE *ǣwiell* + *tūn* with the later addition of OE *cærse*.

Carsington Derbys. *Ghersintune* 1086 (DB). Probably 'farmstead where cress grows'. OE **cærsen* + *tūn*.

Carswell Marsh Oxon. *Chersvelle* 1086 (DB), *Carsewell Merssh* 1467. '(Marsh at) the spring or stream where watercress grows'. OE *cærse* + *wella* with the later addition of OE *mersc*.

Carterton Oxon., a recent name for the village founded by one William *Carter* in 1901.

Carthorpe N. Yorks. *Caretorp* 1086 (DB). 'Outlying farmstead or hamlet of a man called Kári'. OScand. pers. name + *thorp*.

Cartington Northum. *Cretenden* 1220. Probably 'hill associated with a man called *Certa'. OE pers. name + *-ing-* + *dūn*.

Cartmel Cumbria. *C(e)artmel* 12th cent. 'Sandbank by rough stony ground'. OScand. **kartr* + *melr*.

Cary Fitzpaine & Castle Cary Somerset. *Cari* 1086 (DB), *Castelkary* 1237. Named from the River Cary, an ancient Celtic or pre-Celtic river-name. Distinguishing affixes from the *Fitz Payn* family, here in the 13th cent., and from ME *castel* with reference to the Norman castle.

Cassop Durham. *Cazehope* 1183. Possibly 'valley or enclosure frequented by wild-cats'. OE *catt* + *hop*.

Casterton, 'farmstead near the (Roman) fort', OE *cæster* + *tūn*: **Casterton** Cumbria. *Castretune* 1086 (DB). **Casterton, Great & Little** Leics. *Castretone* 1086 (DB).

Castle as affix, see main name, e.g. for **Castle Bolton** (N. Yorks) see BOLTON.

Castleford W. Yorks. *Ceaster forda* late 11th cent. 'Ford by the Roman fort'. OE *cæster* + *ford*.

Castlemorton Heref. & Worcs. *Mortun* 1235, *Castell Morton* 1346. 'Farmstead in the marshy ground'. OE *mōr* + *tūn*, with the later addition of *castel* 'castle'.

Castleton, 'farmstead or village by a castle', from OE *castel* + *tūn*: **Castleton** Derbys. *Castelton* 13th cent. **Castleton** Gtr. Manch. *Castelton* 1246. **Castleton** N. Yorks. *Castleton* 1577.

Castley N. Yorks. *Castelai* 1086 (DB). 'Wood or clearing by a heap of stones'. OE *ceastel* + *lēah*.

Caston Norfolk. *Catestuna* 1086 (DB). 'Farmstead or estate of a man called *Catt or Káti'. OE or OScand. pers. name + OE *tūn*.

Castor Cambs. *Cæstre* 948, *Castre* 1086 (DB). 'The Roman fort'. OE *cæster*.

Catcleugh Northum. *Cattechlow* 1279. 'Deep valley or ravine frequented by wild-cats'. OE *catt* + **clōh*.

Catcott Somerset. *Cadicote* 1086 (DB). 'Cottage of a man called Cada'. OE pers. name + *cot*.

Caterham Surrey. *Catheham* 1179. Probably 'homestead or enclosure at the hill called *Cadeir*', from Celtic **cadeir* (literally 'chair' but used of lofty places) + OE *hām* or *hamm*. Alternatively 'homestead or enclosure of a man called *Catta', with an OE pers. name as first element.

Catesby Northants. *Catesbi* 1086 (DB). 'Farmstead or village of a man called Kátr or Káti'. OScand. pers. name + *bý*.

Catfield Norfolk. *Catefelda* 1086 (DB). 'Open land frequented by wild-cats'. OE *catt* + *feld*.

Catford Gtr. London. *Catford* 1254. 'Ford frequented by wild-cats'. OE *catt* + *ford*.

Catforth Lancs. *Catford* 1332. Identical in origin with the previous name.

Catherington Hants. *Cateringatune* c.1015. Possibly 'farmstead of the people living by the hill called *Cadeir*', from Celtic **cadeir* 'chair' + *-inga-* + *tūn*. Alternatively 'farmstead of the family or followers of a man called *Cat(t)or', from OE pers. name + *-inga-* + *tūn*.

Catherston Leweston Dorset. *Chartreston* 1268, *Lesterton* 1316. Originally names of adjacent estates belonging to families called *Charteray* and *Lester* respectively, from OE *tūn*.

Catherton Shrops. *Carderton* 1316. OE *tūn* 'farmstead, village' with an obscure first element.

Catmore Berks. *Catmere* 10th cent., 1086 (DB). 'Pool frequented by wild-cats'. OE *catt* + *mere*.

Caton Lancs. *Catun* 1086 (DB). 'Farmstead or village of a man called Káti'. OScand. pers. name + OE *tūn*.

Catsfield E. Sussex. *Cedesfeld* (*sic*) 1086

(DB), *Cattesfeld* 12th cent. 'Open land of a man called *Catt or frequented by wild-cats'. OE pers. name or OE *catt* + *feld*.

Catshill Heref. & Worcs. *Catteshull* 1199. 'Hill of a man called *Catt or frequented by wild-cats'. OE pers. name or OE *catt* + *hyll*.

Cattal N. Yorks. *Catale* 1086 (DB). Probably 'nook of land frequented by wild-cats'. OE *catt* + *halh*.

Cattawade Suffolk. *Cattiwad* 1247. 'Ford frequented by wild-cats'. OE *catt* + *(ge)wæd*.

Catterall Lancs. *Catrehala* 1086 (DB). Possibly OScand. *kattar-hali* 'cat's tail' with reference to the shape of some lost feature. Alternatively OE *halh* 'nook of land' with an obscure first element.

Catterick N. Yorks. *Katouraktónion* c.150, *Catrice* 1086 (DB). From Latin *cataracta* 'waterfall', though apparently through a misunderstanding of the original Celtic place-name meaning '(place of) battle ramparts'.

Catterlen Cumbria. *Kaderleng* 1158. Celtic **cadeir* 'chair' (here 'hill') with an obscure second element, possibly a pers. name.

Catterton N. Yorks. *Cadretune* 1086 (DB). Probably 'farmstead at the hill called *Cadeir*'. Celtic **cadeir* 'chair' + OE *tūn*.

Catthorpe Leics. *Torp* 1086 (DB), *Torpkat* 1276. OScand. *thorp* 'outlying farmstead or hamlet', with a manorial addition from a family called *le Cat(t)*.

Cattishall Suffolk. *Catteshale* 1187. Probably 'nook of land of a man called *Catt or frequented by wild-cats'. OE pers. name or OE *catt* + *halh*.

Cattistock Dorset. *Stoche* 1086 (DB), *Cattestok* 1288. OE *stoc* 'outlying farm buildings, secondary settlement', with a manorial addition from a person or family called *Cat(t)*.

Catton, usually 'farmstead of a man called Catta or Káti', OE or OScand. pers. name + OE *tūn*: **Catton** Norfolk. *Catetuna* 1086 (DB). **Catton** N. Yorks. *Catune* 1086 (DB). **Catton, High & Low** Humber. *Caton, Cattune* 1086 (DB).
However the following has a different origin: **Catton** Northum. *Catteden* 1229. 'Valley frequented by wild-cats'. OE *catt* + *denu*.

Catwick Humber. *Catingeuuic* 1086 (DB). 'Dwelling or (dairy) farm associated with a man called Catta'. OE pers. name (+ *-ing-*) + *wīc*.

Catworth Cambs. *Catteswyrth* 10th cent., *Cateuuorde* 1086 (DB). 'Enclosure of a man called *Catt or Catta'. OE pers. name + *worth*.

Caulcott Oxon. *Caldecot* 1199. Identical in origin with CALDECOTE.

Cauldon Staffs. *Celfdun* 1002, *Caldone* 1086 (DB). 'Hill where calves graze'. OE *cælf* + *dūn*.

Cauldwell Derbys. *Caldewællen* 942, *Caldewelle* 1086 (DB). 'Cold spring or stream'. OE *cald* + *wella*.

Caundle, Bishop's & Purse Dorset. *Candel* 1086 (DB), *Purscaundel* 1241, *Caundel Bishops* 1294. The meaning of Caundle is obscure, though it may have been a name for the chain of hills here. The affix *Bishop's* is from the possession of this manor by the Bishop of Salisbury, *Purse* is probably a manorial addition from a family of this name.

Caunton Notts. *Calnestune* 1086 (DB). Probably 'farmstead of a man called *Cal(u)nōth'. OE pers. name + *tūn*.

Causey Park Northum. *La Chauce* 1242. ME *cauce* 'embankment, raised way'.

Cave, North & South Humber. *Cave* 1086 (DB). Probably from the stream here, 'the fast flowing one', from OE *cāf* 'quick'.

Cavendish Suffolk. *Kauanadisc* 1086 (DB). 'Enclosure or enclosed park of a man called *Cāfna'. OE pers. name + *edisc*.

Cavenham Suffolk. *Kanauaham (sic)* 1086 (DB), *Cauenham* 1198. 'Homestead or enclosure of a man called *Cāfna'. OE pers. name + *hām* or *hamm*.

Caversfield Oxon. *Cavrefelle* 1086 (DB). 'Open land of a man called *Cāfhere'. OE pers. name + *feld*.

Caversham Oxon. *Caueresham* 1086 (DB). 'Homestead or enclosure of a man called *Cāfhere'. OE pers. name + *hām* or *hamm*.

Caverswall Staffs. *Cavreswelle* 1086 (DB). 'Spring or stream of a man called *Cāfhere'. OE pers. name + *wella*.

Cavil Humber. *Cafeld* 959, *Cheuede* 1086 (DB). 'Open land frequented by jackdaws'. OE **cā* + *feld*.

Cawkwell Lincs. *Calchewelle* 1086 (DB). 'Chalk spring or stream'. OE *calc* + *wella*.

Cawood N. Yorks. *Kawuda* 963. 'Wood frequented by jackdaws'. OE **cā* + *wudu*.

Cawston, 'farmstead or village of a man called Kalfr', OScand. pers. name + OE *tūn*: **Cawston** Norfolk. *Cau(p)stuna* 1086 (DB). **Cawston** Warwicks. *Calvestone* 1086 (DB).

Cawthorne S. Yorks. *Caltorne* 1086 (DB). 'Cold (i.e. exposed) thorn-tree'. OE *cald* + *thorn*.

Cawthorpe, 'outlying farmstead or hamlet of a man called Kali', OScand. pers. name + *thorp*: **Cawthorpe** Lincs. *Caletorp* 1086 (DB). **Cawthorpe, Little** Lincs. *Calthorp* 1241.

Cawton N. Yorks. *Caluetun* 1086 (DB). 'Farm where calves are reared'. OE *calf* + *tūn*.

Caxton Cambs. *Caustone* (*sic*) 1086 (DB), *Kakestune* c.1150. Probably 'farmstead of a man called *Kakkr'. OScand. pers. name + OE *tūn*.

Caynham Shrops. *Caiham* 1086 (DB). Probably 'homestead or enclosure of a man called *Cǣga'. OE pers. name (genitive *-n*) + *hām* or *hamm*.

Caythorpe, 'outlying farmstead or hamlet of a man called Káti', OScand. pers. name + *thorp*: **Caythorpe** Lincs. *Catorp* 1086 (DB). **Caythorpe** Notts. *Cathorp* 1177.

Cayton N. Yorks. *Caitun(e)* 1086 (DB). 'Farmstead of a man called *Cǣga'. OE pers. name + *tūn*.

Cerne Abbas Dorset. *Cernel* 1086 (DB), *Cerne Abbatis* 1288. Named from the River Cerne, an old Celtic river-name from Celtic **carn* 'cairn, heap of stones'. Affix is Latin *abbas* 'an abbot', with reference to the abbey here.

Cerne, Nether & Up Dorset. *Nudernecerna* 1206, *Obcerne* 1086 (DB). Named from the same river as Cerne Abbas. OE *neotherra* 'lower down' and OE *upp* 'higher up' with reference to their situation on the river.

Cerney, North & South, Cerney Wick Glos. *Cyrnea* 852, *Cernei* 1086 (DB), *Northcerneye* 1291, *Suthcerney* 1285, *Cernewike* 1220. Named from the River Churn (an old Celtic river-name derived from the same root as the first element of CIRENCESTER) + OE *ēa* 'stream'. Wick is from OE *wīc* 'farm, dairy farm'.

Chaceley Glos. *Ceatewesleah* 972. Possibly a derivative of Celtic **cę̄d* 'wood' + OE *lēah* 'wood, clearing'.

Chackmore Bucks. *Chakemore* 1241. Possibly 'marshy ground of a man called *Ceacca'. OE pers. name + *mōr*. Alternatively the first element may be OE **ceacce* 'hill'.

Chacombe Northants. *Cewecumbe* 1086 (DB). 'Valley of a man called *Ceawa'. OE pers. name + *cumb*.

Chadderton Gtr. Manch. *Chaderton* c.1200. Possibly 'farmstead at the hill called *Cadeir*'. Celtic **cadeir* 'chair' (here 'hill') + OE *tūn*.

Chaddesden Derbys. *Cedesdene* 1086 (DB). 'Valley of a man called *Ceadd'. OE pers. name + *denu*.

Chaddesley Corbett Heref. & Worcs. *Ceadresleahge* 816, *Cedeslai* 1086 (DB). Possibly 'wood or clearing at the hill called *Cadeir*'. Celtic **cadeir* 'chair' + OE *lēah*, with manorial addition from the *Corbet* family here in the 12th cent.

Chaddleworth Berks. *Ceadelanwyrth* 960, *Cedeledorde* (*sic*) 1086 (DB). 'Enclosure of a man called *Ceadela'. OE pers. name + *worth*.

Chadlington Oxon. *Cedelintone* 1086 (DB). 'Estate associated with a man called *Ceadela'. OE pers. name + *-ing-* + *tūn*.

Chadshunt Warwicks. *Ceadeles funtan* 949, *Cedeleshunte* 1086 (DB). 'Spring of a man called *Ceadel'. OE pers. name + **funta*.

Chadwell, 'cold spring or stream', OE *c(e)ald* + *wella*: **Chadwell** Leics. *Caldeuuelle* 1086 (DB). **Chadwell St Mary** Essex. *Celdeuuella* 1086 (DB).

Affix from the dedication of the church.

Chadwick Green Mersey. *Chaddewyk* c.1180. '(Dairy) farm of a man called Ceadda'. OE pers. name + *wīc*.

Chaffcombe Somerset. *Caffecome* 1086 (DB). Probably valley of a man called *Ceaffa'. OE pers. name + *cumb*.

Chagford Devon. *Chageford* 1086 (DB). 'Ford where broom or gorse grows'. OE **ceacga* + *ford*.

Chailey E. Sussex. *Cheagele* 11th cent. 'Clearing where broom or gorse grows'. OE **ceacga* + *lēah*.

Chalbury Dorset. *Cheoles burge* 946. 'Fortified place associated with a man called Cēol'. OE pers. name + *burh*.

Chaldon, 'hill where calves graze', OE *cealf* + *dūn*: **Chaldon** Surrey. *Calvedone* 1086 (DB). **Chaldon Herring or East Chaldon** Dorset. *Celvedune* 1086 (DB), *Chaluedon Hareng* 1243. Manorial affix from the *Harang* family, here from the 12th cent.

Chale I. of Wight. *Cela* 1086 (DB). OE *ceole* 'throat' used in a topographical sense 'gorge, ravine'.

Chalfont St Giles & St Peter Bucks. *Celfunte* 1086 (DB), *Chalfund Sancti Egidii* 1237, *Chalfhunte Sancti Petri* 1237–40. 'Spring frequented by calves'. OE *cealf* + **funta*, with distinguishing affixes from the dedications of the churches at the two places.

Chalford, 'chalk or limestone ford', OE *cealc* + *ford*: **Chalford** Glos. *Chalforde* c.1250. **Chalford** Oxon. *Chalcford* 1185–6.

Chalgrave Beds. *Cealhgræfan* 926, *Celgraue* 1086 (DB). 'Chalk pit'. OE *cealc* + *græf*.

Chalgrove Oxon. *Celgrave* 1086 (DB). Identical in origin with the previous name.

Chalk, Chalke, '(place on) the chalk', OE *cealc*: **Chalk** Kent. *Cealca* 10th cent., *Celca* 1086 (DB). **Chalke, Broad & Bowerchalke** Wilts. *Ceolcum* 955, *Chelche* 1086 (DB), *Brode Chalk* 1380, *Burchelke* 1225. Distinguishing affixes are OE *brād* 'great' and *(ge)būra* 'of the peasants' or *burh* 'fortified place'.

Challacombe Devon, near Lynton. *Celdecomba* 1086 (DB). 'Cold valley'. OE *ceald* + *cumb*.

Challock Lees Kent. *Cealfalocum* 824. 'Enclosure(s) for calves'. OE *cealf* + *loca*, with the later addition of *lǣs* 'pasture'.

Challow, East & West Oxon. *Ceawanhlæwe* 947, *Ceveslane (sic)* 1086 (DB). 'Tumulus of a man called *Ceawa'. OE pers. name + *hlǣw, hlāw*.

Chalton Beds., near Toddington. *Chaltun* 1131. 'Farm where calves are reared'. OE *cealf* + *tūn*.

Chalton Hants. *Cealctun* 1015, *Ceptune* 1086 (DB). 'Farmstead on chalk'. OE *cealc* + *tūn*.

Chalvington E. Sussex. *Calvintone* 1086 (DB). 'Estate associated with a man called *Cealf(a)'. OE pers. name + *-ing-* + *tūn*.

Chandler's Ford Hants., on record from 1759, named from the *Chaundler* family, in the area from the 14th cent.

Chapel as affix, see main name, e.g. for **Chapel Allerton** (W. Yorks.) see ALLERTON.

Chapel en le Frith Derbys. *Capella de le Frith* 1272. 'Chapel in the sparse woodland'. ME *chapele* + OE *fyrhth*, with retention of OFrench preposition and definite article.

Chapeltown S. Yorks. *Le Chapel* 13th cent., *Chappeltown* 1707. '(Hamlet by) the chapel'. ME *chapel*.

Chapmanslade Wilts. *Chepmanesled* 1245. 'Valley of the merchants'. OE *ceap-mann* + *slæd*.

Chard, South Chard Somerset. *Cerdren* 1065, *Cerdre* 1086 (DB). Possibly 'house or building in rough ground'. OE *ceart* + *ærn*.

Chardstock Devon. *Cerdestoche* 1086 (DB). 'Secondary settlement belonging to CHARD'. OE *stoc*.

Charfield Avon. *Cirvelde* 1086 (DB). 'Open land by a bending road, or with a rough surface'. OE **cearr(e)* or *ceart* + *feld*.

Charford, North Hants. *Cerdicesford* late 9th cent., *Cerdeford* 1086 (DB). 'Ford associated with the chieftain called Cerdic'. OE pers. name + *ford*.

Charing Kent. *Ciorrincg* 799, *Cheringes* 1086 (DB). Probably OE **cerring* 'a bend in a road'. Alternatively 'place associated with a man called Ceorra', OE pers. name + *-ing*.

Charing Cross Gtr. London. *Cyrring c.*1000, *La Charryngcros* 1360. From OE **cerring* (see previous name), with reference either to a bend in the Roman road to the West or in the River Thames. There was a 'Queen Eleanor cross' here in the 14th cent., see WALTHAM CROSS.

Charingworth Glos. *Chevringavrde* 1086 (DB). 'Enclosure of the family or followers of a man called *Ceafor'. OE pers. name + *-inga-* + *worth*.

Charlbury Oxon. *Ceorlingburh c.*1000. 'Fortified place associated with a man called Ceorl'. OE pers. name + *-ing-* + *burh* (dative *byrig*).

Charlcombe Avon. *Cerlecume* 1086 (DB). 'Valley of the freemen or peasants'. OE *ceorl* + *cumb*.

Charlecote Warwicks. *Cerlecote* 1086 (DB). 'Cottage(s) of the freemen or peasants'. OE *ceorl* + *cot*.

Charles Devon. *Carmes* (*sic*) 1086 (DB), *Charles* 1244. Possibly 'rock-court'. Cornish *carn* + **lys*.

Charlesworth Derbys. *Cheuenwrde* (*sic*) 1086 (DB), *Chauelisworth* 1286. Probably 'enclosure of a man called *Ceafl', OE pers. name + *worth*. Alternatively the first element may be OE *ceafl* 'jaw' here used in the sense 'ravine'.

Charleton Devon. *Cherletone* 1086 (DB). 'Farmstead of the freemen or peasants'. OE *ceorl* + *tūn*.

Charlinch Somerset. *Cerdeslinc* 1086 (DB). Possibly 'ridge of a man called Cēolrēd'. OE pers. name + *hlinc*.

Charlton, a common place-name, usually 'farmstead of the freemen or peasants', from OE *ceorl* (genitive plural *-a*) + *tūn*; examples include: **Charlton** Gtr. London. *Cerletone* 1086 (DB). **Charlton** Hants. *Cherleton* 1192. **Charlton** Wilts., near Malmesbury. *Ceorlatunæ* 10th cent., *Cerletone* 1086 (DB). **Charlton Abbots** Glos. *Cerletone* 1086 (DB), *Charleton Abbatis* 1535. Affix from its possession by Winchcomb Abbey. **Charlton Adam** Somerset. *Cerletune* 1086 (DB), *Cherleton Adam* 13th cent. Manorial addition from the *fitz Adam* family, here in the 13th cent. **Charlton Horethorne** Somerset. *Ceorlatun c.*950. Affix from the old Hundred of Horethorne, meaning 'grey thorn-bush' from OE *hār* + *thyrne*. **Charlton Kings** Glos. *Cherletone* 1160, *Kynges Cherleton* 1245. Affix 'Kings' because it was ancient demesne of the Crown. **Charlton Mackerell** Somerset. *Cerletune* 1086 (DB), *Cherletun Makerel* 1243. Manorial affix from the *Makerel* family. **Charlton Marshall** Dorset. *Cerletone* 1086 (DB), *Cherleton Marescal* 1288. Manorial addition from the *Marshall* family, here in the 13th cent. **Charlton Musgrove** Somerset. *Cerletone* 1086 (DB), *Cherleton Mucegros* 1225. Manorial addition from the *Mucegros* family, here in the 13th cent. **Charlton, North & South** Northum. *Charleton del North*, *Charleton del Suth* 1242. **Charlton on Otmoor** Oxon. *Cerlentone* 1086 (DB), *Cherleton upon Ottemour* 1314. Affix from nearby Ot Moor, 'marshy ground of a man called *Otta', from OE pers. name + *mōr*. **Charlton, Queen** Avon. *Cherleton* 1291. Affix because given to Queen Catherine Parr by Henry VIII.

However the following has a different origin: **Charlton** Surrey. *Cerdentone* 1086 (DB). Probably 'estate associated with a man called Cēolrēd'. OE pers. name + *-ing-* + *tūn*.

Charlwood Surrey. *Cherlewde* 12th cent. 'Wood of the freemen or peasants'. OE *ceorl* + *wudu*.

Charminster Dorset. *Cerminstre* 1086 (DB). 'Church on the River Cerne'. Celtic river-name (see CERNE) + OE *mynster*.

Charmouth Dorset. *Cernemude* 1086 (DB). 'Mouth of the River Char'. Celtic river-name (identical in origin with CERNE) + OE *mūtha*.

Charndon Bucks. *Credendone* (*sic*) 1086 (DB), *Charendone* 1227. Probably 'hill called *Carn*'. Celtic hill-name (from **carn* 'cairn, heap of stones') + OE *dūn*.

Charney Bassett Oxon. *Ceornei* 821, *Cernei* 1086 (DB). 'Island on a river called *Cern*'. Lost Celtic river-name (identical in origin with CERNE) + OE *ēg*, with manorial addition from a family called *Bass*(*es*).

Charnock Richard Lancs. *Chernoch* 1194, *Chernok Ricard* 1288. Possibly a derivative of Celtic **carn* 'cairn, heap of stones' + manorial addition from a certain *Richard* here in the 13th cent.

Charnwood Leics. *Cernewoda* 1129. 'Wood in rocky country'. Celtic **carn* + OE *wudu*.

Charsfield Suffolk. *Ceresfelda* 1086 (DB). OE *feld* 'tract of open country', possibly with a Celtic river-name *Char* as first element.

Chart, Great & Little Kent. *Cert* 762, *Certh, Litelcert* 1086 (DB). OE *cert* 'rough ground'.

Charterhouse Somerset. *Chartuse* 1243. OFrench *chartrouse* 'a house of Carthusian monks'.

Chartham Kent. *Certham c.*871, *Certeham* 1086 (DB). 'Homestead in rough ground'. OE *cert* + *hām*.

Chartridge Bucks. *Charderuge* 1191–4. Possibly 'ridge of a man called *Cærda'. OE pers. name + *hrycg*.

Chart Sutton Kent. *Cært* 814, *Certh* 1086 (DB), *Chert juxta Suthon* 1280. OE *cert* 'rough ground'. Affix from nearby SUTTON VALENCE.

Charwelton Northants. *Cerweltone* 1086 (DB). 'Farmstead on the River Cherwell'. River-name (probably 'winding stream' from OE **cearr(e)* + *wella*) + OE *tūn*.

Chastleton Oxon. *Ceastelton* 777, *Cestitone* 1086 (DB). 'Farmstead by the ruined prehistoric camp'. OE *ceastel* + *tūn*.

Chatburn Lancs. *Chatteburn* 1242. 'Stream of a man called Ceatta'. OE pers. name + *burna*.

Chatcull Staffs. *Ceteruille* (*sic*) 1086 (DB), *Chatculne* 1199. 'Kiln of a man called Ceatta'. OE pers. name + *cyln*.

Chatham, 'homestead or village in or by the wood', Celtic **cę̄d* + OE *hām*: **Chatham** Kent. *Cetham* 880, *Ceteham* 1086 (DB). **Chatham Green** Essex. *Cetham* 1086 (DB).

Chattenden Kent. *Chatendune c.*1100. Possibly 'hill of a man called Ceatta'. OE pers. name (genitive *-n*) + *dūn*.

Chatteris Cambs. *Cæateric* 974, *Cietriz* 1086 (DB). Probably 'raised strip or ridge of a man called Ceatta'. OE pers. name + **ric*. However the first element may be Celtic **cę̄d* 'wood'.

Chattisham Suffolk. *Cetessam* 1086 (DB). Probably 'homestead or enclosure of a man called *Ceatt'. OE pers. name + *hām* or *hamm*.

Chatton Northum. *Chetton* 1178. 'Farmstead of a man called Ceatta'. OE pers. name + *tūn*.

Chatwell, Great Staffs. *Chattewell* 1203. 'Well or spring of a man called Ceatta'. OE pers. name + *wella*.

Chawleigh Devon. *Calvelie* 1086 (DB). 'Clearing where calves are pastured'. OE *cealf* + *lēah*.

Chawston Beds. *Calnestorne* (*sic*) 1086 (DB), *Caluesterne* 1167. 'Thorn-tree of a man called *Cealf'. OE pers. name + *thyrne*.

Chawton Hants. *Celtone* 1086 (DB). 'Farmstead where calves are reared', or 'farmstead on chalk'. OE *cealf* or *cealc* + *tūn*.

Cheadle, from Celtic **cę̄d* 'wood' to which an explanatory OE *lēah* 'wood' has been added: **Cheadle** Gtr. Manch. *Cedde* 1086 (DB), *Chedle c.*1165. **Cheadle** Staffs. *Celle* 1086 (DB).

Cheadle Hulme Gtr. Manch. *Hulm* 12th cent. 'Water-meadow belonging to CHEADLE'. OScand. *holmr*.

Cheam Gtr. London. *Cegham* 967, *Ceiham* 1086 (DB). Probably 'homestead or village by the tree-stumps'. OE **ceg* + *hām*.

Chearsley Bucks. *Cerdeslai* 1086 (DB). 'Wood or clearing of a man called Cēolrēd'. OE pers. name + *lēah*.

Chebsey Staffs. *Cebbesio* 1086 (DB). 'Island, or dry ground in marsh, of a man called *Cebbi'. OE pers. name + *ēg*.

Checkendon Oxon. *Cecadene* 1086 (DB). 'Valley of a man called *Ceacca', or 'valley by the hill'. OE pers. name or OE **ceacce* (genitive *-an*) + *denu*.

Checkley Ches. *Chackileg* 1252. 'Wood or clearing of a man called *Ceaddica'. OE pers. name + *lēah*.

Checkley Heref. & Worcs. *Chakkeleya* 1195. 'Wood or clearing of a man called *Ceacca', or 'wood or clearing on or near a hill'. OE pers. name or OE **ceacce* + *lēah*.

Checkley Staffs. *Cedla* (*sic*) 1086 (DB), *Checkeleg* 1196. Identical in origin with the previous name.

Chedburgh Suffolk. *Cedeberia* 1086 (DB). 'Hill of a man called Cedda'. OE pers. name + *beorg*.

Cheddar Somerset. *Ceodre* c.880, *Cedre* 1086 (DB). Probably OE **cēodor* 'ravine', with reference to Cheddar Gorge.

Cheddington Bucks. *Cete(n)done* 1086 (DB). 'Hill of a man called *Cetta'. OE pers. name (genitive *-n*) + *dūn*.

Cheddleton Staffs. *Celtetone* 1086 (DB), *Chetilton* 1201. 'Farmstead in a valley'. OE *cetel* + *tūn*.

Cheddon Fitzpaine Somerset. *Succedene* (*sic*) 1086 (DB), *Chedene* 1182. OE *denu* 'valley', possibly with Celtic **cę̄d* 'wood'. Manorial addition from the *Fitzpaine* family, here in the 13th cent.

Chedgrave Norfolk. *Scatagraua* 1086 (DB), *Chategrave* 1165–70. Probably 'pit of a man called Ceatta'. OE pers. name + *græf*.

Chedington Dorset. *Chedinton* 1194. 'Estate associated with a man called *Cedd or Cedda'. OE pers. name + *-ing-* + *tūn*.

Chediston Suffolk. *Cedestan* 1086 (DB). 'Stone of a man called *Cedd'. OE pers. name + *stān*.

Chedworth Glos. *Ceddanwryde* 862, *Cedeorde* 1086 (DB). 'Enclosure of a man called Cedda'. OE pers. name + *worth*.

Chedzoy Somerset. *Chedesie* 729. 'Island, or dry ground in marsh, of a man called *Cedd'. OE pers. name + *ēg*.

Cheetham Gtr. Manch. *Cheteham* late 12th cent. 'Homestead or village by the wood called *Chet*'. Celtic **cę̄d* 'forest' + OE *hām*.

Cheetwood Gtr. Manch. *Chetewode* 1489. Near CHEETHAM; an explanatory *wudu* 'wood' has been added to the same first element.

Chelborough Dorset. *Celberge* 1086 (DB). Probably 'hill of a man called Cēola'. OE pers. name + *beorg*. Alternatively the first element may be OE *ceole* 'throat, gorge' or *cealc* 'chalk'.

Cheldon Barton Devon. *Chadeledona* 1086 (DB). 'Hill of a man called *Ceadela'. OE pers. name + *dūn*. Barton is from OE *bere-tūn* 'barley-farm, demesne farm'.

Chelford Ches. *Celeford* 1086 (DB). Probably 'ford of a man called Cēola'. OE pers. name + *ford*. Alternatively the first element could be OE *ceole* 'throat', used in a topographical sense 'channel, gorge'.

Chellaston Derbys. *Celerdestune* 1086 (DB). 'Farmstead of a man called Cēolheard'. OE pers. name + *tūn*.

Chell Heath Staffs. *Chelle* 1227. Probably 'wood of a man called Cēola'. OE pers. name + *lēah*.

Chellington Beds. *Chelewentone* 1219. 'Farmstead of a woman called Cēolwynn'. OE pers. name + *tūn*.

Chelmarsh Shrops. *Celmeres* 1086 (DB). 'Marsh marked out with posts or poles'. OE **cegel* + *mersc*.

Chelmondiston Suffolk. *Chelmundeston* 1174. 'Farmstead of a man called Cēolmund'. OE pers. name + *tūn*.

Chelmorton Derbys. *Chelmerdon(e)* 12th cent. Probably 'hill of a man called Cēolmǣr'. OE pers. name + *dūn*.

Chelmsford Essex. *Celmeresfort* 1086 (DB). 'Ford of a man called Cēolmǣr'. OE pers. name + *ford*. The river-name Chelmer is a 'back-formation' from the place-name.

Chelsea Gtr. London. *Celchyth* 789, *Chelchede* 1086 (DB). Possibly 'landing-place for chalk or limestone'. OE *cealc* + *hȳth*. Alternatively the first element may be OE *cælic* 'cup, chalice' used in some topographical sense.

Chelsfield Gtr. London. *Cillesfelle* 1086 (DB). 'Open land of a man called Cēol'. OE pers. name + *feld*.

Chelsworth Suffolk. *Ceorleswyrthe* 962, *Cerleswrda* 1086 (DB). 'Enclosure of the freeman or of a man called Ceorl'. OE *ceorl* or OE pers. name + *worth*.

Cheltenham Glos. *Celtanhomme* 803, *Chinteneham* (*sic*) 1086 (DB). Probably 'enclosure or river-meadow by a hill-slope called **Celte*'. OE or pre-English hill-name + *hamm*.

Alternatively the first element may be an OE pers. name *Celta.

Chelveston Northants. *Celuestone* 1086 (DB). 'Farmstead of a man called Cēolwulf'. OE pers. name + *tūn*.

Chelvey Avon. *Calviche* 1086 (DB). 'Farm where calves are reared'. OE *cealf* + *wīc*.

Chelwood Avon. *Celeworde* 1086 (DB). 'Enclosure of a man called Cēola'. OE pers. name + *worth*.

Chenies Bucks. *Isenhamstede* 12th cent., *Ysenamstud Cheyne* 13th cent. Probably 'homestead of a man called *Īsa'. OE pers. name + *hām-stede* + manorial addition (which is now used alone) from the *Cheyne* family, here in the 13th cent. Alternatively the first element may be an old river-name.

Cherhill Wilts. *Ciriel* 1155. Possibly Celtic **ial* 'fertile upland' with a Celtic river-name as first element.

Cherington, probably 'village with a church', OE *cirice* + *tūn*: **Cherington** Glos. *Cerintone* 1086 (DB). **Cherington** Warwicks. *Chiriton* 1199.

Cheriton, 'village with a church', OE *cirice* + *tūn*: **Cheriton** Devon. *Ciretone* 1086 (DB). **Cheriton** Hants. *Cherinton* 1167. **Cheriton, North & South** Somerset. *Ciretona, Cherintone* 1086 (DB). **Cheriton Bishop** Devon. *Ceritone* 1086 (DB), *Bishops Churyton* 1370. Affix from the Bishop of Exeter, granted land here in the 13th cent. **Cheriton Fitzpaine** Devon. *Cerintone* 1086 (DB), *Cheriton Fitz Payn* 1335. Manorial addition from the *Fitzpayn* family, here in the 13th cent.

Cherrington Shrops. *Cerlintone* 1086 (DB), *Cherington* 1230. Probably 'estate associated with a man called Ceorra'. OE pers. name + *-ing-* + *tūn*.

Cherry Burton Humber., see BURTON.

Cherry Hinton Cambs., see HINTON.

Cherry Willingham Lincs., see WILLINGHAM.

Chertsey Surrey. *Cerotaesei* 731, *Certesy* 1086 (DB). 'Island of a man called *Cerot'. Celtic pers. name + OE *ēg*.

Cherwell (river) Northants.-Oxon., see CHARWELTON.

Cheselbourne Dorset. *Chiselburne* 869, *Ceseburne* 1086 (DB). 'Gravel stream'. OE *cisel* + *burna*.

Chesham, Chesham Bois Bucks. *Cæstæleshamme* 1012, *Cestreham* 1086 (DB), *Chesham Boys* 1339. 'River-meadow by a heap of stones'. OE *ceastel* + *hamm*, with manorial affix from the *de Bois* family, here in the 13th cent.

Cheshire (the county). *Cestre Scire* 1086 (DB). 'Province of the city of CHESTER'. OE *scīr* 'district'.

Cheshunt Herts. *Cestrehunt* 1086 (DB). Probably 'spring by the old (Roman) fort'. OE *ceaster* + **funta*.

Chesil Beach Dorset. *Chisille bank* c.1540. From OE *cisel* 'shingle'.

Cheslyn Hay Staffs. *Haya de Chistlin* 1236. Probably 'coffin ridge', i.e. 'ridge where a coffin was found'. OE *cest* + *hlinc*, with *hæg* 'enclosure'.

Chessington Gtr. London. *Cisendone* 1086 (DB). 'Hill of a man called Cissa'. OE pers. name (genitive *-n*) + *dūn*.

Chester Ches. *Deoua* c.150, *Legacæstir* 735, *Cestre* 1086 (DB). OE *ceaster* 'Roman town or city'. Originally called *Deoua* from its situation on the River DEE, later *Legacæstir* meaning 'city of the legions'.

Chesterblade Somerset. *Cesterbled* 1065. OE *ceaster* 'old fortification', possibly with OE *blæd* 'blade' in a topographical sense 'ledge'.

Chesterfield Derbys. *Cesterfelda* 955, *Cestrefeld* 1086 (DB). 'Open land near a Roman fort or settlement'. OE *ceaster* + *feld*.

Chesterford, Great & Little Essex. *Ceasterford* 1004, *Cestreforda* 1086 (DB). 'Ford by a Roman fort'. OE *ceaster* + *ford*.

Chester le Street Durham. *Cestra* c.1160, *Cestria in Strata* 1400. 'Roman fort on the Roman road'. OE *ceaster* + *strǣt* (Latin *strata*). The French definite article *le* remains after loss of the preposition.

Chesterton, 'farmstead or village by a Roman fort or town', OE *ceaster* + *tūn*: **Chesterton** Cambs. *Cestretone* 1086 (DB). **Chesterton** Oxon. *Cestertune* 1005, *Cestretone* 1086 (DB). **Chesterton** Staffs. *Cestreton* 1214. **Chesterton**

Warwicks. *Cestretune* 1043, *Cestretone* 1086 (DB).

Cheswardine Shrops. *Ciseworde* 1086 (DB). Probably 'enclosure where cheese is made'. OE *cēse* + *worthign*.

Cheswick Northum. *Chesewic* 1208–10. 'Farm where cheese is made'. OE *cēse* + *wīc*.

Chetnole Dorset. *Chetenoll* 1242. 'Hill-top or hillock of a man called Ceatta'. OE pers. name + *cnoll*.

Chettiscombe Devon. *Chetelescome* 1086 (DB). Probably OE *cetel* 'deep valley' + explanatory OE *cumb* 'valley'.

Chettisham Cambs. *Chetesham c.*1170. Probably 'enclosure of a man called *Ceatt'. OE pers. name + *hamm*. Alternatively the first element may be Celtic **cę̄d* 'wood'.

Chettle Dorset. *Ceotel* 1086 (DB). Probably OE **ceotol* 'deep valley'.

Chetton Shrops. *Catinton* 1086 (DB). Probably 'estate associated with a man called Ceatta'. OE pers. name + *-ing-* + *tūn*.

Chetwode Bucks. *Cetwuda* 949, *Ceteode* 1086 (DB). Celtic **cę̄d* 'wood' to which has been added an explanatory OE *wudu* 'wood'.

Chetwynd Aston Shrops. *Catewinde* 1086 (DB). Probably 'winding ascent of a man called Ceatta'. OE pers. name + *(ge)wind*. Aston is 'east farmstead', OE *ēast* + *tūn*.

Cheveley Cambs. *Cæafle c.*1000, *Chauelai* 1086 (DB). 'Wood full of fallen twigs'. OE *ceaf* + *lēah*.

Chevening Kent. *Chivening* 1199. Possibly '(settlement of) the dwellers at the ridge'. Celtic **cevn* + OE *-ingas*.

Cheverell, Great & Little Wilts. *Chevrel* 1086 (DB). An unexplained name, obscure in origin and meaning.

Chevington, West Northum. *Chiuingtona* 1236. 'Estate associated with a man called *Cifa'. OE pers. name + *-ing-* + *tūn*.

Cheviot (Hills) Northum. *Chiuiet* 1181. A pre-English name of unknown origin and meaning.

Chevithorne Devon. *Cheuetorna* 1086 (DB). 'Thorn-tree of a man called Ceofa'. OE pers. name + *thorn*.

Chew Magna Avon. *Ciw* 1065, *Chiwe* 1086 (DB). Named from the River Chew, which is a Celtic river-name, with affix from Latin *magna* 'great'.

Chew Stoke Avon. *Stoche* 1086 (DB). 'Secondary settlement belonging to CHEW', from OE *stoc*.

Chewton Mendip Somerset. *Ciwtun c.*880, *Ciwetune* 1086 (DB), *Cheuton by Menedep* 1313. 'Estate on the River Chew'. Celtic river-name (see CHEW) + OE *tūn* + affix from the MENDIP HILLS.

Chicheley Bucks. *Cicelai* 1086 (DB). 'Wood or clearing of a man called *Cicca'. OE pers. name + *lēah*.

Chichester W. Sussex. *Cisseceastre* 895, *Cicestre* 1086 (DB). 'Roman town of a chieftain called Cissa'. OE pers. name + *ceaster*.

Chickerell Dorset. *Cicherelle* 1086 (DB). This name remains obscure in origin and meaning.

Chicklade Wilts. *Cytlid c.*912. Possibly 'gate or slope by the wood'. Celtic **cę̄d* + OE *hlid* or **hlid*.

Chidden Hants. *Cittandene* 956. 'Valley of a man called *Citta'. OE pers. name + *denu*.

Chiddingfold Surrey. *Chedelingefelt* (*sic*) 1130, *Chidingefaud* 12th cent. Possibly 'fold of the family or followers of a man called *Cid(d)el or Cid(d)a'. OE pers. name + *-inga-* + *fald*.

Chiddingly E. Sussex. *Cetelingei* (*sic*) 1086 (DB), *Chitingeleghe c.*1230. Probably 'wood or clearing of the family or followers of a man called *Citta'. OE pers. name + *-inga-* + *lēah*.

Chiddingstone Kent. *Cidingstane c.*1110. Possibly 'stone associated with a man called *Cidd or Cidda'. OE pers. name + *-ing-* + *stān*.

Chideock Dorset. *Cidihoc* 1086 (DB). 'Wooded place', from a derivative of Celtic **cę̄d* 'wood'.

Chidham W. Sussex. *Chedeham* 1193. Probably 'homestead or peninsula near the bay'. OE *cēod(e)* + *hām* or *hamm*.

Chieveley Berks. *Cifanlea* 951, *Civelei* 1086 (DB). 'Wood or clearing of a man called *Cifa'. OE pers. name + *lēah*.

Chignall St James & Smealy Essex. *Cingehala* 1086 (DB), *Chikenhale Iacob*

1254, *Chigehale Smetheleye* 1279. Probably 'nook of land of a man called *Cicca'. OE pers. name (genitive *-n*) + *halh*. Affixes from the dedication of the church to St James (Latin *Jacobus*), and from a nearby place meaning 'smooth clearing' from OE *smēthe* + *lēah*.

Chigwell Essex. *Cingheuuella* 1086 (DB), *Chiggewell* 1187. Possibly 'spring or stream of a man called *Cicca'. OE pers. name + *wella*.

Chilbolton Hants. *Ceolboldingtun* 909, *Cilbode(n)tune* 1086 (DB). 'Estate associated with a man called Cēolbeald'. OE pers. name + *-ing-* + *tūn*.

Chilcombe Dorset. *Ciltecombe* 1086 (DB). Possibly 'valley at a hill-slope called **Cilte*'. OE or pre-English hill-name + OE *cumb*.

Chilcompton Avon. *Comtuna* 1086 (DB), *Childecumpton* 1227. 'Valley farmstead or village of the young men'. OE *cild* + *cumb* + *tūn*.

Chilcote Leics. *Cildecote* 1086 (DB). 'Cottage(s) of the young men'. OE *cild* + *cot*.

Childer Thornton Ches., see THORNTON.

Child Okeford Dorset, see OKEFORD.

Childrey Oxon. *Cillarithe* 950, *Celrea* 1086 (DB). Named from Childrey Brook which probably means 'stream of a man called *Cilla or of a woman called Cille'. OE pers. name + *rīth*. Alternatively the first element may be an OE **cille* 'a spring'.

Child's Ercall Shrops., see ERCALL.

Childswickham Heref. & Worcs. *Childeswicwon* 706, *Wicvene* 1086 (DB). Possibly OWelsh **guic* 'lodge, wood' + **guoun* 'plain, meadow, moor', with OE *cild* 'young man'.

Childwall Mersey. *Cildeuuelle* 1086 (DB). 'Spring or stream where young people assemble'. OE *cild* + *wella*.

Chilfrome Dorset. *Frome* 1086 (DB), *Childefrome* 1206. 'Estate on the River Frome belonging to the young men'. Celtic river-name (see FROME) with OE *cild*.

Chilgrove W. Sussex. *Chelegrave* 1200. 'Grove in a gorge or gulley', or 'grove of a man called Cēola'. OE *ceole* or OE pers. name + *grāf*.

Chilham Kent. *Cilleham* 1032, 1086 (DB). 'Homestead or village of a man called *Cilla or of a woman called Cille'. OE pers. name + *hām*. Alternatively the first element may be an OE **cille* 'a spring'.

Chillenden Kent. *Ciollandene* c.833, *Cilledene* 1086 (DB). 'Valley, or woodland pasture, of a man called Ciolla'. OE pers. name (genitive *-n*) + *denu* or *denn*.

Chillerton I. of Wight. *Celertune* 1086 (DB). 'Farmstead of a man called Cēolheard' or 'enclosed farmstead in a valley'. OE pers. name + *tūn*, or OE *ceole* + *geard* + *tūn*.

Chillesford Suffolk. *Ceseforda* 1086 (DB), *Chiselford* 1211. 'Gravel ford'. OE *ceosol* + *ford*.

Chillingham Northum. *Cheulingeham* 1187. 'Homestead or village of the family or followers of a man called *Ceofel'. OE pers. name + *-inga-* + *hām*.

Chillington Devon. *Cedelintone* 1086 (DB). 'Estate associated with a man called *Ceadela'. OE pers. name + *-ing-* + *tūn*.

Chillington Somerset. *Cheleton* 1261. 'Farmstead of a man called Cēola'. OE pers. name + *tūn*.

Chilmark Wilts. *Cigelmerc* 984, *Chilmerc* 1086 (DB). 'Boundary mark consisting of a pole'. OE **cigel* + *mearc*.

Chilson Oxon. *Cildestuna* c.1200. 'Farmstead of the young man'. OE *cild* + *tūn*.

Chilsworthy Devon. *Chelesworde* 1086 (DB). 'Enclosure of a man called Cēol'. OE pers. name + *worth*.

Chiltern Hills Bucks. *Ciltern* 1009. Probably identical in origin with the following name, here used of a district.

Chilthorne Domer Somerset. *Cilterne* 1086 (DB), *Chilterne Dunmere* 1280. Possibly a derivative of an OE or pre-English word **celte* or **cilte* which may have meant 'hill-slope'. Manorial addition from the *Dummere* family, here in the 13th cent.

Chiltington, East E. Sussex. *Childetune* 1086 (DB). Probably identical with the following name.

Chiltington, West W. Sussex. *Cillingtun* 969 *Cilletone* 1086 (DB). Possibly 'farmstead at a hill-slope called **Cilte*'. OE or pre-English hill-name + *-ing* or *-ing-* + *tūn*. Alternatively the first element may be an ancient district-name *Ciltine* derived from the same word.

Chilton, a place-name found in various counties, usually 'farm of the young (noble)men', from OE *cild* + *tūn*; for example: **Chilton** Bucks. *Ciltone* 1086 (DB). **Chilton** Durham. *Ciltona* 1091. **Chilton** Oxon. *Cylda tun c.*895, *Cilletone* 1086 (DB). **Chilton Cantelo** Somerset. *Childeton* 1201, *Chiltone Cauntilo* 1361. Manorial addition from the *Cantelu* family, here in the 13th cent. **Chilton Foliat** Wilts. *Cilletone* 1086 (DB), *Chilton Foliot* 1221. Manorial addition from the *Foliot* family, here in the 13th cent. **Chilton Street** Suffolk. *Chilton* 1254. Affix *street* probably has the sense 'straggling village'. **Chilton Trinity** Somerset. *Cildetone* 1086 (DB), *Chilton Sancte Trinitatis* 1431. Affix from the dedication of the church.

However the following Chilton has a different origin: **Chilton Polden** Somerset. *Ceptone* 1086 (DB), *Chauton* 1303. Possibly 'farmstead on chalk or limestone', from OE *cealc* + *tūn*, with affix from the nearby Polden Hill (*Poeldune* 725, from OE *dūn* 'hill' added to a Celtic name *Bouelt* 705 which probably means 'cow pasture').

Chilwell Notts. *Chideuuelle* 1086 (DB). 'Spring or stream where young people assemble'. OE *cild* + *wella*.

Chilworth, 'enclosure of a man called Cēola', OE pers. name + *worth*: **Chilworth** Hants. *Celeorde* 1086 (DB). **Chilworth** Surrey. *Celeorde* 1086 (DB).

Chimney Oxon. *Ceommanyg* 1069. 'Island, or dry ground in marsh, of a man called *Ceomma'. OE pers. name (genitive *-n*) + *ēg*.

Chineham Hants. *Chineham* 1086 (DB). 'Homestead or enclosure in a deep valley'. OE *cinu* + *hām* or *hamm*.

Chingford Gtr. London. *Cingefort* (*sic*) 1086 (DB), *Chingelford c.*1243. 'Shingle ford'. OE **cingel* + *ford*.

Chinley Derbys. *Chynleye* 1285. 'Wood or clearing in a deep valley'. OE *cinu* + *lēah*.

Chinnock, East & West Somerset. *Cinnuc c.*950, *Cinioch* 1086 (DB). Possibly a derivative of OE *cinu* 'deep valley', but perhaps an old hill-name of Celtic origin.

Chinnor Oxon. *Chennore* 1086 (DB). 'Slope of a man called *Ceonna'. OE pers. name + *ōra*.

Chipnall Shrops. *Ceppacanole* 1086 (DB). 'Knoll of a man called *Cippa', or 'knoll where logs are got'. OE pers. name or OE *cipp* + *cnoll*.

Chippenham, probably 'river-meadow of a man called *Cippa', OE pers. name (genitive *-n*) + *hamm*: **Chippenham** Cambs. *Chipeham* 1086 (DB). **Chippenham** Wilts. *Cippanhamme c.*900, *Chipeham* 1086 (DB).

Chipperfield Herts. *Chiperfeld* 1375. Probably 'open land where traders or merchants meet'. OE *cēapere* + *feld*.

Chipping Lancs. *Chippin* 1203. OE *cēping* 'a market, a market-place'.

Chipping as affix, see main name, e.g. for **Chipping Barnet** (Gtr. London) see BARNET.

Chipstead, 'market-place', OE *cēap-stede*: **Chipstead** Kent. *Chepsteda* 1191. **Chipstead** Surrey. *Tepestede* (*sic*) 1086 (DB), *Chepstede* 1100–29.

Chirbury Shrops. *Cyricbyrig* mid 11th cent., *Cireberie* 1086 (DB). 'Fortified place with a church'. OE *cirice* + *burh* (dative *byrig*).

Chirton Wilts. *Ceritone* 1086 (DB). 'Village with a church'. OE *cirice* + *tūn*.

Chisbury Wilts. *Cheseberie* 1086 (DB). 'Pre-English earthwork associated with a man called Cissa'. OE pers. name + *burh* (dative *byrig*).

Chiselborough Somerset. *Ceoselbergon* 1086 (DB). 'Gravel mound or hill'. OE *cisel* + *beorg*.

Chiseldon Wilts. *Cyseldene c.*880, *Chiseldene* 1086 (DB). 'Gravel valley'. OE *cisel* + *denu*.

Chisenbury Wilts. *Chesigeberie* 1086 (DB). Probably 'stronghold of the dwellers on the gravel'. OE **cis* + *-inga-* + *burh* (dative *byrig*).

Chishill, Great & Little Cambs. *Cishella* 1086 (DB). 'Gravel hill'. OE **cis* + *hyll*.

Chislehampton Oxon. *Hentone* 1086 (DB), *Chiselentona* 1147. Originally 'high farm, farm situated on high land'. OE *hēah* (dative *hēan*) + *tūn*, with the later addition of OE *cisel* 'gravel'.

Chislehurst Gtr. London. *Cyselhyrst* 973. 'Gravelly wooded hill'. OE *cisel* + *hyrst*.

Chislet Kent. *Cistelet* 605, 1086 (DB). Possibly OE **cistelet* 'a chestnut copse'. Alternatively the name may be a compound of OE **cist* 'chestnut tree' or *cist, cyst* 'chest, container' with *(ge)lǣt* 'water-conduit'.

Chiswellgreen Herts., first recorded in 1782, but possibly 'the gravelly spring or stream', from OE **cis* + *wella*, with the later addition of *green*.

Chiswick Gtr. London. *Ceswican* c.1000. 'Farm where cheese is made'. OE **cīese* + *wīc*.

Chisworth Derbys. *Chisewrde* 1086 (DB). 'Enclosure of a man called Cissa'. OE pers. name + *worth*.

Chithurst W. Sussex. *Titesherste* (*sic*) 1086 (DB), *Chyteherst* 1279. Possibly 'wooded hill of a man called *Citta'. OE pers. name + *hyrst*. Alternatively the first element may be Celtic **cę̄d* 'wood'.

Chitterne Wilts. *Chetre* 1086 (DB), *Chytterne* 1268. Possibly a derivative of Celtic **cę̄d* 'wood'.

Chittlehamholt Devon. *Chitelhamholt* 1288. 'Wood of the dwellers in the valley'. OE *cietel* + *hǣme* + *holt*.

Chittlehampton Devon. *Citremetona* 1086 (DB), *Chitelhamtone* 1176. 'Farmstead of the dwellers in the valley'. OE *cietel* + *hǣme* + *tūn*.

Chittoe Wilts. *Chetewe* 1167. Possibly a derivative of Celtic **cę̄d* 'wood'.

Chobham Surrey. *Cebeham* 1086 (DB). 'Homestead or enclosure of a man called *Ceabba'. OE pers. name + *hām* or *hamm*.

Cholderton Wilts. *Celdretone* 1086 (DB). 'Estate associated with a man called Cēolhere or Cēolrēd'. OE pers. name + *-ing-* + *tūn*.

Chollerton Northum. *Choluerton* c.1175. Probably 'farmstead of a man called Cēolferth'. OE pers. name + *tūn*.

Cholsey Oxon. *Ceolesig* c.895, *Celsei* 1086 (DB). 'Island, or dry ground in marsh, of a man called Cēol'. OE pers. name + *ēg*.

Cholstrey Heref. & Worcs. *Cerlestreu* 1086 (DB). 'Tree of the freeman or of a man called Ceorl'. OE *ceorl* or OE pers. name + *trēow*.

Choppington Northum. *Cebbington* c.1050. 'Estate associated with a man called *Ceabba'. OE pers. name + *-ing-* + *tūn*.

Chopwell Tyne & Wear. *Cheppwell* c.1155. Probably 'spring where trading takes place'. OE *cēap* + *wella*.

Chorley, 'clearing of the freemen or peasants', OE *ceorl* (genitive plural *-a*) + *lēah*: **Chorley** Ches., near Nantwich. *Cerlere* 1086 (DB). **Chorley** Lancs. *Cherleg* 1246. **Chorley** Staffs. *Cherlec* 1231.

Chorleywood Herts. *Cherle* 1278, *Charlewoode* 1524. 'Clearing of the freemen or peasants'. OE *ceorl* (genitive plural *-a*) + *lēah*, with the later addition of *wood*.

Chorlton, usually 'farmstead of the freemen or peasants', OE *ceorl* (genitive plural *-a*) + *tūn*: **Chorlton** Ches., near Nantwich. *Cerletune* 1086 (DB). **Chorlton Lane** Ches. *Cherlton* 1283. **Chorlton, Chapel** Staffs. *Cerletone* 1086 (DB).

However the following Chorlton has a different origin: **Chorlton cum Hardy** Lancs. *Cholreton* 1243. 'Farmstead of a man called Cēolfrith'. OE pers. name + *tūn*. Now united with Hardy (*Hardey* 1555, possibly 'hard island' from OE *heard* + *ēg*) as indicated by the Latin preposition *cum* 'with'.

Chowley Ches. *Celelea* 1086 (DB). 'Wood or clearing of a man called Cēola'. OE pers. name + *lēah*.

Chrishall Essex. *Cristeshala* 1086 (DB). 'Nook of land dedicated to Christ'. OE *Crist* + *halh*.

Christchurch Dorset. *Christecerce*

c.1125. 'Church of Christ'. OE *Crist* + *cirice*. Earlier called *Twynham*, 'place between the rivers', OE *betwēonan* + *ēa* (dative plural *ēam*).

Christian Malford Wilts. *Cristemaleford* 937, *Cristemeleford* 1086 (DB). 'Ford by a cross'. OE *cristel-mǣl* + *ford*.

Christleton Ches. *Cristetone* 1086 (DB), *Cristentune* 12th cent. 'Christian farmstead', or 'farmstead of the Christians'. OE *Cristen* (as adjective or noun) + *tūn*.

Christon Somerset. *Crucheston* 1197. 'Farmstead at the hill'. Celtic **crūg* + OE *tūn*.

Christow Devon. *Cristinestowe* 1244. 'Christian place'. OE *Cristen* + *stōw*.

Chudleigh Devon. *Ceddelegam c*.1150. 'Clearing of a man called Ciedda', or 'clearing in a hollow'. OE pers. name or OE *cēod(e)* + *lēah*.

Chulmleigh Devon. *C(h)almonleuga* 1086 (DB). 'Clearing of a man called Cēolmund'. OE pers. name + *lēah*.

Chunal Derbys. *Ceolhal* 1086 (DB). 'Nook of land of a man called Cēola', or 'nook of land near the ravine'. OE pers. name or OE *ceole* + *halh*.

Church Lancs. *Chirche* 1202. '(Place at) the church'. OE *cirice*.

Churcham Glos. *Hamme* 1086 (DB), *Churchehamme* 1200. OE *hamm* 'river meadow' with the later addition of *cirice* 'church'.

Churchdown Glos. *Circesdune* 1086 (DB). Celtic **crūg* 'hill' with explanatory OE *dūn* 'hill'.

Church Fenton N. Yorks., see FENTON.

Churchill, usually from Celtic **crūg* 'hill' with explanatory OE *hyll* 'hill'; examples include: **Churchill** Avon. *Cherchille* 1201. **Churchill** Devon, near Barnstaple. *Cercelle* 1086 (DB). **Churchill** Heref. & Worcs., near Kidderminster. *Cercehalle* (*sic*) 1086 (DB), *Circhul* 11th cent. **Churchill** Oxon. *Cercelle* 1086 (DB).

Church Knowle Dorset. *Cnolle* 1086 (DB), *Churchecnolle* 1346. OE *cnoll* 'hill-top' with the later addition of *cirice* 'church'.

Churchover Warwicks. *Wavre* 1086 (DB), *Chirchewavre* 12th cent. Originally a river-name (an earlier name for the River Swift) meaning 'winding stream' from OE *wæfre* 'wandering', with the later addition of *cirice* 'church'.

Churchstanton Somerset. *Stantone* 1086 (DB), *Cheristontone* 13th cent. 'Farmstead on stony ground'. OE *stān* + *tūn*, with later addition of OE *cirice* 'church' or ME *chiri* 'cherry'.

Churchstow Devon. *Churechestowe* 1242. 'Place with a church'. OE *cirice* + *stōw*.

Churn (river) Glos., see CERNEY.

Churt Surrey. *Cert* 685–7. OE *cert* 'rough ground'.

Churton Ches. *Churton* 12th cent. 'Village with a church'. OE *cirice* + *tūn*.

Churwell W. Yorks. *Cherlewell* 1226. 'Spring or stream of the freemen or peasants'. OE *ceorl* + *wella*.

Cinderford Glos. *Sinderford* 1258. 'Ford built up with cinders or slag (from iron-smelting)'. OE *sinder* + *ford*.

Cirencester Glos. *Korinion c*.150, *Cirenceaster c*.900, *Cirecestre* 1086 (DB). 'Roman camp or town called *Corinion*'. OE *ceaster* added to the reduced form of a Celtic name of uncertain origin and meaning.

Clacton on Sea Essex. *Claccingtune c*.1000, *Clachintune* 1086 (DB). 'Estate associated with a man called *Clacc'. OE pers. name + *-ing-* + *tūn*.

Claines Heref. & Worcs. *Cleinesse* 11th cent. 'Clay headland'. OE *clǣg* + *næss*.

Clandon, East & West Surrey. *Clanedun* 1086 (DB). 'Clean hill', i.e. 'hill free from weeds or other unwanted growth'. OE *clǣne* + *dūn*.

Clanfield, 'clean open land', i.e. 'open land free from weeds or other unwanted growth', OE *clǣne* + *feld*: **Clanfield** Hants. *Clanefeld* 1207. **Clanfield** Oxon. *Chenefelde* (*sic*) 1086 (DB), *Clenefeld* 1196.

Clanville Hants. *Clavesfelle* (*sic*) 1086 (DB), *Clanefeud* 1259. Identical in origin with the previous names.

Clapham, usually 'homestead or enclosure near a hill or hills', OE **clopp(a)* + *hām* or *hamm*: **Clapham**

Beds. *Cloppham* 1060, *Clopeham* 1086 (DB). **Clapham** Gtr. London. *Cloppaham c.*880, *Clopeham* 1086 (DB). **Clapham** W. Sussex. *Clopeham* 1086 (DB).

However the following Clapham has a different origin: **Clapham** N. Yorks. *Clapeham* 1086 (DB). 'Homestead or enclosure by the noisy stream'. OE **clæpe* + *hām* or *hamm*.

Clappersgate Cumbria. *Clappergate* 1588. 'Road or gate by the rough bridge'. ME *clapper* + OScand. *gata* or OE *geat*.

Clapton, 'farmstead or village near a hill or hills', OE **clopp(a)* + *tūn*; examples include: **Clapton** Glos. *Clopton* 1171–83. **Clapton** Northants. *Cloptun c.*960, *Clotone* 1086 (DB). **Clapton** Somerset, near Crewkerne. *Clopton* 1243. **Clapton in Gordano** Avon. *Clotune* (*sic*) 1086 (DB), *Clopton* 1225. Gordano is an old district name (*Gordeyne* 1270), probably 'dirty or muddy valley', OE *gor* + *denu*.

Clarborough Notts. *Claureburg* 1086 (DB). 'Old fortification overgrown with clover'. OE *clǣfre* + *burh*.

Clare Suffolk. *Clara* 1086 (DB). Perhaps originally an old river-name of Celtic origin, identical with that found in HIGHCLERE.

Clatford, Goodworth & Upper Hants. *Cladford, Godorde* 1086 (DB). 'Ford where burdock grows'. OE *clāte* + *ford*. Goodworth (originally a separate name) means 'enclosure of a man called Gōda', OE pers. name + *worth*.

Clatworthy Somerset. *Clateurde* 1086 (DB), *Clatewurthy* 1243. 'Enclosure where burdock grows'. OE *clāte* + *worth* (replaced by *worthig*).

Claughton, 'farmstead on or by a hill'. OE **clacc* + *tūn*: **Claughton** Lancs., near Garstang. *Clactune* 1086 (DB). **Claughton** Lancs., near Lancaster. *Clactun* 1086 (DB).

Claverham Avon. *Claveham* 1086 (DB). 'Homestead or enclosure where clover grows'. OE *clǣfre* + *hām* or *hamm*.

Clavering Essex. *Clæfring c.*1000, *Clauelinga* 1086 (DB). 'Place where clover grows'. OE *clǣfre* + *-ing*.

Claverley Shrops. *Claverlege* 1086 (DB). 'Clearing where clover grows'. OE *clǣfre* + *lēah*.

Claverton Avon. *Clatfordtun c.*1000, *Claftertone* 1086 (DB). 'Farmstead by the ford where burdock grows'. OE *clāte* + *ford* + *tūn*.

Clawson, Long Leics. *Clachestone* 1086 (DB). 'Farmstead on a hill, or of a man called Klakkr'. OE **clacc* or OScand. pers. name + OE *tūn*.

Clawton Devon. *Clavetone* 1086 (DB). 'Farmstead at the tongue of land'. OE *clawu* + *tūn*.

Claxby, 'farmstead on a hill, or of a man called Klakkr', OScand. *klakkr* or pers. name + *bý*: **Claxby** Lincs., near Alford. *Clachesbi* 1086 (DB). **Claxby** Lincs., near Market Rasen. *Clachesbi* 1086 (DB).

Claxton, 'farmstead on a hill, or of a man called Klakkr', OE **clacc* or OScand. pers. name + OE *tūn*: **Claxton** Norfolk. *Clakestona* 1086 (DB). **Claxton** N. Yorks. *Claxtorp* 1086 (DB), *Clakeston* 1176. Second element originally OScand. *thorp* 'outlying farmstead'.

Claybrooke Magna Leics. *Clæg broc* 962, *Claibroc* 1086 (DB). 'Clayey brook'. OE *clǣg* + *brōc*, with Latin affix *magna* 'great'.

Clay Coton Northants. *Cotes* 12th cent., *Cleycotes* 1284. 'Cottages in the clayey district'. OE *cot* (dative plural *cotum* or a ME plural *coten*) with the later addition of *clǣg*.

Clay Cross Derbys., a late name, first recorded in 1734, probably named from a local family called *Clay*.

Claydon, 'clayey hill', OE *clǣgig* + *dūn*: **Claydon** Oxon. *Cleindona* 1109. **Claydon** Suffolk. *Clainduna* 1086 (DB). **Claydon, Botolph, East, & Middle** Bucks. *Claindone* 1086 (DB), *Botle Cleidun* 1224, *Est Cleydon* 1247, *Middelcleydon* 1242. Affixes from OE *bōtl* 'house, building', *ēast* 'east', and *middel* 'middle'. **Claydon, Steeple** Bucks. *Claindone* 1086 (DB), *Stepel Cleydon* 13th cent. Affix from OE *stēpel* 'steeple, tower'.

Claygate Surrey. *Claigate* 1086 (DB). 'Gate or gap in the clayey district'. OE *clǣg* + *geat*.

Clayhanger W. Mids. *Cleyhungre* 13th cent. 'Clayey wooded slope'. OE *clǣg* + *hangra*. The same name occurs in Ches. and Devon.

Clayhidon Devon. *Hidone* 1086 (DB), *Cleyhidon* 1485. 'Hill where hay is made'. OE *hī(e)g* + *dūn*, with the later addition of OE *clǣg* 'clay'.

Claypole Lincs. *Claipol* 1086 (DB). 'Clayey pool'. OE *clǣg* + *pōl*.

Clayton, 'farmstead on clayey soil', OE *clǣg* + *tūn*; examples include: **Clayton** S. Yorks. *Claitone* 1086 (DB). **Clayton** Staffs. *Claitone* 1086 (DB). **Clayton** W. Sussex. *Claitune* 1086 (DB). **Clayton** W. Yorks. *Claitone* 1086 (DB). **Clayton-le-Moors** Lancs. *Cleyton* 1243. Affix 'on the moorland' from OE *mōr*, the French definite article *le* remaining after loss of the preposition. **Clayton-le-Woods** Lancs. *Cleitonam* 1160. Affix 'in the woodland' from OE *wudu*, with French *le* as in previous name. **Clayton West** W. Yorks. *Claitone* 1086 (DB).

Clayworth Notts. *Clauorde* 1086 (DB). 'Enclosure on the low curving hill'. OE *clawu* + *worth*.

Cleadon Tyne & Wear. *Clyvedon* 1280. 'Hill of the cliffs'. OE *clif* (genitive plural *clifa*) + *dūn*.

Clearwell Glos. *Clouerwalle* c.1282. 'Spring or stream where clover grows'. OE *clāfre* + *wella*.

Cleasby N. Yorks. *Clesbi* 1086 (DB). 'Farmstead or village of a man called Kleppr or *Kleiss'. OScand. pers. name + *bý*.

Cleatlam Durham. *Cletlinga* c.1050, *Cletlum* 1271. '(Place at) the clearings where burdock grows'. OE **clǣte* + *lēah* (dative plural *lēaum*), with *-ingas* 'dwellers at' in the earliest form.

Cleator (Moor) Cumbria. *Cletergh* c.1200. 'Hill pasture among the rocks'. OScand. *klettr* + *erg*.

Cleckheaton W. Yorks. *Hetun* 1086 (DB), *Claketon* 1285. 'High farmstead, farmstead situated on high land'. OE *hēah* + *tūn*. The affix *Cleck-* is from OScand. *klakkr* 'a hill'.

Clee St Margaret Shrops. *Cleie* 1086 (DB), *Clye Sancte Margarete* 1285. Named from the Clee Hills, probably an OE **clēo* 'ball-shaped, rounded hill'. Affix from the dedication of the church.

Cleethorpes Humber., not recorded before the 17th cent., meaning 'hamlets near Clee'; the latter is *Cleia* in 1086 (DB), from OE *clǣg* 'clay' with reference to the soil.

Cleeton St Mary Shrops. *Cleotun* 1241. 'Farmstead by the hills called Clee', see CLEE ST MARGARET. OE *tūn*.

Cleeve, Cleve, '(place) at the cliff or bank', OE *clif* (dative *clife*); examples include: **Cleeve** Avon. *Clive* 1243. **Cleeve, Bishop's** Glos. *Clife* 8th cent., *Clive* 1086 (DB), *Bissopes Clive* 1284. Affix from its early possession by the Bishops of Worcester. **Cleeve, Old** Somerset. *Clive* 1086 (DB). **Cleeve Prior** Heref. & Worcs. *Clive* 1086 (DB), *Clyve Prior* 1291. Affix from its early possession by the Prior of Worcester.

Clehonger Heref. & Worcs. *Cleunge* 1086 (DB). 'Clayey wooded slope'. OE *clǣg* + *hangra*.

Clench Wilts. *Clenche* 1289. OE **clenc* 'hill'.

Clenchwarton Norfolk. *Ecleuuartuna* (*sic*) 1086 (DB), *Clenchewarton* 1196. Probably 'farmstead or village of the dwellers at the hill'. OE **clenc* + *-ware* + *tūn*.

Clent Heref. & Worcs. *Clent* 1086 (DB). OE **clent* 'rock, rocky hill'.

Cleobury Mortimer & North Shrops. *Claiberie* 1086 (DB), *Clebury Mortimer* 1272, *Northclaibiry* 1222. 'Fortified place or manor near the hills called Clee', see CLEE ST MARGARET. OE *burh* (dative *byrig*). Manorial addition from the *Mortemer* family, here in the 11th cent.

Clerkenwell Gtr. London. *Clerkenwell* c.1150. 'Well or spring frequented by students'. ME *clerc* (plural *-en*) + OE *wella*.

Clevancy Wilts. *Clive* 1086 (DB), *Clif Wauncy* 1231. '(Place) at the cliff', from OE *clif* (dative *clife*), with manorial addition from the *de Wancy* family, here in the 13th cent.

Clevedon Avon. *Clivedon* 1086 (DB). 'Hill of the cliffs'. OE *clif* (genitive plural *clifa*) + *dūn*.

Cleveland (new county). *Clivelanda*

*c.*1110. 'District of cliffs, hilly district'. OE *clif* (genitive plural *clifa*) + *land.*

Cleveleys Lancs., not on record before early this cent., probably a manorial name from a family called *Cleveley* who may have come from Cleveley near Garstang (*Cliueleye c.*1180, 'woodland clearing near a cliff or bank', OE *clif* + *lēah*).

Clewer Somerset. *Cliveware* 1086 (DB). 'The dwellers on a river-bank'. OE *clif* + *-ware.* The same name occurs in Berks.

Cley next the Sea Norfolk. *Claia* 1086 (DB). OE *clǣg* 'clay, place with clayey soil'.

Cliburn Cumbria. *Clibbrun c.*1140. 'Stream by the cliff or bank'. OE *clif* + *burna.*

Cliddesden Hants. *Cleresden* (*sic*) 1086 (DB), *Cledesdene* 1194. Possibly 'valley of the rock or rocky hill'. OE **clȳde* + *denu.*

Cliff, Cliffe, '(place at) the cliff or bank', OE *clif*; examples include: **Cliffe** Kent. *Cliua* 10th cent., *Clive* 1086 (DB). **Cliffe** N. Yorks. *Clive* 1086 (DB). **Cliffe, King's** Northants. *Clive* 1086 (DB), *Kyngesclive* 1305. A royal manor in 1086. **Cliffe, North & South** Humber. *Cliue* 1086 (DB). **Cliffe, West** Kent. *Wesclive* 1086 (DB). With OE *west* 'west'.

Clifford, 'ford at a cliff or bank', OE *clif* + *ford*: **Clifford** Heref. & Worcs. *Cliford* 1086 (DB). **Clifford** W. Yorks. *Cliford* 1086 (DB). **Clifford Chambers** Glos. *Clifforda* 922, *Clifort* 1086 (DB), *Chaumberesclifford* 1388. Affix from the chamberlain (ME *chamberere*) of St Peter's Gloucester, given the manor in 1099.

Clifton, a common place-name, 'farmstead on or near a cliff or bank', OE *clif* + *tūn*; examples include: **Clifton** Avon. *Clistone* 1086 (DB). **Clifton** Beds. *Cliftune* 10th cent., *Cliftone* 1086 (DB). **Clifton** Cumbria. *Clifton* 1204. **Clifton** Derbys. *Cliftune* 1086 (DB). **Clifton** Notts. *Cliftone* 1086 (DB). **Clifton Campville** Staffs. *Clyfton* 942, *Cliftune* 1086 (DB). Manorial addition from the *de Camvill* family, here in the 13th cent. **Clifton Hampden** Oxon. *Cliftona* 1146. The affix first occurs in 1836, and may be from a family called *Hampden.* **Clifton, North & South** Notts. *Cliftone* 1086 (DB), *Nort Clifton c.*1160, *Suth Clifton* 1280. **Clifton Reynes** Bucks. *Cliftone* 1086 (DB), *Clyfton Reynes* 1383. Manorial addition from the *de Reynes* family, here in the early 14th cent. **Clifton upon Dunsmore** Warwicks. *Cliptone* 1086 (DB), *Clifton super Donesmore* 1306. For the affix, see RYTON-ON-DUNSMORE. **Clifton upon Teme** Heref. & Worcs. *Cliftun ultra Tamedam* 934, *Clistune* (*sic*) 1086 (DB). Teme is an old Celtic river-name, see TENBURY WELLS.

Cliftonville Kent, a modern name invented for this 19th cent. resort.

Climping W. Sussex. *Clepinges* (*sic*) 1086 (DB), *Clympinges* 1228. '(Settlement of) the family or followers of a man called *Climp'. OE pers. name + *-ingas.*

Clint N. Yorks. *Clint* 1208. OScand. *klint* 'a rocky cliff, a steep bank'.

Clippesby Norfolk. *Clepesbei* 1086 (DB). 'Farmstead or village of a man called Klyppr or *Klippr'. OScand. pers. name + *bý.*

Clipsham Leics. *Kilpesham* 1203. Probably 'homestead or enclosure of a man called *Cylp'. OE pers. name + *hām* or *hamm.*

Clipston(e), 'farmstead of a man called Klyppr or *Klippr', OScand. pers. name + OE *tūn*: **Clipston** Northants. *Clipestune* 1086 (DB). **Clipston** Notts. *Cliston* 1198. **Clipstone** Notts. *Clipestune* 1086 (DB).

Clitheroe Lancs. *Cliderhou* 1102. 'Hill with loose stones'. OE **clȳder, *clider* + OE *hōh* or OScand. *haugr.*

Clive Shrops. *Cliua* 1176. '(Place) at the cliff or bank'. OE *clif* (dative *clife*).

Clodock Heref. & Worcs. *Ecclesia Sancti Clitauci c.*1150. '(The church of) St. Clydog'. From the patron saint of the church.

Clophill Beds. *Clopelle* 1086 (DB). 'Lumpy hill'. OE **clopp(a)* + *hyll.*

Clopton Suffolk. *Clop(e)tuna* 1086 (DB). 'Farmstead or village near a hill or hills'. OE **clopp(a)* + *tūn.*

Clothall Herts. *Clatheala c.*1060, *Cladhele* 1086 (DB). 'Nook of land where burdock grows'. OE *clāte* + *healh.*

Clotton Ches. *Clotone* 1086 (DB). 'Farmstead at a dell or deep valley'. OE **clōh* + *tūn*.

Cloud, Temple Avon. *La Clude* 1199. 'The (rocky) hill'. OE *clūd*. Affix probably refers to lands here held by the Knights Templars.

Cloughton N. Yorks. *Cloctune* 1086 (DB). 'Farmstead at a dell or deep valley'. OE **clōh* + *tūn*.

Clovelly Devon. *Cloveleia* 1086 (DB). Probably 'ravine or crevice near the hill thought to resemble a felly or wheel-rim'. OE *clofa* + *felg*.

Clowne Derbys. *Clune* c.1002, 1086 (DB). Named from the river which rises nearby; it is an old river-name identical with that in the following name.

Clun Shrops. *Clune* 1086 (DB). Named from the River Clun, which is an ancient pre-English river-name of uncertain meaning.

Clunbury Shrops. *Cluneberie* 1086 (DB). 'Fortified place on the River Clun'. Pre-English river-name + OE *burh* (dative *byrig*).

Clungunford Shrops. *Clone* 1086 (DB), *Cloune Goneford* 1242. 'Estate on the River Clun held by a man called Gunward'. Pre-English river-name + manorial addition from the name of the lord of the manor in the time of Edward the Confessor.

Clunton Shrops. *Clutone* (*sic*) 1086 (DB), *Cluntune* 12th cent. 'Farmstead or village on the River Clun'. Pre-English river-name + OE *tūn*.

Clutton, 'farmstead or village at a hill', from OE *clūd* + *tūn*: **Clutton** Ches. *Clutone* 1086 (DB). **Clutton** Somerset *Cluttone* 851, *Clutone* 1086 (DB).

Clyst Honiton Devon, see HONITON.

Clyst Hydon Devon. *Clist* 1086 (DB), *Clist Hydone* 1268. 'Estate on the River Clyst held by the *de Hidune* family' (here in the 13th cent.). Celtic river-name (probably meaning 'clean stream') + manorial addition.

Clyst St George Devon. *Clisewic* 1086 (DB), *Clystwik Sancti Georgii* 1327. Originally 'dairy farm on the River Clyst'. Celtic river-name + OE *wīc*, with addition from the dedication of the church.

Clyst St Lawrence Devon. *Clist* 1086 (DB), *Clist Sancti Laurencii* 1203. 'Estate on the River Clyst', with addition from the dedication of the church.

Clyst St Mary Devon. *Clist Sancte Marie* 1242. Identical in origin with the previous name.

Coalbrookdale Shrops. *Caldebrok* 1250. '(Valley of) the cold brook'. OE *cald* + *brōc* with the later addition of *dale*.

Coaley Glos. *Couelege* 1086 (DB). 'Clearing with a hut or shelter'. OE *cofa* + *lēah*.

Coalville Leics., a name of 19th cent. origin, so called because it is in a coal-mining district.

Coate Wilts., near Devizes. *Cotes* 1255. 'The cottage(s) or hut(s)'. OE *cot*.

Coates, 'the cottages or huts', from OE *cot*; examples include: **Coates** Cambs. *Cotes* c.1280. **Coates** Glos. *Cota* 1175. **Coates** Notts. *Cotes* 1200. **Coates, Great** Humber. *Cotes* 1086 (DB). **Coates, North** Lincs. *Nordcotis* c.1115.

Coatham Cleveland. *Cotum* 1123–8. '(Place) at the cottages or huts'. OE *cot* in a dative plural form *cotum*.

Coatham Mundeville Durham. *Cotum* 12th cent., *Cotum Maundevill* 1344. Identical in origin with the previous name. Manorial affix from the *de Amundevilla* family, here in the 13th cent.

Coberley Glos. *Culberlege* 1086 (DB). 'Wood or clearing of a man called Cūthbeorht'. OE pers. name + *lēah*.

Cobham Kent. *Cobba hammes mearce* 939, *Cobbeham* 1197. 'Enclosure or homestead of a man called *Cobba'. OE pers. name + *hamm* or *hām*. The early form contains OE *mearc* 'boundary'.

Cobham Surrey. *Covenham* 1086 (DB). 'Homestead or enclosure of a man called *Cofa, or with a hut or shelter'. OE pers. name or OE *cofa* + *hām* or *hamm*.

Cockayne Hatley Beds., see HATLEY.

Cockerham Lancs. *Cocreham* 1086 (DB). 'Homestead or enclosure on the River Cocker'. Celtic river-name (with a meaning 'crooked') + OE *hām* or *hamm*.

Cockerington, North & South Lincs. *Cocrintone* 1086 (DB). Possibly 'farmstead by a stream called *Cocker*'. Celtic river-name (perhaps an earlier name for the River Lud) + *-ing-* + *tūn*.

Cockermouth Cumbria. *Cokyrmoth* c.1150. 'Mouth of the River Cocker'. Celtic river-name (with a meaning 'crooked') + *mūtha*.

Cockfield Durham. *Kokefeld* 1223. 'Open land frequented by cocks (of wild birds), or belonging to a man called *Cocca'. OE *cocc* or OE pers. name + *feld*.

Cockfield Suffolk. *Cochanfelde* 10th cent. 'Open land of a man called *Cohha'. OE pers. name + *feld*.

Cockfosters Gtr. London. *Cokfosters* 1524. 'House or estate of the chief forester'. ME *for(e)ster*.

Cocking W. Sussex. *Cochinges* 1086 (DB). 'Dwellers at the hillock', or '(settlement of) the family or followers of a man called *Cocc(a)'. OE **cocc* or OE pers. name + *-ingas*.

Cockington Devon. *Cochintone* 1086 (DB). Probably 'estate associated with a man called *Cocc(a)'. OE pers. name + *-ing-* + *tūn*.

Cockley Cley Norfolk. *Cleia* 1086 (DB), *Coclikleye* 1324. OE *clǣg* 'clay, place with clayey soil' + affix which may be manorial from a family called *Cockley* or a local name meaning 'wood frequented by woodcocks' from OE *cocc* + *lēah*.

Cockthorpe Norfolk. *Torp* 1086 (DB), *Coketorp* 1254. Originally OScand. *thorp* 'secondary settlement, outlying farmstead' + affix which may be manorial from a family called *Co(c)ke*, or indicate 'where cocks are reared' from OE *cocc*.

Coddenham Suffolk. *Codenham* 1086 (DB). 'Homestead or enclosure of a man called *Cod(d)a'. OE pers. name (genitive *-n*) + *hām* or *hamm*.

Coddington, 'estate associated with a man called Cot(t)a', from OE pers. name + *-ing-* + *tūn*: **Coddington** Ches. *Cotintone* 1086 (DB). **Coddington** Heref. & Worcs. *Cotingtune* 1086 (DB). **Coddington** Notts. *Cotintone* 1086 (DB).

Codford St Mary & St Peter Wilts. *Codan ford* 901, *Coteford* 1086 (DB), *Codeford Sancte Marie, Sancti Petri* 1291. 'Ford of a man called *Cod(d)a'. OE pers. name + *ford*. Affixes from the dedications of the churches.

Codicote Herts. *Cutheringcoton* 1002, *Codicote* 1086 (DB). 'Cottage(s) associated with a man called Cūthhere'. OE pers. name + *-ing-* + *cot*.

Codnor Derbys. *Cotenoure* 1086 (DB). 'Ridge of a man called *Cod(d)a'. OE pers. name (genitive *-n*) + **ofer*.

Codrington Glos. *Cuderintuna* 12th cent. 'Estate associated with a man called Cūthhere'. OE pers. name + *-ing-* + *tūn*.

Codsall Staffs. *Codeshale* 1086 (DB). 'Nook of land of a man called *Cōd'. OE pers. name + *halh*.

Coffinswell Devon. *Willa* 1086 (DB), *Coffineswell* 1249. '(Place at) the spring or stream'. OE *w(i)ella* + manorial addition from the *Coffin* family, here in the 12th cent.

Cofton Hackett Heref. & Worcs. *Coftune* 8th cent., *Costune* (*sic*) 1086 (DB), *Corfton Hakett* 1431. 'Farmstead with a hut or shelter'. OE *cofa* + *tūn* + manorial addition from the *Haket* family, here in the 12th cent.

Cogenhoe Northants. *Cugenho* 1086 (DB). 'Hill-spur of a man called *Cugga'. OE pers. name (genitive *-n*) + *hōh*.

Cogges, High Cogges Oxon. *Coges* 1086 (DB). 'The hills', from OE **cogg*.

Coggeshall Essex. *Cogheshala* 1086 (DB). 'Nook of land of a man called *Cogg'. OE pers. name + *halh*.

Coker, East, North, & West Somerset. *Cocre* 1086 (DB). Originally the name of the stream here, a Celtic river-name with a meaning 'crooked, winding'.

Colan Cornwall. *Sanctus Colanus* 1205. 'Church of St Colan'. From the patron saint of the church.

Colaton Raleigh Devon. *Coletone* 1086 (DB), *Coleton Ralegh* 1316. 'Farmstead of a man called Cola'. OE pers. name +

tūn + manorial addition from the *de Ralegh* family, here in the 13th cent.

Colburn N. Yorks. *Corburne (sic)* 1086 (DB), *Coleburn* 1198. 'Cool stream'. OE *cōl* + *burna*.

Colby Cumbria. *Collebi* 12th cent. 'Farmstead of a man called Kolli', or 'hill farmstead'. OScand. pers. name or *kollr* + *bý*.

Colby Norfolk. *Colebei* 1086 (DB). 'Farmstead or village of a man called Koli'. OScand. pers. name + *bý*.

Colchester Essex. *Colneceastre* early 10th cent., *Colecestra* 1086 (DB). 'Roman town on the River Colne'. Ancient pre-English river-name (see COLNE ENGAINE) + OE *ceaster*. Alternatively the first element may be a reduced form of Latin *colonia* 'Roman colony for retired legionaries' (the Romano-British name of Colchester being *Colonia Camulodunum*).

Cold as affix, see main name, e.g. for **Cold Brayfield** (Bucks.) see BRAYFIELD.

Coldham Cambs. *Coldham* 1251. 'Cold enclosure'. OE *cald* + *hamm*.

Coldred Kent. *Colret* 1086 (DB). 'Clearing where coal is found, or where charcoal is made'. OE *col* + **ryde*.

Coldridge Devon. *Colrige* 1086 (DB). 'Ridge where charcoal is made'. OE *col* + *hrycg*.

Coldwaltham W. Sussex. *Waltham* 10th cent., *Cold Waltham* 1340. 'Homestead or village in a forest'. OE *w(e)ald* + *hām*, with later affix meaning 'bleak, exposed'.

Cole Somerset. *Colna* 1212. Originally the name of the stream here, a pre-English river-name of uncertain meaning.

Colebatch Shrops. *Colebech* 1176. Probably 'stream-valley of a man called Cola'. OE pers. name + *bece*.

Colebrook Devon, near Cullompton. *Colebroca* 1086 (DB). 'Cool brook'. OE *cōl* + *brōc*.

Colebrooke Devon. *Colebroc* 12th cent. Identical in origin with the previous name.

Coleby Humber. *Colebi* 1086 (DB). 'Farmstead or village of a man called Koli'. OScand. pers. name + *bý*.

Coleford Devon. *Colbrukeforde* 1330. 'Ford at COLEBROOKE'. OE *ford*.

Coleford Glos. *Coleforde* 1282. 'Ford across which coal is carried'. OE *col* + *ford*.

Coleford Somerset, near Frome. *Culeford* 1234. 'Ford across which coal or charcoal is carried'. OE *col* + *ford*.

Colehill Dorset. *Colhulle* 1431. OE *hyll* 'hill' with either *col* 'charcoal' or **coll* 'hill'.

Colemere Shrops. *Colesmere (sic)* 1086 (DB), *Culemere* 1203. Probably 'pool of a man called *Cūla'. OE pers. name + *mere*.

Coleorton Leics. *Ovretone* 1086 (DB), *Cole Orton* 1571. Probably 'higher farmstead'. OE *uferra* + *tūn*. Affix is OE *col* 'coal' with reference to mining here.

Colerne Wilts. *Colerne* 1086 (DB). 'Building where charcoal is made or stored'. OE *col* + *ærn*.

Colesbourne Glos. *Col(l)esburnan* 9th cent., *Colesborne* 1086 (DB). 'Stream of a man called *Col or Coll'. OE pers. name + *burna*.

Coleshill Bucks. *Coleshulle* 1279. Possibly identical in origin with the following name.

Coleshill Oxon. *Colleshylle* 10th cent., *Coleselle* 1086 (DB). Probably OE **coll* 'hill' with the addition of explanatory OE *hyll*, alternatively 'hill of a man called Coll', from OE pers. name + *hyll*.

Coleshill Warwicks. *Colleshyl* 799, *Coleshelle* 1086 (DB). Possibly identical in origin with the previous names, but more likely 'hill on the River Cole', Celtic river-name (of uncertain meaning) + OE *hyll*.

Colkirk Norfolk. *Colechirca* 1086 (DB). 'Church of a man called Cola or Koli'. OE or OScand. pers. name + *kirkja*.

Collaton St Mary Devon. *Coletone* 1261. 'Farmstead of a man called Cola'. OE pers. name + *tūn* + affix from the dedication of the church.

Collingbourne Ducis & Kingston Wilts. *Colengaburnam* 903,

Colingeburne 1086 (DB). Probably 'stream of the family or followers of a man called *Col or Cola'. OE pers. name + *-inga-* + *burna*. Manorial additions from possession by the Dukes of Lancaster (Latin *ducis* 'of the duke') and the king (OE *cyning* + *tūn*).

Collingham, 'homestead or village of the family or followers of a man called *Col or Cola', OE pers. name + *-inga-* + *hām*: **Collingham** Notts. *Colingeham* 1086 (DB). **Collingham** W. Yorks. *Col(l)ingeham* 1167.

Collington Heref. & Worcs. *Col(l)intune* 1086 (DB). 'Estate associated with a man called *Col or Cola'. OE pers. name + *-ing-* + *tūn*.

Collingtree Northants. *Colentreu* 1086 (DB). 'Tree of a man called Cola'. OE pers. name (genitive *-n*) + *trēow*.

Collyweston Northants. *Westone* 1086 (DB), *Colynweston* 1309. 'West farmstead'. OE *west* + *tūn* + manorial affix from *Nicholas* (of which *Colin* is a pet-form) *de Segrave*, here in the 13th cent.

Colmworth Beds. *Colmeworde* 1086 (DB). Possibly 'enclosure of a man called *Culma'. OE pers. name + *worth*.

Colnbrook Bucks. *Colebroc* 1107. 'Cool brook', or 'brook near the River Colne'. OE *cōl* or pre-English river-name + OE *brōc*.

Colne Cambs. *Colne* 1086 (DB). Originally the name (now lost) of the stream here, a pre-English river-name of uncertain meaning.

Colne Lancs. *Calna* 1124. '(Place by) the River Colne'. A pre-English river-name of uncertain meaning, identical with River CALNE in Wilts.

Colne Engaine, Earls Colne, & Wakes Colne Essex. *Colne c.*950, *Colun* 1086 (DB), *Colum Engayne* 1254, *Erlescolne* 1358, *Colne Wake* 1375. '(Places by) the River Colne', an ancient pre-English river-name of uncertain meaning. Manorial additions from possession in medieval times by the *Engayne* family, the *Earls* of Oxford, and the *Wake* family.

Colney Norfolk. *Coleneia* 1086 (DB). 'Island, or dry ground in marsh, of a man called Cola'. OE pers. name (genitive *-n*) + *ēg*.

Colney, London Herts. *Colnea* 1209-35, *London Colney* 1555. 'Island by the River Colne'. Pre-English river-name + OE *ēg*, with affix from its situation on the main road to London.

Coln Rogers, St Aldwyns, & St Dennis Glos. *Cungle* 962, *Colne* 1086 (DB), *Culna Rogeri* 13th cent., *Culna Sancti Aylwini* 12th cent., *Colne Seint Denys* 1287. '(Places by) the River Coln'. Pre-English river-name of uncertain origin. Additions from possession by *Roger* de Gloucester (died 1106), from church dedication to *St Athelwine*, and from possession by the church of *St Denis* of Paris (in the 11th cent.).

Colsterdale N. Yorks. *Colserdale* 1301. 'Valley of the charcoal burners'. OE **colestre* + OE *dæl* or ON *dalr*.

Colsterworth Lincs. *Colsteuorde* 1086 (DB). 'Enclosure of the charcoal burners'. OE **colestre* + *worth*.

Colston, 'farmstead of a man called Kolr', OScand. pers. name + OE *tūn*: **Colston, Car** Notts. *Colestone* 1086 (DB), *Kyrcoluiston* 1242. Affix from OScand. *kirkja* 'church'. **Colston Bassett** Notts. *Coletone* 1086 (DB), *Coleston Bassett* 1228. Manorial addition from the *Basset* family, here in the 12th cent.

Coltishall Norfolk. *Coketeshala* 1086 (DB). 'Nook of land of a man called *Cohhede or *Coccede'. OE pers. name + *halh*.

Colton Cumbria. *Coleton* 1202. 'Farmstead on a river called *Cole*'. Celtic river-name (of uncertain meaning) + OE *tūn*.

Colton Norfolk. *Coletuna* 1086 (DB). 'Farmstead of a man called Cola or Koli'. OE or OScand. pers. name + OE *tūn*.

Colton N. Yorks. *Coletune* 1086 (DB). Probably identical in origin with the previous name.

Colton Staffs. *Coltone* 1086 (DB). Probably 'farmstead of a man called Cola'. OE pers. name + *tūn*.

Colwall Heref. & Worcs. *Colewelle* 1086 (DB). 'Cool spring or stream'. OE *cōl* + *wælla*.

Colwell Northum. *Colewel* 1236. 'Cool spring or stream'. OE *cōl* + *wella*.

Colwich Staffs. *Colewich* 1240. Probably 'building where charcoal is made or stored'. OE *col* + *wīc*.

Colworth W. Sussex. *Coleworth* 10th cent. 'Enclosure of a man called Cola'. OE pers. name + *worth*.

Colyford Devon. *Culyford* 1244. 'Ford over the River Coly'. Celtic river-name (possibly 'narrow')+ OE *ford*.

Colyton Devon. *Culintona* 946, *Colitone* 1086 (DB). 'Farmstead by the River Coly'. Celtic river-name + OE *tūn*.

Combe, Coombe, 'the valley', from OE *cumb*, a common place-name, especially in the South West; examples include: **Combe** Oxon. *Cumbe* 1086 (DB). **Combe, Abbas** Somerset. *Cumbe* 1086 (DB), *Coumbe Abbatisse* 1327. Manorial addition from Latin *abbatisse* 'of the abbess', alluding to early possession by Shaftesbury Abbey. **Combe, Castle** Wilts. *Come* 1086 (DB), *Castelcumbe* 1270. Affix *castel* referring to the Norman castle here. **Combe Florey** Somerset. *Cumba* 12th cent., *Cumbeflori* 1291. Manorial addition from the *de Flury* family, here in the 12th cent. **Combe Hay** Avon. *Come* 1086 (DB), *Cumbehawya* 1249. Manorial addition from the family of *de Haweie*, here in the 13th cent. **Combeinteignhead** Devon. *Comba* 1086 (DB), *Cumbe in Tenhide* 1227. Affix from a district called *Tenhide* because it contained 'ten hides of land' (OE *tēn* + *hīd*). **Combe Martin** Devon. *Comba* 1086 (DB), *Cumbe Martini* 1265. Manorial addition from one *Martin* whose son held the manor in 1133. **Combe, Monkton** Avon. *Cume* 1086 (DB). Affix means 'estate of the monks' (OE *munuc* + *tūn*). **Combe Raleigh** Devon. *Cumba* 1237, *Comberalegh* 1383. Manorial addition from the *de Ralegh* family, here in the 13th cent. **Combe St Nicholas** Somerset. *Cumbe* 1086 (DB). Affix from its possession by the Priory of St Nicholas in Exeter. **Combe, Temple** Somerset. *Come* 1086 (DB), *Cumbe Templer* 1291. Affix from its possession by the Knights Templars at an early date. **Coombe** Hants. *Cumbe* 1086 (DB). **Coombe Bissett** Wilts. *Come* 1086 (DB), *Coumbe Byset* 1288. Manorial addition from the *Biset* family, here in the 12th cent. **Coombe Keynes** Dorset. *Cume* 1086 (DB), *Combe Kaynes* 1299. Manorial addition from the *de Cahaignes* family, here in the 12th cent.

Comberbach Ches. *Combrebeche* 12th cent. 'Valley or stream of the Britons or of a man called Cumbra'. OE **Cumbre* or OE pers. name + *bece*.

Comberford Staffs. *Cumbreford* 1187. 'Ford of the Britons'. OE **Cumbre* + *ford*.

Comberton Cambs. *Cumbertone* 1086 (DB). 'Farmstead of a man called Cumbra'. OE pers. name + *tūn*.

Comberton, Great & Little Heref. & Worcs. *Cumbrincgtun* 972, *Cumbrintune* 1086 (DB). 'Estate associated with a man called Cumbra'. OE pers. name + *-ing-* + *tūn*.

Combrook Warwicks. *Cumbroc* 1217. 'Brook in a valley'. OE *cumb* + *brōc*.

Combs Derbys. *Cumbes* 1251. 'The valleys'. OE *cumb*.

Combs Suffolk. *Cambas* 1086 (DB). 'The hill-crests or ridges'. OE *camb*.

Commondale N. Yorks. *Colemandale* 1272. 'Valley of a man called Colman'. OIrish pers. name + OScand. *dalr*.

Compton, a common place-name, 'farmstead or village in a valley', from OE *cumb* + *tūn*; examples include: **Compton** Berks. *Contone* 1086 (DB). **Compton** Hants. *Cuntone* 1086 (DB). **Compton** Surrey, near Guildford. *Contone* 1086 (DB). **Compton Abbas** Dorset. *Cumtune* 956, *Cuntone* 1086 (DB), *Cumpton Abbatisse* 1293. Manorial addition from Latin *abbatisse* 'of the abbess', alluding to early possession by Shaftesbury Abbey. **Compton Abdale** Glos. *Contone* 1086 (DB), *Apdale Compton* 1504. Affix probably manorial from a family called *Apdale*. **Compton Bassett** Wilts. *Contone* 1086 (DB), *Cumptone Basset* 1228. Manorial addition from the *Basset* family, here in the 13th cent. **Compton Beauchamp** Oxon. *Cumtune* 955, *Contone* 1086 (DB), *Cumton Beucamp* 1236. Manorial addition from the *de Beauchamp* family, here in the 13th cent. **Compton Bishop** Somerset. *Cumbtune* 1067, *Compton Episcopi* 1332.

Affix *Bishop* (Latin *episcopus*) from its early possession by the Bishop of Wells. **Compton Chamberlayne** Wilts. *Contone* 1086 (DB), *Compton Chamberleyne* 1316. Manorial affix from a family called *Chamberlain*, here from the 13th cent. **Compton Dando** Avon. *Contone* 1086 (DB), *Cumton Daunon* 1256. Manorial addition from the *de Auno* or *Dauno* family, here in the 12th cent. **Compton, Fenny** Warwicks. *Contone* 1086 (DB), *Fennicumpton* 1221. The affix is OE *fennig* 'muddy, marshy'. **Compton, Little** Warwicks. *Contone parva* 1086 (DB). The affix *Little* (Latin *parva*) distinguishes it from Long Compton. **Compton, Long** Warwicks. *Cuntone* 1086 (DB), *Long Compton* 1299. The affix *Long* refers to the length of the village. **Compton Martin** Avon. *Comtone* 1086 (DB), *Cumpton Martin* 1228. Manorial addition from one *Martin* de Tours, whose son held the manor in the early 12th cent. **Compton, Nether & Over** Dorset. *Cumbtun* 998, *Contone* 1086 (DB), *Nethercumpton* 1288, *Ouerecumton* 1268. The additions *Nether* and *Over* are from OE *neotherra* 'lower' and *uferra* 'higher'. **Compton Pauncefoot** Somerset. *Cuntone* 1086 (DB), *Cumpton Paunceuot* 1291. Manorial addition from a family called *Pauncefote*. **Compton Valence** Dorset. *Contone* 1086 (DB), *Compton Valance* 1280. Manorial addition from William *de Valencia*, Earl of Pembroke, here in the 13th cent. **Compton, West** Dorset. *Comptone* 934, *Contone* 1086 (DB). Earlier called Compton Abbas but now called West Compton to distinguish it from the other Dorset place of this name.

Conderton Heref. & Worcs. *Cantuaretun* 875, *Canterton* 1201. 'Farmstead of the Kent dwellers or Kentishmen'. OE *Cantware* + *tūn*.

Condicote Glos. *Cundicotan c.*1052, *Condicote* 1086 (DB). 'Cottage associated with a man called Cunda'. OE pers. name + *-ing-* + *cot*.

Condover Shrops. *Conedoure* 1086 (DB). 'Promontory by Cound Brook'. Celtic river-name (see COUND) + OE **ofer*.

Coneysthorpe N. Yorks. *Coningestorp* 1086 (DB). 'The king's farmstead or hamlet'. OScand. *konungr* + *thorp*.

Coney Weston Suffolk. *Cunegestuna* 1086 (DB). 'The king's manor, the royal estate'. OScand. *konungr* + OE *tūn*.

Congerstone Leics. *Cuningestone* 1086 (DB). Identical in origin with the previous name.

Congham Norfolk. *Congheham* 1086 (DB). Possibly 'homestead or village at the hill'. OE **cung* + *hām*.

Congleton Ches. *Cogeltone* (*sic*) 1086 (DB), *Congulton* 13th cent. Probably 'farmstead at the round-topped hill'. OE **cung* + *hyll* + *tūn*.

Congresbury Avon. *Cungresbyri* 9th cent., *Cungresberie* 1086 (DB). 'Fortified place or manor associated with a saint called Congar'. Celtic pers. name + OE *burh* (dative *byrig*).

Coningsby Lincs. *Cuningesbi* 1086 (DB). 'The king's manor or village'. OScand. *konungr* + *bý*.

Conington, 'the king's manor, the royal estate', OScand. *konungr* + OE *tūn*: **Conington** Cambs., near St Ives. *Cunictune* 10th cent., *Coninctune* 1086 (DB). **Conington** Cambs., near Sawtry. *Cunningtune* 10th cent., *Cunitone* 1086 (DB).

Conisbrough S. Yorks. *Cunugesburh c.*1003, *Coningesburg* 1086 (DB). 'The king's fortification'. OScand. *konungr* + OE *burh*.

Conisclifffe, High & Low Durham. *Cingcesclife c.*1050. 'The king's cliff or bank'. OE *cyning* + *clif*.

Conisholme Lincs. *Cuninggesolm* 1195. 'Island, or dry ground in marsh, belonging to the king'. OScand. *konungr* + *holmr*.

Coniston, Conistone, 'the king's manor, the royal estate', OScand. *konungr* + OE *tūn*: **Coniston** Cumbria. *Coningeston* 12th cent. **Coniston** Humber. *Coningesbi* (*sic*) 1086 (DB), *Cuningeston* 1190. OE *tūn* replaced OScand. *bý* 'village' as second element. **Coniston Cold** N. Yorks. *Cuningestone* 1086 (DB), *Calde Cuningeston* 1202. Affix *Cold* (from OE *cald*) from its exposed situation. **Conistone** N. Yorks. *Cunestune* 1086 (DB).

Cononley N. Yorks. *Cutnelai* 1086 (DB), *Conanlia* 12th cent. OE *lēah* 'wood, clearing' with an uncertain first element, possibly an old Celtic river-name or an OIrish pers. name.

Consett Durham. *Covekesheued* 1183, *Conekesheued* 1228. Probably 'headland or promontory of a hill called *Conek*'. Celtic or pre-Celtic **cunāco-* + OE *hēafod*.

Constable Burton N. Yorks., see BURTON.

Constantine Cornwall. *Sanctus Constantinus* 1086 (DB). 'Church of St Constantine'. From the patron saint of the church.

Cookbury Devon. *Cukebyr* 1242. 'Fortification of a man called *Cuca'. OE pers. name + *burh* (dative *byrig*).

Cookham Berks. *Coccham* 798, *Cocheham* 1086 (DB). Possibly 'cook village', i.e. 'village noted for its cooks'. OE *cōc* + *hām*. However the first element may be an OE **cōc(e)* 'hill'.

Cookham Dean Berks. *la Dene* 1220. 'The valley (at COOKHAM)'. OE *denu*.

Cookhill Heref. & Worcs. *Cochilla* 1156. OE **cōc(e)* 'hill' with explanatory OE *hyll*.

Cookley Heref. & Worcs. *Culnan clif* 964, *Culleclive* 11th cent. 'Cliff of a man called *Cūlna'. OE pers. name + *clif*.

Cookley Suffolk. *Cokelei* 1086 (DB). 'Wood or clearing of a man called *Cuca'. OE pers. name + *lēah*.

Cooling Kent. *Culingas* 808, *Colinges* 1086 (DB). '(Settlement of) the family or followers of a man called *Cūl or *Cūla'. OE pers. name + *-ingas*.

Coombe, see COMBE.

Copdock Suffolk. *Coppedoc* 1195. 'Pollarded oak-tree, i.e. oak-tree with its top removed'. OE **coppod* + *āc*.

Copford Green Essex. *Coppanforda* 995, *Copeforda* 1086 (DB). 'Ford of a man called *Coppa'. OE pers. name + *ford* with the later addition of *grēne* 'a green'.

Cople Beds. *Cochepol* 1086 (DB). 'Pool of a man called *Cocca', or 'pool frequented by cocks (of wild birds)'. OE pers. name or *cocc* + *pōl*.

Copmanthorpe N. Yorks. *Copeman Torp* 1086 (DB). 'Outlying farmstead or hamlet belonging to the merchants'. OScand. *kaup-mathr* (genitive plural *-manna*) + *thorp*.

Coppenhall Staffs. *Copehale* 1086 (DB). 'Nook of land of a man called *Coppa'. OE pers. name (genitive *-n*) + *halh*.

Coppingford Cambs. *Copemaneforde* 1086 (DB). 'Ford used by merchants'. OScand. *kaup-mathr* (genitive plural *-manna*) + OE *ford*.

Copplestone Devon. *Copelan stan* 974. 'Peaked or towering stone'. OE **copel* + *stān*.

Coppull Lancs. *Cophill* 1218. 'Hill with a peak'. OE *copp* + *hyll*.

Copt Hewick N. Yorks., see HEWICK.

Copthorne W. Sussex. *Coppethorne* 1437. 'Pollarded thorn-tree, i.e. thorn-tree with its top removed'. OE **coppod* + *thorn*.

Corbridge Northum. *Corebricg* c.1050. 'Bridge near Corchester'. OE *brycg* 'bridge' with a shortened form of the old Celtic name of Corchester (*Corstopitum*) which is near here.

Corby Northants. *Corbei* 1086 (DB). 'Farmstead or village of a man called Kori'. OScand. pers. name + *bý*.

Corby Glen Lincs. *Corbi* 1086 (DB). Identical in origin with the previous name. The affix is presumably *glen* 'a valley'.

Corby, Great Cumbria. *Chorkeby* c.1115. 'Farmstead or village of a man called Corc'. OIrish pers. name + OScand. *bý*.

Coreley Shrops. *Cornelie* 1086 (DB). 'Woodland clearing frequented by cranes or herons'. OE *corn* + *lēah*.

Corfe, 'the cutting, the gap or pass', from OE **corf*: **Corfe** Somerset. *Corf* 1243. **Corfe Castle** Dorset. *Corf* 955, *Corffe Castell* 1302. The affix refers to the Norman castle here. **Corfe Mullen** Dorset. *Corf* 1086 (DB), *Corf le Mulin* 1176. The affix is from OFrench *molin* 'a mill'.

Corfton Shrops. *Cortune* 1086 (DB). 'Farmstead or village in the valley called Corve Dale'. OE **corf* 'a pass' + *tūn*.

Corhampton Hants. *Cornhamton* 1201. 'Home farm or settlement where grain is produced'. OE *corn* + *hām-tūn*.

Corley Warwicks. *Cornelie* 1086 (DB). 'Clearing frequented by cranes or herons'. OE *corn* + *lēah*.

Cornard, Great Suffolk. *Cornerda* 1086 (DB). 'Cultivated land used for corn'. OE *corn* + *erth*.

Corney Cumbria. *Corneia* 12th cent. 'Island frequented by cranes or herons'. OE *corn* + *ēg*.

Cornforth Durham. *Corneford* 1196. 'Ford frequented by cranes or herons'. OE *corn* + *ford*.

Cornhill-on-Tweed Northum. *Cornehale* 12th cent. 'Nook of land frequented by cranes or herons'. OE *corn* + *halh*. For the river-name, see TWEEDMOUTH.

Cornsay Durham. *Corneshowe* 1183. 'Hill-spur frequented by cranes or herons'. OE *corn* + *hōh*.

Cornwall (the county). *Cornubia* c.705, *Cornwalas* 891, *Cornualia* 1086 (DB). '(Territory of) the Britons or Welsh of the *Cornovii* tribe'. Celtic tribal name (meaning 'peninsula people') + OE *walh* (plural *walas*).

Cornwell Oxon. *Cornewelle* 1086 (DB). 'Stream frequented by cranes or herons'. OE *corn* + *wella*.

Cornwood Devon. *Cornehuda* (*sic*) 1086 (DB), *Curnwod* 1242. Probably 'wood frequented by cranes'. OE *corn* + *wudu*.

Cornworthy Devon. *Corneorda* 1086 (DB). 'Enclosure frequented by cranes, or where corn is grown'. OE *corn* + *worth*, *worthig*.

Corpusty Norfolk. *Corpestih* 1086 (DB). 'Raven path', or 'path of a man called Korpr'. OScand. *korpr* or pers. name + *stígr*.

Corringham Essex. *Currincham* 1086 (DB). 'Homestead of the family or followers of a man called *Curra'. OE pers. name + *-inga-* + *hām*.

Corringham Lincs. *Coringeham* 1086 (DB). 'Homestead of the family or followers of a man called *Cora'. OE pers. name + *-inga-* + *hām*.

Corscombe Dorset. *Corigescumb* 1014, *Coriescumbe* 1086 (DB). Possibly 'valley of the road in the pass'. OE **corf* + *weg* + *cumb*. Alternatively the first element may be an old name of the stream here.

Corsham Wilts. *Coseham* 1001, *Cosseham* 1086 (DB). 'Homestead or village of a man called *Cosa or *Cossa'. OE pers. name + *hām*.

Corsley Wilts. *Corselie* 1086 (DB). 'Wood or clearing by the marsh'. Celtic **cors* + OE *lēah*.

Corston Avon. *Corsantune* 941, *Corstune* 1086 (DB). 'Farmstead or estate on the River Corse'. Old river-name (from Celtic **cors* 'marsh') + OE *tūn*.

Corston Wilts. *Corstuna* 1065, *Corstone* 1086 (DB). 'Farmstead or estate on Gauze Brook'. Old river-name (from Celtic **cors* 'marsh') + OE *tūn*.

Corton Suffolk. *Karetuna* 1086 (DB). 'Farmstead of a man called Kári'. OScand. pers. name + OE *tūn*.

Corton Wilts. *Cortitone* 1086 (DB). 'Estate associated with a man called *Cort(a)'. OE pers. name + *-ing-* + *tūn*.

Corton Denham Somerset. *Corfetone* 1086 (DB). 'Farmstead or village at a pass'. OE **corf* + *tūn* + manorial affix from the *de Dinan* family, here in the early 13th cent.

Coryton Devon. *Cur(r)itun* c.970, *Coriton* 1086 (DB). Probably 'farmstead on the River *Curi*'. Pre-English river-name (an old name for the River Lyd) + OE *tūn*.

Cosby Leics. *Cossebi* 1086 (DB). 'Farmstead or village of a man called *Cossa'. OE pers. name + OScand. *bý*.

Coseley W. Mids. *Colseley* 1357. Possibly 'clearing of the charcoal burners'. OE **colestre* + *lēah*.

Cosgrove Northants. *Covesgrave* 1086 (DB). 'Grove of a man called *Cōf'. OE pers. name + *grāf*.

Cosham Hants. *Cos(s)eham* 1086 (DB). 'Homestead or enclosure of a man called *Cossa'. OE pers. name + *hām* or *hamm*.

Cossall Notts. *Coteshale* 1086 (DB). 'Nook of land of a man called *Cott'. OE pers. name + *halh*.

Cossington, 'estate associated with a man called *Cosa or Cusa', OE pers. name + *-ing-* + *tūn*: **Cossington** Leics. *Cosintone* 1086 (DB). **Cossington**

Somerset. *Cosingtone* 729, *Cosintone* 1086 (DB).

Costessey Norfolk. *Costeseia* 1086 (DB). 'Island, or dry ground in marsh, of a man called *Cost'. OE (or OScand.) pers. name + OE *ēg*.

Costock Notts. *Cortingestoche* 1086 (DB). 'Outlying farmstead of the family or followers of a man called *Cort'. OE pers. name + *-inga-* + *stoc*.

Coston Leics. *Castone* 1086 (DB). Probably 'farmstead of a man called Kátr'. OScand. pers. name + OE *tūn*.

Cotes, 'the cottages or huts', from OE *cot*: **Cotes** Leics. *Cothes* 12th cent. **Cotes** Staffs. *Cota* 1086 (DB).

Cotesbach Leics. *Cotesbece* 1086 (DB). 'Stream or valley of a man called *Cott'. OE pers. name + *bece, bæce*.

Cotgrave Notts. *Godegrave* (*sic*) 1086 (DB), *Cotegrava* 1094. 'Grove or copse of a man called Cotta'. OE pers. name + *grāf*.

Cotham Notts. *Cotune* 1086 (DB). '(Place at) the cottages or huts'. OE *cot* in a dative plural form *cotum*.

Cothelstone Somerset. *Cothelestone* 1327. 'Farmstead of a man called Cūthwulf'. OE pers. name + *tūn*.

Cotherstone Durham. *Codrestune* 1086 (DB). 'Farmstead of a man called Cūthhere'. OE pers. name + *tūn*.

Cotleigh Devon. *Coteleia* 1086 (DB). 'Clearing of a man called Cotta'. OE pers. name + *lēah*.

Coton, '(place at) the cottages or huts', from OE *cot* in the dative plural form *cotum* (though some may be from a ME plural *coten*): **Coton** Cambs. *Cotis* 1086. **Coton** Northants. *Cote* 1086 (DB). **Coton** Staffs., near Milwich. *Cote* 1086 (DB). **Coton Clanford** Staffs. *Cote* 1086 (DB). Affix from a local place-name, probably 'clean ford' from OE *clǣne* + *ford*. **Coton in the Elms** Derbys. *Cotune* 1086 (DB). Affix from the abundance of elm-trees here.

Cotswolds Glos./Worcs. *Codesuualt* 12th cent. 'High forest land of a man called *Cōd'. OE pers. name + *wald*.

Cottam, '(place at) the cottages or huts', from OE *cot* in a dative plural form *cotum*: **Cottam** Humber. *Cottun* 1086 (DB). **Cottam** Lancs. *Cotun* 1227. **Cottam** Notts. *Cotum* 1274.

Cottenham Cambs. *Cotenham* 948, *Coteham* 1086 (DB). 'Homestead or village of a man called Cot(t)a'. OE pers. name (genitive *-n*) + *hām*.

Cottered Herts. *Chodrei* (*sic*) 1086 (DB), *Codreth* 1220. OE *rīth* 'stream' with an uncertain first element, possibly a pers. name or an OE **cōd* 'spawn of fish'.

Cotterstock Northants. *Codestoche* 1086 (DB). Probably 'place with a sick house or hospital'. OE **coth-ærn* + *stoc*.

Cottesbrooke Northants. *Cotesbroc* 1086 (DB). 'Brook of a man called *Cott'. OE pers. name + *brōc*.

Cottesmore Leics. *Cottesmore* c.976, *Cotesmore* 1086 (DB). 'Moor of a man called *Cott'. OE pers. name + *mōr*.

Cottingham, 'homestead of the family or followers of a man called *Cott or Cotta', OE pers. name + *-inga-* + *hām*: **Cottingham** Humber. *Cotingeham* 1086 (DB). **Cottingham** Northants. *Cotingeham* 1086 (DB).

Cottingwith Humber. *Coteuuid* (*sic*) 1086 (DB), *Cotingwic* 1195. 'Dairy-farm associated with a man called *Cott or Cotta'. OE pers. name + *-ing-* + *wīc* (replaced by OScand. *vithr* 'wood').

Cottisford Oxon. *Cotesforde* 1086 (DB). 'Ford of a man called *Cott'. OE pers. name + *ford*.

Cotton, Far Northants. *Cotes* 1196. 'The cottages or huts'. OE *cot* in a plural form. Affix *Far* to distinguish it from other places with this name.

Cotwalton Staffs. *Cotewaltun* 1002, *Cotewoldestune* 1086 (DB). Possibly 'farmstead at the wood or stream of a man called Cotta'. OE pers. name + *wald* or *wælla* + *tūn*.

Coughton Warwicks. *Coctune* 1086 (DB). Probably 'farmstead near the hillock'. OE **cocc* + *tūn*.

Coulsdon Gtr. London. *Cudredesdune* 967, *Colesdone* 1086 (DB). 'Hill of a man called Cūthrǣd'. OE pers. name + *dūn*.

Coulston, East & West Wilts. *Covelestone* 1086 (DB). 'Farmstead of a man called *Cufel'. OE pers. name + *tūn*.

Coulton N. Yorks. *Coltune* 1086 (DB).

Probably 'farmstead where charcoal is made'. OE *col* + *tūn*.

Cound Shrops. *Cuneet* 1086 (DB). Named from Cound Brook, a Celtic river-name of uncertain meaning.

Coundon Durham. *Cundun* 1196. Probably 'hill where cows are pastured'. OE *cū* (genitive plural *cūna*) + *dūn*.

Countesthorpe Leics. *Torp* 1209–35, *Cuntastorp* 1242. 'Outlying farmstead or hamlet belonging to a countess'. OScand. *thorp* with manorial affix from ME *contesse*.

Countisbury Devon. *Contesberie* 1086 (DB). 'Fortified place at a hill called *Cunet*'. Celtic name (of uncertain meaning) + OE *burh* (dative *byrig*).

Coupland Northum. *Coupland* 1242. 'Purchased land'. OScand. *kaupa-land*.

Courteenhall Northants. *Cortenhale* 1086 (DB). 'Nook of land of a man called *Corta or *Curta'. OE pers. name (genitive *-n*) + *halh*.

Cove, from OE *cofa* which meant 'hut or shelter', also 'recess or cove': **Cove** Devon. *La Kove* 1242. **Cove** Hants. *Coue* 1086 (DB). **Cove, North** Suffolk. *Cove* 1204. **Cove, South** Suffolk. *Coua* 1086 (DB).

Covehithe Suffolk. *Coveheith* 1523. 'Harbour near (South) COVE', from OE *hȳth*.

Coven Staffs. *Cove* 1086 (DB). '(Place at) the huts or shelters'. OE *cofa* in the dative plural form *cofum*.

Coveney Cambs. *Coueneia* c.1060. 'Island of a man called *Cofa', or 'cove island'. OE pers. name or OE *cofa* (genitive *-n*) + *ēg*.

Covenham St Bartholomew & St Mary Lincs. *Covenham* 1086 (DB). 'Homestead of a man called *Cofa', or 'homestead with a hut or shelter'. OE pers. name or OE *cofa* (genitive *-n*) + *hām*. Affixes from the dedications of the churches.

Coventry W. Mids. *Couentre* 1043, *Couentreu* 1086 (DB). 'Tree of a man called *Cofa'. OE pers. name (genitive *-n*) + *trēow*.

Coverack Cornwall. *Covrack* 1588. Probably originally the name of the stream here, meaning unknown.

Coverham N. Yorks. *Covreham* 1086 (DB). 'Homestead or village on the River Cover'. Celtic river-name + OE *hām*.

Covington Cambs. *Covintune* 1086 (DB). 'Estate associated with a man called *Cofa'. OE pers. name + *-ing-* + *tūn*.

Cowarne, Much & Little Heref. & Worcs. *Cuure* (*sic*) 1086 (DB), *Couern* 1255. 'Cow house, dairy farm'. OE *cū* + *ærn*. Affix *Much* is from OE *mycel* 'great'.

Cowden Kent. *Cudena* c.1100. 'Pasture for cows'. OE *cū* + *denn*.

Cowden, Great Humber. *Coledun* 1086 (DB). 'Hill where charcoal is made'. OE *col* + *dūn*.

Cowes I. of Wight, from the two sandbanks in the river estuary called *Estcowe* and *Westcowe* in 1413, so named from their fancied resemblance to animals. OE *cū* 'a cow'.

Cowesby N. Yorks. *Cahosbi* 1086 (DB). 'Farmstead or village of a man called Kausi'. OScand. pers. name + *bý*.

Cowfold W. Sussex. *Coufaud* 1232. 'Small enclosure for cows'. OE *cū* + *fald*.

Cow Honeybourne Heref. & Worcs., see HONEYBOURNE.

Cowick, East & West Humber. *Cuwich* 1197. 'Cow farm, dairy farm'. OE *cū* + *wīc*.

Cowley Devon, near Exeter. *Couelegh* 1237. 'Clearing of a man called *Cofa or Cufa'. OE pers. name + *lēah*.

Cowley Glos. *Kulege* 1086 (DB). 'Clearing where cows are pastured'. OE *cū* + *lēah*.

Cowley Gtr. London. *Cofenlea* 959, *Covelie* 1086 (DB). 'Clearing of a man called *Cofa'. OE pers. name + *lēah*.

Cowley Oxon. *Couelea* 1004, *Covelie* 1086 (DB). 'Clearing of a man called *Cofa or Cufa'. OE pers. name + *lēah*.

Cowling N. Yorks., near Bedale. *Collinghe* 1086 (DB). 'Place characterized by a hill'. OE *coll + *-ing*.

Cowling N. Yorks., near Glusburn.

Torneton 1086 (DB), *Thornton Colling* 1202. Originally 'farmstead where thorn-trees grow' from OE *thorn* + *tūn*, with manorial affix from a person or family called *Colling*. The first part of the name went out of use in the 15th cent.

Cowlinge Suffolk. *Culinge* 1086 (DB). Probably 'place associated with a man called *Cūl or *Cūla'. OE pers. name + *-ing*.

Cowpen Bewley Cleveland. *Cupum* c.1150. '(Place by) the coops or baskets (for catching fish)'. OE **cūpe* in a dative plural form **cūpum*. Affix from its possession by the manor of Bewley ('beautiful place', OFrench *beau* + *lieu*).

Cowplain Hants., recorded from 1859, self-explanatory.

Cowton, East & North N. Yorks. *Cudtone, Cotun* 1086 (DB). Probably 'cow farm, dairy farm'. OE *cū* + *tūn*.

Coxhoe Durham. *Cockishow* 1277. Possibly 'hill-spur of a man called *Cocc'. OE pers. name + *hōh*.

Coxley Somerset. *Cokesleg* 1207. 'Wood or clearing belonging to the cook'. OE *cōc* + *lēah*. The wife of a cook in the royal household is recorded as holding lands near Wells in 1086 (DB).

Coxwold N. Yorks. *Cuhawalda* 758, *Cucualt* 1086 (DB). 'Woodland of a man called *Cuha'. OE pers. name + *wald*.

Crackenthorpe Cumbria. *Cracantorp* late 12th cent. 'Outlying farmstead or hamlet of a man called *Krakandi, or one frequented by crows or ravens'. OScand. pers. name or OE **crāca* (genitive plural *-ena*) + OScand. *thorp*.

Cracoe N. Yorks. *Crakehou* 12th cent. 'Spur of land or hill frequented by crows or ravens'. OScand. *kráka* + OE *hōh* or OScand. *haugr*.

Cradley Heref. & Worcs. *Credelaie* 1086 (DB). 'Woodland clearing of a man called Creoda'. OE pers. name + *lēah*.

Crakehall, Great & Little N. Yorks. *Crachele* 1086 (DB). 'Nook of land frequented by crows or ravens'. OScand. *kráka* or *krákr* + OE *halh*.

Crambe N. Yorks. *Crambom* 1086 (DB). '(Place at) the river-bends'. OE **cramb* in a dative plural form **crambum*.

Cramlington Northum. *Cramlingtuna* c.1130. Possibly 'farmstead of the people living at the cranes' stream'. OE *cran* + *wella* + *-inga-* + *tūn*.

Cranage Ches. *Croeneche* (*sic*) 1086 (DB), *Cranlach* 12th cent. 'Boggy place or stream frequented by crows'. OE *crāwe* (genitive plural *crāwena*) + **læc(c)*.

Cranborne Dorset. *Creneburne* 1086 (DB). 'Stream frequented by cranes or herons'. OE *cran* + *burna*.

Cranbrook Kent. *Cranebroca* 11th cent. 'Brook frequented by cranes or herons'. OE *cran* + *brōc*.

Cranfield Beds. *Crangfeldæ* 1060, *Cranfelle* 1086 (DB). 'Open land frequented by cranes or herons'. OE *cran, cranuc* + *feld*.

Cranford, 'ford frequented by cranes or herons', OE *cran* + *ford*: **Cranford** Gtr. London. *Cranforde* 1086 (DB). **Cranford St Andrew & St John** Northants. *Craneford* 1086 (DB), *Craneford Sancti Andree, Craneford Sancti Iohannis* 1254. Affixes from the dedications of the churches.

Cranham Glos. *Craneham* 12th cent. 'Enclosure or river-meadow frequented by cranes or herons'. OE *cran* + *hamm*.

Cranham Gtr. London. *Craohv* (*sic*) 1086 (DB), *Crawenho* 1201. 'Spur of land frequented by crows'. OE *crāwe* (genitive plural *crāwena*) + *hōh* (the later spelling perhaps reflecting a dative plural *hōum*).

Cranleigh Surrey. *Cranlea* 1166. 'Woodland clearing frequented by cranes or herons'. OE *cran* + *lēah*.

Cranmore, East & West Somerset. *Cranemere* 10th cent., *Crenemelle* (*sic*) 1086 (DB). 'Pool frequented by cranes or herons'. OE *cran* + *mere*.

Cranoe Leics. *Craweho* 1086 (DB). 'Spur of land frequented by crows'. OE *crāwe* (genitive plural *crāwena*) + *hōh*.

Cransford Suffolk. *Craneforda* 1086 (DB). 'Ford frequented by cranes or herons'. OE *cran* + *ford*.

Cransley, Great Northants. *Cranslea* 956, *Craneslea* 1086 (DB). 'Woodland clearing frequented by cranes or herons'. OE *cran* + *lēah*.

Cranswick Humber., see HUTTON CRANSWICK.

Crantock Cornwall. *Sanctus Carentoch* 1086 (DB). 'Church of St Carantoc'. From the patron saint of the church.

Cranwell Lincs. *Craneuuelle* 1086 (DB). 'Spring or stream frequented by cranes or herons'. OE *cran* + *wella*.

Cranwich Norfolk. *Cranewisse* 1086 (DB). 'Marshy meadow frequented by cranes or herons'. OE *cran* + *wisc*.

Cranworth Norfolk. *Cranaworda* 1086 (DB). 'Enclosure frequented by cranes or herons'. OE *cran* + *worth*.

Craster Northum. *Craucestre* 1242. 'Old fortification or earthwork haunted by crows'. OE *crāwe* + *ceaster*.

Craswall Heref. & Worcs. *Cressewell* 1231. 'Spring or stream where water-cress grows'. OE *cærse* + *wella*.

Cratfield Suffolk. *Cratafelda* 1086 (DB). 'Open land of a man called *Crǣta'. OE pers. name + *feld*.

Crathorne N. Yorks. *Cratorne* 1086 (DB). Possibly 'thorn-tree in a nook of land'. OScand. *krá* + *thorn*.

Craven (district) N. Yorks. *Crave* 1086 (DB), *Cravena* 12th cent. Probably an old Celtic name meaning 'garlic place'.

Crawcrook Tyne & Wear. *Crawecroca* 1130. 'Bend (in a road) or nook of land frequented by crows'. OE *crāwe* + OScand. *krókr* or OE **crōc*.

Crawley, usually 'wood or clearing frequented by crows', OE *crāwe* + *lēah*; examples include: **Crawley** Hants. *Crawanlea* 909, *Crawelie* 1086 (DB). **Crawley** Oxon. *Croule* 1214. **Crawley** W. Sussex. *Crauleia* 1203. **Crawley Down,** *Crauledun* 1272, has the addition of OE *dūn* 'hill, down'. **Crawley, North** Bucks. *Crauelai* 1086 (DB).

Crawshaw Booth Lancs. *Croweshagh* 1324. 'Small wood or copse frequented by crows'. OE *crāwe* + *sc(e)aga*, with the later addition of OScand. *bōth* 'cowhouse, herdsman's hut'.

Cray, Foots, North, St Mary, & St Pauls Gtr. London. *Crǣga(n)* 10th cent., *Crai(e)* 1086 (DB), *Fotescraei*, *Northcraei* c.1100, *Creye sancte Marie* 1257, *Creypaulin* 1291. Named from the River Cray, a Celtic river-name meaning 'fresh, clean'. Foots Cray was held by a man called *Fot* at the time of Domesday. The affixes in St Mary & St Pauls Cray are from the dedications of the churches to St Mary and St Paulinus.

Crayford Gtr. London. *Creiford* 1199. 'Ford over the River Cray'. Celtic river-name + OE *ford*.

Crayke N. Yorks. *Creic* 10th cent., 1086 (DB). Celtic **creig* 'a rock, a cliff'.

Creacombe Devon. *Crawecome* 1086 (DB). 'Valley frequented by crows'. OE *crāwe* + *cumb*.

Creake, North & South Norfolk. *Creic*, *Suthcreich* 1086 (DB), *Northcrec* 1211. Celtic **creig* 'a rock, a cliff'.

Creaton Northants. *Cretone* 1086 (DB). Probably 'farmstead at the rock or cliff'. Celtic **creig* + OE *tūn*.

Credenhill Heref. & Worcs. *Cradenhille* 1086 (DB). 'Hill of a man called Creoda'. OE pers. name (genitive *-n*) + *hyll*.

Crediton Devon. *Cridiantune* 930, *Chritetona* 1086 (DB). 'Farmstead or estate on the River Creedy'. Celtic river-name (meaning 'the winding river') + OE *tūn*.

Creech, from Celtic **crūg* 'a mound or hill': **Creech, East** Dorset. *Criz* 1086 (DB). Referring originally to Creech Barrow. **Creech St Michael** Somerset. *Crice* 1086 (DB). Affix from the dedication of the church.

Creed Cornwall. *Sancta Crida* c.1250. 'Church of St Cride'. From the patron saint of the church.

Creedy (river) Devon, see CREDITON.

Creeting St Mary Suffolk. *Cratingas* 1086 (DB), *Creting Sancte Marie* 1254. '(Settlement of) the family or followers of a man called *Crǣta'. OE pers. name + *-ingas*, with affix from the dedication of the church.

Creeton Lincs. *Cretone* 1086 (DB). Probably 'farmstead of a man called *Crǣta'. OE pers. name + *tūn*.

Crendon, Long Bucks. *Credendone* 1086 (DB). 'Hill of a man called Creoda'. OE pers. name (genitive *-n*) + *dūn*. Affix (in use since 17th cent.) refers to length of village.

Cressage Shrops. *Cristesache* 1086 (DB). 'Christ's oak-tree'. OE *Crist* + *āc* (dative *ǣc*), probably with reference to a spot where preaching took place.

Cressing Essex. *Cressyng* 1136. 'Place where water-cress grows'. OE **cærsing*.

Cressingham, Great & Little Norfolk. *Cressingaham* 1086 (DB). Possibly 'homestead of the family or followers of a man called *Cressa'. OE pers. name + *-inga-* + *hām*. Alternatively 'homestead with cress-beds', with a first element OE **cærsing*.

Cresswell, Creswell, 'spring or stream where water-cress grows', from OE *cærse* + *wella*: **Cresswell** Northum. *Kereswell* 1234. **Cresswell** Staffs. *Cressvale* 1086 (DB). **Creswell** Derbys. *Cressewella* 1176.

Cretingham Suffolk. *Gretingaham* 1086 (DB). 'Homestead of the people from a gravelly district'. OE *grēot* + *-inga-* + *hām*.

Crewe Ches. *Creu* 1086 (DB). Celtic **crïu* 'a fish-trap, a weir'.

Crewe Ches., near Farndon. *Creuhalle* 1086 (DB). Identical in origin with the previous name + OE *hall* 'a hall, a manor house'.

Crewkerne Somerset. *Crucern* 9th cent., *Cruche* 1086 (DB). Probably 'house or building at the hill', Celtic **crūg* + OE *ærn*, although *-ern* may rather represent a Celtic suffix.

Crich Derbys. *Cryc* 1009, *Crice* 1086 (DB). Celtic **crūg* 'a mound or hill'.

Crichel, Long & Moor Dorset. *Circel* 1086 (DB), *Langecrechel* 1208, *Mor Kerchel* 1212. 'Hill called *Crich*'. Celtic **crūg* 'hill' + explanatory OE *hyll*. Affixes are OE *lang* 'long' and OE *mōr* 'marshy ground'.

Crick Northants. *Crec* 1086 (DB). Celtic **creig* 'a rock, a cliff'.

Cricket St Thomas Somerset. *Cruche* 1086 (DB), *Cruk Thomas* 1291. Celtic **crūg* 'a mound or hill' with the later addition of OFrench *-ette* 'little'. Affix from the dedication of the church.

Crickheath Shrops. *Gruchet* 1272. Probably Celtic **crūg* 'hill' + OE *hǣth* 'heath'.

Cricklade Wilts. *Cracgelade* 10th cent., *Crichelade* 1086 (DB). 'River-crossing at the rock or hill'. Celtic **creig* or **crūg* + OE *(ge)lād*.

Cricklewood Gtr. London. *Le Crikeldwode* 1294. 'The curved wood'. ME *crikeled* + *wode*.

Cridling Stubbs N. Yorks. *Credeling* 12th cent., *Credlingstubbes* 1480. 'Place of a man called *Cridela'. OE pers. name + *-ing*, with the later addition of Stubbs, 'tree-stumps', from OE *stubb*.

Crigglestone W. Yorks. *Crigestone* 1086 (DB). 'Farmstead at the hill called *Crik*'. Celtic **crūg* 'hill' + explanatory OE *hyll* + OE *tūn*.

Crimplesham Norfolk. *Crepelesham* (*sic*) 1086 (DB), *Crimplesham* 1200. 'Homestead of a man called *Crympel'. OE pers. name + *hām*.

Cringleford Norfolk. *Kringelforda* 1086 (DB). 'Ford by the round hill'. OScand. *kringla* + OE *ford*.

Crockerton Wilts. *Crokerton* 1249. 'Estate of the potters or of a family called *Crocker*'. OE **croccere* or ME surname + OE *tūn*.

Croft, usually from OE *croft* 'a small enclosed field'; examples include: **Croft** Lincs. *Croft* 1086 (DB). **Croft** N. Yorks. *Croft* 1086 (DB).

However the following has a different origin: **Croft** Leics. *Craeft* 836, *Crebre* (*sic*) 1086 (DB). OE *cræft* 'a machine, an engine', perhaps referring to some kind of mill.

Crofton Gtr. London. *Croptun* 8th cent. 'Farmstead near a hill'. OE *crop(p)* + *tūn*.

Crofton W. Yorks. *Scroftune* (*sic*) 1086 (DB), *Croftona* 12th cent. 'Farmstead with a croft or enclosure'. OE *croft* + *tūn*.

Croglin Cumbria. *Crokelyn* *c.*1140. 'Torrent with a bend in it'. OE **crōc* + *hlynn*.

Cromer Norfolk. *Crowemere* 13th cent. 'Lake frequented by crows'. OE *crāwe* + *mere*.

Cromford Derbys. *Crunforde* 1086 (DB). 'Ford by the river bend'. OE **crumbe* + *ford*.

Cromhall Avon. *Cromhal* 1086 (DB).

'Nook of land in the river bend'. OE **crumbe* + *halh*.

Cromwell Notts. *Crunwelle* 1086 (DB). 'Crooked stream'. OE *crumb* + *wella*.

Crondall Hants. *Crundellan* c.880, *Crundele* 1086 (DB). '(Place at) the chalk-pits or quarries'. OE *crundel* in a dative plural form.

Cronton Mersey. *Crohinton* 1242. Possibly 'farmstead at the place with a nook'. OE **crōh* + *-ing* + *tūn*.

Crook Cumbria. *Croke* 12th cent. OScand. *krókr* or OE **crōc* 'land in a bend, secluded corner of land'.

Crook Durham. *Cruketona* 1267, *Crok* 1304. Identical in origin with the previous name, originally with OE *tūn* 'farmstead, estate'.

Crookham Berks. *Crocheham* 1086 (DB). Probably 'homestead or village by the river bends'. OE **crōc* + *hām*.

Crookham Northum. *Crucum* 1244. '(Place) at the river bends'. OScand. *krókr* in a dative plural form.

Crookham, Church Hants. *Crocham* 1248. Identical in origin with CROOKHAM (Berks.).

Croome, Earls Heref. & Worcs. *Cromman* 10th cent., *Crumbe* 1086 (DB), *Erlescrombe* 1495. Originally the name of the stream here, a Celtic river-name meaning 'the crooked or winding one'. Manorial affix from its early possession by the Earls of Warwick.

Cropredy Oxon. *Cropelie* (*sic*) 1086 (DB), *Croprithi* c.1275. 'Small stream of a man called *Croppa, or near a hill'. OE pers. name or *crop(p)* + *rīthig*.

Cropston Leics. *Cropeston* 12th cent. 'Farmstead of a man called *Cropp or Kroppr'. OE or OScand. pers. name + OE *tūn*. Alternatively the first element may be OE *crop(p)* 'hill'.

Cropthorne Heref. & Worcs. *Croppethorne* 8th cent., *Cropetorn* 1086 (DB). 'Thorn-tree near a hill'. OE *crop(p)* + *thorn*.

Cropton N. Yorks. *Croptune* 1086 (DB). 'Farmstead near a hill'. OE *crop(p)* + *tūn*.

Cropwell Bishop & Butler Notts. *Crophille* 1086 (DB), *Bischopcroppehill* 1280, *Croppill Boteiller* 1265. 'Rounded hill'. OE *crop(p)* + *hyll*. Manorial additions from possession by the Archbishop of York and by the *Butler* family, here from the 12th cent.

Crosby, usually 'village where there are crosses', from OScand. *krossa-bý*; examples include: **Crosby** Cumbria, near Maryport. *Crosseby* 12th cent. **Crosby, Great & Little Crosby** Mersey. *Crosebi* 1086 (DB), *Magna Crossby* c.1190, *Parva Crosseby* 1242. Affixes are Latin *magna* 'great' and *parva* 'little'. **Crosby Garrett** Cumbria. *Crosseby* 1200, *Crossebi Gerard* 1206. Manorial affix from a person or family called *Gerard*. **Crosby, Low** Cumbria. *Crossebi* c.1200. **Crosby Ravensworth** Cumbria. *Crosseby Raveneswart* 12th cent. Manorial affix from the OScand. pers. name *Rafnsvartr*.
However the following has a different origin: **Crosby** Humber. *Cropesbi* (*sic*) 1086 (DB), *Crochesbi* 12th cent. 'Farmstead or village of a man called Krókr, or in a nook'. OScand. pers. name or *krókr* + *bý*.

Crosscanonby Cumbria. *Crosseby Canoun* 1285. 'Village where there are crosses'. OScand. *krossa-bý*. *Canon* refers to lands here given to the canons of Carlisle.

Crossens Mersey. *Crossenes* c.1250. 'Headland or promontory with crosses'. OScand. *kross* + *nes*.

Crosthwaite Cumbria. *Crosthwait* 12th cent. 'Clearing with a cross'. OScand. *kross* + *thveit*.

Croston Lancs. *Croston* 1094. 'Farmstead or village with a cross'. OScand. *kross* or OE *cros* + *tūn*.

Crostwick Norfolk. *Crostueit* 1086 (DB). 'Clearing with a cross'. OScand. *kross* + *thveit*.

Crostwight Norfolk. *Crostwit* 1086 (DB). Identical in origin with the previous name.

Crouch (river) Essex, see BURNHAM ON CROUCH.

Croughton Northants. *Creveltone* 1086 (DB). 'Farmstead or village on the fork of land'. OE **creowel* + *tūn*.

Crowan Cornwall. *Eggloscrauuen* c.1170. 'Church of St Cravenna'. From the patron saint of the church (in the early spelling with Cornish *eglos* 'church').

Crowborough E. Sussex. *Cranbergh* (*sic*, for *Craubergh*) 1292. 'Hill or mound frequented by crows'. OE *crāwe* + *beorg*.

Crowcombe Somerset. *Crawancumb* 10th cent., *Crawecumbe* 1086 (DB). 'Valley frequented by crows'. OE *crāwe* + *cumb*.

Crowdecote Derbys. *Crudecote* 13th cent. 'Cottage of a man called *Crūda'. OE pers. name + *cot*.

Crowfield Suffolk. *Crofelda* 1086 (DB). Probably 'open land near the nook or corner'. OE **crōh* + *feld*.

Crowhurst E. Sussex. *Croghyrste* 772, *Croherst* 1086 (DB). Probably 'wooded hill near the nook or corner'. OE **crōh* + *hyrst*.

Crowhurst Surrey. *Crouhurst* 12th cent. 'Wooded hill frequented by crows'. OE *crāwe* + *hyrst*.

Crowland Lincs. *Cruwland* 8th cent., *Croiland* 1086 (DB). Possibly 'estate or tract of land at the river bend'. OE **crūw* + *land*.

Crowle Heref. & Worcs. *Crohlea* 9th cent., *Croelai* 1086 (DB). 'Woodland clearing by the nook or corner'. OE **crōh* + *lēah*.

Crowle Humber. *Crule* 1086 (DB). Originally the name of a river here (now gone through draining), an OE river-name meaning 'winding'.

Crowmarsh Gifford Oxon. *Cravmares* 1086 (DB), *Cromershe Giffard* 1316. 'Marsh frequented by crows'. OE *crāwe* + *mersc*, with manorial affix from a man called *Gifard* who held the manor in 1086.

Crownthorpe Norfolk. *Congrethorp*, *Cronkethor* 1086 (DB). OScand. *thorp* 'outlying farmstead or hamlet' with an uncertain first element, possibly a pers. name.

Crowthorne Berks., first recorded in 1607, 'thorn-tree frequented by crows'.

Crowton Ches. *Crouton* 1260. 'Farmstead frequented by crows'. OE *crāwe* + *tūn*.

Croxall Staffs. *Crokeshalle* 942, *Crocheshalle* 1086 (DB). 'Nook of land of a man called Krókr, or near a bend'. OScand. pers. name or OE **crōc* + OE *halh*.

Croxdale Durham. *Crokesteil* 1195. 'Projecting piece of land of a man called Krókr'. OScand. pers. name + OE *tægl*.

Croxden Staffs. *Crochesdene* 1086 (DB). Possibly 'valley of a man called Krókr'. OScand. pers. name + OE *denu*. Alternatively the first element may be OE **crōc* 'nook, bend'.

Croxley Green Herts. *Crokesleya* 1166. 'Woodland clearing of a man called Krókr'. OScand. pers. name + OE *lēah*.

Croxton, 'farmstead in a nook, or of a man called Krókr', from OE **crōc* or OScand. pers. name + OE *tūn*: **Croxton** Cambs. *Crochestone* 1086 (DB). **Croxton** Humber. *Crochestune* 1086 (DB). **Croxton** Norfolk, near Thetford. *Crokestuna* 1086 (DB). **Croxton** Staffs. *Crochestone* 1086 (DB). **Croxton Kerrial** Leics. *Crohtone* 1086 (DB), *Croxton Kyriel* 1247. Manorial addition from the *Kyriel* family, here in the 13th cent. **Croxton, South** Leics. *Crochestone* 1086 (DB), *Sudcroxton* 1212. OE *sūth* 'south'.

Croyde Devon. *Crideholda* (*sic*) 1086 (DB), *Crideho* 1242. 'The headland', from OE **crȳde* referring to the promontory called Croyde Hoe (with explanatory OE *hōh* 'hill-spur').

Croydon Cambs. *Crauuedene* 1086 (DB). 'Valley frequented by crows'. OE *crāwe* + *denu*.

Croydon Gtr. London. *Crogedene* 809, *Croindene* 1086 (DB). 'Valley where wild saffron grows'. OE *croh*, **crogen* + *denu*.

Cruckmeole Shrops. *Meole* 1327. Named from Meole Brook (see MEOLE BRACE), first element as in following name.

Cruckton Shrops. *Croctun* 1272. Possibly 'farmstead by a hill'. Celtic **crūg* + OE *tūn*.

Crudgington Shrops. *Crugetone* (*sic*) 1086 (DB), *Crugelton* 12th cent. Probably 'farmstead by a hill called *Cruc*'. Celtic **crūg* + explanatory OE *hyll* + OE *tūn*.

Crudwell Wilts. *Croddewelle* 9th cent., *Credvelle* 1086 (DB). 'Spring or stream of a man called Creoda'. OE pers. name + *wella*.

Crundale Kent. *Crundala c.*1100. OE *crundel* 'a chalk-pit, a quarry'.

Crux Easton Hants., see EASTON.

Cubbington Warwicks. *Cobintone* 1086 (DB). 'Estate associated with a man called *Cubba'. OE pers. name + *-ing-* + *tūn*.

Cubert Cornwall. *Sanctus Cubertus* 1269. 'Church of St Cuthbert'. From the patron saint of the church.

Cublington Bucks. *Coblincote* (*sic*) 1086 (DB), *Cubelintone* 12th cent. 'Estate associated with a man called *Cubbel'. OE pers. name + *-ing-* + *tūn* (with alternative *cot* 'cottage' in the Domesday spelling).

Cuckfield W. Sussex. *Kukefeld c.*1095. Probably 'open land of a man called *Cuca'. OE pers. name + *feld*.

Cucklington Somerset. *Cocintone* (*sic*) 1086 (DB), *Cukelingeton* 1212. 'Estate associated with a man called *Cucol or *Cucola'. OE pers. name + *-ing-* + *tūn*.

Cuddesdon Oxon. *Cuthenesdune* 956, *Codesdone* 1086 (DB). 'Hill of a man called *Cūthen'. OE pers. name + *dūn*.

Cuddington, 'estate associated with a man called Cud(d)a', OE pers. name + *-ing-* + *tūn*: **Cuddington** Bucks. *Cudintuna* 12th cent. **Cuddington** Ches. *Codynton c.*1235. **Cuddington Heath** Ches. *Cuntitone* 1086 (DB), *Cudyngton Hethe* 1532.

Cudham Gtr. London. *Codeham* 1086 (DB). 'Homestead or village of a man called Cuda'. OE pers. name + *hām*.

Cudworth Somerset. *Cudeworde* 1086 (DB). 'Enclosure of a man called Cuda'. OE pers. name + *worth*.

Cudworth S. Yorks. *Cutheworthe* 12th cent. 'Enclosure of a man called Cūtha'. OE pers. name + *worth*.

Cuffley Herts. *Kuffele* 1255. Probably 'woodland clearing of a man called *Cuffa'. OE pers. name + *lēah*.

Culcheth Ches. *Culchet* 1201. Probably 'narrow wood'. Celtic **cūl* + **cęd*.

Culford Suffolk. *Culeforda* 1086 (DB). 'Ford of a man called *Cūla'. OE pers. name + *ford*.

Culgaith Cumbria. *Culgait* 12th cent. Identical in origin with CULCHETH.

Culham Oxon. *Culanhom* 821. 'River-meadow of a man called *Cūla'. OE pers. name + *hamm*.

Culkerton Glos. *Cvlcortone* 1086 (DB). 'Farmstead with a water-hole, or belonging to a man called *Culcere'. OE **culcor* or OE pers. name + *tūn*.

Cullercoats Tyne & Wear. *Culvercoats c.*1600. 'Dove-cots'. OE *culfre* + *cot*.

Cullingworth W. Yorks. *Colingauuorde* 1086 (DB). 'Enclosure of the family or followers of a man called *Cūla'. OE pers. name + *-inga-* + *worth*.

Cullompton Devon. *Columtune c.*880, *Columb* (*sic*) 1086 (DB). 'Farmstead on the Culm river'. Celtic river-name (meaning 'winding stream') + OE *tūn*.

Culmington Shrops. *Comintone* (*sic*) 1086 (DB), *Culminton* 1197. Probably 'estate associated with a man called Cūthhelm'. OE pers. name + *-ing-* + *tūn*.

Culmstock Devon. *Culumstocc* 938, *Culmestoche* 1086 (DB). 'Outlying farmstead on the Culm river'. Celtic river-name (see CULLOMPTON) + OE *stoc*.

Culverthorpe Lincs. *Torp* 1086 (DB), *Calewarthorp* 1275. Originally simply 'outlying farmstead or hamlet' from OScand. *thorp*, later with the name of an owner added, form uncertain.

Culworth Northants. *Culeorde* 1086 (DB). 'Enclosure of a man called *Cūla'. OE pers. name + *worth*.

Cumberland (old county). *Cumbra land* 945. 'Region of the *Cymry* or Cumbrian Britons'. OE **Cumbre* + *land*.

Cumberworth, 'enclosure of a man called Cumbra, or of the Britons', OE pers. name or OE **Cumbre* + *worth*: **Cumberworth** Lincs. *Combreuorde* 1086 (DB). **Cumberworth, Lower & Upper** W. Yorks. *Cumbreuurde* 1086 (DB).

Cumbria (new county). *Cumbria* 8th cent. 'Territory of the *Cymry* or Cumbrian Britons'. A latinization of the Primitive Welsh form of *Cymry* 'the Welsh'.

Cummersdale Cumbria. *Cumbredal* 1227. 'Valley of the Cumbrian Britons'. OE **Cumbre* (genitive plural *-a*) + OScand. *dalr*.

Cumnor Oxon. *Cumanoran* 931, *Comenore* 1086 (DB). 'Hill-slope of a man called *Cuma'. OE pers. name (genitive *-n*) + *ōra*.

Cumrew Cumbria. *Cumreu* c.1200. 'Valley by the hill-slope'. Celtic **cumm* + **riu*.

Cumwhinton Cumbria. *Cumquintina* c.1155. 'Valley of a man called Quintin'. Celtic **cumm* + OFrench pers. name.

Cumwhitton Cumbria. *Cumwyditon* 1278. 'Valley at a place called *Whytington* (estate associated with a man called Hwīta)'. Celtic **cumm* added to an English place-name (from OE pers. name + *-ing-* + *tūn*).

Cundall N. Yorks. *Cundel* 1086 (DB). Probably originally OE *cumb* 'valley', later with the addition of an explanatory OScand. *dalr* 'valley'.

Curbridge Oxon. *Crydan brigce* 956. 'Bridge of a man called Creoda'. OE pers. name + *brycg*.

Curdridge Hants. *Cuthredes hricgæ* 901. 'Ridge of a man called Cūthrǣd'. OE pers. name + *hrycg*.

Curland Somerset. *Curiland* 1252. Probably 'cultivated land belonging to CURRY'. OE *land*.

Curry Mallet & Rivel, North Curry Somerset. *Curig* 9th cent., *Curi*, *Nortcuri* 1086 (DB), *Curi Malet*, *Curry Revel* 1225. 'Estates on the river called *Curi*'. Pre-English river-name (of uncertain origin and meaning), with distinguishing affixes from families called *Malet* and *Revel*, here from the late 12th cent., and from OE *north*.

Curthwaite, East & West Cumbria. *Kyrkthwate* 1272. 'Clearing near or belonging to a church'. OScand. *kirkja* + *thveit*.

Cury Cornwall. *Egloscuri* 1219. 'Church of St Cury' (a pet-form of St Corentin). From the patron saint of the church, with Cornish *eglos* 'church' in the early form.

Cusop Heref. & Worcs. *Cheweshope* 1086 (DB). OE *hop* 'small enclosed valley', first element possibly a lost Celtic river-name *Cyw*.

Cutsdean Glos. *Codestune* 10th cent., 1086 (DB), *Cottesdena* 12th cent. 'Farmstead and/or valley of a man called *Cōd'. OE pers. name + *tūn* and/or *denu*.

Cuxham Oxon. *Cuces hamm* 995, *Cuchesham* 1086 (DB). 'River-meadow of a man called *Cuc'. OE pers. name + *hamm*.

Cuxton Kent. *Cucolanstan* 880, *Coclestane* 1086 (DB). '(Boundary) stone of a man called *Cucola'. OE pers. name + *stān*.

Cuxwold Lincs. *Cucualt* 1086 (DB). 'Woodland of a man called *Cuca'. OE pers. name + *wald*.

D

Dacorum (district) Herts. *Danais* 1086 (DB), *hundredo Dacorum* 1196. '(Hundred) belonging to the Danes', from the genitive plural of Latin *Daci* 'the Dacians' (erroneously used of the Danes in medieval times).

Dacre Cumbria. *Dacor c.*1125. Named from the stream called Dacre Beck, a Celtic river-name meaning 'the trickling one'.

Dacre N. Yorks. *Dacre* 1086 (DB). Originally a Celtic river-name for the stream here, identical in origin with the previous name.

Dadford Bucks. *Dodeforde* 1086 (DB). 'Ford of a man called Dodda'. OE pers. name + *ford*.

Dadlington Leics. *Dadelintona c.*1190. Probably 'estate associated with a man called *Dæd(d)el'. OE pers. name + *-ing-* + *tūn*.

Dagenham Gtr. London. *Dæccanhaam c.*690. 'Homestead or village of a man called *Dæcca'. OE pers. name (genitive *-n*) + *hām*.

Daglingworth Glos. *Daglingworth c.*1150. 'Enclosure of the family or followers of a man called *Dæggel or *Dæccel', or 'enclosure associated with the same man'. OE pers. name + *-inga-* or *-ing-* + *worth*.

Dagnall Bucks. *Dagenhale* 1196. 'Nook of land of a man called *Dægga'. OE pers. name (genitive *-n*) + *healh*.

Dalby, 'farmstead or village in a valley', OScand. *dalr* + *bý*; examples include: **Dalby, Great & Little** Leics. *Dalbi* 1086 (DB). **Dalby, Low** N. Yorks. *Dalbi* 1086 (DB).

Dalderby Lincs. *Dalderby c.*1150. Possibly 'farmstead or village in a small valley', from OScand. *dæld* (genitive *-ar*) + *bý*. Alternatively 'valley farmstead where deer are kept', from OScand. *dalr* + *djúr* + *bý*.

Dale Derbys. *La Dale* late 12th cent. '(Place in) the valley'. OE *dæl*.

Dalham Suffolk. *Dalham* 1086 (DB). 'Homestead or village in a valley'. OE *dæl* + *hām*.

Dalling, Field & Wood Norfolk. *Dallinga* 1086 (DB), *Fildedalling* 1272, *Wode Dallinges* 1198. '(Settlement of) the family or followers of a man called Dalla'. OE pers. name + *-ingas*. The distinguishing affixes are *feld* or **filden* (denoting 'in the open country') and *wudu* (denoting 'in the woodland').

Dallinghoo Suffolk. *Dallingahou* 1086 (DB). 'Hill-spur of the family or followers of a man called Dalla'. OE pers. name + *-inga-* + *hōh*.

Dallington E. Sussex. *Dalintone* 1086 (DB). 'Estate associated with a man called Dalla'. OE pers. name + *-ing-* + *tūn*.

Dalston Cumbria. *Daleston* 1187. Probably 'farmstead of a man called *Dall'. OE pers. name + *tūn*.

Dalston Gtr. London. *Derleston* 1294. 'Farmstead of a man called Dēorlāf'. OE pers. name + *tūn*.

Dalton, a common place-name in the northern counties, 'farmstead or village in a valley', from OE *dæl* + *tūn*; examples include: **Dalton** Lancs. *Daltone* 1086 (DB). **Dalton** Northum., near Hexham. *Dalton* 1256. **Dalton** Northum., near Stamfordham. *Dalton* 1201. **Dalton** N. Yorks., near Richmond. *Daltun* 1086 (DB). **Dalton** N. Yorks., near Thirsk. *Deltune* 1086 (DB). **Dalton** S. Yorks. *Daltone* 1086 (DB). **Dalton in Furness** Cumbria. *Daltune* 1086 (DB), *Dalton in Fournais* 1332. For the district name Furness, see BARROW IN FURNESS. **Dalton-le-Dale** Durham. *Daltun* 8th cent. The addition means 'in the valley', from OE *dæl*. **Dalton,** North Humber. *Dalton* 1086 (DB), *Northdaltona c.*1155. **Dalton-on-Tees**

N. Yorks. *Dalton* 1204. On the River Tees. **Dalton Piercy** Cleveland. *Daltun c.*1150, *Dalton Percy* 1370. Manorial affix from the *Percy* family, here up to the 14th cent. **Dalton, South** Humber. *Delton* 1086 (DB), *Suthdalton* 1260.

Dalwood Devon. *Dalewude* 1195. 'Wood in a valley'. OE *dæl* + *wudu*.

Damerham Hants. *Domra hamme c.*880, *Dobreham* (*sic*) 1086 (DB). 'Enclosure or river-meadow of the judges'. OE *dōmere* + *hamm*.

Danbury Essex. *Danengeberiam* 1086 (DB). Probably 'stronghold of the family or followers of a man called Dene'. OE pers. name + *-inga-* + *burh* (dative *byrig*).

Danby N. Yorks. *Danebi* 1086 (DB). 'Farmstead or village of the Danes'. OScand. *Danir* (genitive plural *Dana*) + *bý*.

Danby Wiske N. Yorks. *Danebi* 1086 (DB), *Daneby super Wiske* 13th cent. Identical in origin with the previous name. Situated on the River Wiske (see APPLETON WISKE).

Dane (river) Ches., see DAVENHAM.

Danehill E. Sussex. *Denne* 1279, *Denhill* 1437. 'Hill by the woodland pasture'. OE *denn* with the later addition of *hyll*.

Darcy Lever Gtr. Manch., see LEVER.

Darenth Kent. *Daerintan* 10th cent., *Tarent* 1086 (DB). '(Estate on) the River Darent'. Darent is a Celtic river-name meaning 'river where oak-trees grow'.

Daresbury Ches. *Deresbiria* 12th cent. 'Stronghold of a man called Dēor'. OE pers. name + *burh* (dative *byrig*).

Darfield S. Yorks. *Dereuueld* 1086 (DB). 'Open land frequented by deer'. OE *dēor* + *feld*.

Darlaston W. Mids. *Derlaveston* 1262. 'Farmstead or village of a man called Dēorlāf'. OE pers. name + *tūn*.

Darley, 'woodland clearing frequented by deer or wild animals', OE *dēor* + *lēah*: **Darley Abbey** Derbys. *Derlega* 12th cent. **Darley Dale** Derbys. *Dereleie* 1086 (DB).

Darlingscott Warwicks. *Derlingescot* 1210. 'Cottage(s) of a man called *Dēorling'. OE pers. name + *cot*.

Darlington Durham. *Dearthingtun c.*1009. 'Estate associated with a man called Dēornōth'. OE pers. name + *-ing-* + *tūn*.

Darliston Shrops. *Derloueston* 1199. 'Farmstead of a man called Dēorlāf'. OE pers. name + *tūn*.

Darlton Notts. *Derluuetun* 1086 (DB). 'Farmstead of a woman called *Dēorlufu'. OE pers. name + *tūn*.

Darrington W. Yorks. *Darni(n)tone* 1086 (DB). Probably 'estate associated with a man called Dēornōth'. OE pers. name + *-ing-* + *tūn*.

Darsham Suffolk. *Dersham* 1086 (DB). 'Homestead or village of a man called Dēor'. OE pers. name + *hām*.

Dartford Kent. *Tarentefort* 1086 (DB). 'Ford over the River Darent'. Celtic river-name (see DARENTH) + OE *ford*.

Dartington Devon. *Dertrintona* 1086 (DB). 'Farmstead on the River Dart'. Celtic river-name (meaning 'river where oak-trees grow') + *-ing-* + *tūn*.

Dartmoor Devon. *Dertemora* 1182. 'Moor in the Dart valley'. Celtic river-name (see DARTINGTON) + OE *mōr*.

Dartmouth Devon. *Dertamuthan* 11th cent. 'Mouth of the River Dart'. Celtic river-name (see DARTINGTON) + OE *mūtha*.

Darton S. Yorks. *Dertun* 1086 (DB). 'Enclosure for deer, deer park'. OE *dēor-tūn*.

Darwen Lancs. *Derewent* 1208. '(Estate on) the River Darwen'. Darwen is a Celtic river-name meaning 'river where oak-trees grow'.

Dassett, Avon & Burton Warwicks. *Derceto(ne)* 1086 (DB), *Afnedereceth* 1185, *Burton Dassett* 1604. Probably 'fold or shelter for deer or other animals'. OE *dēor* + (*ge*)*set* or *cēte*. The distinguishing affixes are from the old Celtic name of the stream here (*Avon* meaning 'river, water') and from a nearby place (Burton is from OE *burh-tūn* 'fortified farmstead').

Datchet Berks. *Deccet* 10th cent., *Daceta* 1086 (DB). Probably an old Celtic name of uncertain meaning.

Datchworth Herts. *Decewrthe* 969,

Daceuuorde 1086 (DB). 'Enclosure of a man called *Dæcca'. OE pers. name + *worth*.

Dauntsey Wilts. *Dometesig* 850, *Dantesie* 1086 (DB). Probably 'island or well-watered land of a man called *Dōmgeat'. OE pers. name + *ieg*.

Davenham Ches. *Deveneham* 1086 (DB). 'Homestead or village on the River Dane'. Celtic river-name (meaning 'trickling stream') + OE *hām*.

Daventry Northants. *Daventrei* 1086 (DB). 'Tree of a man called *Dafa'. OE pers. name (genitive *-n*) + *trēow*.

Davidstow Cornwall. 'Church of *Sanctus David* (*alias Dewstow*)' 1269. 'Holy place of St David'. Saint's name (Cornish *Dewy*) + OE *stōw*.

Dawley Shrops. *Dalelie* 1086 (DB). 'Woodland clearing of a man called Dalla'. OE pers. name + *lēah*.

Dawlish Devon. *Douelis* 1086 (DB). Originally the name of the stream here, a Celtic river-name meaning 'dark stream'.

Daylesford Glos. *Dæglesford* 718, *Eilesford* (*sic*) 1086 (DB). 'Ford of a man called *Dægel'. OE pers. name + *ford*.

Deal Kent. *Addelam* (*sic*) 1086 (DB), *Dela* 1158. '(Place at) the hollow or valley', from OE *dæl* (with Latin preposition *ad* 'at' prefixed in the earliest spelling).

Dean, Deane, a common place-name, '(place in) the valley', from OE *denu*: **Dean** Cumbria. *Dene* c.1170. **Deane** Gtr. Manch. *Dene* 1292. **Deane** Hants. *Dene* 1086 (DB). **Dean, East & West** Hants. *Dene* 1086 (DB). **Dean, East & West** W. Sussex. *Dene* 8th cent., *Estdena, Westdena* 1150. **Dean, Forest of** Glos. *foresta de Dene* 12th cent. **Dean, Lower & Upper** Beds. *Dene* 1086 (DB), *Netherdeane, Overdeane* 1539. OE *neotherra* 'lower' and *uferra* 'upper'. **Dean Prior** Devon. *Denu* 1086 (DB), *Dene Pryour* 1415. Affix from its possession by Plympton Priory from the 11th cent.

Dearham Cumbria. *Derham* c.1160. 'Homestead or enclosure where deer are kept'. OE *dēor* + *hām* or *hamm*.

Dearne (river) S. Yorks., see BOLTON UPON DEARNE.

Debach Suffolk. *Depebecs* 1086 (DB). 'Valley of, or ridge by, the deep river'. OE *dēope* + *bece* or *bæc* (dative **bece*).

Debden Essex. *Deppedana* 1086 (DB). 'Deep valley'. OE *dēop* + *denu*.

Debden (Green) Essex. *Tippedene* 1062, *Tippedana* 1086 (DB). 'Valley of a man called *Tippa'. OE pers. name + *denu*, with the addition of *green* from the 18th cent.

Debenham Suffolk. *Depbenham* 1086 (DB). 'Homestead or village by the deep river'. OE *dēope* + *hām*.

Deddington Oxon. *Dædintun* 1050-2, *Dadintone* 1086 (DB). 'Estate associated with a man called Dǣda'. OE pers. name + *-ing-* + *tūn*.

Dedham Essex. *Delham* (*sic*) 1086 (DB), *Dedham* 1166. 'Homestead or village of a man called *Dydda'. OE pers. name + *hām*.

Dee (river) Ches. *Deoua* c.150. An ancient Celtic river-name meaning 'the goddess, the holy one'.

Deene Northants. *Den* 1065, *Dene* 1086 (DB). '(Place in) the valley'. OE *denu*.

Deenethorpe Northants. *Denetorp* 1169. 'Outlying farmstead or secondary settlement dependent on DEENE'. OScand. *thorp*.

Deepdale Cumbria. *Depedale* 1433. 'Deep valley'. OE *dēop* + *dæl*.

Deeping Gate Cambs. *Depynggate* 1390. 'Road to DEEPING' (see next name). OScand. *gata*.

Deeping St James & St Nicholas, Market & West Deeping Lincs. *Estdepinge, West Depinge* 1086 (DB). 'Deep or low place'. OE **dēoping*. Distinguishing affixes from the dedications of the churches, and from *market, east*, and *west*.

Deerhurst Glos. *Deorhyrst* 804, *Derheste* (*sic*) 1086 (DB). 'Wooded hill frequented by deer'. OE *dēor* + *hyrst*.

Defford Heref. & Worcs. *Deopanforda* 972, *Depeford* 1086 (DB). 'Deep ford'. OE *dēop* + *ford*.

Deighton, 'farmstead surrounded by a ditch', from OE *dīc* + *tūn*: **Deighton** N. Yorks., near Northallerton. *Dictune* 1086 (DB). **Deighton** N. Yorks., near York. *Distone* (*sic*) 1086 (DB), *Dicton* 1176. **Deighton, Kirk & North**

N. Yorks. *Distone* (*sic*) 1086 (DB), *Kirke Dighton* 14th cent., *Northdictun* 12th cent. Distinguishing affixes are OScand. *kirkja* 'church' and OE *north*.

Delamere Ches., named from the ancient Forest of Delamere, *foresta de la Mare* 13th cent., 'forest of the lake', from OE *mere* with the OFrench preposition and article *de la*.

Dembleby Lincs. *Dembelbi* 1086 (DB). 'Farmstead or village with a pool'. OScand. **dembil* + *bý*.

Denbury Devon. *Deveneberie* 1086 (DB). 'Earthwork or fortress of the Devon people'. OE *Defnas* (from Celtic *Dumnonii*) + *burh* (dative *byrig*).

Denby Derbys. *Denebi* 1086 (DB). 'Farmstead or village of the Danes'. OE *Dene* (genitive plural *Dena*) + OScand. *bý*.

Denby Dale W. Yorks. *Denebi* 1086 (DB). Identical in origin with the previous name, with the later addition of *dale* 'valley'.

Denchworth Oxon. *Deniceswurthe* 947, *Dencheswo rde* 1086 (DB). 'Enclosure of a man called *Denic'. OE pers. name + *worth*.

Denford Northants. *Deneforde* 1086 (DB). 'Ford in a valley'. OE *denu* + *ford*.

Denge Marsh Kent, see DUNGENESS.

Dengie Essex. *Deningei c.*707, *Daneseia* 1086 (DB). Probably 'island or well-watered land associated with a man called Dene, or of Dene's people'. OE pers. name + *-ing-* or *-inga-* + *ēg*.

Denham, 'homestead or village in a valley', OE *denu* + *hām*: **Denham** Bucks. *Deneham* 1066, *Daneham* 1086 (DB). **Denham** Suffolk, near Bury St Edmunds. *Denham* 1086 (DB). **Denham** Suffolk, near Eye. *Denham* 1086 (DB).

Denholme W. Yorks. *Denholme* 1252. 'Water-meadow in the valley'. OE *denu* + OScand. *holmr*.

Denmead Hants. *Denemede* 1205. 'Meadow in the valley'. OE *denu* + *mǣd*.

Dennington Suffolk. *Dingifetuna* 1086 (DB). 'Farmstead of a woman called *Denegifu'. OE pers. name + *tūn*.

Denston Suffolk. *Danerdestuna* 1086 (DB). 'Farmstead of a man called Deneheard'. OE pers. name + *tūn*.

Denstone Staffs. *Denestone* 1086 (DB). 'Farmstead of a man called Dene'. OE pers. name + *tūn*.

Dent Cumbria. *Denet* 1202–8. Possibly an old river-name, origin and meaning uncertain.

Denton, a common place-name, usually 'farmstead or village in a valley', from OE *denu* + *tūn*; examples include: **Denton** Cambs. *Dentun* 10th cent., *Dentone* 1086 (DB). **Denton** Durham. *Denton* 1200. **Denton** E. Sussex. *Denton* 9th cent. **Denton** Gtr. Manch. *Denton c.*1220. **Denton** Kent, near Dover. *Denetun* 799, *Danetone* 1086 (DB). **Denton** Lincs. *Dentune* 1086 (DB). **Denton** Norfolk. *Dentuna* 1086 (DB). **Denton** N. Yorks. *Dentun c.*972, 1086 (DB). **Denton** Oxon. *Denton* 1122. **Denton, Upper & Nether** Cumbria. *Denton* 1169.

However the following Denton has a different origin: **Denton** Northants. *Dodintone* 1086 (DB). 'Estate associated with a man called Dodda or Dudda'. OE pers. name + *-ing-* + *tūn*.

Denver Norfolk. *Danefella* (*sic*) 1086 (DB); *Denever* 1200. 'Ford or passage used by the Danes'. OE *Dene* (genitive plural *Dena*) + *fær*.

Denwick Northum. *Den(e)wyc* 1242. 'Dwelling or dairy-farm in a valley'. OE *denu* + *wīc*.

Deopham Norfolk. *Depham* 1086 (DB). 'Homestead or village near the deep place or lake'. OE *dēope* + *hām*.

Depden Suffolk. *Depdana* 1086 (DB). 'Deep valley'. OE *dēop* + *denu*.

Deptford, 'deep ford', OE *dēop* + *ford*: **Deptford** Gtr. London. *Depeforde* 1293. **Deptford** Wilts. *Depeford* 1086 (DB).

Derby Derbys. *Deoraby* 10th cent., *Derby* 1086 (DB). 'Farmstead or village where deer are kept'. OScand. *djúr* + *bý*. **Derbyshire** (OE *scīr* 'district') is first referred to in the 11th cent.

Derby, West Mersey. *Derbei* 1086 (DB), *Westderbi* 1177. Identical in origin with the previous name.

Dereham, East & West Norfolk. *Der(e)ham* 1086 (DB), *Estderham* 1428, *Westderham* 1203. 'Homestead or enclosure where deer are kept'. OE *dēor* + *hām* or *hamm*.

Derrington Staffs. *Dodintone* 1086 (DB). 'Estate associated with a man called Dod(d)a or Dud(d)a'. OE pers. name + *-ing-* + *tūn*.

Derrythorpe Humber. *Dodithorp* 1263. Probably 'outlying farmstead or hamlet of a man called Dod(d)ing'. OE pers. name + OScand. *thorp*.

Dersingham Norfolk. *Dersincham* 1086 (DB). 'Homestead of the family or followers of a man called Dēorsige'. OE pers. name + *-inga-* + *hām*.

Derwent (river), four examples, in Cumbria, Derbys., Durham, and Yorks.; a Celtic river-name recorded from the 8th cent. in the form *Deruuentionis fluvii* 'river where oak-trees grow abundantly'.

Desborough Northants. *Dereburg* (*sic*) 1086 (DB), *Deresburc* 1166. 'Stronghold or fortress of a man called Dēor'. OE pers. name + *burh*.

Desford Leics. *Deresford* 1086 (DB). 'Ford of a man called Dēor'. OE pers. name + *ford*.

Detchant Northum. *Dichende* 1166. 'End of the ditch or dike'. OE *dīc* + *ende*.

Detling Kent. *Detlinges* 11th cent. '(Settlement of) the family or followers of a man called *Dyttel'. OE pers. name + *-ingas*.

Devizes Wilts. *Divises* 11th cent. '(Place on) the boundaries'. OFrench *devise*.

Devon (the county). *Defena, Defenascir* late 9th cent. '(Territory of) the Devonians, earlier called the *Dumnonii*'. OE tribal name *Defnas* (from Celtic *Dumnonii*) + *scīr* 'district'.

Devonport Devon, a modern self-explanatory name only in use since 1824.

Dewchurch, Much & Little Heref. & Worcs. *Lann Deui* 7th cent., *Dewischirche* c.1150. 'Church of St Dewi'. Saint's name (the Welsh form of David) + OE *cirice* (with OWelsh *lann* in the early form). Distinguishing affixes are OE *micel* 'great' and *lȳtel* 'little'.

Dewlish Dorset. *Devenis* (*sic*) 1086 (DB), *Deueliz* 1194. Originally the name of the stream here, a Celtic river-name meaning 'dark stream'.

Dewsbury W. Yorks. *Deusberia* 1086 (DB). 'Stronghold of a man called Dewi'. OWelsh pers. name + OE *burh* (dative *byrig*).

Dibden (Purlieu) Hants. *Depedene* 1086 (DB). 'Deep valley'. OE *dēop* + *denu*. The addition is from ME *purlewe* 'outskirts of a forest'.

Dicker, Lower & Upper E. Sussex. *Diker* 1229. From ME *dyker* 'ten', probably alluding to a plot of land for which this number of iron rods was paid in rent.

Dickleburgh Norfolk. *Dicclesburc* 1086 (DB). Possibly 'stronghold of a man called *Dicel or *Dicla'. OE pers. name + *burh*.

Didbrook Glos. *Duddebrok* 1248. 'Brook of a man called *Dyd(d)a'. OE pers. name + *brōc*.

Didcot Oxon. *Dudecota* 1206. 'Cottage(s) of a man called Dud(d)a'. OE pers. name + *cot*.

Diddington Cambs. *Dodinctun* 1086 (DB). 'Estate associated with a man called Dod(d)a or Dud(d)a'. OE pers. name + *-ing-* + *tūn*.

Diddlebury Shrops. *Dudelebire* 1167. 'Stronghold or manor of a man called *Dud(d)ela'. OE pers. name + *burh* (dative *byrig*).

Didley Heref. & Worcs. *Dodelegie* 1086 (DB). 'Woodland clearing of a man called Dod(d)a or Dud(d)a'. OE pers. name + *lēah*.

Didmarton Glos. *Dydimeretune* 972, *Dedmertone* 1086 (DB). 'Boundary farmstead of a man called Dyd(d)a'. OE pers. name + *mǣre* + *tūn*.

Didsbury Gtr. Manch. *Dedesbiry* 1246. 'Stronghold of a man called *Dyd(d)i'. OE pers. name + *burh* (dative *byrig*).

Digby Lincs. *Dicbi* 1086 (DB). 'Farmstead or village at the ditch'. OE *dīc* or OScand. *díki* + *bý*.

Dilham Norfolk. *Dilham* 1086 (DB). 'Homestead or enclosure where dill grows'. OE *dile* + *hām* or *hamm*.

Dilhorne Staffs. *Dulverne* 1086 (DB). 'House or building by a pit or quarry'. OE **dylf* + *ærn*.

Dilston Northum. *Deuelestune* 1172. 'Farmstead by the dark stream'. Celtic river-name + OE *tūn*.

Dilton Marsh Wilts. *Dulinton* 1190. Probably 'farmstead of a man called *Dulla'. OE pers. name (genitive *-n*) + *tūn*.

Dilwyn Heref. & Worcs. *Dilven* 1086 (DB). '(Settlement at) the shady or secret places'. OE *dīgle* in a dative plural form *dīglum*.

Dinchope Shrops. *Doddinghop* 12th cent. 'Enclosed valley associated with a man called Dudda', or 'valley at Dudda's place'. OE pers. name + *-ing-* or *-ing* + *hop*.

Dinder Somerset. *Dinre* 1174. Probably 'hill with a fort'. Celtic **din* + **breȝ*.

Dinedor Heref. & Worcs. *Dunre* 1086 (DB). Identical in origin with the previous name.

Dingley Northants. *Dinglei* 1086 (DB). Possibly 'woodland clearing with hollows'. OE *lēah* with ME *dingle*.

Dinmore Heref. & Worcs., see HOPE.

Dinnington Somerset. *Dinnitone* 1086 (DB). 'Estate associated with a man called Dynne'. OE pers. name + *-ing-* + *tūn*.

Dinnington S. Yorks. *Dunintone* 1086 (DB). 'Estate associated with a man called Dunn(a)'. OE pers. name + *-ing-* + *tūn*.

Dinnington Tyne & Wear. *Donigton* 1242. Probably identical in origin with the previous name.

Dinsdale, Low Durham. *Ditneshall* c.1185. 'Nook of land belonging to DEIGHTON (N. Yorks)'. OE *halh*.

Dinton, 'estate associated with a man called Dunn(a)', OE pers. name + *-ing-* + *tūn*: **Dinton** Bucks. *Danitone* (*sic*) 1086 (DB), *Duninton* 1208. **Dinton** Wilts. *Domnitone* (*sic*) 1086 (DB), *Dunyngtun* 12th cent.

Diptford Devon. *Depeforde* 1086 (DB). 'Deep ford'. OE *dēop* + *ford*.

Dipton Durham. *Depeden* 1339. 'Deep valley'. OE *dēop* + *denu*.

Diptonmill Northum. *Depeden* 1269. Identical in origin with the previous name, with the later addition of *mill*.

Diseworth Leics. *Digtheswyrthe* c.972, *Diwort* 1086 (DB). 'Enclosure of a man called *Digoth'. OE pers. name + *worth*.

Dishforth N. Yorks. *Disforde* 1086 (DB). 'Ford across a ditch'. OE *dīc* + *ford*.

Disley Ches. *Destesleg* c.1251. OE *lēah* 'wood, woodland clearing' with an obscure first element, possibly an OE **dystels* 'mound or heap'.

Diss Norfolk. *Dice* 1086 (DB). '(Place at) the ditch or dike'. OE *dīc*.

Distington Cumbria. *Dustinton* c.1230. OE *tūn* 'farmstead, estate' with an obscure first element, possibly a pers. name.

Ditchburn Northum. *Dicheburn* 1236. 'Ditch stream'. OE *dīc* + *burna*.

Ditcheat Somerset. *Dichesgate* 842, *Dicesget* 1086 (DB). 'Gap in the dyke or earthwork'. OE *dīc* + *geat*.

Ditchingham Norfolk. *Dicingaham* 1086 (DB). 'Homestead of the dwellers at a ditch or dyke', or 'homestead of the family or followers of a man called *Dic(c)a or *Dīca'. OE *dīc* or OE pers. name + *-inga-* + *hām*.

Ditchling E. Sussex. *Dicelinga* 765, *Dicelinges* 1086 (DB). '(Settlement of) the family or followers of a man called *Dīcel'. OE pers. name + *-ingas*.

Dittisham Devon. *Didasham* 1086 (DB). 'Enclosure or promontory of a man called *Dyddi'. OE pers. name + *hamm*.

Ditton, usually 'farmstead by a ditch or dike', OE *dīc* + *tūn*: **Ditton** Ches. *Ditton* 1194. **Ditton** Kent. *Dictun* 10th cent., *Dictune* 1086 (DB). **Ditton, Fen** Cambs. *Dictunæ* c.975, *Fen Dytton* 1286. Affix is OE *fenn* 'fen, marshland'. **Ditton, Long & Thames** Surrey. *Dictun* 1005, *Ditune* 1086 (DB), *Longa Dittone* 1242, *Temes Ditton* 1235. Distinguishing affixes are OE *lang* 'long' (alluding to the length of the village) and THAMES from the river.

However the following has a different origin: **Ditton Priors** Shrops. *Dodintone* 1086 (DB). 'Estate associated with a man called Dod(d)a or Dud(d)a'. OE pers. name + *-ing-* + *tūn*. Manorial affix from its possession by Wenlock Priory.

Dixton Glos. *Dricledone* 1086 (DB), *Diclisdon* 1169. Probably 'down of the hill with dikes or earthworks'. OE *dīc* + *hyll* + *dūn*. Alternatively the first element may be an OE pers. name **Dīcel* or **Diccel*.

Docking Norfolk. *Doccynge* c.1035, *Dochinga* 1086 (DB). 'Place where docks or water-lilies grow'. OE *docce* + *-ing*.

Docklow Heref. & Worcs. *Dockelawe* 1291. 'Mound or hill where docks grow'. OE *docce* + *hlāw*.

Dockray Cumbria. *Docwra* 1278. 'Nook of land where docks or water-lilies grow'. OE *docce* + OScand. *vrá*.

Doddinghurst Essex. *Doddenhenc* (*sic*) 1086 (DB), *Duddingeherst* 1218. 'Wooded hill of the family or followers of a man called Dudda or Dodda'. OE pers. name + *-inga-* + *hyrst*.

Doddington, Dodington, 'estate associated with a man called Dud(d)a or Dod(d)a', OE pers. name + *-ing-* + *tūn*: **Doddington** Cambs. *Dundingtune* (*sic*) c.975, *Dodinton* 1086 (DB). **Doddington** Kent. *Duddingtun* c.1100. **Doddington** Lincs. *Dodin(c)tune* 1086 (DB). **Doddington** Northum. *Dodinton* 1207. **Doddington** Shrops. *Dodington* 1285. **Doddington, Dry** Lincs. *Dodintune* 1086 (DB). Affix from OE *drȳge* 'dry'. **Doddington, Great** Northants. *Dodintone* 1086 (DB), *Great Dodington* 1290. **Dodington** Avon. *Dodintone* 1086 (DB).

Doddiscombsleigh Devon. *Leuga* 1086 (DB), *Doddescumbeleghe* 1309. Originally 'the woodland clearing', OE *lēah*. Later addition from the *Doddescumb* family, here in the 13th cent.

Dodford, 'ford of a man called Dodda', OE pers. name + *ford*: **Dodford** Heref. & Worcs. *Doddeford* 1232. **Dodford** Northants. *Doddanford* 944, *Dodeforde* 1086 (DB).

Dodington Avon, see DODDINGTON.

Dodleston Ches. *Dodestune* (*sic*) 1086 (DB), *Dodleston* 1153. 'Farmstead of a man called *Dod(d)el'. OE pers. name + *tūn*.

Dodworth S. Yorks. *Dodesuu(o)rde* 1086 (DB). 'Enclosure of a man called Dod(d) or Dod(d)a'. OE pers. name + *worth*.

Dogdyke Lincs. *Dockedic* 12th cent. 'Ditch where docks or water-lilies grow'. OE *docce* + *dīc*.

Dolphinholme Lancs. *Dolphineholme* 1591. 'Island or water-meadow of a man called Dolgfinnr'. OScand. pers. name + *holmr*.

Dolton Devon. *Duueltone* 1086 (DB). Possibly 'farmstead in the open country frequented by doves'. OE *dūfe* + *feld* + *tūn*.

Doncaster S. Yorks. *Doneceastre* 1002, *Donecastre* 1086 (DB). 'Roman fort on the River Don'. Celtic river-name (meaning simply 'water, river') + OE *ceaster*.

Donhead St Andrew & St Mary Wilts. *Dunheved* 871, *Duneheve* 1086 (DB), *Dounheved Sanct Andree* 1302, *Donheved Sancte Marie* 1298. 'Head or end of the down'. OE *dūn* + *hēafod*. Affixes from the dedications of the churches.

Donington, Donnington, usually 'estate associated with a man called Dun(n) or Dun(n)a', OE pers. name + *-ing-* + *tūn* (possibly in some cases 'estate at the hill-place', OE **dūning* + *tūn*); examples include: **Donington** Lincs. *Dunictune* 1086 (DB). **Donington, Castle** Leics. *Duni(n)tone* 1086 (DB), *Castel Donyngton* 1428. Affix refers to a former castle here. **Donington le Heath** Leics. *Duntone* 1086 (DB), *Donygton super le heth* 1462. Affix means 'on the heath', from OE *hǣth*. **Donington on Bain** Lincs. *Duninctune* 1086 (DB), *Donygton super Beyné* 13th cent. Affix from its situation on the River Bain ('the short one', from OScand. *beinn*). **Donnington** Berks. *Deritone* (*sic*) 1086 (DB), *Dunintona* 1086 (DB). **Donnington** Glos. *Doninton* c.1195. **Donnington** Heref. & Worcs. *Dunninctune* 1086 (DB). **Donnington** Shrops., near Eaton Constantine. *Dunniton* 1180. **Donnington** Shrops., near Oakengates. *Donnyton* 1272.

However the following has a different origin: **Donnington** W. Sussex. *Dunketone* 966, *Cloninctune* (*sic*) 1086 (DB). 'Farmstead of a man called *Dunnuca'. OE pers. name + *tūn*.

Donisthorpe Leics. *Durandestorp* 1086 (DB). 'Outlying farmstead or hamlet of a man called Durand'. OFrench pers. name + OScand. *thorp*.

Donnington, see DONINGTON.

Donyatt Somerset. *Duunegete* 8th cent., *Doniet* 1086 (DB). Probably 'gate or gap of a man called Dun(n)a'. OE pers. name + *geat.*

Dorchester Dorset. *Durnovaria* 4th cent., *Dornwaraceaster* 864, *Dorecestre* 1086 (DB). 'Roman town called *Durnovaria*'. Reduced form of Celtic name (perhaps meaning 'place with fist-sized pebbles') + OE *ceaster.*

Dorchester Oxon. *Dorciccaestræ* 731, *Dorchecestre* 1086 (DB). 'Roman town called *Dorcic*'. Celtic name (obscure in origin and meaning) + OE *ceaster.*

Dordon Warwicks. *Derdon* 13th cent. 'Hill frequented by deer or other wild animals'. OE *dēor* + *dūn.*

Dore S. Yorks. *Dore* late 9th cent., 1086 (DB). '(Place at) the gate or narrow pass'. OE *dor.*

Dore, Abbey Heref. & Worcs. *Dore* 1147. Named from the River Dore, a Celtic river-name meaning simply 'the waters'. Affix from the former Cistercian Abbey here.

Dorking Surrey. *Dorchinges* 1086 (DB). '(Settlement of) the family or followers of a man called *Deorc'. OE pers. name + *-ingas.*

Dormans Land Surrey. *Deremanneslond* 1263. 'Cultivated land or estate of the *Dereman* family'. OE *land,* with the surname of a local family.

Dormanstown Cleveland, a modern name for a new town planned in 1918 for the employees of the manufacturing firm Dorman Long.

Dormington Heref. & Worcs. *Dorminton* 1206. 'Estate associated with a man called Dēormōd or Dēormund'. OE pers. name + *-ing-* + *tūn.*

Dorney Bucks. *Dornei* 1086 (DB). 'Island, or dry ground in marsh, frequented by bumble-bees'. OE *dora* (genitive plural *dorena*) + *ēg.*

Dorridge W. Mids. *Derrech* 1400. 'Ridge frequented by deer or wild animals'. OE *dēor* + *hrycg.*

Dorrington Lincs. *Derintone* 1086 (DB). 'Estate associated with a man called Dēor(a)'. OE pers. name + *-ing-* + *tūn.*

Dorrington Shrops., near Condover. *Dodinton* 1198. 'Estate associated with a man called Dod(d)a'. OE pers. name + *-ing-* + *tūn.*

Dorset (the county). *Dornsætum* late 9th cent. '(Territory of) the people around *Dorn*'. Reduced form of *Dornwaraceaster* (see DORCHESTER) + OE *sǣte.*

Dorsington Warwicks. *Dorsintune* 1086 (DB). 'Estate associated with a man called Dēorsige'. OE pers. name + *-ing-* + *tūn.*

Dorstone Heref. & Worcs. *Dodintune* (*sic*) 1086 (DB), *Dorsington* c.1138. Possibly identical in origin with the previous name.

Dorton Bucks. *Dortone* 1086 (DB). 'Farmstead or village at the narrow pass'. OE *dor* + *tūn.*

Dosthill Staffs. *Dercelai* (*sic*) 1086 (DB), *Dercetehill* 1242. Possibly 'hill with a fold or shelter for deer or other animals'. OE *dēor* + (*ge*)*set* or *cēte* + *hyll.*

Doughton Glos. *Ductune* 775–8. 'Duck farmstead'. OE *dūce* + *tūn.*

Doulting Somerset. *Dulting* 725, *Doltin* 1086 (DB). Originally the old name of the River Sheppey on which Doulting stands, probably of Celtic origin but of unknown meaning.

Dovenby Cumbria. *Duuaneby* 1230. 'Farmstead or village of a man called Dufan'. OIrish pers. name + OScand. *bý.*

Dover Kent. *Dubris* 4th cent., *Dofras* c.700, *Dovere* 1086 (DB). Named from the stream here, now called the Dour, a Celtic river-name **dubrās* meaning simply 'the waters'.

Dovercourt Essex. *Douorcortae* c.1000, *Druurecurt* (*sic*) 1086 (DB). Possibly 'enclosed farmyard by the river called *Dover*'. Celtic river-name (meaning 'the waters') + OE **cort(e)* (perhaps from Latin *cohors, cohortem*).

Doverdale Heref. & Worcs. *Douerdale* 706, *Lunvredele* 1086 (*sic*) (DB). 'Valley of the river called *Dover*'. Celtic river-name (meaning 'the waters') + OE *dæl.*

Doveridge Derbys. *Dubrige* 1086 (DB), *Duvebruge* 1252. 'Bridge over the River

Dove'. Celtic river-name (meaning 'the dark one') + OE *brycg*.

Dowdeswell Glos. *Dogodeswellan* 8th cent., *Dodesuuelle* 1086 (DB). 'Spring or stream of a man called *Dogod'. OE pers. name + *wella*.

Dowland Devon. *Duuelande* 1086 (DB). Possibly 'estate in the open country frequented by doves'. OE *dūfe* + *feld* + *land*.

Dowlish Wake Somerset. *Duuelis* 1086 (DB), *Duueliz Wak* 1243. Named from the stream here, a Celtic river-name meaning 'dark stream'. Manorial addition from the *Wake* family, here in the 12th cent.

Down Ampney Glos., see AMPNEY.

Down, Downe, '(place at) the hill', OE *dūn*: **Down, East & West** Devon. *Duna* 1086 (DB), *Estdoune* 1260, *Westdone* 1273. **Down St Mary** Devon. *Done* 1086 (DB), *Dune St Mary* 1297. Affix from the dedication of the church. **Downe** Gtr. London. *Doune* 1316.

Downham, usually 'homestead on or near a hill', OE *dūn* + *hām*: **Downham** Cambs. *Duneham* 1086 (DB). **Downham** Essex. *Dunham* 1168. **Downham Market** Norfolk. *Dunham* c.1050, 1086 (DB). Affix from the market here, referred to as early as the 11th cent.

However the following have a different origin, '(place at) the hills', from OE *dūn* in the dative plural form *dūnum*: **Downham** Lancs. *Dunum* 1194. **Downham** Northum. *Dunum* 1186.

Down Hatherley Glos., see HATHERLEY.

Downhead Somerset. *Duneafd* 851, *Dunehefde* 1086 (DB). 'Head or end of the down'. OE *dūn* + *hēafod*.

Downholme N. Yorks. *Dune* 1086 (DB), *Dunum* 12th cent. '(Place at) the hills'. OE *dūn* in a dative plural form *dūnum*.

Downton, 'farmstead on or by the hill or down', OE *dūn* + *tūn*: **Downton** Wilts. *Duntun* 672, *Duntone* 1086 (DB). **Downton on the Rock** Heref. & Worcs. *Duntune* 1086 (DB). Affix from ME *rokke* 'a rock or peak'.

Dowsby Lincs. *Dusebi* 1086 (DB). 'Farmstead or village of a man called Dúsi'. OScand. pers. name + *bý*.

Doxey Staffs. *Dochesig* 1086 (DB). 'Island, or dry ground in marsh, of a man called *Docc'. OE pers. name + *ēg*.

Doynton Avon. *Didintone* 1086 (DB). 'Estate associated with a man called *Dydda'. OE pers. name + *-ing-* + *tūn*.

Draughton, 'farmstead on a slope used for dragging down timber and the like', OScand. *drag* + OE *tūn*: **Draughton** Northants. *Dractone* 1086 (DB). **Draughton** N. Yorks. *Dractone* 1086 (DB).

Drax N. Yorks. *Drac* 1086 (DB), *Drachs* 11th cent. 'The portages, or places where boats are dragged overland or pulled up from the water'. OScand. *drag*.

Drax, Long N. Yorks. *Langrak* 1208. 'Long stretch of river'. OE *lang* + **racu*.

Draycote, Draycott, a common place-name, probably 'shed where drays or sledges are kept', OE *dræg* + *cot*; examples include: **Draycote** Warwicks. *Draicote* 1203. **Draycott** Derbys. *Draicot* 1086 (DB). **Draycott** Somerset, near Cheddar. *Draicote* 1086 (DB). **Draycott in the Clay** Staffs. *Draicote* 1086 (DB). Affix 'in the clayey district', from OE *clǣg*. **Draycott in the Moors** Staffs. *Draicot* 1251. Affix 'in the moorland', from OE *mōr*.

Drayton, a common place-name, 'farmstead at or near a portage or slope used for dragging down loads', or 'farmstead where drays or sledges are used', OE *dræg* + *tūn*; examples include: **Drayton** Norfolk. *Draituna* 1086 (DB). **Drayton** Oxon., near Banbury. *Draitone* 1086 (DB). **Drayton** Oxon., near Didcot. *Draitune* 958, *Draitone* 1086 (DB). **Drayton** Somerset, near Curry Rivel. *Drayton* 1243. **Drayton Bassett** Staffs. *Draitone* 1086 (DB), *Drayton Basset* 1301. Manorial affix from the *Basset* family, here in the 12th cent. **Drayton Beauchamp** Bucks. *Draitone* 1086 (DB), *Drayton Belcamp* 1239. Manorial affix from the *Beauchamp* family, here in the 13th cent. **Drayton, Dry** Cambs. *Draitone* 1086 (DB), *Driedraiton* 1218. Affix from OE *drȳge* to distinguish it from FEN DRAYTON. **Drayton, East & West** Notts. *Draitone, Draitun* 1086 (DB), *Est Draiton* 1276, *West Draytone* 1269.

Drayton, Fen Cambs. *Drægtun* 1012, *Draitone* 1086 (DB), *Fendreiton* 1188. Affix from OE *fenn* 'marshland' in contrast to DRY DRAYTON. **Drayton, Fenny** Leics. *Draitone* 1086 (DB), *Fenedrayton* 1465. Affix is OE *fennig* 'muddy, marshy'. **Drayton, Market** Shrops. *Draitune* 1086 (DB). Affix from the important market here. **Drayton Parslow** Bucks. *Draitone* 1086 (DB), *Drayton Passelewe* 1254. Manorial affix from the *Passelewe* family, here in the 11th cent. **Drayton, West** Gtr. London. *Drægtun* 939, *Draitone* 1086 (DB), *Westdrayton* 1465.

Drewsteignton Devon. *Taintone* 1086 (DB), *Teyngton Drue* 1275. 'Farmstead or village on the River Teign'. Celtic river-name (see TEIGNMOUTH) + OE *tūn* + manorial affix from a man called *Drew*, here in the 13th cent.

Driby Lincs. *Dribi* 1086 (DB). 'Dry farmstead or village'. OE *drȳge* + OScand. *bý*.

Driffield, 'open land characterized by dirt, or by stubble', OE *drit* or *drīf* + *feld*: **Driffield** Glos. *Drifelle* (*sic*) 1086 (DB), *Driffeld* 1190. **Driffield, Great & Little** Humber. *Drifeld* 1086 (DB).

Drigg Cumbria. *Dreg* 12th cent. 'The portage, or place where boats are dragged overland or pulled up from the water'. OScand. **dræg*.

Drighlington W. Yorks. *Dreslin(g)tone* (*sic*) 1086 (DB), *Drichtlington* 1202. 'Estate associated with a man called *Dryhtel or *Dyrhtla'. OE pers. name + *-ing-* + *tūn*.

Drimpton Dorset. *Dremeton* 1244. 'Farmstead of a man called *Drēama'. OE pers. name + *tūn*.

Drinkstone Suffolk. *Drincestune* c.1050, *Drencestuna* 1086 (DB). 'Farmstead of a man called *Dremic'. OE pers. name + *tūn*.

Drointon Staffs. *Dregetone* (*sic*) 1086 (DB), *Drengeton* 1199. Probably 'farmstead of the free tenants'. OScand. *drengr* + OE *tūn*.

Droitwich Heref. & Worcs. *Wich* 1086 (DB), *Drihtwych* 1347. 'Dirty or muddy salt-works'. OE *wīc* with the later addition of OE *drit* 'dirt'.

Dronfield Derbys. *Dranefeld* 1086 (DB). 'Open land infested with drones'. OE *drān* + *feld*.

Droxford Hants. *Drocenesforda* 826, *Drocheneford* 1086 (DB). OE *ford* 'ford', with an obscure first element, possibly an OE **drocen* 'dry place'.

Droylsden Gtr. Manch. *Driilisden* c.1250. Possibly 'valley of the dry spring or stream'. OE *drȳge* + *well(a)* + *denu*.

Drybeck Cumbria. *Dribek* 1256. 'Stream which sometimes dries up'. OE *drȳge* + OScand. *bekkr*.

Drybrook Glos. *Druybrok* 1282. 'Brook which sometimes dries up'. OE *drȳge* + *brōc*.

Dry Doddington Lincs., see DODDINGTON.

Dry Drayton Cambs., see DRAYTON.

Duckington Ches. *Dochintone* 1086 (DB). 'Estate associated with a man called *Ducc(a)'. OE pers. name + *-ing-* + *tūn*.

Ducklington Oxon. *Duclingtun* 958, *Dochelintone* 1086 (DB). Probably 'estate associated with a man called *Ducel'. OE pers. name + *-ing-* + *tūn*.

Duckmanton, Long Derbys. *Ducemannestune* c.1002, *Dochemanestun* 1086 (DB). 'Farmstead of a man called *Ducemann'. OE pers. name + *tūn*.

Duddenhoe End Essex. *Dudenho* 12th cent. 'Spur of land or ridge of a man called Dudda'. OE pers. name (genitive *-n*) + *hōh*, with the addition of *end* 'district' from the 18th cent.

Duddington Northants. *Dodintone* 1086 (DB). 'Estate associated with a man called Dud(d)a or Dod(d)a'. OE pers. name + *-ing-* + *tūn*.

Duddo Northum. *Dudehou* 1208–10. 'Spur of land or ridge of a man called Dud(d)a'. OE pers. name + *hōh*.

Duddon Ches. *Dudedun* 1185. 'Hill of a man called Dud(d)a'. OE pers. name + *dūn*.

Duddon (river) Lancs., Cumbria, see DUNNERDALE.

Dudleston Shrops. *Dodeleston* 1267. 'Farmstead of a man called Dud(d)el or *Dod(d)el'. OE pers. name + *tūn*.

Dudley W. Mids. *Dudelei* 1086 (DB).

'Woodland clearing of a man called Dud(d)a'. OE pers. name + *lēah*.

Duffield, 'open land frequented by doves', OE *dūfe* + *feld*: **Duffield** Derbys. *Duvelle* (*sic*) 1086 (DB), *Duffeld* 12th cent. **Duffield, North & South** N. Yorks. *Dufeld, Nortdufelt, Suddufeld* 1086 (DB).

Dufton Cumbria. *Dufton* 1256. 'Farmstead where doves are kept'. OE *dūfe* + *tūn*.

Duggleby N. Yorks. *Difgelibi* 1086 (DB). 'Farmstead or village of a man called Dubgall or Dubgilla'. OIrish pers. name + OScand. *bý*.

Dukinfield Gtr. Manch. *Dokenfeld* 12th cent. 'Open land where ducks are found'. OE *dūce* (genitive plural *dūcena*) + *feld*.

Dullingham Cambs. *Dullingham* c.1045, *Dullingeham* 1086 (DB). 'Homestead of the family or followers of a man called *Dull(a)'. OE pers. name + *-inga-* + *hām*.

Duloe Cornwall. *Dulo* 1283. 'Place between the two rivers called Looe'. Cornish *dew* 'two' + river-names from Cornish **logh* 'pool'.

Dulverton Somerset. *Dolvertune* 1086 (DB). Possibly 'farmstead near the hidden ford'. OE *dīegel* + *ford* + *tūn*.

Dulwich Gtr. London. *Dilwihs* 967. 'Marshy meadow where dill grows'. OE *dile* + *wisc*.

Dumbleton Glos. *Dumbeltun* 995, *Dubentune* (*sic*) 1086 (DB). Probably 'farmstead near a shady glen or hollow'. OE **dumbel* + *tūn*.

Dummer Hants. *Dunmere* 1086 (DB). 'Pond on a hill'. OE *dūn* + *mere*.

Dunchurch Warwicks. *Donecerce* (*sic*) 1086 (DB), *Duneschirche* c.1150. Probably 'church of a man called Dun(n)'. OE pers. name + *cirice*.

Duncote Northants. *Dunecote* 1227. 'Cottage(s) of a man called Dun(n)a'. OE pers. name + *cot*.

Duncton W. Sussex. *Donechitone* 1086 (DB). 'Farmstead of a man called *Dunnuca'. OE pers. name + *tūn*.

Dundon Somerset. *Dondeme* (*sic*) 1086 (DB), *Dunden* 1236. 'Valley by the hill'. OE *dūn* + *denu*.

Dundraw Cumbria. *Drumdrahrigg* 1194. 'Slope of the ridge'. Celtic *drum* + OScand. *drag* (with OScand. *hryggr* 'ridge' in the 12th cent. form).

Dundry Avon. *Dundreg* 1065. Possibly 'slope of the hill (used for dragging down loads)', OE *dūn* + *dræg*. Alternatively perhaps a Celtic name for Dundry Hill from **din* 'fort' with another element.

Dungeness Kent. *Dengenesse* 1335. 'Headland (OE *næss*) near Denge Marsh', the latter being *Dengemersc* 774, 'marsh of the valley district' from OE *denu* + **gē* + *mersc*.

Dunham, 'homestead or village at a hill', OE *dūn* + *hām*: **Dunham** Notts. *Duneham* 1086 (DB). **Dunham, Great & Little** Norfolk. *Dunham* 1086 (DB). **Dunham on the Hill** Ches. *Doneham* 1086 (DB), *Dunham on the Hill* 1534. Affix from OE *hyll*. **Dunham Town** Gtr. Manch. *Doneham* 1086 (DB).

Dunhampton Heref. & Worcs. *Dunhampton* 1222. 'Homestead or home farm by the hill'. OE *dūn* + *hām-tūn*.

Dunholme Lincs. *Duneham* 1086 (DB). 'Homestead or village at a hill'. OE *dūn* + *hām*.

Dunkeswell Devon. *Doducheswelle* (*sic*) 1086 (DB), *Dunekeswell* 1219. 'Spring or stream of a man called Duduc or *Dunnuc'. OE pers. name + *wella*.

Dunmow, Great & Little Essex. *Dunemowe* 951, *Dommawa* 1086 (DB). 'Meadow on the hill'. OE *dūn* + **māwe*.

Dunnerdale, Hall Cumbria. *Dunerdale* 1293. 'Valley of the River Duddon'. River-name of uncertain origin and meaning + OScand. *dalr*. Affix probably *hall* 'manor house'.

Dunnington Humber. *Dodintone* 1086 (DB). 'Estate associated with a man called Dud(d)a'. OE pers. name + *-ing-* + *tūn*.

Dunnington N. Yorks. *Donniton* 1086 (DB). 'Estate associated with a man called Dun(n)a'. OE pers. name + *-ing-* + *tūn*.

Dunnockshaw Lancs. *Dunnockschae* 1296. 'Small wood or copse frequented by hedge-sparrows'. OE **dunnoc* + *sceaga*.

Dunsby Lincs., near Rippingale. *Dunesbi* 1086 (DB). 'Farmstead or village of a man called Dun(n)'. OE pers. name + OScand. *bý*.

Dunsden Green Oxon. *Dunesdene* 1086 (DB), *Donsden grene* 1589. 'Valley of a man called Dyn(n)e'. OE pers. name + *denu*, with *grēne* 'village green' added from the 16th cent.

Dunsfold Surrey. *Duntesfaude* 1259. 'Fold or small enclosure of a man called *Dunt'. OE pers. name + *fald*.

Dunsford Devon. *Dun(n)esforda* 1086 (DB). 'Ford of a man called Dun(n)'. OE pers. name + *ford*.

Dunsforth, Lower & Upper N. Yorks. *Doneford(e)*, *Dunesford* 1086 (DB). Identical in origin with the previous name.

Dunsley N. Yorks. *Dunesle* 1086 (DB). 'Woodland clearing of a man called Dun(n)'. OE pers. name + *lēah*.

Dunsmore (old district) Warwicks., see RYTON-ON-DUNSMORE.

Dunstable Beds. *Dunestaple* 1123. 'Boundary post of a man called Dun(n)a'. OE pers. name + *stapol*.

Dunstall Staffs. *Tunstall* 13th cent. 'Site of a farm, a farmstead'. OE **tūn-stall*.

Dunstan Northum. *Dunstan* 1242. 'Stone or rock on a hill'. OE *dūn* + *stān*.

Dunster Somerset. *Torre* 1086 (DB), *Dunestore* 1138. 'Craggy hill-top of a man called Dun(n)'. OE pers. name + *torr*.

Duns Tew Oxon., see TEW.

Dunston, 'farmstead of a man called Dun(n)', OE pers. name + *tūn*: **Dunston** Lincs. *Dunestune* 1086 (DB). **Dunston** Norfolk. *Dunestun* 1086 (DB). **Dunston** Staffs. *Dunestone* 1086 (DB).

Dunterton Devon. *Dondritone* 1086 (DB). OE *tūn* 'farmstead', possibly added to an old Celtic name meaning 'fort village' (**din* + *tre*).

Duntisbourne Abbots, Leer, & Rouse Glos. *Duntesburne* 1055, *Dantesborne*, *Tantesborne*, *Duntesborne* 1086 (DB), *Duntesbourn Abbatis* 1291, *Duntesbourn Lyre* 1307, *Duntesbourn Rus* 1287. 'Stream of a man called *Dunt'. OE pers. name + *burna*. Manorial affixes from possession in medieval times by the Abbot of St Peter's Abbey at Gloucester, by the Abbey of Lire in Normandy, and by the family of *le Rous*.

Duntish Dorset. *Dunhethis* 1249. 'Pasture on a hill'. OE *dūn* + **etisc*.

Dunton Beds. *Donitone* 1086 (DB). Probably 'farmstead on a hill'. OE *dūn* + *tūn*.

Dunton Bucks. *Dodintone* 1086 (DB). 'Estate associated with a man called Dud(d)a or Dod(d)a'. OE pers. name + *-ing-* + *tūn*.

Dunton Norfolk. *Dontuna* 1086 (DB). 'Farmstead on a hill'. OE *dūn* + *tūn*.

Dunton Bassett Leics. *Donitone* 1086 (DB), *Dunton Basset* 1418. Probably identical with the previous name. Manorial affix from the *Basset* family, here in the 12th cent.

Dunton Green Kent. *Dunington* 1244. 'Estate associated with a man called Dun(n) or Dun(n)a'. OE pers. name + *-ing-* + *tūn*.

Dunwich Suffolk. *Domnoc* 731, *Duneuuic* 1086 (DB). An old Celtic name possibly meaning 'deep water' to which OE *wīc* 'harbour, village' was later added.

Durdle Door Dorset. *Dirdale Door* 1811. In spite of the lack of early spellings the first element may be OE *thyrelod* 'pierced' with *duru* 'door, opening'.

Durham Durham. *Dunholm c.*1000. 'Island with a hill'. OE *dūn* + OScand. *holmr*.

Durleigh Somerset. *Derlege* 1086 (DB). 'Wood or clearing frequented by deer'. OE *dēor* + *lēah*.

Durley Hants. *Deorleage* 901, *Derleie* 1086 (DB). Identical in origin with the previous name.

Durnford, Great Wilts. *Diarneford* 1086 (DB). 'Hidden ford'. OE *dierne* + *ford*.

Durrington, 'estate associated with a man called Dēor(a)', OE pers. name + *-ing-* + *tūn*: **Durrington** W. Sussex. *Derentune* 1086 (DB). **Durrington** Wilts. *Derintone* 1086 (DB).

Dursley Glos. *Dersilege* 1086 (DB). 'Woodland clearing of a man called Dēorsige'. OE pers. name + *lēah*.

Durston Somerset. *Derstona* 1086 (DB). 'Farmstead of a man called Dēor'. OE pers. name + *tūn*.

Durweston Dorset. *Derwinestone* 1086 (DB). 'Farmstead of a man called Dēorwine'. OE pers. name + *tūn*.

Duston Northants. *Dustone* 1086 (DB). 'Farmstead on a mound', or 'farmstead with dusty soil'. OE **dus* or *dūst* + *tūn*.

Dutton Ches. *Duntune* 1086 (DB). 'Farmstead at a hill'. OE *dūn* + *tūn*.

Duxford Cambs. *Dukeswrthe c.*950, *Dochesuuorde* 1086 (DB). 'Enclosure of a man called *Duc(c)'. OE pers. name + *worth*.

Dyke Lincs. *Dic* 1086 (DB). '(Place at) the ditch or dike'. OE *dīc*.

Dymchurch Kent. *Deman circe c.*1100. 'Church of the judge, or of a man called *Dema'. OE *dēma* or OE pers. name + *cirice*.

Dymock Glos. *Dimoch* 1086 (DB). Possibly from Celtic **din* 'fort' + adjectival suffix.

Dyrham Avon. *Deorhamme* 950, *Dirham* 1086 (DB). 'Enclosed valley frequented by deer'. OE *dēor* + *hamm*.

E

Eagle Lincs. *Aclei, Aycle* 1086 (DB). 'Wood where oak-trees grow'. OE *āc* (replaced by OScand. *eik*) + OE *lēah*.

Eaglesfield Cumbria. *Eglesfeld c.*1170. 'Open land near a Romano-British Christian church'. Celtic **eglēs* + OE *feld*.

Eakring Notts. *Ecringhe* 1086 (DB). 'Ring or circle of oak-trees'. OScand. *eik* + *hringr*.

Ealand Humber. *Aland* 1316. 'Cultivated land by water or by a river'. OE *ēa-land*.

Ealing Gtr. London. *Gillingas c.*698. '(Settlement of) the family or followers of a man called *Gilla'. OE pers. name + *-ingas*.

Eamont Bridge Cumbria. *Eamotum* 11th cent., *Amotbrig* 1362. 'Bridge at the river-confluences'. OE *ēa-mōt* (replaced by OScand. *á-mót*) + *brycg*.

Earby Lancs. *Eurebi* 1086 (DB). 'Upper farmstead', or 'farmstead of a man called Jǫfurr'. OScand. *efri* or pers. name + *bý*.

Eardington Shrops. *Eardigtun c.*1030, *Ardintone* 1086 (DB). 'Estate associated with a man called *Earda'. OE pers. name + *-ing-* + *tūn*.

Eardisland Heref. & Worcs. *Lene* 1086 (DB), *Erleslen* 1230. 'Nobleman's estate in *Leon*'. OE *eorl* added to old Celtic name for the district (see LEOMINSTER).

Eardisley Heref. & Worcs. *Herdeslege* 1086 (DB). 'Woodland clearing of a man called Ægheard'. OE pers. name + *lēah*.

Eardiston Heref. & Worcs. *Eardulfestun c.*957, *Ardolvestone* 1086 (DB). 'Farmstead of a man called Eardwulf'. OE pers. name + *tūn*.

Earith Cambs. *Herheth* 1244. 'Muddy or gravelly landing place'. OE *ēar* + *hȳth*.

Earle Northum. *Yherdhill* 1242. 'Hill with a fence or enclosure'. OE *geard* + *hyll*.

Earlham Norfolk. *Erlham* 1086 (DB). Possibly 'homestead of a nobleman'. OE *eorl* + *hām*.

Earl or **Earl's** as affix, see main name, e.g. for **Earl's Barton** (Northants.) see BARTON.

Earnley W. Sussex. *Earneleagh* 8th cent. 'Wood or woodland clearing where eagles are seen'. OE *earn* + *lēah*.

Earsdon Tyne & Wear. *Erdesdon* 1233. Probably 'hill of a man called Ēanrǣd or Eorǣd'. OE pers. name + *dūn*.

Earsham Norfolk. *Ersam* 1086 (DB). Possibly 'homestead or village of a man called Ēanhere'. OE pers. name + *hām*.

Earswick N. Yorks. *Edresuuic* (*sic*) 1086 (DB), *Etherícewyk* 13th cent. 'Dwelling or farm of a man called Æthelrīc'. OE pers. name + *wīc*.

Eartham W. Sussex. *Ercheham* (*sic*) 12th cent., *Ertham* 1279. 'Homestead or enclosure with ploughed land'. OE *erth* + *hām* or *hamm*.

Easby N. Yorks., near Stokesley. *Esebi* 1086 (DB). 'Farmstead or village of a man called Ēsi'. OScand. pers. name + *bý*.

Easebourne W. Sussex. *Eseburne* 1086 (DB). 'Stream of a man called Ēsa'. OE pers. name + *burna*.

Easenhall Warwicks. *Esenhull* 1221. 'Hill of a man called Ēsa'. OE pers. name (genitive *-n*) + *hyll*.

Easington, usually 'estate associated with a man called Ēsa', OE pers. name + *-ing-* + *tūn*: **Easington** Bucks. *Hesintone* 1086 (DB). **Easington** Cleveland. *Esingetun* 1086 (DB). **Easington** Durham. *Esingtun c.*1050. **Easington** Humber. *Esintone* 1086 (DB). However the following have different origins: **Easington** Northum. *Yesington* 1242. Possibly an old name for the stream here + OE *tūn* 'farmstead'. **Easington** Oxon., near Cuxham. *Esidone* 1086 (DB). 'Hill of a man called Ēsa'. OE pers. name (genitive *-n*) + *dūn*.

Easingwold N. Yorks. *Eisincewald* 1086 (DB). 'High forest-land of the family or followers of a man called Ēsa'. OE pers. name + *-inga-* + *wald*.

Easole Street Kent. *Oesewalum* 824, *Eswalt* 1086 (DB). Possibly 'ridges or banks associated with a god or gods'. OE *ēs, ōs* + *walu*.

East as affix, see main name, e.g. for **East Allington** (Devon) see ALLINGTON.

Eastbourne E. Sussex. *Burne* 1086 (DB), *Estbourne* 1310. '(Place at) the stream'. OE *burna*, with the later addition of *ēast* 'east' to distinguish it from WESTBOURNE.

Eastburn W. Yorks. *Estbrune* 1086 (DB). 'East stream', or '(land lying) east of the stream'. OE *ēast* or *ēastan* + *burna*.

Eastbury Berks. *Eastbury c.*1090. 'East manor'. OE *ēast* + *burh* (dative *byrig*).

Eastchurch Kent. *Eastcyrce c.*1100. 'East church'. OE *ēast* + *cirice*.

Eastcote, Eastcott, 'eastern cottage(s)', OE *ēast* + *cot*; examples include: **Eastcote** Gtr. London. *Estcotte* 1248. **Eastcott** Wilts., near Potterne. *Estcota* 1167.

Eastcourt Wilts., near Crudwell. *Escote* 901. Identical in origin with the previous two names.

Eastdean E. Sussex. *Esdene* 1086 (DB). 'East valley'. OE *ēast* + *denu*.

Easter, Good & High Essex. *Estre* 11th cent., *Estra* 1086 (DB), *Godithestre* 1200, *Heyestre* 1254. '(Place at) the sheep-fold'. OE *eowestre*. Distinguishing affixes from possession in Anglo-Saxon times by a woman called Gōdgȳth or Gōdgifu, and from OE *hēah* 'high'.

Eastergate W. Sussex. *Gate* 1086 (DB), *Estergat* 1263. '(Place at) the gate or gap'. OE *geat*, with the later addition of *ēasterra* 'more easterly' to distinguish it from WESTERGATE.

Easterton Wilts. *Esterton* 1348. 'More easterly farmstead'. OE *ēasterra* + *tūn*.

Eastham Mersey. *Estham* 1086 (DB). 'East homestead or enclosure'. OE *ēast* + *hām* or *hamm*.

Easthampstead Berks. *Lachenestede* 1086 (DB), *Yethamstede* 1176. 'Homestead by the gate or gap'. OE *geat* + *hām-stede*.

Easthope Shrops. *Easthope* 901, *Stope* (*sic*) 1086 (DB). 'Eastern enclosed valley'. OE *ēast* + *hop*.

Easthorpe Essex. *Estorp* 1086 (DB). 'Eastern outlying farmstead or hamlet'. OE *ēast* + OScand. *thorp*.

Eastington Glos., near Stonehouse. *Esteueneston* 1220. 'Farmstead of a man called Ēadstān'. OE pers. name + *tūn*.

Eastleach Martin & Turville Glos. *Lecche* 862, *Lec(c)e* 1086 (DB), *Estleche Sancti Martini* 1291, *Estleche Roberti de Tureuill* 1221. 'Eastern estate on the River Leach'. OE *ēast* + river-name from OE **læc(c), *lece* 'stream flowing through boggy land'. Affixes from the dedication of the church and from the *de Turville* family, here from the 13th cent.

Eastleigh Hants. *East lea* 932, *Estleie* 1086 (DB). 'East wood or clearing'. OE *ēast* + *lēah*.

Eastling Kent. *Eslinges* 1086 (DB). '(Settlement of) the family or followers of a man called Ēsla'. OE pers. name + *-ingas*.

Eastney Hants. *Esteney* 1242. '(Place in) the east of the island'. OE *ēastan* + *ēg*.

Eastnor Heref. & Worcs. *Astenofre* 1086 (DB). '(Place to) the east of the ridge'. OE *ēastan* + **ofer*.

Eastoft Humber. *Eschetoft c.*1170. 'Homestead or curtilage where ash-trees grow'. OScand. *eski* + *toft*.

Easton, a very common place-name, usually 'east farmstead or village', i.e. one to the east of another settlement, OE *ēast* + *tūn*; examples include: **Easton** Cambs. *Estone* 1086 (DB). **Easton** Cumbria, near Netherby. *Estuna* 12th cent. **Easton** Hants., near Winchester. *Eastun* 825, *Estune* 1086 (DB). **Easton** I. of Wight. *Estetune* 1244. **Easton** Lincs. *Estone* 1086 (DB). **Easton** Norfolk. *Estuna* 1086 (DB). **Easton**

Suffolk, near Framlingham. *Estuna* 1086 (DB). **Easton, Crux** Hants. *Eastun* 801, *Estune* 1086 (DB), *Eston Croc* 1242. Manorial addition from a family called *Croc(h)*, here in the 11th cent. **Easton, Great** Leics. *Estone* 1086 (DB). **Easton Grey** Wilts. *Estone* 1086 (DB), *Eston Grey* 1281. Manorial addition from the *de Grey* family, here in the 13th cent. **Easton in Gordano** Avon. *Estone* 1086 (DB), *Eston in Gordon* 1293. Affix is an old district name, see CLAPTON. **Easton Maudit** Northants. *Estone* 1086 (DB), *Estonemaudeut* 1298. Manorial affix from the *Mauduit* family, here in the 12th cent. **Easton on the Hill** Northants. *Estone* 1086 (DB). Affix from its situation on the brow of a hill. **Easton Royal** Wilts. *Estone* 1086 (DB). Affix from OFrench *roial* 'royal' referring to its situation on the edge of an old royal forest. **Easton, Ston** Somerset. *Estone* 1086 (DB), *Stonieston* 1230. Affix from OE *stānig* 'stony' referring to stony ground.

However some Eastons have a different origin, among them: **Easton, Great & Little** Essex. *E(i)stanes* 1086 (DB). Probably 'stones by the island or well-watered land'. OE *ēg* + *stān*.

Eastrea Cambs. *Estereie c.*1020. 'Eastern part of the island (of WHITTLESEY)'. OE **ēastor* + *ēg*.

Eastrington Humber. *Eastringatun* 959, *Estrincton* 1086 (DB). Probably 'farmstead of those living to the east (of HOWDEN)'. OE **ēastor* + *-inga-* + *tūn*.

Eastry Kent. *Eastorege* 9th cent., *Estrei* 1086 (DB). 'Eastern district or region'. OE **ēastor* + **gē*.

Eastwell Leics. *Estwelle* 1086 (DB). 'Eastern spring or stream'. OE *ēast* + *wella*.

Eastwick Herts. *Esteuuiche* 1086 (DB). 'East dwelling or (dairy) farm'. OE *ēast* + *wīc*.

Eastwood Essex. *Estuuda* 1086 (DB). 'Eastern wood'. OE *ēast* + *wudu*.

Eastwood Notts. *Estewic* (*sic*) 1086 (DB), *Estweit* 1165. 'East clearing'. OE *ēast* + OScand. *thveit*.

Eathorpe Warwicks. *Ethorpe* 1232. 'Outlying farmstead or hamlet on the river'. OE *ēa* + OScand. *thorp*.

Eaton, a common place-name with two different origins. Most are 'farmstead by a river', from OE *ēa* + *tūn*, among them: **Eaton** Ches., near Congleton. *Yeiton c.*1262. **Eaton** Norfolk. *Ettune* 1086 (DB). **Eaton** Notts. *Etune* 1086 (DB). **Eaton** Oxon. *Eatun* 9th cent., *Eltune* (*sic*) 1086 (DB). **Eaton** Shrops., near Bishop's Castle. *Eton* 1252. **Eaton** Shrops., near Ticklerton. *Eton* 1227. **Eaton Bishop** Heref. & Worcs. *Etune* 1086 (DB), *Eton Episcopi* 1316. Affix from its possession by the Bishop (Latin *episcopus*) of Hereford. **Eaton, Castle** Wilts. *Ettone* 1086 (DB). The affix is found from the 15th cent. **Eaton Constantine** Shrops. *Etune* 1086 (DB), *Eton Costentyn* 1285. Manorial affix from the *de Costentin* family, here in the 13th cent. **Eaton Hastings** Oxon. *Etone* 1086 (DB), *Eton Hastinges* 1298. Manorial affix from the *de Hastinges* family, here in the 12th cent. **Eaton Socon** Cambs. *Etone* 1086 (DB). Affix from OE *sōcn* 'district with a right of jurisdiction'. **Eaton upon Tern** Shrops. *Eton c.*1223. On the River Tern, a Celtic river-name meaning 'the strong one'.

However other Eatons have a different origin, 'farmstead on dry ground in marsh, or on well-watered land', from OE *ēg* + *tūn*, among them: **Eaton** Ches., near Tarporley. *Eyton* 1240. **Eaton** Leics. *Aitona c.*1125. **Eaton Bray** Beds. *Eitone* 1086 (DB). Manorial affix from the *Bray* family, here in the 15th cent. **Eaton, Little** Derbys. *Detton* (*sic*) 1086 (DB), *Little Eton* 1392. **Eaton, Long** Derbys. *Aitune* 1086 (DB), *Long Eyton* 1288. Affix refers to length of village.

Ebberston N. Yorks. *Edbriztune* 1086 (DB). 'Farmstead of a man called Ēadbeorht'. OE pers. name + *tūn*.

Ebbesbourne Wake Wilts. *Eblesburna* 826, *Eblesborne* 1086 (DB), *Ebbeleburn Wak* 1249. Probably 'stream of a man called *Ebbel'. OE pers. name + *burna*, with manorial affix from the *Wake* family, here in the 12th cent.

Ebchester Durham. *Ebbecestr* 1230. 'Roman fort of a man called Ebba or Ebbe'. OE pers. name + *ceaster*.

Ebrington Glos. *Bristentune* (*sic*) 1086 (DB), *Edbrihttona* 1155. 'Farmstead of a man called Ēadbeorht'. OE pers. name + *tūn*.

Ecchinswell Hants. *Eccleswelle* 1086 (DB). Possibly 'stream of a man called *Eccel'. OE pers. name + *wella*. Alternatively the first element may be Celtic **eglēs* 'Romano-British Christian church'.

Eccles, from Celtic **eglēs* 'Romano-British Christian church'; examples include: **Eccles** Gtr. Manch. *Eccles* c.1200. **Eccles** Kent. *Æcclesse* c.975, *Aiglessa* 1086 (DB).

Ecclesfield S. Yorks. *Eclesfeld* 1086 (DB). 'Open land near a Romano-British Christian church'. Celtic **eglēs* + OE *feld*.

Eccleshall Staffs. *Ecleshelle* (*sic*) 1086 (DB), *Eccleshale* 1227. 'Nook of land near a Romano-British Christian church'. Celtic **eglēs* + OE *halh*.

Eccleston, 'farmstead by a Romano-British Christian church', Celtic **eglēs* + OE *tūn*: **Eccleston** Ches. *Eclestone* 1086 (DB). **Eccleston** Lancs. *Aycleton* 1094. **Eccleston** Mersey. *Ecclistona* 1190. **Eccleston, Great & Little** Lancs. *Eglestun* 1086 (DB), *Great Ecleston* 1285, *Parua Eccliston* 1261.

Eccup W. Yorks. *Echope* 1086 (DB). 'Enclosed valley of a man called Ecca'. OE pers. name + *hop*.

Eckington, 'estate associated with a man called Ecca or Ecci', OE pers. name + *-ing-* + *tūn*: **Eckington** Derbys. *Eccingtune* c.1002, *Eckintune* 1086 (DB). **Eckington** Heref. & Worcs. *Eccyncgtun* 972, *Aichintune* 1086 (DB).

Ecton Northants. *Echentone* 1086 (DB). 'Farmstead of a man called Ecca'. OE pers. name + *tūn*.

Edale Derbys. *Aidele* 1086 (DB). 'Valley with an island or well-watered land'. OE *ēg* + *dæl*.

Edburton W. Sussex. *Eadburgeton* 12th cent. 'Farmstead of a woman called Ēadburh'. OE pers. name + *tūn*.

Edenbridge Kent. *Eadelmesbregge* c.1100. 'Bridge of a man called Ēadhelm'. OE pers. name + *brycg*. The river-name Eden is a 'back-formation' from the place-name.

Eden, Castle Durham. *Iodene* c.1050. Named from Eden Burn, a Celtic river-name meaning simply 'water' (with OE *burna* 'stream'). The later affix presumably refers to the 18th cent. mansion here.

Edenfield Gtr. Manch. *Aytounfeld* 1324. 'Open land by the island farmstead, or by the farmstead on well-watered land'. OE *ēg* + *tūn* + *feld*.

Edenhall Cumbria. *Edenhal* 1159. 'Nook of land by the River Eden'. Celtic river-name (meaning simply 'water') + OE *halh*.

Edenham Lincs. *Edeneham* 1086 (DB). 'Homestead or enclosure of a man called Ēada'. OE pers. name (genitive *-n*) + *hām* or *hamm*.

Edensor Derbys. *Edensoure* 1086 (DB). 'Sloping bank or ridge of a man called *Ēadin'. OE pers. name + **ofer*.

Edgbaston W. Mids. *Celboldestone* (*sic*) 1086 (DB), *Egbaldestone* 1184. 'Farmstead of a man called Ecgbald'. OE pers. name + *tūn*.

Edgcott Bucks. *Achecote* 1086 (DB). Probably 'cottage(s) made of oak'. OE *ǣcen* + *cot*.

Edge Shrops. *Egge* 1276. '(Place at) the edge or escarpment'. OE *ecg*.

Edgefield Norfolk. *Edisfelda* 1086 (DB). 'Open land by an enclosure or enclosed park'. OE *edisc* + *feld*.

Edgmond Shrops. *Edmendune* (*sic*) 1086 (DB), *Egmendon* 1165. 'Hill of a man called Ecgmund'. OE pers. name + *dūn*.

Edgton Shrops. *Egedune* 1086 (DB). 'Hill with an edge or escarpment, or of a man called Ecga'. OE *ecg* or pers. name + *dūn*.

Edgware Gtr. London. *Ægces wer* c.975. 'Weir or fishing-enclosure of a man called Ecgi'. OE pers. name + *wer*.

Edgworth Lancs. *Eggewrthe* 1212. Probably 'enclosure on an edge or hillside'. OE *ecg* + *worth*.

Edingale Staffs. *Ednunghale* 1086 (DB). 'Nook of land of the family or followers of a man called *Ēadin'. OE pers. name + *-inga-* + *halh*.

Edingley Notts. *Eddyngleia* c.1180. 'Woodland clearing associated with a man called Eddi'. OE pers. name + *-ing-* + *lēah*.

Edingthorpe Norfolk. *Edmestorp* 1198. Probably 'outlying farmstead or hamlet of a man called Ēadhelm'. OE pers. name + OScand. *thorp*.

Edington Somerset. *Eduuintone* 1086 (DB). 'Farmstead of a man called Ēadwine or of a woman called Ēadwynn'. OE pers. name + *tūn*.

Edington Wilts. *Ethandune* late 9th cent., *Edendone* 1086 (DB). 'Uncultivated hill', or 'hill of a man called Ētha'. OE *ēthe* (genitive *-an*) or OE pers. name (genitive *-n*) + *dūn*.

Edith Weston Leics., see WESTON.

Edlesborough Bucks. *Eddinberge* (*sic*) 1086 (DB), *Eduluesberga* 1163. 'Hill or barrow of a man called Ēadwulf'. OE pers. name + *beorg*.

Edlingham Northum. *Eadwulfincham* *c*.1050. 'Homestead of the family or followers of a man called Ēadwulf', or 'homestead at Ēadwulf's place'. OE pers. name + *-inga-* or *-ing* + *hām*.

Edlington, 'estate associated with a man called *Ēdla', OE pers. name + *-ing-* + *tūn*: **Edlington** Lincs. *Ellingetone* (*sic*) 1086 (DB), *Edlingtuna* *c*.1115. **Edlington** S. Yorks. *Ellintone* (*sic*) 1086 (DB), *Edelington* 1194–9.

Edmondsham Dorset. *Amedesham* 1086 (DB). 'Homestead or enclosure of a man called *Ēadmōd or Ēadmund'. OE pers. name + *hām* or *hamm*.

Edmondthorpe Leics. *Edmerestorp* 1086 (DB). 'Outlying farmstead or hamlet of a man called Ēadmǣr'. OE pers. name + OScand. *thorp*.

Edmonton Gtr. London. *Adelmetone* 1086 (DB). 'Farmstead of a man called Ēadhelm'. OE pers. name + *tūn*.

Edstaston Shrops. *Stanestune* (*sic*) 1086 (DB), *Edestaneston* 1256. 'Farmstead of a man called Ēadstān'. OE pers. name + *tūn*.

Edstone, Great N. Yorks. *Micheledestun* 1086 (DB). 'Farmstead of a man called *Ēadin'. OE pers. name + *tūn*. Affix in the early form is OE *micel* 'great'.

Edvin Loach Heref. & Worcs. *Gedeuen* 1086 (DB), *Yedefen Loges* 1242. 'Fen or marshland of a man called *Gedda'. OE pers. name + *fenn*. Manorial affix from the *de Loges* family, here in the 13th cent.

Edwalton Notts. *Eduvoltone* 1086 (DB). 'Farmstead of a man called Ēadweald'. OE pers. name + *tūn*.

Edwardstone Suffolk. *Eduardestuna* 1086 (DB). 'Farmstead of a man called Ēadweard'. OE pers. name + *tūn*.

Edwinstowe Notts. *Edenestou* 1086 (DB). 'Holy place of St Ēadwine'. OE pers. name + *stōw*.

Effingham Surrey. *Epingeham* (*sic*) 1086 (DB), *Effingeham* 1180. 'Homestead of the family or followers of a man called *Effa'. OE pers. name + *-inga-* + *hām*.

Egerton Kent. *Eardingtun* (*sic*) *c*.1100, *Egarditon* 1203. 'Estate associated with a man called Ecgheard'. OE pers. name + *-ing-* + *tūn*.

Egerton Green Ches. *Eggerton* 1259. Probably 'farmstead of a man called Ecghere'. OE pers. name + *tūn*. *Green* is added from the 18th cent.

Eggborough, High & Low N. Yorks. *Egeburg* 1086 (DB). 'Stronghold of a man called Ecga'. OE pers. name + *burh*.

Egg Buckland Devon, see BUCKLAND.

Eggington Beds. *Ekendon* 1195. Probably 'hill of a man called Ecca'. OE pers. name (genitive *-n*) + *dūn*.

Egginton Derbys. *Ecgintune* 1012, *Eghintune* 1086 (DB). 'Estate associated with a man called Ecga'. OE pers. name + *-ing-* + *tūn*.

Egglescliffe Cleveland. *Eggascliff* 1085. Probably 'cliff or bank near a Romano-British Christian church'. Celtic **eglęs* + OE *clif*.

Eggleston Durham. *Egleston* 1196. Probably 'farmstead of a man called *Ecgel'. OE pers. name + *tūn*.

Egham Surrey. *Egeham* 933, 1086 (DB). 'Homestead or village of a man called Ecga'. OE pers. name + *hām*.

Egleton Leics. *Egoluestun* 1218. 'Farmstead of a man called Ecgwulf'. OE pers. name + *tūn*.

Eglingham Northum. *Ecgwulfincham* *c*.1050. 'Homestead of the family or followers of a man called Ecgwulf', or 'homestead at Ecgwulf's place'. OE pers. name + *-inga-* or *-ing* + *hām*.

Egloshayle Cornwall. *Egloshail* 1166. 'Church on an estuary'. Cornish *eglos* + **heyl*.

Egloskerry Cornwall. *Egloskery* c.1145. 'Church of St Keri'. Cornish *eglos* + saint's name.

Egmanton Notts. *Agemuntone* 1086 (DB). 'Farmstead of a man called Ecgmund'. OE pers. name + *tūn*.

Egremont Cumbria. *Egremont* c.1125. 'Sharp-pointed hill'. OFrench *aigre* + *mont*.

Egton N. Yorks. *Egetune* 1086 (DB). 'Farmstead of a man called Ecga'. OE pers. name + *tūn*.

Elberton Avon. *Eldbertone* (*sic*) 1086 (DB), *Albricton* 1186. 'Farmstead of a man called Æthelbeorht'. OE pers. name + *tūn*.

Elburton Devon. *Aliberton* 1254. Identical in origin with the previous name.

Elcombe Wilts. *Elecome* 1086 (DB). 'Valley where elder-trees grow', or 'valley of a man called Ella'. OE *elle(n)* or OE pers. name + *cumb*.

Eldersfield Heref. & Worcs. *Yldresfeld* 972, *Edresfelle* (*sic*) 1086 (DB). 'Open land of the elder-tree, or of a man called Ealdhere'. OE *elle(n)* or pers. name + *feld*.

Eldwick W. Yorks. *Helguic* 1086 (DB). 'Dwelling or (dairy) farm of a man called Helgi'. OScand. pers. name + OE *wīc*.

Eleigh, Brent & Monks Suffolk. *Illanlege* c.995, *Illeleia* 1086 (DB), *Brendeylleye* 1312, *Monekesillegh* 1304. 'Woodland clearing of a man called *Illa'. OE pers. name + *lēah*. Affixes are from ME *brende* 'burnt, destroyed by fire' and OE *munuc* 'a monk' (alluding to possession by St Paul's in London).

Elford, 'ford where elder-trees grow', or 'ford of a man called Ella', OE *elle(n)* or OE pers. name + *ford*: **Elford** Northum. *Eleford* 1256. **Elford** Staffs. *Elleford* 1002, *Eleford* 1086 (DB).

Elham Kent. *Alham* 1086 (DB). 'Homestead or enclosure where eels are found'. OE *ǣl* + *hām* or *hamm*.

Eling Hants. *Edlinges* 1086 (DB). '(Settlement of) the family or followers of a man called *Ēadla or Æthel'. OE pers. name + *-ingas*.

Elkesley Notts. *Elchesleie* 1086 (DB). 'Woodland clearing of a man called Ēalāc'. OE pers. name + *lēah*.

Elkington, North & South Lincs. *Alchinton* 1086 (DB), *Northalkinton* 12th cent., *Sudhelkinton* early 13th cent. 'Estate associated with a man called Ēalāc'. OE pers. name + *-ing-* + *tūn*.

Elkstone Glos. *Elchestane* 1086 (DB). 'Boundary stone of a man called Ēalāc'. OE pers. name + *stān*.

Elkstone, Lower & Upper Staffs. *Elkesdon* 1227. 'Hill of a man called Ēalāc'. OE pers. name + *dūn*.

Ella, Kirk & West Humber. *Aluengi* (*sic*) 1086 (DB), *Kirk Elley* 15th cent., *Westeluelle* 1305. 'Woodland clearing of a man called Ælf(a)'. OE pers. name + *lēah*. Distinguishing affixes are from OScand. *kirkja* 'church' and *west*.

Elland W. Yorks. *Elant* 1086 (DB). 'Cultivated land, or estate, by the river'. OE *ēa-land*.

Ellastone Staffs. *Edelachestone* 1086 (DB). 'Farmstead of a man called Ēadlāc'. OE pers. name + *tūn*.

Ellenhall Staffs. *Linehalle* (*sic*) 1086 (DB), *Ælinhale* c.1200. Possibly 'nook of land associated with a man called Ælle or Ella', from OE pers. name + *-ing-* + *halh*. Alternatively 'nook (by the river) where flax is grown', from OE *līn* + *halh* with the later addition of *ēa*.

Ellerbeck N. Yorks. *Elrebec* 1086 (DB). 'Stream where alders grow'. OScand. *elri* + *bekkr*.

Ellerby N. Yorks. *Elwordebi* 1086 (DB). 'Farmstead or village of a man called Ælfweard'. OE pers. name + OScand. *bý*.

Ellerdine Heath Shrops. *Elleurdine* 1086 (DB). 'Enclosure of a man called Ella'. OE pers. name + *worthign*, with the later addition of *heath*.

Ellerker Humber. *Alrecher* 1086 (DB). 'Marsh where alders grow'. OScand. *elri* + *kjarr*.

Ellerton Humber. *Elreton* 1086 (DB). 'Farmstead by the alders'. OScand. *elri* + OE *tūn*.

Ellerton Shrops. *Athelarton* 13th cent. 'Farmstead of a man called Æthelheard'. OE pers. name + *tūn*.

Ellesborough Bucks. *Esenberge* (*sic*) 1086 (DB), *Eselbergh* 1195. Probably 'hill where asses are pastured'. OE *esol* + *beorg*.

Ellesmere Shrops. *Ellesmeles* (*sic*) 1086 (DB), *Ellesmera* 1172. 'Lake or pool of a man called Elli'. OE pers. name + *mere*.

Ellesmere Port Ches., a modern name, only in use since the early 19th cent., so called because the Ellesmere Canal (from the previous name) joins the Mersey here.

Ellingham, 'homestead of the family or followers of a man called Ella', or 'homestead at Ella's place', OE pers. name + *-inga-* or *-ing* + *hām*: **Ellingham** Norfolk. *Elincham* 1086 (DB). **Ellingham, Great & Little** Norfolk. *Elin(c)gham* 1086 (DB), *Magna Elingham*, *Parva Elingham* 1242. Distinguishing affixes are Latin *magna* 'great' and *parva* 'little'. **Ellingham** Northum. *Ellingeham* c.1130.

Ellingstring N. Yorks. *Elingestrengge* 1198. 'Water-course at the place where eels are caught', or 'water-course at the place associated with a man called Ella or Eli'. OScand. *strengr* with either OE *ǣl*, *ēl* + *-ing* or OE pers. name + *-ing*.

Ellington, 'farmstead at the place where eels are caught', or 'farmstead associated with a man called Ella or Eli', OE *tūn* with either OE *ǣl*, *ēl* + *-ing* or OE pers. name + *-ing-*: **Ellington** Cambs. *Elintune* 1086 (DB). **Ellington** Northum. *Elingtona* 1166. **Ellington, High & Low** N. Yorks. *Ellintone* 1086 (DB).

Ellisfield Hants. *Esewelle* (*sic*) 1086 (DB), *Elsefeld* 1167. Probably 'open land of a man called *Ielfsa'. OE pers. name + *feld*.

Ellough Suffolk. *Elga* 1086 (DB). '(Place at) the heathen temple'. OScand. **elgr*.

Elloughton Humber. *Elgendon* 1086 (DB). 'Hill with a heathen temple', or 'hill of a man called Helgi'. OScand. **elgr* or pers. name + OE *dūn*.

Elm, '(place at) the elm-tree(s)', OE *elm* (dative plural *elmum*): **Elm** Cambs. *Elm*, *Eolum* 10th cent. **Elm, Great** Somerset. *Telma* 1086 (DB). *T-* in the early form is from the OE preposition *æt* 'at'.

Elmbridge Heref. & Worcs. *Elmerige* 1086 (DB). 'Ridge where elm-trees grow'. OE *elm*, **elmen* + *hrycg*.

Elmdon Essex. *Elmenduna* 1086 (DB). 'Hill where elm-trees grow'. OE **elmen* + *dūn*.

Elmesthorpe Leics. *Ailmerestorp* 1207. 'Outlying farmstead or hamlet of a man called Æthelmǣr'. OE pers. name + OScand. *thorp*.

Elmet (old district) W. Yorks., see BARWICK IN ELMET.

Elmham, 'homestead or village where elm-trees grow', OE *elm*, **elmen* + *hām*: **Elmham, North** Norfolk. *Ælmham* c.1035, *Elmenham* 1086 (DB). **Elmham, South** Norfolk. *Almeham* 1086 (DB). The parishes of All Saints, St James, St Margaret and St Michael South Elmham are named from the dedications of the churches. However the affix in St Cross South Elmham is from *Sancroft* 1254, 'sandy enclosure', OE *sand* + *croft*.

Elmley, 'elm-tree wood or clearing', OE *elm* + *lēah*: **Elmley Castle** Heref. & Worcs. *Elmlege* 780, *Castel Elmeleye* 1327. Affix from the former castle here. **Elmley Lovett** Heref. & Worcs. *Ælmeleia* 1086 (DB), *Almeleye Lovet* 1275. Manorial addition from the *Lovett* family, here in the 13th cent.

Elmore Glos. *Elmour* 1176. 'River-bank or ridge where elm-trees grow'. OE *elm* + *ōfer* or **ofer*.

Elmsall, North & South W. Yorks. *Ermeshale* (*sic*) 1086 (DB), *North Elmesale* 1320, *Suthelmeshal* 1230. 'Nook of land by the elm-tree'. OE *elm* + *halh*.

Elmsett Suffolk. *Ylmesæton* c.995, *Elmeseta* 1086 (DB). '(Settlement of) the dwellers among the elm-trees'. OE **elme* + *sǣte*.

Elmstead Gtr. London. *Elmsted* 1320. 'Place by the elm-trees'. OE *elm* + *stede*.

Elmstead Market Essex. *Elmesteda*

1086 (DB), *Elmested Market* 1475. 'Place where elm-trees grow'. OE **elme* or **elmen* + *stede*. Affix *market* from the important early market here.

Elmsted Kent. *Elmanstede* 811. 'Homestead by the elm-trees'. OE *elm* + *hām-stede*.

Elmstone Kent. *Ailmereston* 1203. 'Farmstead of a man called Æthelmǣr'. OE pers. name + *tūn*.

Elmstone Hardwicke Glos. *Almundestan* 1086 (DB). 'Boundary stone of a man called Alhmund'. OE pers. name + *stān*. Hardwicke has been added from a nearby place, see HARDWICKE.

Elmswell Suffolk. *Elmeswella* 1086 (DB). 'Spring or stream where elm-trees grow'. OE *elm* + *wella*.

Elmton Derbys. *Helmetune* 1086 (DB). 'Farmstead where elm-trees grow'. OE *elm*, **elmen* + *tūn*.

Elsdon Northum. *Eledene* 1226. Probably 'valley of a man called El(l)i'. OE pers. name + *denu*.

Elsenham Essex. *Elsenham* 1086 (DB). 'Homestead or village of a man called Elesa'. OE pers. name (genitive *-n*) + *hām*.

Elsfield Oxon. *Esefelde* 1086 (DB), *Elsefeld* c.1130. 'Open land of a man called Elesa'. OE pers. name + *feld*.

Elsham Humber. *Elesham* 1086 (DB). 'Homestead or village of a man called El(l)i'. OE pers. name + *hām*.

Elsing Norfolk. *Helsinga* 1086 (DB). '(Settlement of) the family or followers of a man called Elesa'. OE pers. name + *-ingas*.

Elslack N. Yorks. *Eleslac* 1086 (DB). 'Stream or valley of a man called El(l)i'. OE pers. name + *lacu* or OScand. *slakki*.

Elstead Surrey. *Helestede* 1128. 'Place where elder-trees grow'. OE *elle(n)* + *stede*.

Elsted W. Sussex. *Halestede* (*sic*) 1086 (DB), *Ellesteda* 1180. Identical in origin with the previous name.

Elston Notts. *Elvestune* 1086 (DB). Probably 'farmstead of a man called Eiláfr'. OScand. pers. name + *tūn*.

Elstow Beds. *Elnestou* 1086 (DB). 'Assembly place of a man called *Ællen'. OE pers. name + *stōw*.

Elstree Herts. *Tithulfes treow* 11th cent. 'Boundary tree of a man called Tīdwulf'. OE pers. name + *trēow*. Initial *T-* disappeared in the 13th cent. due to confusion with the preposition *at*.

Elstronwick Humber. *Asteneuuic* (*sic*) 1086 (DB), *Elstanwik* c.1265. 'Dwelling or (dairy) farm of a man called Ælfstān'. OE pers. name + *wīc*.

Elswick Lancs. *Edelesuuic* 1086 (DB). 'Dwelling or (dairy) farm of a man called Æthelsige'. OE pers. name + *wīc*.

Elsworth Cambs. *Eleswurth* 974, *Elesuuorde* 1086 (DB). 'Enclosure of a man called El(l)i'. OE pers. name + *worth*.

Elterwater Cumbria. *Heltewatra* c.1160. 'Lake frequented by swans'. OScand. *elptr* + OE *wæter*.

Eltham Gtr. London. *Elteham* 1086 (DB). 'Homestead or river-meadow frequented by swans', or 'of a man called *Elta'. OE *elfitu* or OE pers. name + *hām* or *hamm*.

Eltisley Cambs. *Hecteslei* (*sic*) 1086 (DB), *Eltesle* 1228. 'Woodland clearing of a man called *Elti'. OE pers. name + *lēah*.

Elton, sometimes probably 'farmstead where eels are got', OE *ǣl* + *tūn*: **Elton** Ches., near Ellesmere Port. *Eltone* 1086 (DB). **Elton** Cleveland. *Eltun* c.1090. **Elton** Derbys. *Eltune* 1086 (DB).

However other Eltons have a different origin: **Elton** Cambs. *Æthelingtun* 10th cent., *Adelintune* 1086 (DB). 'Farmstead of the princes', or 'farmstead associated with a man called Æthel'. OE *ætheling* + *tūn*, or OE pers. name + *-ing-* + *tūn*. **Elton** Heref. & Worcs. *Elintune* 1086 (DB). Probably 'farmstead of a man called Ella'. OE pers. name + *tūn*. **Elton** Notts. *Ailetone* (*sic*) 1086 (DB), *Elleton* 1088. Probably identical with the previous name.

Elvaston Derbys. *Ælwoldestune* 1086 (DB). 'Farmstead of a man called Æthelweald'. OE pers. name + *tūn*.

Elveden Suffolk. *Eluedena* 1086 (DB).

'Swan valley' or 'valley haunted by elves or fairies'. OE *elfitu* or *elf* (genitive plural *-a*) + *denu*.

Elvington N. Yorks. *Aluuintone* 1086 (DB). 'Farmstead of a man called Ælfwine or a woman called Ælfwynn'. OE pers. name + *tūn*.

Elwick Cleveland. *Ailewic* c.1150. 'Dwelling or (dairy) farm of a man called *Ægla or Ella'. OE pers. name + *wīc*.

Elwick Northum. *Ellewich* 12th cent. 'Dwelling or (dairy) farm of a man called Ella'.

Elworth Ches. *Ellewrdth* 1282. 'Enclosure of a man called Ella'. OE pers. name + *worth*.

Elworthy Somerset. *Elwrde* 1086 (DB). 'Enclosure of a man called Ella'. OE pers. name + *worth* (later replaced by *worthig*).

Ely Cambs. *Elge* 731, *Elyg* 1086 (DB). 'District where eels are to be found'. OE *ǣl, ēl* + **gē*.

Emberton Bucks. *Ambretone* 1086 (DB). 'Farmstead of a man called Ēanbeorht'. OE pers. name + *tūn*.

Embleton Cumbria. *Emelton* 1195. 'Farmstead of a man called Ēanbald'. OE pers. name + *tūn*.

Embleton Northum. *Emlesdone* 1212. 'Hill infested by caterpillars', or 'hill of a man called Æmele'. OE *emel* or OE pers. name + *dūn*.

Emborough Somerset. *Amelberge* (*sic*) 1086 (DB), *Emeneberge* 1200. 'Flat-topped mound or hill'. OE *emn* + *beorg*.

Embsay N. Yorks. *Embesie* 1086 (DB). Probably 'enclosure of a man called Embe'. OE pers. name + *hæg*.

Emley W. Yorks. *Ameleie* 1086 (DB). 'Woodland clearing of a man called *Em(m)a'. OE pers. name + *lēah*.

Emmington Oxon. *Amintone* 1086 (DB). 'Estate associated with a man called Eama'. OE pers. name + *-ing-* + *tūn*.

Emneth Norfolk. *Anemetha* 1170. Possibly 'river-confluence of a man called Ēana'. OE pers. name + *(ge)mȳthe*. Alternatively the second element may be OE *mǣth* 'mowing grass, meadow'.

Empingham Leics. *Epingeham* (*sic*) 1086 (DB), *Empingeham* 12th cent. 'Homestead of the family or followers of a man called *Empa'. OE pers. name + *-inga-* + *hām*.

Empshott Hants. *Hibesete* (*sic*) 1086 (DB), *Himbeset* c.1170. 'Corner of land frequented by swarms of bees'. OE *imbe* + *scēat* or **scīete*.

Emsworth Hants. *Emeleswurth* 1224. 'Enclosure of a man called Æmele'. OE pers. name + *worth*.

Enborne Berks. *Aneborne* (*sic*) 1086 (DB), *Enedburn* 1220. 'Duck stream'. OE *ened* + *burna*.

Enderby Leics. *Endrebie* 1086 (DB). Probably 'farmstead or village of a man called Eindrithi'. OScand. pers. name + *bý*.

Enderby, Bag, Mavis, & Wood Lincs. *Andrebi, Endrebi* 1086 (DB), *Bagenderby* 1291, *Enderby Malbys* 1302, *Wodenderby* 1198. Probably identical in origin with the previous name. The affix *Mavis* is manorial, from the *Malebisse* family here in the 13th cent. *Bag* may also be a manorial affix from a family so named. *Wood* (from OE *wudu* 'wood') indicates a situation in a once wooded area.

Endon Staffs. *Enedun* 1086 (DB). 'Hill of a man called Ēana, or where lambs are reared'. OE pers. name or OE **ēan* + *dūn*.

Enfield Gtr. London. *Enefelde* 1086 (DB). 'Open land of a man called Ēana, or where lambs are reared'. OE pers. name or OE **ēan* + *feld*.

Enford Wilts. *Enedford* 934, *Enedforde* 1086 (DB). 'Duck ford'. OE *ened* + *ford*.

England *Englaland* c.890. 'Land of the Angles'. OE *Engle* (genitive plural Engla) 'the Angles' (i.e. the people from the Continental homeland of *Angel* in Schleswig) + *land*.

Englefield Berks. *Englafelda* c.900, *Englefel* 1086 (DB). 'Open land of the Angles'. OE *Engle* + *feld*.

Englefield Green Surrey. *Ingelfeld* 1282. Possibly 'open land of a man called *Ingel or Ingweald'. OE pers. name + *feld*. *Green* is added from the 17th cent.

English Bicknor Glos., see BICKNOR.

Englishcombe Avon. *Ingeliscuma* 1086 (DB). Probably 'valley of a man called *Ingel or Ingweald'. OE pers. name + *cumb*.

English Frankton Shrops., see FRANKTON.

Enham Alamein Hants. *Eanham* early 11th cent., *Etham (sic)* 1086 (DB). 'Homestead or enclosure where lambs are reared'. OE **ēan* + *hām* or *hamm*. Affix from 1945, commemorating the battle of El Alamein and referring to the centre for disabled ex-servicemen here.

Enmore Somerset. *Animere* 1086 (DB). 'Duck pool'. OE *ened* + *mere*.

Ennerdale Bridge Cumbria. *Anenderdale* c.1135, *Eghnerdale* 1321. 'Valley of a man called Anundr'. OScand. pers. name (genitive *-ar*) + *dalr*. Later the first element was replaced by the river-name Ehen (of obscure origin).

Enstone Oxon. *Henestan* 1086 (DB). 'Boundary stone of a man called Enna'. OE pers. name + *stān*.

Enville Staffs. *Efnefeld* 1086 (DB). 'Smooth or level open land'. OE *efn* + *feld*.

Epperstone Notts. *Eprestone* 1086 (DB). Probably 'farmstead of a man called Eorphere'. OE pers. name + *tūn*.

Epping Essex. *Eppinges* 1086 (DB). Probably '(settlement of) the people of the ridge used as a look-out place'. OE *yppe* + *-ingas*.

Eppleby N. Yorks. *Aplebi* 1086 (DB). 'Farmstead where apple-trees grow'. OE *æppel* or OScand. *epli* + *bý*.

Epsom Surrey. *Ebbesham* c.973, *Evesham (sic)* 1086 (DB). 'Homestead or village of a man called Ebbe or Ebbi'. OE pers. name + *hām*.

Epwell Oxon. *Eoppan wyllan* 956. 'Spring or stream of a man called Eoppa'. OE pers. name + *wella*.

Epworth Humber. *Epeurde* 1086 (DB). 'Enclosure of a man called Eoppa'. OE pers. name + *worth*.

Ercall, Child's & High Shrops. *Arcalun (sic), Archelov* 1086 (DB), *Childes Ercalewe, Magna Ercalewe* 1327. Origin and meaning obscure. Affixes are OE *cild* 'son of a noble family' and Latin *magna* 'great'.

Erdington W. Mids. *Hardintone* 1086 (DB). 'Estate associated with a man called *Earda'. OE pers. name + *-ing-* + *tūn*.

Eridge Green E. Sussex. *Ernerigg* 1202. 'Ridge frequented by eagles'. OE *earn* + *hrycg*.

Eriswell Suffolk. *Hereswella* 1086 (DB). Possibly 'spring or stream of a man called *Here'. OE pers. name + *wella*.

Erith Gtr. London. *Earhyth* c.960, *Erhede* 1086 (DB). 'Muddy or gravelly landing place'. OE *ēar* + *hȳth*.

Erlestoke Wilts. *Erlestoke* 12th cent. 'Outlying farmstead belonging to the nobleman'. OE *eorl* + *stoc*.

Ermine Street (Roman road from London to the Humber). *Earninga stræt* 955. 'Roman road of the family or followers of a man called *Earn(a)'. OE pers. name + *-inga-* + *strǣt*. No doubt originally applied to a stretch of the road near ARRINGTON (Cambs.) before the name was extended to the whole length. The name Ermine Street was later transferred to another Roman road, that from Silchester to Gloucester.

Ermington Devon. *Ermentona* 1086 (DB). Probably 'estate associated with a man called *Earma'. OE pers. name + *-ing-* + *tūn*.

Erpingham Norfolk. *Erpingaham* 1086 (DB). 'Homestead of the family or followers of a man called *Eorp'. OE pers. name + *-inga-* + *hām*.

Erwarton Suffolk. *Eurewardestuna* 1086 (DB). 'Farmstead of a man called *Eoforweard'. OE pers. name + *tūn*.

Eryholme N. Yorks. *Argun* 1086 (DB). '(Place at) the shielings or summer pastures'. OScand. *erg* in a dative plural form *ergum*.

Escrick N. Yorks. *Ascri (sic)* 1086 (DB), *Escric* 1169. 'Strip of land or narrow ridge where ash-trees grow'. OScand. *eski* + OE **ric*.

Esh Durham. *Esse* 12th cent. '(Place at) the ash-tree'. OE *æsc*.

Esher Surrey. *Æscæron* 1005, *Aissele*

(*sic*) 1086 (DB). 'District where ash-trees grow'. OE *æsc* + *scearu*.

Eshott Northum. *Esseta* 1187. 'Clump of ash-trees' from OE **æscet*, or 'corner of land growing with ash-trees' from OE *æsc* + *scēat*.

Eshton N. Yorks. *Estune* 1086 (DB). 'Farmstead by the ash-tree(s)'. OE *æsc* + *tūn*.

Eskdale Green Cumbria. *Eskedal* 1294. 'Valley of the River Esk'. Celtic river-name (meaning simply 'the water') + OScand. *dalr*.

Esprick Lancs. *Eskebrec* c.1210. 'Hill slope where ash-trees grow'. OScand. *eski* + *brekka*.

Essendine Leics. *Esindone* (*sic*) 1086 (DB), *Esenden* 1230. 'Valley of a man called Ēsa'. OE pers. name (genitive *-n*) + *denu*.

Essendon Herts. *Eslingadene* 11th cent. 'Valley of the family or followers of a man called *Ēsla'. OE pers. name + *-inga-* + *denu*.

Essex (the county). *East Seaxe* late 9th cent., *Exsessa* 1086 (DB). '(Territory of) the East Saxons'. OE *ēast* + *Seaxe*.

Essington Staffs. *Esingetun* 996, *Eseningetone* 1086 (DB). 'Farmstead of the family or followers of a man called Esne'. OE pers. name + *-inga-* + *tūn*.

Eston Cleveland. *Astun* 1086 (DB). 'East farmstead or village'. OE *ēast* + *tūn*.

Etal Northum. *Ethale* 1232. Probably 'nook of land used for grazing'. OE *ete* + *halh*.

Etchilhampton Wilts. *Echesatingetone* 1086 (DB), *Ehelhamton* 1196. Possibly 'farmstead of the dwellers at the oak-tree hill'. OE *āc* (genitive *ǣc*) + *hyll* + *hǣme* (earlier *sǣte*) + *tūn*.

Etchingham E. Sussex. *Hechingeham* 1158. 'Homestead or enclosure of the family or followers of a man called Ecci'. OE pers. name + *-inga-* + *hām* or *hamm*.

Eton Berks. *Ettone* 1086 (DB). 'Farmstead by the river'. OE *ēa* + *tūn*.

Etton, probably 'farmstead of a man called Ēata', OE pers. name + *tūn*: **Etton** Cambs. *Ettona* 1125–8. **Etton** Humber. *Ettone* 1086 (DB).

Etwall Derbys. *Etewelle* 1086 (DB). Probably 'spring or stream of a man called Ēata'. OE pers. name + *wella*.

Euston Suffolk. *Euestuna* 1086 (DB). 'Farmstead of a man called Efe'. OE pers. name + *tūn*.

Euxton Lancs. *Eueceston* 1187. 'Farmstead of a man called Æfic'. OE pers. name + *tūn*.

Evedon Lincs. *Evedune* 1086 (DB). 'Hill of a man called Eafa'. OE pers. name + *dūn*.

Evenley Northants. *Evelaia* (*sic*) 1086 (DB), *Euenlai* 1147. 'Level woodland clearing'. OE *efen* + *lēah*.

Evenlode Glos. *Euulangelade* 772, *Eunilade* 1086 (DB). 'Water-course or river-crossing of a man called *Eowla'. OE pers. name (genitive *-n*) + (*ge*)*lād*.

Evenwood Durham. *Efenwuda* c.1050. 'Level woodland'. OE *efen* + *wudu*.

Evercreech Somerset. *Evorcric* 1065, *Evrecriz* 1086 (DB). Celtic **crūg* 'hill' with an uncertain first element, possibly OE *eofor* 'wild boar' or a Celtic word meaning 'yew-tree'.

Everdon, Great Northants. *Eferdun* 944, *Everdone* 1086 (DB). 'Hill frequented by wild boars'. OE *eofor* + *dūn*.

Everingham Humber. *Yferingaham* c.972, *Evringham* 1086 (DB). 'Homestead of the family or followers of a man called Eofor'. OE pers. name + *-inga-* + *hām*.

Everleigh Wilts. *Eburleagh* 704. 'Wood or clearing frequented by wild boars'. OE *eofor* + *lēah*.

Everley N. Yorks. *Eurelai* 1086 (DB). Identical in origin with the previous name.

Eversden, Great & Little Cambs. *Euresdone* 1086 (DB), *Everesdon Magna, Parva* 1240. 'Hill of the wild boar, or of a man called Eofor'. OE *eofor* or OE pers. name + *dūn*. Affixes are Latin *magna* 'great', *parva* 'little'.

Eversholt Beds. *Eureshot* (*sic*) 1086 (DB), *Euresholt* 1185. 'Wood of the wild boar'. OE *eofor* + *holt*.

Evershot Dorset. *Teversict* (*sic*) 1202, *Evershet* 1286. Probably 'corner of land frequented by wild boars'. OE *eofor* + *scēat* or **scīete*. Initial *T-* in the first form may be from the preposition *at*.

Eversley Hants. *Euereslea c.*1050, *Evreslei* 1086 (DB). 'Wood or clearing of the wild boar, or of a man called Eofor'. OE *eofor* or OE pers. name + *lēah*.

Everton, 'farmstead where wild boars are seen', OE *eofor* + *tūn*: **Everton** Beds. *Euretone* 1086 (DB). **Everton** Mersey. *Evretona* 1094. **Everton** Notts. *Evretone* 1086 (DB).

Evesham Heref. & Worcs. *Eveshomme* 709, *Evesham* 1086 (DB). 'Land in a river-bend belonging to a man called Ēof'. OE pers. name + *hamm*.

Evington Leics. *Avintone* 1086 (DB). 'Estate associated with a man called Eafa'. OE pers. name + *-ing-* + *tūn*.

Ewell Surrey. *Euuelle* 933, *Etwelle* (*sic*) 1086 (DB). '(Place at) the river-source'. OE *ǣwell*.

Ewell Minnis & Temple Ewell Kent. *Æwille c.*772, *Ewelle* 1086 (DB). Identical in origin with the previous name. The affix *Minnis* is from OE *mǣnnes* 'common land', *Temple* alludes to possession by the Knights Templars from the 12th cent.

Ewelme Oxon. *Auuilme* 1086 (DB). '(Place at) the river-source'. OE *ǣwelm*.

Ewen Glos. *Awilme* 931. Identical in origin with the previous name.

Ewerby Lincs. *Ieresbi* 1086 (DB). 'Farmstead or village of a man called Ívarr'. OScand. pers. name + *bý*.

Ewhurst Surrey. *Iuherst* 1179. 'Yew-tree wooded hill'. OE *īw* + *hyrst*.

Ewyas Harold Heref. & Worcs. *Euwias c.*1150, *Euuiasharold* 1176. A Welsh name meaning 'sheep district'. Affix from a nobleman called *Harold* who held the manor in the 11th cent.

Exbourne Devon. *Hechesburne* (*sic*) 1086 (DB), *Yekesburne* 1242. 'Stream of the cuckoo, or of a man called *Gēac'. OE *gēac* or OE pers. name + *burna*.

Exbury Hants. *Teocreberie* (*sic*) 1086 (DB), *Ykeresbirie* 1196. 'Fortified place of a man called *Eohhere'. OE pers. name + *burh* (dative *byrig*).

Exe, Nether & Up Devon. *Niresse* (*sic*), *Ulpesse* (*sic*) 1086 (DB), *Nitherexe* 1196, *Uphexe* 1238. Named from the River Exe, a Celtic river-name meaning simply 'the water'. Affixes are OE *neotherra* 'lower (down river)' and *upp* 'higher up (river)'.

Exebridge Somerset. *Exebrigge* 1255. 'Bridge over the River Exe'. Celtic river-name + OE *brycg*.

Exelby N. Yorks. *Aschilebi* 1086 (DB). 'Farmstead or village of a man called Eskil'. OScand. pers. name + *bý*.

Exeter Devon. *Iska c.*150, *Exanceaster c.*900, *Execestre* 1086 (DB). 'Roman town on the River Exe'. Celtic river-name (see EXE) + OE *ceaster*.

Exford Somerset. *Aisseford* (*sic*) 1086 (DB), *Exeford* 1243. 'Ford over the River Exe'. Celtic river-name + OE *ford*.

Exminster Devon. *Exanmynster c.*880, *Esseminstre* 1086 (DB). 'Monastery by the River Exe'. Celtic river-name + OE *mynster*.

Exmoor Devon. *Exemora* 1204. 'Moorland on the River Exe'. Celtic river-name + OE *mōr*.

Exmouth Devon. *Exanmutha c.*1025. 'Mouth of the River Exe'. Celtic river-name + OE *mūtha*.

Exning Suffolk. *Essellinge* (*sic*) 1086 (DB), *Exningis* 1158. '(Settlement of) the family or followers of a man called *Gyxen'. OE pers. name + *-ingas*.

Exton Devon. *Exton* 1242. 'Farmstead on the River Exe'. Celtic river-name + OE *tūn*.

Exton Hants. *East Seaxnatune* 940, *Essessentune* 1086 (DB). 'Farmstead of the East Saxons'. OE *Ēastseaxe* + *tūn*.

Exton Leics. *Exentune* 1086 (DB). Probably 'farmstead where oxen are kept'. OE *oxa* (genitive plural **exna*) + *tūn*.

Exton Somerset. *Exton* 1216. 'Farmstead on the River Exe'. Celtic river-name + OE *tūn*.

Eyam Derbys. *Aiune* 1086 (DB). '(Place at) the islands, or the pieces of land between streams'. OE *ēg* in a dative plural form *ēgum*.

Eydon Northants. *Egedone* 1086 (DB). 'Hill of a man called *Æga'. OE pers. name + *dūn*.

Eye, '(place at) the island, or well-watered land, or dry ground in marsh', OE *ēg*: **Eye** Cambs. *Ege* 10th cent. **Eye** Heref. & Worcs. *Eia c.*1175. **Eye** Suffolk. *Eia* 1086 (DB).

Eyke Suffolk. *Eik* 1185. '(Place at) the oak-tree'. OScand. *eik*.

Eynesbury Cambs. *Eanulfesbyrig c.*1000, *Einuluesberie* 1086 (DB). 'Stronghold of a man called Ēanwulf'. OE pers. name + OE *burh* (dative *byrig*).

Eynsford Kent. *Æinesford c.*960. 'Ford of a man called *Ægen'. OE pers. name + *ford*.

Eynsham Oxon. *Egenes homme* 864, *Eglesham* 1086 (DB). Possibly 'enclosure or river-meadow of a man called *Ægen'. OE pers. name + *hamm*.

Eype Dorset. *Yepe* 1365. 'Steep place'. OE **gēap*.

Eythorne Kent. *Heagythethorne* 9th cent. 'Thorn-tree of a woman called *Hēahgȳth'. OE pers. name + *thorn*.

Eyton upon the Weald Moors Shrops. *Etone* 1086 (DB), *Eyton super le Wildmore* 1344. 'Farmstead on dry ground in marsh, or on well-watered land'. OE *ēg* + *tūn*. The affix means 'in the wild moorland', from OE *wilde* + *mōr*.

F

Faccombe Hants. *Faccancumb* 863, *Facumbe* 1086 (DB). 'Valley of a man called *Facca'. OE pers. name + *cumb*.

Faceby N. Yorks. *Feizbi* 1086 (DB). 'Farmstead or village of a man called Feitr'. OScand. pers. name + *bý*.

Faddiley Ches. *Fadilee c*.1220. 'Woodland clearing of a man called *Fad(d)a'. OE pers. name + *lēah*.

Fadmoor N. Yorks. *Fademora* 1086 (DB). 'Moor of a man called *Fad(d)a'. OE pers. name + *mōr*.

Failsworth Gtr. Manch. *Fayleswrthe* 1212. Possibly 'enclosure with a special kind of fence'. OE **fēgels* + *worth*.

Fairburn N. Yorks. *Farenburne c*.1030, *Fareburne* 1086 (DB). 'Stream where ferns grow'. OE *fearn* + *burna*.

Fairfield Heref. & Worcs. *Forfeld* 817. 'Open land where hogs are pastured'. OE *fōr* + *feld*.

Fairford Glos. *Fagranforda* 862, *Fareforde* 1086 (DB). 'Fair or clear ford'. OE *fæger* + *ford*.

Fairlight E. Sussex. *Farleghe c*.1175. 'Woodland clearing where ferns grow'. OE *fearn* + *lēah*.

Fairstead Essex. *Fairstedam* 1086 (DB). 'Fair or pleasant place'. OE *fæger* + *stede*.

Fakenham, 'homestead of a man called *Facca', OE pers. name (genitive *-n*) + *hām*: **Fakenham** Norfolk. *Fachenham* 1086 (DB). **Fakenham, Little** Suffolk. *Litla Fachenham* 1086 (DB). Affix is OE *lȳtel* 'little'.

Faldingworth Lincs. *Falding(e)urde* 1086 (DB). 'Enclosure for folding livestock'. OE **falding* + *worth*.

Falfield Avon. *Falefeld* 1227. 'Pale brown or fallow open land'. OE *fealu* + *feld*.

Falkenham Suffolk. *Faltenham* 1086 (DB). Probably 'homestead of a man called *Falta'. OE pers. name (genitive *-n*) + *hām*.

Falmer E. Sussex. *Falemere* 1086 (DB). Probably 'fallow-coloured pool'. OE *fealu* + *mere*.

Falmouth Cornwall. *Falemuth* 1235. 'Mouth of the River Fal'. River-name (of uncertain origin and meaning) + OE *mūtha*.

Fambridge, North & South Essex. *Fanbruge* 1086 (DB), *North Fambregg*, *Suthfambregg* 1291. 'Bridge by a fen or marsh'. OE *fenn* + *brycg*.

Fangdale Beck N. Yorks. *Fangedala* 12th cent. 'Stream in the valley good for fishing'. OScand. *fang* + *dalr* + *bekkr*.

Fangfoss Humber. *Frangefos* (*sic*) 1086 (DB), *Fangefosse* 12th cent. Possibly 'ditch used for fishing'. OScand. *fang* + OE **foss*.

Farcet Cambs. *Faresheued* 10th cent. 'Bull's headland or hill'. OE *fearr* + *hēafod*.

Far Cotton Northants., see COTTON.

Fareham Hants. *Fearnham c*.970, *Fernham* 1086 (DB). 'Homestead where ferns grow'. OE *fearn* + *hām*.

Farewell Staffs. *Fagerwell* 1200. 'Pleasant spring or stream'. OE *fæger* + *wella*.

Faringdon Oxon. *Færndunæ c*.971, *Ferendone* 1086 (DB). 'Fern-covered hill'. OE *fearn* + *dūn*.

Farington Lancs. *Farinton* 1149. 'Farmstead where ferns grow'. OE *fearn* + *tūn*.

Farleigh, 'woodland clearing growing with ferns', OE *fearn* + *lēah*: **Farleigh** Gtr. London. *Ferlega* 1086 (DB). **Farleigh, East & West** Kent. *Fearnlege* 9th cent., *Ferlaga* 1086 (DB). **Farleigh Hungerford** Somerset. *Fearnlæh* 987, *Ferlege* 1086 (DB),

Farlegh Hungerford 1404. Affix from the *Hungerford* family, here in the 14th cent. **Farleigh, Monkton** Wilts. *Farnleghe* 1001, *Farlege* 1086 (DB), *Monekenefarlegh* 1321. Affix means 'of the monks' from OE *munuc*, alluding to a priory founded here in 1125. **Farleigh Wallop** Hants. *Ferlege* 1086 (DB). Affix from the *Wallop* family, here in the 14th cent.

Farlesthorpe Lincs. *Farlestorp* 1190. 'Outlying farmstead or hamlet of a man called Faraldr'. OScand. pers. name + *thorp*.

Farleton Cumbria. *Farelton* 1086 (DB). 'Farmstead of a man called *Færela or Faraldr'. OE or OScand. pers. name + OE *tūn*.

Farley, 'woodland clearing growing with ferns', OE *fearn* + *lēah*; examples include: **Farley** Staffs. *Fernelege* 1086 (DB). **Farley Hill** Berks. *Ferlega* 1167.

Farlington N. Yorks. *Ferlintun* 1086 (DB). Probably 'estate associated with a man called *Færela'. OE pers. name + *-ing-* + *tūn*.

Farlow Shrops. *Ferlau* 1086 (DB). 'Fern-covered mound or hill'. OE *fearn* + *hlāw*.

Farmborough Avon. *Fearnberngas* (*sic*) 901, *Ferenberge* 1086 (DB). 'Hill(s) or mound(s) growing with ferns'. OE *fearn* + *beorg*.

Farmcote Glos. *Fernecote* 1086 (DB). 'Cottage(s) among the ferns'. OE *fearn* + *cot*.

Farmington Glos. *Tormentone* (*sic*) 1086 (DB), *Tormerton* 1182. Probably 'farmstead near the pool where thorn-trees grow'. OE *thorn* + *mere* + *tūn*.

Farnborough, 'hill(s) or mound(s) growing with ferns', OE *fearn* + *beorg*: **Farnborough** Berks. *Fearnbeorgan* c.935, *Fermeberge* 1086 (DB). **Farnborough** Gtr. London. *Ferenberga* 1180. **Farnborough** Hants. *Ferneberga* 1086 (DB). **Farnborough** Warwicks. *Feornebeorh* c.1015, *Ferneberge* 1086 (DB).

Farncombe Surrey. *Fernecome* 1086 (DB). 'Valley where ferns grow'. OE *fearn* + *cumb*.

Farndon, 'hill growing with ferns', OE *fearn* + *dūn*: **Farndon** Ches. *Fearndune* 924, *Ferentone* (*sic*) 1086 (DB). **Farndon** Notts. *Farendune* 1086 (DB). **Farndon, East** Northants. *Ferendone* 1086 (DB).

Farne Islands Northum. *Farne* c.700. Possibly a derivative of the OE word *fearn* 'fern', but perhaps more probably of Celtic origin.

Farnham, 'homestead or enclosure where ferns grow', OE *fearn* + *hām* or *hamm*: **Farnham** Dorset. *Fernham* 1086 (DB). **Farnham** Essex. *Phernham* 1086 (DB). **Farnham** N. Yorks. *Farneham* 1086 (DB). **Farnham** Suffolk. *Farnham* 1086 (DB). **Farnham** Surrey. *Fernham* c.686, *Ferneham* 1086 (DB). The second element of this name is probably OE *hamm* in the sense 'river-meadow'. **Farnham Royal** Bucks. *Ferneham* 1086 (DB), *Fernham Riall* 1477. Affix (from OFrench *roial*) because it was held by the grand serjeanty of supporting the king's right arm at his coronation.

Farningham Kent. *Ferningeham* 1086 (DB). Possibly 'homestead of the dwellers among the ferns'. OE *fearn* + *-inga-* + *hām*.

Farnley, 'woodland clearing growing with ferns', OE *fearn* + *lēah*: **Farnley** N. Yorks. *Fernleage* c.1030, *Fernelai* 1086 (DB). **Farnley** W. Yorks. *Fernelei* 1086 (DB). **Farnley Tyas** W. Yorks. *Fereleia* (*sic*) 1086 (DB), *Farnley Tyas* 1322. Manorial affix from the family of *le Tyeis*, here in the 13th cent.

Farnsfield Notts. *Fearnesfeld* 958, *Farnesfeld* 1086 (DB). 'Open land where ferns grow'. OE *fearn* + *feld*.

Farnworth, 'enclosure where ferns grow', OE *fearn* + *worth*: **Farnworth** Ches. *Farneword* 1324. **Farnworth** Gtr. Manch. *Farnewurd* 1185.

Farringdon Devon. *Ferhendone* 1086 (DB). 'Fern-covered hill'. OE *fearn* + *dūn*.

Farrington Gurney Avon. *Ferentone* 1086 (DB). 'Farmstead where ferns grow'. OE *fearn* + *tūn*. Manorial affix from the *de Gurnay* family, here in the 13th cent.

Far Sawrey Cumbria, see SAWREY.

Farsley W. Yorks. *Ferselleia* 1086 (DB).

Possibly 'clearing used for heifers'. OE **fers* + *lēah*.

Farthinghoe Northants. *Ferningeho* 1086 (DB). Probably 'hill-spur of the dwellers among the ferns'. OE *fearn* + *-inga-* + *hōh*.

Farthingstone Northants. *Fordinestone* 1086 (DB). Probably 'farmstead of a man called Farthegn'. OScand. pers. name + OE *tūn*.

Farway Devon. *Farewei* 1086 (DB). Probably '(place at) the road way'. OE *fær* + *weg*.

Faulkbourne Essex. *Falcheburna* 1086 (DB). 'Stream frequented by falcons'. OE **falca* + *burna*.

Faulkland Somerset. *Fouklande* 1243. 'Folk-land', i.e. 'land held according to folk-right'. OE *folc-land*.

Faversham Kent. *Fefresham* 811, *Faversham* 1086 (DB). 'Homestead or village of the smith'. OE **fæfer* + *hām*.

Fawkham Green Kent. *Fealcnaham* 10th cent., *Fachesham* (*sic*) 1086 (DB). 'Homestead or village of a man called *Fealcna'. OE pers. name + *hām*.

Fawler Oxon. *Fauflor* 1205. 'Variegated floor', i.e. 'tessellated pavement'. OE *fāg* + *flōr*.

Fawley Berks. *Faleslei* 1086 (DB). Probably 'wood frequented by the fallow deer'. OE *fealu* (used as noun) + *lēah*.

Fawley Bucks. *Falelie* 1086 (DB). 'Fallow-coloured woodland clearing', or 'clearing with ploughed land'. OE *fealu* or *fealg* + *lēah*.

Fawley Hants. *Falegia*, *Falelei* 1086 (DB). Probably identical in origin with the previous name.

Fawley Chapel Heref. & Worcs. *Falileiam* 1142. 'Woodland clearing where hay is made'. OE *fælethe* + *lēah*.

Faxfleet Humber. *Faxflete* 1190. 'Stream of a man called Faxi', or 'stream near which coarse grass grows'. OScand. pers. name or OE *feax* + *flēot*.

Fazeley Staffs. *Faresleia c.*1142. 'Clearing used for bulls'. OE *fearr* + *lēah*.

Fearby N. Yorks. *Federbi* 1086 (DB). OScand. *bý* 'farmstead, village' with a doubtful first element, possibly OE *fether*, OScand. *fjǫthr* 'feather' (perhaps referring to a place frequented by flocks of birds).

Fearnhead Ches. *Ferneheued* 1292. 'Fern-covered hill'. OE *fearn* + *hēafod*.

Featherstone, '(place at) the four stones, i.e. a tetralith', OE *feother-* + *stān*: **Featherstone** Staffs. *Feother(e)stan* 10th cent., *Ferdestan* 1086 (DB). **Featherstone** W. Yorks. *Fredestan* 1086 (DB).

Feckenham Heref. & Worcs. *Feccanhom* 804, *Fecheham* 1086 (DB). 'Enclosure or water-meadow of a man called *Fecca'. OE pers. name + *hamm*.

Feering Essex. *Feringas* 1086 (DB). '(Settlement of) the family or followers of a man called *Fēra'. OE pers. name + *-ingas*.

Feetham N. Yorks. *Fytun* 1242. '(Place at) the riverside meadows'. OScand. *fit* in a dative plural form *fitjum*.

Felbridge Surrey. *Feltbruge* 12th cent. 'Bridge by the open land'. OE *feld* + *brycg*.

Felbrigg Norfolk. *Felebruge* 1086 (DB). 'Bridge made of planks'. OScand. *fjǫl* + OE *brycg*.

Felixkirk N. Yorks. *Felicekirke* 13th cent. 'Church dedicated to St Felix'. Saint's name + OScand. *kirkja*.

Felixstowe Suffolk. *Filchestou* 1254. Probably 'holy place or meeting place of a man called *Filica'. OE pers. name + *stōw*. The pers. name was later associated with that of St Felix, first Bishop of East Anglia.

Felling Tyne & Wear. *Fellyng c.*1220. OE **felling* 'woodland clearing' or *felging* 'fallow land'.

Felmersham Beds. *Falmeresham* 1086 (DB). 'Homestead or enclosure by a fallow-coloured pool, or of a man called *Feolomǣr'. OE *fealu* + *mere* or OE pers. name + *hām* or *hamm*.

Felmingham Norfolk. *Felmincham* 1086 (DB). 'Homestead of the family or followers of a man called *Feolma'. OE pers. name + *-inga-* + *hām*.

Felpham W. Sussex. *Felhhamm c.*880, *Falcheham* 1086 (DB). 'Enclosure with fallow land'. OE **felh* + *hamm*.

Felsham Suffolk. *Fealsham* 1086 (DB). 'Homestead or village of a man called *Fæle'. OE pers. name + *hām*.

Felsted Essex. *Felstede* 1086 (DB). 'Open-land place'. OE *feld* + *stede*.

Feltham Gtr. London. *Feltham* 969, *Felteham* 1086 (DB). Probably 'homestead or enclosure where mullein or a similar plant grows'. OE *felte* + *hām* or *hamm*. Alternatively the first element may be OE *feld* 'open land'.

Felthorpe Norfolk. *Felethorp* 1086 (DB). Probably 'outlying farmstead or hamlet of a man called *Fæla'. OE pers. name + OScand. *thorp*.

Felton, usually 'farmstead or village in open country', OE *feld* + *tūn*; examples include: **Felton** Heref. & Worcs. *Felton* 1086 (DB). **Felton** Northum. *Feltona* 1167. **Felton Butler** Shrops. *Feltone* 1086 (DB), *Felton Butiler* 13th cent. Manorial affix from the *Buteler* family, here in the 12th cent. **Felton, West** Shrops. *Feltone* 1086 (DB).

Feltwell Norfolk. *Feltuuella* 1086 (DB). Probably 'spring or stream where mullein or a similar plant grows'. OE *felte* + *wella*.

Fen Ditton Cambs., see DITTON.

Fen Drayton Cambs., see DRAYTON.

Fenham Northum., near Fenwick. *Fennum* c.1085. '(Place in) the fens'. OE *fenn* in a dative plural form *fennum*.

Feniton Devon. *Finetone* 1086 (DB). 'Farmstead by Vine Water'. Celtic river-name (meaning 'boundary stream') + OE *tūn*.

Fenny as affix, see main name, e.g. for **Fenny Bentley** (Derbys.) see BENTLEY.

Fenrother Northum. *Finrode* 1189. 'Clearing by a mound or heap'. OE *fīn* + *rother.

Fenstanton Cambs. *Stantun* 1012, *Stantone* 1086 (DB), *Fenstanton* 1260. 'Farmstead on stony ground in a marshy district'. OE *fen* + *stān* + *tūn*.

Fenton, 'farmstead or village in a fen or marshland', OE *fenn* + *tūn*; examples include: **Fenton** Cambs. *Fentun* 1236. **Fenton** Lincs., near Claypole. *Fentun* 1212. **Fenton** Lincs., near Kettlethorpe. *Fentuna* c.1115. **Fenton** Staffs. *Fentone* 1086 (DB). **Fenton, Church & Little** N. Yorks. *Fentune* 963, *Fentun* 1086 (DB), *Kirkfenton* 1338. Affix from OE *cirice*, OScand. *kirkja*. **Fenton Town** Northum. *Fenton* 1242.

Fenwick, 'dwelling or (dairy) farm in a fen or marsh', OE *fenn* + *wīc*: **Fenwick** Northum., near Kyloe. *Fenwic* 1208. **Fenwick** Northum., near Stamfordham. *Fenwic* 1242. **Fenwick** S. Yorks. *Fenwic* 1166.

Feock Cornwall. *Lanfioc* 12th cent. 'Church of St Fioc'. From the patron saint of the church, with Cornish *lann in the early form.

Ferndown Dorset. *Fyrne* 1321. OE *fergen* 'wooded hill' or **fierne* 'ferny place', with the later addition of *dūn* 'down, hill'.

Fernham Oxon. *Fernham* 9th cent. 'River-meadow where ferns grow'. OE *fearn* + *hamm*.

Fernhurst W. Sussex. *Fernherst* c.1200. 'Fern-covered wooded hill'. OE *fearn* + *hyrst*.

Fernilee Derbys. *Ferneley* 12th cent. 'Woodland clearing where ferns grow'. OE *fearn* + *lēah*.

Ferrensby N. Yorks. *Feresbi* (*sic*) 1086 (DB), *Feringesby* 13th cent. Probably 'farmstead or village of the man from the Faroe Islands'. OScand. *færeyingr* + *bý*.

Ferriby, North & South Humber. *Ferebi* 1086 (DB), *North Feribi* 1284, *Suthferebi* c.1130. 'Farmstead or village near the ferry'. OScand. *ferja* + *bý*. *North* and *South* with reference to their situation on opposite banks of the Humber.

Ferring W. Sussex. *Ferring* 765, *Feringes* 1086 (DB). Probably '(settlement of) the family or followers of a man called *Fēra'. OE pers. name + *-ingas*.

Ferryhill Durham. *Feregenne* 10th cent., *Ferye on the Hill* 1316. OE *fergen* 'wooded hill', with the later addition of *hyll* 'hill'.

Fersfield Norfolk. *Fersafeld* c.1035, *Ferseuella* (*sic*) 1086 (DB). Possibly 'open land where heifers graze'. OE **fers* + *feld*.

Fetcham Surrey. *Fecham* 10th cent., *Feceham* 1086 (DB). Probably 'homestead or village of a man called *Fecca'. OE pers. name + *hām*.

Fewston N. Yorks. *Fostune* 1086 (DB). 'Farmstead of a man called Fótr'. OScand. pers. name + OE *tūn*.

Fiddington Glos. *Fittingtun* 1004, *Fitentone* 1086 (DB). 'Estate associated with a man called *Fita'. OE pers. name + *-ing-* + *tūn*.

Fiddington Somerset. *Fitintone* 1086 (DB). Probably identical in origin with the previous name.

Fiddleford Dorset. *Fitelford* 1244. 'Ford of a man called Fitela'. OE pers. name + *ford*.

Field Staffs. *Felda* 1130. '(Place at) the open land'. OE *feld*.

Field Dalling Norfolk, see DALLING.

Fifehead Magdalen & Neville Dorset. *Fifhide* 1086 (DB), *Fifyde Maudaleyne* 1388, *Fyfhud Neuyle* 1287. '(Estate of) five hides of land'. OE *fīf* + *hīd*. Affix *Magdalen* from the dedication of the church, *Neville* from the *de Nevill* family, here in the 13th cent.

Fifield, '(estate of) five hides of land', OE *fīf* + *hīd*: **Fifield** Berks. *Fifhide* 1316. **Fifield** Oxon. *Fifhide* 1086 (DB). **Fifield Bavant** Wilts. *Fifhide* 1086 (DB), *Fiffehyde Beaufaunt* 1436. Manorial affix from the *de Bavent* family, here in the 14th cent.

Figheldean Wilts. *Fisgledene* (*sic*) 1086 (DB), *Figelden* 1227. 'Valley of a man called *Fygla'. OE pers. name + *denu*.

Filby Norfolk. *Filebey* 1086 (DB). 'Farmstead or village of a man called *Fili or Fīla'. OScand. or OE pers. name + *bý*. Alternatively the first element may be OScand. **fili* 'planks' (perhaps referring to a bridge or other structure).

Filey N. Yorks. *Fiuelac* (*sic*) 1086 (DB), *Fivelai* 12th cent. Possibly 'promontory shaped like a sea monster'. OE *fīfel* + *ēg*. The allusion would be to Filey Brigg (OScand. *bryggja* 'jetty'), a ridge of rock, half a mile long, projecting into the sea. Alternatively 'the five clearings', from OE *fīf* + *lēah*.

Filgrave Bucks. *Filegrave* 1241. 'Pit or grove of a man called *Fygla'. OE pers. name + *græf* or *grāf*.

Filkins Oxon. *Filching* 12th cent. Probably '(settlement of) the family or followers of a man called *Filica'. OE pers. name + *-ingas*.

Filleigh Devon, near Barnstaple. *Filelei* 1086 (DB). Probably 'woodland clearing where hay is made'. OE *filethe* + *lēah*.

Fillingham Lincs. *Figelingeham* 1086 (DB). 'Homestead of the family or followers of a man called *Fygla'. OE pers. name + *-inga-* + *hām*.

Fillongley Warwicks. *Filingelei* 1086 (DB). 'Woodland clearing of the family or followers of a man called *Fygla'. OE pers. name + *-inga-* + *lēah*.

Filton Avon. *Filton* 1187. 'Farm or estate where hay is made'. OE *filethe* + *tūn*.

Fimber Humber. *Fym(m)ara* 12th cent. 'Pool by a wood pile, or amidst the coarse grass'. OE *fīn* or **finn* + *mere*.

Finborough Suffolk. *Fineberga* 1086 (DB). 'Hill or mound frequented by woodpeckers'. OE *fīna* + *beorg*.

Fincham Norfolk. *P(h)incham* 1086 (DB). 'Homestead or enclosure frequented by finches'. OE *finc* + *hām* or *hamm*.

Finchampstead Berks. *Finchamestede* 1086 (DB). 'Homestead frequented by finches'. OE *finc* + *hām-stede*.

Finchingfield Essex. *Fincingefelda* 1086 (DB). 'Open land of the family or followers of a man called Finc'. OE pers. name + *-inga-* + *feld*.

Finchley Gtr. London. *Finchelee* c.1208. 'Woodland clearing frequented by finches'. OE *finc* + *lēah*.

Findern Derbys. *Findre* 1086 (DB). An obscure name, still not satisfactorily explained.

Findon W. Sussex. *Findune* 1086 (DB). 'Hill with a mound or heap of wood on it'. OE *fīn* + *dūn*.

Finedon Northants. *Tingdene* 1086 (DB). 'Valley where assemblies meet'. OE *thing* + *denu*.

Fingest Bucks. *Tingeherst* 12th cent. 'Wooded hill where assemblies are held'. OE *thing* + *hyrst*.

Finghall N. Yorks. *Finegala* (*sic*) 1086 (DB), *Finyngale* 1157. Probably 'nook of land of the family or followers of a man called *Fīn(a)'. OE pers. name + *-inga-* + *halh*.

Fingringhoe Essex. *Fingringaho* 10th cent. Possibly 'hill-spur of the dwellers on the finger of land'. OE *finger* + *-inga-* + *hōh*.

Finmere Oxon. *Finemere* 1086 (DB). 'Pool frequented by woodpeckers'. OE *fīna* + *mere*.

Finningham Suffolk. *Finingaham* 1086 (DB). 'Homestead of the family or followers of a man called *Fīn(a)'. OE pers. name + *-inga-* + *hām*.

Finningley S. Yorks. *Feniglei* (*sic*) 1086 (DB), *Feningelay* 1175. 'Woodland clearing of the dwellers in the fen'. OE *fenn* + *-inga-* + *lēah*.

Finsbury Gtr. London. *Finesbire* 1235. 'Manor-house of a man called Finn'. OScand. pers. name + ME *bury* (from OE *byrig*, dative of *burh*).

Finsthwaite Cumbria. *Fynnesthwayt* 1336. 'Clearing of a man called Finn'. OScand. pers. name + *thveit*.

Finstock Oxon. *Finestochia* 12th cent. 'Outlying farmstead frequented by woodpeckers'. OE *fīna* + *stoc*.

Firbeck S. Yorks. *Fritebec* 12th cent. 'Woodland stream'. OE *fyrhth* + OScand. *bekkr*.

Firle, West E. Sussex. *Ferle* 1086 (DB). 'Place where oak-trees grow'. OE **fierel*.

Firsby Lincs., near Spilsby. *Frisebi* 1202. 'Farmstead or village of the Frisians'. OScand. *Frísir* (genitive *Frísa*) + *bý*.

Fishbourne, Fishburn, 'fish stream, stream where fish are caught', OE *fisc* + *burna*: **Fishbourne** I. of Wight. *Fisseburne* 1267. **Fishbourne** W. Sussex. *Fiseborne* 1086 (DB). **Fishburn** Durham. *Fisseburne* c.1190.

Fishlake S. Yorks. *Fiscelac* 1086 (DB). 'Fish stream'. OE *fisc* + *lacu*.

Fishtoft Lincs. *Toft* 1086 (DB). OScand. *toft* 'building site, curtilage'. The later addition *Fish-* may be a surname or indicate a connection with fishing.

Fiskerton, 'farmstead or village of the fishermen', OE *fiscere* (replaced by OScand. *fiskari*) + *tūn*: **Fiskerton** Lincs. *Fiskertuna* 1060, *Fiscartone* 1086 (DB). **Fiskerton** Notts. *Fiscertune* 956, *Fiscartune* 1086 (DB).

Fittleton Wilts. *Viteletone* 1086 (DB). 'Farmstead of a man called Fitela'. OE pers. name + *tūn*.

Fittleworth W. Sussex. *Fitelwurtha* 1168. 'Enclosure of a man called Fitela'. OE pers. name + *worth*.

Fitz Shrops. *Witesot* (*sic*) 1086 (DB), *Fittesho* 1194. 'Hill-spur of a man called *Fitt'. OE pers. name + *hōh*.

Fitzhead Somerset. *Fifhida* 1065. '(Estate of) five hides'. OE *fīf* + *hīd*.

Fivehead Somerset. *Fifhide* 1086 (DB). Identical in origin with the previous name.

Flackwell Heath Bucks. *Flakewelle* 1227. Possibly 'spring or stream of a man called *Flæcca'. OE pers. name + *wella*.

Fladbury Heref. & Worcs. *Fledanburg* late 7th cent., *Fledebirie* 1086 (DB). 'Stronghold or manor house of a woman called *Flǣde'. OE pers. name + *burh* (dative *byrig*).

Flagg Derbys. *Flagun* 1086 (DB). Probably 'place where turfs are cut'. OScand. *flag* in a dative plural form *flagum*.

Flamborough Humber. *Flaneburg* 1086 (DB). 'Stronghold of a man called Fleinn'. OScand. pers. name + OE *burh*. Flamborough Head (from OE *hēafod* 'headland') is first recorded in the 14th cent.

Flamstead Herts. *Fleamstede* 990, *Flamestede* 1086 (DB). 'Place of refuge'. OE *flēam* + *stede*.

Flansham W. Sussex. *Flennesham* 1220. OE *hām* 'homestead' or *hamm* 'enclosure' with an obscure first element, probably a pers. name.

Flasby N. Yorks. *Flatebi* 1086 (DB). 'Farmstead or village of a man called Flatr'. OScand. pers. name + *bý*.

Flaunden Herts. *Flawenden* 13th cent. Probably 'flag-stone valley'. OE **flage* + *denu*.

Flawborough Notts. *Flodberge* (*sic*) 1086 (DB), *Flouberge* 12th cent. 'Hill with stones'. OE *flōh* + *beorg*.

Flawith N. Yorks. *Flathwayth* c.1190. Possibly 'ford of the female troll or witch'. OScand. *flagth* + *vath*. Alternatively the first element may be

OScand. *flatha 'flat meadow' or OE *fleathe 'water-lily'.

Flaxby N. Yorks. *Flatesbi* 1086 (DB). 'Farmstead or village of a man called Flatr'. OScand. pers. name + *bý*.

Flaxley Glos. *Flaxlea* 1163. 'Clearing where flax is grown'. OE *fleax* + *lēah*.

Flaxton N. Yorks. *Flaxtune* 1086 (DB). 'Farmstead where flax is grown'. OE *fleax* + *tūn*.

Fleckney Leics. *Flechenie* 1086 (DB). Possibly 'well-watered land of a man called *Flecca'. OE pers. name (genitive *-n*) + *ēg*.

Flecknoe Warwicks. *Flechenho* 1086 (DB). Possibly 'hill-spur of a man called *Flecca'. OE pers. name (genitive *-n*) + *hōh*.

Fleet, '(place at) the stream, pool, or creek', OE *flēot*; examples include: **Fleet** Hants. *Flete* 1313. **Fleet** Lincs. *Fleot* 1086 (DB).

Fleetwood Lancs., a modern name, from Sir Peter Fleetwood who laid out the town in 1836.

Flempton Suffolk. *Flemingtuna* 1086 (DB). Possibly 'farmstead of the Flemings (people from Flanders)'. OE *Fleming* + *tūn*.

Fletching E. Sussex. *Flescinge(s)* 1086 (DB). '(Settlement of) the family or followers of a man called *Flecci'. OE pers. name + *-ingas*.

Fletton, Old Cambs. *Fletun* 1086 (DB). 'Farmstead on a stream'. OE *flēot* + *tūn*.

Flimby Cumbria. *Flemyngeby* 12th cent. 'Farmstead or village of the Flemings (people from Flanders)'. OScand. *Flǽmingr* + *bý*.

Flintham Notts. *Flintham* 1086 (DB). 'Homestead or enclosure of a man called *Flinta'. OE pers. name + *hām* or *hamm*.

Flinton Humber. *Flintone* 1086 (DB). 'Farmstead where flints are found'. OE *flint* + *tūn*.

Flitcham Norfolk. *Flicham* 1086 (DB). 'Homestead or village where flitches of bacon are produced'. OE *flicce* + *hām*.

Flitton Beds. *Flittan c.*985, *Flictham (sic)* 1086 (DB). Obscure in origin and meaning.

Flitwick Beds. *Flicteuuiche* 1086 (DB). OE *wīc* 'dwelling, (dairy) farm' with an uncertain first element.

Flixborough Humber. *Flichesburg* 1086 (DB). 'Stronghold of a man called Flík'. OScand. pers. name + OE *burh*.

Flixton, 'farmstead or village of a man called Flík', OScand. pers. name + OE *tūn*: **Flixton** Gtr. Manch. *Flixton* 1177. **Flixton** N. Yorks. *Fleustone (sic)* 1086 (DB), *Flixtona* 12th cent. **Flixton** Suffolk, near Bungay. *Flixtuna* 1086 (DB).

Flockton W. Yorks. *Flochetone* 1086 (DB). 'Farmstead of a man called Flóki'. OScand. pers. name + OE *tūn*.

Flodden Northum. *Floddoun* 1517. Possibly 'hill with stones'. OE *flōh* + *dūn*.

Flookburgh Cumbria. *Flokeburg* 1246. Probably 'stronghold of a man called Flóki'. OScand. pers. name + OE *burh*.

Floore Northants. *Flore* 1086 (DB). '(Place at) the floor', probably with reference to a lost tessellated pavement. OE *flōr(e)*.

Flordon Norfolk. *Florenduna* 1086 (DB). Probably 'hill with a floor or pavement'. OE *flōre* + *dūn*.

Flotterton Northum. *Flotweyton* 12th cent. Possibly 'farmstead by the road liable to flood'. OE *flot* + *weg* + *tūn*.

Flowton Suffolk. *Flochetuna* 1086 (DB). 'Farmstead of a man called Flóki'. OScand. pers. name + OE *tūn*.

Flyford Flavell Heref. & Worcs. *Fleferth* 10th cent. OE *fyrhth* 'sparse woodland' with an uncertain first element. The affix *Flavell* is simply a Normanized form of Flyford, added to distinguish this place from GRAFTON FLYFORD.

Fobbing Essex. *Phobinge* 1086 (DB). '(Settlement of) the family or followers of a man called *Fobba', or '*Fobba's place'. OE pers. name + *-ingas* or *-ing*.

Fockerby Humber. *Fulcwardby* 12th cent. 'Farmstead or village of a man called Folcward'. OGerman pers. name + OScand. *bý*.

Foggathorpe Humber. *Fulcartorp* 1086 (DB). 'Outlying farmstead or hamlet of a man called Folcward'. OGerman pers. name + OScand. *thorp*.

Foleshill W. Mids. *Focheshelle* (*sic*) 1086 (DB), *Folkeshulla* 12th cent. 'Hill of the people', or 'hill of a man called *Folc'. OE *folc* or OE pers. name + *hyll*.

Folke Dorset. *Folk* 1244. '(Land held by) the people'. OE *folc*.

Folkestone Kent. *Folcanstan c*.697, *Fulchestan* 1086 (DB). Probably 'stone (marking a hundred meeting-place) of a man called *Folca'. OE pers. name + *stān*.

Folkingham Lincs. *Folchingeham* 1086 (DB). 'Homestead of the family or followers of a man called *Folc(a)'. OE pers. name + *-inga-* + *hām*.

Folkington E. Sussex. *Fochintone* (*sic*) 1086 (DB), *Folkintone c*.1150. 'Estate associated with a man called *Folc(a)'. OE pers. name + *-ing-* + *tūn*.

Folksworth Cambs. *Folchesworde* 1086 (DB). 'Enclosure of a man called *Folc'. OE pers. name + *worth*.

Folkton N. Yorks. *Fulcheton* 1086 (DB). 'Farmstead of a man called Folki or *Folca'. OScand. or OE pers. name + *tūn*.

Follifoot N. Yorks. *Pholifet* 12th cent. '(Place of) the horse-fighting' (alluding to a Viking sport). OE *fola* + *feoht*.

Fonthill Bishop & Gifford Wilts. *Funtial* 901, *Fontel* 1086 (DB), *Fontel Episcopi, Fontel Giffard* 1291. Possibly a Celtic river-name (meaning 'stream in fertile upland'). Manorial affixes from possession by the Bishop (Latin *episcopus*) of Winchester and the *Gifard* family at the time of Domesday.

Fontmell Magna Dorset. *Funtemel* 877, *Fontemale* 1086 (DB), *Magnam Funtemell* 1391. Originally a Celtic river-name (meaning 'stream by the bare hill'). Affix is Latin *magna* 'great'.

Foolow Derbys. *Foulowe* 1269. Probably 'hill frequented by birds'. OE *fugol* + *hlāw*.

Foots Cray Gtr. London, see CRAY.

Forcett N. Yorks. *Forset* 1086 (DB). Probably 'fold by a ford'. OE *ford* + *set*.

Ford, a common name, '(place by) the ford', from OE *ford*; examples include: **Ford** Northum. *Forda* 1224. **Ford** Shrops. *Forde* 1086 (DB). **Ford** W. Sussex. *Fordes c*.1194. In this name the form was originally plural.

Fordham, 'homestead or enclosure by a ford', OE *ford* + *hām* or *hamm*: **Fordham** Cambs. *Fordham* 10th cent., *Fordeham* 1086 (DB). **Fordham** Essex. *Fordeham* 1086 (DB). **Fordham** Norfolk. *Fordham* 1086 (DB).

Fordingbridge Hants. *Fordingebrige* 1086 (DB). 'Bridge of the people living by the ford'. OE *ford* + *-inga-* + *brycg*.

Fordon Humber. *Fordun* 1086 (DB). '(Place) in front of the hill'. OE *fore* + *dūn*.

Fordwich Kent. *Fordeuuicum* 675, *Forewic* 1086 (DB). 'Dwelling or (dairy) farm near the ford'. OE *ford* + *wīc*.

Foreland, North Kent. *Forland* 1326. 'Promontory', OE *fore* + *land*. **South Foreland** near Dover has the same origin.

Foremark Derbys. *Fornewerche* 1086 (DB). 'Old fortification'. OScand. *forn* + *verk*.

Forest Hill Oxon. *Fostel* (*sic*) 1086 (DB), *Forsthulle* 1122. 'Hill with a ridge'. OE **forst* + *hyll*.

Forest Row E. Sussex. *Forstrowe* 1467. 'Row (of trees or houses) in ASHDOWN FOREST'. ME *forest* + *row*.

Formby Mersey. *Fornebei* 1086 (DB). 'Old farmstead', or 'farmstead of a man called Forni'. OScand. *forn* or OScand. pers. name + *bý*.

Forncett St Mary & St Peter Norfolk. *Fornesseta* 1086 (DB). 'Dwelling or fold of a man called Forni'. OScand. pers. name + OE (*ge*)*set*. Affixes from the dedications of the churches.

Fornham All Saints & St Martin Suffolk. *Fornham* 1086 (DB), *Fornham Omnium Sanctorum, Fornham Sancti Martini* 1254. 'Homestead or village where trout are caught'. OE *forne* + *hām*. Affixes from the church dedications.

Forsbrook Staffs. *Fotesbroc* 1086 (DB). 'Brook of a man called Fótr'. OScand. pers. name + OE *brōc*.

Forston Dorset. *Fosardeston* 1236. 'Estate of the *Forsard* family'. OE *tūn*.

This family was here from the early 13th cent.

Forthampton Glos. *Forhelmentone* 1086 (DB). 'Estate associated with a man called Forthhelm'. OE pers. name + *-ing-* + *tūn*.

Forton, 'farmstead or village by a ford', OE *ford* + *tūn*: **Forton** Hants. *Forton* 1312. **Forton** Lancs. *Fortune* 1086 (DB). **Forton** Shrops. *Fordune* 1086 (DB). **Forton** Staffs. *Forton* 1198.

Fosbury Wilts., near Tidcombe. *Fostesberge* 1086 (DB). 'Stronghold of the ridge'. OE **forst* + *burh* (dative *byrig*).

Fosdyke Lincs. *Fotesdic* 1183. 'Ditch of a man called Fótr'. OScand. pers. name + OE *dīc*.

Fosse Way (Roman road from Lincoln to Bath). *Foss* 8th cent. From OE **foss* 'ditch', so called from its having had a prominent ditch on either side.

Foston, 'farmstead or village of a man called Fótr', OScand. pers. name + *tūn*: **Foston** Derbys. *Fostun* 12th cent. Recorded as *Farulveston* 1086 (DB), 'farmstead of a man called Farulfr', OScand. pers. name + OE *tūn*. **Foston** Lincs. *Foztun* 1086 (DB). **Foston** N. Yorks. *Fostun* 1086 (DB). **Foston on the Wolds** Humber. *Fodstone* 1086 (DB), *Foston on le Wolde* 1609. For the affix, see WOLDS.

Fotherby Lincs. *Fodrebi* 1086 (DB). 'Farmstead of a man called Fótr', or 'farmstead which supplies fodder'. OScand. pers. name or *fóthr* + *bý*.

Fotheringhay Northants. *Fodringeia* 1086 (DB). Probably 'island or well-watered land used for grazing'. OE **fōdring* + *ēg*.

Foulden Norfolk. *Fugalduna* 1086 (DB). 'Hill frequented by birds'. OE *fugol* + *dūn*.

Foulness Essex. *Fughelnesse* 1215. 'Promontory frequented by birds'. OE *fugol* + *næss*.

Foulridge Lancs. *Folric* 1219. 'Ridge where foals graze'. OE *fola* + *hrycg*.

Foulsham Norfolk. *Folsham* 1086 (DB). 'Homestead of a man called Fugol'. OE pers. name + *hām*.

Fourstones Northum. *Fourstanys* 1236. 'Four stones', here describing a tetralith. OE *fēower* + *stān*.

Fovant Wilts. *Fobbefunte* 901, *Febefonte* (*sic*) 1086 (DB). 'Spring of a man called *Fobba'. OE pers. name + **funta*.

Fowey Cornwall. *Fawi* c.1223. Named from the River Fowey, a Cornish name probably meaning 'beech-tree river'.

Fowlmere Cambs. *Fuglemære* 1086 (DB). 'Mere or lake frequented by birds'. OE *fugol* + *mere*.

Fownhope Heref. & Worcs. *Hope* 1086 (DB), *Faghehope* 1242. OE *hop* 'small enclosed valley' with the later addition of *fāg* (dative *fāgan*) 'variegated, multi-coloured'.

Foxearth Essex. *Focsearde* 1086 (DB). 'The fox's earth, the fox-hole'. OE *fox* + *eorthe*.

Foxham Wilts. *Foxham* 1065. 'Homestead or enclosure where foxes are seen'. OE *fox* + *hām* or *hamm*.

Foxholes N. Yorks. *Fox(o)hole* 1086 (DB). 'The fox-hole(s), the fox's earth(s)'. OE *fox-hol*.

Foxley, 'woodland clearing frequented by foxes', OE *fox* + *lēah*: **Foxley** Norfolk. *Foxle* 1086 (DB). **Foxley** Wilts. *Foxelege* 1086 (DB).

Foxt Staffs. *Foxwiss* 1176. 'The fox's den'. OE *fox* + *wist*.

Foxton, usually 'farmstead where foxes are often seen', OE *fox* + *tūn*: **Foxton** Cambs. *Foxetune* 1086 (DB). **Foxton** Leics. *Foxtone* 1086 (DB).

However the following has a different second element: **Foxton** Durham. *Foxedene* c.1170. 'Valley frequented by foxes'. OE *fox* + *denu*.

Foxwist Green Ches. *Foxwyste* 1475. 'The fox's den'. OE *fox* + *wist*, with *Green* added from the 19th cent.

Foy Heref. & Worcs. *Lann Timoi* c.1150. '(Church of) St Moi'. From the patron saint of the church, originally with Welsh *llan* 'church'.

Fradswell Staffs. *Frodeswelle* 1086 (DB). 'Spring or stream of a man called Frōd'. OE pers. name + *wella*.

Fraisthorpe Humber. *Frestintorp* 1086 (DB). 'Outlying farmstead or hamlet of a man called *Freistingr or

Freysteinn'. OScand. pers. name + *thorp*.

Framfield E. Sussex. *Framelle* (*sic*) 1086 (DB), *Fremefeld* 1257. 'Open land of a man called *Frem(m)a or *Fremi'. OE pers. name + *feld*.

Framilode Glos. *Framilade* 1086 (DB). 'Crossing over the River Frome'. Celtic river-name (meaning 'fair, fine') + OE *gelād*.

Framingham Earl & Pigot Norfolk. *Framingaham* 1086 (DB), *Framelingham Comitis, Framelingham Picot* 1254. 'Homestead of the family or followers of a man called Fram'. OE pers. name + *-inga-* + *hām*. Manorial affixes from early possession by the Earl of Norfolk (Latin *comitis* 'of the earl') and by the *Picot* family.

Framlingham Suffolk. *Fram(e)lingaham* 1086 (DB). 'Homestead of the family or followers of a man called *Framela'. OE pers. name + *-inga-* + *hām*.

Framlington, Long Northum. *Fremelintun* 1166. 'Estate associated with a man called *Framela'. OE pers. name + *-ing-* + *tūn*. Affix from the length of the village.

Frampton, usually 'farmstead or village on the River Frome' (of which there are several), Celtic river-name (meaning 'fair, fine') + OE *tūn*: **Frampton** Dorset. *Frantone* 1086 (DB). **Frampton Cotterell** Avon. *Frantone* 1086 (DB), *Frampton Cotell* 1257. Manorial affix from the *Cotel* family, here in the 12th cent. **Frampton Mansell** Glos. *Frantone* 1086 (DB), *Frompton Maunsel* 1368. Manorial affix from the *Maunsel* family, here in the 13th cent. **Frampton on Severn** Glos. *Frantone* 1086 (DB), *Fromton upon Severne* 1311.

However the following has a different origin: **Frampton** Lincs. *Franetone* 1086 (DB). Probably 'farmstead of a man called *Fráni'. OScand. pers. name + *tūn*.

Framsden Suffolk. *Framesdena* 1086 (DB). 'Valley of a man called Fram'. OE pers. name + *denu*.

Framwellgate Moor Durham. *Framwelgat* 1352. 'Street by the strongly gushing spring'. OE *fram* + *wella* + OScand. *gata*.

Franche Heref. & Worcs. *Frenesse* 1086 (DB). 'Ash-tree of a man called *Frēa'. OE pers. name (genitive *-n*) + *æsc*.

Frankby Mersey. *Frankeby* 13th cent. 'Farm belonging to a Frenchman or to a man called *Franki'. OE *Franca* or OScand. pers. name + *bý*.

Frankley Heref. & Worcs. *Franchelie* 1086 (DB). 'Woodland clearing of a man called Franca'. OE pers. name + *lēah*.

Frankton, 'farmstead or village of a man called Franca', OE pers. name + *tūn*: **Frankton** Warwicks. *Franchetone* 1086 (DB). **Frankton, English & Welsh** Shrops. *Franchetone* 1086 (DB). The distinguishing affixes are self-explanatory, Welsh Frankton being some five miles nearer to the Welsh border.

Fransham Norfolk. *Frandesham* 1086 (DB). OE *hām* 'homestead' or *hamm* 'enclosure' with a pers. name of uncertain form.

Frant E. Sussex. *Fyrnthan* 956. 'Place overgrown with fern or bracken'. OE **fiernthe*.

Frating Green Essex. *Fretinge* c.1060, *Fratinga* 1086 (DB). '(Settlement of) the family or followers of a man called *Fræt(a)', or '*Fræt(a)'s place'. OE pers. name + *-ingas* or *-ing*.

Fratton Hants. *Frodin(c)gtune* 982, *Frodinton* 1086 (DB). 'Estate associated with a man called Frōda'. OE pers. name + *-ing-* + *tūn*.

Freckenham Suffolk. *Frekeham* 895, *Frakenaham* 1086 (DB). 'Homestead or village of a man called *Freca'. OE pers. name (genitive *-n*) + *hām*.

Freckleton Lancs. *Frecheltun* 1086 (DB). Probably 'farmstead of a man called *Frecla'. OE pers. name + *tūn*.

Freeby Leics. *Fredebi* 1086 (DB). 'Farmstead or village of a man called Fræthi'. OScand. pers. name + *bý*.

Freethorpe Norfolk. *Frietorp* 1086 (DB). 'Outlying farmstead or hamlet of a man called Fræthi'. OScand. pers. name + *thorp*.

Fremington, 'estate associated with a man called *Fremi or *Frem(m)a', OE pers. name + *-ing-* + *tūn*: **Fremington** Devon. *Framintone* 1086 (DB). **Fremington** N. Yorks. *Fremington* 1086 (DB).

Frensham Surrey. *Fermesham* 10th cent. 'Homestead or village of a man called *Fremi'. OE pers. name + *hām*.

Freshfield Mersey., a recent name, apparently called after a man named *Fresh* who reclaimed the land after encroachment by sand.

Freshwater I. of Wight. *Frescewatre* 1086 (DB). 'River with fresh water'. OE *fersc* + *wæter*.

Fressingfield Suffolk. *Fessefelda (sic)* 1086 (DB), *Frisingefeld* 1185. Possibly 'open land of the family or followers of a man called *Frīsa ('the Frisian')'. OE pers. name + *-inga-* + *feld*.

Frettenham Norfolk. *Fretham* 1086 (DB). 'Homestead or village of a man called *Frǣta'. OE pers. name (genitive *-n*) + *hām*.

Fridaythorpe Humber. *Fridagstorp* 1086 (DB). Probably 'outlying farmstead or hamlet of a man called *Frīgedæg'. OE pers. name + *thorp*.

Friern Barnet Gtr. London, see BARNET.

Frilford Oxon. *Frieliford* 1086 (DB). 'Ford of a man called *Frithela'. OE pers. name + *ford*.

Frilsham Berks. *Frilesham* 1086 (DB). 'Homestead or village of a man called *Frithel'. OE pers. name + *hām*.

Frimley Surrey. *Fremle* 1203. 'Woodland clearing of a man called *Frem(m)a'. OE pers. name + *lēah*.

Frindsbury Kent. *Freondesberiam* 764, *Frandesberie* 1086 (DB). 'Stronghold of a man called *Frēond'. OE pers. name + *burh* (dative *byrig*).

Fring Norfolk. *Frainghes* 1086 (DB). Probably '(settlement of) the family or followers of a man called *Frēa'. OE pers. name + *-ingas*.

Fringford Oxon. *Feringeford* 1086 (DB). Probably 'ford of the family or followers of a man called *Fēra'. OE pers. name + *-inga-* + *ford*.

Frinsted Kent. *Fredenestede* 1086 (DB). 'Place of protection'. OE **frithen* + *stede*.

Frinton on Sea Essex. *Frientuna* 1086 (DB). 'Farmstead of a man called *Fritha', or 'protected farmstead'. OE pers. name (genitive *-n*) or OE **frithen* + *tūn*.

Frisby on the Wreake Leics. *Frisebie* 1086 (DB). 'Farmstead or village of the Frisians'. OScand. *Frísir* (genitive *Frísa*) + *bý*. Wreake is an OScand. river-name meaning 'twisted, winding'.

Friskney Lincs. *Frischenei* 1086 (DB). 'River with fresh water'. OE *fersc* (dative *-an*) + *ēa*.

Friston E. Sussex. *Friston* 1200. Possibly 'farmstead of a man called *Frēo'. OE pers. name + *tūn*.

Friston Suffolk. *Frisetuna* 1086 (DB). 'Farmstead or village of the Frisians'. OE *Frīsa* + *tūn*.

Fritham Hants. *Friham* 1212. Probably 'enclosure in sparse woodland'. OE *fyrhth* + *hamm*.

Frithelstock Devon. *Fredeletestoc* 1086 (DB). 'Outlying farmstead of a man called *Frithulāc'. OE pers. name + *stoc*.

Frithville Lincs. *Le Frith* 1331. OE *fyrhth* 'sparse woodland' with the later addition of *-ville* (from French *ville* 'village, town').

Frittenden Kent. *Friththingden* 9th cent. 'Woodland pasture associated with a man called Frith'. OE pers. name + *-ing-* + *denn*.

Fritton, 'farmstead offering safety or protection', or 'farmstead of a man called Frithi', OE *frith* or OScand. pers. name + OE *tūn*: **Fritton** Norfolk, near Gorleston. *Fridetuna* 1086 (DB). **Fritton** Norfolk, near Morningthorpe. *Fridetuna* 1086 (DB).

Fritwell Oxon. *Fertwelle* 1086 (DB). Probably 'wishing well'. OE *freht* + *wella*.

Frizington Cumbria. *Frisingaton* c.1160. Probably 'estate of the family or followers of a man called *Frīsa ('the Frisian')'. OE pers. name + *-inga-* + *tūn*.

Frocester Glos. *Frowecestre* 1086 (DB). 'Roman town on the River Frome'. Celtic river-name (meaning 'fair, fine') + OE *ceaster*.

Frodesley Shrops. *Frodeslege* 1086 (DB). 'Woodland clearing of a man called Frōd'. OE pers. name + *lēah*.

Frodingham, 'homestead of the family or followers of a man called Frōd(a)', OE pers. name + *-inga-* + *hām*: **Frodingham** Humber., near Scunthorpe. *Frodingham* 12th cent. **Frodingham, North** Humber. *Frotingham* 1086 (DB), *North Frothyngham* 1297.

Frodsham Ches. *Frotesham* 1086 (DB). 'Homestead or promontory of a man called Frōd'. OE pers. name + *hām* or *hamm*.

Frogmore, usually 'pool frequented by frogs', OE *frogga* + *mere*; for example **Frogmore** Hants. *Frogmore* 1294.

Frome, named from the River Frome (of which there are several), a Celtic river-name meaning 'fair, fine, brisk': **Frome** Somerset. *Froom* 8th cent. **Frome, Bishop's, Canon, & Castle** Heref. & Worcs. *Frome* 1086 (DB), *Frume al Evesk* 1252, *Froma Canonicorum*, *Froma Castri* 1242. Affixes 'Bishop's' (OFrench *eveske*) and 'Canon' (Latin *Canonicorum* 'of the canons') refer to possession by the Bishop of Hereford and the canons of Lanthony in medieval times, 'Castle' refers to a Norman castle. **Frome St Quintin** Dorset. *Litelfrome* 1086 (DB), *Fromequintin* 1288. At first called 'little' (OE *lȳtel*) to distinguish it from other manors on the same river, later given a manorial affix from the *St Quintin* family, here in the 13th cent.

Frostenden Suffolk. *Froxedena* 1086 (DB). Probably 'valley frequented by frogs'. OE *frosc* + *denu*.

Frosterley Durham. *Forsterlegh* 1239. 'Woodland clearing of the forester'. ME *forester* + OE *lēah*.

Froxfield, 'open land frequented by frogs', OE *frosc* + *feld*: **Froxfield** Wilts. *Forscanfeld* 9th cent. **Froxfield Green** Hants. *Froxafelda* 10th cent.

Fryerning Essex. *Inga* 1086 (DB), *Friering* 1469. Originally '(settlement of) the people of the district'. OE **gē* + *-ingas*. Later distinguished from other manors so called by the affix *Freren-* 'of the brethren' (from ME *frere*) referring to possession by the Knights Hospitallers in the 12th cent.

Fryston, Monk N. Yorks. *Fristun* c.1030, *Munechesfryston* 1166. 'Farmstead of the Frisians'. OE *Frīsa* + *tūn*. Affix from OE *munuc* 'monk' referring to possession by Selby Abbey in the 11th cent.

Fryton N. Yorks. *Frideton* 1086 (DB). 'Farmstead offering safety or protection', or 'farmstead of a man called Frithi'. OE *frith* or OScand. pers. name + OE *tūn*.

Fulbeck Lincs. *Fulebec* 1086 (DB). 'Foul or dirty stream'. OE *fūl* + OScand. *bekkr*.

Fulbourn Cambs. *Fuulburne* c.1050, *Fuleberne* 1086 (DB). 'Stream frequented by birds'. OE *fugol* + *burna*.

Fulbrook Oxon. *Fulebroc* 1086 (DB). 'Foul or dirty brook'. OE *fūl* + *brōc*.

Fulford, 'foul or dirty ford', OE *fūl* + *ford*: **Fulford** N. Yorks. *Fuleford* 1086 (DB). **Fulford** Somerset. *Fuleforde* 1327. **Fulford** Staffs. *Fuleford* 1086 (DB).

Fulham Gtr. London. *Fulanham* c.705, *Fuleham* 1086 (DB). 'Land in a river-bend of a man called *Fulla'. OE pers. name + *hamm*.

Fulking W. Sussex. *Fochinges* (*sic*) 1086 (DB), *Folkinges* c.1100. '(Settlement of) the family or followers of a man called *Folca'. OE pers. name + *-ingas*.

Fullerton Hants. *Fugelerestune* 1086 (DB). 'Farmstead or village of the fowlers or bird-catchers'. OE *fuglere* + *tūn*.

Fulletby Lincs. *Fullobi* 1086 (DB). OScand. *bý* 'farmstead, village' with an obscure first element, possibly a pers. name.

Full Sutton Humber., see SUTTON.

Fulmer Bucks. *Fugelmere* 1198. 'Mere or lake frequented by birds'. OE *fugol* + *mere*.

Fulmodeston Norfolk. *Fulmotestuna* 1086 (DB). 'Farmstead of a man called Fulcmod'. OGerman pers. name + *tūn*.

Fulnetby Lincs. *Fulnedebi* 1086 (DB). OScand. *bý* 'farmstead, village' with an uncertain first element, possibly OScand. **full-nautr* 'one who has a full share'.

Fulstow Lincs. *Fugelestou* 1086 (DB). 'Holy place or meeting place of a man called Fugol'. OE pers. name + *stōw*. Alternatively the first element may be OE *fugol* 'bird'.

Fulwell Tyne & Wear. *Fulewella* 12th cent. 'Foul or dirty spring or stream'. OE *fūl* + *wella*.

Fulwood, 'foul or dirty wood', OE *fūl* + *wudu*: **Fulwood** Lancs. *Fulewde* 1199. **Fulwood** Notts. *Folewode* 13th cent.

Funtington W. Sussex. *Fundintune* 12th cent. Possibly 'farmstead at the place with a spring'. OE **funta* + *-ing* + *tūn*.

Furness (old district) Cumbria, see BARROW IN FURNESS.

Fyfield, '(estate of) five hides of land', OE *fīf* + *hīd*: **Fyfield** Essex. *Fifhidam* 1086 (DB). **Fyfield** Glos. *Fishide* 12th cent. **Fyfield** Hants. *Fifhidon* 975, *Fifhide* 1086 (DB). **Fyfield** Oxon. *Fif Hidum* 956, *Fivehide* 1086 (DB). **Fyfield** Wilts. *Fifhide* 1086 (DB).

Fylde (district) Lancs., see POULTON-LE-FYLDE.

G

Gaddesby Leics. *Gadesbi* 1086 (DB). 'Farmstead or village of a man called Gaddr'. OScand. pers. name + *bý*. Alternatively the first element may be OScand. *gaddr* 'spur of land'.

Gaddesden, Great & Little Herts. *Gætesdene* 10th cent., *Gatesdene* 1086 (DB). 'Valley of a man called *Gǣte(n)'. OE pers. name + *denu*.

Gagingwell Oxon. *Gadelingwelle* c.1173. 'Spring or stream of the kinsmen or companions'. OE *gædeling* + *wella*.

Gailey Staffs. *Gageleage* c.1002, *Gragelie* (*sic*) 1086 (DB). 'Woodland clearing where bog-myrtle grows'. OE *gagel* + *lēah*.

Gainford Durham. *Geg(e)nforda* c.1040. 'Direct ford', i.e. 'ford on a direct route'. OE *gegn* + *ford*.

Gainsborough Lincs. *Gainesburg* 1086 (DB). 'Stronghold of a man called *Gegn'. OE pers. name + *burh*.

Gaisgill Cumbria. *Gasegille* 1310. 'Ravine frequented by wild geese'. OScand. *gás* + *gil*.

Galgate Lancs. *Galwaithegate* c.1190. Possibly '(place by) the Galloway road', i.e. 'the road used by cattle drovers from Galloway'. Scottish place-name (meaning 'territory of the stranger-Gaels') + OScand. *gata*.

Galhampton, Galmpton, 'farmstead of rent-paying peasants', OE **gafol-mann* + *tūn*: **Galhampton** Somerset. *Galmeton* 1199. **Galmpton** Devon, near Brixham. *Galmentone* 1086 (DB). **Galmpton** Devon, near Salcombe. *Walementone* 1086 (DB).

Galphay N. Yorks. *Galghagh* 12th cent. 'Enclosure where a gallows stands'. OE *galga* + *haga*.

Gamblesby Cumbria. *Gamelesbi* 1177. 'Farmstead or village of a man called Gamall'. OScand. pers. name + *bý*.

Gamlingay Cambs. *Gamelingei* 1086 (DB). 'Enclosure or well-watered land associated with a man called *Gamela, or of *Gamela's people'. OE pers. name + *-ing-* or *-inga-* + *hæg* or *ēg*.

Gamston, 'farmstead of a man called Gamall', OScand. pers. name + OE *tūn*: **Gamston** Notts., near East Retford. *Gamelestune* 1086 (DB). **Gamston** Notts., near Nottingham. *Gamelestune* 1086 (DB).

Ganarew Heref. & Worcs. *Genoreu* c.1150. 'Opening or pass of the hill'. Welsh *genau* + *rhiw*.

Ganstead Humber. *Gagenestad* 1086 (DB). Probably 'homestead of a man called *Gagni or *Gagne'. OScand. pers. name + *stathr*.

Ganthorpe N. Yorks. *Gameltorp* (*sic*) 1086 (DB), *Galmestorp* 1169. 'Outlying farmstead or hamlet of a man called Galmr'. OScand. pers. name + *thorp*.

Ganton N. Yorks. *Galmeton* 1086 (DB). Probably 'farmstead of a man called Galmr'. OScand. pers. name + OE *tūn*.

Garboldisham Norfolk. *Gerboldesham* 1086 (DB). 'Homestead or village of a man called *Gǣrbald'. OE pers. name + *hām*.

Garford Oxon. *Garanforda* 940, *Wareford* (*sic*) 1086 (DB). 'Ford of a man called *Gāra', or 'ford at the triangular plot of ground'. OE pers. name or *gāra* + *ford*.

Garforth W. Yorks. *Gereford* 1086 (DB). 'Ford of a man called *Gǣra', or 'ford at the triangular plot of ground'. OE pers. name or *gāra* (influenced by OScand. *geiri*) + *ford*.

Gargrave N. Yorks. *Geregraue* 1086 (DB). 'Grove in a triangular plot of ground'. OScand. *geiri* (replacing OE *gār*) + OE *grāf*.

Garrigill Cumbria. *Gerardgile* 1232. 'Deep valley of a man called Gerard'. OGerman pers. name + OScand. *gil*.

Garron (river) Heref. & Worcs., see LLANGARRON.

Garsdale Cumbria. *Garcedale* c.1240. 'Valley of a man called Garthr', or 'grass valley'. OScand. pers. name + *dalr*, or OE *gærs* + *dæl*.

Garsdon Wilts. *Gersdune* 701, *Gardone* 1086 (DB). 'Grass hill'. OE *gærs* + *dūn*.

Garshall Green Staffs. *Garnonshale* 1310. Possibly 'nook of land of a family called *Garnon*'. ME surname + OE *halh*.

Garsington Oxon. *Gersedun* 1086 (DB). 'Grassy hill'. OE **gærsen* + *dūn*.

Garstang Lancs. *Cherestanc* (*sic*) 1086 (DB), *Gairstang* c.1195. 'Pole (marking a boundary or meeting-place) shaped like a spear, or by a triangular plot'. OScand. *geirr* or *geiri* + *stǫng*.

Garston Mersey. *Gerstan* 1094. Possibly 'the great stone'. OE *grēat* + *stān*.

Garston, East Berks. *Esgareston* 1180. 'Estate of a man called Esgar'. OScand. pers. name + OE *tūn*. The modern form is a 'folk etymology' that completely disguises the original meaning of the name.

Garswood Mersey. *Grateswode* 1367. OE *wudu* 'wood' with an obscure first element, possibly a pers. name.

Garthorpe Humber. *Gerulftorp* 1086 (DB). 'Outlying farmstead or hamlet of a man called Geirulfr or Gairulf'. OScand. or OGerman pers. name + OScand. *thorp*.

Garthorpe Leics. *Garthorp* 12th cent. Possibly 'outlying farmstead or hamlet of a man called *Gāra'. OE pers. name + OScand. *thorp*. Alternatively the first element may be OE *gāra* 'triangular plot of ground'.

Garton, 'farmstead in or near the triangular plot of ground', OE *gāra* + *tūn*: **Garton** Humber. *Gartun* 1086 (DB). **Garton on the Wolds** Humber. *Gartune* 1086 (DB), *Garton in Wald* 1347. For the affix, see WOLDS.

Garvestone Norfolk. *Gerolfestuna* 1086 (DB). 'Farmstead or village of a man called Geirulfr or Gairulf'. OScand. or OGerman pers. name + OE *tūn*.

Garway Heref. & Worcs. *Garou* 1137, *Langarewi* 1189. Probably 'church of a man called Guoruoe'. Welsh *llan* + pers. name.

Gastard Wilts. *Gatesterta* 1154. 'Tail of land where goats are kept'. OE *gāt* + *steort*.

Gasthorpe Norfolk. *Gadesthorp* 1086 (DB). 'Outlying farmstead or hamlet of a man called Gaddr'. OScand. pers. name + *thorp*.

Gatcombe I. of Wight. *Gatecome* 1086 (DB). 'Valley where goats are kept'. OE *gāt* + *cumb*.

Gateforth N. Yorks. *Gæiteford* c.1030. 'Goats' ford', i.e. 'ford used when moving goats'. OScand. *geit* + OE *ford*.

Gate Helmsley N. Yorks., see HELMSLEY.

Gateley Norfolk. *Gatelea* 1086 (DB). 'Clearing or pasture where goats are kept'. OE *gāt* + *lēah*.

Gatenby N. Yorks. *Ghetenesbi* 1086 (DB). Possibly 'farmstead or village of a man called Gaithan'. OIrish pers. name + OScand. *bý*.

Gateshead Tyne & Wear. *Gatesheued* 1196. 'Goat's headland or hill'. OE *gāt* + *hēafod*.

Gathurst Gtr. Manch. *Gatehurst* 1547. Probably 'wooded hill where goats are kept'. OE *gāt* + *hyrst*.

Gatley Gtr. Manch. *Gateclyve* 1290. 'Cliff or bank where goats are kept'. OE *gāt* + *clif*.

Gatwick Surrey. *Gatwik* 1241. 'Farm where goats are kept'. OE *gāt* + *wīc*.

Gaunless (river) Durham, see AUCKLAND.

Gautby Lincs. *Goutebi* 1196. 'Farmstead or village of a man called Gauti'. OScand. pers. name + *bý*.

Gawber S. Yorks. *Galgbergh* 1304. 'Gallows hill'. OE *galga* + *beorg*.

Gawcott Bucks. *Chauescote* (*sic*) 1086 (DB), *Gauecota* 1090. 'Cottage(s) for which rent is payable'. OE *gafol* + *cot*.

Gawsworth Ches. *Govesurde* 1086 (DB). Probably 'enclosure of the smith'. Welsh *gof* + OE *worth*.

Gaydon Warwicks. *Gaidone* 1194. 'Hill of a man called *Gæga'. OE pers. name + *dūn*.

Gayhurst Bucks. *Gateherst* 1086 (DB).

'Wooded hill where goats are kept'. OE *gāt* + *hyrst*.

Gayles N. Yorks. *Gales* 1534. '(Place at) the ravines'. OScand. *geil*.

Gayton, usually 'farmstead where goats are kept', from OScand. *geit* + *tún*: **Gayton** Mersey. *Gaitone* 1086 (DB). **Gayton** Norfolk. *Gaituna* 1086 (DB). **Gayton le Marsh** Lincs. *Geiton* 1206. Affix means 'in the marsh' from OE *mersc* with loss of preposition. **Gayton le Wold** Lincs. *Gettone* 1086 (DB). Affix means 'on the wold(s)' with loss of preposition, see WOLDS.
However the following have a different origin, 'farmstead of a man called *Gǣga', from OE pers. name + *tūn*: **Gayton** Northants. *Gaiton* 1162. **Gayton** Staffs. *Gaitone* 1086 (DB).

Gayton Thorpe Norfolk. *Torp* 1086 (DB), *Geytonthorp* 1402. 'Outlying farmstead or hamlet dependent on GAYTON'. OScand. *thorp*.

Gaywood Norfolk. *Gaiuude* 1086 (DB). 'Wood of a man called *Gǣga'. OE pers. name + *wudu*.

Gazeley Suffolk. *Gaysle* 1219. 'Woodland clearing of a man called *Gǣgi'. OE pers. name + *lēah*.

Gedding Suffolk. *Gedinga* 1086 (DB). '(Settlement of) the family or followers of a man called *Gydda'. OE pers. name + *-ingas*.

Geddington Northants. *Geitentone* 1086 (DB). Possibly 'estate associated with a man called *Gæte or Geiti. OE or OScand. pers. name + OE *-ing-* + *tūn*.

Gedney Lincs. *Gadenai* 1086 (DB). Probably 'island or well-watered land of a man called *Gǣda or *Gydda'. OE pers. name (genitive *-n*) + *ēg*.

Geldeston Norfolk. *Geldestun* 1242. 'Farmstead or village of a man called *Gyldi'. OE pers. name + *tūn*.

Gelston Lincs. *Cheuelestune* 1086 (DB). Probably 'farmstead or village of a man called *Gjǫfull'. OScand. pers. name + OE *tūn*.

Georgeham Devon. *Hama* 1086 (DB), *Hamme Sancti Georgii* 1356. Originally 'the well-watered valley' from OE *hamm*. Later affix from the dedication of the church to St George.

George Nympton Devon, see NYMPTON.

Germansweek Devon. *Wica* 1086 (DB), *Wyke Germyn* 1458. Originally 'the dwelling or (dairy) farm' from OE *wīc*. Later affix from the dedication of the church to St Germanus.

Germoe Cornwall. 'Chapel of *Sanctus Germoch*' 12th cent. From the patron saint of the chapel.

Gerrans Cornwall. 'Church of *Sanctus Gerentus*' 1202. 'Church of St. Gerent'. From the patron saint of the church.

Gerrards Cross Bucks. *Gerards Cross* 1692. Named from a local family called *Jarrard* or *Gerrard*.

Gestingthorpe Essex. *Gyrstlingathorpe* late 10th cent., *Ghestingetorp* 1086 (DB). 'Outlying farmstead of the family or followers of a man called *Gyrstel'. OE pers. name + *-inga-* + *throp*.

Gidding, Great, Little, & Steeple Cambs. *Geddinge* 1086 (DB), *Magna Giddinge* 1220, *Gydding Parva* 13th cent., *Stepelgedding* 1260. Probably '(settlement of) the family or followers of a man called *Gydda'. OE pers. name + *-ingas*. Distinguishing affixes are Latin *magna* 'great', *parva* 'little' and OE *stēpel* 'steeple, tower'.

Gidea Park Gtr. London. *La Gidiehall* 1258, *Guydie hall parke* 1668. Literally 'the foolish or crazy hall', from ME *gidi* + *hall*, perhaps alluding to a building of unusual design or construction.

Gidleigh Devon. *Gideleia* 1156. 'Woodland clearing of a man called *Gydda'. OE pers. name + *lēah*.

Giggleswick N. Yorks. *Ghigeleswic* 1086 (DB). 'Dwelling or (dairy) farm of a man called Gikel or Gichel'. OE or ME pers. name (probably a short form of the biblical name *Judichael*) + *wīc*.

Gilberdyke Humber. *Dyc* 1234, *Gilbertdike* 1376. '(Place at) the ditch or dike'. OE *dīc* with manorial addition from a person or family called *Gilbert*.

Gilcrux Cumbria. *Killecruce* c.1175. Probably 'retreat by a hill'. Celtic **cil* + **crūg*.

Gildersome W. Yorks. *Gildehusum* 1181. '(Place at) the guild-houses'. OScand. *gildi-hús* in a dative plural form.

Gildingwells S. Yorks. *Gildanwell* 13th

cent. Probably 'gushing spring'. OE **gyldande* + *wella*.

Gillamoor N. Yorks. *Gedlingesmore* (*sic*) 1086 (DB), *Gillingamor* late 12th cent. 'Moorland belonging to the family or followers of a man called *Gȳthla or *Gētla'. OE pers. name + *-inga-* + *mōr*.

Gilling, '(settlement of) the family or followers of a man called *Gȳthla or *Gētla', OE pers. name + *-ingas*: **Gilling East** N. Yorks. *Ghellinge* 1086 (DB). **Gilling West** N. Yorks. *Ingetlingum* 731, *Ghellinges* 1086 (DB).

Gillingham, 'homestead of the family or followers of a man called *Gylla', OE pers. name + *-inga-* + *hām*: **Gillingham** Dorset. *Gelingeham* 1086 (DB). **Gillingham** Kent. *Gyllingeham* 10th cent., *Gelingeham* 1086 (DB). **Gillingham** Norfolk. *Kildincham* (*sic*) 1086 (DB), *Gelingeham* 12th cent.

Gilmorton Leics. *Mortone* 1086 (DB), *Gilden Morton* 1327. 'Farmstead in marshy ground'. OE *mōr* + *tūn*, with later affix from OE *gylden* 'wealthy, splendid'.

Gilsland Cumbria. *Gillesland* 12th cent. 'Estate of a man called Gille or Gilli'. OIrish or OScand. pers. name + *land*.

Gilston Herts. *Gedeleston* 1197. 'Farmstead or village of a man called *Gēdel or *Gydel'. OE pers. name + *tūn*.

Gimingham Norfolk. *Gimingeham* 1086 (DB). 'Homestead of the family or followers of a man called *Gymi or *Gymma'. OE pers. name + *-inga-* + *hām*.

Ginge, East & West Oxon. *Gæging* 10th cent., *Gainz* 1086 (DB), *Estgeyng*, *Westgenge* 13th cent. Originally an OE river-name meaning 'one that turns aside', from the stem of OE *gǣgan* + *-ing*.

Girsby N. Yorks. *Grisebi* 1086 (DB). 'Farmstead of a man called Gríss', or 'farmstead where young pigs are reared'. OScand. pers. name or OScand. *gríss* + *bý*.

Girton, 'farmstead or village on gravelly ground', OE *grēot* + *tūn*: **Girton** Cambs. *Grittune* c.1060, *Gretone* 1086 (DB). **Girton** Notts. *Gretone* 1086 (DB).

Gisburn Lancs. *Ghiseburne* (*sic*) 1086 (DB), *Giselburn* 12th cent. Probably 'gushing stream'. OE **gysel* + *burna*.

Gisleham Suffolk. *Gisleham* 1086 (DB). 'Homestead or village of a man called *Gysla'. OE pers. name + *hām*.

Gislingham Suffolk. *Gyselingham* c.1060, *Gislingaham* 1086 (DB). 'Homestead of the family or followers of a man called *Gysla'. OE pers. name + *-inga-* + *hām*.

Gissing Norfolk. *Gessinga* 1086 (DB). '(Settlement of) the family or followers of a man called *Gyssa or *Gyssi'. OE pers. name + *-ingas*.

Gittisham Devon. *Gidesham* 1086 (DB). 'Homestead or enclosure of a man called *Gyddi'. OE pers. name + *hām* or *hamm*.

Givendale, Great Humber. *Ghiuedale* 1086 (DB). Probably 'valley of a river called *Gævul'. OScand. river-name (meaning 'good for fishing') + *dalr*.

Glaisdale N. Yorks. *Glasedale* 12th cent. 'Valley of a river called **Glas*'. Celtic river-name (meaning 'grey-green') + OScand. *dalr*.

Glandford Norfolk. *Glamforda* 1086 (DB). Probably 'ford where people assemble for revelry or games'. OE *glēam* + *ford*.

Glanton Northum. *Glentendon* 1186. 'Hill frequented by birds of prey or used as a look-out place'. OE **glente* + *dūn*.

Glanvilles Wootton Dorset, see WOOTTON.

Glapthorn Northants. *Glapethorn* 12th cent. 'Thorn-tree of a man called Glappa'. OE pers. name + *thorn*.

Glapwell Derbys. *Glappewelle* 1086 (DB). 'Stream of a man called Glappa', or 'stream where the plant buckbean grows'. OE pers. name or OE *glæppe* + *wella*.

Glascote Staffs. *Glascote* 12th cent. 'Hut where glass is made'. OE *glæs* + *cot*.

Glasson Cumbria. *Glassan* 1259. Probably a Celtic river-name containing a derivative of *glas* 'grey-green'.

Glasson Lancs. *Glassene* c.1265. Perhaps originally a river-name meaning 'clear or bright one' from OE **glǣsne* or **glǣsen*.

Glassonby Cumbria. *Glassanebi* 1177. 'Farmstead or village of a man called Glassán'. OIrish pers. name + OScand. *bý*.

Glaston Leics. *Gladestone* 1086 (DB). Probably 'farmstead of a man called *Glathr'. OScand. pers. name + OE *tūn*.

Glastonbury Somerset. *Glastingburi* 725, *Glæstingeberia* 1086 (DB). 'Stronghold of the people living at *Glaston*'. Celtic name (possibly meaning 'woad place') + OE *-inga-* + *burh* (dative *byrig*).

Glatton Cambs. *Glatune* 1086 (DB). 'Pleasant farmstead'. OE *glæd* + *tūn*.

Glazebrook Ches. *Glasbroc* 1227. Named from Glaze Brook, a Celtic river-name (meaning 'grey-green') + OE *brōc*.

Glazebury Ches., a late name of recent origin formed from GLAZEBROOK.

Glazeley Shrops. *Gleslei* 1086 (DB). Probably 'bright clearing'. OE **glǣs* + *lēah*.

Gleadless S. Yorks. *Gledeleys* 13th cent. Probably 'woodland clearings frequented by kites'. OE *gleoda* + *lēah*.

Gleaston Cumbria. *Glassertun* (*sic*) 1086 (DB), *Gleseton* 1269. Probably 'bright farmstead or village'. OE **glǣs* + *tūn*. The first element may be used as a stream-name 'the bright one'.

Glemham, Great & Little Suffolk. *Glaimham* 1086 (DB). Probably 'homestead or village noted for its revelry or games'. OE *glēam* + *hām*.

Glemsford Suffolk. *Glemesford c.*1050, *Clamesforda* (*sic*) 1086 (DB). Probably 'ford where people assemble for revelry or games'. OE *glēam* + *ford*.

Glen Parva & Great Glen Leics. *Glenne* 849, *Glen* 1086 (DB), *Parva Glen* 1242, *Magna Glen* 1247. '(Place at) the valley'. OE **glenn* (from Celtic **glĭnn*). Distinguishing affixes are Latin *parva* 'small' and *magna* 'great'.

Glenfield Leics. *Clanefelde* 1086 (DB). 'Clean open land', i.e. 'open land free from weeds or other unwanted growth'. OE *clǣne* + *feld*.

Glentham Lincs. *Glentham* 1086 (DB). 'Homestead frequented by birds of prey or at a look-out place'. OE **glente* + *hām*.

Glentworth Lincs. *Glentewrde* 1086 (DB). 'Enclosure frequented by birds of prey or at a look-out place'. OE **glente* + *worth*.

Glinton Cambs. *Clinton* 1060, *Glintone* 1086 (DB). Possibly 'fenced farmstead'. OE **glind* + *tūn*.

Glooston Leics. *Glorstone* 1086 (DB). 'Farmstead of a man called Glōr'. OE pers. name + *tūn*.

Glossop Derbys. *Glosop* 1086 (DB), *Glotsop* 1219. 'Valley of a man called *Glott'. OE pers. name + *hop*.

Gloucester Glos. *Coloniae Glev'* 2nd cent., *Glowecestre* 1086 (DB). 'Roman town called *Glevum*'. Celtic name (meaning 'bright place') + OE *ceaster*. The early form contains Latin *colonia* 'Roman colony for retired legionaries'. **Gloucestershire** (OE *scīr* 'district') is first referred to in the 11th cent.

Glusburn N. Yorks. *Glusebrun* 1086 (DB). '(Place at) the bright or shining stream'. OScand. **glus(s)* + *brunnr*.

Glympton Oxon. *Glimtuna c.*1050, *Glintone* 1086 (DB). 'Farmstead on the River Glyme'. Celtic river-name (meaning 'bright stream') + OE *tūn*.

Glynde E. Sussex. *Glinda* 1165. '(Place at) the fence or enclosure'. OE **glind*.

Glyndebourne E. Sussex. *Burne juxta Glynde* 1288. 'Stream near GLYNDE'. OE *burna*.

Gnosall Staffs. *Geneshale* (*sic*) 1086 (DB), *Gnowesala* 1140. OE *halh* 'nook of land' with an uncertain first element, probably an OE or OScand. pers. name.

Goadby, 'farmstead or village of a man called Gauti', OScand. pers. name + *bý*: **Goadby** Leics. *Goutebi* 1086 (DB). **Goadby Marwood** Leics. *Goutebi* 1086 (DB). Manorial affix from the *Maureward* family, here in the 14th cent.

Goathill Dorset. *Gatelme* (*sic*) 1086 (DB), *Gathulla* 1176. 'Hill where goats are pastured'. OE *gāt* + *hyll*.

Goathland N. Yorks. *Godelandia c.*1110. 'Cultivated land of a man called Gōda', or 'good cultivated land'. OE pers. name or OE *gōd* + *land*.

Goathurst Somerset. *Gahers (sic)* 1086 (DB), *Gothurste* 1292. 'Wooded hill where goats are kept'. OE *gāt* + *hyrst*.

Godalming Surrey. *Godelmingum c.*880, *Godelminge* 1086 (DB). '(Settlement of) the family or followers of a man called *Godhelm'. OE pers. name + *-ingas*.

Goddington Gtr. London. *Godinton* 1240. 'Estate associated with a man called Gōda'. OE pers. name + *-ing-* + *tūn*.

Godmanchester Cambs. *Godmundcestre* 1086 (DB). 'Roman station associated with a man called Godmund'. OE pers. name + *ceaster*.

Godmanstone Dorset. *Godemanestone* 1166. 'Farmstead of a man called Godmann'. OE pers. name + *tūn*.

Godmersham Kent. *Godmeresham* 822, *Gomersham* 1086 (DB). 'Homestead or village of a man called Godmǣr'. OE pers. name + *hām*.

Godney Somerset. *Godeneia* 10th cent. 'Island or well-watered land of a man called Gōda'. OE pers. name (genitive *-n*) + *ēg*.

Godolphin Cross Cornwall. *Wulgholgan* 1194. An obscure name, origin and meaning uncertain.

Godshill, 'hill associated with a heathen god or with the Christian God', OE *god* + *hyll*: **Godshill** Hants. *Godeshull* 1230. **Godshill** I. of Wight. *Godeshella* 12th cent.

Godstone Surrey. *Godeston* 1248, *Codeston* 1279. Probably 'farmstead of a man called *Cōd'. OE pers. name + *tūn*.

Golborne Gtr. Manch. *Goldeburn* 1187. 'Stream where marsh marigolds grow'. OE *golde* + *burna*.

Golcar W. Yorks. *Gudlagesarc* 1086 (DB). 'Shieling or hill-pasture of a man called Guthleikr or Guthlaugr'. OScand. pers. name + *erg*.

Goldhanger Essex. *Goldhangra* 1086 (DB). Probably 'wooded slope where marigolds or other yellow flowers grow'. OE *golde* + *hangra*.

Golding Shrops. *Goldene* 1086 (DB). Probably 'valley where marigolds grow'. OE *golde* + *denu*.

Goldsborough N. Yorks., near Knaresborough. *Godenesburg (sic)* 1086 (DB), *Godelesburc* 1170. 'Stronghold of a man called Godel'. OE (or OGerman) pers. name + *burh*.

Goldthorpe S. Yorks. *Goldetorp* 1086 (DB). 'Outlying farmstead or hamlet of a man called Golda'. OE pers. name + OScand. *thorp*.

Gomeldon Wilts. *Gomeledona* 1189. 'Hill of a man called *Gumela'. OE pers. name + *dūn*.

Gomersal W. Yorks. *Gomershale* 1086 (DB). 'Nook of land of a man called *Gūthmǣr'. OE pers. name + *halh*.

Gomshall Surrey. *Gomeselle (sic)* 1086 (DB), *Gumeselva* 1168. 'Shelf or terrace of land of a man called *Guma'. OE pers. name + *scelf*.

Gonalston Notts. *Gunnulvestune* 1086 (DB). 'Farmstead of a man called Gunnulf'. OScand. pers. name + OE *tūn*.

Gonerby, Great Lincs. *Gunfordebi* 1086 (DB). 'Farmstead or village of a man called Gunnfrøthr'. OScand. pers. name + *bý*.

Good Easter Essex, see EASTER.

Gooderstone Norfolk. *Godestuna (sic)* 1086 (DB), *Gutherestone* 1254. 'Farmstead of a man called Gūthhere'. OE pers. name + *tūn*.

Goodleigh Devon. *Godelege* 1086 (DB). 'Woodland clearing of a man called Gōda'. OE pers. name + *lēah*.

Goodmanham Humber. *Godmunddingaham* 731, *Gudmundham* 1086 (DB). 'Homestead of the family or followers of a man called Gōdmund'. OE pers. name + *-inga-* + *hām*.

Goodmayes Gtr. London. *Goodmayes* 1456. Named from the *Godemay* family who had lands here in the 14th cent.

Goodnestone, 'farmstead of a man called Gōdwine', OE pers. name + *tūn*: **Goodnestone** Kent, near Aylesham. *Godwineston* 1196. **Goodnestone** Kent, near Faversham. *Godwineston* 1208.

Goodrich Heref. & Worcs. *Castellum Godric* 1102. Originally 'castle of a man called Gōdrīc'. OE pers. name (that of a land-holder in 1086 (DB)) with Latin *castellum*.

Goodrington Devon. *Godrintone* 1086 (DB). 'Estate associated with a man called Gōdhere'. OE pers. name + *-ing-* + *tūn*.

Goodworth Clatford Hants., see CLATFORD.

Goole Humber. *Gulle* 1362. 'The stream or channel'. ME *goule*.

Goosey Oxon. *Goseie* 9th cent., *Gosei* 1086 (DB). 'Goose island'. OE *gōs* + *ēg*.

Goosnargh Lancs. *Gusansarghe* 1086 (DB). 'Shieling or hill-pasture of a man called Gussān'. OIrish pers. name + OScand. *erg*.

Gordano (old district) Avon, see CLAPTON IN GORDANO.

Gore Kent. *Gore* 1198. '(Place at) the triangular plot of ground'. OE *gāra*. The same name occurs in other counties.

Goring, '(settlement of) the family or followers of a man called *Gāra', OE pers. name + *-ingas*: **Goring** Oxon. *Garinges* 1086 (DB). **Goring by Sea** W. Sussex. *Garinges* 1086 (DB).

Gorleston on Sea Norfolk. *Gorlestuna* 1086 (DB). Probably 'farmstead of a man called *Gurl'. OE pers. name + *tūn*.

Gorran Cornwall. *Sanctus Goranus* 1086 (DB). '(Church of) St Goran'. From the patron saint of the church.

Gorsley Glos. *Gorstley* 1228. 'Woodland clearing where gorse grows'. OE *gorst* + *lēah*.

Gorton Gtr. Manch. *Gorton* 1282. 'Dirty farmstead'. OE *gor* + *tūn*.

Gosbeck Suffolk. *Gosebech* 1179. 'Stream frequented by geese'. OE *gōs* + OScand. *bekkr*.

Gosberton Lincs. *Gosebertechirche* 1086 (DB). 'Church of a man called Gosbert'. OGerman pers. name + OE *cirice* (replaced by *tūn* 'village').

Gosfield Essex. *Gosfeld* 1198. 'Open land frequented by (wild) geese'. OE *gōs* + *feld*.

Gosford, 'ford frequented by geese', OE *gōs* + *ford*; for example **Gosford** Devon. *Goseford* 1249.

Gosforth, 'ford frequented by geese', OE *gōs* + *ford*: **Gosforth** Cumbria. *Goseford* c.1150. **Gosforth** Tyne & Wear. *Goseford* 1166.

Gosport Hants. *Goseport* 1250. 'Market town where geese are sold'. OE *gōs* + *port*.

Goswick Northum. *Gossewic* 1202. 'Farm where geese are kept'. OE *gōs* + *wīc*.

Gotham Notts. *Gatham* 1086 (DB). 'Homestead or enclosure where goats are kept'. OE *gāt* + *hām* or *hamm*.

Gotherington Glos. *Godrinton* 1086 (DB). 'Estate associated with a man called Gūthhere'. OE pers. name + *-ing-* + *tūn*.

Goudhurst Kent. *Guithyrste* 11th cent. Probably 'wooded hill of a man called Gūtha'. OE pers. name + *hyrst*.

Goulceby Lincs. *Colchesbi* 1086 (DB). 'Farmstead or village of a man called *Kolkr'. OScand. pers. name + *bý*.

Gowdall Humber. *Goldale* 12th cent. 'Nook of land where marigolds grow'. OE *golde* + *halh*.

Goxhill, possibly 'hill or clearing of the cuckoo, or of a man called Gaukr', OScand. *gaukr* or pers. name + OE *hyll* or *lēah*: **Goxhill** Humber., near Barrow upon Humber. *Golse* (*sic*) 1086 (DB), *Gousele* 1212. **Goxhill** Humber., near Hornsea. *Golse* (*sic*) 1086 (DB), *Gousle* 12th cent.

Graffham W. Sussex. *Grafham* 1086 (DB). 'Homestead or enclosure in or by a grove'. OE *grāf* + *hām* or *hamm*.

Grafham Cambs. *Grafham* 1086 (DB). Identical in origin with the previous name.

Grafton, a common name, usually 'farmstead in or by a grove', OE *grāf* + *tūn*; examples include: **Grafton** Heref. & Worcs., near Hereford. *Crafton* 1303. **Grafton** N. Yorks. *Graftune* 1086 (DB). **Grafton** Oxon. *Graptone* (*sic*) 1086 (DB), *Graftona* 1130. **Grafton, East & West** Wilts. *Graftone* 1086 (DB). **Grafton Flyford** Heref. & Worcs. *Graftun* 9th cent., *Garstune* (*sic*) 1086 (DB). Affix from the nearby FLYFORD FLAVELL. **Grafton Regis** Northants. *Grastone* (*sic*) 1086 (DB), *Graftone* 12th cent. Latin affix *regis* 'of the king' because it was a royal manor. **Grafton Underwood**

Northants. *Grastone (sic)* 1086 (DB), *Grafton Underwode* 1367. Affix 'under or near the wood' (OE *under* + *wudu*) refers to Rockingham Forest.

However the following has a different origin: **Grafton, Temple** Warwicks. *Greftone* 10th cent., *Grastone (sic)* 1086 (DB), *Temple Grafton* 1363. 'Farmstead by the pit or trench'. OE *græf* + *tūn*. Affix refers to early possession by the Knights Templars or Hospitallers.

Grain Kent. *Grean c.*1100. 'Gravelly, sandy ground'. OE **grēon*.

Grainsby Lincs. *Grenesbi* 1086 (DB). Probably 'farmstead or village of a man called Grein'. OScand. pers. name + *bý*.

Grainthorpe Lincs. *Germund(s)torp* 1086 (DB). 'Outlying farmstead of a man called Geirmundr or Germund'. OScand. or OGerman pers. name + OScand. *thorp*.

Grampound Cornwall. *Grauntpount* 1302. '(Place at) the great bridge'. OFrench *grant* + *pont*.

Granborough Bucks. *Grenebeorge c.*1060, *Grenesberga (sic)* 1086 (DB). 'Green hill'. OE *grēne* + *beorg*.

Granby Notts. *Granebi* 1086 (DB). 'Farmstead or village of a man called Grani'. OScand. pers. name + *bý*.

Grange-over-Sands Cumbria. *Grange* 1491. ME *grange* 'outlying farm belonging to a religious house' (in this case Cartmel Priory). Affix means 'across the sands of Morecambe Bay'.

Grangetown Cleveland, 19th cent. iron and steel town, named from nearby ESTON Grange which belonged to Fountains Abbey (for *grange* see previous name).

Gransden, Great & Little Cambs. *Grantandene* 973, *Grante(s)dene* 1086 (DB). 'Valley of a man called *Granta or *Grante'. OE pers. name + *denu*.

Gransmoor Humber. *Grentesmor* 1086 (DB). 'Marshland of a man called *Grante or *Grentir'. OE or OScand. pers. name + OE *mōr* or OScand. *mór*.

Grantchester Cambs. *Granteseta* 1086 (DB). 'Settlers on the River Granta'. Celtic river-name (etymology obscure) + OE *sǣte*.

Grantham Lincs. *Grantham* 1086 (DB). Probably 'homestead or village of a man called *Granta'. OE pers. name + *hām*. Alternatively the first element may be OE **grand* 'gravel'.

Grantley, High N. Yorks. *Grantelege c.*1030, *Grentelai* 1086 (DB). 'Woodland clearing of a man called *Granta or *Grante'. OE pers. name + *lēah*.

Grappenhall Ches. *Gropenhale* 1086 (DB). 'Nook of land at a ditch or drain'. OE **grōpe* (genitive *-an*) + *halh*.

Grasby Lincs. *Gros(e)bi* 1086 (DB). Possibly 'farmstead or village on gravelly ground'. OScand. *grjót* + *bý*.

Grasmere Cumbria. *Gressemere* 1245. Probably 'mere called grass lake'. OE *gres* + *sǣ* 'lake' with explanatory *mere*.

Grassendale Mersey. *Gresyndale* 13th cent. 'Grassy valley', or 'valley used for grazing'. OE **gærsen* or **gærsing* + *dæl* or OScand. *dalr*.

Grassington N. Yorks. *Ghersintone* 1086 (DB). 'Grazing or pasture farm'. OE **gærsing* + *tūn*.

Grassthorpe Notts. *Grestorp* 1086 (DB). 'Grass farmstead or hamlet'. OScand. *gres* + *thorp*.

Grately Hants. *Greatteleiam* 929. 'Great wood or clearing'. OE *grēat* + *lēah*.

Gratwich Staffs. *Crotewiche (sic)* 1086 (DB), *Grotewic* 1176. '(Dairy) farm by the gravelly place'. OE **grēote* + *wīc*.

Graveley Herts. *Gravelai* 1086 (DB). 'Clearing by a grove or copse'. OE *grǣfe* or *grāf(a)* + *lēah*.

Gravely Cambs. *Greflea* 10th cent., *Gravelei* 1086 (DB). Possibly 'woodland clearing by the pit or trench'. OE *græf* + *lēah*. Alternatively identical in origin with the previous name.

Graveney Kent. *Grafonaea* 9th cent. '(Place at) the ditch stream'. OE **grafa* (genitive *-n*) + *ēa*.

Gravenhurst Beds. *Grauenhurst* 1086 (DB). 'Wooded hill with a coppice or a ditch'. OE *grāfa* or **grafa* (genitive *-n*) + *hyrst*.

Gravesend Kent. *Gravesham (sic)* 1086 (DB), *Grauessend* 1157. '(Place at) the end of the grove or copse'. OE *grāf* + *ende*.

Grayingham Lincs. *Graingeham* 1086 (DB). 'Homestead of the family or followers of a man called *Grǣg(a)'. OE pers. name + *-inga-* + *hām*.

Grayrigg Cumbria. *Grarigg* 12th cent. 'Grey ridge'. OScand. *grár* + *hryggr*.

Grays Essex. *Turruc* 1086 (DB), *Turrokgreys* 1248. Originally Grays THURROCK, with manorial affix from the *de Grai* family, here in the 12th cent.

Grayshott Hants. *Grauesseta* 1185. 'Corner of land near a grove'. OE *grāf* + *scēat*.

Grazeley Berks. *Grægsole c.*950. 'Badgers' wallowing-place'. OE **græg* + *sol*.

Greasbrough S. Yorks. *Gersebroc* 1086 (DB). Probably 'grassy brook'. OE *gærs*, **gærsen* + *brōc*.

Greasby Mersey. *Gravesberie* 1086 (DB), *Grauisby c.*1100. 'Stronghold at a grove or copse'. OE *grǣfe* + *burh* (dative *byrig*) (replaced by OScand. *bý* 'farmstead').

Great as affix, see main name, e.g. for **Great Abington** (Cambs.) see ABINGTON.

Greatford Lincs. *Greteford* 1086 (DB). 'Gravelly ford'. OE *grēot* + *ford*.

Greatham, 'gravelly homestead or enclosure', OE *grēot* + *hām* or *hamm*: **Greatham** Cleveland. *Gretham* 1196. **Greatham** Hants. *Greteham* 1086 (DB).

Greatworth Northants. *Grentevorde* (*sic*) 1086 (DB), *Gretteworth* 12th cent. 'Gravelly enclosure'. OE *grēot* + *worth*.

Greenford Gtr. London. *Grenan forda* 845, *Greneforde* 1086 (DB). '(Place at) the green ford'. OE *grēne* + *ford*.

Greenham Berks. *Greneham* 1086 (DB). 'Green enclosure or river-meadow'. OE *grēne* + *hamm*.

Green Hammerton N. Yorks., see HAMMERTON.

Greenhaugh Northum. *Le Grenehalgh* 1326. 'The green nook of land'. OE *grēne* + *halh*.

Greenhead Northum. *Le Greneheued* 1290. 'The green hill'. OE *grēne* + *hēafod*.

Greenhithe Kent. *Grenethe* 1264. 'Green landing place'. OE *grēne* + *hȳth*.

Greenhow Hill N. Yorks. *Grenehoo* 1540. 'Green mound or hill'. OE *grēne* + OScand. *haugr*, with the later addition of *hill*.

Greenodd Cumbria. *Green Odd* 1774. 'Green point or tongue of land'. From OScand. *oddi*.

Greens Norton Northants., see NORTON.

Greenstead Essex. *Grenstede* 10th cent., *Grenesteda* 1086 (DB). 'Green place' i.e. 'pasture used for grazing'. OE *grēne* + *stede*.

Greensted Essex. *Gernesteda* 1086 (DB). Identical in origin with the previous name.

Greenwich Gtr. London. *Grenewic* 964, *Grenviz* 1086 (DB). 'Green port or harbour'. OE *grēne* + *wīc*.

Greet Glos. *Grete* 12th cent. 'Gravelly place'. OE **grēote*.

Greete Shrops. *Grete* 1183. Identical in origin with the previous name.

Greetham, 'gravelly homestead or enclosure', OE *grēot* + *hām* or *hamm*: **Greetham** Leics. *Gretham* 1086 (DB). **Greetham** Lincs. *Gretham* 1086 (DB).

Greetland W. Yorks. *Greland* (*sic*) 1086 (DB), *Greteland* 13th cent. 'Rocky cultivated land'. OScand. *grjót* + *land*.

Greinton Somerset. *Graintone* 1086 (DB). 'Farmstead of a man called *Grǣga'. OE pers. name (genitive *-n*) + *tūn*.

Grendon, usually 'green hill', OE *grēne* + *dūn*: **Grendon** Northants. *Grendone* 1086 (DB). **Grendon** Warwicks. *Grendone* 1086 (DB). **Grendon Underwood** Bucks. *Grennedone* 1086 (DB). Affix means 'in or near the wood'.
However the following has a different second element: **Grendon** Heref. & Worcs. *Grenedene* 1086 (DB). 'Green valley'. OE *grēne* + *denu*.

Gresham Norfolk. *Gressam* 1086 (DB). 'Grass homestead or enclosure'. OE *gærs* + *hām* or *hamm*.

Gresley, Castle & Church Derbys. *Gresele c.*1125, *Castelgresele* 1252, *Churchegreseleye* 1363. OE *lēah* 'woodland clearing' with an uncertain first element, possibly OE *grēosn* 'gravel'. Distinguishing affixes from the former castle and the church here.

Gressenhall Norfolk. *Gressenhala* 1086

(DB). 'Grassy or gravelly nook of land'. OE **gærsen* or *grēosn* + *halh.*

Gressingham Lancs. *Ghersinctune* 1086 (DB), *Gersingeham* 1183. 'Homestead or enclosure with grazing or pasture'. OE **gærsing* + *hām* or *hamm* (replaced by *tūn* 'farmstead' in the Domesday form).

Greta (river), three examples, in Cumbria, Lancs., and N. Yorks.; an OScand. river-name recorded from the 13th cent., 'stony stream', from OScand. *grjót* + *á.*

Gretton Glos. *Gretona* 1175. 'Farmstead near GREET'. OE *tūn.*

Gretton Northants. *Gretone* 1086 (DB). 'Gravel farmstead'. OE *grēot* + *tūn.*

Gretton Shrops. *Grotintune* 1086 (DB). 'Farmstead on gravelly ground'. OE **grēoten* + *tūn.*

Grewelthorpe N. Yorks. *Torp* 1086 (DB), *Gruelthorp* 1281. OScand. *thorp* 'outlying farmstead' with later manorial affix from a family called *Gruel.*

Greysouthen Cumbria. *Craykesuthen c.*1187. 'Rock or cliff of a man called Suthán'. Celtic **creig* + OIrish pers. name.

Greystoke Cumbria. *Creistoc* 1167. Probably 'secondary settlement by a river once called *Cray*'. Lost Celtic river-name (meaning 'fresh, clean') + OE *stoc.*

Greywell Hants. *Graiwella* 1167. Probably 'spring or stream frequented by badgers'. OE **grǣg* + *wella.*

Griff Warwicks. *Griva* 12th cent. '(Place at) the deep valley or hollow'. OScand. *gryfja.*

Grimley Heref. & Worcs. *Grimanleage* 9th cent., *Grimanleh* 1086 (DB). 'Wood or glade haunted by a spectre or goblin'. OE *grīma* + *lēah.*

Grimoldby Lincs. *Grimoldbi* 1086 (DB). 'Farmstead or village of a man called Grimald'. OGerman pers. name + OScand. *bý.*

Grimsargh Lancs. *Grimesarge* 1086 (DB). 'Hill-pasture of a man called Grímr'. OScand. pers. name + *erg.*

Grimsby, 'farmstead or village of a man called Grímr', OScand. pers. name + *bý*: **Grimsby** Humber. *Grimesbi* 1086 (DB). **Grimsby, Little** Lincs. *Grimesbi* 1086 (DB).

Grimscote Northants. *Grimescote* 12th cent. 'Cottage(s) of a man called Grímr'. OScand. pers. name + OE *cot.*

Grimstead, East & West Wilts. *Gremestede* 1086 (DB). Probably 'green homestead'. OE *grēne* + *hām-stede.*

Grimsthorpe Lincs. *Grimestorp* 1212. 'Outlying farmstead or hamlet of a man called Grímr'. OScand. pers. name + *thorp.*

Grimston, 'farmstead or estate of a man called Grímr', OScand. pers. name + OE *tūn*; examples include: **Grimston** Leics. *Grimestone* 1086 (DB). **Grimston** Norfolk. *Grimastun c.*1035, *Grimestuna* 1086 (DB). **Grimston, North** N. Yorks. *Grimeston* 1086 (DB).

Grindale Humber. *Grendele* 1086 (DB). 'Green valley'. OE *grēne* + *dæl.*

Grindleton Lancs. *Gretlintone* 1086 (DB) *Grenlington* 1251. Probably 'farmstead, near the gravelly stream'. OE **grendel* + *-ing* + *tūn.*

Grindley Staffs. *Grenleg* 1251. 'Green woodland clearing'. OE *grēne* + *lēah.*

Grindlow Derbys. *Grenlawe* 1199. 'Green hill or mound'. OE *grēne* + *hlāw.*

Grindon, 'green hill', OE *grēne* + *dūn*: **Grindon** Northum. *Grandon* 1210. **Grindon** Staffs. *Grendone* 1086 (DB).

Gringley on the Hill Notts. *Gringeleia* 1086 (DB). Possibly 'woodland clearing of the people living at the green place'. OE *grēne* + *-inga-* + *lēah.*

Grinsdale Cumbria. *Grennesdale c.*1180. Probably 'valley by the green promontory'. OE *grēne* + *næss* + OScand. *dalr.*

Grinshill Shrops. *Grivelesul* (*sic*) 1086 (DB), *Grineleshul* 1242. OE *hyll* 'hill' with an uncertain first element.

Grinstead, 'green place' i.e. 'pasture used for grazing', OE *grēne* + *stede*: **Grinstead, East** W. Sussex. *Grenesteda* 1121, *Estgrenested* 1271. **Grinstead, West** W. Sussex. *Grenestede* 1086 (DB), *Westgrenested* 1280.

Grinton N. Yorks. *Grinton* 1086 (DB). 'Green farmstead'. OE *grēne* + *tūn.*

Gristhorpe N. Yorks. *Grisetorp* 1086 (DB). 'Outlying farmstead or hamlet of a man called Gríss, or where young pigs are reared'. OScand. pers. name or *gríss* + *thorp*.

Griston Norfolk. *Gristuna* 1086 (DB). Possibly 'farmstead of a man called Gríss, or where young pigs are reared'. OScand. pers. name or *gríss* + OE *tūn*. Alternatively the first element may be OE *gres* 'grass'.

Grittenham Wilts. *Gruteham* 850. 'Gravelly homestead or enclosure'. OE **grīeten* + *hām* or *hamm*.

Grittleton Wilts. *Grutelington* 940, *Gretelintone* 1086 (DB). Possibly 'estate associated with a man called *Grytel'. OE pers. name + *-ing-* + *tūn*.

Grizebeck Cumbria. *Grisebek* 13th cent. 'Brook by which young pigs are kept'. OScand. *gríss* + *bekkr*.

Grizedale Cumbria. *Grysdale* 1336. 'Valley where young pigs are kept'. OScand. *gríss* + *dalr*.

Groby Leics. *Grobi* 1086 (DB). Probably 'farmstead near a hollow or pit'. OScand. *gróf* + *bý*.

Groombridge Kent. *Gromenebregge* 1239. 'Bridge where young men congregate'. ME *grome* (genitive plural *-ene*) + OE *brycg*.

Grosmont N. Yorks. *Grosmunt* 1228. Originally the name of the priory here, in turn named from the mother Priory of Grosmont in France ('big hill' from OFrench *gros* + *mont*).

Groton Suffolk. *Grotena* 1086 (DB). Probably 'sandy or gravelly stream'. OE **groten* + *ēa*.

Grove, a common name, '(place at) the grove or copse', OE *grāf(a)*; examples include: **Grove** Notts. *Grava* 1086 (DB). **Grove** Oxon. *la Graue* 1188.

Grundisburgh Suffolk. *Grundesburch* 1086 (DB). 'Stronghold on or near the foundation of a building'. OE *grund* + *burh*.

Guestling E. Sussex. *Gestelinges* 1086 (DB). '(Settlement of) the family or followers of a man called *Gyrstel'. OE pers. name + *-ingas*.

Guestwick Norfolk. *Geghestueit* 1086 (DB). 'Clearing belonging to GUIST'. OScand. *thveit*.

Guilden Morden Cambs., see MORDEN.

Guilden Sutton Ches., see SUTTON.

Guildford Surrey. *Gyldeforda c.*880, *Gildeford* 1086 (DB). Probably 'ford by the gold-coloured (i.e. sandy) hill', from OE **gylde* + *ford*, see HOG'S BACK.

Guilsborough Northants. *Gildesburh c.*1070, *Gisleburg* (*sic*) 1086 (DB). 'Stronghold of a man called *Gyldi'. OE pers. name + *burh*.

Guisborough Cleveland. *Ghigesburg* 1086 (DB). Probably 'stronghold of a man called Gígr'. OScand. pers. name + OE *burh*.

Guiseley W. Yorks. *Gislicleh c.*972, *Gisele* 1086 (DB). 'Woodland clearing of a man called *Gīslic'. OE pers. name + *lēah*.

Guist Norfolk. *Gæssæte c.*1035, *Gegeseta* 1086 (DB). Possibly 'dwelling of a man called *Gǣga or *Gǣgi'. OE pers. name + *sǣte*.

Guiting Power & Temple Guiting Glos. *Gythinge* 814, *Getinge* 1086 (DB), *Gettinges Poer* 1220, *Guttinges Templar* 1221. Originally a river-name, 'running stream, stream with a good current', OE *gyte* + *-ing*. Manorial affixes from early possession by the *le Poer* family and by the Knights Templars.

Guldeford, East E. Sussex. *Est Guldeford* 1517. Named from the *Guldeford* family (so called because they came from GUILDFORD).

Gulval Cornwall. 'Church of *Sancta Welvela*' 1328. '(Church of) St Gwelvel'. From the patron saint of the church.

Gumley Leics. *Godmundesleah* 8th cent., *Godmundelai* 1086 (DB). 'Woodland clearing of a man called Godmund'. OE pers. name + *lēah*.

Gunby Humber. *Gunelby* 1066–9. 'Farmstead or village of a woman called Gunnhildr'. OScand. pers. name + *bý*.

Gunby Lincs. *Gunnebi* 1086 (DB). 'Farmstead or village of a man called Gunni'. OScand. pers. name + *bý*.

Gunnersbury Gtr. London. *Gounyldebury* 1334. 'Manor house of a woman called Gunnhildr'. OScand.

pers. name + ME *bury* (from OE *byrig*, dative of *burh*).

Gunnerton Northum. *Gunwarton* 1170. Probably 'farmstead of a woman called Gunnvǫr'. OScand. pers. name + OE *tūn*.

Gunness Humber. *Gunnesse* 1199. 'Headland of a man called Gunni'. OScand. pers. name + *nes*.

Gunnislake Cornwall. *Gonellake* 1485. Probably 'stream of a man called Gunni'. OScand. pers. name + OE *lacu*.

Gunthorpe, usually 'outlying farmstead of a man called Gunni', OScand. pers. name + *thorp*: **Gunthorpe** Cambs. *Gunetorp* 1130. **Gunthorpe** Norfolk. *Gunestorp* 1086 (DB).

However the following has a different origin: **Gunthorpe** Notts. *Gulnetorp* 1086 (DB). 'Outlying farmstead of a woman called Gunnhildr'. OScand. pers. name + *thorp*.

Gunwalloe Cornwall. 'Chapel of *Sanctus Wynwolaus*' 1332. From the patron saint of the church or chapel, St Winwaloe.

Gussage All Saints & St Michael Dorset. *Gyssic* 10th cent., *Gessic* 1086 (DB), *Gussich All Saints* 1245, *Gussich St Michael* 1297. Probably 'gushing stream', originally the name of the river here. OE **gyse* + *sīc*. Affixes from the dedications of the churches.

Guston Kent. *Gocistone* 1086 (DB). 'Farmstead of a man called *Gūthsige'. OE pers. name + *tūn*.

Guyhirn Cambs. *La Gyerne* 1275. OE *hyrne* 'angle or corner of land' with OFrench *guie* 'a guide' (with reference to controlling tidal flow) or 'a salt-water ditch'.

Guyzance Northum. *Gynis* 1242. A manorial name, 'estate of the family called *Guines*'.

Gweek Cornwall. *Wika* 1201. Cornish **gwig* 'village' or OE *wīc* 'hamlet'.

Gwennap Cornwall. 'Church of *Sancta Wenappa*' 1269. '(Church of) St Wynup'. From the patron saint of the church.

Gwithian Cornwall. 'Parish of *Sanctus Goythianus*' 1334. From the patron saint of the church, St Gothian.

H

Habblesthorpe Notts. *Happelesthorp* 1154. Probably 'outlying farmstead of a man called *Hæppel'. OE pers. name + OScand. *thorp*.

Habrough Humber. *Haburne* (*sic*) 1086 (DB), *Haburg* 1202. 'High or chief stronghold'. OE *hēah* (replaced by OScand. *hár*) + *burh*.

Habton, Great N. Yorks. *Habetun* 1086 (DB). 'Farmstead of a man called *Hab(b)a'. OE pers. name + *tūn*.

Haceby Lincs. *Hazebi* 1086 (DB), *Hathsebi* 1115. 'Farmstead or village of a man called Haddr'. OScand. pers. name + *bý*.

Hacheston Suffolk. *Hacestuna* 1086 (DB). 'Farmstead of a man called Hæcci'. OE pers. name + *tūn*.

Hackford Norfolk, near Wymondham. *Hakeforda* 1086 (DB). 'Ford with a hatch or by a bend'. OE *hæcc* or *haca* + *ford*.

Hackforth N. Yorks. *Acheford* 1086 (DB). Identical in origin with the previous name.

Hackleton Northants. *Hachelintone* 1086 (DB). 'Estate associated with a man called *Hæccel'. OE pers. name + *-ing-* + *tūn*.

Hackness N. Yorks. *Hacanos* 731, *Hagenesse* 1086 (DB). 'Hook-shaped or projecting headland'. OE *haca* + *nose*.

Hackney Gtr. London. *Hakeneia* 1198. 'Island, or dry ground in marsh, of a man called *Haca'. OE pers. name (genitive *-n*) + *ēg*.

Hackthorn Lincs. *Hagetorne* 1086 (DB). '(Place at) the hawthorn or prickly thorn-tree'. OE *hagu-thorn* or **haca-thorn*.

Hackthorpe Cumbria. *Hakatorp c.*1150. Possibly 'outlying farmstead or hamlet of a man called Haki'. OScand. pers. name + *thorp*. Alternatively the first element may be OScand. *haki* or OE *haca* 'hook-shaped promontory'.

Haconby Lincs. *Hacunesbi* 1086 (DB). 'Farmstead or village of a man called Hákon'. OScand. pers. name + *bý*.

Haddenham, 'homestead or village of a man called Hǣda', OE pers. name + *hām*: **Haddenham** Bucks. *Hedreham* (*sic*) 1086 (DB), *Hedenham* 1142. **Haddenham** Cambs. *Hædan ham* 970, *Hadreham* 1086 (DB).

Haddington Lincs. *Hadinctune* 1086 (DB). 'Estate associated with a man called Headda or Hada'. OE pers. name + *-ing-* + *tūn*.

Haddiscoe Norfolk. *Hadescou* 1086 (DB). 'Wood of a man called Haddr or Haddi'. OScand. pers. name + *skógr*.

Haddlesey, Chapel & West N. Yorks. *Hathel-sæ c.*1030, *Chappel Haddlesey* 1605, *Westhathelsay* 1280. Probably 'marshy pool in a hollow'. OE **hathel* + *sǣ*. Distinguishing affixes from ME *chapel* and *west*.

Haddon, usually 'heath hill, hill where heather grows', OE *hǣth* + *dūn*: **Haddon, East & West** Northants. *Eddone, Hadone* 1086 (DB), *Esthaddon* 1220, *Westhaddon* 12th cent. **Haddon, Nether & Over** Derbys. *Hadun(e)* 1086 (DB), *Nethir Haddon* 1248, *Uverehaddon* 1206. Distinguishing affixes are OE *neotherra* 'lower' and *uferra* 'higher'.
However the following may have a different origin: **Haddon** Cambs. *Haddedun* 951, *Adone* 1086 (DB). Probably 'hill of a man called Headda'. OE pers. name + *dūn*.

Hadfield Derbys. *Hetfelt* 1086 (DB). 'Heathy open land, or open land where heather grows'. OE *hǣth* + *feld*.

Hadham, Much & Little Herts. *Hædham* 957, *Hadam, Parva Hadam* 1086 (DB), *Muchel Hadham* 1373. Probably 'heath homestead'. OE *hǣth* + *hām*. Distinguishing affixes from OE *mycel* 'great' and *lȳtel* 'little' (Latin *parva*).

Hadleigh, Hadley, 'heath clearing, clearing where heather grows', OE *hǣth* + *lēah*: **Hadleigh** Essex. *Hæthlege* c.1000, *Leam* (*sic*) 1086 (DB). **Hadleigh** Suffolk. *Hædleage* c.995, *Hetlega* 1086 (DB). **Hadley** Shrops. *Hatlege* 1086 (DB). **Hadley, Monken** Gtr. London. *Hadlegh* 1248, *Monken Hadley* 1489. Affix means 'of the monks' (from OE *munuc*) referring to early possession by Walden Abbey.

Hadlow Kent. *Haslow* (*sic*) 1086 (DB), *Hadlou* 1235. Probably 'mound or hill where heather grows'. OE *hǣth* + *hlāw*.

Hadlow Down E. Sussex. *Hadleg* 1254. Probably 'woodland clearing where heather grows'. OE *hǣth* + *lēah*.

Hadnall Shrops. *Hadehelle* (*sic*) 1086 (DB), *Hadenhale* 1242. 'Nook of land of a man called Headda'. OE pers. name (genitive *-n*) + *halh*.

Hadstock Essex. *Hadestoc* 11th cent. 'Outlying farmstead of a man called Hada'. OE pers. name + *stoc*.

Hadzor Heref. & Worcs. *Hadesore* 1086 (DB). 'Bank or ridge of a man called *Headd'. OE pers. name + *ōfer* or **ofer*.

Hagbourne, East & West Oxon. *Haccaburna* c.895, *Hacheborne* 1086 (DB). Probably '(place by) the stream of a man called *Hacca'. OE pers. name + *burna*.

Haggerston Gtr. London. *Hergotestane* 1086 (DB). 'Boundary stone of a man called Hærgod'. OE pers. name + *stān*.

Haggerston Northum. *Agardeston* 1196. Probably 'estate of a family called *Hagard*'. ME (from OFrench) surname + OE *tūn*.

Hagley Heref. & Worcs. *Hageleia* 1086 (DB). 'Woodland clearing where haws grow'. OE **hagga* + *lēah*.

Hagworthingham Lincs. *Hacberdingeham* (*sic*) 1086 (DB), *Hagwrthingham* 1198. 'Homestead of the people from the hawthorn enclosure'. OE **hagga* + *worth* + *-inga-* + *hām*.

Haigh, 'the enclosure', OScand. *hagi* or OE *haga*: **Haigh** Gtr. Manch. *Hage* 1194. **Haigh** S. Yorks. *Hagh* 1379.

Haighton Green Lancs. *Halctun* 1086 (DB). 'Farmstead in a nook of land'. OE *halh* + *tūn*.

Hailes Glos. *Heile* 1086 (DB). Perhaps originally the name of the stream here, a Celtic river-name possibly meaning 'dirty stream'.

Hailey, 'clearing where hay is made', OE *hēg* + *lēah*: **Hailey** Herts. *Hailet* (*sic*) 1086 (DB), *Heile* 1235. **Hailey** Oxon. *Haylegh* 1241.

Hailsham E. Sussex. *Hamelesham* (*sic*) 1086 (DB), *Helesham* 1189. 'Homestead or enclosure of a man called *Hægel'. OE pers. name + *hām* or *hamm*.

Hail Weston Cambs., see WESTON.

Hainford Norfolk. *Hanforda* 1086 (DB), *Heinford* 12th cent. 'Ford near an enclosure'. OE **hægen* + *ford*.

Hainton Lincs. *Haintone* 1086 (DB). 'Farmstead in an enclosure'. OE **hægen* + *tūn*.

Haisthorpe Humber. *Ascheltorp* 1086 (DB). 'Outlying farmstead of a man called Hǫskuldr'. OScand. pers. name + *thorp*.

Halam Notts. *Healum* 958. '(Place at) the nooks or corners of land'. OE *halh* in a dative plural form *halum*.

Halberton Devon. *Halsbretone* 1086 (DB). Possibly 'farmstead by a hazel wood'. OE *hæsel* + *bearu* + *tūn*.

Halden, High Kent. *Hadinwoldungdenne* c.1100. 'Woodland pasture associated with a man called Heathuwald'. OE pers. name + *-ing-* + *denn*.

Hale, a common name, '(place at) the nook or corner of land', OE *halh* (dative *hale*); examples include: **Hale** Ches. *Halas* 1094. Originally in a plural form. **Hale** Gtr. Manch. *Hale* 1086 (DB). **Hale** Hants. *Hala* 1161. **Hale, Great & Little** Lincs. *Hale* 1086 (DB).

Hales, 'the nooks or corners of land', OE *halh* in a plural form: **Hales** Norfolk. *Hals* 1086 (DB). **Hales** Staffs. *Hales* 1291.

Halesowen W. Mids. *Hala* 1036 (DB), *Hales Ouweyn* 1276. 'Nooks or corners of land'. OE *halh* in a plural form, with manorial affix from the Welsh prince called *Owen* who held the manor in the early 13th cent.

Halesworth Suffolk. *Healesuurda* 1086

(DB). Probably 'enclosure of a man called *Hæle'. OE pers. name + *worth*.

Halewood Mersey. *Halewode* c.1200. 'Wood near HALE'. OE *wudu*.

Halford Shrops. *Hauerford* 1155. Possibly 'ford used by hawkers'. OE *hafocere* + *ford*.

Halford Warwicks. *Halchford* 12th cent. 'Ford by a nook or corner of land'. OE *halh* + *ford*.

Halifax W. Yorks. *Halyfax* c.1095. Possibly 'area of coarse grass in a nook of land'. OE *halh* + **gefeaxe*.

Hallam S. Yorks. *Hallun* 1086 (DB). Possibly identical in origin with the next name, but alternatively '(place at) the rocks', from OScand. *hallr* or OE *hall* in a dative plural form *hallum*.

Hallam, Kirk & West Derbys. *Halun* 1086 (DB), *Kyrkehallam* 12th cent., *Westhalum* 1230. '(Place at) the nooks of land'. OE *halh* in a dative plural form *halum*. Distinguishing affixes from OScand. *kirkja* 'church' and OE *west*.

Hallaton Leics. *Alctone* 1086 (DB). 'Farmstead in a nook of land or narrow valley'. OE *halh* + *tūn*.

Hallatrow Avon. *Helgetrev* 1086 (DB). '(Place by) the holy tree'. OE *hālig* + *trēow*.

Halling Kent. *Hallingas* 8th cent., *Hallinges* 1086 (DB). '(Settlement of) the family or followers of a man called *Heall'. OE pers. name + *-ingas*.

Hallingbury, Great & Little Essex. *Hallingeberiam* 1086 (DB). 'Stronghold of the family or followers of a man called *Heall'. OE pers. name + *-inga-* + *burh* (dative *byrig*).

Hallington Northum. *Halidene* 1247. 'Holy valley'. OE *hālig* + *denu*.

Halloughton Notts. *Healhtune* 958. 'Farmstead in a nook of land or narrow valley'. OE *halh* + *tūn*.

Hallow Heref. & Worcs. *Halhagan* 9th cent., *Halhegan* 1086 (DB). 'Enclosures in a nook or corner of land'. OE *halh* + *haga*.

Halnaker W. Sussex. *Helnache* 1086 (DB). 'Half an acre'. OE *healf* (dative *-an*) + *æcer*.

Halsall Lancs. *Heleshale* 1086 (DB). Probably 'nook of land of a man called *Hæle'. OE pers. name + *halh*.

Halse Northants. *Hasou* (*sic*) 1086 (DB), *Halsou* c.1160. 'Neck of land forming a ridge'. OE *hals* + *hōh*.

Halse Somerset. *Halse* 1086 (DB). '(Place at) the neck of land'. OE *hals*.

Halsham Humber. *Halsaham* 1033, *Halsam* 1086 (DB). 'Homestead on the neck of land'. OE *hals* + *hām*.

Halstead, 'place of refuge or shelter', OE *h(e)ald* + *stede*: **Halstead** Essex. *Haltesteda* 1086 (DB). **Halstead** Kent. *Haltesteda* c.1100. **Halstead** Leics. *Elstede* 1086 (DB).

Halstock Dorset. *Halganstoke* 998. 'Outlying farmstead belonging to a religious foundation'. OE *hālig* + *stoc*.

Halstow, 'holy place', OE *hālig* + *stōw*: **Halstow, High** Kent. *Halgesto* c.1100. **Halstow, Lower** Kent. *Halgastaw* c.1100.

Haltham Lincs. *Holtham* 1086 (DB). 'Homestead by or in a wood'. OE *holt* + *hām*.

Halton, a common name, usually 'farmstead in a nook or corner of land', OE *halh* + *tūn*: **Halton** Bucks. *Healtun* c.1033, *Haltone* 1086 (DB). **Halton** Lancs. *Haltune* 1086 (DB). **Halton** W. Yorks. *Halletune* 1086 (DB). **Halton, East** Lincs. *Haltune* 1086 (DB). **Halton East** N. Yorks. *Haltone* 1086 (DB). **Halton Holegate** Lincs. *Haltun* 1086 (DB). Affix means 'road in a hollow', OScand. *holr* + *gata*. **Halton, West** Lincs. *Haltone* 1086 (DB). **Halton West** N. Yorks. *Halctun* 12th cent.

However the following have a different origin: **Halton** Ches. *Heletune* 1086 (DB), *Hethelton* 1174. Possibly 'farmstead at a heathery place'. OE **hāthel* + *tūn*. **Halton** Northum. *Haulton* 1161. Possibly 'farmstead at the look-out hill'. OE **hāw* + *hyll* + *tūn*.

Haltwhistle Northum. *Hautwisel* 1240. OE *twisla* 'junction of two streams', possibly with OFrench *haut* 'high'.

Halvergate Norfolk. *Halfriate* 1086 (DB). Possibly 'land for which a half heriot (a feudal service or payment) is due'. OE *half* + *here-geatu*.

Halwell Devon. *Halganwylle* 10th cent. 'Holy spring'. OE *hālig* + *wella*.

Halwill Devon. *Halgewilla* 1086 (DB). Identical in origin with the previous name.

Ham, a common name, from OE *hamm* which had various meanings, including 'enclosure, land hemmed in by water or higher ground, land in a river-bend'; examples include: **Ham** Glos. *Hamma* 1194. **Ham** Gtr. London. *Hama c.*1150. **Ham** Kent. *Hama* 1086 (DB). **Ham** Wilts. *Hamme* 931, *Hame* 1086 (DB). **Ham, East & West** Gtr. London. *Hamme* 958, *Hame* 1086 (DB), *Est Hammes c.*1250, *Westhamma* 1186. **Ham, High** Somerset. *Hamme* 973, *Hame* 1086 (DB).

Hamble Hants. *Hamele* 1165. Named from the River Hamble on which it stands, 'crooked river', i.e. 'river with bends in it', from OE **hamel* + *ēa*.

Hambleden Bucks. *Hamelan dene* 1015, *Hanbledene* 1086 (DB). 'Crooked or undulating valley'. OE **hamel* + *denu*.

Hambledon, 'crooked or irregularly-shaped hill', OE **hamel* + *dūn*: **Hambledon** Hants. *Hamelandunæ* 956, *Hamledune* 1086 (DB). **Hambledon** Surrey. *Hameledune* 1086 (DB).

Hambleton, usually 'farmstead at the crooked hill', OE **hamel* + *tūn*: **Hambleton** Lancs. *Hameltune* 1086 (DB). **Hambleton** N. Yorks., near Selby. *Hameltun* 1086 (DB).

However the following has the same origin as HAMBLEDON: **Hambleton, Upper** Leics. *Hameldun* 1086 (DB).

Hambrook Avon. *Hanbroc* 1086 (DB). Probably 'brook by the stone'. OE *hān* + *brōc*.

Hameringham Lincs. *Hameringam* 1086 (DB). Probably 'homestead of the dwellers at the cliff or steep hill'. OE *hamor* + *-inga-* + *hām*.

Hamerton Cambs. *Hambertune* 1086 (DB). 'Farmstead with a smithy', or 'farmstead where a plant such as hammer-sedge grows'. OE *hamor* + *tūn*.

Hammersmith Gtr. London. *Hamersmythe* 1294. '(Place with) a hammer smithy or forge'. OE *hamor* + *smiththe*.

Hammerton, Green & Kirk N. Yorks. *Hambretone* 1086 (DB), *Grenhamerton* 1176, *Kyrkehamerton* 1226. Probably identical in origin with HAMERTON (Cambs.). Distinguishing affixes from OE *grēne* 'village green' and OScand. *kirkja* 'church'.

Hammerwich Staffs. *Humeruuich* (*sic*) 1086 (DB), *Hamerwich* 1191. Probably 'building with a smithy'. OE *hamor* + *wīc*.

Hammoon Dorset. *Hame* 1086 (DB), *Hamme Moun* 1280. 'Enclosure or land in a river-bend'. OE *hamm*, with manorial affix from the *Moion* family which held the manor in 1086.

Hampden, Great & Little Bucks. *Hamdena* 1086 (DB). Probably 'valley with an enclosure'. OE *hamm* + *denu*.

Hampnett Glos. *Hantone* 1086 (DB), *Hamtonett* 1213. 'High farmstead'. OE *hēah* (dative *hēan*) + *tūn*, with the addition of OFrench *-ette* 'little'.

Hampole S. Yorks. *Hanepole* 1086 (DB). 'Pool of a man called Hana', or 'pool frequented by cocks (of wild birds)'. OE pers. name or OE *hana* + *pōl*.

Hampshire (the county). *Hamtunscir* late 9th cent. 'District based on *Hamtun* (i.e. SOUTHAMPTON)'. OE *scīr*.

Hampstead, Hamstead, 'the homestead', OE *hām-stede*: **Hampstead** Gtr. London. *Hemstede* 959, *Hamestede* 1086 (DB). **Hampstead Norris** Berks. *Hanstede* 1086 (DB), *Hampstede Norreys* 1517. Manorial affix from the *Norreys* family who bought the manor in 1448. **Hamstead** I. of Wight. *Hamestede* 1086 (DB). **Hamstead** W. Mids. *Hamsted* 1227. **Hamstead Marshall** Berks. *Hamestede* 1086 (DB), *Hamsted Marchal* 1284. Manorial affix from the *Marshal* family, here in the 13th cent.

Hampsthwaite N. Yorks. *Hamethwayt c.*1180. 'Clearing of a man called Hamr or Hamall'. OScand. pers. name + *thveit*.

Hampton, a common name, has no less than three different origins. Some are from OE *hām-tūn* 'home farm, homestead': **Hampton Lovett** Heref. & Worcs. *Hamtona* 716, *Hamtune* 1086 (DB). Manorial affix from the *Luvet* family, here in the 13th cent. **Hampton, Meysey** Glos. *Hantone* 1086 (DB), *Meseishampton* 1287. Manorial addition from the *de Meisi* family, here from the 12th cent. **Hampton Poyle** Oxon. *Hantone* 1086 (DB), *Hampton*

Poile 1428. Manorial affix from the *de la Puile* family, here in the 13th cent.

Other Hamptons are 'farmstead in an enclosure or river-bend', OE *hamm* + *tūn*: **Hampton** Gtr. London. *Hamntone* 1086 (DB). **Hampton Bishop** Heref. & Worcs. *Hantune* 1086 (DB), *Homptone* 1240. Manorial affix from early possession by the Bishop of Hereford. **Hampton Lucy** Warwicks. *Homtune* 781, *Hantone* 1086 (DB). Manorial affix from its possession by the *Lucy* family in the 16th cent.

Other Hamptons are 'high farmstead', OE *hēah* (dative *hēan*) + *tūn*: **Hampton** Heref. & Worcs., near Evesham. *Heantune* 780, *Hantun* 1086 (DB). **Hampton** Shrops. *Hempton* 1391. **Hampton on the Hill** Warwicks. *Hamtone* 12th cent.

Hams, South (district) Devon. *Southammes* 1396. Possibly 'cultivated areas of land to the south (of Dartmoor)'. OE *sūth* + *hamm*.

Hamsey E. Sussex. *Hamme* 961, *Hame* 1086 (DB), *Hammes Say* 1306. 'The enclosure, the land in a river-bend'. OE *hamm* with manorial addition from the *de Say* family, here in the 13th cent.

Hamstead, see HAMPSTEAD.

Hamsterley Durham. *Hamsteleie* c.1190. 'Clearing infested with corn-weevils'. OE **hamstra* + *lēah*.

Hamstall Ridware Staffs., see RIDWARE.

Hamworthy Dorset. *Hamme* 1236, *Hamworthy* 1463. OE *hamm* 'enclosure', here possibly 'peninsula', with the later addition of *worthig* 'enclosure'.

Hanborough, Church & Long Oxon. *Haneberge* 1086 (DB). 'Hill of a man called Hagena or Hana'. OE pers. name + *beorg*.

Hanbury, 'high or chief fortified place', OE *hēah* (dative *hēan*) + *burh* (dative *byrig*): **Hanbury** Heref. & Worcs. *Heanburh* c.765, *Hambyrie* 1086 (DB). **Hanbury** Staffs. *Hambury* c.1185.

Hanchurch Staffs. *Hancese* (*sic*) 1086 (DB), *Hanchurche* 1212. 'High church'. OE *hēah* (dative *hēan*) + *cirice*.

Handbridge Ches. *Bruge* 1086 (DB), *Honebrugge* c.1150. 'Bridge at the rock'. OE *hān* + *brycg*.

Handforth Ches. *Haneford* 12th cent. 'Ford frequented by cocks (of wild birds)', or 'ford at the stones (used as markers)'. OE *hana* or *hān* + *ford*.

Handley, 'high wood or clearing', OE *hēah* (dative *hēan*) + *lēah*: **Handley** Ches. *Hanlei* 1086 (DB). **Handley, Sixpenny** Dorset. *Hanlee* 877, *Hanlege* 1086 (DB), *Sexpennyhanley* 1575. Affix added in 16th cent. from an old Hundred name *Sexpene* 'hill of the Saxons', from OE *Seaxe* + Celtic **penn*. **Handley, West** Derbys. *Henleie* 1086 (DB).

Handsacre Staffs. *Hadesacre* (*sic*) 1086 (DB), *Handesacra* 1196. 'Arable plot of a man called *Hand'. OE pers. name + *æcer*.

Handsworth S. Yorks. *Handesuuord* 1086 (DB). 'Enclosure of a man called *Hand'. OE pers. name + *worth*.

Handsworth W. Mids. *Honesworde* 1086 (DB). 'Enclosure of a man called Hūn'. OE pers. name + *worth*.

Hanford Staffs. *Heneford* (*sic*) 1086 (DB), *Honeford* 1212. 'Ford frequented by cocks (of wild birds)', or 'ford at the stones'. OE *hana* or *hān* + *ford*.

Hanham Avon. *Hanun* 1086 (DB). '(Place at) the rocks'. OE *hān* in a dative plural form *hānum*.

Hankelow Ches. *Honcolawe* 12th cent. 'Mound or hill of a man called *Haneca'. OE pers. name + *hlāw*.

Hankerton Wilts. *Hanekyntone* 680. 'Estate associated with a man called *Haneca'. OE pers. name + *-ing-* + *tūn*.

Hankham E. Sussex. *Hanecan hamme* 947, *Henecham* 1086 (DB). 'Enclosure, or dry ground in marsh, of a man called *Haneca'. OE pers. name + *hamm*.

Hanley, 'high wood or clearing', OE *hēah* (dative *hēan*) + *lēah*: **Hanley** Staffs. *Henle* 1212. **Hanley Castle** Heref. & Worcs. *Hanlege* 1086 (DB). Affix from the early 13th cent. castle here. **Hanley Child & William** Heref. & Worcs. *Hanlege* 1086 (DB), *Cheldreshanle* 1255, *Williames Henle* 1275. Affixes from OE *cild* (plural *cildra*) 'young monk, noble-born son', and from a *William* de la Mare who held one of the manors in 1242.

Hanlith N. Yorks. *Hangelif* (*sic*) 1086

(DB), *Hahgenlid* 12th cent. 'Slope or hill-side of a man called Hagni or Hǫgni'. OScand. pers. name + *hlíth*.

Hanney, East & West Oxon. *Hannige* 956, *Hannei* 1086 (DB). 'Island, or land between streams, frequented by cocks (of wild birds)'. OE *hana* + *ēg*.

Hanningfield, East, South, & West Essex. *Hamningefelde* c.1036, *Haningefelda* 1086 (DB). Probably 'open land of the family or followers of a man called Hana'. OE pers. name + *-inga-* + *feld*.

Hannington Hants. *Hanningtun* 1023, *Hanitune* 1086 (DB). 'Estate associated with a man called Hana'. OE pers. name + *-ing-* + *tūn*.

Hannington Northants. *Hanintone* 1086 (DB). Identical in origin with the previous name.

Hannington Wilts. *Hanindone* 1086 (DB). 'Hill frequented by cocks (of wild birds)', or 'hill of a man called Hana'. OE *hana* (genitive plural *hanena*) or OE pers. name (genitive *-n*) + *dūn*.

Hanslope Bucks. *Hamslape* 1086 (DB). 'Muddy place or slope of a man called Hāma'. OE pers. name + **slǣp*.

Hanthorpe Lincs. *Hermodestorp* 1086 (DB). 'Outlying farmstead or hamlet of a man called Heremōd or Hermóthr'. OE or OScand. pers. name + OScand. *thorp*.

Hanwell Gtr. London. *Hanewelle* 959, *Hanewelle* 1086 (DB). 'Spring or stream frequented by cocks (of wild birds)'. OE *hana* + *wella*.

Hanwell Oxon. *Hanewege* 1086 (DB), *Haneuell* 1236. 'Way (and stream) of a man called Hana'. OE pers. name + *weg* (replaced by *wella* in the 13th cent.).

Hanwood, Great Shrops. *Hanewde* 1086 (DB). 'Wood frequented by cocks (of wild birds)'. OE *hana* + *wudu*.

Hanworth Gtr. London. *Haneworde* 1086 (DB). 'Enclosure of a man called Hana'. OE pers. name + *worth*.

Hanworth Norfolk. *Haganaworda* 1086 (DB). 'Enclosure of a man called Hagena'. OE pers. name + *worth*.

Hanworth, Cold Lincs. *Haneurde* 1086 (DB), *Calthaneworth* 1322. 'Enclosure of a man called Hana'. OE pers. name + *worth*. Affix is OE *cald* 'cold, exposed'.

Happisburgh Norfolk. *Hapesburc* 1086 (DB). 'Stronghold of a man called *Hæp'. OE pers. name + *burh*.

Hapsford Ches. *Happesford* 13th cent. 'Ford of a man called *Hæp'. OE pers. name + *ford*.

Hapton Lancs. *Apton* 1242. 'Farmstead by a hill'. OE *hēap* + *tūn*.

Hapton Norfolk. *Habetuna* 1086 (DB). 'Farmstead of a man called *Hab(b)a'. OE pers. name + *tūn*.

Harberton Devon. *Herburnaton* 1108. 'Farmstead on the River Harbourne'. OE river-name ('pleasant stream' from OE *hēore* + *burna*) + *tūn*.

Harbledown Kent. *Herebolddune* 1175. 'Hill of a man called Herebeald'. OE pers. name + *dūn*.

Harborne W. Mids. *Horeborne* 1086 (DB). 'Dirty or muddy stream'. OE *horu* + *burna*.

Harborough Magna Warwicks. *Herdeberge* 1086 (DB), *Hardeburgh Magna* 1498. 'Hill of the flocks or herds'. OE *heord* + *beorg*. Affix is Latin *magna* 'great'.

Harborough, Market Leics. *Haverbergam* 1153, *Mercat Heburgh* 1312. Probably 'hill where oats are grown'. OScand. *hafri* or OE **hæfera* + OScand. *berg* or OE *beorg*. Alternatively the first element may be OE *hæfer* or OScand. *hafr* 'a he-goat'. Affix (ME *merket*) from the important market here.

Harbottle Northum. *Hirbotle* c.1220. Probably 'dwelling of the hireling'. OE *hȳra* + *bōthl*.

Harbourne (river) Devon, see HARBERTON.

Harbury Warwicks. *Hereburgebyrig* 1002, *Erburgeberie* 1086 (DB). 'Stronghold or manor-house of a woman called Hereburh'. OE pers. name + *burh* (dative *byrig*).

Harby, 'farmstead of a man called Herrøthr' or 'farmstead with a herd or flock', OScand. pers. name or OScand. *hjǫrth* + *bý*: **Harby** Leics. *Herdebi* 1086 (DB). **Harby** Notts. *Herdrebi* 1086 (DB).

Harden W. Yorks. *Hareden* late 12th cent. 'Rock valley', or 'valley frequented by hares'. OE **hær* or *hara* + *denu.*

Hardham W. Sussex. *Heriedeham* 1086 (DB). 'Homestead or river-meadow of a woman called Heregȳth'. OE pers. name + *hām* or *hamm.*

Hardingham Norfolk. *Hardingeham* 1161. 'Homestead of the family or followers of a man called *Hearda'. OE pers. name + *-inga-* + *hām.*

Hardingstone Northants. *Hardingestone* 1086 (DB), *Hardingesthorn* 12th cent. 'Thorn-tree of a man called Hearding'. OE pers. name + *thorn.*

Hardington, 'estate associated with a man called *Hearda', OE pers. name + *-ing-* + *tūn*: **Hardington** Somerset. *Hardintone* 1086 (DB). **Hardington Mandeville** Somerset. *Hardintone* 1086 (DB). Manorial affix from its possession by the *de Mandeville* family from the 12th cent.

Hardley Hants. *Hardelie* 1086 (DB). 'Hard clearing'. OE *heard* + *lēah.*

Hardley Street Norfolk. *Hardale* 1086 (DB). Probably identical in origin with the previous name.

Hardmead Bucks. *Herulfmede* 1086 (DB). Probably 'meadow of a man called Heoruwulf or Herewulf'. OE pers. name + *mǣd.*

Hardres, Upper Kent. *Haredum* 785, *Hardes* 1086 (DB). '(Place at) the woods'. OE **harad* in a plural form.

Hardstoft Derbys. *Hertestaf (sic)* 1086 (DB), *Hertistoft* 1257. 'Homestead of a man called *Heort or Hjǫrtr'. OE or OScand. pers. name + OScand. *toft.*

Hardwick, Hardwicke, a common name, 'herd farm, farm for livestock', OE *heorde-wīc*: **Hardwick** Bucks. *Harduich* 1086 (DB). **Hardwick** Cambs. *Hardwic c.*1050, *Harduic* 1086 (DB). **Hardwick** Norfolk, near King's Lynn. *Herdwic* 1242. **Hardwick** Northants. *Heordewican c.*1067, *Herdewiche* 1086 (DB). **Hardwick** Oxon., near Bicester. *Hardewich* 1086 (DB). **Hardwick** Oxon., near Witney. *Herdewic* 1199. **Hardwick, East & West** W. Yorks. *Harduic* 1086 (DB). **Hardwick, Priors** Warwicks. *Herdewyk* 1043, *Herdewiche* 1086 (DB), *Herdewyk Priour* 1310. Affix from its possession by Coventry Priory in the 11th cent. **Hardwicke** Glos., near Stroud. *Herdewike* 12th cent. **Hardwicke** Glos., near Tewkesbury. *Herdeuuic* 1086 (DB). **Hardwicke** Heref. & Worcs., near Clifford. *La Herdewyk* 14th cent.

Hardy Lancs., see CHORLTON.

Hareby Lincs. *Harebi* 1086 (DB). Probably 'farmstead or village of a man called Hári'. OScand. pers. name + *bý.*

Harefield Gtr. London. *Herefelle (sic)* 1086 (DB), *Herefeld* 1206. Probably 'open land used by an army (perhaps a Viking army)'. OE *here* + *feld.*

Harewood W. Yorks. *Harawuda* 10th cent., *Hareuuode* 1086 (DB). 'Grey wood', or 'wood by the rocks', or 'wood frequented by hares'. OE *hār* or **hær* or *hara* + *wudu.*

Harford Devon, near Ivybridge. *Hereford* 1086 (DB). 'Ford suitable for the passage of an army'. OE **here-ford.*

Hargrave, probably 'hoar grove, or grove on a boundary', OE *hār* + *grāf* or *grǣfe*: **Hargrave** Ches. *Haregrave* 1086 (DB). **Hargrave** Northants. *Haregrave* 1086 (DB). **Hargrave** Suffolk. *Haragraua* 1086 (DB).

Harkstead Suffolk. *Herchesteda* 1086 (DB). Probably 'pasture or homestead of a man called Hereca'. OE pers. name + *stede.*

Harlaston Staffs. *Heorelfestun* 1002, *Horulvestone* 1086 (DB). 'Farmstead of a man called Heoruwulf'. OE pers. name + *tūn.*

Harlaxton Lincs. *Herlavestune* 1086 (DB). 'Farmstead of a man called *Herelāf or *Heorulāf'. OE pers. name + *tūn.*

Harlesden Gtr. London. *Herulvestune* 1086 (DB). 'Farmstead of a man called Heoruwulf or Herewulf'. OE pers. name + *tūn.*

Harleston, Harlestone, 'farmstead of a man called Heoruwulf or Herewulf', OE pers. name + *tūn*: **Harleston** Devon. *Harliston* 1252. **Harleston** Norfolk. *Heroluestuna* 1086 (DB). **Harleston** Suffolk. *Heroluestuna* 1086 (DB). **Harlestone** Northants. *Herolvestune* 1086 (DB).

Harley Shrops. *Harlege* 1086 (DB). 'Rock

clearing', or 'clearing frequented by hares'. OE *hær or hara + lēah.

Harling, East Norfolk. *Herlinge* c.1060, *Herlinga* 1086 (DB). '(Settlement of) the family or followers of a man called *Herela', or 'place of a man called *Herela'. OE pers. name + *-ingas* or *-ing*.

Harlington Beds. *Herlingdone* 1086 (DB). 'Hill of the family or followers of a man called *Herela'. OE pers. name + *-inga-* + *dūn*.

Harlington Gtr. London. *Hygereding tun* 831, *Herdintone* 1086 (DB). 'Estate associated with a man called Hygerēd'. OE pers. name + *-ing-* + *tūn*.

Harlow Essex. *Herlawe* 1045, *Herlaua* 1086 (DB). 'Mound or hill associated with an army (perhaps a Viking army)'. OE *here* + *hlāw*.

Harlow Hill Northum. *Hirlawe* 1242. Possibly identical in origin with the previous name.

Harlsey, East N. Yorks. *Herlesege* 1086 (DB). 'Island, or dry ground in marsh, of a man called *Herel'. OE pers. name + *ēg*.

Harlthorpe Humber. *Herlesthorpia* 1150–60. 'Outlying farmstead of a man called Herleifr or Herlaugr'. OScand. pers. name + *thorp*.

Harlton Cambs. *Herletone* 1086 (DB). 'Farmstead of a man called *Herela'. OE pers. name + *tūn*.

Harmby N. Yorks. *Hernebi* 1086 (DB). 'Farmstead or village of a man called Hjarni'. OScand. pers. name + *bý*.

Harmondsworth Gtr. London. *Hermodesworde* 1086 (DB). 'Enclosure of a man called Heremōd'. OE pers. name + *worth*.

Harmston Lincs. *Hermodestune* 1086 (DB). 'Farmstead of a man called Heremōd or Hermóthr'. OE or OScand. pers. name + OE *tūn*.

Harnham, East & West Wilts. *Harnham* 1115. Probably 'enclosure frequented by hares'. OE *hara* (genitive plural *harena*) + *hamm*.

Harnhill Glos. *Harehille* 1086 (DB). 'Grey hill' or 'hill frequented by hares'. OE *hār* (dative *-an*) or *hara* (genitive plural *-ena*) + *hyll*.

Harold Hill Gtr. London, named from HAROLD WOOD.

Harold Wood Gtr. London. *Horalds Wood* c.1237. Named from Earl Harold, king of England until his defeat at Hastings in 1066; he held the nearby manor of Havering.

Harome N. Yorks. *Harum* 1086 (DB). '(Place at) the rocks or stones'. OE *hær in a dative plural form *harum.

Harpenden Herts. *Herpedene* c.1060. 'Valley of the harp'. OE *hearpe* (genitive *-an*) + *denu*. Alternatively the first element may be a reduced form of OE *here-pæth* 'highway or main road'.

Harpford Devon. *Harpeford* 1167. 'Ford on a highway or main road'. OE *here-pæth* + *ford*.

Harpham Humber. *Arpen* (*sic*) 1086 (DB), *Harpam* 1100–15. 'Homestead where the harp is played'. OE *hearpe* + *hām*. Alternatively the first element may have the sense 'salt-harp, sieve for making salt'.

Harpley, 'clearing of the harp', perhaps 'harp-shaped clearing', OE *hearpe* + *lēah*: **Harpley** Norfolk. *Herpelai* 1086 (DB). **Harpley** Heref. & Worcs. *Hoppeleia* (*sic*) 1222, *Harpele* 1275.

Harpole Northants. *Horpol* 1086 (DB). 'Dirty or muddy pool'. OE *horu* + *pōl*.

Harpsden Oxon. *Harpendene* 1086 (DB). 'Valley of the harp'. OE *hearpe* (genitive *-an*) + *denu*.

Harpswell Lincs. *Herpeswelle* 1086 (DB). 'Spring or stream of the harp or harper'. OE *hearpe* or *hearpere* + *wella*.

Harptree, East & West Avon. *Harpetreu* 1086 (DB). Probably 'tree by a highway or main road'. OE *here-pæth* + *trēow*.

Harpurhey Gtr. Manch. *Harpourhey* 1320. 'Enclosure of a man called *Harpour*'. OE *hæg* with the surname of a 14th cent. landowner.

Harrietsham Kent. *Herigeardes hamm* 10th cent., *Hariardesham* 1086 (DB). 'River-meadow of a man called Heregeard, or near army quarters'. OE pers. name (or OE *here* + *geard*) + *hamm*.

Harringay Gtr. London, see HORNSEY.

Harrington Cumbria. *Haueringtona*

c.1160. 'Estate associated with a man called *Hæfer'. OE pers. name + *-ing-* + *tūn*.

Harrington Lincs. *Haringtona* 12th cent. Possibly 'farmstead of a man called *Hæring', from OE pers. name + *tūn*, or the first element may be an OE **hæring* 'stony place' or **hāring* 'grey wood'.

Harrington Northants. *Arintone* (*sic*) 1086 (DB), *Hederingeton* 1184. Possibly 'estate associated with a man called *Heathuhere'. OE pers. name + *-ing-* + *tūn*.

Harringworth Northants. *Haringwrth* *c*.1060, *Haringeworde* 1086 (DB). Possibly 'enclosure of the dwellers at a stony place'. OE **hær* + *-inga-* + *worth*.

Harrogate N.Yorks. *Harwegate* 1332. '(Place at) the road to the cairn or heap of stones'. OScand. *hǫrgr* + *gata*.

Harrold Beds. *Hareuuelle* (*sic*) 1086 (DB), *Harewolda* 1163. Probably 'high forest-land on a boundary'. OE *hār* + *weald*.

Harrow Gtr. London. *Hearge* 825, *Herges* 1086 (DB). 'Heathen shrine or temple'. OE *hearg*.

Harrow Weald Gtr. London. *Welde* 1282, *Harewewelde* 1388. 'Woodland near HARROW'. OE *weald*.

Harrowden, Great & Little Northants. *Hargedone* 1086 (DB). 'Hill of the heathen shrines or temples'. OE *hearg* + *dūn*.

Harston Cambs. *Herlestone* 1086 (DB). Probably 'farmstead of a man called *Herel'. OE pers. name + *tūn*.

Harston Leics. *Herstan* 1086 (DB). 'Grey or boundary stone'. OE *hār* + *stān*.

Hart Cleveland. *Heruteu* 8th cent. 'Island or peninsula frequented by harts or stags'. OE *heorot* + *ēg*.

Hartburn, East Cleveland. *Herteburna* *c*.1190. 'Stream frequented by harts or stags'. OE *heorot* + *burna*.

Hartest Suffolk. *Hertest* *c*.1050, *Herterst* 1086 (DB). 'Wooded hill frequented by harts or stags'. OE *heorot* + *hyrst*.

Hartfield E. Sussex. *Hertevel* (*sic*) 1086 (DB), *Hertefeld* 12th cent. 'Open land frequented by harts or stags'. OE *heorot* + *feld*.

Hartford, usually 'ford frequented by harts or stags', OE *heorot* + *ford*: **Hartford** Ches. *Herford* (*sic*) 1086 (DB), *Hartford* late 12th cent. **Hartford, East** Northum. *Hertford* 1198.

However the following has a different origin: **Hartford** Cambs. *Hereforde* 1086 (DB). 'Ford suitable for the passage of an army'. OE **here-ford*.

Harthill, 'hill frequented by harts or stags', OE *heorot* + *hyll*: **Harthill** Ches. *Herthil* 1259. **Harthill** S. Yorks. *Hertil* 1086 (DB).

Harting, East & South W. Sussex. *Hertingas* 970, *Hertinges* 1086 (DB). '(Settlement of) the family or followers of a man called *Heort'. OE pers. name + *-ingas*.

Hartington Derbys. *Hortedun* 1086 (DB). Probably 'hill of the harts or stags'. OE *heorot* + *dūn*.

Hartland Devon. *Heortigtun* *c*.880, *Hertitona* 1086 (DB), *Hertilanda* 1130. 'Farmstead (or estate) on the peninsula frequented by harts or stags'. OE *heorot* + *īeg* + *tūn* (later *land*).

Hartlebury Heref. & Worcs. *Heortlabyrig* 817, *Huerteberie* 1086 (DB). 'Stronghold of a man called *Heortla'. OE pers. name + *burh* (dative *byrig*).

Hartlepool Cleveland. *Herterpol* *c*.1170. 'Pool or bay near the stag peninsula'. OE *heorot* + *ēg* + *pōl*.

Hartley, usually 'wood or clearing frequented by harts or stags', OE *heorot* + *lēah*; examples include: **Hartley** Kent, near Cranbrook. *Heoratleag* 843. **Hartley** Kent, near Longfield. *Erclei* (*sic*) 1086 (DB), *Hertle* 1253. **Hartley Westpall** Hants. *Harlei* 1086 (DB), *Hertlegh Waspayl* *c*.1270. Manorial addition from early possession by the *Waspail* family. **Hartley Wintney** Hants. *Hurtlege* 12th cent., *Hertleye Wynteneye* 13th cent. Manorial addition from its possession by the Priory of Wintney in the 13th cent.

However other Hartleys have different origins: **Hartley** Cumbria. *Harteclo* 1176. Probably 'hard ridge of land'. OE *heard* + *clā*. **Hartley** Northum. *Hertelawa* 1167. 'Mound or hill frequented by harts or stags'. OE *heorot* + *hlāw*.

Hartlip Kent. *Heordlyp* 11th cent. 'Gate

or fence over which harts or stags can leap'. OE *heorot* + *hlīep*.

Harton N. Yorks. *Heretune* 1086 (DB). Probably 'farmstead by the rocks or stones'. OE **hær* + *tūn*.

Harton Tyne & Wear. *Heortedun* 1104–8. 'Hill frequented by harts or stags'. OE *heorot* + *dūn*.

Hartpury Glos. *Hardepiry* 12th cent. 'Pear-tree with hard fruit'. OE *heard* + *pirige*.

Hartshill Warwicks. *Ardreshille* (*sic*) 1086 (DB), *Hardredeshella* 1151. 'Hill of a man called Heardrēd'. OE pers. name + *hyll*.

Hartshorne Derbys. *Heorteshorne* 1086 (DB). 'Hart's horn', i.e. 'hill thought to resemble a hart's horn'. OE *heorot* + *horn*.

Hartwell Northants. *Hertewelle* 1086 (DB). 'Spring or stream frequented by harts or stags'. OE *heorot* + *wella*.

Harvington Heref. & Worcs. *Herverton* 709, *Herferthun* 1086 (DB). 'Farmstead near the ford suitable for the passage of an army'. OE **here-ford* + *tūn*.

Harwell Oxon. *Haranwylle* 956, *Harvvelle* 1086 (DB). 'Spring or stream by the hill called *Hāra* (the grey one)'. OE hill-name from *hār* 'grey' + *wella*.

Harwich Essex. *Herewic* 1248. 'Army camp', probably that of a Viking army. OE *here-wīc*.

Harwood, 'grey wood', 'wood by the rocks', or 'wood frequented by hares', OE *hār* or **hær* or *hara* + *wudu*: **Harwood** Gtr. Manch. *Harewode* 1212. **Harwood Dale** N. Yorks. *Harewode* 1301, *Harwoddale* 1577. With OScand. *dalr* 'valley'. **Harwood, Great** Lancs. *Majori Harewuda* early 12th cent. Affix is Latin *maior* 'greater'.

Harworth Notts. *Hareworde* 1086 (DB). Probably 'enclosure on the boundary'. OE *hār* + *worth*.

Hascombe Surrey. *Hescumb* 1232. Possibly 'the witch's valley'. OE *hægtesse* + *cumb*.

Haselbech Northants. *Esbece* (*sic*) 1086 (DB), *Haselbech* 12th cent. 'Valley-stream where hazels grow'. OE *hæsel* + *bece*.

Haselbury Plucknett Somerset. *Halberge* (*sic*) 1086 (DB), *Haselbare Ploukenet* 1431. 'Hazel wood or grove'. OE *hæsel* + *bearu*. Manorial affix from its possession by the *de Plugenet* family in the 13th cent.

Haseley, Great & Little Oxon. *Haselie* 1086 (DB). 'Hazel wood or clearing'. OE *hæsel* + *lēah*.

Haselor Warwicks. *Haseloue* 1086 (DB). 'Slope or hill where hazels grow'. OE *hæsel* + **ofer*.

Hasfield Glos. *Hasfelde* 1086 (DB). 'Open land where hazels grow'. OE *hæsel* + *feld*.

Hasketon Suffolk. *Haschetuna* 1086 (DB). 'Farmstead of a man called *Haseca'. OE pers. name + *tūn*.

Hasland Derbys. *Haselont* 1129–38. 'Hazel grove'. OScand. *hasl* + *lundr*.

Haslemere Surrey. *Heselmere* 1221. 'Pool where hazels grow'. OE *hæsel* + *mere*.

Haslingden Lancs. *Heselingedon* 1241. 'Valley growing with hazels'. OE *hæslen* + *denu*.

Haslingfield Cambs. *Haslingefeld* 1086 (DB). Probably 'open land of the family or followers of a man called *Hæsel(a)'. OE pers. name + *-inga-* + *feld*.

Haslington Ches. *Hasillinton* early 13th cent. 'Farmstead where hazels grow'. OE *hæslen* + *tūn*.

Hassall Ches. *Eteshale* (*sic*) 1086 (DB), *Hatishale* 13th cent. 'The witch's nook of land'. OE *hægtesse* + *halh*.

Hassingham Norfolk. *Hasingeham* 1086 (DB). 'Homestead of the family or followers of a man called *Hasu'. OE pers. name + *-inga-* + *hām*.

Hassocks W. Sussex, a modern settlement named from a field called *Hassocks*, from OE *hassuc* 'clump of coarse grass'.

Hassop Derbys. *Hetesope* 1086 (DB). Probably 'the witch's valley'. OE *hægtesse* + *hop*.

Hastingleigh Kent. *Hæstingalege* 993, *Hastingelai* 1086 (DB). 'Woodland clearing of the family or followers of a man called *Hǣsta'. OE pers. name + *-inga-* + *lēah*.

Hastings E. Sussex. *Hastinges* 1086 (DB). '(Settlement of) the family or followers of a man called *Hæsta'. OE pers. name + *-ingas*. Earlier *Hæstingaceaster* c.915, 'Roman town of *Hæsta's people', from OE *ceaster*.

Haswell Durham. *Hessewella* 1131. Probably 'spring or stream where hazels grow'. OE *hæsel* + *wella*.

Hatch, a common name, from OE *hæcc* 'a hatch-gate (leading to a forest)' or 'floodgate (in a stream)'; examples include: **Hatch** Beds. *La Hache* 1232. **Hatch** Hants. *Heche* 1086 (DB). **Hatch** Wilts. *Hache* 1200. **Hatch Beauchamp** Somerset. *Hache* 1086 (DB), *Hache Beauchampe* 1243. Manorial affix from its possession by the *Beauchamp* family in the 13th cent. **Hatch, West** Somerset. *Hache* 1201, *Westhache* 1243.

Hatch End Gtr. London. *Le Hacchehend* 1448. 'District by the gate' (probably a gate to Pinner Park). OE *hæcc* + *ende*.

Hatcliffe Humber. *Hadecliue* 1086 (DB). 'Cliff or bank of a man called Headda'. OE pers. name + *clif*.

Hatfield, a common name, 'heathy open land, or open land where heather grows', OE *hǣth* + *feld*; examples include: **Hatfield** Heref. & Worcs., near Kempsey. *Hadfeld* 1182. **Hatfield** Heref. & Worcs., near Pudlestone. *Hetfelde* 1086 (DB). **Hatfield** Herts. *Haethfelth* 731, *Hetfelle* 1086 (DB). **Hatfield** S. Yorks. *Haethfelth* 731, *Hedfeld* 1086 (DB). **Hatfield Broad Oak** Essex. *Hadfelda* 1086 (DB), *Hatfeld Brodehoke* c.1130. Affix from a large oak-tree, OE *brād* + *āc*. **Hatfield, Great & Little** Humber. *Haifeld, Heifeld* 1086 (DB), *Haitefeld* 12th cent. First element influenced by OScand. *heithr* 'heath'. **Hatfield Peverel** Essex. *Hadfelda* 1086 (DB), *Hadfeld Peurell* 1166. Manorial affix from its possession by Ralph *Peverel* in 1086.

Hatford Oxon. *Hevaford* (*sic*) 1086 (DB), *Hauetford* 1176. 'Ford near a headland or hill'. OE *hēafod* + *ford*.

Hatherden Hants. *Hetherden* 1193. Probably 'hawthorn valley'. OE *hagu-thorn* + *denu*.

Hatherleigh Devon. *Hadreleia* 1086 (DB). Probably identical in origin with the next name.

Hatherley, Down & Up Glos. *Athelai* 1086 (DB), *Dunheytherleye* 1273, *Hupheberleg* 1221. 'Hawthorn clearing'. OE *hagu-thorn* + *lēah*. Distinguishing affixes from OE *dūne* 'lower downstream' and *upp* 'higher upstream'.

Hathern Leics. *Avederne* (*sic*) 1086 (DB), *Hacthurne* 1230. '(Place at) the hawthorn'. OE *hagu-thyrne*.

Hatherop Glos. *Etherope* 1086 (DB). Probably 'high outlying farmstead'. OE *hēah* + *throp*.

Hathersage Derbys. *Hereseige* (*sic*) 1086 (DB), *Hauersegg* c.1220. 'He-goat's ridge', or 'ridge of a man called *Hæfer'. OE *hæfer* or OE pers. name + *ecg*.

Hatherton Ches. *Haretone* (*sic*) 1086 (DB), *Hatherton* 1262. 'Farmstead where hawthorn grows'. OE *hagu-thorn* + *tūn*.

Hatherton Staffs. *Hagenthorndun* 996, *Hargedone* 1086 (DB). 'Hill where hawthorn grows'. OE *hagu-thorn* + *dūn*.

Hatley, probably 'woodland clearing on the hill', OE *hætt* + *lēah*: **Hatley, Cockayne** Beds. *Hattenleia* c.960, *Hatelai* 1086 (DB), *Cocking Hatley* 1576. Manorial affix from the *Cockayne* family, here in the 15th cent. **Hatley, East & Hatley St George** Cambs. *Hatelai* 1086 (DB), *Esthatteleia* 1199, *Hattele de Sancto Georgio* 1279. Distinguishing affixes from OE *ēast* 'east' and from possession by the family *de Sancto Georgio* here in the 13th cent.

Hattingley Hants. *Hattingele* 1204. Probably 'woodland clearing at the hill place'. OE *hætt* + *-ing* + *lēah*.

Hatton, 'farmstead on a heath', OE *hǣth* + *tūn*; examples include: **Hatton** Ches. *Hattone* c.1230. **Hatton** Derbys. *Hatune* 1086 (DB). **Hatton** Gtr. London. *Hatone* 1086 (DB). **Hatton** Lincs. *Hatune* 1086 (DB). **Hatton** Shrops. *Hatton* 1212. **Hatton, Cold & High** Shrops. *Hatune, Hetune* 1086 (DB), *Colde Hatton* 1233, *Heye Hatton* 1327. Distinguishing affixes from OE *cald* 'cold, exposed' and *hēah* 'high, chief'. **Hatton Heath** Ches. *Etone* (*sic*) 1086 (DB), *Hettun* 1185.

Haugham Lincs. *Hecham* 1086 (DB). Probably 'high or chief homestead'. OE *hēah* + *hām*.

Haughley Suffolk. *Hagele* c.1040,

Hagala 1086 (DB). 'Wood or clearing with a hedge, or where haws grow'. OE *haga* + *lēah*.

Haughton, usually 'farmstead in or by a nook of land', OE *halh* + *tūn*: **Haughton** Shrops., near Oswestry. *Halchton* 1285. **Haughton** Shrops., near Shifnal. *Halghton* 1281. **Haughton** Shrops., near Shrewsbury. *Haustone* 1086 (DB). **Haughton** Staffs. *Haltone* 1086 (DB). **Haughton Green** Gtr. Manch. *Halghton* 1307. **Haughton-le-Skerne** Durham. *Halhtun* c.1050. On the River Skerne (for the origin of this river-name see SKERNE with which it is identical in meaning).

However the following has a different origin: **Haughton** Notts. *Hoctun* 1086 (DB). 'Farmstead on a spur of land'. OE *hōh* + *tūn*.

Haunton Staffs. *Hagnatun* 942. 'Farmstead of a man called Hagena'. OE pers. name + *tūn*.

Hautbois, Little Norfolk. *Hobbesse* 1044–7, *Hobuisse* 1086 (DB). Probably 'marshy meadow with tussocks or hummocks'. OE **hobb* + *wisc*, **wisse*.

Hauxley Northum. *Hauekeslaw* 1204. 'Mound of the hawk, or of a man called *Hafoc'. OE *hafoc* or pers. name + *hlāw*.

Hauxton Cambs. *Hafucestune* c.975, *Hauochestun* 1086 (DB). 'Farmstead of a man called *Hafoc'. OE pers. name + *tūn*.

Hauxwell, East N. Yorks. *Hauocheswelle* 1086 (DB). 'Spring of the hawk, or of a man called *Hafoc'. OE *hafoc* or pers. name + *wella*.

Havant Hants. *Hamanfuntan* 935, *Havehunte* 1086 (DB). 'Spring of a man called Hāma'. OE pers. name + **funta*.

Havenstreet I. of Wight. *Hethenestrete* 1255. 'Street made or used by heathens'. OE *hǣthen* + *strǣt*.

Haverhill Suffolk. *Hauerhella* 1086 (DB). Probably 'hill where oats are grown'. OScand. *hafri* + OE *hyll*.

Haverigg Cumbria. *Haverig* c.1180. 'Ridge where oats are grown, or where he-goats graze'. OScand. *hafri* or *hafr* + *hryggr*.

Havering-atte-Bower Gtr. London. *Haueringas* 1086 (DB), *Hauering atte Bower* 1272. '(Settlement of) the family or followers of a man called *Hæfer'. OE pers. name + *-ingas*. Affix means 'at the bower or royal residence' from OE *būr*.

Haversham Bucks. *Hæfæresham* 10th cent., *Havresham* 1086 (DB). 'Homestead or river-meadow of a man called *Hæfer'. OE pers. name + *hām* or hamm.

Haverthwaite Cumbria. *Haverthwayt* 1336. 'Clearing where oats are grown'. OScand. *hafri* + *thveit*.

Hawes N. Yorks. *Hawes* 1614. '(Place at) the pass between the hills'. OE *hals*.

Hawkchurch Devon. *Hauekechierch* 1196. 'Church of a man called *Hafoc'. OE pers. name + *cirice*.

Hawkedon Suffolk. *Hauokeduna* 1086 (DB). Probably 'hill frequented by hawks'. OE *hafoc* + *dūn*.

Hawkesbury Avon. *Havochesberie* 1086 (DB). 'Stronghold of the hawk, or of a man called *Hafoc'. OE *hafoc* or OE pers. name + *burh* (dative *byrig*).

Hawkhill Northum. *Hauechil* 1178. 'Hill frequented by hawks'. OE *hafoc* + *hyll*.

Hawkhurst Kent. *Hauekehurst* 1254. 'Wooded hill frequented by hawks'. OE *hafoc* + *hyrst*.

Hawkinge Kent. *Hauekinge* 1204. 'Place frequented by hawks', or 'place of a man called *Hafoc'. OE *hafoc* or pers. name + *-ing*.

Hawkley Hants. *Hauecle* 1207. 'Woodland clearing frequented by hawks'. OE *hafoc* + *lēah*.

Hawkridge Somerset. *Hauekerega* 1194. 'Ridge frequented by hawks'. OE *hafoc* + *hrycg*.

Hawkshead Cumbria. *Hovkesete* c.1200. 'Mountain pasture of a man called Haukr'. OScand. pers. name + *sǣtr*.

Hawkswick N. Yorks. *Hochesuuic* (*sic*) 1086 (DB), *Haukeswic* 1176. 'Dwelling or (dairy) farm of a man called Haukr'. OScand. pers. name + OE *wīc*.

Hawksworth Notts. *Hochesuorde* 1086 (DB). 'Enclosure of a man called Hōc'. OE pers. name + *worth*.

Hawksworth W. Yorks. *Hafecesweorthe* c.1030, *Hauocesorde* 1086 (DB).

'Enclosure of a man called *Hafoc'. OE pers. name + *worth*.

Hawkwell Essex. *Hacuuella* 1086 (DB). 'Winding stream'. OE *haca* + *wella*.

Hawley Hants. *Hallee, Halely* 1248. Possibly 'woodland clearing near a hall or large house'. OE *heall* + *lēah*. Alternatively the first element may be *healh* 'nook or corner of land'.

Hawley Kent. *Hagelei* (*sic*) 1086 (DB), *Halgeleg* 1203. 'Holy wood or clearing'. OE *hālig* + *lēah*.

Hawling Glos. *Hallinge* 1086 (DB). '(Settlement of) the people from HALLOW', or '(settlement of) the people at the nook of land'. OE *halh* + *-ingas*. Alternatively, identical in origin with HALLING (Kent).

Hawnby N. Yorks. *Halm(e)bi* 1086 (DB). 'Farmstead or village of a man called Halmi'. OScand. pers. name + *bý*. Alternatively the first element may be OScand. *halmr* 'straw'.

Haworth W. Yorks. *Hauewrth* 1209. 'Enclosure with a hedge'. OE *haga* + *worth*.

Hawsker, High N. Yorks. *Houkesgarth* *c*.1125. 'Enclosure of a man called Haukr'. OScand. pers. name + *garthr*.

Hawstead Suffolk. *Haldsteda* 1086 (DB). 'Place of refuge or shelter'. OE *h(e)ald* + *stede*.

Hawthorn Durham. *Hagethorn* 1155. '(Place at) the hawthorn'. OE *hagu-thorn*.

Hawton Notts. *Holtone* 1086 (DB). Probably 'farmstead in a hollow'. OE *hol* + *tūn*.

Haxby N. Yorks. *Haxebi* 1086 (DB). 'Farmstead or village of a man called Hákr'. OScand. pers. name + *bý*.

Haxey Humber. *Acheseia* 1086 (DB). 'Island, or dry ground in marsh, of a man called Hákr'. OScand. pers. name + OE *ēg* or OScand. *ey*

Haydock Mersey. *Hedoc* 1169. Probably a Welsh name meaning 'barley place, corn farm'.

Haydon, usually 'hill or down where hay is made', OE *hēg* + *dūn*: **Haydon** Dorset. *Heydone* 1163. **Haydon Wick** Wilts. *Haydon* 1242, *Haydonwyk* 1249. The addition is OE *wīc* 'dairy farm'.

However the following has a different second element: **Haydon Bridge** Northum. *Hayden* 1236. 'Valley where hay is made'. OE *hēg* + *denu*.

Hayes, 'land overgrown with brushwood', OE **hǣs(e)*: **Hayes** Gtr. London, near Bromley. *Hesa* 1177. **Hayes** Gtr. London, near Hillingdon. *Hæse* 831, *Hesa* 1086 (DB).

Hayfield Derbys. *Hedfelt* (*sic*) 1086 (DB), *Heyfeld* 1285. 'Open land where hay is obtained'. OE *hēg* + *feld*.

Hayle Cornwall. *Heyl* 1265. Named from the River Hayle, a Celtic name meaning 'estuary'.

Hayling Island Hants. *Heglingaigæ* 956, *Halingei* 1086 (DB). 'Island of the family or followers of a man called *Hægel'. OE pers. name + *-inga-* + *ēg*.

Hayling, North & South Hants. *Hailinges* *c*.1140. '(Settlement of) the family or followers of a man called *Hægel'. OE pers. name + *-ingas*.

Haynes Beds. *Hagenes* 1086 (DB). 'The enclosures'. OE **hægen*, **hagen* in a plural form.

Hayton, 'farmstead where hay is made or stored', OE *hēg* + *tūn*: **Hayton** Cumbria, near Brampton. *Hayton* *c*.1170. **Hayton** Humber. *Haiton* 1086 (DB). **Hayton** Notts. *Heiton* 1175.

Haywards Heath W. Sussex. *Heyworth* 1261, *Haywards Hoth* 1544. 'Heath by the enclosure with a hedge'. OE *hege* + *worth*, with the later addition of *hǣth*.

Haywood, 'enclosed wood', OE *hæg* or *hege* + *wudu*: **Haywood** Heref. & Worcs. *Haywode* 1276. **Haywood, Great & Little** Staffs. *Haiwode* 1086 (DB). **Haywood Oaks** Notts. *Heywod* 1232. The affix no doubt refers to some notable oak-trees.

Hazelbury Bryan Dorset. *Hasebere* 1201, *Hasilbere Bryan* 1547. 'Hazel wood or grove'. OE *hæsel* + *bearu*. Manorial affix from the *Bryene* family, here in the 14th cent.

Hazeley Hants. *Heishulla* 1167. 'Brushwood hill'. OE **hǣs* + *hyll*.

Hazel Grove Gtr. Manch. *Hesselgrove* 1690. 'Hazel copse'. OE *hæsel* + *grāf*.

Hazelwood Derbys. *Haselwode* 1306. 'Hazel wood'. OE *hæsel* + *wudu*.

Hazlemere Bucks. *Heselmere* 13th cent. 'Pool where hazels grow'. OE *hæsel* + *mere*.

Hazleton Glos. *Hasedene* (*sic*) 1086 (DB), *Haselton* 12th cent. 'Farmstead where hazels grow'. OE *hæsel* + *tūn*.

Heacham Norfolk. *Hecham* 1086 (DB). 'Homestead with a hedge or hatch-gate'. OE *hecg* or *hecc* + *hām*.

Headcorn Kent. *Hedekaruna* c.1100. Possibly 'tree-trunk (used as a footbridge) of a man called *Hydeca'. OE pers. name + *hruna*.

Headingley W. Yorks. *Hedingeleia* 1086 (DB). 'Woodland clearing of the family or followers of a man called Head(d)a'. OE pers. name + *-inga-* + *lēah*.

Headington Oxon. *Hedenandun* 1004, *Hedintone* 1086 (DB). 'Hill of a man called *Hedena'. OE pers. name (genitive *-n*) + *dūn*.

Headlam Durham. *Hedlum* c.1190. '(Place at) the woodland clearings where heather grows'. OE *hǣth* + *lēah* (in a dative plural form *lēaum*).

Headley, 'woodland clearing where heather grows', OE *hǣth* + *lēah*; examples include: **Headley** Hants. *Hallege* 1086 (DB), *Hetliga* c.1190. **Headley** Surrey. *Hallega* 1086 (DB).

Headon Notts. *Hedune* 1086 (DB). Probably 'high hill'. OE *hēah* + *dūn*.

Heage Derbys. *Heyheg* 1251. 'High edge or ridge'. OE *hēah* + *ecg*.

Healaugh, Healey, 'high clearing or wood', OE *hēah* + *lēah*: **Healaugh** N. Yorks. *Hale* (*sic*) 1086 (DB), *Helagh* 1200. **Healey** Northum., near Hexham. *Heley* 1268. **Healey** N. Yorks. *Helagh* c.1280.

Healing Humber. *Hegelinge* 1086 (DB). '(Settlement of) the family or followers of a man called *Hægel'. OE pers. name + *-ingas*.

Heanor Derbys. *Hainoure* 1086 (DB). '(Place at) the high ridge'. OE *hēah* (dative *hēan*) + **ofer*.

Heanton Punchardon Devon. *Hantone* 1086 (DB), *Heanton Punchardun* 1297. 'High (or chief) farm'. OE *hēah* (dative *hēan*) + *tūn*. Manorial affix from its possession by the *Punchardon* family (from the 11th cent.).

Heapham Lincs. *Iopeham* 1086 (DB). 'Homestead or enclosure where rose-hips or brambles grow'. OE *hēope* or *hēopa* + *hām* or *hamm*.

Heath, a common name, '(place at) the heath', OE *hǣth*; examples include: **Heath and Reach** Beds. *La Hethe* 1276. See REACH. **Heath** Derbys. *Heth* 1257. Earlier called *Lunt* 1086 (DB) from OScand. *lundr* 'small wood, grove'.

Heathcote Derbys. *Hedcote* late 12th cent. 'Cottage(s) on a heath'. OE *hǣth* + *cot*.

Heather Leics. *Hadre* 1086 (DB). 'Place where heather grows'. OE **hǣddre*.

Heathfield, 'heathy open land, open land overgrown with heather', OE *hǣth* + *feld*: **Heathfield** E. Sussex. *Hadfeld* 12th cent. **Heathfield** Somerset. *Hafella* (*sic*) 1086 (DB), *Hathfeld* 1159.

Heath Hayes Staffs. *Hethhey* 1570. 'Heathy enclosure(s)'. OE *hǣth* + *hæg*.

Heathrow Gtr. London. *La Hetherewe* c.1410. 'Row of houses on or near a heath'. OE *hǣth* + *rǣw*.

Heatley Ches. *Heyteley* 1525. 'Woodland clearing where heather grows'. OE *hǣth* + *lēah*.

Heaton, a common name, 'high farmstead', OE *hēah* + *tūn*; examples include: **Heaton** Tyne & Wear. *Heton* 1256. **Heaton** W. Yorks. *Hetun* 1160. **Heaton, Castle** Northum. *Heton* 1183. Affix may refer to a hall-house here in medieval times. **Heaton, Earls** W. Yorks. *Etone* 1086 (DB), *Erlesheeton* 1308. Manorial affix from possession by the Earls of Warren.

Hebburn Tyne & Wear. *Heabyrm* 1104–8. 'High burial place or tumulus'. OE *hēah* + *byrgen*.

Hebden, 'valley where rose-hips or brambles grow', OE *hēope* or *hēopa* + *denu*: **Hebden** N. Yorks. *Hebedene* 1086 (DB). **Hebden Bridge** W. Yorks. *Hepdenbryge* 1399. With OE *brycg* 'bridge' (over Hebden Water).

Hebron Northum. *Heburn* 1242. Probably identical in origin with HEBBURN.

Heck, Great N. Yorks. *Hech* 1153–5. 'The hatch or gate'. OE *hæcc*.

Heckfield Hants. *Hechfeld* 1207. Possibly 'open land by a hedge or hatch-gate'. OE *hecg* or *hecc* + *feld*.

Heckington Lincs. *Hechintune* 1086 (DB). 'Estate associated with a man called Heca'. OE pers. name + *-ing-* + *tūn*.

Heckmondwike W. Yorks. *Hedmundewic* (*sic*) 1086 (DB), *Hecmundewik* 13th cent. 'Dwelling or (dairy) farm of a man called Hēahmund'. OE pers. name + *wīc*.

Heddington Wilts. *Edintone* 1086 (DB). 'Estate associated with a man called Hedde'. OE pers. name + *-ing-* + *tūn*.

Heddon, 'hill where heather grows', OE *hǣth* + *dūn*: **Heddon, Black** Northum. *Hedon* 1271. **Heddon on the Wall** Northum. *Hedun* 1175. Affix from its situation on Hadrian's Wall.

Hedenham Norfolk. *Hedenaham* 1086 (DB). 'Homestead of a man called *Hedena'. OE pers. name + *hām*.

Hedge End Hants. *Cutt Hedge End* 1759. Self-explanatory, with *cut* 'clipped' in the 18th cent. form.

Hedgerley Bucks. *Huggeleg* 1195. 'Woodland clearing of a man called *Hycga'. OE pers. name + *lēah*.

Hedingham, Castle & Sible Essex. *Hedingham* 1086 (DB), *Heyngham Sibille* 1231, *Hengham ad castrum* 1254. Probably 'homestead of the family or followers of a man called *Hyth(a), or of the dwellers at the landing-place'. OE pers. name or *hȳth* + *-inga-* + *hām*. Distinguishing affixes from ME *castel* (Latin *castrum*) 'castle' and from the family of a lady called *Sibil* who held land here in the 13th cent.

Hedley on the Hill Northum. *Hedley* 1242. 'Woodland clearing where heather grows'. OE *hǣth* + *lēah*.

Hednesford Staffs. *Hedenesford* 13th cent. 'Ford of a man called *Heddīn'. OE pers. name + *ford*.

Hedon Humber. *Hedon* 12th cent. 'Hill where heather grows'. OE *hǣth* + *dūn*.

Heigham, Potter Norfolk. *Echam* 1086 (DB), *Hegham Pottere* 1182. Possibly 'homestead with a hedge or hatch-gate'. OE *hecg* or *hecc* + *hām*. Alternatively the first element may be OE *hēah* 'high' in the sense 'chief'. The affix (from OE *pottere*) must allude to pot-making here at an early date.

Heighington Durham. *Heghyngtona* 1183. Probably 'estate associated with a man called Heca'. OE pers. name + *-ing-* + *tūn*.

Heighington Lincs. *Hictinton* 1242. Probably 'estate associated with a man called *Hyht'. OE pers. name + *-ing-* + *tūn*.

Heighton, South E. Sussex. *Hectone* 1086 (DB), *Sutheghton* 1327. 'High farmstead'. OE *hēah* + *tūn*, with OE *sūth* 'south'.

Helford Cornwall. *Helleford* 1230. 'Estuary crossing-place'. Cornish **heyl* + OE *ford*.

Helhoughton Norfolk. *Helgatuna* 1086 (DB). 'Farmstead of a man called Helgi'. OScand. pers. name + OE *tūn*.

Helions Bumpstead Essex, see BUMPSTEAD.

Helland Cornwall. *Hellaunde* 1284. 'Old church-site'. Cornish **hen-lann*.

Hellesdon Norfolk. *Hægelisdun* c.985, *Hailesduna* 1086 (DB). 'Hill of a man called *Hægel'. OE pers. name + *dūn*.

Hellidon Northants. *Elliden* 12th cent. 'Holy, healthy, or prosperous valley'. OE *hǣlig* + *denu*.

Hellifield N. Yorks. *Helgefeld* 1086 (DB). Probably 'open land of a man called Helgi'. OScand. pers. name + OE *feld*.

Hellingly E. Sussex. *Hellingeleghe* 13th cent. 'Woodland clearing of the family or followers of a man called *Hielle, or of the hill dwellers'. OE pers. name or OE *hyll* + *-inga-* + *lēah*.

Hellington Norfolk. *Halgatune* 1086 (DB). 'Farmstead of a man called Helgi'. OScand. pers. name + OE *tūn*.

Hellvellyn Cumbria. *Helvillon* 1574. Of unknown origin and meaning.

Helmdon Northants. *Elmedene* 1086 (DB). 'Valley of a man called *Helma'. OE pers. name + *denu*.

Helmingham Suffolk. *Helmingheham* 1086 (DB). 'Homestead of the family or followers of a man called Helm'. OE pers. name + *-inga-* + *hām*.

Helmshore Lancs. *Hellshour* 1510. 'Steep slope with a cattle shelter'. OE *helm* + **scora*.

Helmsley N. Yorks. *Elmeslac* (*sic*) 1086 (DB), *Helmesley* 12th cent. 'Woodland clearing of a man called Helm'. OE pers. name + *lēah*.

Helmsley, Gate & Upper N. Yorks. *Hamelsec(h)* 1086 (DB), *Gatehemelsay* 1438, *Over Hemelsey* 1301. 'Island, or dry ground in marsh, of a man called Hemele'. OE pers. name + *ēg*. Distinguishing affixes from OScand. *gata* 'road' (here a Roman road) and OE *uferra* 'upper'.

Helperby N. Yorks. *Helperby* 972, *Helprebi* 1086 (DB). 'Farmstead or village of a woman called Hjalp'. OScand. pers. name (genitive *-ar*) + *bý*.

Helperthorpe N. Yorks. *Elpetorp* 1086 (DB). 'Outlying farmstead or hamlet of a woman called Hjalp'. OScand. pers. name (genitive *-ar*) + *thorp*.

Helpringham Lincs. *Helperi(n)cham* 1086 (DB). 'Homestead of the family or followers of a man called Helprīc'. OE pers. name + *-inga-* + *hām*.

Helpston Cambs. *Hylpestun* 948. 'Farmstead of a man called *Help'. OE pers. name + *tūn*.

Helsby Ches. *Helesbe* (*sic*) 1086 (DB), *Hellesbi* late 12th cent. 'Farmstead or village on a ledge'. OScand. *hjallr* + *bý*.

Helston, Helstone, 'estate at an old court', Cornish **hen-lys* + OE *tūn*: **Helston** Cornwall. *Henlistone* 1086 (DB). **Helstone** Cornwall. *Henliston* 1086 (DB).

Helton Cumbria. *Helton c.*1160. Probably 'farmstead on a slope'. OE *helde* + *tūn*.

Hemblington Norfolk. *Hemelingetun* 1086 (DB). 'Estate associated with a man called Hemele'. OE pers. name + *-ing-* + *tūn*.

Hemel Hempstead Herts., see HEMPSTEAD.

Hemingbrough N. Yorks. *Hemingburgh* 1080–6, *Hamiburg* 1086 (DB). Probably 'stronghold of a man called Hemingr'. OScand. pers. name + OE *burh*.

Hemingby Lincs. *Hamingebi* 1086 (DB). 'Farmstead or village of a man called Hemingr'. OScand. pers. name + *bý*.

Hemingford Abbots & Grey Cambs. *Hemmingeford* 974, *Emingeford* 1086 (DB), *Hemingford Abbatis* 1276, *Hemingford Grey* 1316. 'Ford of the family or followers of a man called Hemma or Hemmi'. OE pers. name + *-inga-* + *ford*. Distinguishing affixes from early possession by the Abbot of Ramsey and the *de Grey* family.

Hemingstone Suffolk. *Hamingestuna* 1086 (DB). 'Farmstead of a man called Hemingr'. OScand. pers. name + OE *tūn*.

Hemington, 'estate associated with a man called Hemma or Hemmi', OE pers. name + *-ing-* + *tūn*: **Hemington** Leics. *Aminton c.*1125. **Hemington** Northants. *Hemmingtune* 1077, *Hemintone* 1086 (DB). **Hemington** Somerset. *Hammingtona* 1086 (DB).

Hemley Suffolk. *Helmelea* 1086 (DB). 'Woodland clearing of a man called *Helma'. OE pers. name + *lēah*.

Hempholme Humber. *Hempholm* 12th cent. 'Raised ground in marshland where hemp is grown'. OE *hænep* + OScand. *holmr*.

Hempnall Norfolk. *Hemenhala* 1086 (DB). 'Nook of land of a man called Hemma'. OE pers. name (genitive *-n*) + *halh*.

Hempstead, usually 'the homestead', OE *hām-stede, hæm-stede*: **Hempstead** Essex. *Hamesteda* 1086 (DB). **Hempstead** Norfolk, near Lessingham. *Hemsteda* 1086 (DB). **Hempstead, Hemel** Herts. *Hamelamestede* 1086 (DB). Hemel is an old district-name first recorded *c.*705 meaning 'broken, undulating' from OE **hamel*.

However the following has a different origin: **Hempstead** Norfolk, near Holt. *Henepsteda* 1086 (DB). 'Place where hemp is grown'. OE *hænep* + *stede*.

Hempsted Glos. *Hechanestede* 1086 (DB). 'High homestead'. OE *hēah* + *hām-stede*.

Hempton Norfolk. *Hamatuna* 1086 (DB). 'Farmstead or village of a man called Hemma'. OE pers. name + *tūn*.

Hempton Oxon. *Henton* 1086 (DB). 'High farm'. OE *hēah* (dative *hēan*) + *tūn*.

Hemsby Norfolk. *Heimesbei* 1086 (DB). Probably 'farmstead or village of a man called *Hēmer'. OScand. pers. name + *bý*.

Hemswell Lincs. *Helmeswelle* 1086 (DB). 'Spring or stream of a man called Helm'. OE pers. name + *wella*.

Hemsworth W. Yorks. *Hamelesuurde* (*sic*) 1086 (DB), *Hymeleswrde* 12th cent. 'Enclosure of a man called *Hymel'. OE pers. name + *worth*.

Hemyock Devon. *Hamihoc* 1086 (DB). Possibly a Celtic river-name meaning 'summer stream', otherwise 'river-bend of a man called Hemma', from OE pers. name + *hōc*.

Henbury Avon. *Heanburg* 692, *Henberie* 1086 (DB). 'High or chief fortified place'. OE *hēah* (dative *hēan*) + *burh* (dative *byrig*).

Henbury Ches. *Hameteberie* 1086 (DB). 'Stronghold or manor-house where a community lives'. OE *hǣmed* + *burh* (dative *byrig*).

Hendon Gtr. London. *Heandun* c.975, *Handone* 1086 (DB). '(Place at) the high hill'. OE *hēah* (dative *hēan*) + *dūn*.

Hendon Tyne & Wear. *Hynden* 1382. 'Valley frequented by hinds'. OE *hind* + *denu*.

Hendred, East & West Oxon. *Hennarith* 956, *Henret* 1086 (DB). 'Stream frequented by hens (of wild birds)'. OE *henn* + *rīth*.

Henfield W. Sussex. *Hanefeld* 770, *Hamfelde* 1086 (DB). Probably 'open land characterized by stones or rocks'. OE *hān* + *feld*.

Hengrave Suffolk. *Hemegretham* (*sic*) 1086 (DB), *Hemegrede* c.1095. 'Grassy meadow of a man called Hemma'. OE pers. name + **grēd* (with *hām* 'homestead' in the Domesday form).

Henham Essex. *Henham* c.1045, 1086 (DB). 'High homestead or enclosure'. OE *hēah* (dative *hēan*) + *hām* or *hamm*.

Henley, usually 'high (or chief) wood or clearing', OE *hēah* (dative *hēan*) + *lēah*; examples include: **Henley** Somerset. *Henleighe* 973. **Henley** Suffolk. *Henleia* 1086 (DB). **Henley-in-Arden** Warwicks. *Henle* c.1180. Affix refers to the medieval Forest of Arden (*Eardene* 1088), possibly a Celtic name meaning 'high district'. **Henley-on-Thames** Oxon. *Henleiam* c.1140. See THAMES.

However the following has a different origin: **Henley** Shrops. *Haneleu* 1086 (DB). 'Wood or clearing frequented by hens (of wild birds)'. OE *henn* + *lēah*.

Henlow Beds. *Haneslauue* 1086 (DB). 'Hill or mound frequented by hens (of wild birds)'. OE *henn* + *hlāw*.

Hennock Devon. *Hainoc* 1086 (DB). '(Place at) the high oak-tree'. OE *hēah* (dative *hēan*) + *āc*.

Henny, Great Essex. *Heni* 1086 (DB). 'High island or land partly surrounded by water'. OE *hēah* (dative *hēan*) + *ēg*.

Hensall N. Yorks. *Edeshale* (*sic*) 1086 (DB), *Hethensale* 12th cent. 'Nook of land of a man called *Hethīn or Hethinn'. OE or OScand. pers. name + OE *halh*.

Henshaw Northum. *Hedeneshalch* 12th cent. Identical in origin with the previous name.

Henstead Suffolk. *Henestede* 1086 (DB). Probably 'place frequented by hens (of wild birds)'. OE *henn* + *stede*.

Henstridge Somerset. *Hengstesrig* 956, *Hengest(e)rich* 1086 (DB). 'Ridge where stallions are kept' or 'ridge of a man called Hengest'. OE *hengest* or OE pers. name + *hrycg*.

Henton Oxon. *Hentone* 1086 (DB). 'High (or chief) farmstead'. OE *hēah* (dative *hēan*) + *tūn*.

Henton Somerset. *Hentun* 1065. Identical in origin with previous name, or 'farmstead where hens are kept', OE *henn* + *tūn*.

Hepburn Northum. *Hybberndune* c.1050. Probably identical in origin with HEBBURN (and with the addition of OE *dūn* 'hill' in the early spelling).

Hepple Northum. *Hephal* 1205. 'Nook of land where rose-hips or brambles grow'. OE *hēope* or *hēopa* + *halh*.

Hepscott Northum. *Hebscot* 1242. 'Cottage(s) of a man called *Hebbi'. OE pers. name + *cot*.

Heptonstall W. Yorks. *Heptonstall* 1253. 'Farmstead where rose-hips or bra- -'es grow'. OE *hēope* or *hēopa* + *tūn-stall*.

Hepworth, probably 'enclosure of a man called *Heppa', OE pers. name + *worth*: **Hepworth** Suffolk. *Hepworda* 1086 (DB). **Hepworth** W. Yorks. *Heppeuuord* 1086 (DB).

Hereford, 'ford suitable for the passage of an army', OE **here-ford*: **Hereford** Heref. & Worcs. *Hereford* 958, 1086 (DB). **Herefordshire** (OE *scīr* 'district') is first referred to in the 11th cent. **Hereford, Little** Heref. & Worcs. *Lutelonhereford* 1086 (DB). Affix is OE *lȳtlan*, dative of *lȳtel* 'little'.

Hergest Heref. & Worcs. *Hergest(h)* 1086 (DB). Probably a Welsh name, but obscure in origin and meaning.

Herne, Herne Bay Kent. *Hyrnan* c.1100. '(Place at) the angle or corner of land'. OE *hyrne*.

Hernhill Kent. *Haranhylle* c.1100. '(Place at) the grey hill'. OE *hār* (dative *-an*) + *hyll*.

Herriard Hants. *Henerd* (*sic*) 1086 (DB), *Herierda* c.1160. Probably 'army quarters' (perhaps of a Viking army), OE *here* + *geard*. Alternatively this may be a Celtic name meaning 'long ridge' from *hyr* + **garth*.

Herringfleet Suffolk. *Herlingaflet* 1086 (DB). 'Stream of the family or followers of a man called *Herela'. OE pers. name + *-inga-* + *flēot*.

Herringswell Suffolk. *Hyrningwella* 1086 (DB). 'Spring or stream at the corner of land'. OE *hyrne* + *-ing* + *wella*.

Herrington, East Tyne & Wear. *Erinton* 1196. Possibly 'estate associated with a man called *Here'. OE pers. name + *-ing-* + *tūn*.

Hersham Surrey. *Hauerichesham* 1175. 'Homestead or river-meadow of a man called *Hæferic'. OE pers. name + *hām* or *hamm*.

Herstmonceux E. Sussex. *Herst* 1086 (DB), *Herstmonceus* 1287. OE *hyrst* 'wooded hill' + manorial affix from possession by the *Monceux* family in the 12th cent.

Hertford Herts. *Herutford* 731, *Hertforde* 1086 (DB). 'Ford frequented by harts or stags'. OE *heorot* + *ford*.

Hertfordshire (OE *scīr* 'district') is first referred to in the 11th cent.

Hertingfordbury Herts. *Herefordingberie* (*sic*) 1086 (DB), *Hertfordingeberi* 1220. 'Stronghold of the people of HERTFORD'. OE *-inga-* + *burh* (dative *byrig*).

Hesket, Hesketh, probably 'boundary land where horses graze', but possibly 'race course for horses', OScand. *hestr* + *skeith*; examples include: **Hesket, High & Low** Cumbria. *Hescayth* 1285. **Hesketh** Lancs. *Heschath* 1288.

However the following has a different origin: **Hesket Newmarket** Cumbria. *Eskeheued* 1227. 'Hill growing with ash-trees'. OScand. *eski* + OE *hēafod*. Affix first found in the 18th cent. refers to the market here.

Heskin Green Lancs. *Heskyn* 1257. A Welsh name meaning 'wet ground growing with sedge or coarse grass'.

Hesleden Durham. *Heseldene* c.1050. 'Valley where hazels grow'. OE *hæsel* + *denu*.

Heslerton, East & West N. Yorks. *Heslerton* 1086 (DB). 'Farmstead where hazels grow'. OE **hæsler* + *tūn*.

Heslington N. Yorks. *Haslinton* 1086 (DB). 'Farmstead by the hazel wood'. OE **hæsling* + *tūn*.

Hessay N. Yorks. *Hesdesai* (*sic*) 1086 (DB), *Heslesaia* 12th cent. 'Marshland, or island, where hazels grow'. OE *hæsel* (influenced by OScand. *hesli*) + *sǣ* or *ēg*.

Hessett Suffolk. *Heteseta* (*sic*) 1086 (DB), *Heggeset* 1225. 'Fold (for animals) with a hedge'. OE *hecg* + *(ge)set*.

Hessle Humber. *Hase* (*sic*) 1086 (DB), *Hesel* 12th cent. '(Place at) the hazel-tree'. OE *hæsel* (influenced by OScand. *hesli*).

Hest Bank Lancs. *Hest* 1177. OE **hǣst* 'undergrowth, brushwood'.

Heston Gtr. London. *Hestone* c.1125. 'Farmstead among the brushwood'. OE **hǣs* + *tūn*.

Heswall Mersey. *Eswelle* (*sic*) 1086 (DB), *Haselwell* c.1200. 'Spring where hazels grow'. OE *hæsel* + *wella*.

Hethe Oxon. *Hedha* 1086 (DB). OE *hǣth* 'heath, uncultivated land'.

Hethersett Norfolk. *Hederseta* 1086 (DB). Probably '(settlement of) the dwellers among the heather'. OE **hǣddre* + *sǣte*.

Hett Durham. *Het* c.1168. '(Place at) the hat-shaped hill'. OE *hætt* or OScand. *hetti* (dative of *hǫttr*).

Hetton N. Yorks. *Hetune* 1086 (DB). 'Farmstead on a heath'. OE *hǣth* + *tūn*.

Hetton le Hole Tyne & Wear. *Heppedun* 1180. 'Hill where rose-hips or brambles grow'. OE *hēope* or *hēopa* + *dūn*. Affix means 'in the hollow'.

Heugh Northum. *Hou* 1279. '(Place at) the ridge or spur of land'. OE *hōh*.

Heveningham Suffolk. *Heueniggeham* 1086 (DB). 'Homestead of the family or followers of a man called *Hefin'. OE pers. name + *-inga-* + *hām*.

Hever Kent. *Heanyfre* 814. '(Place at) the high edge or hill-brow'. OE *hēah* (dative *hēan*) + *yfer*.

Heversham Cumbria. *Hefresham* c.1050, *Eureshaim* 1086 (DB). Probably 'homestead of a man called Hēahfrith'. OE pers. name + *hām*.

Hevingham Norfolk. *Heuincham* 1086 (DB). 'Homestead of the family or followers of a man called Hefa'. OE pers. name + *-inga-* + *hām*.

Hewelsfield Glos. *Hiwoldestone* 1086 (DB), *Hualdesfeld* c.1145. 'Open land of a man called Hygewald'. OE pers. name + *feld* (replacing earlier *tūn* 'farmstead').

Hewick, Bridge & Copt N. Yorks. *Heawic* 1086 (DB), *Hewik atte brigg* 1309, *Coppedehaiwic* 1208. 'High (or chief) dairy-farm'. OE *hēah* (dative *hēan*) + *wīc*. Distinguishing affixes 'at the bridge' (from OE *brycg*) and 'with a peak or hill-top' (OE *coppede*).

Hewish, 'measure of land that would support a family', OE *hīwisc*: **Hewish** Somerset. *Hywys* 1327. **Hewish, East & West** Avon. *Hiwis* 1198.

Hexham Northum. *Hagustaldes ham* 685. 'The warrior's homestead'. OE *hagustald* + *hām*.

Hexton Herts. *Hegestanestone* 1086 (DB). 'Farmstead of a man called Hēahstān'. OE pers. name + *tūn*.

Heybridge Essex. *Heaghbregge* c.1200. 'High (or chief) bridge'. OE *hēah* + *brycg*.

Heydon Cambs. *Haidenam* 1086 (DB). 'Valley where hay is made', or 'valley with an enclosure'. OE *hēg* or *hæg* + *denu*.

Heydon Norfolk. *Heidon* 1196. 'Hill where hay is made'. OE *hēg* + *dūn*.

Heyford, 'hay ford', i.e. 'ford used chiefly at hay-making time', OE *hēg* + *ford*: **Heyford, Lower & Upper** Oxon. *Hegford* 1086 (DB). **Heyford, Nether & Upper** Northants. *Heiforde* 1086 (DB).

Heysham Lancs. *Hessam* 1086 (DB). 'Homestead or village among the brushwood'. OE **hǣs* + *hām*.

Heyshott W. Sussex. *Hethsete* c.1100. 'Corner of land where heather grows'. OE *hǣth* + *scēat*.

Heytesbury Wilts. *Hestrebe* (*sic*) 1086 (DB), *Hehtredeberia* c.1115. 'Stronghold of a woman called *Hēahthrȳth'. OE pers. name + *burh* (dative *byrig*).

Heythrop Oxon. *Edrope* (*sic*) 1086 (DB), *Hethrop* 11th cent. 'High hamlet or outlying farmstead'. OE *hēah* + *throp*.

Heywood Gtr. Manch. *Heghwode* 1246. 'High (or chief) wood'. OE *hēah* + *wudu*.

Heywood Wilts. *Heiwode* 1225. 'Enclosed wood'. OE *hæg* + *wudu*.

Hibaldstow Humber. *Hiboldestou* 1086 (DB). 'Holy place where St Hygebald is buried'. OE pers. name + *stōw*.

Hickleton S. Yorks. *Icheltone* 1086 (DB). Probably 'farmstead frequented by woodpeckers'. OE *hicol* + *tūn*.

Hickling, '(settlement of) the family or followers of a man called *Hicel', OE pers. name + *-ingas*: **Hickling** Norfolk. *Hikelinga* 1086 (DB). **Hickling** Notts. *Hikelinge* c.1000, *Hechelinge* 1086 (DB).

Hidcote Boyce Glos. *Hudicota* 716, *Hedecote* 1086 (DB), *Hudicote Boys* 1327. 'Cottage of a man called *Hydeca or Huda'. OE pers. name + *cot*. Manorial affix from a family called *de Bosco* or *Bois*, here in the 13th cent.

Hiendley, South W. Yorks. *Hindeleia* 1086 (DB). 'Wood or clearing frequented by hinds or does'. OE *hind* + *lēah*.

High as affix, see main name, e.g. for **High Ackworth** (W. Yorks.) see ACKWORTH.

Higham, 'high (or chief) homestead or enclosure', OE *hēah* + *hām* or *hamm*; examples include: **Higham** Derbys. *Hehham* 1155. **Higham** Kent. *Hegham* 1242. **Higham** Lancs. *Hegham* 1296. **Higham** Suffolk, near Stratford St Mary. *Hecham* c.1050, *Heihham* 1086 (DB). **Higham, Cold** Northants. *Hecham* 1086 (DB), *Colehigham* 1541. Affix is OE *cald* 'cold, exposed'. **Higham Ferrers** Northants. *Hecham* 1086 (DB), *Heccham Ferrar* 1279. Manorial affix from the *Ferrers* family, here in the 12th cent. **Higham Gobion** Beds. *Echam* 1086 (DB), *Heygham Gobyon* 1291. Manorial affix from the *Gobion* family, here from the 12th cent. **Higham on the Hill** Leics. *Hecham* 1220–35. The affix is found from the 16th cent. **Higham Upshire** Kent. *Heahhaam* c.765, *Hecham* 1086 (DB). The affix means 'higher district' from OE *upp* + *scīr*.

Highampton Devon. *Hantone* 1086 (DB), *Heghanton* 1303. 'High farmstead'. OE *hēah* (dative *hēan*) + *tūn*, with the later addition of ME *heghe* 'high' after the meaning of the original first element had been forgotten.

High Beach Essex. *Highbeach-green* 1670. Probably named from the beech-trees here.

Highbridge Somerset. *Highbridge* 1324. 'High (or chief) bridge'. OE *hēah* + *brycg*.

Highbury Gtr. London. *Heybury* c.1375. 'High manor'. OE *hēah* + *burh* (dative *byrig*).

Highclere Hants. *Clere* 1086 (DB), *Alta Clera* c.1270. Perhaps originally a Celtic river-name meaning 'bright stream', with the later addition of *high* (Latin *alta*).

Higher as affix, see main name, e.g. for **Higher Ansty** (Dorset) see ANSTY.

Highcliffe Dorset. *High Clift* 1759, earlier *Black Cliffe* 1610. Self-explanatory.

Highgate Gtr. London. *Le Heighgate* 1354. 'High tollgate'. OE *hēah* + *geat*.

Highleadon Glos. *Hineledene* 13th cent. 'Estate on the River Leadon belonging to a religious community'. OE *hīwan* (genitive plural *hīgna*) + Celtic river-name (meaning 'broad stream').

Highley Shrops. *Hugelei* 1086 (DB). 'Woodland clearing of a man called *Hugga'. OE pers. name + *lēah*.

Highnam Glos. *Hamme* 1086 (DB), *Hinehamme* 12th cent. OE *hamm* 'river-meadow' with the later addition of OE *hīwan* (genitive plural *hīgna*) 'a religious community'.

Hightown Ches., a late name, meaning simply 'the high part of the town' (of CONGLETON).

Highway Wilts. *Hiwei* 1086 (DB). 'Road used for carrying hay'. OE *hēg* + *weg*.

Highworth Wilts. *Wrde* 1086 (DB), *Hegworth* 1232. OE *worth* 'enclosure, farmstead' with the later addition of *hēah* 'high'.

Hilborough Norfolk. *Hildeburhwella* 1086 (DB), *Hildeburwrthe* 1242. 'Stream or enclosure of a woman called Hildeburh'. OE pers. name + *wella* or *worth*.

Hildenborough Kent. *Hyldenn* 1240, *Hildenborough* 1389. Probably 'woodland pasture on or by a hill'. OE *hyll* + *denn* with the later addition of *burh* 'manor, borough'.

Hildersham Cambs. *Hildricesham* 1086 (DB). 'Homestead of a man called *Hildrīc'. OE pers. name + *hām*.

Hilderstone Staffs. *Hidulvestune* 1086 (DB). 'Farmstead of a man called Hildulfr or Hildwulf'. OScand. or OE pers. name + *tūn*.

Hilderthorpe Humber. *Hilgertorp* 1086 (DB). 'Outlying farmstead of a man called Hildiger or a woman called Hildigerthr'. OScand. pers. name + *thorp*.

Hilfield Dorset. *Hylfelde* 934. 'Open land by a hill'. OE *hyll* + *feld*.

Hilgay Norfolk. *Hillingeiæ* 974, *Hidlingheia* 1086 (DB). 'Island, or dry ground in marsh, of the family or followers of a man called *Hȳthla or *Hydla'. OE pers. name + *-inga-* + *ēg*.

Hill Avon. *Hilla* 1086 (DB). '(Place at) the hill'. OE *hyll*.

Hill, North & South Cornwall. *Henle* 1238, *Northhindle* 1260, *Suthhulle* 1270,

Suthhynle 1306. 'High wood or clearing' or 'hinds' wood or clearing'. OE *hēah* (dative *hēan*) or *hind* + *lēah*, with later replacement by *hyll* 'hill'.

Hillam N. Yorks. *Hillum* 963. '(Place at) the hills'. OE *hyll* in a dative plural form *hyllum*.

Hillesden Bucks. *Hildesdun* 949, *Ilesdone* 1086 (DB). 'Hill of a man called Hild'. OE pers. name + *dūn*.

Hillfarance Somerset. *Hilla* 1086 (DB), *Hull Ferun* 1253. '(Place at) the hill'. OE *hyll*. Manorial addition from the *Furon* family, here in the 12th cent.

Hill Head Hants., a recent name, self-explanatory.

Hillingdon Gtr. London. *Hildendune* c.1080, *Hillendone* 1086 (DB). 'Hill of a man called Hilda'. OE pers. name (genitive *-n*) + *dūn*.

Hillington Norfolk. *Helingetuna* 1086 (DB). 'Farmstead of the family or followers of a man called *Hȳthla or *Hydla'. OE pers. name + *-inga-* + *tūn*.

Hillmorton Warwicks. *Mortone* 1086 (DB), *Hulle and Morton* 1247. Originally two distinct names, now combined. *Hill* is '(place at) the hill' from OE *hyll*. *Morton* is 'marshland farmstead' from OE *mōr* + *tūn*.

Hilmarton Wilts. *Helmerdingtun* 962, *Helmerintone* 1086 (DB). 'Estate associated with a man called *Helmheard'. OE pers. name + *-ing-* + *tūn*.

Hilperton Wilts. *Help(e)rinton* 1086 (DB). 'Estate associated with a man called *Hylprīc'. OE pers. name + *-ing-* + *tūn*.

Hilton, usually 'farmstead or village on or near a hill', OE *hyll* + *tūn*: **Hilton** Cambs. *Hiltone* 1196. **Hilton** Cleveland. *Hiltune* 1086 (DB). **Hilton** Derbys. *Hiltune* 1086 (DB).

However other Hiltons have a different origin: **Hilton** Cumbria. *Helton* 1289. Probably 'farmstead on a slope'. OE *helde* + *tūn*. **Hilton** Dorset. *Eltone* 1086 (DB). 'Farmstead on a slope or where tansy grows'. OE *h(i)elde* or *helde* + *tūn*.

Himbleton Heref. & Worcs. *Hymeltun* 816, *Himeltun* 1086 (DB). 'Farmstead where the hop plant (or some similar plant) grows'. OE *hymele* + *tūn*.

Himley Staffs. *Himelei* 1086 (DB). 'Woodland clearing where the hop plant (or some similar plant) grows'. OE *hymele* + *lēah*.

Hincaster Cumbria. *Hennecastre* 1086 (DB). 'Old fortification or earthwork haunted by hens (of wild birds)'. OE *henn* + *ceaster*.

Hinckley Leics. *Hinchelie* 1086 (DB). 'Woodland clearing of a man called Hȳnca'. OE pers. name + *lēah*.

Hinderclay Suffolk. *Hilderclea* 1086 (DB). 'Tongue of land where elder-trees grow'. OE **hyldre* + *clēa*.

Hinderwell N. Yorks. *Hildrewell* 1086 (DB). Possibly 'spring or well associated with St Hild'. OE pers. name (with Scandinavianized genitive *-ar*) + *wella*. Alternatively the first element may be OE **hyldre* or **hylder* 'elder-tree'.

Hindhead Surrey. *Hyndehed* 1571. 'Hill frequented by hinds or does'. OE *hind* + *hēafod*.

Hindley Gtr. Manch. *Hindele* 1212. 'Wood or clearing frequented by hinds or does'. OE *hind* + *lēah*.

Hindolveston Norfolk. *Hidolfestuna* 1086 (DB). 'Farmstead of a man called Hildwulf'. OE pers. name + *tūn*.

Hindon Wilts. *Hynedon* 1268. Probably 'hill belonging to a religious community'. OE *hīwan* (genitive plural *hīgna*) + *dūn*.

Hindringham Norfolk. *Hindringaham* 1086 (DB). Possibly 'homestead of the people living behind (the hills)'. OE *hinder* + *-inga-* + *hām*.

Hingham Norfolk. *Hincham* 1086 (DB), *Heingeham* 1173. Probably 'homestead of the family or followers of a man called Hega'. OE pers. name + *-inga-* + *hām*.

Hinksey, North & South Oxon. *Hengestesige* 10th cent. 'Island or well-watered land of the stallion or of a man called Hengest'. OE *hengest* or OE pers. name + *ēg*.

Hinstock Shrops. *Stoche* 1086 (DB), *Hinestok* 1242. 'Outlying farmstead belonging to a religious community'. OE *hīwan* (genitive plural *hīgna*) + *stoc*.

Hintlesham Suffolk. *Hintlesham* 1086

(DB). 'Homestead or enclosure of a man called *Hyntel'. OE pers. name + *hām* or *hamm*.

Hinton, a very common name, has two different origins. Sometimes 'high (or chief) farmstead' from OE *hēah* (dative *hēan*) + *tūn*: **Hinton** Avon, near Dyrham. *Heanton* 13th cent. **Hinton Ampner** Hants. *Heantun* 1045, *Hentune* 1086 (DB), *Hinton Amner* 13th cent. Affix is OFrench *aumoner* 'almoner', from its early possession by the almoner of St Swithun's Priory at Winchester. **Hinton Blewett** Avon. *Hantone* 1086 (DB), *Hentun Bluet* 1246. Manorial affix from its early possession by the *Bluet* family. **Hinton, Broad** Wilts. *Hentone* 1086 (DB), *Brodehenton* 1319. Affix is OE *brād* 'large'. **Hinton Charterhouse** Avon. *Hantone* 1086 (DB), *Henton Charterus* 1273. Affix is OFrench *chartrouse* 'a house of Carthusian monks' referring to a priory founded in the early 13th cent. **Hinton, Great** Wilts. *Henton* 1216. **Hinton St George** Somerset. *Hantone* 1086 (DB), *Hentun Sancti Georgii* 1246. Affix from the dedication of the church. **Hinton St Mary** Dorset. *Hamtune* 944, *Haintone* 1086 (DB), *Hinton Marye* 1627. Affix from the possession of the manor by the Abbey of St Mary at Shaftesbury. **Hinton Waldrist** Oxon. *Hentone* 1086 (DB), *Hinton Walrush* 1676. Manorial affix from the family *de Sancto Walerico*, here in the 12th cent.

However many Hintons mean 'farmstead belonging to a religious community', from OE *hīwan* (genitive plural *hīgna*) + *tūn*: **Hinton** Heref. & Worcs., near Peterchurch. *Hinetune* 1086 (DB). **Hinton** Northants. *Hintone* 1086 (DB). **Hinton, Cherry** Cambs. *Hintone* 1086 (DB), *Cheryhynton* 1576. Affix is ME *chiri* 'cherry' from the number of cherry-trees formerly growing here. **Hinton in the Hedges** Northants. *Hintone* 1086 (DB). Affix (meaning 'among the hedges') is from OE *hecg*. **Hinton, Little** Wilts. *Hinneton* 1205. **Hinton Martell** Dorset. *Hinetone* 1086 (DB), *Hineton Martel* 1226. Manorial affix from the *Martell* family, here in the 13th cent. **Hinton on the Green** Heref. & Worcs. *Hinetune* 1086 (DB). Affix is OE *grēne* 'village green'.

Hints, '(place on) the roads or paths', Welsh *hynt*: **Hints** Shrops. *Hintes* 1242. **Hints** Staffs. *Hintes* 1086 (DB).

Hinwick Beds. *Heneuuic(h)* 1086 (DB). 'Farm where hens are kept'. OE *henn* + *wīc*.

Hinxhill Kent. *Haenostesyle* c.1100. 'Hill of the stallion or of a man called Hengest'. OE *hengest* or OE pers. name + *hyll*.

Hinxton Cambs. *Hestitone (sic)* 1086 (DB), *Hengstiton* 1202. 'Estate associated with a man called Hengest'. OE pers. name + *-ing-* + *tūn*.

Hinxworth Herts. *Haingesteuuorde* 1086 (DB). Probably 'enclosure where stallions are kept'. OE *hengest* + *worth*.

Hipperholme W. Yorks. *Huperun* 1086 (DB). '(Place among) the osiers'. OE **hyper* in a dative plural form **hyperum*.

Hirst Courtney, Temple Hirst N. Yorks. *Hyrst* c.1030, *Hirst Courtenay* 1303, *Templehurst* 1316. '(Place at) the wooded hill'. OE *hyrst*. Distinguishing affixes from possession by the *Courtney* family (here in the 13th cent.) and by the Knights Templars (here in the 12th cent.).

Histon Cambs. *Histone* 1086 (DB). Possibly 'farmstead of the sons or young men'. OE *hys(s)e* + *tūn*.

Hitcham Suffolk. *Hecham* 1086 (DB). 'Homestead with a hedge or hatch-gate'. OE *hecg* or *hecc* + *hām*.

Hitchin Herts. *Hiccam* c.945, *Hiz* 1086 (DB). '(Place in the territory of) the tribe called *Hicce*'. Old tribal name (possibly derived from a Celtic river-name meaning 'dry') in a dative plural form *Hiccum*.

Hittisleigh Devon. *Hitenesleia* 1086 (DB). 'Woodland clearing of a man called *Hyttīn'. OE pers. name + *lēah*.

Hixon Staffs. *Hustedone (sic)* 1086 (DB), *Huchtesdona* 1130. 'Hill of a man called *Hyht'. OE pers. name + *dūn*.

Hoar Cross Staffs. *Horcros* 1230. 'Grey or boundary cross'. OE *hār* + *cros*.

Hoarwithy Heref. & Worcs. *La Horewythy* 13th cent. '(Place at) the whitebeam'. OE *hār* + *wīthig*.

Hoath Kent. *La hathe* 13th cent. '(Place at) the heath'. OE **hāth*.

Hoathly, 'heathy woodland clearing' or 'woodland clearing where heather grows', OE **hāth* + *lēah*: **Hoathly, East** E. Sussex. *Hodlegh* 1287. **Hoathly, West** W. Sussex. *Hadlega* 1121.

Hoby Leics. *Hobie* 1086 (DB). 'Farmstead or village on a spur of land'. OE *hōh* + OScand. *bý*.

Hockering Norfolk. *Hokelinka* (*sic*) 1086 (DB), *Hokeringhes* 12th cent. '(Settlement of) the people at the rounded hill'. OE **hocer* + *-ingas*.

Hockerton Notts. *Hocretone* 1086 (DB). 'Farmstead at the hump or rounded hill'. OE **hocer* + *tūn*.

Hockham, Great Norfolk. *Hocham* 1086 (DB). 'Homestead of a man called Hocca, or where hocks or mallows grow'. OE pers. name or OE *hocc* + *hām*.

Hockley Essex. *Hocheleia* 1086 (DB). 'Woodland clearing of a man called Hocca, or where hocks or mallows grow'. OE pers. name or OE *hocc* + *lēah*.

Hockley Heath W. Mids. *Huckeloweheth c.*1280. 'Heath near the mound or hill of a man called *Hucca'. OE pers. name + *hlāw* + *hǣth*.

Hockliffe Beds. *Hocgan clif* 1015, *Hocheleia* (*sic*) 1086 (DB). Probably 'steep hill-side of a man called *Hocga'. OE pers. name + *clif*.

Hockwold cum Wilton Norfolk. *Hocuuella* (*sic*) 1086 (DB), *Hocwolde* 1242. 'Wooded area where hocks or mallows grow'. OE *hocc* + *wald*. See WILTON.

Hockworthy Devon. *Hocoorde* 1086 (DB). 'Enclosure of a man called Hocca'. OE pers. name + *worth*.

Hoddesdon Herts. *Hodesdone* 1086 (DB). 'Hill of a man called *Hod'. OE pers. name + *dūn*.

Hoddlesden Lancs. *Hoddesdene* 1296. 'Valley of a man called *Hod or *Hodel'. OE pers. name + *denu*.

Hodnet Shrops. *Odenet* 1086 (DB). Probably a Welsh name meaning 'pleasant valley'.

Hoe Norfolk. *Hou* 1086 (DB). '(Place at) the ridge or spur of land'. OE *hōh* (dative *hōe*).

Hoff Cumbria. *Houf* 1179. 'The heathen temple or sanctuary'. OScand. *hof*.

Hoggeston Bucks. *Hochestone* (*sic*) 1086 (DB), *Hoggeston* 1200. 'Farmstead of a man called *Hogg'. OE pers. name + *tūn*.

Hoghton Lancs. *Hoctonam c.*1160. 'Farmstead on or near a hill-spur'. OE *hōh* + *tūn*.

Hognaston Derbys. *Ochenavestun* 1086 (DB). Possibly 'grazing farm of a man called Hocca'. OE pers. name + *ǣfesn* + *tūn*.

Hog's Back Surrey, first so called (from its shape) in 1823, earlier *Geldedon* 1195, probably 'hill called *Gylde* (the gold-coloured one)', from OE **gylde* + *dūn*, see GUILDFORD.

Hogsthorpe Lincs. *Hocgestorp* 12th cent. 'Outlying farmstead or hamlet of a man called *Hogg'. OE pers. name + OScand. *thorp*.

Holbeach Lincs. *Holebech* 1086 (DB). 'Hollow stream' or 'hollow ridge'. OE *hol* + *bece* or *bæc* (locative **bece*).

Holbeck Notts. *Holebek c.*1180. 'Hollow stream, stream in a hollow'. OScand. *holr* or *hol* + *bekkr*.

Holbeton Devon. *Holbouton* 1229. 'Farmstead in the hollow bend'. OE *hol* + *boga* + *tūn*.

Holborn Gtr. London. *Holeburne* 1086 (DB). 'Hollow stream, stream in a hollow'. OE *hol* + *burna*.

Holbrook, 'hollow brook, brook in a hollow', OE *hol* + *brōc*: **Holbrook** Derbys. *Holebroc* 1086 (DB). **Holbrook** Suffolk. *Holebroc* 1086 (DB).

Holbury Hants., near Fawley. *Holeberi* 1187. 'Hollow stronghold', or 'stronghold in a hollow'. OE *hol* + *burh* (dative *byrig*).

Holcombe, a common name, 'deep or hollow valley', OE *hol* + *cumb*; examples include: **Holcombe** Devon, near Dawlish. *Holacumba c.*1070, *Holcomma* 1086 (DB). **Holcombe** Gtr. Manch. *Holecumba* early 13th cent. **Holcombe** Somerset. *Holecumbe* 1243. **Holcombe Burnell** Devon. *Holecumba* 1086 (DB), *Holecumbe Bernard* 1263.

Manorial affix (later modified to the modern form) from a man called *Bernard* whose son held the manor in 1242. **Holcombe Rogus** Devon. *Holecoma* 1086 (DB), *Holecombe Roges* 1281. Manorial affix from one *Rogo* who held the manor in 1086.

Holcot Northants. *Holecote* 1086 (DB). 'Cottage(s) in the hollow(s)'. OE *hol* + *cot*.

Holden Lancs. *Holedene* 1086 (DB). 'Hollow valley'. OE *hol* + *denu*.

Holdenby Northants. *Aldenesbi* 1086 (DB). 'Farmstead or village of a man called Halfdan'. OScand. pers. name + *bý*.

Holderness (district) Humber. *Heldernesse* 1086 (DB). 'Headland ruled by a high-ranking yeoman'. OScand. *hǫldr* + *nes*.

Holdgate Shrops. *Castellum Hologoti* 1185. 'Castle of a man called Helgot'. OFrench pers. name with Latin *castellum*.

Holdingham Lincs. *Haldingeham* 1202. 'Homestead of the family or followers of a man called *Hald'. OE pers. name + *-inga-* + *hām*.

Holford Somerset. *Holeforde* 1086 (DB). 'Hollow ford, ford in a hollow'. OE *hol* + *ford*.

Holker Cumbria. *Holecher* 1086 (DB). 'Hollow marsh, marsh in a hollow'. OScand. *holr* or *hol* + *kjarr*.

Holkham Norfolk. *Holcham* 1086 (DB). 'Homestead in or near a hollow'. OE *holc* + *hām*.

Hollacombe Devon. *Holecome* 1086 (DB). 'Deep or hollow valley'. OE *hol* + *cumb*.

Holland, 'cultivated land by a hill-spur', OE *hōh* + *land*: **Holland on Sea** Essex. *Holande c.*1000, *Holanda* 1086 (DB). **Holland, Up** Lancs. *Hoiland* 1086 (DB). Affix is OE *upp* 'higher up'.
However the following, although an identical compound, may have a somewhat different meaning: **Holland** Lincs. *Hoiland* 1086 (DB). Probably 'district characterized by hill-spurs'.

Hollesley Suffolk. *Holeslea* 1086 (DB). 'Woodland clearing in a hollow, or of a man called *Hōl'. OE *hol* or OE pers. name + *lēah*.

Hollingbourne Kent. *Holingeburna* 10th cent., *Holingeborne* 1086 (DB). 'Stream of the family or followers of a man called *Hōla, or of the people dwelling in the hollow'. OE pers. name or *hol* + *-inga-* + *burna*.

Hollington, 'farmstead where holly grows', OE *holegn* + *tūn*: **Hollington** Derbys. *Holintune* 1086 (DB). **Hollington** E. Sussex. *Holintune* 1086 (DB). **Hollington** Staffs. *Holyngton* 13th cent.

Hollingworth Gtr. Manch. *Holisurde* (*sic*) 1086 (DB), *Holinewurth* 13th cent. 'Holly enclosure'. OE *holegn* + *worth*.

Holloway Gtr. London. *Le Holeweye* 1307. 'The road in a hollow'. OE *hol* + *weg*.

Hollowell Northants. *Holewelle* 1086 (DB). 'Spring or stream in a hollow'. OE *hol* + *wella*.

Hollym Humber. *Holam* 1086 (DB). Probably 'homestead or enclosure in or near the hollow'. OE *hol* + *hām* or *hamm*. Alternatively '(place at) the hollows', from OE *hol* or OScand. *holr* in a dative plural form *holum*.

Holme, a common place-name, usually from OScand. *holmr* 'island, dry ground in marsh, water-meadow': **Holme** Cambs. *Hulmo* 1167. **Holme** Cumbria. *Holme* 1086 (DB). **Holme** N. Yorks. *Hulme* 1086 (DB). **Holme** Notts. *Holme* 1203. **Holme Chapel** Lancs. *Holme* 1305. **Holme Hale** Norfolk. *Holm* 1086 (DB), *Holmhel* 1267. Second element is OE *halh* (dative *hale*) 'nook of land'. **Holme next the Sea** Norfolk. *Holm c.*1035, 1086 (DB). **Holme Pierrepont** Notts. *Holmo* 1086 (DB), *Holme Peyrpointe* 1571. Manorial affix from the *de Perpount* family, here in the 14th cent. **Holme St Cuthbert** Cumbria. *Sanct Cuthbert Chappell* 1538. Named from the dedication of the chapel. **Holme, South** N.Yorks. *Holme* 1086 (DB), *Southolme* 1301. **Holme upon Spalding Moor** Humber. *Holme* 1086 (DB), *Holm in Spaldingmor* 1293. Spalding Moor is an old district-name meaning 'moor of the people called *Spaldingas*', from the tribe who gave their name to SPALDING (Lincs.) + OE *mōr*.
However some examples of Holme have other origins: **Holme** W. Yorks,

near Holmfirth. *Holne* 1086 (DB). '(Place at) the holly tree'. OE *holegn*. **Holme, East & West** Dorset. *Holne* 1086 (DB), *Estholn, Westholn* 1288. Identical in origin with the previous name. **Holme Lacy** Heref. & Worcs. *Hamme* 1086 (DB), *Homme Lacy* 1221. OE *hamm* 'enclosure, land in a river-bend'. Manorial affix from its possession by the *de Laci* family from 1086. **Holme on the Wolds** Humber. *Hougon* 1086 (DB), *Holme super Wolde* 1578. '(Place at) the mounds or hills'. OScand. *haugr* in a dative plural form *haugum*. The affix is from OE *wald* 'high forest-land'.

Holmer, 'pool in a hollow', OE *hol* + *mere*: **Holmer** Heref. & Worcs. *Holemere* 1086 (DB). **Holmer Green** Bucks. *Holemere* 1208.

Holmes Chapel Ches. *Hulm* 12th cent., *Holme chapell* 1400–5. 'Chapel at the place called *Hulme* or *Holme*'. OScand. *holmr* 'water-meadow' with the later addition of ME *chapel*.

Holmesfield Derbys. *Holmesfelt* 1086 (DB). Probably 'open land near a place called *Holm*'. OE *feld* with a lost place-name *Holm* from OScand. *holmr* 'island, dry ground in marsh'.

Holmfirth W. Yorks. *Holnefrith* 1274. 'Sparse woodland belonging to HOLME'. OE *fyrhth*.

Holmpton Humber. *Holmetone* 1086 (DB). 'Farmstead near the shore-meadows'. OScand. *holmr* + OE *tūn*.

Holmwood, North & South Surrey. *Homwude* 1241. 'Wood in or near an enclosure or river-meadow'. OE *hamm* + *wudu*.

Holne Devon. *Holle* (*sic*) 1086 (DB), *Holna* 1178. '(Place at) the holly tree'. OE *holegn*.

Holnest Dorset. *Holeherst* 1185. 'Wooded hill where holly grows'. OE *holegn* + *hyrst*.

Holsworthy Devon. *Haldeurdi* 1086 (DB). 'Enclosure of a man called *Heald'. OE pers. name + *worthig*.

Holt, a common name, '(place at) the wood or thicket', OE *holt*; examples include: **Holt** Dorset. *Winburneholt* 1185, *Holte* 1372. Originally 'wood near WIMBORNE [MINSTER]'. **Holt** Heref. & Worcs. *Holte* 1086 (DB). **Holt** Norfolk. *Holt* 1086 (DB). **Holt** Wilts. *Holt* 1242. **Holt End** Hants. *Holt* 1167.

Holtby N. Yorks, near York. *Holtebi* 1086 (DB). Probably 'farmstead or village of a man called Holti'. OScand. pers. name + *bý*.

Holton, a common name, has a number of different origins: **Holton** Lincs., near Beckering. *Houtune* 1086 (DB). 'Farmstead on a spur of land'. OE *hōh* + *tūn*. **Holton** Oxon. *Healhtun* 956, *Eltone* 1086 (DB). 'Farmstead in a nook of land'. OE *healh* + *tūn*. **Holton** Somerset. *Healhtun c.*1000. Identical in origin with the previous name. **Holton** Suffolk. *Holetuna* 1086 (DB). 'Farmstead near a hollow, or of a man called *Hōla'. OE *hol* or OE pers. name + *tūn*. **Holton Heath** Dorset. *Holtone* 1086 (DB). 'Farmstead near a hollow, or near a wood'. OE *hol* or *holt* + *tūn*. **Holton le Clay** Lincs. *Holtun* (*sic*) 1086 (DB), *Houtuna c.*1115. 'Farmstead on a spur of land'. OE *hōh* + *tūn*. Affix means 'in the clayey district' from OE *clǣg*. **Holton le Moor** Lincs. *Hoctune* 1086 (DB). Identical in origin with the previous name. Affix means 'in the moorland' from OE *mōr*. **Holton St Mary** Suffolk. *Holetuna* 1086 (DB). 'Farmstead near a hollow, or of a man called *Hōla'. OE *hol* or OE pers. name + *tūn*. Affix from the dedication of the church.

Holwell, a common name, has several different origins: **Holwell** Dorset, near Sherborne. *Holewala* 1188. 'Ridge or bank in a hollow'. OE *hol* + *walu*. **Holwell** Herts. *Holewelle* 969, 1086 (DB). 'Spring or stream in a hollow'. OE *hol* + *wella*. **Holwell** Leics. *Holewelle* 1086 (DB). Identical in origin with the previous name. **Holwell** Oxon. *Haliwell* 1222. 'Holy spring or stream'. OE *hālig* + *wella*.

Holwick Durham. *Holewyk* 1235. Probably 'dwelling or farm in a hollow'. OE *hol* + *wīc*.

Holworth Dorset. *Holewertthe* 934, *Holverde* 1086 (DB). 'Enclosure in a hollow'. OE *hol* + *worth*.

Holybourne Hants. *Haliburne* 1086 (DB). 'Holy stream'. OE *hālig* + *burna*.

Holy Island Northum. *Halieland* 1195. 'Holy island' (from its association with early Christian missionaries). OE *hālig* + *ēg-land*. See LINDISFARNE.

Holyport Berks. *Horipord* 1220. 'Muddy or dirty market town'. OE *horig* + *port*. The first element was intentionally changed to *holy* by the late 14th cent.

Holystone Northum. *Halistan* 1242. 'Holy stone' (perhaps one at which the gospel was preached). OE *hālig* + *stān*.

Holywell Cambs. *Haliewelle* 1086 (DB). 'Holy spring or stream'. OE *hālig* + *wella*.

Homersfield Suffolk. *Humbresfelda* 1086 (DB). 'Open land of a man called Hūnbeorht'. OE pers. name + *feld*.

Homerton Gtr. London. *Humburton* 1343. 'Farmstead of a woman called Hūnburh'. OE pers. name + *tūn*.

Homington Wilts. *Hummingtun* 956, *Humitone* 1086 (DB). 'Estate associated with a man called *Humma'. OE pers. name + *-ing-* + *tūn*.

Honeybourne, Church & Cow Heref. & Worcs. *Huniburna* 709, *Huniburne, Heniberge* (*sic*) 1086 (DB), *Churchoniborne* 1535, *Calewe Honiburn* 1374. '(Places on) the stream by which honey is found'. OE *hunig* + *burna*. Affixes from OE *cirice* 'church' and *calu* 'bare, lacking vegetation'.

Honeychurch Devon. *Honechercha* 1086 (DB). Probably 'church of a man called Hūna'. OE pers. name + *cirice*.

Honiley Warwicks. *Hunilege* 1208. 'Woodland clearing where honey is found'. OE *hunig* + *lēah*.

Honing Norfolk. *Haninga* 1086 (DB). Probably '(settlement of) the people at the rock or hill'. OE *hān* + *-ingas*.

Honingham Norfolk. *Hunincham* 1086 (DB). 'Homestead of the family or followers of a man called Hūn(a)'. OE pers. name + *-inga-* + *hām*.

Honington Lincs. *Hundintone* 1086 (DB). Probably 'estate associated with a man called *Hund'. OE pers. name + *-ing-* + *tūn*.

Honington Suffolk. *Hunegetuna* 1086 (DB). Probably 'farmstead of the family or followers of a man called Hūn(a)'. OE pers. name + *-inga-* + *tūn*.

Honington Warwicks. *Hunitona* 1043, *Hunitone* 1086 (DB). 'Farmstead where honey is produced'. OE *hunig* + *tūn*.

Honiton Devon. *Honetone* 1086 (DB). 'Farmstead of a man called Hūna'. OE pers. name + *tūn*.

Honiton, Clyst Devon. *Hinatune* c.1100, *Clysthynetone* 1281. 'Farmstead (on the River Clyst) belonging to a religious community' (in this case Exeter Cathedral). OE *hīwan* (genitive plural *hīgna*) + *tūn*, to which the Celtic river-name (see CLYST) was later added.

Honley W. Yorks. *Haneleia* 1086 (DB). 'Woodland clearing where woodcock abound, or where there are stones and rocks'. OE *hana* or *hān* + *lēah*.

Hoo, Hooe, '(place at) the spur of land', OE *hōh* (dative *hōe*): **Hoo, St Mary's Hoo** Kent. *Hoge* c.687, *How* 1086 (DB), *Ho St. Mary* 1272. Affix St Mary from the dedication of the church. **Hoo Green** Suffolk. *Ho* c.1050, *Hou* 1086 (DB). **Hooe** Devon. *Ho* 1086 (DB). **Hooe** E. Sussex. *Hou* 1086 (DB).

Hook, Hooke, usually '(place at) the hook of land, or bend in a river or hill', OE *hōc*: **Hook** Gtr. London. *Hoke* 1227. **Hook** Hants., near Basingstoke. *Hoc* 1223. **Hook** Wilts. *La Hok* 1238. **Hooke** Dorset. *Lahoc* 1086 (DB). With the French definite article *la* in the early form.

However the following have a different origin: **Hook** Humber. *Huck* 12th cent. OE **hūc* 'river-bend'. **Hook Norton** Oxon. *Hocneratune* early 10th cent. Possibly 'farmstead of a tribe called **Hoccanēre*'. OE tribal name (meaning 'people at Hocca's hill-slope' from OE pers. name and *ōra*) + *tūn*.

Hoole Ches. *Hole* 1119. '(Place at) the hollow'. OE *hol*.

Hoole, Much Lancs. *Hulle* 1204, *Magna Hole* c.1235. OE *hulu* 'a shed, a hovel'. Affix is OE *mycel* 'great' (earlier Latin *magna*).

Hooton, 'farmstead on a spur of land', OE *hōh* + *tūn*: **Hooton** Ches. *Hotone* 1086 (DB). **Hooton Levitt** S. Yorks. *Hotone* 1086 (DB). Manorial affix from the *Livet* family, here in the 13th cent. **Hooton Pagnell** S. Yorks. *Hotun* 1086 (DB), *Hotton Painel* 1192. Manorial affix from its possession by the *Painel* family from the 11th cent. **Hooton**

Roberts S. Yorks. *Hotun* 1086 (DB), *Hoton Robert* 1285. Manorial affix from its possession by a man called *Robert* in the 13th cent.

Hope, a common name, from OE *hop* 'small enclosed valley, enclosed plot of land'; examples include: **Hope** Derbys. *Hope* 926, 1086 (DB). **Hope** Devon. *La Hope* 1281. **Hope** Shrops. *Hope* 1242. **Hope Bowdler** Shrops. *Fordritishope* 1086 (DB), *Hop* 1201, *Hopebulers* 1273. Held by a man called *Forthrǣd* in 1086, but later manorial affix from the *de Bulers* family, here in the 12th cent. **Hope Green** Ches. *Hope* 1282. With the later addition of *grēne* 'village green'. **Hope Mansell** Heref. & Worcs. *Hope* 1086 (DB), *Hoppe Maloisel* 12th cent. Manorial affix from early possession by the *Maloisel* family. **Hope, Sollers** Heref. & Worcs. *Hope* 1086 (DB), *Hope Solers* 1242. Manorial affix from the *de Solariis* family, here in the 13th cent. **Hope under Dinmore** Heref. & Worcs. *Hope* 1086 (DB), *Hope sub' Dinnemor* 1291. Dinmore may be a Welsh name *din mawr* meaning 'great fort', or alternatively 'marsh of a man called *Dynna' from OE pers. name + *mōr*.

Hopton, 'farmstead in a small enclosed valley or enclosed plot of land', OE *hop* + *tūn*: **Hopton** Shrops., near Hodnet. *Hotune* (*sic*) 1086 (DB), *Hopton* 1242. **Hopton** Staffs. *Hoptuna* 1167. **Hopton** Suffolk, near Thetford. *Hopetuna* 1086 (DB). **Hopton Cangeford** Shrops. *Hopton* 1242, *Hopton Cangefot* 1315. Manorial affix from its early possession by the *Cangefot* family. **Hopton Castle** Shrops. *Opetune* 1086 (DB). Affix from the Norman castle here. **Hopton Wafers** Shrops. *Hoptone* 1086 (DB), *Hopton Wafre* 1236. Manorial affix from its early possession by the *Wafre* family.

Hopwas Staffs. *Opewas* 1086 (DB). 'Marshy or alluvial land near an enclosure'. OE *hop* + **wæsse*.

Hopwood, 'wood near an enclosure or in a small enclosed valley', OE *hop* + *wudu*: **Hopwood** Gtr. Manch. *Hopwode* 1278. **Hopwood** Heref. & Worcs. *Hopwuda* 849.

Horbling Lincs. *Horbelinge* 1086 (DB). Probably 'muddy settlement of the family or followers of a man called Bill or *Billa'. OE *horu* + OE pers. name + *-ingas*.

Horbury W. Yorks. *Horberie* 1086 (DB). 'Stronghold on muddy land'. OE *horu* + *burh* (dative *byrig*).

Horden Durham. *Horedene c.*1050. 'Dirty or muddy valley'. OE *horu* + *denu*.

Hordle Hants. *Herdel* (*sic*) 1086 (DB), *Hordhull* 1242. 'Hill where treasure was found'. OE *hord* + *hyll*.

Hordley Shrops. *Hordelei* 1086 (DB). 'Woodland clearing where treasure was found'. OE *hord* + *lēah*.

Horham Suffolk. *Horham c.*950. 'Muddy homestead'. OE *horu* + *hām*.

Horkesley, Great & Little Essex. *Horchesleia c.*1130. 'Woodland clearing with a shelter', or 'dirty, muddy clearing'. OE **horc* or *horsc* + *lēah*.

Horkstow Humber. *Horchetou* 1086 (DB). Probably 'shelter for animals or people'. OE **horc* + *stōw*.

Horley, probably 'woodland clearing in a horn-shaped piece of land', OE *horn*, **horna* + *lēah*: **Horley** Oxon. *Hornelie* 1086 (DB). **Horley** Surrey. *Horle* 12th cent.

Hormead, Great Herts. *Horemede* 1086 (DB). 'Muddy meadow'. OE *horu* + *mǣd*.

Hornblotton Green Somerset. *Hornblawertone* 851, *Horblawetone* 1086 (DB). 'Farmstead of the hornblowers or trumpeters'. OE *horn-blāwere* + *tūn*.

Hornby, 'farmstead or village on a horn-shaped piece of land, or of a man called Horn or *Horni', OScand. *horn* or pers. name + *bý*: **Hornby** Lancs. *Hornebi* 1086 (DB). **Hornby** N. Yorks., near Great Smeaton. *Hornebia* 1086 (DB). **Hornby** N. Yorks., near Hackforth. *Hornebi* 1086 (DB).

Horncastle Lincs. *Hornecastre* 1086 (DB). 'Roman station or fortification on a horn-shaped piece of land'. OE **horna* + *ceaster*.

Hornchurch Gtr. London. *Hornechurch* 1233. 'Church with horn-like gables'. OE *horn*, *hornede* + *cirice*.

Horncliffe Northum. *Hornecliff* 1210.

'Slope of the horn-shaped hill or piece of land'. OE *horna + clif.*

Horndon on the Hill Essex. *Hornindúna* 1086 (DB). 'Horn-shaped hill'. OE **horning* + *dūn*.

Horne Surrey. *Horne* 1208. '(Place at) the horn-shaped hill or piece of land'. OE *horn* or **horna*.

Horning Norfolk. *Horningga* early 11th cent., *Horninga* 1086 (DB). '(Settlement of) the people living at the horn-shaped hill or piece of land'. OE *horn*, **horna* + *-ingas*.

Horninghold Leics. *Horniwale* (*sic*) 1086 (DB), *Horningewald* 1163. 'Woodland of the people living at the horn-shaped piece of land'. OE *horn*, **horna* + *-inga-* + *wald*.

Horninglow Staffs. *Horninglow* 12th cent. 'Mound at the horn-shaped hill or piece of land'. OE **horning* + *hlāw*.

Horningsea Cambs. *Horninges ige c.*975, *Horningesie* 1086 (DB). 'Island, or dry ground in marsh, of a man called *Horning or by the horn-shaped hill'. OE pers. name or **horning* + *ēg*.

Horningsham Wilts. *Horningesham* 1086 (DB). Probably 'homestead of a man called *Horning'. OE pers. name + *hām*. Alternatively the first element may be OE **horning* 'horn-shaped hill or piece of land'.

Horningtoft Norfolk. *Horninghetoft* 1086 (DB). 'Homestead of the people living at the horn-shaped hill or piece of land'. OE *horn*, **horna* + *-inga-* + OScand. *toft*.

Hornsby Cumbria. *Ormesby c.*1210. 'Farmstead or village of a man called Ormr'. OScand. pers. name + *bý*.

Hornsea Humber. *Hornessei* 1086 (DB). 'Lake with a horn-shaped peninsula'. OScand. *horn* + *nes* + *sǽr*.

Hornsey Gtr. London. *Haringeie* 1201, *Haringesheye* 1243. 'Enclosure in the grey wood' or 'of a man called *Hæring'. OE **hāring* or OE pers. name + *hæg*. Nearby HARRINGAY is a different development of the same name.

Hornton Oxon. *Hornigeton* 1194. 'Farmstead near the horn-shaped piece of land'. OE **horning* + *tūn*, or *horn(a)* + *-ing-* + *tūn*.

Horrabridge Devon. *Horebrigge* 1345. 'Grey or boundary bridge'. OE *hār* + *brycg*.

Horringer Suffolk. *Horningeserda* 1086 (DB). 'Ploughed land at the bend or headland' or 'of a man called *Horning'. OE **horning* or OE pers. name + *erth*.

Horrington, East & West Somerset. *Hornningdun* 1065. Possibly 'horn-shaped hill', OE **horning* + *dūn*. Alternatively 'hill of the people living at the horn-shaped piece of land', OE *horn* or **horna* + *-inga-* + *dūn*.

Horseheath Cambs. *Horseda c.*1080, *Horsei* (*sic*) 1086 (DB). 'Heath where horses are kept'. OE *hors* + *hǣth*.

Horsell Surrey. *Horisell* 13th cent. 'Shelter for animals in a muddy place'. OE *horu* + *(*ge*)sell.

Horsey Norfolk. *Horseia* 1086 (DB). 'Island, or dry ground in marsh, where horses are kept'. OE *hors* + *ēg*.

Horsford Norfolk. *Hosforda* 1086 (DB). 'Ford which horses can cross'. OE *hors* + *ford*.

Horsforth W. Yorks. *Horseford* 1086 (DB). Identical in origin with the previous name.

Horsham, 'homestead or village where horses are kept', OE *hors* + *hām*: **Horsham** W. Sussex. *Horsham* 947. **Horsham St Faith** Norfolk. *Horsham* 1086 (DB). Affix from the dedication of the church.

Horsington Lincs. *Horsintone* 1086 (DB). 'Estate associated with a man called Horsa'. OE pers. name + *-ing-* + *tūn*.

Horsington Somerset. *Horstenetone* 1086 (DB). 'Farmstead of the horsekeepers or grooms'. OE *hors-thegn* + *tūn*.

Horsley, 'clearing or pasture where horses are kept', OE *hors* + *lēah*: **Horsley** Derbys. *Horselei* 1086 (DB). **Horsley** Glos. *Horselei* 1086 (DB). **Horsley** Northum. *Horseley* 1242. **Horsley, East & West** Surrey. *Horsalæge* 9th cent., *Horslei*, *Orselei* 1086 (DB).

Horsmonden Kent. *Horsbundenne c.*1100. Probably 'woodland pasture near the stream where horses drink'. OE *hors* + *burna* + *denn*.

Horstead, Horsted, 'place where horses are kept', OE *hors* + *stede*: **Horstead** Norfolk. *Horsteda* 1086 (DB). **Horsted Keynes** W. Sussex. *Horstede* 1086 (DB), *Horsted Kaynes* 1307. Manorial affix from its possession by William *de Cahainges* in 1086. **Horsted, Little** E. Sussex. *Horstede* 1086 (DB), *Little Horstede* 1307.

Horton, a common name, usually 'dirty or muddy farmstead', OE *horu* + *tūn*; examples include: **Horton** Bucks., near Ivinghoe. *Hortone* 1086 (DB). **Horton** Dorset. *Hortun* 1033, *Hortune* 1086 (DB). **Horton** Northants. *Hortone* 1086 (DB). **Horton** Oxon. *Hortun* 1005–12, *Hortone* 1086 (DB). **Horton** Shrops., near Wem. *Hortune* 1086 (DB). **Horton** Staffs. *Horton* 1239. **Horton** Surrey. *Horton* 1178. **Horton** Wilts. *Horton* 1158. **Horton Green** Ches. *Horton c.*1240. **Horton-in-Ribblesdale** N. Yorks. *Hortune* 1086 (DB), *Horton in Ribbelesdale* 13th cent. Affix means 'valley of the River Ribble', OE river-name (see RIBBLETON) + OE *dæl* or OScand. *dalr*. **Horton Kirby** Kent. *Hortune* 1086 (DB), *Horton Kyrkeby* 1346. Manorial affix from its possession by the *de Kirkeby* family in the 13th cent.
However the following has a different origin: **Horton** Avon. *Horedone* 1086 (DB). 'Hill frequented by harts or stags'. OE *heorot* + *dūn*.

Horwich Gtr. Manch. *Horewic* 1221. '(Place at) the grey wych-elm(s)'. OE *hār* + *wice*.

Horwood Devon. *Horewode, Hareoda* 1086 (DB). 'Grey wood or muddy wood'. OE *hār* or *horu* + *wudu*.

Horwood, Great & Little Bucks. *Horwudu* 792, *Hereworde* (*sic*) 1086 (DB). 'Dirty or muddy wood'. OE *horu* + *wudu*.

Hose Leics. *Hoches, Howes* 1086 (DB). 'The spurs of land'. OE *hōh* in a plural form *hō(h)as*.

Hotham Humber. *Hode* 963, *Hodhum* 1086 (DB). '(Place at) the shelters'. OE **hōd* in a dative plural form **hōdum*.

Hothfield Kent. *Hathfelde c.*1100. 'Heathy open land'. OE **hāth* + *feld*.

Hoton Leics. *Hohtone* 1086 (DB). 'Farmstead on a spur of land'. OE *hōh* + *tūn*.

Hough, 'the ridge or spur of land', OE *hōh*: **Hough** Ches., near Willaston. *Hohc* 1241. **Hough** Ches., near Wilmslow. *Le Hogh* 1289.

Hougham Lincs. *Hacham* 1086 (DB). Probably 'river-meadow belonging to HOUGH-ON-THE-HILL'. OE *hamm*.

Hough-on-the-Hill Lincs. *Hach, Hag* 1086 (DB). OE *haga* 'enclosure'.

Houghton, a common name, usually 'farmstead on or near a ridge or hill-spur', OE *hōh* + *tūn*: **Houghton** Cambs. *Hoctune* 1086 (DB). **Houghton** Cumbria. *Hotton* 1246. **Houghton** Hants. *Hohtun* 982, *Houstun* (*sic*) 1086 (DB). **Houghton** W. Sussex. *Hohtun* 683. **Houghton Conquest** Beds. *Houstone* 1086 (DB), *Houghton Conquest* 1316. Manorial affix from the *Conquest* family, here in the 13th cent. **Houghton, Great & Little** Northants. *Hohtone* 1086 (DB), *Magna Houtona* 1199, *Parva Houtone* 1233. Distinguishing affixes are Latin *magna* 'great' and *parva* 'little'. **Houghton le Side** Durham. *Hoctona* 1200. Affix means 'by the hill slope' from OE *sīde*. **Houghton le Spring** Tyne & Wear. *Hoctun, Hoghton Springes c.*1220. Manorial affix from the *Spring* family, here in the 13th cent. **Houghton on the Hill** Leics. *Hohtone* 1086 (DB). The affix is recorded from the 17th cent. **Houghton Regis** Beds. *Houstone* 1086 (DB), *Kyngeshouton* 1287. Latin affix *regis* 'of the king' because it was a royal manor at an early date. **Houghton St Giles** Norfolk. *Hohttune* 1086 (DB). Affix from the dedication of the church.
However the following have a different origin, 'farmstead in a nook of land', OE *halh* + *tūn*: **Houghton, Great** S. Yorks. *Haltun* 1086 (DB), *Magna Halghton* 1303. Affix is Latin *magna* 'great'. **Houghton, Little** S. Yorks. *Haltone* 1086 (DB), *Parva Halghton* 1303. Affix is Latin *parva* 'little'.

Hound Green Hants. *Hune* 1086 (DB). 'Place where the plant hoarhound grows'. OE *hūne*.

Hounslow Gtr. London. *Honeslaw* (*sic*) 1086 (DB), *Hundeslawe* 1217. 'Mound or tumulus of the hound, or of a man called *Hund'. OE *hund* or OE pers. name + *hlāw*.

Hove E. Sussex. *La Houue* 1288. OE *hūfe* 'hood-shaped hill' or 'shelter'.

Hoveringham Notts. *Horingeham* (*sic*) 1086 (DB), *Houeringeham* 1167. 'Homestead of the people living at the hump-shaped hill'. OE *hofer* + *-inga-* + *hām*.

Hoveton Norfolk. *Houetuna* 1086 (DB). 'Farmstead of a man called Hofa, or where the plant ale-hoof grows'. OE pers. name or OE *hōfe* + *tūn*.

Hovingham N. Yorks. *Hovingham* 1086 (DB). 'Homestead of the family or followers of a man called Hofa'. OE pers. name + *-inga-* + *hām*.

Howden Humber. *Heafuddene* 959, *Hovedene* 1086 (DB). 'Valley by the headland or spit of land'. OE *hēafod* (replaced by OScand. *hǫfuth*) + *denu*.

Howe Norfolk. *Hou* 1086 (DB). '(Place at) the hill or barrow'. OScand. *haugr*.

Howell Lincs. *Huuelle* 1086 (DB). Second element OE *wella* 'spring, stream', first element doubtful, possibly OE **hugol* 'mound, hillock' or *hūne* 'hoarhound'.

Howle Shrops. *Hugle* 1086 (DB). '(Place at) the mound or hillock'. OE **hugol*.

Howsham, '(place at) the houses or buildings', OE *hūs* or OScand. *hús* in a dative plural form: **Howsham** Humber. *Usun* 1086 (DB). **Howsham** N. Yorks. *Huson* 1086 (DB).

Howton Heref. & Worcs. *Huetune* c.1184. Probably 'estate of a man called Hugh'. OFrench pers. name + OE *tūn*.

Hoxne Suffolk. *Hoxne* c.950, *Hoxana* 1086 (DB). Possibly 'hock-shaped spur of land'. OE *hōhsinu*.

Hoxton Gtr. London. *Hochestone* 1086 (DB). 'Farmstead of a man called *Hōc'. OE pers. name + *tūn*.

Hoylake Mersey. *Hyle Lake* 1687. 'Tidal lake or channel at the hillock or sandbank'. OE **hygel* + ME *lake* or OE *lacu*.

Hoyland, 'cultivated land on or near a hill-spur', OE *hōh* + *land*: **Hoyland, High** S. Yorks. *Holand* 1086 (DB), *Heyholand* 1283. Affix is OE *hēah* 'high'. **Hoyland Nether** S. Yorks. *Ho(i)land* 1086 (DB), *Nether Holand* 1390. Affix is OE *neotherra* 'lower'. **Hoyland Swaine** S. Yorks. *Holande* 1086 (DB), *Holandeswayn* 1266. Manorial affix from possession in the 12th cent. by a man called *Swein* (OScand. *Sveinn*).

Hubberholme N. Yorks. *Huburgheham* 1086 (DB). 'Homestead of a woman called Hūnburh'. OE pers. name + *hām*.

Huby N. Yorks., near Easingwold. *Hobi* 1086 (DB). 'Farmstead on the spur of land'. OE *hōh* + OScand. *bý*.

Huby N. Yorks., near Stainburn. *Huby* 1198. 'Farmstead of a man called Hugh'. OFrench pers. name + OScand. *bý*.

Hucclecote Glos. *Hochilicote* 1086 (DB). 'Cottage associated with a man called *Hucel(a)'. OE pers. name + *-ing-* + *cot*.

Hucking Kent. *Hugginges* 1195. '(Settlement of) the family or followers of a man called *Hucca'. OE pers. name + *-ingas*.

Hucklow, Great & Little Derbys. *Hochelai* 1086 (DB), *Magna Hockelawe* 1251, *Parva Hokelawe* 13th cent. 'Mound or hill of a man called *Hucca'. OE pers. name + *hlāw*. Affixes are Latin *magna* 'great' and *parva* 'little'.

Hucknall, 'nook of land of a man called *Hucca', OE pers. name (genitive *-n*) + *halh*: **Hucknall** Notts. *Hochenale* 1086 (DB). **Hucknall, Ault** Derbys. *Hokenhale* 1291, *Haulte Huknall* 1535. Affix is OFrench *haut* 'high'.

Huddersfield W. Yorks. *Odresfeld* 1086 (DB). 'Open land of a man called *Hudræd'. OE pers. name + *feld*. Alternatively the first element may be an OE **hūder* 'a shelter'.

Huddington Heref. & Worcs. *Hudintune* 1086 (DB). 'Estate associated with a man called Hūda'. OE pers. name + *-ing-* + *tūn*.

Hudswell N. Yorks. *Hudreswelle* (*sic*) 1086 (DB), *Hudeleswell* 12th cent. Probably 'spring or stream of a man called *Hūdel'. OE pers. name + *wella*.

Huggate Humber. *Hughete* 1086 (DB). Possibly 'road to or near the mounds'. OScand. **hugr* + *gata*.

Hughenden Valley Bucks. *Huchedene* 1086 (DB). 'Valley of a man called *Huhha'. OE pers. name (genitive *-n*) + *denu*.

Hughley Shrops. *Lega* 12th cent., *Hugh Leghe* 1327. Originally 'the wood or clearing', from OE *lēah*. Later addition from possession by a man called *Hugh* in the 12th cent.

Hugh Town Isles of Scilly, Cornwall. *Hugh Town* 17th cent., named from *the Hew Hill* 1593. Probably OE *hōh* 'spur of land'.

Huish, a common name, 'measure of land that would support a family', OE *hīwisc*; examples include: **Huish** Wilts. *Iwis* 1086 (DB). **Huish Champflower** Somerset. *Hiwis* 1086 (DB), *Hywys Champflur* 1274. Manorial affix from the *Champflur* family, here in the 13th cent. **Huish Episcopi** Somerset. *Hiwissh* 973. Affix is Latin *episcopi* 'bishop's', referring to early possession by the Bishop of Wells. **Huish, North & South** Devon. *Hewis, Heuis* 1086 (DB).

Hulcott Bucks. *Hoccote* 1200, *Hulecote* 1228. Probably 'hovel-like cottages'. OE *hulu* + *cot*.

Hull Humber., see KINGSTON UPON HULL.

Hulland Derbys. *Hoilant* 1086 (DB). 'Cultivated land by a hill-spur'. OE *hōh* + *land*.

Hullavington Wilts. *Hunlavintone* 1086 (DB). 'Estate associated with a man called Hūnlāf'. OE pers. name + *-ing-* + *tūn*.

Hullbridge Essex. *Whouluebregg* 1375. Probably 'bridge with arches'. OE *hwalf* + *brycg*.

Hulme, 'the island, the dry ground in marsh, the water-meadow', OScand. *holmr*: **Hulme** Gtr. Manch. *Hulm* 1246. **Hulme, Cheadle** Gtr. Manch. *Hulm* late 12th cent., *Chedle Hulm* 1345. Within the parish of CHEADLE. **Hulme End** Staffs. *Hulme* 1227. **Hulme Walfield** Ches. *Wallefeld et Hulm* c.1262. Walfield was originally a separate manor, 'open land at a spring', OE *wælla* or *wælm* + *feld*.

Hulton, Abbey Staffs. *Hulton* 1235. 'Farmstead on a hill'. OE *hyll* + *tūn*. Affix from the Cistercian abbey founded here in 1223.

Humber Court Heref. & Worcs. *Humbre* 1086 (DB). Originally the name of Humber Brook, see next name.

Humberside (new county), named from the River Humber, an ancient pre-English river-name of uncertain origin and meaning which occurs elsewhere in England (as in previous name).

Humberston Humber. *Humbrestone* 1086 (DB). '(Place by) the boundary stone in the River Humber'. Ancient river-name (see previous name) + OE *stān*.

Humbleton Humber. *Humeltone* 1086 (DB). 'Farmstead by a rounded hillock, or where hops grow', or 'farmstead of a man called Humli'. OE **humol* or *humele* or OScand. pers. name + OE *tūn*.

Humbleton Northum. *Hameldun* 1170. 'Crooked or scarred hill'. OE **hamel* + *dūn*.

Humshaugh Northum. *Hounshale* 1279. Probably 'nook of land of a man called Hūn'. OE pers. name + *halh*.

Huncoat Lancs. *Hunnicot* 1086 (DB). Possibly 'cottage(s) of a man called Hūna', OE pers. name + *cot*. Alternatively the first element may be OE *hunig* 'honey'.

Huncote Leics. *Hunecote* 1086 (DB). Probably 'cottage(s) of a man called Hūna'. OE pers. name + *cot*.

Hunderthwaite Durham. *Hundredestoit* 1086 (DB). 'Clearing or meadow of a man called Húnrøthr'. OScand. pers. name + *thveit*. Alternatively the first element may be OScand. *hundrath* or OE *hundred* in the sense 'administrative district'.

Hundleby Lincs. *Hundelbi* 1086 (DB). 'Farmstead or village of a man called Hundulfr'. OScand. pers. name + *bý*.

Hundon Suffolk. *Hunedana* 1086 (DB). 'Valley of a man called Hūna'. OE pers. name + *denu*.

Hungerford Berks. *Hungreford* 1101–18. 'Hunger ford', i.e. 'ford leading to poor or unproductive land'. OE *hungor* + *ford*.

Hunmanby N. Yorks. *Hundemanebi* 1086 (DB). 'Farmstead or village of the houndsmen or dog-keepers'. OScand. **hunda-mann* (genitive plural *-a*) + *bý*.

Hunningham Warwicks. *Huningeham* 1086 (DB). 'Homestead of the family or followers of a man called Hūna'. OE pers. name + *-inga-* + *hām*.

Hunsdon Herts. *Honesdone* 1086 (DB). 'Hill of a man called Hūn'. OE pers. name + *dūn*.

Hunsingore N. Yorks. *Hulsingoure* (*sic*) 1086 (DB), *Hunsinghouere* 1194. 'Promontory associated with a man called Hūnsige'. OE pers. name + *-ing-* + **ofer*.

Hunslet W. Yorks. *Hunslet* (*sic*) 1086 (DB), *Hunesflete* 12th cent. 'Inlet or stream of a man called Hūn'. OE pers. name + *flēot*.

Hunsley, High Humber. *Hund(r)eslege* 1086 (DB). 'Woodland clearing of a man called *Hund'. OE pers. name + *lēah*.

Hunsonby Cumbria. *Hunswanby* 1292. 'Farmstead or village of the houndsmen or dog-keepers'. OScand. *hunda-sveinn* + *bý*.

Hunstanton Norfolk. *Hunstanestun* c.1035, *Hunestanestuna* 1086 (DB). 'Farmstead of a man called Hūnstān'. OE pers. name + *tūn*.

Hunstanworth Durham. *Hunstanwortha* 1183. 'Enclosure of a man called Hūnstān'. OE pers. name + *worth*.

Hunston Suffolk. *Hunterstuna* 1086 (DB). 'Farmstead of the hunter'. OE **huntere* + *tūn*.

Hunston W. Sussex. *Hunestan* 1086 (DB). 'Boundary stone of a man called Hūn(a)'. OE pers. name + *stān*.

Huntingdon Cambs. *Huntandun* 973, *Huntedun* 1086 (DB). 'Hill of the huntsman, or of a man called Hunta'. OE *hunta* or pers. name (genitive *-n*) + *dūn*. **Huntingdonshire** (OE *scīr* 'district') is first referred to in the 11th cent.

Huntingfield Suffolk. *Huntingafelde* 1086 (DB). 'Open land of the family or followers of a man called Hunta'. OE pers. name + *-inga-* + *feld*.

Huntington N. Yorks. *Huntindune* 1086 (DB). Probably 'hunting hill', i.e. 'hill where hunting takes place'. OE *hunting* + *dūn*.

Huntington Staffs. *Huntendon* 1167. 'Hill of the huntsmen'. OE *hunta* (genitive plural *huntena*) + *dūn*.

Huntley Glos. *Huntelei* 1086 (DB). 'Huntsman's wood or clearing'. OE *hunta* + *lēah*.

Hunton Kent. *Huntindone* 11th cent. 'Hill of the huntsmen'. OE *hunta* (genitive plural *huntena*) + *dūn*.

Hunton N. Yorks. *Huntone* 1086 (DB). 'Farmstead of a man called Hūna'. OE pers. name + *tūn*.

Huntsham Devon. *Honesham* 1086 (DB). 'Homestead or enclosure of a man called Hūn'. OE pers. name + *hām* or *hamm*.

Huntspill Somerset. *Honspil* 1086 (DB). 'Tidal creek of a man called Hūn'. OE pers. name + *pyll*.

Huntworth Somerset. *Hunteworde* 1086 (DB). 'Enclosure of the huntsman, or of a man called Hunta'. OE *hunta* or pers. name + *worth*.

Hunwick Durham. *Hunewic* c.1050. 'Dwelling or (dairy) farm of a man called Hūna'. OE pers. name + *wīc*.

Hunworth Norfolk. *Hunaworda* 1086 (DB). 'Enclosure of a man called Hūna'. OE pers. name + *worth*.

Hurdsfield Ches. *Hirdelesfeld* 13th cent. Probably 'open land at a hurdle (fence)'. OE *hyrdel*, **hyrdels* + *feld*.

Hurley, 'woodland clearing in a recess in the hills', OE *hyrne* + *lēah*: **Hurley** Berks. *Herlei* 1086 (DB), *Hurnleia* 1106–21. **Hurley** Warwicks. *Hurle* early 11th cent., *Hurnlee* c.1180.

Hurn Dorset. *Herne* 1086 (DB). '(Place at) the angle or corner of land'. OE *hyrne*.

Hursley Hants. *Hurselye* 1171. Probably 'mare's woodland clearing'. OE **hyrse* + *lēah*.

Hurst Berks. *Herst* 1220. '(Place at) the wooded hill'. OE *hyrst*. The same name occurs in other counties.

Hurstbourne Priors & Tarrant Hants. *Hysseburnan* c.880, *Esseborne* 1086 (DB). 'Stream with winding water-plants', or 'stream of the youths'. OE *hysse* + *burna*. Distinguishing affixes from early possession of the two manors by Winchester Priory and Tarrant Abbey.

Hurstpierpont W. Sussex. *Herst* 1086 (DB), *Herst Perepunt* 1279. OE *hyrst* 'wooded hill' + manorial addition from possession by Robert *de Pierpoint* in 1086.

Hurworth Durham. *Hurdewurda* 1158. 'Enclosure made with hurdles'. OE **hurth* + *worth*.

Husbands Bosworth Leics., see BOSWORTH.

Husborne Crawley Beds. *Hysseburnan* 969, *Crawelai* 1086 (DB), *Husseburn Crouleye* 1276. Originally two separate places. 'Stream with winding water-plants', or 'stream frequented by youths', from OE *hysse* + *burna*, and 'wood or clearing frequented by crows' from OE *crāwe* + *lēah*.

Husthwaite N. Yorks. *Hustwait* 1167. 'Clearing with a house or houses built on it'. OScand. *hús* + *thveit*.

Huthwaite Notts. *Hodweit* 1199. 'Clearing on a spur of land'. OE *hōh* + OScand. *thveit*.

Huttoft Lincs. *Hotoft* 1086 (DB). 'Homestead on a spur of land'. OE *hōh* + OScand. *toft*.

Hutton, a common name, 'farmstead on or near a ridge or hill-spur', OE *hōh* + *tūn*: **Hutton** Cumbria. *Hoton* 1291. **Hutton** Essex. *Atahov* 1086 (DB), *Houton* 1200. In DB it is simply '(place) at the ridge or hillspur'. **Hutton** Lancs., near Penwortham. *Hoton* 12th cent. **Hutton** Somerset. *Hotune* 1086 (DB). **Hutton Buscel** N. Yorks. *Hotun* 1086 (DB), *Hoton Buscel* 1253. Manorial affix from the *Buscel* family, here in the 12th cent. **Hutton Conyers** N. Yorks. *Hotone* 1086 (DB), *Hotonconyers* 1198. Manorial affix from the *Conyers* family, here in the early 12th cent. **Hutton Cranswick** Humber. *Hottune* 1086 (DB). Distinguishing affix from its proximity to Cranswick (*Cranzuic* 1086 (DB)) which is possibly '(dairy) farm of a man called *Cranuc', OE pers. name + *wīc*. **Hutton Henry** Durham. *Hoton* c.1050. Affix from its possession by *Henry de Essh* in the 14th cent. **Hutton-le-Hole** N. Yorks. *Hotun* 1086 (DB). Affix means 'in the hollow' from OE *hol*. **Hutton Lowcross** Cleveland. *Hotun* 1086 (DB). Affix from a nearby place (*Loucros* 12th cent.) which may be 'cross of a man called Logi', OScand. pers. name + *cros*. **Hutton Magna** Durham. *Hotton* 1086 (DB), *Magna Hoton* 1157. Latin *magna* 'great'. **Hutton Roof** Cumbria. *Hotunerof* 1278. Affix is probably manorial from some early owner called *Rolf* (OScand. Hrólfr). **Hutton Rudby** N. Yorks. *Hotun* 1086 (DB), *Hoton by Ruddeby* 1310. Affix from a nearby place (*Rodebi* 1086 (DB)) which is 'farmstead of a man called Ruthi', OScand. pers. name + *bý*. **Hutton, Sand** N. Yorks. *Hotone* 1086 (DB), *Sandhouton* 1219. Affix is OE *sand* 'sand'. **Hutton Sessay** N. Yorks. *Hottune* 1086 (DB). Affix from its proximity to SESSAY. **Hutton Wandesley** N. Yorks. *Hoton* c.1200, *Hotun Wandelay* 1253. Affix from a nearby place (*Wandeslage* 1086 (DB)), 'woodland clearing of a man called *Wand or *Wandel', OE pers. name + *lēah*.

Huxley Ches. *Huxelehe* early 13th cent. Probably 'woodland clearing of a man called *Hucc'. OE pers. name + *lēah*.

Huyton Mersey. *Hitune* 1086 (DB). 'Estate with a landing-place'. OE *hȳth* + *tūn*.

Hyde, 'estate assessed at one hide, an amount of land for the support of one free family and its dependants', OE *hīd*; for example **Hyde** Gtr. Manch. *Hyde* early 13th cent.

Hykeham, North & South Lincs. *Hicham* 1086 (DB). OE *hām* 'homestead' or *hamm* 'enclosure' with a doubtful first element, possibly an OE **hīce* 'some kind of small bird'.

Hylton, South Tyne & Wear. *Helton* 1195. 'Farmstead on a slope or hill'. OE *helde* or *hyll* + *tūn*.

Hythe, 'landing-place or harbour', OE *hȳth*: **Hythe** Kent. *Hede* 1086 (DB). **Hythe** Hants. *La Huthe* 1248.

I

Ibberton Dorset. *Abristetone* 1086 (DB). 'Estate associated with a man called Ēadbeorht'. OE pers. name + *-ing-* + *tūn*.

Ible Derbys. *Ibeholon* 1086 (DB). 'Hollow(s) of a man called Ibba'. OE pers. name + *hol*.

Ibsley Hants. *Tibeslei* 1086 (DB), *Ibeslehe* 13th cent. 'Woodland clearing of a man called *Tibbi or *Ibbi'. OE pers. name + *lēah*.

Ibstock Leics. *Ibestoche* 1086 (DB). 'Outlying farmstead or hamlet of a man called Ibba'. OE pers. name + *stoc*.

Ibstone Bucks. *Ebestan* 1086 (DB). 'Boundary stone of a man called Ibba'. OE pers. name + *stān*.

Ickburgh Norfolk. *Iccheburc* 1086 (DB). 'Stronghold of a man called *Ic(c)a'. OE pers. name + *burh*.

Ickenham Gtr. London. *Ticheham* 1086 (DB). 'Homestead or village of a man called Tic(c)a'. OE pers. name (genitive *-n*) + *hām*. Initial *T-* was lost in the 13th cent. due to confusion with the preposition *at*.

Ickford Bucks. *Iforde* (*sic*) 1086 (DB), *Ycford* 1175. 'Ford of a man called *Ic(c)a'. OE pers. name + *ford*.

Ickham Kent. *Ioccham* 785, *Gecham* 1086 (DB). 'Homestead or village comprising a yoke (some fifty acres) of land'. OE *geoc* + *hām*.

Ickleford Herts. *Ikelineford* 12th cent. 'Ford associated with a man called Icel'. OE pers. name + *-ing-* + *ford*.

Icklesham E. Sussex. *Icoleshamme* 770. 'Promontory or river-meadow of a man called Icel'. OE pers. name + *hamm*.

Ickleton Cambs. *Icelingtune* *c*.975, *Hichelintone* 1086 (DB). 'Estate associated with a man called Icel'. OE pers. name + *-ing-* + *tūn*.

Icklingham Suffolk. *Ecclingaham* 1086 (DB). 'Homestead of the family or followers of a man called *Yccel'. OE pers. name + *-inga-* + *hām*.

Icknield Way (prehistoric trackway from Norfolk to Dorset). *Icenhylte* 903. Obscure in origin and meaning. The name was transferred in the 12th cent. to the Roman road from Bourton on the Water to Templeborough near Rotherham, now called Icknield or Ryknild Street.

Ickwell Green Beds. *Ikewelle* *c*.1170. 'Beneficial spring or stream', or 'spring or stream of a man called *Gic(c)a'. OE *gēoc* or OE pers. name + *wella*.

Icomb Glos. *Iccacumb* 781, *Iccumbe* 1086 (DB). 'Valley of a man called *Ic(c)a'. OE pers. name + *cumb*.

Iddesleigh Devon. *Edeslege* (*sic*) 1086 (DB), *Edwislega* 1107. 'Woodland clearing of a man called Ēadwīg'. OE pers. name + *lēah*.

Ide Devon. *Ide* 1086 (DB). Possibly an old river-name of pre-English origin.

Ideford Devon. *Yudaforda* 1086 (DB). 'Ford of a man called *Giedda', or 'ford where people assemble for speeches or songs'. OE pers. name or OE *giedd* + *ford*.

Iden E. Sussex. *Idene* 1086 (DB). 'Woodland pasture where yew-trees grow'. OE **īg* + *denn*.

Idlicote Warwicks. *Etelincote* 1086 (DB). 'Cottage(s) associated with a man called *Yttel(a)'. OE pers. name + *-ing-* + *cot*.

Idmiston Wilts. *Idemestone* 947. 'Farmstead of a man called *Idmǣr or *Idhelm'. OE pers. name + *tūn*.

Idridgehay Derbys. *Edrichesei* 1230. 'Enclosure of a man called Ēadrīc'. OE pers. name + *hæg*.

Idstone Oxon. *Edwineston* 1199.

'Farmstead of a man called Ēadwine'. OE pers. name + *tūn*.

Ifield W. Sussex. *Ifelt* 1086 (DB). 'Open land where yew-trees grow'. OE **īg* + *feld*.

Ifold W. Sussex. *Ifold* 1296. Probably 'fold or enclosure in well-watered land'. OE *īeg* + *fald*.

Iford E. Sussex. *Niworde* (*sic*) 1086 (DB), *Yford* late 11th cent. 'Ford in well-watered land', or 'where yew-trees grow'. OE *īeg* or **īg* + *ford*.

Ifton Heath Shrops. *Iftone* 1272. Possibly 'farmstead of a man called Ifa'. OE pers. name + *tūn*.

Ightfield Shrops. *Istefelt* 1086 (DB). OE *feld* 'open land' with an obscure first element, possibly a pre-English river-name *Ight*.

Ightham Kent. *Ehteham c.*1100. 'Homestead or village of a man called *Ehta'. OE pers. name + *hām*.

Iken Suffolk. *Ykene* 1212. Perhaps originally a river-name, 'stream of a man called *Ica', OE pers. name (genitive *-n*) + *ēa*.

Ilam Staffs. *Hilum* 1002. Possibly a Celtic river-name (an early name for River Manifold) meaning 'trickling stream'. Alternatively the name may be '(place at) the pools', from OScand. *hylr* in a dative plural form *hylum*.

Ilchester Somerset. *Givelcestre* 1086 (DB). 'Roman town on the River *Gifl*'. Celtic river-name (meaning 'forked river') + OE *ceaster*. *Gifl* was an earlier name for the River Yeo.

Ilderton Northum. *Ildretona c.*1125. 'Farmstead where elder-trees grow'. OE **hyldre* + *tūn*.

Ilford Gtr. London. *Ilefort* 1086 (DB). 'Ford over the river called *Hyle*'. Celtic river-name (meaning 'trickling stream') + OE *ford*. *Hyle* was an early name for the River Roding below Ilford.

Ilfracombe Devon. *Alfreincome* 1086 (DB). 'Valley associated with a man called Ælfrēd'. OE pers. name + *-ing-* + *cumb*.

Ilkeston Derbys. *Tilchestune* (*sic*) 1086 (DB), *Elkesdone* early 11th cent. 'Hill of a man called Ēalāc'. OE pers. name + *tūn*.

Ilketshall St Andrew & St Margaret Suffolk. *Ilcheteleshala* 1086 (DB). 'Nook of land of a man called *Ylfketill'. OScand. pers. name + OE *halh*. Distinguishing affixes from the dedications of the churches.

Ilkley W. Yorks. *Hillicleg c.*972, *Illiclei* 1086 (DB). Possibly 'woodland clearing of a man called *Yllica or *Illica'. OE pers. name + *lēah*.

Illingworth W. Yorks. *Illingworthe* 1276. 'Enclosure associated with a man called *Illa or Ylla'. OE pers. name + *-ing-* + *worth*.

Illogan Cornwall. 'Church of *Sanctus Illoganus*' 1291. 'Church of St Illogan'. From the patron saint of the church.

Illston on the Hill Leics. *Elvestone* 1086 (DB). Possibly 'farmstead of a man called Iólfr or *Elf'. OScand. or OE pers. name + OE *tūn*.

Ilmer Bucks. *Imere* (*sic*) 1086 (DB), *Ilmere* 1161–3. Probably 'pool where leeches are found'. OE *īl* + *mere*.

Ilmington Warwicks. *Ylmandun* 978, *Ilmedone* 1086 (DB). 'Hill growing with elm-trees'. OE **ylme* (genitive *-an*) + *dūn*.

Ilminster Somerset. *Illemynister* 995, *Ileminstre* 1086 (DB). 'Large church on the River Isle'. Celtic river-name (of uncertain meaning) + OE *mynster*.

Ilsington Devon. *Ilestintona* 1086 (DB). 'Estate associated with a man called *Ielfstān'. OE pers. name + *-ing-* + *tūn*.

Ilsley, East & West Berks. *Hildeslei* 1086 (DB). 'Woodland clearing of a man called Hild'. OE pers. name + *lēah*.

Ilton N. Yorks. *Ilcheton* 1086 (DB). 'Farmstead of a man called *Yllica or *Illica'. OE pers. name + *tūn*.

Ilton Somerset. *Atiltone* (*sic*) 1086 (DB), *Ilton* 1243. 'Farmstead on the River Isle'. Celtic river-name (of uncertain meaning) + OE *tūn*.

Immingham Humber. *Imungeham* 1086 (DB). 'Homestead of the family or followers of a man called Imma'. OE pers. name + *-inga-* + *hām*.

Impington Cambs. *Impintune c.*1050, *Epintone* 1086 (DB). 'Estate associated with a man called *Empa or *Impa'. OE pers. name + *-ing-* + *tūn*.

Ince, 'the island', OWelsh **inis*: **Ince** Ches. *Inise* 1086 (DB). **Ince** Gtr. Manch. *Ines* 1202. **Ince Blundell** Mersey. *Hinne (sic)* 1086 (DB), *Ins Blundell* 1332. Manorial affix from the *Blundell* family, here in the early 13th cent.

Ingatestone Essex. *Gynges Atteston* 1283. 'Manor called *Ing* (for which see FRYERNING) at the stone'. One of a group of places so called, this one distinguished by reference to a Roman milestone, OE *stān*.

Ingbirchworth S. Yorks. *Berceuuorde* 1086 (DB), *Yngebyrcheworth* 1424. 'Enclosure where birch-trees grow'. OE *birce* + *worth* with the later addition of OScand. *eng* 'meadow'.

Ingham, possibly 'homestead or village of a man called Inga', OE pers. name + *hām*, although it has recently been suggested that the first element of these names may be a word meaning 'the Inguione', a member of the ancient Germanic tribe called the *Inguiones*: **Ingham** Lincs. *Ingeham* 1086 (DB). **Ingham** Norfolk. *Hincham* 1086 (DB). **Ingham** Suffolk. *Ingham* 1086 (DB).

Ingleby, 'farmstead or village of the Englishmen'. OScand. *Englar* + *bý*: **Ingleby** Derbys. *Englaby* 1009, *Englebi* 1086 (DB). **Ingleby** Lincs. *Englebi* 1086 (DB). **Ingleby Arncliffe** N. Yorks. *Englebi* 1086 (DB). Affix is from a nearby place (*Erneclive* 1086), 'eagles' cliff', OE *earn* + *clif*. **Ingleby Greenhow** N. Yorks. *Englebi* 1086 (DB). Affix is from a nearby place (*Grenehou* 12th cent.), 'green mound', OE *grēne* + OScand. *haugr*.

Inglesham Wilts. *Inggeneshamme c.*950. 'Enclosure or river-meadow of a man called *Ingen or *Ingīn'. OE pers. name + *hamm*.

Ingleton Durham. *Ingeltun c.*1050. Probably 'farmstead of a man called Ingeld or Ingwald'. OE pers. name + *tūn*.

Ingleton N. Yorks. *Inglestune* 1086 (DB). 'Farmstead near the hill or peak'. OE **ingel* + *tūn*.

Ingoe Northum. *Hinghou* 1229. Probably OE **ing* 'hill, peak' with the addition of *hōh* 'spur of land'.

Ingoldisthorpe Norfolk. *Torp* 1086 (DB), *Ingaldestorp* 1203. 'Outlying farmstead or hamlet of a man called Ingjaldr'. OScand. pers. name + *thorp*.

Ingoldmells Lincs. *in Guldelsmere (sic)* 1086 (DB), *Ingoldesmeles* 1180. 'Sand-banks of a man called Ingjaldr'. OScand. pers. name + *melr*.

Ingoldsby Lincs. *Ingoldesbi* 1086 (DB). 'Farmstead or village of a man called Ingjaldr'. OScand. pers. name + *bý*.

Ingram Northum. *Angerham* 1242. 'Homestead or enclosure with grassland'. OE **anger* + *hām* or *hamm*.

Ingrave Essex. *Ingam* 1086 (DB), *Gingeraufe* 1276. 'Manor called *Ing* (for which see FRYERNING) held by a man called Ralf (OGerman Radulf)'. He was a tenant in 1086.

Ingworth Norfolk. *Inghewurda* 1086 (DB). Probably 'enclosure of a man called Inga'. OE pers. name + *worth*.

Inkberrow Heref. & Worcs. *Intanbeorgas* 789, *Inteberge* 1086 (DB). 'Hills or mounds of a man called Inta'. OE pers. name + *beorg* (plural *-as*).

Inkpen Berks. *Ingepenne c.*935, *Hingepene* 1086 (DB). OE **ing* 'hill, peak' with either Celtic **penn* 'hill' or OE *penn* 'enclosure, fold'.

Inskip Lancs. *Inscip* 1086 (DB). Probably OWelsh **inis* 'island' with OE *cȳpe* 'osier-basket for catching fish'.

Instow Devon. *Johannesto* 1086 (DB). 'Holy place of St John'. Saint's name + OE *stōw*. The church here is dedicated to St John the Baptist.

Inwardleigh Devon. *Lega* 1086 (DB), *Inwardlegh* 1235. 'Woodland clearing'. OE *lēah*, with manorial addition from the man called *Inwar* (OScand. *Ingvar*) who held the manor in 1086.

Inworth Essex. *Inewrth* 1206. 'Enclosure of a man called Ina'. OE pers. name + *worth*.

Iping W. Sussex. *Epinges* 1086 (DB). '(Settlement of) the family or followers of a man called *Ipa'. OE pers. name + *-ingas*.

Ipplepen Devon. *Iplanpenne* 956,

Iplepene 1086 (DB). 'Fold or enclosure of a man called *Ipela'. OE pers. name + *penn*.

Ipsden Oxon. *Yppesdene* 1086 (DB). 'Valley near the upland'. OE *yppe* + *denu*.

Ipstones Staffs. *Yppestan* 1175. Probably 'stone in the high place or upland'. OE *yppe* + *stān*.

Ipswich Suffolk. *Gipeswic* c.975, 1086 (DB). 'Harbour of a man called *Gip'. OE pers. name + *wīc*.

Irby, Ireby, 'farmstead or village of the Irishmen', OScand. *Írar* + *bý*: **Irby** Mersey. *Irreby* c.1100. **Irby in the Marsh** Lincs. *Irebi* c.1115. **Irby upon Humber** Humber. *Iribi* 1086 (DB). For the river-name, see HUMBERSIDE. **Ireby** Cumbria. *Irebi* c.1160. **Ireby** Lancs. *Irebi* 1086 (DB).

Irchester Northants. *Yranceaster* 973, *Irencestre* 1086 (DB). 'Roman station associated with a man called Ira or *Yra'. OE pers. name + *ceaster*.

Ireby, see IRBY.

Ireleth Cumbria. *Irlid* 1190. 'Hill-slope of the Irishmen'. OScand. *Írar* + *hlíth*.

Ireton, Kirk Derbys. *Hiretune* 1086 (DB). *Kirkirton* 1370. 'Farmstead of the Irishmen'. OScand. *Írar* + OE *tūn*. Affix is OScand. *kirkja* 'church'.

Irlam Gtr. Manch. *Urwelham* c.1190. 'Homestead or enclosure on the River Irwell'. OE river-name ('winding stream' from OE *irre* + *wella*) + OE *hām* or *hamm*.

Irnham Lincs. *Gerneham* 1086 (DB). 'Homestead or village of a man called *Georna'. OE pers. name + *hām*.

Iron Acton Avon, see ACTON.

Iron-Bridge Shrops., a late name, so called from the famous iron bridge built here across the River Severn in 1779.

Irthington Cumbria. *Irthinton* 1169. 'Farmstead on the River Irthing'. Celtic river-name + OE *tūn*.

Irthlingborough Northants. *Yrtlingaburg* 780, *Erdi(n)burne* (*sic*) 1086 (DB). Probably 'fortified manor belonging to the ploughmen'. OE *erthling*, *yrthling* + *burh*.

Irton N. Yorks. *Iretune* 1086 (DB). 'Farmstead of the Irishmen'. OScand. *Írar* + *tūn*.

Irwell (river) Lancs., see IRLAM.

Isfield E. Sussex. *Isefeld* 1214. 'Open land of a man called *Isa'. OE pers. name + *feld*.

Isham Northants. *Ysham* 974, *Isham* 1086 (DB). 'Homestead or promontory by the River Ise'. Celtic river-name (meaning 'water') + OE *hām* or *hamm*.

Isle Abbotts & Brewers Somerset. *Yli* 966, *I(s)le* 1086 (DB), *Ile Abbatis* 1291, *Ile Brywer* 1275. Named from the River Isle, which is a Celtic river-name of uncertain meaning. Distinguishing affixes from early possession by Muchelney Abbey (Latin *abbatis* 'of the abbot') and by the *Briwer* family.

Isleworth Gtr. London. *Gislheresuuyrth* 677, *Gisteleswarde* 1086 (DB). 'Enclosure of a man called Gīslhere'. OE pers. name + *worth*.

Islington Gtr. London. *Gislandune* c.1000, *Iseldone* 1086 (DB). 'Hill of a man called *Gīsla'. OE pers. name (genitive *-n*) + *dūn*.

Islip Northants. *Isslepe* 10th cent., *Islep* 1086 (DB). 'Slippery place by the River Ise'. Pre-English river-name (meaning 'water') + OE **slǣp*.

Islip Oxon. *Githslepe* c.1050, *Letelape* (*sic*) 1086 (DB). 'Slippery place by the River *Ight* (an old name for the River Ray)'. Pre-English river-name (of uncertain meaning) + OE **slǣp*.

Itchen Abbas Hants. *Icene* 1086 (DB), *Ichene Monialium* 1167. Named from the River Itchen, an ancient pre-Celtic river-name of unknown origin and meaning. The Latin affix in the 12th cent. form means 'of the nuns', the later affix *Abbas* is a reduced form of Latin *abbatissa* 'abbess', both referring to possession by the Abbey of St Mary, Winchester.

Itchen Stoke Hants. *Stoche* 1086 (DB), *Ichenestoke* 1185. 'Secondary settlement from ITCHEN [ABBAS]'. OE *stoc*.

Itchenor, East & West W. Sussex. *Iccannore* 683, *Icenore* 1086 (DB). 'Shore of a man called *Icca'. OE pers. name (genitive *-n*) + *ōra*.

Itchington Avon. *Icenantune* 967, *Icetune* 1086 (DB). 'Farmstead by a stream called *Itchen*'. Lost pre-Celtic river-name (of unknown meaning) + OE *tūn*.

Itchington, Bishops & Long Warwicks. *Yceantune* 1001, *Ice(n)tone* 1086 (DB), *Bisshopesychengton* 1384, *Longa Hichenton* c.1185. 'Farmstead on the River Itchen'. Pre-Celtic river-name (of unknown meaning) + OE *tūn*. Distinguishing affixes from possession by the Bishop of Coventry and Lichfield and from OE *lang* 'long'.

Itteringham Norfolk. *Utrincham* 1086 (DB). Probably 'homestead of the family or followers of a man called *Ytra or *Ytri'. OE pers. name + *-inga-* + *hām*.

Ivegill Cumbria. *Yuegill* 1361. 'Deep narrow valley of the River Ive'. OScand. river-name (meaning 'yew stream') + *gil*.

Ivel (river) Beds., Herts., see NORTHILL.

Iver Bucks. *Evreham* 1086 (DB), *Eura* c.1130. '(Place by) the brow of a hill or the tip of a promontory'. OE *yfer* (*-am* in the Domesday spelling is a Latin ending).

Iveston Durham. *Ivestan* 1183. 'Boundary stone of a man called Ifa'. OE pers. name + *stān*.

Ivinghoe Bucks. *Evinghehou* 1086 (DB). 'Hill-spur of the family or followers of a man called Ifa'. OE pers. name + *-inga-* + *hōh*.

Ivington Heref. & Worcs. *Ivintune* 1086 (DB). 'Estate associated with a man called Ifa'. OE pers. name + *-ing-* + *tūn*.

Ivybridge Devon. *Ivebrugge* 1292. 'Ivy-covered bridge'. OE *īfig* + *brycg*.

Ivychurch Kent. *Iue circe* 11th cent. 'Ivy-covered church'. OE *īfig* + *cirice*.

Iwade Kent. *Ywada* 1179. 'Ford where yew-trees grow'. OE *īw* + *(ge)wæd*.

Iwerne Courtney or Shroton, Iwerne Minster Dorset. *Ywern* 877, *Werne, Evneministre* 1086 (DB), *Iwerne Courteney alias Shyrevton* 1403. Named from the River Iwerne, a Celtic river-name possibly meaning 'yew river' or referring to a goddess. Distinguishing affixes from the *Courtenay* family, here in the 13th cent., and from OE *mynster* 'church of a monastery' in allusion to early possession by Shaftesbury Abbey. Shroton means 'sheriff's estate', OE *scīr-rēfa* + *tūn*.

Ixworth Suffolk. *Gyxeweorde* c.1025, *Giswortha* 1086 (DB). 'Enclosure of a man called *Gicsa or *Gycsa'. OE pers. name + *worth*.

Ixworth Thorpe Suffolk. *Torp* 1086 (DB), *Ixeworth thorp* 1305. 'Secondary settlement dependent on IXWORTH'. OScand. *thorp*.

J

Jacobstow, Jacobstowe, 'holy place of St James', saint's name (Latin *Jacobus*) + OE *stōw*: **Jacobstow** Cornwall. *Jacobestowe* 1270. **Jacobstowe** Devon. *Jacopstoue* 1331.

Jarrow Tyne & Wear. *Gyruum* c.730. '(Settlement of) the fen people'. OE tribal name *Gyrwe* derived from OE *gyr* 'mud, marsh'.

Jaywick Sands Essex. *Clakyngeywyk* 1438, *Gey wyck* 1584. 'Dwelling or (dairy) farm at the place associated with a man called *Clacc'. OE pers. name + *-ing* + *wīc*. The first part of the name (probably taken to be a local form of CLACTON) was dropped in the 16th cent.

Jevington E. Sussex. *Lovingetone* (*sic*) 1086 (DB), *Govingetona* 1189. 'Farmstead of the family or followers of a man called *Geofa'. OE pers. name + *-inga-* + *tūn*.

Jodrell Bank Ches., recorded from 1831, 'bank or hill-side belonging to the *Jodrell* family', land-owners here in the 19th cent.

Johnby Cumbria. *Johannebi* 1200. 'Farmstead or village of a man called Johan'. OFrench pers. name + OScand. *bý*.

K

Kaber Cumbria. *Kaberge* late 12th cent. 'Hill frequented by jackdaws'. OE **cā* + *beorg*, or OScand. **ká* + *berg*.

Kea, Old Kea Cornwall. *Sanctus Che* 1086 (DB). '(Church of) St Kea'. From the dedication of the church.

Keal, East & West Lincs. *Estrecale, Westrecale* 1086 (DB). 'The ridge of hills'. OScand. *kjǫlr*. Distinguishing affixes are OE *ēasterra* 'more easterly' and *westerra* 'more westerly'.

Kearsley Gtr. Manch. *Cherselawe* 1187, *Kersleie* c.1220. 'Clearing where cress grows'. OE *cærse* + *lēah*.

Kearstwick Cumbria. *Kesthwaite* 1547. 'Valley clearing'. OScand. *kjóss* + *thveit*.

Kearton N. Yorks. *Karretan* (*sic*) 13th cent., *Kirton* 1298. Possibly 'farmstead of a man called Kærir'. OScand. pers. name + OE *tūn*.

Keddington Lincs. *Cadinton* (*sic*) 1086 (DB), *Kedingtuna* 12th cent. Probably 'farmstead associated with a man called Cydda'. OE pers. name + *-ing-* + *tūn*.

Kedington Suffolk. *Kydington* 1043–5, *Kidituna* 1086 (DB). Identical in origin with the previous name.

Kedleston Derbys. *Chetelestune* 1086 (DB). 'Farmstead of a man called Ketill'. OScand. pers. name + OE *tūn*.

Keelby Lincs. *Chelebi* 1086 (DB). 'Farmstead or village on or near a ridge'. OScand. *kjǫlr* + *bý*.

Keele Staffs. *Kiel* 1169. 'Hill where cows graze'. OE *cȳ* + *hyll*.

Keevil Wilts. *Kefle* 964, *Chivele* 1086 (DB). Probably 'woodland clearing in a hollow'. OE *cȳf* + *lēah*.

Kegworth Leics. *Cacheworde* (*sic*) 1086 (DB), *Caggworth* c.1125. Possibly 'enclosure of a man called *Cægga'. OE pers. name + *worth*.

Keighley W. Yorks. *Chichelai* 1086 (DB). 'Woodland clearing of a man called *Cyhha'. OE pers. name + *lēah*.

Keinton Mandeville Somerset. *Chintune* 1086 (DB), *Kyngton Maundevill* 1280. 'Royal manor'. OE *cyne-* + *tūn*. Manorial affix from the *Maundevill* family, here in the 13th cent.

Keisby Lincs. *Chisebi* 1086 (DB). 'Farmstead or village of a man called Kisi'. OScand. pers. name + *bý*. Alternatively the first element may be OScand. **kīs* 'gravel, coarse sand'.

Kelbrook Lancs. *Chelbroc* 1086 (DB). Probably 'brook flowing in a ravine'. OE *ceole* (with Scand. *k-*) + *brōc*.

Kelby Lincs. *Chelebi* 1086 (DB). Probably 'farmstead or village on or near a ridge or wedge-shaped piece of land'. OScand. *kjǫlr* or **kæl* + *bý*.

Keldholme N. Yorks. *Keldeholm* 12th cent. 'Island or river-meadow near the spring'. OScand. *kelda* + *holmr*.

Kelfield, 'open land where chalk was spread, or by a cup-shaped feature', OE **celce* or *cælc* + *feld*: **Kelfield** Lincs. *Kelkefeld* 12th cent. **Kelfield** N. Yorks. *Chelchefeld* 1086 (DB).

Kelham Notts. *Calun* (*sic*) 1086 (DB), *Kelum* 1156. '(Place at) the ridges'. OScand. *kjǫlr* in a dative plural form.

Kelk, Great Humber. *Chelche* 1086 (DB). 'Chalky ground'. OE **celce*.

Kellet, Nether & Over Lancs. *Chellet* 1086 (DB). 'Slope with a spring'. OScand. *kelda* + *hlíth*.

Kelleth Cumbria. *Keldelith* 12th cent. Identical in origin with the previous name.

Kelling Norfolk. *Chillinge* c.970, *Kellinga* 1086 (DB). '(Settlement of) the family or followers of a man called *Cylla or Ceolla'. OE pers. name + *-ingas*.

Kellington N. Yorks. *Chellinctone* 1086 (DB). 'Estate associated with a man called Ceolla'. OE pers. name (with Scand. k-) + *-ing-* + *tūn*.

Kelloe Durham. *Kelflau* c.1170. 'Hill where calves graze'. OE *celf* + *hlāw*.

Kelly Devon. *Chenleie* (*sic*) 1086 (DB), *Chelli* 1166. Probably Cornish *kelli* 'grove, small wood'.

Kelmarsh Northants. *Keilmerse* 1086 (DB). Probably 'marsh marked out by poles or posts'. OE **cegel* (with Scand. *k-*) + *mersc*.

Kelmscot Oxon. *Kelmescote* 1234. 'Cottage(s) of a man called Cēnhelm'. OE pers. name + *cot*.

Kelsale Suffolk. *Keleshala* 1086 (DB). 'Nook of land of a man called *Cēl(i) or Cēol'. OE pers. name + *halh*.

Kelsall Ches. *Kelsale* 1257. 'Nook of land of a man called Kell'. ME pers. name + *halh*.

Kelsey, North & South Lincs. *Chelsi*, *Northchelesei* 1086 (DB), *Suthkelleseye* 1262. Possibly 'island, or dry ground in marsh, of a man called Cēol'. OE pers. name + *ēg*. Alternatively the first element may be OScand. **kæl* 'wedge-shaped piece of land'.

Kelshall Herts. *Keleshelle* c.1050, *Cheleselle* 1086 (DB). 'Hill of a man called *Cylli'. OE pers. name + *hyll*.

Kelston Avon. *Calveston* 1178. OE *tūn* 'farmstead, estate' with a doubtful first element, possibly an OE pers. name *C(e)alf.

Kelvedon Essex. *Cynlauedyne* 998, *Chelleuedana* 1086 (DB). 'Valley of a man called Cynelāf'. OE pers. name + *denu*.

Kelvedon Hatch Essex. *Kylewendune* 1066, *Keluenduna* 1086 (DB), *Kelwedon Hacche* 1276. 'Speckled hill'. OE *cylu* (dative *cylwan*) + *dūn*, with the later addition of *hæcc* 'gate'.

Kemberton Shrops. *Chenbritone* 1086 (DB). 'Farmstead of a man called Cēnbeorht'. OE pers. name + *tūn*.

Kemble Glos. *Kemele* 682, *Chemele* 1086 (DB). Probably a Celtic place-name meaning 'border, edge'.

Kemerton Heref. & Worcs. *Cyneburgingctun* 840, *Chenemertune* 1086 (DB). 'Farmstead associated with a woman called Cyneburg'. OE pers. name + *-ing-* + *tūn*.

Kempley Glos. *Chenepelei* 1086 (DB). Probably 'woodland clearing of a man called *Cenep'. OE pers. name + *lēah*.

Kempsey Heref. & Worcs. *Kemesei* 799, *Chemesege* 1086 (DB). 'Island, or dry ground in marsh, of a man called *Cymi'. OE pers. name + *ēg*.

Kempsford Glos. *Cynemæres forda* 9th cent., *Chenemeresforde* 1086 (DB). 'Ford of a man called Cynemǣr'. OE pers. name + *ford*.

Kempston Beds. *Kemestan* 1060, *Camestone* 1086 (DB). Possibly 'farmstead at the bend'. A derivative of Celtic **camm* 'crooked' + OE *tūn*.

Kempton Shrops. *Chenpitune* 1086 (DB). 'Farmstead of the warrior or of a man called *Cempa'. OE *cempa* or OE pers. name + *tūn*.

Kemsing Kent. *Cymesing* 822. 'Place of a man called *Cymesa'. OE pers. name + *-ing*.

Kenardington Kent. *Kynardingtune* 11th cent. 'Estate associated with a man called Cyneheard'. OE pers. name + *-ing-* + *tūn*.

Kenchester Heref. & Worcs. *Chenecestre* 1086 (DB). 'Roman fort or town associated with a man called Cēna'. OE pers. name + *ceaster*.

Kencot Oxon. *Chenetone* (*sic*) 1086 (DB), *Chenicota* c.1130. 'Cottage of a man called Cēna'. OE pers. name + *cot* (in the first form *tūn* 'farmstead').

Kendal Cumbria. *Cherchebi* 1086 (DB), *Kircabikendala* c.1095, *Kendale* 1452. 'Village with a church in the valley of the River Kent'. Originally OScand. *kirkju-bý* with the addition of a district name (Celtic river-name of uncertain meaning + OScand. *dalr*) which now alone survives.

Kenilworth Warwicks. *Chinewrde* (*sic*) 1086 (DB), *Chenildeworda* early 12th cent. 'Enclosure of a woman called Cynehild'. OE pers. name + *worth*.

Kenley, 'woodland clearing of a man called Cēna', OE pers. name + *lēah*:
Kenley Gtr. London. *Kenele* 1255.
Kenley Shrops. *Chenelie* 1086 (DB).

Kenn, originally the name of the streams on which the places stand, a pre-English river-name of uncertain origin and meaning: **Kenn** Devon. *Chent* 1086 (DB). **Kenn** Avon. *Chen(t)* 1086 (DB).

Kennerleigh Devon. *Kenewarlegh* 1219. 'Woodland clearing of a man called Cyneweard'. OE pers. name + *lēah*.

Kennett Cambs. *Chenet* 1086 (DB). Named from the River Kennett, a Celtic river-name of doubtful meaning.

Kennett, East & West Wilts. *Cynetan* 939, *Chenete* 1086 (DB). Named from the River Kennet, a river-name identical in origin with that in the previous name.

Kennford Devon. *Keneford* 1300. 'Ford over the River Kenn'. Pre-English river-name (of uncertain origin and meaning) + OE *ford*.

Kenninghall Norfolk. *Keninchala* 1086 (DB). Probably 'nook of land of the family or followers of a man called Cēna'. OE pers. name + *-inga-* + *halh*.

Kennington Gtr. London. *Chenintune* 1086 (DB). 'Farmstead associated with a man called Cēna'. OE pers. name + *-ing-* + *tūn*.

Kennington Kent. *Chenetone* 1086 (DB). 'Royal manor'. OE *cyne-* + *tūn*.

Kennington Oxon. *Chenitun* 821, 1086 (DB). 'Farmstead associated with a man called Cēna'. OE pers. name + *-ing-* + *tūn*.

Kennythorpe N. Yorks. *Cheretorp* (*sic*) 1086 (DB), *Kinnerthorp* c.1180. Probably 'outlying farmstead or hamlet of a man called Cēnhere'. OE pers. name + OScand. *thorp*.

Kensal Green Gtr. London. *Kingisholte* 1253, *Kynsale Green* 1550. 'The king's wood'. OE *cyning* + *holt*, with the later addition of *grēne* 'village green'.

Kensington Gtr. London. *Chenesitun* 1086 (DB). 'Estate associated with a man called Cynesige'. OE pers. name + *-ing-* + *tūn*.

Kensworth Beds. *Ceagnesworthe* 975, *Canesworde* 1086 (DB). 'Enclosure of a man called *Cægīn'. OE pers. name + *worth*.

Kent (the county). *Cantium* 51 BC. An ancient Celtic name, often explained as 'coastal district' but possibly 'land of the hosts or armies'.

Kent (river) Lancs., Cumbria, see KENDAL.

Kentchurch Heref. & Worcs. *Lan Cein* c.1130, *Keynchirche* 1341. 'Church of St Ceina'. Female saint's name + OE *cirice* (with OWelsh **lann* in the early form).

Kentford Suffolk. *Cheneteforde* 11th cent. 'Ford over the River Kennett'. Celtic river-name (of uncertain origin and meaning) + OE *ford*.

Kentisbeare Devon. *Chentesbere* (*sic*) 1086 (DB), *Kentelesbere* 1242. 'Wood or grove of a man called *Centel'. OE pers. name + *bearu*.

Kentisbury Devon. *Chentesberie* (*sic*) 1086 (DB), *Kentelesberi* 1260. 'Stronghold of a man called *Centel'. OE pers. name + *burh* (dative *byrig*).

Kentish Town Gtr. London. *Kentisston* 1208. Probably 'estate held by a family called *Kentish*'. ME surname (meaning 'man from Kent') + OE *tūn*.

Kentmere Cumbria. *Kentemere* 13th cent. 'Pool by the River Kent'. Celtic river-name (of uncertain meaning) + OE *mere*.

Kenton Devon. *Chentone* 1086 (DB). 'Farmstead on the River Kenn'. Pre-English river-name (of uncertain origin and meaning) + OE *tūn*.

Kenton Gtr. London. *Keninton* 1232. 'Estate associated with a man called Cēna'. OE pers. name + *-ing-* + *tūn*.

Kenton Suffolk. *Chenetuna* 1086 (DB). Probably 'royal manor'. OE *cyne-* + *tūn*. Alternatively the first element may be the OE pers. name *Cēna*.

Kenwick Shrops. *Kenewic* 1203. 'Dwelling or (dairy) farm of a man called Cēna'. OE pers. name + *wīc*.

Kenwyn Cornwall. *Keynwen* 1259. Probably 'white ridge'. OCornish *keyn* + *gwynn*.

Kenyon Gtr. Manch. *Kenien* 1212. Possibly a shortened form of an OWelsh name *Cruc Einion* 'mound of a man called Einion'.

Kepwick N. Yorks. *Chipuic* 1086 (DB). 'Hamlet with a market'. OE *cēap* (with Scand. *k-*) + *wīc*.

Keresley W. Mids. *Keresleia* c.1144. Possibly 'woodland clearing of a man called Cēnhere'. OE pers. name + *lēah*.

Kerne Bridge Heref. & Worcs. *Kernebrigges* 1272. Probably 'bridge(s) by a mill'. OE *cweorn* + *brycg*.

Kersall Notts. *Cherueshale* 1086 (DB), *Kyrneshale* 1196. Possibly 'nook of land of a man called Cynehere'. OE pers. name + *halh*.

Kersey Suffolk. *Cæresige* c.995, *Careseia* 1086 (DB). 'Island where cress grows'. OE *cærse* + *ēg*.

Kersoe Heref. & Worcs. *Criddesho* 780. 'Hill-spur of a man called *Criddi'. OE pers. name + *hōh*.

Kesgrave Suffolk. *Gressegraua (sic)* 1086 (DB), *Kersigrave* 1231. 'Ditch where cress grows'. OE *cærse* + *græf*.

Kessingland Suffolk. *Kessingalanda* 1086 (DB). 'Cultivated land of the family or followers of a man called *Cyssi'. OE pers. name + *-inga-* + *land*.

Kesteven Lincs. *Ceoftefne* c.1000, *Chetsteven* 1086 (DB). Probably 'wood meeting-place'. Celtic **cęd* + OScand. *stefna*.

Keston Gtr. London. *Cysse stan* 973, *Chestan* 1086 (DB). 'Boundary stone of a man called *Cyssi'. OE pers. name + *stān*.

Keswick, 'farm where cheese is made', OE *cēse* (with Scand. *k-*) + *wīc*: **Keswick** Cumbria. *Kesewic* c.1240. **Keswick** Norfolk, near Bacton. *Casewic* c.1150. **Keswick** Norfolk, near Norwich. *Chesewic* 1086 (DB). **Keswick, East** W. Yorks. *Chesuic* 1086 (DB).

Kettering Northants. *Cytringan* 956, *Cateringe* 1086 (DB). Probably '(settlement of) the family or followers of a man called *Cytra'. OE pers. name + *-ingas*.

Ketteringham Norfolk. *Keteringham* c.1060, *Keterincham* 1086 (DB). 'Homestead of the family or followers of a man called *Cytra'. OE pers. name + *-inga-* + *hām*.

Kettlebaston Suffolk. *Kitelbeornastuna* 1086 (DB). 'Farmstead of a man called Ketilbjǫrn'. OScand. pers. name + OE *tūn*.

Kettleburgh Suffolk. *Ketelbiria* 1086 (DB). 'Hill of a man called Ketil, or hill by a deep valley'. OScand. pers. name or OE *cetel* (with Scand. *k-*) + OE *beorg* or OScand. *berg*.

Kettleby, Ab Leics. *Chetelbi* 1086 (DB), *Abeketleby* 1236. 'Farmstead or village of a man called Ketil'. OScand. pers. name + *bý*, with manorial affix from early possession by a man called Abba.

Kettleshulme Ches. *Ketelisholm* 1285. 'Island or water-meadow of a man called Ketil'. OScand. pers. name + *holmr*.

Kettlesing N. Yorks. *Ketylsyng* 1379. 'Meadow of a man called Ketil'. OScand. pers. name + *eng*.

Kettlestone Norfolk. *Ketlestuna* 1086 (DB). 'Farmstead of a man called Ketil'. OScand. pers. name + OE *tūn*.

Kettlethorpe Lincs. *Ketelstorp* 1220. 'Outlying farmstead or hamlet of a man called Ketil'. OScand. pers. name + *thorp*.

Kettlewell N. Yorks. *Cheteleuuelle* 1086 (DB). 'Spring or stream in a deep valley'. OE *cetel* (with Scand. *k-*) + *wella*.

Ketton Leics. *Chetene* 1086 (DB). An old river-name, possibly a derivative of Celtic **cęd* 'wood' + OE *ēa* 'river'.

Kew Gtr. London. *Cayho* 1327. 'Key-shaped spur of land, or spur of land near a quay'. OE *cǣg* or ME *key* + OE *hōh*.

Kewstoke Avon. *Chiwestoch* 1086 (DB). OE *stoc* 'secondary settlement' with the addition of the Celtic saint's name *Kew*.

Kexbrough S. Yorks. *Cezeburg (sic)* 1086 (DB), *Kesceburg* c.1170. Probably 'stronghold of a man called Keptr'. OScand. pers. name + OE *burh*.

Kexby Lincs. *Cheftesbi* 1086 (DB). 'Farmstead or village of a man called Keptr'. OScand. pers. name + *bý*.

Kexby N. Yorks. *Kexebi* 12th cent. Probably 'farmstead or village of a man called Keikr'. OScand. pers. name + *bý*.

Keyham Leics. *Caiham* 1086 (DB). Possibly 'homestead or village of a man called *Cǣga', OE pers. name + *hām*. Alternatively the first element may be OE *cǣg* 'key' (used of a place that could be locked) or **cæg* 'stone, boulder'.

Keyhaven Hants. *Kihavene c.*1170. 'Harbour where cows are shipped'. OE *cū* (genitive *cȳ*) + *hæfen*.

Keyingham Humber. *Caingeham* 1086 (DB). 'Homestead of the family or followers of a man called *Cǣga'. OE pers. name + *-inga-* + *hām*.

Keymer W. Sussex. *Chemere* 1086 (DB). 'Cow's pond'. OE *cū* (genitive *cȳ*) + *mere*.

Keynsham Avon. *Cægineshamme c.*1000, *Cainesham* 1086 (DB). 'Land in a river-bend belonging to a man called *Cǣgin'. OE pers. name + *hamm*.

Keysoe Beds. *Caissot* 1086 (DB). Probably 'key-shaped spur of land'. OE *cǣg* + *hōh*. Alternatively the first element may be **cǣg* 'a stone, a boulder'.

Keyston Cambs. *Chetelestan* 1086 (DB). 'Boundary stone of a man called Ketil'. OScand. pers. name + OE *stān*.

Keyworth Notts. *Caworde* 1086 (DB). OE *worth* 'enclosure' with an uncertain first element, probably a pers. name.

Kibblesworth Tyne & Wear. *Kibleswrthe* 1185. 'Enclosure of a man called *Cybbel'. OE pers. name + *worth*.

Kibworth Beauchamp & Harcourt Leics. *Chiburde* 1086 (DB), *Kybeworth Beauchamp* 1315, *Kibbeworth Harecourt* 13th cent. 'Enclosure of a man called *Cybba'. Manorial affixes from early possession by the *de Beauchamp* and *de Harewecurt* families.

Kidbrooke Gtr. London. *Ketebroc* 1202. 'Brook where kites are seen'. OE *cȳta* + *brōc*.

Kidderminster Heref. & Worcs. *Chideminstre* (*sic*) 1086 (DB), *Kedeleministre* 1154. 'Monastery of a man called *Cydela'. OE pers. name + *mynster*.

Kiddington Oxon. *Chidintone* 1086 (DB). 'Estate associated with a man called Cydda'. OE pers. name + *-ing-* + *tūn*.

Kidlington Oxon. *Chedelintone* 1086 (DB). 'Estate associated with a man called *Cydela'. OE pers. name + *-ing-* + *tūn*.

Kielder Northum. *Keilder* 1326. Named from the river here, a Celtic river-name meaning 'rapid stream'.

Kilburn Derbys. *Kileburn* 1179. Possibly 'stream of a man called *Cylla'. OE pers. name + *burna*.

Kilburn Gtr. London. *Cuneburna c.*1130. Possibly 'cows' stream'. OE *cū* (genitive plural *cūna*) + *burna*.

Kilburn N. Yorks. *Chileburne* 1086 (DB). Perhaps identical in origin with KILBURN (Derbys).

Kilby Leics. *Cilebi* 1086 (DB). Probably 'farmstead or village of the young men'. OE *cild* (with Scand. *k-*) + OScand. *bý*.

Kilcot Glos. *Chilecot* 1086 (DB). 'Cottage of a man called *Cylla'. OE pers. name + *cot*.

Kildale N. Yorks. *Childale* 1086 (DB). Probably 'narrow valley'. OScand. *kíll* + *dalr*.

Kildwick W. Yorks. *Childeuuic* 1086 (DB). 'Dairy-farm of the young men or attendants'. OE *cild* (with Scand. *k-*) + *wīc*.

Kilham, '(place at) the kilns', OE *cyln* in a dative plural form *cylnum*: **Kilham** Humber. *Chillun* 1086 (DB). **Kilham** Northum. *Killum* 1177.

Kilkhampton Cornwall. *Chilchetone* 1086 (DB). Probably Cornish **kylgh* 'a circle' (perhaps referring to a lost archaeological feature) with the addition of OE *tūn* 'farmstead'.

Killamarsh Derbys. *Chinewoldemaresc* 1086 (DB). 'Marsh of a man called Cynewald'. OE pers. name + *mersc*.

Killerby Durham. *Culuerdebi* 1091. Probably 'farmstead or village of a man called *Ketilfrøthr'. OScand. pers. name + *bý*.

Killinghall N. Yorks. *Chilingale* 1086 (DB). 'Nook of land of the family or followers of a man called *Cylla'. OE pers. name + *-inga-* + *halh*.

Killingholme Lincs. *Chelvingeholm* 1086 (DB). Probably 'homestead of the family or followers of a man called Cēolwulf'. OE pers. name + *-inga-* + *hām* (replaced by OScand. *holmr* 'island, dry ground in marsh').

Killington Cumbria. *Killintona* 1175.

'Estate associated with a man called *Cylla'. OE pers. name + *-ing-* + *tūn*.

Kilmersdon Somerset. *Kunemersdon* 951, *Chenemeresdone* 1086 (DB). 'Hill of a man called Cynemǣr'. OE pers. name + *dūn*.

Kilmeston Hants. *Cenelemestune* 961, *Chelmestune* 1086 (DB). 'Farmstead of a man called Cēnhelm'. OE pers. name + *tūn*.

Kilmington, 'estate associated with a man called Cynehelm', OE pers. name + *-ing-* + *tūn*: **Kilmington** Devon. *Chenemetone* 1086 (DB). **Kilmington** Wilts. *Cilemetone* 1086 (DB).

Kilnhurst S. Yorks. *Kilnhirst* 12th cent. 'Wooded hill with a kiln'. OE *cyln* + *hyrst*.

Kilnsea Humber. *Chilnesse* 1086 (DB). 'Pool near the kiln'. OE *cyln* + *sǣ*.

Kilnsey N. Yorks. *Chileseie* (*sic*) 1086 (DB), *Kilnesey* 1162. Probably 'marsh near the kiln'. OE *cyln* + **sǣge*.

Kilnwick Humber. *Chileuuit* (*sic*) 1086 (DB), *Killingwic* late 12th cent. 'Farm associated with a man called *Cylla'. OE pers. name + *-ing-* + *wīc*. Alternatively the first element may be OE *cyln* 'a kiln'.

Kilnwick Percy Humber. *Chelingewic* 1086 (DB). 'Farm of the family or followers of a man called *Cylla'. OE pers. name + *-inga-* + *wīc*.

Kilpeck Heref. & Worcs. *Chipeete* 1086 (DB). Welsh *cil* 'corner, nook' with an obscure second element.

Kilpin Humber. *Celpene* 959, *Chelpin* 1086 (DB). Probably 'enclosure for calves'. OE *celf* (with Scand. *k-*) + *penn*.

Kilsby Northants. *Kildesbig* 1043, *Chidesbi* 1086 (DB). 'Farmstead or village of the young nobleman, or of a man called Cild'. OE *cild* or pers. name (with Scand. *k-*) + OScand. *bý*.

Kilton Somerset. *Cylfantun* c.880, *Chilvetune* 1086 (DB). 'Farmstead near the club-shaped hill'. OE **cylfe* + *tūn*.

Kilve Somerset. *Clive* 1086 (DB), *Kylve* 1243. 'Club-shaped hill'. OE **cylfe*.

Kilvington, 'estate associated with a man called *Cylfa or Cynelāf', OE pers. name + *-ing-* + *tūn*: **Kilvington** Notts. *Chelvinctune* 1086 (DB). **Kilvington, North** N. Yorks. *Chelvintun* 1086 (DB). **Kilvington, South** N. Yorks. *Chelvinctune* 1086 (DB).

Kilworth, North & South Leics. *Chivelesworde* 1086 (DB), *Kiuelingwurda* 1191. 'Enclosure associated with a man called *Cyfel'. OE pers. name + *-ing-* + *worth*.

Kimberley Norfolk. *Chineburlai* 1086 (DB). 'Woodland clearing of a woman called Cyneburg'. OE pers. name + *lēah*.

Kimberley Notts. *Chinemarleie* 1086 (DB). 'Woodland clearing of a man called Cynemǣr'. OE pers. name + *lēah*.

Kimble, Great & Little Bucks. *Chenebelle* 1086 (DB). 'Royal bell-shaped hill'. OE *cyne-* + *belle*.

Kimblesworth Durham. *Kymliswrth* 13th cent. 'Enclosure of a man called Cynehelm'. OE pers. name + *worth*.

Kimbolton, 'farmstead of a man called Cynebald', OE pers. name + *tūn*: **Kimbolton** Cambs. *Chenebaltone* 1086 (DB). **Kimbolton** Heref. & Worcs. *Kimbalton* 13th cent.

Kimcote Leics. *Chenemundescote* 1086 (DB). 'Cottage(s) of a man called Cynemund'. OE pers. name + *cot*.

Kimmeridge Dorset. *Cameric* (*sic*) 1086 (DB), *Kimerich* 1212. 'Convenient track or strip of land, or one belonging to a man called Cȳma'. OE *cȳme* or OE pers. name + **ric*.

Kimmerston Northum. *Kynemereston* 1244. 'Farmstead of a man called Cynemǣr'. OE pers. name + *tūn*.

Kimpton, 'farmstead associated with a man called Cȳma', OE pers. name + *-ing-* + *tūn*: **Kimpton** Hants. *Chementune* 1086 (DB). **Kimpton** Herts. *Kamintone* 1086 (DB).

Kineton Glos. *Kinton* 1191. 'Royal manor'. OE *cyne-* + *tūn*.

Kineton Warwicks. *Cyngtun* 969, *Quintone* 1086 (DB). 'The king's manor'. OE *cyning* + *tūn*.

Kingham Oxon. *Caningeham* (*sic*) 1086 (DB), *Keingaham* 11th cent. 'Homestead of the family or followers of a man called *Cǣga'. OE pers. name + *-inga-* + *hām*.

King's as affix, see main name, e.g. for **King's Bromley** (Staffs.) see BROMLEY.

Kingsbridge Devon. *Cinges bricge* 962. 'The king's bridge'. OE *cyning* + *brycg*.

Kingsbury, 'the king's manor', OE *cyning* + *burh* (dative *byrig*): **Kingsbury** Gtr. London. *Kynges Byrig* 1044, *Chingesberie* 1086 (DB). **Kingsbury Episcopi** Somerset. *Cyncgesbyrig* 1065, *Chingesberie* 1086 (DB). Latin affix *episcopi* 'of the bishop' from its early possession by the Bishop of Bath.

Kingsclere Hants. *Kyngeclera* early 12th cent. OE *cyning* 'king' (denoting a royal manor) added to the original name found also in HIGHCLERE.

Kingsdon, Kingsdown, 'the king's hill', OE *cyning* + *dūn*: **Kingsdon** Somerset. *Kingesdon* 1194. **Kingsdown** Kent, near Deal. *Kyngesdoune* 1318. **Kingsdown, West** Kent. *Kingesdon* 1199.

Kingsey Bucks. *Eya* 1174, *Kingesie* 1197. 'The king's island'. OE *cyning* + *ēg*.

Kingsford Heref. & Worcs. *Cenungaford* 964. 'Ford of the family or followers of a man called Cēna'. OE pers. name + *-inga-* + *ford*.

Kingskerswell Devon. *Carsewelle* 1086 (DB), *Kyngescharsewell* 1270. 'Spring or stream where water-cress grows'. OE *cærse* + *wella*. The manor belonged to the king in 1086.

Kingsland Heref. & Worcs. *Lene* 1086 (DB), *Kingeslan* 1213. 'The king's estate in *Leon*'. OE *cyning* with old Celtic name for the district (see LEOMINSTER).

Kingsley, 'the king's wood or clearing', OE *cyning* + *lēah*: **Kingsley** Ches. *Chingeslie* 1086 (DB). **Kingsley** Hants. *Kyngesly c.*1210. **Kingsley** Staffs. *Chingeslei* 1086 (DB).

King's Lynn Norfolk, see LYNN.

Kingsnorth Kent. *Kingesnade* 1226. 'Detached piece of land or woodland belonging to the king'. OE *cyning* + *snād*.

Kingstanding W. Mids., from ME *standing* 'a hunter's station from which to shoot game', although according to tradition the mound here was where Charles I reviewed his troops in 1642. The same name occurs in other counties.

Kingsteignton Devon. *Teintona* 1086 (DB), *Kingestentone* 1274. 'Farmstead on the River Teign'. Celtic river-name (see TEIGNMOUTH) + OE *tūn*, with affix from its possession by the king in 1086.

Kingsthorpe Northants. *Torp* 1086 (DB), *Kingestorp* 1190. 'Outlying farmstead or hamlet belonging to the king'. OE *cyning* + OScand. *thorp*.

Kingston, a common name, usually 'the king's manor or estate', OE *cyning* + *tūn*; examples include: **Kingston** Hants. *Kingeston* 1194. **Kingston Bagpuize** Oxon. *Cyngestun c.*976, *Chingestune* 1086 (DB), *Kingeston Bagepuz* 1284. Manorial affix from the *de Bagpuize* family who held the manor from 1086. **Kingston Blount** Oxon. *Chingestone* 1086 (DB), *Kyngestone Blont* 1379. Manorial affix from the *le Blund* family, here in the 13th cent. **Kingston Deverill** Wilts. *Devrel* 1086 (DB), *Deverel Kyngeston* 1249. For the original river-name *Deverill* see BRIXTON DEVERILL. **Kingston Lacy** Dorset. *Kingestune* 1170, *Kynggestone Lacy* 1319. Manorial affix from the *de Lacy* family who held the manor in the 13th cent. **Kingston upon Hull** Humber. *Kyngeston* 1256, alternatively called simply **Hull** from the River Hull from early times (*Hul* 1228), the river-name being either OScand. (meaning 'deep one') or Celtic (meaning 'muddy one'). **Kingston upon Thames** Gtr. London. *Cyninges tun* 838, *Chingestune* 1086 (DB). See THAMES.

However the following has a different origin: **Kingston on Soar** Notts. *Chinestan* 1086 (DB). 'The royal stone'. OE *cyne-* + *stān*. For the river-name, see BARROW UPON SOAR.

Kingstone Heref. & Worcs., near Hereford. *Chingestone* 1086 (DB). 'The king's manor or estate'. OE *cyning* + *tūn*.

Kingstone Somerset. *Chingestana* 1086 (DB). 'The king's boundary stone'. OE *cyning* + *stān*.

Kingswear Devon. *Kingeswere* 12th

cent. 'The king's weir'. OE *cyning* + *wer*.

Kingswinford W. Mids. *Svinesford* 1086 (DB), *Kyngesswynford* 1322. 'Pig ford'. OE *swīn* + *ford*. Affix from its being a royal manor.

Kingswood, 'the king's wood', OE *cyning* + *wudu*: **Kingswood** Avon. *Kingeswode* 1231. **Kingswood** Glos. *Kingeswoda* 1166. **Kingswood** Surrey. *Kingeswode* c.1180.

Kington, 'royal manor or estate', OE *cyne-* (replaced by *cyning*) + *tūn*: **Kington** Heref. & Worcs., near Inkberrow. *Cyngtun* 972, *Chintune* 1086 (DB). **Kington** Heref. & Worcs., near Lyonshall. *Chingtune* 1086 (DB). **Kington Magna** Dorset. *Chintone* 1086 (DB), *Magna Kington* 1243. Affix is Latin *magna* 'great'. **Kington St Michael** Wilts. *Kingtone* 934, *Chintone* 1086 (DB), *Kyngton Michel* 1279. Affix from the dedication of the church. **Kington, West** Wilts. *Westkinton* 1195.

Kinlet Shrops. *Chinlete* 1086 (DB). 'Royal share or lot'. OE *cyne-* + *hlēt*. The manor was held in 1066 by Queen Edith, widow of Edward the Confessor.

Kinnerley, Kinnersley, 'woodland clearing of a man called Cyneheard', OE pers. name + *lēah*: **Kinnerley** Shrops. *Chenardelei* 1086 (DB). **Kinnersley** Heref. & Worcs., near Malvern. *Chinardeslege* 1123. **Kinnersley** Heref. & Worcs., near Weobley. *Cyrdes leah* c.1030, *Curdeslege* 1086 (DB).

Kinnerton, Lower Ches. *Kynarton* 1240. 'Farmstead of a man called Cyneheard'. OE pers. name + *tūn*.

Kinoulton Notts. *Kinildetune* c.1000, *Chineltune* 1086 (DB). 'Farmstead of a woman called Cynehild'. OE pers. name + *tūn*.

Kinsley W. Yorks. *Chineslai* 1086 (DB). 'Woodland clearing of a man called Cyne'. OE pers. name + *lēah*.

Kintbury Berks. *Cynetanbyrig* c.935, *Cheneteberie* 1086 (DB). 'Fortified place on the River Kennet'. Celtic river-name (see KENNETT) + OE *burh* (dative *byrig*).

Kinver Staffs. *Cynibre* 736, *Chenevare* 1086 (DB). Celtic **breȝ* 'hill' with an obscure first element.

Kippax W. Yorks. *Chipesch* 1086 (DB). 'Ash-tree of a man called *Cippa or *Cyppa'. OE pers. name (with Scand. *K-*) + OE *æsc* (replaced by OScand. *askr*).

Kirby, a common name in the Midlands and North, usually 'village with a church', OScand. *kirkju-bý*; examples include: **Kirby Bedon** Norfolk. *Kerkebei* 1086 (DB), *Kirkeby Bydon* 1291. Manorial affix from the *de Bidun* family, here in the 12th cent. **Kirby Bellars** Leics. *Chirchebi* 1086 (DB), *Kirkeby Belers* 1428. Manorial affix from the *Beler* family, here from the 12th cent. **Kirby Grindalythe** N. Yorks. *Chirchebi* 1086 (DB), *Kirkby in Crendalith* 1367. Affix is an old district name meaning 'slope of the valley frequented by cranes', from OE *cran* + *dæl* + OScand. *hlíth*. **Kirby le Soken** Essex. *Kyrkebi* 1181, *Kirkeby in the Sokne* 1385. Affix is from OE *sōcn* 'district with special jurisdiction'. **Kirby, West** Mersey. *Cherchebia* 1081.
However the following have a different origin, 'farmstead or village of a man called Kærir', OScand. pers. name + *bý*: **Kirby, Cold** N. Yorks. *Carebi* 1086 (DB). The affix means 'bleak, exposed'. **Kirby Muxloe** Leics. *Carbi* 1086 (DB). The affix (found from the 17th cent.) is manorial, from lands here held by a family of that name.

Kirdford W. Sussex. *Kinredeford* 1228. 'Ford of a woman called Cynethrȳth or a man called Cynerēd'. OE pers. name + *ford*.

Kirk as affix, see main name, e.g. for **Kirk Bramwith** (S. Yorks.) see BRAMWITH.

Kirkandrews upon Eden Cumbria. *Kirkandres* c.1200. 'Church of St Andrew'. OScand. *kirkja*, named from the dedication of the church. Eden is a Celtic river-name.

Kirkbampton Cumbria. *Banton* c.1185, *Kyrkebampton* 1292. 'Farmstead made of beams or by a tree'. OE *bēam* + *tūn*. Later affix is OScand. *kirkja* 'church'.

Kirkbride Cumbria. *Chirchebrid* 1163. 'Church of St Bride or Brigid'. OScand. *kirkja* + Irish saint's name.

Kirkburn Humber. *Westburne* 1086 (DB), *Kirkebrun* 1272. '(Place on) the spring or stream'. OE *burna* with OScand. *kirkja* 'church'.

Kirkburton W. Yorks. *Bertone* 1086 (DB). 'Farmstead near or belonging to a fortification'. OE *byrh-tūn*, with affix OScand. *kirkja* 'church' from the 16th cent.

Kirkby, a common name in the Midlands and North, 'village with a church', OScand. *kirkju-bý*; examples include: **Kirkby** Mersey. *Cherchebi* 1086 (DB). **Kirkby in Ashfield** Notts. *Chirchebi* 1086 (DB), *Kirkeby in Esfeld* 1216. The affix is an old district name, see ASHFIELD. **Kirkby Lonsdale** Cumbria. *Cherchebi* 1086 (DB), *Kircabi Lauenesdale* 1090–7. The affix means 'in the valley of the River Lune', Celtic river-name (see LANCASTER) + OScand. *dalr*. **Kirkby Malzeard** N. Yorks. *Chirchebi* 1086 (DB), *Kirkebi Malesard* c.1105. The affix means 'poor clearing', from OFrench *mal* + *assart*. **Kirkby Overblow** N. Yorks. *Cherchebi* 1086 (DB), *Kirkeby Oreblowere* 1211. The affix is from OE **or-blāwere* 'ore-blower' alluding to the early smelting of iron ore here. **Kirkby, South** W. Yorks. *Cherchebi* 1086 (DB), *Sudkirkebi* c.1124. Affix 'south' to distinguish this place from another Kirkby (now lost) in Pontefract. **Kirkby Stephen** Cumbria. *Cherkaby Stephan* c.1094. Affix from the dedication of the church or from the name of an early owner. **Kirkby Thore** Cumbria. *Kirkebythore* 1179. Manorial affix probably from the name (OScand. *Thórir*) of some early owner.

Kirkbymoorside N. Yorks. *Chirchebi* 1086 (DB), *Kirkeby Moresheved* c.1170. Identical in origin with the previous names, with affix meaning 'head or top of the moor', OE *mōr* + *hēafod*.

Kirkcambeck Cumbria. *Camboc* c.1177, *Kirkecamboc* c.1280. 'Place on Cam Beck with a church'. Celtic river-name (meaning 'crooked stream') with the addition of OScand. *kirkja*.

Kirkham, 'homestead or village with a church', OE *cirice* (replaced by OScand. *kirkja*) + OE *hām*: **Kirkham** Lancs. *Chicheham* (*sic*) 1086 (DB), *Kyrkham* 1094. **Kirkham** N. Yorks. *Cherchan* 1086 (DB).

Kirkharle Northum. *Herle* 1177, *Kyrkeherl* 1242. Possibly 'woodland clearing of a man called *Herela'. OE pers. name + *lēah*.

Kirkheaton, 'high farmstead', OE *hēah* + *tūn* with the later addition of OScand. *kirkja* 'church': **Kirkheaton** Northum. *Heton* 1242. **Kirkheaton** W. Yorks. *Heptone* (*sic*) 1086 (DB), *Kirkheton* 13th cent.

Kirkland, 'estate belonging to a church', OScand. *kirkja* + *land*: **Kirkland** Cumbria, near Blencarn. *Kyrkeland* c.1140. **Kirkland** Cumbria, near Lamplugh. *Kirkland* 1586.

Kirkleatham Cleveland. *Westlidum* 1086 (DB), *Kyrkelidun* 1181. '(Place at) the slopes'. OE *hlith* or OScand. *hlíth* in a dative plural form. Affix is OE *west* replaced by OScand. *kirkja* 'church'.

Kirklevington Cleveland. *Levetona* 1086 (DB). 'Farmstead on the River Leven'. Celtic river-name (possibly meaning 'smooth') + OE *tūn*, with later addition of OScand. *kirkja* 'church'.

Kirkley Suffolk. *Kirkelea* 1086 (DB). 'Woodland clearing near or belonging to a church'. OScand. *kirkja* + OE *lēah*.

Kirklington, 'estate associated with a man called *Cyrtla', OE pers. name + *-ing-* + *tūn*: **Kirklington** N. Yorks. *Cherdinton* (*sic*) 1086 (DB), *Chirtlintuna* c.1150. **Kirklington** Notts. *Cyrlingtune* 958, *Cherlinton* 1086 (DB).

Kirklinton Cumbria. *Leuenton* c.1170, *Kirkeleuinton* 1278. 'Farmstead by the River Lyne'. Celtic river-name (possibly 'the smooth one') + OE *tūn*, with later affix from OScand. *kirkja* 'church'.

Kirknewton Northum. *Niwetona* 12th cent. 'New farmstead'. OE *nīwe* + *tūn*, with later affix from OScand. *kirkja* 'church'.

Kirkoswald Cumbria. *Karcoswald* 1167. 'Church of St Oswald'. From the dedication of the church (OScand. *kirkja*) to this saint, a 7th cent. king of Northumbria.

Kirksanton Cumbria. *Santacherche* 1086 (DB), *Kirkesantan* c.1150. 'Church of St Sanctán'. OScand. *kirkja* with Irish saint's name.

Kirkwhelpington Northum. *Welpinton*

1176. 'Estate associated with a man called *Hwelp'. OE pers. name + *-ing-* + *tūn*, with later affix from OScand. *kirkja* 'church'.

Kirmington Humber. *Chernitone* 1086 (DB). Possibly 'estate associated with a man called Cynehere'. OE pers. name + *-ing-* + *tūn*.

Kirmond le Mire Lincs. *Chevremont* 1086 (DB). 'Goat hill'. OFrench *chèvre* + *mont*. Affix means 'in the marshy ground', from OScand. *mýrr*.

Kirstead Green Norfolk. *Kerkestede* c.1095. 'Site of a church'. OE *cirice* (replaced by OScand. *kirkja*) + OE *stede*.

Kirtling Cambs. *Chertelinge* 1086 (DB). 'Place associated with a man called *Cyrtla'. OE pers. name + *-ing*.

Kirtlington Oxon. *Kyrtlingtune* c.1000, *Certelintone* 1086 (DB). 'Estate associated with a man called *Cyrtla'. OE pers. name + *-ing-* + *tūn*.

Kirton, 'village with a church', OScand. *kirkja* (probably replacing OE *cirice*) + OE *tūn*: **Kirton** Lincs. *Chirchetune* 1086 (DB). **Kirton** Notts. *Circeton* 1086 (DB). **Kirton** Suffolk. *Kirketuna* 1086 (DB). **Kirton in Lindsey** Humber. *Chirchetone* 1086 (DB). See LINDSEY.

Kislingbury Northants. *Ceselingeberie* 1086 (DB). 'Stronghold of the dwellers on the gravel, or of the family or followers of a man called *Cysel'. OE *cisel* or pers. name + *-inga-* + *burh* (dative *byrig*).

Kiveton Park S. Yorks. *Ciuetone* 1086 (DB). Probably 'farmstead by a tub-shaped feature'. OE *cӯf* + *tūn*.

Knaith Lincs. *Cheneide* 1086 (DB). 'Landing-place by a river-bend'. OE *cnēo* + *hӯth*.

Knaphill Surrey. *La Cnappe* 1225, *Knephull* 1440. 'The hill'. OE *cnæpp*, with later explanatory *hyll*.

Knapton, 'the servant's farmstead', or 'farmstead of a man called Cnapa', OE *cnapa* or pers. name + *tūn*: **Knapton** Norfolk. *Kanapatone* 1086 (DB). **Knapton** N. Yorks. *Cnapetone* 1086 (DB). **Knapton, East & West** N. Yorks. *Cnapetone* 1086 (DB).

Knapwell Cambs. *Cnapwelle* c.1045, *Chenepewelle* 1086 (DB). 'Spring or stream of the servant, or of a man called Cnapa'. OE *cnapa* or pers. name + *wella*.

Knaresborough N. Yorks. *Chenaresburg* 1086 (DB). Probably 'stronghold of a man called Cēnheard'. OE pers. name + *burh*.

Knarsdale Northum. *Knaresdal* 1254. 'Valley of the rugged rock'. OE *cnearr* + OScand. *dalr*.

Knayton N. Yorks. *Cheniueton* 1086 (DB). 'Farmstead of a woman called Cēngifu'. OE pers. name + *tūn*.

Knebworth Herts. *Chenepeworde* 1086 (DB). 'Enclosure of a man called Cnebba'. OE pers. name + *worth*.

Kneesall Notts. *Cheneshale* (*sic*) 1086 (DB), *Cneshala* 1175. Possibly 'nook of land of a man called Cynehēah'. OE pers. name + *halh*.

Kneesworth Cambs. *Cnesworth* c.1218. Possibly 'enclosure of a man called Cynehēah'. OE pers. name + *worth*.

Kneeton Notts. *Cheniueton* 1086 (DB). 'Farmstead of a woman called Cēngifu'. OE pers. name + *tūn*.

Knightcote Warwicks. *Knittecote* 1242. 'Cottage(s) of the young retainers'. OE *cniht* + *cot*.

Knighton, a fairly common name, 'farmstead or village of the young thanes or retainers', OE *cniht* + *tūn*; examples include: **Knighton** Leics. *Cnihtetone* 1086 (DB). **Knighton** Staffs., near Eccleshall. *Chnitestone* 1086 (DB). **Knighton, West** Dorset. *Chenistetone* 1086 (DB).

Knightsbridge Gtr. London. *Cnihtebricge* c.1050. 'Bridge of the young men', i.e. where they congregate. OE *cniht* + *brycg*.

Knill Heref. & Worcs. *Chenille* 1086 (DB). '(Place at) the hillock'. OE *cnylle*.

Knipton Leics. *Gniptone* 1086 (DB). 'Farmstead by a steep rock or peak'. OScand. gnípa + OE *tūn*.

Knitsley Durham. *Knyhtheley* 1303. 'Woodland clearing of the retainers'. OE *cniht* + *lēah*.

Kniveton Derbys. *Cheniuetun* 1086 (DB). 'Farmstead of a woman called Cēngifu'. OE pers. name + *tūn*.

Knock Cumbria. *Chonoc* 12th cent. OIrish *cnocc* 'a hillock'.

Knockholt Kent. *Ocholt* 1197, *Nocholt* 1353. '(Place at) the oak wood'. OE *āc* + *holt*, with initial *N-* from the OE definite article.

Knockin Shrops. *Cnochin* 1165. Celtic **cnöccïn* 'a little hillock'.

Knodishall Suffolk. *Cnotesheala* 1086 (DB). 'Nook of land of a man called *Cnott'. OE pers. name + *halh*.

Knook Wilts. *Cunuche* 1086 (DB). Probably OWelsh **cnucc* 'a hillock'.

Knossington Leics. *Nossitone* (*sic*) 1086 (DB), *Cnossintona* 12th cent. Probably 'estate associated with a man called *Cnossa'. OE pers. name + *-ing-* + *tūn*.

Knott End on Sea Lancs. *Cnote* 13th cent. ME *knot* 'a hillock'.

Knotting Beds. *Chenotinga* 1086 (DB). Probably '(settlement of) the family or followers of a man called *Cnotta'. OE pers. name + *-ingas*.

Knottingley W. Yorks. *Notingeleia* 1086 (DB). 'Woodland clearing of the family or followers of a man called *Cnotta'. OE pers. name + *-inga-* + *lēah*.

Knowle, '(place at) the hill-top or hillock', OE *cnoll*; examples include:
Knowle Avon. *Canole* 1086 (DB).
Knowle W. Mids. *La Cnolle* 1221.
Knowle, Church Dorset. *C(he)nolle* 1086 (DB), *Churchecnolle* 1346. Later addition is OE *cirice* 'church'.

Knowlton Kent. *Chenoltone* 1086 (DB). 'Farmstead by a hillock'. OE *cnoll* + *tūn*.

Knowsley Mersey. *Chenulueslei* 1086 (DB). 'Woodland clearing of a man called Cēnwulf or Cynewulf'. OE pers. name + *lēah*.

Knowstone Devon. *Chenutdestana* 1086 (DB). 'Boundary stone of a man called Knútr'. OScand. pers. name + OE *stān*.

Knoyle, East & West Wilts. *Cnugel* 948, *Chenvel* 1086 (DB). '(Place at) the knuckle-shaped hill'. OE **cnugel*.

Knutsford Ches. *Cunetesford* 1086 (DB). Probably 'ford of a man called Knútr'. OScand. pers. name + OE *ford*.

Kyloe Northum. *Culeia* 1195. 'Clearing or pasture for cows'. OE *cū* + *lēah*.

Kyme, North & South Lincs. *Chime* 1086 (DB). '(Place at) the hollow'. OE **cymbe*.

Kyre Magna Heref. & Worcs. *Cuer* 1086 (DB). Named from the stream here, a pre-English river-name of uncertain origin and meaning.

L

Laceby Humber. *Levesbi* 1086 (DB). 'Farmstead or village of a man called Leifr'. OScand. pers. name + *bý*.

Lach Dennis Ches. *Lece* 1086 (DB), *Lache Deneys* 1260. 'The boggy stream'. OE **lece*, with manorial affix from ME *danais* 'Danish' referring to a man called *Colben* who held the manor in 1086.

Lackford Suffolk. *Lecforda* 1086 (DB). 'Ford where leeks grow'. OE *lēac* + *ford*.

Ladbroke Warwicks. *Hlodbroc* 998, *Lodbroc* 1086 (DB). Possibly 'brook used for divination'. OE *hlod* + *brōc*.

Ladock Cornwall. 'Church of *Sancta Ladoca*' 1268. From the patron saint of the church.

Laindon Essex. *Ligeandune* c.1000, *Leienduna* 1086 (DB). Probably 'hill by a stream called *Lea*'. Lost Celtic river-name (possibly meaning 'light river') + OE *dūn*.

Lake Wilts. *Lake* 1289. OE *lacu* 'small stream'.

Lakenham, Old & New Norfolk. *Lakemham* 1086 (DB). Probably 'homestead or village of a man called *Lāca'. OE pers. name (genitive *-n*) + *hām*.

Lakenheath Suffolk. *Lacingahith* 945, *Lakingahethe* 1086 (DB). 'Landing-place of the people living by streams'. OE *lacu* + *-inga-* + *hȳth*.

Laleham Surrey. *Læleham* 1042–66, *Leleham* 1086 (DB). 'Homestead or enclosure where twigs or brushwood are found'. OE *lǣl* + *hām* or *hamm*.

Lamarsh Essex. *Lamers* 1086 (DB). 'Loam marsh'. OE *lām* + *mersc*.

Lamas Norfolk. *Lamers* 1086 (DB). Identical in origin with the previous name.

Lamberhurst Kent. *Lamburherste* c.1100. 'Wooded hill where lambs graze'. OE *lamb* (genitive plural *lambra*) + *hyrst*.

Lambeth Gtr. London. *Lamhytha* 1088. 'Landing-place for lambs'. OE *lamb* + *hȳth*.

Lambley, 'clearing or pasture for lambs', OE *lamb* + *lēah*: **Lambley** Northum. *Lambeleya* 1201. **Lambley** Notts. *Lambeleia* 1086 (DB).

Lambourn, Lambourne, probably 'stream where lambs are washed', OE *lamb* + *burna*: **Lambourn, Upper Lambourn** Berks. *Lambburnan* c.880, *Lamborne* 1086 (DB), *Uplamburn* 1182. Distinguishing affix is OE *upp* 'higher upstream'. **Lambourne** Essex. *Lamburna* 1086 (DB).

Lambrook, East Somerset. *Landbroc* 1065. OE *brōc* 'brook' with OE *land* 'cultivated ground, estate'.

Lamerton Devon. *Lambretona* 1086 (DB). 'Farmstead on the lamb stream or loam stream'. OE *lamb* or *lām* + *burna* + *tūn*.

Lamesley Tyne & Wear. *Lamelay* 1297. 'Clearing or pasture for lambs'. OE *lamb* + *lēah*.

Lamonby Cumbria. *Lambeneby* 1257. 'Farmstead or village of a man called Lambin'. ME pers. name + OScand. *bý*.

Lamorran Cornwall. *Lannmoren* 969. 'Church-site of St Moren'. From Cornish **lann* with the patron saint of the church.

Lamplugh Cumbria. *Lamplou* c.1150. 'Bare valley'. Celtic *nant* + *blwch*.

Lamport Northants. *Langeport* 1086 (DB). 'Long village or market-place'. OE *lang* + *port*.

Lamyatt Somerset. *Lambageate* late 10th cent., *Lamieta* 1086 (DB). 'Gate for lambs'. OE *lamb* (genitive plural *-a*) + *geat*.

Lancaster Lancs. *Loncastre* 1086 (DB). 'Roman fort on the River Lune'. Celtic river-name (probably meaning 'healthy, pure') + OE *cæster*. **Lancashire** (the county) is a reduced form of *Lancastreshire* 14th cent., from Lancaster + OE *scīr* 'district'.

Lanchester Durham. *Langecestr* 1196. Apparently 'long Roman fort or stronghold'. OE *lang* + *ceaster*. The first element may however preserve a reduced form of its old Romano-British name *Longovicium* (probably 'place of the ship-fighters' from Celtic **longo-* 'ship').

Lancing W. Sussex. *Lancinges* 1086 (DB). '(Settlement of) the family or followers of a man called *Wlanc'. OE pers. name + *-ingas*.

Landbeach Cambs. *Bece* 1086 (DB), *Landebeche* 1218. OE *bece* 'stream, valley' or *bæc* (locative **bece*) 'low ridge', with the later addition of *land* 'dry land' to distinguish it from WATERBEACH.

Landcross Devon. *Lanchers* 1086 (DB). Possibly OE *ears* 'buttock-shaped hill' with OE *hlanc* 'long, narrow'. Alternatively a Celtic name meaning 'church by the fen', from **lann* + **cors*.

Landford Wilts. *Langeford* (*sic*) 1086 (DB), *Laneford* 1242. 'Ford crossed by a lane'. OE *lanu* + *ford*.

Landkey Devon. *Landechei* 1166. 'Church-site of St Ke'. Cornish **lann* + saint's name.

Landrake Cornwall. *Landerhtun* late 11th cent. Cornish *lannergh* 'a clearing' (with OE *tūn* 'farmstead' in the early spelling).

Land's End Cornwall. *Londeseynde* 1337. 'End of the mainland'. OE *land* + *ende*.

Landulph Cornwall. *Landelech* 1086 (DB). 'Church-site of Dilic'. Cornish **lann* + saint's name.

Landwade Cambs. *Landuuade* 11th cent. Probably 'estate or district ford'. OE *land* + *wæd*.

Laneast Cornwall. *Lanast* 1076. Cornish **lann* 'church-site' with an obscure second element, probably a pers. name.

Laneham, Church Laneham Notts. *Lanun* 1086 (DB). '(Place at) the lanes'. OE *lanu* in a dative plural form *lanum*.

Lanercost Cumbria. *Lanrecost* 1169. Celtic **lannerch* 'glade, clearing', perhaps with the pers. name *Aust* (from Latin *Augustus*).

Langar Notts. *Langare* 1086 (DB). 'Long gore or point of land'. OE *lang* + *gāra*.

Langcliffe N. Yorks. *Lanclif* 1086 (DB). 'Long cliff or bank'. OE *lang* + *clif*.

Langdale, Little Cumbria. *Langedenelittle* c.1160. 'Long valley'. OE *lang* + *denu* (replaced by OScand. *dalr*).

Langdon, 'long hill or down', OE *lang* + *dūn*: **Langdon, East & West** Kent. *Langandune* 861, *Estlangedoun, Westlangedone* 1291. **Langdon Hills** Essex. *Langenduna* 1086 (DB), *Langdon Hilles* 1485.

Langenhoe Essex. *Langhou* 1086 (DB). 'Long hill-spur'. OE *lang* (dative *-an*) + *hōh*.

Langford, usually 'long ford', OE *lang* + *ford*; examples include: **Langford** Beds. *Longaford* 944–6, *Langeford* 1086 (DB). **Langford** Essex. *Langheforda* 1086 (DB). **Langford Budville** Somerset. *Langeford* 1212, *Langeford Budevill* 1305. Manorial affix from the *de Buddevill* family, here in the 13th cent.

However the following has a different origin: **Langford** Notts. *Landeforde* 1086 (DB). Possibly 'ford of a man called *Landa', OE pers. name + *ford*; alternatively the first element may be OE *land* in a sense such as 'boundary or district'.

Langham, usually 'long homestead or enclosure', OE *lang* + *hām* or *hamm*: **Langham** Leics. *Langham* 1202. **Langham** Norfolk. *Langham* 1086 (DB). **Langham** Suffolk. *Langham* 1086 (DB).

However the following has a different origin: **Langham** Essex. *Laingaham* 1086 (DB). Possibly 'homestead of the family or followers of a man called *Lahha'. OE pers. name + *-inga-* + *hām*.

Langho Lancs. *Langale* 13th cent. 'Long nook of land'. OE *lang* + *halh*.

Langley, a fairly common name, 'long wood or clearing', OE *lang* + *lēah*; examples include: **Langley** Bucks.

Langeley 1208. **Langley** Kent. *Longanleag* 814, *Langvelei* 1086 (DB). **Langley, Abbots & Kings** Herts. *Langalege c.*1060, *Langelai* 1086 (DB), *Abbotes Langele* 1263, *Kyngeslangeley* 1436. Distinguishing affixes refer to early possession by the Abbot of St Albans and the King. **Langley Burrell** wilts. *Langelegh* 940, *Langhelei* 1086 (DB), *Langele Burel* 1309. Manorial affix from the *Burel* family, here from the 13th cent. **Langley, Kington** Wilts. *Langhelei* 1086 (DB). Affix *Kington*, first added in the 17th cent., is from KINGTON ST MICHAEL nearby. **Langley, Kirk** Derbys. *Langelei* 1086 (DB), *Kyrkelongeleye* 1269. Affix is OScand. *kirkja* 'church'. **Langley Park** Durham. *Langeleye* 1232.

Langney E. Sussex. *Langelie* (*sic*) 1086 (DB), *Langania* 1121. 'Long island, or long piece of dry ground in marsh'. OE *lang* (dative *-an*) + *ēg*.

Langold Notts. *Langalde* 1246. 'Long shelter or place of refuge'. OE *lang* + *hald*.

Langport Somerset. *Longport* 10th cent., *Lanport* 1086 (DB). 'Long market-place'. OE *lang* + *port*.

Langrick Lincs. *Langrak* 1243. 'Long stretch of river'. OE *lang* + **racu*.

Langridge Avon. *Lancheris* (*sic*) 1086 (DB), *Langerig* 1225. 'Long ridge'. OE *lang* + *hrycg*.

Langrigg Cumbria. *Langrug* 1189. 'Long ridge'. OScand. *langr* + *hryggr*.

Langrish Hants. *Langerishe* 1236. 'Long rush-bed'. OE *lang* + **rysce*.

Langsett S. Yorks. *Langeside* 12th cent. 'Long hill-slope'. OE *lang* + *sīde*.

Langstone Hants. *Langeston* 1289. 'Long (or tall) stone'. OE *lang* + *stān*.

Langthorne N. Yorks. *Langetorp* (*sic*) 1086 (DB), *Langethorn c.*1100. 'Tall thorn-tree'. OE *lang* + *thorn*.

Langthorpe N. Yorks. *Torp* 1086 (DB), *Langliuetorp* 12th cent. 'Outlying farmstead or hamlet of a woman called Langlíf'. OScand. pers. name + *thorp*.

Langthwaite N. Yorks. *Langethwait* 1167. 'Long clearing'. OScand. *langr* + *thveit*.

Langtoft, 'long homestead or curtilage', OScand. *langr* + *toft*: **Langtoft** Humber. *Langetou* (*sic*) 1086 (DB), *Langetoft c.*1165. **Langtoft** Lincs. *Langetof* 1086 (DB).

Langton, a fairly common name, usually 'long farmstead or estate', OE *lang* + *tūn*; examples include: **Langton, Church & East** Leics. *Lang(e)tone* 1086 (DB), *Chirch Langeton* 1316, *Estlangeton* 1327. **Langton, Great** N. Yorks. *Langeton* 1086 (DB), *Great Langeton* 1223. **Langton Herring** Dorset. *Langetone* 1086 (DB), *Langeton Heryng* 1336. Manorial affix from the *Harang* family, here in the 13th cent. **Langton Matravers** Dorset. *Langeton* 1165, *Langeton Mawtravers* 1428. Manorial addition from the *Mautravers* family, here from the 13th cent.

However the following have a different origin: **Langton** Durham. *Langadun c.*1050. 'Long hill or down'. OE *lang* + *dūn*. **Langton, Tur** Leics. *Terlintone* 1086 (DB). Probably 'estate associated with a man called Tyrhtel or *Tyrli'. OE pers. name + *-ing-* + *tūn*. The name was later remodelled under the influence of nearby CHURCH & EAST LANGTON.

Langtree Devon. *Langtrewa* 1086 (DB). 'Tall tree'. OE *lang* + *trēow*.

Langwathby Cumbria. *Langwadebi* 1159. 'Farmstead or village by the long ford'. OScand. *langr* + *vath* + *bý*.

Langwith, 'long ford', OScand. *langr* + *vath*: **Langwith, Nether** Notts. *Languath c.*1179, *Netherlangwat* 1252. Affix is OE *neotherra* 'lower (down-stream)' to distinguish it from the next name. **Langwith, Upper** Derbys. *Langwath* 1208.

Langworth Lincs., near Wragby. *Longwathe c.*1055. Identical in origin with the previous names.

Lanivet Cornwall. *Lannived* 1268. 'Church-site at the pagan sacred place'. Cornish **lann* + *neved*.

Lanlivery Cornwall. *Lanliveri* 12th cent. 'Church-site of *Livri'. Cornish **lann* + pers. name.

Lanreath Cornwall. *Lanredoch* 1086 (DB). 'Church-site of Reydhogh'. Cornish **lann* + pers. name.

Lansallos Cornwall. *Lansaluus* 1086

(DB). 'Church-site of *Salwys'. Cornish *lann + pers. name.

Lanteglos Cornwall, near Fowey. *Lanteglos* 1249. 'Valley of the church'. Cornish *nans* + *eglos*.

Lanton Northum. *Langeton* 1242. 'Long farmstead or estate'. OE *lang* + *tūn*.

Lapford Devon. *Slapeforda* (*sic*) 1086 (DB), *Lapeford* 1107. Probably 'ford of a man called *Hlappa'. OE pers. name + *ford*.

Lapley Staffs. *Lappeley* 1061, *Lepelie* 1086 (DB). 'Woodland clearing at the end of the estate or parish'. OE *læppa* + *lēah*.

Lapworth Warwicks. *Hlappawurthin* 816, *Lapeforde* (*sic*) 1086 (DB). 'Enclosure in a detached district, or belonging to a man called *Hlappa'. OE *læppa* or pers. name + *worthign* (replaced by *worth*).

Larkfield Kent. *Lavrochesfel* 1086 (DB). 'Open land frequented by larks'. OE *lāwerce* + *feld*.

Larling Norfolk. *Lurlinga* 1086 (DB). '(Settlement of) the family or followers of a man called *Lyrel'. OE pers. name + *-ingas*.

Lartington Durham. *Lyrtingtun* c.1050, *Lertinton* 1086 (DB). 'Estate associated with a man called *Lyrti'. OE pers. name + *-ing-* + *tūn*.

Lasham Hants. *Esseham* (*sic*) 1086 (DB), *Lasham* 1175. 'Smaller homestead, or homestead of a man called *Leassa'. OE *lǣssa* or pers. name + *hām*.

Lastingham N. Yorks. *Lestingeham* 1086 (DB). 'Homestead of the family or followers of a man called *Lǣsta'. OE pers. name + *-inga-* + *hām*.

Latchingdon Essex. *Læcendune* c.1050, *Lacenduna* 1086 (DB). Probably 'hill by the well-watered ground'. OE **læcen* + *dūn*.

Lathbury Bucks. *Lateberie* 1086 (DB). 'Fortification built with laths or beams'. OE *lætt* + *burh* (dative *byrig*).

Latimer Bucks. *Yselhamstede* 1220, *Isenhampstede Latymer* 1389. For its original name, see CHENIES. The manorial addition (now used alone) is from the *Latymer* family, here in the 14th cent.

Latteridge Avon. *Laderugga* 1176. Possibly 'ridge by a water-course'. OE *lād* + *hrycg*.

Lattiford Somerset. *Lodereforda* 1086 (DB). 'Ford frequented by beggars'. OE *loddere* + *ford*.

Latton Wilts. *Latone* 1086 (DB). 'Leek or garlic enclosure, herb garden'. OE *lēac-tūn*.

Laughterton Lincs. *Leuggtricdun* c.680, *Lactertun* 1227. 'Hill or farmstead where lettice grows'. OE *leahtric* + *dūn* or *tūn*.

Laughton, usually 'leek or garlic enclosure, herb garden', OE *lēac-tūn*: **Laughton** E. Sussex. *Lestone* 1086 (DB). **Laughton** Leics. *Lachestone* 1086 (DB). **Laughton en le Morthen** S. Yorks. *Lastone* 1086 (DB), *Latton in Morthing* 1230. Affix means 'in the (district called) Morthen', a name first recorded in the 12th cent. from OE or OScand. *mōr* 'moorland' + *thing* 'assembly'.

However the following has a different origin: **Laughton** Lincs., near Folkingham. *Loctone* 1086 (DB). 'Enclosure that can be locked'. OE *loc* + *tūn*.

Launcells Cornwall. *Landseu* (*sic*) 1086 (DB), *Lanceles* 1204. Cornish **lann* 'church-site' with an uncertain second element.

Launceston Cornwall. *Lanscavetone* 1086 (DB). 'Estate near the church-site of St Stephen'. Cornish **lann* + saint's name + OE *tūn*.

Launton Oxon. *Langtune* c.1050, *Lantone* 1086 (DB). 'Long farmstead or estate'. OE *lang* + *tūn*.

Lavant, East Lavant W. Sussex. *Loventone* 1086 (DB), *Lavent* 1227. Originally 'farmstead on the River Lavant', with OE *tūn*, later taking name from the river alone, a Celtic river-name meaning 'gliding one'.

Lavendon Bucks. *Lavendene* 1086 (DB). 'Valley of a man called Lāfa'. OE pers. name (genitive *-n*) + *denu*.

Lavenham Suffolk. *Lauanham* c.995, *Lauenham* 1086 (DB). 'Homestead of a man called Lāfa'. OE pers. name (genitive *-n*) + *hām*.

Laver, High, Little, & Magdalen Essex. *Lagefare* c.1010, *Lagafara* 1086 (DB), *Laufar la Magdelene* 1263. 'Water passage or crossing'. OE *lagu* + *fær*. Affix *Magdalen* from the dedication of the church.

Laverstock Wilts. *Lavvrecestoches* 1086 (DB). 'Outlying farmstead or hamlet frequented by larks'. OE *lāwerce* + *stoc*.

Laverstoke Hants. *Lavrochestoche* 1086 (DB). Identical in origin with the previous name.

Laverton, usually probably 'farmstead frequented by larks', OE *lāwerce* + *tūn*: **Laverton** Glos. *Lawertune c.*1160. **Laverton** Somerset. *Lavretone* 1086 (DB).

However the following has a different origin: **Laverton** N. Yorks. *Lavretone* 1086 (DB). 'Farmstead on the River Laver'. Celtic river-name (meaning 'babbling brook') + OE *tūn*.

Lavington, probably 'estate associated with a man called Lāfa', OE pers. name + *-ing-* + *tūn*: **Lavington, East & West** W. Sussex. *Levitone* 1086 (DB). **Lavington, Market & West** Wilts. *Laventone* 1086 (DB). Distinguishing affixes *market* and *west* first found in the 17th cent.

Lawford, probably 'ford of a man called *Lealla', OE pers. name + *ford*: **Lawford** Essex. *Lalleford* 1045, *Laleforda* 1086 (DB). **Lawford, Church & Long** Warwicks. *Lelleford* 1086 (DB), *Chirche Lalleford, Long Lalleford* 1235. Distinguishing affixes are OE *cirice* 'church' and *lang* 'long'.

Lawhitton Cornwall. *Landuuithan* 10th cent., *Languitetone* 1086 (DB). Probably 'valley or church-site of a man called Gwethen', Cornish *nans* or **lann* + pers. name, with the later addition of OE *tūn* 'farmstead'.

Lawkland N. Yorks. *Laukeland* 12th cent. 'Arable land where leeks are grown'. OScand. *laukr* + *land*.

Lawley Shrops. *Lavelei* 1086 (DB). 'Woodland clearing of a man called Lāfa'. OE pers. name + *lēah*.

Lawshall Suffolk. *Lawessela* 1086 (DB). 'Dwelling or shelter by a hill or mound'. OE *hlāw* + *sele* or **sell*.

Lawton, 'farmstead by a hill or mound', OE *hlāw* + *tūn*: **Lawton** Heref. & Worcs. *Lavtune* 1086 (DB). **Lawton, Church** Ches. *Lautune* 1086 (DB), *Church Laughton* 1331.

Laxfield Suffolk. *Laxefelda* 1086 (DB). 'Open land of a man called *Leaxa'. OE pers. name + *feld*.

Laxton, 'estate associated with a man called *Leaxa', OE pers. name + *-ing-* + *tūn*: **Laxton** Humber. *Laxinton* 1086 (DB). **Laxton** Notts. *Laxintune* 1086 (DB).

However the following may have a slightly different meaning: **Laxton** Northants. *Lastone* 1086 (DB). '*Leaxa's estate'. OE pers. name + *tūn*.

Laycock W. Yorks. *Lacoc* 1086 (DB). 'The small stream'. OE **lacuc*.

Layer Breton, Layer de la Haye Essex. *Legra* 1086 (DB), *Leyre Bretoun* 1254, *Legra de Haya* 1236. Probably originally a river-name *Leire* of Celtic origin. Distinguishing affixes from early possession by families called *Breton* and *de Haia*.

Layham Suffolk. *Hligham c.*995, *Leiham* 1086 (DB). 'Homestead with a shelter'. OE **hlīg* + *hām*.

Laytham Humber. *Ladon* 1086 (DB). '(Place at) the barns'. OScand. *hlatha* in a dative plural form *hlathum*.

Layton, East & West N. Yorks. *Latton, Lastun* 1086 (DB). 'Leek enclosure, herb garden'. OE *lēac-tūn*.

Lazenby Cleveland. *Lesingebi* 1086 (DB). 'Farmstead of the freedmen, or of a man called *Leysingr'. OScand. *leysingi* or pers. name + *bý*.

Lazonby Cumbria. *Leisingebi* 1165. Identical in origin with the previous name.

Lea (river) Beds., Herts., Essex, see LEYTON.

Lea, '(place at) the wood or woodland clearing', OE *lēah*; examples include: **Lea** Derbys. *Lede* (*sic*) 1086 (DB), *Lea c.*1155. **Lea** Heref. & Worcs. *Lecce* (*sic*) 1086 (DB), *La Lee* 1219. **Lea** Lincs. *Lea* 1086 (DB). **Lea** Wilts. *Lia* 1190. **Lea Town** Lancs. *Lea* 1086 (DB).

Leach (river) Glos., see EASTLEACH.

Leadenham Lincs. *Ledeneham* 1086 (DB). Probably 'homestead or village of a man called *Lēoda'. OE pers. name (genitive *-n*) + *hām*.

Leaden Roding Essex, see RODING.

Leadgate Durham. *Lidgate* 1590. OE *hlid-geat* 'a swing-gate'.

Leadon (river) Glos., Heref. & Worcs., see HIGHLEADON.

Leafield Oxon. *La Felde* 1213. 'The open land'. OE *feld* with the OFrench definite article.

Leagrave Beds. *Littegraue* 1224. 'Light-coloured, or lightly wooded, grove'. OE *lēoht* + *grāf*.

Leake, '(place at) the brook', OScand. *lœkr*: **Leake** Lincs. *Leche* 1086 (DB). **Leake** N. Yorks. *Lec(h)e* 1086 (DB). **Leake, East & West** Notts. *Lec(c)he* 1086 (DB).

Lealholm N. Yorks. *Lelun* 1086 (DB). '(Place among) the twigs or brushwood'. OE *lǣl* in a dative plural form *lǣlum*.

Leamington, 'farmstead on the River Leam', Celtic river-name (meaning 'elm river', or 'marshy river') + OE *tūn*: **Leamington Hastings** Warwicks. *Lunnitone* 1086 (DB), *Lemyngton Hasting* 1285. Manorial affix from the *Hastinges* family, here in the 13th cent. **Royal Leamington Spa** Warwicks. *Lamintone* 1086 (DB). The affix was granted by Queen Victoria in 1838, *Spa* referring to the medicinal springs here.

Learmouth, East & West Northum. *Leuremue* 1177. 'Mouth of the stream where rushes grow'. OE *lǣfer* + *mūtha*.

Leasingham Lincs. *Leuesingham* 1086 (DB). 'Homestead of the family or followers of a man called Lēofsige'. OE pers. name + *-inga-* + *hām*.

Leatherhead Surrey. *Leodridan* c.880, *Leret* (*sic*) 1086 (DB). 'Grey ford'. Celtic **lę̄d* + **rïd*.

Leathley N. Yorks. *Ledelai* 1086 (DB). 'Woodland clearing on the slopes'. OE *hlith* (genitive plural *hleotha*) + *lēah*.

Leaton Shrops. *Letone* 1086 (DB). OE *tūn* 'farmstead' with an uncertain first element.

Leaveland Kent. *Levelant* 1086 (DB). 'Cultivated land of a man called Lēofa'. OE pers. name + *land*.

Leavening N. Yorks. *Ledlinghe* (*sic*) 1086 (DB), *Leyingges* 1242. Possibly '(settlement of) the family or followers of a man called Lēofhēah'. OE pers. name + *-ingas*.

Lebberston N. Yorks. *Ledbeztun* 1086 (DB). 'Farmstead of a man called Lēodbriht'. OE pers. name + *tūn*.

Lechlade Glos. *Lecelade* 1086 (DB). Probably 'river-crossing near the River Leach'. River-name (from OE **læc(c)*, **lece* 'boggy stream') + *gelād*.

Leckford Hants. *Leahtforda* 947, *Lechtford* 1086 (DB). 'Ford at or over a channel'. OE **leaht* + *ford*.

Leckhampstead, 'homestead where leeks are grown', OE *lēac* + *hām-stede*: **Leckhampstead** Berks. *Lechamstede* 956–9, *Lecanestede* 1086 (DB). **Leckhampstead** Bucks. *Lechamstede* 1086 (DB).

Leckhampton Glos. *Lechametone* 1086 (DB). 'Home farm where leeks are grown'. OE *lēac* + *hām-tūn*.

Leconfield Humber. *Lachinfeld* 1086 (DB). OE *feld* 'open land' with an uncertain first element, possibly a derivative of OE **læc(c)*, **lece* 'boggy stream'.

Ledburn Bucks. *Leteburn* 1212. 'Stream with a conduit, or by a cross-roads'. OE *(ge)lǣt(e)* + *burna*.

Ledbury Heref. & Worcs. *Liedeberge* 1086 (DB). Probably 'fortified place on the River Leadon'. Celtic river-name (see HIGHLEADON) + OE *burh* (dative *byrig*).

Ledsham Ches. *Levetesham* 1086 (DB). 'Homestead of a man called Lēofede'. OE pers. name + *hām*.

Ledsham W. Yorks. *Ledesham* c.1030, 1086 (DB). 'Homestead within the district of LEEDS'. OE *hām*.

Ledston W. Yorks. *Ledestune* 1086 (DB). 'Farmstead within the district of LEEDS'. OE *tūn*.

Ledwell Oxon. *Ledewelle* 1086 (DB). 'Spring or stream called the loud one'. OE **hlȳde* + *wella*.

Lee, '(place at) the wood or woodland clearing', OE *lēah*; examples include: **Lee** Gtr. London. *Lee* 1086 (DB). **Lee** Hants. *Ly* 1236. **Lee** Shrops. *Lee* 1327. **Lee Brockhurst** Shrops. *Lege* 1086 (DB), *Leye under Brochurst* 1285. Affix from a nearby place, 'wooded hill frequented by badgers', OE *brocc* + *hyrst*. **Lee on the Solent** Hants. *Lie* 1212. See SOLENT.

Leebotwood Shrops. *Botewde* 1086 (DB), *Leg de Bottewud* 1212. 'Wood of a man called Botta', OE pers. name + *wudu*, with the later addition of *lēah* 'clearing'.

Leece Cumbria. *Lies* 1086 (DB). Probably from Celtic **līss* 'a hall, a court, the chief house in a district'.

Leeds Kent. *Esledes* 1086 (DB), *Hledes* c.1100. Possibly from a stream-name, OE **hlȳde* 'the loud one'.

Leeds W. Yorks. *Loidis* 731, *Ledes* 1086 (DB). A Celtic name, originally *Lādenses*, meaning 'people living by the strongly flowing river'.

Leek Staffs. *Lec* 1086 (DB). '(Place at) the brook'. OScand. *lœkr*.

Leek Wootton Warwicks., see WOOTTON.

Leeming N. Yorks. *Leming* 12th cent. Named from Leeming Beck, a river-name possibly of OE origin and meaning 'bright stream'.

Lees Gtr. Manch. *The Leese* 1604. 'The woods or woodland clearings'. OE *lēah* (plural *lēas*).

Legbourne Lincs. *Lecheburne* 1086 (DB). Probably 'boggy stream'. OE **læc(c)*, **lece* + *burna*.

Legsby Lincs. *Lagesbi* 1086 (DB). 'Farmstead or village of a man called Leggr'. OScand. pers. name + *bý*.

Leicester Leics. *Ligera ceaster* early 10th cent., *Ledecestre* 1086 (DB). 'Roman town of the people called *Ligore*'. Tribal name (of uncertain origin and meaning) + OE *ceaster*. **Leicestershire** (OE *scīr* 'district') is first referred to in the 11th cent.

Leigh, a common name, '(place at) the wood or woodland clearing', OE *lēah*; examples include: **Leigh** Gtr. Manch. *Legh* 1276. **Leigh** Heref. & Worcs. *Beornothesleah* 972, *Lege* 1086 (DB). 'Belonging to a man called Beornnōth' in the 10th cent. spelling. **Leigh** Kent. *Lega* c.1100. **Leigh** Surrey. *Leghe* late 12th cent. **Leigh, Abbots** Avon. *Lege* 1086 (DB). Affix from its early possession by the Abbot of St Augustine's, Bristol. **Leigh, Bessels** Oxon. *Leie* 1086 (DB), *Bessilles Lee* 1538. Manorial affix from the *Besyles* family, here in the 15th cent. **Leigh, North & South** Oxon. *Lege* 1086 (DB), *Northleg* 1225, *Suthleye* early 13th cent. **Leigh-on-Sea** Essex. *Legra (sic)* 1086 (DB), *Legha* 1226. **Leigh Sinton** Heref. & Worcs., see SINTON.

Leighs, Great & Little Essex. *Lega* 1086 (DB), *Leyes* 1271. OE *lēah* 'wood, woodland clearing'.

Leighterton Glos. *Lettrintone* 12th cent. 'Farmstead where lettuce grows'. OE *leahtric* + *tūn*.

Leighton, 'leek or garlic enclosure, herb garden', OE *lēac-tūn*: **Leighton** Shrops. *Lestone* 1086 (DB). **Leighton Bromswold** Cambs. *Lectone* 1086 (DB), *Letton super Bruneswald* 1254. Affix is from a nearby place, 'high forest-land of a man called Brūn', OE pers. name + *weald*. **Leighton Buzzard** Beds. *Lestone* 1086 (DB), *Letton Busard* 1254. Manorial affix is from a family called *Busard*, no doubt landowners here in the 13th cent.

Leinthall Earls & Starkes Heref. & Worcs. *Lentehale* 1086 (DB), *Leintall Comites* 1275, *Leinthale Starkare* 13th cent. 'Nook of land by the River *Lent*'. Lost Celtic river-name (meaning 'torrent, stream') + OE *halh*. Manorial affixes from early possession by an *earl* (Latin *comitis* 'of the earl') and a man called *Starker*.

Leintwardine Heref. & Worcs. *Lenteurde* 1086 (DB). 'Enclosure on the River *Lent*'. Lost Celtic river-name (see previous name) + *worth* (replaced by *worthign*).

Leire Leics. *Legre* 1086 (DB). Probably an ancient pre-English river-name for the small tributary of the River Soar on which the place stands.

Leiston Suffolk. *Leistuna* 1086 (DB). Possibly 'farmstead near a beacon-fire'. OE *lēg* + *tūn*.

Lelant Cornwall. *Lananta* c.1170. 'Church-site of Anta'. Cornish **lann* + female saint's name.

Lelley Humber. *Lelle* 1246. 'Wood or clearing where twigs or brushwood are found'. OE *læ̅l* + *lēah*.

Lemington, Lower Glos. *Limentone*

1086 (DB). Probably 'farmstead near a stream called *Limen*'. Lost Celtic river-name (meaning 'elm river') + OE *tūn*.

Lench, from OE **hlenc* 'an extensive hill-slope', originally the name of a district and giving name to: **Lench, Abbots** Heref. & Worcs. *Abeleng* 1086 (DB). Manorial affix originally from possession by a man with the OE pers. name *Abba*. **Lench, Atch** Heref. & Worcs. *Achelenz* 1086 (DB). Manorial affix from possession by a man with the OE pers. name *Æcci*. **Lench, Church** Heref. & Worcs. *Lench* 9th cent., *Chirichlench* 1054. Affix is OE *cirice* 'church'. **Lench, Rous** Heref. & Worcs. *Lenc* 983, *Biscopesleng* 1086 (DB), *Rous Lench* 1445. Manorial affix from the *Rous* family, here in the 14th cent. (held by the Bishop of Worcester in 1086).

Lenham Kent. *Leanaham* 858, *Lerham* (*sic*) 1086 (DB). 'Homestead or village of a man called *Lēana'. OE pers. name + *hām*. The river-name Len is a 'back-formation' from the place-name.

Lenton Lincs. *Lofintun* c.1067, *Lavintone* 1086 (DB). Probably 'estate associated with a man called Lēofa'. OE pers. name + *-ing-* + *tūn*.

Lenwade Norfolk. *Langewade* 1199. 'Ford crossed by a lane'. OE *lanu* + *gewæd*.

Leominster Heref. & Worcs. *Leomynster* 10th cent., *Leominstre* 1086 (DB). 'Church in *Leon*'. Old Celtic name for the district (meaning 'at the streams') + OE *mynster*.

Leonard Stanley Glos., see STANLEY.

Leppington N. Yorks. *Lepinton* 1086 (DB). 'Estate associated with a man called Leppa'. OE pers. name + *-ing-* + *tūn*.

Lepton W. Yorks. *Leptone* 1086 (DB). 'Farmstead on a hill-slope'. OE **hlēp* + *tūn*.

Lesbury Northum. *Lechesbiri* c.1190. 'Fortified house of the leech or physician'. OE *lǣce* + *burh* (dative *byrig*).

Lesnewth Cornwall. *Lisniwen* (*sic*) 1086 (DB), *Lisneweth* 1201. 'New court'. Cornish **lys* + *nowydh*.

Lessingham Norfolk. *Losincham* 1086 (DB). Possibly 'homestead of the family or followers of a man called Lēofsige'. OE pers. name + *-inga-* + *hām*.

Letchworth Herts. *Leceworde* 1086. Probably 'enclosure that can be locked'. OE **lycce* + *worth*.

Letcombe Bassett & Regis Oxon. *Ledecumbe* 1086 (DB). 'Valley of a man called *Lēoda'. OE pers. name + *cumb*. Distinguishing affixes from early possession by the *Bassett* family and by the Crown.

Letheringham Suffolk. *Letheringaham* 1086 (DB). Probably 'homestead of the family or followers of a man called Lēodhere'. OE pers. name + *-inga-* + *hām*.

Letheringsett Norfolk. *Leringaseta* 1086 (DB). Probably 'dwelling or fold of the family or followers of a man called Lēodhere'. OE pers. name + *-inga-* + *(ge)set*.

Letton, probably 'leek enclosure, herb garden', OE *lēac-tūn*: **Letton** Heref. & Worcs., near Eardisley. *Letune* 1086 (DB). **Letton** Heref. & Worcs., near Walford. *Lectune* 1086 (DB).

Letwell S. Yorks. *Lettewelle* c.1150. Possibly 'spring or stream with an obstructed flow'. ME *lette* + OE *wella*.

Leven (river) Cleveland, see KIRKLEVINGTON.

Leven Humber. *Leuene* 1086 (DB). Probably originally the name of the stream here, a lost Celtic river-name possibly meaning 'smooth one'.

Levens Cumbria. *Lefuenes* 1086 (DB). Probably 'promontory of a man called Lēofa'. OE pers. name (genitive *-n*) + *næss*.

Levenshulme Gtr. Manch. *Lewyneshulm* 1246. 'Island of a man called Lēofwine'. OE pers. name + OScand. *holmr*.

Lever, Darcy & Little Gtr. Manch. *Parua Lefre* 1212, *Darcye Lever* 1590. 'Place where rushes grow'. OE *lǣfer*. Distinguishing affixes are from possession by the *D'Arcy* family, here c.1500, and from Latin *parva* 'little'.

Leverington Cambs. *Leverington* c.1130. 'Estate associated with a man called

Lēofhere'. OE pers. name + *-ing-* + *tūn*.

Leverton Lincs. *Leuretune* 1086 (DB). Probably 'farmstead where rushes grow'. OE *lǣfer* + *tūn*.

Leverton, North & South Notts. *Legretone* 1086 (DB). Probably 'farmstead on a stream called *Legre*'. Celtic river-name (of uncertain meaning) + OE *tūn*.

Levington Suffolk. *Leuentona* 1086 (DB). Probably 'farmstead of a man called Lēofa'. OE pers. name (genitive *-n*) + *tūn*.

Levisham N. Yorks. *Leuecen* (*sic*) 1086 (DB), *Leuezham* c.1230. Probably 'homestead or village of a man called Lēofgēat'. OE pers. name + *hām*.

Lew Oxon. *Hlæwe* 984, *Lewa* 1086 (DB). '(Place at) the mound or tumulus'. OE *hlǣw*.

Lewannick Cornwall. *Lanwenuc* c.1125. 'Church-site of Gwenek'. Cornish **lann* + pers. name.

Lewes E. Sussex. *Læwes* c.959, *Lewes* 1086 (DB). 'The burial-mounds or tumuli'. OE *hlǣw* in a plural form.

Lewisham Gtr. London. *Levesham* 1086 (DB). 'Homestead or village of a man called *Lēofsa'. OE pers. name + *hām*. Also referred to earlier in the phrase *Liofshema mearc* 862 'boundary of the people of Lewisham'.

Lewknor Oxon. *Leofecanoran* 990, *Levecanole* (*sic*) 1086 (DB). 'Hill-slope of a man called Lēofeca'. OE pers. name (genitive *-n*) + *ōra*.

Lewtrenchard Devon. *Lewe* 1086 (DB), *Lyu Trencharde* 1261. Originally the name of the river here, a Celtic river-name meaning 'bright one'. Manorial affix from the *Trenchard* family, here in the 13th cent.

Lexham, East & West Norfolk. *Lecesham* 1086 (DB). 'Homestead or village of the leech or physician'. OE *lǣce* + *hām*.

Leybourne Kent. *Lillanburna* 10th cent., *Leleburne* 1086 (DB). 'Stream of a man called *Lylla'. OE pers. name + *burna*.

Leyburn N. Yorks. *Leborne* 1086 (DB). OE *burna* 'stream', possibly with **hlēg* 'shelter'.

Leyland Lancs. *Lailand* 1086 (DB). 'Estate with untilled ground'. OE **lǣge* + *land*.

Leysdown on Sea Kent. *Legesdun* c.1100. Probably 'hill with a beacon-fire'. OE *lēg* + *dūn*.

Leyton Gtr. London. *Lugetune* c.1050, *Leintune* 1086 (DB). 'Farmstead on the River Lea'. Celtic river-name (possibly meaning 'light river') + OE *tūn*.

Lezant Cornwall. *Lansant* c.1125. 'Church-site of Sant'. Cornish **lann* + pers. name.

Lichfield Staffs. *Licitfelda* c.710–20. 'Open land near *Letocetum*'. OE *feld* added to a Celtic place-name meaning 'grey wood'.

Liddington Wilts. *Lidentune* 940, *Ledentone* 1086 (DB). 'Farmstead on the noisy stream'. OE **hlȳde* + *tūn*.

Lidgate Suffolk. *Litgata* 1086 (DB). '(Place at) the swing-gate'. OE *hlid-geat*.

Lidlington Beds. *Litincletone* 1086 (DB). 'Farmstead of the family or followers of a man called *Lȳtel'. OE pers. name + *-inga-* + *tūn*.

Lifton Devon. *Liwtune* c.880, *Listone* (*sic*) 1086 (DB). 'Farmstead on the River Lew'. Celtic river-name (see LEWTRENCHARD) + OE *tūn*.

Lighthorne Warwicks. *Listecorne* (*sic*) 1086 (DB), *Litthethurne* 1235. 'Light-coloured thorn-tree'. OE *lēoht* + *thyrne*.

Lilbourne Northants. *Lilleburne* 1086 (DB). 'Stream of a man called Lilla'. OE pers. name + *burna*.

Lilburn Northum. *Lilleburn* 1170. Identical in origin with the previous name.

Lilleshall Shrops. *Linleshelle* (*sic*) 1086 (DB), *Lilleshull* 1162. 'Hill of a man called Lill'. OE pers. name + *hyll*.

Lilley Herts. *Linleia* 1086 (DB). 'Woodland clearing where flax is grown'. OE *līn* + *lēah*.

Lilling, East & West N. Yorks. *Lilinge* 1086 (DB). '(Settlement of) the family or followers of a man called Lilla'. OE pers. name + *-ingas*.

Lillingstone Dayrell & Lovell Bucks. *Lillingestan* 1086 (DB), *Litlingestan Daireli* 1166. 'Boundary stone of the family or followers of a man called *Lȳtel'. OE pers. name + *-inga-* + *stān*. Manorial affixes from early possession by the *Dayrell* and *Lovell* families.

Lillington Dorset. *Lilletone* 1166. 'Estate associated with a man called *Lylla'. OE pers. name + *-ing-* + *tūn*.

Lilstock Somerset. *Lulestoch* 1086 (DB). 'Outlying farmstead or hamlet of a man called *Lylla'. OE pers. name + *stoc*.

Lim (river) Devon, Dorset, see LYME REGIS.

Limber, Great Lincs. *Lindbeorhge* c.1067, *Limberge* 1086 (DB). 'Hill where lime-trees grow'. OE *lind* + *beorg*.

Limbury Beds. *Lygeanburg* late 9th cent. 'Stronghold on the River Lea'. Celtic river-name (see LEYTON) + OE *burh* (dative *byrig*).

Limehouse Gtr. London. *Le Lymhostes* 1367. 'The lime oasts or kilns'. OE *līm* + *āst*.

Limpenhoe Norfolk. *Limpeho* 1086 (DB). 'Hill-spur of a man called *Limpa'. OE pers. name (genitive *-n*) + *hōh*.

Limpsfield Surrey. *Limenesfelde* 1086 (DB). 'Open land at *Limen*'. OE *feld* added to a Celtic place-name meaning 'elm wood'.

Linby Notts. *Lidebi* (*sic*) 1086 (DB), *Lindebi* 1163. 'Farmstead or village where lime-trees grow'. OScand. *lind* + *bý*.

Linchmere W. Sussex. *Wlenchemere* 1186. 'Pool of a man called *Wlenca'. OE pers. name + *mere*.

Lincoln Lincs. *Lindon* c.150, *Lindum colonia* late 7th cent., *Lincolia* 1086 (DB). 'Roman colony (for retired legionaries) by the pool', referring to the broad pool in the River Witham. Celtic **lindo-* + Latin *colonia*. **Lincolnshire** (OE *scīr* 'district') is first referred to in the 11th cent.

Lindal in Furness Cumbria. *Lindale* c.1220. 'Valley where lime-trees grow'. OScand. *lind* + *dalr*. For the old district name Furness, see BARROW IN FURNESS.

Lindale Cumbria. *Lindale* 1246. Identical in origin with the previous name.

Lindfield W. Sussex. *Lindefeldia* c.765. 'Open land where lime-trees grow'. OE *linden* + *feld*.

Lindisfarne Northum. *Lindisfarnae* c.700. Possibly 'island of the travellers from LINDSEY', from OE *fara* (genitive plural *-ena*) + *ēg*. Also called HOLY ISLAND.

Lindrick (old district) Notts., see CARLTON IN LINDRICK.

Lindridge Heref. & Worcs. *Lynderycge* 11th cent. 'Ridge where lime-trees grow'. OE *lind* + *hrycg*.

Lindsell Essex. *Lindesela* 1086 (DB). 'Dwelling among lime-trees'. OE *lind* + *sele*.

Lindsey Lincs. (*prouincia*) *Lindissi* c.730, *Lindesi* 1086 (DB). Ancient district name, probably a Celtic derivative of the old name for LINCOLN (*Lindon* from Celtic **lindo-* 'pool').

Lindsey Suffolk. *Lealeseia* c.1095. 'Island, or dry ground in marsh, of a man called *Lelli'. OE pers. name + *ēg*.

Linford, Great Bucks. *Linforde* 1086 (DB). Probably 'ford where maple-trees grow'. OE *hlyn* + *ford*.

Lingen Heref. & Worcs. *Lingen* 704–9, *Lingham* 1086 (DB). Probably originally the name of the brook here, perhaps a Celtic name meaning 'clear stream'.

Lingfield Surrey. *Leangafelda* 9th cent. Probably 'open land of the dwellers in the wood or clearing'. OE *lēah* + *-inga-* + *feld*.

Lingwood Norfolk. *Lingewode* 1199. 'Wood on a bank or slope'. OE *hlinc* + *wudu*.

Linkenholt Hants. *Linchehou* (*sic*) 1086 (DB), *Lynkeholte* c.1145. 'Wood by the banks or ledges'. OE *hlinc*, **hlincen* + *holt*.

Linkinhorne Cornwall. *Lankinhorn* c.1175. 'Church-site of a man called Kenhoarn'. Cornish **lann* + pers. name.

Linley Shrops., near Norbury. *Linlega* c.1150. 'Woodland clearing where flax is grown'. OE *līn* + *lēah*.

Linshiels Northum. *Lynsheles* 1292.

Probably 'shieling(s) where lime-trees grow'. OE *lind* + **scēla*.

Linslade Beds. *Hlincgelad* 966, *Lincelada* 1086 (DB). 'River-crossing near a bank'. OE *hlinc* + *gelād*.

Linstead Magna & Parva Suffolk. *Linestede* 1086 (DB). 'Place where flax is grown, or where maple-trees grow'. OE *līn* or *hlyn* + *stede*. Affixes are Latin *magna* 'great' and *parva* 'little'.

Linstock Cumbria. *Linstoc* 1212. 'Outlying farmstead or hamlet where flax is grown'. OE *līn* + *stoc*.

Linthwaite W. Yorks. *Lindthait* late 12th cent. 'Clearing where flax is grown, or where lime-trees grow'. OScand. *lín* or *lind* + *thveit*.

Linton, usually 'farmstead where flax is grown', OE *līn* + *tūn*; examples include: **Linton** Cambs. *Lintune* 1008, *Lintone* 1086 (DB). **Linton** Derbys. *Lintone* 942, *Linctune* (*sic*) 1086 (DB). **Linton** Heref. & Worcs., near Ross. *Lintune* 1086 (DB). **Linton** N. Yorks. *Lipton* (*sic*) 1086 (DB), *Linton* 12th cent. Alternatively the first element may be OE *hlynn* 'rushing stream'. **Linton** W. Yorks. *Lintone* 1086 (DB). **Linton-on-Ouse** N. Yorks. *Luctone* (*sic*) 1086 (DB), *Linton* 1176. For the river-name, see OUSEBURN.
However the following has a quite different origin: **Linton** Kent. *Lilintuna* c.1100. 'Estate associated with a man called Lill or Lilla'. OE pers. name + *-ing-* + *tūn*.

Linwood, 'lime-tree wood', OE *lind* + *wudu*: **Linwood** Hants. *Lindwude* 1200. **Linwood** Lincs., near Market Rasen. *Lindude* 1086 (DB).

Liphook Hants. *Leophok* 1364. Probably 'angle of land by the deer-leap or steep slope'. OE *hlīep* + *hōc*.

Liscard Mersey. *Lisnekarke* c.1260. 'Court at the rock'. Celtic **līs* + **en* 'the' + **carreg*.

Liskeard Cornwall. *Lys Cerruyt* c.1010, *Liscarret* 1086 (DB). Probably 'court of a man called Kerwyd'. Cornish **lys* + pers. name.

Liss Hants. *Lis* 1086 (DB). Celtic **līs* 'a court, chief house in a district'.

Lissett Humber. *Lessete* 1086 (DB). Probably 'dwelling near the pasture-land'. OE *lǣs* + (*ge*)*set*.

Lissington Lincs. *Lessintone* 1086 (DB). Probably 'estate associated with a man called Lēofsige'. OE pers. name + *-ing-* + *tūn*.

Litcham Norfolk. *Licham* 1086 (DB). Possibly 'homestead or village with an enclosure'. OE **lycce* + *hām*.

Litchborough Northants. *Liceberge* 1086 (DB). Probably 'hill with an enclosure'. OE **lycce* + *beorg*.

Litchfield Hants. *Liveselle* (*sic*) 1086 (DB), *Lieueselva* 1168. Possibly 'shelf of land with a shelter'. OE **hlīf* + *scelf* or *scylf*.

Litherland Mersey. *Liderlant* 1086 (DB). 'Cultivated land on a slope'. OScand. *hlíth* (genitive *-ar*) + *land*.

Litlington Cambs. *Litlingeton* 1183, *Lidlingtone* 1086 (DB). 'Farmstead of the family or followers of a man called *Lȳtel'. OE pers. name + *-inga-* + *tūn*.

Litlington E. Sussex. *Litlinton* 1191. 'Little farmstead' from OE *lȳtel* (dative *-an*) + *tūn*, or 'farmstead associated with a man called *Lȳtel(a)' from OE pers. name + *-ing-* + *tūn*.

Little as affix, see main name, e.g. for **Little Abington** (Cambs.) see ABINGTON.

Littleborough, 'little fort or stronghold', OE *lȳtel* + *burh*: **Littleborough** Gtr. Manch. *Littlebrough* 1577. **Littleborough** Notts. *Litelburg* 1086 (DB).

Littlebourne Kent. *Littelburne* 696, *Liteburne* 1086 (DB). 'Little estate on the *Bourn* (the earlier name for the Little Stour river)'. OE *lȳtel* + *burna* 'stream'.

Littlebredy Dorset, see BREDY.

Littlebury Essex. *Lytlanbyrig* c.1000, *Litelbyria* 1086 (DB). 'Little fort or stronghold'. OE *lȳtel* + *burh* (dative *byrig*).

Littledean Glos. *Dene* 1086 (DB), *Parva Dene* 1220. OE *denu* 'valley', with later affix *little* (Latin *parva*) to distinguish this place from MITCHELDEAN.

Littleham Devon, near Exmouth. *Lytlanhamme* 1042, *Liteham* 1086 (DB).

'Little enclosure or river-meadow'. OE *lȳtel* + *hamm*.

Littlehampton W. Sussex. *Hantone* 1086 (DB), *Lyttelhampton* 1482. OE *hām-tūn* 'home farm, homestead' with the later addition of *little* perhaps to distinguish it from SOUTHAMPTON.

Littlehempston Devon. *Hamistone* 1086 (DB), *Parua Hæmeston* 1176. 'Farmstead of a man called *Hǣme or Hemme'. OE pers. name + *tūn*. Affix *little* (Latin *parva*) to distinguish this place from BROADHEMPSTON.

Littlehoughton Northum. *Houcton Parva* 1242. 'Farmstead on or near a ridge or hill-spur'. OE *hōh* + *tūn*. Affix *little* (Latin *parva*) to distinguish this place from LONGHOUGHTON.

Littlemore Oxon. *Luthlemoria* c.1130. 'Little marsh'. OE *lȳtel* + *mōr*.

Littleover Derbys. *Parva Ufre* 1086 (DB). '(Place at) the ridge'. OE **ofer* with the affix *little* (Latin *parva*) to distinguish this place from MICKLEOVER.

Littleport Cambs. *Litelport* 1086 (DB). 'Little (market) town'. OE *lȳtel* + *port*.

Littleton, 'little farmstead or estate', OE *lȳtel* + *tūn*; examples include: **Littleton** Ches. *Litelton* 1435. Earlier *Parva Cristentona* c.1125, 'the smaller part of CHRISTLETON'. **Littleton** Hants., near Winchester. *Lithleton* 1285. **Littleton** Somerset. *Liteltone* 1086 (DB). **Littleton Drew** Wilts. *Liteltone* 1086 (DB), *Littleton Dru* 1311. Manorial affix from the *Driwe* family, here in the 13th cent. **Littleton, High** Avon. *Liteltone* 1086 (DB), *Heghelitleton* 1324. Affix is OE *hēah* 'high'. **Littleton, Middle, North, & South** Heref. & Worcs. *Litletona* 709, *Liteltune* 1086 (DB). **Littleton Pannell** Wilts. *Liteltone* 1086 (DB), *Lutleton Paynel* 1317. Manorial affix from the *Paynel* family, here in the 13th cent. **Littleton upon Severn** Avon. *Lytletun* 986, *Liteltone* 1086 (DB). For the river-name, see SEVERN.

Littlewick Green Berks. *Lidlegewik* c.1060. 'Farm by the woodland clearing with a gate or on a slope'. OE *hlid* or **hlid* + *lēah* + *wīc*.

Littleworth Oxon. *Wyrthæ* c.971, *Ordia* (*sic*) 1086 (DB), *Lytleworth* 1284. OE *worth* 'enclosure', later with the affix *lȳtel* 'little' to distinguish this place from LONGWORTH.

Litton Derbys. *Litun* 1086 (DB). Possibly 'farmstead on a slope'. OE *hlith* + *tūn*.

Litton N. Yorks. *Litone* 1086 (DB). Probably identical in origin with the previous name.

Litton Somerset. *Hlytton* c.1060, *Litune* 1086 (DB). Possibly 'farmstead at a gate or by a slope'. OE *hlid* or **hlid* + *tūn*.

Litton Cheney Dorset. *Lideton* 1204. Probably 'farmstead by a noisy stream'. OE **hlȳde* + *tūn*. Manorial affix from the *Cheyne* family, here in the 14th cent.

Livermere, Great Suffolk. *Leuuremer* c.1050, *Liuermera* 1086 (DB). 'Liver-shaped pool, or pool with thick or muddy water'. OE *lifer* + *mere*.

Liverpool Mersey. *Liuerpul* c.1190. 'Pool or creek with thick or muddy water'. OE *lifer* + *pōl*.

Liversedge W. Yorks. *Livresec* 1086 (DB). Probably 'edge or ridge of a man called Lēofhere'. OE pers. name + *ecg*.

Liverton Cleveland. *Liuretun* 1086 (DB). 'Farmstead of a man called Lēofhere, or on a stream with thick or muddy water'. OE pers. name or *lifer* + *tūn*.

Lizard Cornwall. *Lisart* 1086 (DB). 'Court on a height'. Cornish **lys* + **ardh*.

Llandinabo Heref. & Worcs. *Lann Hunapui* c.1130. 'Church-site of a man called Iunapui'. Welsh *llan* + pers. name.

Llangarron Heref. & Worcs. *Lann Garan* c.1130. 'Church-site on the River Garron'. Welsh *llan* + Celtic river-name meaning 'crane stream'.

Llangrove Heref. & Worcs. *Longe grove* 1372. 'Long grove or copse'. OE *lang* + *grāf*.

Llanrothal Heref. & Worcs. *Lann Ridol* c.1130. Welsh *llan* 'church-site', probably with a pers. name.

Llanvair Waterdine Shrops. *Watredene* 1086 (DB), *Thlanveyr* 1284. 'St Mary's church in the river valley'. Welsh *llan* + saint's name, with the addition from OE *wæter* + *denu*.

Llanwarne Heref. & Worcs. *Ladgvern* (*sic*) 1086 (DB), *Lann Guern* c.1130.

'Church by the alder grove'. Welsh *llan* + *gwern*.

Llanymynech Shrops. *Llanemeneych* 1254. 'Church-site of the monks'. Welsh *llan* + *mynach*.

Load, Long Somerset. *La Lade* 1285. 'The watercourse or drainage channel'. OE *lād*.

Lockeridge Wilts. *Locherige* 1086 (DB). Possibly 'ridge with folds or enclosures'. OE *loc(a)* + *hrycg*.

Lockerley Hants. *Locherlega* 1086 (DB). Probably 'woodland clearing of a keeper or shepherd'. OE **lōcere* + *lēah*.

Locking Avon. *Lockin* 1212. 'Place associated with a man called Locc', OE pers. name + *-ing*, or from an OE **locing* 'fold or enclosure'.

Lockington Humber. *Locheton* 1086 (DB). 'Estate associated with a man called *Loca'. OE pers. name + *-ing-* + *tūn*. Alternatively the first element may be an OE **locing* 'fold, enclosure'.

Lockton N. Yorks. *Lochetun* 1086 (DB). Probably 'farmstead of a man called *Loca', OE pers. name + *tūn*. Alternatively the first element may be OE *loca* 'enclosure'.

Loddington Leics. *Ludintone* 1086 (DB). Probably 'estate associated with a man called Luda'. OE pers. name + *-ing-* + *tūn*.

Loddington Northants. *Lodintone* 1086 (DB). 'Estate associated with a man called Lod(a)'. OE pers. name + *-ing-* + *tūn*.

Loddiswell Devon. *Lodeswille* 1086 (DB). 'Spring or stream of a man called *Lod'. OE pers. name + *wella*.

Loddon (river) Berks., Hants., see SHERFIELD.

Loddon Norfolk. *Lodne* 1043, *Lotna* 1086 (DB). Originally a Celtic river-name (possibly meaning 'muddy stream'), an old name for the River Chet.

Lode Cambs. *Lada* 12th cent. OE *lād* 'watercourse or drainage channel'.

Loders Dorset. *Lodre(s)* 1086 (DB). Probably originally a Celtic river-name (meaning 'pool stream'), an old name for the River Asker.

Lodsworth W. Sussex. *Lodesorde* 1086 (DB). 'Enclosure of a man called *Lod'. OE pers. name + *worth*.

Lofthouse W. Yorks., near Leeds. *Loftose* 1086 (DB). 'House(s) with a loft or upper floor'. OScand. *loft-hús* in a dative plural form.

Loftus Cleveland. *Loctehusum* 1086 (DB). Identical in origin with the previous name.

Lolworth Cambs. *Lollesworthe* 1034, *Lolesuuorde* 1086 (DB). 'Enclosure of a man called *Loll or Lull'. OE pers. name + *worth*.

Loman (river) Devon, see UPLOWMAN.

Londesborough Humber. *Lodenesburg* 1086 (DB). 'Stronghold of a man called Lothinn'. OScand. pers. name + OE *burh*.

London *Londinium c.*115. An ancient name often explained as 'place belonging to a man called Londinos', from a Celtic pers. name with adjectival suffix, but now considered obscure in origin and meaning.

London Colney Herts., see COLNEY.

Londonthorpe Lincs. *Lundertorp* 1086 (DB). 'Outlying farmstead or hamlet by a grove'. OScand. *lundr* (genitive *lundar*) + *thorp*.

Long as affix, see under main name, e.g. for **Long Ashton** (Avon) see ASHTON.

Longbenton Tyne & Wear. *Bentune c.*1190, *Magna Beneton* 1256. 'Farmstead where bent-grass grows, or where beans are grown'. OE *beonet* or *bēan* + *tūn*, with later affix *long*.

Longborough Glos. *Langeberge* 1086 (DB). 'Long hill or barrow'. OE *lang* + *beorg*.

Longbridge W. Mids., a self-explanatory name of recent origin.

Longbridge Deverill Wilts. *Devrel* 1086 (DB), *Deverill Langebrigge* 1316. 'Estate on the River *Deverill* with the long bridge'. OE *lang* + *brycg* with Celtic river-name (for which see BRIXTON DEVERILL).

Longburton Dorset. *Burton* 1244, *Langebourton* 1460. 'Fortified farm', or 'farm near a fortification'. OE *burh-tūn*. Affix is OE *lang* referring to the length of the village.

Longcot Oxon. *Cotes* 1233, *Longcote* 1332.

'The cottages', from OE *cot*, with the later addition of *lang* 'long'.

Longden Shrops. *Langedune* 1086 (DB). 'Long hill or down'. OE *lang* + *dūn*.

Longdendale Derbys., Gtr. Manch., see MOTTRAM.

Longdon, 'long hill or down', OE *lang* + *dūn*: **Longdon** Heref. & Worcs. *Longandune* 969, *Longedun* 1086 (DB). **Longdon** Staffs. *Langandune* 1002. **Longdon upon Tern** Shrops. *Languedune* 1086 (DB). For the river-name, see EATON UPON TERN.

Longfield Kent. *Langafelda* 10th cent., *Langafel* 1086 (DB). 'Long stretch of open country'. OE *lang* + *feld*.

Longford, 'long ford', OE *lang* + *ford*: **Longford** Derbys. *Langeford* 1197. **Longford** Glos. *Langeford* 1107. **Longford** Shrops., near Market Drayton. *Langeford* 13th cent. **Longford** Shrops., near Newport. *Langanford* 1002, *Langeford* 1086 (DB).

Longham Norfolk. *Lawingham* 1086 (DB). Probably 'homestead of the family or followers of a man called *Lāwa'. OE pers. name + *-inga-* + *hām*.

Longhirst Northum. *Langherst* 1200. 'Long wooded hill'. OE *lang* + *hyrst*.

Longhope Glos. *Hope* 1086 (DB), *Langehope* 1248. 'The valley'. OE *hop* with the later addition of *lang* 'long'.

Longhorsley Northum. *Horsleg* 1196. 'Woodland clearing where horses are kept'. OE *hors* + *lēah*, with the later affix *long*.

Longhoughton Northum. *Houcton Magna* 1242. 'Farmstead on or near a ridge or hill-spur'. OE *hōh* + *tūn*. Affix *long* (earlier Latin *magna* 'great') to distinguish this place from LITTLEHOUGHTON.

Longleat Wilts. *Langelete* 1235. 'Long stream or channel'. OE *lang* + (*ge*)*lǣt*.

Longney Glos. *Longanege* 972, *Langenei* 1086 (DB). 'Long island'. OE *lang* (dative *-an*) + *ēg*.

Longnor Shrops. *Longenalra* c.1170. 'Tall alder-tree', or 'long alder-copse'. OE *lang* (dative *-an*) + *alor*.

Longnor Staffs., near Buxton. *Langenoure* 1227. 'Long ridge'. OE *lang* (dative *-an*) + **ofer*.

Longparish Hants. *Langeparisshe* 1389. Self-explanatory. Earlier called Middleton, *Middeltune* 1086 (DB), 'middle farmstead or estate', from OE *middel* + *tūn*.

Longridge Lancs. *Langrig* 1246. 'Long ridge'. OE *lang* + *hrycg*.

Longsdon Staffs. *Longesdon* 1242. Probably 'hill called *Lang* ('the long one')'. OE *lang* + *dūn*.

Longstock Hants. *Stoce* 982, *Stoches* 1086 (DB), *Langestok* 1233. OE *stoc* 'outlying farm or hamlet', with the later addition of *lang* 'long'.

Longstone, Great & Little Derbys. *Langesdune* 1086 (DB). Probably 'hill called *Lang* ('the long one')'. OE *lang* + *dūn*.

Longton, Longtown, 'long farmstead or estate'. OE *lang* + *tūn*: **Longton** Lancs. *Langetuna* c.1155. **Longton** Staffs. *Longeton* 1212. **Longtown** Cumbria. *Longeton* 1267. **Longtown** Heref. & Worcs. *Longa villa* 1540, earlier *Ewias* 1086 (DB), *Ewyas Lascy* 13th cent. (manorial affix from Roger *de Laci*, owner in 1086, see EWYAS HAROLD).

Longville in the Dale Shrops. *Longefewd* 1255. 'Long stretch of open country'. OE *lang* + *feld*, with later affix from *dæl* 'valley'.

Longwitton Northum. *Wttun* 1236, *Langwotton* 1340. 'Farmstead in or by a wood'. OE *wudu* + *tūn*, with later affix *lang* 'long'.

Longworth Oxon. *Wurthe* 958, *Langewrth* 1284. OE *worth* or *wyrth* 'enclosure', with the later addition of *lang* 'long'.

Looe, East & West Cornwall. *Loo* c.1220. Cornish **logh* 'pool, inlet'.

Loose Kent. *Hlose* 11th cent. '(Place at) the pig-sty'. OE *hlōse*.

Loosley Row Bucks. *Losle* 1241. 'Woodland clearing with a pig-sty'. OE *hlōse* + *lēah*.

Lopen Somerset. *Lopen(e)* 1086 (DB). Celtic **penn* 'hill' or OE *penn* 'fold, enclosure' with an uncertain first element.

Lopham, North & South Norfolk. *Lopham* 1086 (DB). 'Homestead or village of a man called *Loppa'. OE pers. name + *hām*.

Loppington Shrops. *Lopitone* 1086 (DB). 'Estate associated with a man called *Loppa'. OE pers. name + *-ing-* + *tūn*.

Lorton, High & Low Cumbria. *Loretona* c.1150. Probably 'farmstead on a stream called **Hlóra*'. OScand. river-name (meaning 'roaring one') + OE *tūn*.

Loscoe Derbys. *Loscowe* 1277. 'Wood with a lofthouse'. OScand. *loft* + *skógr*.

Lostock, 'outlying farmstead with a pig-sty', OE *hlōse* + *stoc*: **Lostock** Gtr. Manch., near Bolton. *Lostok* 1205. **Lostock Gralam** Ches. *Lostoch* c.1100, *le Lostoke Graliam* 1288. Manorial affix from a 12th cent. owner called *Gralam*.

Lostwithiel Cornwall. *Lostwetell* 1194. 'Tail-end of the woodland'. Cornish *lost* + *gwydhyel*.

Loudwater Bucks. *La Ludewatere* 1241. Originally a river-name, 'the noisy stream', OE *hlūd* + *wæter*.

Loughborough Leics. *Lucteburne* (*sic*) 1086 (DB), *Lucteburga* 12th cent. 'Fortified house of a man called Luhhede'. OE pers. name + *burh*.

Loughton Bucks. *Lochintone* 1086 (DB). 'Estate associated with a man called Luhha'. OE pers. name (+ *-ing-*) + *tūn*.

Loughton Essex. *Lukintone* 1062, *Lochetuna* 1086 (DB). 'Estate associated with a man called Luca'. OE pers. name (+ *-ing-*) + *tūn*.

Loughton Shrops. *Luchton* c.1138. Possibly 'estate of a man called Luhha'. OE pers. name + *tūn*.

Lound, 'small wood or grove', OScand. *lundr*: **Lound** Lincs. *Lund* 1086 (DB). **Lound** Notts. *Lund* 1086 (DB). **Lound** Suffolk. *Lunda* 1086 (DB). **Lound, East** Humber. *Lund* 1086 (DB), *Estlound* 1370. Addition is OE *ēast* 'east'.

Louth Lincs. *Lude* 1086 (DB). Named from the River Lud, OE **Hlūde* 'the loud one, the noisy stream'.

Loversall S. Yorks. *Loureshale* 1086 (DB). 'Nook of a man called Lēofhere'. OE pers. name + *halh*.

Lovington Somerset. *Lovintune* 1086 (DB). 'Estate associated with a man called Lufa'. OE pers. name + *-ing-* + *tūn*.

Low as affix, see main name, e.g. for **Low Ackworth** (W. Yorks.) see ACKWORTH.

Lowdham Notts. *Ludham* 1086 (DB). 'Homestead or village of a man called *Hlūda'. OE pers. name + *hām*.

Lower as affix, see main name, e.g. for **Lower Aisholt** (Somerset) see AISHOLT.

Lowesby Leics. *Glowesbi* (*sic*) 1086 (DB), *Lousebia* c.1125. Possibly 'farmstead or village of a man called Lauss or Lausi'. OScand. pers. name + *bý*.

Lowestoft Suffolk. *Lothu Wistoft* 1086 (DB). 'Homestead of a man called Hlothvér'. OScand. pers. name + *toft*.

Loweswater Cumbria. *Lousewater* c.1160. Named from the lake, 'leafy lake', from OScand. *lauf* + *sǽr* with the addition of OE *wæter* 'expanse of water'.

Lowick Cumbria. *Lofwik* 1202. Probably 'leafy creek or river-bend'. OScand. *lauf* + *vík*.

Lowick Northants. *Luhwic* 1086 (DB). 'Dwelling or (dairy) farm of a man called Luhha or *Luffa'. OE pers. name + *wīc*.

Lowick Northum. *Lowich* 1181. 'Dwelling or (dairy) farm on the River Low'. River-name (probably from OE *luh* 'pool') + OE *wīc*.

Lowther Cumbria. *Lauder* c.1175. Named from the River Lowther, possibly an OScand. river-name meaning 'foamy river', OScand. *lauthr* + *á*, but perhaps Celtic in origin.

Lowthorpe Humber. *Log(h)etorp* 1086 (DB). 'Outlying farmstead or hamlet of a man called Lági or Logi'. OScand. pers. name + *thorp*.

Lowton Gtr. Manch. *Lauton* 1202. 'Farmstead by a mound or hill'. OE *hlāw* + *tūn*.

Loxbeare Devon. *Lochesbere* 1086 (DB). 'Wood or grove of a man called Locc'. OE pers. name + *bearu*.

Loxhore Devon. *Lochesore* 1086 (DB). 'Hill-slope of a man called Locc'. OE pers. name + *ōra*.

Loxley Warwicks. *Locheslei* 1086 (DB).

'Woodland clearing of a man called Locc'. OE pers. name + *lēah*.

Loxton Avon. *Lochestone* 1086 (DB). 'Farmstead on the stream called Lox Yeo'. Celtic river-name (of uncertain meaning) + OE *ēa* + *tūn*.

Lubenham Leics. *Lubanham, Lobenho* 1086 (DB). 'Hill-spur(s) of a man called *Lubba'. OE pers. name (genitive *-n*) + *hōh* (dative plural *hōum*).

Luccombe, probably 'valley of a man called Lufa', OE pers. name + *cumb*: **Luccombe** Somerset. *Locumbe* 1086 (DB). **Luccombe Village** I. of Wight. *Lovecumbe* 1086 (DB).

Lucker Northum. *Lucre* 1170. Probably 'the hollows', OScand. *lúka* in a plural form *lúkur*.

Luckington Wilts. *Lochintone* 1086 (DB). 'Estate associated with a man called *Luca'. OE pers. name + *-ing-* + *tūn*.

Lucton Heref. & Worcs. *Lugton* 1185. 'Farmstead on the River Lugg'. Celtic river-name (see LUGWARDINE) + OE *tūn*.

Ludborough Lincs. *Ludeburg* 1086 (DB). 'Stronghold on the River Lud'. OE river-name **Hlūde* 'noisy stream' + OE *burh*.

Luddesdown Kent. *Hludesduna* 10th cent., *Ledesdune* 1086 (DB). 'Hill of a man called *Hlūd'. OE pers. name + *dūn*.

Luddington Humber. *Ludintone* 1086 (DB). 'Estate associated with a man called Luda'. OE pers. name + *-ing-* + *tūn*.

Ludford Shrops. *Ludeford* 1086 (DB). 'Ford near a rapid'. OE **hlūde* + *ford*.

Ludgershall, 'nook with a trapping-spear', OE **lūte-gār* + *halh*: **Ludgershall** Bucks. *Lotegarser* (*sic*) 1086 (DB), *Lutegareshale* 1164. **Ludgershall** Wilts. *Lutegaresheale* 1015, *Litlegarselę* (*sic*) 1086 (DB).

Ludgvan Cornwall. *Luduhan* 1086 (DB). Possibly 'place of ashes, burnt place'. Cornish *lusow, ludw* + suffix.

Ludham Norfolk. *Ludham* 1021–4, 1086 (DB). 'Homestead or village of a man called Luda'. OE pers. name + *hām*.

Ludlow Shrops. *Ludelaue* 1138. 'Hill or tumulus by a rapid'. OE **hlūde* + *hlāw*.

Ludwell Wilts. *Luddewell* early 12th cent. 'Loud spring or stream'. OE *hlūd* + *wella*.

Ludworth Durham. *Ludeuurthe* 12th cent. 'Enclosure of a man called Luda'. OE pers. name + *worth*.

Luffenham, North & South Leics. *Lufenham* 1086 (DB). 'Homestead or village of a man called *Luffa'. OE pers. name + *hām*.

Luffincott Devon. *Lughyngecot* 1242. 'Cottage(s) of the family or followers of a man called Luhha'. OE pers. name + *-inga-* + *cot*.

Lugwardine Heref. & Worcs. *Lucvordine* 1086 (DB). 'Enclosure on the River Lugg'. Celtic river-name (meaning 'bright stream') + OE *worthign*.

Lullington, 'estate associated with a man called Lulla', OE pers. name + *-ing-* + *tūn*: **Lullington** Derbys. *Lullitune* 1086 (DB). **Lullington** Somerset. *Loligtone* 1086 (DB).

Lulsley Heref. & Worcs. *Lulleseia* 12th cent. 'Island, or dry ground in marsh, of a man called Lull'. OE pers. name + *ēg*.

Lulworth, East & West Dorset. *Lulvorde* 1086 (DB). 'Enclosure of a man called Lulla'. OE pers. name + *worth*.

Lumb Lancs. *Le Lome* 1534. 'The pool'. OE **lumm*.

Lumby N. Yorks. *Lundby* 963. 'Farmstead in or near a grove'. OScand. *lundr* + *bý*.

Lumley, Great Durham. *Lummalea* c.1050. 'Woodland clearing by the pools.' OE **lumm* + *lēah*.

Lund, 'small wood or grove', OScand. *lundr*: **Lund** Humber. *Lont* 1086 (DB). **Lund** N. Yorks., near Barlby. *Lund* 1066–9, *Lont* 1086 (DB).

Lune (river) Lancs., Cumbria, see LANCASTER.

Lunt Mersey. *Lund* 1251. Identical in origin with LUND.

Luppitt Devon. *Lovapit* 1086 (DB). 'Pit or hollow of a man called *Lufa'. OE pers. name + *pytt*.

Lupton Cumbria. *Lupetun* 1086 (DB). 'Farmstead of a man called *Hluppa'. OE pers. name + *tūn*.

Lurgashall W. Sussex. *Lutegareshale* 12th cent. 'Nook with a trapping-spear'. OE **lūte-gār* + *halh*.

Lusby Lincs. *Luzebi* 1086 (DB). 'Farmstead or village of a man called Lútr'. OScand. pers. name + *bý*.

Lustleigh Devon. *Leuestelegh* 1242. Probably 'woodland clearing of a man called *Lēofgiest'. OE pers. name + *lēah*.

Luston Heref. & Worcs. *Lustone* 1086 (DB). Probably 'insignificant, or louse-infested, farmstead'. OE *lūs* + *tūn*.

Luton Beds. *Lygetun* 792, *Loitone* 1086 (DB). 'Farmstead on the River Lea'. Celtic river-name (see LEYTON) + OE *tūn*.

Luton Devon, near Ideford. *Leueton* 1238. Possibly 'farmstead of a woman called Lēofgifu'. OE pers. name + *tūn*.

Luton Kent. *Leueton* 1240. 'Farmstead of a man called Lēofa'. OE pers. name + *tūn*.

Lutterworth Leics. *Lutresurde* 1086 (DB). Possibly 'enclosure on a stream called **Hlūtre* (the clear or pure one)'. OE river-name (perhaps an earlier name for the River Swift) + *worth*.

Lutton Lincs. *Luctone* 1086 (DB). 'Farmstead by a pool'. OE *luh* + *tūn*.

Lutton Northants. *Lundingtun* (*sic*) *c*.970, *Luditone* 1086 (DB). 'Estate associated with a man called Luda'. OE pers. name + *-ing-* + *tūn*.

Lutton, East & West N. Yorks. *Ludton* 1086 (DB). Probably 'estate of a man called Luda'. OE pers. name + *tūn*.

Luxborough Somerset. *Lolochesberie* 1086 (DB). 'Stronghold, or hill, of a man called Lulluc'. OE pers. name + *burh* or *beorg*.

Luxulyan Cornwall. *Luxulian* 1282. 'Chapel of Sulyen'. Cornish **log* + pers. name.

Lydbrook, Upper Glos. *Luidebroc* 1224. 'Brook called **Hlȳde* or the loud one'. OE river-name + *brōc*.

Lydbury North Shrops. *Lideberie* 1086 (DB). Possibly 'fortified house with gates or by slopes'. OE *hlid* or **hlid* + *burh* (dative *byrig*).

Lydd Kent. *Hlidum* 774. Probably '(place at) the gates or the slopes'. OE *hlid* or **hlid* in a dative plural form.

Lydden (river) Dorset, see LYDLINCH.

Lydden Kent, near Dover. *Hleodaena* *c*.1100. Probably 'valley with a shelter, or sheltered valley'. OE *hlēo* + *denu*.

Lyde Heref. & Worcs. *Lude* 1086 (DB). Named from the stream here, OE **Hlȳde* 'the loud one'.

Lydeard St Lawrence & Bishop's Lydeard Somerset. *Lidegeard* 854, *Lidiard*, *Lediart* 1086 (DB). Celtic **garth* 'ridge' with an uncertain first element, possibly **lęd* 'grey'. Distinguishing affixes from the dedication of the church and from early possession by the Bishop of Wells.

Lydford Devon. *Hlydanforda* *c*.1000, *Lideforda* 1086 (DB). 'Ford over the River Lyd'. OE river-name (from **hlȳde* 'noisy stream') + *ford*.

Lydford Somerset. *Lideford* 1086 (DB). 'Ford over the noisy stream'. OE **hlȳde* + *ford*.

Lydham Shrops. *Lidum* 1086 (DB). Possibly '(place at) the gates or the slopes'. OE *hlid* or **hlid* in a dative plural form.

Lydiard Millicent Wilts. *Lidgeard* 901, *Lidiarde* 1086 (DB), *Lidiard Milisent* 1275. Identical in origin with LYDEARD. Manorial affix from a woman called *Millisent*, here in the late 12th cent.

Lydiate Lancs. *Leiate* (*sic*) 1086 (DB), *Liddigate* 1202. '(Place at) the swing-gate'. OE *hlid-geat*.

Lydlinch Dorset. *Lidelinz* 1182. 'Ridge by, or bank of, the River Lydden'. Celtic river-name (probably meaning 'the broad one') + OE *hlinc*.

Lydney Glos. *Lideneg* *c*.853, *Ledenei* 1086 (DB). 'Island or river-meadow of the sailor, or of a man called *Lida'. OE *lida* or pers. name (genitive *-n*) + *ēg*.

Lye, Lower Heref. & Worcs. *Lege* 1086 (DB). '(Place at) the wood or woodland clearing'. OE *lēah*.

Lyford Oxon. *Linforda* 944, *Linford* 1086 (DB). 'Ford where flax grows'. OE *līn* + *ford*.

Lyme (old district and forest) Lancs., Ches., Staffs., see ASHTON-UNDER-LYNE, NEWCASTLE UNDER LYME.

Lyme Regis Dorset. *Lim* 774, *Lime* 1086 (DB), *Lyme Regis* 1285. Named from the River Lim, a Celtic river-name meaning simply 'stream'. Affix is Latin *regis* 'of the king'.

Lyminge Kent. *Liminge* 689, *Leminges* 1086 (DB). 'District around LYMPNE'. Ancient Celtic place-name + OE **gē*.

Lymington Hants. *Lentune* (*sic*) 1086 (DB), *Limington* 1186. Probably 'farmstead on a river called *Limen*'. Lost Celtic river-name (meaning 'elm river' or 'marshy river') + OE *tūn*.

Lyminster W. Sussex. *Lullyngmynster* c.880, *Lolinminstre* 1086 (DB). 'Monastery or large church associated with a man called Lulla'. OE pers. name + *-ing-* + *mynster*.

Lymm Ches. *Lime* 1086 (DB). 'The noisy stream or torrent'. OE *hlimme*.

Lympne Kent. *Lemanis* 4th cent. 'Elm-wood place', or 'marshy place'. Celtic place-name related to the River *Limen* (the old name for the East Rother), a Celtic river-name meaning 'elm-wood river' or 'marshy river'.

Lympsham Somerset. *Limpelesham* 1189. OE *hām* 'homestead' or *hamm* 'enclosure' with an uncertain first element, possibly an OE pers. name **Limpel*.

Lympstone Devon. *Levestone* (*sic*) 1086 (DB), *Leveneston* 1238. 'Farmstead of a man called Lēofwine'. OE pers. name + *tūn*.

Lyndhurst Hants. *Linhest* 1086 (DB). 'Wooded hill growing with lime-trees'. OE *lind* + *hyrst*.

Lyndon Leics. *Lindon* 1167. 'Hill where flax is grown, or where lime-trees grow'. OE *līn* or *lind* + *dūn*.

Lyne (river) Cumbria, see KIRKLINTON.

Lyne Surrey, near Chertsey. *La Linde* 1208. 'The lime-tree'. OE *lind*.

Lyneham, 'homestead or enclosure where flax is grown', OE *līn* + *hām* or *hamm*: **Lyneham** Oxon. *Lineham* 1086 (DB). **Lyneham** Wilts. *Linham* 1224.

Lynemouth Northum. *Lynmuth* 1342. 'Mouth of the River Lyne'. Celtic river-name (meaning 'stream') + OE *mūtha*.

Lyng Norfolk. *Ling* 1086 (DB). Probably OE *hlinc* 'bank or ridge'.

Lyng Somerset. *Lengen* c.910, *Lege* (*sic*) 1086 (DB). Possibly OE **hlenc* 'hill-slope'.

Lynmouth Devon. *Lymmouth* 1330. 'Mouth of the River Lyn'. OE river-name (from *hlynn* 'torrent') + *mūtha*.

Lynn, King's & West Norfolk. *Lena*, *Lun* 1086 (DB). 'The pool'. Celtic **linn*. Affix *King's* dates from the 16th cent.

Lynton Devon. *Lintone* 1086 (DB). 'Farmstead on the River Lyn'. OE river-name (see LYNMOUTH) + *tūn*.

Lyonshall Heref. & Worcs. *Lenehalle* 1086 (DB). 'Nook of land in *Leon*'. Celtic district name (meaning 'at the streams') + OE *halh*.

Lytchett Matravers & Minster Dorset. *Lichet* 1086 (DB), *Lichet Mautrauers* 1280, *Licheminster* 1244. 'Grey wood'. Celtic **lēd* + **cēd*. Distinguishing affixes from the *Maltrauers* family, here in 1086, and from OE *mynster* 'large church'.

Lytham St Anne's Lancs. *Lidun* 1086 (DB). '(Place at) the slopes or dunes'. OE *hlith* in a dative plural form *hlithum*. Affix from the dedication of the church.

Lythe N. Yorks. *Lid* 1086 (DB). 'The slope'. OScand. *hlíth*.

M

Mabe Burnthouse Cornwall. *Lavabe* 1524, *Mape* 1549. 'Church-site of Mab'. Cornish **lann* + pers. name. Addition *Burnthouse*, no doubt alluding to a fire here, is first found in early 19th cent.

Mablethorpe Lincs. *Malbertorp* 1086 (DB). 'Outlying farmstead of a man called Malbert'. OGerman pers. name + OScand. *thorp*.

Macclesfield Ches. *Maclesfeld* 1086 (DB). Probably 'open country of a man called *Maccel'. OE pers. name + *feld*.

Mackworth Derbys. *Macheuorde* 1086 (DB). 'Enclosure of a man called *Macca'. OE pers. name + *worth*.

Madehurst W. Sussex. *Medliers* 1188, *Medhurst* 1255. Possibly 'wooded hill near meadow-land', OE *mǣd* + *hyrst*. Alternatively the first element may be OE *mæthel* 'assembly, meeting'.

Madeley, 'woodland clearing of a man called *Māda', OE pers. name + *lēah*: **Madeley** Shrops. *Madelie* 1086 (DB). **Madeley** Staffs., near Newcastle. *Madanlieg* 975, *Madelie* 1086 (DB).

Madingley Cambs. *Madingelei* 1086 (DB). 'Woodland clearing of the family or followers of a man called *Māda'. OE pers. name + *-inga-* + *lēah*.

Madresfield Heref. & Worcs. *Madresfeld* c.1086, *Metheresfeld* 1192. 'Open land of the mower or of a man called Mǣthhere'. OE *mǣthere* or pers. name + *feld*.

Madron Cornwall. '(Church of) *Sanctus Madernus*' 1203. From the patron saint of the church.

Maer Staffs. *Mere* 1086 (DB). '(Place at) the pool'. OE *mere*.

Maesbrook Shrops. *Meresbroc* 1086 (DB). Probably 'brook near the boundary'. OE *mǣre* + *brōc*. The reference in this and the next name may be to Offa's Dyke.

Maesbury Shrops. *Meresberie* 1086 (DB). 'Fortified place near the boundary'. OE *mǣre* + *burh* (dative *byrig*).

Magdalen Laver Essex, see LAVER.

Maghull Mersey. *Magele (sic)* 1086 (DB), *Maghal* 1219. Probably 'nook of land where mayweed grows'. OE *mægthe* + *halh*.

Maiden as affix, see main name, e.g. for **Maiden Bradley** (Wilts.) see BRADLEY.

Maidenhead Berks. *Maidenhee* 1202. 'Landing-place of the maidens'. OE *mægden* + *hȳth*.

Maidenwell Lincs. *Welle* 1086 (DB), *Maidenwell* 1212. Originally '(place at) the spring or stream', from OE *wella*, with the later addition of *mægden* 'maiden'.

Maidford Northants. *Merdeford (sic)* 1086 (DB), *Maideneford* 1166. 'Ford of the maidens, i.e. where they gathered'. OE *mægden* + *ford*.

Maids Moreton Bucks., see MORETON.

Maidstone Kent. *Mægthan stan* late 10th cent., *Meddestane* 1086 (DB). Probably 'stone of the maidens, i.e. where they gathered'. OE *mægth*, *mægden* + *stān*.

Maidwell Northants. *Medewelle* 1086 (DB). 'Spring or stream of the maidens, i.e. where they gathered'. OE *mægden* + *wella*.

Maisemore Glos. *Mayesmora* 1138. Probably 'the great field'. Welsh *maes* + *mawr*.

Makerfield (old district) Lancs., see ASHTON-IN-MAKERFIELD.

Malborough Devon. *Malleberge* 1249. 'Hill or mound of a man called *Mǣrla, or where gentian grows'. OE pers. name or *meargealla* + *beorg*.

Malden, New Gtr. London. *Meldone* 1086 (DB). 'Hill with a crucifix'. OE *mǣl* + *dūn*.

Maldon Essex. *Mældune* early 10th

cent., *Malduna* 1086 (DB). Identical in origin with the previous name.

Malham N. Yorks. *Malgun* 1086 (DB). '(Settlement) by the gravelly places'. OScand. **malgi* in a dative plural form.

Malling, '(settlement of) the family or followers of a man called *Mealla', OE pers. name + *-ingas*: **Malling, East & West** Kent. *Meallingas* 942–6, *Mellingetes* (*sic*) 1086 (DB). **Malling, South** E. Sussex. *Mallingum* 838, *Mellinges* 1086 (DB).

Malmesbury Wilts. *Maldumesburg* 685, *Malmesberie* 1086 (DB). 'Stronghold of a man called Maeldub'. OIrish pers. name + OE *burh* (dative *byrig*).

Malpas Ches. *Malpas* c.1125. 'The difficult passage'. OFrench *mal* + *pas*. The same name occurs in other counties.

Maltby, 'farmstead or village of a man called Malti, or where malt is made', OScand. pers. name or *malt* + *bý*: **Maltby** Cleveland. *Maltebi* 1086 (DB). **Maltby** S. Yorks. *Maltebi* 1086 (DB). **Maltby le Marsh** Lincs. *Maltebi* 1086 (DB). Affix 'in the marshland' from OE *mersc*.

Malton N. Yorks. *Maltune* 1086 (DB). Possibly 'farmstead where an assembly was held'. OE *mæthel* + *tūn*. Alternatively the first element may be OScand. *methal* 'middle'.

Malvern, Great & Little Heref. & Worcs. *Mælfern* c.1030, *Malferna* 1086 (DB). 'Bare hill'. Celtic **moil* + **brïnn*. **Malvern Link**, *Link* 1215, is from OE *hlinc* 'ledge, terrace'.

Mamble Heref. & Worcs. *Mamele* 1086 (DB). Probably a derivative of Celtic **mamm* 'breast-like hill'.

Manaccan Cornwall. '(Church of) *Sancta Manaca*' 1309. Probably from the patron saint of the church.

Manaton Devon. *Manitone* 1086 (DB). 'Farmstead held communally, or by a man called Manna'. OE *(ge)mǣne* or pers. name + *tūn*.

Manby Lincs., near Louth. *Mannebi* 1086 (DB). 'Farmstead or village of a man called Manni, or of the men'. OScand. pers. name or *mann* (genitive plural *-a*) + *bý*.

Mancetter Warwicks. *Manduessedum* 4th cent., *Manacestre* 1195. OE *ceaster* 'Roman fort or town' added to a reduced form of the original Celtic name which probably means 'horse chariot' (perhaps alluding to a topographical feature).

Manchester Gtr. Manch. *Mamucio* 4th cent., *Mamecestre* 1086 (DB). OE *ceaster* 'Roman fort or town' added to a reduced form of the original Celtic name (meaning obscure, but possibly containing Celtic **mamm* 'breast-like hill').

Manea Cambs. *Moneia* 1177. OE *ēg* 'island, well-watered land' with a doubtful first element, possibly OE *(ge)mǣne* 'held in common'.

Manfield N. Yorks. *Mannefelt* 1086 (DB). 'Open land of a man called Manna, or held communally'. OE pers. name or OE *(ge)mǣne* + *feld*.

Mangotsfield Avon. *Manegodesfelle* 1086 (DB). 'Open land of a man called Mangod'. OGerman pers. name + OE *feld*.

Manley Ches. *Menlie* 1086 (DB). 'Common wood or clearing'. OE *(ge)mǣne* + *lēah*.

Manningford Bohune & Bruce Wilts. *Maningaford* 987, *Maniford* 1086 (DB), *Manyngeford Bon*, *Manyngeford Breuse* 1279. 'Ford of the family or followers of a man called Manna'. OE pers. name + *-inga-* + *ford*. Manorial additions from the *Boun* and *Breuse* families, here in the 13th cent.

Mannington Dorset. *Manitone* 1086 (DB). 'Estate associated with a man called Manna'. OE pers. name + *-ing-* + *tūn*.

Manningtree Essex. *Manitre* 1248. 'Many trees', or 'tree of a man called Manna'. OE *manig* or OE pers. name + *trēow*.

Mansell Gamage & Lacy Heref. & Worcs. *Mælueshylle* c.1045, *Malveselle* 1086 (DB), *Maumeshull Gamages*, *Maumeshull Lacy* 1242. Probably 'hill of the gravel ridge'. OE **malu* + *hyll*. Manorial affixes from the *de Gamagis* family, here in the 12th cent., and from the *de Lacy* family, here in 1086.

Mansfield Notts. *Mamesfelde* 1086 (DB). 'Open land by the River Maun'. Celtic river-name (from Celtic *mamm 'breast-like hill') + OE *feld*.

Mansfield Woodhouse Notts. *Wodehuse* 1230, *Mamesfeud Wodehus* 1280. 'Woodland hamlet near MANSFIELD'. OE *wudu* + *hūs*.

Manston, 'farmstead of a man called Mann', OE pers. name + *tūn*: **Manston** Dorset. *Manestone* 1086 (DB). **Manston** Kent. *Manneston* 1254.

Manthorpe Lincs., near Thurlby. *Mannetorp* 1086 (DB). 'Outlying farmstead or village of a man called Manni, or of the men'. OScand. pers. name or *mann* (genitive plural *-a*) + *thorp*.

Manton Humber. *Malmetun* 1060–6, *Mameltune* 1086 (DB). 'Farmstead on sandy or chalky ground'. OE **malm* + *tūn*.

Manton Leics. *Manatona* c.1130. 'Farmstead held communally, or by a man called Manna'. OE *(ge)mǣne* or OE pers. name + *tūn*.

Manton Wilts. *Manetune* 1086 (DB). Identical in origin with the previous name.

Manuden Essex. *Magghedana* (*sic*) 1086 (DB), *Manegedan* c.1130. Probably 'valley of the family or followers of a man called Manna'. OE pers. name + *-inga-* + *denu*.

Maplebeck Notts. *Mapelbec* 1086 (DB). 'Stream where maple-trees grow'. OE **mapel* + OScand. *bekkr*.

Mapledurham Oxon. *Mapeldreham* 1086 (DB). 'Homestead where maple-trees grow'. OE *mapuldor* + *hām*.

Mapledurwell Hants. *Mapledrewell* 1086 (DB). 'Spring or stream where maple-trees grow'. OE *mapuldor* + *wella*.

Maplestead, Great & Little Essex. *Mapulderstede* 1042, *Mapledestedam* 1086 (DB). 'Place where maple-trees grow'. OE *mapuldor* + *stede*.

Mapperley Derbys. *Maperlie* 1086 (DB). 'Maple-tree wood or clearing'. OE *mapuldor* + *lēah*.

Mapperton Dorset, near Beaminster. *Malperetone* 1086 (DB). 'Farmstead where maple-trees grow'. OE *mapuldor* + *tūn*.

Mappleborough Green Warwicks. *Mepelesbarwe* 848, *Mapelberge* 1086 (DB). 'Hill where maple-trees grow'. OE **mapel* + *beorg*.

Mappleton Humber. *Mapletone* 1086 (DB). 'Farmstead where maple-trees grow'. OE **mapel* + *tūn*.

Mappowder Dorset. *Mapledre* 1086 (DB). '(Place at) the maple-tree'. OE *mapuldor*.

Marazion Cornwall. *Marghasbigan* c.1265. 'Little market'. Cornish *marghas* + *byghan*.

Marbury Ches., near Whitchurch. *Merberie* 1086 (DB). 'Fortified place near a lake'. OE *mere* + *burh* (dative *byrig*).

March Cambs. *Merche* 1086 (DB). '(Place at) the boundary'. OE *mearc* in an old locative form.

Marcham Oxon. *Merchamme* 900, *Merceham* 1086 (DB). 'Enclosure or river-meadow where smallage (wild celery) grows'. OE *merece* + *hamm*.

Marchamley Shrops. *Marcemeslei* 1086 (DB). Possibly 'woodland clearing of a man called Merchelm'. OE pers. name + *lēah*.

Marchington Staffs. *Mærchamtun* 1002, *Merchametone* 1086 (DB). Probably 'farmstead of the dwellers at a homestead where smallage (wild celery) grows'. OE *merece* + *hǣme* + *tūn*.

Marchwood Hants. *Merceode* 1086 (DB). 'Wood where smallage (wild celery) grows'. OE *merece* + *wudu*.

Marcle, Much & Little Heref. & Worcs. *Merchelai* 1086 (DB). 'Wood or clearing on a boundary'. OE *mearc* + *lēah*. Affix *Much* is from OE *mycel* 'great'.

Marden Heref. & Worcs. *Maurdine* (*sic*) 1086 (DB), *Magewurdin* 1177. 'Enclosed settlement in the district called MAUND'. OE *worthign*.

Marden Kent. *Maeredaen* c.1100. 'Woodland pasture for mares, or near a boundary'. OE *mere* or *(ge)mǣre* + *denn*.

Marden Wilts. *Mercdene* 941, *Meresdene*

1086 (DB). Probably 'boundary valley'. OE *mearc* + *denu*.

Marden, East, North, & West W. Sussex. *Meredone* 1086 (DB). 'Boundary hill'. OE *(ge)mǣre* + *dūn*.

Marefield Leics. *Merdefelde* 1086 (DB). 'Open land frequented by martens or weasels'. OE *mearth* + *feld*.

Mareham le Fen & Mareham on the Hill Lincs. *Marun, Meringhe* 1086 (DB), *Marum* c.1200. '(Place at) the pools' from OE *mere* in a dative plural form *merum*, in early sources alternating with '(settlement of) the dwellers by the pools' from OE *mere* + *-ingas*. Affix *le Fen* means 'in the marshland'.

Maresfield E. Sussex. *Mersfeld* 1234. 'Open land by a marsh or pool'. OE *mersc* or *mere* + *feld*.

Marfleet Humber. *Mereflet* 1086 (DB). 'Pool stream'. OE *mere* + *flēot*.

Margaret Roding Essex, see RODING.

Margaretting Essex. *Ginga* 1086 (DB), *Gynge Margarete* 1291. 'Manor called *Ing* (for which see FRYERNING) of St Margaret'. From the dedication of the church.

Margate Kent. *Meregate* 1254. Probably 'gate or gap leading to the sea'. OE *mere* + *geat*.

Marham Norfolk. *Merham* c.1050, *Marham* 1086 (DB). 'Homestead by or with a pond'. OE *mere* + *hām*.

Marhamchurch Cornwall. *Maronecirce* 1086 (DB). 'Church of St Marwen or Merwenn'. Female saint's name + OE *cirice*.

Marholm Cambs. *Marham* c.1060. 'Homestead by or with a pond'. OE *mere* + *hām*.

Mariansleigh Devon. *Lege* 1086 (DB), *Marinelegh* 1238. 'The wood or clearing' from OE *lēah*, with the later addition of the saint's name *Marina* or *Marion* (a diminutive of *Mary*).

Marishes, High & Low N. Yorks. *Aschilesmares, Chiluesmares, Ouduluesmersc* 1086 (DB). 'The marshes', from OE *mersc*. Different manors originally distinguished by the names of early owners, OScand. *Ásketill, Ketilfrøthr*, and *Authulfr*.

Mark Somerset. *Mercern* 1065. 'House or building near a boundary'. OE *mearc* + *ærn*.

Markby Lincs. *Marchebi* 1086 (DB). Possibly 'farmstead or village of a man called Marki'. OScand. pers. name + *bý*. Alternatively the first element may be OScand. *mǫrk* 'frontier area, wilderness'.

Market as affix, see main name, e.g. for **Market Bosworth** (Leics.) see BOSWORTH.

Markfield Leics. *Merchenefeld* 1086 (DB). 'Open land of the Mercians'. OE *Merce* (genitive plural *Mercna*) + *feld*.

Markham, East & West Notts. *Marcham* 1086 (DB), *Estmarcham* 1192. 'Homestead or village on a boundary'. OE *mearc* + *hām*.

Markington N. Yorks. *Mercingtune* c.1030, *Merchinton* 1086 (DB). Possibly 'farmstead of the Mercians', OE *Merce* (genitive plural *Mercna*) + *tūn*. Alternatively 'farmstead of the boundary-dwellers, or by a boundary', OE *(ge)merce* (with Scand. *-k-*) + *-inga-* or *-ing* + *tūn*.

Marksbury Avon. *Merkesburi* 936, *Mercesberie* 1086 (DB). Possibly 'stronghold of a man called *Mǣrec or *Mearc'. OE pers. name + *burh* (dative *byrig*). Alternatively the first element may be OE *mearc* 'boundary' (perhaps with reference to the Wansdyke).

Markyate Herts. *Markȝate* 12th cent. 'Gate at the (county) boundary'. OE *mearc* + *geat*.

Marland, Peters Devon. *Mirlanda* 1086 (DB). 'Cultivated land by a pool'. OE *mere* + *land*.

Marlborough Wilts. *Merleberge* 1086 (DB). 'Hill or mound of a man called *Mǣrla, or where gentian grows'. OE pers. name or *meargealla* + *beorg*.

Marlcliff Warwicks. *Mearnanclyfe* 872. 'Cliff of a man called *Mearna'. OE pers. name + *clif*.

Marldon Devon. *Mergheldone* 1307. 'Hill where gentian grows'. OE *meargealla* + *dūn*.

Marlesford Suffolk. *Merlesforda* 1086 (DB). Probably 'ford of a man called *Mǣrel'. OE pers. name + *ford*.

Marlingford Norfolk. *Marthingforth c.*1000, *Merlingeforda, Marthingeforda* 1086 (DB). Possibly 'ford of the family or followers of a man called *Mearthel'. OE pers. name + *-inga-* + *ford*.

Marlow Bucks. *Merelafan* 1015, *Merlaue* 1086 (DB). 'Land remaining after the draining of a pool'. OE *mere* + *lāf*.

Marnham, High & Low Notts. *Marneham* 1086 (DB). 'Homestead or village of a man called *Mearna'. OE pers. name + *hām*.

Marnhull Dorset. *Marnhulle* 1267. Probably 'hill of a man called *Mearna'. OE pers. name + *hyll*.

Marple Gtr. Manch. *Merpille* early 13th cent. 'Pool or stream at the boundary'. OE *(ge)mǣre* + *pyll*.

Marr S. Yorks. *Marra* 1086 (DB). '(Place at) the marsh'. OScand. *marr*.

Marrick N. Yorks. *Marige* 1086 (DB). 'Boundary ridge'. OE *(ge)mǣre* + *hrycg*.

Marsden W. Yorks. *Marchesden* 12th cent. Probably 'boundary valley'. OE *mercels* + *denu*.

Marsh, '(place at) the marsh', OE *mersc*: **Marsh** Shrops. *Mersse* 1086 (DB). **Marsh Gibbon** Bucks. *Merse* 1086 (DB), *Mersh Gibwyne* 1292. Manorial affix from the *Gibwen* family, here in the 12th cent.

Marsh Baldon Oxon., see BALDON.

Marsham Norfolk. *Marsam* 1086 (DB). 'Homestead or village by a marsh'. OE *mersc* + *hām*.

Marshfield Avon. *Meresfelde* 1086 (DB). Probably 'open land on the boundary'. OE *(ge)mǣre* + *feld*. Alternatively the first element may be OE *mersc* 'marsh'.

Marshwood Dorset. *Merswude* 1188. 'Wood by a marsh'. OE *mersc* + *wudu*.

Marske, '(place at) the marsh', OE *mersc* (with Scand. *-sk*): **Marske** N. Yorks. *Mersche* 1086 (DB). **Marske-by-the-Sea** Cleveland. *Mersc* 1086 (DB).

Marston, a common name, 'farmstead in or by a marsh', OE *mersc* + *tūn*; examples include: **Marston** Oxon. *Mersttune c.*1069. **Marston Meysey** Wilts. *Merston* 1199, *Merston Meysi* 1259. Manorial affix from the *de Meysi* family, here in the 13th cent. **Marston Moretaine** Beds. *Merestone* 1086 (DB), *Merston Morteyn* 1383. Manorial affix from its early possession by the *Morteyn* family. **Marston, Priors** Warwicks. *Merston* 1236, *Prioris Merston* 1316. The manor was held by the Prior of Coventry in 1242. **Marston Trussell** Northants. *Mersitone* 1086 (DB), *Merston Trussel* 1235. Manorial affix from the *Trussel* family, here in the 13th cent.

Marstow Heref. & Worcs. *Lann Martin c.*1130, *Martinestowe* 1291. 'Church or holy place of St Martin'. Saint's name + OE *stōw* (replacing Welsh *llan* in the early form).

Marsworth Bucks. *Mæssanwyrth* 10th cent., *Missevorde* (*sic*) 1086 (DB). 'Enclosure of a man called *Mæssa'. OE pers. name + *worth*.

Marten Wilts. *Mertone* 1086 (DB). 'Farmstead near a boundary, or by a pool'. OE *(ge)mǣre* or *mere* + *tūn*.

Marthall Ches. *Marthale* late 13th cent. 'Nook of land frequented by martens or weasels'. OE *mearth* + *halh*.

Martham Norfolk. *Martham* 1086 (DB). 'Homestead or enclosure frequented by martens or weasels'. OE *mearth* + *hām* or *hamm*.

Martin, 'farmstead near a boundary, or by a pool', OE *(ge)mǣre* or *mere* + *tūn*; examples include: **Martin** Hants. *Mertone* 946. **Martin** Lincs., near Horncastle. *Mærtune* 1060, *Martone* 1086 (DB). **Martin** Lincs., near Metheringham. *Martona* 12th cent. **Martin Hussingtree** Heref. & Worcs. *Meretun, Husantreo* 972, *Husentre* 1086 (DB), *Marten Hosentre* 1535. Originally two separate manors, Hussingtree being 'tree of a man called Hūsa', from OE pers. name (genitive *-n*) + *trēow*.

Martinhoe Devon. *Matingeho* 1086 (DB). 'Hill-spur of the family or followers of a man called *Matta'. OE pers. name + *-inga-* + *hōh*.

Martinscroft Ches. *Martinescroft* 1332. 'Enclosure of a man called Martin'. ME pers. name + *croft*.

Martinstown Dorset. *Wintreburne* 1086 (DB), *Wynterburn Seynt Martyn* 1280, *Martyn towne* 1494. Originally 'estate on the River WINTERBORNE with a church dedicated to St Martin'. The alternative name came into use in the late 15th cent.

Martlesham Suffolk. *Merlesham* (*sic*) 1086 (DB), *Martlesham* 1254. Possibly 'homestead by a woodland clearing frequented by martens'. OE *mearth* + *lēah* + *hām*. Alternatively the first element may be an OE pers. name *Mertel.

Martock Somerset. *Mertoch* 1086 (DB). Possibly 'outlying farmstead or hamlet by a pool'. OE *mere* + *stoc*.

Marton, a common name, usually 'farmstead by a pool, OE *mere* + *tūn*, although some names may be 'farmstead near a boundary' with OE (*ge*)*mǣre* as first element; examples include: **Marton** Lincs. *Martone* 1086 (DB). **Marton** Warwicks. *Mortone* (*sic*) 1086 (DB), *Merton* 1151. **Marton-le-Moor** N. Yorks. *Marton* 1198, *Marton on the Moor* 1292. Affix is from OE *mōr* 'moor'. **Marton, Long** Cumbria. *Meretun c.*1170. Affix refers to the length of the parish.

Marwood Devon. *Mereuda* 1086 (DB). Probably 'wood near a boundary'. OE (*ge*)*mǣre* + *wudu*.

Marylebone Gtr. London. *Maryburne* 1453. '(Place by) St Mary's stream'. OE *burna*. Named from the dedication of the church built in the 15th cent. The *-le-* is intrusive and dates from the 17th cent.

Maryport Cumbria. *Mary-port* 1762. A modern name, the harbour here built in the 18th cent by Humphrey Senhouse being named after his wife Mary.

Marystow Devon. *Sancte Marie Stou* 1266. 'Holy place of St Mary'. OE *stōw*.

Mary Tavy Devon, see TAVY.

Masham N. Yorks. *Massan* (*sic*) 1086 (DB), *Masham* 1153. 'Homestead or village of a man called *Mæssa'. OE pers. name + *hām*.

Mashbury Essex. *Maisseberia* 1068, *Massebirig* 1086 (DB). 'Stronghold of a man called *Mæssa or *Mæcca'. OE pers. name + *burh* (dative *byrig*).

Massingham, Great & Little Norfolk. *Masingeham* 1086 (DB). 'Homestead of the family or followers of a man called *Mæssa'. OE pers. name + *-inga-* + *hām*.

Matching Essex. *Matcinga* 1086 (DB). '(Settlement of) the family or followers of a man called *Mæcca', or '*Mæcca's place'. OE pers. name + *-ingas* or *-ing*.

Matfen Northum. *Matefen* 1159. Probably 'fen of a man called *Matta'. OE pers. name + *fenn*.

Matfield Kent. *Mattefeld c.*1230. 'Open land of a man called *Matta'. OE pers. name + *feld*.

Mathon Heref. & Worcs. *Matham* 1014, *Matma* 1086 (DB). 'The treasure or gift'. OE *māthm*.

Matlask Norfolk. *Matelasc* 1086 (DB). 'Ash-tree where meetings are held'. OE *mæthel* + *æsc* or OScand. *askr*.

Matlock Derbys. *Meslach* (*sic*) 1086 (DB), *Matlac* 1196. 'Oak-tree where meetings are held'. OE *mæthel* + *āc*.

Matterdale End Cumbria. *Mayerdale* (*sic*) *c.*1250, *Matherdal* 1323. 'Valley where madder grows'. OScand. *mathra* + *dalr*.

Mattersey Notts. *Madressei* 1086 (DB). 'Island, or well-watered land, of a man called Mǣthhere'. OE pers. name + *ēg*.

Mattingley Hants. *Matingelege* 1086 (DB). 'Woodland clearing of the family or followers of a man called *Matta'. OE pers. name + *-inga-* + *lēah*.

Mattishall Norfolk. *Mateshala* 1086 (DB). Probably 'nook of land of a man called *Matt'. OE pers. name + *halh*.

Maugersbury Glos. *Meilgaresbyri* 714, *Malgeresberie* 1086 (DB). 'Stronghold of a man called *Mæthelgār'. OE pers. name + *burh* (dative *byrig*).

Maulden Beds. *Meldone* 1086 (DB). 'Hill with a crucifix'. OE *mǣl* + *dūn*.

Maulds Meaburn Cumbria, see MEABURN.

Maun (river) Notts., see MANSFIELD.

Maunby N. Yorks. *Mannebi* 1086 (DB). 'Farmstead or village of a man called Magni'. OScand. pers. name + *bý*.

Maund Bryan Heref. & Worcs. *Magene* 1086 (DB), *Magene Brian* 1242. A difficult name, but possibly '(place at) the hollows', from OE *maga* 'stomach' (used in a topographical sense) in a dative plural form. Alternatively Maund (also a district-name) may represent the survival of an ancient Celtic name *Magnis* (probably 'the rocks'). Manorial affix from a 12th cent. owner called *Brian*.

Mautby Norfolk. *Malteby* 1086 (DB). 'Farmstead or village of a man called Malti, or where malt is made'. OScand. pers. name or *malt* + *bý*.

Mavis Enderby Lincs., see ENDERBY.

Mawdesley Lancs. *Madesle* 1219. 'Woodland clearing of a woman called Maud'. OFrench pers. name (from OGerman *Mahthildis*) + OE *lēah*.

Mawgan Cornwall. *Scanctus Mawan* 1086 (DB). '(Church of) St Mawgan'. From the patron saint of the church.

Mawnan Cornwall. '(Church of) *Sanctus Maunanus*' 1281. From the patron saint of the church.

Maxey Cambs. *Macuseige* c.963. 'Island, or dry ground in marsh, of a man called Maccus'. OScand. pers. name + *ēg*.

Mayfield E. Sussex. *Magavelda* 12th cent. 'Open land where mayweed grows'. OE *mægthe* + *feld*.

Mayfield Staffs. *Medevelde* (*sic*) 1086 (DB), *Matherfeld* c.1180. 'Open land where madder grows'. OE *mæddre* + *feld*.

Mayford Surrey. *Maiford* 1212. Possibly 'maidens' ford', or 'ford where mayweed grows'. OE *mægth* or *mægthe* + *ford*.

Mayland Essex. *La Mailanda* 1188. Possibly 'land or estate where mayweed grows', from OE *mægthe* + *land*. Alternatively '(place at) the island', from OE *ēg-land*, with *M-* from the dative case of the OE definite article.

Meaburn, King's & Maulds Cumbria. *Maiburne* 12th cent., *Meburne Regis* 1279, *Meburnemaud* 1278. 'Meadow stream'. OE *mǣd* + *burna*. Distinguishing affixes from possession by the Crown (Latin *regis* 'of the king') and by a woman called *Maud* here in the 12th cent.

Meare Somerset. *Mere* 1086 (DB). '(Place at) the pool or lake'. OE *mere*.

Mears Ashby Northants., see ASHBY.

Measham Leics. *Messeham* 1086 (DB). 'Homestead or village on the River Mease'. OE river-name ('mossy river' from OE *mēos*) + *hām*.

Meathop Cumbria. *Midhop* c.1185. 'Middle enclosure in marsh'. OE *midd* (replaced by OScand. *mithr*) + *hop*.

Meaux Humber. *Melse* 1086 (DB). 'Sand-bank pool'. OScand. *melr* + *sǽr*.

Meavy Devon. *Mæwi* 1031, *Mewi* 1086 (DB). Named from the River Meavy, probably a Celtic river-name meaning 'lively stream'.

Medbourne Leics. *Medburne* 1086 (DB). 'Meadow stream'. OE *mǣd* + *burna*.

Meddon Devon. *Madone* 1086 (DB). 'Meadow hill'. OE *mǣd* + *dūn*.

Medina I. of Wight, district named from the River Medina, *Medine* 1196, 'the middle one', from OE *medume*.

Medmenham Bucks. *Medmeham* 1086 (DB). 'Middle or middle-sized homestead or enclosure'. OE *medume* (dative *-an*) + *hām* or *hamm*.

Medstead Hants. *Medested* 1202. 'Meadow place', or 'place of a man called *Mēde'. OE *mǣd* or pers. name + *stede*.

Medway (river) Sussex-Kent. *Medeuuæge* 8th cent. Ancient pre-English river-name *Wey* (of obscure etymology), possibly compounded with Celtic or OE *medu* 'mead' with reference to the colour or the sweetness of the water.

Meerbrook Staffs. *Merebroke* 1338. 'Boundary brook'. OE *(ge)mǣre* + *brōc*.

Meesden Herts. *Mesdone* 1086 (DB). 'Mossy or boggy hill'. OE *mēos* + *dūn*.

Meeth Devon. *Meda* 1086 (DB). OE *(ge)mȳthe* 'confluence of rivers' or *mǣth* 'place where corn or grass is cut'.

Melbourn Cambs. *Meldeburna* 970, *Melleburne* 1086 (DB). Possibly 'stream where orach or a similar plant grows'. OE *melde* + *burna*.

Melbourne Derbys. *Mileburne* 1086 (DB). Probably 'mill stream'. OE *myln* + *burna*.

Melbourne Humber. *Middelburne* 1086

(DB). 'Middle stream'. OE *middel* (replaced by OScand. *methal*) + OE *burna*.

Melbury, probably 'multi-coloured fortified place', OE *mǣle* + *burh* (dative *byrig*): **Melbury Abbas** Dorset. *Meleburge* 956, *Meleberie* 1086 (DB), *Melbury Abbatisse* 1291. Affix is Latin *abbatissa* 'abbess' from its early possession by Shaftesbury Abbey. **Melbury Bubb, Osmond, & Sampford** Dorset. *Mele(s)berie* 1086 (DB), *Melebir Bubbe* 1244, *Melebur Osmund* 1283, *Melebury Saunford* 1312. Manorial affixes from the *Bubbe* family, from a man called *Osmund*, and from the *Saunford* family, all here in the 13th cent.

Melchbourne Beds. *Melceburne* 1086 (DB). 'Stream by pastures yielding good milk'. OE **melce* + *burna*.

Melcombe Regis Dorset. *Melecumb* 1223. Probably 'valley where milk is produced'. OE *meoluc* + *cumb*.

Meldon Devon. *Meledon* 1175. 'Multi-coloured hill'. OE *mǣle* + *dūn*.

Meldon Northum. *Meldon* 1242. 'Hill with a crucifix'. OE *mǣl* + *dūn*.

Meldreth Cambs. *Melrede* 1086 (DB). 'Mill stream'. OE *myln* + *rīth*.

Melford, Long Suffolk. *Melaforda* 1086 (DB). Probably 'ford by a mill'. OE *myln* + *ford*.

Melkinthorpe Cumbria. *Melcanetorp* c.1150. 'Outlying farmstead or hamlet of a man called Maelchon'. OIrish pers. name + OScand. *thorp*.

Melkridge Northum. *Melkrige* 1279. 'Ridge where milk is produced'. OE *meoluc* + *hrycg*.

Melksham Wilts. *Melchesham* 1086 (DB). Possibly 'homestead or enclosure where milk is produced'. OE *meoluc* + *hām* or *hamm*.

Melling, probably '(settlement of) the family or followers of a man called *Mealla', or '*Mealla's place', OE pers. name + *-ingas* or *-ing*: **Melling** Lancs. *Mellinge* 1086 (DB). **Melling** Mersey. *Melinge* 1086 (DB).

Mellis Suffolk. *Melles* 1086 (DB). 'The mills'. OE *myln*.

Mellor, 'bare or smooth-topped hill', Celtic **męl* + **brez*: **Mellor** Gtr. Manch. *Melver* 1283. **Mellor** Lancs. *Malver* c.1130.

Mells Somerset. *Milne* 942, *Mulle* 1086 (DB). 'The mill(s)'. OE *myln*.

Melmerby, 'farmstead or village of a man called Maelmuire', OIrish pers. name + OScand. *bý*: **Melmerby** Cumbria. *Malmerbi* 1201. **Melmerby** N. Yorks., near Coverham. *Melmerbi* 1086 (DB). **Melmerby** N. Yorks., near Ripon. *Malmerbi* 1086 (DB). First element alternatively OScand. *malmr* 'sandy field'.

Melplash Dorset. *Melpleys* 1155. Probably 'multi-coloured pool'. OE *mǣle* + **plæsc*.

Melsonby N. Yorks. *Malsenebi* 1086 (DB). Possibly 'farmstead or village of a man called Maelsuithan'. OIrish pers. name + OScand. *bý*.

Meltham W. Yorks. *Meltham* 1086 (DB). Possibly 'homestead or village where smelting is done'. OE **melt* + *hām*.

Melton, usually 'middle farmstead', OE *middel* (replaced by OScand. *methal*) + *tūn*: **Melton, Great & Little** Norfolk. *Middilton* c.1060, *Meltuna* 1086 (DB). **Melton, High** S. Yorks. *Middeltun* 1086 (DB). **Melton Mowbray** Leics. *Medeltone* 1086 (DB), *Melton Moubray* 1284. Manorial affix from the *de Moubray* family, here in the 12th cent. **Melton Ross** Humber. *Medeltone* 1086 (DB), *Melton Roos* 1402. Manorial affix from the *de Ros* family, here in the 14th cent.

However the following may have a different origin: **Melton** Suffolk. *Meltune* c.1050, *Meltuna* 1086 (DB). Perhaps rather 'farmstead with a crucifix', OE *mǣl* + *tūn*. **Melton Constable** Norfolk. *Maeltuna* 1086 (DB), *Melton Constable* 1320. Possibly identical with the previous name. Manorial affix from possession by the *constable* of the Bishop of Norwich in the 12th cent.

Melverley Shrops. *Melevrlei* (*sic*) 1086 (DB), *Milverlegh* 1311. Probably 'woodland clearing by the mill ford'. OE *myln* + *ford* + *lēah*.

Membury Devon. *Manberia* 1086 (DB). OE *burh* (dative *byrig*) 'fortified place' with an uncertain first element, possibly Celtic **main* 'stone' or OE *mǣne* 'common'.

Mendham Suffolk. *Myndham c.*950, *Mendham* 1086 (DB). 'Homestead or village of a man called *Mynda'. OE pers. name + *hām*.

Mendip Hills Somerset. *Menedepe* 1185. Probably Celtic **mönïth* 'mountain, hill' with an uncertain second element, perhaps OE *yppe* in the sense 'upland, plateau'.

Mendlesham Suffolk. *Mundlesham* 1086 (DB). 'Homestead or village of a man called *Myndel'. OE pers. name + *hām*.

Menheniot Cornwall. *Mahiniet* 1260. 'Land or plain of *Hynyed'. Cornish **ma* + pers. name.

Menston W. Yorks. *Mensinctun c.*972, *Mersintone* 1086 (DB). 'Estate associated with a man called *Mensa'. OE pers. name + *-ing-* + *tūn*.

Mentmore Bucks. *Mentemore* 1086 (DB). 'Moor of a man called *Menta'. OE pers. name + *mōr*.

Meole Brace Shrops. *Melam* 1086 (DB), *Melesbracy* 1273. Named from Meole Brook, possibly itself derived from Celtic **mẹ̄l* 'bare (hill)'. Manorial affix from the *de Braci* family, here in the 13th cent.

Meols, Great & Little Mersey. *Melas* 1086 (DB). 'The sandhills'. OScand. *melr*.

Meon, East & West Hants. *Meone c.*880, *Mene, Estmeone* 1086 (DB). Named from the River Meon, a Celtic river-name of uncertain origin and meaning, possibly 'swift one'.

Meonstoke Hants. *Menestoche* 1086 (DB). 'Outlying farmstead on the River Meon or dependent on MEON'. OE *stoc*.

Meopham Kent. *Meapaham* 788, *Mepeham* 1086 (DB). 'Homestead or village of a man called *Mēapa'. OE pers. name + *hām*.

Mepal Cambs. *Mepahala* 12th cent. 'Nook of land of a man called *Mēapa'. OE pers. name + *halh*.

Meppershall Beds. *Maperteshale* 1086 (DB). Probably 'nook of the maple-tree'. OE *mæpel-trēow* + *halh*.

Mere, '(place at) the pool or lake', OE *mere*: **Mere** Ches. *Mera* 1086 (DB). **Mere** Wilts. *Mere* 1086 (DB).

Mereworth Kent. *Meranworth* 843, *Marovrde* 1086 (DB). 'Enclosure of a man called *Mǣra'. OE pers. name + *worth*.

Meriden W. Mids. *Mereden* 1230. 'Pleasant valley', or 'valley where merry-making takes place'. OE *myrge* + *denu*.

Merrington Shrops. *Muridon* 1254. 'Pleasant hill', or 'hill where merry-making takes place'. OE *myrge* + *dūn*.

Merrington, Kirk Durham. *Mærintun c.*1085, *Kyrke Merington* 1331. 'Estate associated with a man called *Mǣra'. OE pers. name + *-ing-* + *tūn*. Affix is OScand. *kirkja* 'church'.

Merriott Somerset. *Meriet* 1086 (DB). Possibly 'boundary gate'. OE *mǣre* + *geat*.

Merrow Surrey. *Marewe* 1185. Possibly OE *mearg* 'marrow' in a figurative sense such as 'fertile ground'.

Mersea, East & West Essex. *Meresig* early 10th cent., *Meresai* 1086 (DB). 'Island of the pool'. OE *mere* (genitive *-s*) + *ēg*.

Merseyside (new county), named from the River Mersey, *Mærse* 1002, 'boundary river' from OE *mǣre* (genitive *-s*) + *ēa*.

Mersham Kent. *Mersaham* 858, *Merseham* 1086 (DB). 'Homestead or village of a man called *Mǣrsa'. OE pers. name + *hām*.

Merstham Surrey. *Mearsætham* 947, *Merstan* 1086 (DB). 'Homestead near a trap for martens or weasels'. OE *mearth* + *sǣt* + *hām*.

Merston W. Sussex. *Mersitone* 1086 (DB). 'Farmstead on marshy ground'. OE *mersc* + *tūn*.

Merstone I. of Wight. *Merestone* 1086 (DB). Identical in origin with the previous name.

Merther Cornwall. *Eglosmerthe* 1201. 'Church at the saint's grave'. Cornish *eglos* + **merther*.

Merton, 'farmstead by the pool', OE *mere* + *tūn*: **Merton** Devon. *Mertone* 1086 (DB). **Merton** Gtr. London.

Mertone 967, *Meretone* 1086 (DB). **Merton** Norfolk. *Meretuna* 1086 (DB). **Merton** Oxon. *Meretone* 1086 (DB).

Meshaw Devon. *Mauessart* 1086 (DB). Probably 'bad or infertile clearing'. OFrench *mal* + *assart*.

Messing Essex. *Metcinges* 1086 (DB). '(Settlement of) the family or followers of a man called *Mæcca'. OE pers. name + *-ingas*.

Metfield Suffolk. *Medefeld* 1214. 'Open land with meadow'. OE *mǣd* + *feld*.

Metheringham Lincs. *Medricesham* 1086 (DB), *Mederingeham* 1193. Possibly 'homestead of a man called *Mæthelrīc or of his people'. OE pers. name (+ *-inga-*) + *hām*.

Methley W. Yorks. *Medelai* 1086 (DB). 'Clearing where grass is mown', OE *mǣth* + *lēah*, or 'middle land between rivers', OScand. *methal* + OE *ēg*.

Methwold Norfolk. *Medelwolde* c.1050, *Methelwalde* 1086 (DB). 'Middle forest'. OScand. *methal* + OE *wald*.

Methwold Hythe Norfolk. *Methelwoldehythe* 1277. 'Landing-place near METHWOLD'. OE *hȳth*.

Mettingham Suffolk. *Metingaham* 1086 (DB). Probably 'homestead of the family or followers of a man called *Metti'. OE pers. name + *-inga-* + *hām*.

Mevagissey Cornwall. *Meffagesy* c.1400. From the patron saints of the church, Saints Meva and Issey (the medial *-ag-* in the place-name being from Cornish *hag* 'and').

Mexborough S. Yorks. *Mechesburg* 1086 (DB). 'Stronghold of a man called *Mēoc or Mjúkr'. OE or OScand. pers. name + OE *burh*.

Meysey Hampton Glos., see HAMPTON.

Michaelchurch, 'church dedicated to St Michael', saint's name + OE *cirice*: **Michaelchurch** Heref. & Worcs. *Lann mihacgel* c.1150. Welsh *llan* 'church'. **Michaelchurch Escley** Heref. & Worcs. *Michaeleschirche* c.1275. Affix is from Escley Brook, probably a Celtic river-name *Esk* ('the water') + OE *hlynn* 'torrent'.

Michaelstow Cornwall. *Mighelestowe* 1302. 'Holy place of St Michael'. Saint's name + OE *stōw*.

Micheldever Hants. *Mycendefr* 862, *Miceldevere* 1086 (DB). Named from the stream here, probably a Celtic name meaning 'boggy waters', the second element being the Celtic word found in DOVER. At an early date, the first element was confused with OE *micel* 'great'.

Michelmersh Hants. *Miclamersce* 985. 'Large marsh'. OE *micel* + *mersc*.

Mickfield Suffolk. *Mucelfelda* 1086 (DB). 'Large tract of open country'. OE *micel* + *feld*.

Mickleby N. Yorks. *Michelbi* 1086 (DB). 'Large farmstead'. OScand. *mikill* + *bý*.

Mickleham Surrey. *Micleham* 1086 (DB). 'Large homestead or river-meadow'. OE *micel* + *hām* or *hamm*.

Mickleover Derbys. *Vfre* 1011, *Ufre* 1086 (DB), *Magna Oufra* c.1100. '(Place at) the ridge'. OE **ofer*, with the affix *micel* 'great' (earlier Latin *magna*) to distinguish this place from LITTLEOVER.

Mickleton, 'large farmstead', OE *micel* + *tūn*: **Mickleton** Durham. *Micleton* 1086 (DB). **Mickleton** Glos. *Micclantun* 1005, *Muceltvne* 1086 (DB).

Mickle Trafford Ches., see TRAFFORD.

Mickley Northum. *Michelleie* c.1190. 'Large wood or clearing'. OE *micel* + *lēah*.

Middle as affix, see main name, e.g. for **Middle Assendon** (Oxon.) see ASSENDON.

Middleham, 'middle homestead or enclosure', OE *middel* + *hām* or *hamm*: **Middleham** N. Yorks. *Medelai* (*sic*) 1086 (DB), *Midelham* 12th cent. **Middleham, Bishop** Durham. *Middelham* 12th cent. Affix from early possession by the Bishop of Durham.

Middlesbrough Cleveland. *Midelesburc* c.1165. 'Middlemost stronghold'. OE *midlest* + *burh*.

Middlesex (the county). *Middelseaxan* 704, *Midelsexe* 1086 (DB). '(Territory of) the Middle Saxons', originally a tribal name from OE *middel* + *Seaxe*.

Middlestown W. Yorks. *Midle Shitlington* 1325, *Myddleston* 1551. A contracted form of 'Middle Shitlington' (now SITLINGTON), which is *Schelintone* 1086 (DB), 'estate associated with a man called *Scyttel', OE pers. name + *-ing-* + *tūn*.

Middleton, a very common name, usually 'middle farmstead or estate', OE *middel* + *tūn*; examples include: **Middleton** Gtr. Manch. *Middelton* 1194. **Middleton** Norfolk. *Mideltuna* 1086 (DB). **Middleton Cheney** Northants. *Mideltone* 1086 (DB), *Middelton Cheyndut* 1342. Manorial affix from the *de Chendut* family, here in the 12th cent. **Middleton in Teesdale** Durham. *Middeltun c.*1164. Affix means 'in the valley of the River Tees', Celtic river-name ('surging river') + OScand. *dalr*. **Middleton on Sea** W. Sussex. *Middeltone* 1086 (DB). **Middleton on the Wolds** Humber. *Middeltun* 1086 (DB). See WOLDS. **Middleton St George** Durham. *Middlinton* 1238. Affix from the dedication of the church. **Middleton Scriven** Shrops. *Middeltone* 1086 (DB). Manorial affix is probably the ME surname *Scriven* from a family of this name with lands here. **Middleton Tyas** N. Yorks. *Middeltun* 1086 (DB), *Midilton Tyas* 14th cent. Manorial affix from the *le Tyeis* family who may have had lands here at an early date.

However the following have a different origin: **Middleton on the Hill** Heref. & Worcs. *Miceltune* 1086 (DB). 'Large farmstead or estate'. OE *micel* + *tūn*. **Middleton Priors** Shrops. *Mittilton c.*1200. First element uncertain. Affix from its early possession by Wenlock Priory.

Middlewich Ches. *Wich, Mildestuich* 1086 (DB). 'Middlemost salt-works'. OE *midlest* + *wīc*.

Middlezoy Somerset. *Soweie* 725, *Sowi* 1086 (DB), *Middlesowy* 1227. 'Island on the River *Sow*'. Lost pre-English river-name (of doubtful etymology) with the later affix *middle*.

Midge Hall Lancs. *Miggehalgh* 1390. 'Nook of land infested with midges'. OE *mycg* + *halh*.

Midgham Berks. *Migeham* 1086 (DB). 'Homestead or enclosure infested with midges'. OE *mycg* + *hām* or *hamm*.

Midgley, 'wood or clearing infested with midges', OE *mycg* + *lēah*: **Midgley** W. Yorks., near Crigglestone. *Migelaia* 12th cent. **Midgley** W. Yorks., near Halifax. *Micleie* 1086 (DB).

Midhurst W. Sussex. *Middeherst* 1186. 'Middle wooded hill'. OE *midd* + *hyrst*.

Midsomer Norton Avon, see NORTON.

Milborne, Milbourne, Milburn, 'mill stream', OE *myln* + *burna*: **Milborne Port** Somerset. *Mylenburnan c.*880, *Meleburne* 1086 (DB), *Milleburnport* 1249. Affix is OE *port* 'market town'. **Milborne St Andrew** Dorset. *Muleburne* 934, *Meleburne* 1086 (DB), *Muleburne St Andrew* 1294. Affix from the dedication of the church. **Milbourne** Northum. *Meleburna* 1158. **Milburn** Cumbria. *Milleburn* 1178.

Milcombe Oxon. *Midelcumbe* 1086 (DB). 'Middle valley'. OE *middel* + *cumb*.

Milden Suffolk. *Mellinga* (*sic*) 1086 (DB), *Meldinges c.*1130. '(Settlement of) the family or followers of a man called *Melda', OE pers. name + *-ingas*, or 'place where orach grows', OE *melde* + *-ing*.

Mildenhall Suffolk. *Mildenhale c.*1050, *Mitdenehalla* 1086 (DB). Possibly 'middle nook of land', OE *middel* + *halh*, but perhaps identical in origin with the next name.

Mildenhall Wilts. *Mildanhald* 803-5, *Mildenhalle* 1086 (DB). 'Nook of land of a man called *Milda'. OE pers. name (genitive *-n*) + *halh*.

Mile End, '(place at) the end of a mile', OE *mīl* + *ende*: **Mile End** Essex. *Milende* 1156-80. **Mile End** Gtr. London. *La Mile Ende* 1288.

Mileham Norfolk. *Meleham* 1086 (DB). 'Homestead or village with a mill'. OE *myln* + *hām*.

Milford, 'ford by a mill', OE *myln* + *ford*: **Milford** Derbys. *Muleford* 1086 (DB). **Milford** Surrey. *Muleford* 1235. **Milford on Sea** Hants. *Melleford* 1086 (DB). **Milford, South** N. Yorks. *Myleford c.*1030.

Millbrook, 'brook by a mill', OE *myln* + *brōc*: **Millbrook** Beds. *Melebroc* 1086 (DB). **Millbrook** Hants. *Melebroce* 956, *Melebroc* 1086 (DB).

Millington Humber. *Milleton* 1086 (DB). 'Farmstead with a mill'. OE *myln* + *tūn*.

Millmeece Staffs. *Mess* 1086 (DB), *Mulnemes* 1289. 'Mossy or boggy place'. OE *mēos* with the later addition of *myln* 'mill'.

Millom Cumbria. *Millum* c.1180. '(Place at) the mills'. OE *myln* in a dative plural form *mylnum*.

Milnrow Gtr. Manch. *Mylnerowe* 1554. 'Row of houses by a mill'. OE *myln* + *rāw*.

Milnthorpe Cumbria. *Milntorp* 1272. 'Outlying farmstead or hamlet with a mill'. OE *myln* + OScand. *thorp*.

Milson Shrops. *Mulstone* 1086 (DB). Possibly 'farmstead of a man called *Myndel'. OE pers. name + *tūn*.

Milstead Kent. *Milstede* late 11th cent. Possibly 'middle place'. OE *middel* + *stede*.

Milston Wilts. *Mildestone* 1086 (DB). Probably 'middlemost farmstead'. OE *midlest* + *tūn*.

Milton, a very common name, usually 'middle farmstead or estate', OE *middel* + *tūn*; examples include: **Milton** Cambs. *Middeltune* c.975, *Middeltone* 1086 (DB). **Milton Abbas** Dorset. *Middeltone* 934, *Mideltune* 1086 (DB), *Middelton Abbatis* 1268. Latin affix means 'of the abbot' with reference to the abbey here. **Milton Bryan** Beds. *Middelton* 1086 (DB), *Mideltone Brian* 1303. Manorial affix from a 12th cent. owner called *Brian*. **Milton Clevedon** Somerset. *Mideltune* 1086 (DB), *Milton Clyvedon* 1408. Manorial affix from a family called *de Clyvedon*, here c.1200. **Milton Damerel** Devon. *Mideltone* 1086 (DB), *Middelton Aubemarle* 1301. Manorial affix from Robert *de Albemarle* who held the manor in 1086. **Milton Ernest** Beds. *Middeltone* 1086 (DB), *Middelton Orneys* 1330. Manorial affix from early possessions here of a man called *Erneis*. **Milton Keynes** Bucks. *Middeltone* 1086 (DB), *Middeltone Kaynes* 1227. Manorial affix from the *de Cahaignes* family, here from the 12th cent. **Milton under Wychwood** Oxon. *Mideltone* 1086 (DB). For the affix, see ASCOTT.

However some Miltons have a different origin, 'farmstead or village with a mill', OE *myln* + *tūn*; examples include: **Milton** Cumbria. *Milneton* 1285. **Milton** Staffs. *Mulneton* 1227.

Milverton Somerset. *Milferton* 11th cent., *Milvertone* 1086 (DB). 'Farmstead by the mill ford'. OE *myln* + *ford* + *tūn*.

Milwich Staffs. *Mulewiche* 1086 (DB). 'Farmstead with a mill'. OE *myln* + *wīc*.

Mimms, North & South Herts. *Mimes* 1086 (DB). Possibly '(territory of) a tribe called the *Mimmas*', although this tribal name is obscure in origin and meaning.

Minchinhampton Glos. *Hantone* 1086 (DB), *Minchenhamtone* 1221. 'High farmstead'. OE *hēah* (dative *hēan*) + *tūn*, with affix *myncena* 'of the nuns' (with reference to possession by the nunnery of Caen in the 11th cent.).

Mindrum Northum. *Minethrum* c.1050. 'Mountain ridge'. Celtic **mönïth* + **drum*.

Minehead Somerset. *Mynheafdon* 1046, *Maneheve* 1086 (DB). Pre-English hill-name (possibly Celtic **mönïth* 'mountain') + OE *hēafod* 'projecting hill-spur'.

Minety Wilts. *Mintig* 844. 'Island, or dry ground in marsh, where mint grows'. OE *minte* + *ēg*.

Miningsby Lincs. *Melingesbi* (*sic*) 1086 (DB), *Mithingesbia* 1142. Probably 'farmstead or village of a man called Mithjungr'. OScand. pers. name + *bý*.

Minshull, Church Ches. *Maneshale* (*sic*) 1086 (DB), *Chirchemunsulf* late 13th cent. 'Shelf or shelving terrain of a man called Monn'. OE pers. name + *scelf*. Affix is OE *cirice* 'church'.

Minskip N. Yorks. *Minescip* 1086 (DB). OE (*ge*)*mǣnscipe* 'a community, a communal holding'.

Minstead Hants. *Mintestede* 1086 (DB). 'Place where mint grows or is grown'. OE *minte* + *stede*.

Minster, 'the monastery or large church', OE *mynster*: **Minster** Kent, near Ramsgate. *Menstre* 694. **Minster** Kent, near Sheerness. *Menstre* 1203. **Minster Lovell** Oxon. *Minstre* 1086 (DB), *Ministre Lovel* 1279. Manorial affix from the *Luvel* family, here in the 13th cent.

Minsterley Shrops. *Menistrelie* 1086 (DB). 'Woodland clearing near or belonging to a minster church'. OE *mynster* + *lēah*.

Minsterworth Glos. *Mynsterworthig* c.1030. 'Enclosure of the monastery' (here St Peter's Gloucester). OE *mynster* + *worth* (*worthig* in the early form).

Minterne Magna Dorset. *Minterne* 987. 'House near the place where mint grows'. OE *minte* + *ærn*. Affix is Latin *magna* 'great'.

Minting Lincs. *Mentinges* 1086 (DB). '(Settlement of) the family or followers of a man called *Mynta'. OE pers. name + *-ingas*.

Minton Shrops. *Munetune* 1086 (DB). 'Farmstead or estate by the mountain (Long Mynd)'. Welsh *mynydd* + OE *tūn*.

Mirfield W. Yorks. *Mirefeld* 1086 (DB). 'Pleasant open land', or 'open land where festivities are held'. OE *myrge* or *myrgen* + *feld*.

Miserden Glos. *Musardera* 1186. 'Musard's manor'. OFrench surname + suffix *-ere*. In 1086 (DB) the manor (then called *Grenhamstede* 'the green homestead' from OE *grēne* + *hām-stede*) was already held by the *Musard* family.

Missenden, Great & Little Bucks. *Missedene* 1086 (DB). Probably 'valley where water-plants or marsh-plants grow'. OE **mysse* + *denu*.

Misson Notts. *Misne* 1086 (DB). Possibly 'mossy or marshy place', from a derivative of OE *mos* 'moss, marsh'.

Misterton, 'farmstead or estate with a church or belonging to a monastery', OE *mynster* + *tūn*: **Misterton** Leics. *Minstretone* 1086 (DB). **Misterton** Notts. *Ministretone* 1086 (DB). **Misterton** Somerset. *Mintreston* 1199.

Mistley Essex. *Mitteslea* (*sic*) 1086 (DB), *Misteleg* 1225. Probably 'wood or clearing where mistletoe grows'. OE *mistel* + *lēah*.

Mitcham Gtr. London. *Michelham* 1086 (DB). 'Large homestead or village'. OE *micel* + *hām*.

Mitcheldean Glos. *Dena* 1220, *Muckeldine* 1224. '(Place at) the valley'. OE *denu* with the later addition of *micel* 'great'.

Mitchell Cornwall. *Meideshol* 1239. Probably 'maiden's hollow'. OE *mægd(en)* + *hol*.

Mitford Northum. *Midford* 1196. 'Ford where two streams join'. OE *(ge)mȳthe* + *ford*.

Mitton, 'farmstead where two rivers join', OE *(ge)mȳthe* + *tūn*; examples include: **Mitton, Great** Lancs. *Mitune* 1086 (DB). **Mitton, Upper** Heref. & Worcs. *Myttun* 841, *Mettune* 1086 (DB).

Mixbury Oxon. *Misseberie* 1086 (DB). 'Fortified place near a dunghill'. OE *mixen* + *burh* (dative *byrig*).

Mobberley Ches. *Motburlege* 1086 (DB). 'Clearing at the fortification where meetings are held'. OE *mōt* + *burh* + *lēah*.

Moccas Heref. & Worcs. *Mochros* c.1130, *Moches* 1086 (DB). 'Moor where swine are kept'. Welsh *moch* + *rhos*.

Mockerkin Cumbria. *Moldcorkyn* 1208. Probably 'hill-top of a man called Corcán'. OIrish pers. name + OScand. **moldi*.

Modbury Devon. *Motberia* 1086 (DB). 'Fortification where meetings are held'. OE *mōt* + *burh* (dative *byrig*).

Moddershall Staffs. *Modredeshale* 1086 (DB). 'Nook of a man called Mōdrēd'. OE pers. name + *halh*.

Mogerhanger Beds. *Mogarhangre* 1216. OE *hangra* 'wooded slope' with an uncertain first element.

Molescroft Humber. *Molescroft* 1086 (DB). 'Enclosure of a man called Mūl'. OE pers. name + *croft*.

Molesey, East & West Surrey. *Muleseg* 672–4, *Molesham* (*sic*) 1086 (DB). 'Island, or dry ground in marsh, of a man called Mūl'. OE pers. name + *ēg*. The river-name Mole is a 'back-formation' from the place-name.

Molesworth Cambs. *Molesworde* 1086 (DB). 'Enclosure of a man called Mūl'. OE pers. name + *worth*.

Molland Devon. *Mollande* 1086 (DB). OE *land* 'cultivated land, estate' with an uncertain first element, possibly a pre-English hill-name.

Mollington, 'estate associated with a man called Moll', OE pers. name + *-ing-* + *tūn*: **Mollington** Ches.

Molintone 1086 (DB). **Mollington** Oxon. *Mollintune*, c.1015, *Mollitone* 1086 (DB).

Molton, North & South Devon. *Nortmoltone, Sudmoltone* 1086 (DB). OE *tūn* 'farmstead, estate' with the same first element as in MOLLAND. Distinguishing affixes are OE *north* and *sūth*.

Monewden Suffolk. *Munegadena* 1086 (DB). Probably 'valley of the family or followers of a man called *Munda'. OE pers. name + *-inga-* + *denu*.

Mongeham, Great & Little Kent. *Mundelingeham* 761, *Mundingeham* 1086 (DB). 'Homestead of the family or followers of a man called *Mundel', or 'homestead at *Mundel's place'. OE pers. name + *-inga-* or *-ing* + *hām*.

Monk as affix, see main name, e.g. for **Monk Bretton** (S. Yorks.) see BRETTON.

Monkhopton Shrops. *Hopton* c.1180. 'Farmstead in a valley'. OE *hop* + *tūn*. Later affix from its possession by Wenlock Priory.

Monkland Heref. & Worcs. *Leine* 1086 (DB), *Munkelen* c.1180. 'Estate in *Leon* held by the monks'. Old Celtic name for the district (see LEOMINSTER) with OE *munuc*. The manor belonged before 1086 to Conches Abbey in Normandy.

Monkleigh Devon. *Lega* 1086 (DB), *Munckenelegh* 1244. 'Wood or clearing of the monks'. OE *munuc* + *lēah*, with reference to possession by Montacute Priory from the 12th cent.

Monkokehampton Devon. *Monacochamentona* 1086 (DB). 'Estate on the River Okement held by the monks'. OE *munuc* + Celtic river-name (possibly 'swift stream') + OE *tūn*. It once belonged to Glastonbury Abbey.

Monks as affix, see main name, e.g. for **Monks Eleigh** (Suffolk) see ELEIGH.

Monkseaton Tyne & Wear. *Seton Monachorum* 1380. 'Farmstead by the sea'. OE *sǣ* + *tūn*. Affix 'of the monks' (Latin *monachorum* in the early form) from its early possession by the monks of Tynemouth.

Monksilver Somerset. *Selvere* 1086 (DB), *Monkesilver* 1249. Probably an old river-name from OE *seolfor* 'silver', i.e. 'clear or bright stream'. Affix is OE *munuc* alluding to early possession by the monks of Goldcliff Priory.

Monkton, 'farmstead of the monks', OE *munuc* + *tūn*; examples include: **Monkton** Devon. *Muneketon* 1244. **Monkton** Kent. *Munccetun* c.960, *Monocstune* 1086 (DB). **Monkton, Bishop** N. Yorks. *Munecatun* c.1030, *Monucheton* 1086 (DB). Affix from its possession by the Archbishops of York. **Monkton, Moor & Nun** N. Yorks. *Monechetone* 1086 (DB), *Moremonketon* 1402, *Nunmonkton* 1397. Distinguishing affixes are OE *mōr* 'moor' and *nunne* 'nun' (from the nunnery founded here in the 12th cent.). **Monkton, West** Somerset. *Monechetone* 1086 (DB).

Monkton as affix, see main name, e.g. for **Monkton Combe** (Avon), see COMBE.

Monkwearmouth Tyne & Wear. *Uuiremutha* c.730, *Wermuth Monachorum* 1291. 'The mouth of the River Wear'. Celtic or pre-Celtic river-name (probably meaning simply 'water, river') + OE *mūtha*. Affix *Monk-* (Latin *monachorum* 'of the monks') refers to early possession by the monks of Durham.

Monnington on Wye Heref. & Worcs. *Manitune* 1086 (DB). 'Estate held communally, or by a man called Manna'. OE *(ge)mǣne* or pers. name (genitive *-n*) + *tūn*. For the river-name, see ROSS ON WYE.

Montacute Somerset. *Montagud* 1086 (DB). 'Pointed hill'. OFrench *mont* + *aigu*.

Montford Shrops. *Maneford* 1086 (DB). 'Communal ford', or 'ford of the community'. OE *(ge)mǣne* or *mann* (genitive plural *-a*) + *ford*.

Monxton Hants. *Anna de Becco* c.1270, *Monkestone* 15th cent. 'Estate (on the River *Ann*) held by the monks (of Bec Abbey)'. OE *munuc* + *tūn*, see ANN.

Monyash Derbys. *Maneis* 1086 (DB). 'Many ash-trees'. OE *manig* + *æsc*.

Moorby Lincs. *Morebi* 1086 (DB). 'Farmstead or village in the moor or marshland'. OScand. *mór* + *bý*.

Moor Crichel Dorset, see CRICHEL.

Moore Ches. *Mora* 12th cent. 'The marsh'. OE *mōr*.

Moorlinch Somerset. *Mirieling* 971. 'Pleasant ledge or terrace'. OE *myrge* + *hlinc*.

Moor Monkton N. Yorks., see MONKTON.

Moors, West Dorset. *La More* 1310, *Moures* 1407. 'The marshy ground(s)'. OE *mōr*.

Moorsholm Cleveland. *Morehusum* 1086 (DB). '(Place at) the houses on the moor'. OE *mōr* + *hūs*, or OScand. *mór* + *hús*, in a dative plural form in *-um*.

Moorsley, Low Tyne & Wear. *Moreslau* 12th cent. Probably 'hill of the moor'. OE *mōr* + *hlāw*.

Morborne Cambs. *Morburne* 1086 (DB). 'Marsh stream'. OE *mōr* + *burna*.

Morchard, 'great wood or forest', Celtic **mọ̄r* + **cẹd*: **Morchard Bishop** Devon. *Morchet* 1086 (DB), *Bisschoppesmorchard* 1311. Affix from its possession by the Bishop of Exeter in 1086. **Morchard, Cruwys** Devon. *Morchet* 1086 (DB), *Cruwys Morchard* c.1260. Manorial affix from the *de Crues* family, here in the 13th cent.

Morcombelake Dorset. *Morecomblake* 1558. 'Stream in the marshy valley'. OE *mōr* + *cumb* + *lacu*.

Morcott Leics. *Morcote* 1086 (DB). 'Cottage(s) in the marshland'. OE *mōr* + *cot*.

Morden, 'hill in marshland', OE *mōr* + *dūn*: **Morden** Dorset. *Mordune* 1086 (DB). **Morden** Gtr. London. *Mordune* 969, *Mordone* 1086 (DB). **Morden, Guilden & Steeple** Cambs. *Mordune* 1015, *Mordune* 1086 (DB), *Gildene Mordon* 1204, *Stepelmordun* 1242. Distinguishing affixes are OE *gylden* 'wealthy, splendid' and *stēpel* 'church steeple'.

Mordiford Heref. & Worcs. *Mord(e)ford* 12th cent. OE *ford* 'a ford' with an uncertain first element.

Mordon Durham. *Mordun* c.1050. 'Hill in marshland'. OE *mōr* + *dūn*.

More Shrops. *La Mora* 1181. 'The marsh'. OE *mōr*.

Morebath Devon. *Morbatha* 1086 (DB). 'Bathing-place in marshy ground'. OE *mōr* + *bæth*.

Morecambe Lancs., a modern revival of an old Celtic name for the Lune estuary, *Morikámbē* 'the curved inlet', first recorded c.150 AD.

Moreleigh Devon. *Morlei* 1086 (DB). 'Woodland clearing on or near a moor'. OE *mōr* + *lēah*.

Moresby Cumbria. *Morèsceby* c.1160. 'Farmstead or village of a man called Maurice'. OFrench pers. name + OScand. *bý*.

Morestead Hants. *Morstede* 1172. 'Place by a moor'. OE *mōr* + *stede*.

Moreton, Morton, a common name, 'farmstead in moorland or marshy ground', OE *mōr* + *tūn*; examples include: **Moreton** Mersey. *Moreton* 1278. **Moreton-in-Marsh** Glos. *Mortun* 714, *Mortune* 1086 (DB), *Morton in Hennemersh* 1253. Affix is an old district-name meaning 'marsh frequented by wild hen-birds (moorhens or the like)', OE *henn* + *mersc*. **Moreton, Maids** Bucks. *Mortone* 1086 (DB), *Maidenes Morton* c.1488. Affix from the tradition that the church here was built by two maiden ladies in the 15th cent. **Moreton Morrell** Warwicks. *Mortone* 1086 (DB), *Merehull* 1279, *Morton Merehill* 1285. Originally two distinct names first combined in the 13th cent. Morrell means 'boundary hill', OE *(ge)mǣre* + *hyll*. **Moreton Pinkney** Northants. *Mortone* 1086 (DB). Manorial affix (first used in the 16th cent.) from the *de Pinkeny* family who held the manor in the 13th cent. **Moreton Say** Shrops. *Mortune* 1086 (DB), *Morton de Say* 1255. Manorial affix from the *de Sai* family, here in 1199. **Morton** Derbys. *Mortun* 956, *Mortune* 1086 (DB). **Morton** Lincs., near Bourne. *Mortun* 1086 (DB). **Morton** Lincs., near Gainsborough. *Mortune* 1086 (DB). **Morton Bagot** Warwicks. *Mortone* 1086 (DB), *Morton Bagod* 1262. Manorial affix from the *Bagod* family, here from the 12th cent.

Moretonhampstead Devon. *Mortone* 1086 (DB), *Morton Hampsted* 1493. Identical in origin with the previous names, with a later addition which may be a family name or from a nearby place (from OE *hām-stede* 'homestead').

Morland Cumbria. *Morlund* c.1140.

'Grove in the moor or marsh'. OScand. *mór* + *lundr*.

Morley, 'woodland clearing in or near a moor or marsh', OE *mōr* + *lēah*: **Morley** Derbys. *Morlege* 1002, *Morleia* 1086 (DB). **Morley** Durham. *Morley* 1312. **Morley** Norfolk. *Morlea* 1086 (DB). **Morley** W. Yorks. *Moreleia* 1086 (DB).

Morningthorpe Norfolk. *Torp, Maringatorp* 1086 (DB). Possibly 'outlying farmstead of the dwellers by the lake or by the boundary'. OE *mere* or *mǣre* + *-inga-* + OScand. *thorp*.

Morpeth Northum. *Morthpath c.*1200. 'Path where a murder took place'. OE *morth* + *pæth*.

Morston Norfolk. *Merstona* 1086 (DB). 'Farmstead by a marsh'. OE *mersc* + *tūn*.

Mortehoe Devon. *Morteho* 1086 (DB). Possibly 'hill-spur called *Mort* or the stump'. OE **mort* + *hōh*.

Mortimer Berks., from the manorial affix of STRATFIELD MORTIMER.

Mortlake Gtr. London. *Mortelage* 1086 (DB). Probably 'stream of a man called *Morta'. OE pers. name + *lacu*. Alternatively the first element may be OE **mort* 'young salmon or similar fish'.

Morton, see MORETON.

Morvah Cornwall. *Morveth* 1327. 'Grave by the sea'. Cornish *mor* + *bedh*.

Morval Cornwall. *Morval* 1238. Probably Cornish *mor* 'sea' with an obscure second element.

Morville Shrops. *Membrefelde* 1086 (DB). OE *feld* 'open land' with an uncertain first element, possibly an old name of Mor Brook.

Morwenstow Cornwall. *Morwestewe* 1201. 'Holy place of St Morwenna'. Cornish saint's name + OE *stōw*.

Mosborough S. Yorks. *Moresburh c.*1002, *Moresburg* 1086 (DB). 'Fortified place in the moor'. OE *mōr* + *burh*.

Mosedale Cumbria. *Mosedale* 1285. 'Valley with a bog'. OScand. *mosi* + *dalr*.

Moseley Heref. & Worcs. *Museleie* 1086 (DB). 'Woodland clearing infested with mice'. OE *mūs* + *lēah*.

Moseley W. Mids. *Moleslei* 1086 (DB). 'Woodland clearing of a man called Moll'. OE pers. name + *lēah*.

Moss S. Yorks. *Mose* 1416. 'The swamp or bog'. OE *mos* or OScand. *mosi*.

Mossley Gtr. Manch. *Moselegh* 1319. 'Woodland clearing by a swamp or bog'. OE *mos* or OScand. *mosi* + OE *lēah*.

Mosterton Dorset. *Mortestorne* 1086 (DB). 'Thorn-tree of a man called *Mort'. OE pers. name + *thorn*.

Moston, usually 'moss or marsh farmstead', OE *mos* + *tūn*; for example **Moston** Shrops. *Mostune* 1086 (DB).

Motcombe Dorset. *Motcumbe* 1244. 'Valley where meetings are held'. OE *mōt* + *cumb*.

Mottingham Gtr. London. *Modingeham* 1044. 'Homestead or enclosure of the family or followers of a man called *Mōda'. OE pers. name + *-inga-* + *hām* or *hamm*.

Mottisfont Hants. *Mortesfunde* (*sic*) 1086 (DB), *Motesfont* 1167. 'Spring near a river-confluence', or 'spring where meetings are held'. OE *mōt* + **funta*.

Mottistone I. of Wight. *Modrestan* 1086 (DB). 'Stone of the speaker(s) at a meeting'. OE *mōtere* + *stān*.

Mottram, possibly 'speakers' place' or 'place where meetings are held', OE *mōtere* or *mōt* + *rūm*: **Mottram in Longdendale** Gtr. Manch. *Mottrum c.*1220, *Mottram in Longedenedale* 1308. Affix is a district name, 'dale of the long valley', OE *lang* + *denu* + OScand. *dalr*. **Mottram St Andrew** Ches. *Motre* (*sic*) 1086 (DB), *Motromandreus* 1351. Affix is probably manorial from some early owner called *Andrew*.

Mouldsworth Ches. *Moldeworthe* 12th cent. 'Enclosure at a hill'. OE *molda* + *worth*.

Moulsecoomb E. Sussex. *Mulescumba c.*1100. 'Valley of a man called Mūl'. OE pers. name + *cumb*.

Moulsford Oxon. *Muleforda c.*1110. Probably 'ford of a man called Mūl'. OE pers. name + *ford*.

Moulsoe Bucks. *Moleshou* 1086 (DB).

'Hill-spur of a man called Mūl'. OE pers. name + *hōh*.

Moulton, 'farmstead of a man called Mūla, or where mules are kept', OE pers. name or OE *mūl* + *tūn*: **Moulton** Ches. *Moletune* 1086 (DB). **Moulton** Lincs. *Multune* 1086 (DB). **Moulton** Northants. *Multone* 1086 (DB). **Moulton** N. Yorks. *Moltun* 1086 (DB). **Moulton** Suffolk. *Muletuna* 1086 (DB). **Moulton St Michael** Norfolk. *Mulantun c.*1035, *Muletuna* 1086 (DB). Affix from the dedication of the church.

Mount Bures Essex, see BURES.

Mountfield E. Sussex. *Montifelle* (*sic*) 1086 (DB), *Mundifeld* 12th cent. 'Open land of a man called *Munda'. OE pers. name + *feld*.

Mountnessing Essex. *Ginga* 1086 (DB), *Gynges Munteny* 1237. 'Manor called *Ing* (for which see FRYERNING) held by the *de Mounteney* family'.

Mountsorrel Leics. *Munt Sorel* 1152. 'Sorrel-coloured hill', referring to the pinkish-brown stone here. OFrench *mont* + *sorel*.

Mousehole Cornwall. *Musehole* 1284. Self-explanatory, OE *mūs* + *hol*, originally referring to a large cave here.

Mow Cop Ches./Staffs. *Mowel c.*1270, *Mowle-coppe* 1621. 'Heap hill'. OE *mūga* + *hyll* with the later addition of *copp* 'hill top'.

Mowsley Leics. *Muselai* 1086 (DB). 'Wood or clearing infested with mice'. OE *mūs* + *lēah*.

Much as affix, see main name, e.g. for **Much Birch** (Heref. & Worcs.) see BIRCH.

Mucking Essex. *Muc(h)inga* 1086 (DB). '(Settlement of) the family or followers of a man called Mucca', or 'Mucca's place'. OE pers. name + *-ingas* or *-ing*.

Mucklestone Staffs. *Moclestone* 1086 (DB). 'Farmstead of a man called Mucel'. OE pers. name + *tūn*.

Muckton Lincs. *Machetone* (*sic*) 1086 (DB), *Muketun* 12th cent. 'Farmstead of a man called Muca'. OE pers. name + *tūn*.

Mudford Somerset. *Mudiford* 1086 (DB). 'Muddy ford'. OE **muddig* + *ford*.

Mudgley Somerset. *Mudesle* 1157. OE *lēah* 'wood or clearing' with an uncertain first element, possibly a pers. name.

Mugginton Derbys. *Mogintun* 1086 (DB). 'Estate associated with a man called *Mogga or *Mugga'. OE pers. name + *-ing-* + *tūn*.

Muggleswick Durham. *Muclingwic* c.1170. 'Farmstead of a man called Mucel'. OE pers. name (+ *-ing-*) + *wīc*.

Muker N. Yorks. *Meuhaker* 1274. 'Narrow cultivated plot'. OScand. *mjór* + *akr*.

Mulbarton Norfolk. *Molkebertuna* 1086 (DB). 'Outlying farm where milk is produced'. OE *meoluc* + *bere-tūn*.

Mullion Cornwall. 'Church of *Sanctus Melanus*' 1262. From the patron saint of the church.

Mumby Lincs. *Mundebi* 1086 (DB). Possibly 'farmstead or village of a man called Mundi'. OScand. pers. name + *bý*. Alternatively the first element may be OE or OScand. *mund* in the sense 'protection' or 'hedge'.

Mundesley Norfolk. *Muleslai* 1086 (DB). 'Woodland clearing of a man called Mūl or *Mundel'. OE pers. name + *lēah*.

Mundford Norfolk. *Mundeforda* 1086 (DB). 'Ford of a man called *Munda'. OE pers. name + *ford*.

Mundham, 'homestead or enclosure of a man called *Munda', OE pers. name + *hām* or *hamm*: **Mundham** Norfolk. *Mundaham* 1086 (DB). **Mundham** W. Sussex. *Mundhame c.*692, *Mundreham* 1086 (DB).

Mundon Essex. *Munduna* 1086 (DB). 'Protection hill', i.e. probably 'raised ground safe from flooding, or protected by fencing'. OE *mund* + *dūn*.

Mungrisdale Cumbria. *Grisedale* 1285, *Mounge Grieesdell* 1600. 'Valley where young pigs are kept'. OScand. *gríss* + *dalr*, with the later addition of the saint's name *Mungo* from the dedication of the church.

Munsley Heref. & Worcs. *Muleslage*, *Muneslai* 1086 (DB). 'Woodland clearing of a man called Mūl or *Mundel'. OE pers. name + *lēah*.

Munslow Shrops. *Mulselawa* 12th cent., *Munsselawe* 1256. OE *hlāw* 'mound, tumulus', with an uncertain first element.

Murcott Oxon. *Morcot c.*1191. 'Cottage(s) in marshy ground'. OE *mōr* + *cot*.

Murrow Cambs. *Morrowe* 1376. 'Row (of houses) in marshy ground'. OE *mōr* + *rāw*.

Mursley Bucks. *Muselai* (*sic*) 1086 (DB), *Murselai* 12th cent. Probably 'woodland clearing of a man called *Myrsa'. OE pers. name + *lēah*.

Murton, 'farmstead in moorland or marshy ground', OE *mōr* + *tūn*: **Murton** Cumbria. *Morton* 1235. **Murton** Durham, near Seaham. *Mortun* 1155. **Murton** Northum. *Morton* 1204. **Murton** N. Yorks., near York. *Mortun* 1086 (DB).

Musbury Devon. *Musberia* 1086 (DB). 'Old fortification infested with mice'. OE *mūs* + *burh* (dative *byrig*).

Muscoates N. Yorks. *Musecote c.*1160. 'Cottages infested with mice'. OE *mūs* + *cot*.

Musgrave, Great & Little Cumbria. *Musegrave* 12th cent. 'Grove or copse infested with mice'. OE *mūs* + *grāf*.

Muskham, North & South Notts. *Muscham, Nordmuscham* 1086 (DB). Possibly 'homestead or village of a man called *Musca'. OE pers. name + *hām*.

Muston Leics. *Mustun* 12th cent. 'Mouse-infested farmstead'. OE *mūs* + *tūn*.

Muston N. Yorks. *Mustone* 1086 (DB). Identical with previous name, or 'farmstead of a man called Músi', OScand. pers. name + OE *tūn*.

Muswell Hill Gtr. London. *Mosewella c.*1155. 'Mossy spring'. OE *mēos* + *wella*, with the addition of *hill* from the 17th cent.

Mylor Bridge Cornwall. 'Church of *Sanctus Melorus*' 1258. From the patron saint of the church.

Myndtown Shrops. *Munete* 1086 (DB). 'Place at the mountain (Long Mynd)'. Welsh *mynydd*, with the later addition of *town*.

Mytholmroyd W. Yorks. *Mithomrode* late 13th cent. 'Clearing at the river-mouths'. OE (*ge*)*mȳthe* (dative plural (*ge*)*mȳthum*) + **rodu*.

Myton, Mytton, 'farmstead where two rivers join', OE (*ge*)*mȳthe* + *tūn*: **Myton on Swale** N. Yorks. *Mytun* 972, *Mitune* 1086 (DB). On the River Swale (probably OE **swalwe* 'rushing water') near to where it joins the Ure. **Mytton** Shrops. *Mutone* 1086 (DB).

N

Naburn N. Yorks. *Naborne* 1086 (DB). Possibly 'stream called the narrow one'. OE *naru* + *burna*.

Nackington Kent. *Natyngdun* late 10th cent, *Latintone* (*sic*) 1086 (DB). 'Hill at the wet place'. OE **næt* + *-ing* + *dūn*.

Nacton Suffolk. *Nachetuna* 1086 (DB). Possibly 'farmstead of a man called Hnaki'. OScand. pers. name + OE *tūn*.

Nafferton Humber. *Nadfartone* 1086 (DB). Probably 'farmstead of a man called Náttfari'. OScand. pers. name + OE *tūn*.

Nailsea Avon. *Nailsi* 1196. 'Island, or dry ground in marsh, of a man called *Nægl'. OE pers. name + *ēg*.

Nailstone Leics. *Naylestone* 1225. 'Farmstead of a man called *Nægl'. OE pers. name + *tūn*.

Nailsworth Glos. *Nailleswurd* 1196. 'Enclosure of a man called *Nægl'. OE pers. name + *worth*.

Nantwich Ches. *Wich* 1086 (DB), *Nametwihc* 1194. 'The salt-works'. OE *wīc* with the later addition of ME *named* 'renowned, famous'.

Nappa N. Yorks., near Hellifield. *Napars* (*sic*) 1086 (DB), *Nappai* 1182. Possibly 'enclosure in a bowl-shaped hollow'. OE *hnæpp* + *hæg*.

Napton on the Hill Warwicks. *Neptone* 1086 (DB). Possibly 'farmstead on a hill thought to resemble an inverted bowl'. OE *hnæpp* + *tūn*.

Narborough Leics. *Norburg c.*1220. 'North stronghold'. OE *north* + *burh*.

Narborough Norfolk. *Nereburh* 1086 (DB). Possibly 'stronghold near a narrow place or pass'. OE **neru* + *burh*.

Naseby Northants. *Navesberie* 1086 (DB). 'Stronghold of a man called Hnæf'. OE pers. name + *burh* (dative *byrig*), replaced by OScand. *bý* 'village' in the 12th cent.

Nash, 'place at the ash-tree', OE *æsc*, with initial *N-* from ME *atten* 'at the'; examples include: **Nash** Bucks. *Esse* 1231. **Nash** Heref. & Worcs. *Nasche* 1239. **Nash** Shrops. *Eshse* 13th cent.

Nassington Northants. *Nassingtona* 1017–34, *Nassintone* 1086 (DB). Probably 'farmstead on the promontory'. OE *næss* + *-ing* + *tūn*.

Nateby, 'farmstead or village where nettles grow, or of a man called *Nati', OScand. **nata* or pers. name + *bý*: **Nateby** Cumbria. *Nateby* 1242. **Nateby** Lancs. *Nateby* 1204.

Nately, Up Hants. *Nataleie* 1086 (DB), *Upnateley* 1274. 'Wet wood or clearing'. OE **næt* + *lēah*. Affix is OE *upp* 'higher up'.

Natland Cumbria. *Natalund c.*1175. 'Grove where nettles grow, or of a man called *Nati'. OScand. **nata* or pers. name + *lundr*.

Naughton Suffolk. *Nawelton c.*1150. Possibly 'farmstead of a man called Nagli'. OScand. pers. name + OE *tūn*.

Naunton, 'new farmstead or estate', OE *nīwe* (dative *nīwan*) + *tūn*: **Naunton** Glos., near Winchcombe. *Niwetone* 1086 (DB). **Naunton** Heref. & Worcs. *Newentone c.*1120. **Naunton Beauchamp** Heref. & Worcs. *Niwantune* 972, *Newentune* 1086 (DB), *Newenton Beauchamp* 1370. Manorial affix from the *Beauchamp* family, here from the 11th cent.

Navenby Lincs. *Navenebi* 1086 (DB). 'Farmstead or village of a man called Nafni'. OScand. pers. name + *bý*.

Navestock Essex. *Nasingestok* 867, *Nassestoca* 1086 (DB). Probably 'outlying farmstead on the promontory'. OE *næss* + *-ing* + *stoc*. Alternatively 'outlying farmstead belonging to the promontory people or to NAZEING'.

Nawton N. Yorks. *Nagletune* 1086 (DB). 'Farmstead of a man called Nagli'. OScand. pers. name + OE *tūn*.

Nayland Suffolk. *Eilanda* 1086 (DB), *Neiland* 1227. '(Place at) the island'. OE *ēg-land*, with *N-* from ME *atten* 'at the'.

Nazeing Essex. *Nassingan* 1062, *Nasinga* 1086 (DB). '(Settlement of) the people of the promontory'. OE *næss* + *-ingas*.

Near Sawrey Cumbria, see SAWREY.

Neasden Gtr. London. *Neosdune c.*1000. 'Nose-shaped hill'. OE **neosu* + *dūn*.

Neasham Durham. *Nesham* 1158. 'Homestead or enclosure by the projecting piece of land in a river-bend'. OE **neosu* + *hām* or *hamm*.

Neatishead Norfolk. *Netheshird* 1020–22, *Snateshirda* (*sic*) 1086 (DB). Probably 'household of a retainer'. OE *genēat* + *hīred*.

Necton Norfolk. *Nechetuna* 1086 (DB). Probably 'farmstead by a neck of land'. OE *hnecca* + *tūn*.

Nedging Tye Suffolk. *Hnyddinge c.*995, *Niedinga* 1086 (DB). 'Place associated with a man called *Hnydda'. OE pers. name + *-ing*. Later affix is *tye* 'common pasture'.

Needham, 'poor or needy homestead', OE *nēd* + *hām*: **Needham** Norfolk. *Nedham* 1352. **Needham Market** Suffolk. *Nedham* 13th cent., *Nedeham Markett* 1511. **Needham Street** Suffolk. *Nedham c.*1185. Affix *street* here means 'hamlet'.

Needingworth Cambs. *Neddingewurda* 1161. 'Enclosure of the family or followers of a man called *Hnydda'. OE pers. name + *-inga-* + *worth*.

Needwood Staffs. *Nedwode* 1248. 'Poor wood', or 'wood resorted to in need (as a refuge)'. OE *nēd* + *wudu*.

Neen Savage & Sollars Shrops. *Nene* 1086 (DB), *Nenesauvage* 13th cent., *Nen Solers* 1274. Originally the Celtic or pre-Celtic name of the river here (an old name for the River Rea). Manorial affixes from the *le Savage* family here in the 13th cent., and from the *de Solers* family here in the late 12th cent.

Neenton Shrops. *Newentone* (*sic*) 1086 (DB), *Nenton* 1242. Probably 'farmstead on the River *Neen*', OE *tūn*, see previous name. However the Domesday spelling suggests 'new farmstead', from OE *nīwe* (dative *-an*) + *tūn*, and this may represent its original meaning.

Nelson Lancs., a 19th cent. name for the new textile town, taken from the Lord Nelson Inn.

Nempnett Thrubwell Avon. *Emnet c.*1200, *Trubewel* 1201. Originally two places. Nempnett is '(place at) the level ground' from OE *emnet* with *N-* from ME *atten* 'at the'. Thrubwell is from OE *wella* 'spring, stream' with an uncertain first element.

Nene (river) Northants–Lincs. *Nyn* 948. An ancient Celtic or pre-Celtic name, of obscure etymology.

Nenthead Cumbria. *Nentheade* 1631. 'Place at the source of the River Nent'. Celtic river-name (from *nant* 'a glen') + OE *hēafod*.

Nesbit Northum., near Doddington. *Nesebit* 1242. 'Promontory river-bend'. OE **neosu* + *byht*.

Ness, '(place at) the promontory or projecting ridge', OE *næss*: **Ness** Ches. *Nesse* 1086 (DB). **Ness, East & West** N. Yorks. *Ne(i)sse* 1086 (DB). **Ness, Great & Little** Shrops. *Nessham*, *Nesse* 1086 (DB).

Neston Ches. *Nestone* 1086 (DB). 'Farmstead near the promontory'. OE *næss* + *tūn*.

Nether as affix, see main name, e.g. for **Nether Broughton** (Leics.) see BROUGHTON.

Netheravon Wilts. *Nigravre* (*sic*) 1086 (DB), *Nederauena c.*1150. '(Settlement) lower down the River Avon'. OE *neotherra* + Celtic river-name (meaning simply 'river').

Netherbury Dorset. *Niderberie* 1086 (DB). 'Lower fortified place'. OE *neotherra* + *burh* (dative *byrig*).

Netherfield E. Sussex. *Nedrefelle* 1086 (DB). 'Open land infested with adders'. OE *nǣddre* + *feld*.

Netherhampton Wilts. *Notherhampton*

1242. 'Lower homestead'. OE *neotherra* + *hām-tūn*.

Netherseal & Overseal Derbys. *Scel(l)a* 1086 (DB), *Nether Scheyle, Overe Scheyle* 13th cent. 'Small wood or copse'. OE **scegel*. Distinguishing affixes are OE *neotherra* 'lower' and *uferra* 'upper'.

Netherthong W. Yorks. *Thoying* 13th cent., *Nethyrthonge* 1448. 'Narrow strip of land'. OE *thwang*, with *neotherra* 'lower' to distinguish it from UPPERTHONG.

Netherton, a common name, 'lower farmstead or estate', OE *neotherra* + *tūn*; examples include: **Netherton** Heref. & Worcs., near Evesham. *Neotheretun* 780, *Neotheretune* 1086 (DB). **Netherton** Northum. *Nedertun* c.1050.

Netley Hants. *Lætanlia* 955–8, *Latelei* 1086 (DB). Probably 'neglected clearing, or clearing left fallow'. OE **lǣte* + *lēah*, with change to initial *N-* only from the 14th cent. perhaps through confusion with the following name.

Netley Marsh Hants. *Natanleaga* late 9th cent., *Nutlei* (*sic*) 1086 (DB). Probably 'wet wood or clearing'. OE **næt* + *lēah*.

Nettlebed Oxon. *Nettlebed* 1246. 'Plot of ground overgrown with nettles'. OE *netele* + *bedd*.

Nettlecombe Dorset. *Netelcome* 1086 (DB). 'Valley where nettles grow'. OE *netele* + *cumb*.

Nettleham Lincs. *Netelham* 1086 (DB). 'Homestead or enclosure where nettles grow'. OE *netele* + *hām* or *hamm*.

Nettlestead Kent. *Netelamstyde* 9th cent., *Nedestede* (*sic*) 1086 (DB). 'Homestead where nettles grow'. OE *netele* + *hām-stede*.

Nettlestone I. of Wight. *Hoteleston* (*sic*) 1086 (DB), *Nutelastone* 1248. 'Farmstead by the nut pasture or nut wood'. OE *hnutu* + *lǣs* or *lēah* (genitive *lēas*) + *tūn*.

Nettleton Lincs. *Neteltone* 1086 (DB). 'Farmstead where nettles grow'. OE *netele* + *tūn*.

Nettleton Wilts. *Netelingtone* 940, *Niteletone* 1086 (DB). 'Farmstead at the place overgrown with nettles'. OE *netele* + *-ing* + *tūn*.

Nevendon Essex. *Nezendena* (*sic*) 1086 (DB), *Neuendene* 1218. '(Place at) the level valley'. OE *efen* + *denu*, with *N-* from ME *atten* 'at the'.

New as affix, see main name, e.g. for **New Alresford** (Hants.) see ALRESFORD.

Newark, 'new fortification or building', OE *nīwe* + *weorc*: **Newark** Cambs. *Nieuyrk* 1189. **Newark on Trent** Notts. *Niweweorce* c.1080, *Neuuerche* 1086 (DB). For the river-name, see TRENTHAM.

Newbald, North Humber. *Neoweboldan* 972, *Niuuebold* 1086 (DB). 'New building'. OE *nīwe* + *bold*.

Newbiggin, a common name in the North, 'new building or house', OE *nīwe* + ME *bigging*; examples include: **Newbiggin** Cumbria, near Appleby. *Neubigging* 1179. **Newbiggin** Durham, near Middleton. *Neubigging* 1316. **Newbiggin by the Sea** Northum. *Niwebiginga* 1187.

Newbold, a common name in the Midlands, 'new building', OE *nīwe* + *bold*; examples include: **Newbold** Derbys. *Newebold* 1086 (DB). **Newbold** Leics. *Neoboldia* 12th cent. **Newbold on Avon** Warwicks. *Neobaldo* 1077, *Newebold* 1086 (DB). Avon is a Celtic river-name meaning simply 'river'. **Newbold on Stour** Warwicks. *Nioweboldan* 991. Stour is a Celtic or OE river-name probably meaning 'the strong one'. **Newbold Pacey** Warwicks. *Niwebold* 1086 (DB), *Neubold Pacy* 1235. Manorial affix from the *de Pasci* family, here in the 13th cent.

Newborough Staffs. *Neuboreg* 1280. 'New fortification'. OE *nīwe* + *burh*.

Newbottle, 'new building', OE *nīwe* + *bōthl*: **Newbottle** Northants. *Niwebotle* 1086 (DB). **Newbottle** Tyne & Wear. *Neubotl* 1196.

Newbourn Suffolk. *Neubrunna* 1086 (DB). 'New stream', i.e. 'stream which has changed course'. OE *nīwe* + *burna*.

Newbrough Northum. *Nieweburc* 1203. 'New fortification'. OE *nīwe* + *burh*.

Newburgh Lancs. *Neweburgh* 1431. 'New market town or borough'. OE *nīwe* + *burh*.

Newburn Tyne & Wear. *Neuburna* 1121–9. 'New stream', i.e. 'stream which has changed course'. OE *nīwe* + *burna*.

Newbury Berks. *Neuberie c*.1080. 'New market town or borough'. OE *nīwe* + *burh* (dative *byrig*).

Newby, a common name in the North, 'new farmstead or village', OE *nīwe* + OScand. *bý*; examples include: **Newby** Cumbria, near Appleby. *Neubi* 12th cent. **Newby East** Cumbria. *Neuby c*.1190. **Newby West** Cumbria. *Neuby c*.1200. **Newby Wiske** N. Yorks. *Neuby* 1157. Affix from the River Wiske, see APPLETON WISKE.

Newcastle, 'new castle', OE *nīwe* + *castel* (often in Latin in early spellings): **Newcastle** Shrops. *Novum castrum* 1284. **Newcastle under Lyme** Staffs. *Novum castellum subtus Lymam* 1173. *Lyme* is an old Celtic district name, probably meaning 'elm-tree region'. **Newcastle upon Tyne** Tyne & Wear. *Novem Castellum* 1130. For the river-name, see TYNEMOUTH.

Newchurch, 'new church', OE *nīwe* + *cirice*: **Newchurch** I. of Wight. *Niechirche* 12th cent. **Newchurch** Kent. *Nevcerce* 1086 (DB).

Newdigate Surrey. *Niudegate c*.1167. 'Gate by the new wood'. OE *nīwe* + *wudu* + *geat*.

Newenden Kent. *Newedene* 1086 (DB). 'New woodland pasture'. OE *nīwe* (dative *-an*) + *denn*.

Newent Glos. *Noent* 1086 (DB). Probably a Celtic name meaning 'new place'.

New Forest Hants. *Nova Foresta* 1086 (DB). 'The new forest' created by William the Conqueror in the 11th cent. for hunting game.

Newhall, 'new hall or manor house', OE *nīwe* + *hall*: **Newhall** Ches. *La Nouehall* 1252. **Newhall** Derbys. *Niewehal* 1197.

Newham Gtr. London, a recent name created for the new London borough comprising EAST & WEST HAM.

Newham Northum., near Bamburgh. *Neuham* 1242. 'New homestead or enclosure'. OE *nīwe* + *hām* or *hamm*.

Newhaven E. Sussex. *Newehaven* 1587. 'New harbour'. OE *nīwe* + *hæfen*.

Newholm N. Yorks. *Neueham* 1086 (DB). 'New homestead or enclosure'. OE *nīwe* + *hām* or *hamm*.

Newick E. Sussex. *Niwicha* 1121. 'New dwelling or farm'. OE *nīwe* + *wīc*.

Newington, 'the new farmstead or estate', OE *nīwe* (dative *nīwan*) + *tūn*: **Newington** Kent, near Hythe. *Neventone* 1086 (DB). **Newington** Kent, near Sittingbourne. *Newetone* 1086 (DB). **Newington** Oxon. *Niwantun c*.1045, *Nevtone* 1086 (DB). **Newington, North** Oxon. *Newinton* 1200. **Newington, South** Oxon. *Niwetone* 1086 (DB). **Newington, Stoke** Gtr. London. *Neutone* 1086, *Neweton Stoken* 1274. Affix means 'by the tree-stumps' or 'made of logs', from OE *stoccen*.

Newland, Newlands, 'new arable land', OE *nīwe* + *land*: **Newland** Heref. & Worcs. *La Newelande* 1221. **Newland** N. Yorks. *Newland* 1234. **Newlands** Northum. *Neuland* 1343.

Newlyn Cornwall. *Nulyn* 1279, *Lulyn* 1290. Probably 'pool for a fleet of boats'. Cornish *lu* + *lynn*.

Newlyn East Cornwall. 'Church of *Sancta Niwelina*' 1259. From the patron saint of the church.

Newmarket Suffolk. *Novum Forum* 1200, *la Newmarket* 1418. 'New market town'. ME *market* (rendered by Latin *forum* in the earliest form).

New Mills Derbys. *New Miln* 1625. Self-explanatory, although the plural form is recent. Earlier called *Midelcauel* 1306, 'the middle allotment of land', from ME *cauel*.

Newnham, a fairly common name, 'the new homestead or enclosure', OE *nīwe* (dative *-an*) + *hām* or *hamm*; examples include: **Newnham** Glos. *Nevneham* 1086 (DB). **Newnham** Herts. *Neuham* 1086 (DB). **Newnham** Northants. *Niwanham* 1021–3.

Newnton, North Wilts. *Northniwetune* 892, *Newetone* 1086 (DB). 'New farmstead'. OE *nīwe* (dative *nīwan*) + *tūn*.

Newport, 'new market town', OE *nīwe* + *port*: **Newport** Devon. *Neuport* 1295. **Newport** Essex. *Neuport* 1086 (DB). **Newport** I. of Wight. *Neweport* 1202. **Newport** Shrops. *Novus Burgus* 12th cent., *Newport* 1237. **Newport Pagnell** Bucks. *Neuport* 1086 (DB), *Neuport*

Paynelle 1220. Manorial affix from the *Paynel* family, here in the 12th cent.

Newquay Cornwall. *Newe Kaye* 1602. Named from the new quay (ME *key*) built here in the 15th cent.

Newsham, Newsholme, a fairly common name in the North, '(place at) the new houses', OE *nīwe* + *hūs* in a dative plural form *nīwum hūsum*; examples include: **Newsham** Northum. *Neuhusum* 1207. **Newsham** N. Yorks., near Ravensworth. *Neuhuson* 1086 (DB). **Newsholme** Humber., near Howden. *Neuhusam* 1086 (DB). **Newsholme** Lancs., near Barnoldswick. *Neuhuse* 1086 (DB).

Newstead Northum. *Novus Locus* 13th cent., *Newstede* 1339. 'New farmstead'. OE *nīwe* + *stede*.

Newstead Notts. *Novus Locus* 12th cent., *Newstede* 1302. 'New monastic site'. OE *nīwe* + *stede*.

Newthorpe N. Yorks. *Niwan-thorp* c.1030. 'New outlying farm'. OE *nīwe* + OScand. *thorp*.

Newton, a very common name, 'the new farmstead, estate, or village', OE *nīwe* + *tūn*; examples include: **Newton Abbot** Devon. *Nyweton* c.1200, *Nyweton Abbatis* 1270. The Latin affix meaning 'of the abbot' refers to its possession by Torre Abbey in the 12th cent. **Newton Arlosh** Cumbria. *Arlosk* 1185, *Neutonarlosk* 1345. Arlosh is probably a Celtic name meaning 'burnt place'. **Newton Blossomville** Bucks. *Niwetone* 1175, *Newenton Blosmevill* 1254. Manorial affix from the *de Blosseville* family, here in the 13th cent. **Newton Burgoland** Leics. *Neutone* 1086 (DB), *Neuton Burgilon* 1390. Manorial affix from early possession of lands here by the *Burgilon* family. **Newton Ferrers** Devon. *Niwetone* 1086 (DB), *Neweton Ferers* 1303. Manorial affix from the *de Ferers* family, here in the 13th cent. **Newton-le-Willows** Mersey. *Neweton* 1086 (DB). Affix means 'by the willow-trees'. **Newton, Maiden** Dorset. *Newetone* 1086 (DB), *Maydene Neweton* 1288. Addition means 'of the maidens', perhaps referring to early possession of the manor by nuns. **Newton Poppleford** Devon. *Poplesford* 1226, *Neweton Popilford* 1305. Poppleford means 'pebble ford', OE **popel* + *ford*.

In contrast to the above 'new settlements' of medieval origin, the following makes use of the old name-type for a modern development: **Newton Aycliffe** Durham, a recent 'new town' named from AYCLIFFE.

Nibley, 'woodland clearing near the peak', OE **hnybba* + *lēah*: **Nibley** Avon. *Nubbelee* 1189. **Nibley, North** Glos. *Hnibbanlege* 940.

Nidd N. Yorks. *Nith* 1086 (DB). Named from the River Nidd, a Celtic or pre-Celtic river-name of uncertain etymology.

Ninebanks Northum. *Ninebenkes* 1228. 'The nine banks or hills'. OE *nigon* + *benc*.

Ninfield E. Sussex. *Nerewelle* (*sic*) 1086 (DB), *Nimenefeld* 1255. 'Newly taken-in open land'. OE *nīwe* + *numen* + *feld*.

Niton I. of Wight. *Neeton* 1086 (DB). 'New farmstead'. OE *nīwe* + *tūn*.

Nobottle Northants. *Neubote* (*sic*) 1086 (DB), *Neubottle* 12th cent. 'New building'. OE *nīwe* + *bōthl*.

Nocton Lincs. *Nochetune* 1086 (DB). Probably 'farmstead where wether sheep are kept'. OE *hnoc* + *tūn*.

Noke Oxon. *Ac(h)am* 1086 (DB), *Noke* 1382. '(Place at) the oak-tree'. OE *āc*, with *N-* from ME *atten* 'at the'.

Nonington Kent. *Nunningitun* c.1100. 'Estate associated with a man called Nunna'. OE pers. name + *-ing-* + *tūn*.

Norbiton Gtr. London. *Norberton* 1205. 'Northern grange or outlying farm'. OE *north* + *bere-tūn*. See SURBITON.

Norbury, 'northern stronghold or manor-house', OE *north* + *burh* (dative *byrig*): **Norbury** Ches., near Marbury. *Norberie* 1086 (DB). **Norbury** Derbys. *Nortberie* 1086 (DB). **Norbury** Gtr. London. *Northbury* 1359. **Norbury** Shrops. *Norbir* 1237. **Norbury** Staffs. *Nortberie* 1086 (DB).

Norfolk (the county). *Nordfolc* 1086 (DB). '(Territory of) the northern people (of the East Angles)'. OE *north* + *folc*, see SUFFOLK.

Norham Northum. *Northham* c.1050. 'Northern homestead or enclosure'. OE *north* + *hām* or *hamm*.

Norley Ches. *Northleg* 1239. 'Northern glade or clearing'. OE *north* + *lēah*.

Normanby, 'farmstead or village of the Northmen or Norwegian Vikings', OE *Northman* + OScand. *bý*: **Normanby** Cleveland. *Northmannabi c.*1050. **Normandy** Humber. *Normanebi* 1086 (DB). **Normanby** Lincs. *Normanebi* 1086 (DB). **Normanby** N. Yorks. *Normanebi* 1086 (DB). **Normanby le Wold** Lincs. *Normane(s)bi* 1086 (DB). Affix means 'on the wolds', from OE *wald* 'high forest land'.

Normanton, a fairly common name, 'farmstead of the Northmen or Norwegian Vikings', OE *Northman* + *tūn*; examples include: **Normanton** Derbys. *Normantun* 1086 (DB). **Normanton** W. Yorks. *Normantone* 1086 (DB). **Normanton, South** Derbys. *Normentune* 1086 (DB). **Normanton, Temple** Derbys. *Normantune* 1086 (DB), *Normanton Templer* 1330. Manorial affix from its possession by the Knights Templars in the late 12th cent.

Norrington Common Wilts. *Northinton* 1227. '(Place lying) north in the village'. OE *north* + *in* + *tūn*.

North as affix, see main name, e.g. for **North Anston** (S. Yorks.) see ANSTON.

Northallerton N. Yorks. *Aluretune* 1086 (DB), *North Alverton* 1293. 'Farmstead of a man called Ælfhere'. OE pers. name + *tūn*, with the affix *north* from the 13th cent.

Northam, 'northern enclosure or promontory', OE *north* + *hamm*: **Northam** Devon. *Northam* 1086 (DB). **Northam** Hants. *Northam* 1086 (DB).

Northampton Northants. *Hamtun* early 10th cent., *Northantone* 1086 (DB). 'Home farm, homestead'. OE *hām-tūn*, with prefix *north* to distinguish this place from SOUTHAMPTON (which has a different origin). **Northamptonshire** (OE *scīr* 'district') is first referred to in the 11th cent.

Northaw Herts. *North Haga* 11th cent. 'Northern enclosure'. OE *north* + *haga*.

Northborough Cambs. *Northburh* 12th cent. 'Northern fortification'. OE *north* + *burh*.

Northbourne Kent. *Nortburne* 618, *Norborne* 1086 (DB). 'Northern stream'. OE *north* + *burna*.

Northfield W. Mids. *Nordfeld* 1086 (DB). 'Open land lying to the north' (relative to King's Norton). OE *north* + *feld*.

Northfleet Kent. *Flyote* 10th cent., *Norfluet* 1086 (DB). '(Place at) the stream'. OE *flēot* with the addition of *north* to distinguish it from SOUTHFLEET.

Northiam E. Sussex. *Hiham* 1086 (DB), *Nordhyam c.*1200. Probably 'promontory where hay is grown'. OE *hīg* + *hamm*, with the later addition of *north*. Alternatively the original first element may be OE *hēah* 'high'.

Northill Beds. *Nortgiuele* 1086 (DB). 'Northern settlement of the tribe called *Gifle*', see SOUTHILL. OE *north* + tribal name derived from the River Ivel, a Celtic river-name meaning 'forked stream'.

Northington Hants. *Northametone* 903. 'Farmstead of the dwellers to the north' (of Alresford or Winchester). OE *north* + *hǣme* + *tūn*.

Northleach Glos. *Lecce* 1086 (DB), *Northlecche* 1200. 'Northern estate on the River Leach'. OE *north* + river-name (see EASTLEACH).

Northleigh Devon. *Lege* 1086 (DB), *Northleghe* 1291. '(Place at) the wood or clearing'. OE *lēah*, with *north* to distinguish it from SOUTHLEIGH.

Northlew Devon. *Leuia* 1086 (DB), *Northlyu* 1282. Named from the River Lew, a Celtic river-name meaning 'bright stream'.

Northmoor Oxon. *More* 1059, *Northmore* 1367. 'The marsh'. OE *mōr* with the later addition of *north*.

Northolt Gtr. London. *Northhealum* 960, *Northala* 1086 (DB). 'Northern nook(s) of land'. OE *north* + *halh*, see SOUTHALL.

Northowram W. Yorks. *Ufrun* 1086 (DB), *Northuuerum* 1202. '(Place at) the ridges'. OE **ofer*, **ufer* in a dative plural form **uferum*, with *north* to distinguish it from SOUTHOWRAM.

Northrepps Norfolk. *Norrepes* 1086 (DB), *Nordrepples* 1185. Possibly 'north strips of land'. OE *north* + **reopul*.

Northumberland (the county). *Norhumberland* 1130. 'Territory of the *Northhymbre* (i.e. those living north of the River Humber)'. OE tribal name + *land*. In Anglo-Saxon times the territory of the tribe and kingdom of the *Northymbre* was much larger than the present county.

Northwich Ches. *Wich, Norwich* 1086 (DB). 'North salt-works'. OE *north* + *wīc*.

Northwick Avon. *Northwican* 955–9. 'Northern (dairy) farm'. OE *north* + *wīc*.

Northwold Norfolk. *Northuuold* 970, *Nortwalde* 1086 (DB). 'Northern forest'. OE *north* + *wald*.

Northwood, 'northern wood', OE *north* + *wudu*: **Northwood** Gtr. London. *Northwode* 1435. **Northwood** I. of Wight. *Northewde* early 13th cent.

Norton, a very common name, 'north farmstead or village', i.e. one to the north of another settlement, OE *north* + *tūn*; examples include: **Norton** N. Yorks. *Nortone* 1086 (DB). **Norton Bavant** Wilts. *Nortone* 1086 (DB), *Nortonbavent* 1381. Manorial affix from the *de Bavent* family, here in the 14th cent. **Norton, Blo** Norfolk. *Nortuna* 1086 (DB), *Blonorton* 1291. Affix is probably OE *blāw* 'bleak, exposed'. **Norton, Brize** Oxon. *Nortone* 1086 (DB), *Northone Brun* c.1266. Manorial affix from a William *le Brun* who had land here in 1200. **Norton Canon** Heref. & Worcs. *Nortune* 1086 (DB), *Norton Canons* 1327. Affix from its early possession by the canons of Hereford Cathedral. **Norton, Chipping & Over** Oxon. *Nortone* 1086 (DB), *Chepingnorthona* 1224, *Overenorton* 1302. Distinguishing affixes are OE *cēping* 'market' and *uferra* 'higher'. **Norton Disney** Lincs. *Nortune* 1086 (DB), *Norton Isny* 1331. Manorial affix from the *de Isney* family, here in the 12th cent. **Norton Fitzwarren** Somerset. *Nortone* 1086 (DB). Manorial affix from lands here held by a family called *Fitzwarren*. **Norton, Greens** Northants. *Nortone* 1086 (DB), *Grenesnorton* 1465. Manorial affix from the *Grene* family, here in the 14th cent. **Norton, King's** W. Mids. *Nortune* 1086 (DB), *Kinges Norton* 1221. A royal manor at the time of Domesday Book. **Norton, Midsomer** Avon. *Midsomeres Norton* 1248. Affix from the festival of St John the Baptist, patron saint of the church, on Midsummer Day. **Norton-in-the-Moors** Staffs. *Nortone* 1086 (DB), *Norton super le Mores* 1285. Affix is from OE *mōr* 'moor, marshy ground'.

Norton, Hook Oxon., see HOOK.

Norwell Notts. *Nortwelle* 1086 (DB). 'North spring or stream'. OE *north* + *wella*.

Norwich Norfolk. *Northwic* 10th cent., *Noruic* 1086 (DB). 'North port or harbour'. OE *north* + *wīc*.

Norwood, 'north wood', OE *north* + *wudu*: **Norwood Green** Gtr. London. *Northuuda* 832. **Norwood Hill** Surrey. *Norwode* 1250. **Norwood, South & West** Gtr. London. *Norwude* 1176.

Nosterfield N. Yorks. *Nostrefeld* 1204. 'Open land with a sheep-fold or by a hillock'. OE *eowestre* or **ōster* + *feld*, with *N-* from ME *atten* 'at the'.

Notgrove Glos. *Natangrafum* 716–43, *Nategraua* 1086 (DB). 'Wet grove or copse'. OE **næt* + *grāf*.

Notley, Black & White Essex. *Hnutlea* 998, *Nutlea* 1086 (DB), *Blake Nuteleye* 1252, *White Nuteleye* 1235. 'Wood or clearing where nut-trees grow'. OE *hnutu* + *lēah*. Distinguishing affixes *blæc* and *hwīt* may refer to soil colour or vegetation.

Nottingham Notts. *Snotengaham* late 9th cent., *Snotingeham* 1086 (DB). 'Homestead of the family or followers of a man called Snot'. OE pers. name + *-inga-* + *hām*, with loss of *S-* in the 12th cent. due to Norman influence. **Nottinghamshire** (OE *scīr* 'district') is first referred to in the 11th cent.

Notting Hill Gtr. London. *Knottynghull* 1356. Possibly 'hill at the place associated with a man called *Cnotta'. OE pers. name + *-ing* + *hyll*. Alternatively Notting may be a family name from KNOTTING (Beds.).

Nottington Dorset. *Notinton* 1212. 'Estate associated with a man called *Hnotta'. OE pers. name + *-ing-* + *tūn*.

Notton W. Yorks. *Notone* 1086 (DB).

'Farmstead where wether sheep are kept'. OE *hnoc* + *tūn*.

Notton Wilts. *Natton* 1232. 'Cattle farm'. OE *nēat* + *tūn*.

Nuffield Oxon. *Tofeld* c.1181. Probably 'tough open land'. OE *tōh* + *feld*, with change to initial *N-* only from the 14th cent.

Nunburnholme Humber. *Brunha'* 1086 (DB), *Nonnebrynholme* 1530. '(Place at) the springs or streams'. OScand. *brunnr* in a dative plural form *brunnum*, with later affix from the Benedictine nunnery here.

Nuneaton Warwicks. *Etone* 1086 (DB), *Nonne Eton* 1247. 'Farmstead by a river'. OE *ēa* + *tūn*, with later affix from the Benedictine nunnery founded here in the 12th cent.

Nuneham Courtenay Oxon. *Neuham* 1086 (DB), *Newenham Courteneye* 1320. 'New homestead or village'. OE *nīwe* (dative *nīwan*) + *hām*. Manorial affix from the *Curtenay* family, here in the 13th cent.

Nun Monkton N. Yorks., see MONKTON.

Nunney Somerset. *Nuni* 954, *Nonin* (*sic*) 1086 (DB). Probably 'island, or dry ground in marsh, of a man called Nunna', OE pers. name + *ēg*. Alternatively the first element may be OE *nunne* 'a nun'.

Nunnington N. Yorks. *Noningtune* 1086 (DB). 'Estate associated with a man called Nunna'. OE pers. name + *-ing-* + *tūn*.

Nunthorpe Cleveland. *Torp* 1086 (DB), *Nunnethorp* 1240. 'Outlying farmstead or hamlet of the nuns'. OScand. *thorp*, with later affix from the medieval nunnery here.

Nursling Hants. *Nhutscelle* c.800, *Notesselinge* 1086 (DB). 'Nutshell place', probably indicating a small abode or settlement. OE *hnutu* + *scell* + *-ing*.

Nutbourne W. Sussex, near Pulborough. *Nordborne* 1086 (DB). 'North stream'. OE *north* + *burna*.

Nutfield Surrey. *Notfelle* 1086 (DB). 'Open land where nut-trees grow'. OE *hnutu* + *feld*.

Nuthall Notts. *Nutehale* 1086 (DB). 'Nook of land where nut-trees grow'. OE *hnutu* + *halh*.

Nuthampstead Herts. *Nuthamstede* c.1150. 'Homestead where nut-trees grow'. OE *hnutu* + *hām-stede*.

Nuthurst W. Sussex. *Nothurst* 1228. 'Wooded hill where nut-trees grow'. OE *hnutu* + *hyrst*.

Nutley E. Sussex. *Nutleg* 1249. 'Wood or clearing where nut-trees grow'. OE *hnutu* + *lēah*.

Nyetimber W. Sussex, near Pagham. *Neuetunbra* 12th cent. 'New timbered building'. OE *nīwe* + *timbre*.

Nymet Rowland & Tracey Devon. *Nymed* 974, *Limet* (*sic*) 1086 (DB), *Nimet Rollandi* 1242, *Nemethe Tracy* 1270. Celtic *nimet* 'holy place' (probably also an old name of the River Yeo). Manorial affixes from possession by a man called *Roland* in the 12th cent. and by the *de Trascy* family in the 13th.

Nympsfield Glos. *Nymdesfelda* 862, *Nimdesfelde* 1086 (DB). 'Open land by the holy place'. Celtic *nimet* + OE *feld*.

Nympton, 'farmstead near the river called *Nymet*' (probably an old name for the River Mole), Celtic *nimet* 'holy place' + OE *tūn*: **Nympton, Bishop's** Devon. *Nimetone* 1086 (DB), *Bysshopes Nymet* 1334. Affix from its possession by the Bishop of Exeter in 1086. **Nympton, George** Devon. *Nimet* 1086 (DB), *Nymeton Sancti Georgij* 1291. Affix from the dedication of the church. **Nympton, King's** Devon. *Nimetone* 1086 (DB), *Kyngesnemeton* 1254. Affix from its status as a royal manor in 1066.

Nynehead Somerset. *Nigon Hidon* 11th cent., *Nichehede* 1086 (DB). '(Estate of) nine hides'. OE *nigon* + *hīd*.

Nyton W. Sussex. *Nyton* 1327. Probably 'new farmstead', OE **nīge* + *tūn*, or 'farmstead on an island of dry ground in marsh' if the first element is *īeg* (with *N-* from ME *atten* 'at the').

O

Oadby Leics. *Oldebi* (*sic*) 1086 (DB), *Outheby* 1199. Probably 'farmstead or village of a man called Authi'. OScand. pers. name + *bý*.

Oake Somerset. *Acon* 11th cent., *Acha* 1086 (DB). '(Place at) the oak-trees'. OE *āc* in a dative plural form *ācum*.

Oaken Staffs. *Ache* 1086 (DB). Identical in origin with the previous name.

Oakengates Shrops. *Lee Okynyate* 1535. 'The gate or gap where oak-trees grow'. OE *ācen* + *geat*.

Oakenshaw W. Yorks. *Akescahe* 1246. 'Copse where oak-trees grow'. OE *ācen* + *sceaga*.

Oakford Devon. *Alforda* (*sic*) 1086 (DB), *Acford* 1166. 'Ford by the oak-tree(s)'. OE *āc* + *ford*.

Oakham Leics. *Ocham* 1067, *Ocheham* 1086 (DB). 'Homestead or enclosure of a man called Oc(c)a'. OE pers. name + *hām* or *hamm*.

Oakhanger Hants. *Acangre* 1086 (DB). 'Wooded slope where oak-trees grow'. OE *āc* + *hangra*.

Oakington Cambs. *Hochinton* 1086 (DB). 'Estate associated with a man called Hocca'. OE pers. name + *-ing-* + *tūn*.

Oakle Street Glos. *Acle* c.1270. 'Wood or clearing where oak-trees grow'. OE *āc* + *lēah*. Later affix *street* probably refers to its situation on a Roman road.

Oakley, a fairly common name, 'wood or clearing where oak-trees grow', OE *āc* + *lēah*; examples include: **Oakley** Beds. *Achelai* 1086 (DB). **Oakley** Dorset. *Ocle* 1327. **Oakley, Great** Essex. *Accleia* 1086 (DB).

Oakmere Ches. *Ocmare* 1277. '(Place at) the lake where oak-trees grow'. OE *āc* + *mere*.

Oaksey Wilts. *Wochesie* 1086 (DB). 'Island, or well-watered land, of a man called *Wocc'. OE pers. name + *ēg*.

Oakthorpe Leics. *Achetorp* 1086 (DB). 'Outlying farmstead or hamlet of a man called Áki'. OScand. pers. name + *thorp*.

Oakworth W. Yorks. *Acurde* 1086 (DB). 'Oak-tree enclosure'. OE *āc* + *worth*.

Oare, '(place at) the shore or hill-slope', OE *ōra*: **Oare** Kent. *Ore* 1086 (DB). **Oare** Wilts. *Oran* 934.

Oborne Dorset. *Womburnan* 975, *Wocburne* 1086 (DB). '(Place at) the crooked or winding stream'. OE *wōh* + *burna*.

Occlestone Green Ches. *Aculuestune* 1086 (DB). 'Farmstead of a man called Ācwulf'. OE pers. name + *tūn*.

Occold Suffolk. *Acholt* c.1050, *Acolt* 1086 (DB). 'Oak-tree wood'. OE *āc* + *holt*.

Ockbrook Derbys. *Ochebroc* 1086 (DB). 'Brook of a man called Occa'. OE pers. name + *brōc*.

Ockendon, North (Gtr. London) **& South** (Essex). *Wokendune* c.1070, *Wochenduna* 1086 (DB). 'Hill of a man called *Wocca'. OE pers. name (genitive *-n*) + *dūn*.

Ockham Surrey. *Bocheham* (*sic*) 1086 (DB), *Hocham* 1170. Possibly 'homestead or enclosure of a man called Occa'. OE pers. name + *hām* or *hamm*.

Ockley Surrey. *Hoclei* 1086 (DB). Probably 'woodland clearing of a man called Occa'. OE pers. name + *lēah*.

Ocle Pychard Heref. & Worcs. *Aclea* c.1030, *Acle* 1086 (DB), *Acle Pichard* 1242. 'Oak-tree wood or clearing'. OE *āc* + *lēah*. Manorial affix from the *Pichard* family, here in the 13th cent.

Odcombe Somerset. *Udecome* 1086 (DB). Probably 'valley of a man called Uda'. OE pers. name + *cumb*.

Oddingley Heref. & Worcs. *Oddingalea* 816, *Oddunclei* 1086 (DB). 'Woodland clearing of the family or followers of a man called *Odda'. OE pers. name + *-inga-* + *lēah*.

Oddington Oxon. *Otendone* 1086 (DB). 'Hill of a man called *Otta'. OE pers. name (genitive *-n*) + *dūn*.

Odell Beds. *Wadehelle* 1086 (DB). 'Hill where woad is grown'. OE *wād* + *hyll*.

Odiham Hants. *Odiham* 1086 (DB). 'Wooded homestead or enclosure'. OE *wudig* + *hām* or *hamm*.

Odstock Wilts. *Odestoche* 1086 (DB). 'Outlying farmstead or hamlet of a man called *Od(d)a'. OE pers. name + *stoc*.

Odstone Leics. *Odestone* 1086 (DB). Probably 'farmstead of a man called Oddr'. OScand. pers. name + OE *tūn*.

Offchurch Warwicks. *Offechirch* 1139. 'Church of a man called Offa'. OE pers. name + *cirice*.

Offenham Heref. & Worcs. *Offeham* 709, *Offenham* 1086 (DB). 'Homestead of a man called Offa or Uffa'. OE pers. name (genitive *-n*) + *hām*.

Offham E. Sussex. *Wocham* c.1092. Probably 'crooked homestead or enclosure'. OE *wōh* + *hām* or *hamm*.

Offham Kent. *Offaham* 10th cent. 'Homestead of a man called Offa'. OE pers. name + *hām*.

Offley, 'woodland clearing of a man called Offa', OE pers. name + *lēah*: **Offley, Bishops & High** Staffs. *Offeleia* 1086 (DB). Affix *Bishops* is from early possession by the Bishop of Lichfield. **Offley, Great** Herts. *Offanlege* 944–6, *Offelei* 1086 (DB).

Offord Cluny & Darcy Cambs. *Upeforde, Opeforde* 1086 (DB), *Offord Clunye* 1257, *Offord Willelmi Daci* 1220. 'Upper ford'. OE *upp(e)* + *ford*. Manorial affixes from early possession by the monks of Cluny Abbey in France and by the *Dacy* (or *le Daneys*) family.

Offton Suffolk. *Offetuna* 1086 (DB). 'Farmstead of a man called Offa'. OE pers. name + *tūn*.

Offwell Devon. *Offewille* 1086 (DB). 'Spring or stream of a man called Uffa'. OE pers. name + *wella*.

Ogbourne St Andrew & St George Wilts. *Oceburnan* 10th cent., *Ocheburne* 1086 (DB), *Okeborne Sancti Andree* 1289, *Okeburne Sancti Georgii* 1332. 'Stream of a man called Occa'. OE pers. name + *burna*. Distinguishing affixes from the church dedications.

Ogle Northum. *Hoggel* 1170. Possibly 'hill of a man called Ocga'. OE pers. name + *hyll*.

Ogwell, East & West Devon. *Wogganwylle* 956, *Wogewille* 1086 (DB). 'Spring or stream of a man called *Wocga'. OE pers. name + *wella*.

Okeford, Child, & Okeford Fitzpaine Dorset. *Acford* 1086 (DB), *Childacford* 1227, *Ocford Fitz Payn* 1321. 'Oak-tree ford'. OE *āc* + *ford*. Affixes are from OE *cild* 'noble-born son' (probably with reference to some early owner) and from the *Fitz Payn* family, here from the 13th cent.

Okehampton Devon. *Ocmundtun* c.970, *Ochenemitona* 1086 (DB). 'Farmstead on the River Okement'. Celtic river-name (possibly 'swift stream') + OE *tūn*.

Old as affix, see main name, e.g. for **Old Alresford** (Hants.) see ALRESFORD.

Old Northants. *Walda* 1086 (DB). '(Place at) the woodland or forest'. OE *wald*.

Oldberrow Warwicks. *Ulenbeorge* 709, *Oleberge* 1086 (DB). 'Hill or mound of a man called *Ulla'. OE pers. name + *beorg*.

Oldbury, 'old fortification or stronghold', OE *(e)ald* + *burh* (dative *byrig*): **Oldbury** Kent. *Ealdebery* 1302. **Oldbury** Shrops. *Aldeberie* 1086 (DB). **Oldbury** Warwicks. *Aldburia* 12th cent. **Oldbury** W. Mids. *Aldeberia* 1174. **Oldbury on the Hill** Glos. *Ealdanbyri* 972, *Aldeberie* 1086 (DB). Affix 'on the Hill' first used in the 18th cent. **Oldbury upon Severn** Glos. *Aldeburhe* 1185.

Oldham Gtr. Manch. *Aldholm* 1226–8. 'Old promontory'. OE *ald* + OScand. *holmr*.

Old Hurst Cambs. *Waldhirst* 1227. 'Wooded hill by the wold or forest'. OE *wald* + *hyrst*.

Oldland Avon. *Aldelande* 1086 (DB). 'Old or long-used cultivated land'. OE *ald* + *land*.

Ollerton, 'farmstead where alder-trees grow', OE *alor* + *tūn*: **Ollerton** Ches.

Alretune 1086 (DB). **Ollerton** Notts. *Alretun* 1086 (DB).

Olney Bucks. *Ollanege* 979, *Olnei* 1086 (DB). 'Island, or dry ground in marsh, of a man called *Olla'. OE pers. name (genitive *-n*) + *ēg*.

Olton W. Mids. *Alton* 1221. Possibly 'old farmstead'. OE *ald* + *tūn*.

Olveston Avon. *Ælvestune* 955–9, *Alvestone* 1086 (DB). 'Farmstead of a man called Ælf'. OE pers. name + *tūn*.

Ombersley Heref. & Worcs. *Ambreslege* 706. 'Woodland clearing of a man called *Ambre'. OE pers. name + *lēah*.

Ompton Notts. *Almuntone* 1086 (DB). 'Farmstead of a man called Alhmund'. OE pers. name + *tūn*.

Onecote Staffs. *Anecote* 1199. 'Lonely cottage(s)'. OE *āna* + *cot*.

Ongar, Chipping & High Essex. *Aungre* 1045, *Angra* 1086 (DB), *Chepyngaungre* 1314, *Heyghangre* 1339. 'Pasture land'. OE **anger*, with distinguishing affixes *cēping* 'market' and *hēah* 'high'.

Onibury Shrops. *Aneberie* 1086 (DB). 'Stronghold or manor on the River Onny'. River-name (possibly 'ash-tree stream') + OE *burh* (dative *byrig*).

Onn, High Staffs. *Otne* (*sic*) 1086 (DB), *Onna* c.1130. Probably Welsh *onn* 'ash-trees'.

Onneley Staffs. *Anelege* 1086 (DB). 'Woodland clearing of a man called Onna', or 'isolated clearing'. OE pers. name or *āna* + *lēah*.

Orby Lincs. *Heresbi* (*sic*) 1086 (DB), *Orreby* c.1115. 'Farmstead or village of a man called Orri'. OScand. pers. name + *bý*.

Orchard, East & West Dorset. *Archet* 939. '(Place) beside the wood'. Celtic *ar* + **cę̄d*.

Orchard Portman Somerset. *Orceard* 854. OE *orceard* 'a garden or orchard'. Manorial affix from the *Portman* family, here in the 15th cent.

Orcheston Wilts. *Orc(h)estone* 1086 (DB). Probably 'farmstead of a man called Ordrīc'. OE pers. name + *tūn*.

Orcop Heref. & Worcs. *Orcop* 1138. 'Top of the slope or ridge'. OE *ōra* + *copp*.

Ord, East Northum. *Horde* 1196. 'Projecting ridge'. OE *ord*.

Ore E. Sussex. *Ora* 1121-5. '(Place at) the hill-slope or ridge'. OE *ōra*.

Orford Ches. *Orford* 1332. Possibly 'upper ford'. OE *uferra* + *ford*.

Orford Suffolk. *Oreford* 1164. Possibly 'ford near the shore'. OE *ōra* + *ford*.

Orgreave Staffs. *Ordgraue* 1195. Probably 'pointed grove or copse'. OE *ord* + *grǣfe*.

Orleton Heref. & Worcs., near Leominster. *Alretune* 1086 (DB). 'Farmstead where alder-trees grow'. OE *alor* + *tūn*.

Orlingbury Northants. *Ordinbaro* (*sic*) 1086 (DB), *Ordelinberg* 1202. Probably 'hill associated with a man called *Ordla'. OE pers. name + *-ing-* + *beorg*.

Ormesby, Ormsby, usually 'farmstead or village of a man called Ormr', OScand. pers. name + *bý*: **Ormesby** Cleveland. *Ormesbi* 1086 (DB). **Ormesby** Norfolk. *Ormisby* c.1025, *Ormesbei* 1086 (DB). **Ormsby, North** Lincs. *Urmesbyg* c.1067, *Ormesbi* 1086 (DB).

However the following has a different origin: **Ormsby, South** Lincs. *Ormesbi* 1086 (DB), *Ormeresbi* early 12th cent. 'Farmstead of a man called Ormarr'. OScand. pers. name + *bý*.

Ormside, Great & Little Cumbria. *Ormesheued* c.1140. 'Headland of a man called Ormr'. OScand. pers. name + OE *hēafod*. Alternatively the first element may be OScand. *ormr* 'snake'.

Ormskirk Lancs. *Ormeschirche* c.1190. 'Church of a man called Ormr'. OScand. pers. name + *kirkja*.

Orpington Gtr. London. *Orpedingtun* 1032, *Orpinton* 1086 (DB). 'Estate associated with a man called *Orped'. OE pers. name + *-ing-* + *tūn*.

Orrell, possibly 'hill where ore is dug', OE *ōra* + *hyll*: **Orrell** Gtr. Manch. *Horhill* 1202. **Orrell** Mersey. *Orhul* 1299.

Orsett Essex. *Orseathan* 957, *Orseda* 1086 (DB). '(Place at) the pits where (iron) ore is dug'. OE *ōra* + *sēath* (dative plural *-um*).

Orston Notts. *Oschintone* 1086 (DB). Probably 'estate associated with a man called *Ōsica'. OE pers. name + *-ing-* + *tūn*.

Orton, usually 'higher farmstead', or 'farmstead by a ridge or bank', OE *uferra* or **ofer* or *ōfer* + *tūn*: **Orton** Cumbria. *Overton* 1239. **Orton** Northants. *Overtone* 1086 (DB). **Orton Longueville & Waterville** Cambs. *Ofertune* 958, *Ovretune* 1086 (DB), *Ouerton Longavill* 1247, *Ouertone Wateruile* 1248. Manorial affixes from the *de Longauilla* and *de Waltervilla* families, here in the 12th cent. **Orton on the Hill** Leics. *Wortone* (*sic*) 1086 (DB), *Overton* c.1215.

However the following has a different origin: **Orton, Great & Little** Cumbria. *Orreton* 1210. 'Farmstead of a man called Orri'. OScand. pers. name + OE *tūn*.

Orwell Cambs. *Ordeuuelle* 1086 (DB). 'Spring by a pointed hill'. OE *ord* + *wella*.

Orwell (river) Suffolk. *Arewan* 11th cent., *Orewell* 1341. An ancient Celtic or pre-Celtic river-name meaning simply 'stream', to which has been added OE *wella*, also 'stream'.

Osbaldeston Lancs. *Ossebaldiston* c.1200. 'Farmstead of a man called Ōsbald'. OE pers. name + *tūn*.

Osbaston Leics. *Sbernestun* (*sic*) 1086 (DB), *Osberneston* 1200. 'Farmstead of a man called Ásbjǫrn'. OScand. pers. name + OE *tūn*.

Osbournby Lincs. *Osbernebi* 1086 (DB). 'Farmstead or village of a man called Ásbjǫrn'. OScand. pers. name + *bý*.

Osgathorpe Leics. *Osgodtorp* 1086 (DB). 'Outlying farmstead or hamlet of a man called Ásgautr'. OScand. pers. name + *thorp*.

Osgodby, 'farmstead or village of a man called Ásgautr', OScand. pers. name + *bý*: **Osgodby** Lincs., near Market Rasen. *Osgotebi* 1086 (DB). **Osgodby** N. Yorks. *Asgozbi* 1086 (DB).

Osmaston Derbys., near Derby. *Osmundestune* 1086 (DB). 'Farmstead of a man called Ōsmund'. OE pers. name + *tūn*.

Osmington Dorset. *Osmingtone* 934, *Osmentone* 1086 (DB). 'Estate associated with a man called Ōsmund'. OE pers. name + *-ing-* + *tūn*.

Osmotherley N. Yorks. *Asmundrelac* (*sic*) 1086 (DB), *Osmunderle* 1088. 'Woodland clearing of a man called Ásmundr'. OScand. pers. name (genitive *-ar*) + OE *lēah*.

Ospringe Kent. *Ospringes* 1086 (DB). Possibly '(place at) the spring'. OE **or-spring* or **of-spring*.

Ossett W. Yorks. *Osleset* 1086 (DB). 'Fold of a man called *Ōsla, or 'fold frequented by blackbirds'. OE pers. name or OE *ōsle* + *set*.

Ossington Notts. *Oschintone* 1086 (DB). Probably 'estate associated with a man called *Ōsica'. OE pers. name + *-ing-* + *tūn*.

Osterley Gtr. London. *Osterle* 1274. 'Woodland clearing with a sheepfold'. OE *eowestre* + *lēah*.

Oswaldkirk N. Yorks. *Oswaldescherca* 1086 (DB). 'Church dedicated to St Ōswald'. OE pers. name + *cirice* (replaced by OScand. *kirkja*).

Oswaldtwistle Lancs. *Oswaldestwisel* 1246. 'River-junction of a man called Ōswald'. OE pers. name + *twisla*.

Oswestry Shrops. *Osewaldstreu* c.1190. 'Tree of a man called Ōswald'. OE pers. name + *trēow*. The traditional connection with St Oswald, 7th cent. king of Northumbria, is uncertain.

Otford Kent. *Otteford* 832, *Otefort* 1086 (DB). 'Ford of a man called *Otta'. OE pers. name + *ford*.

Otham Kent. *Oteham* 1086 (DB). 'Homestead or village of a man called *Otta'. OE pers. name + *hām*.

Othery Somerset. *Othri* 1225. Probably 'the other or second island'. OE *ōther* + *ēg*.

Otley, 'woodland clearing of a man called *Otta', OE pers. name + *lēah*: **Otley** Suffolk. *Otelega* 1086 (DB). **Otley** W. Yorks. *Ottanlege* c.972, *Otelai* 1086 (DB).

Otterbourne, Otterburn, 'stream frequented by otters', OE *oter* + *burna*: **Otterbourne** Hants. *Oterburna* c.970, *Otreburne* 1086 (DB). **Otterburn** Northum. *Oterburn* 1217. **Otterburn** N. Yorks. *Otreburne* 1086 (DB).

Otterham Cornwall. *Otrham* 1086 (DB). Probably 'enclosure or river-meadow by the River Ottery'. OE river-name ('otter stream', OE *oter* + *ēa*) + *hamm*.

Otterington, North & South N. Yorks. *Otrinctun* 1086 (DB). 'Estate associated with a man called *Oter'. OE pers. name + *-ing-* + *tūn*.

Ottershaw Surrey. *Otershaghe c*.890. 'Small wood frequented by otters'. OE *oter* + *sceaga*.

Otterton Devon. *Otritone* 1086 (DB). 'Farmstead by the River Otter'. OE river-name (see OTTERY) + *tūn*.

Ottery St Mary Devon. *Otri* 1086 (DB), *Otery Sancte Marie* 1242. Named from the River Otter, 'stream frequented by otters', OE *oter* + *ēa*. Affix from the dedication of the church.

Ottery, Venn Devon. *Fenotri* 1156. 'Marshy land by the River Otter'. OE *fenn*, see previous name.

Ottringham Humber. *Otringeham* 1086 (DB). 'Homestead of the family or followers of a man called Oter'. OE pers. name + *-inga-* + *hām*.

Oughtibridge S. Yorks. *Uhtiuabrigga* 1161. Probably 'bridge of a woman called *Ūhtgifu'. OE pers. name + *brycg*.

Oulston N. Yorks. *Uluestun* 1086 (DB). 'Farmstead of a man called Wulf or Ulfr'. OE or OScand. pers. name + OE *tūn*.

Oulton Cumbria. *Ulveton c*.1200. 'Farmstead of a man called Wulfa'. OE pers. name + *tūn*.

Oulton Norfolk. *Oulstuna* 1086 (DB). Probably 'farmstead of a man called Authulfr'. OScand. pers. name + OE *tūn*.

Oulton Suffolk. *Aleton* 1203. 'Farmstead of a man called Áli', or 'old farmstead'. OScand. pers. name or OE *ald* + *tūn*. **Oulton Broad** contains *broad* in the sense 'extensive piece of water', see BROADS.

Oulton W. Yorks. *Aleton* 1180. Identical in origin with the previous name.

Oundle Northants. *Undolum c*.710–20, *Undele* 1086 (DB). '(Settlement of) the tribe called *Undalas*'. OE tribal name (meaning possibly 'those without a share' or 'undivided').

Ousby Cumbria. *Uluesbi* 1195. 'Farmstead or village of a man called Ulfr'. OScand. pers. name + *bý*.

Ousden Suffolk. *Uuesdana* 1086 (DB). 'Valley frequented by owls'. OE *ūf* + *denu*.

Ouseburn, Great & Little N. Yorks. *Useburne* 1086 (DB). '(Place at) the stream flowing into the River Ouse'. Celtic or pre-Celtic river-name (meaning simply 'water') + OE *burna*.

Ousefleet Humber. *Useflete* 1100–8. '(Place at) the channel of the River Ouse'. OE *flēot*, see previous name.

Ouston Durham. *Vlkilstan* 1244–9. 'Boundary stone of a man called Ulfkell'. OScand. pers. name + OE *stān*.

Out Newton Humber., see NEWTON.

Out Rawcliffe Lancs., see RAWCLIFFE.

Outwell Norfolk. *Wellan* 963, *Utuuella* 1086 (DB). '(Place at) the spring or stream'. OE *wella*, with affix *ūte* 'outer, lower downstream' to distinguish it from UPWELL.

Ovenden W. Yorks. *Ovenden* 1219. Probably 'valley of a man called Ōfa'. OE pers. name (genitive *-n*) + *denu*.

Over as affix, see main name, e.g. for **Over Compton** (Dorset) see COMPTON.

Over, '(place at) the ridge or slope', OE **ofer*: **Over** Avon. *Ofre* 1005. **Over** Cambs. *Ouer* 1060, *Ovre* 1086 (DB). **Over** Ches. *Ovre* 1086 (DB).

Overbury Heref. & Worcs. *Uferebiri* 875, *Ovreberie* 1086 (DB). 'Upper fortification'. OE *uferra* + *burh* (dative *byrig*).

Overseal Derbys., see NETHERSEAL.

Overstone Northants. *Oveston* 12th cent. Probably 'farmstead of a man called Ufic'. OE pers. name + *tūn*.

Overstrand Norfolk. *Othestranda* (*sic*) 1086 (DB), *Overstrand* 1231. 'Land along the shore'. OE *ōfer* + *strand*.

Overton, a fairly common name, usually 'higher farmstead', OE *uferra* + *tūn*; examples include: **Overton** Hants. *Uferantun* 909, *Ovretune* 1086 (DB). **Overton, West** Wilts. *Uferantune*

939, *Ovretone* 1086 (DB).

However some Overtons may have a different origin, 'farmstead by a ridge or bank', OE **ofer* or *ōfer* + *tūn*; examples include: **Overton** Lancs. *Ouretun* 1086 (DB). **Overton** N. Yorks. *Ovretun* 1086 (DB).

Oving, '(settlement of) the family or followers of a man called Ūfa', OE pers. name + *-ingas*: **Oving** Bucks. *Olvonge* (*sic*) 1086 (DB), *Vuinges* 12th cent. **Oving** W. Sussex. *Uuinges* 956.

Ovingdean E. Sussex. *Hovingedene* 1086 (DB). Probably 'valley of the family or followers of a man called Ūfa'. OE pers. name + *-inga-* + *denu*.

Ovingham Northum. *Ovingeham* 1238. 'Homestead of the family or followers of a man called Ōfa', or 'homestead at Ōfa's place'. OE pers. name + *-inga-* or *-ing* + *hām*.

Ovington, usually 'estate associated with a man called Ūfa', OE pers. name + *-ing-* + *tūn*: **Ovington** Essex. *Ouituna* 1086 (DB). **Ovington** Hants. *Ufinctune* c.970. **Ovington** Norfolk. *Uvinton* 1202.

However the following have a different origin: **Ovington** Durham. *Ulfeton* 1086 (DB). 'Estate associated with a man called Wulfa'. OE pers. name + *-ing-* + *tūn*. **Ovington** Northum. *Ofingadun* 699–705. 'Hill of the family or followers of a man called Ōfa'. OE pers. name + *-inga-* + *dūn*.

Ower Hants., near Copythorne. *Hore* 1086 (DB). '(Place at) the bank or slope'. OE *ōra*.

Owermoigne Dorset. *Ogre* 1086 (DB), *Oure Moyngne* 1314. Probably '(place at) the slope or ridge'. OE **ofer*, with manorial affix from the *Moigne* family, here in the 13th cent.

Owersby, North & South Lincs. *Aresbi, Oresbi* 1086 (DB). Possibly 'farmstead or village of a man called Ávarr or *Aurr'. OScand. pers. name + *bý*.

Owmby, probably 'farmstead or village of a man called Authunn', OScand. pers. name + *bý*, though alternatively the first element may be OScand. *authn* 'uncultivated land, deserted farm': **Owmby** Lincs. *Odenebi* 1086 (DB). **Owmby-by-Spital** Lincs. *Ounebi* 1086 (DB). See SPITAL.

Owslebury Hants. *Oselbyrig* c.970. 'Stronghold of a man called *Ōsla', or 'stronghold frequented by blackbirds'. OE pers. name or OE *ōsle* + *burh* (dative *byrig*).

Owston Leics. *Osulvestone* 1086 (DB). 'Farmstead of a man called Ōswulf'. OE pers. name + *tūn*.

Owston S. Yorks. *Aust(h)un* 1086 (DB). 'East farmstead'. OScand. *austr* + OE *tūn*.

Owston Ferry Humber. *Ostone* 1086 (DB). Identical in origin with the previous name.

Owstwick Humber. *Osteuuic* 1086 (DB). 'Eastern outlying farm'. OScand. *austr* (possibly replacing OE *ēast*) + OE *wīc*.

Owthorpe Notts. *Ovetorp* 1086 (DB). 'Outlying farmstead or hamlet of a man called Úfi or Ūfa'. OScand. or OE pers. name + OScand. *thorp*.

Oxborough Norfolk. *Oxenburch* 1086 (DB). 'Fortification where oxen are kept'. OE *oxa* + *burh*.

Oxendon, Great Northants. *Oxendone* 1086 (DB). 'Hill where oxen are pastured'. OE *oxa* (genitive plural *oxna*) + *dūn*.

Oxenholme Cumbria. *Oxinholme* 1274. 'River-meadow where oxen are pastured'. OE *oxa* (genitive plural *oxna*) + OScand. *holmr*.

Oxenhope W. Yorks. *Hoxnehop* 12th cent. 'Valley where oxen are kept'. OE *oxa* (genitive plural *oxna*) + *hop*.

Oxenton Glos. *Oxendone* 1086 (DB). 'Hill where oxen are pastured'. OE *oxa* (genitive plural *oxna*) + *dūn*.

Oxford Oxon. *Oxnaforda* 10th cent., *Oxeneford* 1086 (DB). 'Ford used by oxen'. OE *oxa* (genitive plural *oxna*) + *ford*. **Oxfordshire** (OE *scīr* 'district') is first referred to in the 11th cent.

Oxhey Herts. *Oxangehæge* 1007. 'Enclosure for oxen'. OE *oxa* (genitive plural *oxna*) + *(ge)hæg*.

Oxhill Warwicks. *Octeselve* 1086 (DB). 'Shelf or ledge of a man called Ohta'. OE pers. name + *scelf*.

Oxley W. Mids. *Oxelie* 1086 (DB).

'Woodland clearing where oxen are pastured'. OE *oxa* + *lēah*.

Oxshott Surrey. *Okesseta* 1179. 'Projecting piece of land of a man called Ocga'. OE pers. name + *scēat*.

Oxspring S. Yorks. *Ospring* (*sic*) 1086 (DB), *Oxspring* 1154. 'Spring frequented by oxen'. OE *oxa* + *spring*.

Oxted Surrey. *Acstede* 1086 (DB). 'Place where oak-trees grow'. OE *āc* + *stede*.

Oxton Notts. *Oxetune* 1086 (DB). 'Farmstead where oxen are kept'. OE *oxa* + *tūn*.

Oxwick Norfolk. *Ossuic* (*sic*) 1086 (DB), *Oxewic* 1242. 'Farm where oxen are kept'. OE *oxa* + *wīc*.

P

Packington Leics. *Pakinton* 1043, *Pachintone* 1086 (DB). 'Estate associated with a man called *Pac(c)a'. OE pers. name + *-ing-* + *tūn*.

Padbury Bucks. *Pateberie* 1086 (DB). 'Fortified place of a man called Padda'. OE pers. name + *burh* (dative *byrig*).

Paddington Gtr. London. *Padington* c.1050. 'Estate associated with a man called Padda'. OE pers. name + *-ing-* + *tūn*.

Paddlesworth Kent, near Folkestone. *Peadleswurthe* 11th cent. 'Enclosure of a man called *Pæddel'. OE pers. name + *worth*.

Paddock Wood Kent. *Parrok* 1279. OE *pearroc* 'small enclosure, paddock'.

Padiham Lancs. *Padiham* 1251. Possibly 'homestead or enclosure associated with a man called Padda'. OE pers. name + *-ing-* + *hām* or *hamm*.

Padley, Upper & Nether Derbys. *Paddeley* c.1230. 'Woodland clearing of a man called Padda', or 'one frequented by toads'. OE pers. name or OE **padde* + *lēah*.

Padstow Cornwall. *Sancte Petroces stow* 11th cent. 'Holy place of St Petroc'. Cornish saint's name + OE *stōw*.

Padworth Berks. *Peadanwurthe* 956, *Peteorde* 1086 (DB). 'Enclosure of a man called Peada'. OE pers. name + *worth*.

Pagham W. Sussex. *Pecganham* 680, *Pageham* 1086 (DB). 'Homestead or promontory of a man called *Pæcga'. OE pers. name + *hām* or *hamm*.

Paglesham Essex. *Paclesham* 1066, *Pachesham* (*sic*) 1086 (DB). 'Homestead or village of a man called *Pæccel'. OE pers. name + *hām*.

Paignton Devon. *Peintone* 1086 (DB). Probably 'estate associated with a man called Pǣga'. OE pers. name + *-ing-* + *tūn*.

Pailton Warwicks. *Pallentuna* 1077. 'Estate associated with a man called *Pægel'. OE pers. name + *-ing-* + *tūn*.

Painswick Glos. *Wiche* 1086 (DB), *Painswike* 1237. 'The dwelling or dairy farm', OE *wīc*. Later manorial affix from *Pain* Fitzjohn who held the manor in the early 12th cent.

Pakefield Suffolk. *Paggefella* 1086 (DB). 'Open land of a man called *Pacca'. OE pers. name + *feld*.

Pakenham Suffolk. *Pakenham* c.950, *Pachenham* 1086 (DB). 'Homestead or village of a man called *Pacca'. OE pers. name (genitive *-n*) + *hām*.

Palgrave Suffolk. *Palegrave* 962, *Palegraua* 1086 (DB). Probably 'grove where poles are got'. OE *pāl* + *grāf*.

Palgrave, Great Norfolk. *Pag(g)raua* 1086 (DB). Possibly 'grove of a man called Paga'. OE pers. name + *grāf*.

Palling, Sea Norfolk. *Pallinga* 1086 (DB). '(Settlement of) the family or followers of a man called Pælli'. OE pers. name + *-ingas*.

Palterton Derbys. *Paltertune* c.1002, *Paltretune* 1086 (DB). OE *tūn* 'farmstead' with an uncertain first element.

Pamber Hants. *Penberga* 1165. Probably 'hill with a fold or enclosure'. OE *penn* + *beorg*.

Pamphill Dorset. *Pamphilla* 1168. Possibly 'hill of a man called *Pampa or *Pempa', OE pers. name + *hyll*, but the first element may be an OE word **pamp* meaning 'hill'.

Pampisford Cambs. *Pampesuuorde* 1086 (DB). Probably 'enclosure of a man called *Pamp'. OE pers. name + *worth*.

Pancrasweek Devon. *Pancradeswike* 1197. 'Hamlet with a church dedicated to St Pancras'. OE *wīc*.

Panfield Essex. *Penfelda* 1086 (DB). 'Open land by the River Pant'. Celtic river-name (meaning 'valley') + OE *feld*.

Pangbourne Berks. *Pegingaburnan* 844, *Pangeborne* 1086 (DB). 'Stream of the family or followers of a man called Pǣga'. OE pers. name + *-inga-* + *burna*.

Pannal N. Yorks. *Panhal* 1170. 'Pan-shaped nook of land'. OE *panne* + *halh*.

Panton Lincs. *Pantone* 1086 (DB). Possibly 'farmstead near a hill or pan-shaped feature'. OE **pamp* or *panne* + *tūn*.

Panxworth Norfolk. *Pankesford* 1086 (DB). OE *ford* 'a ford' with an uncertain first element, possibly a pers. name.

Papcastle Cumbria. *Pabecastr* 1260. 'Roman fort occupied by a hermit'. OScand. *papi* + OE *cæster*.

Papplewick Notts. *Papleuuic* 1086 (DB). 'Dwelling or (dairy) farm in the pebbly place'. OE **papol* + *wīc*.

Papworth Everard & St Agnes Cambs. *Pappawyrthe* 1012, *Papeuuorde* 1086 (DB), *Pappewrth Everard* 1254, *Anneys Papwrth* 1241. 'Enclosure of a man called *Pappa'. OE pers. name + *worth*. Manorial affixes from 12th cent. owners called *Evrard* and *Agnes*.

Parbold Lancs. *Perebold* 1200. 'Dwelling where pears grow'. OE *peru* + *bold*.

Pardshaw Cumbria. *Perdishaw* c.1205. 'Hill or mound of a man called *Perd(i)'. OE pers. name + OScand. *haugr*.

Parham Suffolk. *Perreham* 1086 (DB). Probably 'homestead or enclosure where pears grow'. OE *peru* + *hām* or *hamm*.

Parkham Devon. *Percheham* 1086 (DB). Probably 'enclosure with paddocks'. OE *pearroc* + *hamm*.

Parley, West Dorset. *Perlai* 1086 (DB). 'Wood or clearing where pears grow'. OE *peru* + *lēah*.

Parndon, Great Essex. *Perenduna* 1086 (DB). 'Hill where pears grow'. OE **peren* + *dūn*.

Parson Drove Cambs. *Personesdroue* 1324. 'Cattle road used by or belonging to a parson'. ME *persone* + *drove*.

Partington Gtr. Manch. *Partinton* 1260. 'Estate associated with a man called *Pearta'. OE pers. name + *-ing-* + *tūn*.

Partney Lincs. *Peartaneu* 731, *Partenay* 1086 (DB). 'Island, or dry ground in marsh, of a man called *Pearta'. OE pers. name (genitive *-n*) + *ēg*.

Parwich Derbys. *Piowerwic* 963, *Pevrewic* 1086 (DB). Possibly 'dairy farm on the River *Pever*'. Lost Celtic river-name (meaning 'bright stream') + OE *wīc*.

Passenham Northants. *Passanhamme* early 10th cent., *Passeham* 1086 (DB). 'River-meadow of a man called Passa'. OE pers. name (genitive *-n*) + *hamm*.

Paston Norfolk. *Pastuna* 1086 (DB). Possibly 'farmstead of a man called *Pæcci', OE pers. name + *tūn*. Alternatively the first element may be an OE **pæsc(e)* 'muddy place, pool'.

Patcham E. Sussex. *Piceham* (*sic*) 1086 (DB), *Peccham* c.1090. Possibly 'homestead of a man called *Pæcca'. OE pers. name + *hām*.

Patching W. Sussex. *Pæccingas* 960, *Petchinges* 1086 (DB). '(Settlement of) the family or followers of a man called *Pæcc(i)'. OE pers. name + *-ingas*.

Patchway Avon. *Petshagh* 1276. 'Enclosure of a man called Pēot'. OE pers. name + *haga*.

Pateley Bridge N. Yorks. *Pathlay* 1202. 'Woodland clearing near the path(s)'. OE *pæth* + *lēah*.

Patney Wilts. *Peattanige* 963. 'Island or well-watered land of a man called *Peatta'. OE pers. name (genitive *-n*) + *ēg*.

Patrick Brompton N. Yorks., see BROMPTON.

Patrington Humber. *Patringtona* 1033, *Patrictone* 1086 (DB). OE *tūn* 'farmstead, estate' with an uncertain first element, probably a pers. name or folk-name.

Patrixbourne Kent. *Borne* 1086 (DB), *Patricburn* 1215. '(Place at) the stream'. OE *burna*, with later affix from William *Patricius* who held the manor in the 12th cent.

Patterdale Cumbria. *Patrichesdale* c.1180. 'Valley of a man called Patric'. OIrish pers. name + OScand. *dalr*.

Pattingham Staffs. *Patingham* 1086

(DB). 'Homestead of the family or followers of a man called *P(e)atta', or 'homestead at *P(e)atta's place'. OE pers. name + *-inga-* or *-ing* + *hām*.

Pattishall Northants. *Pascelle* (*sic*) 1086 (DB), *Patesshille* 12th cent. 'Hill of a man called *Pætti'. OE pers. name + *hyll*.

Paulerspury Northants. *Pirie* 1086 (DB), *Pirye Pavely* c.1280. Originally '(place at) the pear-tree', from OE *pirige*. Manorial affix from the *de Pavelli* family who held the manor from 1086, thus distinguishing this place from neighbouring POTTERSPURY.

Paull Humber. *Pagele* 1086 (DB). '(Place at) the stake (marking a landing-place)'. OE **pagol*.

Paulton Avon. *Palton* 1171. 'Farmstead on a ledge or hill-slope'. OE **peall* + *tūn*.

Pavenham Beds. *Pabeneham* 1086 (DB). 'Homestead or river-meadow of a man called *Papa'. OE pers. name (genitive *-n*) + *hām* or *hamm*.

Paxton, Great & Little Cambs. *Pachstone* 1086 (DB). Probably 'farmstead of a man called *Pæcc'. OE pers. name + *tūn*.

Payhembury Devon. *Hanberie* 1086 (DB), *Paihember* 1236. 'High or chief fortified place'. OE *hēah* (dative *hēan*) + *burh* (dative *byrig*). Later manorial affix from possession by a man called *Pæga*.

Paythorne Lancs. *Pathorme* 1086 (DB). Possibly 'thorn-tree of a man called Pái'. OScand. pers. name + *thorn*.

Peacehaven E. Sussex, a recent name for this new resort, chosen to commemorate the end of the First World War.

Peak District Derbys. *Pecsætna lond* 7th cent., *Pec* 1086. OE **pēac* 'a peak, a pointed hill', once applied to some particular hill but used of a larger area from early times. The first form means 'land of the peak dwellers', with OE *sǣte* + *land*.

Peakirk Cambs. *Pegecyrcan* 1016. 'Church of St Pega'. OE female saint's name + OE *cirice* (replaced by OScand. *kirkja*).

Peasemore Berks. *Praxemere* (*sic*) 1086 (DB), *Pesemere* 1166. 'Pond by which peas grow'. OE *pise* + *mere*.

Peasenhall Suffolk. *Pesehala* 1086 (DB). 'Nook of land where peas grow'. OE **pisen* + *halh*.

Peatling Magna & Parva Leics. *Petlinge* 1086 (DB). '(Settlement of) the family or followers of a man called *Pēotla'. OE pers. name + *-ingas*.

Pebmarsh Essex. *Pebeners* 1086 (DB). 'Ploughed field of a man called Pybba'. OE pers. name (genitive *-n*) + *ersc*.

Pebworth Heref. & Worcs. *Pebewrthe* 848, *Pebeworde* 1086 (DB). 'Enclosure of a man called *Peobba'. OE pers. name + *worth*.

Peckforton Ches. *Pevreton* 1086 (DB). 'Farmstead at the ford by a peak or hill'. OE **pēac* + *ford* + *tūn*.

Peckham, 'homestead by a peak or hill', OE **pēac* + *hām*: **Peckham** Gtr. London. *Pecheham* 1086 (DB). Peckham Rye (*-Rithe* 1520) is from OE *rīth* 'stream'. **Peckham, East & West** Kent. *Peccham* 10th cent., *Pecheham* 1086 (DB).

Peckleton Leics. *Pechintone* (*sic*) 1086 (DB), *Petlington* 1180. 'Estate associated with a man called *Peohtel'. OE pers. name + *-ing-* + *tūn*.

Pedmore W. Mids. *Pevemore* (*sic*) 1086 (DB), *Pubemora* 1176. 'Marsh of a man called Pybba'. OE pers. name + *mōr*.

Pegswood Northum. *Peggiswrth* 1242. 'Enclosure of a man called *Pecg'. OE pers. name + *worth*.

Pelaw Tyne & Wear. *Pellowe* 1242. Possibly 'mound or hill of a man called *Pēola'. OE pers. name + *hlāw*.

Peldon Essex. *Piltendone* c.950, *Peltenduna* 1086 (DB). Probably 'hill of a man called *Pylta'. OE pers. name (genitive *-n*) + *dūn*.

Pelham, Brent, Furneaux, & Stocking Herts. *Peleham* 1086 (DB), *Barndepelham* 1230, *Pelham Furnelle* 1240, *Stokenepelham* 1235. 'Homestead or village of a man called *Pēola'. OE pers. name + *hām*. Distinguishing affixes from OE *bærned* 'burnt, destroyed by fire', from the *de Fornellis* family here in the 13th cent., and from OE *stoccen* 'made of logs' or 'by the tree-stumps'.

Pelsall W. Mids. *Peoleshale* 996, *Peleshale* 1086 (DB). 'Nook of land of a man called *Pēol'. OE pers. name + *halh*.

Pelton Durham. *Pelton* 1312. Possibly 'farmstead of a man called *Pēola'. OE pers. name + *tūn*.

Pelynt Cornwall. *Plunent* 1086 (DB). 'Parish of Nennyd'. Cornish *plu* + saint's name.

Pembridge Heref. & Worcs. *Penebruge* 1086 (DB). Possibly 'bridge of a man called *Pena or *Pægna'. OE pers. name + *brycg*.

Pembury Kent. *Peppingeberia* c.1100. Possibly 'fortified place of the family or followers of a man called *Pepa or the like'. OE (?) pers. name + *-inga-* + *burh* (dative *byrig*).

Penare Cornwall. *Pennarth* 1284. 'The headland'. Cornish **penn-ardh*.

Pencombe Heref. & Worcs. *Pencumbe* 12th cent. Probably 'valley with an enclosure'. OE *penn* + *cumb*.

Pencoyd Heref. & Worcs. *Pencoyt* 1291. 'Wood's end'. Celtic **penn* + **coid*.

Pencraig Heref. & Worcs. *Penncreic* c.1150. 'Top of the crag or rocky hill'. Celtic **penn* + **creig*.

Pendlebury Gtr. Manch. *Penelbiri* 1202. 'Manor by the hill called *Penn*'. Celtic **penn* 'hill' + explanatory OE *hyll* + *burh* (dative *byrig*).

Pendleton Lancs. *Peniltune* 1086 (DB). 'Farmstead by the hill called *Penn* (Pendle Hill)'. Celtic **penn* 'hill' + explanatory OE *hyll* + *tūn*.

Pendock Heref. & Worcs. *Penedoc* 875, 1086 (DB). Possibly 'hill where barley is grown'. Celtic **penn* + **heiddiog*.

Penge Gtr. London. *Penceat* 1067. 'Wood's end', or 'chief wood'. Celtic **penn* + **cę̄d*.

Penhurst E. Sussex. *Penehest* (*sic*) 1086 (DB), *Peneherste* 12th cent. Possibly 'wooded hill of a man called *Pena'. OE pers. name + *hyrst*.

Penistone S. Yorks. *Pengestone* 1086 (DB), *Peningeston* 1199. Probably 'farmstead by a hill called *Penning*'. Celtic **penn* 'hill' + OE *-ing* + *tūn*.

Penketh Ches. *Penket* 1242. 'Wood's end'. Celtic **penn* + **cę̄d*.

Penkridge Staffs. *Pennocrucium* 4th cent., *Pancriz* 1086 (DB). 'Chief mound or tumulus'. Celtic **penn* + **crūg*.

Penn, '(place at) the hill', Celtic **penn*: **Penn** Bucks. *Penna* 1188. **Penn, Lower** (Staffs.) **& Upper** (W. Mids.) *Penne* 1086 (DB).

Pennard, East & West Somerset. *Pengerd* 681, *Pennarminstre* 1086 (DB). Celtic **penn* 'hill' with either **garth* 'ridge' or *ardd* 'high'. The Domesday form contains OE *mynster* 'large church'.

Pennines, The, a name first appearing in the 18th cent. and of unknown origin, perhaps based partly on the Celtic element **penn* 'hill' or an invention influenced by the name Apennines for the Italian mountain range.

Pennington, probably 'farmstead paying a penny rent', OE *pening* + *tūn*: **Pennington** Cumbria. *Pennigetun* 1086 (DB). **Pennington, Lower** Hants. *Penyton* 12th cent.

Penny Bridge Cumbria, a recent name, from a local family called *Penny*.

Penrith Cumbria. *Penrith* c.1100. 'Hill ford' or 'chief ford'. Celtic **penn* + **rïd*.

Penruddock Cumbria. *Penreddok* 1278. Celtic **penn* 'hill' or 'chief', with an uncertain second element.

Penryn Cornwall. *Penryn* 1236. 'The promontory or headland'. Cornish *penn rynn*.

Pensax Heref. & Worcs. *Pensaxan* 11th cent. 'Hill of the Anglo-Saxons'. Celtic **penn* + **Sachson*. The order of elements is Celtic.

Pensby Mersey. *Penisby* c.1229. 'Farmstead or village at a hill called *Penn*'. Celtic **penn* 'hill' + OScand. *bý*.

Penselwood Somerset. *Penne* 1086 (DB), *Penne in Selewode* 1345. Celtic **penn* 'hill' with the later addition 'in SELWOOD'.

Pensford Avon. *Pensford* 1400. OE *ford* 'a ford' with an uncertain first element, possibly a pers. name.

Penshurst Kent. *Pensherst* 1072. Possibly 'wooded hill of a man called *Pefen'. OE pers. name + *hyrst*.

Pentire, West Pentire Cornwall. *Pentir c.*1270. 'The headland'. Cornish *penn tir*.

Pentney Norfolk. *Penteleiet (sic)* 1086 (DB), *Pentenay* 1200. Possibly 'island, or dry ground in marsh, of a man called *Penta'. OE pers. name (genitive *-n*) + *ēg*.

Penton Mewsey Hants. *Penitone* 1086 (DB), *Penitune Meysi* 1264. 'Farmstead paying a penny rent'. OE *pening* + *tūn*. Manorial affix from the *de Meisy* family, here in the 13th cent.

Pentrich Derbys. *Pentric* 1086 (DB). 'Hill of the boar'. Celtic **penn* + **tyrch*.

Pentridge Dorset. *Pentric* 762, 1086 (DB). Identical in origin with the previous name.

Penwith Cornwall, see ST JUST.

Penwortham, Higher & Lower Lancs. *Peneverdant (sic)* 1086 (DB), *Penuertham* 1149. Probably 'enclosed homestead at a hill called *Penn*'. Celtic **penn* 'hill' + OE *worth* + *hām*.

Penzance Cornwall. *Pensans* 1284. 'Holy headland'. Cornish *penn* + *sans*.

Peopleton Heref. & Worcs. *Piplincgtun* 972, *Piplintune* 1086 (DB). Probably 'estate associated with a man called *Pyppel'. OE pers. name + *-ing-* + *tūn*.

Peover, Lower Ches. *Pevre* 1086 (DB). Named from the River Peover, a Celtic river-name meaning 'the bright one'.

Peper Harow Surrey. *Pipereherge* 1086 (DB). Probably 'heathen temple of the pipers'. OE *pīpere* + *hearg*.

Perivale Gtr. London. *Pyryvale* 1508. 'Pear-tree valley'. ME *perie* + *vale*.

Perranarworthal Cornwall. *Arewethel* 1181, 'church of *Sanctus Pieranus* in *Arwothel*' 1388. 'Parish of St Piran (in the place) beside the marsh'. Cornish saint's name + **ar* + **goethel*.

Perranporth Cornwall. *St Perins creeke* 1577, *Perran Porth* 1810. 'Cove or harbour of St Piran's parish', from English dialect *porth*, with reference to PERRANZABULOE.

Perranuthnoe Cornwall. *Odenol* 1086 (DB), 'church of *Sanctus Pieranus* of *Udno*' 1373. 'Parish of St Piran in the manor of *Uthno*' (meaning obscure).

Perranzabuloe Cornwall. *Lanpiran* 1086 (DB), *Peran in Zabulo* 1535. 'Parish of St Piran in the sand'. Cornish saint's name (with **lann* 'church-site' in the first form) + Latin *in sabulo*.

Perrott, named from the River Parrett, a pre-English river-name of obscure origin: **Perrott, North** Somerset. *Peddredan c.*1050, *Peret* 1086 (DB). **Perrott, South** Dorset. *Pedret* 1086 (DB), *Suthperet* 1268.

Perry Barr W. Mids. *Pirio* 1086 (DB). '(Place at) the pear-tree'. OE *pirige*. It is close to GREAT BARR.

Pershore Heref. & Worcs. *Perscoran* 972, *Persore* 1086 (DB). 'Slope or bank where osiers grow'. OE **persc* + *ōra*.

Pertenhall Beds. *Partenhale* 1086 (DB). 'Nook of land of a man called *Pearta'. OE pers. name (genitive *-n*) + *halh*.

Perton Staffs. *Pertona* 1167. 'Farmstead where pears grow'. OE *peru* + *tūn*.

Peterborough Cambs. *Burg* 1086 (DB), *Petreburgh* 1333. 'St Peter's town'. OE *burh*, with saint's name from the dedication of the abbey.

Peterchurch Heref. & Worcs. *Petrescherche* 1302. 'Church dedicated to St Peter'. OE *cirice*.

Peterlee Durham, a recent name, created to commemorate the trade union leader Peter Lee (died 1935).

Petersham Gtr. London. *Patricesham* 1086 (DB). 'Homestead or river-bend land of a man called *Peohtrīc'. OE pers. name + *hām* or *hamm*.

Petersfield Hants. *Peteresfeld* 1182. Probably '(settlement at) the open land with a church dedicated to St Peter'. OE *feld*.

Peters Marland Devon, see MARLAND.

Peterstow Heref. & Worcs. *Peterestow* 1207. 'Holy place of St Peter'. OE *stōw*.

Peter Tavy Devon, see TAVY.

Petham Kent. *Pettham c.*961, *Piteham* 1086 (DB). 'Homestead or enclosure in a hollow'. OE *pytt* + *hām* or *hamm*.

Petherick, Little Cornwall. 'Parish of *Sanctus Petrocus Minor*' 1327. From the dedication of the church to St Petrock.

Petherton, 'farmstead on the River Parrett', pre-English river-name of obscure origin + OE *tūn*: **Petherton,**

North Somerset. *Nordperet, Peretune* 1086 (DB). **Petherton, South** Somerset. *Sudperetone* 1086 (DB).

Petherwin, '(church of) Padern the blessed', from the Cornish patron saint of the church + *gwynn* 'blessed': **Petherwin, North** Cornwall. *North Piderwine* 1259. **Petherwin, South** Cornwall. *Suthpydrewyn* 1269.

Petrockstow Devon. *Petrochestou* 1086 (DB). 'Holy place of St Petrock'. Cornish saint's name + OE *stōw*.

Pett E. Sussex. *Pette* 1195. '(Place at) the pit'. OE *pytt*.

Pettaugh Suffolk. *Petehaga* 1086 (DB). 'Enclosure of a man called Pēota'. OE pers. name + *haga*.

Pettistree Suffolk. *Petrestre* 1253. 'Tree of a man called Peohtrēd'. OE pers. name + *trēow*.

Petton Devon. *Petetona c.*1150. 'Farmstead of a man called *Peatta'. OE pers. name + *tūn*.

Petton Shrops. *Pectone* 1086 (DB). 'Farmstead by a hill or point'. OE **pēac* + *tūn*.

Petworth W. Sussex. *Peteorde* 1086 (DB). 'Enclosure of a man called Pēota'. OE pers. name + *worth*.

Pevensey E. Sussex. *Pefenesea* 947, *Pevenesel* 1086 (DB). 'River of a man called *Pefen'. OE pers. name + *ēa*.

Pewsey Wilts. *Pefesigge c.*880, *Pevesie* 1086 (DB). 'Island or well-watered land of a man called *Pefe'. OE pers. name + *ēg*.

Pexall, Lower Ches. *Pexhull* 1274. 'Hill called *Pēac*'. OE **pēac* 'hill' + *hyll*.

Phillack Cornwall. 'Church of *Sancta Felicitas*' (*sic*) 1259, *Felok* 1388. From the dedication of the church to a St Felek.

Philleigh Cornwall. 'Church of *Sanctus Filius*' 1312. From the dedication of the church to a St Fily.

Pickenham, North & South Norfolk. *Pichenham* 1086 (DB). Probably 'homestead or village of a man called *Pīca'. OE pers. name (genitive *-n*) + *hām*.

Pickering N. Yorks. *Picheringa* 1086 (DB). Possibly '(settlement of) the family or followers of a man called *Pīcer'. OE pers. name + *-ingas*.

Pickhill N. Yorks. *Picala* 1086 (DB). 'Nook of land by the pointed hills', or 'nook of a man called *Pīca'. OE *pīc* or pers. name + *halh*.

Picklescott Shrops. *Pikelescote c.*1230. 'Cottage(s) of a man called Pīcel'. OE pers. name + *cot*.

Pickmere Ches. *Pichemere* 12th cent. 'Lake where pike are found'. OE *pīc* + *mere*.

Pickwell Leics. *Pichewell* 1086 (DB). 'Spring or stream by the pointed hill(s)'. OE *pīc* + *wella*.

Pickworth, 'enclosure of a man called *Pīca', OE pers. name + *worth*: **Pickworth** Leics. *Pikeworda c.*1215. **Pickworth** Lincs. *Picheuuorde* 1086 (DB).

Picton, 'farmstead of a man called *Pīca', OE pers. name + *tūn*: **Picton** Ches. *Picheton* 1086 (DB). **Picton** N. Yorks. *Piketon* 1200.

Piddinghoe E. Sussex. *Pidingeho* 12th cent. 'Hill-spur of the family or followers of a man called *Pyda'. OE pers. name + *-inga-* + *hōh*.

Piddington, 'estate associated with a man called *Pyda', OE pers. name + *-ing-* + *tūn*: **Piddington** Northants. *Pidentone* 1086 (DB). **Piddington** Oxon. *Petintone* 1086 (DB).

Piddlehinton Dorset. *Pidele* 1086 (DB), *Pidel Hineton* 1244. 'Estate on the River Piddle belonging to a religious community'. OE river-name (**pidele* 'a marsh or fen') + *hīwan* + *tūn*.

Piddle, North & Wyre Heref. & Worcs. *Pidele(t)* 1086 (DB), *Northpidele* 1271, *Wyre Pidele* 1208. Named from Piddle Brook (OE **pidele* 'a marsh or fen'). Affix *Wyre* is probably from WYRE FOREST.

Piddletrenthide Dorset. *Uppidelen* 966, *Pidrie* 1086 (DB), *Pidele Trentehydes* 1212. 'Estate on the River Piddle assessed at thirty hides'. OE river-name (see PIDDLEHINTON) + OFrench *trente* + OE *hīd*.

Pidley Cambs. *Pydele* 1228. 'Woodland clearing of a man called *Pyda'. OE pers. name + *lēah*.

Piercebridge Durham. *Persebrigc c.*1050. Probably 'bridge where osiers grow'. OE **persc* + *brycg*.

Pigdon Northum. *Pikedenn* 1205. 'Valley of a man called *Pīca, or by the pointed hills'. OE pers. name or OE *pīc* + *denu*.

Pilgrims Hatch Essex. *Pylgremeshacch* 1483. 'Hatch-gate used by pilgrims' (to the chapel of St Thomas). ME *pilegrim* + OE *hæcc*.

Pilham Lincs. *Pileham* 1086 (DB). Probably 'homestead or enclosure made with stakes'. OE *pīl* + *hām* or *hamm*.

Pillaton Cornwall. *Pilatona* 1086 (DB). 'Farmstead made with stakes'. OE *pīl* + *tūn*.

Pillerton Hersey Warwicks. *Pilardintone* 1086 (DB), *Pilardinton Hersy* 1247. 'Estate associated with a man called Pīlheard'. OE pers. name + *-ing-* + *tūn*. Manorial affix from the *de Hersy* family, here in the 13th cent.

Pilley S. Yorks. *Pillei* 1086 (DB). 'Wood or clearing where stakes are obtained'. OE *pīl* + *lēah*.

Pilling Lancs. *Pylin c.*1195. Named from the River Pilling, probably OE *pyll* 'creek' + *-ing*.

Pilsbury Derbys. *Pilesberie* 1086 (DB). 'Fortified place of a man called *Pīl'. OE pers. name + *burh* (dative *byrig*).

Pilsdon Dorset. *Pilesdone* 1086 (DB). Probably 'hill with a peak', or 'hill marked by a stake'. OE *pīl* + *dūn*.

Pilsley Derbys., near Clay Cross. *Pilleslege c.*1002, *Pinneslei* 1086 (DB). Possibly 'woodland clearing of a man called *Pinnel'. OE pers. name + *lēah*.

Pilton Leics. *Pilton* 1202. Probably 'farmstead by a stream'. OE *pyll* + *tūn*.

Pilton Northants. *Pilchetone* 1086 (DB). 'Farmstead of a man called *Pīleca'. OE pers. name + *tūn*.

Pilton Somerset. *Piltune* 725, *Piltone* 1086 (DB). Identical in origin with PILTON (Leics.).

Pimperne Dorset. *Pimpern* 935, *Pinpre* 1086 (DB). Possibly 'five trees' from Celtic **pimp* + *prenn*, or 'place among the hills' from a derivative of an OE word **pimp* 'hill'.

Pinchbeck Lincs. *Pincebec* 1086 (DB). 'Minnow stream', or 'finch ridge'. OE **pinc* or **pinca* + *bece* (influenced by OScand. *bekkr*) or *bæc* (locative **bece*).

Pinhoe Devon. *Peonho c.*1050, *Pinnoc* 1086 (DB). 'Hill-spur called *Pen*'. Celtic **penn* 'hill' + OE *hōh*.

Pinner Gtr. London. *Pinnora* 1232. 'Peg-shaped or pointed ridge or bank'. OE *pinn* + *ōra*. The river-name Pinn is a 'back-formation' from the place-name.

Pinvin Heref. & Worcs. *Pendefen* 1187. 'Fen of a man called Penda'. OE pers. name + *fenn*.

Pinxton Derbys. *Penkeston* 1208. Possibly 'farmstead of a man called *Penec'. OE pers. name + *tūn*.

Pipe Heref. & Worcs. *Pipe* 1086 (DB). OE *pīpe* 'a pipe, a conduit', originally referring to the stream here.

Pipe Ridware Staffs., see RIDWARE.

Pipewell Northants. *Pipewelle* 1086 (DB). 'Spring or stream with a pipe or conduit'. OE *pīpe* + *wella*.

Pirbright Surrey. *Perifrith* 1166. 'Sparse woodland where pear-trees grow'. OE *pirige* + *fyrhth*.

Pirton, 'pear orchard, or farmstead where pear-trees grow', OE *pirige* + *tūn*: **Pirton** Heref. & Worcs. *Pyritune* 972, *Peritune* 1086 (DB). **Pirton** Herts. *Peritone* 1086 (DB).

Pishill Oxon. *Pesehull* 1195. 'Hill where peas grow'. OE *pise* + *hyll*.

Pitchcott Bucks. *Pichecote* 1176. 'Cottage or shed where pitch is made or stored'. OE *pic* + *cot*.

Pitchford Shrops. *Piceforde* 1086 (DB). 'Ford near a place where pitch is found'. OE *pic* + *ford*.

Pitcombe Somerset. *Pidecombe* 1086 (DB). Probably 'marsh valley'. OE **pide* + *cumb*.

Pitminster Somerset. *Pipingmynstre* 938, *Pipeminstre* 1086 (DB). 'Church associated with a man called Pippa'. OE pers. name + *-ing-* + *mynster*.

Pitney Somerset. *Petenie* 1086 (DB). 'Island, or dry ground in marsh, of a man called *Pytta or Pēota'. OE pers. name (genitive *-n*) + *ēg*.

Pitsea Essex. *Piceseia* 1086 (DB). 'Island

or dry ground in marsh, of a man called Pīc'. OE pers. name + *ēg*.

Pitsford Northants. *Pitesford* 1086 (DB). 'Ford of a man called *Peoht'. OE pers. name + *ford*.

Pitstone Bucks. *Pincelestorne* (*sic*) 1086 (DB), *Pichelesthorne* 1220. 'Thorn-tree of a man called Pīcel'. OE pers. name + *thorn*.

Pittington Durham. *Pittindun* c.1085. 'Hill associated with a man called *Pytta'. OE pers. name + *-ing-* + *dūn*.

Pitton Wilts. *Putenton* 1165. 'Farmstead of a man called Putta, or one frequented by hawks'. OE pers. name or OE *putta* + *tūn*.

Plaish Shrops. *Plesc*, *Plæsc* 963, *Plesha* 1086 (DB). '(Place at) the shallow pool'. OE **plæsc*.

Plaistow W. Sussex. *La Pleyestowe* 1271. 'Place for play or sport'. OE *pleg-stōw*. The same name occurs in other counties.

Plaitford Hants. *Pleiteford* 1086 (DB). Probably 'ford where play or sport takes place'. OE **pleget* + *ford*.

Plawsworth Durham. *Plauworth* 1297. Possibly 'enclosure for play or sport'. OE *plaga* + *worth*, but the first element might be a pers. name.

Plaxtol Kent. *Plextole* 1386. 'Place for play or sport'. OE *pleg-stōw*.

Playden E. Sussex. *Pleidena* 1086 (DB). 'Woodland pasture where play or sport takes place'. OE *plega* + *denn*.

Playford Suffolk. *Plegeforda* 1086 (DB). 'Ford where play or sport takes place'. OE *plega* + *ford*.

Plealey Shrops. *Pleyleye* 1308. 'Woodland clearing where play or sport takes place'. OE *plega* + *lēah*.

Pleasington Lancs. *Plesigtuna* 1196. 'Estate associated with a man called Plēsa'. OE pers. name + *-ing-* + *tūn*.

Pleasley Derbys. *Pleseleia* 1166. 'Woodland clearing of a man called Plēsa'. OE pers. name + *lēah*.

Plenmeller Northum. *Playnmelor* 1279. Probably 'top of the bare hill'. Celtic **blain* + **mēl* + **brez*.

Pleshey Essex. *Plaseiz* c.1150. OFrench *plaisseis* 'an enclosure made with interlaced fencing'.

Plowden Shrops. *Plaueden* 1252. 'Valley where play or sport takes place'. OE *plaga* + *denu*.

Pluckley Kent. *Pluchelei* 1086 (DB). 'Woodland clearing of a man called Plucca'. OE pers. name + *lēah*.

Plumbland Cumbria. *Plumbelund* c.1150. 'Plum-tree grove'. OE *plūme* + OScand. *lundr*.

Plumley Ches. *Plumleia* 1119. 'Plum-tree wood or clearing'. OE *plūme* + *lēah*.

Plumpton, 'farmstead where plum-trees grow', OE *plūme* + *tūn*: **Plumpton** Cumbria. *Plumton* 1212. **Plumpton** E. Sussex. *Pluntune* 1086 (DB). **Plumpton, Great & Little** Lancs. *Pluntun* 1086 (DB).

Plumstead, 'place where plum-trees grow', OE *plūme* + *stede*: **Plumstead** Gtr. London. *Plumstede* 961–9, *Plumestede* 1086 (DB). **Plumstead** Norfolk, near Holt. *Plumestede* 1086 (DB). **Plumstead, Great & Little** Norfolk. *Plumesteda* 1086 (DB).

Plumtree Notts. *Pluntre* 1086 (DB). '(Place at) the plum-tree'. OE *plūm-trēow*.

Plungar Leics. *Plungar* c.1125. 'Triangular plot where plum-trees grow'. OE *plūme* + *gāra*.

Plush Dorset. *Plyssch* 891. '(Place at) the shallow pool'. OE **plysc*.

Plymouth Devon. *Plymmue* 1230. 'Mouth of the River Plym'. OE *mūtha* with a river-name formed from the next name by the process of 'back-formation'.

Plympton Devon. *Plymentun* c.905, *Plintona* 1086 (DB). 'Farmstead of the plum-tree'. OE *plȳme* + *tūn*.

Plymstock Devon. *Plemestocha* 1086. Probably 'outlying farmstead or hamlet connected with PLYMPTON'. OE *stoc*.

Plymtree Devon. *Plumtrei* 1086 (DB). '(Place at) the plum-tree'. OE **plȳm-trēow*.

Pockley N. Yorks. *Pochelac* (*sic*) 1086 (DB), *Pokelai* c.1190. 'Woodland clearing of a man called *Poca'. OE pers. name + *lēah*.

Pocklington Humber. *Poclinton* 1086 (DB). 'Estate associated with a man called *Pocela'. OE pers. name + *-ing-* + *tūn*.

Podimore Somerset, probably identical in origin with PODMORE.

Podington Beds. *Podintone* 1086 (DB). 'Estate associated with a man called Poda or Puda'. OE pers. name + *-ing-* + *tūn*.

Podmore Staffs. *Podemore* 1086 (DB). 'Marsh frequented by toads or frogs'. ME *pode* + OE *mōr*.

Pointon Lincs. *Pochinton* 1086 (DB). 'Estate associated with a man called Pohha'. OE pers. name + *-ing-* + *tūn*.

Polden Hill Somerset, see CHILTON POLDEN.

Polebrook Northants. *Pochebroc* 1086 (DB). 'Brook by a pouch-shaped feature', OE *pohha* + *brōc*. Alternatively the first element may be an OE **poc(c)e* 'frog'.

Polesworth Warwicks. *Polleswyrth* c.1000. 'Enclosure of a man called *Poll'. OE pers. name + *worth*.

Poling W. Sussex. *Palinges* 1199. '(Settlement of) the family or followers of a man called *Pāl'. OE pers. name + *-ingas*.

Pollicott, Upper Bucks. *Policote* 1086 (DB). Possibly 'cottage(s) associated with a man called *Poll'. OE pers. name + *-ing-* + *cot*.

Pollington Humber. *Pouelington* c.1185. 'Farmstead associated with a piece of ground called *Pofel*'. OE **pofel* (of uncertain meaning) + *-ing-* + *tūn*.

Polperro Cornwall. *Portpira* 1303. Probably 'harbour of a man called *Pyra'. Cornish *porth* + pers. name.

Polruan Cornwall. *Porthruan* 1284. 'Harbour of a man called Ruveun'. Cornish *porth* + pers. name.

Polsham Somerset. *Paulesham* 1065. 'Enclosure of a man called Paul'. ME pers. name + OE *hamm*.

Polstead Suffolk. *Polstede* c.975, *Polesteda* 1086 (DB). 'Place by a pool'. OE *pōl* + *stede*.

Poltimore Devon. *Pultimore* 1086 (DB). Possibly 'marshy ground of a man called *Pulta'. OE pers. name + *mōr*.

Pontefract W. Yorks. *Pontefracto* 1090. 'Broken bridge'. Latin *pons* + *fractus*.

Ponteland Northum. *Punteland* 1203. 'Cultivated land by the river called Pont'. Celtic river-name (meaning 'valley') + OE *ēa-land*.

Pontesbury Shrops. *Pantesberie* 1086 (DB). Possibly 'fortified place of a man called Pant', OE pers. name + *burh* (dative *byrig*), but the first element could be an old Celtic river-name meaning 'valley'.

Ponton, Great & Little Lincs. *Pamptune* 1086 (DB). Probably 'farmstead by a hill'. OE **pamp* + *tūn*.

Pool, Poole, usually '(place at) the pool or creek', OE *pōl*: **Poole** Dorset. *Pole* 1183. **Poole Keynes** Glos. *Pole* 10th cent., 1086 (DB). **Pool, South** Devon. *Pole* 1086 (DB).

However the following has a different origin: **Pool** W. Yorks. *Pofle* c.1030, *Pouele* 1086 (DB). From an OE word **pofel* of uncertain meaning.

Pooley Bridge Cumbria. *Pulhoue* 1252. 'Hill or mound by a pool'. OE *pōl* + OScand. *haugr*.

Poorton, North & South Dorset. *Pourtone* 1086 (DB). OE *tūn* 'farmstead' with an obscure first element which may be an old river-name.

Popham Hants. *Popham* 903, *Popeham* 1086 (DB). OE *hām* 'homestead' or *hamm* 'enclosure' with an uncertain first element, possibly an OE **pop(p)* 'pebble'.

Poplar Gtr. London. *Popler* 1327. '(Place at) the poplar tree'. ME *popler*.

Poppleton, Upper N. Yorks. *Popeltune* c.972, *Popletone* 1086 (DB). 'Farmstead on pebbly soil'. OE **popel* + *tūn*.

Poringland, East Norfolk. *Porringalanda* 1086 (DB). 'Cultivated land or estate of a tribe called the *Porringas*'. Obscure first element (probably an OE pers. name) + *-inga-* + *land*.

Porlock Somerset. *Portloca* 10th cent., *Portloc* 1086 (DB). 'Enclosure by the harbour'. OE *port* + *loca*.

Portbury Avon. *Porberie* 1086 (DB). 'Fortified place near the harbour'. OE *port* + *burh* (dative *byrig*).

Portchester Hants. *Porteceaster c.*960, *Portcestre* 1086 (DB). 'Roman fort by the harbour'. OE *port* + *ceaster*.

Portesham Dorset. *Porteshamme* 1024, *Portesham* 1086 (DB). 'Enclosure or valley near a harbour or market town'. OE *port* + *hamm*.

Port Gate Northum. *Portyate* 1269. OE *port* 'gate' with explanatory OE *geat* 'gate', referring to the gap in Hadrian's Wall where Watling Street runs through it.

Porthallow Cornwall, near Manaccan. *Worthalaw* (*sic*) 967, *Porthaleu* 1333. 'Cove or harbour by a stream called *Alaw*'. Cornish *porth* + river-name (probably pre-Celtic) of uncertain meaning.

Portington Humber. *Portinton* 1086 (DB). 'Farmstead belonging to a market town'. OE *port* + *-ing-* + *tūn*.

Portinscale Cumbria. *Porqeneschal c.*1160. 'Shielings of the harlots'. OE *port-cwēn* + OScand. *skáli*.

Portishead Avon. *Portesheve* (*sic*) 1086 (DB), *Portesheved* 1200. 'Headland by the harbour'. OE *port* + *hēafod*.

Portland, Isle of Dorset. *Port* 9th cent., *Portlande* 862, *Porland* 1086 (DB). 'Estate by the harbour'. OE *port* + *land*. Portland Bill, recorded from 1649, is from OE *bile* 'a bill, a beak' used topographically for 'promontory'.

Portlemouth, East Devon. *Porlamuta* (*sic*) 1086 (DB), *Porthelemuthe* 1308. Possibly 'harbour estuary', from Cornish *porth* + **heyl* with OE *mūtha* 'mouth'. Alternatively 'mouth of the harbour stream', from OE *port* + *wella* + *mūtha*.

Porton Wilts. *Portone* 1086 (DB). Probably identical in origin with POORTON (Dorset).

Portsdown Hants. *Portesdone* 1086 (DB). 'Hill by the harbour'. OE *port* + *dūn*.

Portsea Hants. *Portesig* 982. 'Harbour island'. OE *port* + *ēg*.

Portslade by Sea E. Sussex. *Porteslage* (*sic*) 1086 (DB), *Portes Ladda c.*1095. Probably 'crossing-place near the harbour'. OE *port* + *gelād*.

Portsmouth Hants. *Portesmuthan* late 9th cent. 'Mouth of the harbour'. OE *port* + *mūtha*.

Port Sunlight Mersey., a modern name for the late 19th-cent. model village, called after the brand-name of the soap made here.

Portswood Hants. *Porteswuda* 1045. 'Wood belonging to the market town'. OE *port* + *wudu*.

Poslingford Suffolk. *Poslingeorda* 1086 (DB). 'Enclosure of the family or followers of a man called *Possel'. OE pers. name + *-inga-* + *worth*.

Postling Kent. *Postingas* (*sic*) 1086 (DB), *Postlinges* 1212. Possibly '(settlement of) the family or followers of a man called *Possel'. OE pers. name + *-ingas*.

Postwick Norfolk. *Possuic* 1086 (DB). 'Dwelling or (dairy) farm of a man called *Possa'. OE pers. name + *wīc*.

Potsgrove Beds. *Potesgrave* 1086 (DB). 'Grove near a pit or pot-hole'. OE *pott* + *grāf*.

Potter Brompton N. Yorks., see BROMPTON.

Potterhanworth Lincs. *Haneworde* 1086 (DB). 'Enclosure of a man called Hana'. OE pers. name + *worth*, the later affix referring to pot-making here.

Potter Heigham Norfolk, see HEIGHAM.

Potterne Wilts. *Poterne* 1086 (DB). 'Building where pots are made'. OE *pott* + *ærn*.

Potters Bar Herts. *Potterys Barre* 1509. 'Forest-gate of a family called *Potter*'. ME surname + *barre*.

Potterspury Northants. *Perie* 1086 (DB), *Potterispirye* 1287. Originally '(place at) the pear-tree', from OE *pirige*, with later affix *Potters-* 'of the pot-maker(s)' from the pottery here. See PAULERSPURY.

Potter Street Essex. *Potters streete* 1594. Named from a family called *le Pottere* ('the potmaker') here in the 13th cent.

Potto N. Yorks. *Pothow* 1202. 'Mound or hill by a pit or where pots were found'. OE *pott* + OScand. *haugr*.

Potton Beds. *Pottun c.*960, *Potone* 1086 (DB). 'Farmstead where pots are made'. OE *pott* + *tūn*.

Pott Shrigley Ches., see SHRIGLEY.

Poughill Cornwall. *Pochehelle (sic)* 1086 (DB), *Pochewell* 1227. 'Spring or stream by a feature resembling a pouch or bag', or 'spring or stream of a man called Pohha'. OE *pohha* or pers. name + *wella*.

Poughill Devon. *Pochehille* 1086 (DB). 'Bag-shaped hill', or 'hill of a man called Pohha'. OE *pohha* or pers. name + *hyll*.

Poulshot Wilts. *Paveshou (sic)* 1086 (DB), *Paulesholt* 1187. 'Wood of a man called Paul'. ME pers. name + OE *holt*.

Poulton, 'farmstead by a pool or creek', OE **pull* or *pōl* + *tūn*: **Poulton** Glos. *Pultune* 855. **Poulton** Mersey., near Seacombe. *Pulton* 1260. **Poulton-le-Fylde** Lancs. *Poltun* 1086 (DB). Affix means 'in the district called The Fylde', from OE *filde* 'a plain' (recorded as *Filde* 1246).

Poundon Bucks. *Paundon* 1255. OE *dūn* 'hill' with an uncertain first element.

Poundstock Cornwall. *Pondestoch* 1086 (DB). 'Outlying farmstead or hamlet with a pound for animals'. OE **pund* + *stoc*.

Powderham Devon. *Poldreham* 1086 (DB). 'Promontory in reclaimed marshland'. OE **polra* + *hamm*.

Powerstock Dorset. *Povrestoch* 1086 (DB). OE *stoc* 'outlying farmstead' with the same obscure first element as in POORTON.

Powick Heref. & Worcs. *Poincguuic* 972, *Poiwic* 1086 (DB). 'Dwelling or farm associated with a man called Pohha'. OE pers. name + *-ing-* + *wīc*.

Poxwell Dorset. *Poceswylle* 987, *Pocheswelle* 1086 (DB). 'Steeply rising ground of a man called *Poca', or 'spring of a man called *Poc'. OE pers. name + **swelle* or *wella*.

Poynings W. Sussex. *Puningas* 960, *Poninges* 1086 (DB). '(Settlement of) the family or followers of a man called *Pūn(a)'. OE pers. name + *-ingas*.

Poyntington Dorset. *Ponditone* 1086 (DB). 'Estate associated with a man called *Punt'. OE pers. name + *-ing-* + *tūn*.

Poynton Ches. *Povinton* 1249. 'Estate associated with a man called *Pofa'. OE pers. name + *-ing-* + *tūn*.

Poynton Green Shrops. *Peventone* 1086 (DB). 'Estate associated with a man called *Pēofa'. OE pers. name + *-ing-* + *tūn*.

Prawle, East Devon. *Prenla (sic)* 1086 (DB), *Prahulle* 1204. Probably 'look-out hill'. OE **prāw* + *hyll*.

Preen, Church Shrops. *Prene* 1086 (DB), *Chirche Prene* 1301. OE *prēon* 'a brooch, a pin', perhaps used figuratively of the hill here, with later affix OE *cirice*.

Prees Shrops. *Pres* 1086 (DB). '(Place by) the brushwood or thicket'. OWelsh *pres*.

Preesall Lancs. *Pressouede* 1086 (DB). 'Brushwood headland'. OWelsh *pres* + OScand. *hǫfuth* or OE *hēafod*.

Prendwick Northum. *Prendewic* 1242. 'Dwelling or farm of a man called Prend'. OE pers. name + *wīc*.

Prenton Mersey. *Prestune (sic)* 1086 (DB), *Prenton* 1260. 'Farmstead of a man called Præn'. OE pers. name + *tūn*.

Prescot(t), 'priests' cottage(s)', OE *prēost* + *cot*; for example **Prescot** Mersey. *Prestecota* 1178.

Prestbury, 'manor of the priests', OE *prēost* + *burh* (dative *byrig*): **Prestbury** Ches. *Presteberi* 1181. **Prestbury** Glos. *Preosdabyrig c.*900, *Presteberie* 1086 (DB).

Presthope Shrops. *Presthope* 1167. 'Valley of the priests'. OE *prēost* + *hop*.

Preston, a common name, 'farmstead of the priests', OE *prēost* + *tūn*; examples include: **Preston** Dorset. *Prestun* 1228. **Preston** E. Sussex. *Prestetone* 1086 (DB). **Preston** Humber. *Prestone* 1086 (DB). **Preston** Lancs. *Prestune* 1086 (DB). **Preston** Northum. *Preston* 1242. **Preston Bissett** Bucks. *Prestone* 1086 (DB), *Preston Byset* 1327. Manorial affix from the *Biset* family, holders of the manor from the 12th cent. **Preston Capes** Northants. *Prestetone* 1086 (DB), *Preston Capes* 1300. Manorial affix from the *de Capes* family, here in the 13th cent. **Preston Gubbals** Shrops. *Prestone* 1086 (DB), *Preston Gobald* 1292. Manorial affix from a priest called *Godebold* who held the manor in 1086. **Preston, Long** N. Yorks. *Prestune* 1086

(DB). Affix refers to the length of the village. **Preston-under-Scar** N. Yorks. *Prestun* 1086 (DB), *Preston undescar* 1568. Affix means 'under the rocky hill' from OScand. *sker*. **Preston Wynne** Heref. & Worcs. *Prestetune* 1086 (DB). Manorial affix from a family called *la Wyne* here in the 14th cent.

Preston Candover Hants., see CANDOVER.

Prestwich Gtr. Manch. *Prestwich* 1194. 'Dwelling or farm of the priest(s)'. OE *prēost* + *wīc*.

Prestwick Northum. *Prestwic* 1242. Identical in origin with the previous name.

Priddy Somerset. *Pridia* 1182. Probably 'earth house'. Celtic **prith* + **tïȝ*.

Primethorpe Leics. *Torp* 1086 (DB), *Prymesthorp* 1316. 'Outlying farmstead or hamlet of a man called Prim'. OE pers. name + OScand. *thorp*.

Princes Risborough Bucks., see RISBOROUGH.

Princethorpe Warwicks. *Prandestorpe* 1221. 'Outlying farmstead or hamlet of a man called Præn or Pren'. OE pers. name + OScand. *thorp*.

Princetown Devon, a modern name, called after the Prince Regent, later George IV (1820-30).

Priors Hardwick Warwicks., see HARDWICK.

Priors Marston Warwicks., see MARSTON.

Priston Avon. *Prisctun* 931, *Prisctone* 1086 (DB). 'Farmstead near the brushwood or copse'. OWelsh **prisc* + OE *tūn*.

Prittlewell Essex. *Pritteuuella* 1086 (DB). 'Babbling spring or stream'. OE **pritol* + *wella*.

Privett Hants. *Pryfetes flodan* late 9th cent. '(Place at) the privet copse'. OE *pryfet* (with *flōde* 'channel, gutter' in the early form).

Probus Cornwall. *Sanctus Probus* 1086 (DB). From the dedication of the church to St Probus.

Prudhoe Northum. *Prudho* 1173. 'Hill-spur of a man called *Prūda'. OE pers. name + *hōh*.

Puckeridge Herts. *Pucherugge* 1294. 'Raised strip or ridge haunted by a goblin'. OE *pūca* + **ric* or *hrycg*.

Puckington Somerset. *Pokintuna* 1086 (DB). 'Estate associated with a man called *Pūca'. OE pers. name + *-ing-* + *tūn*.

Pucklechurch Avon. *Pucelancyrcan* 950, *Pulcrecerce* 1086 (DB). 'Church of a man called *Pūcela'. OE pers. name + *cirice*.

Puddington, 'estate associated with a man called Put(t)a', OE pers. name + *-ing-* + *tūn*: **Puddington** Ches. *Potitone* 1086 (DB). **Puddington** Devon. *Potitone* 1086 (DB).

Puddletown Dorset. *Pitretone* (*sic*) 1086 (DB), *Pideleton* 1212. 'Farmstead on the River Piddle'. OE river-name (**pidele* 'a marsh or fen') + *tūn*.

Pudleston Heref. & Worcs. *Pillesdune* (*sic*) 1086 (DB), *Putlesdone* 1212. 'Hill of the mouse-hawk or of a man called Pyttel'. OE *pyttel* or pers. name + *dūn*.

Pudsey W. Yorks. *Podechesaie* 1086 (DB). Probably 'enclosure of a man called *Pudoc, or by the hill called "the Wart" '.OE pers. name or *puduc* + *hæg*.

Pulborough W. Sussex. *Poleberge* 1086 (DB). 'Hill or mound by the pools'. OE *pōl*, **pull* + *beorg*.

Pulford Ches. *Pulford* 1086 (DB). 'Ford by a pool or on a stream'. OE *pōl* or **pull* + *ford*.

Pulham, 'homestead or enclosure by the pools or streams', OE *pōl* or **pull* + *hām* or *hamm*: **Pulham** Dorset. *Poleham* 1086 (DB). **Pulham** Norfolk. *Polleham* c.1050, *Pullaham* 1086 (DB).

Pulloxhill Beds. *Polochessele* 1086 (DB). 'Hill of a man called *Pulloc'. OE pers. name + *hyll*.

Pulverbatch, Church Shrops. *Polrebec* 1086 (DB), *Chirchpolrebache* 1301. Possibly 'valley of a stream called *Pulre*'. Lost OE river-name (perhaps 'babbling one') + *bece*. Affix is OE *cirice*.

Puncknowle Dorset. *Pomacanole* 1086 (DB). Probably 'hillock of a man called *Puma'. OE pers. name + *cnoll*.

Purbeck, Isle of Dorset. *Purbicinga*

948, *Porbi* 1086 (DB). 'Beak-shaped ridge frequented by the bittern or snipe'. OE *pūr* + **bic*. In the earliest spelling the name is combined with a form of OE *-ingas* 'dwellers in'.

Purbrook Hants. *Pukebrok* 1248. 'Brook haunted by a goblin'. OE *pūca* + *brōc*.

Purfleet Essex. *Purteflyete* 1285. 'Creek or stream of a man called *Purta'. OE pers. name + *flēot*.

Puriton Somerset. *Peritone* 1086 (DB). 'Pear orchard, or farmstead where pear-trees grow'. OE *pirige* + *tūn*.

Purleigh Essex. *Purlea* 998, *Purlai* 1086 (DB). 'Wood or clearing frequented by the bittern or snipe'. OE *pūr* + *lēah*.

Purley Berks. *Porlei* 1086 (DB). Identical in origin with the previous name.

Purley Gtr. London. *Pirlee* 1200. 'Wood or clearing where pear-trees grow'. OE *pirige* + *lēah*.

Purse Caundle Dorset, see CAUNDLE.

Purslow Shrops. *Possalau* 1086 (DB). 'Tumulus of a man called *Pussa'. OE pers. name + *hlāw*.

Purston Jaglin W. Yorks. *Preston* 1086 (DB), *Preston Jakelin* 1269. 'Farmstead of the priests'. OE *prēost* + *tūn*. Manorial affix from some early feudal tenant called *Jakelyn*.

Purton, 'pear orchard, or farmstead where pear-trees grow', OE *pirige* + *tūn*: **Purton** Glos., near Berkeley. *Piritone* 1297. **Purton** Glos., near Lydney. *Peritone* 1086 (DB). **Purton** Wilts. *Puritone* 796, *Piritone* 1086 (DB).

Pusey Oxon. *Pesei* 1086 (DB). 'Island, or dry ground in marsh, where peas grow'. OE *pise* + *ēg*.

Putford, West Devon. *Poteforda* 1086 (DB). 'Ford of a man called Putta, or one frequented by hawks'. OE pers. name or OE **putta* + *ford*.

Putley Heref. & Worcs. *Poteslepe* (*sic*) 1086 (DB), *Putelega c.*1180. 'Woodland clearing of a man called Putta, or one frequented by hawks'. OE pers. name or OE **putta* + *lēah*.

Putney Gtr. London. *Putelei* (*sic*) 1086 (DB), *Puttenhuthe* 1279. 'Landing-place of a man called Putta, or one frequented by hawks'. OE pers. name or OE **putta* (genitive *-n*) + *hӯth*.

Puttenham, 'homestead or enclosure of a man called Putta, or one frequented by hawks', OE pers. name or OE **putta* (genitive *-n*) + *hām* or *hamm*: **Puttenham** Herts. *Puteham* 1086 (DB). **Puttenham** Surrey. *Puteham* 1199.

Puxton Avon. *Pukereleston* 1212. 'Estate of a family called *Pukerel*'. OFrench surname + OE *tūn*.

Pyecombe W. Sussex. *Picumba* late 11th cent. 'Valley infested with gnats or other insects'. OE *pīe* + *cumb*.

Pylle Somerset. *Pil* 705, *Pille* 1086 (DB). 'The tidal creek'. OE *pyll*.

Pyon, Canon & Kings Heref. & Worcs. *Pionie* 1086 (DB), *Pyone canonicorum* 1221, *Kings Pyon* 1285. 'Island infested with gnats or other insects'. OE *pīe* (genitive plural *pēona*) + *ēg*. Distinguishing affixes from early possession by the canons of Hereford and the Crown.

Pyrford Surrey. *Pyrianforda* 956, *Peliforde* (*sic*) 1086 (DB). 'Ford by a pear-tree'. OE *pirige* + *ford*.

Pyrton Oxon. *Pirigtune* 987, *Peritone* 1086 (DB). 'Pear orchard, or farmstead where pear-trees grow'. OE *pirige* + *tūn*.

Pytchley Northants. *Pihteslea* 956, *Pihteslea* 1086 (DB). 'Woodland clearing of a man called *Peoht'. OE pers. name + *lēah*.

Pyworthy Devon. *Paorda* (*sic*) 1086 (DB), *Peworthy* 1239. 'Enclosure infested with gnats or other insects'. OE *pīe* + *worthig*.

Q

Quadring Lincs. *Quedhaveringe* 1086 (DB). 'Muddy settlement of the family or followers of a man called *Hæfer'. OE *cwēad* + OE pers. name + *-ingas.*

Quainton Bucks. *Chentone (sic)* 1086 (DB), *Quentona* 1167. 'The queen's farmstead or estate'. OE *cwēn* + *tūn.*

Quantock Hills Somerset. *Cantucuudu* 682. Celtic hill name, possibly a derivative of an element **canto-* 'border or district', with OE *wudu* 'wood' in the early form.

Quantoxhead, East & West Somerset. *Cantocheve* 1086 (DB). 'Projecting ridge of the QUANTOCK HILLS'. Celtic hill name + OE *hēafod.*

Quarley Hants. *Cornelea* 1167. Probably 'woodland clearing with a mill or where mill-stones are obtained'. OE *cweorn* + *lēah.*

Quarndon Derbys. *Cornun (sic)* 1086 (DB), *Querendon c.*1200. 'Hill where mill-stones are obtained'. OE *cweorn* + *dūn.*

Quarrington Lincs. *Corninctun* 1086 (DB). Probably 'farmstead at the mill-stone place'. OE *cweorn* + *-ing* + *tūn.*

Quarrington Hill Durham. *Querendune c.*1190. 'Hill where mill-stones are obtained'. OE *cweorn* + *dūn.*

Quatford Shrops. *Quatford* 1086 (DB). OE *ford* 'ford' with an obscure first element.

Quatt Shrops. *Quatone* 1086 (DB), *Quatte* 1212. From the same element as in previous name, with OE *tūn* 'farmstead' in the Domesday form.

Quedgeley Glos. *Quedesleya c.*1140. Possibly 'woodland clearing of a man called *Cwēod'. OE pers. name + *lēah.*

Queenborough Kent. *Queneburgh* 1376. 'Borough named after Queen Philippa'. OE *cwēn* + *burh*. Philippa was the wife of Edward III.

Queen Camel Somerset, see CAMEL.

Queen Charlton Avon, see CHARLTON.

Queensbury W. Yorks., a modern name created in 1863; earlier the village was known as *Queen's Head*, the name of an inn here.

Quendon Essex. *Kuenadana* 1086 (DB). Probably 'valley of the women'. OE *cwene* (genitive plural *cwenena*) + *denu.*

Queniborough Leics. *Cuinburg (sic)* 1086 (DB), *Queniburg* 12th cent. 'The queen's fortified manor'. OE *cwēn* + *burh.*

Quenington Glos. *Qvenintone* 1086 (DB). 'Farmstead of the women', or 'farmstead associated with a woman called *Cwēn'. OE *cwene* (genitive plural *cwenena*) + *tūn*, or OE pers. name + *-ing-* + *tūn.*

Quernmore Lancs. *Quernemor* 1228. 'Moor where mill-stones are obtained'. OE *cweorn* + *mōr.*

Quethiock Cornwall. *Quedoc* 1201. 'Wooded place'. OCornish *cuidoc.*

Quidenham Norfolk. *Cuidenham* 1086 (DB). 'Homestead or village of a man called *Cwida'. OE pers. name (genitive *-n*) + *hām.*

Quidhampton, 'muddy home farm', or 'home farm with good manure', OE *cwēad* + *hām-tūn*: **Quidhampton** Hants. *Quedementun* 1086 (DB). **Quidhampton** Wilts. *Quedhampton* 1249.

Quinton, Lower & Upper Warwicks. *Quentone* 848, *Quenintune* 1086 (DB). 'The queen's farmstead or estate.' OE *cwēn* + *tūn.*

Quorndon Leics. *Querendon c.*1220. 'Hill where mill-stones are obtained'. OE *cweorn* + *dūn.*

Quy Cambs., see STOW CUM QUY.

R

Raby Mersey. *Rabie* 1086 (DB). 'Farmstead or village at a boundary'. OScand. *rá* + *bý*.

Rackenford Devon. *Racheneforda* 1086 (DB). Probably 'ford suitable for riding, by a stretch of river'. OE **racu* + *ærne* + *ford*.

Rackham W. Sussex. *Recham* 1166. Possibly 'homestead or enclosure with a rick or ricks'. OE *hrēac* + *hām* or *hamm*.

Rackheath Norfolk. *Racheitha* 1086 (DB). Probably 'landing-place near a gully or water-course'. OE *hraca* or **racu* + *hȳth*.

Radcliffe, Radclive, 'the red cliff or bank', OE *rēad* + *clif*: **Radcliffe** Gtr. Manch. *Radecliue* 1086 (DB). **Radcliffe on Trent** Notts. *Radeclive* 1086 (DB). For the river-name Trent, see NEWARK. **Radclive** Bucks. *Radeclive* 1086 (DB).

Radcot Oxon. *Rathcota* 1163. 'Red cottage' or 'reed cottage' (i.e. with a roof thatched with reeds). OE *rēad* or *hrēod* + *cot*.

Radford Semele Warwicks. *Redeford* 1086 (DB), *Radeford Symely* 1314. 'Red ford', i.e. where the soil is red. OE *rēad* + *ford*. Manorial affix from the *Simely* family, here in the 12th cent.

Radipole Dorset. *Retpole* 1086 (DB). 'Reedy pool'. OE *hrēod* + *pōl*.

Radlett Herts. *Radelett* 1453. 'Junction of roads'. OE *rād* + *(ge)lǣt*.

Radley Oxon. *Radelege c.*1180. 'Red wood or clearing'. OE *rēad* + *lēah*.

Radnage Bucks. *Radenhech* 1162. '(Place at) the red oak-tree'. OE *rēad* + *āc* (dative *ǣc*).

Radstock Avon. *Stoche* 1086 (DB), *Radestok* 1221. 'Outlying farmstead by the road' (here the Fosse Way). OE *rād* + *stoc*.

Radstone Northants. *Rodestone* 1086 (DB). '(Place at) the rood-stone or stone cross'. OE **rōd-stān*.

Radwell Beds. *Radeuuelle* 1086 (DB). 'Red spring or stream'. OE *rēad* + *wella*.

Radwinter Essex. *Redeuuintra* 1086 (DB). Possibly 'red vineyard', from OE *rēad* + **winter*. Alternatively 'tree of a woman called *Rǣdwynn', OE pers. name + *trēow*.

Ragdale Leics. *Ragendele* (*sic*) 1086 (DB), *Rachedal c.*1125. Probably 'valley of the gully or narrow pass'. OE *hraca* + OE *dæl*.

Ragnall Notts. *Ragenehil* 1086 (DB). 'Hill of a man called Ragni'. OScand. pers. name + OE *hyll*.

Rainford Mersey. *Raineford* 1198. 'Ford of a man called *Regna', or 'boundary ford'. OE pers. name or OScand. *rein* + OE *ford*.

Rainham Gtr. London. *Renaham* 1086 (DB). Possibly identical in origin with the next name. Alternatively 'homestead of a man called *Regna', OE pers. name + *hām*.

Rainham Kent. *Roegingaham* 811. Probably 'homestead of the *Roegingas*'. OE tribal name (of uncertain meaning) + *hām*.

Rainhill Mersey. *Raynhull c.*1190. 'Hill of a man called *Regna', or 'boundary hill'. OE pers. name or OScand. *rein* + OE *hyll*.

Rainow Ches. *Rauenouh* 1285. 'Hill-spur frequented by ravens'. OE *hræfn* + *hōh*.

Rainton, 'estate associated with a man called *Rægen or *Regna', OE pers. name + *-ing-* + *tūn*: **Rainton** N. Yorks. *Rainincton* 1086 (DB). **Rainton, East** (Tyne & Wear) **& West** (Durham). *Reiningtone c.*1170.

Rainworth Notts. *Reynwath* 1268.

'Clean ford', or 'boundary ford'. OScand. *hreinn* or *rein* + *vath*.

Raithby Lincs., near Louth. *Radresbi* 1086 (DB). 'Farmstead or village of a man called *Hreithi'. OScand. pers. name + *bý*.

Raithby Lincs., near Spilsby. *Radebi* 1086 (DB). 'Farmstead or village of a man called Hrathi'. OScand. pers. name + *bý*.

Rake W. Sussex. *Rake* 1296. '(Place at) the hollow or pass'. OE *hraca*.

Rame Cornwall, near Plymouth. *Rame* 1086 (DB). Possibly '(place at) the barrier', perhaps alluding to a fortress. OE **hrama*.

Rampisham Dorset. *Ramesham* 1086 (DB). 'Wild-garlic enclosure', or 'enclosure of the ram or of a man called Ramm'. OE *hramsa* or *ramm* or pers. name + *hamm*.

Rampside Cumbria. *Rameshede* 1292. 'Headland of the ram', perhaps from a fancied resemblance to the animal. OE *ramm* + *hēafod*.

Rampton Cambs. *Rantone* 1086 (DB). 'Farmstead where rams are kept'. OE *ramm* + *tūn*.

Rampton Notts. *Rametone* 1086 (DB). Probably identical in origin with the previous name.

Ramsbottom Gtr. Manch. *Romesbothum* 1324. 'Valley of the ram, or where wild garlic grows'. OE *ramm* or *hramsa* + **bothm*.

Ramsbury Wilts. *Rammesburi* 947, *Ramesberie* 1086 (DB). 'Fortification of the raven, or of a man called *Hræfn'. OE *hræfn* or pers. name + *burh* (dative *byrig*).

Ramsden, probably 'valley where wild garlic grows', OE *hramsa* + *denu*: **Ramsden** Oxon. *Rammesden* 1246. **Ramsden Bellhouse** Essex. *Ramesdana* 1086 (DB), *Ramesden Belhous* 1254. Manorial affix from the *de Belhus* family, here in the 13th cent.

Ramsey, probably 'island where wild garlic grows', OE *hramsa* + *ēg*: **Ramsey** Cambs. *Hramesege c.*1000. **Ramsey** Essex. *Rameseia* 1086 (DB).

Ramsgate Kent. *Remmesgate* 1275. 'Gap (in the cliffs) of the raven, or of a man called *Hræfn'. OE *hræfn* or pers. name + *geat*.

Ramsgill N. Yorks. *Ramesgile* 1198. 'Ravine of the ram, or where wild garlic grows'. OE *ramm* or *hramsa* + OScand. *gil*.

Ramshorn Staffs. *Rumesoura* 1197. 'The ram's ridge', or 'ridge where wild garlic grows'. OE *ramm* or *hramsa* + **ofer*.

Ranby Notts. *Ranebi* 1086 (DB). 'Farmstead or village of a man called Hrani'. OScand. pers. name + *bý*.

Rand Lincs. *Rande* 1086 (DB). '(Place at) the border or edge'. OE *rand*.

Randwick Glos. *Rendewiche* 1121. Probably 'dwelling or farm on the edge or border'. OE **rend* + *wīc*.

Rangeworthy Avon. *Rengeswurda* 1167. 'Enclosure of a man called *Hrencga', or 'enclosure made of stakes'. OE pers. name or OE **hrynge* + *worthig*.

Ranskill Notts. *Raveschel* (*sic*) 1086 (DB), *Ravenskelf* 1275. 'Shelf or ridge frequented by ravens, or of a man called Hrafn'. OScand. *hrafn* or pers. name + *skjalf*.

Ranton Staffs. *Rantone* 1086 (DB). Possibly 'farmstead where rams are kept'. OE *ramm* + *tūn*.

Ranworth Norfolk. *Randwrthe c.*1045, *Randuorda* 1086 (DB). 'Enclosure by an edge or border', or 'enclosure of a man called Randi'. OE *rand* or OScand. pers. name + OE *worth*.

Rasen, Market, Middle, & West Lincs. *Resne* 1086 (DB). '(Place at) the plank-bridge'. OE *ræsn*.

Raskelf N. Yorks. *Raschel* 1086 (DB). 'Shelf or ridge frequented by roe-deer'. OScand. *rá* + *skjalf*.

Rastrick W. Yorks. *Rastric* 1086 (DB). Probably 'raised strip or ridge with a resting-place'. OScand. *rǫst* + OE **ric*.

Ratby Leics. *Rotebie* 1086 (DB). 'Farmstead or village of a man called Rōta'. OE pers. name + OScand. *bý*.

Ratcliffe, 'red cliff or bank', OE *rēad* + *clif*: **Ratcliffe Culey** Leics. *Redeclive* 1086 (DB). Manorial affix from the *de Culy* family, here in the 13th cent. **Ratcliffe on Soar** Notts. *Radeclive*

1086 (DB). For the river-name, see BARROW UPON SOAR. **Ratcliffe on the Wreake** Leics. *Radeclive* 1086 (DB). For the river-name, see FRISBY ON THE WREAKE.

Rathmell N. Yorks. *Rodemele* 1086 (DB). 'Red sandbank'. OScand. *rauthr* + *melr*.

Ratley Warwicks. *Rotelei* 1086 (DB). 'Pleasant clearing', or 'clearing of a man called Rōta'. OE *rōt* or pers. name + *lēah*.

Ratlinghope Shrops. *Rotelingehope* 1086 (DB). 'Enclosed valley associated with a man called *Rōtel', or 'valley at *Rōtel's place'. OE pers. name + *-ing-* or *-ing* + *hop*.

Rattery Devon. *Ratreu* 1086 (DB). '(Place at) the red tree'. OE *rēad* + *trēow*.

Rattlesden Suffolk. *Ratlesdena* 1086 (DB). OE *denu* 'valley' with an uncertain first element, possibly a pers. name.

Rauceby, North & South Lincs. *Rosbi, Roscebi* 1086 (DB). 'Farmstead or village of a man called Rauthr'. OScand. pers. name + *bý*.

Raughton Head Cumbria. *Ragton* 1182, *Raughtonheved* 1367. Probably 'farmstead where moss or lichen grows'. OE *ragu* + OE *tūn*, with the later addition of *hēafod* 'headland, hill'.

Raunds Northants. *Randan c.*980, *Rande* 1086 (DB). '(Place at) the borders or edges'. OE *rand* in a plural form.

Raveley, Great & Little Cambs. *Ræflea c.*1060. Possibly 'woodland clearing frequented by ravens'. OE *hræfn* + *lēah*.

Ravendale, East Humber. *Ravenedal* 1086 (DB). 'Valley frequented by ravens'. OE *hræfn* + *dæl* or OScand. *hrafn* + *dalr*.

Ravenfield S. Yorks. *Rauenesfeld* 1086 (DB). 'Open land of a man called *Hræfn, or frequented by ravens'. OE pers. name or OE *hræfn* + *feld*.

Ravenglass Cumbria. *Rengles c.*1180. 'Lot or share of a man called Glas'. OIrish *rann* + pers. name.

Raveningham Norfolk. *Rauenicham* 1086 (DB). 'Homestead of the family or followers of a man called *Hræfn'. OE pers. name + *-inga-* + *hām*.

Ravenscar N. Yorks. *Rauenesere* 1312. 'Rock frequented by ravens'. OScand. *hrafn* + *sker*.

Ravensden Beds. *Rauenesden c.*1150. 'Valley of the raven, or of a man called *Hræfn'. OE *hræfn* or pers. name + *denu*.

Ravensthorpe, 'outlying farmstead or hamlet of a man called Hrafn', OScand. pers. name + *thorp*: **Ravensthorpe** Northants. *Ravenestorp* 1086 (DB). **Ravensthorpe** W. Yorks. *Rauenestorp* 1086 (DB).

Ravenstone, 'farmstead of a man called *Hræfn or Hrafn', OE or OScand. pers. name + *tūn*: **Ravenstone** Bucks. *Raveneston* 1086 (DB). **Ravenstone** Leics. *Ravenestun* 1086 (DB).

Ravenstonedale Cumbria. *Rauenstandale* 12th cent. 'Valley of the raven stone'. OE *hræfn* + *stān* + OScand. *dalr*.

Ravensworth N. Yorks. *Raveneswet* (*sic*) 1086 (DB), *Raveneswad* 1157. 'Ford of a man called Hrafn'. OScand. pers. name + *vath*.

Rawcliffe, 'red cliff or bank', OScand. *rauthr* + *klif*: **Rawcliffe** Humber. *Routheclif c.*1080. **Rawcliffe** N. Yorks., near York. *Roudeclife* 1086 (DB). **Rawcliffe, Out** Lancs. *Rodeclif* 1086 (DB). Affix is OE *ūte* 'outer'.

Rawdon W. Yorks. *Roudun* 1086 (DB). 'Red hill'. OScand. *rauthr* + OE *dūn*.

Rawmarsh S. Yorks. *Rodemesc* (*sic*) 1086 (DB), *Rowmareis c.*1200. 'Red marsh'. OScand. *rauthr* + OE *mersc*.

Rawreth Essex. *Raggerea* 1177. 'Stream frequented by herons'. OE *hrāgra* + *rīth*.

Rawtenstall Lancs. *Routonstall* 1324. 'Rough farmstead or cow-pasture'. OE *rūh* + **tūn-stall*.

Raydon Suffolk. *Reindune* 1086 (DB). 'Hill where rye is grown'. OE *rygen* + *dūn*.

Rayleigh Essex. *Ragheleia* 1086 (DB). 'Woodland clearing frequented by female roe-deer or by she-goats'. OE *rǣge* + *lēah*.

Rayne Essex. *Hrægenan c.*1000, *Raines*

1086 (DB). Possibly '(place at) the shelter or eminence'. OE **hrægene*.

Raynham Norfolk. *Reineham* 1086 (DB). Possibly 'homestead or village of a man called *Regna'. OE pers. name + *hām*.

Reach, '(place at) the raised strip of land or other linear feature', OE **rǣc*: **Reach** Beds. *Reche c.*1220. **Reach** Cambs. *Reche* 1086.

Read Lancs. *Revet* 1202. 'Headland frequented by female roe-deer or by she-goats'. OE *rǣge* + *hēafod*.

Reading Berks. *Readingum c.*900, *Reddinges* 1086 (DB). '(Settlement of) the family or followers of a man called *Rēad(a)'. OE pers. name + *-ingas*.

Reagill Cumbria. *Reuegile* 1176. 'Ravine frequented by foxes'. OScand. *refr* + *gil*.

Rearsby Leics. *Redresbi* 1086 (DB). 'Farmstead or village of a man called Hreitharr'. OScand. pers. name + *bý*.

Reculver Kent. *Regulbium c.*425, *Roculf* 1086 (DB). An ancient Celtic name meaning 'great headland'.

Redbourn, Redbourne, 'reedy stream', OE *hrēod* + *burna*: **Redbourn** Herts. *Reodburne c.*1060, *Redborne* 1086 (DB). **Redbourne** Humber. *Radburne* 1086 (DB).

Redcar Cleveland. *Redker c.*1170. 'Red or reedy marsh'. OE *rēad* or *hrēod* + OScand. *kjarr*.

Redcliff Bay Avon. *Radeclive c.*1180. 'Red cliff or bank'. OE *rēad* + *clif*.

Redbridge Gtr. London, borough named from an old bridge across the River Roding first recorded as *Red Bridge* in 1777.

Reddish Gtr. Manch. *Rediche* 1212. 'Reedy ditch'. OE *hrēod* + *dīc*.

Redditch Heref. & Worcs. *La Rededich* 1247. 'Red or reedy ditch'. OE *rēad* or *hrēod* + *dīc*.

Rede Suffolk. *Reoda* 1086 (DB). Probably '(place at) the reed bed'. OE *hrēod*.

Redenhall Norfolk. *Redanahalla* 1086 (DB). Probably 'nook of land where reeds grow'. OE **hrēoden* + *halh*.

Redgrave Suffolk. *Redgrafe* 11th cent. 'Reedy pit' from OE *hrēod* + *græf*, or 'red grove' from OE *rēad* + *grāf*.

Redhill Avon. *Ragiol* 1086 (DB). Possibly 'hill at roe-deer edge'. OE *rā* + *ecg* + *hyll*.

Redhill Surrey. *Redehelde* 1301. 'Red slope'. OE *rēad* + *helde*.

Redisham Suffolk. *Redesham* 1086 (DB). Probably 'homestead or village of a man called *Rēad'. OE pers. name + *hām*.

Redland Avon. *Thriddeland* 1209. Probably 'third part of an estate'. OE *thridda* + *land*.

Redlingfield Suffolk. *Radinghefelda* (*sic*) 1086 (DB), *Radlingefeld* 1166. 'Open land of the family or followers of a man called Rǣdel or *Rǣdla'. OE pers. name + *-inga-* + *feld*.

Redlynch Somerset. *Redlisc* 1086 (DB). 'Reedy marsh'. OE *hrēod* + **lisc*.

Redmarley D'Abitot Glos. *Reodemæreleage* 963, *Ridmerlege* 1086 (DB), *Rudmarleye Dabetot* 1324. 'Woodland clearing with a reedy pond'. OE *hrēod* + *mere* + *lēah*. Manorial affix from the *d'Abitot* family, here in 1086.

Redmarshall Cleveland. *Rodmerehil* 1208–10. 'Hill by a red (i.e. sandy) pond'. OE *rēad* + *mere* + *hyll*.

Redmire N. Yorks. *Ridemare* 1086 (DB). 'Reedy pool'. OE *hrēod* + *mere*.

Redruth Cornwall. *Ridruth* 1259. 'Red ford'. OCornish *rid* + *rudh*.

Redwick Avon. *Hreodwican* 955–9, *Redeuuiche* 1086 (DB). 'Dairy farm among the reeds'. OE *hrēod* + *wīc*.

Redworth Durham. *Redwortha* 1183. 'Enclosure where reeds grow'. OE *hrēod* + *worth*.

Reed Herts. *Retth* 1086 (DB). Probably OE **rȳ(h)th* 'a rough piece of ground'.

Reedham Norfolk. *Redham* 1044–7, *Redeham* 1086 (DB). 'Homestead or enclosure where reeds grow'. OE *hrēod* + *hām* or *hamm*.

Reedness Humber. *Rednesse c.*1170. 'Reedy headland'. OE *hrēod* + *næss*.

Reepham, 'manor held or run by a reeve', OE *rēfa* + *hām*: **Reepham** Lincs. *Refam* 1086 (DB). **Reepham** Norfolk. *Refham* 1086 (DB).

Reeth N. Yorks. *Rie* 1086 (DB), *Rithe* 1184.

Probably '(place at) the stream'. OE *rīth*.

Reigate Surrey. *Reigata c.*1170. 'Gate for female roe-deer'. OE *rǣge* + *geat*.

Reighton N. Yorks. *Rictone* 1086 (DB). 'Farmstead by the straight ridge'. OE **ric* + *tūn*.

Remenham Berks. *Rameham* 1086 (DB). Probably 'homestead or enclosure by the river-bank'. OE *reoma* (genitive *-n*) + *hām* or *hamm*.

Rempstone Notts. *Rampestune* 1086 (DB). Probably 'farmstead of a man called *Hrempi'. OE pers. name + *tūn*.

Rendcomb Glos. *Rindecumbe* 1086 (DB). 'Valley of a stream called *Hrinde*'. OE river-name (meaning 'the pusher') + *cumb*.

Rendham Suffolk. *Rimdham, Rindham* 1086 (DB). 'Cleared homestead', or 'homestead by a hill'. OE *rȳmed* or **rind(e)* + *hām*.

Renhold Beds. *Ranhale* 1220. Probably 'nook of land frequented by roe-deer'. OE *rā* (genitive plural *rāna*) + *halh*.

Rennington Northum. *Reiningtun* 12th cent. 'Estate associated with a man called *Regna'. OE pers. name + *-ing-* + *tūn*.

Renwick Cumbria. *Rauenwich* 1178. Probably 'dwelling or farm of a man called Hrafn or *Hræfn'. OScand. or OE pers. name + *wīc*.

Repps Norfolk. *Repes* 1086 (DB), *Repples* 1191. Possibly 'the strips of land'. OE **reopul*.

Repton Derbys. *Hrypadun* 730–40, *Rapendune* 1086 (DB). 'Hill of the tribe called *Hrype*'. Old tribal name (see RIPON) + OE *dūn*.

Reston, North & South Lincs. *Ristone* 1086 (DB). 'Farmstead near or among brushwood'. OE *hrīs* + *tūn*.

Restormel Cornwall. *Rostormel* 1310. Possibly 'moor at the bare hill'. Cornish **ros* + *tor* + **moyl*.

Retford, East & West Notts. *Redforde* 1086 (DB). 'Red ford'. OE *rēad* + *ford*.

Rettendon Essex. *Rettendun c.*1000, *Ratenduna* 1086 (DB). Probably 'hill infested with rats'. OE **rætten* + *dūn*.

Revesby Lincs. *Resuesbi* 1086 (DB). 'Farmstead or village of a man called Refr'. OScand. pers. name + *bý*.

Rewe Devon. *Rewe* 1086 (DB). 'Row of houses'. OE *rǣw*.

Reydon Suffolk. *Rienduna* 1086 (DB). 'Hill where rye is grown'. OE *rygen* + *dūn*.

Reymerston Norfolk. *Raimerestùna* 1086 (DB). 'Farmstead of a man called Raimar'. OGerman pers. name + OE *tūn*.

Ribbesford Heref. & Worcs. *Ribbedford* 1023, *Ribeford* 1086 (DB). 'Ford by a bed of ribwort or hound's-tongue'. OE *ribbe* + *bedd* + *ford*.

Ribbleton Lancs. *Ribleton* 1201. 'Farmstead on the River Ribble'. OE river-name (from **ripel* 'tearing' or 'boundary') + *tūn*.

Ribchester Lancs. *Ribelcastre* 1086 (DB). 'Roman fort on the River Ribble'. OE river-name (see previous name) + *ceaster*.

Ribston, Great & Little N. Yorks. *Ripestan* 1086. Probably 'rock or stone by which ribwort or hound's-tongue grows'. OE *ribbe* + *stān*.

Riby Lincs. *Ribi* 1086 (DB). 'Farmstead where rye is grown'. OE *ryge* + OScand. *bý*.

Riccall N. Yorks. *Richale* 1086 (DB). 'Nook of land of a man called *Rīca'. OE pers. name + *halh*.

Richards Castle Shrops. *Castri Ricardi* 1212. Named from the castle (Latin *castrum*) probably built by a Frenchman called *Richard* Scrope who held land in the area in the 11th cent.

Richborough Kent. *Routoupiae c.*150, *Ratteburg* 1197. 'Stronghold called **Repta*'. Reduced form of ancient Celtic name (probably 'muddy waters or estuary') + OE *burh*.

Richmond Gtr. London. *Richemount* 1502. Earlier called SHEEN, renamed by Henry VII from the following place.

Richmond N. Yorks. *Richemund c.*1110. 'Strong hill'. OFrench *riche* + *mont*.

Rickinghall Inferior & Superior Suffolk. *Rikinghale* 10th cent., *Rikingahala* 1086 (DB). 'Nook of the family or followers of a man called *Rīca'. OE pers. name + *-inga-* + *halh*.

Rickling Essex. *Richelinga* 1086 (DB). '(Settlement of) the family or followers of a man called *Rīcela or a woman called Rīcola'. OE pers. name + *-ingas*.

Rickmansworth Herts. *Prichemareworde* (*sic*) 1086 (DB), *Richemaresworthe* c.1180. 'Enclosure of a man called *Rīcmǣr'. OE pers. name + *worth*.

Riddlesden W. Yorks. *Redelesden* 1086 (DB). 'Valley of a man called Rēthel or Hrēthel'. OE pers. name + *denu*.

Ridge Herts. *La Rigge* 1248. 'The ridge'. OE *hrycg*.

Ridgewell Essex. *Rideuuella* 1086 (DB). Probably 'spring or stream where reeds grow'. OE *hrēod* + *wella*.

Ridgmont Beds. *Rugemund* 1227. 'Red hill'. OFrench *rouge* + *mont*.

Riding, East, North, & West (old tripartite division of Yorkshire). *Estreding*, *Nortreding*, *Westreding* 1086 (DB). From OScand. *thrithjungr* 'a third part', the initial *th-* having coalesced with the final consonant of *ēast*, *north*, and *west* to give *Riding*.

Riding Mill Northum. *Ryding* 1262. OE **ryding* 'a clearing'.

Ridlington, 'estate associated with a man called Rēthel or Hrēthel', OE pers. name + *-ing-* + *tūn*: **Ridlington** Leics. *Redlinctune* 1086 (DB). **Ridlington** Norfolk. *Ridlinketuna* 1086 (DB).

Ridware, Hamstall & Pipe Staffs. *Rideware* 1004, 1086 (DB), *Hamstal Ridewar* 1242, *Pipe Ridware* 14th cent. Probably '(settlement of) the dwellers at the ford'. Celtic **rïd* + OE *-ware*. Distinguishing affixes are from OE *hām-stall* 'homestead' and from the *Pipe* family, holders of the manor in the 13th cent.

Rievaulx N. Yorks. *Rievalle* 1157. 'Valley of the River Rye'. Celtic river-name (probably meaning 'stream') + OFrench *val(s)*.

Rillington N. Yorks. *Redlintone* 1086 (DB). 'Estate associated with a man called Rēthel or Hrēthel'. OE pers. name + *-ing-* + *tūn*.

Rimington Lancs. *Renitone* (*sic*) 1086 (DB), *Rimingtona* 1182–5. 'Farmstead on the boundary stream'. OE *rima* + *-ing* + *tūn*.

Rimpton Somerset. *Rimtune* 938, *Rintone* 1086 (DB). 'Farmstead on the boundary'. OE *rima* + *tūn*.

Rimswell Humber. *Rimeswelle* 1086 (DB). Possibly 'spring or stream of a man called Hrímr or *Rȳmi'. OScand. or OE pers. name + OE *wella*.

Ringland Norfolk. *Remingaland* 1086 (DB). Probably 'cultivated land of the family or followers of a man called *Rȳmi'. OE pers. name + *-inga-* + *land*.

Ringmer E. Sussex. *Ryngemere* 1276. 'Circular pool', or 'pool near a circular feature'. OE *hring* + *mere*.

Ringmore Devon, near Bigbury. *Reimore* (*sic*) 1086 (DB), *Redmore* 1242. 'Reedy moor'. OE *hrēod* + *mōr*.

Ringsfield Suffolk. *Ringesfelda* 1086 (DB). 'Open land of a man called *Hring, or near a circular feature'. OE pers. name or OE *hring* + *feld*.

Ringshall Suffolk. *Ringeshala* 1086 (DB). Possibly 'nook of land of a man called *Hring, or near a circular feature'. OE pers. name or OE *hring* + *halh*.

Ringstead, 'circular enclosure, or place near a circular feature', OE *hring* + *stede*: **Ringstead** Norfolk. *Ringstyde* c.1050, *Rincsteda* 1086 (DB). **Ringstead** Northants. *Ringstede* 12th cent.

Ringwood Hants. *Rimucwuda* 955, *Rincvede* 1086 (DB). Probably 'wood on a boundary'. OE **rimuc* + *wudu*.

Ringwould Kent. *Roedligwealda* 861. Probably 'woodland of the family or followers of a man called Rēthel or Hrēthel'. OE pers. name + *-inga-* + *weald*.

Ripe E. Sussex. *Ripe* 1086 (DB). '(Place at) the edge or strip of land'. OE **rip*.

Ripley, usually 'strip-shaped woodland clearing', OE **ripel* + *lēah*: **Ripley** Derbys. *Ripelei* 1086 (DB). **Ripley** Hants. *Riple* 1086 (DB). **Ripley** Surrey. *Ripelia* 1204.

However the following may have a different origin: **Ripley** N. Yorks. *Ripeleia* 1086 (DB). Probably 'woodland clearing of the tribe called *Hrype*'. Old tribal name (see RIPON) + OE *lēah*.

Riplingham Humber. *Ripingham* (*sic*) 1086 (DB), *Ripplingeham* 1180. 'Homestead associated with a man called *Rip(p)el', or 'homestead by the strip of land'. OE pers. name or OE **ripel* + *-ing-* + *hām*.

Ripon N. Yorks. *Hrypis c.*715, *Ripum* 1086 (DB). '(Place in the territory of) the tribe called *Hrype*'. Old tribal name (origin and meaning obscure) in a dative plural form *Hrypum*.

Rippingale Lincs. *Repingale* 806, *Repinghale* 1086 (DB). 'Nook of the family or followers of a man called *Hrepa'. OE pers. name + *-inga-* + *halh*.

Ripple, '(place at) the strip of land', OE **ripel*: **Ripple** Heref. & Worcs. *Rippell* 780, *Rippel* 1086 (DB). **Ripple** Kent. *Ryple* 1086.

Ripponden W. Yorks. *Ryburnedene* 1307. 'Valley of the River Ryburn'. OE river-name ('fierce or reedy stream') + *denu*.

Ripton, Abbot's & King's Cambs. *Riptone c.*960, *Riptune* 1086 (DB). 'Farmstead by a strip of land'. OE **rip* + *tūn*. Affixes from early possession by the Abbot of Ramsey and the King.

Risborough, Monks & Princes Bucks. *Hrisanbyrge* 903, *Riseberge* 1086 (DB). 'Hill(s) where brushwood grows'. OE **hrīsen* + *beorg*. Manorial affixes from early possession by the monks of Christchurch, Canterbury and by the Black Prince.

Risbury Heref. & Worcs. *Riseberia* 1086 (DB). 'Fortress among the brushwood'. OE *hrīs* + *burh* (dative *byrig*).

Risby, 'farmstead or village among the brushwood or by a clearing', OScand. *hrís* or *ryth* + *bý*: **Risby** Humber. *Risebi* 1086 (DB). **Risby** Suffolk. *Risebi* 1086 (DB).

Rise Humber. *Risun* 1086 (DB). '(Place among) the brushwood'. OE *hrīs* in a dative plural form *hrīsum*.

Riseley, 'brushwood clearing', OE *hrīs* + *lēah*: **Riseley** Beds. *Riselai* 1086 (DB). **Riseley** Berks. *Rysle* 1300.

Rishangles Suffolk. *Risangra* 1086 (DB). 'Wooded slope where brushwood grows'. OE *hrīs* + *hangra*.

Rishton Lancs. *Riston c.*1205. 'Farmstead where rushes grow'. OE *risc* + *tūn*.

Rishworth W. Yorks. *Risseworde* 12th cent. 'Enclosure where rushes grow'. OE *risc* + *worth*.

Rising, Castle Norfolk. *Risinga* 1086 (DB), *Castel Risinge* 1254. Probably '(settlement of) the family or followers of a man called *Risa'. OE pers. name + *-ingas*, with the later addition of *castel* from the Norman castle here. Alternatively 'dwellers in the brushwood', OE *hrīs* + *-ingas*.

Risley, 'brushwood clearing', OE *hrīs* + *lēah*: **Risley** Ches. *Ryselegh* 1284. **Risley** Derbys. *Riselei* 1086 (DB).

Rissington, Great & Little Glos. *Rise(n)dune* 1086 (DB). 'Hill where brushwood grows'. OE **hrīsen* + *dūn*.

Riston, Long Humber. *Ristune* 1086 (DB). 'Farmstead near or among brushwood'. OE *hrīs* + *tūn*.

Rivenhall End Essex. *Reuenhala* 1068, *Ruenhale* 1086 (DB). Probably 'rough or rugged nook of land'. OE *hrēof* (dative *-an*) + *halh*.

Riverhead Kent. *Reddride* 1278. 'Landing-place for cattle'. OE *hrīther* + *hȳth*.

Rivington Lancs. *Revington* 1202. 'Farmstead at the rough or rugged hill'. OE *hrēof* + *-ing* + *tūn*.

Roade Northants. *Rode* 1086 (DB). '(Place at) the clearing'. OE **rod*.

Robertsbridge E. Sussex. *Pons Roberti* 1176, *Robartesbregge* 1445. Named from *Robert* de St Martin, founder of the 12th cent. abbey here. The earliest form has Latin *pons* 'bridge'.

Robin Hood's Bay N. Yorks. *Robin Hoode Baye* 1532. A late name which probably arose from the popular ballads about this legendary outlaw.

Roborough Devon. *Raweberge* 1086 (DB). 'Rough hill'. OE *rūh* + *beorg*.

Roby Mersey. *Rabil* (*sic*) 1086 (DB), *Rabi* 1185. 'Farmstead or village at a boundary'. OScand. *rá* + *bý*.

Rocester Staffs. *Rowcestre* 1086 (DB). OE *ceaster* 'Roman fort', possibly with *rūh* 'rough' or an unidentified pers. name.

Rochdale Gtr. Manch. *Recedham* 1086 (DB), *Rachedal c.*1195. 'Valley of the River Roch'. River-name + OScand. *dalr*. The river-name itself is a 'back-formation' from the old name *Recedham* 'homestead with a hall', OE *reced* + *hām*.

Roche Cornwall. *La Roche* 1233. 'The rock'. OFrench *roche*.

Rochester Kent. *Hrofaescaestir* 731, *Rovecestre* 1086 (DB). Probably 'Roman town or fort called *Hrofi*'. Ancient Celtic name (reduced from *Durobrivis* 4th cent. 'the walled town with the bridges') + OE *ceaster*.

Rochester Northum. *Rucestr* 1242. Possibly 'rough earthwork or fort'. OE *rūh* + *ceaster*.

Rochford, 'ford of the hunting-dog', OE *ræcc* + *ford*: **Rochford** Essex. *Rochefort* 1086 (DB). **Rochford** Heref. & Worcs. *Recesford* 1086 (DB).

Rock Heref. & Worcs. *Ak* 1224, *Roke* 1259. '(Place at) the oak-tree'. OE *āc*, with *R-* from ME *atter* 'at the'.

Rock Northum. *Rok* 1242. Probably ME *rokke* 'a rock, a peak'.

Rockbeare Devon. *Rochebere* 1086 (DB). 'Grove frequented by rooks'. OE *hrōc* + *bearu*.

Rockbourne Hants. *Rocheborne* 1086 (DB). 'Stream frequented by rooks'. OE *hrōc* + *burna*.

Rockcliffe Cumbria. *Rodcliua* 1185. 'Red cliff or bank'. OScand. *rauthr* + OE *clif*.

Rockhampton Avon. *Rochemtune* 1086 (DB). 'Homestead by the rock, or frequented by rooks'. OE *rocc* or *hrōc* + *hām-tūn*.

Rockingham Northants. *Rochingeham* 1086 (DB). 'Homestead of the family or followers of a man called *Hrōc(a)'. OE pers. name + *-inga-* + *hām*.

Rockland, 'grove frequented by rooks', OScand. *hrókr* + *lundr*: **Rockland All Saints & St Peter** Norfolk. *Rokelund* 1086 (DB). Distinguishing affixes from the church dedications. **Rockland St Mary** Norfolk. *Rokelund* 1086 (DB). Affix from the church dedication.

Rockley Wilts. *Rochelie* 1086 (DB) 'Wood or clearing frequented by rooks'. OE *hrōc* + *lēah*.

Rodbourne, 'reedy stream', OE *hrēod* + *burna*: **Rodbourne** Wilts., near Malmesbury. *Reodburna* 701.

Rodbourne Cheney Wilts. *Redborne* 1086 (DB), *Rodburne Chanu* 1304. Manorial affix from Ralph *le Chanu*, here in 1242.

Rodd Heref. & Worcs. *La Rode* 1220. 'The clearing'. OE **rod*.

Roddam Northum. *Rodun* 1201. '(Place at) the clearings'. OE **rod* in a dative plural form **rodum*.

Rode, 'the clearing', OE **rod*: **Rode Heath** Ches. *Rode* 1086 (DB), *Rodeheze* 1280. With the later addition of OE *hǣth* 'heath'. **Rode, North** Ches. *Rodo* 1086 (DB).

Roden Shrops. *Rodene* 1242. Named from the River Roden, a Celtic river-name probably meaning 'swift river'.

Roding, Abbess, Aythorpe, Beauchamp, High, Leaden, Margaret, & White Essex. *Rodinges* c.1050, 1086 (DB), *Roinges Abbatisse* 1237, *Roeng Aytrop* 1248, *Roynges Beuchamp* 1238, *High Roinges* 1224, *Ledeineroing* 1248, *Roinges Sancte Margaret* c.1245, *White Roeng* 1248. '(Settlement of) the family or followers of a man called *Hrōth(a)'. OE pers. name + *-ingas*. The affixes *Abbess*, *Aythorpe*, and *Beauchamp* are all manorial, from early possession by the Abbess of Barking, by a man called *Aitrop*, and by the *de Beauchamp* family respectively. *High* Roding refers to its situation, *Leaden* (OE *lēaden*) to the lead roof of the church, *Margaret* to the dedication of the church, and *White* to the colour of the church walls.

Rodington Shrops. *Rodintone* 1086 (DB). 'Farmstead on the River Roden'. Celtic river-name (see RODEN) + OE *tūn*.

Rodley Glos. *Rodele* 1086 (DB). 'Clearing amongst the reeds'. OE *hrēod* + *lēah*.

Rodley W. Yorks. *Rothelaye* 1246. Probably 'woodland clearing of a man called Hrōthwulf or *Róthulfr'. OE or OScand. pers. name + OE *lēah*.

Rodmarton Glos. *Redmertone* 1086 (DB). 'Farmstead by a reedy pool', or 'boundary farmstead where reeds grow'. OE *hrēod* + *mere* or *mǣre* + *tūn*.

Rodmell E. Sussex. *Redmelle* (*sic*) 1086 (DB), *Radmelde* 1202. Probably '(place with) red soil'. OE *rēad* + **mylde*.

Rodmersham Kent. *Rodmaeresham* c.1100. 'Homestead or village of a man called *Hrōthmǣr'. OE pers. name + *hām*.

Rodney Stoke Somerset, see STOKE.

Rodsley Derbys. *Redeslei* 1086 (DB). OE *lēah* 'woodland clearing', possibly with OE *hrēod* 'reed bed'.

Roehampton Gtr. London. *Rokehampton* 1350. 'Home farm frequented by rooks'. OE *hrōc* + *hām-tūn*.

Roffey W. Sussex. *La Rogheye* 1281. Probably 'the fence or enclosure for roe-deer', OE *rāh-hege*, but 'the rough enclosure' if the first element is OE *rūh*.

Rogate W. Sussex. *Ragata* 12th cent. 'Gate for roe-deer'. OE *rā* + *geat*.

Rollesby Norfolk. *Rotholfuesby* 1086 (DB). 'Farmstead or village of a man called Hrólfr'. OScand. pers. name + *bý*.

Rolleston Leics. *Rovestone* 1086 (DB). 'Farmstead of a man called Hrōthwulf or Hrólfr'. OE or OScand. pers. name + OE *tūn*.

Rolleston Notts. *Roldestun* 1086 (DB). 'Farmstead of a man called Hróaldr'. OScand. pers. name + OE *tūn*.

Rolleston Staffs. *Rothulfeston* 941, *Rolvestune* 1086 (DB). Identical in origin with ROLLESTON (Leics.).

Rollright, Great & Little Oxon. *Rollandri* (*sic*) 1086 (DB), *Rollendricht* 1091. Probably 'property of a man called *Hrolla'. OE pers. name + *land-riht*.

Rolvenden Kent. *Rovindene* (*sic*) 1086 (DB), *Ruluinden* 1185. 'Woodland pasture associated with a man called Hrōthwulf'. OE pers. name + *-ing-* + *denn*.

Romaldkirk Durham. *Rumoldesc(h)erce* 1086 (DB). 'Church dedicated to St Rūmwald'. OE pers. name + OScand. *kirkja*.

Romanby N. Yorks. *Romundrebi* 1086 (DB). 'Farmstead or village of a man called Róthmundr'. OScand. pers. name + *bý*.

Romansleigh Devon. *Liega* 1086 (DB), *Reymundesle* 1228. 'The wood or clearing'. OE *lēah*, with the later addition of the Celtic saint's name *Rumon* from the dedication of the church.

Romford Gtr. London. *Romfort* 1177. Probably 'wide or spacious ford'. OE *rūm* + *ford*. The river-name Rom is a 'back-formation' from the place-name.

Romiley Gtr. Manch. *Rumelie* 1086 (DB). 'Spacious woodland clearing'. OE *rūm* + *lēah*.

Romney, New Kent. *Rumenea* 11th cent., *Romenel* 1086 (DB). Originally a river-name, from OE *ēa* 'river' and an uncertain first element.

Romsey Hants. *Rummæsig* c.970, *Romesy* 1086 (DB). 'Island, or dry ground in marsh, of a man called *Rūm'. OE pers. name + *ēg*.

Romsley, probably 'woodland clearing where wild garlic grows', OE *hramsa* + *lēah*: **Romsley** Heref. & Worcs. *Romesle* 1270. **Romsley** Shrops. *Hremesleage* 1002, *Rameslege* 1086 (DB).

Rookhope Durham. *Rochop* 1242. 'Valley frequented by rooks'. OE *hrōc* + *hop*.

Rookley I. of Wight. *Roclee* 1202. 'Wood or clearing frequented by rooks'. OE *hrōc* + *lēah*.

Roos Humber. *Rosse* 1086 (DB). Celtic **ros* 'a moor, a heath'.

Roose Cumbria. *Rosse* 1086 (DB). Identical in origin with the previous name.

Ropley Hants. *Roppele* 1172. 'Woodland clearing of a man called *Hroppa'. OE pers. name + *lēah*.

Ropsley Lincs. *Ropeslai* 1086 (DB). Probably 'woodland clearing of a man called *Hropp'. OE pers. name + *lēah*.

Rorrington Shrops. *Roritune* 1086 (DB). 'Estate associated with a man called *Hrōr'. OE pers. name + *-ing-* + *tūn*.

Roseacre Lancs. *Raysacre* 1283. 'Cultivated land with a cairn'. OScand. *hreysi* + *akr*.

Rose Ash Devon. *Aissa* 1086 (DB), *Assherowes* 1281. '(Place at) the ash-tree'. OE *æsc*, with later manorial affix from possession by a man called *Ralph* in the late 12th cent.

Rosedale Abbey N. Yorks. *Russedal*

c.1140. 'Valley of the horses, or of a man called Rossi'. OScand. *hross* or pers. name + *dalr*.

Roseden Northum. *Russeden* 1242. 'Valley where rushes grow'. OE **rysc* + *denu*.

Roseland Cornwall, see ST JUST.

Rosgill Cumbria. *Rossegile* late 12th cent. 'Ravine of the horses'. OScand. *hross* + *gil*.

Rosley Cumbria. *Rosseleye* 1272. 'Woodland clearing where horses are kept'. OScand. *hross* + OE *lēah*.

Rosliston Derbys. *Redlauestun* 1086 (DB). Probably 'farmstead of a man called Hrōthlāf'. OE pers. name + *tūn*.

Ross, 'hill-spur, moor, heathy upland', Celtic **ros*: **Ross** Northum. *Rosse* 1208–10. **Ross on Wye** Heref. & Worcs. *Rosse* 1086 (DB). Wye is an ancient pre-English river-name of unknown origin and meaning.

Rossington S. Yorks. *Rosington c*.1190. Probably 'farmstead at the moor'. Celtic **ros* + OE *-ing-* + *tūn*.

Rostherne Ches. *Rodestorne* 1086 (DB). 'Thorn-tree of a man called Rauthr'. OScand. pers. name + OE *thorn* or *thyrne*.

Roston Derbys. *Roschintone* 1086 (DB). Possibly 'estate associated with a man called *Hrōthsige'. OE pers. name + *-ing-* + *tūn*.

Rothbury Northum. *Routhebiria c*.1125. 'Stronghold of a man called *Hrōtha'. OE pers. name + *burh* (dative *byrig*). Alternatively the first element may be OScand. *rauthr* 'red' (from the colour of the bed-rock in the area).

Rotherby Leics. *Redebi* 1086 (DB). 'Farmstead or village of a man called Hreitharr or *Hreithi'. OScand. pers. name + *bý*.

Rotherfield, 'open land where cattle graze', OE *hrȳther* + *feld*: **Rotherfield** E. Sussex. *Hrytheranfeld c*.880, *Reredfelle* (*sic*) 1086 (DB). **Rotherfield Greys & Peppard** Oxon. *Redrefeld* 1086 (DB), *Retherfeld Grey* 1313, *Ruderefeld Pippard* 1255. Manorial affixes from early possession by the *de Gray* and *Pipard* families.

Rotherham S. Yorks. *Rodreham* 1086 (DB). 'Homestead or village on the River Rother'. Celtic river-name (meaning 'chief river') + OE *hām*.

Rotherhithe Gtr. London. *Rederheia c*.1105. 'Landing-place for cattle'. OE *hrȳther* + *hȳth*.

Rothersthorpe Northants. *Torp* 1086 (DB), *Retherestorp* 1231. 'Outlying farm or hamlet of the counsellor or advocate'. OScand. *thorp* with the later addition of OE *rǣdere*.

Rotherwick Hants. *Hrytheruuica c*.1100. 'Cattle farm'. OE *hrȳther* + *wīc*.

Rothley, probably 'wood with clearings', OE **roth* + *lēah*: **Rothley** Leics. *Rodolei* 1086 (DB). **Rothley** Northum. *Rotheley* 1233.

Rothwell, 'spring or stream by the clearing(s)', OE **roth* + *wella*: **Rothwell** Lincs. *Rodewelle* 1086 (DB). **Rothwell** Northants. *Rodewelle* 1086 (DB). **Rothwell** W. Yorks. *Rodewelle* 1086 (DB).

Rotsea Humber. *Rotesse* 1086 (DB). 'Pool with scum on it', or 'pool of a man called Rōta'. OE *hrot* or pers. name + *sǣ*.

Rottingdean E. Sussex. *Rotingedene* 1086 (DB). Probably 'valley of the family or followers of a man called Rōta'. OE pers. name + *-inga-* + *denu*.

Rottington Cumbria. *Rotingtona c*.1125. 'Estate associated with a man called Rōt(a)'. OE pers. name + *-ing-* + *tūn*.

Rougham, probably 'homestead or village on rough ground', OE *rūh* + *hām*: **Rougham** Norfolk. *Ruhham* 1086 (DB). **Rougham Green** Suffolk. *Rucham c*.950, *Ruhham* 1086 (DB).

Roughton Lincs. *Rocstune* 1086 (DB). 'Rough farm', or 'rye farm'. OE *rūh* or OScand. *rugr* (replacing OE *ryge*) + OE *tūn*.

Roughton Norfolk. *Rugutune* 1086 (DB). Identical in origin with the previous name.

Roughton Shrops. *Roughton* 1316. 'Farmstead on rough ground'. OE *rūh* + *tūn*.

Roundhay W. Yorks. *La Rundehaia c*.1180. 'Round enclosure'. OFrench *rond* + OE *hæg*.

Roundway Wilts. *Rindweiam* 1149.

Probably 'cleared way'. OE *rȳmed* + *weg*.

Rounton, East & West N. Yorks. *Rontun*, *Runtune* 1086 (DB), *Rungtune* c.1130. 'Farmstead enclosed with poles, or near a causeway made with poles'. OE *hrung* + *tūn*.

Rousdon Devon. *Done* 1086 (DB), *Rawesdon* 1285. '(Place at) the hill'. OE *dūn*, with manorial affix from the family of *Ralph* here from the 12th cent.

Rous Lench Heref. & Worcs., see LENCH.

Routh Humber. *Rutha* 1086 (DB). Possibly 'rough shaly ground'. OScand. *hrúthr*.

Rowde Wilts. *Rode* 1086 (DB). Probably '(place at) the reed bed'. OE *hrēod*.

Rowhedge Essex. *Rouhegy* 1346. 'Rough hedge or enclosure'. OE *rūh* + *hecg*.

Rowland Derbys. *Ralunt* 1086 (DB). 'Boundary grove', or 'grove frequented by roe-deer'. OScand. *rá* + *lundr*.

Rowley, 'rough wood or clearing', OE *rūh* + *lēah*: **Rowley** Humber. *Rulee* 12th cent. **Rowley Hill** W. Yorks. *Ruleia* c.1180. **Rowley Regis** W. Mids. *Roelea* 1173. Affix is Latin *regis* 'of the king' from early possession by the Crown.

Rowsham Bucks. *Rollesham* 1170. 'Homestead or village of a man called Hrōthwulf'. OE pers. name + *hām*.

Rowsley Derbys. *Reuslege* (*sic*) 1086 (DB), *Rolvesle* 1204. 'Woodland clearing of a man called Hrōthwulf or Hrólfr'. OE or OScand. pers. name + OE *lēah*.

Rowston Lincs. *Rouestune* 1086 (DB). Possibly 'farmstead of a man called Hrólfr'. OScand. pers. name + OE *tūn*. Alternatively the first element may be OE *hrōf* 'roof', perhaps in some topographical sense.

Rowton Ches. *Rowa Christletona* 12th cent., *Roweton* 13th cent. 'The rough part of CHRISTLETON'. OE *rūh* + *tūn*.

Rowton Shrops., near High Ercall. *Routone* (*sic*) 1086 (DB), *Rowelton* 1195. Possibly 'farmstead by a rough hill'. OE *rūh* + *hyll* + *tūn*.

Roxby Humber. *Roxebi* 1086 (DB). 'Farmstead or village of a man called Hrókr'. OScand. pers. name + *bý*.

Roxby N. Yorks., near Hinderwell. *Roscebi* 1086 (DB). 'Farmstead or village of a man called Rauthr'. OScand. pers. name + *bý*.

Roxton Beds. *Rochesdone* 1086 (DB). Probably 'hill of a man called *Hrōc'. OE pers. name + *dūn*.

Roxwell Essex. *Rokeswelle* 1291. Probably 'spring or stream of a man called *Hrōc'. OE pers. name + *wella*.

Royal Leamington Spa Warwicks., see LEAMINGTON.

Roydon Essex. *Ruindune* 1086 (DB). 'Hill where rye is grown'. OE *rygen* + *dūn*.

Roydon Norfolk, near Diss. *Rygedune* c.1035, *Regadona* 1086 (DB). 'Rye hill'. OE *ryge* + *dūn*.

Royston Herts. *Roiston* 1286. Originally called *Crux Roaisie* 1184 'cross (Latin *crux*) of a woman called Rohesia', later simply *Roeys* to which *tūn* 'village' was added in the 13th cent.

Royston S. Yorks. *Rorestone* 1086 (DB). 'Farmstead of a man called *Hrōr or Róarr'. OE or OScand. pers. name + OE *tūn*.

Royton Gtr. Manch. *Ritton* 1226. 'Farmstead where rye is grown'. OE *ryge* + *tūn*.

Ruan, named from the patron saint of the parish, St Ruan or Rumon: **Ruan Lanihorne** Cornwall. *Lanryhorn* 1270, 'parish of *Sanctus Rumonus* of *Lanyhorn*' 1327. The second part of the name means 'church-site of a man called *Rihoarn', Cornish **lann* + pers. name. **Ruan Minor** Cornwall. 'Church of *Sanctus Rumonus Parvus*' 1277. Affix is Latin *minor* 'smaller' (earlier *parvus* 'small') to distinguish it from the adjacent parish of Ruan Major.

Ruardean Glos. *Rwirdin* 1086 (DB). 'Rye or hill enclosure'. OE *ryge* or Celtic **riu* + OE *worthign*.

Rubery Heref. & Worcs. *Robery Hills* 1650. 'Rough mound or hill'. OE *rūh* + *beorg*.

Ruckcroft Cumbria. *Rucroft* 1211. 'Rye enclosure'. OScand. *rugr* + OE *croft*.

Ruckinge Kent. *Hroching* 786, *Rochinges* 1086 (DB). 'Place characterized by rooks', or 'place associated with a man called *Hrōc'. OE *hrōc* or pers. name + *-ing*.

Ruckland Lincs. *Rocheland* (*sic*) 1086 (DB), *Roclund* 12th cent. 'Grove frequented by rooks'. OScand. *hrókr* + *lundr*.

Ruddington Notts. *Roddintone* 1086 (DB). 'Estate associated with a man called Rudda'. OE pers. name + *-ing-* + *tūn*.

Rudge Shrops. *Rigge* 1086 (DB). '(Place at) the ridge'. OE *hrycg*.

Rudgwick W. Sussex. *Regwic* 1210. 'Dwelling or farm on a ridge'. OE *hrycg* + *wīc*.

Rudham, East & West Norfolk. *Rudeham* 1086 (DB). 'Homestead or village of a man called Rudda'. OE pers. name + *hām*.

Rudston Humber. *Rodestan* 1086 (DB). '(Place at) the rood-stone or stone cross'. OE **rōd-stān*.

Rudyard Staffs. *Rudegeard* 1002, *Rudierd* 1086 (DB). Probably 'yard or enclosure where rue is grown'. OE *rūde* + *geard*.

Rufford Lancs. *Ruchford* 1212. 'Rough ford'. OE *rūh* + *ford*.

Rufforth N. Yorks. *Ruford* 1086 (DB). Identical in origin with the previous name.

Rugby Warwicks. *Rocheberie* 1086 (DB), *Rokebi* 1200. 'Fortified place of a man called *Hrōca'. OE pers. name + *burh* (dative *byrig*) replaced by OScand. *bý* 'village'. Alternatively 'fort frequented by rooks', with OE *hrōc* as first element.

Rugeley Staffs. *Rugelie* 1086 (DB). 'Woodland clearing on or near a ridge'. OE *hrycg* + *lēah*.

Ruishton Somerset. *Risctun* 9th cent. 'Farmstead where rushes grow'. OE **rysc* + *tūn*.

Ruislip Gtr. London. *Rislepe* 1086 (DB). Probably 'leaping-place (across the river) where rushes grow'. OE **rysc* + *hlȳp*.

Rumburgh Suffolk. *Romburch c.*1050, *Ramburc* (*sic*) 1086 (DB). 'Wide stronghold, or stronghold built of tree-trunks'. OE *rūm* or **hruna* + *burh*.

Runcorn Ches. *Rumcofan c.*1000. 'Wide bay or creek'. OE *rūm* + *cofa*.

Runcton W. Sussex. *Rochintone* 1086 (DB). 'Estate associated with a man called *Hrōc(a)'. OE pers. name + *-ing-* + *tūn*.

Runcton, North & South, Runcton Holme Norfolk. *Runghetuna* 1086 (DB), *Rungeton Holm* 1276. 'Farmstead enclosed with poles, or near a causeway made with poles'. OE *hrung* + *tūn*. Holme is probably OScand. *holmr* 'island, raised ground in marsh'.

Runfold Surrey. *Hrunigfeall* 974. 'Place where trees have been felled'. OE **hruna* + *(ge)feall*.

Runhall Norfolk. *Runhal* 1086 (DB). Possibly 'nook of land where there are tree-trunks'. OE **hruna* + *halh*.

Runham Norfolk. *Ronham* 1086 (DB). Possibly 'homestead or enclosure of a man called *Rūna', OE pers. name + *hām* or *hamm*. Alternatively the first element may be OE **hruna* 'tree-trunk'.

Runnington Somerset. *Runetone* 1086 (DB). Probably 'farmstead of a man called *Rūna'. OE pers. name (genitive *-n*) + *tūn*.

Runnymede Surrey. *Ronimede* 1215. 'Meadow at the island where councils are held'. OE *rūn* + *ēg* + *mǣd*.

Runswick N. Yorks. *Reneswike* 1273. Possibly 'creek of a man called Reinn'. OScand. pers. name + *vík*.

Runton, East & West Norfolk. *Runetune* 1086 (DB). 'Farmstead of a man called *Rūna or Rúni'. OE or OScand. pers. name + OE *tūn*.

Runwell Essex. *Runewelle c.*940, *Runewella* 1086 (DB). 'Council spring', i.e. probably 'wishing-well'. OE *rūn* + *wella*.

Ruscombe Berks. *Rothescamp* 1091. 'Enclosed land of a man called *Rōt'. OE pers. name + *camp*.

Rushall Norfolk. *Riuessala* 1086 (DB). OE *halh* 'nook of land' with an uncertain first element, probably a pers. name.

Rushall Wilts. *Rusteselve* (*sic*) 1086 (DB),

Rusteshala 1160. Probably 'nook of land of a man called *Rust'. OE pers. name + *halh*.

Rushbrooke Suffolk. *Ryssebroc c.*950, *Ryscebroc* 1086 (DB). 'Brook where rushes grow'. OE **rysc* + *brōc*.

Rushden, 'valley where rushes grow', OE **ryscen* + *denu*: **Rushden** Herts. *Risendene* 1086 (DB). **Rushden** Northants. *Risedene* 1086 (DB).

Rushford Suffolk. *Rissewrth c.*1060, *Rusceuuorda* 1086 (DB). 'Enclosure where rushes grow'. OE **rysc* + *worth*.

Rushmere, 'pool where rushes grow', OE **rysc* + *mere*: **Rushmere** Suffolk. *Ryscemara* 1086 (DB). **Rushmere St Andrew** Suffolk. *Ryscemara* 1086 (DB). Affix from the dedication of the church.

Rushock Heref. & Worcs. *Russococ* (*sic*) 1086 (DB), *Rossoc* 1166. Probably 'rushy place, rush-bed'. OE **ryscuc*.

Rusholme Gtr. Manch. *Russum* 1235. '(Place at) the rushes'. OE **rysc* in a dative plural form **ryscum*.

Rushton, 'farmstead where rushes grow', OE **rysc* + *tūn*: **Rushton** Ches. *Rusitone* 1086 (DB). **Rushton** Northants. *Risetone* 1086 (DB). **Rushton Spencer** Staffs. *Risetone* 1086 (DB). Manorial affix from early possession by the *Spencer* family.

Rushwick Heref. & Worcs. *Russewyk* 1275. 'Dairy farm among the rushes'. OE **rysc* + *wīc*.

Ruskington Lincs. *Rischintone* 1086 (DB). 'Farmstead where rushes grow'. OE **ryscen* (with Scand. *-sk-*) + *tūn*.

Rusland Cumbria. *Rolesland* 1336. 'Cultivated land of a man called Hrólfr or Hróaldr'. OScand. pers. name + *land*.

Rusper W. Sussex. *Rusparre* 1219. '(Place at) the rough spar or beam of wood'. OE *rūh* + **spearr*.

Rustington W. Sussex. *Rustinton* 1180. 'Estate associated with a man called *Rust(a)'. OE pers. name + *-ing-* + *tūn*.

Ruston N. Yorks. *Rostune* 1086 (DB). Possibly 'farmstead distinguished by its roof-beams or rafters'. OE **hrōst* + *tūn*.

Ruston, East & Sco Norfolk. *Ristuna* 1086 (DB), *Estriston* 1405, *Skouriston* 1425. 'Farmstead near or among brushwood'. OE *hrīs* + *tūn*. Distinguishing affixes are OE *ēast* and OScand. *skógr* 'wood'.

Ruston Parva Humber. *Roreston* 1086 (DB). 'Farmstead of a man called *Hrōr or Róarr'. OE or OScand. pers. name + OE *tūn*.

Ruswarp N. Yorks. *Risewarp c.*1146. Possibly 'silted land overgrown with brushwood'. OE *hrīs* + *wearp*.

Rutland (former county). *Roteland c.*1060, 1086 (DB). 'Estate of a man called Rōta'. OE pers. name + *land*.

Ruyton-XI-Towns Shrops. *Ruitone* 1086 (DB). 'Farmstead where rye is grown'. OE *ryge* + *tūn*. The parish was formerly composed of eleven townships.

Ryal Northum. *Ryhill* 1242. 'Hill where rye is grown'. OE *ryge* + *hyll*.

Ryarsh Kent. *Riesce* (*sic*) 1086 (DB), *Rierssh* 1242. 'Ploughed field used for rye'. OE *ryge* + *ersc*.

Ryburgh, Great & Little Norfolk. *Reie(n)burh* 1086 (DB). Probably 'old encampment used for growing rye'. OE *ryge(n)* + *burh*.

Rydal Cumbria. *Ridale* 1240. 'Valley where rye is grown'. OE *ryge* + OScand. *dalr*.

Ryde I. of Wight. *La Ride* 1257. 'The small stream'. OE *rīth*.

Rye E. Sussex. *Ria* 1130. '(Place at) the island or dry ground in marsh'. OE *īeg*, with initial *R-* from ME *atter* 'at the'.

Rye (river) N. Yorks., see RIEVAULX.

Ryhall Leics. *Riehale* 1086 (DB). 'Nook of land where rye is grown'. OE *ryge* + *halh*.

Ryhill, 'hill where rye is grown', OE *ryge* + *hyll*: **Ryhill** Humber. *Ryel c.*1155. **Ryhill** W. Yorks. *Rihella* 1086 (DB).

Ryhope Tyne & Wear. *Reofhoppas c.*1050. Possibly 'rough valleys or enclosures', OE *hrēof* + *hop* (originally in a plural form). Alternatively the first element may be OE *rēfa* 'a reeve, a bailiff'.

Ryle, Great & Little Northum. *Rihull*

1212. 'Hill where rye is grown'. OE *ryge* + *hyll*.

Rylstone N. Yorks. *Rilestun* 1086 (DB). OE *tūn* 'farmstead' with an uncertain first element, possibly OE *rynel* 'a small stream'.

Ryme Intrinseca Dorset. *Rima* 1160. '(Place at) the edge or border'. OE *rima*. Latin affix means 'inner', distinguishing this place from the former manor of Ryme Extrinseca ('outer').

Ryther N. Yorks. *Ridre* 1086 (DB). '(Place at) the clearing'. OE **ryther*.

Ryton, usually 'farm where rye is grown', OE *ryge* + *tūn*: **Ryton** Shrops. *Ruitone* 1086 (DB). **Ryton** Tyne & Wear. *Ritona* 1183. **Ryton, Great** Shrops. *Rutton* 1250. **Ryton-on-Dunsmore** Warwicks. *Ruyton c.*1045, *Rietone* 1086 (DB). Dunsmore (*Dunesmore* 12th cent.) is an old district name meaning 'moor of a man called Dunn', OE pers. name + *mōr*.

However the following has a different origin: **Ryton** N. Yorks. *Ritun* 1086 (DB). 'Farmstead on the River Rye'. Celtic river-name (see RIEVAULX) + OE *tūn*.

S

Sabden Lancs. *Sapeden* c.1140. 'Valley where fir-trees grow'. OE *sæppe* + *denu*.

Sacombe Herts. *Sueuecampe* 1086 (DB). 'Enclosed land of a man called *Swǣfa'. OE pers. name + *camp*.

Sacriston Durham. *Segrysteynhogh* 1312. 'Hill-spur of the sacristan (of Durham)'. ME *secrestein* + OE *hōh*.

Sadberge Durham. *Sadberge* 1169. OScand. *set-berg* 'a flat-topped hill'.

Saddington Leics. *Sadintone* 1086 (DB). OE *tūn* 'farmstead, estate' with an uncertain first element, possibly a reduced form of an OE pers. name such as Sǣgēat or *Sǣhæth with *-ing-*, or OE *sēath* 'pit' with *-ing*.

Saddle Bow Norfolk. *Sadelboge* 1198. 'The saddle-bow', referring to some arched or curved feature. OE *sadol* + *boga*.

Saddleworth Gtr. Manch. *Sadelwrth* late 12th cent. 'Enclosure on a saddle-shaped ridge'. OE *sadol* + *worth*.

Saffron Walden Essex, see WALDEN.

Saham Toney Norfolk. *Saham* 1086 (DB), *Saham Tony* 1498. 'Homestead by the pool'. OE *sǣ* + *hām*. Manorial affix from the *de Toni* family, here in the late 12th cent.

Saighton Ches. *Saltone* 1086 (DB). 'Farmstead where willow-trees grow'. OE *salh* + *tūn*.

St Agnes Cornwall. 'Parish of *Sancta Agnes*' 1327. From the dedication of the church to St Agnes.

St Albans Herts. *Sancte Albanes stow* 1007, *Villa Sancti Albani* 1086 (DB). 'Holy place of St Alban', from the saint martyred here in AD 209. The early spellings contain OE *stōw* 'holy place' and Latin *villa* 'town'. See also WATLING STREET.

St Austell Cornwall. 'Church of *Austol*' c.1150. From the dedication of the parish church to St Austol.

St Bees Cumbria. 'Church of *Sancta Bega*' c.1135. Named from St Bega, a female saint.

St Breock Cornwall. 'Church of *Sanctus Briocus*' 1259. From the patron saint of the church, St Brioc.

St Breward Cornwall. 'Church of *Sanctus Brewveredus*' c.1190. From the patron saint of the church, St Breward.

St Briavels Glos. '(Castle of) *Sanctus Briauel*' 1130. Named from the Welsh saint Briavel.

St Budeaux Devon. *Seynt Bodokkys* 1520. From the dedication of the church to the Celtic saint Budoc. Earlier *Bucheside* 1086 (DB), 'St Budoc's hide of land', OE *hīd*.

Saintbury Glos. *Svineberie* (*sic*) 1086 (DB), *Seinesberia* 1186. 'Fortified place of a man called Sǣwine'. OE pers. name + *burh* (dative *byrig*).

St Buryan Cornwall. 'Church of *Sancta Beriana*' c.939, *Sancta Berriona* 1086 (DB). Named from St Beryan, a female saint.

St Cleer Cornwall. 'Church of *Sanctus Clarus*' 1212. From the patron saint of the church, St Cleer.

St Columb Major & Minor Cornwall. 'Church of *Sancta Columba*' c.1240. Named from St Columba, a female saint.

St Cross South Elmham Suffolk, see ELMHAM.

St Devereux Heref. & Worcs. 'Church of *Sanctus Dubricius*' 1291. Named from St Dyfrig, a male Welsh saint.

St Endellion Cornwall. 'Church of *Sancta Endelienta*' 1260. Named from St Endilient, a female saint.

St Germans Cornwall. 'Church of

Sanctus Germanus' 1086 (DB). From the patron saint of the church.

St Giles in the Wood Devon. *Stow St Giles* 1330. 'Holy place of St Giles', from OE *stōw* and the patron saint of the church.

St Giles on the Heath Devon. 'Chapel of *Sanctus Egidius*' 1202, *St Gylses en le Hethe* 1585. From the dedication of the church to St Giles (Latin *Egidius*), with affix 'on the heath' from OE *hǣth*.

St Helens I. of Wight. *Sancta Elena* 12th cent. From the dedication of the church to St Helena.

St Helens Mersey., named from the chapel of St Helen, first recorded in 1552.

St Issey Cornwall. *Sanctus Ydi* 1195. From the dedication of the church to St Idi.

St Ive Cornwall. *Sanctus Yvo* 1201. From the dedication of the church to St Ivo, see next name.

St Ives Cambs. *Sancto Ivo de Slepe* 1110. Named from St Ivo whose relics were found here in the 10th cent. The earlier name *Slepe* is from OE **slǣp* 'slippery place'.

St Ives Cornwall. *Sancta Ya* 1284. From the dedication of the church to St Ya, a female saint.

St Ives Dorset. *Iuez* 1167. 'Place overgrown with ivy'. OE **Ifet*. *Saint* was only added in recent times on the analogy of the previous names.

St Just Cornwall. 'Church of *Sanctus Justus*' 1291. From the dedication of the church to St Just. Often called **St Just in Penwith**, this last (*Penwid* 1186, probably 'end-district') being an old Cornish name for the Land's End peninsula.

St Just in Roseland Cornwall. 'Church of *Sanctus Justus*' *c*.1070. Identical in origin with the previous name. Roseland (*Roslande* 1259) is an old district name meaning 'promontory land', Cornish *ros* + OE *land*.

St Keverne Cornwall. *Sanctus Achebrannus* 1086 (DB). From the patron saint of the church, St Aghevran.

St Kew Cornwall. *Sanctus Cheus* 1086 (DB). From the patron saint of the church, St Kew.

St Keyne Cornwall. 'Church of *Sancta Keyna*' 1291. Named from St Keyn, a female saint.

St Leonards E. Sussex. *Villa de Sancto Leonardo juxta Hasting* ('manor of St Leonard near to Hastings') 1288. Named from the dedication of the church.

St Leonards, Chapel Lincs., a late name, from the dedication of the chapel.

St Margaret's at Cliffe Kent. *Sancta Margarita* 1086 (DB), *Cliue c*.1100. 'Church dedicated to St Margaret near the cliff' (OE *clif*).

St Mary Bourne Hants., see BOURNE.

St Mary Cray Gtr. London, see CRAY.

St Mary's Bay Kent, named from St Mary in the Marsh (*Seyntemariecherche* 1240), with affix from OE *mersc*.

St Mary's Hoo Kent, see HOO.

St Mawes Cornwall. 'Town of *Sanctus Maudetus*' 1284. From the patron saint of the church, St Maudyth.

St Mellion Cornwall. 'Church of *Sanctus Melanus*' 1259. From the patron saint of the church, St Melaine.

St Merryn Cornwall. *Sancta Marina* 1259. Apparently named from St Marina (a female saint), but possibly from St Merin (a male).

St Mewan Cornwall. 'Church of *Sanctus Mawanus*' 1291. From the dedication of the church to St Mewan.

St Michael Caerhays Cornwall. 'Chapel of *Sanctus Michael de Karihaes*' 1259. From the dedication of the church to St Michael the Archangel. The distinguishing affix is from the manor of Caerhays, a name obscure in origin and meaning.

St Michael Penkevil Cornwall. 'Church of *Sanctus Michael de Penkevel*' 1261. From the same dedication as previous name. The affix is from the manor of Penkevil, a Cornish name probably meaning 'horse headland'.

St Michael's on Wyre Lancs. *Michelescherche* 1086 (DB). 'Church of St Michael', with OE *cirice* in the early spelling. Wyre is a Celtic river-name meaning 'winding one'.

St Neot Cornwall. *Sanctus Neotus* 1086 (DB). From the patron saint of the church, St Neot.

St Neots Cambs. *S' Neod* 12th cent. Also named from St Neot, whose relics were brought here from Cornwall in the 10th cent.

St Nicholas at Wade Kent. *Villa Sancti Nicholai* 1254. Named from the dedication of the church. Wade is from OE *wæd* 'a ford'.

St Osyth Essex. *Seynte Osithe* 1046. From the dedication of a priory here to St Ōsgȳth, a 7th-century princess. Its early name *Cice* 1086 (DB) is from OE **cicc* 'a bend'.

St Paul's Cray Gtr. London, see CRAY.

St Peter's Kent. *Borgha sancti Petri* ('borough of St Peter') 1254. Named from the dedication of the church.

St Tudy Cornwall. *Hecglostudic* 1086 (DB). From the dedication of the church to St Tudy, with Cornish *eglos* 'church' in the early spelling.

St Weonards Heref. & Worcs. *Lann Sant Guainerth* c.1130. 'Church of St Gwennarth', with OWelsh **lann* 'church' in the early spelling.

Salcombe, 'salt valley', OE *sealt* + *cumb*: **Salcombe** Devon. *Saltecumbe* 1244. **Salcombe Regis** Devon. *Sealtcumbe* c.1060, *Selcome* 1086 (DB). Affix is Latin *regis* 'of the king'.

Salcott Essex. *Saltcot* c.1200. 'Building where salt is made or stored'. OE *sealt* + *cot*.

Sale Gtr. Manch. *Sale* c.1205. '(Place at) the sallow-tree'. OE *salh* in a dative form *sale*.

Saleby Lincs. *Salebi* 1086 (DB). Possibly 'farmstead or village of a man called Sali'. OScand. pers. name + *bý*. Alternatively the first element may be OE *salh* 'sallow, willow'.

Salehurst E. Sussex. *Salhert* (*sic*) 1086 (DB), *Salhirst* c.1210. 'Wooded hill where sallow-trees grow'. OE *salh* + *hyrst*.

Salesbury Lancs. *Sale(s)byry* 1246. 'Fortified place or manor where sallow-trees grow'. OE *salh* + *burh* (dative *byrig*).

Salford Beds. *Saleford* 1086 (DB). 'Ford where sallow-trees grow'. OE *salh* + *ford*.

Salford Gtr. Manch. *Salford* 1086 (DB). Identical in origin with the previous name.

Salford Oxon. *Saltford* 777, *Salford* 1086 (DB). 'Ford over which salt is carried'. OE *salt* + *ford*.

Salford Priors & Abbots Salford Warwicks. *Saltford* 714, *Salford* 1086 (DB). Identical in origin with the previous name. Affixes from early possession by Kenilworth Priory and Evesham Abbey.

Salfords Surrey. *Salford* 1279. 'Ford where sallow-trees grow'. OE *salh* + *ford*.

Salhouse Norfolk. *Salhus* 1291. Probably 'the sallow-trees'. OE *salh* in a plural form.

Saling, Great Essex. *Salinges* 1086 (DB). Probably '(settlement of) the dwellers among the sallow-trees'. OE *salh* + *-ingas*.

Salisbury Wilts. *Searobyrg* c.900, *Sarisberie* 1086 (DB). 'Stronghold at *Sorvio*'. OE *burh* (dative *byrig*) added to reduced form of original Celtic name *Sorviodunum* (obscure word + Celtic **dūno-* 'fort').

Salkeld, Great & Little Cumbria. *Salchild* c.1110. 'Sallow-tree wood'. OE *salh* + **hylte*.

Salle Norfolk. *Salla* 1086 (DB). 'Wood or clearing where sallow-trees grow'. OE *salh* + *lēah*.

Salmonby Lincs. *Salmundebi* 1086 (DB). 'Farmstead or village of a man called Salmundr'. OScand. pers. name + *bý*.

Salop (the county), see SHROPSHIRE.

Salperton Glos. *Salpretune* 1086 (DB). Probably 'farmstead on a salt-way'. OE *salt* + *here-pæth* + *tūn*.

Salt Staffs. *Selte* 1086 (DB). OE **selte* 'a salt-pit, a salt-works'.

Saltash Cornwall. *Esse* 1201, *Saltehasche* 1302. Originally '(place at) the ash-tree', OE *æsc*. Later addition *salt* from the production of salt here.

Saltburn-by-the-Sea Cleveland. *Salteburnam* c.1185. '(Place by) the salt stream'. OE *salt* + *burna*.

Saltby Leics. *Saltebi* 1086 (DB). Possibly 'farmstead or village of a man called *Salti or Salt'. OScand. pers. name + *bý*. Alternatively the first element may be OScand. *salt* 'salt'.

Salter Lancs. *Salterge* c.1150. 'Shieling where salt is found or kept'. OE *salt* + OScand. *erg*.

Salterforth Lancs. *Salterford* 13th cent. 'Ford used by salt-merchants'. OE *saltere* + *ford*.

Salterton, Budleigh Devon. *Saltre* 1210, *Salterne* 1405. OE *salt-ærn* 'building where salt is made or sold'. Affix from nearby BUDLEIGH.

Salterton, Woodbury Devon. *Salterton* 1306. 'Farmstead of the salt-workers or salt-merchants'. OE *saltere* + *tūn*. Affix from nearby WOODBURY.

Saltfleet Lincs. *Salfluet* 1086 (DB). '(Place by) the salt stream'. OE *salt* + *flēot*.

Saltfleetby Lincs. *Salflatebi* 1086 (DB). 'Farmstead or village by the salt stream'. OE *salt* + *flēot* + OScand. *bý*.

Saltford Avon. *Sanford* (*sic*) 1086 (DB), *Salford* 1229, *Saltford* 1291. Probably 'salt-water ford', OE *salt* + *ford*, but the first element may originally have been *salh* 'sallow, willow'.

Salthouse Norfolk. *Salthus* 1086 (DB). 'Building for storing salt'. OE *salt* + *hūs*.

Saltmarshe Humber. *Saltemersc* 1086 (DB). 'Salty or brackish marsh'. OE *salt* + *mersc*.

Saltney Ches. *Salteney* c.1230. 'Salty island or dry ground in marsh'. OE *salt* (dative *-an*) + *ēg*.

Salton N. Yorks. *Saletun* 1086 (DB). 'Farmstead where sallow-trees grow'. OE *salh* + *tūn*.

Saltwood Kent. *Sealtwuda* c.1000, *Salteode* 1086 (DB). 'Wood where salt is made or stored'. OE *sealt* + *wudu*.

Salvington W. Sussex. *Saluinton* 1249. 'Estate associated with a man called Sǣlāf or Sǣwulf'. OE pers. name + *-ing-* + *tūn*.

Salwarpe Heref. & Worcs. *Salouuarpe* 817, *Salewarpe* 1086 (DB). Probably 'dark-coloured silted land'. OE *salu* + *wearp*.

Sambourne Warwicks. *Samburne* 714, *Sandburne* 1086 (DB). 'Sandy stream'. OE *sand* + *burna*.

Sambrook Shrops. *Semebre* (*sic*) 1086 (DB), *Sambrok* 1285. 'Sandy brook'. OE *sand* + *brōc*.

Samlesbury Lancs. *Samelesbure* 1188. Probably 'stronghold near a shelf or ledge of land'. OE *scamol* + *burh* (dative *byrig*).

Sampford, 'sandy ford', OE *sand* + *ford*: **Sampford Arundel** Somerset. *Sanford* 1086 (DB), *Samford Arundel* 1240. Manorial affix from Roger *Arundel*, tenant in 1086. **Sampford Brett** Somerset. *Sanford* 1086 (DB), *Saunford Bret* 1306. Manorial affix from the *Bret* family, here in the 12th cent. **Sampford Courtenay** Devon. *Sanfort* 1086 (DB), *Saunforde Curtenay* 1262. Manorial affix from the *Curtenay* family, here in the 13th cent. **Sampford Peverell** Devon. *Sanforda* 1086 (DB), *Saunford Peverel* 1275. Manorial affix from the *Peverel* family, here in the 12th cent. **Sampford Spiney** Devon. *Sanforda* 1086 (DB), *Saundford Spyneye* 1304. Manorial affix from the *Spiney* family, here in the 13th cent.

Sancreed Cornwall. 'Church of *Sanctus Sancretus*' 1235. From the patron saint of the church, St Sancred.

Sancton Humber. *Santun* 1086 (DB). 'Farmstead with sandy soil'. OE *sand* + *tūn*.

Sandall, Kirk S. Yorks. *Sandala* 1086 (DB), *Kirke Sandale* 1261. 'Sandy nook of land'. OE *sand* + *halh*. Affix is OScand. *kirkja* 'church'.

Sandbach Ches. *Sanbec* 1086 (DB). 'Sandy valley-stream'. OE *sand* + *bæce*.

Sanderstead Surrey. *Sondenstede* c.880, *Sandestede* 1086 (DB). 'Sandy homestead'. OE *sand* + *hǣm-styde*.

Sandford, 'sandy ford', OE *sand* + *ford*: **Sandford** Cumbria. *Saunford* c.1210. **Sandford** Devon. *Sandforda* 930. **Sandford** Shrops. *Sanford* 1086 (DB). **Sandford on Thames** Oxon. *Sandforda* 1050, *Sanford* 1086 (DB).

Sandford Orcas Dorset. *Sanford* 1086 (DB), *Sandford Horscoys* 1372. Manorial affix from the *Orescuils* family, here from the 12th cent. **Sandford St Martin** Oxon. *Sanford* 1086 (DB). Affix from the dedication of the church.

Sandgate Kent. *Sandgate* 1256. 'Gap or gate leading to the sandy shore'. OE *sand* + *geat*.

Sandhoe Northum. *Sandho* 1225. 'Sandy hill-spur'. OE *sand* + *hōh*.

Sandhurst, 'sandy wooded hill', OE *sand* + *hyrst*: **Sandhurst** Berks. *Sandherst* 1175. **Sandhurst** Glos. *Sanher* (*sic*) 1086 (DB), *Sandhurst* 12th cent. **Sandhurst** Kent. *Sandhyrste* c.1100.

Sandhutton N. Yorks. *Hotune* 1086 (DB), *Sandhoton* 12th cent. 'Farmstead on a sandy spur of land'. OE *sand* + *hōh* + *tūn*.

Sand Hutton N. Yorks., see HUTTON.

Sandiacre Derbys. *Sandiacre* 1086 (DB). 'Sandy cultivated land'. OE *sandig* + *æcer*.

Sandon, 'sandy hill', OE *sand* + *dūn*: **Sandon** Essex. *Sandun* 1199. **Sandon** Herts. *Sandune* c.1000, *Sandone* 1086 (DB). **Sandon** Staffs. *Sandone* 1086 (DB).

Sandown I. of Wight. *Sande* (*sic*) 1086 (DB), *Sandham* 1271. 'Sandy enclosure or river-meadow'. OE *sand* + *hamm*.

Sandown Park Surrey. *Sandone* 1235. 'Sandy hill or down'. OE *sand* + *dūn*.

Sandridge Herts. *Sandrige* 1086 (DB). 'Sandy ridge'. OE *sand* + *hrycg*. The same name occurs in Devon.

Sandringham Norfolk. *Santdersincham* 1086 (DB). 'The sandy part of DERSINGHAM'. The affix is OE *sand*.

Sandtoft Humber. *Sandtofte* 1157. 'Sandy building plot or curtilage'. OScand. *sandr* + *toft*.

Sandwell W. Mids. *Saundwell* 13th cent. 'Sandy spring'. OE *sand* + *wella*.

Sandwich Kent. *Sandwicæ* c.710–20, *Sandwice* 1086 (DB). 'Sandy harbour or hamlet'. OE *sand* + *wīc*.

Sandwith Cumbria. *Sandwath* 1260. 'Sandy ford'. OScand. *sandr* + *vath*.

Sandy Beds. *Sandeie* 1086 (DB). 'Sandy island'. OE *sand* + *ēg*.

Sankey, Great Ches. *Sonchi* c.1180. Named from the River Sankey, a pre-English river-name of uncertain origin and meaning.

Santon, 'farmstead with sandy soil', OE *sand* + *tūn*: **Santon Bridge** Cumbria. *Santon* c.1235. **Santon, Low** Humber. *Santone* 1086 (DB).

Sapcote Leics. *Scepecote* 1086 (DB). 'Shed or shelter for sheep'. OE *scēap* + *cot*.

Sapey, Lower & Upper Heref. & Worcs. *Sapian* 781, *Sapie* 1086 (DB). Probably from OE *sæpig* 'sappy, juicy', originally applied to Sapey Brook.

Sapiston Suffolk. *Sapestuna* 1086 (DB). OE *tūn* 'farmstead' with an uncertain first element, possibly a pers. name.

Sapley Cambs. *Sappele* 1227. 'Wood or clearing where fir-trees grow'. OE *sæppe* + *lēah*.

Sapperton, 'farmstead of the soap-makers or soap-merchants', OE **sāpere* + *tūn*: **Sapperton** Glos. *Sapertun* c.1075, *Sapletorne* (*sic*) 1086 (DB). **Sapperton** Lincs. *Sapretone* 1086 (DB).

Sarnesfield Heref. & Worcs. *Sarnesfelde* 1086 (DB). 'Open land by a road'. OWelsh *sarn* + OE *feld*.

Sarratt Herts. *Syreth* c.1085. Possibly 'dry or barren place'. OE **sīeret*.

Sarre Kent. *Serræ* 761. Obscure in origin and meaning, but possibly an old pre-English name for the River Wantsum.

Sarsden Oxon. *Secendene* (*sic*) 1086 (DB), *Cerchesdena* c.1180. Probably 'valley of the church'. OE *cirice* + *denu*.

Satley Durham. *Sateley* 1228. Possibly 'woodland clearing with a stable or fold'. OE *set* + *lēah*.

Satterleigh Devon. *Saterlei* 1086 (DB). 'Woodland clearing of the robbers'. OE *sǣtere* + *lēah*.

Satterthwaite Cumbria. *Saterthwayt* 1336. Probably 'clearing by a hut or shieling'. OScand. *sǽtr* + *thveit*.

Saughall, Great & Little Ches. *Salhale* 1086 (DB). 'Nook of land where sallow-trees grow'. OE *salh* + *halh*.

Saul Glos. *Salle* 12th cent. 'Wood or clearing where sallow-trees grow'. OE *salh* + *lēah*.

Saundby Notts. *Sandebi* 1086 (DB). Probably 'farmstead or village of a man called Sandi'. OScand. pers. name + *bý*. Alternatively the first element may be OScand. *sandr* 'sand'.

Saunderton Bucks. *Santesdune* 1086 (DB), *Santredon* 1196. OE *dūn* 'hill' with an uncertain first element.

Savernake Forest Wilts. *Safernoc* 934. Probably 'district of a river called *Sabrina* or *Severn*', from a derivative of an ancient pre-English river-name (perhaps applied originally to the River Bedwyn) of unknown origin and meaning.

Sawbridgeworth Herts. *Sabrixteworde* 1086 (DB). 'Enclosure of a man called Sǣbeorht'. OE pers. name + *worth*.

Sawdon N. Yorks. *Saldene* early 13th cent. 'Valley where sallow-trees grow'. OE *salh* + *denu*.

Sawley Derbys. *Salle* (*sic*) 1086 (DB), *Sallawa* 1166. 'Hill or mound where sallow-trees grow'. OE *salh* + *hlāw*.

Sawley Lancs. *Sotleie* (*sic*) 1086 (DB), *Sallaia* 1147. 'Woodland clearing where sallow-trees grow'. OE *salh* + *lēah*.

Sawley N. Yorks. *Sallege c.*1030. Identical in origin with the previous name.

Sawrey, Far & Near Cumbria. *Sourer* 1336. 'The sour or muddy grounds'. OScand. *saurr* in a plural form *saurar*.

Sawston Cambs. *Salsingetune* 970, *Salsiton* 1086 (DB). 'Farmstead of the family or followers of a man called *Salse'. OE pers. name + *-inga-* + *tūn*.

Sawtry Cambs. *Saltreiam* 974, *Saltrede* 1086 (DB). 'Salty stream'. OE *salt* + *rīth*.

Saxby, probably 'farmstead or village of a man called Saksi', OScand. pers. name + *bý*, but alternatively the first element may be OScand. *Saksar* 'Saxons': **Saxby** Leics. *Saxebi* 1086 (DB). **Saxby** Lincs. *Sassebi* 1086 (DB). **Saxby All Saints** Humber. *Saxebi* 1086 (DB). Affix from the dedication of the church.

Saxelby Leics. *Saxelbie* 1086 (DB). Probably 'farmstead or village of a man called Saksulfr'. OScand. pers. name + *bý*.

Saxham, Great & Little Suffolk. *Saxham* 1086 (DB). Probably 'homestead of the Saxons'. OE *Seaxe* + *hām*.

Saxilby Lincs. *Saxebi* (*sic*) 1086 (DB), *Saxlabi c.*1115. Identical in origin with SAXELBY.

Saxlingham, 'homestead of the family or followers of a man called *Seaxel or Seaxhelm', OE pers. name + *-inga-* + *hām*: **Saxlingham** Norfolk. *Saxelingaham* 1086 (DB). **Saxlingham Nethergate** Norfolk. *Seaxlingaham* 1046, *Saiselingaham* 1086 (DB). The affix, first found in the 13th cent., means 'lower gate or street'.

Saxmundham Suffolk. *Sasmundeham* 1086 (DB). 'Homestead of a man called *Seaxmund'. OE pers. name + *hām*.

Saxondale Notts. *Saxeden* 1086 (DB), *Saxendala c.*1130. 'Valley of the Saxons'. OE *Seaxe* + *dæl* (replacing *denu*).

Saxtead Suffolk. *Saxteda* 1086 (DB). Probably 'place of a man called Seaxa'. OE pers. name + *stede*.

Saxthorpe Norfolk. *Saxthorp* 1086 (DB). 'Outlying farmstead or hamlet of a man called Saksi'. OScand. pers. name + *thorp*.

Saxton N. Yorks. *Saxtun* 1086 (DB). 'Farmstead of the Saxons, or of a man called Saksi'. OE *Seaxe* or OScand. pers. name + OE *tūn*.

Scackleton N. Yorks. *Scacheldene* 1086 (DB). Probably 'valley by a point of land'. OE *scacol* (with Scand. *sk-*) + *denu*.

Scaftworth Notts. *Scafteorde* 1086 (DB). Probably 'enclosure of a man called *Sceafta or Skapti', OE or OScand. pers. name + OE *worth*. Alternatively 'enclosure made with poles', OE *sceaft* (with Scand. *sk-*) + *worth*.

Scagglethorpe N. Yorks. *Scachetorp* 1086 (DB). Probably 'outlying farmstead or hamlet of a man called Skakull or Skakli'. OScand. pers. name + *thorp*.

Scalby, 'farmstead or village of a man called Skalli', OScand. pers. name + *bý*: **Scalby** Humber. *Scalleby* 1230. **Scalby** N. Yorks. *Scallebi* 1086 (DB).

Scaldwell Northants. *Scaldewelle* 1086 (DB). 'Shallow spring or stream'. OE **scald* (with Scand. *sk-*) + *wella*.

Scaleby Cumbria. *Schaleby c.*1235. 'Farmstead or village near the huts or shielings'. OScand. *skáli* + *bý*.

Scales, a common name in the North, 'the temporary huts or sheds', OScand. *skáli*; examples include: **Scales** Cumbria, near Aldingham. *Scales* 1269. **Scales** Cumbria, near Threlkeld. *Skales* 1323. **Scales** Lancs., near Newton. *Skalys* 1501.

Scalford Leics. *Scaldeford* 1086 (DB). 'Shallow ford'. OE **scald* (with Scand. *sk-*) + *ford*.

Scamblesby Lincs. *Scamelesbi* 1086 (DB). Probably 'farmstead or village of a man called Skammel'. OScand. pers. name + *bý*.

Scampston N. Yorks. *Scameston* 1086 (DB). 'Farmstead of a man called Skammr or Skammel'. OScand. pers. name + OE *tūn*.

Scampton Lincs. *Scantone* 1086 (DB). 'Short farmstead, or farmstead of a man called Skammi'. OScand. *skammr* or pers. name + OE *tūn*.

Scarborough N. Yorks. *Escardeburg c.*1160. Probably 'stronghold of a man called Skarthi'. OScand. pers. name + OE *burh*.

Scarcliffe Derbys. *Scardeclif* 1086 (DB). 'Cliff or steep slope with a gap'. OE *sceard* (with Scand. *sk-*) + *clif*.

Scarcroft W. Yorks. *Scardecroft* 1166. Probably 'enclosure in a gap'. OE *sceard* (with Scand. *sk-*) + *croft*.

Scargill Durham. *Scracreghil* 1086 (DB). Probably 'ravine frequented by mergansers or similar seabirds'. OScand. *skraki* + *gil*.

Scarisbrick Lancs. *Scharisbrec c.*1200. Possibly 'hill-side or slope by a hollow'. OScand. *skar* + *brekka*.

Scarle, North (Lincs.) **& South** (Notts.). *Scornelei* 1086 (DB). 'Mud or dung clearing'. OE *scearn* (with Scand. *sk-*) + *lēah*.

Scarning Norfolk. *Scerninga* 1086 (DB). Probably 'the muddy or dirty place'. OE *scearn* (with Scand. *sk-*) + *-ing*.

Scarrington Notts. *Scarintone* 1086 (DB). Possibly 'muddy or dirty farmstead'. OE **scearnig* (with Scand. *sk-*) + *tūn*. Alternatively the first element may be OE **scearning* 'dirty place'.

Scartho Humber. *Scarhou* 1086 (DB). 'Mound near a gap, or one frequented by cormorants'. OScand. *skarth* or *skarfr* + *haugr*.

Scawby Humber. *Scallebi* 1086 (DB). Probably 'farmstead or village of a man called Skalli'. OScand. pers. name + *bý*.

Scawton N. Yorks. *Scaltun* 1086 (DB). 'Farmstead in a hollow or with a shieling'. OScand. *skál* or *skáli* + OE *tūn*.

Scholar Green Ches. *Scholehalc* late 13th cent. 'Nook of land with a hut or shieling'. OScand. *skáli* + OE *halh*.

Scholes, a common name in the North, 'the temporary huts or sheds', OScand. *skáli*; examples include: **Scholes** W. Yorks., near Holmfirth. *Scholes* 1284. **Scholes** W. Yorks., near Leeds. *Skales* 1258.

Scilly Isles Cornwall. *Sully* 12th cent. An ancient pre-English name first recorded in the first century AD, of unknown origin and meaning.

Scole Norfolk. *Escales* 1191. 'The temporary huts or sheds'. OScand. *skáli*.

Scopwick Lincs. *Scapeuic* 1086 (DB). 'Sheep farm'. OE *scēap* (with Scand. *sk-*) + *wīc*.

Scorborough Humber. *Scogerbud* 1086 (DB). 'Booth or shelter in a wood'. OScand. *skógr* + *búth*.

Scorton, 'farmstead near a ditch or ravine', OScand. *skor* + OE *tūn*: **Scorton** Lancs. *Scourton c.*1550. **Scorton** N. Yorks. *Scortone* 1086 (DB).

Sco Ruston Norfolk, see RUSTON.

Scotby Cumbria. *Scoteby* 1130. 'Farmstead or village of the Scots'. OScand. *Skoti* + *bý*.

Scotch Corner N. Yorks., road junction on the Great North Road so called because the main road to SW Scotland via Carlisle branches off here.

Scotforth Lancs. *Scozforde* 1086 (DB). 'Ford used by the Scot or Scots'. OE *Scot* (with Scand. *sk-*) + *ford*.

Scothern Lincs. *Scotstorne* 1086 (DB).

'Thorn-tree of the Scot or Scots'. OE *Scot* (with Scand. *sk-*) + *thorn*.

Scotter Lincs. *Scot(e)re* 1086 (DB). Possibly 'tree of the Scots'. OE *Scot* (with Scand. *sk-*) + *trēow*.

Scotterthorpe Lincs. *Scaltorp* 1086 (DB). Probably 'outlying farmstead or hamlet of a man called Skalli'. OScand. pers. name + *thorp*.

Scotton, 'farmstead of the Scots', OE *Scot* (with Scand. *sk-*) + *tūn*: **Scotton** Lincs. *Scottun* 1060–6, *Scotone* 1086 (DB). **Scotton** N. Yorks., near Knaresborough. *Scotone* 1086 (DB). **Scotton** N. Yorks., near Richmond. *Scottune* 1086 (DB).

Scottow Norfolk. *Scoteho* 1044–7, *Scotohou* 1086 (DB). 'Hill-spur of the Scots'. OE *Scot* (with Scand. *sk-*) + *hōh*.

Scoulton Norfolk. *Sculetuna* 1086 (DB). 'Farmstead of a man called Skúli'. OScand. pers. name + OE *tūn*.

Scrafton, West N. Yorks. *Scraftun* 1086 (DB). 'Farmstead near a hollow'. OE *scræf* (with Scand. *sk-*) + *tūn*.

Scrainwood Northum. *Scravenwod* 1242. 'Wood frequented by shrewmice or villains'. OE *scrēawa* (genitive plural *-ena* and with Scand. *sk-*) + *wudu*.

Scrane End Lincs. *Screinga* 12th cent. '(Settlement of) the family or followers of a man called *Scīrhēah' from an OE pers. name + *-ingas*, or 'structure(s) made of poles' from an OE **scræging* (with Scand. *sk-*).

Scraptoft Leics. *Scraptoft* 1043, *Scrapentot* (*sic*) 1086 (DB). Probably 'homestead of a man called Skrápi'. OScand. pers. name + *toft*.

Scratby Norfolk. *Scroutebi* c.1020, *Scroteby* 1086 (DB). 'Farmstead or village of a man called Skrauti'. OScand. pers. name + *bý*.

Scrayingham N. Yorks. *Screngham*, *Escraingham* 1086 (DB). 'Homestead of the family or followers of a man called *Scīrhēah' from OE pers. name + *-inga-* + *hām*, or 'homestead with a structure of poles' from an OE **scræging* (with Scand. *sk-*) + *hām*.

Scredington Lincs. *Scredinctun* 1086 (DB). Possibly 'estate associated with a man called Scīrheard'. OE pers. name (with Scand. *sk-*) + *-ing-* + *tūn*.

Scremby Lincs. *Screnbi* 1086 (DB). 'Farmstead or village of a man called *Skræma'. OScand. pers. name + *bý*.

Scremerston Northum. *Schermereton* 1196. 'Estate of the *Skermer* family'. ME surname + OE *tūn*.

Scriven N. Yorks. *Scrauing(h)e* 1086 (DB). 'Hollow place with pits'. OE **screfen* (with Scand. *sk-*).

Scrooby Notts. *Scrobi* 1086 (DB). Possibly 'farmstead or village of a man called Skropi'. OScand. pers. name + *bý*.

Scropton Derbys. *Scrotun* (*sic*) 1086 (DB), *Scropton* c.1141. Probably 'farmstead of a man called Skropi'. OScand. pers. name + OE *tūn*.

Scruton N. Yorks. *Scurvetone* 1086 (DB). 'Farmstead of a man called Skurfa'. OScand. pers. name + OE *tūn*.

Sculthorpe Norfolk. *Sculatorpa* 1086 (DB). 'Outlying farmstead or hamlet of a man called Skúli'. OScand. pers. name + *thorp*.

Scunthorpe Humber. *Escumetorp* 1086 (DB). 'Outlying farmstead or hamlet of a man called Skúma'. OScand. pers. name + *thorp*.

Seaborough Dorset. *Seveberge* 1086 (DB). 'Seven hills or barrows'. OE *seofon* + *beorg*.

Seacombe Mersey. *Secumbe* c.1277. 'Valley by the sea'. OE *sǣ* + *cumb*.

Seacroft W. Yorks. *Sacroft* 1086 (DB). 'Enclosure by a pool or marsh'. OE *sǣ* + *croft*.

Seaford E. Sussex. *Saforde* 12th cent. 'Ford by the sea'. OE *sǣ* + *ford*. The River Ouse flowed into the sea here until the 16th cent.

Seaforth Mersey., a recent name, from *Seaforth House* in Litherland which was named after Lord Seaforth in the early 19th cent.

Seagrave Leics. *Setgraue* 1086 (DB). Possibly 'grove with or near a pit'. OE *sēath* + *grāf*.

Seagry, Upper Wilts. *Segrete* 1086 (DB). 'Stream where sedge grows'. OE *secg* + *rīth*.

Seaham Durham. *Sæham* c.1050. 'Homestead or village by the sea'. OE *sǣ* + *hām*.

Seal Kent. *La Sela* 1086 (DB). Probably 'the hall or dwelling', OE *sele*. Alternatively 'the sallow-tree copse', OE **sele*.

Seamer, 'lake or marsh pool', OE *sǣ* + *mere*: **Seamer** N. Yorks., near Scarborough. *Semær* 1086 (DB). **Seamer** N. Yorks., near Stokesley. *Semer* 1086 (DB).

Sea Palling Norfolk, see PALLING.

Searby Lincs. *Seurebi* 1086 (DB). 'Farmstead or village of the seafarers, or of a man called Sæfari'. OScand. **sæfari* or pers. name + *bý*.

Seasalter Kent. *Seseltre* 1086 (DB). 'Salt-works on the sea'. OE *sǣ* + *sealt-ærn*.

Seascale Cumbria. *Sescales c.*1165. 'Shieling(s) or hut(s) by the sea'. OScand. *sǽr* + *skáli*.

Seathwaite Cumbria, near Borrowdale. *Seuethwayt* 1292. 'Sedge clearing'. OScand. *sef* + *thveit*.

Seathwaite Cumbria., near Ulpha. *Seathwhot* 1592. 'Lake clearing'. OScand. *sǽr* + *thveit*.

Seaton, usually 'farmstead by the sea or by an inland pool', OE *sǣ* + *tūn*; examples include: **Seaton** Devon. *Seton* 1238. **Seaton** Cumbria, near Workington. *Setona c.*1174. **Seaton Carew** Cleveland. *Setona* late 12th cent., *Seton Carrowe* 1345. Manorial affix from the *Carou* family, here in the 12th cent. **Seaton Delaval** Northum. *Seton de la Val* 1270. Manorial affix from the *de la Val* family, here in the 13th cent. **Seaton Ross** Humber. *Seton* 1086 (DB), *Seaton Rosse* 1618. Manorial affix from the *Ross* family who held the vill from the 12th cent.

However the following has a different origin: **Seaton** Leics. *Seieton* 1086 (DB). Possibly 'farmstead of a man called *Sǣga'. OE pers. name + *tūn*.

Seavington St Michael & St Mary Somerset. *Seofenempton c.*1025, *Sevenehantune* 1086 (DB). 'Village of seven homesteads'. OE *seofon* + *hām-tun*. Distinguishing affixes from the dedications of the churches here.

Sebergham Cumbria. *Saburgham* 1223. Probably 'homestead of a woman called Sǣburh'. OE pers. name + *hām*.

Seckington Warwicks. *Seccandun* late 9th cent., *Sechintone* 1086 (DB). 'Hill of a man called Secca'. OE pers. name (genitive *-an*) + *dūn*.

Sedbergh Cumbria. *Sedberge* 1086 (DB). OScand. *set-berg* 'a flat-topped hill'.

Sedgeberrow Heref. & Worcs. *Segcgesbearuue* 777, *Seggesbarue* 1086 (DB). 'Grove of a man called *Secg'. OE pers. name + *bearu*.

Sedgebrook Lincs. *Sechebroc* 1086 (DB). 'Brook where sedge grows'. OE *secg* + *brōc*.

Sedgefield Durham. *Ceddesfeld c.*1050. 'Open land of a man called *Cedd or *Secg'. OE pers. name + *feld*.

Sedgeford Norfolk. *Secesforda* 1086 (DB). Possibly 'ford of a man called *Secci'. OE pers. name + *ford*.

Sedgehill Wilts. *Seghulle* early 12th cent. 'Hill of a man called Secga, or near where sedge grows'. OE pers. name or OE *secg* + *hyll*.

Sedgley W. Mids. *Secgesleage* 985, *Segleslei (sic)* 1086 (DB). 'Woodland clearing of a man called *Secg'. OE pers. name + *lēah*.

Sedgwick Cumbria. *Sigghiswic c.*1185. 'Dwelling or farm of a man called *Sicg'. OE pers. name + *wīc*.

Sedlescombe E. Sussex. *Selescome (sic)* 1086 (DB), *Sedelescumbe c.*1210. Probably 'valley with a house or dwelling'. OE *sedl* + *cumb*.

Seend Wilts. *Sinda* 1190. Probably 'sandy place'. OE **sende*.

Seer Green Bucks. *La Sere* 1223. 'The dry or barren place'. OE *sēar*.

Seething Norfolk. *Sithinges* 1086 (DB). Probably '(settlement of) the family or followers of a man called *Sīth(a)'. OE pers. name + *-ingas*.

Sefton Mersey. *Sextone (sic)* 1086 (DB), *Sefftun c.*1220. 'Farmstead where rushes grow'. OScand. *sef* + OE *tūn*.

Seghill Northum. *Syghal* 1198. Possibly 'nook of land by a stream called **Sige*'. OE river-name (meaning 'slow-moving') + *halh*.

Seighford Staffs. *Cesteforde* 1086 (DB). 'Ford by an old fortification'. OE *ceaster* + *ford*.

Selattyn Shrops. *Sulatun* 1254. Probably 'farmstead with ploughs or ploughlands'. OE *sulh* + *tūn*.

Selborne Hants. *Seleborne* 903, *Selesburne* 1086 (DB). 'Stream by (a copse of) sallow-trees'. OE *sealh* or **sele* + *burna*.

Selby N. Yorks. *Seleby* c.1030, *Salebi* 1086 (DB). 'Farmstead or village near (a copse of) sallow-trees'. OE **sele* or OScand. *selja* + OScand. *bý*.

Selham W. Sussex. *Seleham* 1086 (DB). 'Homestead by a copse of sallow-trees'. OE **sele* + *hām*.

Sellack Heref. & Worcs. *Lann Suluc* c.1130. 'Church of Suluc (a pet-form of Suliau)'. From the dedication of the church (OWelsh **lann*).

Sellafield Cumbria. *Sellofeld* 1576. Probably 'land by the willow-tree mound'. OScand. *selja* + *haugr* + OE *feld*.

Sellindge Kent. *Sedlinges* 1086 (DB). Probably '(settlement of) those sharing a house or building', from OE *sedl* + *-ingas*. Alternatively 'place at a house or building', OE *sedl* + *-ing*.

Selling Kent. *Setlinges* 1086 (DB). Identical in origin with the previous name.

Selly Oak W. Mids. *Escelie* (*sic*) 1086 (DB), *Selvele* 1204. 'Woodland clearing on a shelf or ledge'. OE *scelf* + *lēah*, with the later addition *oak*.

Selmeston E. Sussex. *Sielmestone* 1086 (DB). 'Farmstead of a man called Sigehelm'. OE pers. name + *tūn*.

Selsdon Gtr. London. *Selesdune* c.880. 'Hill of a man called *Sele or *Seli'. OE pers. name + *dūn*.

Selsey W. Sussex. *Seolesiae* c.715, *Seleisie* 1086 (DB). 'Island of the seal'. OE *seolh* + *ēg*. Selsey Bill, not recorded until the 18th cent., is from OE *bile* 'a bill, a beak' used topographically for 'promontory'.

Selston Notts. *Salestune* 1086 (DB). Probably 'farmstead of a man called *Sele or *Seli'. OE pers. name + *tūn*.

Selwood Somerset. *Seluudu* c.894. 'Wood where sallow-trees grow'. OE *sealh* + *wudu*.

Selworthy Somerset. *Seleuurde* 1086 (DB). 'Enclosure by a copse of sallow-trees'. OE **sele* + *worth*(*ig*).

Semer Suffolk. *Seamera* 1086 (DB). 'Lake or marsh pool'. OE *sǣ* + *mere*.

Semington Wilts. *Semneton* 13th cent. 'Farmstead on the stream called *Semnet*'. Pre-English river-name (of uncertain meaning) + OE *tūn*.

Semley Wilts. *Semeleage* 955. 'Woodland clearing on the River Sem'. Pre-English river-name (of uncertain meaning) + OE *lēah*.

Send Surrey. *Sendan* 960–2, *Sande* 1086 (DB). 'Sandy place'. OE **sende*.

Sennen Cornwall. 'Parish of *Sancta Senana*' 1327. From the female patron saint of the church.

Sessay N. Yorks. *Sezai* 1086 (DB). 'Island or well-watered land where sedge grows'. OE *secg* + *ēg*.

Setchey Norfolk. *Seche* (*sic*) 1086 (DB), *Sechithe* 13th cent. Possibly 'landing-place of a man called *Secci'. OE pers. name + *hȳth*.

Settle N. Yorks. *Setel* 1086 (DB). 'The house or dwelling'. OE *setl*.

Settrington N. Yorks. *Sendriton* (*sic*) 1086 (DB), *Seteringetune* c.1090. Possibly 'estate associated with a robber or with a man called *Sǣtere'. OE *sǣtere* or OE pers. name + *-ing-* + *tūn*.

Seven (river) N. Yorks., see SINNINGTON.

Sevenhampton, 'village of seven homesteads', OE *seofon* + *hām-tūn*: **Sevenhampton** Glos. *Sevenhamtone* 1086 (DB). **Sevenhampton** Wilts. *Sevamentone* 1086 (DB).

Sevenoaks Kent. *Seouenaca* c.1100. '(Place by) seven oak-trees'. OE *seofon* + *āc*.

Severn (river) Shrops.–Somerset. *Sabrina* 2nd cent. AD, *Sauerna* 1086 (DB). An ancient pre-English river-name of doubtful etymology.

Sevington Kent. *Seivetone* 1086 (DB). 'Farmstead of a woman called Sǣgifu'. OE pers. name + *tūn*.

Sewerby Humber. *Siuuardbi* 1086 (DB). 'Farmstead or village of a man called Sigvarthr'. OScand. pers. name + *bý*.

Sewstern Leics. *Sewesten* (*sic*) 1086 (DB), *Seustern* c.1125. Possibly 'seven properties', OE *seofon* + **sterne*. Alternatively 'pool of a man called Sǣwig', OE pers. name + OScand. *tjǫrn*.

Sezincote Glos. *Ch(i)esnecote* 1086 (DB). 'Gravelly cottage(s)'. OE **cisen* + *cot*.

Shabbington Bucks. *Sobintone* 1086 (DB). 'Estate associated with a man called *Sc(e)obba'. OE pers. name + *-ing-* + *tūn*.

Shackerstone Leics. *Sacrestone* 1086 (DB). 'The robber's farmstead'. OE *scēacere* + *tūn*.

Shadforth Durham. *Shaldeford* 1183. 'Shallow ford'. OE **sc(e)ald* + *ford*.

Shadingfield Suffolk. *Scadenafella* 1086 (DB). Possibly 'open land by the boundary valley'. OE *scēad* + *denu* + *feld*.

Shadoxhurst Kent. *Schettokesherst* 1239. OE *hyrst* 'wooded hill' with an uncertain first element, probably a pers. name or surname.

Shaftesbury Dorset. *Sceaftesburi* 877, *Sceftesberie* 1086 (DB). 'Fortified place of a man called *Sceaft, or on a shaft-shaped hill'. OE pers. name or OE *sceaft* + *burh* (dative *byrig*).

Shafton S. Yorks. *Sceptun* (*sic*) 1086 (DB), *Scaftona* c.1160. 'Farmstead marked by a pole, or made with poles'. OE *sceaft* + *tūn*.

Shalbourne Wilts. *Scealdeburnan* 955, *Scaldeburne* 1086 (DB). 'Shallow stream'. OE **sceald* + *burna*.

Shalcombe I. of Wight. *Eseldecome* 1086 (DB). 'Shallow valley'. OE **sceald* + *cumb*.

Shalden Hants. *Scealdeden* 1046, *Seldene* 1086 (DB). 'Shallow valley'. OE **sceald* + *denu*.

Shalfleet I. of Wight. *Scealdan fleote* 838, *Seldeflet* 1086 (DB). 'Shallow stream or creek'. OE **sceald* + *flēot*.

Shalford, 'shallow ford', OE *sceald + *ford*: **Shalford** Essex. *Scaldefort* 1086 (DB). **Shalford** Surrey. *Scaldefor* 1086 (DB).

Shalstone Bucks. *Celdestone* 1086 (DB). Possibly 'farmstead at the shallow place or stream'. OE **sceald* (used as a noun) + *tūn*.

Shangton Leics. *Sanctone* 1086 (DB). 'Farmstead by a hill-spur, or of a man called *Scanca'. OE *scanca* or pers. name + *tūn*.

Shanklin I. of Wight. *Sencliz* 1086 (DB). 'Bank by the drinking cup' (referring to the waterfall here). OE *scenc* + *hlinc*.

Shap Cumbria. *Hep* c.1190. 'The heap of stones' (referring to an ancient stone circle). OE *hēap*.

Shapwick, 'sheep farm', OE *scēap* + *wīc*: **Shapwick** Dorset. *Scapeuuic* 1086 (DB). **Shapwick** Somerset. *Sapwic* 725, *Sapeswich* 1086 (DB).

Shardlow Derbys. *Serdelau* 1086 (DB). 'Mound with a notch or indentation'. OE *sceard* + *hlāw*.

Shareshill Staffs. *Servesed* (*sic*) 1086 (DB), *Sarueshull* 1213, *Sarushulf* 1298. Probably 'hill (or shelf of land) of a man called *Scearf'. OE pers. name + *hyll* (alternating with OE *scylf* in the early forms).

Sharlston W. Yorks. *Scharueston* c.1180. Possibly 'farmstead of a man called *Scearf'. OE pers. name + *tūn*.

Sharnbrook Beds. *Scernebroc* 1086 (DB). 'Dirty or muddy brook'. OE *scearn* + *brōc*.

Sharow N. Yorks. *Sharou* c.1130. 'Boundary hill-spur'. OE *scearu* + *hōh*.

Sharpenhoe Beds. *Scarpeho* 1197. 'Sharp or steep hill-spur'. OE *scearp* (dative *-an*) + *hōh*.

Sharperton Northum. *Scharberton* 1242. Possibly 'farmstead by the steep hill'. OE *scearp* + *beorg* + *tūn*.

Sharpness Glos. *Nesse* 1086 (DB), *Schobbenasse* 1368. 'Headland of a man called *Scobba'. OE pers. name + *næss*.

Sharrington Norfolk. *Scarnetuna* 1086 (DB). 'Dirty or muddy farmstead'. OE *scearn* (dative *-an*) + *tūn*.

Shaugh Prior Devon. *Scage* 1086 (DB). 'Small wood or copse'. OE *sc(e)aga*. Affix from its early possession by Plympton Priory.

Shavington Ches. *Santune* (*sic*) 1086 (DB), *Shawynton* 1260. 'Estate associated with a man called Scēafa'. OE pers. name + *-ing-* + *tūn*.

Shaw, 'small wood or copse', OE

sc(e)aga: **Shaw** Berks. *Essages (sic)* 1086 (DB), *Shage* 1167. **Shaw** Gtr. Manch. *Shaghe* 1555. **Shaw** Wilts. *Schawe* 1256.

Shawbury Shrops. *Sawesberie* 1086 (DB). 'Manor house by a small wood or copse'. OE *sc(e)aga* + *burh* (dative *byrig*).

Shawell Leics. *Sawelle (sic)* 1086 (DB), *Schadewelle* 1224. 'Boundary spring or stream'. OE *scēath* + *wella*.

Shawford Hants. *Scaldeforda* 1208. 'Shallow ford'. OE **sceald* + *ford*.

Sheaf (river) Derbys., S. Yorks., see SHEFFIELD.

Shearsby Leics. *Svevesbi* 1086 (DB). Possibly 'farmstead or village of a man called Swǣf or Skeifr'. OE or OScand. pers. name + OScand. *bý*.

Shebbear Devon. *Sceftbeara* 1050–73, *Sepesberie* 1086 (DB). 'Grove where shafts or poles are got'. OE *sceaft* + *bearu*.

Shebdon Staffs. *Schebbedon* 1267. 'Hill of a man called *Sceobba'. OE pers. name + *dūn*.

Shedfield Hants. *Scidafelda* 956. 'Open land where planks of wood are got, or where they are used as foot-bridges'. OE *scīd* + *feld*.

Sheen, 'the sheds or shelters', OE **scēo* in a plural form **scēon*: **Sheen** Staffs. *Sceon* 1002, 1086 (DB). **Sheen, East, North, & West** Gtr. London. *Sceon* c.950. West Sheen was the earlier name for RICHMOND.

Sheepstor Devon. *Sitelestorra* 1168. Possibly 'craggy hill thought to resemble a bar or bolt', OE *scytels* + *torr*. Alternatively the first element may be an OE **scitels* 'dung'.

Sheepwash Devon. *Schepewast* 1166. 'Place where sheep are dipped'. OE *scēap-wæsce*.

Sheepy Magna & Parva Leics. *Scepehe* 1086 (DB). 'Island, or dry ground in marsh, where sheep graze'. OE *scēap* + *ēg*. Distinguishing affixes are Latin *magna* 'great' and *parva* 'little'.

Sheering Essex. *Sceringa* 1086 (DB). Probably '(settlement of) the family or followers of a man called *Scear(a)'. OE pers. name + *-ingas*.

Sheerness Kent. *Scerhnesse* 1203. Probably 'bright headland'. OE *scīr* + *næss*. Alternatively the first element may be OE *scear* 'plough-share' alluding to the shape of the headland.

Sheet Hants. *Syeta* c.1210. 'Projecting piece of land, corner or nook'. OE **scīete*.

Sheffield S. Yorks. *Scafeld* 1086 (DB). 'Open land by the River Sheaf'. OE river-name (from *scēath* 'boundary') + *feld*.

Sheffield Bottom Berks. *Sewelle (sic)* 1086 (DB). *Scheaffelda* 1167. 'Open land with a shelter'. OE **scēo* + *feld*.

Sheffield Green E. Sussex. *Sifelle (sic)* 1086 (DB), *Shipfeud* 1272. 'Open land where sheep graze'. OE *scēap* + *feld*.

Shefford, 'ford used for sheep', OE *scēap* or **scīep* + *ford*: **Shefford** Beds. *Sepford* 1220. **Shefford, East & Great** Berks. *Siford (sic)* 1086 (DB), *Schipforda* 1167.

Sheinton Shrops. *Scentune* 1086 (DB). Probably 'beautiful farmstead'. OE *scēne* + *tūn*.

Sheldon Derbys. *Scelhadun* 1086 (DB). Probably 'heathy hill with a shelf or ledge'. OE *scelf* + *hǣth* + *dūn*.

Sheldon Devon. *Sildene* 1086 (DB). 'Valley with steeply shelving sides'. OE *scylf* + *denu*.

Sheldon W. Mids. *Scheldon* 1189. 'Shelf hill'. OE *scelf* + *dūn*.

Sheldwich Kent. *Scilduuic* 784. 'Dwelling or farm with a shelter'. OE *sceld* + *wīc*.

Shelf W. Yorks. *Scelf* 1086 (DB). 'Shelving terrain'. OE *scelf*.

Shelfanger Norfolk. *Sceluangra* 1086 (DB). 'Wood on sloping ground'. OE *scelf* + *hangra*.

Shelfield, 'hill with a shelf or plateau', OE *scelf* + *hyll*: **Shelfield** Warwicks. *Shelfhulle* 1221. **Shelfield** W. Mids. *Scelfeld (sic)* 1086 (DB), *Schelfhul* 1271.

Shelford, 'ford at a shallow place', OE **sceldu* + *ford*: **Shelford** Notts. *Scelforde* 1086 (DB). **Shelford, Great & Little** Cambs. *Scelford* c.1050, *Escelforde* 1086 (DB).

Shelley W. Yorks. *Scelneleie* (*sic*) 1086 (DB), *Shelfleie* 1198. 'Woodland clearing on shelving terrain'. OE *scelf* + *lēah*.

Shellingford Oxon. *Scaringaford* 931, *Serengeford* 1086 (DB). 'Ford of the family or followers of a man called *Scear'. OE pers. name + *-inga-* + *ford*.

Shellow Bowells Essex. *Scelga* 1086 (DB), *Scheuele Boueles* 1303. 'Winding river' (with reference to the River Roding). OE **Sceolge* from *sceolh* 'twisted'. Manorial affix from the *de Bueles* family, here in the 13th cent.

Shelton, 'farmstead on a shelf of flat or sloping ground', OE *scelf* + *tūn*: **Shelton** Beds. *Eseltone* 1086 (DB). **Shelton** Norfolk. *Sceltuna* 1086 (DB). **Shelton** Notts. *Sceltun* 1086 (DB). **Shelton** Shrops. *Saltone* (*sic*) 1086 (DB), *Shelfton* 1221.

Shelve Shrops. *Schelfe* 1180. 'Shelf of level ground'. OE *scelf*.

Shelwick Heref. & Worcs. *Scelwiche* 1086 (DB). 'Dwelling or farm with a shelter'. OE *sceld* + *wīc*.

Shenfield Essex. *Scenefelda* 1086 (DB). 'Beautiful open land'. OE *scēne* + *feld*.

Shenington Oxon. *Senendone* 1086 (DB). 'Beautiful hill'. OE *scēne* (dative *-an*) + *dūn*.

Shenley, 'bright or beautiful woodland glade', OE *scēne* + *lēah*: **Shenley** Bucks. *Senelai* 1086 (DB). **Shenley** Herts. *Scenlai* 1086 (DB).

Shenstone Staffs. *Seneste* (*sic*) 1086 (DB), *Scenstan* 11th cent. 'Beautiful stone'. OE *scēne* + *stān*.

Shenton Leics. *Scenctun* 1002, *Scentone* 1086 (DB). 'Farmstead on the River Sence'. OE river-name (from *scenc* 'drinking cup') + *tūn*.

Shepley W. Yorks. *Scipelei* 1086 (DB). 'Clearing where sheep are kept'. OE *scēap* + *lēah*.

Shepperton Surrey. *Scepertune* 959, *Scepertone* 1086 (DB). Probably 'farmstead of the shepherd(s)'. OE *scēap-hirde* + *tūn*.

Sheppey, Isle of Kent. *Scepeig* 696–716, *Scape* 1086 (DB). 'Island where sheep are kept'. OE *scēap* + *ēg*.

Shepreth Cambs. *Esceprid* 1086 (DB). 'Sheep stream'. OE *scēap* + *rīth*.

Shepshed Leics. *Scepeshefde* 1086 (DB). 'Sheep headland'. OE *scēap* + *hēafod*.

Shepton, 'sheep farm', OE *scēap* + *tūn*: **Shepton Beauchamp** Somerset. *Sceptone* 1086 (DB), *Septon Belli campi* 1266. Manorial affix from the *de Beauchamp* (Latin *de Bello campo*) family, here in the 13th cent. **Shepton Mallet** Somerset. *Sepetone* 1086 (DB), *Scheopton Malet* 1228. Manorial affix from the *Malet* family, here in the 12th cent. **Shepton Montague** Somerset. *Sceptone* 1086 (DB), *Schuptone Montagu* 1285. Manorial affix from Drogo *de Montacute*, tenant in 1086.

Sheraton Durham. *Scurufatun c.*1040. Probably 'farmstead of a man called Skurfa'. OScand. pers. name + OE *tūn*.

Sherborne, Sherbourne, Sherburn, '(place at) the bright or clear stream', OE *scīr* + *burna*: **Sherborne** Dorset. *Scireburnan* 864, *Scireburne* 1086 (DB). **Sherborne** Glos. *Scireburne* 1086 (DB). **Sherborne St John & Monk Sherborne** Hants. *Sireburne, Sireborne* 1086 (DB), *Shireburna Johannis* 1167, *Schireburne Monachorum c.*1270. Distinguishing affixes from possession by Robert *de Sancto Johanne* in the 13th cent., and from the priory here (Latin *monachorum* 'of the monks'). **Sherbourne** Warwicks. *Scireburne* 1086 (DB). **Sherburn** Durham. *Scireburne c.*1170. **Sherburn** N. Yorks. *Scire(s)burne* 1086 (DB). **Sherburn in Elmet** N. Yorks. *Scirburnan c.*900, *Scireburne* 1086 (DB). For the old district name Elmet, see BARWICK.

Shere Surrey. *Essira* 1086 (DB). '(Place at) the bright or clear stream'. OE *scīr*.

Shereford Norfolk. *Sciraford* 1086 (DB). 'Bright or clear ford'. OE *scīr* + *ford*.

Sherfield, probably 'bright open land', i.e. having sparse vegetation, OE *scīr* + *feld*: **Sherfield English** Hants. *Sirefelle* 1086 (DB). Manorial affix from *le Engleis* family, here in the 14th cent. **Sherfield on Loddon** Hants. *Schirefeld* 1179. Loddon is a Celtic river-name (possibly meaning 'muddy stream').

Sherford Devon. *Scireford c.*1050, *Sirefort* 1086 (DB). 'Bright or clear ford'. OE *scīr* + *ford*.

Sheriffhales Shrops. *Halas* 1086 (DB), *Shiruehales* 1301. 'Nooks of land', OE *halh* in a plural form. Affix is OE *scīr-rēfa* from possession by the Sheriff of Shropshire in 1086.

Sheriff Hutton N. Yorks., see HUTTON.

Sheringham Norfolk. *Silingeham* (*sic*) 1086 (DB), *Scheringham* 1242. 'Homestead of the family or followers of a man called Scīra'. OE pers. name + *-inga-* + *hām*.

Sherington Bucks. *Serintone* 1086 (DB). 'Estate associated with a man called Scīra'. OE pers. name + *-ing-* + *tūn*.

Shernborne Norfolk. *Scernebrune* 1086 (DB). 'Dirty or muddy stream'. OE *scearn* + *burna*.

Sherrington Wilts. *Scearntune* 968, *Scarentone* 1086 (DB). 'Dirty or muddy farmstead'. OE **scearn* + *tūn*.

Sherston Wilts. *Scorranstan* 896, *Sorestone* 1086 (DB). 'Stone or rock on a steep slope'. OE **scora* + *stān*.

Sherwood Forest Notts. *Scirwuda* 955. 'Wood belonging to the shire'. OE *scīr* + *wudu*.

Shevington Gtr. Manch. *Shefinton* c.1225. Probably 'farmstead near a hill called *Shevin*'. Celtic **cevn* 'ridge' + OE *tūn*.

Sheviock Cornwall. *Savioch* 1086 (DB). Possibly 'strawberry place'. Cornish *sevi* + suffix *-ek*.

Shields, 'temporary sheds or huts (used by fisherman)', ME *schele*: **Shields, North** Tyne & Wear. *Chelis* 1268. **Shields, South** Tyne & Wear. *Scheles* 1235.

Shifnal Shrops. *Scuffanhalch* 12th cent. 'Nook of a man called *Scuffa'. OE pers. name (genitive *-n*) + *halh*.

Shilbottle Northum. *Schipplingbothill* 1242. Probably 'dwelling of the men of SHIPLEY'. Place-name + OE *-inga-* + *bōtl*.

Shildon Durham. *Sciluedon* 1214. 'Shelf hill'. OE *scylfe* + *dūn*.

Shillingford, probably 'ford of the family or followers of a man called *Sciell(a)', OE pers. name + *-inga-* + *ford*, but an OE stream-name **Scielling* 'the noisy one' may be an alternative first element: **Shillingford** Devon. *Sellingeford* 1179. **Shillingford** Oxon. *Sillingeforda* 1156. **Shillingford St George** Devon. *Selingeforde* 1086 (DB). Affix from the dedication of the church.

Shillingstone Dorset. *Akeford Skelling* 1220, *Shillyngeston* 1444. 'Schelin's estate (in OKEFORD)'. OE *tūn* with the name of the tenant in 1086 (DB).

Shillington Beds. *Scytlingedune* 1060, *Sethlindone* 1086 (DB). 'Hill of the family or followers of a man called *Scyttel'. OE pers. name + *-inga-* + *dūn*.

Shilton, 'farmstead on a shelf or ledge', OE *scylf(e)* + *tūn*: **Shilton** Oxon. *Scylftune* 1044. **Shilton** Warwicks. *Scelftone* 1086 (DB). **Shilton, Earl** Leics. *Sceltone* 1086 (DB). Affix from its early possession by the Earls of Leicester.

Shimpling, probably '(settlement of) the family or followers of a man called *Scimpel', OE pers. name + *-ingas*: **Shimpling** Norfolk. *Simplingham* c.1035, *Simplinga* 1086 (DB). Sometimes with OE *hām* 'homestead' in early spellings. **Shimpling** Suffolk. *Simplinga* 1086 (DB).

Shinfield Berks. *Selingefelle* (*sic*) 1086 (DB), *Schiningefeld* 1167. 'Open land of the family or followers of a man called *Scīene'. OE pers. name + *-inga-* + *feld*.

Shipbourne Kent. *Sciburna* (*sic*) c.1100, *Scipburn* 1198. 'Sheep stream'. OE *scēap* + *burna*.

Shipdham Norfolk. *Scipdham* 1086 (DB). 'Homestead with a flock of sheep'. OE **scīpde* + *hām*.

Shiplake Oxon. *Siplac* 1163. 'Sheep stream'. OE *scēap* + *lacu*.

Shipley, 'clearing or pasture where sheep are kept', OE *scēap* + *lēah*; examples include: **Shipley** Northum. *Schepley* 1236. **Shipley** Shrops. *Sciplei* 1086 (DB). **Shipley** W. Sussex. *Scapeleia* 1073, *Sepelei* 1086 (DB). **Shipley** W. Yorks. *Scipeleia* 1086 (DB).

Shipmeadow Suffolk. *Scipmedu* 1086 (DB). 'Meadow for sheep'. OE *scēap* + *mǣd* (dative *mǣdwe*).

Shippon Oxon. *Sipene* 1086 (DB). OE *scypen* 'a cattle-shed'.

Shipston on Stour Warwicks.

Scepuuæisctune c.770, *Scepwestun* 1086 (DB). 'Farmstead by the sheep-wash'. OE *scēap-wæsce* + *tūn*. Stour is a Celtic or OE river-name probably meaning 'the strong one'.

Shipton, usually 'sheep farm', OE *scēap* or **sclep* + *tūn*; examples include: **Shipton** Shrops. *Scipetune* 1086 (DB). **Shipton Bellinger** Hants. *Sceptone* 1086 (DB), *Shupton Berenger* 14th cent. Manorial affix from the *Berenger* family, here in the 13th cent. **Shipton Gorge** Dorset. *Sepetone* 1086 (DB), *Shipton Gorges* 1594. Manorial addition from the *de Gorges* family, here in the 13th cent. **Shipton Moyne** Glos. *Sciptone* 1086 (DB), *Schipton Moine* 1287. Manorial affix from the *Moygne* family, here from the 13th cent. **Shipton under Wychwood** Oxon. *Sciptone* 1086 (DB). Wychwood is an old forest-name, see ASCOTT UNDER WYCHWOOD.

However the following has a different origin: **Shipton** N. Yorks. *Hipton* 1086 (DB). 'Farmstead where rose-hips grow'. OE *hēope* + *tūn*.

Shirburn Oxon. *Scireburne* 1086 (DB). 'Bright or clear stream'. OE *scīr* + *burna*.

Shirebrook Derbys. *Scirebroc* 1202. 'Boundary brook' or 'bright brook'. OE *scīr* (as noun or adjective) + *brōc*.

Shireoaks Notts. *Shirakes* 12th cent. 'Oak-trees on the (county) boundary'. OE *scīr* + *āc*. In the similar name **Shire Oak** (W. Mids.) the meaning is rather 'oak-tree marking the site of the shire assembly'.

Shirland Derbys. *Sirelunt* 1086 (DB). Probably 'bright or sparsely wooded grove'. OE *scīr* + OScand. *lundr*.

Shirley, 'bright woodland clearing' or perhaps sometimes 'shire clearing', OE *scīr* + *lēah*: **Shirley** Derbys. *Sirelei* 1086 (DB). **Shirley** Gtr. London. *Shirleye* 1314. **Shirley** Hants. *Sirelei* 1086 (DB). **Shirley** W. Mids. *Syrley* c.1240.

Shirrell Heath Hants. *Scirhiltæ* 826. Probably 'bright or sparsely wooded grove'. OE *scīr* + **hylte*, with the addition of *heath* from the 17th cent.

Shirwell Devon. *Sirewelle* 1086 (DB). 'Bright or clear spring or stream'. OE *scīr* + *wella*.

Shobdon Heref. & Worcs. *Scepedune* (*sic*) 1086 (DB), *Scobbedun* 1242. 'Hill of a man called *Sceobba'. OE pers. name + *dūn*.

Shobrooke Devon. *Sceocabroc* 938, *Sotebroca* 1086 (DB). 'Brook haunted by an evil spirit'. OE *sceocca* + *brōc*.

Shocklach Ches. *Socheliche* 1086 (DB). 'Boggy stream haunted by an evil spirit'. OE *sceocca* + **læcc*.

Shoeburyness, North Shoebury Essex. *Sceobyrig* early 10th cent., *Soberia* 1086 (DB), *Shoberynesse* 16th cent. 'Fortress providing shelter'. OE **scēo* + *burh* (dative *byrig*), with the later addition of *næss* 'promontory'.

Sholden Kent. *Shoueldune* 1176. Possibly 'hill thought to resemble a shovel'. OE *scofl* + *dūn*.

Sholing Hants. *Sholling* 1251. Possibly 'uneven or sloping place'. OE *sceolh* + *-ing*.

Shoreditch Gtr. London. *Soredich* c.1148. 'Ditch by a steep bank or slope'. OE **scora* + *dīc*.

Shoreham, 'homestead by a steep bank or slope', OE **scora* + *hām*: **Shoreham** Kent. *Scorham* 822. **Shoreham by Sea** W. Sussex. *Sorham* 1073, *Soreham* 1086 (DB).

Shorncote Glos. *Schernecote* 1086 (DB). 'Cottage(s) in a dirty or muddy place'. OE *scearn* + *cot*.

Shorne Kent. *Scorene* c.1100. 'Steep place'. OE **scoren*.

Shorwell I. of Wight. *Sorewelle* 1086 (DB). 'Spring or stream by a steep slope'. OE **scora* + *wella*.

Shotesham Norfolk. *Shotesham* 1044–7, *Scotesham* 1086 (DB). 'Homestead of a man called Scot'. OE pers. name + *hām*.

Shotley, possibly 'clearing frequented by pigeons, or where shooting takes place', OE **sceote* or *sceot* + *lēah*: **Shotley** Suffolk. *Scoteleia* 1086 (DB). **Shotley Bridge** Northum. *Schotley* 1242.

Shottermill Surrey. *Shottover* 1537, *Schotouermyll* 1607. Probably 'mill of a family called *Shotover*'. ME surname + *myln*.

Shottery Warwicks. *Scotta rith* 699–709.

Probably 'stream of the Scots'. OE *Scot* (genitive plural *-a*) + *rīth*. Alternatively the first element may be OE *sc(e)ota* 'trout'.

Shotteswell Warwicks. *Soteswell c.*1140. Probably 'spring or stream of a man called Scot'. OE pers. name + *wella*.

Shottisham Suffolk. *Scotesham* 1086 (DB). 'Homestead of a man called Scot or *Scēot'. OE pers. name + *hām*.

Shottle Derbys. *Sothelle (sic)* 1086 (DB), *Schethell* 1191. Probably 'hill with a steep slope'. OE **scēot* + *hyll*.

Shotton Durham, near Peterlee. *Sotton c.*1165. Possibly 'farmstead on or near a steep slope'. OE **scēot* + *tūn*.

Shotton Northum., near Mindrum. *Scotadun c.*1050. 'Hill of the Scots'. OE *Scot* (genitive plural *-a*) + *dūn*.

Shotwick Ches. *Sotowiche* 1086 (DB). 'Dwelling or farm at a steep promontory'. OE **scēot* + *hōh* + *wīc*.

Shouldham Norfolk. *Sculdeham* 1086 (DB). Probably 'homestead owing a debt or obligation'. OE **sculd* + *hām*.

Shoulton Heref. & Worcs. *Scolegeton c.*1220. Possibly 'farmstead at the stream called **Sceolge*'. OE river-name (meaning 'winding') + *tūn*.

Shrawardine Shrops. *Saleurdine (sic)* 1086 (DB), *Shrawurdin* 1166. Possibly 'enclosure near a hollow or hovel'. OE *scræf* + *worthign*.

Shrawley Heref. & Worcs. *Scræfleh* 804. 'Woodland clearing near a hollow or hovel'. OE *scræf* + *lēah*.

Shrewsbury Shrops. *Scrobbesbyrig* 11th cent., *Sciropesberie* 1086 (DB). 'Fortified place of the scrubland region'. Old district name (from an OE **scrobb*) + OE *burh* (dative *byrig*).

Shrewton Wilts. *Wintreburne* 1086 (DB), *Winterbourne Syreveton* 1232. 'The sheriff's manor on the stream formerly called *Wintreburne*'. OE *scīr-rēfa* + *tūn*. The 'winter stream' (OE *winter* + *burna*) is now called Till.

Shrigley, Pott Ches. *Schriggeleg* 1285, *Potte Shryggelegh* 1354. Two distinct names. Pott is from ME *potte* 'a deep hole'. Shrigley is 'woodland clearing frequented by missel-thrushes', OE *scrīc* + *lēah*.

Shrivenham Oxon. *Scrifenanhamme c.*950, *Seriveham* 1086 (DB). 'River-meadow allotted by decree (to the church)'. OE *scrifen* + *hamm*.

Shropham Norfolk. *Screpham* 1086 (DB). OE *hām* 'homestead' with an uncertain first element, possibly a pers. name.

Shropshire (the county). *Sciropescire* 1086 (DB). Shortened form of old spelling for SHREWSBURY + OE *scīr* 'district'. The form **Salop** (now adopted as the name of the 'new' county) is a revival of an old Norman contracted spelling of the name Shropshire.

Shroton Dorset, see IWERNE COURTNEY.

Shuckburgh Warwicks. *Socheberge* 1086 (DB). 'Hill or mound haunted by an evil spirit'. OE *scucca* + *beorg*.

Shucknall Heref. & Worcs. *Shokenhulle* 1377. 'Hill haunted by an evil spirit'. OE *scucca* (genitive *-n*) + *hyll*.

Shudy Camps Cambs., see CAMPS.

Shurdington Glos. *Surditona c.*1150. Possibly 'estate associated with a man called *Scyrda'. OE pers. name + *-ing-* + *tūn*.

Shurton Somerset. *Shureveton* 1219. 'The sheriff's manor'. OE *scīr-rēfa* + *tūn*.

Shute Devon. *Schieta c.*1200. 'The corner or angle of land'. OE **scīete*.

Shutford Oxon. *Schiteford c.*1160. Probably 'ford of a man called *Scytta'. OE pers. name + *ford*.

Shutlanger Northants. *Shitelhanger* 1162. 'Wooded slope where shuttles or wooden bars are obtained'. OE *scytel* + *hangra*.

Shuttington Warwicks. *Cetitone (sic)* 1086 (DB), *Schetintuna c.*1160. 'Estate associated with a man called *Scytta'. OE pers. name + *-ing-* + *tūn*.

Sibbertoft Northants. *Sibertod (sic)* 1086 (DB), *Sibertoft* 1198. 'Homestead of a man called Sigebeorht or Sigbjorn'. OE or OScand. pers. name + *toft*.

Sibdon Carwood Shrops. *Sibetune* 1086 (DB). 'Farmstead of a man called Sibba'. OE pers. name + *tūn*. Carwood is a nearby place with name of uncertain meaning, possibly 'rocky wood' from OE *carr* + *wudu*.

Sibford Ferris & Gower Oxon.

Sibeford 1086 (DB), *Sibbard Ferreys* early 18th cent., *Sibbeford Goyer* 1220. 'Ford of a man called Sibba'. OE pers. name + *ford*. Manorial affixes from early possession by the *de Ferrers* and *Guher* families.

Sible Hedingham Essex, see HEDINGHAM.

Sibsey Lincs. *Sibolci* 1086 (DB). 'Island of a man called Sigebald'. OE pers. name + *ēg*.

Sibson Cambs. *Sibestune* 1086 (DB). 'Farmstead of a man called Sibbi'. OScand. pers. name + OE *tūn*.

Sibson Leics. *Sibetesdone* 1086 (DB). 'Hill of a man called Sigebed'. OE pers. name + *dūn*.

Sibthorpe Notts. *Sibetorp* 1086 (DB). 'Outlying farm of a man called Sibba or Sibbi'. OE or OScand. pers. name + OScand. *thorp*.

Sibton Suffolk. *Sibbetuna* 1086 (DB). 'Farmstead of a man called Sibba'. OE pers. name + *tūn*.

Sicklinghall N. Yorks. *Sidingale* (*sic*) 1086 (DB), *Sicclinhala* c.1150. 'Nook of land of the family or followers of a man called *Sicel'. OE pers. name + *-inga-* + *halh*.

Sidbury Devon. *Sideberia* 1086 (DB). 'Fortified place by the River Sid'. OE river-name (from *sīd* 'broad') + *burh* (dative *byrig*).

Sidbury Shrops. *Sudberie* 1086 (DB). 'Southern fortified place or manor'. OE *sūth* + *burh* (dative *byrig*).

Sidcup Gtr. London. *Cetecopp* 1254. Probably 'seat-shaped or flat-topped hill'. OE **set-copp*.

Siddington Ches. *Sudendune* 1086 (DB). '(Place) south of the hill'. OE *sūthan* + *dūn*.

Siddington Glos. *Sudintone* 1086 (DB). '(Land) south in the township'. OE *sūth* + *in* + *tūn*.

Sidestrand Norfolk. *Sistran* (*sic*) 1086 (DB), *Sidestrande* late 12th cent. 'Broad shore'. OE *sīd* + *strand*.

Sidford Devon. *Sideford* 1238. 'Ford on the River Sid'. OE river-name (see SIDBURY) + *ford*.

Sidlesham W. Sussex. *Sidelesham* 683. 'Homestead of a man called *Sidel'. OE pers. name + *hām*.

Sidmouth Devon. *Sedemuda* 1086 (DB). 'Mouth of the River Sid'. OE river-name (see SIDBURY) + *mūtha*.

Siefton Shrops. *Sireton* (*sic*) 1086 (DB), *Siveton* 1257. Possibly 'farmstead of a woman called Sigegifu'. OE pers. name + *tūn*.

Sigglesthorne Humber. *Siglestorne* 1086 (DB). 'Thorn-tree of a man called Sigulfr'. OScand. pers. name + *thorn*.

Silchester Hants. *Silcestre* 1086 (DB). Possibly 'Roman station by a willow copse'. OE **siele* + *ceaster*. Alternatively the first element may be a reduced form of *Calleva* 'place in the woods', the original Celtic name of this Roman city first recorded in the 2nd cent. AD.

Sileby Leics. *Siglebi* 1086 (DB). 'Farmstead or village of a man called Sigulfr'. OScand. pers. name + *bý*.

Silecroft Cumbria. *Selecroft* 1211. 'Enclosure where willows grow'. OScand. *selja* + OE *croft*.

Silkstone S. Yorks. *Silchestone* 1086 (DB). 'Farmstead of a man called Sigelāc'. OE pers. name + *tūn*.

Silksworth Tyne & Wear. *Sylceswurthe* c.1050. 'Enclosure of a man called Sigelāc'. OE pers. name + *worth*.

Silk Willoughby Lincs., see WILLOUGHBY.

Silloth Cumbria. *Selathe* 1292. 'Barn(s) by the sea'. OScand. *sǽr* or OE *sǣ* + OScand. *hlatha*.

Silpho N. Yorks. *Silfhou* c.1160. 'Flat-topped hill-spur'. OE *scylfe* + *hōh*.

Silsden W. Yorks. *Siglesdene* 1086 (DB). 'Valley of a man called Sigulfr'. OScand. pers. name + OE *denu*.

Silsoe Beds. *Siuuilessou* 1086 (DB). 'Hill-spur of a man called *Sifel'. OE pers. name + *hōh*.

Silton, Nether & Over N. Yorks. *Silftune* 1086 (DB). 'Farmstead by a shelf or ledge', or 'farmstead of a man called Sylfa'. OE *scylfe* or OScand. pers. name + OE *tūn*.

Silverdale Lancs. *Selredal* (*sic*) 1199, *Celverdale* 1292. 'Silver-coloured valley' (from the grey limestone here). OE *seolfor* + *dæl*.

Silverstone Northants. *Sulueston* 942, *Silvestone* 1086 (DB). Probably 'farmstead of a man called Sǣwulf or Sigewulf'. OE pers. name + *tūn*.

Silverton Devon. *Sulfretone* 1086 (DB). Probably 'farmstead near the gully ford'. OE *sulh* + *ford* + *tūn*.

Simonburn Northum. *Simundeburn* 1229. 'Stream of a man called Sigemund'. OE pers. name + *burna*.

Simonstone Lancs. *Simondestan* 1278. 'Boundary stone of a man called Sigemund'. OE pers. name + *stān*.

Simpson Bucks. *Siwinestone* 1086 (DB). 'Farmstead of a man called Sigewine'. OE pers. name + *tūn*.

Sinderby N. Yorks. *Senerebi* 1086 (DB). 'Southern farmstead or village', or 'farmstead or village of a man called Sindri'. OScand. *syndri* or pers. name + *bý*.

Sindlesham Berks. *Sindlesham* 1220. Possibly 'homestead or enclosure of a man called *Synnel'. OE pers. name + *hām* or *hamm*.

Singleborough Bucks. *Sincleberia* 1086 (DB). 'Shingle hill'. OE **singel* + *beorg*.

Singleton Lancs. *Singletun* 1086 (DB). 'Farmstead with shingled roof'. OE **scingol* + *tūn*.

Singleton W. Sussex. *Silletone* (*sic*) 1086 (DB), *Sengelton* 1185. Probably 'farmstead by a burnt clearing'. OE **sengel* + *tūn*.

Sinnington N. Yorks. *Siuenintun* 1086 (DB). 'Farmstead near the River Seven'. Pre-English river-name (of uncertain meaning) + OE *-ing-* + *tūn*.

Sinton, Leigh Heref. & Worcs. *Sothyntone in Lega* 13th cent. '(Place) south in the village (of LEIGH)'. OE *sūth* + *in* + *tūn*.

Sipson Gtr. London. *Sibwineston* c.1150. 'Farmstead of a man called Sibwine'. OE pers. name + *tūn*.

Sissinghurst Kent. *Saxingherste* c.1180. 'Wooded hill of the family or followers of a man called Seaxa'. OE pers. name + *-inga-* + *hyrst*.

Siston Avon. *Sistone* 1086 (DB). 'Farmstead of a man called *Sige'. OE pers. name + *tūn*.

Sithney Cornwall. *St Sythyn* 1230. From the patron saint of the parish church, St Sithny.

Sitlington W. Yorks., see MIDDLESTOWN.

Sittingbourne Kent. *Sidingeburn* 1200. Probably 'stream of the dwellers on the slope'. OE *sīde* + *-inga-* + *burna*.

Sixhills Lincs. *Sisse* (*sic*) 1086 (DB), *Sixlei* 1196. 'Six woodland clearings'. OE *six* + *lēah*.

Sixpenny Handley Dorset, see HANDLEY.

Sizewell Suffolk. *Syreswell* 1240. Probably 'spring or stream of a man called Sigehere'. OE pers. name + *wella*.

Skeeby N. Yorks. *Schirebi* (*sic*) 1086 (DB), *Schittebi* 1187. Probably 'farmstead or village of a man called Skíthi'. OScand. pers. name + *bý*.

Skeffington Leics. *Sciftitone* 1086 (DB). Probably 'estate associated with a man called *Sceaft'. OE pers. name (with Scand. *sk-*) + *-ing-* + *tūn*.

Skeffling Humber. *Sckeftling* 12th cent. Probably '(settlement of) the family or followers of a man called *Sceaftel'. OE pers. name (with Scand. *sk-*) + *-ingas*.

Skegby Notts., near Mansfield. *Schegebi* 1086 (DB). 'Farmstead or village of a man called Skeggi, or on a beard-shaped promontory'. OScand. pers. name or *skegg* + *bý*.

Skegness Lincs. *Sceggenesse* 12th cent. 'Beard-shaped promontory', or 'promontory of a man called Skeggi'. OScand. *skegg* or pers. name + *nes*.

Skellingthorpe Lincs. *Scheldinchope* 1086 (DB). 'Enclosure in marsh associated with a man called *Sceld' from OE pers. name + *-ing-* + *hop*, or 'enclosure in marsh by a shield-shaped hill' from OE *sceld* + *-ing* + *hop*. Initial *Sk-* through Scand. influence.

Skellow S. Yorks. *Scanhalle* (*sic*) 1086 (DB), *Scalehale* c.1190. 'Nook of land with a shieling or hut'. OE **scēla* (influenced by OScand. *skáli*) + *halh*.

Skelmanthorpe W. Yorks. *Scelmertorp* 1086 (DB). 'Outlying farmstead of a man called *Skjaldmarr'. OScand. pers. name + *thorp*.

Skelmersdale Lancs. *Schelmeresdele* 1086 (DB). 'Valley of a man called *Skjaldmarr'. OScand. pers. name + *dalr*.

Skelton, 'farmstead on a shelf or ledge', OE *scelf* (with Scand. *sk-*) + *tūn*: **Skelton** Cleveland. *Scheltun* 1086 (DB). **Skelton** Cumbria. *Sheltone* c.1160. **Skelton** Humber. *Schilton* 1086 (DB). **Skelton** N. Yorks., near Richmond. *Scelton* 12th cent. **Skelton** N. Yorks., near York. *Scheltun* 1086 (DB).

Skelwith Bridge Cumbria. *Schelwath* 1246. 'Ford by the waterfall'. OScand. *skjallr* 'resounding' + *vath*.

Skendleby Lincs. *Scheueldebi* (*sic*) 1086 (DB), *Schendelebia* c.1150. OScand. *bý* 'farmstead, village' possibly added to a place-name meaning 'beautiful slope' from OE *scēne* (with Scand. *sk-*) + *helde*.

Skerne Humber. *Schirne* 1086 (DB). Named from Skerne Beck, 'the clear or pure stream', from OScand. *skírn*, or (perhaps more likely) from OE *scīr* (dative *-an*) + *ēa* with initial *sk-* through Scand. influence.

Skewsby N. Yorks. *Scoxebi* 1086 (DB). 'Farmstead or village in the wood'. OScand. *skógr* + *bý*.

Skeyton Norfolk. *Scegutuna* 1086 (DB). 'Farmstead of a man called Skeggi'. OScand. pers. name + *tūn*.

Skidbrooke Lincs. *Schitebroc* 1086 (DB). 'Dirty brook'. OE *scite* (with Scand. *sk-*) + *brōc*.

Skidby Humber. *Scyteby* 972, *Schitebi* 1086 (DB). 'Farmstead or village of a man called Skyti', or 'dirty farmstead or village'. OScand. pers. name or *skítr* + *bý*.

Skilgate Somerset. *Schiligata* 1086 (DB). Possibly 'stony or shaly gate or gap'. OE **scilig* + *geat*.

Skillington Lincs. *Schillintune* 1086 (DB). Possibly 'estate associated with a man called *Scill(a)', OE pers. name + *-ing-* + *tūn*. Alternatively the first element may be OE *scilling* 'shilling' alluding to a rent. Initial *Sk-* through Scand. influence.

Skinburness Cumbria. *Skyneburg* 1175, *Skynburneyse* 1298. 'Promontory near the demon-haunted stronghold'. OE *scinna* (with Scand. *sk-*) + *burh* + OScand. *nes*.

Skinningrove Cleveland. *Scineregrive* c.1175. 'Pit used by skinners or tanners'. OScand. *skinnari* + *gryfja*.

Skipsea Humber. *Skipse* 1160. 'Lake used for ships'. OScand. *skip* + *sǽr*.

Skipton, 'sheep farm', OE *scīp* (with Scand. *sk-*) + *tūn*: **Skipton** N. Yorks. *Scipton* 1086 (DB). **Skipton on Swale** N. Yorks. *Schipetune* 1086 (DB). Swale is an OE river-name probably meaning 'rushing water'.

Skipwith N. Yorks. *Schipewic* 1086 (DB). 'Sheep farm'. OE *scīp* (with Scand. *sk-*) + *wīc* (replaced by OScand. *vithr* 'wood').

Skirlaugh, North & South Humber. *Schirelai* 1086 (DB). 'Bright woodland clearing'. OE *scīr* (with Scand. *sk-*) + *lēah*.

Skirmett Bucks. *La Skiremote* c.1307. 'Meeting-place of the shire-court'. OE *scīr* (with Scand *sk-*) + *(ge)mōt*.

Skirpenbeck Humber. *Scarpenbec* 1086 (DB). Probably 'stream which sometimes dries up'. OScand. **skerpin* + *bekkr*.

Skirwith Cumbria. *Skirewit* 1205. 'Wood belonging to the shire'. OE *scīr* (with Scand. *sk-*) + OScand. *vithr*.

Slaggyford Northum. *Slaggiford* 13th cent. 'Muddy ford'. ME **slaggi* + *ford*.

Slaidburn Lancs. *Slateborne* 1086 (DB). 'Stream by the sheep-pasture'. OE **slæget* + *burna*.

Slaithwaite W. Yorks. *Sladweit* 1178, *Sclagtwayt* 1277. Probably 'clearing where timber was felled'. OScand. *slag* + *thveit*.

Slaley Northum. *Slaveleia* 1166. 'Muddy woodland clearing'. OE **slæf* + *lēah*.

Slapton, 'farmstead by a slippery place' or 'muddy farmstead', OE **slǣp* or **slæp* + *tūn*: **Slapton** Bucks. *Slapetone* 1086 (DB). **Slapton** Devon. *Sladone* (*sic*) 1086 (DB), *Slapton* 1244. **Slapton** Northants. *Slaptone* 1086 (DB).

Slaugham W. Sussex. *Slacham* c.1100. 'Homestead or enclosure where sloes grow'. OE *slāh* + *hām* or *hamm*.

Slaughter, Lower & Upper Glos. *Sclostre* 1086 (DB). Probably 'muddy place'. OE **slōhtre*.

Slawston Leics. *Slagestone* 1086 (DB). Probably 'farmstead of a man called Slagr'. OScand. pers. name + OE *tūn*.

Sleaford Lincs. *Slioford* 852, *Eslaforde* 1086 (DB). 'Ford over the River Slea'. OE river-name (meaning 'muddy stream') + *ford*.

Sleagill Cumbria. *Slegill* c.1190. 'Ravine of the trickling stream, or of a man called *Slefa'. OScand. *slefa* or pers. name + *gil*.

Sledmere Humber. *Slidemare* 1086 (DB). 'Pool in the valley'. OE *slæd* + *mere*.

Sleekburn, East & West Northum. *Sliceburne* c.1050. 'Smooth stream, or muddy stream'. OE **slicu* or **slīc* + *burna*.

Sleightholme Durham. *Slethholm* 1234. Probably 'level raised ground'. OScand. *sléttr* + *holmr*.

Sleights N. Yorks. *Sleghtes* c.1223. 'Smooth or level fields'. OScand. *slétta*.

Slimbridge Glos. *Heslinbruge* (*sic*) 1086 (DB), *Slimbrugia* c.1153. 'Bridge or causeway over a muddy place'. OE *slīm* + *brycg*.

Slindon, probably 'sloping hill', OE **slinu* + *dūn*: **Slindon** Staffs. *Slindone* 1086 (DB). **Slindon** W. Sussex. *Eslindone* 1086 (DB).

Slingsby N. Yorks. *Selungesbi* 1086 (DB). 'Farmstead or village of a man called Slengr'. OScand. pers. name + *bý*.

Slipton Northants. *Sliptone* 1086 (DB). Probably 'muddy farmstead'. OE *slipa* + *tūn*.

Sloley Norfolk. *Slaleia* 1086 (DB). 'Woodland clearing where sloes grow'. OE *slāh* + *lēah*.

Sloothby Lincs. *Slodebi* 1086 (DB). Probably 'farmstead or village of a man called Slóthi'. OScand. pers. name + *bý*.

Slough Berks. *Slo* 1195. 'The slough or miry place'. OE *slōh*.

Slyne Lancs. *Sline* 1086 (DB). From OE **slinu* 'a slope'.

Smallburgh Norfolk. *Smaleberga* 1086 (DB). 'Hill or mound by the narrow stream'. Old name for the River Ant (from OE *smæl* 'narrow') + OE *beorg*.

Smalley Derbys. *Smælleage* 1009, *Smalei* 1086 (DB). 'Narrow woodland clearing'. OE *smæl* + *lēah*.

Smardale Cumbria. *Smeredal* 1190. Probably 'valley where butter is produced'. OScand. *smjǫr* or OE *smeoru* + OScand. *dalr*.

Smarden Kent. *Smeredaenne* c.1100. 'Woodland pasture where butter is produced'. OE *smeoru* + *denn*.

Smeaton, 'farmstead of the smiths', OE *smith* + *tūn*: **Smeaton, Great** N. Yorks. *Smithatune* 966–72, *Smidetune* 1086 (DB). **Smeaton, Kirk & Little** N. Yorks. *Smedetone* 1086 (DB). Distinguishing affix is OScand. *kirkja* 'church'.

Smeeth Kent. *Smitha* 1018. From OE *smiththe* 'a smithy'.

Smethwick W. Mids. *Smedeuuich* 1086 (DB). 'Dwelling or building of the smiths'. OE *smith* (genitive plural **smeotha*) + *wīc*.

Smisby Derbys. *Smidesbi* 1086 (DB). 'The smith's farmstead'. OScand. *smithr* + *bý*.

Snailwell Cambs. *Sneillewelle* c.1050, *Snelleuuelle* 1086 (DB). 'Spring or stream infested with snails'. OE *snægl* + *wella*.

Snainton N. Yorks. *Snechintune* 1086 (DB). Possibly 'farmstead associated with a man called *Snoc'. OE pers. name + *-ing-* + *tūn*.

Snaith Humber. *Snaith* c.1080, *Esneid* 1086 (DB). 'Piece of land cut off'. OScand. *sneith*.

Snape, from OE **snæp* 'boggy piece of land' or OScand. *snap* 'poor pasture'; examples include: **Snape** N. Yorks. *Snape* 1154. **Snape** Suffolk. *Snapes* 1086 (DB).

Snarestone Leics. *Snarchetone* 1086 (DB). 'Farmstead of a man called *Snar(o)c'. OE pers. name + *tūn*.

Snarford Lincs. *Snerteforde* 1086 (DB). 'Ford of a man called Snǫrtr'. OScand. pers. name + OE *ford*.

Snargate Kent. *Snergathe* c.1197. Probably 'gate or gap where snares for animals are placed'. OE *sneare* + *geat*.

Snave Kent. *Snaues* 1182. Possibly 'the spits or strips of land'. OE **snafa*.

Sneaton N. Yorks. *Snetune* 1086 (DB). 'Farmstead of a man called Snær, or with a detached piece of land'. OScand. pers. name or OE *snǣd* + *tūn*.

Snelland Lincs. *Sneleslunt* 1086 (DB). 'Grove of a man called Snjallr'. OScand. pers. name + *lundr*.

Snelston Derbys. *Snellestune* 1086 (DB). 'Farmstead of a man called Snell'. OE pers. name + *tūn*.

Snettisham Norfolk. *Snetesham* 1086 (DB). 'Homestead of a man called *Snǣt or *Sneti'. OE pers. name + *hām*.

Snitter Northum. *Snitere* 1176. Possibly 'weather-beaten place' from a word related to ME *sniteren* 'to snow'.

Snitterby Lincs. *Snetrebi* 1086 (DB). Probably 'farmstead or village of a man called *Snytra'. OE pers. name + OScand. *bý*.

Snitterfield Warwicks. *Snitefeld* 1086 (DB). 'Open land frequented by snipe'. OE *snīte* + *feld*.

Snodhill Heref. & Worcs. *Snauthil* 1195. Probably 'snowy hill'. OE **snāwede* + *hyll*.

Snodland Kent. *Snoddingland* 838, *Esnoiland* (*sic*) 1086 (DB). 'Cultivated land associated with a man called *Snodd'. OE pers. name + *-ing-* + *land*.

Snoreham Essex. *Snorham* 1238. Probably 'homestead or enclosure by a rough hill'. OE **snōr* + *hām* or *hamm*.

Snoring, Great & Little Norfolk. *Snaringes* 1086 (DB). Probably '(settlement of) the family or followers of a man called *Snear'. OE pers. name + *-ingas*.

Snowshill Glos. *Snawesille* 1086 (DB). 'Hill where the snow lies long'. OE *snāw* + *hyll*.

Soar (river) Warwicks.-Leics.-Notts., see BARROW UPON SOAR.

Soberton Hants. *Sudbertune* 1086 (DB). 'Southern grange or outlying farm'. OE *sūth* + *bere-tūn*.

Sodbury, Chipping & Old Avon. *Soppanbyrig* 872–915, *Sopeberie* 1086 (DB), *Cheping Sobbyri* 1269, *Olde Sobbury* 1346. 'Fortified place of a man called *Soppa'. OE pers. name + *burh* (dative *byrig*). Distinguishing affixes from OE *cēping* 'market' and *ald* 'old'.

Soham Cambs. *Sægham c.*1000, *Saham* 1086 (DB). 'Homestead by a swampy pool'. OE **sǣge* + *hām*.

Soham, Earl & Monk Suffolk. *Saham* 1086 (DB). 'Homestead by a pool'. OE *sǣ* or **sā* + *hām*. Distinguishing affixes from early possession by the Earl of Norfolk and the monks of Bury St Edmunds.

Soho Gtr. London. *So Ho* 1632. A hunting cry, from the early association of this area with hunting.

Solent, The Hants. *Soluente* 731. An ancient pre-English name of uncertain origin and meaning.

Solihull W. Mids. *Solihull* 12th cent. 'Muddy hill'. OE **sylig*, **solig* + *hyll*. Alternatively the first element may be OE **sulig* 'pig-stye'.

Sollers Hope Heref. & Worcs., see HOPE.

Sollom Lancs. *Solayn c.*1200. 'Muddy enclosure' from OScand. *sol* + **hegn*, or 'sunny slope' from OScand. *sól* + *hlein*.

Solway Firth Cumbria, see BOWNESS-ON-SOLWAY.

Somborne, King's, Little, & Upper Hants. *Swinburnan* 909, *Sunburne* 1086 (DB). 'Pig stream'. OE *swīn* + *burna*. Affix *King's* from its having been a royal estate.

Somerby, probably 'farmstead or village of a man called Sumarlithi', OScand. pers. name + *bý*: **Somerby** Leics. *Sumerlidebie* 1086 (DB). **Somerby** Lincs., near Brigg. *Sumertebi* 1086 (DB).

Somercotes, 'huts or cottages used in summer', OE *sumor* + *cot*: **Somercotes** Derbys. *Somercotes* 1276. **Somercotes, North & South** Lincs. *Summercotes* 1086 (DB).

Somerford, 'ford usable in summer', OE *sumor* + *ford*: **Somerford, Great & Little** Wilts. *Sumerford* 937, *Sumreford* 1086 (DB). **Somerford Keynes** Glos. *Sumerford* 685, *Somerford Keynes* 1291. Manorial affix from the *de Kaynes* family, here in the 13th cent.

Somerleyton Suffolk. *Sumerledetuna*

1086 (DB). 'Farmstead of a man called Sumarlithi'. OScand. pers. name + OE *tūn*.

Somersal Herbert Derbys. *Summersale* 1086 (DB), *Somersale Herbert* c.1300. 'Nook of land of a man called *Sumor'. OE pers. name + *halh*. Manorial affix from the *Fitzherbert* family, here in the 13th cent.

Somersby Lincs. *Summerdebi* 1086 (DB). Probably 'farmstead or village of a man called Sumarlithi'. OScand. pers. name + *bý*.

Somerset (the county). *Sumersæton* 12th cent. '(District of) the settlers around Somerton'. Reduced form of SOMERTON + OE *sǣte*.

Somersham Cambs. *Summeresham* c.1000, *Sumersham* 1086 (DB). Probably 'homestead of a man called *Sumor or *Sunmǣr'. OE pers. name + *hām*.

Somersham Suffolk. *Sumersham* 1086 (DB). 'Homestead of a man called *Sumor'. OE pers. name + *hām*.

Somerton, usually 'farmstead used in summer', OE *sumor* + *tūn*: **Somerton** Norfolk. *Somertuna* 1086 (DB). **Somerton** Oxon. *Sumertone* 1086 (DB). **Somerton** Somerset. *Sumortun* 901–24, *Summertone* 1086 (DB).

However the following has a different origin: **Somerton** Suffolk. *Sumerledetuna* 1086 (DB). 'Farmstead of a man called Sumarlithi'. OScand. pers. name + OE *tūn*.

Sompting W. Sussex. *Suntinga* 956, *Sultinges* 1086 (DB). '(Settlement of) the dwellers at the marsh'. OE **sumpt* + *-ingas*.

Sonning Berks. *Soninges* 1086 (DB). '(Settlement of) the family or followers of a man called *Sunna'. OE pers. name + *-ingas*.

Sopley Hants. *Sopelie* 1086 (DB). Possibly 'woodland clearing of a man called *Soppa'. OE pers. name + *lēah*. Alternatively the first element may be an OE **soppa* 'marsh'.

Sopworth Wilts. *Sopeworde* 1086 (DB). 'Enclosure of a man called *Soppa'. OE pers. name + *worth*.

Sotby Lincs. *Sotebi* 1086 (DB). 'Farmstead or village of a man called Sóti'. OScand. pers. name + *bý*.

Sotterley Suffolk. *Soterlega* 1086 (DB). OE *lēah* 'woodland clearing' with an uncertain first element, possibly a pers. name.

Soudley, Upper Glos. *Suleie* 1221. 'South woodland clearing'. OE *sūth* + *lēah*.

Soulbury Bucks. *Soleberie* 1086 (DB). 'Stronghold by a gully'. OE *sulh* + *burh* (dative *byrig*).

Soulby, 'farmstead of a man called Súla, or one made of posts', OScand. pers. name or *súla* + *bý*: **Soulby** Cumbria, near Brough. *Sulebi* c.1160. **Soulby** Cumbria, near Penrith. *Suleby* 1235.

Souldern Oxon. *Sulethorne* c.1160. 'Thorn-tree in or near a gully'. OE *sulh* + *thorn*.

Souldrop Beds. *Sultrop* 1196. 'Outlying farmstead near a gully'. OE *sulh* + *throp*.

Sourton Devon. *Swurantune* c.970, *Surintone* 1086 (DB). 'Farmstead by a neck of land or col'. OE *swēora* + *tūn*.

South as affix, see main name, e.g. for **South Acre** (Norfolk) see ACRE.

Southall Gtr. London. *Suhaull* 1198. 'Southern nook(s) of land'. OE *sūth* + *halh*, see NORTHOLT.

Southam, 'southern homestead or land in a river-bend', OE *sūth* + *hām* or *hamm*: **Southam** Glos. *Suth-ham* c.991, *Surham* (*sic*) 1086 (DB). **Southam** Warwicks. *Suthham* 998, *Sucham* (*sic*) 1086 (DB).

Southampton Hants. *Homtun* 825, *Suthhamtunam* 962, *Hantone* 1086 (DB). 'Estate on a promontory'. OE *hamm* + *tūn*, with prefix *sūth* to distinguish this place from NORTHAMPTON (which has a different origin).

Southborough Kent. 'Borough of *Suth*' 1270, *la South Burgh* 1450. 'Southern borough' (of TONBRIDGE). OE *sūth* + *burh*.

Southbourne Dorset, like Northbourne and Westbourne, a name of recent creation for a suburb of BOURNEMOUTH.

Southburgh Norfolk. *Berc* (*sic*) 1086 (DB), *Suthberg* 1291. 'South hill'. OE *sūth* + *beorg*.

Southchurch Essex. *Suthcyrcan* 1042–

66, *Sudcerca* 1086 (DB). 'Southern church'. OE *sūth* + *cirice*.

Southease E. Sussex. *Sueise* 966, *Suesse* 1086 (DB). 'Southern land overgrown with brushwood'. OE *sūth* + **hǣs(e)*.

Southend on Sea Essex. *Sowthende* 1481. 'The southern end (of Prittlewell parish)'. ME *south* + *ende*.

Southery Norfolk. *Suthereye* 942, *Sutreia* 1086 (DB). 'Southerly island'. OE *sūtherra* + *ēg*.

Southfleet Kent. *Suthfleotes* 10th cent., *Sudfleta* 1086 (DB). 'Southern place at the stream'. OE *sūth* + *flēot*.

Southgate Gtr. London. *Suthgate* 1370. 'Southern gate' (to Enfield Chase). OE *sūth* + *geat*.

Southill Beds. *Sudgiuele* 1086 (DB). 'Southern settlement of the tribe called *Gifle*'. OE *sūth* + old tribal name, see NORTHILL.

Southleigh Devon. *Lege* 1086 (DB), *Suthlege* 1228. '(Place at) the wood or clearing'. OE *lēah* with *sūth* to distinguish it from NORTHLEIGH.

Southminster Essex. *Suthmynster* c.1000, *Sudmunstra* 1086 (DB). 'Southern church'. OE *sūth* + *mynster*.

Southoe Cambs. *Sutham* (*sic*) 1086 (DB), *Sudho* 1186. 'Southern hill-spur'. OE *sūth* + *hōh*.

Southolt Suffolk. *Sudholda* 1086 (DB). 'South wood'. OE *sūth* + *holt*.

Southorpe Cambs. *Sudtorp* 1086 (DB). 'Southern outlying farmstead'. OScand. *súthr* + *thorp*.

Southowram W. Yorks. *Overe* 1086 (DB), *Sudhouerum* c.1275. '(Place at) the ridges'. OE **ofer*, **ufer* in a dative plural form **uferum*, with *sūth* to distinguish it from NORTHOWRAM.

Southport Mersey., a modern artificial name, first bestowed on the place in 1798.

Southrepps Norfolk. *Sutrepes* 1086 (DB), *Sutrepples* 1209. Possibly 'south strips of land'. OE *sūth* + **reopul*.

Southrey Lincs. *Sutreie* 1086 (DB). 'Southerly island'. OE *sūtherra* + *ēg*.

Southrop Glos. *Sudthropa* c.1140. 'Southern outlying farmstead'. OE *sūth* + *throp*.

Southsea Hants. *Southsea Castle* c.1600. Self-explanatory. The present place grew up round the castle built by Henry VIII in 1540.

Southwaite Cumbria, near Hesket. *Thouthweyt* 1272. 'Clay clearing'. OE *thōh* + OScand. *thveit*.

Southwark Gtr. London. *Sudwerca* 1086 (DB). 'Southern defensive work or fort'. OE *sūth* + *weorc*. Earlier called *Suthriganaweorc* 10th cent., 'fort of the men of SURREY'.

Southwell Notts. *Suthwellan* 958, *Sudwelle* 1086 (DB). 'South spring'. OE *sūth* + *wella*.

Southwick, 'southern dwelling or (dairy) farm', OE *sūth* + *wīc*: **Southwick** Hants. *Sudwic* c.1140. **Southwick** Northants. *Suthwycan* c.980. **Southwick** Tyne & Wear. *Suthewich* 12th cent. **Southwick** W. Sussex. *Sudewic* 1073. **Southwick** Wilts. *Sudwich* 1196.

Southwold Suffolk. *Sudwolda* 1086 (DB). 'South forest'. OE *sūth* + *wald*.

Southwood Norfolk. *Sudwda* 1086 (DB). 'Southern wood'. OE *sūth* + *wudu*.

Sow (river) Somerset, see MIDDLEZOY.

Sowe (river) W. Mids., see WALSGRAVE.

Sowerby, 'farmstead on sour ground', OScand. *saurr* + *bý*; examples include: **Sowerby** N. Yorks., near Thirsk. *Sorebi* 1086 (DB). **Sowerby, Sowerby Bridge** W. Yorks. *Sorebi* 1086 (DB), *Sourebybrigge* 15th cent. The bridge is across the River Calder. **Sowerby, Brough** Cumbria. *Sowreby* 1235, *Soureby by Burgh* 1314. It is near to BROUGH. **Sowerby, Temple** Cumbria. *Sourebi* 1179, *Templessoureby* 1292. Affix from its early possession by the Knights Templars.

Sowton Devon. *Southton* 1420. 'South farmstead or village'. OE *sūth* + *tūn*. Its earlier name was *Clis* 1086 (DB), one of several places named from the River Clyst, see CLYST HYDON.

Spalding Lincs. *Spallinge* 1086 (DB), *Spaldingis* c.1115. '(Settlement of) the dwellers in *Spald*'. Old district name (possibly from OE **spald* 'ditch or trench') + *-ingas*.

Spaldington Humber. *Spellinton* 1086 (DB). 'Farmstead of the tribe called

Spaldingas' (who give name to SPALDING). OE tribal name (genitive plural *-inga-*) + *tūn*.

Spaldwick Cambs. *Spalduice* 1086 (DB). Possibly 'dwelling or farm by a trickling stream or ditch'. OE *spāld* or **spald* + *wīc*.

Spalford Notts. *Spaldesforde* 1086 (DB). Possibly 'ford over a trickling stream or ditch'. OE *spāld* or **spald* + *ford*.

Sparham Norfolk. *Sparham* 1086 (DB). 'Homestead or enclosure made with spars or shafts'. OE **spearr* + *hām* or *hamm*.

Sparkford Somerset. *Sparkeforda* 1086 (DB). 'Brushwood ford'. OE **spearca* + *ford*.

Sparkwell Devon. *Spearcanwille* c.1070, *Sperchewelle* 1086 (DB). 'Spring or stream where brushwood grows'. OE **spearca* + *wella*.

Sparsholt, 'wood of the spear' (perhaps referring to a spear-trap for wild animals or to a wood where spear-shafts are obtained), OE *spere* + *holt*: **Sparsholt** Berks. *Speresholte* 963, *Spersolt* 1086 (DB). **Sparsholt** Hants. *Speoresholte* 901. Alternatively the first element of this name may be OE **spearr* 'a spar, a rafter'.

Spaunton N. Yorks. *Spantun* 1086 (DB). 'Farmstead with shingled roof'. OScand. *spánn* + OE *tūn*.

Spaxton Somerset. *Spachestone* 1086 (DB). Probably 'farmstead of a man called Spakr'. OScand. pers. name + OE *tūn*.

Speen Berks. *Spene* 821, *Spone* 1086 (DB). Probably 'place where wood-chips are found'. OE **spēne*. This OE name represents an adaptation of the older Latin name *Spinis* 'at the thorn bushes' (recorded in the 4th cent.).

Speeton N. Yorks. *Specton* 1086 (DB). Possibly 'enclosure where meetings are held'. OE *spēc* + *tūn*.

Speke Mersey. *Spec* 1086 (DB). Possibly OE *spēc* 'branches, brushwood'.

Speldhurst Kent. *Speldhirst* 8th cent. 'Wooded hill where wood-chips are found'. OE *speld* + *hyrst*.

Spelsbury Oxon. *Speolesbyrig* early 11th cent., *Spelesberie* 1086 (DB). 'Stronghold of a man called *Spēol'. OE pers. name + *burh* (dative *byrig*).

Spen, High Tyne & Wear. *Le Spen* 1312. ME *spenne* 'a fence, an enclosure'.

Spennithorne N. Yorks. *Speningetorp* (*sic*) 1086 (DB), *Speningthorn* 1184. Probably 'thorn-tree by the fence or enclosure'. OE or OScand. **spenning* + *thorn*.

Spennymoor Durham. *Spendingmor* c.1336. Probably 'moor with a fence or enclosure'. OE or OScand. **spenning* + *mōr*.

Spetchley Heref. & Worcs. *Spæclea* 967, *Speclea* 1086 (DB). 'Woodland clearing where meetings are held'. OE *spēc* + *lēah*.

Spetisbury Dorset. *Spehtesberie* 1086 (DB). 'Pre-English earthwork frequented by the green woodpecker'. OE **speoht* + *burh* (dative *byrig*).

Spexhall Suffolk. *Specteshale* 1197. 'Nook of land frequented by the green woodpecker'. OE **speoht* + *halh*.

Spilsby Lincs. *Spilesbi* 1086 (DB). 'Farmstead or village of a man called *Spillir'. OScand. pers. name + *bý*.

Spindlestone Northum. *Spindlestan* 1187. 'Stone or rock thought to resemble a spindle'. OE *spinele* + *stān*.

Spital in the Street Lincs. *Hospitale* 1204, *Spitelenthestrete* 1322. 'The hospital or religious house on the Roman road (Ermine Street)'. ME *spitel* (from OFrench *hospitale*) with OE *strǣt*.

Spithead Hants., not recorded before the 17th cent., 'headland of the sand-spit or pointed sandbank'. OE *spitu* + *hēafod*.

Spixworth Norfolk. *Spikesuurda* 1086 (DB). Probably 'enclosure of a man called *Spic'. OE pers. name + *worth*.

Spofforth N. Yorks. *Spoford* (*sic*) 1086 (DB), *Spotford* 1218. 'Ford by a small plot of ground'. OE **spot* + *ford*.

Spondon Derbys. *Spondune* 1086 (DB). 'Hill where wood-chips or shingles are got'. OE *spōn* + *dūn*.

Sporle Norfolk. *Sparlea* 1086 (DB). Probably 'wood or clearing where spars or shafts are obtained'. OE **spearr* + *lēah*.

Spratton Northants. *Spretone* 1086 (DB). Probably 'farmstead made of poles'. OE *sprēot* + *tūn*.

Spreyton Devon. *Spreitone* 1086 (DB). 'Farmstead amongst brushwood'. OE **spræ̆g* + *tūn*.

Spridlington Lincs. *Spredelintone* 1086 (DB). Probably 'estate associated with a man called *Sprytel'. OE pers. name + *-ing-* + *tūn*.

Springthorpe Lincs. *Springetorp* 1086 (DB). 'Outlying farmstead by a spring'. OE *spring* + OScand. *thorp*.

Sproatley Humber. *Sprotele* 1086 (DB). 'Woodland clearing where young shoots grow'. OE *sprota* + *lēah*.

Sproston Green Ches. *Sprostune* 1086 (DB). 'Farmstead of a man called Sprow'. OE pers. name + *tūn*.

Sprotbrough S. Yorks. *Sproteburg* 1086 (DB). 'Stronghold of a man called *Sprota', or 'stronghold overgrown with shoots'. OE pers. name or *sprota* + *burh*.

Sproughton Suffolk. *Sproeston* 1191. Probably 'farmstead of a man called Sprow'. OE pers. name + *tūn*.

Sprowston Norfolk. *Sprowestuna* 1086 (DB). 'Farmstead of a man called Sprow'. OE pers. name + *tūn*.

Sproxton, 'farmstead of a man called *Sprok', or 'brushwood farmstead', OScand. pers. name or **sprogh* + OE *tūn*: **Sproxton** Leics. *Sprotone* (*sic*) 1086 (DB), *Sproxcheston* c.1125. **Sproxton** N. Yorks. *Sprostune* 1086 (DB).

Spurn Head Humber. *Ravenserespourne* 1399. From ME **spurn* 'a spur, a projecting piece of land', in the early spelling with the place-name *Ravenser* which means 'sandbank of a man called Hrafn', OScand. pers. name + *eyrr*.

Spurstow Ches. *Spuretone* (*sic*) 1086 (DB), *Sporstow* c.1200. 'Meeting place on a trackway, or by a spur of land'. OE *spor* or *spura* + *stōw*.

Stadhampton Oxon. *Stodeham* c.1135. 'Enclosure or river meadow where horses are kept'. OE *stōd* + *hamm*. The *-ton* is a late addition.

Staffield Cumbria. *Stafhole* c.1225. 'Round hill with a staff or post'. OScand. *stafr* + *hóll*.

Stafford Staffs. *Stæfford* mid 11th cent., *Stadford* 1086 (DB). 'Ford by a landing-place'. OE *stæth* + *ford*. **Staffordshire** (OE *scīr* 'district') is first referred to in the 11th cent.

Stafford, West Dorset. *Stanford* 1086 (DB). 'Stony ford'. OE *stān* + *ford*.

Stagsden Beds. *Stachedene* 1086 (DB). 'Valley of stakes or boundary posts'. OE *staca* + *denu*.

Stainburn N. Yorks. *Stanburne* c.972, *Sta(i)nburne* 1086 (DB). 'Stony stream'. OE *stān* (replaced by OScand. *steinn*) + *burna*.

Stainby Lincs. *Stigandebi* 1086 (DB). 'Farmstead or village of a man called Stígandi'. OScand. pers. name + *bý*.

Staincross S. Yorks. *Staincros* 1086 (DB). 'Stone cross'. OScand. *steinn* + *kros*.

Staindrop Durham. *Standropa* c.1040. Probably 'valley with stony ground'. OE *stǣner* + *hop*.

Staines Surrey. *Stane* 11th cent., *Stanes* 1086 (DB). '(Place at) the stone(s)'. OE *stān*.

Stainfield Lincs., near Bardney. *Steinfelde* 1086 (DB). 'Stony open land'. OE *stān* (replaced by OScand. *steinn*) + *feld*.

Stainfield Lincs., near Rippingale. *Stentvith* 1086 (DB). 'Stony clearing'. OScand. *steinn* + *thveit*.

Stainforth, 'stony ford', OE *stān* (replaced by OScand. *steinn*) + *ford*: **Stainforth** N. Yorks. *Stainforde* 1086 (DB). **Stainforth** S. Yorks. *Steinforde* 1086 (DB).

Staining Lancs. *Staininghe* 1086 (DB). Possibly '(settlement of) the family or followers of a man called *Stān, or the dwellers in a stony district'. OE pers. name or *stān* (with Scand. influence) + *-ingas*. Alternatively 'stony place', OE **stāning*.

Stainland W. Yorks. *Stanland* 1086 (DB). 'Stony cultivated land'. OE *stān* (replaced by OScand. *steinn*) + *land*.

Stainley, 'stony woodland clearing', OE *stān* (replaced by OScand. *steinn*) + *lēah*: **Stainley, North** N. Yorks.

*Stanleh c.*972, *Nordstanlaia* 1086 (DB). **Stainley, South** N. Yorks. *Stanlai* 1086 (DB), *Southstainlei* 1198.

Stainmore, North Cumbria. *Stanmoir c.*990. 'Rocky or stony moor'. OE *stān* (replaced by OScand. *steinn*) + *mōr*.

Stainsacre N. Yorks. *Stainsaker* 1090–6. 'Cultivated land of a man called Steinn'. OScand. pers. name + *akr*.

Stainton, a frequent name in the North, usually 'farmstead on stony ground', OE *stān* (replaced by OScand. *steinn*) + *tūn*; examples include: **Stainton** Durham. *Staynton c.*1150. **Stainton** S. Yorks. *Stantone* 1086 (DB). **Stainton, Market** Lincs. *Staintone* 1086 (DB), *Steynton Market* 1286. Affix is ME *merket*. **Stainton le Vale** Lincs. *Staintone* 1086 (DB). Affix means 'in the valley' from ME *vale*.

However the following has a different origin: **Stainton, Great & Little** Durham. *Staninctona* 1091. 'Farmstead at the stony place, or one associated with a man called *Stān'. OE **stāning* + *tūn*, or OE pers. name + *-ing-* + *tūn*.

Staintondale N. Yorks. *Steintun* 1086 (DB), *Staynton Dale* 1562. 'Farmstead on stony ground'. OE *stān* (replaced by OScand. *steinn*) + *tūn*, with the later addition of *dale* 'valley'.

Staithes N. Yorks. *Setonstathes* 1415. 'The landing-places'. OE *stæth*. Seaton ('sea farmstead') is a nearby place.

Stalbridge Dorset. *Stapulbreicge* 998, *Staplebrige* 1086 (DB). 'Bridge built on posts or piles'. OE *stapol* + *brycg*.

Stalham Norfolk. *Stalham* 1086 (DB). Probably 'homestead by the fishing pool'. OE *stall* + *hām*.

Stalisfield Green Kent. *Stanefelle* (*sic*) 1086 (DB), *Stealesfelde c.*1100. Probably 'open land with a stall or stable'. OE *steall* + *feld*.

Stallingborough Humber. *Stalingeburg* 1086 (DB). Possibly 'stronghold of the dwellers near a stall or stable'. OE *stall* + *-inga-* + *burh*.

Stalling Busk N. Yorks. *Stalunesbusc* 1218. 'The stallion's bush'. ME *stalun* + OScand. **buski*.

Stalmine Lancs. *Stalmine* 1086 (DB). Probably 'mouth of the stream or pool'. OE *stæll* + OScand. *mynni*.

Stalybridge Gtr. Manch. *Stauelegh* 13th cent., *Stalybridge* 1687. 'Bridge at the wood where staves are got'. OE *stæf* + *lēah*, with the later addition of *bridge*.

Stambourne Essex. *Stanburna* 1086 (DB). 'Stony stream'. OE *stān* + *burna*.

Stambridge, Great Essex. *Stanbruge* 1086 (DB). 'Stone bridge'. OE *stān* + *brycg*.

Stamford, 'stone ford' or 'stony ford', OE *stān* + *ford*: **Stamford** Lincs. *Steanford* 10th cent., *Stanford* 1086 (DB). **Stamford Bridge** Humber. *Stanford brycg c.*1075. The ford here was replaced by a bridge at an early date.

Stamfordham Northum. *Stanfordham* 1188. 'Homestead or village at the stone ford'. OE *stān* + *ford* + *hām*.

Stamford Hill Gtr. London. *Saundfordhull* 1294. 'Hill by a sandy ford'. OE *sand* + *ford* + *hyll*.

Stanbridge Beds. *Stanbrugge* 1165. 'Stone bridge'. OE *stān* + *brycg*.

Standish Gtr. Manch. *Stanesdis* 1178. 'Stony pasture or enclosure'. OE *stān* + *edisc*.

Standlake Oxon. *Stanlache c.*1155. 'Stony stream or channel'. OE *stān* + *lacu*.

Standon, 'stony hill', OE *stān* + *dūn*: **Standon** Herts. *Standune* 944–6, *Standone* 1086 (DB). **Standon** Staffs. *Stantone* (*sic*) 1086 (DB), *Standon* 1190.

Stanfield Norfolk. *Stanfelda* 1086 (DB). 'Stony open land'. OE *stān* + *feld*.

Stanford, found in various counties, 'stone ford' or 'stony ford', OE *stān* + *ford*; examples include: **Stanford** Kent. *Stanford* 1035. **Stanford Bishop** Heref. & Worcs. *Stanford* 1086 (DB). Affix from its early possession by the Bishop of Hereford. **Stanford Dingley** Berks. *Stanworde* 1086 (DB), *Staneford Deanly* 1535. Manorial affix from the *Dyngley* family, here in the 15th cent. **Stanford in the Vale** Oxon. *Stanford* 1086 (DB), *Stanford in le Vale* 1496. Affix from its situation in the VALE OF WHITE HORSE. **Stanford le Hope** Essex. *Staunford* 1267, *Stanford in the Hope* 1361. Affix means 'in the bay' from ME *hope*. **Stanford Rivers** Essex. *Stanford* 1068, *Stanfort* 1086 (DB), *Stanford Ryueres*

1289. Manorial affix from the *Rivers* family, here in the 13th cent.

Stanhoe Norfolk. *Stanhou* 1086 (DB). 'Stony hill-spur'. OE *stān* + *hōh*.

Stanhope Durham. *Stanhopa* 1183. 'Stony valley'. OE *stān* + *hop*.

Stanion Northants. *Stanere* (*sic*) 1086 (DB), *Stanerna* 1162. 'Stone house(s) or building(s)'. OE *stān* + *ærn*.

Stanley, 'stony woodland clearing', OE *stān* + *lēah*; examples include: **Stanley** Derbys. *Stanlei* 1086 (DB). **Stanley** Durham. *Stanley* 1297. **Stanley** Staffs. *Stanlega* 1130. **Stanley** W. Yorks. *Stanlei* 1086 (DB). **Stanley, King's & Leonard** Glos. *Stanlege* 1086 (DB), *Kingestanleg* 1220, *Stanllegh Leonardi* 1285. Affixes from ownership by the Crown and from the former dedication of the church to St Leonard.

Stanmer E. Sussex. *Stanmere* 765, 1086 (DB). 'Stony pool'. OE *stān* + *mere*.

Stanmore Gtr. London. *Stanmere* 1086 (DB). Identical in origin with the previous name.

Stanney Ches. *Stanei* 1086 (DB). 'Stone or rock island'. OE *stān* + *ēg*.

Stannington Northum. *Stanigton* 1242. 'Farmstead at the stony place, or one associated with a man called *Stān'. OE **stāning* + *tūn*, or OE pers. name + *-ing-* + *tūn*.

Stansfield Suffolk. *Stanesfelda* 1086 (DB). Probably 'open land of a man called *Stān'. OE pers. name + *feld*.

Stanstead, Stansted, 'stony place', OE *stān* + *stede*: **Stanstead** Suffolk. *Stanesteda* 1086 (DB). **Stanstead Abbots** Herts. *Stanestede* 1086 (DB), *Stanstede Abbatis de Wautham* 1247. Affix from early possession by the Abbot of Waltham. **Stansted** Kent. *Stansted* 1231. **Stansted Mountfitchet** Essex. *Stanesteda* 1086 (DB), *Stansted Mounfichet* c.1290. Manorial affix from the *Muntfichet* family, here in the 12th cent.

Stanton, a common name, usually 'farmstead on stony ground', occasionally 'farmstead near standing stones', OE *stān* + *tūn*; examples include: **Stanton** Glos. *Stantone* 1086 (DB). **Stanton** Suffolk. *Stantuna* 1086 (DB). **Stanton Drew** Avon. *Stantone* 1086 (DB), *Stanton Drogonis* 1253. Manorial affix from possession by one *Drogo* or *Drew* in 1225. **Stanton Harcourt** Oxon. *Stantone* 1086 (DB), *Stantone Harecurt* c.1275. Manorial affix from the *de Harecurt* family, here in the 12th cent. **Stanton, Long** Cambs. *Stantune* 1086 (DB), *Long Stanton* 1282. Affix refers to the length of the village. **Stanton St Quintin** Wilts. *Stantone* 1086 (DB), *Staunton St Quintin* 1283. Manorial affix from the *de Sancto Quintino* family, here in the 13th cent. **Stanton upon Hine Heath** Shrops. *Stantune* 1086 (DB), *Staunton super Hyne Heth* 1327. Affix means 'on the heath belonging to the religious community', OE *hīwan* + *hǣth*.

Stanwardine Shrops. *Staurdine* 1086 (DB). 'Enclosure made of stones, or stony ground'. OE *stān* + *worthign*.

Stanway, 'stony road', OE *stān* + *weg*: **Stanway** Essex. *Stanwægun* c.1000, *Stanwega* 1086 (DB). **Stanway** Glos. *Stanwege* 12th cent.

Stanwell Surrey. *Stanwelle* 1086 (DB). 'Stony spring or stream'. OE *stān* + *wella*.

Stanwick Northants. *Stanwigga* 10th cent., *Stanwige* 1086 (DB). 'The rocking- or logan-stone'. OE *stān* + *wigga*.

Stapeley Ches. *Steple* (*sic*) 1086 (DB), *Stapeleg* 1260. Probably 'wood or clearing where posts are got'. OE *stapol* + *lēah*.

Stapenhill Staffs. *Stapenhille* 1086 (DB). '(Place at) the steep hill'. OE *stēap* (dative *-an*) + *hyll*.

Staple, '(place at) the pillar of wood or stone', OE *stapol*: **Staple** Kent. *Staples* 1205. **Staple Fitzpaine** Somerset. *Staple* 1086 (DB). Manorial affix from the *Fitzpaine* family, here in the 14th cent.

Stapleford, 'ford marked by a post', OE *stapol* + *ford*; examples include: **Stapleford** Cambs. *Stapelforda* 956, *Stapleforde* 1086 (DB). **Stapleford** Notts. *Stapleford* 1086 (DB). **Stapleford Abbots & Tawney** Essex. *Staplefort* 1086 (DB), *Staplford Abbatis Sancti Edmundi* 1255, *Stapilford Thany* 1291. Distinguishing affixes from early possession by the Abbot of Bury St Edmunds and by the *de Tany* family.

Staplegrove Somerset. *Stapilgrove* 1327. 'Grove where posts are got'. OE *stapol* + *grāf*.

Staplehurst Kent. *Stapelherst* 1226. 'Wooded hill where posts are got'. OE *stapol* + *hyrst*.

Stapleton, usually 'farmstead by a post or built on posts', OE *stapol* + *tūn*; examples include: **Stapleton** Avon. *Stapleton* 1215. **Stapleton** Leics. *Stapletone* 1086 (DB).
However the following probably mean 'farmstead by a steep slope', OE *stēpel* + *tūn*: **Stapleton** Heref. & Worcs. *Stepeltone* 1286. **Stapleton** Shrops. *Stepleton* 12th cent.

Staploe Beds. *Stapelho* 1203. 'Hill-spur marked by, or shaped like, a post'. OE *stapol* + *hōh*.

Starbotton N. Yorks. *Stamphotne* (*sic*) 1086 (DB), *Stauerboten* 12th cent. 'Valley where stakes are got'. OE **stæfer* (replacing OScand. *stafn* in the first form) + OScand. *botn*.

Starston Norfolk. *Sterestuna* 1086 (DB). 'Farmstead or village of a man called Styrr'. OScand. pers. name + OE *tūn*.

Startforth Durham. *Stretford* c.1050, *Stradford* 1086 (DB). 'Ford on a Roman road'. OE *strǣt* + *ford*.

Start Point Devon. *La Sterte* 1310. OE *steort* 'tongue of land, promontory'.

Stathe Somerset. *Stathe* 1233. 'The landing-place'. OE *stæth*.

Stathern Leics. *Stachedirne* 1086 (DB). 'Stake thorn-tree', i.e. 'thorn-tree marking a boundary'. OE *staca* + *thyrne*.

Staughton, Great (Cambs.) **& Little** (Beds.). *Stoctun* c.1000, *Tochestone*, *Estone* (*sic*) 1086 (DB). 'Farmstead at an outlying hamlet'. OE *stoc* + *tūn*.

Staunton, usually 'farmstead on stony ground, or one near a standing stone', OE *stān* + *tūn*; examples include: **Staunton** Glos., near Hartpury. *Stantun* 972, 1086 (DB). **Staunton on Arrow** Heref. & Worcs. *Stantun* 958, *Stantune* 1086 (DB). Arrow is a Celtic river-name probably meaning 'bright stream'.
However the following has a different origin: **Staunton on Wye** Heref. & Worcs. *Standune* 1086 (DB). 'Stony hill'. OE *stān* + *dūn*. For the river-name, see ROSS ON WYE.

Staveley, 'wood or clearing where staves are got', OE *stæf* + *lēah*: **Staveley** Cumbria. *Staueleye* c.1200. **Staveley** Derbys. *Stavelie* 1086 (DB). **Staveley** N. Yorks. *Stanlei* (*sic*) 1086 (DB), *Staflea* 1167. **Staveley-in-Cartmel** Cumbria. *Stavelay* 1282. See CARTMEL.

Staverton, usually 'farmstead made of or marked by stakes', OE *stæfer* + *tūn*: **Staverton** Glos. *Staruenton* 1086 (DB). **Staverton** Northants. *Stæfertun* 944, *Stavertone* 1086 (DB). **Staverton** Wilts. *Stavretone* 1086 (DB).
However the following has a different origin: **Staverton** Devon. *Stofordtune* c.1070, *Stovretona* 1086 (DB). 'Farmstead by a stony ford'. OE *stān* + *ford* + *tūn*.

Stawell Somerset. *Stawelle* 1086 (DB). 'Stony spring or stream'. OE *stān* + *wella*.

Staxton N. Yorks. *Stacstone* 1086 (DB). 'Farmstead or village of a man called Stakkr'. OScand. pers. name + OE *tūn*.

Stearsby N. Yorks. *Stirsbi* 1086 (DB). 'Farmstead or village of a man called Styrr'. OScand. pers. name + *bý*.

Stebbing Essex. *Stibinga* 1086 (DB). '(Settlement of) the family or followers of a man called *Stybba, or the dwellers among the tree-stumps'. OE pers. name or *stybb* + *-ingas*.

Stedham W. Sussex. *Steddanham* 960, *Stedeham* 1086 (DB). 'Homestead or enclosure of the stallion, or of a man called *Stedda'. OE *stēda* or pers. name + *hām* or *hamm*.

Steep Hants. *Stepe* 12th cent. 'The steep place'. OE **stīepe*.

Steeping, Great & Little Lincs. *Stepinge* 1086 (DB). Probably '(settlement of) the family or followers of a man called Stēapa'. OE pers. name + *-ingas*.

Steeple, 'steep place', OE *stēpel*: **Steeple** Dorset. *Stiple* 1086 (DB). **Steeple** Essex. *Stepla* 1086 (DB).

Steeple as affix, see main name, e.g. for **Steeple Ashton** (Wilts.) see ASHTON.

Steeton W. Yorks., near Keighley. *Stiuetune* 1086 (DB). Probably 'farmstead built of or amongst tree-stumps'. OE **styfic* + *tūn*.

Stelling Minnis Kent. *Stellinges* 1086 (DB). Possibly '(settlement of) the family or followers of a man called *Stealla'. OE pers. name + *-ingas*. Affix is from OE *mǣnnes* 'common land'.

Stepney Gtr. London. *Stybbanhythe* c.1000, *Stibanhede* 1086 (DB). Probably 'landing-place of a man called *Stybba'. OE pers. name (genitive *-n*) + *hȳth*.

Steppingley Beds. *Stepigelai* 1086 (DB). 'Woodland clearing of the family or followers of a man called Stēapa'. OE pers. name + *-inga-* + *lēah*.

Sternfield Suffolk. *Sternesfelda* 1086 (DB). Possibly 'open land of a man called *Sterne'. OE pers. name + *feld*.

Stert Wilts. *Sterte* 1086 (DB). 'Projecting piece of land'. OE *steort*.

Stetchworth Cambs. *Steuicheswrthe* c.1050, *Stiuicesuuorde* 1086 (DB). 'Enclosure amongst the tree-stumps, or of a man called *Styfic'. OE **styfic* or pers. name + *worth*.

Stevenage Herts. *Stithenæce* c.1060, *Stigenace* 1086 (DB). Probably '(place at) the strong oak-tree'. OE *stīth* (dative *-an*) + *āc* (dative *ǣc*).

Steventon, 'estate associated with a man called *Stīf(a)', OE pers. name + *-ing-* + *tūn*, or possibly 'farmstead at the tree-stump place', OE **styf(ic)ing* + *tūn*: **Steventon** Hants. *Stivetune* 1086 (DB). **Steventon** Oxon. *Stivetune* 1086 (DB).

Stevington Beds. *Stiuentone* 1086 (DB). Probably identical in origin with the previous two names.

Stewartby Beds., a recent name for a 'new village' built in 1935 for employees in the brick-making industry, named from Halley *Stewart*, chairman of a local brick company.

Stewkley Bucks. *Stiuelai* (*sic*) 1086 (DB), *Stiuecelea* 1182. 'Woodland clearing with tree-stumps'. OE **styfic* + *lēah*.

Stewton Lincs. *Stivetone* 1086. Probably 'farmstead built of or amongst tree-stumps'. OE **styfic* + *tūn*.

Steyning W. Sussex. *Stæningum* c.880, *Staninges* 1086 (DB). Probably '(settlement of) the family or followers of a man called *Stān, or the dwellers at the stony place'. OE pers. name or OE *stān* or **stǣne* + *-ingas*.

Stibbard Norfolk. *Stabyrda* (*sic*) 1086 (DB), *Stiberde* 1202. 'Bank beside a path, a road-side'. OE *stīg* + **byrde*.

Stibbington Cambs. *Stebintune* 1086 (DB). Probably 'estate associated with a man called *Stybba'. OE pers. name + *-ing-* + *tūn*. Alternatively the first element may be OE **stybbing* 'tree-stump clearing'.

Stickford Lincs. *Stichesforde* 1086 (DB). 'Ford by the long strip of land'. OE *sticca* + *ford*.

Sticklepath Devon. *Stikelepethe* 1280. 'Steep path'. OE *sticol* + *pæth*.

Stickney Lincs. *Stichenai* 1086 (DB). 'Long strip of land between streams'. OE *sticca* (genitive *-n*) + *ēg*.

Stiffkey Norfolk. *Stiuekai* 1086 (DB). 'Island, or dry ground in marsh, with tree-stumps'. OE **styfic* + *ēg*.

Stillingfleet N. Yorks. *Steflingefled* 1086 (DB). 'Stretch of river belonging to the family or followers of a man called *Stȳfel'. OE pers. name + *-inga-* + *flēot*.

Stillington, probably 'estate associated with a man called *Stȳfel', OE pers. name + *-ing-* + *tūn*: **Stillington** Cleveland. *Stilligtune* c.1190. **Stillington** N. Yorks. *Stiuelinctun* 1086 (DB).

Stilton Cambs. *Stichiltone* 1086 (DB). 'Farmstead or village at a stile or steep ascent'. OE *stigel* + *tūn*.

Stinchcombe Glos. *Stintescombe* c.1155. 'Valley frequented by the sandpiper or dunlin'. OE **stint* + *cumb*.

Stinsford Dorset. *Stincteford* 1086 (DB). 'Ford frequented by the sandpiper or dunlin'. OE **stint* + *ford*.

Stirchley Shrops. *Styrcleage* 1002. 'Clearing or pasture for young bullocks'. OE *styrc* + *lēah*.

Stisted Essex. *Stistede* 1086 (DB), *Stidsted* 1198. Probably 'place where lamb's cress or nettles grow'. OE *stīthe* + *stede*.

Stithians Cornwall. *Sancta Stethyana* 1268. From the dedication of the church to St Stithian, a female saint.

Stittenham, High N. Yorks. *Stidnun* (*sic*) 1086 (DB), *Stiklum c.*1260. Probably '(place at) the steep ascents'. OE **sticel(e)* in a dative plural form **sticelum*.

Stivichall W. Mids. *Stivichall c.*1144. 'Nook of land with tree-stumps'. OE **styfic* + *halh*.

Stixwould Lincs. *Stigeswalde* 1086 (DB). 'Forest of a man called Stígr'. OScand. pers. name + OE *wald*.

Stoborough Dorset. *Stanberge* 1086 (DB). 'Stony hill or barrow'. OE *stān* + *beorg*.

Stock Essex. *Herewardestoc* 1234, *Stocke* 1337. 'Outlying farmstead or hamlet of a man called Hereweard'. OE pers. name + *stoc*. The longer name remained in use until the 17th cent.

Stockbridge Hants. *Stocbrugge* 1221. 'Bridge made of logs'. OE *stocc* + *brycg*. The same name occurs in other counties.

Stockbury Kent. *Stochingeberge* 1086 (DB). 'Woodland pasture of the dwellers at the outlying farmstead'. OE *stoc* + *-inga-* + *bǣr*.

Stockerston Leics. *Stoctone* (*sic*) 1086 (DB), *Stocfaston c.*1130. 'Stronghold built of logs'. OE *stocc* + *fæsten*.

Stock Green & Wood Heref. & Worcs. *La Stokke* 1271. 'The tree-stump'. OE *stocc*.

Stockingford Warwicks. *Stoccingford* 1157. 'Ford by the tree-stump clearing'. OE **stoccing* + *ford*.

Stocking Pelham Herts., see PELHAM.

Stockland, 'cultivated land of the outlying farmstead', OE *stoc* + *land*: **Stockland** Devon. *Stocland* 998. **Stockland Bristol**. Somerset. *Stocheland* 1086 (DB). Manorial affix from its possession by the chamber of Bristol.

Stockleigh English & Pomeroy Devon. *Stochelie* 1086 (DB), *Stokeley Engles* 1268, *Stokelegh Pomeray* 1261. Probably 'woodland clearing with tree-stumps'. OE *stocc* + *lēah*. Manorial affixes from early possession by the *Engles* and *de Pomerei* families.

Stockport Gtr. Manch. *Stokeport c.*1170. 'Market-place at an outlying hamlet'. OE *stoc* + *port*.

Stocksbridge S. Yorks., not on record before 1841, probably identical in origin with STOCKBRIDGE.

Stocksfield Northum. *Stokesfeld* 1242. 'Open land belonging to an outlying hamlet'. OE *stoc* + *feld*.

Stockton, a name found in several counties, probably 'farmstead at an outlying hamlet' from OE *stoc* + *tūn*, although some may be 'farmstead built of logs', OE *stocc* + *tūn*; examples include: **Stockton** Warwicks. *Stocton* 1249. **Stockton Heath** Ches. *Stocton c.*1200, *Stoaken Heath* 1682. **Stockton on Tees** Cleveland. *Stocton* 1196. Tees is a Celtic or pre-Celtic river-name, possibly meaning 'surging river'.

Stockwell Gtr. London. *Stokewell* 1197. 'Spring or stream by a tree-stump'. OE *stocc* + *wella*.

Stockwith, East (Lincs.) **& West** (Notts.). *Stochithe* 12th cent. 'Landing-place made of logs or tree-stumps'. OE *stocc* + *hȳth*.

Stodmarsh Kent. *Stodmerch* 675. 'Marsh where a herd of horses is kept'. OE *stōd* + *mersc*.

Stoford, 'stony ford', OE *stān* + *ford*: **Stoford** Somerset, near Yeovil. *Stafford* 1225. **Stoford** Wilts. *Stanford* 943.

Stogumber Somerset. *Stoke Gunner* 1225. 'Outlying farmstead or hamlet'. OE *stoc*, with pers. name or surname *Gumer* of an early owner.

Stogursey Somerset. *Stoche* 1086 (DB), *Stok Curcy* 1212. 'Outlying farmstead or hamlet'. OE *stoc*, with manorial affix from the *de Curci* family, here in the 12th cent.

Stoke, a very common name, from OE *stoc* 'outlying farmstead or hamlet, secondary settlement'; examples include: **Stoke-by-Nayland** Suffolk. *Stoke c.*950, *Stokeneylond* 1272. See NAYLAND. **Stoke Climsland** Cornwall. *Stoke* 1266, *Stok in Clymeslond* 1302. Affix is from OE *land* 'estate' with an obscure first element. **Stoke D'Abernon** Surrey. *Stoche* 1086 (DB), *Stokes de Abernun* 1253. Manorial affix from the *de Abernun* family, here in the 12th cent. **Stoke Ferry** Norfolk.

Stoches 1086 (DB), *Stokeferie* 1248. Affix is OScand. *ferja*, referring to a ferry over the River Wissey. **Stoke Fleming** Devon. *Stoc* 1086 (DB), *Stokeflemeng* 1270. Manorial affix from the family of *le Flemeng*, here in the 13th cent. **Stoke Gabriel** Devon. *Stoke* 1307, *Stokegabriel* 1309. Affix from the dedication of the church to St Gabriel. **Stoke Gifford** Glos. *Stoche* 1086 (DB), *Stokes Giffard* 1243. Manorial affix from the *Gifard* family, here from the 11th to the 14th cent. **Stoke Mandeville** Bucks. *Stoches* 1086 (DB), *Stoke Mandeville* 1284. Manorial affix from the *Mandeville* family who held the manor in the 13th cent. **Stoke on Trent** Staffs. *Stoche* 1086 (DB): For the river-name, see TRENTHAM. **Stoke Poges** Bucks. *Stoches* 1086 (DB), *Stokepogeis* 1292. Manorial affix from the family of *le Pugeis*, here in the 13th cent. **Stoke, Rodney** Somerset. *Stoches* 1086 (DB). Manorial affix from the *de Rodeney* family, here in the early 14th cent. **Stoke St Gregory** Somerset. *Stokes* 1225. Affix from the dedication of the church. **Stoke sub Hamdon** Somerset. *Stoca* 1086 (DB), *Stokes under Hamden* 1248. Affix refers to Hamdon Hill, possibly 'hill of the enclosures' from OE *hamm* + *dūn*.

Stokeham Notts. *Estoches* 1086 (DB), *Stokum* 1242. '(Place at) the outlying farmsteads'. OE *stoc* in a dative plural form *stocum*.

Stokeinteignhead Devon. *Stoches* 1086 (DB), *Stokes in Tynhide* 1279. Originally 'outlying farmstead or hamlet', from OE *stoc*. Affix means 'in the district consisting of ten hides of land', from OE *tēn* + *hīd*.

Stokenchurch Bucks. *Stockenechurch* *c.*1200. 'Church made of logs'. OE *stoccen* + *cirice*.

Stoke Newington Gtr. London, see NEWINGTON.

Stokenham Devon. *Stokes* 1242, *Stok in Hamme* 1276. 'Outlying farmstead or hamlet in the area of cultivated ground'. OE *stoc* + *in* + *hamm*.

Stokesay Shrops. *Stoches* 1086 (DB), *Stoksay* 1256. Originally 'outlying farmstead or hamlet', from OE *stoc*. Manorial affix from the *de Sei* family, here in the 12th cent.

Stokesby Norfolk. *Stokesbei* 1086 (DB). 'Village with an outlying farmstead or pasture'. OE *stoc* + OScand. *bý*.

Stokesley N. Yorks. *Stocheslage* 1086 (DB). 'Woodland clearing belonging to an outlying farmstead or hamlet'. OE *stoc* + *lēah*.

Stondon, 'stony hill', OE *stān* + *dūn*: **Stondon Massey** Essex. *Staundune* 1062, *Standon de Marcy* 1238. Manorial affix from the *de Marci* family, here in the 13th cent. **Standon, Upper** Beds. *Standone* 1086 (DB).

Stone, 'place at the stone or stones', OE *stān*; examples include: **Stone** Bucks. *Stanes* 1086 (DB). **Stone** Glos. *Stane* 1204. **Stone** Kent, near Dartford. *Stane* 10th cent., *Estanes* 1086 (DB). **Stone** Staffs. *Stanes* 1187.

Ston Easton Somerset, see EASTON.

Stonegrave N. Yorks. *Staningagrave* 757–8, *Stainegrif* 1086 (DB). 'Quarry of the people living by the stone or rock'. OE *stān* + *-inga-* + *græf* (influenced by OScand. *gryfja*).

Stonehenge Wilts. *Stanenges c.*1130. 'Stone gallows' (from a fancied resemblance of the monument to such). OE *stān* + *hengen*.

Stonehouse Glos. *Stanhus* 1086 (DB). 'The stone-built house'. OE *stān* + *hūs*.

Stoneleigh Warwicks. *Stanlei* 1086 (DB). 'Stony woodland clearing'. OE *stān* + *lēah*.

Stonely Cambs. *Stanlegh* 1260. Identical in origin with the previous name.

Stonesby Leics. *Stovenebi* 1086 (DB). Probably 'farmstead or village by a tree-stump'. OE or OScand. *stofn* + *bý*.

Stonesfield Oxon. *Stuntesfeld* 1086 (DB). 'Open land of a man called *Stunt'. OE pers. name + *feld*.

Stonham Aspal & Little Stonham Suffolk. *Stonham c.*1040, *Stanham* 1086 (DB). 'Homestead by a stone or with stony ground'. OE *stān* + *hām*. Aspal is a manorial affix from the *de Aspale* family, here in the 13th cent.

Stonnall Staffs. *Stanahala* 1143. 'Stony nook of land'. OE *stān* + *halh*.

Stonor Oxon. *Stanora* late 10th cent. 'Stony hill-slope'. OE *stān* + *ōra*.

Stonton Wyville Leics. *Stantone* 1086

(DB), *Staunton Wyvile* 1265. 'Farmstead on stony ground'. OE *stān* + *tūn*. Manorial affix from the *de Wivill* family, here in the 13th cent.

Stony Stratford Bucks., see STRATFORD.

Stoodleigh Devon. *Stodlei* 1086 (DB). 'Woodland clearing where a herd of horses is kept'. OE *stōd* + *lēah*.

Stopham W. Sussex. *Stopeham* 1086 (DB). 'Homestead or river-meadow of a man called *Stoppa, or by a hollow'. OE pers. name or OE *stoppa* + *hām* or *hamm*.

Stopsley Beds. *Stoppelee* 1198. 'Woodland clearing of a man called *Stoppa, or by a hollow'. OE pers. name or OE *stoppa* + *lēah*.

Storeton Mersey. *Stortone* 1086 (DB). 'Large farmstead', or 'farmstead near a young wood'. OScand. *stórr* or *storth* + OE *tūn*.

Storridge Heref. & Worcs. *Storugge* 13th cent. 'Stony ridge'. OE *stān* + *hrycg*.

Storrington W. Sussex. *Storgetune* 1086 (DB). Probably 'farmstead or village visited by storks'. OE *storc* + *tūn*.

Stortford, Bishop's Herts. *Storteford* 1086 (DB). 'Ford by the tongues of land'. OE *steort* + *ford*. Affix from its early possession by the Bishop of London.

Storth Cumbria. *Storthes* 1349. 'Brushwood, plantation'. OScand. *storth*.

Stotfold Beds. *Stodfald* 1007, *Stotfalt* 1086 (DB). 'The stud-fold or enclosure for horses'. OE *stōd-fald*.

Stottesdon Shrops. *Stodesdone* 1086 (DB). Probably 'hill where a herd of horses is kept'. OE *stōd* + *dūn*.

Stoughton, 'farmstead at an outlying hamlet', OE *stoc* + *tūn*: **Stoughton** Leics. *Stoctone* 1086 (DB). **Stoughton** Surrey. *Stoctune* 12th cent. **Stoughton** W. Sussex. *Estone* (*sic*) 1086 (DB), *Stoctona* 1121.

Stoulton Heref. & Worcs. *Stoltun* 840, 1086 (DB). 'Farmstead or village with a seat (used at meetings of the Hundred)'. OE *stōl* + *tūn*.

Stourbridge W. Mids. *Sturbrug* 1255. 'Bridge over the River Stour'. Celtic or OE river-name (probably meaning 'the strong one') + OE *brycg*. There are no less than five major rivers in England called Stour, see following names.

Stour, East & West Dorset. *Sture* 1086 (DB). Named from the Dorset/Hants. River Stour, see STOURBRIDGE.

Stourmouth Kent. *Sturmutha* late 11th cent. 'Mouth of the River Stour'. Celtic or OE river-name (see STOURBRIDGE) + OE *mūtha*.

Stourpaine Dorset. *Sture* 1086 (DB), *Stures Paen* 1243. 'Estate on the River Stour held by the *Payn* family' (here in the 13th cent.), see STOUR, EAST & WEST.

Stourport-on-Severn Heref. & Worcs. *Stourport c.*1775. 'Port at the confluence of the Rivers Stour and Severn'. A recent name.

Stour Provost Dorset. *Stur* 1086 (DB), *Sture Preauus* 1270. 'Estate on the River Stour held by the Norman Abbey of Préaux' (during the 12th and 13th centuries), see STOUR, EAST & WEST.

Stourton, 'farmstead or village on one of the rivers called Stour', Celtic or OE river-name (probably meaning 'the strong one') + OE *tūn*: **Stourton** Staffs. *Sturton* 1227. **Stourton** Warwicks. *Sturton* 1206. **Stourton** Wilts. *Stortone* 1086 (DB).

Stourton Caundle Dorset, see CAUNDLE.

Stoven Suffolk. *Stouone* 1086 (DB). '(Place at) the tree-stump(s)'. OE or OScand. *stofn*.

Stow, Stowe, a common name, from OE *stōw* 'place of assembly' or 'holy place'; examples include: **Stow Bardolph** Norfolk. *Stou* 1086 (DB). Manorial affix from the *Bardulf* family, here in the 13th cent. **Stow Bedon** Norfolk. *Stou* 1086 (DB), *Stouwebidun* 1287. Manorial affix from the *de Bidun* family, here in the 13th cent. **Stow cum Quy** Cambs. *Stoua* 1086, *Stowe cum Quey* 1316. Quy is *Coeia* in 1086 (DB), 'cow island' from OE *cū* + *ēg*. Latin *cum* is 'with'. **Stowe** Staffs. *Stowe* 1242. **Stow Maries** Essex. *Stowe* 1222, *Stowe Mareys* 1420. Manorial affix from the *Mareys* family, here in the 13th cent. **Stow on the Wold** Glos. *Eduuardesstou* 1086 (DB), *Stoua* 1213, *Stowe on the Olde* 1574. Originally 'St

Edward's holy place'. Later affix is from OE *wald* 'high ground cleared of forest'.

Stowell, 'stony spring or stream', OE *stān* + *wella*: **Stowell** Somerset. *Stanwelle* 1086 (DB). **Stowell, West** Wilts. *Stawelle* 1176.

Stowey, Nether & Over Somerset. *Stawei* 1086 (DB). 'Stone way'. OE *stān* + *weg*.

Stowford, 'stony ford', OE *stān* + *ford*; examples include: **Stowford** Devon, near Portgate. *Staford* 1086 (DB). **Stowford, East** Devon. *Staveford* 1086 (DB).

Stowlangtoft Suffolk. *Stou* 1086 (DB), *Stowelangetot* 13th cent. OE *stōw* 'place of assembly or holy place', with manorial affix from the *de Langetot* family, here in the 13th cent.

Stowmarket Suffolk. *Stou* 1086 (DB), *Stowmarket* 1268. OE *stōw* as in previous name, here with later addition referring to the important market here.

Stowting Kent. *Stuting* 1044, *Stotinges* 1086 (DB). Probably 'place characterized by a lumpy hillock', OE **stūt* + *-ing*. Alternatively 'place associated with a man called *Stūt', with an OE pers. name as first element.

Stradbroke Suffolk. *Statebroc* (*sic*) 1086 (DB), *Stradebroc* 1168. Possibly 'brook by a paved road'. OE *strǣt* + *brōc*.

Stradsett Norfolk. *Strateseta* 1086 (DB). 'Dwelling or fold on a Roman road'. OE *strǣt* + *(ge)set*.

Stragglethorpe Lincs. *Stragerthorp* 1242. OScand. *thorp* 'outlying farmstead or hamlet' with an uncertain first element, possibly the pers. name or surname of some early owner.

Stramshall Staffs. *Stagrigesholle* (*sic*) 1086 (DB), *Strangricheshull* 1227. Possibly 'hill of a man called *Strangrīc'. OE pers. name + *hyll*.

Strangeways Gtr. Manch. *Strangwas* 1322. Probably '(place by) a stream with a strong current'. OE *strang* + *(ge)wæsc*.

Stratfield, 'open land by a Roman road', OE *strǣt* + *feld*: **Stratfield Mortimer** Berks. *Stradfeld* 1086 (DB), *Stratfeld Mortimer* 1275. Manorial affix from the *de Mortemer* family, here from 1086. **Stratfield Saye & Turgis** Hants. *Stratfeld* c.1060, *Stradfelle* 1086 (DB), *Stratfeld Say* 1277, *Stratfeld Turgys* 1289. Manorial affixes from the *de Say* and *Turgis* families, here in the 13th cent.

Stratford, 'ford on a Roman road', OE *strǣt* + *ford*; examples include: **Stratford** Gtr. London. *Stratford* 1177. **Stratford, Fenny** Bucks. *Fenni Stratford* 1252. Affix is OE *fennig* 'marshy'. **Stratford St Andrew** Suffolk. *Straffort* 1086 (DB). Affix from the dedication of the church. **Stratford, Stony** Bucks. *Stani Stratford* 1202. Affix is OE *stānig* 'stony'. **Stratford Tony** Wilts. *Stretford* 672, *Stradford* 1086 (DB), *Stratford Touny* 14th cent. Manorial affix from the *de Touny* family, here in the 13th cent. **Stratford upon Avon** Warwicks. *Stretfordæ* c.700, *Stradforde* 1086 (DB). Avon is a Celtic river-name meaning simply 'river'. **Stratford, Water** Bucks. *Stradford* 1086 (DB), *West Watrestretford* 1383. Affix is OE *wæter* 'river, stream'.

Stratton, usually 'farmstead or village on a Roman road', OE *strǣt* + *tūn*; examples include: **Stratton Audley** Oxon. *Stratone* 1086 (DB), *Stratton Audeley* 1318. Manorial affix from the *de Alditheleg* family, here in the 13th cent. **Stratton, East & West** Hants. *Strattone* 903, *Stratune* 1086 (DB). **Stratton on the Fosse** Somerset. *Stratone* 1086 (DB). On the great Roman road called FOSSE WAY. **Stratton St Margaret** Wilts. *Stratone* 1086 (DB). Affix from the dedication of the church. **Stratton St Michael & Long Stratton** Norfolk. *Stratuna*, *Stretuna* 1086 (DB). Distinguishing affixes from the dedication of the church and from the length of the village. **Stratton Strawless** Norfolk. *Stratuna* 1086 (DB), *Stratton Streles* 1446. The affix means literally 'lacking in straw', from OE *strēaw* + *-lēas*.

However the following has a different origin: **Stratton** Cornwall. *Strætneat* c.880, *Stratone* 1086 (DB). 'Valley of the River Neet'. Celtic river-name (of uncertain meaning) + Cornish *stras*, with the later addition of OE *tūn* 'village'.

Streat E. Sussex. *Estrat* 1086 (DB). '(Place on or near) a Roman road'. OE *strǣt*.

Streatham Gtr. London. *Estreham* (*sic*) 1086 (DB), *Streteham* 1247. 'Homestead or village on a Roman road'. OE *strǣt* + *hām*.

Streatley, 'woodland clearing by a Roman road', OE *strǣt* + *lēah*: **Streatley** Beds. *Strætlea* c.1053, *Stradlei* 1086 (DB). **Streatley** Berks. *Stretlea* c.690, *Estralei* 1086 (DB).

Street, '(place on or near) a Roman road or other paved highway', OE *strǣt*; for example **Street** (Somerset, near Glastonbury): *Stret* 725.

Streethay Staffs. *Stretheye* 1262. 'Enclosure on a Roman road'. OE *strǣt* + *hæg*.

Streetly, 'woodland clearing by a Roman road', OE *strǣt* + *lēah*: **Streetly** W. Mids. *Strætlea* 957. **Streetly End** Cambs. *Stradleia* 1086.

Strefford Shrops. *Straford* 1086 (DB). 'Ford on a Roman road'. OE *strǣt* + *ford*.

Strensall N. Yorks. *Strenshale* 1086 (DB). Possibly 'nook of land given as a reward, or one used for love-making'. OE *strēon* + *halh*.

Strensham Heref. & Worcs. *Strengesho* 972, *Strenchesham* c.1086. 'Homestead or enclosure of a man called *Strenge'. OE pers. name + *hām* or *hamm* (alternating with *hōh* 'promontory' in the early spelling).

Strete Devon. *Streta* 1194. '(Place on) the Roman road'. OE *strǣt*.

Stretford Gtr. Manch. *Stretford* 1212. 'Ford on a Roman road'. OE *strǣt* + *ford*.

Strethall Essex. *Strathala* 1086 (DB). 'Nook of land by a Roman road'. OE *strǣt* + *halh*.

Stretham Cambs. *Stratham* c.970, *Stradham* 1086 (DB). 'Homestead or village on a Roman road'. OE *strǣt* + *hām*.

Strettington W. Sussex. *Stratone* 1086 (DB), *Estretementona* 12th cent. 'Farmstead or village of the dwellers by the Roman road'. OE *strǣt* + *hǣme* + *tūn*.

Stretton, 'farmstead or village on a Roman road', OE *strǣt* + *tūn*; examples include: **Stretton** Derbys. *Strættune* c.1002, *Stratune* 1086 (DB). **Stretton, All & Church** Shrops. *Stratun* 1086 (DB), *Alured Stretton* 1262, *Chirchestretton* 1337. Distinguishing affixes from the name of an early owner called *Alfred* and from OE *cirice* 'church'. **Stretton Grandison** Heref. & Worcs. *Stratune* 1086 (DB), *Stretton Graundison* 1350. Manorial affix from the *Grandison* family, here in the 14th cent. **Stretton-on-Dunsmore** Warwicks. *Stratone* 1086 (DB). For Dunsmore, see RYTON. **Stretton Sugwas** Heref. & Worcs. *Stratone* 1086 (DB), *Strattone by Sugwas* 1334. Sugwas is 'alluvial land frequented by sparrows', or 'marshy alluvial land', OE **sugge* or **sugga* + **wæsse*.

Strickland, Great & Little Cumbria. *Stircland* late 12th cent. 'Cultivated land where young bullocks are kept'. OE *stirc* + *land*.

Stringston Somerset. *Strengestune* 1086 (DB). 'Farmstead or village of a man called *Strenge'. OE pers. name + *tūn*.

Strixton Northants. *Strixton* 12th cent. 'Farmstead or village of a man called Stríkr'. OScand. pers. name + *tūn*.

Strood, Stroud, 'marshy land overgrown with brushwood', OE *strōd*; examples include: **Strood** Kent, near Rochester. *Strod* 889. **Stroud** Glos. (*La*) *Strode* 1200. **Stroud Green** Gtr. London, near Highbury. *Strode* 1407.

Strubby Lincs., near Alford. *Strobi* 1086 (DB). Probably 'farmstead or village of a man called Strútr'. OScand. pers. name + *bý*.

Strumpshaw Norfolk. *Stromessaga* 1086 (DB). 'Tree-stump wood or copse'. OE **strump* + *sceaga*.

Stubbington Hants. *Stubitone* 1086 (DB). 'Estate associated with a man called *Stubba', OE pers. name + *-ing-* + *tūn*, or 'farmstead at the tree-stump clearing', OE **stubbing* + *tūn*.

Stubbins Gtr. Manch. *Stubbyng* 1563. OE **stubbing* 'place with tree-stumps, a clearing'.

Stubbs, Walden N. Yorks. *Istop* (*sic*) 1086 (DB), *Stubbis* c.1180, *Stubbes Walding* 1280. 'The tree-stumps'. OE *stubb*. Manorial affix from an early owner called *Walding*, here in the 12th cent.

Stubton Lincs. *Stubetune* 1086 (DB). 'Farmstead or village of a man called *Stubba, or where there are tree-stumps'. OE pers. name or *stubb* + *tūn*.

Studdal, East Kent. *Stodwalde* 1240. 'Forest where a herd of horses is kept'. OE *stōd* + *weald*.

Studham Beds. *Stodham* 1053–66, *Estodham* 1086 (DB). 'Homestead or enclosure where a herd of horses is kept'. OE *stōd* + *hām* or *hamm*.

Studland Dorset. *Stollant* 1086 (DB). 'Cultivated land where a herd of horses is kept'. OE *stōd* + *land*.

Studley, 'woodland clearing or pasture where a herd of horses is kept', OE *stōd* + *lēah*: **Studley** Oxon. *Stodleya* c.1185. **Studley** Warwicks. *Stodlei* 1086 (DB). **Studley** Wilts. *Stodleia* 12th cent. **Studley Roger** N. Yorks. *Stodlege* c.1030, *Stollai* 1086 (DB), *Stodelay Roger* 1228. Manorial affix from early possession by *Roger de Mowbray* or by Archbishop *Roger* of York.

Stukeley, Great & Little Cambs. *Stivecle* 1086 (DB). 'Woodland clearing with tree-stumps'. OE **styfic* + *lēah*.

Stuntney Cambs. *Stuntenei* 1086 (DB). 'Steep island'. OE *stunt* (dative *-an*) + *ēg*.

Sturmer Essex. *Sturmere* c.1000, 1086 (DB). 'Pool on the River Stour'. Celtic or OE river-name (probably 'the strong one') + OE *mere*.

Sturminster Marshall Dorset. *Sture minster* 9th cent., *Sturminstre* 1086 (DB), *Sturminìstre Marescal* 1268. 'Church on the River Stour'. Celtic or OE river-name (see STOUR, EAST & WEST) + OE *mynster*. Manorial affix from the *Mareschal* family, here in the 13th cent.

Sturminster Newton Dorset. *Nywetone, at Stoure* 968, *Newentone* 1086 (DB), *Sturminstr Nyweton* 1291. Originally two separate names for places on opposite sides of the river, 'new farmstead or village' from OE *nīwe* + *tūn*, and 'church on the River Stour' (see previous name).

Sturry Kent. *Sturgeh* 678, *Esturai* 1086 (DB). 'District by the River Stour'. Celtic or OE river-name (see STOURMOUTH) + OE **gē*.

Sturton, 'farmstead or village on a Roman road', OE *strǣt* + *tūn*: **Sturton by Stow** Lincs. *Stratone* 1086 (DB). **Sturton, Great** Lincs. *Stratone* 1086 (DB). **Sturton le Steeple** Notts. *Estretone* 1086 (DB). Affix *le Steeple*, first found in the 18th cent., refers to the tower of the church.

Stuston Suffolk. *Stutestuna* 1086 (DB). Probably 'farmstead or village of a man called *Stūt'. OE pers. name + *tūn*.

Stutton N. Yorks. *Stouetun* 1086 (DB). 'Farmstead of a man called Stúfr', or 'one built of or amongst tree-stumps'. OScand. pers. name or *stúfr* + OE *tūn*.

Stutton Suffolk. *Stuttuna* 1086 (DB). 'Farmstead or village infested with gnats, or where bullocks are kept'. OE *stūt* or OScand. *stútr* + OE *tūn*.

Styal Ches. *Styhale* c.1200. 'Nook of land with a pigsty, or by a path'. OE *stigu* or *stīg* + *halh*.

Suckley Heref. & Worcs. *Suchelei* 1086 (DB). 'Woodland clearing frequented by sparrows'. OE **succa* + *lēah*.

Sudborough Northants. *Sutburg* 1086 (DB). 'Southern fortification'. OE *sūth* + *burh*.

Sudbourne Suffolk. *Sutborne* c.1050, *Sutburna* 1086 (DB). 'Southern stream'. OE *sūth* + *burna*.

Sudbrooke Lincs., near Lincoln. *Sutbroc* 1086 (DB). 'Southern brook'. OE *sūth* + *brōc*.

Sudbury, 'southern fortification', OE *sūth* + *burh* (dative *byrig*): **Sudbury** Derbys. *Sudberie* 1086 (DB). **Sudbury** Gtr. London. *Suthbery* 1292. Here the second element may mean 'manor'. **Sudbury** Suffolk. *Suthbyrig* c.995, *Sutberia* 1086 (DB).

Suffield Norfolk. *Sudfelda* 1086 (DB). 'Southern open land'. OE *sūth* + *feld*.

Suffolk (the county). *Suthfolchi* 895, *Sudfulc* 1086 (DB). '(Territory of) the southern people (of the East Angles)'. OE *sūth* + *folc*, see NORFOLK.

Sugnall Staffs. *Sotehelle* (*sic*) 1086 (DB), *Sugenhulle* 1222. 'Hill frequented by sparrows'. OE *sugge (genitive plural -ena) + hyll.

Sulgrave Northants. *Sulgrave* 1086 (DB). 'Grove near a gully or narrow valley'. OE *sulh* + *grāf*.

Sulham Berks. *Soleham* 1086 (DB). Probably 'homestead by a gully'. OE *sulh* + *hām*.

Sulhamstead Berks. *Silamested* 1198. 'Homestead by a gully or narrow valley'. OE *sulh* (genitive *sylh*) + *hām-stede*.

Sullington W. Sussex. *Sillinctune* 959, *Sillintone* 1086 (DB). Possibly 'farmstead or village by a willow copse'. OE **sieling* + *tūn*. Alternatively the first element may be OE **sielling* 'gift', denoting land given as a gift.

Summerseat Gtr. Manch. *Sumersett* 1556. 'Hut or shieling used in summer'. OScand. *sumarr* + *sǽtr*.

Sunbury Surrey. *Sunnanbyrg* 960, *Sunneberie* 1086 (DB). 'Stronghold of a man called *Sunna'. OE pers. name + *burh* (dative *byrig*).

Sunderland, usually 'detached estate', OE *sundor-land*: **Sunderland** Cumbria. *Sonderland* 1278. **Sunderland** Tyne & Wear. *Sunderland* c.1168.

However the following has a different origin: **Sunderland, North** Northum. *Sutherlannland* 12th cent. 'Southern cultivated land'. OE *sūtherra* + *land*.

Sundon Beds. *Sunnandune* c.1050, *Sonedone* 1086 (DB). 'Hill of a man called *Sunna'. OE pers. name + *dūn*.

Sundridge Kent. *Sondresse* 1086 (DB). 'Separate or detached ploughed field'. OE *sundor* + *ersc*.

Sunningdale Berks., a parish-name formed in the 19th cent. from the following name.

Sunninghill Berks. *Sunningehull* 1190. 'Hill of the family or followers of a man called *Sunna'. OE pers. name + *-inga-* + *hyll*.

Sunningwell Oxon. *Sunningauuille* 9th cent., *Soningeuuel* 1086 (DB). 'Spring or stream of the family or followers of a man called *Sunna'. OE pers. name + *-inga-* + *wella*.

Surbiton Gtr. London. *Suberton* 1179. 'Southern grange or outlying farm'. OE *sūth* + *bere-tūn*. See NORBITON.

Surfleet Lincs. *Sverefelt* (*sic*) 1086 (DB), *Surfliet* 1167. 'Sour stream'. OE *sūr* + *flēot*.

Surlingham Norfolk. *Sutherlingaham* 1086 (DB). Probably 'homestead of the family or followers of a man called *Herela', from OE pers. name + *-inga-* + *hām*, with *sūth* 'south'. Alternatively 'homestead of the people living to the south (of Norwich)', OE *sūther* + *-linga-* + *hām*.

Surrey (the county). *Suthrige* 722, *Sudrie* 1086 (DB). 'Southerly district' (relative to MIDDLESEX). OE *sūther* + **gē*.

Sussex (the county). *Suth Seaxe* late 9th cent., *Sudsexe* 1086 (DB). '(Territory of) the South Saxons'. OE *sūth* + *Seaxe*.

Sustead Norfolk. *Sutstede* 1086 (DB). 'Southern place'. OE *sūth* + *stede*.

Sutcombe Devon. *Sutecome* 1086 (DB). 'Valley of a man called *Sutta'. OE pers. name + *cumb*.

Sutterton Lincs. *Suterton* 1200. Probably 'farmstead or village of the shoe-maker(s)'. OE *sūtere* + *tūn*.

Sutton, a very common place-name, 'south farmstead or village', i.e. one to the south of another settlement, OE *sūth* + *tūn*; examples include: **Sutton** Cambs. *Sudtone* 1086 (DB). **Sutton** Gtr. London. *Sudtone* 1086 (DB). **Sutton** Suffolk. *Suthtuna* 1086 (DB). **Sutton Bonington** Notts. *Sudtone, Bonniton* 1086 (DB). Originally two separate manors, Bonington being 'estate associated with a man called Buna', OE pers. name + *-ing-* + *tūn*. **Sutton Bridge** Lincs. named from LONG SUTTON. **Sutton Coldfield** W. Mids. *Sutone* 1086 (DB), *Sutton in Colefeud* 1269. Coldfield is 'open land where charcoal is produced', OE *col* + *feld*. **Sutton Courtenay** Oxon. *Suthtun* c.870, *Sudtone* 1086 (DB), *Suttone Curteney* 1284. Manorial affix from the *Curtenai* family, here in the 12th cent. **Sutton, Full** Humber. *Sudtone* 1086 (DB), *Fulesutton* 1234. Affix is OE *fūl* 'dirty'. **Sutton, Guilden** Ches. *Sudtone* 1086 (DB), *Guldenesutton* c.1200. Affix is OE *gylden* 'splendid, wealthy'. **Sutton in Ashfield** Notts. *Sutone* 1086 (DB),

Sutton in Essefeld 1276. Affix is an old district name, see ASHFIELD. **Sutton, Long** Lincs. *Sudtone* 1086 (DB). Affix refers to the length of the village. **Sutton on Hull** Humber. *Sudtone* 1086 (DB), *Sutune iuxta Hul* 1172. See KINGSTON UPON HULL. **Sutton on Sea** Lincs. *Sudtone* 1086 (DB). **Sutton on Trent** Notts. *Sudtone* 1086 (DB). **Sutton Valence** Kent. *Suthtun* 814, *Sudtone* 1086 (DB), *Sutton Valence* 1316. Manorial affix from the *Valence* family, here in the 13th cent.

Swaby Lincs. *Suabi* 1086 (DB). 'Farmstead or village of a man called Sváfi'. OScand. pers. name + *bý*.

Swadlincote Derbys. *Sivardingescotes* 1086 (DB). Probably 'cottage(s) of a man called *Sweartling or *Svartlingr'. OE or OScand. pers. name + OE *cot*.

Swaffham, 'homestead of the Swabians', OE *Swǣfe* + *hām*: **Swaffham** Norfolk. *Suafham* 1086 (DB). **Swaffham Bulbeck & Prior** Cambs. *Suafham c.*1050, 1086 (DB), *Swafham Bolebek* 1218, *Swafham Prior* 1261. Manorial affixes from early possession by the *de Bolebech* family and by the Prior of Ely.

Swafield Norfolk. *Suafelda* (*sic*) 1086 (DB), *Suathefeld c.*1150. 'Open land characterized by swathes or tracks'. OE *swæth* + *feld*.

Swainby N. Yorks., near Whorlton. *Swaneby* 1314. Probably 'farmstead or village of the young men'. OScand. *sveinn* + *bý*.

Swainsthorpe Norfolk. *Sueinestorp* 1086 (DB). 'Outlying farmstead or hamlet of a man called Sveinn'. OScand. pers. name + *thorp*.

Swalcliffe Oxon. *Sualewclive c.*1166. 'Cliff or slope frequented by swallows'. OE *swealwe* + *clif*.

Swale (river), two examples identical in origin: i) Kent, see SWALECLIFFE, ii) N. Yorks., see BROMPTON ON SWALE.

Swalecliffe Kent. *Swalewanclife* 949, *Soaneclive* (*sic*) 1086 (DB). 'Swallow's river-bank', OE *swealwe* + *clif*, or 'bank by the River Swale' if the first element is the river-name (from OE **swealwe* 'rushing water').

Swallow Lincs. *Sualun* 1086 (DB). Probably '(place on) the rushing stream'. OE **swalwe*.

Swallowcliffe Wilts. *Swealewanclif* 940, *Svaloclive* 1086 (DB). 'Swallow's cliff or slope'. OE *swealwe* + *clif*.

Swallowfield Berks. *Sualefelle* 1086 (DB). 'Open land on the rushing stream'. OE **swealwe* + *feld*.

Swanage Dorset. *Swanawic* late 9th cent., *Swanwic* 1086 (DB). 'Farm of the herdsmen, or farm where swans are reared'. OE *swān* or *swan* + *wīc*.

Swanbourne Bucks. *Suanaburna* 792, *Sueneborne* 1086 (DB). 'Stream frequented by swans'. OE *swan* + *burna*.

Swanland Humber. *Suenelund* 1189. 'Grove of a man called Svanr or Sveinn'. OScand. pers. name + *lundr*.

Swanley Kent, near Farningham. *Swanleg* 1203. Probably 'woodland clearing of the herdsmen'. OE *swān* + *lēah*.

Swanmore Hants. *Suanemere* 1205. 'Pool frequented by swans'. OE *swan* + *mere*.

Swannington, probably 'estate associated with a man called *Swan', OE pers. name + *-ing-* + *tūn*: **Swannington** Leics. *Suaninton* late 12th cent. **Swannington** Norfolk. *Sueningatuna* 1086 (DB).

Swanscombe Kent. *Suanescamp* 695, *Svinescamp* 1086 (DB). 'Enclosed land of the herdsman'. OE *swān* + *camp*.

Swanton, 'farmstead or village of the herdsmen', OE *swān* + *tūn*: **Swanton Abbot** Norfolk. *Suanetuna* 1086 (DB). Affix from early possession by Holme Abbey. **Swanton Morley** Norfolk. *Suanetuna* 1086 (DB). Manorial affix from the *de Morle* family, here in the 14th cent. **Swanton Novers** Norfolk. *Suanetuna* 1086 (DB). Manorial affix from the *de Nuiers* family, here in the 13th cent.

Swanwick, '(dairy) farm of the herdsmen', OE *swān* + *wīc*: **Swanwick** Derbys. *Swanwyk* late 13th cent. **Swanwick** Hants. *Suanewic* 1185.

Swarby Lincs. *Svarrebi* 1086 (DB). 'Farmstead or village of a man called Svarri'. OScand. pers. name + *bý*.

Swardeston Norfolk. *Suerdestuna* 1086 (DB). 'Farmstead or village of a man called *Sweord'. OE pers. name + *tūn*.

Swarkestone Derbys. *Suerchestune* 1086 (DB). Probably 'farmstead or village of a man called Swerkir'. OScand. pers. name + OE *tūn*.

Swarland Northum. *Swarland* 1242. 'Heavy cultivated land'. OE *swǣr* + *land*.

Swaton Lincs. *Svavetone* 1086 (DB). 'Farmstead or village of a man called *Swāfa or Sváfi'. OE or OScand. pers. name + OE *tūn*.

Swavesey Cambs. *Suauesye* 1086 (DB). 'Landing-place of a man called *Swǣf'. OE pers. name ('the Swabian') + *hӯth*.

Sway Hants. *Sueia* 1086 (DB). Possibly an OE river-name meaning 'noisy stream', or from OE *swæth* 'swathe, track'.

Swayfield Lincs. *Suafeld* (*sic*) 1086 (DB), *Suathefeld* 1206. 'Open land characterized by swathes or tracks'. OE *swæth* + *feld*.

Swaythling Hants. *Swætheling e* 909. Probably an old name of the stream here, uncertain in origin and meaning but possibly an OE **swætheling* meaning 'misty stream'.

Swefling Suffolk. *Sueflinga* 1086 (DB), *Sueftlinges c.*1150. Probably '(settlement of) the family or followers of a man called *Swiftel'. OE pers. name + *-ingas*.

Swell, Lower & Upper Glos. *Swelle* 706, *Svelle* 1086 (DB). OE **swelle* 'rising ground or hill'.

Swepstone Leics. *Scopestone* (*sic*) 1086 (DB), *Swepeston c.*1125. 'Farmstead or village of a man called *Sweppi'. OE pers. name + *tūn*.

Swerford Oxon. *Surford* 1086 (DB), *Swereford* 1194. 'Ford by a neck of land or col'. OE *swēora* + *ford*.

Swettenham Ches. *Suetenham* late 12th cent. 'Homestead or enclosure of a man called Swēta'. OE pers. name (genitive *-n*) + *hām* or *hamm*.

Swilland Suffolk. *Suinlanda* 1086 (DB). 'Cultivated land where pigs are kept'. OE *swīn* + *land*.

Swillington W. Yorks. *Suillintune* 1086 (DB). Possibly 'farmstead near the pig hill (or clearing)'. OE *swīn* + *hyll* (or *lēah*) + *-ing-* + *tūn*.

Swimbridge Devon. *Birige* 1086 (DB), *Svimbrige* 1225. '(Place at) the bridge held by a man called Sǣwine'. OE pers. name (of the tenant in 1086) + *brycg*.

Swinbrook Oxon. *Svinbroc* 1086 (DB). 'Pig brook'. OE *swīn* + *brōc*.

Swinderby Lincs. *Sunderby*, *Suindrebi* 1086 (DB). Possibly 'southern farmstead or village', OScand. *sundri* + *bý*. Alternatively 'animal farmstead where pigs are kept', OScand. *svín* + *djúr* + *bý*.

Swindon, 'hill where pigs are kept', OE *swīn* + *dūn*: **Swindon** Glos. *Svindone* 1086 (DB). **Swindon** Staffs. *Swineduna* 1167. **Swindon** Wilts. *Svindune* 1086 (DB).

Swine Humber. *Suuine* 1086 (DB). '(Place at) the creek or channel'. OE **swin*.

Swinefleet Humber. *Swyneflet c.*1195. Probably 'stretch of river where pigs are kept'. OE *swīn* + *flēot*.

Swineshead, 'pig's headland or hill', OE *swīn* + *hēafod*: **Swineshead** Beds. *Suineshefet* 1086 (DB). **Swineshead** Lincs. *Suinesheabde* 786–96.

Swinford, 'pig ford', OE *swīn* + *ford*: **Swinford** Leics. *Svineford* 1086 (DB). **Swinford** Oxon. *Swynford* 931.

Swingfield Minnis Kent. *Suinafeld c.*1100. 'Open land where pigs are kept'. OE *swīn* + *feld*. Affix is OE *mǣnnes* 'common land'.

Swinhoe Northum. *Swinhou* 1242. 'Swine headland'. OE *swīn* + *hōh*.

Swinhope Lincs. *Suinhope* 1086 (DB). 'Valley where pigs are kept'. OE *swīn* + *hop*.

Swinithwaite N. Yorks. *Swiningethwait* 1202. 'Place cleared by burning'. OScand. *svithningr* + *thveit*.

Swinscoe Staffs. *Swyneskow* 1248. 'Swine wood'. OScand. *svín* + *skógr*.

Swinstead Lincs. *Suinhamstede* 1086 (DB). 'Homestead where pigs are kept'. OE *swīn* + *hām-stede*.

Swinton, 'pig farm', OE *swīn* + *tūn*: **Swinton** Gtr. Manch. *Suinton* 1258. **Swinton** N. Yorks., near Masham. *Suinton* 1086 (DB). **Swinton** S. Yorks. *Suintone* 1086 (DB).

Swithland Leics. *Swithellund c.*1215. 'Grove by the burnt clearing'. OScand. *svitha* + *lundr*.

Swynnerton Staffs. *Sulvertone* (*sic*) 1086 (DB), *Suinuerton* 1242. 'Farmstead by the pig ford'. OE *swīn* + *ford* + *tūn*.

Swyre Dorset. *Suere* 1086 (DB). OE *swēora* 'a neck of land, a col'.

Syde Glos. *Side* 1086 (DB). 'Long hill-slope'. OE *sīde*.

Sydenham Gtr. London. *Chipeham* 1206. Probably 'homestead or enclosure of a man called *Cippa'. OE pers. name (genitive *-n*) + *hām* or *hamm*.

Sydenham Oxon. *Sidreham* (*sic*) 1086 (DB), *Sidenham* 1216. 'Broad or extensive enclosure'. OE *sīd* (dative *-an*) + *hamm*.

Sydenham Damerel Devon. *Sidelham* (*sic*) 1086 (DB), *Sydenham Albemarlie* 1297. Identical in origin with the previous name. Manorial affix from the *de Albemarle* family, here in the 13th cent.

Syderstone Norfolk. *Cidesterna* 1086 (DB). Possibly 'broad or extensive property', OE *sīd* + **sterne*. Alternatively 'pool of a man called *Siduhere', OE pers. name + OScand. *tjǫrn*.

Sydling St Nicholas Dorset. *Sidelyng* 934, *Sidelince* 1086 (DB). 'Broad ridge'. OE *sīd* + *hlinc*. Affix from the dedication of the church.

Sydmonton Hants. *Sidemanestone* 1086 (DB). 'Farmstead or village of a man called Sidumann'. OE pers. name + *tūn*.

Syerston Notts. *Sirestune* 1086 (DB). 'Farmstead or village of a man called Sigehere'. OE pers. name + *tūn*.

Sykehouse S. Yorks. *Sikehouse* 1404. 'House(s) by the stream'. OScand. *sík* + *hús*.

Symondsbury Dorset. *Simondesberge* 1086 (DB). 'Hill or barrow of a man called Sigemund'. OE pers. name + *beorg*.

Syresham Northants. *Sigresham* 1086 (DB). 'Homestead or enclosure of a man called Sigehere'. OE pers. name + *hām* or *hamm*.

Syston Leics. *Sitestone* 1086 (DB). Possibly 'farmstead or village of a man called Sigehæth'. OE pers. name + *tūn*.

Syston Lincs. *Sidestan* 1086 (DB). 'Broad stone'. OE *sīd* + *stān*.

Sywell Northants. *Siwella* 1086 (DB). 'Seven springs'. OE *seofon* + *wella*.

T

Tabley, Over Ches. *Stabelei* (*sic*) 1086 (DB), *Thabbelewe* 12th cent. 'Woodland clearing of a man called Tæbba'. OE pers. name + *lēah*.

Tackley Oxon. *Tachelie* 1086 (DB). 'Woodland clearing of a man called *Tæcca, or where young sheep are kept'. OE pers. name or OE **tacca* + *lēah*.

Tacolneston Norfolk. *Tacoluestuna* 1086 (DB). 'Farmstead or village of a man called Tātwulf'. OE pers. name + *tūn*.

Tadcaster N. Yorks. *Tatecastre* 1086 (DB). 'Roman town of a man called Tāta or *Tāda'. OE pers. name + *cæster*.

Taddington Derbys. *Tadintune* 1086 (DB). 'Estate associated with a man called *Tāda'. OE pers. name + *-ing-* + *tūn*.

Tadley Hants. *Tadanleage* 909. Probably 'woodland clearing of a man called *Tāda'. OE pers. name + *lēah*.

Tadlow Cambs. *Tadeslaue c.*1080, *Tadelai* 1086 (DB). 'Tumulus of a man called *Tāda'. OE pers. name + *hlāw*.

Tadmarton Oxon. *Tademærtun* 956, *Tademertone* 1086 (DB). Probably 'farmstead by a pool frequented by toads'. OE **tāde* + *mere* + *tūn*.

Tadworth Surrey. *Thæddeuurthe* 1062, *Tadeorde* 1086 (DB). Possibly 'enclosure of a man called *Thædda'. OE pers. name + *worth*.

Takeley Essex. *Tacheleia* 1086 (DB). 'Woodland clearing of a man called *Tæcca, or where young sheep are kept'. OE pers. name or OE **tacca* + *lēah*.

Talaton Devon. *Taletone* 1086 (DB). 'Farmstead or village on the River Tale'. OE river-name (meaning 'the swift one') + *tūn*.

Talke Staffs. *Talc* 1086 (DB). Possibly an old name for the ridge here, but of obscure origin.

Talkin Cumbria. *Talcan c.*1195. Probably a Celtic name meaning 'white brow (of a hill)'.

Tallentire Cumbria. *Talentir c.*1160. Probably a Celtic name meaning 'end of the land'.

Tallington Lincs. *Talintune* 1086 (DB). Probably 'estate associated with a man called *Tæl or *Tala'. OE pers. name + *-ing-* + *tūn*.

Tame (river), three examples, see THAMES.

Tamerton, 'farmstead or village on the River Tamar', Celtic river-name (possibly 'the dark one' or simply 'river') + OE *tūn*: **Tamerton Foliot** Devon. *Tambretone* 1086 (DB), *Tamereton Foliot* 1262. Manorial affix from the *Foliot* family, here from the 13th cent. **Tamerton, North** Cornwall. *Tamerton* 1180.

Tamworth Staffs. *Tamouuorthig* 781, *Tamuuorde* 1086 (DB). 'Enclosure on the River Tame'. Celtic river-name (possibly 'the dark one' or simply 'river') + OE *worthig* (replaced by *worth*).

Tandridge Surrey. *Tenhric c.*965, *Tenrige* 1086 (DB). OE *hrycg* 'ridge, hill' with an uncertain first element.

Tanfield Durham. *Tamefeld* 1179. 'Open land on the River Team'. Celtic river-name (possibly 'the dark one' or simply 'river') + OE *feld*.

Tanfield, East & West N. Yorks. *Tanefeld* 1086 (DB). Possibly 'open land where shoots or osiers grow'. OE *tān* + *feld*.

Tangley Hants. *Tangelea* 1175. Possibly 'woodland clearing at the spits of land'. OE *tang* + *lēah*.

Tangmere W. Sussex. *Tangmere* 680,

Tangemere 1086 (DB). Possibly 'tongs-shaped pool'. OE *tang* + *mere*.

Tankersley S. Yorks. *Tancresleia* 1086 (DB). 'Woodland clearing of a man called Thancrēd'. OE (or OGerman) pers. name + *lēah*.

Tannington Suffolk. *Tatintuna* 1086 (DB). 'Estate associated with a man called Tāta'. OE pers. name + *-ing-* + *tūn*.

Tansley Derbys. *Taneslege* 1086 (DB). Probably 'woodland clearing of a man called *Tān', OE pers. name + *lēah*. Alternatively the first element may be OE *tān* 'branch' (perhaps used of 'a valley branching off from the main valley').

Tansor Northants. *Tanesovre* 1086 (DB). Probably 'promontory or bank of a man called *Tān', OE pers. name + **ofer* or *ōfer*. Alternatively the first element may be OE *tān* 'branch' as in previous name.

Tanton N. Yorks. *Tametun* 1086 (DB). 'Farmstead or village on the River Tame'. Celtic river-name (possibly 'the dark one' or simply 'river') + OE *tūn*.

Taplow Bucks. *Thapeslau* 1086 (DB). 'Tumulus of a man called *Tæppa'. OE pers. name + *hlāw*.

Tarbock Green Mersey. *Torboc* 1086 (DB), *Thornebrooke* c.1240. Probably 'thorn-tree brook'. OE *thorn* + *brōc*.

Tarlton Glos. *Torentune* (*sic*) 1086 (DB), *Torleton* 1204. Probably 'farmstead at the thorn-tree clearing'. OE *thorn* + *lēah* + *tūn*.

Tarporley Ches. *Torpelei* 1086 (DB), *Thorperlegh* 1281. Possibly 'woodland clearing of the peasants or cottagers'. OE **thorpere* + *lēah*.

Tarrant, Celtic river-name possibly meaning 'the trespasser', i.e. 'river liable to floods', and giving name to the following: **Tarrant Crawford** Dorset. *Tarente* 1086 (DB), *Little Craweford* 1280. Distinguishing affix from *Craveford* 1086 (DB), 'ford frequented by crows', OE *crāwe* + *ford*. **Tarrant Gunville** Dorset. *Tarente* 1086 (DB), *Tarente Gundevill* 1233. Manorial affix from the *Gundeville* family, here in the 12th cent. **Tarrant Hinton** Dorset. *Terente* 9th cent., *Tarente* 1086 (DB), *Tarente Hyneton* 1280. 'Estate on the River Tarrant belonging to a religious community (Shaftesbury Abbey)'. OE *hīwan* + *tūn*. **Tarrant Keyneston** Dorset. *Tarente* 1086 (DB), *Tarente Kahaines* 1225. 'Estate held by the *Cahaignes* family', here from the 12th cent. **Tarrant Launceston** Dorset. *Tarente* 1086 (DB), *Tarente Louweniston* 1280. 'Estate held by a man called *Lēofwine* or a family called *Lowin*'. **Tarrant Monkton** Dorset. *Tarente* 1086 (DB), *Tarent Moneketon* 1280. 'Estate belonging to the monks (of Tewkesbury Abbey)'. OE *munuc* + *tūn*. **Tarrant Rawston** Dorset. *Tarente* 1086 (DB), *Tarrant Rawston alias Antyocke* 1535. 'Ralph's estate', earlier 'estate held by the *Antioch* family'. **Tarrant Rushton** Dorset. *Tarente* 1086 (DB), *Tarente Russeus* 1280. 'Estate held by the *de Rusceaus* family', here in the 13th cent.

Tarring Neville E. Sussex. *Toringes* 1086 (DB), *Thoring Nevell* 1339. Possibly '(settlement of) the family or followers of a man called *Teorra', OE pers. name + *-ingas*. Alternatively 'dwellers at the rocky hill', OE *torr* + *-ingas*. Manorial affix from the *de Neville* family, here in the 13th cent.

Tarrington Heref. & Worcs. *Tatintune* 1086 (DB). 'Estate associated with a man called Tāta'. OE pers. name + *-ing-* + *tūn*.

Tarvin Ches. *Terve* (*sic*) 1086 (DB), *Teruen* 1185. Celtic river-name meaning 'boundary (stream)', the old name of the River Gowy.

Tasburgh Norfolk. *Taseburc* 1086 (DB). Probably 'stronghold of a man called *Tǣsa'. OE pers. name + *burh*.

Tasley Shrops. *Tasselegh* 1230. OE *lēah* 'wood, clearing' with an uncertain first element.

Tatenhill Staffs. *Tatenhyll* 942. 'Hill of a man called Tāta'. OE pers. name (genitive *-n*) + *hyll*.

Tatham Lancs. *Tathaim* 1086 (DB). 'Homestead of a man called Tāta'. OE pers. name + *hām*.

Tathwell Lincs. *Tadewelle* 1086 (DB). 'Spring or stream frequented by toads'. OE **tāde* + *wella*.

Tatsfield Surrey. *Tatelefelle* 1086 (DB).

'Open land of a man called Tātel'. OE pers. name + *feld*.

Tattenhall Ches. *Tatenale* 1086 (DB). 'Nook of land of a man called Tāta'. OE pers. name (genitive *-n*) + *halh*.

Tatterford Norfolk. *Taterforda* 1086 (DB). 'Ford of a man called Tāthere'. OE pers. name + *ford*.

Tattersett Norfolk. *Tatessete* 1086 (DB). 'Fold of a man called Tāthere'. OE pers. name + *set*.

Tattershall Lincs. *Tateshale* 1086 (DB). 'Nook of land of a man called Tāthere'. OE pers. name + *halh*.

Tattingstone Suffolk. *Tatistuna* (*sic*) 1086 (DB), *Tatingeston* 1219. Possibly 'farmstead of a man called *Tāting', OE pers. name + *tūn*. Alternatively 'farmstead at the place associated with a man called Tāta', OE pers. name + *-ing* + *tūn*.

Taunton Somerset. *Tantun* 737, *Tantone* 1086 (DB). 'Farmstead or village on the River Tone'. Celtic river-name (possibly 'roaring stream') + OE *tūn*.

Taverham Norfolk. *Taverham* 1086 (DB). 'Red-lead homestead or enclosure', perhaps referring to a red-painted building or to soil colour. OE *tēafor* + *hām* or *hamm*.

Tavistock Devon. *Tauistoce* 981, *Tavestoc* 1086 (DB). 'Outlying farmstead or hamlet by the River Tavy'. Celtic river-name (possibly 'dark stream') + OE *stoc*.

Tavy, Mary & Peter Devon. *Tavi*, *Tawi* 1086 (DB), *Tavymarie* 1412, *Petri Tavy* 1270. Named from the River Tavy, see previous name. Distinguishing affixes from the dedications of their churches.

Tawstock Devon. *Tauestoca* 1086 (DB). 'Outlying farmstead or hamlet on the River Taw'. Celtic river-name (see next name) + OE *stoc*.

Tawton, 'farmstead or village on the River Taw', Celtic river-name (possibly 'strong or silent stream') + OE *tūn*: **Tawton, Bishop's** Devon. *Tautona* 1086 (DB), *Tautone Episcopi* 1284. Affix from its possession by the Bishop (Latin *episcopus*) of Exeter in 1086. **Tawton, North & South** Devon. *Tawetone*, *Tavetone* 1086 (DB).

Taxal Derbys. *Tackeshale* c.1251. Possibly 'nook of land held on lease'. ME *tak* + OE *halh*.

Taynton Glos. *Tetinton* 1086 (DB). 'Estate associated with a man called Tǣta'. OE pers. name + *-ing-* + *tūn*.

Tealby Lincs. *Tavelesbi* 1086 (DB). Possibly 'farmstead or village at a square or flat piece of land'. OScand. *tafl* or OE **tefli* + OScand. *bý*.

Team (river) Durham, gives name to TANFIELD, see THAMES.

Tean, Lower & Upper Staffs. *Tene* 1086 (DB). Named from the River Tean, a Celtic river-name probably meaning simply 'stream'.

Tebay Cumbria. *Tibeia* c.1160. 'Island of a man called Tiba'. OE pers. name + *ēg*.

Tebworth Beds. *Teobbanwyrthe* 962. 'Enclosure of a man called *Teobba'. OE pers. name (genitive *-n*) + *worth*.

Tedburn St Mary Devon. *Teteborne* 1086 (DB). '(Place at) the stream of a woman called Tette or a man called *Tetta'. OE pers. name + *burna*.

Teddington Glos. *Teottingtun* 780, *Teotintune* 1086 (DB). 'Estate associated with a man called *Teotta'. OE pers. name + *-ing-* + *tūn*.

Teddington Gtr. London. *Tudintun* 969. 'Estate associated with a man called Tuda'. OE pers. name + *-ing-* + *tūn*.

Tedstone Delamere & Wafre Heref. & Worcs. *Tedesthorne* 1086 (DB), *Teddesthorn la Mare*, *Teddesthorne Wafre* 1249. Probably 'thorn-tree of a man called *Tēod'. OE pers. name + *thorn*. Manorial affixes from early possession by the *de la Mare* and *le Wafre* families.

Tees (river) Cumbria-Cleveland, see STOCKTON ON TEES.

Teeton Northants. *Teche* (*sic*) 1086 (DB), *Teacne* 1195. '(Hill with) a beacon'. OE **tǣcne*.

Teffont Evias & Magna Wilts. *Tefunte* 860, *Tefonte* 1086 (DB), *Teffunt Ewyas* 1275. 'Boundary spring'. OE **tēo* + **funta*. Manorial affix from possession by the barons of *Ewyas* in the 13th cent.; the other affix is Latin *magna* 'great'.

Teigh Leics. *Tie* 1086 (DB). OE *tēag* 'a small enclosure'.

Teigngrace Devon. *Taigne* 1086 (DB), *Teyngegras* 1331. Named from the River Teign, a Celtic river-name meaning simply 'stream'. Manorial affix from the *Gras* family, here in the 14th cent.

Teignmouth Devon. *Tengemutha* 1044. 'Mouth of the River Teign'. Celtic river-name (see previous name) + OE *mūtha*.

Telford Shrops., a modern name commemorating the engineer Thomas *Telford* (1757–1834), famous for his bridges, roads, and canals.

Tellisford Somerset. *Tefleforth* 1001, *Tablesford* 1086 (DB). Possibly 'ford at a flat or level place', OE **tefli* + *ford*. Alternatively the first element may be the OE pers. name *Theabul*.

Telscombe E. Sussex. *Titelescumbe* 966. 'Valley of a man called *Titel'. OE pers. name + *cumb*.

Teme (river) Shrops.–Heref. & Worcs., see TENBURY WELLS.

Temple as affix, see main name, e.g. for **Temple Cloud** (Avon) see CLOUD.

Templeton Devon. *Templum* 1206, *Templeton* 1334. 'Manor held by the Knights Templars'. ME *temple* + OE *tūn*.

Tenbury Wells Heref. & Worcs. *Tamedeberie* 1086 (DB). 'Stronghold on the River Teme'. Celtic river-name (possibly 'the dark one') + OE *burh*. The addition *Wells* referring to the spa here is only recent.

Tendring Essex. *Tendringa* 1086 (DB). Possibly 'place where tinder or fuel is gathered'. OE *tynder* + *-ing*.

Tenterden Kent. *Tentwardene* 1179. 'Woodland pasture of the Thanet dwellers'. THANET + OE *-ware* + *denn*.

Terling Essex. *Terlinges* 1017–35, *Terlingas* 1086 (DB). '(Settlement of) the family or followers of a man called Tyrhtel'. OE pers. name + *-ingas*.

Tern (river) Shrops., see EATON UPON TERN.

Terrington N. Yorks. *Teurinctune* 1086 (DB). Possibly 'estate associated with a man called *Teofer'. OE pers. name + *-ing-* + *tūn*.

Terrington St Clement & St John Norfolk. *Tilinghetuna* 1086 (DB), *Terintona* 1121. 'Farmstead of the family or followers of a man called *Tīr(a)'. OE pers. name + *-inga-* + *tūn*. Distinguishing affixes from the dedications of the churches.

Teston Kent. *Terstan* 10th cent., *Testan* 1086 (DB). 'Stone with a gap or hole'. OE *tær* + *stān*.

Testwood Hants. *Lesteorde* (*sic*) 1086 (DB), *Terstewode* c.1185. 'Wood by the River Test'. Celtic or pre-Celtic river-name (obscure in origin and meaning) + OE *wudu*.

Tetbury Glos. *Tettanbyrg* c.900, *Teteberie* 1086 (DB). 'Fortified place of a woman called Tette'. OE pers. name + *burh* (dative *byrig*).

Tetcott Devon. *Tetecote* 1086 (DB). 'Cottage of a woman called Tette or of a man called *Tetta'. OE pers. name + *cot*.

Tetford Lincs. *Tedforde* 1086 (DB). 'People's or public ford'. OE *thēod* + *ford*.

Tetney Lincs. *Tatenai* 1086 (DB). 'Island of a man called Tǣta'. OE pers. name (genitive *-n*) + *ēg*.

Tetsworth Oxon. *Tetleswrthe* c.1150. 'Enclosure of a man called *Tǣtel'. OE pers. name + *worth*.

Tettenhall W. Mids. *Teotanheale* early 10th cent., *Totenhale* 1086 (DB). 'Nook of land of a man called *Tēotta'. OE pers. name (genitive *-n*) + *halh*.

Teversal Notts. *Tevreshalt* 1086 (DB). 'Shelter of the painter or sorcerer, or of a man called *Teofer'. OE *tīefrere* or pers. name + *hald*.

Teversham Cambs. *Teuersham* 1086 (DB). 'Homestead of the painter or sorcerer, or of a man called *Teofer'. OE *tīefrere* or pers. name + *hām*.

Tew, Great & Little, Duns Tew Oxon. *Tiwan* 1004, *Tewe*, *Teowe* 1086 (DB), *Donestiua* c.1210. Possibly an OE **tīewe* 'row or ridge'. Manorial affix from early possession by a man called *Dunn*.

Tewin Herts. *Tiwingum* 944–6, *Teuuinge* 1086 (DB). Possibly '(settlement of) the family or followers of a man called *Tīwa'. OE pers. name + *-ingas*.

Tewkesbury Glos. *Teodekesberie* 1086 (DB). 'Fortified place of a man called *Tēodec'. OE pers. name + *burh* (dative *byrig*).

Tey, Great & Marks Essex. *Tygan* c.950, *Teia* 1086 (DB), *Merkys Teye* 1475. From OE **tīege* 'enclosure'. Manorial affix from possession by the *de Merck* family.

Teynham Kent. *Teneham* 798, *Therham* (*sic*) 1086 (DB). Probably 'homestead of a man called *Tēna'. OE pers. name + *hām*.

Thakeham W. Sussex. *Taceham* 1086 (DB). 'Homestead with a thatched roof'. OE *thaca* + *hām*.

Thame Oxon. *Tame* c.1000, 1086 (DB). Named from the River Thame, a Celtic river-name, see THAMES.

Thames (river) Glos.-London. *Tamesis* 51 BC. An ancient Celtic river-name possibly meaning 'dark one' or simply 'river'. The river-names **Tame** (three examples, N. Yorks., Warwicks.-Staffs., W. Yorks.-Ches.), **Team** (Durham), **Thame** (Bucks.-Oxon.), and (with a different ending) **Tamar** (Cornwall-Devon) are from the same root and probably have a similar meaning.

Thames Ditton Surrey, see DITTON.

Thamesmead Gtr. London, a recent name for a new development by the Thames.

Thanet Kent. *Tanatus* 3rd cent., *Tanet* 1086 (DB). A Celtic name possibly meaning 'bright island', perhaps with reference to a beacon.

Thanington Kent. *Tanningtune* 833. Possibly 'estate associated with a man called *Tān'. OE pers. name + *-ing-* + *tūn*.

Tharston Norfolk. *Therstuna* 1086 (DB). 'Farmstead or village of a man called Therir'. OScand. pers. name + OE *tūn*.

Thatcham Berks. *Thæcham* c.954, *Taceham* 1086 (DB). 'Thatched homestead, or river-meadow where thatching materials are got'. OE **thæcce* + *hām* or *hamm*.

Thatto Heath Mersey. *Thetwall* 12th cent. 'Spring or stream with a water-pipe'. OE *thēote* + *wella*.

Thaxted Essex. *Tachesteda* 1086 (DB). 'Place where thatching materials are got'. OE *thæc* + *stede*.

Theakston N. Yorks. *Eston* (*sic*) 1086 (DB), *Thekeston* 1157. Probably 'farmstead or village of a man called *Thēodec'. OE pers. name + *tūn*.

Thealby Humber. *Tedulfbi* 1086 (DB). 'Farmstead or village of a man called Thjóthulfr'. OScand. pers. name + *bý*.

Theale, 'the planks' (referring to a bridge or building), OE *thel* in a plural form *thelu*: **Theale** Berks. *Teile* 1208. **Theale** Somerset. *Thela* 1176.

Thearne Humber. *Thoren* 1297. 'The thorn-tree'. OE *thorn*.

Theberton Suffolk. *Thewardetuna* (*sic*) 1086 (DB), *Tiberton* 1178. 'Farmstead or village of a man called Thēodbeorht'. OE pers. name + *tūn*.

Thedden Grange Hants. *Tedena* (*sic*) 1168, *Thetdene* 1234. 'Valley with a water-pipe'. OE *thēote* + *denu*.

Theddingworth Leics. *Tedingesworde* (*sic*) 1086 (DB), *Tedingewrth* 1206. Probably 'enclosure of the family or followers of a man called *Thēoda'. OE pers. name + *-inga-* + *worth*.

Theddlethorpe Lincs. *Tedlagestorp* 1086 (DB). Possibly 'outlying farmstead or hamlet of a man called *Thēodlāc'. OE pers. name + OScand. *thorp*.

Thelbridge Devon. *Talebrige* 1086 (DB). 'Plank bridge'. OE *thel* + *brycg*.

Thelnetham Suffolk. *Thelueteham* 1086 (DB). Possibly 'enclosure frequented by swans near a plank bridge'. OE *thel* + *elfitu* + *hamm*.

Thelwall Ches. *Thelwæle* 923. 'Pool by a plank bridge'. OE *thel* + *wēl*.

Themelthorpe Norfolk. *Timeltorp* 1203. 'Outlying farmstead or hamlet of a man called *Thȳmel or *Thymill'. OE or OScand. pers. name + *thorp*.

Thenford Northants. *Taneford* 1086 (DB). 'Ford of the thegns or retainers'. OE *thegn* + *ford*.

Therfield Herts. *Therefeld* 1060, *Derevelde* 1086 (DB). 'Dry open land'. OE *thyrre* + *feld*.

Thetford, 'people's or public ford', OE *thēod* + *ford*: **Thetford** Norfolk. *Theodford* late 9th cent., *Tedfort* 1086 (DB). **Thetford, Little** Cambs.

Thiutforda c.972, *Liteltedford* 1086 (DB). Affix is OE *lȳtel.*

Theydon Bois Essex. *Thecdene* 1062, *Teidana* 1086 (DB), *Teidon Boys* 1257. Probably 'valley where thatching materials are got'. OE *thæc* + *denu.* Manorial affix from the *de Bosco* or *de Boys* family, here in the 12th cent.

Thimbleby, 'farmstead or village of a man called *Thymill or *Thymli', OScand. pers. name + *bý*: **Thimbleby** Lincs. *Stimblebi* (*sic*) 1086 (DB), *Timblebi* c.1115. **Thimbleby** N. Yorks. *Timbelbi* 1086 (DB).

Thingwall Mersey. *Tinguelle* 1086 (DB). 'Field where an assembly meets'. OScand. *thing-vǫllr.*

Thirkleby N. Yorks. *Turchilebi* 1086 (DB). 'Farmstead or village of a man called Thorkell'. OScand. pers. name + *bý.*

Thirlby N. Yorks. *Trillebia* 1187. 'Farmstead or village of a man called *Thrylli, or of the thralls'. OScand. pers. name or *thrǽll* + *bý.*

Thirn N. Yorks. *Thirne* 1086 (DB). 'The thorn-tree'. OE *thyrne.*

Thirsk N. Yorks. *Tresch* 1086 (DB). OScand. **thresk* 'a marsh'.

Thirston, East Northum. *Thrasfriston* 1242. Possibly 'farmstead or village of a man called *Thræsfrith'. OE pers. name + *tūn.*

Thistleton, 'farmstead or village where thistles grow', OE *thistel* + *tūn*: **Thistleton** Lancs. *Thistilton* 1212. **Thistleton** Leics. *Tisteltune* 1086 (DB).

Thixendale N. Yorks. *Sixtendale* 1086 (DB). 'Valley of a man called Sigsteinn'. OScand. pers. name + *dalr.*

Tholthorpe N. Yorks. *Turulfestorp* 1086 (DB). 'Outlying farmstead or hamlet of a man called Thórulfr'. OScand. pers. name + *thorp.*

Thompson Norfolk. *Tomestuna* 1086 (DB). 'Farmstead or village of a man called Tumi'. OScand. pers. name + OE *tūn.*

Thong Kent. *Thuange* c.1200. 'Narrow strip of land'. OE *thwang.*

Thoralby N. Yorks. *Turoldesbi* 1086 (DB). Probably 'farmstead or village of a man called Thóraldr'. OScand. pers. name + *bý.*

Thoresby Notts. *Thuresby* 958, *Turesbi* 1086 (DB). 'Farmstead or village of a man called Thūrir'. OScand. pers. name + *bý.*

Thoresby, North Lincs. *Toresbi* 1086 (DB). 'Farmstead or village of a man called Thórir'. OScand. pers. name + *bý.*

Thoresby, South Lincs. *Toresbi* 1086 (DB). Identical in origin with the previous name.

Thoresway Lincs. *Toreswe* 1086 (DB). 'Way or road of a man called Thórir'. OScand. pers. name + OE *weg.*

Thorganby, 'farmstead or village of a man called Thorgrímr', OScand. pers. name + *bý*: **Thorganby** Lincs. *Turgrimbi* 1086 (DB). **Thorganby** N. Yorks. *Turgisbi* (*sic*) 1086 (DB), *Turgrimebi* 1192.

Thorington Suffolk. *Torentuna* 1086 (DB). 'Thorn-tree enclosure or farmstead'. OE *thorn* or *thyrne* + *tūn.*

Thorlby N. Yorks. *Toreilderebi* 1086 (DB). 'Farmstead or village of a man called Thóraldr, or of a woman called Thórhildr'. OScand. pers. name + *bý.*

Thorley, 'thorn-tree wood or clearing', OE *thorn* + *lēah*: **Thorley** Herts. *Torlei* 1086 (DB). **Thorley** I. of Wight. *Torlei* 1086 (DB).

Thormanby N. Yorks. *Tormozbi* 1086 (DB). 'Farmstead or village of a man called Thormóthr'. OScand. pers. name + *bý.*

Thornaby on Tees Cleveland. *Tormozbi* 1086 (DB). Identical in origin with the previous name.

Thornage Norfolk. *Tornedis* 1086 (DB). 'Thorn-tree enclosure or pasture'. OE *thorn* + *edisc.*

Thornborough, 'hill where thorn-trees grow', OE *thorn* + *beorg*: **Thornborough** Bucks. *Torneberge* 1086 (DB). **Thornborough** N. Yorks. *Thornbergh* 1198.

Thornbury, 'fortified place where thorn-trees grow', OE *thorn* + *burh* (dative *byrig*): **Thornbury** Avon. *Turneberie* 1086 (DB). **Thornbury** Devon. *Torneberie* 1086 (DB).

Thornbury Heref. & Worcs. *Thornbyrig* c.1000, *Torneberie* 1086 (DB).

Thornby Northants. *Torneberie* 1086 (DB), *Thirnebi* c.1160. 'Farmstead or village where thorn-trees grow'. OScand. *thyrnir* + *bý* (replacing OE *burh* 'stronghold').

Thorncombe, 'valley where thorn-trees grow', OE *thorn* + *cumb*: **Thorncombe** Dorset, near Blandford. *Tornecome* 1086 (DB). **Thorncombe** Dorset, near Holditch. *Tornecoma* 1086 (DB).

Thorndon Suffolk. *Tornduna* 1086 (DB). 'Hill where thorn-trees grow'. OE *thorn* + *dūn*.

Thorne, '(place at) the thorn-tree', OE *thorn*: **Thorne** S. Yorks. *Torne* 1086 (DB). **Thorne St Margaret** Somerset. *Torne* 1086 (DB), *Thorn St Margaret* 1251. Affix from the dedication of the church.

Thorner W. Yorks. *Tornoure* 1086 (DB). 'Ridge or bank where thorn-trees grow'. OE *thorn* + **ofer*.

Thorney, usually 'thorn-tree island', OE *thorn* + *ēg*; examples include: **Thorney** Cambs. *Thornige* c.960, *Torny* 1086 (DB). **Thorney, West** W. Sussex. *Thorneg* 11th cent., *Tornei* 1086 (DB).

However the following has a different origin: **Thorney** Notts. *Torneshaie* 1086 (DB). 'Thorn-tree enclosure'. OE *thorn* + *haga*.

Thornfalcon Somerset. *Torne* 1086 (DB), *Thorn fagun* 1265. '(Place at) the thorn-tree', OE *thorn*. Manorial affix from early possession by a family called *Fagun*.

Thornford Dorset. *Thornford* 951, *Torneford* 1086 (DB). 'Ford where thorn-trees grow'. OE *thorn* + *ford*.

Thorngumbald Humber. *Torne* 1086 (DB), *Thoren Gumbaud* 1297. '(Place at) the thorn-tree'. OE *thorn*. Manorial affix from the *Gumbald* family, here in the 13th cent.

Thornham, 'homestead or village where thorn-trees grow', OE *thorn* + *hām*: **Thornham** Norfolk. *Tornham* 1086 (DB). **Thornham Magna** Suffolk. *Thornham* 1086 (DB). Affix is Latin *magna* 'great'.

Thornhaugh Cambs. *Thornhawe* 1189. 'Thorn-tree enclosure'. OE *thorn* + *haga*.

Thornhill, 'hill where thorn-trees grow', OE *thorn* + *hyll*; examples include: **Thornhill** Derbys. *Tornhull* 1200. **Thornhill** W. Yorks. *Tornil* 1086 (DB).

Thornley Durham, near Crook. *Thornley* 1382. 'Thorn-tree wood or clearing'. OE *thorn* + *lēah*.

Thornley Durham, near Peterlee. *Thornhlawa* 1071–80. 'Thorn-tree hill or mound'. OE *thorn* + *hlāw*.

Thornthwaite, 'thorn-tree clearing', OScand. *thorn* + *thveit*: **Thornthwaite** Cumbria, near Keswick. *Thornthwayt* 1254. **Thornthwaite** N. Yorks. *Tornthueit* 1230.

Thornton, a common name, 'thorn-tree enclosure or farmstead', OE *thorn* + *tūn*; examples include: **Thornton** Lancs. *Torentun* 1086 (DB). **Thornton** W. Yorks. *Torentone* 1086 (DB). **Thornton, Bishop** N. Yorks. *Thorntune* c.1030, *Torentune* 1086 (DB). Affix refers to its early possession by the Archbishop of York. **Thornton, Childer** Ches. *Thorinthun* c.1210, *Childrethornton* 1288. Affix means 'of the young men' (from OE *cild*, genitive plural *cildra*), with reference to the young monks of St Werburgh's Abbey in Chester. **Thornton Dale** N. Yorks. *Torentune* 1086 (DB). Affix is OScand. *dalr* 'valley'. **Thornton Heath** Gtr. London. *Thorneton Hethe* 1511. With OE *hǣth* 'heath'.

Thoroton Notts. *Toruertune* 1086 (DB). 'Farmstead or village of a man called Thorfrøthr'. OScand. pers. name + OE *tūn*.

Thorp, Thorpe, a common name, from OScand. *thorp* 'outlying farmstead or hamlet, dependent secondary settlement', except for a few South Country instances which are from OE *throp* of similar meaning; examples include: **Thorp Arch** W. Yorks. *Torp* 1086 (DB), *Thorp de Arches* 1272. Manorial affix from the *de Arches* family, here in the 11th cent. **Thorpe** Norfolk. *Torpe* 1254. **Thorpe** Surrey. *Thorp* 672–4, *Torp* 1086 (DB). **Thorpe-le-Soken** Essex. *Torp* 12th cent., *Thorpe in ye Sooken* 1612. Affix is from OE *sōcn* 'district with special jurisdiction'. **Thorpe on the Hill** Lincs. *Torp* 1086 (DB). **Thorpe St Andrew** Norfolk. *Torp* 1086 (DB). Affix from the dedication of the church. **Thorpe Salvin** S. Yorks. *Torp* 1086 (DB), *Thorpe Saluayn* 1255. Manorial affix from the *Salvain* family, here in the 13th cent. **Thorpe Willoughby** N. Yorks. *Torp* 1086 (DB), *Thorp Wyleby* 1276. Manorial affix from the *de Willeby* family, here in the 13th cent.

Thorrington Essex. *Torinduna* (*sic*) 1086 (DB), *Torritona* 1202. Probably 'thorn-tree enclosure or farmstead'. OE *thorn* or *thyrne* + *tūn*.

Thorverton Devon. *Toruerton* 1182. Probably 'farmstead by the thorn-tree ford'. OE *thorn* + *ford* + *tūn*.

Thrandeston Suffolk. *Thrandeston* c.1035, *Thrandestuna* 1086 (DB). 'Farmstead or village of a man called Thrándr'. OScand. pers. name + OE *tūn*.

Thrapston Northants. *Trapestone* 1086 (DB). 'Farmstead or village of a man called *Thræpst'. OE pers. name + *tūn*.

Threapwood Ches. *Threpewood* 1548. 'Disputed wood'. OE *thrēap* + *wudu*.

Three Bridges W. Sussex. *Le three bridges* 1613. Self-explanatory.

Threlkeld Cumbria. *Trellekell* 1197. 'Spring of the thralls or serfs'. OScand. *thrǣll* + *kelda*.

Threshfield N. Yorks. *Freschefelt* (*sic*) 1086 (DB), *Threskefeld* 12th cent. 'Open land where corn is threshed'. OE **thresc* + *feld*.

Thrigby Norfolk. *Trikebei* 1086 (DB). 'Farmstead or village of a man called *Thrykki'. OScand. pers. name + *bý*.

Thringstone Leics. *Trangesbi* (*sic*) 1086 (DB), *Trengeston* c.1200. 'Farmstead or village of a man called *Thræingr'. OScand. pers. name + OE *tūn* (replacing OScand. *bý*).

Thrintoft N. Yorks. *Tirnetofte* 1086 (DB). 'Thorn-tree homestead'. OScand. *thyrnir* + *toft*. Alternatively the first element may be the OScand. man's name Thyrnir.

Thriplow Cambs. *Tripelan* (*sic*) c.1050, *Trepeslau* 1086 (DB). 'Hill or tumulus of a man called *Tryppa'. OE pers. name + *hlāw*.

Throcking Herts. *Trochinge* 1086 (DB). Possibly 'place where beams are used or obtained'. OE *throc* + *-ing*.

Throckley Tyne & Wear. *Trokelawa* 1177. Possibly 'hill where beams are obtained'. OE *throc* + *hlāw*.

Throckmorton Heref. & Worcs. *Trochemerton* 1176. Possibly 'farmstead by a pool with a beam bridge'. OE *throc* + *mere* + *tūn*.

Throphill Northum. *Trophil* 1166. 'Hamlet hill'. OE *throp* + *hyll*.

Thropton Northum. *Tropton* 1177. 'Estate with an outlying farmstead or hamlet'. OE *throp* + *tūn*.

Throston, High Cleveland. *Thoreston* c.1300. 'Farmstead or village of a man called Thórir or Thórr'. OScand. pers. name + OE *tūn*.

Throwleigh Devon. *Trule* 1086 (DB). 'Woodland clearing with or near a conduit'. OE *thrūh* + *lēah*.

Throwley Kent. *Trevelai* 1086 (DB). Identical in origin with the previous name.

Thrumpton Notts., near Ruddington. *Turmodestun* 1086 (DB). 'Farmstead or village of a man called Thormóthr'. OScand. pers. name + OE *tūn*.

Thrupp, 'outlying farmstead or hamlet', OE *throp*: **Thrupp** Glos. *Trop* 1261. **Thrupp** Oxon. *Trop* 1086 (DB).

Thrushelton Devon. *Tresetone* 1086 (DB). 'Farmstead or village frequented by thrushes'. OE **thryscele* + *tūn*.

Thruxton, 'estate or manor of a man called Thorkell', OScand. pers. name + OE *tūn*: **Thruxton** Hants. *Turkilleston* 1167. **Thruxton** Heref. & Worcs. *Torchestone* (*sic*) 1086 (DB), *Turkelestona* 1160–70.

Thrybergh S. Yorks. *Triberge* 1086 (DB). 'Three hills'. OE *thrī* + *beorg*.

Thundersley Essex. *Thunreslea* 1086 (DB). 'Sacred grove of the heathen god Thunor'. OE god-name + *lēah*.

Thurcaston Leics. *Turchitelestone* 1086 (DB). 'Farmstead or village of a man called Thorketill'. OScand. pers. name + OE *tūn*.

Thurcroft S. Yorks. *Thurscroft* 1319. 'Enclosure of a man called Thórir'. OScand. pers. name + OE *croft*.

Thurgarton, 'farmstead or village of a man called Thorgeirr', OScand. pers. name + OE *tūn*: **Thurgarton** Norfolk. *Thurgartun* 1044–7, *Turgartuna* 1086 (DB). **Thurgarton** Notts. *Turgarstune* 1086 (DB).

Thurgoland S. Yorks. *Turgesland* 1086 (DB). 'Cultivated land of a man called Thorgeirr'. OScand. pers. name + *land*.

Thurlaston, 'farmstead or village of a man called Thorleifr', OScand. pers. name + OE *tūn*: **Thurlaston** Leics. *Turlauestona* 1166. **Thurlaston** Warwicks. *Torlauestone* 1086 (DB).

Thurlby, 'farmstead or village of a man called Thórulfr', OScand. pers. name + *bý*: **Thurlby** Lincs., near Bourne. *Turolvebi* 1086 (DB). **Thurlby** Lincs., near Lincoln. *Turolue(s)bi* 1086 (DB).

Thurleigh Beds. *La Lega* 1086 (DB), *Thyrleye* 1372. '(Place at) the wood or clearing'. From OE *lēah* with the remains of the OE definite article *thǣre* (dative).

Thurlestone Devon. *Thyrelanstane* 847, *Torlestan* 1086 (DB). 'Stone or rock with a hole in it'. OE *thyrel* + *stān*.

Thurlow, Great & Little Suffolk. *Tridlauua* 1086 (DB). Probably 'burial mound of the warriors'. OE *thrȳth* + *hlāw*.

Thurloxton Somerset. *Turlakeston* 1195. 'Farmstead or village of a man called Thorlákr'. OScand. pers. name + OE *tūn*.

Thurlstone S. Yorks. *Turulfestune* 1086 (DB). 'Farmstead or village of a man called Thórulfr'. OScand. pers. name + OE *tūn*.

Thurlton Norfolk. *Thuruertuna* 1086 (DB). 'Farmstead or village of a man called Thorfrithr'. OScand. pers. name + OE *tūn*.

Thurmaston Leics. *Turmodestone* 1086 (DB). 'Farmstead or village of a man called Thormóthr'. OScand. pers. name + OE *tūn*.

Thurnby Leics. *Turneby* 1156. 'Farmstead or village of a man called Thyrnir, or where thorn-bushes grow'. OScand. pers. name or *thyrnir* + *bý*.

Thurnham Lancs. *Tiernun* (*sic*) 1086 (DB), *Thurnum* 1160. '(Place at) the thorn-trees'. OE *thyrne* in a dative plural form *thyrnum*.

Thurning, 'place where thorn-trees grow', OE *thyrne* + *-ing*: **Thurning** Norfolk. *Turninga* 1086 (DB). **Thurning** Northants. *Torninge* 1086 (DB).

Thurnscoe S. Yorks. *Ternusche* 1086 (DB), *Thirnescoh* c.1090. 'Thorn-tree wood'. OScand. *thyrnir* + *skógr*.

Thurrock, Little & West Essex. *Thurroce* 1040–2, *Thurrucca* 1086 (DB). 'Place where filthy water collects'. OE *thurruc*. Originally applied to a stretch of marshland west of Tilbury. See also GRAYS.

Thursby Cumbria. *Thoresby* c.1165. 'Farmstead or village of a man called Thórir'. OScand. pers. name + *bý*.

Thursford Norfolk. *Turesfort* 1086 (DB). 'Ford associated with a giant or demon'. OE *thyrs* + *ford*.

Thursley Surrey. *Thoresle* 1292. Probably 'sacred grove of the heathen god Thunor'. OE god-name + *lēah*.

Thurstaston Mersey. *Turstanetone* 1086 (DB). 'Farmstead or village of a man called Thorsteinn'. OScand. pers. name + OE *tūn*.

Thurston Suffolk, near Bury. *Thurstuna* 1086 (DB). 'Farmstead or village of a man called Thóri'. OScand. pers. name + OE *tūn*.

Thurstonfield Cumbria. *Turstanfeld* c.1210. 'Open land of a man called Thorsteinn'. OScand. pers. name + OE *feld*.

Thurstonland W. Yorks. *Tostenland* 1086 (DB). 'Cultivated land of a man called Thorsteinn'. OScand. pers. name + *land*.

Thurton Norfolk. *Tortuna* 1086 (DB). Probably 'thorn-tree enclosure or farmstead'. OE *thorn* or *thyrne* + *tūn*.

Thurvaston Derbys. *Turverdestune* 1086 (DB). 'Farmstead or village of a man called Thorfrithr'. OScand. pers. name + OE *tūn*.

Thuxton Norfolk. *Turstanestuna* 1086 (DB). 'Farmstead or village of a man called Thorsteinn'. OScand. pers. name + OE *tūn*.

Thwaite, 'the clearing, meadow, or paddock', OScand. *thveit*; examples include: **Thwaite** Suffolk. *Theyt* 1228. **Thwaite St Mary** Norfolk. *Thweit* 1254. Affix from the dedication of the church.

Thwing Humber. *Tuuenc* 1086 (DB). 'Narrow strip of land'. OScand. *thvengr* or OE *thweng*.

Tibberton, 'farmstead or village of a man called Tīdbeorht', OE pers. name + *tūn*: **Tibberton** Glos. *Tebriston* 1086 (DB). **Tibberton** Heref. & Worcs. *Tidbrihtincgtun* 978–92, *Tidbertun* 1086 (DB). **Tibberton** Shrops. *Tetbristone* 1086 (DB).

Tibshelf Derbys. *Tibecel* 1086 (DB), *Tibbeshelf* 1179. 'Shelf or ridge of a man called Tibba'. OE pers. name + *scelf*.

Tibthorpe Humber. *Tibetorp* 1086 (DB). 'Outlying farmstead or hamlet of a man called Tibbi or Tibba'. OScand. or OE pers. name + OScand. *thorp*.

Ticehurst E. Sussex. *Tycheherst* 1248. 'Wooded hill where young goats are kept'. OE *ticce(n)* + *hyrst*.

Tichborne Hants. *Ticceburna c.*909. 'Stream frequented by young goats'. OE *ticce(n)* + *burna*.

Tickencote Leics. *Tichecote* 1086 (DB). 'Shed for young goats'. OE *ticcen* + *cot*.

Tickenham Avon. *Ticaham* 1086 (DB). 'Homestead or enclosure of a man called Tica, or where young goats are kept'. OE pers. name (genitive *-n*) or *ticcen* + *hām* or *hamm*.

Tickhill S. Yorks. *Tikehill* 12th cent. 'Hill of a man called Tica, or where young goats are kept'. OE pers. name or *ticce(n)* + *hyll*.

Ticknall Derbys. *Ticenheale c.*1002. 'Nook of land where young goats are kept'. OE *ticcen* + *halh*.

Tickton Humber. *Tichetone* 1086 (DB). 'Farmstead of a man called Tica, or where young goats are kept'. OE pers. name or *ticce(n)* + *tūn*.

Tidcombe Wilts. *Titicome* 1086 (DB). Probably 'valley of a man called *Titta'. OE pers. name + *cumb*.

Tiddington Oxon. *Titendone* 1086 (DB). 'Hill of a man called *Tytta'. OE pers. name (genitive *-n*) + *dūn*.

Tiddington Warwicks. *Tidinctune* 969. 'Estate associated with a man called Tīda'. OE pers. name + *-ing-* + *tūn*.

Tideford Cornwall. *Tutiford* 1201. 'Ford over the River Tiddy'. Old river-name (of uncertain origin and meaning) + OE *ford*.

Tidenham Glos. *Dyddanhamme* 956, *Tedeneham* 1086 (DB). 'Enclosure of a man called *Dydda'. OE pers. name (genitive *-n*) + *hamm*.

Tideswell Derbys. *Tidesuuelle* 1086 (DB). 'Spring or stream of a man called Tīdi'. OE pers. name + *wella*.

Tidmarsh Berks. *Tedmerse* 1196. 'People's or common marsh'. OE *thēod* + *mersc*.

Tidmington Warwicks. *Tidelminctune* 977, *Tidelmintun* 1086 (DB). 'Estate associated with a man called Tīdhelm'. OE pers. name + *-ing-* + *tūn*.

Tidworth, North (Wilts.) **& South** (Hants.). *Tudanwyrthe c.*990, *Tode(w)orde* 1086 (DB). 'Enclosure of a man called Tuda'. OE pers. name + *worth*.

Tiffield Northants. *Tifelde* 1086 (DB). Possibly 'open land with or near a meeting-place'. OE **tīg* + *feld*.

Tilbrook Cambs. *Tilebroc* 1086 (DB). Probably 'brook of a man called Tila'. OE pers. name + *brōc*.

Tilbury Essex. *Tilaburg* 731, *Tiliberia* 1086 (DB). Probably 'stronghold of a man called Tila'. OE pers. name + *burh* (dative *byrig*). Alternatively the first element may be a lost stream-name **Tila* 'the useful one'.

Tilehurst Berks. *Tigelherst* 1167. 'Wooded hill where tiles are made'. OE *tigel* + *hyrst*.

Tilford Surrey. *Tileford c.*1140. 'Useful ford, or ford of a man called Tila'. OE *til* or pers. name + *ford*.

Tillingham Essex. *Tillingaham c.*1000, *Tillingham* 1086 (DB). 'Homestead of the family or followers of a man called Tilli'. OE pers. name + *-inga-* + *hām*.

Tillington Heref. & Worcs. *Tullinton c.*1180. 'Estate associated with a man called Tulla or *Tylla'. OE pers. name + *-ing-* + *tūn*.

Tillington W. Sussex. *Tullingtun* 960.

'Estate associated with a man called Tulla'. OE pers. name + *-ing-* + *tūn*.

Tilmanstone Kent. *Tilemanestone* 1086 (DB). 'Farmstead or village of a man called Tilmann'. OE pers. name + *tūn*.

Tilney Norfolk. *Tilnea* 1170. 'Useful island, or island of a man called Tila'. OE *til* (dative *-an*) or pers. name (genitive *-n*) + *ēg*.

Tilshead Wilts. *Tidulfhide* 1086 (DB). 'Hide of land of a man called Tīdwulf'. OE pers. name + *hīd*.

Tilstock Shrops. *Tildestok* 1211. 'Outlying farmstead or hamlet of a woman called Tīdhild'. OE pers. name + *stoc*.

Tilston Ches. *Tilleston* 1086 (DB). 'Stone of a man called Tilli or Tilla'. OE pers. name + *stān*.

Tilstone Fearnall Ches. *Tidulstane* 1086 (DB), *Tilston Farnhale* 1427. 'Stone of a man called Tīdwulf'. OE pers. name + *stān*. Affix is the name of a local place now lost, 'fern nook', OE *fearn* + *halh*.

Tilsworth Beds. *Pileworde* (*sic*) 1086 (DB), *Thuleswrthe* 1202. Probably 'enclosure of a man called *Thȳfel or *Tyfel'. OE pers. name + *worth*.

Tilton Leics. *Tiletone* 1086 (DB). 'Farmstead or village of a man called Tila'. OE pers. name + *tūn*.

Timberland Lincs. *Timberlunt* 1086 (DB). 'Grove where timber is obtained'. OE *timber* or OScand. *timbær* + *lundr*.

Timberscombe Somerset. *Timbrecumbe* 1086 (DB). 'Valley where timber is obtained'. OE *timber* + *cumb*.

Timble N. Yorks. *Timmel c*.972, *Timble* 1086 (DB). Possibly from an OE **tymbel* 'a fall of earth' or 'a tumbling stream'.

Timperley Gtr. Manch. *Timperleie* 1211-25. 'Wood or clearing where timber is obtained'. OE *timber* + *lēah*.

Timsbury Avon. *Timesberua* (*sic*) 1086 (DB), *Timberesberwe* 1233. 'Grove where timber is obtained'. OE *timber* + *bearu*.

Timsbury Hants. *Timbreberie* 1086 (DB). 'Timber or wooden fort or manor'. OE *timber* + *burh* (dative *byrig*).

Timworth Green Suffolk. *Timeworda* 1086 (DB). 'Enclosure of a man called *Tima'. OE pers. name + *worth*.

Tincleton Dorset. *Tincladene* 1086 (DB). 'Valley of the small farms'. OE **tȳnincel* + *denu*.

Tindale Cumbria. *Tindale* late 12th cent. 'Valley of the River South Tyne'. Celtic or pre-Celtic river-name (meaning simply 'river') + OScand. *dalr*.

Tingewick Bucks. *Tedinwiche* 1086 (DB). Probably 'dwelling or (dairy) farm at the place associated with a man called Tīda or Tēoda'. OE pers. name + *-ing* + *wīc*.

Tingrith Beds. *Tingrei* (*sic*) 1086 (DB), *Tingrith c*.1215. 'Stream by which assemblies are held'. OE *thing* + *rīth*.

Tinsley S. Yorks. *Tineslauue* 1086 (DB). 'Mound of a man called *Tynni'. OE pers. name + *hlāw*.

Tintagel Cornwall. *Tintagol c*.1137. Probably 'fort by the neck of land'. Cornish **din* + **tagell*.

Tintinhull Somerset. *Tintanhulle* 10th cent., *Tintenella* 1086 (DB). OE *hyll* 'hill' added to an old Celtic name from **din* 'fort' with an uncertain second element.

Tintwistle Derbys. *Tengestvisie* 1086 (DB). Probably 'river-fork of the prince'. OE *thengel* + *twisla*.

Tinwell Leics. *Tedinwelle* (*sic*) 1086 (DB), *Tineguella* 1125-8. Possibly 'spring or stream frequented by goats'. OE **tige* (genitive plural *-ena*) + *wella*.

Tipton W. Mids. *Tibintone* 1086 (DB). 'Estate associated with a man called Tibba'. OE pers. name + *-ing-* + *tūn*.

Tiptree Essex. *Tipentrie* 12th cent. Probably 'tree of a man called *Tippa'. OE pers. name + *trēow*.

Tirley Glos. *Trineleie* 1086 (DB). 'Circular woodland clearing'. OE **trind* + *lēah*.

Tisbury Wilts. *Tyssesburg c*.800, *Tisseberie* 1086 (DB). 'Stronghold of a man called *Tyssi'. OE pers. name + *burh* (dative *byrig*).

Tissington Derbys. *Tizinctun* 1086 (DB). 'Estate associated with a man called Tīdsige'. OE pers. name + *-ing-* + *tūn*.

Tisted, East & West Hants. *Ticcesstede* 932, *Tistede* 1086 (DB). 'Place where young goats are kept'. OE *ticce(n)* + *stede*.

Titchfield Hants. *Ticefelle* 1086 (DB).

'Open land where young goats are kept'. OE *ticce(n)* + *feld*.

Titchmarsh Northants. *Tuteanmersc* 973, *Ticemerse* 1086 (DB). 'Marsh of a man called Ticcea'. OE pers. name + *mersc*.

Titchwell Norfolk. *Ticeswelle c.*1035, *Tigeuuella* 1086 (DB). 'Spring or stream frequented by young goats'. OE *ticce(n)* + *wella*.

Titley Heref. & Worcs. *Titelege* 1086 (DB). Probably 'woodland clearing of a man called *Titta'. OE pers. name + *lēah*.

Titlington Northum. *Titlingtona* 12th cent. Probably 'estate associated with a man called *Titel'. OE pers. name + *-ing-* + *tūn*.

Tittensor Staffs. *Titesovre* (*sic*) 1086 (DB), *Titneshovere* 1236. 'Ridge of a man called *Titten'. OE pers. name + **ofer*.

Tittleshall Norfolk. *Titeshala* (*sic*) 1086 (DB), *Titleshal* 1200. 'Nook of land of a man called *Tyttel'. OE pers. name + *halh*.

Tiverton Ches. *Tevreton* 1086 (DB). 'Red-lead farmstead', perhaps denoting a red-painted building or where red-lead was available. OE *tēafor* + *tūn*.

Tiverton Devon. *Twyfyrde* 880–5, *Tovretona* 1086 (DB). 'Farmstead or village at the double ford'. OE **twī-fyrde* + *tūn*.

Tivetshall Norfolk. *Teueteshala* 1086 (DB). OE *halh* 'nook of land', possibly with an old form of dialect *tewhit* 'lapwing'.

Tixall Staffs. *Ticheshale* 1086 (DB). 'Nook of land where young goats are kept'. OE *ticce(n)* + *halh*.

Tixover Leics. *Tichesovre* 1086 (DB). 'Promontory where young goats are kept'. OE *ticce(n)* + **ofer*.

Tockenham Wilts. *Tockenham* 854, *Tocheham* 1086 (DB). 'Homestead or enclosure of a man called *Toca'. OE pers. name + *hām* or *hamm*.

Tockholes Lancs. *Tocholis c.*1200. 'Hollows of a man called *Toca or Tók(i)'. OE or OScand. pers. name + *hol*.

Tockington Avon. *Tochintune* 1086 (DB). 'Estate associated with a man called *Toca'. OE pers. name + *-ing-* + *tūn*.

Tockwith N. Yorks. *Tocvi* 1086 (DB). 'Wood of a man called Tóki'. OScand. pers. name + *vithr*.

Todber Dorset. *Todeberie* 1086 (DB). Probably 'hill or grove of a man called Tota'. OE pers. name + *beorg* or *bearu*.

Toddington Beds. *Totingedone* 1086 (DB). 'Hill of the family or followers of a man called Tuda'. OE pers. name + *-inga-* + *dūn*.

Toddington Glos. *Todintun* 1086 (DB). 'Estate associated with a man called Tuda'. OE pers. name + *-ing-* + *tūn*.

Todenham Glos. *Todanhom* 804, *Teodeham* 1086 (DB). 'Enclosed valley of a man called Tēoda'. OE pers. name (genitive *-n*) + *hamm*.

Todmorden W. Yorks. *Tottemerden* 1246. 'Boundary valley of a man called Totta'. OE pers. name + *mǣre* + *denu*.

Todwick S. Yorks. *Tatewic* 1086 (DB). 'Dwelling or (dairy) farm of a man called Tāta'. OE pers. name + *wīc*.

Toft, Tofts, from OScand. *toft* 'curtilage or homestead'; examples include: **Toft** Cambs. *Tofth* 1086 (DB). **Toft Monks** Norfolk. *Toft* 1086 (DB). Affix from its possession by the Norman Abbey of Préaux in the 12th cent. **Tofts, West** Norfolk. *Stofftam* (*sic*) 1086 (DB), *Toftes* 1199.

Toftrees Norfolk. *Toftes* 1086 (DB). Identical in origin with the previous name.

Togston Northum. *Toggesdena* 1130. 'Valley of a man called *Tocg'. OE pers. name + *denu*.

Tolland Somerset. *Talanda* 1086 (DB). 'Cultivated land by the River Tone'. Celtic river-name (see TAUNTON) + OE *land*.

Tollard Royal Wilts. *Tollard* 1086 (DB), *Tollard Ryall* 1535. 'Hollow hill'. Celtic **tull* + *ardd*. Affix from lands here held *c.*1200 by King John.

Toller Fratrum & Porcorum Dorset. *Tolre* 1086 (DB), *Tolre Fratrum, Tolre Porcorum* 1340. Named from the River *Toller*, now the River Hooke. *Toller* is an old Celtic river-name meaning 'hollow stream'. The humorously contrasting affixes are Latin *fratrum* 'of the brethren' (with reference to early possession by the Knights Hospitallers) and *porcorum* 'of the pigs' (with reference to its herds of swine).

Tollerton N. Yorks. *Toletun* 972, *Tolentun* 1086 (DB). 'Farmstead or village of the tax-gatherers'. OE *tolnere* + *tūn*.

Tollerton Notts. *Troclauestune* 1086 (DB). 'Farmstead or village of a man called Thorleifr'. OScand. pers. name + OE *tūn*.

Tollesbury Essex. *Tolesberia* 1086 (DB). 'Stronghold of a man called *Toll'. OE pers. name + *burh* (dative *byrig*).

Tolleshunt D'Arcy & Major Essex. *Tollesfuntan* c.1000, *Toleshunta* 1086 (DB). 'Spring of a man called *Toll'. OE pers. name + **funta*. Manorial affixes from possession by the *Darcy* family (here in the 15th cent.) and by a tenant called *Malger* in 1086.

Tolpuddle Dorset. *Pidele* 1086 (DB), *Tollepidele* 1210. 'Estate on the River Piddle belonging to a woman called Tola'. OE river-name (see PIDDLEHINTON) with OE pers. name.

Tolworth Gtr. London. *Taleorde* 1086 (DB). 'Enclosure of a man called *Tala'. OE pers. name + *worth*.

Tonbridge Kent. *Tonebrige* 1086 (DB). Probably 'bridge belonging to the estate or manor'. OE *tūn* + *brycg*.

Tone (river) Somerset, see TAUNTON.

Tong, 'tongs-shaped feature', e.g. 'fork of a river', OE *tang*, **twang*: **Tong** Shrops. *Tweongan* 10th cent., *Tvange* 1086 (DB). **Tong** W. Yorks. *Tuinc* (*sic*) 1086 (DB), *Tange* 1176.

Tonge Leics. *Tunge* 1086 (DB). 'The tongue of land'. OScand. *tunga*.

Tongham Surrey. *Tuangham* 1189. 'Homestead or enclosure by the fork of a river'. OE *tang* or **twang* + *hām* or *hamm*.

Toot Baldon Oxon., see BALDON.

Tooting Bec & Graveney Gtr. London. *Totinge* 675, *Totinges* 1086 (DB), *Totinge de Bek* 1255, *Thoting Gravenel* 1272. Possibly '(settlement of) the family or followers of a man called Tōta', from OE pers. name + *-ingas*. Alternatively 'people of the look-out place', from OE **tōt* + *-ingas*. Distinguishing affixes from early possession by the Norman Abbey of Bec-Hellouin and by the *de Gravenel* family.

Topcroft Norfolk. *Topecroft* 1086 (DB). 'Enclosure of a man called Tópi'. OScand. pers. name + OE *croft*.

Toppesfield Essex. *Topesfelda* 1086 (DB). 'Open land of a man called *Topp'. OE pers. name + *feld*.

Topsham Devon. *Toppeshamme* 937, *Topeshant* (*sic*) 1086 (DB). 'Promontory of a man called *Topp'. OE pers. name + *hamm*.

Torbay Devon. *Torrebay* 1401. 'Bay near TORRE'. ME *bay*.

Torbryan Devon. *Torre* 1086 (DB), *Torre Briane* 1238. 'The rocky hill'. OE *torr*, with manorial affix from the *de Brione* family, here in the 13th cent.

Torksey Lincs. *Turecesieg* 11th cent., *Torchesey* 1086 (DB). 'Island of a man called *Turec'. OE pers. name + *ēg*.

Tormarton Avon. *Tormentone* (*sic*) 1086 (DB), *Tormarton* 1166. 'Boundary farmstead where thorn-trees grow'. OE *thorn* + *mǣre* + *tūn*.

Torpenhow Cumbria. *Torpennoc* 1163. 'Ridge of the hill with a rocky peak'. OE *torr* + Celtic **penn* + OE *hōh*.

Torpoint Cornwall. *Tor-point* 1746. 'Rocky headland'. OE *torr* + ME *point*.

Torquay Devon. *Torrekay* 1591. 'Quay near TORRE', see next name. ME *key*.

Torre Devon. *Torre* 1086 (DB). 'The rocky hill'. OE *torr*.

Torrington, Black, Great, & Little Devon. *Tori(n)tona* 1086 (DB), *Blaketorrintun* 1219. 'Farmstead or village on the River Torridge'. Celtic river-name (meaning 'turbulent stream') + OE *tūn*. Affix is OE *blæc* 'dark-coloured' (referring to the river here).

Torrington, East & West Lincs. *Terintone* 1086 (DB). 'Estate associated with a man called *Tīr(a)'. OE pers. name + *-ing-* + *tūn*.

Torrisholme Lancs. *Toredholme* 1086 (DB). 'Island of a man called Thóraldr'. OScand. pers. name + *holmr*.

Tortington W. Sussex. *Tortinton* 1086 (DB). 'Estate associated with a man called *Torhta'. OE pers. name + *-ing-* + *tūn*.

Tortworth Avon. *Torteword* 1086 (DB). 'Enclosure of a man called *Torhta'. OE pers. name + *worth*.

Torver Cumbria. *Thoruergh* 1190–9. 'Turf-roofed shed or shieling', or 'shieling of a man called *Thorfi'. OScand. *torf* or pers. name + *erg*.

Torworth Notts. *Turdeworde* 1086 (DB). Probably 'enclosure of a man called Thórthr'. OScand. pers. name + OE *worth*.

Toseland Cambs. *Toleslund* 1086 (DB). 'Grove of a man called Tóli'. OScand. pers. name + *lundr*.

Tosson, Great Northum. *Tossan* 1205. Possibly 'look-out stone'. OE **tōt* + *stān*.

Tostock Suffolk. *Totestoc* 1086 (DB). 'Outlying farmstead or hamlet by the look-out place'. OE **tōt* + *stoc*.

Totham, Great & Little Essex. *Totham* c.950, *Tot(e)ham* 1086 (DB). 'Homestead or village by the look-out place'. OE **tōt* + *hām*.

Totland I. of Wight. *Totland* 1608. 'Cultivated land or estate with a look-out place'. OE **tōt* + *land*.

Totley S. Yorks. *Totingelei* 1086 (DB). 'Woodland clearing of the family or followers of a man called Tota'. OE pers. name + *-inga-* + *lēah*.

Totnes Devon. *Totanæs* c.1000, *Toteneis* 1086 (DB). 'Promontory of a man called Totta'. OE pers. name + *næss*.

Tottenham Gtr. London. *Toteham* 1086 (DB). 'Homestead or village of a man called Totta'. OE pers. name (genitive *-n*) + *hām*.

Tottenhill Norfolk. *Tottenhella* 1086 (DB). 'Hill of a man called Totta'. OE pers. name (genitive *-n*) + *hyll*.

Totteridge Gtr. London. *Taderege* c.1150. 'Ridge of a man called Tāta'. OE pers. name + *hrycg*.

Totternhoe Beds. *Totenehou* 1086 (DB). 'Hill-spur with a look-out house'. OE **tōt* + *ærn* + *hōh*.

Tottington Gtr. Manch. *Totinton* 1212. Probably 'estate associated with a man called Tota'. OE pers. name + *-ing-* + *tūn*. Alternatively the first element may be OE **tōt* 'look-out hill'.

Totton Hants. *Totintone* 1086 (DB). Identical in origin with the previous name.

Towcester Northants. *Tofeceaster* early 10th cent., *Tovecestre* 1086 (DB). 'Roman fort on the River Tove'. OE river-name (meaning 'slow') + *ceaster*.

Towednack Cornwall. 'Parish of *Sanctus Tewennocus*' 1327. From the dedication of the church to St Winwaloe (of which name *To-Winnoc* is a pet-form).

Tower Hamlets Gtr. London, term used at least as early as the 18th cent. for 'hamlets under the jurisdiction of the Tower of London'.

Towersey Oxon. *Eie* 1086 (DB), *Turrisey* 1240. 'The island held by the *de Turs* family' (here from the 13th cent.). OE *ēg* with later manorial affix.

Tow Law Durham. *Tollawe* 1423. Possibly 'look-out hill or mound'. OE **tōt* + *hlāw*.

Towthorpe N. Yorks., near Haxby. *Touetorp* 1086 (DB). 'Outlying farmstead or hamlet of a man called Tófi'. OScand. pers. name + *thorp*.

Towton N. Yorks. *Touetun* 1086 (DB). 'Farmstead or village of a man called Tófi'. OScand. pers. name + *tūn*.

Toxteth Mersey. *Stochestede* (*sic*) 1086 (DB), *Tokestath* 1212. 'Landing-place of a man called Tóki or *Tōk'. OScand. pers. name + *stǫth*.

Toynton All Saints & St Peter Lincs. *Totintun(e)* 1086 (DB). 'Estate associated with a man called Tota'. OE pers. name + *-ing-* + *tūn*. Alternatively the first element may be OE **tōt* 'look-out hill'. Affixes from the dedications of the churches.

Toynton, High Lincs. *Tedin-*, *Todintune* 1086 (DB). 'Estate associated with a man called Tēoda'. OE pers. name + *-ing-* + *tūn*.

Trafford, Bridge & Mickle Ches. *Trosford*, *Traford* 1086 (DB). 'Trough ford'. OE *trog* + *ford*. Distinguishing affixes are OE *brycg* and OScand. *mikill* 'great'.

Trafford Park Gtr. Manch. *Stratford* 1206. 'Ford on a Roman road'. OE *strǣt* + *ford*.

Tranmere Mersey. *Tranemul* late 12th cent. 'Sandbank frequented by cranes'. OScand. *trani* + *melr*.

Tranwell Northum. *Trennewell* 1268. 'Spring or stream frequented by cranes'. OScand. *trani* + OE *wella*.

Trawden Lancs. *Trochdene* 1296. 'Trough-shaped valley'. OE *trog* + *denu*.

Treales Lancs. *Treueles* 1086 (DB). 'Farmstead of a court'. Welsh *tref* + *llys*.

Treborough Somerset. *Traberge* 1086 (DB). 'Hill or mound growing with trees'. OE *trēow* + *beorg*.

Tredington Warwicks. *Tredingctun* 757, *Tredinctun* 1086 (DB). 'Estate associated with a man called Tyrdda'. OE pers. name + *-ing-* + *tūn*.

Treeton S. Yorks. *Tretone* 1086 (DB). Probably 'farmstead built with posts'. OE *trēow* + *tūn*.

Tregony Cornwall. *Trefhrigoni* 1049, *Treligani* 1086 (DB). Possibly 'farm of a man called *Rigni'. Cornish *tre* + pers. name.

Tremaine Cornwall. *Tremen c.*1230. 'Farm of the stone'. Cornish *tre* + *men*.

Trematon Cornwall. *Tremetone* 1086 (DB). Cornish *tre* 'farm' + unknown word or pers. name + OE *tūn* 'estate'.

Treneglos Cornwall. *Treneglos* 1269. 'Farm of the church'. Cornish *tre* + *an* 'the' + *eglos*.

Trent Dorset. *Trente* 1086 (DB). Originally the name of the stream here, a Celtic river-name possibly meaning 'the trespasser', i.e. 'river liable to floods'.

Trentham Staffs. *Trenham* 1086 (DB). 'Homestead or river-meadow on the River Trent'. Celtic river-name (identical with previous name) + OE *hām* or *hamm*.

Trentishoe Devon. *Trendesholt* (*sic*) 1086 (DB), *Trenlesho* 1203. 'Round hill-spur'. OE *trendel* + *hōh*.

Tresco Isles of Scilly, Cornwall. *Trescau* 1305. 'Farm of elder-trees'. Cornish *tre* + *scaw*.

Treswell Notts. *Tireswelle* 1086 (DB). 'Spring or stream of a man called *Tīr'. OE pers. name + *wella*.

Tretire Heref. & Worcs. *Rythir* 1212. 'Long ford'. Welsh *rhyd* + *hir*.

Trevose Head Cornwall, first recorded in the 17th cent., named from a farm called Trevose which is *Trenfos* 1302, 'farm by the bank or dyke' (perhaps referring to an earlier fort), from Cornish *tre* + *an* 'the' + *fos*.

Trewhitt, High Northum. *Tirwit* 1150–62. Possibly 'river-bend where resinous wood is obtained'. OScand. *tyri* + OE **wiht*.

Treyford W. Sussex. *Treverde* 1086 (DB). 'Ford marked by a tree or with a tree-trunk bridge'. OE *trēow* + *ford*.

Trimdon Durham. *Tremeldon* 1196. Probably 'hill with a wooden cross'. OE *trēow* + *mǣl* + *dūn*.

Trimingham Norfolk. *Trimingeham* 1185. 'Homestead of the family or followers of a man called *Trymma'. OE pers. name + *-inga-* + *hām*.

Trimley Suffolk. *Tremelaia* 1086 (DB). 'Woodland clearing of a man called *Trymma'. OE pers. name + *lēah*.

Trimpley Heref. & Worcs. *Trinpelei* 1086 (DB). 'Woodland clearing of a man called *Trympa'. OE pers. name + *lēah*.

Tring Herts. *Treunge* (*sic*) 1086 (DB), *Trehangr* 1199. 'Wooded slope'. OE *trēow* + *hangra*.

Tritlington Northum. *Turthlyngton c.*1170. 'Estate associated with a man called Tyrhtel'. OE pers. name + *-ing-* + *tūn*.

Troston Suffolk. *Trostingtun c.*1000, *Trostuna* 1086 (DB). 'Estate associated with a man called *Trost(a)'. OE pers. name + *-ing-* + *tūn*.

Trottiscliffe Kent. *Trottes clyva* 788, *Totesclive* (*sic*) 1086 (DB). 'Cliff or hill-slope of a man called *Trott'. OE pers. name + *clif*.

Trotton W. Sussex. *Traitone* (*sic*) 1086 (DB), *Tratinton* 12th cent. Possibly 'estate associated with a man called *Trætt'. OE pers. name + *-ing-* + *tūn*. Alternatively the first element may be an OE **træding* 'path, stepping-stones'.

Troutbeck, '(place on) the trout stream', OE *truht* + OScand. *bekkr*: **Troutbeck** Cumbria, near Ambleside. *Trutebek* 1272. **Troutbeck** Cumbria, near Penruddock. *Troutbek* 1332.

Trowbridge Wilts. *Straburg* (*sic*) 1086 (DB), *Trobrigge* 1184. 'Tree-trunk bridge'. OE *trēow* + *brycg*.

Trowse Newton Norfolk. *Treus*, *Newotuna* 1086 (DB). Originally two separate names, 'wooden house' from OE *trēow* + *hūs*, and 'new farmstead' from OE *nīwe* + *tūn*.

Trull Somerset. *Trendle* 1225. 'Circular feature'. OE *trendel*.

Trumpington Cambs. *Trumpintune* c.1050, *Trumpintone* 1086 (DB). 'Estate associated with a man called *Trump(a)'. OE pers. name + *-ing-* + *tūn*.

Trunch Norfolk. *Trunchet* 1086 (DB). Possibly a Celtic name meaning 'wood on a spur of land'.

Truro Cornwall. *Triueru* c.1173. Possibly a Cornish name meaning '(place of) great water-turbulence'.

Trusham Devon. *Trisma* 1086 (DB). Possibly 'place overgrown with brushwood' from a derivative of OE *trūs*.

Trusley Derbys. *Trusselai* 1166. Possibly 'brushwood clearing'. OE *trūs* + *lēah*.

Trusthorpe Lincs. *Dreuistorp* 1086 (DB). 'Outlying farmstead or hamlet of a man called Drjúgr or Dreus'. OScand. or OFrench pers. name + OScand. *thorp*.

Trym (river) Glos., see WESTBURY ON TRYM.

Trysull Staffs. *Treslei* 1086 (DB). Named from the River Trysull, possibly a Celtic river-name meaning 'strongly flowing'.

Tubney Oxon. *Tobenie* 1086 (DB). 'Island, or dry ground in marsh, of a man called *Tubba'. OE pers. name (genitive *-n*) + *ēg*.

Tuddenham, 'homestead or village of a man called Tūda', OE pers. name (genitive *-n*) + *hām*: **Tuddenham** Suffolk. *Todenham* 1086 (DB). **Tuddenham, East & North** Norfolk. *East, Nord Tudenham* 1086 (DB).

Tudeley Kent. *Tivedele* 1086 (DB). Possibly 'wood or clearing overgrown with ivy'. OE **īfede* + *lēah*, with initial *T-* from the OE preposition *æt* 'at'.

Tudhoe Durham. *Tudhow* 1279. 'Hill-spur of a man called Tūda'. OE pers. name + *hōh*.

Tuesley Surrey. *Tiwesle* 1086 (DB). Possibly 'wood or clearing dedicated to the heathen god Tīw', from OE god-name + *lēah*. Alternatively the first element may be an OE man's name *Tīwhere.

Tuffley Glos. *Tuffelege* 1086 (DB). 'Woodland clearing of a man called Tuffa'. OE pers. name + *lēah*.

Tufton Hants. *Tochiton* 1086 (DB). 'Estate associated with a man called *Toca or Tucca'. OE pers. name + *-ing-* + *tūn*.

Tugby Leics. *Tochebi* 1086 (DB). 'Farmstead or village of a man called Tóki'. OScand. pers. name + *bý*.

Tugford Shrops. *Dodefort* (*sic*) 1086 (DB), *Tuggeford* c.1138. 'Ford of a man called *Tucga'. OE pers. name + *ford*.

Tumby Lincs. *Tunbi* 1086 (DB). Possibly 'farmstead or village of a man called Tumi'. OScand. pers. name + *bý*. Alternatively the first element may be OE *tūn* or OScand. *tún* 'enclosure'.

Tunbridge Wells Kent, named from TONBRIDGE, *Wells* referring to the medicinal springs here discovered in the 17th cent. The affix Royal was bestowed on the town by Edward VII.

Tunstall, found in various counties, from OE **tūn-stall* 'the site of a farm, a farmstead'; examples include: **Tunstall** Kent. *Tunestelle* 1086 (DB). **Tunstall** Staffs., near Stoke. *Tunstal* 1212. **Tunstall** Suffolk. *Tunestal* 1086 (DB).

Tunstead Norfolk. *Tunstede* 1044–7, *Tunesteda* 1086 (DB). OE *tūn-stede* 'farmstead'.

Tunworth Hants. *Tuneworde* 1086 (DB). Probably 'enclosure of a man called Tunna'. OE pers. name + *worth*.

Tupsley Heref. & Worcs. *Topeslage* 1086 (DB). Possibly 'ram's woodland clearing'. ME *tup* (or a byname formed from this word) + OE *lēah*.

Turkdean Glos. *Turcandene* 716–43,

Turchedene 1086 (DB). 'Valley of a river called *Turce*'. Lost Celtic river-name (probably meaning 'boar') + OE *denu*.

Tur Langton Leics., see LANGTON.

Turnastone Heref. & Worcs. *Thurneistun* 1242. 'Estate of a family called *de Turnei*'. OE *tūn*, with the name of a family recorded in the area in the 12th cent.

Turners Puddle Dorset, see PUDDLE.

Turnworth Dorset. *Torneworde* 1086 (DB). 'Thorn-bush enclosure'. OE *thyrne* + *worth*.

Turton Bottoms Lancs. *Turton* 1212. 'Farmstead or village of a man called Thóri or Thórr'. OScand. pers. name + OE *tūn*. Affix is from OE *botm* 'valley bottom'.

Turvey Beds. *Torueie* 1086 (DB). 'Island with good turf or grass'. OE *turf* + *ēg*.

Turville Bucks. *Thyrefeld* 796. 'Dry open land'. OE *thyrre* + *feld*.

Turweston Bucks. *Turvestone* 1086 (DB). Possibly 'farmstead or village of a man called Thorfrøthr or *Thorfastr'. OScand. pers. name + OE *tūn*.

Tutbury Staffs. *Toteberia* 1086 (DB), *Stutesberia* c.1150. 'Stronghold of a man called Tutta or *Stūt'. OE pers. name + *burh* (dative *byrig*).

Tutnall Heref. & Worcs. *Tothehel* (*sic*) 1086 (DB), *Tottenhull* 1262. 'Hill of a man called Totta'. OE pers. name (genitive *-n*) + *hyll*.

Tuttington Norfolk. *Tutincghetuna* 1086 (DB). 'Estate associated with a man called Tutta'. OE pers. name + *-ing-* + *tūn*.

Tuxford Notts. *Tuxfarne* (*sic*) 1086 (DB), *Tukesford* 12th cent. Possibly 'ford of a man called *Tuk', OScand. pers. name + OE *ford*, but the first element may be an early form of *tusk* 'tussock, tuft of rushes'.

Tweedmouth Northum. *Tuedemue* 1208–10. 'Mouth of the River Tweed'. Celtic or pre-Celtic river-name (possibly meaning 'powerful one') + OE *mūtha*.

Twemlow Green Ches. *Twamlawe* 12th cent. '(Place at) the two tumuli'. OE *twēgen* (dative *twǣm*) + *hlāw*.

Twickenham Gtr. London. *Tuicanhom* 704. Probably 'land in a river-bend of a man called *Twicca'. OE pers. name (genitive *-n*) + *hamm*. Alternatively the first element may be OE **twicce* 'river-fork'.

Twigworth Glos. *Tuiggewrthe* 1216. Probably 'enclosure of a man called Twicga'. OE pers. name + *worth*.

Twineham W. Sussex. *Tuineam* late 11th cent. '(Place) between the streams'. OE *betwēonan* + *ēa* (dative plural *ēam*).

Twinstead Essex. *Tumesteda* (*sic*) 1086 (DB), *Twinstede* 1203. Probably 'double homestead'. OE *twinn* + *stede*.

Twitchen Devon. *Twechon* 1442. OE *twicen(e)* 'cross-roads'.

Twycross Leics. *Tvicros* 1086 (DB). '(Place with) two crosses'. OE *twī-* + *cros*.

Twyford, found in various counties, 'double ford', OE **twī-ford* or **twī-fyrde*; examples include: **Twyford** Berks. *Tuiford* 1170. **Twyford** Hants. *Tuifyrde* c.970, *Tviforde* 1086 (DB).

Twyning Glos. *Bituinæum* 814, *Tveninge* 1086 (DB). Originally '(place) between the rivers' from OE *betwēonan* + *ēa* (dative *ēam*), later 'settlement of those living there' with the addition of OE *-ingas*.

Twywell Northants. *Twiwel* 1013, *Tuiwella* 1086 (DB). 'Double spring or stream'. OE *twī-* + *wella*.

Tydd St Giles (Cambs.) **& St Mary** (Lincs.). *Tid* 1086 (DB). Probably OE **tydd* 'shrubs or brushwood'. Distinguishing affixes from the church dedications.

Tyldesley Gtr. Manch. *Tildesleia* c.1210. 'Woodland clearing of a man called Tilwald'. OE pers. name + *lēah*.

Tyler Hill Kent. *Tylerhelde* 1304. 'Slope of the tile-makers'. OE **tiglere* + *helde*.

Tyne & Wear (new county), named from the Rivers Tyne and Wear, see TYNEMOUTH, MONKWEARMOUTH.

Tyneham Dorset. *Tigeham* 1086 (DB). Probably 'goat's enclosure'. OE **tige* (genitive *-an*) + *hamm*.

Tynemouth Tyne & Wear. *Tinanmuthe* 792. 'Mouth of the River Tyne'. Celtic or pre-Celtic river-name (meaning simply 'river') + OE *mūtha*. The new district-name **Tyneside** is named from the same river.

Tyringham Bucks. *Telingham* (*sic*) 1086 (DB), *Tringeham* 1130. 'Homestead or river-meadow of the family or followers of a man called *Tīr(a)'. OE pers. name + *-inga-* + *hām* or *hamm*.

Tysoe Warwicks. *Tiheshoche* 1086 (DB). Probably 'hill-spur of the heathen god Tīw'. OE god-name + *hōh*.

Tytherington, 'estate associated with a man called *Tydre', OE pers. name + *-ing-* + *tūn*, or 'stock-breeding farmstead', with an OE **tȳd(d)ring* as first element: **Tytherington** Avon. *Tidrentune* 1086 (DB). **Tytherington** Ches. *Tidderington c.*1245. **Tytherington** Wilts. *Tuderinton* 1242.

Tytherleigh Devon. *Tiderlege* 12th cent. Probably 'young wood or clearing', referring to new growth. OE *tīedre* + *lēah*.

Tytherley, East & West Hants. *Tiderlei* 1086 (DB). Identical in origin with the previous name.

Tytherton Lucas & East Tytherton Wilts. *Tedrintone* 1086 (DB). Identical in origin with TYTHERINGTON. Manorial affix from the *Lucas* family, here in the 13th cent.

Tywardreath Cornwall. *Tiwardrai* 1086 (DB). 'House on the beach'. Cornish *ti* + *war* + *treth*.

U

Ubbeston Green Suffolk. *Upbestuna* 1086 (DB). 'Farmstead or village of a man called Ubbi'. OScand. pers. name + OE *tūn*.

Ubley Avon. *Hubbanlege* late 10th cent., *Tumbeli* (*sic*) 1086 (DB). 'Woodland clearing of a man called Ubba'. OE pers. name + *lēah*.

Uckerby N. Yorks. *Ukerby* 1198. 'Farmstead or village of a man called *Úkyrri or *Útkári'. OScand. pers. name + *bý*.

Uckfield E. Sussex. *Uckefeld* 1220. 'Open land of a man called Ucca'. OE pers. name + *feld*.

Uckington Glos. *Hochinton* 1086 (DB). 'Estate associated with a man called Ucca'. OE pers. name + *-ing-* + *tūn*.

Udimore E. Sussex. *Dodimere* (*sic*) 1086 (DB), *Odumer* 12th cent. Possibly 'woody pond'. OE *wudig* + *mere*.

Uffculme Devon. *Offecoma* 1086 (DB). 'Estate on the Culm river held by a man called Uffa'. OE pers. name + Celtic river-name (see CULLOMPTON).

Uffington, 'estate associated with a man called Uffa', OE pers. name + *-ing-* + *tūn*: **Uffington** Lincs. *Offintone* 1086 (DB). **Uffington** Shrops. *Ofitone* 1086 (DB).

Uffington Oxon. *Uffentune* 10th cent., *Offentone* 1086 (DB). 'Estate of a man called Uffa'. OE pers. name (genitive *-n*) + *tūn*.

Ufford, 'enclosure of a man called Uffa', OE pers. name + *worth*: **Ufford** Cambs. *Uffawyrtha* 948. **Ufford** Suffolk. *Uffeworda* 1086 (DB).

Ufton Warwicks. *Hulhtune* 1043, *Ulchetone* 1086 (DB). Possibly 'farmstead with a shed or hut'. OE **huluc* + *tūn*.

Ufton Nervet Berks. *Offetune* 1086 (DB), *Offeton Nernut* 1284. 'Farmstead or village of a man called Uffa'. OE pers. name + *tūn*. Manorial affix from the *Neyrnut* family, here in the 13th cent.

Ugborough Devon. *Ulgeberge* (*sic*) 1086 (DB), *Uggeberge* 1200. 'Hill or mound of a man called *Ugga'. OE pers. name + *beorg*.

Uggeshall Suffolk. *Uggiceheala* 1086 (DB). 'Nook of land of a man called *Uggeca'. OE pers. name + *halh*.

Ugglebarnby N. Yorks. *Ugleberdesbi* 1086 (DB). 'Farmstead or village of a man called *Uglubárthr'. OScand. pers. name + *bý*.

Ugley Essex. *Uggele* c.1041, *Ugghelea* 1086 (DB). 'Woodland clearing of a man called *Ugga'. OE pers. name + *lēah*.

Ugthorpe N. Yorks. *Ughetorp* 1086 (DB). 'Outlying farmstead or hamlet of a man called Uggi'. OScand. pers. name + *thorp*.

Ulceby, 'farmstead or village of a man called Ulfr', OScand. pers. name + *bý*: **Ulceby** Humber. *Ulvesbi* 1086 (DB). **Ulceby** Lincs. *Ulesbi* 1086 (DB).

Ulcombe Kent. *Ulancumbe* 946, *Olecumbe* 1086 (DB). 'Valley of the owl'. OE *ūle* + *cumb*.

Uldale Cumbria. *Ulvesdal* 1216. 'Valley of a man called Ulfr, or one frequented by wolves'. OScand. pers. name or *ulfr* + *dalr*.

Uley Glos. *Euuelege* 1086 (DB). 'Yew-tree wood or clearing'. OE *īw* + *lēah*.

Ulgham Northum. *Wlacam* 1139, *Ulweham* 1242. 'Valley or nook frequented by owls'. OE *ūle* + *hwamm*.

Ullenhall Warwicks. *Holehale* 1086 (DB). 'Nook of land of a man called *Ulla'. OE pers. name (genitive *-n*) + *halh*.

Ulleskelf N. Yorks. *Oleschel* (*sic*) 1086 (DB), *Ulfskelf* 1170–7. 'Shelf or bank of a man called Ulfr'. OScand. pers. name + *skjalf* or OE *scelf* (with Scand. *sk-*).

Ullesthorpe Leics. *Ulestorp* 1086 (DB).

'Outlying farmstead or hamlet of a man called Ulfr'. OScand. pers. name + *thorp*.

Ulley S. Yorks. *Ollei* 1086 (DB). Probably 'woodland clearing frequented by owls'. OE *ūle* + *lēah*.

Ullingswick Heref. & Worcs. *Ullingwic* 1086 (DB). 'Dwelling or (dairy) farm associated with a man called *Ulla'. OE pers. name + *-ing-* + *wīc*.

Ullock Cumbria, near Mockerkin. *Uluelaik* 1279. 'Place where wolves play'. OScand. *ulfr* + *leikr*.

Ullswater Cumbria. *Ulueswater* c.1230. 'Lake of a man called Ulfr'. OScand. pers. name + OE *wæter*.

Ulpha Cumbria, near Coniston. *Wolfhou* 1279. 'Hill frequented by wolves'. OScand. *ulfr* + *haugr*.

Ulrome Humber. *Ulfram* 1086 (DB). Probably 'homestead or village of a man called Wulfhere or a woman called Wulfwaru'. OE pers. name + *hām*.

Ulverston Cumbria. *Ulurestun* 1086 (DB). 'Farmstead or village of a man called Wulfhere or Ulfarr'. OE or OScand. pers. name + OE *tūn*.

Umberleigh Devon. *Umberlei* 1086 (DB), *Wumberlegh* 1270. Possibly 'woodland clearing by the meadow stream'. OE **winn* + *burna* + *lēah*.

Underbarrow Cumbria. *Underbarroe* 1517. '(Place) under the hill'. OE *under* + *beorg*.

Underriver Kent. *Sub le Ryver* 1477. '(Place) under the hill-brow'. OE *under* + *yfer*.

Underwood Notts. *Underwode* 1287. '(Place) within or near a wood'. OE *under* + *wudu*.

Unstone Derbys. *Onestune* 1086 (DB). Probably 'farmstead or village of a man called *Ōn'. OE pers. name + *tūn*.

Unthank Cumbria, near Gamblesby. *Unthank* 1254. '(Land held) without consent', i.e. 'a squatter's holding'. OE *unthanc*. There are other examples of the name in Northumberland and Cumbria.

Up as affix, see main name, e.g. for **Up Cerne** (Dorset) see CERNE.

Upavon Wilts. *Oppavrene* 1086 (DB). '(Settlement) higher up the River Avon'. OE *upp* + Celtic river-name (meaning simply 'river').

Upchurch Kent. *Upcyrcean* c.1100. 'Church standing high up'. OE *upp* + *cirice*.

Upham Hants. *Upham* 1201. 'Upper homestead or enclosure'. OE *upp* + *hām* or *hamm*.

Uphill Somerset. *Opopille* 1086 (DB). '(Place) above the creek'. OE *uppan* + *pyll*.

Upleadon Glos. *Ledene* 1086 (DB), *Upleden* 1253. '(Settlement) higher up the River Leadon'. OE *upp* + Celtic river-name (see HIGHLEADON).

Upleatham Cleveland. *Upelider* 1086 (DB), *Uplithum* c.1150. '(Place at) the upper slopes'. OE *upp* + *hlith*, or OScand. *upp(i)* + *hlíth*, in a dative plural form.

Uplowman Devon. *Oppaluma* 1086 (DB). '(Settlement) higher up the River Loman'. OE *upp* + Celtic river-name (probably meaning 'elm river').

Uplyme Devon. *Lim* 1086 (DB), *Uplim* 1238. '(Settlement) higher up the River Lim'. OE *upp* + Celtic river-name (meaning simply 'stream').

Upminster Gtr. London. *Upmunstra* 1086 (DB). 'Higher minster or church'. OE *upp* + *mynster*.

Upottery Devon. *Upoteri* 1005, *Otri* 1086 (DB). '(Settlement) higher up the River Otter'. OE *upp* + river-name (see OTTERY).

Upper as affix, see main name, e.g. for **Upper Arley** (Heref. & Worcs.) see ARLEY.

Upperthong W. Yorks. *Thwong* 1274, *Overthong* 1286. 'Narrow strip of land'. OE *thwang*, with *uferra* 'upper' to distinguish it from NETHERTHONG.

Uppingham Leics. *Yppingeham* 1067. 'Homestead or village of the hill-dwellers'. OE *yppe* + *-inga-* + *hām*.

Uppington Shrops. *Opetone* 1086 (DB), *Oppinton* 1195. 'Higher farmstead', or 'farmstead at the place higher up'. OE *upp* (+ *-ing*) + *tūn*.

Upsall N. Yorks., near Thirsk. *Upsale* 1086 (DB). 'Higher dwelling(s)'. OScand. *upp* + *salr*.

Upton, a common name, usually 'higher farmstead or village', OE *upp* + *tūn*; examples include: **Upton** Berks., near Slough. *Opetone* 1086 (DB). **Upton** Ches., near Birkenhead. *Optone* 1086 (DB). **Upton** Dorset, near Lytchett. *Upton* 1463. **Upton Cheyney** Avon. *Vppeton* 1190, *Upton Chaune* 1325. Manorial affix from the *Cheyney* family. **Upton Grey** Hants. *Upton* 1202, *Upton Grey* 1281. Manorial affix from the *de Grey* family, here in the 13th cent. **Upton Hellions** Devon. *Uppetone Hyliun* 1270. Manorial affix from the *de Helihun* family, here in the 13th cent. **Upton Pyne** Devon. *Opetone* 1264, *Uppetone Pyn* 1283. Manorial affix from the *de Pyn* family, here in the 13th cent. **Upton St Leonards** Glos. *Optune* 1086 (DB), *Upton Sancti Leonardi* 1287. Affix from the dedication of the church. **Upton Scudamore** Wilts. *Uptune* c.990, *Uptone* 1086 (DB), *Upton Squydemor* 1275. Manorial affix from the *de Skydemore* family, here in the 13th cent. **Upton Snodsbury** Heref. & Worcs. *Snoddesbyri* 972, *Snodesbyrie* 1086 (DB), *Upton juxta Snodebure* 1280. Originally two separate names, the earlier being 'stronghold of a man called *Snodd', OE pers. name + *burh* (dative *byrig*). **Upton upon Severn** Heref. & Worcs. *Uptune* 897, *Uptun* 1086 (DB).

However the following has a different origin: **Upton Lovell** Wilts. *Ubbantun* 957, *Ubbedon Lovell* 1476. 'Farmstead or village of a man called Ubba'. OE pers. name + *tūn*, with manorial affix from the *Lovell* family, here in the 15th cent.

Upwaltham W. Sussex. *Waltham* 1086 (DB), *Up Waltham* 1371. 'Homestead or village in a forest'. OE *w(e)ald* + *hām*, with *upp* 'higher'.

Upwell Norfolk. *Wellan* 963, *Upwell* 1221. '(Place) higher up the stream'. OE *wella* with affix *upp* to distinguish it from OUTWELL.

Upwey Dorset. *Wai(e)* 1086 (DB), *Uppeweie* 1241. '(Settlement) higher up the River Wey'. Pre-English river-name (see WEYMOUTH) with OE *upp*.

Upwood Cambs. *Upwude* 974, *Upehude* (*sic*) 1086 (DB). 'Higher wood'. OE *upp* + *wudu*.

Urchfont Wilts. *Ierchesfonte* 1086 (DB). 'Spring of a man called *Eohrīc'. OE pers. name + **funta*.

Urishay Heref. & Worcs. *Haya Hurri* 1242. 'Enclosure of a man called Wulfrīc'. OE pers. name + *hæg*.

Urmston Gtr. Manch. *Wermeston* 1194. 'Farmstead or village of a man called *Wyrm or Urm'. OE or OScand. pers. name + OE *tūn*.

Urswick, Great & Little Cumbria. *Ursewica* c.1150. 'Dwelling or (dairy) farm by the bison lake'. OE *ūr* + *sǣ* + *wīc*.

Ushaw Moor Durham. *Ulveskahe* 12th cent. Probably 'small wood frequented by wolves'. OE *wulf* + *scaga*.

Usselby Lincs. *Osoluebi* c.1115. 'Farmstead or village of a man called Ōswulf or Ásulfr'. OE or OScand. pers. name + *bý*.

Utterby Lincs. *Uttrebi* 1197. 'Outer or more remote farmstead'. OE *ūterra* + OScand. *bý*.

Uttoxeter Staffs. *Wotocheshede* 1086 (DB). Probably 'heath of a man called *Wuttuc'. OE pers. name + **hǣddre*.

Uxbridge Gtr. London. *Wixebrug* c.1145. 'Bridge of the tribe called *Wixan*'. OE tribal name + *brycg*.

V

Vale of White Horse (district) Oxon. *The vale of Whithors* 1368. Named from the pre-historic figure of a horse cut into the chalk on White Horse Hill.

Vale Royal Ches. *Vallis Regalis* 1277, *Valroyal* 1357. 'Royal valley', the site of a monastery founded by Edward I. OFrench *val* + *roial* (in Latin in the first spelling).

Vange Essex. *Fengge* 963, *Phenge* 1086 (DB). 'Fen or marsh district'. OE *fenn* + **gē*.

Vauxhall Gtr. London. *Faukeshale* 1279. 'Hall or manor of a man called *Falkes*'. OFrench pers. name + OE *hall*.

Venn Ottery Devon, see OTTERY.

Ventnor I. of Wight. '(Farm of) *Vintner*' 1617. Probably a manorial name from a family called *le Vyntener*.

Vernham Dean Hants. *Ferneham* 1210. 'Homestead or enclosure where ferns grow'. OE *fearn* + *hām* or *hamm*, with the later addition of *denu* 'valley'.

Verwood Dorset. *Beuboys* 1288, *Fairwod* 1329. 'Beautiful wood'. OE *fæger* + *wudu* (alternating with OFrench *beu* + *bois* in the earliest spelling).

Veryan Cornwall. *Sanctus Symphorianus* 1281. From the dedication of the church to St Symphorian.

Vexford, Lower Somerset. *Fescheforde* 1086 (DB). Possibly 'fresh-water ford'. OE *fersc* + *ford*.

Vigo Village Kent, modern name apparently commemorating the capture of the Spanish port of Vigo by the British fleet in 1719.

Virginia Water Surrey, first recorded in 1749, originally a fanciful name for the artificial lake created here by the Duke of Cumberland in the previous year.

Virginstow Devon. *Virginestowe* c.1180. 'Holy place of (St Bridget) the Virgin'. Saint's name (from the dedication of the church) + OE *stōw*.

Vobster Somerset. *Fobbestor* 1234. 'Rocky hill of a man called *Fobb'. OE pers. name + *torr*.

Vowchurch Heref. & Worcs. *Fowchirche* 1291. 'Coloured church'. OE *fāh* + *cirice*.

W

Wackerfield Durham. *Wacarfeld c.*1050. Probably 'open land where osiers grow'. OE **wācor* + *feld*.

Wacton Norfolk. *Waketuna* 1086 (DB). 'Farmstead or village of a man called *Waca'. OE pers. name + *tūn*.

Wadborough Heref. & Worcs. *Wadbeorgas* 972, *Wadberge* 1086 (DB). 'Hills where woad grows'. OE *wād* + *beorg*.

Waddesdon Bucks. *Votesdone* 1086 (DB). 'Hill of a man called *Weott'. OE pers. name + *dūn*.

Waddingham Lincs. *Wadingeham* 1086 (DB). 'Homestead of the family or followers of a man called Wada'. OE pers. name + *-inga-* + *hām*.

Waddington, 'estate associated with a man called Wada', OE pers. name + *-ing-* + *tūn*: **Waddington** Lancs. *Widitun* (*sic*) 1086 (DB), *Wadingtun c.*1231. **Waddington** Lincs. *Wadintune* 1086 (DB).

Waddon Gtr. London. *Waddone c.*1115. 'Hill where woad grows'. OE *wād* + *dūn*.

Wadebridge Cornwall. *Wade* 1358, *Wadebrygge* 1478. OE *wæd* 'a ford' with the later addition of *brycg* from the 15th cent. when a bridge was built.

Wadenhoe Northants. *Wadenho* 1086 (DB). 'Hill-spur of a man called Wada'. OE pers. name (genitive *-n*) + *hōh*.

Wadhurst E. Sussex. *Wadehurst* 1253. 'Wooded hill of a man called Wada'. OE pers. name + *hyrst*.

Wadshelf Derbys. *Wadescel* 1086 (DB). 'Shelf or level ground of a man called Wada'. OE pers. name + *scelf*.

Wadworth S. Yorks. *Wadewrde* 1086 (DB). 'Enclosure of a man called Wada'. OE pers. name + *worth*.

Wainfleet All Saints Lincs. *Wenflet* 1086 (DB). 'Stream that can be crossed by a wagon'. OE *wægn* + *flēot*. Affix from the dedication of the church.

Waitby Cumbria. *Watebi c.*1170. 'Wet farmstead'. OScand. *vátr* + *bý*.

Wakefield W. Yorks. *Wachefeld* 1086 (DB). 'Open land where wakes or festivals take place'. OE **wacu* + *feld*.

Wakering, Great & Little Essex. *Wacheringa* 1086 (DB). '(Settlement of) the family or followers of a man called Wacer'. OE pers. name + *-ingas*.

Wakerley Northants. *Wacherlei* 1086 (DB). 'Woodland clearing of the watchful ones, or where osiers grow'. OE *wacor* (genitive plural *wacra*) or **wācor* + *feld*.

Wakes Colne Essex, see COLNE.

Walberswick Suffolk. *Walberdeswike* 1199. 'Dwelling or (dairy) farm of a man called Walbert'. OGerman pers. name + OE *wīc*.

Walberton W. Sussex. *Walburgetone* 1086 (DB). 'Farmstead or village of a woman called Wealdburh or Waldburg'. OE or OGerman pers. name + *tūn*.

Walcot, Walcote, Walcott, 'cottage(s) of the Britons', OE *walh* (genitive plural *wala*) + *cot*; examples include: **Walcot** Lincs., near Folkingham. *Walecote* 1086 (DB). **Walcote** Leics. *Walecote* 1086 (DB). **Walcott** Norfolk. *Walecota* 1086 (DB).

Walden, 'valley of the Britons', OE *walh* (genitive plural *wala*) + *denu*: **Walden** N. Yorks. *Waldene* 1270. **Walden, King's** Herts. *Waledene* 888, *Waldene* 1086 (DB). It was held by the king in 1086. **Walden, Saffron** Essex. *Wealadene c.*1000, *Waledana* 1086 (DB), *Saffornewalden* 1582. Affix (ME *safron*) refers to the cultivation of the saffron plant here.

Walden Stubbs N. Yorks., see STUBBS.

Walderslade Kent. *Waldeslade* 1190. 'Valley in a forest'. OE *weald* + *slæd*.

Walderton W. Sussex. *Walderton* 1168. 'Farmstead or village of a man called Wealdhere'. OE pers. name + *tūn*.

Waldingfield, Great & Little Suffolk. *Wealdingafeld* c.995, *Waldingefelda* 1086 (DB). 'Open land of the forest dwellers'. OE *weald* + *-inga-* + *feld*.

Walditch Dorset. *Waldic* 1086 (DB). 'Ditch with a wall or embankment'. OE *weall* or *walu* + *dīc*.

Waldridge Durham. *Walrigge* 1297. Probably 'ridge with or by a wall'. OE *wall* + *hrycg*.

Waldringfield Suffolk. *Waldringfeld* c.950, *Waldringafelda* 1086 (DB). 'Open land of the family or followers of a man called Waldhere'. OE pers. name + *-inga-* + *feld*.

Waldron E. Sussex. *Waldrene* 1086 (DB). 'House in the forest'. OE *weald* + *ærn*.

Wales S. Yorks. *Wales* 1086 (DB). '(Settlement of) the Britons'. OE *walh* (plural *walas*). This place-name is thus identical in origin with Wales the name of the principality.

Walesby, 'farmstead or village of a man called Valr', OScand. pers. name + *bý*: **Walesby** Lincs. *Walesbi* 1086 (DB). **Walesby** Notts. *Walesbi* 1086 (DB).

Walford Heref. & Worcs., near Ross. *Walecford* 1086 (DB). 'Briton ford'. OE *walh* + *ford*.

Walford Heref. & Worcs., near Wigmore. *Waliforde* 1086 (DB). Probably 'ford near a spring'. OE *wælla* + *ford*.

Walford Shrops. *Waleford* 1086 (DB). Identical in origin with the previous name.

Walgherton Ches. *Walcretune* 1086 (DB). 'Farmstead or village of a man called Walhhere'. OE pers. name + *tūn*.

Walgrave Northants. *Waldgrave* 1086 (DB). 'Grove belonging to OLD'. OE *grāf*.

Walkden Gtr. Manch. *Walkeden* 1325. Possibly 'valley of a man called *Walca'. OE pers. name + *denu*.

Walker Tyne & Wear. *Waucre* 1242. 'Marsh by the (Roman) wall'. OE *wall* + OScand. *kjarr*.

Walkeringham Notts. *Wacheringeham* 1086 (DB). Probably 'homestead of the family or followers of a man called Walhhere'. OE pers. name + *-inga-* + *hām*.

Walkern Herts. *Walchra* (*sic*) 1086 (DB), *Walkern* 1222. 'Building for fulling cloth'. OE **walc* + *ærn*.

Walkhampton Devon. *Walchentone* 1084, *Wachetona* (*sic*) 1086 (DB). Probably 'farmstead of the dwellers on a stream called **Wealce*'. OE river-name (meaning 'the rolling one') + *hǣme* + *tūn*.

Walkington Humber. *Walchinton* 1086 (DB). 'Estate associated with a man called *Walca'. OE pers. name + *-ing-* + *tūn*.

Wall, usually '(place at) the wall' from OE *wall*: **Wall** Northum. *Wal* 1166. With reference to the Roman Wall. **Wall** Staffs. *Walla* 1167. With reference to the Roman town here.

However the following has a different origin: **Wall, East & Wall under Heywood** Shrops. *Walle* 1200, *Walle sub Eywode* 1255. '(Place at) the spring or stream' from OE (Mercian) *wælla*. Affix means 'within or near the enclosed wood', OE *hæg* or *hege* + *wudu*.

Wallasey Mersey. *Walea* 1086 (DB), *Waleyesegh* 1351. 'The island of *Waley* (Britons' island)'. OE *walh* (genitive plural *wala*) + *ēg* with the later addition of a second explanatory *ēg*.

Wallingford Oxon. *Welingaforda* c.895, *Walingeford* 1086 (DB). 'Ford of the family or followers of a man called Wealh'. OE pers. name + *-inga-* + *ford*.

Wallington Gtr. London. *Waletone* 1086 (DB). 'Farmstead or village of the Britons'. OE *walh* (genitive plural *wala*) + *tūn*.

Wallington Hants. *Waletune* 1233. Probably identical in origin with the previous name.

Wallington Herts. *Wallingtone* (*sic*) 1086 (DB), *Wandelingetona* 1280. 'Farmstead of the family or followers of a man called *Wændel'. OE pers. name + *-inga-* + *tūn*.

Wallop, Nether & Over Hants. *Wallope* 1086 (DB). Possibly 'valley with a spring or stream'. OE *wella*, *wælla* +

hop. Alternatively the first element may be OE *weall* 'a wall' or *walu* 'a ridge, an embankment'.

Wallsend Tyne & Wear. *Wallesende* c.1085. 'End of the (Roman) wall'. OE *wall* + *ende*.

Walmer Kent. *Walemere* 1087. 'Pool of the Britons'. OE *walh* (genitive plural *wala*) + *mere*.

Walmersley Gtr. Manch. *Walmeresley* 1262. Possibly 'woodland clearing of a man called Waldmǣr or Walhmǣr'. OE pers. name + *lēah*.

Walmley W. Mids. *Warmelegh* 1232. 'Warm wood or clearing'. OE *wearm* + *lēah*.

Walney, Isle of Cumbria. *Wagneia* 1127. Probably 'killer-whale island', from OScand. *vǫgn* + *ey*. Alternatively the first element may be OE **wagen* 'quaking sands'.

Walpole Norfolk. *Walpola* 1086 (DB). 'Pool by the (Roman) bank'. OE *wall* + *pōl*.

Walpole Suffolk. *Walepola* 1086 (DB). 'Pool of the Britons'. OE *walh* (genitive plural *wala*) + *pōl*.

Walsall W. Mids. *Waleshale* 1163. 'Nook of land or valley of a man called Walh'. OE pers. name + *halh*. Alternatively the first element could be OE *walh* 'Welshman'.

Walsden W. Yorks. *Walseden* 1235. Probably 'valley of a man called *Walsa'. OE pers. name + *denu*.

Walsgrave on Sowe W. Mids. *Sowa* 1086 (DB), *Woldegrove* 1411. 'Grove in or near a forest'. OE *wald* + *grāf*. Originally named from the River Sowe itself, a pre-English river-name of unknown meaning.

Walsham, 'homestead or village of a man called Walh', OE pers. name + *hām*: **Walsham le Willows** Suffolk. *Wal(e)sam* 1086 (DB). Affix means 'among the willow-trees'. **Walsham, North** Norfolk. *Northwalsham* 1044–7, *Walsam* 1086 (DB). **Walsham, South** Norfolk. *Suthwalsham* 1044–7, *Walesham* 1086 (DB).

Walsingham, Great & Little Norfolk. *Walsingaham* c.1035, 1086 (DB). 'Homestead of the family or followers of a man called Wæls'. OE pers. name + *-inga-* + *hām*.

Walsoken Cambs. *Walsocne* 974, *Walsoca* 1086 (DB). 'Jurisdictional district near the (Roman) bank'. OE *wall* + *sōcn*.

Walterstone Heref. & Worcs. *Walterestun* 1249. 'Walter's manor or estate'. OE *tūn*. From its possession by *Walter* de Lacy in the late 11th cent.

Waltham, found in various counties, 'homestead or village in a forest', OE *w(e)ald* + *hām*; examples include: **Waltham** Humber. *Waltham* 1086 (DB). **Waltham Abbey** Essex. *Waltham* 1086 (DB). Affix from the medieval Abbey of Holy Cross here. **Waltham, Bishops** Hants. *Waltham* 904, 1086 (DB). Affix from its early possession by the Bishop of Winchester. **Waltham Cross** Herts. *Walthamcros* 1365. 'Cross near WALTHAM [ABBEY]'. Named from the 'Eleanor Cross' set up here by Edward I in memory of Queen Eleanor in 1290. **Waltham on the Wolds** Leics. *Waltham* 1086 (DB). See WOLDS. **Waltham St Lawrence & White Waltham** Berks. *Wealtham* 940, *Waltham* 1086 (DB), *Waltamia Sancti Laurencii* 1225, *Wytewaltham* 1243. Distinguishing affixes from the dedication of the church and from OE *hwīt* 'white' referring to chalky soil.

Walthamstow Gtr. London. *Wilcumestowe* c.1075, *Wilcumestou* 1086 (DB). 'Place where guests are welcome', or 'holy place of a woman called Wilcume'. OE *wilcuma* or pers. name + *stōw*. The London borough of **Waltham Forest** takes its name (somewhat artificially in view of the etymology above) from this place.

Walton, a common name, often 'farmstead or village of the Britons', from OE *walh* (genitive plural *wala*) + *tūn*; examples include: **Walton** Derbys. *Waletune* 1086 (DB). **Walton** Suffolk. *Waletuna* 1086 (DB). **Walton, Higher** Ches. *Waletona* 1154–60. **Walton-le-Dale** Lancs. *Waletune* 1086 (DB), *Walton in La Dale* 1304. Affix means 'in the valley' from OScand. *dalr*. **Walton-on-Thames** Surrey. *Waletona* 1086 (DB). **Walton on the Naze** Essex. *Walentonie* 11th cent., *Walton at the Naase* 1545. Affix means 'on the promontory', from OE *næss*. **Walton upon Trent** Derbys. *Waletune* 942, 1086 (DB).

However several Waltons have a different origin; examples include: **Walton in Gordano** Avon. *Waltona* 1086 (DB). 'Farmstead in a forest or with a wall'. OE *w(e)ald* or *w(e)all* + *tūn*. For the affix, see CLAPTON. **Walton on the Hill** Surrey. *Waltone* 1086 (DB). Identical in origin with the previous name. **Walton, West** Norfolk. *Waltuna* 1086 (DB). 'Farmstead or village by the (Roman) bank'. OE *w(e)all* + *tūn*. **Walton, Wood** Cambs. *Waltune* 1086 (DB), *Wodewalton* 1300. Probably 'farmstead in a forest'. OE *w(e)ald* + *tūn*, with the later addition of *wudu* 'woodland'.

Walworth, 'enclosure of the Britons', OE *walh* (genitive plural *wala*) + *worth*: **Walworth** Durham. *Walewrth* 1207. **Walworth** Gtr. London. *Wealawyrth* 1001, *Waleorde* 1086 (DB).

Wambrook Somerset. *Wambrook* 1280. '(Place at) the winding brook'. OE *wōh* (dative *wōn*) + *brōc*.

Wanborough Wilts. *Wænbeorgon* 854, *Wemberge* 1086 (DB). '(Place at) the tumour-shaped mounds'. OE *wenn* + *beorg*.

Wandsworth Gtr. London. *Wendleswurthe* 11th cent., *Wandelesorde* 1086 (DB). 'Enclosure of a man called *Wændel'. OE pers. name + *worth*. The river-name **Wandle** is a 'back-formation' from the place-name.

Wangford Suffolk, near Southwold. *Wankeforda* 1086 (DB). 'Ford by the open fields'. OE *wang* + *ford*.

Wanlip Leics. *Anlepe* 1086 (DB). 'The lonely or solitary place'. OE *ānlīepe*.

Wansdyke (ancient embankment, now district-name in Avon). *Wodnes dic* 903. 'Dyke associated with the heathen war-god Wōden'. OE god-name + *dīc*.

Wansford Cambs. *Wylmesforda* 972. 'Ford by a spring or whirlpool'. OE *wylm*, *wælm* + *ford*.

Wansford Humber. *Wandesford* 1176. 'Ford of a man called *Wand or *Wandel'. OE pers. name + *ford*.

Wanstead Gtr. London. *Wænstede* c.1055, *Wenesteda* 1086 (DB). 'Place by a tumour-shaped mound or where waggons are kept'. OE *wænn* or *wǣn* + *stede*.

Wanstrow Somerset. *Wandestreu* 1086 (DB). 'Tree of a man called *Wand or *Wandel'. OE pers. name + *trēow*.

Wantage Oxon. *Waneting* c.880, *Wanetinz* 1086 (DB). '(Place at) the fluctuating stream'. Derivative of OE *wanian* 'to decrease' + *-ing*.

Wapley Avon. *Wapelei* 1086 (DB). 'Woodland clearing by the spring'. OE *wapol* + *lēah*.

Wappenbury Warwicks. *Wapeberie* 1086 (DB). 'Stronghold of a man called *Wæppa'. OE pers. name (genitive *-n*) + *burh* (dative *byrig*).

Wappenham Northants. *Wapeham* 1086 (DB). 'Homestead or enclosure of a man called *Wæppa'. OE pers. name (genitive *-n*) + *hām* or *hamm*.

Wapping Gtr. London. *Wapping* c.1220. Probably '(settlement of) the family or followers of a man called *Wæppa', or '*Wæppa's place'. OE pers. name + *-ingas* or *-ing*.

Warbleton E. Sussex. *Warborgetone* 1086 (DB). 'Farmstead or village of a woman called Wǣrburh'. OE pers. name + *tūn*.

Warborough Oxon. *Wardeberg* 1200. 'Watch or look-out hill'. OE *weard* + *beorg*.

Warboys Cambs. *Weardebusc* 974. Probably 'bush of a man called *Wearda'. OE pers. name + *busc*. Alternatively the first element may be OE *weard* 'watch, protection'.

Warbstow Cornwall. 'Chapel of *Sancta Werburga*' 1282, *Warberstowe* 1309. 'Holy place of St Wǣrburh'. OE female saint's name + *stōw*.

Warburton Gtr. Manch. *Wareburgetune* 1086 (DB). 'Farmstead or village of a woman called Wǣrburh'. OE pers. name + *tūn*.

Warcop Cumbria. *Warthecopp* 1199–1225. 'Look-out hill', or 'hill with a cairn'. OScand. *vǫrthr* (genitive *varthar*) or *vartha* + OE *copp*.

Warden, 'watch or look-out hill', OE *weard* + *dūn*: **Warden** Kent. *Wardon* 1207. **Warden** Northum. *Waredun* c.1175. **Warden, Chipping** Northants.

Waredone 1086 (DB), *Chepyng Wardoun* 1389. Affix is OE *cēping* 'market'.
Warden, Old Beds. *Wardone* 1086 (DB), *Old Wardon* 1495. Affix is OE *eald* 'old'.

Wardington Oxon. *Wardinton* c.1180. Probably 'estate associated with a man called *Wearda or Wǣrheard'. OE pers. name + *-ing-* + *tūn*.

Wardle, 'watch or look-out hill', OE *weard* + *hyll*: **Wardle** Ches. *Warhelle* (*sic*) 1086 (DB), *Wardle* 1184. **Wardle** Gtr. Manch. *Wardhul* c.1193.

Wardley Leics. *Werlea* 1067. Probably 'wood or clearing near a weir', OE *wer* + *lēah*. Alternatively the first element may be OE *weard* 'watch, protection' if the *-d-* spelling (found from 1263) is original.

Wardlow Derbys. *Wardelawe* 1258. 'Watch or look-out hill'. OE *weard* + *hlāw*.

Ware Herts. *Waras* 1086 (DB). 'The weirs'. OE *wær*.

Wareham Dorset. *Werham* late 9th cent., *Warham* 1086 (DB). 'Homestead or river-meadow by a weir'. OE *wer*, *wær* + *hām* or *hamm*.

Warehorne Kent. *Werahorna* 830, *Werahorne* 1086 (DB). 'Horn-shaped piece of land by the weirs'. OE *wer* + **horna*.

Warenford Northum. *Warneford* 1256. 'Ford over Warren Burn'. Celtic river-name (probably 'alder river' with the later addition of OE *burna* 'stream') + OE *ford*.

Waresley Cambs. *Wederesle* (*sic*) 1086 (DB), *Wereslea* 1169. Probably 'woodland clearing of a man called *Wether or *Wǣr'. OE pers. name + *lēah*.

Warfield Berks. *Warwelt* (*sic*) 1086 (DB), *Warefeld* 1171. 'Open land by a weir'. OE *wer*, *wær* + *feld*.

Wargrave Berks. *Weregrave* 1086 (DB). Probably 'grove by the weirs'. OE *wer* + *grāf*.

Warham Norfolk. *Warham* 1086 (DB). 'Homestead or village by a weir'. OE *wær* + *hām*.

Wark, from OE (*ge*)*weorc* 'fortification': **Wark** Northum., near Bellingham. *Werke* 1279. **Wark** Northum., near Cornhill. *Werch* 1158.

Warkleigh Devon. *Warocle* 1100–3, *Wauerkelegh* 1242. Possibly 'spider wood or clearing'. OE **wæferce* + *lēah*.

Warkton Northants. *Wurcingtun* 946, *Werchintone* 1086 (DB). 'Estate associated with a man called *Weorc(a)'. OE pers. name + *-ing-* + *tūn*.

Warkworth Northum. *Werceworthe* c.1050. 'Enclosure of a man called *Weorca'. OE pers. name + *worth*.

Warlaby N. Yorks. *Werlegesbi* 1086 (DB). 'Farmstead or village of the traitor or troth-breaker'. OE *wērloga* + OScand. *bý*.

Warley, Great & Little Essex. *Werle* c.1045, *Wareleia* 1086 (DB). 'Wood or clearing near a weir or subject to a covenant'. OE *wer* or *wǣr* + *lēah*.

Warlingham Surrey. *Warlyngham* 1144. 'Homestead of the family or followers of a man called *Wǣrla'. OE pers. name + *-inga-* + *hām*.

Warmfield W. Yorks. *Warnesfeld* 1086 (DB). 'Open land frequented by wrens, or where stallions are kept'. OE *wærna* or **wǣrna* + *feld*.

Warmingham Ches. *Warmincham* 1259. 'Homestead of the family or followers of a man called Wǣrma or Wǣrmund', or 'homestead at Wǣrma's or Wǣrmund's place'. OE pers. name + *-inga-* or *-ing* + *hām*.

Warmington Northants. *Wyrmingtun* c.980, *Wermintone* 1086 (DB). 'Estate associated with a man called *Wyrma'. OE pers. name + *-ing-* + *tūn*.

Warmington Warwicks. *Warmintone* 1086 (DB). 'Estate associated with a man called Wǣrma or Wǣrmund'. OE pers. name + *-ing-* + *tūn*.

Warminster Wilts. *Worgemynster* c.912, *Guerminstre* 1086 (DB). 'Church on the River Were'. OE river-name (meaning 'winding') + *mynster*.

Warmsworth S. Yorks. *Wermesford* (*sic*) 1086 (DB), *Wermesworth* c.1105. 'Enclosure of a man called *Wǣrmi or Wǣrmund'. OE pers. name + *worth*.

Warmwell Dorset. *Warmewelle* 1086 (DB). 'Warm spring'. OE *wearm* + *wella*.

Warnborough, North & South Hants. *Weargeburnan* 973–4,

Wergeborne 1086 (DB). 'Stream where criminals were drowned'. OE *wearg* + *burna*.

Warnford Hants. *Wernæford* c.1053, *Warneford* 1086 (DB). 'Ford frequented by wrens or one used by stallions'. OE *wærna* or **wǣrna* + *ford*. Alternatively the first element may be an OE man's name *Wǣrna.

Warnham W. Sussex. *Werneham* 1166. 'Homestead or enclosure of a man called *Wǣrna, or where stallions are kept'. OE pers. name or **wǣrna* + *hām* or *hamm*.

Warrington Bucks. *Wardintone* c.1175. Probably 'estate associated with a man called *Wearda or *Wǣrheard'. OE pers. name + *-ing-* + *tūn*.

Warrington Ches. *Walintune* (*sic*) 1086 (DB), *Werington* 1246. 'Farmstead or village by the weir or river-dam'. OE **wering* + *tūn*.

Warsash Hants. *Weresasse* 1272. 'Ash-tree by the weir, or of a man called *Wǣr'. OE *wer* or pers. name + *æsc*.

Warslow Staffs. *Wereslei* (*sic*) 1086 (DB), *Werselow* 1300. Possibly 'hill with a watch-tower'. OE *weard-seld* + *hlāw*.

Warsop Notts. *Wareshope* 1086 (DB). Probably 'enclosed valley of a man called *Wǣr'. OE pers. name + *hop*.

Warter Humber. *Wartre* 1086 (DB). 'The gallows for criminals'. OE *wearg-trēow*.

Warthill N. Yorks. *Wardhilla* 1086 (DB). 'Watch or look-out hill'. OE *weard* + *hyll*.

Wartling E. Sussex. *Werlinges* (*sic*) 1086 (DB), *Wertlingis* 12th cent. '(Settlement of) the family or followers of a man called *Wyrtel'. OE pers. name + *-ingas*.

Wartnaby Leics. *Worcnodebie* 1086 (DB). Possibly 'farmstead or village of a man called *Wærcnōth'. OE pers. name + OScand. *bý*.

Warton Lancs., near Kirkham. *Wartun* 1086 (DB). 'Watch or look-out farmstead'. OE *weard* + *tūn*.

Warton Northum. *Wartun* 1236. Identical in origin with the previous name.

Warton Warwicks. *Wavertune* c.1155. 'Farmstead by a swaying tree or near marshy ground'. OE *wæfre* + *tūn*.

Warwick Cumbria. *Warthwic* 1131. 'Dwelling or farm on the bank'. OE *waroth* + *wīc*.

Warwick Warwicks. *Wærincwicum* 1001, *Warwic* 1086 (DB). 'Dwellings by the weir or river-dam'. OE **wæring* + *wīc*. **Warwickshire** (OE *scīr* 'district') is first referred to in the 11th cent.

Wasdale Head Cumbria. *Wastedale* 1279, *Wascedaleheved* 1334. 'Valley of the water or lake'. OScand. *vatn* (genitive *-s*) + *dalr*, with the later addition of OE *hēafod* 'head, upper end'.

Wash, The Lincs./Norfolk. *The Wasshes* c.1545. OE *wæsc* 'sandbank washed by the sea', originally used of two stretches fordable at low water.

Washbourne Devon. *Waseborne* 1086 (DB). 'Stream used for washing (sheep or clothes)'. OE *wæsce* + *burna*.

Washbourne, Great & Little Glos. *Uassanburnan* 780, *Waseborne* 1086 (DB). 'Stream with alluvial land'. OE **wæsse* + *burna*.

Washfield Devon. *Wasfelte* 1086 (DB). Probably 'open land near a place used for washing (sheep or clothes)'. OE *wæsce* + *feld*.

Washford Somerset. *Wecetford* c.960. 'Ford on the road to WATCHET'. OE *ford*.

Washford Pyne Devon. *Wasforde* 1086 (DB). Probably 'ford at the place for washing (sheep or clothes)'. OE *wæsce* + *ford*. Manorial affix from the *de Pinu* family, here in the 13th cent.

Washingborough Lincs. *Washingeburg* 1086 (DB). Possibly 'stronghold of the dwellers at the place subject to floods or used for washing'. OE *wæsc* or *wæsce* + *-inga-* + *burh*.

Washington Tyne & Wear. *Wassyngtona* 1183. 'Estate associated with a man called *Wassa'. OE pers. name + *-ing-* + *tūn*.

Washington W. Sussex. *Wessingatun* 946–55, *Wasingetune* 1086 (DB). 'Estate of the family or followers of a man called *Wassa'. OE pers. name + *-inga-* + *tūn*.

Wasing Berks. *Walsince* 1086 (DB).

Perhaps originally the name of the stream here, with obscure element + OE *-ing*.

Wasperton Warwicks. *Waspertune* 1043, *Wasmertone* (*sic*) 1086 (DB). Probably 'pear orchard by alluvial land'. OE **wæsse* + *peru* + *tūn*.

Wass N. Yorks. *Wasse* 1541. Probably 'the fords'. OScand. *vath* in a plural form.

Watchet Somerset. *Wæcet* 962, *Wacet* 1086 (DB). Probably 'lower wood' from Celtic **cę̄d* 'wood' with prefix.

Watchfield Oxon. *Wæclesfeld* 931, *Wachenesfeld* 1086 (DB). 'Open land of a man called *Wæcel or *Wæccīn'. OE pers. name + *feld*.

Watendlath Cumbria. *Wattendlane* late 12th cent. Probably 'lane to the end of the lake'. OScand. *vatn* + *endi* with OE *lane* (replaced by OScand. *hlatha* 'barn').

Waterbeach Cambs. *Vtbech* 1086 (DB), *Waterbech* 1237. OE *bece* 'stream, valley' or *bæc* (locative **bece*) 'low ridge', with the addition of OE *ūt* 'outer' and *wæter* 'water' to distinguish it from LANDBEACH.

Waterden Norfolk. *Waterdenna* 1086 (DB). 'Valley with a stream or lake'. OE *wæter* + *denu*.

Waterfall Staffs. *Waterfal* 1201. OE *wæter-gefall* 'place where a stream disappears into the ground'.

Wateringbury Kent. *Uuotryngebyri* 964–95, *Otringeberge* 1086 (DB). Possibly 'stronghold of the family or followers of a man called Ōhthere'. OE pers. name + *-inga-* + *burh* (dative *byrig*).

Waterloo Mersey., named from the *Royal Waterloo Hotel* (founded in 1815 and so called after the famous battle of that year). Similar names commemorating the battle are found in other counties, for example **Waterloo** Gtr. London, **Waterlooville** Hants.

Watermillock Cumbria. *Wethermeloc* early 13th cent. 'Little bare hill where wether-sheep graze'. Celtic **mę̄l* with diminutive suffix, to which OE *wether* has been added.

Waterperry Oxon. *Perie* 1086 (DB), *Waterperi* c.1190. 'Place at the pear-tree(s)'. OE *pyrige* with the later addition of OE *wæter* to distinguish it from WOODPERRY.

Water Stratford Bucks., see STRATFORD.

Watford, 'ford used when hunting', OE *wāth* + *ford*: **Watford** Herts. *Watford* c.945. **Watford** Northants. *Watford* 1086 (DB).

Wath, 'the ford', OScand. *vath*; examples include: **Wath** N. Yorks., near Ripon. *Wat* 1086 (DB). **Wath upon Dearne** S. Yorks. *Wade* 1086 (DB). For the river-name, see BOLTON UPON DEARNE.

Watling Street (Roman road from Dover to Wroxeter). *Wæclinga stræt* late 9th cent. 'Roman road associated with the family or followers of a man called *Wacol'. OE pers. name + *-inga-* + *strǣt*. An early name for ST ALBANS is *Wæclingaceaster* c.900, 'Roman fort of *Wacol's people', and the road-name was no doubt applied to the stretch of road between St Albans and London before it was extended to the whole length. The name Watling Street was later transferred to several other Roman roads.

Watlington Norfolk. *Watlingetun* 11th cent. Possibly 'farmstead of the family or followers of a man called *Hwætel or *Wacol'. OE pers. name + *-inga-* + *tūn*.

Watlington Oxon. *Wæclinctune* 887, *Watelintone* 1086 (DB). Probably 'estate associated with a man called *Wæcel'. OE pers. name + *-ing-* + *tūn*.

Watnall Notts. *Watenot* (*sic*) 1086 (DB), *Watenho* 1202. 'Hill-spur of a man called *Wata'. OE pers. name (genitive *-n*) + *hōh*.

Wattisfield Suffolk. *Watlesfelda* 1086 (DB). 'Open land of a man called *Wacol or *Hwætel'. OE pers. name + *feld*.

Wattisham Suffolk. *Wecesham* 1086 (DB). 'Homestead or village of a man called *Wæcci'. OE pers. name + *hām*.

Watton Humber. *Uetadun* 731, *Wattune* 1086 (DB). 'Wet hill, or hill of the wet places'. OE *wǣt* (as adjective or noun) + *dūn*.

Watton Norfolk. *Wadetuna* 1086 (DB). 'Farmstead of a man called Wada'. OE pers. name + *tūn*.

Watton at Stone Herts. *Wattun* 969,

Wodtone 1086 (DB), *Watton atte Stone* 1311. 'Farmstead where woad is grown'. OE *wād* + *tūn*. Affix 'at the stone' (OE *stān*) from an old stone here.

Wavendon Bucks. *Wafandun* 969, *Wavendone* 1086 (DB). 'Hill of a man called *Wafa'. OE pers. name (genitive *-n*) + *dūn*.

Waverton Ches. *Wavretone* 1086 (DB). 'Farmstead by a swaying tree'. OE *wæfre* + *tūn*.

Waverton Cumbria. *Wauerton* 1183. 'Farmstead by the River Waver'. OE river-name (from *wæfre* 'winding') + *tūn*.

Wawne Humber. *Wagene* 1086 (DB). 'Quaking bog or quagmire'. OE **wagen*.

Waxham Norfolk. *Wacstanesham* 1086 (DB). 'Homestead or village of a man called *Wægstān'. OE pers. name + *hām*.

Waxholme Humber. *Waxham* 1086 (DB). 'Homestead where wax (from bees) is produced'. OE *weax* + *hām*.

Wayford Somerset. *Waiford* 1206. 'Ford on a way or road'. OE *weg* + *ford*.

Weald, 'the woodland or forest', OE *weald*: **Weald Bassett, North** Essex. *Walda* 1086 (DB), *Welde Basset* 1291. Manorial affix from the *Basset* family, here in the 13th cent. **Weald, South** Essex. *Welde* 1062, *Welda* 1086 (DB). **Weald, The** Kent–Hants. *Waldum* (a dative plural form) 1185.

Wealdstone Gtr. London, a late name, 'boundary stone of HARROW WEALD'.

Wear (river) Tyne & Wear, see MONKWEARMOUTH.

Weasenham Norfolk. *Wesenham* 1086 (DB). Possibly 'homestead or village of a man called *Weosa'. OE pers. name (genitive *-n*) + *hām*.

Weaverham Ches. *Wivreham* 1086 (DB). 'Homestead or village by the River Weaver'. OE river-name (from **wēfer* 'winding stream') + *hām*.

Weaverthorpe N. Yorks. *Wifretorp* 1086 (DB). 'Outlying farmstead or hamlet of a man called Víthfari'. OScand. pers. name + *thorp*.

Weddington Warwicks. *Watitune* 1086 (DB). Possibly 'estate associated with a man called *Hwæt'. OE pers. name + *-ing-* + *tūn*.

Wedmore Somerset. *Wethmor* late 9th cent., *Wedmore* 1086 (DB). Possibly 'marsh used for hunting'. OE **wǣthe* + *mōr*.

Wednesbury W. Mids. *Wadnesberie* 1086 (DB). 'Stronghold associated with the heathen god Wōden'. OE god-name + *burh* (dative *byrig*).

Wednesfield W. Mids. *Wodnesfeld* 996, *Wodnesfelde* 1086 (DB). 'Open land of the heathen god Wōden'. OE god-name + *feld*.

Weedon, 'hill with a heathen temple', OE *wēoh* + *dūn*: **Weedon** Bucks. *Weodune* 1066. **Weedon Bec** Northants. *Weodun* 944, *Wedone* 1086 (DB), *Wedon Beke* 1379. Manorial affix from its possession by the Norman Abbey of Bec-Hellouin in the 12th cent. **Weedon Lois** Northants. *Wedone* 1086 (DB), *Leyes Weedon* 1475. The affix is possibly from a 'well of St Loys or Lewis' in the parish, but it may be manorial.

Weeford Staffs. *Weforde* 1086 (DB). Probably 'ford by a heathen temple'. OE *wēoh* + *ford*.

Week, Weeke, 'the dwelling, the specialized farm or trading settlement', OE *wīc*; examples include: **Week St Mary** Cornwall. *Wich* 1086 (DB), *Seintemarywyk* 1321. Affix from the dedication of the church. **Weeke** Hants. *Wike* 1248.

Weekley Northants. *Wiclea* 956, *Wiclei* 1086 (DB). Probably 'wood or clearing near an earlier Romano-British settlement'. OE *wīc* + *lēah*.

Weeley Essex. *Wilgelea* 11th cent., *Wileia* 1086 (DB). 'Wood or clearing where willow-trees grow'. OE **wilig* + *lēah*.

Weeting Norfolk. *Watinge* c.1050, *Wetinge* 1086 (DB). 'Wet or damp place'. OE *wēt* + *-ing*.

Weeton, 'farmstead where willow-trees grow', OE *wīthig* + *tūn*: **Weeton** Humber. *Wideton* 1086 (DB). **Weeton** Lancs. *Widetun* 1086 (DB). **Weeton** N. Yorks. *Widitun* 1086 (DB).

Weighton, Little Humber. *Widetone* 1086 (DB). Identical in origin with the previous names.

Weighton, Market Humber. *Wicstun* 1086 (DB). 'Farmstead by an earlier Romano-British settlement'. OE *wīc* + *tūn*. The affix *Market* first occurs in the early 19th cent.

Welborne, Welbourn, Welburn, 'stream fed by a spring', OE *wella* + *burna*; examples include: **Welborne** Norfolk. *Walebruna* 1086 (DB). **Welbourn** Lincs. *Wellebrune* 1086 (DB). **Welburn** N. Yorks., near Bulmer. *Wellebrune* 1086 (DB).

Welbury N. Yorks. *Welleberge* 1086 (DB). 'Hill with a spring'. OE *wella* + *beorg*.

Welby Lincs. *Wellebi* 1086 (DB). 'Farmstead or village by a spring or stream'. OE *wella* + OScand. *bý*.

Welcombe Devon. *Walcome* 1086 (DB). 'Valley with a spring or stream'. OE *wella* + *cumb*.

Weldon, Great & Little Northants. *Weledone* 1086 (DB). 'Hill with a spring or by a stream'. OE *wella* + *dūn*.

Welford Berks. *Weligforda* 949, *Waliford* 1086 (DB). 'Ford where willow-trees grow'. OE *welig* + *ford*.

Welford Northants. *Wellesford* 1086 (DB). 'Ford by the spring or over the stream'. OE *wella* + *ford*.

Welford on Avon Warwicks. *Welleford* 1086 (DB), *Welneford* 1177. 'Ford by the springs'. OE *wella* (genitive plural *-ena*) + *ford*.

Welham Leics. *Weleham* 1086 (DB). Possibly 'homestead by the stream', OE *wella* + *hām*. Alternatively the first element may be an OE pers. name *Wēola.

Welham Notts. *Wellun* 1086 (DB). '(Place at) the springs'. OE *wella* in a dative plural form *wellum*.

Welhamgreen Herts. *Wethyngham* c.1315, *Whelamgrene* 1467. 'Willow-tree enclosure'. OE **wīthign* + *hamm*, with later *grēne* 'green'.

Well, '(place at) the spring or stream', OE *wella*; examples include: **Well** Lincs. *Welle* 1086 (DB). **Well** N. Yorks. *Welle* 1086 (DB).

Welland (river) Northants.-Lincs. *Weolud* 921. A Celtic or pre-Celtic river-name of uncertain meaning.

Wellesbourne Hastings & Mountford Warwicks. *Welesburnan* 840, *Waleborne* 1086 (DB). Possibly 'stream with a pool'. OE *wēl* + *burna*. Distinguishing affixes from possession by the *de Hastanges* family (from the 14th cent.) and the *de Munford* family (from the 12th cent.).

Welling Gtr. London. *Wellyngs* 1362. A manorial name from the *Welling* or *Willing* family, here in the early 14th cent.

Wellingborough Northants. *Wedlingeberie* 1086 (DB), *Wendlingburch* 1178. 'Stronghold of the family or followers of a man called *Wændel'. OE pers. name + *-inga-* + *burh*.

Wellingham Norfolk. *Walnccham* (*sic*) 1086 (DB), *Uuelingheham* c.1190. 'Homestead of the dwellers by a spring or stream'. OE *wella* + *-inga-* + *hām*.

Wellingore Lincs. *Wellingoure* 1086 (DB). Probably 'promontory of the dwellers by a spring or stream'. OE *wella* + *-inga-* + **ofer*.

Wellington, probably 'estate associated with a man called *Wēola', OE pers. name + *-ing-* + *tūn*: **Wellington** Heref. & Worcs. *Weolintun* early 11th cent., *Walintone* 1086 (DB). **Wellington** Shrops. *Walitone* 1086 (DB). **Wellington** Somerset. *Weolingtun* 904, *Walintone* 1086 (DB).

Wellow Avon. *Weleuue* 1084. Originally the name of the stream here, a Celtic river-name possibly meaning 'winding'.

Wellow I. of Wight. *Welig* c.880, *Welige* 1086 (DB). '(Place at) the willow-tree'. OE *welig*.

Wellow Notts. *Welhag* 1207. 'Enclosure near a spring or stream'. OE *wella* + *haga*.

Wellow, East & West Hants. *Welewe* c.880, *Weleve* 1086 (DB). Identical in origin with WELLOW (Avon).

Wells, 'the springs', OE *wella* in a plural form: **Wells** Somerset. *Willan* c.1050, *Welle* 1086 (DB). **Wells-next-the-Sea** Norfolk. *Guelle* (*sic*) 1086 (DB), *Wellis* 1291.

Wellsborough Leics. *Wethelesberne* (*sic*) 1185, *Weulesbergh* 1285. 'Hill of the wheel', i.e. 'hill with a circular shape or feature'. OE *hweowol* + *beorg*.

Welnetham, Great & Little Suffolk.

Hvelfiham (*sic*) 1086 (DB), *Weluetham* 1170. Possibly 'enclosure frequented by swans near a water-wheel or other circular feature'. OE *hwēol* + *elfitu* + *hamm*.

Welney Norfolk. *Wellenhe c.*14th cent. 'River called *Welle*'. The earlier name of Old Croft River (from OE *wella* 'stream') + OE *ēa*.

Welsh Bicknor Heref. & Worcs., see BICKNOR.

Welsh Frankton Shrops., see FRANKTON.

Welton, usually 'farmstead by a spring or stream', OE *wella* + *tūn*; examples include: **Welton** Humber. *Welleton* 1086 (DB). **Welton le Marsh** Lincs. *Waletune* 1086 (DB). Affix means 'in the marshland'. **Welton le Wold** Lincs. *Welletune* 1086 (DB). Affix means 'on the wold(s)' with loss of preposition, see WOLDS.

Welwick Humber. *Welwic* 1086 (DB). 'Dwelling or (dairy) farm near a spring or stream'. OE *wella* + *wīc*.

Welwyn Herts. *Welingum c.*945, *Welge* 1086 (DB). '(Place at) the willow-trees'. OE *welig* in a dative plural form *weligum*.

Wem Shrops. *Weme* 1086 (DB). 'Dirty or muddy place'. OE **wemm*.

Wembdon Somerset. *Wadmendune* 1086 (DB). Probably 'hill of the huntsmen'. OE **wǣthe-mann* + *dūn*.

Wembley Gtr. London. *Wembalea* 825. 'Woodland clearing of a man called *Wemba'. OE pers. name + *lēah*.

Wembury Devon. *Wenbiria* late 12th cent. Possibly 'holy stronghold'. OE **wēoh* (dative **wēon*) + *burh* (dative *byrig*).

Wembworthy Devon. *Mameorda* (*sic*) 1086 (DB), *Wemeworth* 1207. 'Enclosure of a man called *Wemba'. OE pers. name + *worth*.

Wendens Ambo Essex. *Wendena* 1086 (DB). Probably 'winding valley'. OE **wende* + *denu*. Affix is Latin *ambo* 'both', referring to the union of the two parishes called Wenden in 1662.

Wendlebury Oxon. *Wandesberie* (*sic*) 1086 (DB), *Wendelberi c.*1175. 'Stronghold of a man called *Wændla'. OE pers. name + *burh* (dative *byrig*).

Wendling Norfolk. *Wenlinga* 1086 (DB). Possibly '(settlement of) the family or followers of a man called *Wændel'. OE pers. name + *-ingas*.

Wendover Bucks. *Wændofran c.*970, *Wendoure* 1086 (DB). Originally the name of the stream here, a Celtic river-name meaning 'white waters'.

Wendron Cornwall. 'Church of *Sancta Wendrona*' 1291. Named from the patron saint of the church, a female saint of whom nothing is known.

Wendy Cambs. *Wandei* 1086 (DB). 'Island at a river-bend'. OE **wende* + *ēg*.

Wenham, Great Suffolk. *Wenham* 1086 (DB). Possibly 'homestead or enclosure with pastureland'. OE **wynn* + *hām* or *hamm*.

Wenhaston Suffolk. *Wenadestuna* 1086 (DB). 'Farmstead or village of a man called *Wynhæth'. OE pers. name + *tūn*.

Wenlock, Little & Much Shrops. *Wynloca c.*1000, *Wenloch* 1086 (DB). Possibly 'white monastery'. Celtic **wīnn* + *loc*. Affix is OE *mycel* 'great'.

Wennington Cambs. *Wenintone c.*960. 'Estate associated with a man called *Wenna'. OE pers. name + *-ing-* + *tūn*.

Wennington Gtr. London. *Winintune c.*1100. 'Estate associated with a man called Wynna'. OE pers. name + *-ing-* + *tūn*.

Wennington Lancs. *Wennigetun* 1086 (DB). 'Farmstead on the River Wenning'. OE river-name (meaning 'dark stream') + *tūn*.

Wensley Derbys. *Wodnesleie* 1086 (DB). 'Sacred grove of the heathen god Wōden'. OE god-name + *lēah*.

Wensley N. Yorks. *Wendreslaga* 1086 (DB), *Wendesle* 1203. 'Woodland clearing of a man called *Wændel'. OE pers. name + *lēah*.

Wentbridge W. Yorks. *Wentbrig* 1302. 'Bridge across the River Went'. Pre-English river-name of uncertain origin + OE *brycg*.

Wentnor Shrops. *Wantenovre* 1086 (DB). Probably 'promontory of a man called

*Wanta'. OE pers. name (genitive *-n*) + **ofer*.

Wentworth, probably 'enclosure of a man called Wintra', OE pers. name + *worth*: **Wentworth** Cambs. *Winteuuorde* 1086 (DB). **Wentworth** S. Yorks. *Wintreuuorde* 1086 (DB).

Weobley Heref. & Worcs. *Wibelai* 1086 (DB). 'Woodland clearing of a man called *Wiobba'. OE pers. name + *lēah*.

Were (river) Wilts., see WARMINSTER.

Wereham Norfolk. *Wigreham* 1086 (DB). Probably 'homestead on a stream called *Wigor* (the winding one)'. Celtic river-name (an old name for the River Wissey) + OE *hām*.

Werrington Cambs. *Witheringtun* 972, *Widerintone* 1086 (DB). 'Estate associated with a man called Wither'. OE pers. name + *-ing-* + *tūn*.

Werrington Cornwall. *Ulvredintone* 1086 (DB). 'Estate associated with a man called Wulfrǣd'. OE pers. name + *-ing-* + *tūn*.

Wervin Ches. *Wivrevene* 1086 (DB). 'Cattle fen, or quaking fen'. OE *weorf* or **wifer* + *fenn*.

Wesham Lancs. *Westhusum* 1189. '(Place at) the westerly houses'. OE *west* + *hūs* in a dative plural form.

Wessex (Anglo-Saxon kingdom centred on Winchester). *West Seaxe* late 9th cent. '(Territory of) the West Saxons'. OE *west* + *Seaxe*.

Wessington Derbys. *Wistanestune* 1086 (DB). 'Farmstead or village of a man called Wīgstān'. OE pers. name + *tūn*.

West as affix, see main name, e.g. for **West Acre** (Norfolk) see ACRE.

Westbere Kent. *Westbere* 1212. 'Westerly woodland pasture'. OE *west* + *bǣr*.

Westborough Lincs. *Westburg* 1086 (DB). 'Westerly stronghold'. OE *west* + *burh*.

Westbourne W. Sussex. *Burne* 1086 (DB), *Westbourne* 1305. '(Place at) the stream'. OE *burna*, with the later addition of *west* to distinguish it from EASTBOURNE.

Westbury, 'westerly stronghold or fortified place', OE *west* + *burh* (dative *byrig*); examples include: **Westbury** Shrops. *Wesberie* 1086 (DB). **Westbury** Wilts. *Westberie* 1086 (DB). **Westbury on Severn** Glos. *Wesberie* 1086 (DB). **Westbury on Trym** Avon. *Westbyrig* 791–6, *Hvesberie* (*sic*) 1086 (DB). Trym is an OE river-name (probably 'strong one').

Westby Lancs. *Westbi* 1086 (DB). 'Westerly farmstead or village'. OScand. *vestr* + *bý*.

Westcliffe on Sea Essex, a self-explanatory name of recent origin.

Westcote, Westcott, 'westerly cottage(s)', OE *west* + *cot*; examples include: **Westcote** Glos. *Westcote* 1315. **Westcott** Surrey. *Westcote* 1086 (DB).

West End Hants. *Westend* 1607. Possibly from OE *wēsten* 'waste-land'.

Westerdale N. Yorks. *Westerdale c.*1165. 'More westerly valley'. OScand. *vestari* + *dalr*.

Westerfield Suffolk. *Westrefelda* 1086 (DB). '(More) westerly open land'. OE **wester* or *westerra* + *feld*.

Westergate W. Sussex. *Westgate* 1230. 'More westerly gate or gap'. OE *westerra* + *geat*. See EASTERGATE.

Westerham Kent. *Westarham* 871–89, *Oistreham* (*sic*) 1086 (DB). 'Westerly homestead'. OE **wester* + *hām*.

Westerleigh Avon. *Westerlega* 1176. 'More westerly woodland clearing'. OE *westerra* + *lēah*.

Westfield, 'westerly open land', OE *west* + *feld*: **Westfield** E. Sussex. *Westewelle* (*sic*) 1086 (DB), *Westefelde c.*1115. **Westfield** Norfolk. *Westfelda* 1086 (DB).

Westgate on Sea Kent. *Westgata* 1168. 'Westerly gate or gap'. OE *west* + *geat*.

Westhall Suffolk. *Westhala* 1169. 'Westerly nook of land'. OE *west* + *halh*.

Westham E. Sussex. *Westham* 1222. 'Westerly promontory'. OE *west* + *hamm*.

Westhampnett W. Sussex. *Hentone* 1086 (DB), *Westhamptonette* 1279. Originally 'high farmstead', from OE *hēah* (dative *hēan*) + *tūn*, with the later addition of *west* and OFrench *-ette* 'little'.

Westhead Lancs. *Westhefd c.*1190.

'Westerly headland or ridge'. OE *west* + *hēafod*.

Westhide Heref. & Worcs. *Hide* 1086 (DB), *Westhyde* 1242. 'Westerly hide of land'. OE *west* + *hīd*.

Westhope Shrops. *Weshope* 1086 (DB). 'Westerly valley'. OE *west* + *hop*.

Westhorpe Suffolk. *Westtorp* 1086 (DB). 'Westerly outlying farmstead or hamlet'. OScand. *vestr* + *thorp*.

Westhoughton Gtr. Manch. *Halcton* c.1210, *Westhalcton* c.1240. 'Westerly farmstead in a nook of land'. OE *west* + *halh* + *tūn*.

Westleigh Devon. *Weslega* 1086 (DB). 'Westerly wood or clearing'. OE *west* + *lēah*.

Westleton Suffolk. *Westledestuna* 1086 (DB). 'Farmstead or village of a man called Vestlithi'. OScand. pers. name + OE *tūn*.

Westley, 'westerly wood or clearing', OE *west* + *lēah*: **Westley** Suffolk. *Westlea* 1086 (DB). **Westley Waterless** Cambs. *Westle* c.1045, *Weslai* 1086 (DB), *Westle Waterles* 1285. Affix means 'wet clearings', from OE *wæter* + *lēas* (the plural of *lēah*).

Westlinton Cumbria. *Westlevington* c.1200. 'Farmstead by the River Lyne'. Celtic river-name (possibly 'the smooth one') + OE *tūn*, with *west* to distinguish it from KIRKLINTON.

Westmeston E. Sussex. *Westmæstun* c.765, *Wesmestun* 1086 (DB). 'Most westerly farmstead'. OE *westmest* + *tūn*.

Westmill Herts. *Westmele* 1086 (DB). 'Westerly mill'. OE *west* + *myln*.

Westminster Gtr. London. *Westmynster* c.975. 'West monastery', i.e. to the west of London. OE *west* + *mynster*.

Westmorland (old county). *Westmoringaland* c.1150. 'District of the people living west of the moors' (alluding to the North Yorkshire Pennines). OE *west* + *mōr* + *-inga-* + *land*.

Westnewton Northum. *Niwetona* 12th cent. 'New farmstead'. OE *nīwe* + *tūn*, with *west* to distinguish it from KIRKNEWTON.

Weston, a very common place-name, 'west farmstead or village', i.e. one to the west of another settlement, OE *west* + *tūn*; examples include: **Weston** Herts. *Westone* 1086 (DB). **Weston** Lincs. *Westune* 1086 (DB). **Weston, Buckhorn** Dorset. *Westone* 1086 (DB), *Boukeresweston* 1275. Manorial affix from some medieval owner called *Bouker*. **Weston, Edith** Leics. *Westona* 1167, *Weston Edith* 1275. Affix probably from its possession by Queen Ēadgȳth, wife of Edward the Confessor, in 1086. **Weston, Hail** Cambs. *Heilweston* 1199. Affix is the original Celtic name (meaning 'dirty stream') of the River Kym. **Weston Rhyn** Shrops. *Westone* 1086 (DB). Affix is Welsh *rhyn* 'peak, hill'. **Weston Subedge** Glos. *Westone* 1086 (DB), *Weston sub Egge* 1255. Affix means 'under the edge or escarpment' (of the Cotswolds) from Latin *sub* and OE *ecg*. **Weston super Mare** Avon. *Weston* c.1230, *Weston super Mare* 1349. The Latin affix means 'on the sea'. **Weston Turville** Bucks. *Westone* 1086 (DB), *Westone Turvile* 1302. Manorial affix from the *de Turville* family, here in the 12th cent.

Westoning Beds. *Westone* 1086 (DB), *Westone Ynge* 1365. 'West farmstead', OE *west* + *tūn*, with manorial affix from its possession by the *Ing* family in the 14th cent.

Westonzoyland Somerset. *Sowi* 1086 (DB), *Westsowi* c.1245. 'The westerly manor of the estate called *Sowi*', thus distinguished from MIDDLEZOY and with the later addition of *land* 'estate'.

Westward Cumbria. *Le Westwarde* 1354. 'Western division (of a forest)'. ME *west* + *warde*.

Westward Ho! Devon, modern name commemorating the novel of this name by Charles Kingsley (published in 1855) largely set in this locality.

Westwell, 'westerly spring or stream', OE *west* + *wella*: **Westwell** Kent. *Welle* 1086 (DB), *Westwell* 1226. **Westwell** Oxon. *Westwelle* 1086 (DB).

Westwick, 'westerly dwelling or (dairy) farm', OE *west* + *wīc*: **Westwick** Cambs. *Westuuiche* 1086 (DB). **Westwick** Durham. *Westewic* 1091. **Westwick** Norfolk. *Westuuic* 1086 (DB).

Westwood Wilts. *Westwuda* 987,

Westwode 1086 (DB). 'Westerly wood'. OE *west* + *wudu*.

Wetheral Cumbria. *Wetherhala* c.1100. 'Nook of land where wether-sheep are kept'. OE *wether* + *halh*.

Wetherby W. Yorks. *Wedrebi* 1086 (DB). 'Wether-sheep farmstead'. OScand. *vethr* + *bý*.

Wetherden Suffolk. *Wederdena* 1086 (DB). 'Valley where wether-sheep are kept'. OE *wether* + *denu*.

Wetheringsett Suffolk. *Weddreringesete* c.1035, *Wederingaseta* 1086 (DB). Probably 'fold of the people of WETHERDEN'. Reduced form of previous name + *-inga-* + *set*.

Wethersfield Essex. *Witheresfelda* 1086 (DB). 'Open land of a man called Wihthere or *Wether'. OE pers. name + *feld*.

Wettenhall Ches. *Watenhale* 1086 (DB). 'Wet nook of land'. OE *wēt* (dative *-an*) + *halh*.

Wetton Staffs. *Wettindun* 1252. Possibly 'wet hill'. OE *wēt* (dative *-an*) + *dūn*.

Wetwang N. Yorks. *Wetuuangha* 1086 (DB). Probably 'field for the trial of a legal action'. OScand. *vǽtt-vangr*.

Wetwood Staffs. *Wetewode* 1291. 'Wet wood'. OE *wēt* + *wudu*.

Wexcombe Wilts. *Wexcumbe* 1167. 'Valley where wax (from bees) is found'. OE *weax* + *cumb*.

Weybourne Norfolk. *Wabrune* 1086 (DB). OE *burna* 'spring, stream' with an uncertain first element, possibly an OE or pre-English name of the river from a root **war-* 'water', or an OE **wagu* 'quagmire', or OE *wær* 'weir, river-dam'.

Weybread Suffolk. *Weibrada* 1086 (DB). Probably 'broad stretch of land by a road'. OE *weg* + *brǣdu*.

Weybridge Surrey. *Webruge* 1086. 'Bridge over the River Wey'. Ancient pre-English river-name of unknown origin and meaning + OE *brycg*.

Weyhill Hants. *La Wou* c.1270. Possibly 'the hill-spur climbed by a road'. OE *weg* + *hōh*, with the later addition of *hill*. Alternatively the original name may be from OE *wēoh* '(heathen) temple'.

Weymouth Dorset. *Waimouthe* 934. 'Mouth of the River Wey'. Ancient pre-English river-name of unknown origin and meaning + OE *mūtha*.

Whaddon, usually 'hill where wheat is grown'. OE *hwǣte* + *dūn*; examples include: **Whaddon** Bucks. *Hwætædun* 966–75, *Wadone* 1086 (DB). **Whaddon** Cambs. *Wadone* 1086 (DB).

However the following has a different second element: **Whaddon** Wilts., near Salisbury. *Watedene* 1086 (DB). 'Valley where wheat is grown'. OE *hwǣte* + *denu*.

Whale Cumbria. *Vwal* 1178. OScand. *hváll* 'an isolated round hill'.

Whaley Derbys., near Bolsover. *Walley* 1230. Possibly 'woodland clearing by a spring or stream'. OE *wælla* + *lēah*.

Whaley Bridge Derbys. *Weile* c.1250. 'Woodland clearing by a road'. OE *weg* + *lēah*.

Whalley Lancs. *Hwælleage* 11th cent., *Wallei* 1086 (DB). 'Woodland clearing on or near a round hill'. OE **hwæl* + *lēah*.

Whalton Northum. *Walton* 1203. Possibly 'farmstead by a round hill'. OE **hwæl* + *tūn*.

Whaplode Lincs. *Cappelad* 810, *Copelade* 1086 (DB). 'Watercourse or channel where eelpouts are found'. OE **cwappa* + *lād*.

Wharfe N. Yorks. *Warf* 1224. OScand. *hvarf* or *hverfi* 'a bend or corner'.

Wharfe (river) W. Yorks., see BURLEY IN WHARFEDALE.

Wharles Lancs. *Quarlous* 1249. Probably 'hills or mounds near a stone circle'. OE *hwerfel* + *hlāw*.

Wharncliffe Side S. Yorks. *Querncliffe* 1406, *Wharnetliffe Side* 1634. 'Cliff where querns or millstones are obtained'. OE *cweorn* + *clif*, with the later addition of *sīde* 'hill-side'.

Wharram Percy & le Street N. Yorks. *Warran* 1086 (DB), *Wharrom Percy* 1291, *Warrum in the Strete* 1333. Possibly '(place at) the kettles or cauldrons' (perhaps used in some topographical sense). OE *hwer* in a dative plural form. Distinguishing affixes from early possession by the *de Percy* family and from proximity to an ancient road ('on the street' from OE *strǣt*).

Wharton Ches. *Wanetune* (*sic*) 1086 (DB), *Waverton* 1216. Probably 'farmstead by a swaying tree'. OE *wæfre* + *tūn*.

Whashton N. Yorks. *Whassingetun* c.1160. Probably 'estate associated with a man called *Hwæssa'. OE pers. name + *-ing-* + *tūn*.

Whatcombe Dorset. *Watecumbe* 1288. 'Wet valley', or 'valley where wheat is grown'. OE *wǣt* or *hwǣte* + *cumb*.

Whatcote Warwicks. *Quatercote* (*sic*) 1086 (DB), *Whatcote* 1206. 'Cottage near which wheat is grown'. OE *hwǣte* + *cot*.

Whatfield Suffolk. *Watefelda* 1086 (DB). Probably 'open land where wheat is grown'. OE *hwǣte* + *feld*.

Whatley Somerset, near Chard. *Watelege* 1086 (DB). 'Woodland clearing where wheat is grown'. OE *hwǣte* + *lēah*.

Whatlington E. Sussex. *Watlingetone* 1086 (DB). Probably 'farmstead of the family or followers of a man called *Hwætel'. OE pers. name + *-inga-* + *tūn*.

Whatstandwell Derbys. *Wattestanwell ford* 1390. Named from a certain *Wat* or *Walter Stonewell* who had a house near the ford in 1390.

Whatton, probably 'farmstead where wheat is grown', OE *hwǣte* + *tūn*: **Whatton** Notts. *Watone* 1086 (DB). **Whatton, Long** Leics. *Watton* 1190. Affix (recorded from the 14th cent.) refers to the length of the village.

Wheatacre Norfolk. *Hwateaker* 1086 (DB). 'Cultivated land used for wheat'. OE *hwǣte* + *æcer*.

Wheathampstead Herts. *Wathemestede* c.960, *Watamestede* 1086 (DB). 'Homestead where wheat is grown'. OE *hwǣte* + *hām-stede*.

Wheatley, 'clearing where wheat is grown', OE *hwǣte* + *lēah*; examples include: **Wheatley** Oxon. *Hwatelega* 1163. **Wheatley Lane** Lancs. *Watelei* 1086 (DB). **Wheatley, North & South** Notts. *Wateleie* 1086 (DB).

Wheaton Aston Staffs., see ASTON.

Wheddon Cross Somerset. *Wheteden* 1243. 'Valley where wheat is grown'. OE *hwǣte* + *denu*.

Wheelock Ches. *Hoiloch* 1086 (DB). Named from the River Wheelock, a Celtic river-name meaning 'winding'.

Wheelton Lancs. *Weltona* c.1160. 'Farmstead with a water-wheel or near some other circular feature'. OE *hwēol* + *tūn*.

Whenby N. Yorks. *Quennebi* 1086 (DB). 'Farmstead or village of the women'. OScand. *kona* (genitive plural *kvenna*) + *bý*.

Whepstead Suffolk. *Wepstede* 942–51, *Huepestede* 1086 (DB). Probably 'place where brushwood grows'. OE **hwip(p)e* + *stede*.

Wherstead Suffolk. *Weruesteda* 1086 (DB). 'Place by a wharf or shore'. OE *hwearf* + *stede*.

Wherwell Hants. *Hwerwyl* 955. Probably 'spring provided with a kettle or cauldron'. OE *hwer* + *wella*.

Wheston, Whetstone, from OE *hwet-stān* 'a whetstone', probably referring to places where stone suitable for whetstones was found: **Wheston** Derbys. *Whetstan* 1251. **Whetstone** Gtr. London. *Wheston* 1417. **Whetstone** Leics. *Westham* (*sic*) 1086 (DB), *Whetestan* 12th cent.

Whicham Cumbria. *Witingham* 1086 (DB). 'Homestead of the family or followers of a man called Hwīta', or 'homestead at Hwīta's place'. OE pers. name + *-inga-* or *-ing* + *hām*.

Whichford Warwicks. *Wicford* 1086 (DB), *Wicheforda* c.1130. Probably 'ford of the tribe called the *Hwicce*'. OE tribal name + *ford*.

Whickham Tyne & Wear. *Quicham* 1196. 'Homestead or enclosure with a quickset hedge'. OE **cwic* + *hām* or *hamm*.

Whilton Northants. *Woltone* 1086 (DB). 'Farmstead with a water-wheel, or on a round hill'. OE *hwēol* + *tūn*.

Whimple Devon. *Winple* 1086 (DB). Originally the name of the stream here, a Celtic name meaning 'white pool or stream'.

Whinburgh Norfolk. *Wineberga* 1086

(DB). 'Hill where gorse grows'. OScand. *hvin + OE *beorg*.

Whippingham I. of Wight. *Wippingeham* 735, *Wipingeham* 1086 (DB). 'Homestead of the family or followers of a man called *Wippa'. OE pers. name + *-inga-* + *hām*.

Whipsnade Beds. *Wibsnede* 1202. 'Detached plot of a man called *Wibba'. OE pers. name + *snǣd*.

Whissendine Leics. *Wichingedene* 1086 (DB). 'Valley of the family or followers of a man called *Wic'. OE pers. name + *-inga-* + *denu*. Alternatively the first element of this and the following name may be OE *wīcinga* 'of the pirates'.

Whissonsett Norfolk. *Witcingkeseta* 1086 (DB). 'Fold of the family or followers of a man called *Wic'. OE pers. name + *-inga-* + *set*.

Whistley Green Berks. *Wisclea* 968, *Wiselei* 1086 (DB). 'Marshy-meadow clearing'. OE *wisc* + *lēah*.

Whiston Mersey. *Quistan* 1190. 'The white stone'. OE *hwīt* + *stān*.

Whiston Northants. *Hwiccingtune* 974, *Wicentone* 1086 (DB). 'Farmstead of the tribe called the *Hwicce*'. OE tribal name (genitive plural *-na*) + *tūn*.

Whiston S. Yorks. *Witestan* 1086 (DB). 'The white stone'. OE *hwīt* + *stān*.

Whiston Staffs. *Witestun* c.1002, *Witestone* 1086 (DB). 'Farmstead of a man called *Witi'. OE pers. name + *tūn*.

Whitacre, Nether & Over Warwicks. *Witacre* 1086 (DB). 'White cultivated land'. OE *hwīt* + *æcer*.

Whitbeck Cumbria. *Witebec* c.1160. 'White stream'. OScand. *hvítr* + *bekkr*.

Whitburn Tyne & Wear. *Hwiteberne* c.1190. 'Tumulus or barn of a man called Hwīta'. OE pers. name + *byrgen* or *bere-ærn*.

Whitby Ches. *Witeberia* c.1100. 'White stronghold or manor-house'. OE *hwīt* + *burh* (dative *byrig*).

Whitby N. Yorks. *Witeby* 1086 (DB). 'White farmstead or village, or of a man called Hvíti'. OScand. *hvítr* or pers. name + *bý*.

Whitchurch, 'white church', i.e. probably 'stone-built church', OE *hwīt* + *cirice*; examples include: **Whitchurch** Avon. *Hwitecirce* 1065. **Whitchurch** Hants. *Hwitancyrice* 909. **Whitchurch** Shrops. *Album Monasterium* 1199 (here the name is rendered in Latin), *Whytchyrche* 13th cent. Called *Westune* 'west farmstead' in 1086 (DB). **Whitchurch Canonicorum** Dorset. *Witcerce* 1086 (DB), *Whitchurch Canonicorum* 1262. Latin affix means 'of the canons', referring to early possession by the canons of Salisbury.

White as affix, see main name, e.g. for **White Notley** (Essex) see NOTLEY.

Whitechapel Gtr. London. *Whitechapele* 1340. 'The white chapel', i.e. probably 'stone-built chapel'. OE *hwīt* + ME *chapele*.

Whitefield Gtr. Manch. *Whitefeld* 1292. 'White open land'. OE *hwīt* + *feld*.

Whitegate Ches. *Whytegate* 1540. 'The white gate'. OE *hwīt* + *geat*, referring to the outer gate of Vale Royal Abbey.

Whitehaven Cumbria. *Qwithofhavene* c.1135. 'Harbour near the white headland'. OScand. *hvítr* + *hǫfuth* + *hafn*.

White Ladies Aston Heref. & Worcs., see ASTON.

Whiteparish Wilts. *La Whytechyrche* 1278, *Whyteparosshe* 1289. Originally 'the white church', later replaced by 'parish'. OE *hwīt* + *cirice* and ME *paroche*.

Whitestaunton Somerset. *Stantune* 1086 (DB), *Whitestaunton* 1337. 'Farmstead on stony ground', OE *stān* + *tūn*, with later affix referring to the limestone quarries here.

Whitestone Devon. *Hwitastane* c.1100, *Witestan* 1086 (DB). '(Place at) the white stone'. OE *hwīt* + *stān*.

Whitfield, 'white open land', OE *hwīt* + *feld*: **Whitfield** Kent. *Whytefeld* 1228. **Whitfield** Northants. *Witefelle* 1086 (DB). **Whitfield** Northum. *Witefeld* 1254.

Whitford Devon. *Witefort* 1086 (DB). 'White ford'. OE *hwit* + *ford*.

Whitgift Humber. *Witegift* c.1070. Probably 'dowry land of a man called Hvítr'. OScand. pers. name + *gipt*.

Whitgreave Staffs. *Witegraue* 1193. 'White grove or copse'. OE *hwīt* + *grǣfe*.

Whitley, 'white wood or clearing', OE *hwīt* + *lēah*; examples include: **Whitley** Berks., near Reading. *Witelei* 1086 (DB). **Whitley Bay** Tyne & Wear. *Wyteleya* 12th cent. **Whitley, Higher & Lower** Ches. *Witelei* 1086 (DB).

Whitmore Staffs. *Witemore* 1086 (DB). 'White moor or marsh'. OE *hwīt* + *mōr*.

Whitnash Warwicks. *Witenas* 1086 (DB). '(Place at) the white ash-tree'. OE *hwīt* (dative *-an*) + *æsc*.

Whitney Heref. & Worcs. *Witenie* 1086 (DB). 'White island'. OE *hwīt* (dative *-an*) + *ēg*. Alternatively the first element may be the OE pers. name Hwīta (genitive *-n*).

Whitsbury Hants. *Wiccheberia* c.1130. 'Fortified place where wych-elms grow'. OE *wice* + *burh* (dative *byrig*).

Whitstable Kent. *Witenestaple* 1086 (DB). 'White post', or 'post of the councillors'. OE *hwīt* (dative *-an*) or *wita* (genitive plural *-ena*) + *stapol*.

Whitstone Cornwall. *Witestan* 1086 (DB). 'White stone'. OE *hwīt* + *stān*.

Whittingham Northum. *Hwitincham* c.1050. 'Homestead of the family or followers of a man called Hwīta', or 'homestead at Hwīta's place'. OE pers. name + *-inga-* or *-ing* + *hām*.

Whittingslow Shrops. *Witecheslawe* 1086 (DB). 'Tumulus of a man called Hwittuc'. OE pers. name + *hlāw*.

Whittington, 'estate associated with a man called Hwīta', OE pers. name + *-ing-* + *tūn*; examples include: **Whittington** Shrops. *Wititone* 1086 (DB). **Whittington** Staffs. *Hwituntune* 925. **Whittington, Great** Northum. *Witynton* 1233.

Whittlebury Northants. *Witlanbyrig* c.930. 'Stronghold of a man called *Witla'. OE pers. name + *burh* (dative *byrig*).

Whittle-le-Woods Lancs. *Witul* c.1160. 'White hill'. OE *hwīt* + *hyll*. Later affix means 'in the woodland'.

Whittlesey Cambs. *Witlesig* c.972, *Witesie* 1086 (DB). 'Island of a man called *Wittel'. OE pers. name + *ēg*.

Whittlesford Cambs. *Witelesforde* 1086 (DB). 'Ford of a man called *Wittel'. OE pers. name + *ford*.

Whitton, usually 'white farmstead' or 'farmstead of a man called Hwīta', OE *hwīt* or pers. name + *tūn*, for example: **Whitton** Cleveland. *Wittune* 1208–10. **Whitton** Suffolk. *Widituna* (*sic*) 1086 (DB), *Witton* 1212.

However the following has a different origin: **Whitton** Humber. *Witenai* 1086 (DB). 'White island'. OE *hwīt* (dative *-an*) + *ēg*.

Whittonstall Northum. *Quictunstal* 1242. 'Farmstead with a quickset hedge'. OE **cwic* + *tūn-stall*.

Whitwell, 'white spring or stream', OE *hwīt* + *wella*; examples include: **Whitwell** Derbys. *Hwitewylle* c.1002, *Witewelle* 1086 (DB). **Whitwell** I. of Wight. *Quitewell* 1212.

Whitwick Leics. *Witewic* 1086 (DB). 'White dwelling or (dairy) farm', or 'farm of a man called Hwīta'. OE *hwīt* or pers. name + *wīc*.

Whitwood W. Yorks. *Witewde* 1086 (DB). 'White wood' (referring to colour of tree-bark or blossom). OE *hwīt* + *wudu*.

Whitworth Lancs. *Whiteworth* 13th cent. 'White enclosure'. OE *hwīt* + *worth*.

Whixall Shrops. *Witehala* (*sic*) 1086 (DB), *Whitekeshal* 1241. 'Nook of land of a man called Hwittuc'. OE pers. name + *halh*.

Whixley N. Yorks. *Cucheslage* 1086 (DB). 'Woodland clearing of a man called *Cwic'. OE pers. name + *lēah*.

Whorlton Durham. *Queorningtun* c.1050. Probably 'farmstead at the mill-stone place or the mill stream'. OE *cweorn* + *-ing* + *tūn*.

Whorlton N. Yorks. *Wirveltune* 1086 (DB). 'Farmstead near the round-topped hill'. OE *hwerfel* + *tūn*.

Whyteleafe Surrey, named from *White Leaf Field* 1839, so called from the aspens that grew there.

Wibtoft Leics. *Wibbetofte* 1002, *Wibetot* 1086 (DB). 'Homestead of a man called

Wibba or Vibbi'. OE or OScand. pers. name + *toft*.

Wichenford Heref. & Worcs. *Wiceneford* 11th cent. 'Ford by the wych-elms'. OE *wice* (genitive plural *-ena*) + *ford*.

Wichling Kent. *Winchelesmere* 1086 (DB), *Winchelinge* 1220-4. Probably '(settlement of) the family or followers of a man called *Wincel', OE pers. name + *-ingas*. The alternative name used in the 11th and 12th centuries means '*Wincel's pool or boundary', second element OE *mere* or *mǣre*.

Wick, 'the dwelling, the specialized farm or trading settlement', OE *wīc*; examples include: **Wick** Avon, near Kingswood. *Wike* 1189. **Wick** Heref. & Worcs., near Pershore. *Wiche* 1086 (DB). **Wick St Lawrence** Avon. *Wike* 1225. Affix from the dedication of the church.

Wicken, 'the dwellings, the specialized farm or trading settlement', OE *wīc* in the dative plural form *wīcum* or a ME plural form *wiken*: **Wicken** Cambs. *Wicha* 1086 (DB), *Wiken c.*1200. **Wicken** Northants. *Wiche* 1086 (DB), *Wicne* 1235. **Wicken Bonhunt** Essex. *Wica* 1086 (DB), *Wykes Bonhunte* 1238. Originally two separate names, Bonhunt (*Banhunta* 1086 (DB) possibly being 'place where people were summoned for hunting', OE *bann* + **hunte*.

Wickenby Lincs. *Wichingebi* 1086 (DB). 'Farmstead or village of a man called Víkingr, or of the vikings'. OScand. pers. name or *víkingr* + *bý*.

Wickersley S. Yorks. *Wicresleia* 1086 (DB). 'Woodland clearing of a man called Víkarr'. OScand. pers. name + OE *lēah*.

Wickford Essex. *Wicforda c.*975, *Wicfort* 1086 (DB). Probably 'ford by an earlier Romano-British settlement'. OE *wīc* + *ford*.

Wickham, usually 'homestead associated with a *vicus*, i.e. an earlier Romano-British settlement', OE **wīc-hām*; examples include: **Wickham** Hants. *Wicham* 925-41, *Wicheham* 1086 (DB). **Wickham Bishops** Essex. *Wicham* 1086 (DB), *Wykham Bishops* 1313. Affix from its possession by the Bishop of London. **Wickham Market** Suffolk. *Wikham* 1086 (DB). Affix from the important market here. **Wickham Skeith** Suffolk. *Wichamm* 1086 (DB), *Wicham Skeyth* 1368. Affix is OScand. *skeith* 'a race-course'. **Wickham, West** Gtr. London. *Wichamm* 973, *Wicheham* 1086 (DB). It is possible that in this name the second element is rather OE *hamm* in the sense 'promontory'.

Wickhambreux Kent. *Wicham* 948, *Wicheham* 1086 (DB), *Wykham Breuhuse* 1270. Identical in origin with the previous names. Manorial affix from the *de Brayhuse* family, here in the 13th cent.

Wickhambrook Suffolk. *Wicham* 1086 (DB), *Wichambrok* 1254. Identical in origin with the previous names, but with the later addition of OE *brōc* 'brook'.

Wickhamford Heref. & Worcs. *Wicwona* 709, *Wiquene* 1086 (DB), *Wikewaneford* 1221. 'Ford at the place called *Wicwon*'. OE *ford*, see CHILDSWICKHAM.

Wickhampton Norfolk. *Wichamtuna* 1086 (DB). Probably 'homestead with or near a dairy farm'. OE *wīc* + *hām-tūn*.

Wicklewood Norfolk. *Wikelewuda* 1086 (DB). Possibly 'wood by the dairy-farm clearing'. OE *wīc* + *lēah* + *wudu*.

Wickmere Norfolk. *Wicmera* 1086 (DB). 'Pool by a dwelling or (dairy) farm'. OE *wīc* + *mere*.

Wickwar Avon. *Wichen* 1086 (DB), *Wykewarre* 13th cent. Originally 'the dwellings or specialized farm', from OE *wīc* in a plural form. Later manorial affix from the family of *la Warre*, here from the early 13th cent.

Widcombe, North & South Avon. *Widecomb* 1303. 'Wide valley', or 'willow-tree valley'. OE *wīd* or *wīthig* + *cumb*.

Widdington Essex. *Widintuna* 1086 (DB). 'Farmstead or village where willow-trees grow'. OE **wīthign* + *tūn*.

Widdrington Northum. *Vuderintuna c.*1160. 'Estate associated with a man called *Widuhere'. OE pers. name + *-ing-* + *tūn*.

Widecombe in the Moor Devon. *Widecumba* 12th cent. Probably 'valley where willow-trees grow'. OE *wīthig* +

cumb. Affix refers to its situation on DARTMOOR.

Widford, 'ford where willow-trees grow', OE *wīthig* + *ford*: **Widford** Essex. *Witford* 1202. **Widford** Herts. *Wideford* 1086 (DB).

Widmerpool Notts. *Wimarspol* 1086 (DB). 'Wide lake (or willow-tree lake) pool'. OE *wīd* or *wīthig* + *mere* + *pōl*.

Widnes Ches. *Wydnes* c.1200. 'Wide promontory'. OE *wīd* + *næss*.

Wigan Gtr. Manch. *Wigan* 1199. Probably a shortened form of a Welsh name *Tref Wigan* 'homestead of a man called Wigan'.

Wigborough, Great Essex. *Wicgheberga* 1086 (DB). 'Hill of a man called Wicga'. OE pers. name + *beorg*.

Wiggenhall Norfolk. *Wigrehala* 1086 (DB), *Wiggenhal* 1196. 'Nook of land of a man called Wicga'. OE pers. name (genitive *-n*) + *halh*.

Wigginton, 'farmstead of, or associated with, a man called Wicga', OE pers. name (genitive *-n* or + *-ing-*) + *tūn*: **Wigginton** Herts. *Wigentone* 1086 (DB). **Wigginton** N. Yorks. *Wichintun* 1086 (DB). **Wigginton** Oxon. *Wigentone* 1086 (DB). **Wigginton** Staffs. *Wigetone* 1086 (DB).

Wigglesworth N. Yorks. *Winchelesuuorde* 1086 (DB). 'Enclosure of a man called Wincel'. OE pers. name + *worth*.

Wiggonby Cumbria. *Wygayneby* 1278. 'Farmstead or village of a man called Wigan'. Celtic pers. name + OScand. *bý*.

Wighill N. Yorks. *Duas Wicheles* 1086 (DB), *Wikale* 1219. 'Nook of land with a dairy-farm or by an earlier Romano-British settlement'. OE *wīc* + *halh* (in the plural form in 1086, with Latin *duas* 'two').

Wight, Isle of (the county). *Vectis* c.150, *Wit* 1086 (DB). A Celtic name possibly meaning 'place of the division', referring to its situation between the two arms of the Solent.

Wighton Norfolk. *Wistune* 1086 (DB). 'Dwelling place, farmstead with a dwelling'. OE *wīc-tūn*.

Wigmore Heref. & Worcs. *Wigemore* 1086 (DB). Probably 'quaking marsh'. OE *wigga* + *mōr*.

Wigmore Kent. *Wydemere* 1275. 'Broad pool'. OE *wīd* + *mere*.

Wigsley Notts. *Wigesleie* 1086 (DB). 'Woodland clearing of a man called *Wicg'. OE pers. name + *lēah*.

Wigsthorpe Northants. *Wykingethorp* 1232. 'Outlying farmstead or hamlet of a man called Víkingr'. OScand. pers. name + *thorp*.

Wigston Magna Leics. *Wichingestone* 1086 (DB). 'Farmstead or estate of a man called *Wīcing or Víkingr'. OE or OScand. pers. name + OE *tūn*. Affix is Latin *magna* 'great' to distinguish this place from **Wigston Parva** (*Wicestan* 1086 (DB)) which has a quite different origin, either 'rocking-stone' from OE *wigga* + *stān*, or 'stone of a man called *Wicg' from OE pers. name + *stān*.

Wigtoft Lincs. *Wiketoft* 1187. Probably 'homestead by a (former) creek'. OScand. *vík* + *toft*.

Wigton Cumbria. *Wiggeton* 1163. 'Farmstead or village of a man called Wicga'. OE pers. name + *tūn*.

Wike, 'the dwelling, the specialized farm', OE *wīc*; for example **Wike** W. Yorks., near Harewood *Wich* 1086 (DB).

Wilbarston Northants. *Wilbertestone* 1086 (DB). 'Farmstead or village of a man called Wilbeorht'. OE pers. name + *tūn*.

Wilberfoss Humber. *Wilburcfosa* 1148. 'Ditch of a woman called Wilburh'. OE pers. name + *foss*.

Wilbraham, Great & Little Cambs. *Wilburgeham* c.975, *Wiborgham* 1086 (DB). 'Homestead or village of a woman called Wilburh'. OE pers. name + *hām*.

Wilburton Cambs. *Wilburhtun* 970, *Wilbertone* 1086 (DB). 'Farmstead or village of a woman called Wilburh'. OE pers. name + *tūn*.

Wilby Norfolk. *Willebeih* 1086 (DB). 'Farmstead by the willow-trees', or possibly 'circle of willow-trees'. OE *wilig + OScand. *bý* or OE *bēag*.

Wilby Northants. *Willabyg* c.1067, *Wilebi* 1086 (DB). 'Farmstead of a man called Willa or Villi'. OE or OScand. pers. name + *bý*.

Wilby Suffolk. *Wilebey* 1086 (DB). Probably 'circle of willow-trees'. OE **wilig* + *bēag*.

Wilcot Wilts. *Wilcotum* 940, *Wilcote* 1086 (DB). 'Cottages by the stream or spring'. OE *wiella* + *cot* (dative plural *-um*).

Wilden Beds. *Wildene* 1086 (DB). Possibly 'willow-tree valley'. OE **wilig* + *denu*.

Wilden Heref. & Worcs. *Wineladuna* (*sic*) 1182, *Wiveldon* 1299. Probably 'hill of a man called *Wifela'. OE pers. name + *dūn*.

Wildsworth Lincs. *Winelesworth* (*sic*) 1199, *Wyvelesworth* 1280. Probably 'enclosure of a man called *Wifel'. OE pers. name + *worth*.

Wilford Notts. *Wilesford* 1086 (DB). Probably 'willow-tree ford'. OE **wilig* + *ford*.

Wilkesley Ches. *Wiuelesde* (*sic*) 1086 (DB), *Wivelescle* 1230. 'Tongue of land of a man called *Wifel'. OE pers. name + *clēa*.

Willand Devon. *Willelanda* 1086 (DB). 'Waste land', or 'cultivated land reverted to waste'. OE *wilde* + *land*.

Willaston, 'farmstead or village of a man called Wīglāf', OE pers. name + *tūn*: **Willaston** Ches., near Hooton. *Wilaveston* 1086 (DB). **Willaston** Ches., near Nantwich. *Wilavestune* 1086 (DB).

Willen Bucks. *Wily* 1189. '(Place at) the willow-trees'. OE **wilig* in a dative plural form.

Willenhall W. Mids., near Coventry. *Wilenhala* 12th cent. 'Nook or small valley where willow-trees grow'. OE **wiligen* + *halh*.

Willenhall W. Mids., near Wolverhampton. *Willanhalch* 732, *Winenhale* (*sic*) 1086 (DB). 'Nook or small valley of a man called Willa'. OE pers. name (genitive *-n*) + *halh*.

Willerby, 'farmstead or village of a man called Wilheard', OE pers. name + OScand. *bý*: **Willerby** Humber. *Wilgardi* (*sic*) 1086 (DB), *Willardebi* 1196. **Willerby** N. Yorks. *Willerdebi* 1125–30.

Willersey Glos. *Willerseye* 709, *Willersei* 1086 (DB). 'Island of a man called Wilhere or Wilheard'. OE pers. name + *ēg*.

Willersley Heref. & Worcs. *Willaveslege* 1086 (DB). Probably 'woodland clearing of a man called Wīglāf'. OE pers. name + *lēah*.

Willesborough Kent. *Wifelesberg* 863. 'Hill or mound of a man called *Wifel'. OE pers. name + *beorg*.

Willesden Gtr. London. *Willesdone* 939, *Wellesdone* 1086 (DB). 'Hill with a spring'. OE *wiell* + *dūn*.

Willett Somerset. *Willet* 1086 (DB). Named from the River Willett, an old river-name of uncertain origin and meaning.

Willey, usually 'willow-tree wood or clearing', OE **wilig* + *lēah*; examples include: **Willey** Shrops. *Wilit* (*sic*) 1086 (DB), *Wilileg* 1199. **Willey** Warwicks. *Welei* 1086 (DB).

However the following has a different origin: **Willey** Surrey. *Weoleage* 909. 'Sacred grove with a heathen temple'. OE *wēoh* + *lēah*.

Williamscot Oxon. *Williamescote* 1166. 'Cottage of a man called Willelm or William'. OGerman pers. name + OE *cot*.

Willingale Doe Essex. *Willinghehala* 1086 (DB), *Willingeshale Doe* 1270. 'Nook of land of the family or followers of a man called Willa'. OE pers. name + *-inga-* + *halh*. Manorial affix from the *de Ou* family, here in the 12th cent.

Willingdon E. Sussex. *Willendone* 1086 (DB). Probably 'hill of a man called Willa'. OE pers. name (genitive *-n*) + *dūn*.

Willingham, sometimes 'homestead of the family or followers of a man called *Wifel', OE pers. name + *-inga-* + *hām*: **Willingham** Cambs., near Cambridge. *Vuivlingeham* c.1050, *Wivelingham* 1086 (DB). **Willingham** Lincs. *Wilingeham* 1086 (DB). **Willingham, North** Lincs. *Wiuilingeham* 1086 (DB).

However the following are 'homestead of the family or followers of a man called Willa', OE pers. name + *-inga-* + *hām*: **Willingham, Cherry** Lincs. *Wilingeham* 1086 (DB), *Chyry Wylynham* 1386. Affix is ME *chiri* 'cherry-tree'. **Willingham, South** Lincs. *Ulingeham* 1086 (DB).

Willington Beds. *Welitone* 1086 (DB). 'Willow-tree farmstead'. OE **wilign* + *tūn*.

Willington Derbys. *Willetune* 1086 (DB). Probably identical in origin with the previous name.

Willington Durham. *Wyvelintun c.*1190. 'Estate associated with a man called *Wifel'. OE pers. name + *-ing-* + *tūn*.

Willington Tyne & Wear. *Wiflintun c.*1085. Identical in origin with the previous name.

Willington Warwicks. *Ullavintone* 1086 (DB). 'Estate associated with a man called Wulflāf'. OE pers. name + *-ing-* + *tūn*.

Willington Corner Ches. *Winfletone* 1086 (DB). 'Farmstead or village of a woman called Wynflǣd'. OE pers. name + *tūn*. Affix, first used in the 19th cent., refers to a corner of Delamere Forest.

Willitoft Humber. *Wilgetot* 1086 (DB). 'Willow-tree homestead'. OE **wilig* + OScand. *toft*.

Williton Somerset. *Willettun* 904, *Willetone* 1086 (DB). 'Farmstead or village on the River Willett'. Old river-name (see WILLETT) + OE *tūn*.

Willoughby, usually 'farmstead by the willow-trees', OE **wilig* + OScand. *bý*, although some may be 'circle of willow-trees', OE **wilig* + *bēag*; examples include: **Willoughby** Lincs., near Alford. *Wilgebi* 1086 (DB). **Willoughby** Warwicks. *Wiliabyg* 956, *Wilebei* 1086 (DB). **Willoughby, Silk** Lincs. *Wilgebi* 1086 (DB). Affix is a reduced form of a nearby place *Silkebi* 1212, 'farmstead of a man called Silki, or near a gully', OScand. pers. name or OE **sīoluc* + OScand. *bý*.

Willoughton Lincs. *Wilchetone* 1086 (DB). 'Farmstead or village where willow-trees grow'. OE **wilig* + *tūn*.

Wilmcote Warwicks. *Wilmundigcotan* 1016, *Wilmecote* 1086 (DB). 'Cottage associated with a man called Wilmund'. OE pers. name + *-ing-* + *cot*.

Wilmington Devon. *Wilelmitone* 1086 (DB). 'Estate associated with a man called Wilhelm'. OE pers. name + *-ing-* + *tūn*.

Wilmington E. Sussex. *Wilminte* (*sic*) 1086 (DB), *Wilminton* 1189. 'Estate associated with a man called Wīghelm or Wilhelm'. OE pers. name + *-ing-* + *tūn*.

Wilmington Kent, near Dartford. *Wilmintuna* 1089. 'Estate associated with a man called Wīghelm'. OE pers. name + *-ing-* + *tūn*.

Wilmslow Ches. *Wilmesloe c.*1250. 'Mound of a man called Wīghelm'. OE pers. name + *hlāw*.

Wilnecote Staffs. *Wilmundecote* 1086 (DB). 'Cottage of a man called Wilmund'. OE pers. name + *cot*.

Wilpshire Lancs. *Wlypschyre* 1246. OE *scīr* 'district, estate' with an uncertain first element, possibly a pers. name **Wlips*.

Wilsford, 'ford of a man called *Wifel', OE pers. name + *ford*: **Wilsford** Lincs. *Wivelesforde* 1086 (DB). **Wilsford** Wilts., near Pewsey. *Wifelesford* 892, *Wivlesford* 1086 (DB). **Wilsford** Wilts., near Salisbury. *Wiflesford* 1086 (DB).

Wilsill N. Yorks. *Wifeleshealh c.*1030, *Wifleshale* 1086 (DB). 'Small valley of a man called *Wifel or Vífill'. OE or OScand. pers. name + OE *halh*.

Wilson Leics. *Wiuelestunia* 12th cent. 'Farmstead or village of a man called *Wifel'. OE pers. name + *tūn*.

Wilstone Herts. *Wivelestorn* 1220. 'Thorn-tree of a man called *Wifel'. OE pers. name + *thorn*.

Wilton, usually 'farmstead or village where willow-trees grow', OE **wilig* + *tūn*; examples include: **Wilton** Cleveland. *Wiltune* 1086 (DB). **Wilton** Norfolk. *Wiltuna* 1086 (DB). **Wilton, Bishop** Humber. *Wiltone* 1086 (DB). Affix from its early possession by the Archbishops of York.

However the following have a different origin: **Wilton** Wilts., near Burbage. *Wulton* 1227. Probably 'farmstead near a spring or stream'. OE *wiella* + *tūn*. **Wilton** Wilts., near Salisbury. *Uuiltun* 838, *Wiltune* 1086 (DB). 'Farmstead or village on the River Wylye'. Pre-English river-name (see WYLYE) + OE *tūn*.

Wiltshire (the county). *Wiltunscir* 870, *Wiltescire* 1086 (DB). 'Shire centred on WILTON'. OE *scīr*.

Wimbish Essex. *Winebisc, Wimbisc* c.1040, *Wimbeis* 1086 (DB). Possibly 'bushy copse of a man called Wine'. OE pers. name + *(ge)bysce.

Wimbledon Gtr. London. *Wunemannedune* c.950. Probably 'hill of a man called *Wynnmann'. OE pers. name + *dūn*.

Wimblington Cambs. *Wimblingetune* c.975. Probably 'estate associated with a man called Wynnbald'. OE pers. name + *-ing-* + *tūn*.

Wimborne Minster Dorset. *Winburnan* late 9th cent., *Winburne* 1086 (DB), *Wymburneminstre* 1236. Originally the name of the river here (now called Allen), 'meadow stream' from OE **winn* + *burna*. Affix is OE *mynster* 'monastery (church)'.

Wimbotsham Norfolk. *Winebotesham* 1086 (DB). 'Homestead of a man called Winebald or Winebaud'. OE or OGerman pers. name + OE *hām*.

Wimpstone Warwicks. *Wylmestone* 1313. 'Farmstead of a man called Wilhelm or Wīghelm'. OE pers. name + *tūn*.

Wincanton Somerset. *Wincaletone* 1086 (DB). 'Farmstead on (an arm of) the River Cale'. Celtic river-name (of uncertain origin, but prefixed by **wīnn* 'white') + OE *tūn*.

Winch, East & West Norfolk. *Estwinic, Wesuuinic* 1086 (DB). 'Farmstead with meadowland'. OE **winn* + *wīc*.

Wincham Ches. *Wimundisham* 1086 (DB). 'Homestead of a man called Wīgmund'. OE pers. name + *hām*.

Winchcombe Glos. *Wincelcumbe* c.810, 1086 (DB). 'Valley with a bend in it'. OE **wincel* + *cumb*.

Winchelsea E. Sussex. *Winceleseia* 1130. 'Island by a river-bend'. OE **wincel* + *ēg*.

Winchendon Bucks. *Wincandone* 1004, *Wichendone* 1086 (DB). Possibly 'hill at a bend'. OE *wince* (genitive *-an*) + *dūn*.

Winchester Hants. *Ouenta* c.150, *Uintancæstir* c.730, *Wincestre* 1086 (DB). 'Roman town called *Venta*'. Pre-Celtic name (possibly 'favoured or chief place') + OE *ceaster*.

Winchfield Hants. *Winchelefeld* 1229. 'Open land by a nook or corner'. OE **wincel* + *feld*.

Winchmore Hill Gtr. London. *Wynsemerhull* 1319. Probably 'boundary hill of a man called Wynsige'. OE pers. name + *mǣre* + *hyll*.

Wincle Ches. *Winchul* c.1190. 'Hill of a man called *Wineca or by a bend'. OE pers. name or *wince* + *hyll*.

Windermere Cumbria. *Winandermere* 12th cent. 'Lake of a man called Vinandr'. OScand. pers. name (genitive *-ar*) + OE *mere*.

Winderton Warwicks. *Winterton* 1166. 'Farmstead used in winter'. OE *winter* + *tūn*.

Windlesham Surrey. *Windesham* 1178, *Windlesham* 1227. Probably 'homestead of a man called *Windel'. OE pers. name + *hām*. Alternatively the first element may be OE **windels* 'a windlass'.

Windley Derbys. *Winleg* 12th cent. 'Meadow clearing'. OE **winn* + *lēah*.

Windrush Glos. *Wenric* 1086 (DB). Named from the River Windrush, a Celtic river-name possibly meaning 'white fen'.

Windsor Berks. *Windlesoran* c.1060, *Windesores* 1086 (DB). 'Bank or slope with a windlass'. OE **windels* + *ōra*.

Winestead Humber. *Wifestede* 1086 (DB). 'Homestead of the women, or of a man called *Wīfa'. OE *wīf* or pers. name + *stede*.

Winfarthing Norfolk. *Wineferthinc* 1086 (DB). 'Quarter of an estate belonging to a man called Wina'. OE pers. name + *feorthung*.

Winford Avon. *Wunfrod* c.1000, *Wenfrod* 1086 (DB). A Celtic river-name meaning 'white or bright stream', Celtic **wīnn* + **frud*.

Winforton Heref. & Worcs. *Widferdestune* (*sic*) 1086 (DB), *Wynfreton* 1265. Probably 'farmstead or estate of a man called Winefrith'. OE pers. name + *tūn*.

Winfrith Newburgh Dorset. *Winfrode* 1086 (DB). Identical in origin with WINFORD. Manorial affix from the *Newburgh* family, here from the 12th cent.

Wing Bucks. *Weowungum (sic)* 966–75, *Witehunge* 1086 (DB). Probably '(settlement of) the family or followers of a man called *Wiwa'. OE pers. name + *-ingas*.

Wing Leics. *Wenge* 12th cent. 'The field'. OScand. *vengi*.

Wingate(s), 'wind-swept gap(s) or pass(es)', OE **wind-geat*; examples include: **Wingate** Durham. *Windegatum* 1071–80. **Wingates** Northum. *Wyndegates* 1208.

Wingerworth Derbys. *Wingreurde* 1086 (DB). 'Enclosure of a man called *Winegār'. OE pers. name + *worth*.

Wingfield Beds. *Winfeld c.*1200. 'Open land used for pasture, or by a nook'. OE **winn* or *wince* + *feld*.

Wingfield Suffolk. *Wingefeld c.*1035, *Wighefelda* 1086 (DB). Probably 'open land of the family or followers of a man called Wiga'. OE pers. name + *-inga-* + *feld*. Alternatively the first element may be OE *wīg* 'heathen temple'.

Wingfield, North & South Derbys. *Wynnefeld* 1002, *Winnefelt*, *Winefeld* 1086 (DB). 'Open land used for pasture'. OE **winn* + *feld*.

Wingham Kent. *Uuigincggaham* 834, *Wingheham* 1086 (DB). 'Homestead of the family or followers of a man called Wiga'. OE pers. name + *-inga-* + *hām*. Alternatively the first element may be OE *wīg* 'heathen temple'.

Wingrave Bucks. *Withungrave (sic)* 1086 (DB), *Wiungraua* 1163. Probably 'grove of the family or followers of a man called *Wiwa'. OE pers. name + *-inga-* + *grāf*.

Winkburn Notts. *Wicheburne (sic)* 1086 (DB), *Winkeburna c.*1150. 'Stream of a man called *Wineca, or with bends in it'. OE pers. name or **wincel* (with Scand. *-k-*) + *burna*.

Winkfield Berks. *Winecanfeld* 942, *Wenesfelle* 1086 (DB). 'Open land of a man called *Wineca'. OE pers. name + *feld*.

Winkleigh Devon. *Wincheleia* 1086 (DB). 'Woodland clearing of a man called *Wineca'. OE pers. name + *lēah*.

Winksley N. Yorks. *Wincheslaie* 1086 (DB). 'Woodland clearing of a man called Winuc'. OE pers. name + *lēah*.

Winmarleigh Lancs. *Wynemerislega* 1212. 'Woodland clearing of a man called Winemǣr'. OE pers. name + *lēah*.

Winnersh Berks. *Wenesse* 1190. 'Ploughed field by meadow'. OE **winn* + *ersc*.

Winscales Cumbria. *Wyndscales* 1227. 'Temporary huts in a windy place'. OE *wind* + OScand. *skáli*.

Winscombe Avon. *Winescumbe c.*965, *Winescome* 1086 (DB). 'Valley of a man called Wine'. OE pers. name + *cumb*.

Winsford, 'ford of a man called Wine', OE pers. name + *ford*: **Winsford** Ches. *Wyneford c.*1334. **Winsford** Somerset. *Winesford* 1086 (DB).

Winsham Somerset. *Winesham* 1046, 1086 (DB). 'Homestead or enclosure of a man called Wine'. OE pers. name + *hām* or *hamm*.

Winshill Staffs. *Wineshylle* 1002. 'Hill of a man called Wine'. OE pers. name + *hyll*.

Winskill Cumbria. *Wyndscales* 1292. 'Temporary huts in a windy place'. OE *wind* + OScand. *skáli*.

Winslade Hants. *Winesflot* 1086 (DB). 'Spring or channel of a man called Wine'. OE pers. name + *flōde*.

Winsley Wilts. *Winesleg* 1242. 'Woodland clearing of a man called Wine'. OE pers. name + *lēah*.

Winslow Bucks. *Wineshlauu* 795, *Weneslai* 1086 (DB). 'Mound of a man called Wine'. OE pers. name + *hlāw*.

Winson Glos. *Winestune* 1086 (DB). 'Farmstead or village of a man called Wine'. OE pers. name + *tūn*.

Winster Cumbria. *Winster* 13th cent. Named from the River Winster, a Celtic river-name meaning 'white stream' or an OScand. river-name meaning 'the left one'.

Winster Derbys. *Winsterne* 1086 (DB). 'Thorn-tree of a man called Wine'. OE pers. name + *thyrne*.

Winston, 'farmstead or village of a man called Wine', OE pers. name + *tūn*: **Winston** Durham. *Winestona* 1091. **Winston** Suffolk. *Winestuna* 1086 (DB).

Winstone Glos. *Winestan* 1086 (DB). '(Boundary) stone of a man called Wynna'. OE pers. name + *stān*.

Winterborne, Winterbourne, originally a river-name 'winter stream, i.e. stream flowing most strongly in winter', OE *winter* + *burna*; examples of places named from their situation on the various rivers so called include: **Winterborne Came** Dorset. *Wintreburne* 1086 (DB), *Winterburn Caam* 1280. Affix from its early possession by the Norman Abbey of Caen. **Winterborne Clenston** Dorset. *Wintreburne* 1086 (DB), *Wynterburn Clencheston* 1303. Affix means 'estate (*tūn*) of the Clench family'. **Winterborne Stickland** Dorset. *Winterburne* 1086 (DB), *Winterburn Stikellane* 1203. Affix means '(with a) steep lane', from OE *sticol* + *lane*. **Winterborne Whitechurch** Dorset.. *Wintreburne* 1086 (DB), *Wynterborn Wytecherch* 1268. Affix means '(with a) white, i.e. stone-built, church', OE *hwīt* + *cirice*. **Winterborne Zelston** Dorset. *Wintreborne* 1086 (DB), *Wynterbourn Selyston* 1350. Affix means 'estate (*tūn*) of the *de Seles* family'. **Winterbourne** Avon. *Wintreborne* 1086 (DB). **Winterbourne Abbas** Dorset. *Wintreburne* 1086 (DB), *Wynterburn Abbatis* 1244. Latin affix 'of the abbot' refers to early possession by the Abbey of Cerne. **Winterbourne Bassett & Monkton** Wilts. *Wintreburne* 950, 1086 (DB), *Winterburn Basset* 1242, *Moneke Wynterburn* 1251. Distinguishing affixes from early possession by the *Basset* family and by the monks of Glastonbury Abbey. **Winterbourne Dauntsey, Earls & Gunner** Wilts. *Wintreburne* 1086 (DB), *Wynterburne Dauntesie* 1268, *Winterburne Earls* 1250, *Winterburn Gonor* 1267. Distinguishing affixes from early possession by the *Danteseye* family, by the Earls of Salisbury, and by a lady called *Gunnora* (here in 1249).

Winteringham Humber. *Wintringeham* 1086 (DB). 'Homestead of the family or followers of a man called Wintra'. OE pers. name + *-inga-* + *hām*.

Wintersett W. Yorks. *Wintersete* c.1125. 'Fold used in winter'. OE *winter* + *set*.

Winterton Humber. *Wintringatun* c.1067, *Wintrintune* 1086 (DB). 'Farmstead of the family or followers of a man called Wintra'. OE pers. name + *-inga-* + *tūn*.

Winterton-on-Sea Norfolk. *Wintertun* 1044–7, *Wintretuna* 1086 (DB). 'Farmstead used in winter'. OE *winter* + *tūn*.

Winthorpe Lincs. *Winetorp* 12th cent. 'Outlying farmstead or hamlet of a man called Wina'. OE pers. name + OScand. *thorp*.

Winthorpe Notts. *Wimuntorp* 1086 (DB). 'Outlying farmstead or hamlet of a man called Wīgmund or Vígmundr'. OE or OScand. pers. name + *thorp*.

Winton Cumbria. *Wyntuna* c.1094. Probably 'pasture farmstead'. OE **winn* + *tūn*.

Wintringham N. Yorks. *Wentrigham* 1086 (DB), *Wintringham* 1169. 'Homestead of the family or followers of a man called Wintra'. OE pers. name + *-inga-* + *hām*.

Winwick, 'dwelling or (dairy) farm of a man called Wina', OE pers. name + *wīc*: **Winwick** Cambs. *Wineuuiche* 1086 (DB). **Winwick** Northants. *Winewican* 1043, *Winewiche* 1086 (DB).

Wirksworth Derbys. *Wyrcesuuyrthe* 835, *Werchesworde* 1086 (DB). 'Enclosure of a man called *Weorc'. OE pers. name + *worth*.

Wirral Ches. *Wirhealum, Wirheale* early 10th cent. '(Place at) the nook(s) where bog-myrtle grows'. OE *wīr* + *halh*.

Wirswall Ches. *Wireswelle* 1086 (DB). 'Spring or stream of a man called Wīghere'. OE pers. name + *wella*.

Wisbech Cambs. *Wisbece* 1086 (DB). Possibly 'marshy-meadow valley or ridge'. OE *wisc* or **wisse* + *bece* or *bæc* (locative **bece*). Alternatively the first element may be the River Wissey, itself an OE name meaning 'marshy stream'.

Wisborough Green W. Sussex.

Wisebregh 1227. 'Marshy-meadow hill'. OE *wisc* + *beorg*.

Wiseton Notts. *Wisetone* 1086 (DB). 'Farmstead of a man called Wīsa', or 'marshy-meadow farmstead'. OE pers. name or *wisc* + *tūn*.

Wishford, Great Wilts. *Wicheford* 1086 (DB). 'Ford where wych-elms grow'. OE *wice* + *ford*.

Wiske (river) N. Yorks., see APPLETON WISKE.

Wisley Surrey. *Wiselei* 1086 (DB). 'Marshy-meadow clearing'. OE *wisc* + *lēah*.

Wispington Lincs. *Wispinctune* 1086 (DB). Possibly 'farmstead at the place where brushwood grows'. OE **wisp* + *-ing* + *tūn*.

Wissett Suffolk. *Wisseta* 1086 (DB), *Witseta* 1165. Possibly 'fold of a man called Witta'. OE pers. name + *set*.

Wistanswick Shrops. *Wistaneswick* 1274. 'Dwelling or (dairy) farm of a man called Wīgstān'. OE pers. name + *wīc*.

Wistaston Ches. *Wistanestune* 1086 (DB). 'Farmstead or village of a man called Wīgstān'. OE pers. name + *tūn*.

Wiston W. Sussex. *Wistanestun* 1086 (DB). 'Farmstead or village of a man called Wīgstān or Winestān'. OE pers. name + *tūn*.

Wistow, 'the dwelling place', OE *wīc-stōw*: **Wistow** Cambs. *Wicstoue* 974, *Wistov* 1086 (DB). **Wistow** N. Yorks. *Wicstow* c.1030.

Wiswell Lancs. *Wisewell* 1207. Possibly 'spring or stream near a marshy meadow'. OE *wisc* or **wisse* + *wella*.

Witcham Cambs. *Wichamme* 970, *Wiceham* 1086 (DB). 'Promontory where wych-elms grow'. OE *wice* + *hamm*.

Witchampton Dorset. *Wichemetune* 1086 (DB). Probably 'farmstead of the dwellers at a village associated with an earlier Romano-British settlement'. OE *wīc* + *hǣme* + *tūn*.

Witchford Cambs. *Wiceford* 1086 (DB). 'Ford where wych-elms grow'. OE *wice* + *ford*.

Witcombe, Great Glos. *Wydecomb* 1220. 'Wide valley'. OE *wīd* + *cumb*.

Witham Essex. *Witham* late 9th cent., 1086 (DB). Probably 'homestead near a river-bend'. OE **wiht* + *hām*.

Witham Friary Somerset. *Witeham* 1086 (DB). 'Homestead of a councillor, or of a man called Witta'. OE *wita* or pers. name + *hām*. The affix Friary, found from 16th cent., is possibly from Latin *fraeria* 'guild'.

Witham, North & South Lincs. *Widme* 1086 (DB). Named from the River Witham, a Celtic or pre-Celtic river-name of uncertain origin.

Witham on the Hill Lincs. *Witham* 1086 (DB). Probably 'homestead in a bend'. OE **wiht* + *hām*.

Witheridge Devon. *Wiriga* (*sic*) 1086 (DB), *Wytherigge* 1256. 'Willow-tree ridge', or 'ridge where wether-sheep are kept'. OE *wīthig* or *wether* + *hrycg*.

Witherley Leics. *Wytherdele* c.1204. 'Woodland clearing of a woman called Wīgthrȳth'. OE pers. name + *lēah*.

Withern Lincs. *Widerne* 1086 (DB). Probably 'house in the wood'. OE *widu*, *wudu* + *ærn*.

Withernsea Humber. *Widfornessei* 1086 (DB). Possibly 'lake at the place near the thorn-tree'. OE *with* + *thorn* + *sǣ*.

Withernwick Humber. *Widforneuuic* 1086 (DB). Possibly 'dairy farm of the place near the thorn-tree'. OE *with* + *thorn* + *wīc*.

Withersdale Street Suffolk. *Weresdel* (*sic*) 1086 (DB), *Wideresdala* 1184. 'Valley where wether-sheep are kept'. OE *wether* + *dæl*.

Withersfield Suffolk. *Wedresfelda* 1086 (DB). 'Open land where wether-sheep are kept.' OE *wether* + *feld*.

Witherslack Cumbria. *Witherslake* c.1190. 'Valley of the wood, or of the willow-tree'. OScand. *vithr* (genitive *vithar*) or *víth* (genitive *víthjar*) + *slakki*.

Withiel Cornwall. *Widie* 1086 (DB). 'Wooded place'. Cornish *gwydh* 'trees' with suffix **-yel*.

Withiel Florey Somerset. *Withiglea* 737, *Wythele Flory* 1305. 'Wood or clearing where willow-trees grow'. OE *wīthig* + *lēah*. Manorial affix from the *de Flury* family, here in the 13th cent.

Withington, usually 'farmstead with a willow copse', OE **wīthign* + *tūn*; examples include: **Withington** Ches. *Widinton* 1185. **Withington** Heref. & Worcs. *Widingtune* 1086 (DB).

However the following has a different origin: **Withington** Glos. *Wudiandun* 737, *Widindune* 1086 (DB). 'Hill of a man called Widia'. OE pers. name (genitive *-n*) + *dūn*.

Withnell Lancs. *Withinhull c.*1160. 'Hill where willow-trees grow'. OE **wīthigen* + *hyll*.

Withybrook Warwicks. *Wythibroc* 12th cent. 'Willow-tree brook'. OE *wīthig* + *brōc*.

Withycombe, 'valley where willow-trees grow', OE *wīthig* + *cumb*: **Withycombe** Somerset. *Widicumbe* 1086 (DB). **Withycombe Raleigh** Devon. *Widecome* 1086 (DB), *Widecombe Ralegh* 1465. Manorial affix from the *de Ralegh* family, here in the early 14th cent.

Withyham E. Sussex. *Withiham* 1230. 'Willow-tree enclosure or promontory'. OE *wīthig* + *hamm*.

Withypool Somerset. *Widepolle* 1086 (DB). 'Willow-tree pool'. OE *wīthig* + *pōl*.

Witley Surrey. *Witlei* 1086 (DB). 'Woodland clearing in a bend, or of a man called Witta'. OE **wiht* or pers. name + *lēah*.

Witley, Great & Little Heref. & Worcs. *Wittlæg* 964, *Witlege* 1086 (DB). 'Woodland clearing in a bend'. OE **wiht* + *lēah*.

Witnesham Suffolk. *Witdesham (sic)* 1086 (DB), *Witnesham* 1254. Possibly 'homestead of a man called *Wittīn'. OE pers. name + *hām*.

Witney Oxon. *Wyttanige* 969, *Witenie* 1086 (DB). 'Island, or dry ground in marsh, of a man called Witta'. OE pers. name (genitive *-n*) + *ēg*.

Wittenham, Little & Long Oxon. *Wittanham c.*865, *Witeham* 1086 (DB). 'River-bend land of a man called Witta'. OE pers. name (genitive *-n*) + *hamm*.

Wittering Cambs. *Witheringaeige* 972, *Witheringham* 1086 (DB), *Witeringa* 1167. '(Island or homestead of) the family or followers of a man called Wither'. OE pers. name + *-ingas* (in genitive plural with *ēg* and *hām* in the early forms).

Wittering, East & West W. Sussex. *Wihttringes* 683, *Westringes (sic)* 1086 (DB). '(Settlement of) the family or followers of a man called Wihthere'. OE pers. name + *-ingas*.

Wittersham Kent. *Wihtriceshamme* 1032. 'Promontory of a man called Wihtrīc'. OE pers. name + *hamm*.

Witton, a common name, usually 'farmstead in or by a wood', OE *wudu* or *widu* + *tūn*; for example: **Witton Bridge** Norfolk. *Widituna* 1086 (DB). **Witton, East & West** N. Yorks. *Witun* 1086 (DB). **Witton Gilbert** Durham. *Wyton* 1195. Manorial affix from its possession by *Gilbert* de la Ley in the 12th cent. **Witton-le-Wear** Durham. *Wudutun c.*1050. On the River Wear, for which see MONKWEARMOUTH.

However some Wittons have a different origin: **Witton** Ches. *Witune* 1086 (DB). 'Estate with a salt-works'. OE *wīc* + *tūn*. **Witton, Upper** W. Mids. *Witone* 1086 (DB). Possibly 'farmstead by an earlier Romano-British settlement'. OE *wīc* + *tūn*.

Wiveliscombe Somerset. *Wifelescumb* 854, *Wivelescome* 1086 (DB). 'Valley of a man called *Wifel'. OE pers. name + *cumb*.

Wivelsfield E. Sussex. *Wifelesfeld c.*765. Probably 'open land of a man called *Wifel', OE pers. name + *feld*. Alternatively the first element in this and the previous name may be the noun *wifel* 'weevil' denoting 'weevil-infested land'.

Wivenhoe Essex. *Wiunhov* 1086 (DB). 'Hill-spur of a man called *Wīfa'. OE pers. name (genitive *-n*) + *hōh*.

Wiveton Norfolk. *Wiuentona* 1086 (DB). 'Farmstead or village of a man called *Wīfa'. OE pers. name (genitive *-n*) + *tūn*.

Wix Essex. *Wica* 1086 (DB). 'The dwellings or specialized farm'. OE *wīc* in a ME plural form *wikes*.

Wixford Warwicks. *Wihtlachesforde* 962, *Witelavesford (sic)* 1086 (DB). 'Ford of a man called Wihtlāc'. OE pers. name + *ford*.

Wixoe Suffolk. *Wlteskeou (sic)* 1086 (DB),

Widekeshoo 1205. 'Hill-spur of a man called Widuc'. OE pers. name + *hōh*.

Woburn Beds. *Woburne* 1086 (DB). '(Place at) the crooked or winding stream'. OE *wōh* + *burna*.

Wokefield Park Berks. *Weonfelda* c.950, *Hocfelle* 1086 (DB). Probably 'open land of a man called *Weohha'. OE pers. name + *feld*.

Woking Surrey. *Wocchingas* c.712, *Wochinges* 1086 (DB). '(Settlement of) the family or followers of a man called *Wocc(a)'. OE pers. name + *-ingas*.

Wokingham Berks. *Wokingeham* 1146. 'Homestead of the family or followers of a man called *Wocc(a)'. OE pers. name + *-inga-* + *hām*.

Woldingham Surrey. *Wallingeham* (*sic*) 1086 (DB), *Waldingham* 1204. Probably 'homestead of the forest dwellers', OE *weald* + *-inga-* + *hām*. Alternatively 'homestead of the family or followers of a man called *Wealda', with an OE pers. name as first element.

Wolds, The (upland districts, i. Leics., ii. Lincs., iii. N. Yorks. & Humberside), from OE *wald* 'high forest-land, later cleared', see FOSTON ON THE WOLDS, GARTON ON THE WOLDS, etc.

Wolferton Norfolk. *Wulferton* 1166. 'Farmstead or village of a man called Wulfhere'. OE pers. name + *tūn*.

Wolford, Great & Little Warwicks. *Wolwarde* 1086 (DB). 'Place protected against wolves'. OE *wulf* + *weard*.

Wollaston Northants. *Wilavestone* (*sic*) 1086 (DB), *Wullaueston* 1190. 'Farmstead or village of a man called Wulflāf'. OE pers. name + *tūn*.

Wollaston Shrops. *Willavestune* 1086 (DB). 'Farmstead or village of a man called Wīglāf'. OE pers. name + *tūn*.

Wollerton Shrops. *Ulvretone* 1086 (DB), *Wluruntona* c.1135. 'Farmstead or village of a woman called Wulfrūn'. OE pers. name + *tūn*.

Wolsingham Durham. *Wlsingham* c.1150. 'Homestead of the family or followers of a man called Wulfsige'. OE pers. name + *-inga-* + *hām*.

Wolstanton Staffs. *Wlstanetone* 1086 (DB). 'Farmstead or village of a man called Wulfstān'. OE pers. name + *tūn*.

Wolston Warwicks. *Ulvricetone* 1086 (DB). 'Farmstead or village of a man called Wulfrīc'. OE pers. name + *tūn*.

Wolvercote Oxon. *Ulfgarcote* 1086 (DB). 'Cottage associated with a man called Wulfgār'. OE pers. name + *-ing-* + *cot*.

Wolverhampton W. Mids. *Heantune* 985, *Wolvrenehamptonia* c.1080. Originally 'high farmstead', from OE *hēah* (dative *hēan*) + *tūn*, later with the addition of the OE pers. name *Wulfrūn*, the lady to whom the manor was given in 985.

Wolverley Heref. & Worcs. *Wulfferdinleh* 866, *Ulwardelei* 1086 (DB). 'Woodland clearing associated with a man called Wulfweard'. OE pers. name + *-ing-* + *lēah*.

Wolverton Bucks. *Wluerintone* 1086 (DB). 'Estate associated with a man called Wulfhere'. OE pers. name + *-ing-* + *tūn*.

Wolvey Warwicks. *Ulveia* 1086 (DB). Probably 'enclosure protected against wolves'. OE *wulf* + *hege* or *hæg*.

Wolviston Cleveland. *Oluestona* 1091. 'Farmstead or village of a man called Wulf'. OE pers. name + *tūn*.

Wombleton N. Yorks. *Winbeltun* 1086 (DB). 'Farmstead or village of a man called Wynbald or Winebald'. OE pers. name + *tūn*.

Wombourn Staffs. *Wamburne* 1086 (DB). '(Place at) the crooked or winding stream'. OE *wōh* (dative *wōn*) + *burna*.

Wombwell S. Yorks. *Wanbuelle* 1086 (DB). 'Spring or stream in a hollow, or of a man called *Wamba'. OE *wamb* or pers. name + *wella*.

Womenswold Kent. *Wimlincgawald* 824. Possibly 'forest of the family or followers of a man called *Wīmel'. OE pers. name + *-inga-* + *weald*.

Wonersh Surrey. *Woghenhers* 1199. 'Crooked ploughed field'. OE *wōh* (dative *wōn*) + *ersc*.

Wonston, South Hants. *Wynsigestune* 901, *Wenesistune* 1086 (DB). 'Farmstead or village of a man called Wynsige'. OE pers. name + *tūn*.

Wooburn Bucks. *Waburna* c.1075, *Waborne* 1086 (DB). Probably 'stream with its banks walled up, or with a dam'. OE *wāg* + *burna*. Alternatively the first element may be OE *wōh* 'crooked, winding'.

Wood as affix, see main name, e.g. for **Wood Dalling** (Norfolk) see DALLING.

Woodale N. Yorks. *Wulvedale* 1223. 'Valley frequented by wolves'. OE *wulf* + *dæl*.

Woodbastwick Norfolk. *Bastwik* 1044–7, *Bastuuic* 1086 (DB), *Wodbastwyk* 1253. 'Farm where bast (the bark of the lime-tree used for rope-making) is got'. OE *bæst* + *wīc*, with the later addition of *wudu* 'wood'.

Woodborough Notts. *Udeburg* 1086 (DB). 'Fortified place by the wood'. OE *wudu* + *burh*.

Woodborough Wilts. *Wideberghe* 1208. 'Wooded hill'. OE *wudu* + *beorg*.

Woodbridge Suffolk. *Oddebruge c.*1050, *Wudebrige* 1086 (DB). 'Wooden bridge', or 'bridge near the wood'. OE *wudu* + *brycg*.

Woodburn, East Northum. *Wodeburn* 1265. 'Stream in the wood'. OE *wudu* + *burna*.

Woodbury Devon. *Wodeberia* 1086 (DB). 'Fortified place by the wood'. OE *wudu* + *burh* (dative *byrig*).

Woodbury Salterton Devon, see SALTERTON.

Woodchester Glos. *Uuduceastir* 716–43, *Widecestre* 1086 (DB). 'Roman camp in the wood'. OE *wudu* + *ceaster*.

Woodchurch Kent. *Wuducirce c.*1100. 'Wooden church', or 'church by the wood'. OE *wudu* + *cirice*.

Woodcote, Woodcott, 'cottage(s) in or by a wood', OE *wudu* + *cot*; examples include: **Woodcote** Gtr. London. *Wudecot* 1200. **Woodcote** Oxon. *Wdecote* 1109.

Woodeaton Oxon. *Etone* 1086 (DB), *Wudeetun* 1185. 'Farmstead by a river'. OE *ēa* + *tūn*, with the later affix *wudu* 'wood'.

Woodend, '(place at) the end of the wood', OE *wudu* + *ende*; for example **Woodend** Northants. *Wodende* 1316.

Woodford, 'ford in or by a wood', OE *wudu* + *ford*; examples include: **Woodford** Gtr. London. *Wdefort* 1086 (DB). **Woodford** Gtr. Manch. *Wideforde* 1248. **Woodford** Northants., near Thrapston. *Wodeford* 1086 (DB). **Woodford** Wilts. *Wuduforda* 972. **Woodford Halse** Northants. *Wodeford* 1086 (DB). Affix from the manor of HALSE.

Wood Green Gtr. London. *Wodegrene* 1502. 'Green place near woodland'. OE *wudu* + *grēne*.

Woodhall, 'hall in or by a wood', OE *wudu* + *h(e)all*; for example **Woodhall Spa** Lincs. *Wudehalle* 12th cent. (with recent affix from its reputation as a watering-place).

Woodham, usually 'homestead or village in or by a wood', OE *wudu* + *hām*; examples include: **Woodham** Surrey. *Wodeham* 672–4. **Woodham Ferrers, Mortimer, & Walter** Essex. *Wudaham c.*975, *Udeham, Odeham, Wdeham* 1086 (DB), *Wodeham Ferrers* 1230, *Wodeham Mortimer* 1255, *Wodeham Walter* 1238. Manorial affixes from early possession of estates here by the *de Ferrers, Mortimer*, and *Fitzwalter* families.

Woodhay, East (Hants.) **& West** (Berks.) *Wideheia c.*1150. 'Wide enclosure'. OE *wīd* (dative *-an*) + *hæg*.

Woodhorn Northum. *Wudehorn* 1178. 'Wooded horn of land or promontory'. OE *wudu* + *horn*.

Woodhouse, 'house(s) in or near a wood', OE *wudu* + *hūs*; examples include: **Woodhouse** Leics. *Wodehuses c.*1220. **Woodhouse** S. Yorks. *Wdehus* 1200.

Woodhurst Cambs. *Wdeherst* 1209. Originally OE *hyrst* 'wooded hill' with the later addition of *wudu* 'wood'.

Woodland(s), 'cultivated land in or near a wood', OE *wudu* + *land*; examples include: **Woodland** Devon. *Wodelonde* 1328. **Woodlands** Dorset. *Wodelande* 1244.

Woodleigh Devon. *Wuduleage c.*1010, *Odelie* 1086 (DB). 'Clearing in a wood'. OE *wudu* + *lēah*.

Woodlesford W. Yorks. *Wridelesford* 12th cent. 'Ford near a thicket'. OE **wrīdels* + *ford*.

Woodmancote, Woodmancott, 'cottage(s) of the woodsmen or foresters', OE *wudu-mann* + *cot*;

examples include: **Woodmancote** Glos., near Rendcomb. *Wodemancote* 12th cent. **Woodmancott** Hants. *Woedemancote* 903, *Udemanecote* 1086 (DB).

Woodmansey Humber. *Wodemanse* 1289. 'Pool of the woodsman or forester'. OE *wudu-mann* + *sǣ*.

Woodmansterne Surrey. *Odemerestor* (*sic*) 1086 (DB), *Wudemaresthorne c.*1190. 'Thorn-tree by the boundary of the wood'. OE *wudu* + *mǣre* + *thorn*.

Woodnesborough Kent. *Wanesberge* (*sic*) 1086 (DB), *Wodnesbeorge c.*1100. 'Mound associated with the heathen god Wōden'. OE god-name + *beorg*.

Woodnewton Northants. *Niwetone* 1086 (DB), *Wodeneuton* 1255. 'New farmstead (in woodland)'. OE *nīwe* + *tūn* with the later addition of *wudu*.

Woodplumpton Lancs. *Pluntun* 1086 (DB), *Wodeplumpton* 1327. 'Farmstead (in woodland) where plum-trees grow'. OE *plūme* + *tūn* with the later addition of *wudu*.

Woodrising Norfolk. *Risinga* 1086 (DB), *Woderisingg* 1291. Probably '(settlement of) the family or followers of a man called *Risa'. OE pers. name + *-ingas*, with the later addition of *wudu*.

Woodsetts S. Yorks. *Wodesete* 1324. 'Folds (for animals) in the wood'. OE *wudu* + *set*.

Woodsford Dorset. *Wardesford* 1086 (DB). 'Ford of a man called *Weard'. OE pers. name + *ford*.

Woodstock Oxon. *Wudestoce c.*1000, *Wodestoch* 1086 (DB). 'Settlement in woodland'. OE *wudu* + *stoc*.

Woodthorpe, 'outlying farmstead or hamlet in woodland', OE *wudu* + OScand. *thorp*: **Woodthorpe** Derbys. *Wodethorpe* 1258. **Woodthorpe** Lincs. *Wdetorp* 12th cent.

Woodton Norfolk. *Wodetuna* 1086 (DB). 'Farmstead in or near a wood'. OE *wudu* + *tūn*.

Woodville Derbys., a modern name dating from 1845, until then known as *Wooden-Box* from the wooden hut here for collecting toll at the turnpike.

Woodyates, East & West Dorset. *Wdegeate* 9th cent., *Odiete* 1086 (DB). '(Place at) the gate or gap in the wood'. OE *wudu* + *geat*.

Woofferton Shrops. *Wulfreton* 1221. 'Farmstead of a man called Wulfhere or Wulffrith'. OE pers. name + *tūn*.

Wookey Somerset. *Woky* 1065. '(Place at) the trap or snare for animals', OE *wōcig*, probably originally with reference to Wookey Hole (*Wokyhole* 1065, with OE *hol* 'ravine').

Wool Dorset. *Welle* 1086 (DB). '(Place at) the spring or springs'. OE *wiella*.

Woolacombe Devon. *Wellecome* 1086 (DB). 'Valley with a spring or stream'. OE *wiella* + *cumb*.

Woolaston Glos. *Odelaweston* 1086 (DB). 'Farmstead of a man called Wulflāf'. OE pers. name + *tūn*.

Woolbeding W. Sussex. *Welbedlinge* 1086 (DB). Probably 'place associated with a man called Wulfbeald'. OE pers. name + *-ing*.

Wooler Northum. *Wulloure* 1187. Probably 'spring promontory'. OE *wella* + **ofer*.

Woolfardisworthy Devon, near Crediton. *Ulfaldeshodes* (*sic*) 1086 (DB), *Wolfardesworthi* 1264. 'Enclosure of a man called Wulfheard'. OE pers. name + *worthig*.

Woolhampton Berks. *Ollavintone* 1086 (DB). 'Estate associated with a man called Wulflāf'. OE pers. name + *-ing-* + *tūn*.

Woolhope Heref. & Worcs. *Hope* 1086 (DB), *Wulvivehop* 1234. '(Place at) the valley'. OE *hop*, with later addition from a woman called *Wulfgifu* who gave the manor to Hereford Cathedral in the 11th cent.

Woolland Dorset. *Wonlonde* 934, *Winlande* 1086 (DB). 'Estate with pasture or meadow'. OE **wynn* + *land*.

Woolley, usually 'wood or clearing frequented by wolves', OE *wulf* + *lēah*; examples include: **Woolley** Cambs. *Ciluelai* (*sic*) 1086 (DB), *Wulueleia* 1158. **Woolley** W. Yorks. *Wiluelai* 1086 (DB).

Woolpit Suffolk. *Wlpit* 10th cent., *Wlfpeta* 1086 (DB). 'Pit for trapping wolves'. OE *wulf-pytt*.

Woolscott Warwicks. *Wulscote c.*1235.

Probably 'cottage of a man called Wulfsige'. OE pers. name + *cot.*

Woolstaston Shrops. *Ulestanestune* 1086 (DB). 'Farmstead of a man called Wulfstān'. OE pers. name + *tūn.*

Woolsthorpe Lincs., near Grantham. *Ulestanestorp* 1086 (DB). 'Outlying farmstead or hamlet of a man called Wulfstān'. OE pers. name + OScand. *thorp.*

Woolston Ches. *Ulfitona* 1142. 'Farmstead of a man called Wulfsige'. OE pers. name + *tūn.*

Woolston Devon. *Ulsistone* 1086 (DB). Identical in origin with the previous name.

Woolston Hants. *Olvestune* 1086 (DB). 'Farmstead of a man called Wulf'. OE pers. name + *tūn.*

Woolstone Oxon. *Olvricestone* 1086 (DB). 'Estate of a man called Wulfrīc'. OE pers. name + *tūn.*

Woolstone, Great & Little Bucks. *Wlsiestone* 1086 (DB). 'Farmstead of a man called Wulfsige'. OE pers. name + *tūn.*

Woolton Mersey. *Uluentune* 1086 (DB). 'Farmstead of a man called *Wulfa'. OE pers. name (genitive *-n*) + *tūn.*

Woolverstone Suffolk. *Uluerestuna* 1086 (DB). 'Farmstead of a man called Wulfhere'. OE pers. name + *tūn.*

Woolverton Somerset. *Wulfrinton* 1196. Probably 'estate associated with a man called Wulfhere'. OE pers. name + *-ing-* + *tūn.*

Woolwich Gtr. London. *Uuluuich* 918, *Hulviz* (*sic*) 1086 (DB). 'Port from which wool is shipped.' OE *wull* + *wīc.*

Woore Shrops. *Wavre* 1086 (DB). Possibly '(place by) the swaying tree'. OE *wæfre.*

Wootton, a common name, 'farmstead in or near a wood', OE *wudu* + *tūn*; examples include: **Wootton** Northants. *Witone* 1086 (DB). **Wootton** Oxon., near Abingdon. *Wuttune* 985. **Wootton Bassett** Wilts. *Wdetun* 680, *Wodetone* 1086 (DB), *Wotton Basset* 1272. Manorial affix from the *Basset* family, here in the 13th cent. **Wootton Fitzpaine** Dorset. *Wodetone* 1086 (DB), *Wotton Fitz Payn* 1392. Manorial affix from the *Fitz Payn* family, here in the 14th cent. **Wootton, Glanvilles** Dorset. *Widetone* 1086 (DB), *Wotton Glaunuill* 1288. Manorial affix from the *Glanville* family, here in the 13th cent. **Wootton, Leek** Warwicks. *Wottona* 1122, *Lecwotton* 1285. Affix presumably OE *lēac* 'leek' from their cultivation here. **Wootton Rivers** Wilts. *Wdutun* 804, *Otone* 1086 (DB), *Wotton Ryvers* 1332. Manorial affix from the *de Rivere* family, here in the 13th cent. **Wootton St Lawrence** Hants. *Wudatune* 990, *Odetone* 1086 (DB). Affix from the dedication of the church. **Wootton Wawen** Warwicks. *Uuidutuun* 716–37, *Wotone* 1086 (DB), *Wageneswitona* c.1142. Affix from its possession in the 11th cent. by a man called *Wagen* (OScand. *Vagn*).

Worcester Heref. & Worcs. *Weogorna civitas* 691, *Wigranceastre* 717, *Wirecestre* 1086 (DB). 'Roman town of the *Weogora* tribe'. Pre-English folk-name (possibly from a Celtic river-name meaning 'winding river') + OE *ceaster.* **Worcestershire** (OE *scīr* 'district') is first referred to in the 11th cent.

Wordsley W. Mids. *Wuluardeslea* 12th cent. 'Woodland clearing of a man called Wulfweard'. OE pers. name + *lēah.*

Worfield Shrops. *Wrfeld* 1086 (DB). 'Open land on the River Worfe'. OE river-name (meaning 'winding') + *feld.*

Workington Cumbria. *Wirkynton* c.1125. 'Estate associated with a man called *Weorc'. OE pers. name + *-ing-* + *tūn.*

Worksop Notts. *Werchesope* 1086 (DB). 'Enclosure or valley of a man called *Weorc'. OE pers. name + *hop.*

Worlaby Humber. *Uluricebi* 1086 (DB). 'Farmstead or village of a man called Wulfrīc'. OE pers. name + OScand. *bý.*

Worldham, East & West Hants. *Werildeham* 1086 (DB). Probably 'homestead of a woman called *Wǣrhild'. OE pers. name + *hām.*

Worle Avon. *Worle* 1086 (DB). Probably 'wood or clearing frequented by wood-grouse'. OE **wōr* + *lēah.*

Worleston Ches. *Werblestune* (*sic*) 1086 (DB), *Weruelestona* c.1100. Possibly 'farmstead at the clearing for cattle'. OE *weorf* + *lēah* (genitive *lēas*) + *tūn.*

Worlingham Suffolk. *Werlingaham*

1086 (DB). Probably 'homestead of the family or followers of a man called *Wērel'. OE pers. name + *-inga-* + *hām*.

Worlington Devon. *Ulvredintone* 1086 (DB). 'Estate associated with a man called Wulfrēd'. OE pers. name + *-ing-* + *tūn*.

Worlington Suffolk. *Wirilintona* 1086 (DB), *Wridelingeton* 1201. 'Farmstead by the winding stream'. OE **wride* + *wella* + *-ing-* + *tūn*.

Worlingworth Suffolk. *Wilrincgawertha c.*1035, *Wyrlingwortha* 1086 (DB). 'Enclosure of the family or followers of a man called Wilhere'. OE pers. name + *-inga-* + *worth*.

Wormbridge Heref. & Worcs. *Wermebrig* 1207. 'Bridge on Worm Brook'. Celtic river-name (meaning 'dark stream') + OE *brycg*.

Wormegay Norfolk. *Wermegai* 1086 (DB). 'Island of the family or followers of a man called *Wyrma'. OE pers. name + *-inga-* + *ēg*.

Wormhill Derbys. *Wruenele* (*sic*) 1086 (DB), *Wermehull c.*1105. Probably 'hill of a man called *Wyrma'. OE pers. name + *hyll*.

Wormingford Essex. *Widemondefort* 1086 (DB). 'Ford of a man called *Withermund'. OE pers. name + *ford*.

Worminghall Bucks. *Wermelle* (*sic*) 1086 (DB), *Wirmenhale c.*1218. Probably 'nook of land of a man called *Wyrma'. OE pers. name (genitive *-n*) + *halh*.

Wormington Glos. *Wermetune* 1086 (DB). 'Estate associated with a man called *Wyrma'. OE pers. name + *-ing-* + *tūn*.

Worminster Somerset. *Wormester* 946. 'Rocky hill of the snake or dragon'. OE *wyrm* + *torr*.

Wormleighton Warwicks. *Wilmanlehttune* 956, *Wimelestone* 1086 (DB). 'Herb garden of a man called *Wilma'. OE pers. name + *lēac-tūn*.

Wormley Herts. *Wrmeleia c.*1060, *Wermelai* 1086 (DB). 'Woodland clearing infested with snakes'. OE *wyrm* + *lēah*.

Wormshill Kent. *Godeselle* (*sic*) 1086 (DB), *Wotnesell c.*1225, *Worneshelle* 1254. Possibly 'hill of the heathen god Wōden', OE god-name + *hyll*. Alternatively 'shelter for a herd of pigs', OE *weorn* + **(ge)sell*.

Wormsley Heref. & Worcs. *Wermeslai* 1086 (DB). 'Woodland clearing of a man called *Wyrm', or 'one infested with snakes'. OE pers. name or *wyrm* + *lēah*.

Wormwood Scrubs Gtr. London. *Wermeholte* 1200. 'Snake-infested wood', OE *wyrm* + *holt*, with the later addition of **scrubb* 'scrubland, place overgrown with brushwood'.

Worplesdon Surrey. *Werpesdune* 1086 (DB). 'Hill with a path or track'. OE **werpels* + *dūn*.

Worrall S. Yorks. *Wihale* 1086 (DB), *Wirhal* 1218. Probably 'nook of land where bog-myrtle grows'. OE *wīr* + *halh*.

Worsall, High & Low N. Yorks. *Wirceshel, Wercheshale* 1086 (DB). 'Nook of land of a man called *Weorc'. OE pers. name + *halh*.

Worsbrough S. Yorks. *Wircesburg* 1086 (DB). 'Stronghold of a man called *Wyrc'. OE pers. name + *burh*.

Worsley Gtr. Manch. *Werkesleia* 1196, *Wyrkitheley* 1246. Possibly 'woodland clearing of a woman called *Weorcgȳth or of a man called *Weorchæth'. OE pers. name + *lēah*.

Worstead Norfolk. *Wrthestede* 1044–7, *Wrdesteda* 1086 (DB). 'Site of an enclosure, a farmstead'. OE *worth* + *stede*.

Worsthorne Lancs. *Worthesthorn* 1202. 'Thorn-tree of a man called *Weorth'. OE pers. name + *thorn*.

Worston Lancs. *Wrtheston* 1212. 'Farmstead of a man called *Weorth'. OE pers. name + *tūn*.

Worth, 'the enclosure, the enclosed settlement', OE *worth*; examples include: **Worth** Kent. *Wurth* 1226. **Worth** W. Sussex. *Orde* 1086 (DB). **Worth Matravers** Dorset. *Wirde* 1086 (DB), *Worth Matrauers* 1664. Manorial affix from the *Mautravers* family, here from the 14th cent.

Wortham Suffolk. *Wrtham c.*950, *Wortham* 1086 (DB). 'Homestead with an enclosure'. OE *worth* + *hām*.

Worthen Shrops. *Wrdine* 1086 (DB). 'The enclosure'. OE *worthign*.

Worthing Norfolk. *Worthing* 1282. Probably identical in origin with the previous name.

Worthing W. Sussex. *Ordinges* 1086 (DB). Probably '(settlement of) the family or followers of a man called *Weorth'. OE pers. name + *-ingas*.

Worthington Leics. *Werditone* 1086 (DB). Probably 'estate associated with a man called *Weorth'. OE pers. name + *-ing-* + *tūn*.

Worthy, Headbourne, Kings, & Martyr Hants. *Worthige* 825, *Ordie* 1086 (DB), *Hydeburne Worthy* c.1270, *Chinges Ordia* 1157, *Wordia le Martre* 1243. 'The enclosure(s)'. OE *worthig*. The affix Headbourne is an old stream-name ('stream by the hides of land', OE *hīd* + *burna*), the other affixes being from early possession by the king and the *le Martre* family.

Wortley S. Yorks. *Wirtleie* 1086 (DB). 'Woodland clearing used for growing vegetables'. OE *wyrt* + *lēah*.

Worton Wilts. *Wrton* 1173. 'The vegetable garden'. OE *wyrt-tūn*.

Worton, Nether & Over Oxon. *Ortune* 1050–2, *Hortone* 1086 (DB). 'Farmstead by a bank or slope'. OE *ōra* + *tūn*.

Wotherton Shrops. *Udevertune* 1086 (DB). 'Farmstead by the woodland ford'. OE *wudu* + *ford* + *tūn*.

Wotton, 'farmstead in or near a wood', OE *wudu* + *tūn*; examples include: **Wotton** Surrey. *Wodetone* 1086 (DB). **Wotton under Edge** Glos. *Wudutune* 940, *Vutune* 1086 (DB). Affix refers to its situation under the Cotswold escarpment. **Wotton Underwood** Bucks. *Wudotun* 848, *Oltone* (*sic*) 1086 (DB). Affix means 'within the wood'.

Woughton on the Green Bucks. *Ulchetone* (*sic*) 1086 (DB), *Wocheton* 1163. Probably 'farmstead of a man called *Wēoca'. OE pers. name + *tūn*.

Wouldham Kent. *Uuldaham* 811, *Oldeham* 1086 (DB). 'Homestead of a man called *Wulda'. OE pers. name + *hām*.

Wrabness Essex. *Wrabenasa* 1086 (DB). 'Headland of a man called *Wrabba'. OE pers. name + *næss*.

Wrafton Devon. *Wratheton* 1238. Possibly 'farmstead built on piles or timber supports'. OE *wrathu* + *tūn*.

Wragby, 'farmstead or village of a man called Vragi or *Wraghi', OScand. pers. name + *bý*: **Wragby** Lincs. *Waragebi* 1086 (DB). **Wragby** W. Yorks. *Wraggebi* 1160–70.

Wramplingham Norfolk. *Wranplincham* 1086 (DB). OE *hām* 'homestead' with an uncertain first element, probably a pers. name or tribal name.

Wrangle Lincs. *Werangle* 1086 (DB). 'Crooked stream or other feature'. OE *wrengel* or OScand. *vrengill*.

Wrantage Somerset. *Wrentis* 1199. 'Pasture for stallions'. OE *wrǣna* + *etisc*.

Wratting, 'place where crosswort or hellebore grows', OE *wrætt* + *-ing*: **Wratting, Great & Little** Suffolk. *Wratinga* 1086 (DB). **Wratting, West** Cambs. *Wreattinge* 974, *Waratinge* 1086 (DB).

Wrawby Humber. *Waragebi* 1086 (DB). Probably 'farmstead or village of a man called *Wraghi'. OScand. pers. name + *bý*.

Wraxall, 'nook of land frequented by the buzzard or other bird of prey', OE *wrocc* + *halh*: **Wraxall** Avon. *Werocosale* 1086 (DB). **Wraxall** Dorset. *Brocheshale* (*sic*) 1086 (DB), *Wrokeshal* 1196. **Wraxall, North** Wilts. *Werocheshalle* 1086 (DB). **Wraxall, South** Wilts. *Wroxhal* 1227.

Wray, Wrea, Wreay, 'secluded nook or corner of land', OScand. *vrá*; examples include: **Wray** Lancs. *Wra* 1227. **Wray, High** Cumbria. *Wraye* c.1535. **Wrea Green** Lancs. *Wra* 1201. **Wreay** Cumbria, near Soulby. *Wra* 1487.

Wraysbury Berks. *Wirecesberie* (*sic*) 1086 (DB), *Wiredesbur* 1195. 'Stronghold of a man called Wīgrēd'. OE pers. name + *burh* (dative *byrig*).

Wreake (river) Leics., see FRISBY ON THE WREAKE.

Wrecclesham Surrey. *Wrecclesham* 1225. Probably 'homestead or enclosure of a man called *Wrecel'. OE pers. name + *hām* or *hamm*.

Wrekin, The Shrops., see WROXETER.

Wrelton N. Yorks. *Wereltun* 1086 (DB). Possibly 'farmstead by the hill where criminals are hanged'. OE *wearg* + *hyll* + *tūn*.

Wrenbury Ches. *Wareneberie* 1086 (DB). 'Stronghold of the wren, or of a man called *Wrenna'. OE *wrenna* or pers. name + *burh* (dative *byrig*).

Wreningham Norfolk. *Wreningham* c.1060, *Urnincham* (*sic*) 1086 (DB). Probably 'homestead of the family or followers of a man called *Wrenna'. OE pers. name + *-inga-* + *hām*.

Wrentham Suffolk. *Wretham* (*sic*) 1086 (DB), *Wrentham* 1228. Probably 'homestead of a man called *Wrenta'. OE pers. name + *hām*.

Wressle Humber. *Weresa* (*sic*) 1086 (DB), *Wresel* 1183. From OE **wrǣsel* 'something twisted', perhaps referring to broken ground or a winding river.

Wrestlingworth Beds. *Wrastlingewrd* c.1150. Probably 'enclosure of the family or followers of a man called *Wrǣstel'. OE pers. name + *-inga-* + *worth*.

Wretham, East Norfolk. *Wretham* 1086 (DB). 'Homestead where crosswort or hellebore grows'. OE *wrætt* + *hām*.

Wretton Norfolk. *Wretton* 1198. 'Farmstead where crosswort or hellebore grows'. OE *wrætt* + *tūn*.

Wribbenhall Heref. & Worcs. *Gurberhale* (*sic*) 1086 (DB), *Wrubbenhale* c.1160. 'Nook of land of a man called *Wrybba'. OE pers. name (genitive *-n*) + *halh*.

Wrightington Lancs. *Wrichtington* 1202. Possibly 'farmstead or village of the wrights or carpenters'. OE *wyrhta* (genitive plural *-ena*) + *tūn*.

Wrinehill Staffs. *Wrinehull* 1225. OE *hyll* 'hill' with an uncertain first element, possibly a stream-name or an earlier name for the hill itself.

Wrington Avon. *Wringtone* 926, *Weritone* (*sic*) 1086 (DB). 'Farmstead on the river called *Wring*'. Earlier or alternative name (possibly meaning 'winding stream') for the River Yeo + OE *tūn*.

Writtle Essex. *Writele* 1066–76, *Writelam* 1086 (DB). Originally a river-name from OE **writol* 'babbling', an earlier name for the River Wid.

Wrockwardine Shrops. *Recordine* 1086 (DB), *Wrocwurthin* 1196. 'Enclosure by the hill called the Wrekin'. Celtic name (see WROXETER) + OE *worthign*.

Wroot Humber. *Wroth* 1157. 'Snout-like spur of land'. OE *wrōt*.

Wrotham Kent. *Uurotaham* 788, *Broteham* (*sic*) 1086 (DB). 'Homestead of a man called *Wrōta'. OE pers. name + *hām*.

Wroughton Wilts. *Wervetone* 1086 (DB). 'Farmstead on the river called *Worf*'. Celtic river-name meaning 'winding stream' (an old name of the River Ray) + OE *tūn*.

Wroxall I. of Wight. *Wroccesheale* 1038–44, *Warochesselle* 1086 (DB). 'Nook of land frequented by the buzzard or other bird of prey'. OE **wrocc* + *halh*.

Wroxeter Shrops. *Ouirokónion* c.150, *Rochecestre* 1086 (DB). 'Roman fort at or near *Uriconio* or the Wrekin'. Ancient Celtic name (possibly 'town of Virico') + OE *ceaster*.

Wroxham Norfolk. *Vrochesham* 1086 (DB). 'Homestead or enclosure of the buzzard, or of a man called *Wrocc'. OE **wrocc* or pers. name + *hām* or *hamm*.

Wroxton Oxon. *Werochestan* 1086 (DB). Probably 'stone of the buzzards or other birds of prey'. OE **wrocc* + *stān*.

Wyaston Derbys. *Widerdestune* (*sic*) 1086 (DB), *Wyardestone* 1244. 'Farmstead of a man called Wīgheard'. OE pers. name + *tūn*.

Wyberton Lincs. *Wibertune* 1086 (DB). Possibly 'farmstead of a man called Wīgbeorht or of a woman called Wīgburh'. OE pers. name + *tūn*.

Wyboston Beds. *Wiboldestone* 1086 (DB). 'Farmstead of a man called Wīgbeald'. OE pers. name + *tūn*.

Wychbold Heref. & Worcs. *Uuicbold* 692, *Wicelbold* 1086 (DB). 'Dwelling near the trading settlement'. OE *wīc* + *bold*.

Wychwood (old forest) Oxon., see ASCOTT UNDER WYCHWOOD.

Wycomb Leics. *Wiche* 1086 (DB), *Wicham* 1316. Possibly identical in origin with the next name, but more likely to be from OE **wīc-hām* for which see WICKHAM.

Wycombe, High & West Bucks. *Wicumun* c.970, *Wicumbe* 1086 (DB). '(Place) at the dwellings or settlements'. OE *wīc* in a dative plural form *wīcum*. The river-name Wye here is probably only a 'back-formation' from the place-name.

Wyddial Herts. *Widihale* 1086 (DB). 'Nook of land where willow-trees grow'. OE *wīthig* + *halh*.

Wye (river) Heref. & Worcs., see ROSS ON WYE.

Wye Kent. *Uuiæ* 839, *Wi* 1086 (DB). '(Place at) the heathen temple'. OE *wīg*.

Wyke, 'the dwelling, the specialized farm or trading settlement', OE *wīc*; examples include: **Wyke** Surrey. *Wucha* 1086 (DB). **Wyke Regis** Dorset. *Wike* 984, *Kingeswik* 1242. Anciently a royal manor, hence the Latin affix *Regis* 'of the king'.

Wykeham N. Yorks. *Wicham* 1086 (DB). Probably 'homestead associated with an earlier Romano-British settlement'. OE **wīc-hām*.

Wylam Northum. *Wylum* 12th cent. Probably '(place at) the fish-traps'. OE *wīl* or *wīle* in a dative plural form *wīlum*.

Wylye Wilts. *Wilig* 901, *Wili* 1086 (DB). Named from the River Wylye, a pre-English river-name possibly meaning 'tricky stream', i.e. one liable to flood.

Wymering Hants. *Wimeringes* 1086 (DB). '(Settlement of) the family or followers of a man called Wīgmǣr'. OE pers. name + *-ingas*.

Wymeswold Leics. *Wimundeswald* 1086 (DB). 'Forest of a man called Wīgmund'. OE pers. name + *wald*.

Wymington Beds. *Wimentone* 1086 (DB). Probably 'farmstead of a man called Wīdmund'. OE pers. name + *tūn*.

Wymondham, 'homestead of a man called Wīgmund', OE pers. name + *hām*: **Wymondham** Leics. *Wimundesham* 1086 (DB). **Wymondham** Norfolk. *Wimundham* 1086 (DB).

Wynford Eagle Dorset. *Wenfrot* 1086 (DB), *Wynfrod Egle* 1288. A Celtic river-name meaning 'white or bright stream', Celtic **winn* + **frud*. Manorial affix from the *del Egle* family, here in the 13th cent.

Wyre Forest Heref. & Worcs., Shrops. *Wyre* c.1080. Possibly from a Celtic river-name meaning 'winding river'.

Wyre Piddle Heref. & Worcs., see PIDDLE.

Wyrley, Great & Little Staffs. *Wereleia* 1086 (DB). 'Woodland clearing where bog-myrtle grows'. OE *wīr* + *lēah*.

Wysall Notts. *Wisoc* 1086 (DB). Possibly 'hill-spur of the heathen temple'. OE *wīg* + *hōh*.

Wytham Oxon. *Wihtham* c.957, *Winteham* (*sic*) 1086 (DB). 'Homestead or village in a river-bend'. OE **wiht* + *hām*.

Wytheford, Great Shrops. *Wicford* (*sic*) 1086 (DB), *Widiford* 1195. 'Ford where willow-trees grow'. OE *wīthig* + *ford*.

Wyverstone Suffolk. *Wiuerthestune* 1086 (DB). 'Farmstead of a man called Wīgferth'. OE pers. name + *tūn*.

Y

Yaddlethorpe Humber. *Iadulfestorp* 1086 (DB). 'Outlying farmstead or hamlet of a man called Ēadwulf'. OE pers. name + OScand. *thorp.*

Yafforth N. Yorks. *Iaforde* 1086 (DB). 'Ford over the river (Wiske)'. OE *ēa* + *ford.*

Yalding Kent. *Hallinges* 1086 (DB), *Ealding* 1207. '(Settlement of) the family or followers of a man called Ealda'. OE pers. name + *-ingas.*

Yanworth Glos. *Janeworth* c.1050, *Teneurde (sic)* 1086 (DB). 'Enclosure used for lambs, or of a man called *Gæna'. OE **ēan* or pers. name + *worth.*

Yapham Humber. *Iapun* 1086 (DB). '(Place at) the steep slopes'. OE **gēap* in a dative plural form *gēapum.*

Yapton W. Sussex. *Abbiton* c.1187. 'Estate associated with a man called *Eabba'. OE pers. name + *-ing-* + *tūn.*

Yarburgh Lincs. *Gereburg* 1086 (DB), *Jerdeburc* 12th cent. 'The earthwork, the fortification built of earth'. OE *eorth-burh.*

Yarcombe Devon. *Ercecombe* 10th cent., *Erticoma* 1086 (DB). 'Valley of the River Yarty'. Old river-name of uncertain origin + OE *cumb.*

Yardley, 'wood or clearing where rods or spars are obtained', OE *gyrd* + *lēah*: **Yardley** W. Mids. *Gyrdleah* 972, *Gerlei* 1086 (DB). **Yardley Gobion** Northants. *Gerdeslai* 1086 (DB), *Yerdele Gobioun* 1353. Manorial affix from the *Gubyun* family, here in the 13th cent. **Yardley Hastings** Northants. *Gerdelai* 1086 (DB), *Yerdele Hastinges* 1316. Manorial affix from the *de Hastinges* family, here in the 13th cent.

Yarkhill Heref. & Worcs. *Geardcylle* 811, *Archel* 1086 (DB). 'Kiln with a yard or enclosure'. OE *geard* + *cyln.*

Yarlet Staffs. *Erlide* 1086 (DB). Possibly 'gravelly slope, or eagle slope'. OE *ēar* or *earn* + *hlith.*

Yarlington Somerset. *Gerlincgetuna* 1086 (DB). 'Farmstead of the family or followers of a man called *Gerla'. OE pers. name + *-inga-* + *tūn.*

Yarm Cleveland. *Iarun* 1086 (DB). '(Place at) the fish-weirs'. OE **gear* in a dative plural form **gearum.*

Yarmouth I. of Wight. *Ermud* 1086 (DB), *Ernemuth* 1223. 'Gravelly or muddy estuary'. OE **ēaren* + *mūtha.*

Yarmouth, Great Norfolk. *Gernemwa* 1086 (DB). '(Place at) the mouth of the River Yare'. Celtic river-name (probably 'babbling stream') + OE *mūtha.*

Yarnfield Staffs. *Ernefeld* 1266. 'Open land frequented by eagles'. OE *earn* + *feld.*

Yarnscombe Devon. *Hernescome* 1086 (DB). 'Valley of the eagle'. OE *earn* + *cumb.*

Yarnton Oxon. *Ærdintune* 1005, *Hardintone* 1086 (DB). 'Estate associated with a man called *Earda'. OE pers. name + *-ing-* + *tūn.*

Yarpole Heref. & Worcs. *Iarpol* 1086 (DB). 'Pool with a weir or dam for catching fish'. OE **gear* + *pōl.*

Yarty (river) Devon, see YARCOMBE.

Yarwell Northants. *Jarewelle* 1166. 'Spring by the dam(s) for catching fish'. OE **gear* + *wella.*

Yate Avon. *Geate* 779, *Giete* 1086 (DB). '(Place at) the gate or gap'. OE *geat.*

Yateley Hants. *Yatele* 1248. 'Woodland clearing with or near a gate or gap'. OE *geat* + *lēah.*

Yatesbury Wilts. *Etesberie* 1086 (DB). 'Stronghold of a man called Gēat'. OE pers. name + *burh* (dative *byrig*).

Yattendon Berks. *Etingedene* 1086 (DB). Probably 'valley of the family or followers of a man called Gēat'. OE pers. name + *-inga-* + *denu*.

Yatton Avon. *Iatune* 1086 (DB). 'Farmstead by a river'. OE *ēa* + *tūn*.

Yatton Heref. & Worcs. *Getune* 1086 (DB). 'Farmstead near a gate or gap'. OE *geat* + *tūn*.

Yatton Keynell Wilts. *Getone* 1086 (DB), *Yatton Kaynel* 1289. Identical in origin with the previous name. Manorial affix from the *Caynel* family, here in the 13th cent.

Yaverland I. of Wight. *Ewerelande* 683, *Evreland* 1086 (DB). 'Cultivated land where boars are kept'. OE *eofor* + *land*.

Yaxham Norfolk. *Jachesham* 1086 (DB). 'Homestead or enclosure of the cuckoo or of a man called *Gēac'. OE *gēac* or pers. name + *hām* or *hamm*.

Yaxley, 'wood or clearing of the cuckoo', OE *gēac* + *lēah*: **Yaxley** Cambs. *Geaceslea* 963–84, *Iacheslei* 1086 (DB). **Yaxley** Suffolk. *Jacheslea* 1086 (DB).

Yazor Heref. & Worcs. *Iavesovre* 1086 (DB), *Iagesoure* 1242. 'Ridge of a man called Iago'. Welsh pers. name + OE **ofer*.

Yeading Gtr. London. *Geddinges* 716–57. '(Settlement of) the family or followers of a man called Geddi'. OE pers. name + *-ingas*.

Yeadon W. Yorks. *Iadun* 1086 (DB). Probably 'steep hill'. OE **gǣh* + *dūn*.

Yealand Conyers & Redmayne Lancs. *Jalant* 1086 (DB), *Yeland Coygners* 1301, *Yeland Redman* 1341. 'High cultivated land'. OE *hēah* + *land*. Distinguishing affixes from early possession by the *de Conyers* and *Redeman* families.

Yealmpton Devon. *Elintona* 1086 (DB). 'Farmstead on the River Yealm'. Celtic or pre-Celtic river-name (of doubtful meaning) + OE *tūn*.

Yearsley N. Yorks. *Eureslage* 1086 (DB). 'Wood or clearing of the wild boar, or of a man called *Eofor'. OE *eofor* or pers. name + *lēah*.

Yeaton Shrops. *Aitone* 1086 (DB), *Eton* 1327. 'Farmstead by a river'. OE *ēa* + *tūn*.

Yeaveley Derbys. *Gheveli* 1086 (DB). 'Woodland clearing of a man called *Geofa'. OE pers. name + *lēah*.

Yedingham N. Yorks. *Edingham* 1170–5. 'Homestead of the family or followers of a man called Ēada'. OE pers. name + *-inga-* + *hām*.

Yeldham, Great & Little Essex. *Geldeham* 1086 (DB). Probably 'homestead liable to pay a certain tax'. OE *gield* + *hām*.

Yelford Oxon. *Aieleforde* 1086 (DB). 'Ford of a man called *Ægel'. OE pers. name + *ford*.

Yelling Cambs. *Gillinge* 974, *Gellinge* 1086 (DB). Probably '(settlement of) the family or followers of a man called *Giella'. OE pers. name + *-ingas*.

Yelvertoft Northants. *Gelvrecote (sic)* 1086 (DB), *Gelvertoft* 12th cent. Possibly 'homestead of a man called *Geldfrith'. OE pers. name + OScand. *toft* (replacing OE *cot* 'cottage'). Alternatively the first part of the name may be 'ford at a pool', from an OE **gēol* + *ford*.

Yelverton Devon. *Elleford* 1291, *Elverton* 1765. Originally 'elder-tree ford', from OE *ellen* + *ford*, with the later addition of *tūn* 'village'.

Yeoford Devon. *Ioweford* 1242. 'Ford on the River Yeo'. OE river-name (possibly 'yew stream') + *ford*.

Yeolmbridge Cornwall. *Yambrigge* 13th cent. Possibly 'bridge by the river meadow'. OE *ēa* + *hamm* + *brycg*.

Yeovil Somerset. *Gifle* c.880, *Givele* 1086 (DB). '(Place on) the River *Gifl*'. Celtic river-name (meaning 'forked river'), an earlier name for the River Yeo (the form of which has been influenced by OE *ēa* 'river').

Yeovilton Somerset. *Geveltone* 1086 (DB). 'Farmstead on the River *Gifl*'. Celtic river-name (see YEOVIL) + OE *tūn*.

Yetlington Northum. *Yettlinton* 1187. Possibly 'estate associated with a man called *Gēatela'. OE pers. name + *-ing-* + *tūn*.

Yetminster Dorset. *Etiminstre* 1086 (DB). 'Church of a man called Ēata'. OE pers. name + *mynster*.

Yettington Devon. *Yethemeton* 1242. 'Farmstead of the dwellers by the gate or gap'. OE *geat* + *hǣme* + *tūn*.

Yiewsley Gtr. London. *Wiuesleg* 1235. 'Woodland clearing of a man called *Wifel or *Wīfe'. OE pers. name + *lēah*.

Yockenthwaite N. Yorks. *Yoghannesthweit* 1241. 'Clearing of a man called Eogan'. OIrish pers. name + OScand. *thveit*.

Yockleton Shrops. *Ioclehuile* 1086 (DB). Possibly 'hill by a small manor or estate'. OE *geocled* + *hyll* (later replaced by *tūn*).

Yokefleet Humber. *Iucufled* 1086 (DB). Probably 'creek or stream of a man called Jókell'. OScand. pers. name + *flēot*.

York N. Yorks. *Ebórakon* c.150, *Eboracum, Euruic* 1086 (DB). An ancient Celtic name meaning 'estate of a man called Eburos' or (more probably) 'yew-tree estate'. **Yorkshire** (OE *scīr* 'district') is first referred to in the 11th cent.

York Town Surrey, so named in the early 19th cent. after Frederick, Duke of York, who founded Sandhurst College in 1812.

Yorton Shrops. *Iartune* 1086 (DB). 'Farmstead with a yard'. OE *geard* + *tūn*.

Youlgreave Derbys. *Giolgrave* 1086 (DB). 'Yellow grove or pit'. OE *geolu* + *grǣfe* or *græf*.

Youlthorpe Humber. *Aiulftorp* 1086 (DB), *Joletorp* 1166. 'Outlying farmstead or hamlet of a man called Eyjulfr or Jól(i)'. OScand. pers. name + *thorp*.

Youlton N. Yorks. *Ioletun* 1086 (DB). 'Farmstead of a man called Jóli'. OScand. pers. name + OE *tūn*.

Yoxall Staffs. *Iocheshale* 1086 (DB). Possibly 'nook comprising a yoke or measure of land'. OE *geoc* + *halh*.

Yoxford Suffolk. *Gokesford* 1086 (DB). 'Ford wide enough for a yoke of oxen'. OE *geoc* + *ford*.

Z

Zeal Monachorum Devon. *Seale* 956, *Sele Monachorum* 1275. '(Place at) the sallow-tree'. OE *sealh*. Latin affix 'of the monks' refers to early possession by Buckfast Abbey.

Zeal, South Devon. *La Sele* 1168. 'The hall', or 'the sallow-tree'. OE *sele* or *sealh*.

Zeals Wilts. *Sele* 1086 (DB), *Seles* 1176. 'The sallow-trees'. OE *sealh* in a plural form.

Zennor Cornwall. 'Church of *Sanctus Sinar*' c.1170. From the female patron saint of the church.

Glossary of Some Common Elements in English Place-Names

In this list, OE stands for Old English, ME for Middle English, OFrench for Old French, and OScand. for Old Scandinavian. The OE letters 'thorn' and 'eth' have been rendered *th* throughout. The OE letter *æ* ('ash') represents a sound between *a* and *e*. Elements with an asterisk are postulated or hypothetical forms, that is they are words not recorded in independent use or only found in use at a later date.

á *OScand.* river
āc *OE* oak-tree
ācen *OE* made of oak, growing with oak-trees
ād *OE* funeral pyre, beacon
æcer *OE* plot of cultivated or arable land
ǣl, ēl *OE* eel
æppel *OE* apple-tree
ærn *OE* house, building, dwelling
æsc *OE* ash-tree
æspe *OE* aspen-tree, white poplar
ǣwell *OE* river-source
ǣwelm *OE* river-source
akr *OScand.* plot of cultivated or arable land
ald, eald *OE* old, long used
alor *OE* alder-tree
***anger** *OE* grassland, pasture
ānstiga *OE* narrow or lonely track, track linking other routes
apuldor *OE* apple-tree
askr *OScand.* ash-tree
austr *OScand.* east
bæc *OE* back, ridge
bæce, bece *OE* stream in a valley
bærnet *OE* land cleared by burning
bæth *OE* bath
***bagga** *OE* badger
banke *OScand.* bank, hill-slope
bār *OE* boar
bēacon *OE* beacon, signal
bēam *OE* tree-trunk. beam of timber
bēan *OE* bean
bearu *OE* grove, wood
beau, bel *OFrench* fine, beautiful
bēce *OE* beech-tree
bekkr *OScand.* stream
bēl *OE* fire, funeral pyre
***bel-** *OE* glade, dry ground in marsh
bēo *OE* bee
beofor *OE* beaver
beonet *OE* bent-grass, coarse grass
beorc *OE* birch-tree
beorg, berg *OE* hill, mound, tumulus
***bēos** *OE* bent-grass, rough grass
bere *OE* barley
bere-ærn *OE* barn, store-house for barley
bere-tūn *OE* barley farm, corn farm, *later* outlying grange or demesne farm
bere-wīc *OE* barley farm, *later* outlying part of an estate
berg *OScand.* hill
***bic, *bica** *OE* pointed hill or ridge
***bīc** *OE* nest of bees
bīcere *OE* bee-keeper
bigging *ME* a building
birce *OE* birch-tree
blæc *OE* black, dark-coloured
blá(r) *OScand.* dark, cheerless, exposed
bōc *OE* (i) beech-tree, (ii) book, charter
bōc-land *OE* land granted by charter
boga *OE* bow, arch, bend
***boi(a)** *OE* boy, servant
bóndi *OScand.* peasant landowner
botm, *bothm *OE*, **botn** *OScand.* broad river valley, valley bottom
bōthl, bōtl, bold *OE* special house or building
box *OE* box-tree
brād *OE* broad, spacious
brēc, brǣc *OE* land broken up for cultivation

bred *OE* board, plank
***breȝ** Celtic hill
brekka *OScand.* hill-slope
brēmel, brembel *OE* bramble, blackberry bush
brende *ME* burnt, cleared by burning
brēr *OE* briars
Brettas *OE* Britons
brōc *OE* brook, stream
brocc *OE* badger
brōm *OE* thorny bush, broom
brycg *OE* bridge, *sometimes* causeway
bucc *OE* buck, stag
bucca *OE* he-goat
***bula** *OE* bull
būr *OE* cottage, dwelling
(ge)būr *OE* peasant holding land for rent or services
burh (*dative* **byrig**) *OE* fortified place, stronghold, *variously applied to Iron-Age hill-forts, Roman and Anglo-Saxon fortifications, and fortified houses, later to manors or manor houses and to towns or boroughs*
burna *OE* stream
búth, bōth *OScand.* booth, temporary shelter
bý *OScand.* farmstead, village, settlement
byden *OE* vessel, tub, hollow
***cadeir** *Celtic* chair, lofty place
cærse *OE* cress, water-cress
calc, cealc *OE* chalk, limestone
cald, ceald *OE* cold
calf, cealf *OE* calf
calu *OE* bald, bare, lacking vegetation, *often* bare hill
camb *OE* hill-crest, ridge
camp *OE* enclosed piece of land, *originally* open uncultivated land on the edge of a Romano-British settlement
cat(t) *OE* cat, wild-cat
cēap *OE* trade, market
ceaster, cæster *OE* Roman station or walled town, old fortification or earthwork
***cēd** *Celtic* forest, wood
ceorl *OE* freeman, peasant
cēping, cīeping *OE* market
cēse, *cīese *OE* cheese
cild *OE* child, youth, younger son, young nobleman
cirice *OE* church
cisel, ceosol *OE* gravel, shingle
clǣfre *OE* clover
clǣg *OE* clay, clayey soil
clif *OE* cliff, slope, river-bank
***clōh** *OE* ravine, deep valley
***clopp(a)** *OE* lump, hill
cniht *OE* youth, servant, retainer
cnoll *OE* hill-top, *later* hillock
cocc *OE* (i) heap, hillock, (ii) cock of wild bird, woodcock
cofa *OE* chamber, cave, cove
col *OE* coal, charcoal
cōl *OE* cool
copp *OE* hill-top
cot *OE* cottage, hut, shelter
cran, corn *OE* crane, *also probably* heron *or similar bird*
crāwe *OE* crow
croft *OE* enclosure, small enclosed field
cros *OE* cross
***crûg** *Celtic* hill, mound, tumulus
cū *OE* cow
cumb *OE* coomb, valley, *used particularly of relatively short or broad valleys*
***Cumbre** *OE* the Cymry, the Cumbrian Britons
cwēn *OE* queen
cwene *OE* woman
cweorn *OE* quern, hand-mill
cyln *OE* kiln
cyne- *OE* royal
cyning *OE* king
cȳta *OE* kite
dæl *OE* pit, hollow, valley
dalr *OScand.* valley
denn *OE* woodland pasture, especially for swine
denu *OE* valley, *used particularly of relatively long, narrow valleys*
dēop *OE* deep
dēor *OE* animal, *also* deer
derne, dierne *OE* hidden, overgrown with vegetation
dīc *OE* ditch, dyke, *also* embankment
***djúr, dýr** *OScand.* animal, *also* deer
dræg *OE* a portage or slope used for dragging down loads, *also* a dray, a sledge
dūn *OE* hill, down

Glossary of English Place-Name Elements

ēa *OE* river
earn *OE* eagle
ēast *OE* east, eastern
ecg *OE* edge, escarpment
edisc *OE* enclosure, enclosed park
ēg, īeg *OE* island, land partly surrounded by water, dry ground in marsh, well-watered land, promontory
***eglę̄s** *Celtic* Romano-British Christian church
eik *OScand.* oak-tree
elfitu *OE* swan
elle(r)n *OE* elder-tree
elm *OE* elm-tree
ende *OE*, **endi** *OScand.* end, district of an estate
ened *OE* duck
Engle *OE* the Angles, *later* the English
eofor *OE* wild boar
eorl *OE* nobleman
eowestre *OE* sheep-fold
eowu *OE* ewe
erg, ǽrgi *OScand.* shieling, hill pasture, summer pasture
ersc *OE* ploughed or stubble field
eski *OScand.* place growing with ash-trees
fæger *OE* fair, pleasant
fæsten *OE* stronghold
fāg *OE* variegated, multi-coloured
fald *OE* fold, enclosure for animals
fearn *OE* fern, bracken
feld *OE* open country, tract of land cleared of trees
fenn *OE* fen, marshy ground
fennig *OE* marshy, muddy
ferja *OScand.* ferry
fleax *OE* flax
flēot *OE* estuary, inlet, creek, *also* stream
fola *OE*, **foli** *OScand.* foal
folc *OE* folk, tribe, people
ford *OE* ford, river-crossing
fox *OE* fox
fugol *OE* (wild) fowl, bird
fūl *OE* foul, dirty
***funta** *OE* spring (*a loan-word from Latin* fons, fontis *and therefore possibly used of a spring characterized by Roman building work*)
fyrhth(e) *OE* woodland, *often* sparse woodland or scrub
fyrs *OE* furze
gærs *OE*, **gres** *OScand.* grass
gāra *OE* triangular plot of ground, point of land
garthr *OScand.* enclosure
gāt *OE*, **geit** *OScand.* goat
gata *OScand.* road, street
***gē** *OE* district, region
gēac *OE* cuckoo
geard *OE* yard, enclosure
geat *OE* gate, gap, pass
gil *OScand.* deep narrow valley, ravine
gōs *OE* goose
græf *OE* pit, trench
grǣfe *OE* thicket, brushwood, grove
grāf(a) *OE* grove, copse
grēne *OE* (i) green-coloured, (ii) grassy place, village green
grēot *OE* gravel
hæcc *OE* hatch, hatch-gate, flood-gate
hæg, gehæg *OE* enclosure
hǣme *OE* inhabitants, dwellers
***hær** *OE* rock, heap of stones
***hǣs, *hǣse** *OE* (land overgrown with) brushwood
hæsel *OE* hazel-tree
hǣth *OE* heath, heather, uncultivated land overgrown with heather
hafoc *OE* hawk
haga *OE*, **hagi** *OScand.* hedged enclosure
hagu-thorn *OE* hawthorn
halh *OE* nook or corner of land, *often used of land in a hollow or river-bend*
hālig *OE* holy
hām *OE* homestead, village, manor, estate
hamm *OE* enclosure, land hemmed in by water or marsh or higher ground, land in a river-bend, river-meadow, promontory
***hamol, *hamel** *OE* mutilated, crooked
hām-stede, hǣm-styde *OE* homestead, site of a dwelling
hām-tūn *OE* home farm or settlement, enclosure in which a homestead stands
hana *OE* cock (of wild bird)

hangra *OE* wood on a steep slope
hār *OE* hoar, grey, *also* boundary
hara *OE* hare
***hāth** *OE* heath, heather, uncultivated land
haugr *OScand.* hill, mound, tumulus
hēafod *OE* head, headland, end of a ridge, river-source
hēah *OE* high, *also* chief
hearg *OE* heathen shrine or temple
hecg(e) *OE* hedge
hēg, hīeg *OE* hay
helde, hielde *OE* slope
hengest *OE* stallion
henn *OE* hen (of wild bird)
heorot *OE* hart, stag
here *OE* army
hīd *OE* hide of land, amount of land for the support of one free family and its dependants (*usually about 120 acres*)
hind *OE* hind, doe
hīwan (*genitive* **hīgna**) *OE* household, members of a family or religious community
hīwisc *OE* household, amount of land for the support of a family
hlāw, hlǣw *OE* tumulus, mound, hill
hlinc *OE* ridge, ledge, terrace
hlith *OE*, **hlíth** *OScand.* hill-slope
hlōse *OE* pigsty
hōc *OE* hook or corner of land, land in a bend
hōh *OE* heel of land, projecting hill-spur
hol *OE* (i) *as noun* a hole or hollow, (ii) *as adjective* hollow, deep
holegn *OE* holly
holmr *OScand.* island, raised ground in marsh, river-meadow
holt *OE* wood, thicket
hop *OE* small enclosed valley, enclosure in marsh or moor
horn *OE*, *OScand.*, ***horna** *OE* horn, horn-shaped hill or piece of land
hors *OE* horse
hræfn *OE*, **hrafn** *OScand.* raven
hramsa *OE* garlic
hrēod *OE* reed, rush
hrīs *OE*, **hrís** *OScand.* brushwood, shrubs
hrīther *OE* ox, cattle
hrōc *OE*, **hrókr** *OScand.* rook
hrycg *OE*, **hryggr** *OScand.* ridge
hund *OE* dog
hunig *OE* honey
hunta *OE* huntsman
hūs *OE*, **hús** *OScand.* house
***hvin** *OScand.* gorse
hwǣte *OE* wheat
hwēol *OE* wheel, circular feature
hwerfel, hwyrfel *OE*, **hvirfill** *OScand.* circle, circular feature
hwīt *OE*, **hvítr** *OScand.* white
hyll *OE* hill
hyrst *OE* wooded hill
hȳth *OE* landing-place or harbour, inland port
-ing *OE suffix* place or stream characterized by, place belonging to
-ing- *OE connective particle implying* associated with *or* called after
-inga- *OE genitive (possessive) case of* **-ingas**
-ingas *OE plural suffix* people of, family or followers of, dwellers at
īw, ēow, *īg *OE* yew-tree
kaldr *OScand.* cold
kalfr *OScand.* calf
karl *OScand.* freeman, peasant
kelda *OScand.* spring
kirkja *OScand.* church
kjarr *OScand.* marsh overgrown with brushwood
konungr, kunung *OScand.* king
krók *OScand.* bend, land in a river-bend
kross *OScand.* cross
lacu *OE* stream, water-course
lād *OE* water-course, **gelād** *OE* river-crossing
***læcc, *læce** *OE* stream, bog
lǣs *OE* pasture, meadow-land
lamb *OE* lamb
land *OE* tract of land, estate, cultivated land
***lann** *Cornish*, *OWelsh*, **llan** *Welsh* churchyard, church-site, church
lang *OE*, **langr** *OScand.* long
lāwerce *OE* lark
lēac *OE* leek, garlic
lēah *OE* wood, woodland clearing or glade, *later* pasture, meadow
līn *OE*, **lín** *OScand.* flax
lind *OE* lime-tree

loc, **loca** *OE* lock, fold, enclosure
lundr *OScand.* small wood or grove
lȳtel *OE* little
mǣd *OE* meadow
mægden *OE* maiden
mǣl, **mēl** *OE* cross, crucifix
mǣne, **gemǣne** *OE* held in common, communal
mǣre, **gemǣre** *OE* boundary
***mapel**, ***mapul**, **mapuldor** *OE* maple-tree
marr *OScand.* fen, marsh
mearc *OE* boundary
melr *OScand.* sand-bank, sand-hill
mēos *OE* moss
mere *OE* pond, pool, lake
mersc *OE* marsh, marshland
micel, **mycel** *OE*, **mikill** *OScand.* great
middel *OE* middle
***mōnīth** *Celtic*, **mynydd** *Welsh* mountain, hill
mont *OFrench*, *ME* mount, hill
mōr *OE*, **mór** *OScand.* moor, marshy ground, barren upland
mos *OE*, **mosi** *OScand.* moss, marsh, bog
munuc *OE* monk
mūs *OE*, **mús** *OScand.* mouse
mūtha *OE* river-mouth, estuary
myln *OE* mill
mynster *OE* monastery, church of a monastery, minster or large church
mýrr *OScand.* mire, bog, swampy ground
mȳthe, **gemȳthe** *OE* confluence of rivers
næss, **ness** *OE*, **nes** *OScand.* promontory, headland
nīwe, **nēowe** *OE* new
north *OE* north, northern
ōfer *OE* bank, margin, shore
***ofer**, ***ufer** *OE* flat-topped ridge, hill, promontory
ōra *OE* (i) shore, hill-slope, flat-topped hill, (ii) ore, iron-ore
oter *OE* otter
oxa *OE* ox
pæth *OE* path, track
***penn** *Celtic* head, end, hill, *also* chief (*adjective*)
penn *OE* pen, fold, enclosure for animals
peru *OE* pear
pirige, **pyrige** *OE* pear-tree
plega *OE* play, games, sport
plūme *OE* plum, plum-tree
pōl, ***pull** *OE* pool, pond, creek
port *OE* (i) harbour, (ii) town, market town, market, (iii) gate
prēost *OE* priest
pres, **prys** *Welsh* brushwood, thicket
pyll *OE* tidal creek, pool, stream
pytt *OE* pit, hollow
rá *OScand.* (i) roe, roebuck, (ii) boundary
rauthr *OScand.* red
rēad *OE* red
rēfa *OE* reeve, bailiff
***ric** *OE* raised straight strip of land, narrow ridge
risc, ***rysc** *OE* rush
rīth, **rīthig** *OE* small stream
***rod**, ***rodu** *OE* clearing
***ros** *Celtic* moor, heath, *also* promontory
rūh *OE* rough
ryge *OE*, **rugr** *OScand.* rye
sǣ *OE*, **sǽr** *OScand.* sea, inland lake
sǣte *OE plural* dwellers, settlers
sǽtr *OScand.* shieling, hill pasture, summer pasture
salh, **sealh** *OE* sallow, willow
salt *OE* (i) salt, (ii) salty (*adjective*)
sand *OE*, **sandr** *OScand.* sand
saurr *OScand.* mud, dirt, sour ground
sc̣eaga *OE* small wood, copse
sc̣ēap, **sc̣ēp**, **sc̣īp**, ***sc̣īep** *OE* sheep
sc̣ēat *OE* corner or angle of land, projecting wood or piece of land
***sc̣ēla** *OE* temporary hut or shelter
scelf, **scielf**, **scylfe** *OE* shelf of level or gently sloping ground, ledge
sc̣ēne, **sc̣īene** *OE* bright, beautiful
sc̣īr *OE* (i) shire, district, (ii) bright, clear
scucca *OE* evil spirit, demon
Seaxe *OE* the Saxons
sele *OE* dwelling, house, hall
***sele**, ***siele** *OE* sallow or willow copse
seofon *OE* seven
set, **geset** *OE* dwelling, stable, fold
sīc *OE* small stream
sīd *OE* large, extensive

sīde *OE* hill-side
skáli *OScand.* temporary hut or shed
skógr *OScand.* wood
slæd *OE* valley
***slæp** *OE* slippery muddy place
slakki *OScand.* shallow valley
slōh *OE* slough, mire
sol *OE* muddy place
stæth *OE*, **stǫth** *OScand.* landing-place
stān *OE*, **steinn** *OScand.* stone, rock, boundary stone
stapol *OE* post, pillar of wood or stone
stede *OE* enclosed pasture, place, site
steort *OE* tail or tongue of land
stīg *OE*, **stígr** *OScand.* path, narrow road
stoc *OE* place, outlying farmstead or hamlet, secondary or dependent settlement
stocc *OE*, **stokkr** *OScand.* tree-trunk, stump, log
stōd *OE* stud, herd of horses
stōw *OE* place, assembly place, holy place
strǣt *OE* Roman road, paved road
strōd *OE* marshy land overgrown with brushwood
sumor *OE*, **sumarr** *OScand.* summer
sūth *OE* south, southern
swan *OE* swan
swān *OE* herdsman, peasant
swīn *OE*, **svín** *OScand.* swine, pig
thing *OE*, *OScand.* assembly, meeting
thorn *OE*, *OScand.* thorn-tree
thorp *OScand.* secondary settlement, dependent outlying farmstead or hamlet
throp *OE* dependent outlying farmstead, hamlet
Thunor *OE heathen Saxon god (corresponding to the Scandinavian* Thor)
thveit *OScand.* clearing, meadow, paddock
thyrne *OE*, **thyrnir** *OScand.* thorn-tree
thyrs *OE* giant, demon
ticce(n) *OE* kid, young goat
Tīw, Tig *OE heathen Germanic god*
toft, topt *OScand.* site of a house or building, curtilage, homestead
torr *OE* rock, rocky hill
***tōt(e)** *OE* look-out place
trēo(w) *OE* tree, post, beam
tūn *OE* enclosure, farmstead, village, manor, estate
twī- *OE* double
twisla *OE* fork of a river, junction of streams
upp *OE* higher up
vath *OScand.* ford
vithr *OScand.* wood
vrá, rá *OScand.* nook or corner of land
wād *OE* woad
wæd, gewæd *OE* ford
***wæsse** *OE* riverside land liable to flood
wæter *OE* water, river, lake
wald, weald *OE* woodland, forest, high forest land later cleared
walh, wealh *OE* Briton, Welshman
wall, weall *OE* wall, bank
-ware *OE plural* dwellers
weard *OE* watch, ward, protection
weg *OE* way, track, road
wella, wiella, wælla *OE* spring, strea[m]
weorc, geweorc *OE* building, fortification
wer, wær *OE* weir, river-dam, fishing-enclosure in a river
west *OE* west, western
wēt, wǣt *OE* wet, damp
wether *OE* wether, ram
wīc *OE* earlier Romano-British settlement; dwelling, specialized farm or building, dairy farm; trading or industrial settlement, harbour
wice *OE* wych-elm
***wīc-hām** *OE* homestead associated with an earlier Romano-British settlement
wīd *OE* wide, spacious
wīg, wēoh *OE* heathen shrine or temple
***wilig, welig** *OE* willow-tree
wīthig *OE* withy, willow-tree
Wōden *OE heathen Germanic god (corresponding to the Scandinavian* Othin)
wōh *OE* twisted, crooked
worth, worthig, worthign *OE* enclosure, enclosed settlement

wudu, *earlier* **widu** *OE* wood, forest, *also* timber
wulf *OE*, **ulfr** *OScand.* wolf
wyrm, wurm *OE* reptile, snake, *also* dragon
yfer *OE* edge or brow of a hill

Select Bibliography for Further Reading

Other Dictionaries and Works of Reference

Ekwall, E., *The Concise Oxford Dictionary of English Place-Names*, 4th edition (Oxford 1960).

Field, J., *English Field-Names: a Dictionary* (Newton Abbot 1972, reprinted Gloucester 1989).

Forster, K., *A Pronouncing Dictionary of English Place-Names* (London 1981).

Gelling, M., Nicolaisen, W. F. H., and Richards, M., *The Names of Towns and Cities in Britain* (London 1970, revised reprint 1986).

Padel, O. J., *Cornish Place-Name Elements*, EPNS 56/57 (Cambridge 1985).

Pointon, G. E. (ed.), *BBC Pronouncing Dictionary of British Names*, 2nd edition (Oxford 1983).

Room, A., *A Concise Dictionary of Modern Place-Names in Great Britain and Ireland* (Oxford 1983).

Smith, A. H., *English Place-Name Elements*, EPNS 25, 26 (Cambridge 1956).

Spittal, J. and Field, J., *A Reader's Guide to the Place-Names of the United Kingdom* (Stamford 1990).

County Surveys and Monographs

Armstrong, A. M., Mawer, A., Stenton, F. M., and Dickins, B., *The Place-Names of Cumberland*, EPNS 20-2 (Cambridge 1950-2).

Cameron, K., *The Place-Names of Derbyshire*, EPNS 27-9 (Cambridge 1959).

——, *The Place-Names of Lincolnshire*, EPNS 58 (Cambridge 1985) (several volumes to follow).

Coates, R., *The Place-Names of Hampshire* (London 1989).

Coplestone-Crow, B., *Herefordshire Place-Names*, British Archaeological Reports, British Series 214 (Oxford 1989).

Cox, B., *The Place-Names of Leicestershire and Rutland* (unpublished Ph.D. thesis, Nottingham University, 1971).

Dodgson, J. McN., *The Place-Names of Cheshire*, EPNS 44-8, 54 (Cambridge 1970-81) (one volume to follow).

Duignan, W. H., *Notes on Staffordshire Place-Names* (London 1902).

Ekwall, E., *The Place-Names of Lancashire* (Manchester 1922).

Fägersten, A., *The Place-Names of Dorset* (Uppsala 1933).

Field, J., *Place-Names of Greater London* (London 1980).

Gelling, M., *The Place-Names of Berkshire*, EPNS 49-51 (Cambridge 1973-6).

Gelling, M., *The Place-Names of Oxfordshire*, EPNS 23–4 (Cambridge 1953–4).

——, with Foxall, H. D. G., *The Place-Names of Shropshire*, EPNS 62/3 (Nottingham 1990) (several volumes to follow).

Glover, J., *The Place-Names of Kent* (London 1976).

Gover, J. E. B., Mawer, A., and Stenton, F. M., *The Place-Names of Devon*, EPNS 8, 9 (Cambridge 1931-2).

——, *The Place-Names of Hertfordshire*, EPNS 15 (Cambridge 1938).

——, *The Place-Names of Northamptonshire*, EPNS 10 (Cambridge 1933).

——, *The Place-Names of Nottinghamshire*, EPNS 17 (Cambridge 1940).

——, *The Place-Names of Wiltshire*, EPNS 16 (Cambridge 1939).

——, with Bonner, A., *The Place-Names of Surrey*, EPNS 11 (Cambridge 1934).

——, with Houghton, F. T. S., *The Place-Names of Warwickshire*, EPNS 13 (Cambridge 1936).

——, with Madge, S. J., *The Place-Names of Middlesex (apart from the City of London)*, EPNS 18 (Cambridge 1942).

Kökeritz, H., *The Place-Names of the Isle of Wight* (Uppsala 1940).

Mawer, A., *The Place-Names of Northumberland and Durham* (Cambridge 1920).

—— and Stenton, F. M., *The Place-Names of Bedfordshire and Huntingdonshire*, EPNS 3 (Cambridge 1926).

——, *The Place-Names of Buckinghamshire*, EPNS 2 (Cambridge 1925).

, with Gover, J. E. B., *The Place-Names of Sussex*, EPNS 6, 7 (Cambridge 1929–30).

—— and Houghton, F. T. S., *The Place-Names of Worcestershire*, EPNS 4 (Cambridge 1927).

Mills, A. D., *The Place-Names of Dorset*, EPNS 52, 53, 59/60 (Cambridge 1977–89) (two volumes to follow).

——, *Dorset Place-Names: their Origins and Meanings* (Wimborne 1986, reprinted Southampton 1991).

Mills, D., *The Place-Names of Lancashire* (London 1976).

Oakden, J. P., *The Place-Names of Staffordshire*, EPNS 55 (Cambridge 1984) (several volumes to follow).

Padel, O. J., *A Popular Dictionary of Cornish Place-Names* (Penzance 1988).

Reaney, P. H., *The Place-Names of Cambridgeshire and the Isle of Ely*, EPNS 19 (Cambridge 1943).

——, *The Place-Names of Essex*, EPNS 12 (Cambridge 1935).

Sandred, K. I. and Lindström, B., *The Place-Names of Norfolk*, EPNS 61 (Nottingham 1989) (several volumes to follow).

Skeat, W. W., *The Place-Names of Suffolk* (Cambridge 1913).

Smith, A. H., *The Place-Names of Gloucestershire*, EPNS 38–40 (Cambridge 1964–5).

——, *The Place-Names of the East Riding of Yorkshire and York*, EPNS 14 (Cambridge 1937).
——, *The Place-Names of the North Riding of Yorkshire*, EPNS 5 (Cambridge 1928).
——, *The Place-Names of the West Riding of Yorkshire*, EPNS 30–7 (Cambridge 1961–3).
——, *The Place-Names of Westmorland*, EPNS 42, 43 (Cambridge 1967).
Turner, A. G. C., *The Place-Names of North Somerset* (unpublished typescript, 1950).
Wallenberg, J. K., *Kentish Place-Names* (Uppsala 1931).
——, *The Place-Names of Kent* (Uppsala 1934).

Various Studies on the Interpretation and Significance of Place-Names

Cameron, K., *English Place-Names*, 4th edition (London 1988).
—— (ed.), *Place-Name Evidence for the Anglo-Saxon Invasion and Scandinavian Settlements*, EPNS (Nottingham 1977) (collection of eight essays).
——, 'The Significance of English Place-Names', *Proceedings of the British Academy* 62 (Oxford 1976).
Copley, G. J., *Archaeology and Place-Names in the Fifth and Sixth Centuries*, British Archaeological Reports, British Series 147 (Oxford 1986).
——, *English Place-Names and their Origins* (Newton Abbot 1968).
Ekwall, E., *English Place-Names in -ing*, 2nd edition (Lund 1962).
——, *English River-Names* (Oxford 1928).
——, *Old English wic in Place-Names* (Uppsala 1964).
Fellows-Jensen, G., *Scandinavian Settlement Names in the East Midlands* (Copenhagen 1978).
——, *Scandinavian Settlement Names in the North-West* (Copenhagen 1985).
——, *Scandinavian Settlement Names in Yorkshire* (Copenhagen 1972).
Gelling, M., *Place-Names in the Landscape* (London 1984).
——, *Signposts to the Past*, 2nd edition (Chichester 1988).
Hooke, D., *The Anglo-Saxon Landscape: the Kingdom of the Hwicce* (Manchester 1985).
Jackson, K. H., *Language and History in Early Britain* (Edinburgh 1953).
Mawer, A. and Stenton, F. M. (eds.), *Introduction to the Survey of English Place-Names*, EPNS 1 (Cambridge 1924).
Reaney, P. H., *The Origins of English Place-Names* (London 1960).
Rivet, A. L. F. and Smith, C., *The Place-Names of Roman Britain* (London 1979).
Sandred, K. I., *English Place-Names in -stead* (Uppsala 1963).
Wainwright, F. T., *Archaeology and Place-Names and History* (London 1962).